CLASHING OVER COMMERCE

CLASHING OVER COMMERCE

A History of US Trade Policy

DOUGLAS A. IRWIN

THE UNIVERSITY OF CHICAGO PRESS
CHICAGO AND LONDON

The University of Chicago Press, Chicago 60637
The University of Chicago Press, Ltd., London
© 2017 by The University of Chicago
Published 2017
Paperback edition 2019
Printed in the United States of America

28 27 26 25 24 23 22 21 20 19   1 2 3 4 5

ISBN-13: 978-0-226-39896-9 (cloth)
ISBN-13: 978-0-226-67844-3 (paper)
ISBN-13: 978-0-226-39901-0 (e-book)
DOI: https://doi.org/10.7208/chicago/9780226399010.001.0001

Library of Congress Cataloging-in-Publication Data

Names: Irwin, Douglas A., 1962– author.
Title: Clashing over commerce : a history of US trade policy / Douglas A. Irwin.
Other titles: Markets and governments in economic history
Description: Chicago : The University of Chicago Press, 2017. | Series: Markets and governments in economic history
Identifiers: LCCN 2017021822 | ISBN 9780226398969 (cloth : alk. paper) | ISBN 9780226399010 (e-book)
Subjects: LCSH: United States—Commercial policy—History. | Tariff—United States—History.
Classification: LCC HF3021.I79 2017 | DDC 382/.30973—dc23
LC record available at https://lccn.loc.gov/2017021822

Relation of the Directors to the Work and Publications of the NBER

1. The object of the NBER is to ascertain and present to the economics profession, and to the public more generally, important economic facts and their interpretation in a scientific manner without policy recommendations. The Board of Directors is charged with the responsibility of ensuring that the work of the NBER is carried on in strict conformity with this object.

2. The President shall establish an internal review process to ensure that book manuscripts proposed for publication DO NOT contain policy recommendations. This shall apply both to the proceedings of conferences and to manuscripts by a single author or by one or more coauthors but shall not apply to authors of comments at NBER conferences who are not NBER affiliates.

3. No book manuscript reporting research shall be published by the NBER until the President has sent to each member of the Board a notice that a manuscript is recommended for publication and that in the President's opinion it is suitable for publication in accordance with the above principles of the NBER. Such notification will include a table of contents and an abstract or summary of the manuscript's content, a list of contributors if applicable, and a response form for use by Directors who desire a copy of the manuscript for review. Each manuscript shall contain a summary drawing attention to the nature and treatment of the problem studied and the main conclusions reached.

4. No volume shall be published until forty-five days have elapsed from the above notification of intention to publish it. During this period a copy shall be sent to any Director requesting it, and if any Director objects to publication on the grounds that the manuscript contains policy recommendations, the objection will be presented to the author(s) or editor(s). In case of dispute, all members of the Board shall be notified, and the President shall appoint an ad hoc committee of the Board to decide the matter; thirty days additional shall be granted for this purpose.

5. The President shall present annually to the Board a report describing the internal manuscript review process, any objections made by Directors before publication or by anyone after publication, any disputes about such matters, and how they were handled.

6. Publications of the NBER issued for informational purposes concerning the work of the Bureau, or issued to inform the public of the activities at the Bureau, including but not limited to the NBER Digest and Reporter, shall be consistent with the object stated in paragraph 1. They shall contain a specific disclaimer noting that they have not passed through the review procedures required in this resolution. The Executive Committee of the Board is charged with the review of all such publications from time to time.

7. NBER working papers and manuscripts distributed on the Bureau's Web site are not deemed to be publications for the purpose of this resolution, but they shall be consistent with the object stated in paragraph 1. Working papers shall contain a specific disclaimer noting that they have not passed through the review procedures required in this resolution. The NBER's Web site shall contain a similar disclaimer. The President shall establish an internal review process to ensure that the working papers and the Web site do not contain policy recommendations and shall report annually to the Board on this process and any concerns raised in connection with it.

8. Unless otherwise determined by the Board or exempted by the terms of paragraphs 6 and 7, a copy of this resolution shall be printed in each NBER publication as described in paragraph 2 above.

For Marjorie B. Rose

CONTENTS

In *Federalist 10*, James Madison observed that different economic interests arise in every society and often have sharply conflicting views on government policy. "A landed interest, a manufacturing interest, a mercantile interest, a moneyed interest, with many lesser interests, grow up of necessity in civilized nations, and divide them into different classes, actuated by different sentiments and views," he noted. "The regulation of these various and interfering interests forms the principal task of modern legislation, and involves the spirit of party and faction in the necessary and ordinary operations of the government." Madison illustrated this observation with the example of trade policy: "Shall domestic manufactures be encouraged, and in what degree, by restrictions on foreign manufactures? are questions which would be differently decided by the landed and the manufacturing classes, and probably by neither with a sole regard to justice and the public good." Rather pessimistically, he concluded, "It is in vain to say that enlightened statesmen will be able to adjust these clashing interests, and render them all subservient to the public good."[1]

Time has proven Madison right: trade policy has been the source of bitter political conflict throughout American history. This conflict has been fierce because dollars and jobs are at stake: depending on the policy outcome, some industries, farmers, and workers will suffer, while others will prosper. Madison also correctly anticipated that the fundamental issue in trade policy is the degree to which domestic producers should be protected from foreign competition. This persistent question has pitted different segments of society, regions of the country, and philosophical viewpoints against one another.

This book explores the economic and political factors that have shaped the battle over US trade policy from the colonial period to the present. It considers the economic interests and partisan positions that have influenced the course of trade policy, the historical circumstances that have confronted and constrained policymakers, the policy outcomes that have emerged from the political process, and the economic consequences of those policies. Congress is at the center of the story because it is the principal venue in which trade policy is determined. Producer interests, labor unions, advocacy groups, public intellectuals, and even presidents can demand, protest, denounce, and complain all they want, but to change existing policy requires a majority in Congress and the approval of the executive. If the votes are not lined up, the existing policy will not change.

US trade policy has been directed toward achieving three principal objectives: raising revenue for the government by levying duties on imports, restricting imports to protect domestic producers from foreign competition, and concluding reciprocity agreements to reduce trade barriers and expand exports. These three Rs—revenue, restriction, and reciprocity—have been the main purposes of US trade policy. While all three have been important throughout history, US trade policy can be divided into three eras in which one of them has taken priority. In the first era, from the establishment of the federal government until the Civil War, revenue was the key objective of trade policy. In the second era, from the Civil War until the Great Depression, the restriction of imports to protect domestic producers was the primary goal of trade policy. In the third era, from the Great Depression to the present, reciprocal trade agreements to reduce tariff and non-tariff barriers to trade have been the main priority.

This delineation suggests that there have been only two major exogenous shocks to American trade politics that have produced a transition from one objective to another. The first was the Civil War, which led to a political realignment in favor of the Republicans and a shift from revenue to restriction as the primary goal of trade policy. The second was the Great Depression, which led to a political realignment in favor of the Democrats and a shift from restriction to reciprocity as the primary goal of trade policy. Within each of these three eras, existing policies were heatedly disputed by the two political parties. The status quo never went unchallenged, with one side or the other complaining that the country would be ruined if tariffs were not raised higher or lowered further. Yet, despite all the debate and controversy that different, clashing interests generated, it has proven very difficult to dislodge existing policies once they were established. Within each of the three eras described above, US trade policy has shown remarkable continuity and stability, despite the political and economic conflict that exists at any given point in time.

This stability is built into American trade politics by the country's economic geography and political system. Different regions of the country specialize in different economic activities, the location of which can persist for decades if not centuries. For more than two centuries, cotton has been produced in Mississippi, tobacco in Kentucky and North Carolina, iron and steel in Pennsylvania, and so forth. These specialized regions have different interests with respect to trade: some produce goods that are exported, while others produce goods facing competition from imports. In representing these different regions, members of Congress usually vote on legislation according to the interests of their constituents. As a result, the stable economic geography of the United States leads to a stable political geography of Congressional voting on trade policy.[2] In addition, the American political system makes it very difficult to pass legislation, which biases policy toward maintaining the status quo.

As an economist, I am partial to using economic analysis as a way of understanding the forces operating on policymakers and the consequences of their policy decisions. The last major history of US trade policy by an economist was Frank Taussig's A Tariff History of the United States, first published in 1889 and running through eight editions, the last in 1931. This classic work requires updating for three reasons. First, nearly a century of momentous history has transpired since Taussig completed his last edition just after the passage of the Hawley-Smoot tariff in 1930 but before the depths of the Great Depression had been reached. Since then, the United States has moved from isolationism and protectionism in its trade policy to global leadership in promoting freer trade around the world. Second, empirical analysis has shed new light on many key questions of economic history that Taussig could only speculate about. Such questions include the impact of antebellum tariffs on the South, the role of protection in fostering the growth of infant industries, and the relationship between high trade barriers and the Great Depression. Third, the analytical framework that economists use to think about the political economy of economic policy has advanced significantly since Taussig's day.[3]

Of course, the story of US trade policy involves much more than economics; it is interwoven with the nation's political history. Not surprisingly, political scientists and historians have also made important contributions to understanding the evolution of trade policy.[4] Political scientists examine factors that economists too often ignore, such as how the policymaking process itself can shape policy outcomes. (As Rep. John Dingell of Michigan is reported to have said, "I'll let you write the substance [of legislation], you let me write the procedure [for considering it], and I'll beat you every time"—although he apparently used a more colorful word than "beat.") And historians have provided detailed expositions of the political context in which trade policy debates have taken place.

At the same time, political scientists and historians have never been particularly engrossed by the intricacies of trade policy. Alan Milward (1981, 58) once wrote that "tariffs are extraordinarily uninteresting things unless related to the political events which give them meaning"—implying that only boring economists could ever find them intrinsically worthy of study. And historians, by their own admission, have never shown a deep interest in trade policy. As John Belohlavek (1994, 482) confessed, the tariff has "engendered narcolepsy among generations of American historians. . . . While few of us would contest the importance of the issue, even fewer care to research the confusing maze of rates and duties."

More importantly, political scientists and historians tend to neglect the economic consequences of different trade policies. How did Jefferson's trade embargo in 1808 affect the economy? Did high tariffs promote America's industrialization in the nineteenth century? Did the Hawley-Smoot tariff of 1930 exacerbate or ameliorate the Great Depression? Were liberal trade policies after World War II responsible for the economic prosperity experienced in the postwar period? Did trade with China in the early 2000s destroy jobs in manufacturing and hurt blue collar workers? Although this book focuses more on understanding the political and economic forces that have shaped the formation of trade policy rather than the consequences of any particular policy outcome, these important questions need to be addressed.

This book is organized chronologically, but within each chapter both political and economic developments are analyzed. This introduction provides some background to the chapters that follow. We first examine the main policy outcome that we are seeking to understand: the average tariff on imported goods. The average tariff is usually set to achieve one of the three objectives of trade policy (the three Rs): *revenue* for the government, *restriction* of imports to protect domestic producers from foreign competition, and *reciprocity* to open foreign markets to exports. We then discuss how the economic and political geography of the United States influences the policies that emerge from Congress. Finally, we consider how partisan and ideological factors can also play a role in the formation of trade policy.

THE INSTRUMENTS AND
OBJECTIVES OF TRADE POLICY

International trade consists of exchanging exports of domestic goods and services for imports of foreign goods and services. Governments can either encourage this trade with subsidies or discourage it with taxes. This gives us four possible ways in which governments can intervene in trade: export taxes, export subsidies, import taxes, and import subsidies. Two of these four policies have little relevance to the American experience. For reasons discussed in chapter 1, export taxes are expressly prohibited under article 1, section 9 of the Constitution. Import subsidies, which are government payments to bring foreign goods into the domestic market, are almost never employed by any country, the United States being no exception.

This leaves export subsidies and import taxes. The United States has sometimes used export subsidies, but never on a large scale because of their budgetary cost.[5] By contrast, import taxes—known as tariffs, or customs duties—have been the central focus of trade policy since the establishment of the federal government in 1789. As a result, import tariffs will be the primary focus of this book.[6]

Import tariffs are taxes levied on foreign goods as they enter the United States.[7] Tariffs can take the form of ad valorem duties (a percentage of the imported good's value, such as 30 percent) or specific duties (a fixed charge per unit of the imported good, such as $1 per pound or per unit). An important feature of specific duties is that their percentage (ad valorem) equivalent cannot be determined without reference to the price of the imported good. For example, if a specific duty happens to be $5 per imported shirt, then the ad valorem equivalent is 50 percent on a $10 shirt and 10 percent on a $50 shirt. Thus, the ad valorem equivalent of a specific duty is inversely related to the good's price. Because many tariffs are specific duties, wide swings in import prices have been responsible for large movements in the average tariff during certain periods in history.[8]

The average tariff is the most widely used indicator of a country's policy with respect to imports. Figure I.1 presents the average tariff on total and dutiable imports for the United States from 1790 to 2015.[9] The average tariff on total imports is the broadest measure and includes imports of all goods (dutiable and duty-free), whereas the average tariff on dutiable imports focuses just on goods that are subject to a tariff. A large gap between these two series appeared after the Civil War, when some foreign products were allowed to enter duty-free—usually goods not produced

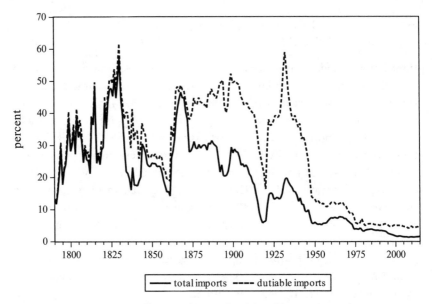

Figure I.1. Average tariff on imports, total and dutiable, 1790–2015. (US Bureau of the Census 1975, series U-211–12 for 1790–1970; US International Trade Commission, "U.S. Imports for Consumption, Duties Collected, and Ratio of Duties to Value, 1891–2015," March 2016, for 1970–2015.)

domestically, such as coffee and tea, where no domestic producer would be harmed. Since the 1980s, free-trade agreements have also allowed some foreign countries to export their goods to the United States without facing any duties. Setting aside such imports, the average tariff on dutiable imports can be interpreted, somewhat simplistically but still usefully, as the average degree of protection given to domestic producers facing foreign competition. In some sense, these protective tariffs are the key "policy outcome" that we focus on throughout this book.

As Figure I.1 shows, these tariffs have fluctuated over time, suggesting that trade policy has been quite volatile. However, this is largely an illusion, and underlying policies have been much more stable than the figure suggests. While some of the movement in the average tariff is due to changes in tariff rates as enacted by Congress or negotiated by the president in trade agreements, most tariff acts and trade agreements only made incremental changes to the existing structure and rate of import duties and thus maintained the continuity of existing policy. By contrast, the largest movements in the average tariff have been driven by changing import prices acting on specific duties. These exogenous fluctuations in import prices have sometimes produced large changes in average tariffs, even when there were no changes in underlying rates of duty set by policymakers and applied to imports.

What objectives have Congress and the president sought to achieve in setting these import tariffs? As already mentioned, policymakers have had three principal goals: raising revenue for the government, restricting imports to protect certain domestic industries from foreign competition, and pursuing reciprocity agreements with other countries to open foreign markets to US exports. In a rough way, the three eras of US trade policy can be seen in Figure I.1. In the first era, from 1790 to 1860, revenue was a key factor in setting import duties because they generated about 90 percent of the federal government's income. Of course, revenue was not the sole consideration: the average tariff rose from about 20 percent in the early 1800s to nearly 60 percent by the late 1820s because some northern states sought to introduce a protective tariff. This bid was eventually defeated by southern states, which wanted "a tariff for revenue only," but only after a major political crisis in which South Carolina threatened to secede from the union. The Compromise of 1833 resolved the matter and put tariffs on a downward path until the outbreak of the Civil War, by which time they were below 20 percent. The average tariffs on total and dutiable imports were similar because almost every imported good was subject to customs duties.[10]

This political equilibrium was disrupted by the Civil War, which shifted political power from the low-tariff Democrats in the South to the high-tariff Republicans in the North. During this second era, from 1860 until 1934, the primary goal of trade policy was the restriction of imports to protect certain industries from foreign competition. This new objective became a priority because the party that controlled the levers of political power changed, as did the strength of different economic interests that got represented in Congress. As a result, the average tariff on dutiable imports jumped from less than 20 percent in 1859 to about 50 percent during the war, where it remained for many decades. During this period, protective tariffs were a major issue in national politics: Proponents argued that they promoted the nation's growth and industrial development, while critics charged that they were inefficient and subsidized some sectors of the economy at the expense of others.

While the average tariff on dutiable imports remained high, the average tariff on total imports fell because some consumer goods (coffee and tea) and raw materials (tin and rubber) were given duty-free treatment. In this period, import tariffs were less important for revenue purposes because other taxes had been introduced. From 1860 to 1913, import duties generated about half of the government's revenue; after the introduction of the income tax in 1913, only a small fraction of government revenue has come from import duties. From 1913 to 1933, tariffs were highly unstable: the average tariff declined sharply during World War I, quickly rose again after the war, then spiked to nearly 60 percent in the early 1930s. These fluctuations reflected not only legislative changes in tariff rates, but the impact of import-price movements on specific duties as well.

This political equilibrium was disrupted by the Great Depression, which shifted political power to the low-tariff Democrats in the election of 1932. In the third era, from 1934 to the present, reciprocity became the principle objective of trade policy, with the goal of opening up foreign markets for US exports. Reciprocity involves the negotiation of agreements with other countries to reduce trade barriers; that is, the United States agrees to reduce its tariff on foreign goods in exchange for foreign tariff reductions on US goods. Up to this point, trade agreements had not been feasible, in general, because Congress wanted to maintain control of the tariff schedule and was reluctant to give negotiating authority to the president. Because high foreign trade barriers were imposed during the Great Depression and were detrimental to US exports, Congress delegated such powers to the president in the Reciprocal Trade Agreements Act of 1934.

This landmark piece of legislation moved the locus of trade policy-making from the legislature to the executive branch and marked the beginning of a new era. Since then, the United States has concluded many agreements, such as the General Agreement on Tariffs and Trade (GATT) in 1947 and the North American Free Trade Agreement (NAFTA) in 1993. Partly as a result of such agreements, tariffs have fallen to historically low levels. After collapsing in the 1940s, largely due to rising import prices during and after World War II, the average tariff on dutiable imports stood at about 10 percent by the early 1950s and then declined to about 5 percent by the late 1970s, about where it stands today.

Thus, over the long sweep of history, there have been only two ruptures that have led to major shifts in US trade policy: the Civil War, which marked the transition from revenue to restriction, and the Great Depression, which marked the transition from restriction to reciprocity. The former was associated with a shift in political power between different regions of the country; the latter was associated with a political realignment along with an important institutional change in the trade policymaking process.

In each of these periods, what guidelines did policymakers use in setting tariffs to raise revenue, restrict imports, and realize reciprocity? In fact, there are no objective, scientific criteria for determining how tariffs should be set to achieve these objectives.[11] The revenue-maximizing tariff rate depends upon the price elasticity of import demand, but Congress never really knows the precise magnitude of that elasticity and, in any event, may not wish to "maximize" revenue. There are no specific rules for determining which industries should be protected from foreign competition or the degree to which they should be protected, or even for determining whether such protection could improve economic welfare. Economists generally believe that trade restrictions reduce national income, but there are theoretical reasons for promoting "infant industries" if certain conditions are met. Yet there are few indicators that help one determine in advance which industries are candidates for such support. And reciprocity involves a political judgment about whether a particular trade agreement constitutes a "good deal" that serves the national interest.

Even if there were practical guidelines in each case, they would likely play little role in the political arena where policy decisions are made. The setting of tariffs is an inherently political exercise. Actual tariffs are "guesswork modified by compromise," as Senator Joseph Foraker of Ohio once put it. Members of Congress usually disagree intensely about using tariffs to achieve any particular objective. The policy outcomes reflect compromises and trade-offs between many different considerations (domestic and foreign) and objectives (political and economic). As House Speaker Thomas Reed (R-ME) quipped, "the only place you can pass a perfectly balanced tariff is in your mind: Congress will never pass one."[12]

As Madison seems to have predicted, restricting imports for protectionist purposes has always been the most contentious part of US trade policy, although in recent years trade agreements have also generated intense controversy. The raising or lowering of protective tariffs has always sparked heated debate because those tariffs affect which sectors of the economy will expand and which will contract.[13] By increasing the domestic price of imported goods, a protective tariff affects the allocation of labor employment and capital investment across different sectors of the economy. For these reasons, rendering these "clashing interests" subservient to the public good, as Madison put it, has always been a difficult challenge for policymakers.

THE ECONOMIC AND POLITICAL
GEOGRAPHY OF US TRADE POLICY

So why has trade policy been so hotly disputed and yet also so stable within each of the three eras discussed above? Political conflict arises because some regional economic interests benefit from exports, while others are harmed by imports. The continuity of trade policy is rooted in the country's stable economic geography (the economic interests located in various regions) along with its stable political geography (the representation of those interests in Congress).

In terms of economic geography, the production of goods that can be traded across countries—the cultivation of agricultural crops, the extraction of mineral resources, and production of manufactured goods—tend to be located in certain parts of the country, where they can remain for decades, if not centuries. The composition of trade—the types of goods exported and imported—also tends to be stable over time. This means that the nation's farmers, miners, and manufacturers have long-standing but conflicting interests over trade: some export to foreign markets and want relatively open trade, while others face foreign competition and want protective tariffs to keep imports out of the domestic market. Thus, different regions of the country, with their different producer interests, tend to have fairly stable preferences for certain trade policies. Because members of Congress usually reflect the interests of their constituents, Congressional voting patterns also show continuity over time.

The logic of this argument is illustrated in Figure I.2: the stable economic geography of production combined with the stable composition of trade gives rise to stable regional producer interests and hence a stable political geography of trade policy in Congress. We shall see throughout this book how this pattern plays out time and again, making it difficult to change existing policies unless a large shock—such as the Civil War or the Great Depression—comes along and produces a major shift in political power. Of course, should an industry's geographic location change or the composition of trade shift, regional economic interests will be affected and Congressional voting patterns will adjust. Let us consider each step in more detail.

The most important economic interests that influence trade policy are domestic producers—namely, firms and the workers they employ. It is often said that the United States has a "producer-driven" trade policy, in that members of Congress and executive branch officials are particularly responsive to the nation's farmers, miners, and manufacturers. These pro-

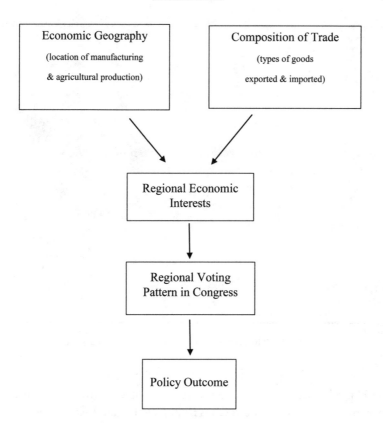

Figure I.2. Schema of the book.

ducer interests are not only deeply engaged in the policy process, but they are often concentrated in certain parts of the country. Different regions have different attributes—soil or climatic conditions in the case of agriculture, geological factors in the case of mining, or proximity to natural resources in the case of manufacturing—which leads them to specialize in producing different agricultural crops, mineral resources, and manufactured goods. For example, one usually associates cotton production with South Carolina, Mississippi, and Texas, iron and steel with Pennsylvania and Ohio, tobacco with Virginia, North Carolina, and Kentucky, wheat with Kansas and Nebraska, automobiles with Michigan, coal with Pennsylvania and West Virginia, financial services with New York, copper with Arizona and New Mexico, high technology goods with California, aircraft with Washington, and so forth.

Figure I.3 presents a stylized depiction of the economic geography of

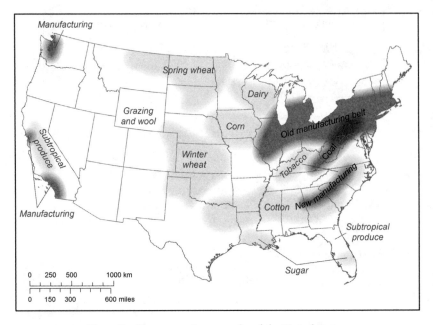

Figure I.3. The economic geography of the United States.

the United States. A long manufacturing belt that first emerged in the early nineteenth century stretches from New England across upstate New York and Pennsylvania and into the upper Midwest. This region encompasses the early textile and woolen manufactures industry (in Massachusetts and Rhode Island), the steel industry (in Pennsylvania and Ohio), and later the automobile industry (in Michigan) and the farm equipment industry (in Ohio and Illinois). Tobacco production has been concentrated in the upper South and cotton production in the lower South. In the Midwest, there is a wheat belt in Minnesota, North Dakota, and Kansas, a corn belt in Iowa, Illinois, and Indiana, and a dairy belt in Wisconsin and Michigan.

This geographic specialization in production can last for many decades, but it is not immutable.[14] For most of the nineteenth century, cotton textile production was located primarily in New England, but it gradually migrated to the South in the early twentieth century when the development of electricity freed the mills from their dependence on water power and allowed them to relocate in search of lower labor costs. Cotton production is concentrated in the South; it started in South Carolina in the 1820s and slowly moved westward toward Mississippi and Texas over the following century. The geographic concentration of iron and steel production in Pennsylvania and Ohio was originally due to local deposits of coal and iron ore, and these two states accounted for about two-thirds of domestic production of iron and steel until the mid-twentieth century. In the 1970s and 1980s, with the intensification of foreign competition, manufacturing belt states with a concentration of heavy industries became known as the Rust Belt when plants shut down or moved to the South, where a new manufacturing belt had developed.[15]

Given that the nation's farms, mines, and factories have tended to be geographically concentrated, what determines the interests of these producers with respect to trade? That depends largely on whether these producers export their goods to foreign markets or face competition from imports. As a broad generalization, producers that face foreign competition want high tariffs on imports, while producers that export to foreign markets want low tariffs on imports. The interests of exporters and import-competing producers are opposed because international trade involves the exchange of exports for imports and any policy intervention that reduces imports also reduces exports, other things being equal.

The interdependence of exports and imports has long been recognized. A proposition known as the Lerner Symmetry Theorem holds that a tax on imports is equivalent to a tax on exports. In effect, by levying a tax to restrict imports, policymakers are also levying a tax that restricts exports.[16] As a result, political conflict over trade policy often pits export-oriented producers against import-competing producers. In fact, exporters tend to be the leading interest group willing to fight against import-competing producers that demand higher tariffs. In the nineteenth century, for example, export-dependent cotton and tobacco producers in the South strongly opposed the high tariffs sought by manufacturing producers in the North.

Producers and consumers within an industry also have conflicting interests over trade. A tariff that protects domestic producers from foreign competition by increasing the price they receive also harms domestic consumers by increasing the price they must pay. In effect, the tariff subsidizes domestic producers competing against imports and taxes domestic consumers of imported goods and their domestic substitutes. And consumers are not only households but also industries that use imported raw materials and intermediate goods in their production processes. Many trade-policy conflicts have pitted producers of raw materials and intermediate goods against producers of final goods. For example, while domestic wool producers (sheep farmers) have demanded high tariffs on imported wool, domestic woolen manufactures wanted low tariffs to keep their production costs down.

These trade-policy interests of producers are stable as long as the composition of trade is stable. The composition of trade—the types of goods exported and imported—is largely determined by a country's natural resources, factor endowments (land, labor, and capital), and technology relative to other countries. Because these underlying attributes are usually slow to change, the composition of trade tends to be stable over time. The United States exported cotton and wheat two centuries ago and continues to do so today. The United States imported clothing, iron and steel goods, and tropical produce two centuries ago and continues to do so today.

Figure I.4 shows the broad commodity composition of (A) exports and (B) imports from 1821 to 2010. Prior to the Civil War, food and raw materials (wheat and cotton) comprised about two-thirds of exports, and manufactured goods (clothing and metal goods) comprised about two-thirds of imports. This pattern reflected the abundance of arable land and the scarcity of labor and capital in the United States compared to Britain and other trading partners. Of course, when a country's natural resources, factor endowments, and technology change, the pattern of trade will change as well. Throughout the nineteenth century, the United States accumulated capital and began exploiting its rich mineral deposits, particularly iron ore. This allowed it to become an exporter of mineral-intensive capital goods, such as iron and steel products, while continuing to import labor-intensive manufactured goods, such as apparel. Manufacturers of capital-intensive goods became less interested in protecting the domestic market from foreign competition and more interested in exporting to foreign markets, while manufacturers of labor-intensive goods continued to face competition from abroad and sought to maintain high tariffs. This evolution in trade patterns had a profound impact on the economic interests of various sectors of the economy and, as we will see, was eventually reflected in Congressional trade politics.

The combination of the slowly changing geographic location of production and the slowly changing composition of trade means that many states have distinctive, long-lasting economic interests with respect to trade policy. Consequently, the lineup of states in the political battle over trade policy has tended to be persistent over time. For most of the nineteenth century and well into the twentieth, there was a distinctive North-South division in Congressional voting on trade issues. Simply put, the North was the location of manufacturing production, and the South was where agricultural crops for export were cultivated.[17] For example, Figure I.5 depicts the geography of the House votes to increase tariffs in 1828 and in 1929. Although these votes are separated by more than a century, the simi-

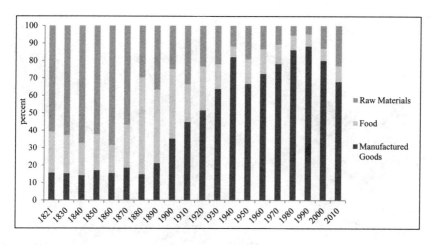

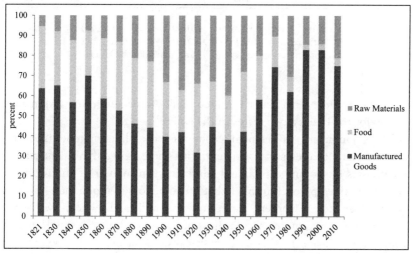

Figure I.4. Commodity composition of (A) exports and (B) imports, 1821–2010 (US Bureau of the Census 1975, series U-213–34; since 1980, from www.bea.gov).

larity in the voting pattern is striking; the correlation between the share of a state's delegates voting for the tariff in the two periods is 0.70. This illustrates how a stable economic geography combined with a stable pattern of trade leads to a stable political geography of Congressional voting. After World War II, however, Congress began voting on presidential negotiating authority and trade agreements rather than on specific tariff rates, and the voting pattern became somewhat more scrambled, with a rough East-West division emerging. Even so, the correlation between voting on the tariff in

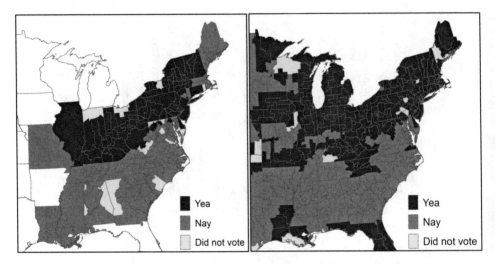

Figure I.5. House voting on tariff bills in 1828 and 1929.
Left: April 22, 1828. *Right*: May 28, 1929. (Map courtesy of Citrin
GIS/Applied Spatial Analysis Lab, Dartmouth College.)

1828 and on the North American Free Trade Agreement (NAFTA) in 1993
is 0.60 for the twenty-two states in the Union in 1828.

This emphasis on regional economic specialization and industry-
specific trade interests is consistent with there being significant adjustment costs in moving capital and labor between industries and regions.[18]
An alternative approach implies that broad factors of production—skilled
workers, unskilled workers, capital owners, and land owners—will have
similar economic interests, regardless of the particular industry in which
they are employed. In this case, political conflict over trade policy will
be based on different factors of production (capital owners against labor,
or skilled workers against unskilled workers) rather than different industries of employment (export-oriented industries against import-competing
industries).[19]

For most of US history, however, there has not been a single, unified
"capital" or "labor" interest regarding trade policy, because there are
many different types of capital and labor that are affected by trade in different ways. Capital owners and workers employed in industries that compete against imports (iron and steel, textiles and apparel) typically have a
much different view of trade policy than the capital owners and workers
employed in industries that export (agriculture, machinery, or aerospace).
In the late nineteenth and early twentieth centuries, national labor unions

generally declined to take a position on tariff policy, because individual unions disagreed over what policy to advocate, depending on the situation facing their particular industry. Therefore, economic interests were usually organized on an industry basis in producer associations (the National Wool Growers Association, the American Iron and Steel Association, and the American Farm Bureau) and labor unions (the United Auto Workers, United Steelworkers, Amalgamated Clothing and Textile Workers Union, and the United Mine Workers). The tariff schedule is also organized by product classification (chemicals, metals, clothing, etc.), not by the primary factors that are used in production (labor-intensive versus capital-intensive goods). Congress debated the tariff on a product-by-product, industry-by-industry basis, which only reinforced the incentive of business and labor groups to organize at the industry level.

That said, since the 1970s, Congress has voted on trade agreements, not tariff rates. In such agreements, specific industry interests have been somewhat less important, and a broader "class" analysis has become more relevant than in the past. The rise of intra-industry trade—as suggested by Figure I.4, in which both exports and imports are now largely manufactured goods—also means that economic interests may be less sharply defined by industry and more by intensity of factor use, since the United States tends to import labor-intensive goods and export skilled-labor and technology-intensive goods. In this case, economic interests will be defined by factor-type, or economic class, and they may form broad, opposing coalitions, such as labor unions (the AFL-CIO) or business groups (the Chamber of Commerce) that cut across different industries. Consequently, in recent decades, production workers and the labor movement, broadly speaking, have opposed trade agreements, whereas multinational firms and capital-owners have supported them.

TRADE POLICY AND POLITICAL INSTITUTIONS

Regardless of how conflicting economic interests are organized, they must thrash out their differences through the political process. So how does the political system affect the resolution of these clashing views? Madison and the framers of the Constitution designed American political institutions to make it difficult to enact large policy changes. They divided power within the federal government to provide checks and balances on the ability of any group to dominate the system. Power was dispersed across three entities—the House of Representatives, the Senate, and the executive—each of which represented a different constituency and would have to approve legislation before it became law. By creating three potential roadblocks (or veto points) to the enactment of legislation, the framers built into the political system a strong status-quo bias. This constitutes another reason for the stability of policy over time.

Article 1 of the Constitution gives Congress the authority to levy duties on imports and regulate foreign commerce. Therefore, Congress is the main forum in which economic interests play out their struggle to influence trade policy. Policy decisions come down to whether a majority of members in the House and Senate support or oppose higher or lower tariffs and accept or reject particular trade agreements.[20] Because members of Congress represent specific geographic areas with distinct economic interests, the votes of members tend to reflect the interests of their constituents, because they are unlikely to be reelected if they do otherwise. "It is easy to formulate general principles," concluded John Sherman (1895, 2:1128), a leading Republican senator in the late nineteenth century, "but when we come to apply them to the great number of articles named on the tariff list, we find that the interests of their constituents control the action of Senators and Members."[21] Thus it is not surprising that representatives from Pennsylvania and Ohio support steel interests, Louisiana and Florida support sugar interests, Mississippi and Texas support cotton interests, California and Washington support aerospace interests, and so forth. Satisfying the demands of these producer interests was the primary mission of Congress. "The dominant congressional opinion on the tariff" for many years, Fetter (1933, 427) notes, was "a tacitly accepted belief that the way to promote the national welfare was to give each group what it wanted to make its members individually prosperous, without any consideration of the relation of such action to larger problems of national policy."

Of course, politicians can also abandon long-held views on trade policy when the interests of their constituents change. Daniel Webster of Massachusetts spoke eloquently in Congress for many years about the importance of free trade and open commerce when his state was dominated by shipping and mercantile interests. When cotton textiles became an important part of the state's economy in the 1820s, Webster adjusted his position and began supporting protective tariffs. (This gave rise to many chortles on the floor of the Senate where his earlier speeches had not been forgotten.)

Because political representation is based on geography, shifts in population have changed the political strength of different regions, and hence of different trade-related interests, over time. Figure I.6 shows the regional share of seats in the House of Representatives due to the admission of new states and the reapportionment of seats after each census. Before the Civil

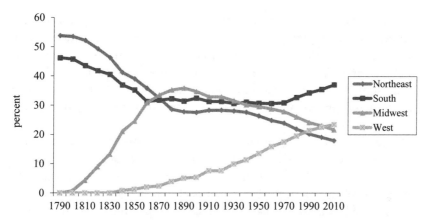

Figure I.6. Regional representation in the House of Representatives, 1790–2010. (http://www.census.gov/population/apportionment/data/2010_apportionment_results.html.)

War, the House was about equally divided between the North and South, but rapid westward expansion soon meant that both sides had to appeal to votes from the Midwest to achieve a majority. The twentieth century saw the rise of the far West. More recently, the North and Midwest have lost seats in the House, making it difficult for heavy industries and unionized workers in the old manufacturing belt to win support for import restrictions or defeat trade agreements.

There is no reason to believe that opposing trade interests—whether export-oriented and import-competing industries, or producers and consumers within an industry—will be equally balanced and wield the same amount of political power in Congress. First of all, trade interests are not equally distributed across regions. For example, in the nineteenth century, exports were highly concentrated in just a few commodities, particularly cotton and tobacco, which came from just a few southern states. Meanwhile, imports consisted of many different types of manufactured goods—cotton and woolen textiles, iron and steel products, pottery and earthenware—that competed against a large number of producers scattered across many states in the Northeast and upper Midwest. Because Congressional representation is based on geography, export interests had fewer advocates in Congress than import-competing interests.

Different groups also have different incentives to organize for political activity. Although the United States exported large amounts of cotton, wheat, and corn in the nineteenth century, the trade interests of these farmers were very uneven: cotton producers were highly dependent on foreign markets (about two thirds of the crop was exported), wheat producers less so (about a quarter of the crop was exported), and corn farmers hardly at all (only a tiny share of the crop was exported). Therefore, the incentive of these exporters to push for open trade policies varied considerably. By contrast, just about any industry competing against imports has a strong incentive to lobby for higher tariffs even if the foreign share of the domestic market was small.

The same is true for producers and consumers of a particular good. Even if the economic stakes facing each are about equal, their political strength can be highly unequal because they have different incentives to engage in political action.[22] The benefits of import restrictions are highly concentrated on a few producers who have a strong incentive to organize and support the policy, while the costs are spread widely across many consumers, who have very little incentive to organize and oppose the policy. As Vilfredo Pareto (1971 [1909], 379) pointed out long ago, "A protectionist measure provides large benefits to a small number of people, and causes a very great number of consumers a slight loss." This makes it relatively easy to impose import duties, as does the legislative practice of logrolling, or vote trading.[23]

Furthermore, once in place, import restrictions are difficult to remove. A reduction in a tariff will bring certain harm to particular groups and uncertain gains for others. As a result, those facing large capital losses will fight against such a policy change much more vigorously than the many potential beneficiaries will fight for the policy change.[24] This makes it difficult for members of Congress to vote for lower tariffs; it has been said that doing so is an "unnatural act" for any politician.[25] For example, although the 1988 US-Canada Free Trade Agreement was relatively uncontroversial, Senator Bob Packwood (R-OR) described how hard it was for many members of Congress to vote for it. If the agreement was opposed by one vocal industry in a senator's home state, he pointed out, that senator was almost certain to vote against it, even if the pact would also benefit ten other special interests in the state. "Those that are hurt are infinitely madder, and have longer memories, than those that are helped," Packwood said. Thus, a "no" vote to protect one industry from damage "is going to be remembered more than a 'yes' that helped ten."[26]

What about the executive branch? In the nineteenth and early twentieth centuries, presidents were expected to defer to Congress on legislative matters and did not play a major role in trade policy. For example, in 1888, Senator John Sherman instructed President-elect Benjamin Harrison that a president "should have no policy distinct from that of his party and that is better represented in Congress than in the executive."[27] Presidents could always propose policy changes, particularly if their party had a legislative majority, but ultimately Congress would decide whether to enact such proposals and what the content of the final legislation would be.

Since the passage of the Reciprocal Trade Agreements Act in 1934, however, presidents have taken a much greater leadership role in the formation of trade policy. This legislation allowed the president to reach trade agreements with foreign countries. Since then, presidents have led Congress in undertaking new trade initiatives, or presidential passivity has led to policy drift. Yet Congress still retains ultimate authority over trade policy. Even though Congress has not passed any general tariff legislation since 1930, Congress has had to approve any trade agreement negotiated by the executive branch since the 1970s. This has sometimes led to epic battles, such as the 1993 debate over the passage of NAFTA.

As the chief executive, the president has a national constituency and thus has a different perspective on trade policy than individual members of Congress. Whereas Congress views trade based on how it affects the interests of their constituents, the president is insulated from the parochial concerns of any particular group of producers. Presidents tend to view international trade based on how it affects the nation as a whole and often use trade policy to achieve foreign-policy goals. As a result, they usually aim to expand trade and see trade agreements as a way of projecting America's power and influence around the world. At the same time, presidents do occasionally support import restrictions for domestic political purposes.

POLITICAL PARTIES AND IDEOLOGY

Of course, trade policy is not simply a matter of how economic interests play out in Congress, because not all regions of the country have sharply defined interests with respect to trade. This means that political parties, ideology, and other factors also have the potential to influence the course of trade policy.

Madison's observation that different economic interests "give rise to the spirit of party and faction" was, of course, prophetic. For most of US history, American politics has been dominated by two political parties, each taking a different stand on trade policy. For more than a century after the advent of the Second Party system in the 1830s, Democrats advocated low import tariffs, and Whigs and Republicans advocated high protective tariffs. This partisan divide had a geographic basis: Democrats originally

drew most of their support from the agrarian South, where farmers produced staple crops for export, and Whigs and Republicans drew most of
their support from the industrial North, where manufacturers faced foreign competition.

Different parties have dominated American politics in different periods, which has helped to establish and maintain a particular trade policy
equilibrium. In the three decades before the Civil War, Democrats were
politically stronger than the Whigs and kept tariffs relatively low, because
they viewed revenue as the main objective of trade policy. After the Civil
War, Republicans were politically stronger than the Democrats and kept
tariffs relatively high because they supported the protection of domestic
industries as the main objective of trade policy. After the Great Depression, the Democrats were politically stronger than the Republicans and
helped push tariffs back down again, because they supported reciprocity as
the main objective of trade policy.

After World War II, the United States entered an unusual period in
which a bipartisan consensus favored reciprocal trade agreements. This
consensus emerged as much for foreign-policy reasons as for economic
ones. Then, in the 1970s, two things began to happen. First, the geographic
regions from which the parties drew most of their support began to shift:
The Democratic base shifted to the North, and the Republican base shifted
to the South and West. Second, the economy became exposed to greater
foreign competition, which particularly affected the industrial heartland
in the upper Midwest. As a result, Democratic support for open trade policies began to weaken, and Republican support for open trade policies began to strengthen.[28] By the 1980s, the parties had largely switched positions on the issue. By the 1990s, the bipartisan consensus on trade policy
had frayed, and it was once again a polarizing issue in American politics.

A timeless question in political science is whether parties matter for
policy outcomes. To some, political parties simply reflect underlying economic interests and therefore do not have an independent effect on policy. "There is much truth in the suggestion that special interests in one
guise or another are more potent in securing the legislation that governs
the country than are the political parties under whose banners the politicians are elected to hold office," Oscar Underwood (1928, 404), an Alabama
Democrat, once conceded. Distinguishing the impact of political parties
and economic interests on policy outcomes is complicated by the fact that
they have a symbiotic relationship: interests are attracted to the party that
comes closest to supporting their views, while the parties are positioning
themselves to gain the support of various interests to boost their electoral

fortunes. Because of this interdependence, a straight party-line vote in Congress does not necessarily mean that only partisan factors are at work.

In fact, constituent interests often take priority over partisan positions when members of Congress face a conflict between the two. "The real struggle in tariff legislation is one of *sections*," John Sherman (1895, 2:1085) noted. "The Republican party affirms that it is for a protective tariff. The Democratic party declares that it is for a tariff for revenue only; but generally, when Republicans and Democrats together are framing a tariff, each Member or Senator consults the interest of his 'deestrict' or state." For example, Louisiana is a case where interests dominated party loyalty: in the nineteenth century, it was a solidly Democratic state whose representatives almost always voted for higher tariffs (against the party's position) because local sugar producers wanted to keep out foreign sugar.

At the same time, political parties care about many other issues beyond trade policy. Not all states have sharply defined economic interests with respect to trade, and yet they are represented in Congress by members of one party or another. These party members are usually willing to vote with their colleagues on trade issues so long as other members vote with them on matters of greater concern to their own constituents. Perhaps for this reason, studies of Congressional voting have shown that political parties do, in fact, have an impact on voting patterns, even after controlling for district-level economic interests.[29]

Because parties matter for legislative outcomes, large swings in political power—which can occur for reasons completely unrelated to changes in trade or trade-related economic interests—often bring about significant changes in trade policy. A sweeping electoral victory by one party can generate such a policy shift because the two parties are dependent on different economic interests. Thus, even when underlying state-level economic interests are unchanged, the political power of those interests can rise or fall when there is a shift in party dominance after an election.

Because the political parties usually take opposing positions on trade issues, the passage of trade legislation often requires a unified government, in which the same party controls the House, Senate, and the presidency. Unified governments were responsible for the passage of every major piece of trade-related legislation from the early 1840s through the 1960s. Changes in unified government from one party to another are fairly rare. In the 150 years since the Civil War, there have been only ten transitions to a new unified government under a different party. These occurred after the elections of 1892, 1896, 1912, 1920, 1932, 1952, 1960, 2000, 2008, and 2016. On average, there is a change in party control only once every fifteen years. Each of these occasions created an opportunity for a different political party to put its stamp on policy, sometimes (but not always) bringing important changes to trade policy. The infrequency with which one party replaces another in controlling government is an important factor in explaining the persistence of existing policies. In fact, about 40 percent of the seventy-seven Congresses since the end of the Civil War have been under divided government, during which time major policy changes were nearly impossible.[30]

While economic interests and shifts in partisan political strength have clearly influenced the course of trade policy, the role of ideology is more difficult to establish.[31] On the one hand, it is easy to dismiss ideology as being something too amorphous to affect Congressional decisions. Some believe that ideas simply provide rhetorical cover for views that are actually rooted in interests. The writer Ambrose Bierce (1911, 258) once defined politics as "a strife of interests masquerading as a contest of principles." Even Alexis de Tocqueville (2004 [1848], 202) supported this interpretation in writing that a politician "first tries to identify his own interests and find out what similar interests might be joined with this. He then casts about to discover whether there might not by chance exist some doctrine or principle around which this new association might be organized, so that it may present itself to the world and gain ready acceptance."

And yet the role of ideas cannot be dismissed entirely, because not every participant in the trade-policy process has an economic stake in the matter. This implies that interests alone provide an incomplete account of political motivation. Ideas are systems of beliefs that allow policymakers to understand and debate the specific policy issues that confront them. The framing of the tariff issue—the rationale or justification for supporting or opposing a particular position—could enhance political support for the status quo or support a change in policy. Many views about trade policy are related to one's political philosophy regarding the goals of government policy. Should the federal government intervene in the economy to achieve certain outcomes? Is the manufacturing sector special and does it deserve protection from foreign competition? Other ideas relate to an economic understanding of cause and effect. Do higher tariffs increase or decrease wages? Do higher tariffs promote industrial development or just subsidize inefficient industries? Do trade agreements help big corporations and hurt workers, or do they promote competition and benefit consumers? The purported answers to these questions help to define which policies are viewed as economically desirable or politically acceptable at any given point in time.

In particular, the lessons drawn from past experience can shape the public debate by influencing what policies are believed to be desirable. For many decades after the Civil War, the economic growth and development of the United States was associated with the policy of high protective tariffs. Regardless of its validity, the perception that protection was responsible for that growth helped shape political reality, making it very difficult for politicians and the public to support a significant change in policy. Later, the public's association of the Hawley-Smoot tariff of 1930 with the Great Depression and the catastrophic collapse of world trade demolished the argument that higher import duties would keep the economy strong. In the post–World War II period, multilateral cooperation to reduce tariffs became identified with expanding trade, a growing economy, and more peaceful international relations. This experience shaped perceptions of the issue among many members of Congress and the public who did not have a direct stake in one particular policy. By the 2000s, job losses and the decline in manufacturing employment were associated with increased trade with Mexico and China and led to demands to limit imports from those countries. Narrow economic interests were not solely responsible for shifts in prevailing opinion; rather, these shifts seemed to arise from broader lessons drawn from experience.

Furthermore, economic interests are sometimes passive until political entrepreneurs, motivated by ideas or driven by ideological passions, recruit them in support of a particular cause. Instead of simply accepting existing policy as they find it, politicians can become leaders who can mobilize dormant interests and form new political coalitions to support a change in policy. During the antebellum period, Henry Clay's notion of an "American System" became an effective way of describing policies to protect domestic producers from foreign competition and develop the home market. This policy was ultimately rooted in economic interests, but a large political coalition in support of it is unlikely to have coalesced without an overarching idea that gave various separate interests a plausible rationale for working together toward a common goal.

Similarly, the outbreak of World War I led a congressman from Tennessee to believe that governments fighting over markets and scrambling to create colonial trade blocs had been an important cause of the conflict. He became convinced that freer world trade could make a positive contribution to world peace. That congressman, Cordell Hull, eventually became Secretary of State (serving from 1933–44) and worked tirelessly to help reduce trade barriers around the world. His purpose was both political (world peace) as well as economic (world prosperity). More than any other individual, Hull was the driving force behind the reciprocal trade agreements program, the framework that guides US trade policy to this day.

Hull's attachment to certain ideas, not the demands of powerful interests, was critical to moving policy in a new direction. Though he came from the traditionally pro-trade South, Hull was not simply acting on behalf of economic interests, and he did little to cultivate them in building political support for his approach. Rather, he simply sought to persuade others about the merits of his views, which is why so many people at the time dismissed his quest as futile. He ultimately played a critical role in changing the direction of US trade policy. As Senator Paul H. Douglas (1972, 476) wrote, "Thus, the shrewd, hillbilly free trader and militia captain from the Tennessee mountains outwitted for beneficent ends the high-priced protectionist lawyers and lobbyists of Pittsburgh and Wall Street."

In fact, the one regime change in US trade policy, the enactment of the Reciprocal Trade Agreements Act of 1934 that authorized the president to undertake trade negotiations, is difficult to explain on the basis of the political strength of various economic interests. There are no compelling interest-group based explanations for the origin of this legislation. Rather, this institutional change in trade policy was tied to shifts in the dominant ideas that guide policy. Jeffrey Legro (2000) argues that changes in collective ideas are likely to occur when a policy generates outcomes that deviate from societal expectations, those outcomes are undesirable, and a viable alternative policy exists. These three conditions were met in the early 1930s. The Hawley-Smoot tariff of 1930 led to foreign retaliation against US exports and a collapse in global trade. This disastrous, and largely unexpected, outcome led politicians and the public to associate high tariffs with the Great Depression. This allowed negotiated tariff reductions to emerge as a credible alternative to existing policy and a potential solution to the problems caused by the collapse of world trade. As a result, an enormous sea change in ideas occurred: the case for protectionism was weakened, and freer trade was gradually accepted as a viable alternative. Hull stepped into power at precisely this moment.

Have the ideas of economists also played a role in promoting more open trade policies? Although economists are widely known for pointing out the gains from trade and the costs of trade restrictions, they have not had much influence in shaping policy outcomes throughout history. Frank Fetter (1933, 413) went so far as to write that "in the field of the tariff, the teachings and writings of American economists have been virtually without effect in the education of public opinion or the formulation of public policy." In June 1930, a petition signed by more than one thousand economists urged President Herbert Hoover not to sign the Hawley-Smoot tariff bill, but of course he signed it anyway. Since the Great Depression, however, economists have played a larger role in economic policy debates and may have had some impact in giving politicians pause before endorsing protectionist policies, although it is difficult to know how influential they have been.

In sum, trade policy has always been controversial because there are clashing economic interests at stake, as Madison understood long ago. While Daniel Webster grumbled that the tariff was "a tedious disagreeable subject" for the legislators forced to deal with it, the political and economic debates about trade policy have always been spirited.[32] Studying past controversies over trade will help us understand whether today's disputes are really different from those in the past. The history of trade policy will also show us the path by which the United States found itself in the globalized world of today.

PART I

Revenue

CHAPTER ONE

The Struggle for Independence, 1763–1789

The regulation of America's foreign trade played an important role in shaping events during the critical period around the country's move toward independence and nationhood. While the conflict between Britain and the thirteen North American colonies was ultimately about political power and sovereignty, many disputes concerned the restrictions and taxes that Britain imposed on colonial commerce. Lacking any political voice in Parliament to influence those policies, the colonists responded by employing the only weapons at their disposal, including economic pressure through the boycott of British goods. After having fought successfully for independence, however, Americans discovered that engaging in trade outside the British Empire was difficult. These problems were compounded by a weak central government under the Articles of Confederation, which prevented Congress from establishing a national trade policy or imposing import duties to raise revenue. These trade-policy difficulties were key factors in setting the stage for the constitutional convention of 1787.

TRADE AND THE AMERICAN COLONIES

For more than a century after the first permanent English settlement in North America was established at Jamestown in 1607, the New World settlers were heavily dependent on foreign trade. Trade was essential to the well-being of the new arrivals, furnishing them with clothing and blankets, nails and firearms, cooking implements and metal goods, and other tools and materials that could not be produced locally. Without these imports, the standard of living of the colonists might have suffered so much that they would not have stayed. As McCusker and Menard (1985, 71) put it, "Overseas commerce did not merely make colonial life comfortable, it made it possible."

Overseas trade with Britain was an integral part of the economic life of the North American colonies, even though they were separated by some three thousand miles across the Atlantic Ocean. Through the seventeenth and eighteenth centuries, the colonists paid for imports of manufactured goods from Britain by exporting cash crops, such as tobacco and rice, and abundant local produce, such as fish and wood. The terms of trade—the price of exported goods relative to the price of imported goods—was a key determinant of economic welfare in the colonies. A rise in the price of tobacco because of increased European demand, for example, would enable the colonists to import more manufactured goods in exchange for those exports. A decline in the price of commodity exports not only made European imports more expensive to procure, but reduced agricultural income and diminished the economic prospects of the colonies. As a result, fluctuations in the prices of exported and imported goods had a pronounced impact on the growth and welfare of the colonial economy.[1]

By the early eighteenth century, New World abundance along with overseas trade allowed the colonists to enjoy a relatively high standard of living. Adjusting for the different price levels between Britain and the colonies (that is, using a purchasing-power comparison), real per capita income in the colonies was at least 50 percent higher than in England between 1700 and 1774.[2] This brought a steady stream of European migrants to America, and the colonies grew in size and economic importance. By 1770, the population of Britain's thirteen North American colonies was 2.1 million, most living near the seacoast. By contrast, the population of Great Britain was just over 7 million at the time. In terms of economic output, the colonial economy was about a third the size of Britain's in 1774. Thus, by the late eighteenth century, North America was by no means a small and insignificant part of the world economy.

The main economic activity in the colonies was the cultivation of agricultural goods and the production of home crafts. About 85 percent of the labor force was employed in the agricultural sector, some producing crops for export but most for local consumption. Even though colonial society was largely rural and agrarian, nearly all Americans were linked in some way to the larger world market. Whether they were raising livestock in New England, wheat and corn in Pennsylvania, tobacco in Virginia, or rice in South Carolina, the colonists did not practice local self-sufficiency

unless circumstances—mainly distance to the market—so dictated.[3] As
Jensen (1969, 108–9) notes,

> The American farmers at the outset of the Revolution were utterly de-
> pendent, therefore, for their growth and prosperity, on the sale of farm
> produce in overseas markets, as were American fishermen and lumber-
> men. Any proper economic map of America at the beginning of the
> Revolution would show America as a mere fringe between the Atlantic
> Ocean and the Appalachian Mountains, with a network of lines criss-
> crossing the Atlantic between America and the West Indies, Africa,
> the Mediterranean, and the British Isles. Most Americans of the eigh-
> teenth century understood this, and they were more concerned with
> what went on in those areas than they were with what went on a hun-
> dred miles inland from the ocean, for it was in the far-flung seaports
> scattered around the Atlantic Ocean that Americans marketed their
> surpluses of tobacco, rice, indigo, wheat, and Indian corn. Hence it was
> that American newspapers were filled with political news, and crop
> and weather conditions even in such far-away places as Turkey and
> Russia, for what happened there might well affect the price of Ameri-
> can wheat and corn.

The North American colonies could be divided into four economic regions, each endowed with different resources and hence specializing in
different productive activities.[4] With its forests and proximity to the sea,
New England was dominated by shipping-related activities, such as shipbuilding, shipping services, fishing, and whaling. Merchant shipping gave
rise to production in related industries, especially wood and lumber (for
masts and ship construction, caskets and barrels), finance, and insurance.
Although many small farms in the region produced corn, wheat, and livestock, New England had relatively poor agricultural land and was a net
importer of food.

The Mid-Atlantic states of New York, Pennsylvania, New Jersey, and
Delaware were more economically diverse. The ports of New York and
Philadelphia were major urban centers and hubs of commerce, but were
linked to the domestic coastal trade as much as overseas trade. New York
was a center for commercial services. Philadelphia, the largest city in colonial America, was the home to small manufacturers and craft production, including iron works and flour mills, making the region's residents
somewhat less dependent upon manufactured imports from Britain. The

area's staple products were grain and flour: many small farms in New York and Pennsylvania grew wheat, corn, barley, and rye, some of which was exported to the British Empire.

The South produced major cash crops for bulk export: the upper South (Maryland, Virginia, and North Carolina) specialized in tobacco, while the lower South (South Carolina and Georgia) produced rice and indigo. These crops were produced on relatively large farms employing slave labor that had been transported from Africa. This region had the highest per capita exports and the strongest dependence on the world market, but also had the least diversified economy and relied on British financing and transport to conduct its trade.

Thus, the different regions of the colonies specialized in the production of different exportable goods: tobacco from Virginia and Maryland, wheat and flour from Pennsylvania and New York, rice and indigo from Carolina, and wood products and fish from New England. The top three commodity exports—tobacco (27 percent), wheat, flour and breadstuffs (19 percent), and rice (11 percent)—comprised well over half of total merchandise exports from 1768 to 1772. New England also provided shipping services and earned more income from the carrying trade and insurance than from exporting any single commodity.[5]

The earnings from merchandise exports and shipping services enabled the colonies to pay for their imports. The port cities were the key points of contact with the rest of the world, and most foreign goods were imported through the seaports of Philadelphia, New York, Boston, and Charleston. About 80 percent of these imports consisted of manufactured goods from Britain. Woolens and linens were among the most important, but imports included a variety of other products, such as paper, glass, and metal goods. Commodities for household consumption, such as tea and alcoholic beverages, also made up a sizeable portion of imports.[6]

The importance of foreign trade in an economy is commonly measured by the ratio of exports or imports to gross domestic product (GDP). In 1774, imports from Britain amounted to roughly 8 to 9 percent of colonial GDP.[7] Because Britain accounted for more than 80 percent of America's imports prior to the Revolutionary War, the ratio of total merchandise imports to GDP was probably about 10 percent. This is an imperfect indicator of the economic importance of trade, because the prices of all traded goods were determined by the world market and thereby had a pervasive effect throughout the colonial economy. These prices connected all households to the world market, either through prices they received for the produce they sold or the prices they paid for the goods they purchased.

THE ECONOMIC CONSEQUENCES
OF THE NAVIGATION ACTS

Although the commodity composition of America's foreign trade was largely determined by regional resource endowments and driven by market forces, the geographic pattern of trade was not. Instead, the British Parliament had enacted the Navigation Acts, which artificially channeled colonial trade through Britain and its territories in the West Indies. These trade regulations and subsequent taxes and customs duties led to friction between Britain and America and helped stimulate colonial demands for independence.

The purpose of the Navigation Acts was to promote Britain's maritime power and ensure that trade within the Empire served its commercial interests. First applied to the American colonies in 1651, the Navigation Acts involved a complex web of government policies. These mercantilist policies—designed to promote British commercial interests by promoting exports and restricting imports—regulated the nationality of the ships and crews employed in British and colonial commerce, restricted the destinations to which colonial goods could be shipped and the sources of colonial imports, favored selected British industries with subsidies, preferential tariffs, charter monopolies, and other encouragements, and prohibited the development of certain industries in the colonies that might harm producers in Britain.

From America's standpoint, the most important regulation was the requirement that almost all its exports and imports be shipped via Britain. In terms of exports, all "enumerated" goods had to pass through a British port before reaching their final destination. About three-quarters of American exports to Britain were enumerated, the most important of which was tobacco. Although American tobacco received preferential treatment in Britain (discriminatory duties were imposed on tobacco imported from Spanish and Portuguese colonies), the overwhelming majority of tobacco exports was reexported to Europe. This indirect routing imposed extra costs on American exporters and reduced the prices received by tobacco planters. If tobacco had not been enumerated and could be sold directly to European customers, the income of tobacco planters would have been anywhere from 15 to 35 percent higher, according to Sawers (1992, 269). Thus, the Navigation Acts imposed a significant burden on a politically influential, trade-dependent group, the Chesapeake tobacco farmers of Maryland and Virginia.

Rice exports were partially enumerated; exports destined for southern

Europe could be shipped directly, but those for northern Europe required passage through Britain. This limited the adverse impact of these regulations on the prices received by planters in South Carolina. Other exports benefited from British bounties (subsidies). These included exports of indigo, naval stores, and lumber, although the benefit to the colonies was not large because the subsidy margin and volume of exports were relatively small. Other agricultural goods, notably wheat and flour, had limited access to the British market but were given preferential access in the British West Indies.

The Navigation Acts did not significantly distort colonial imports. Most of America's imports from Britain were made in Britain, the world's leading producer of manufactured goods. For some of these goods, such as gunpowder, linen, sailcloth, silk, and refined sugar, the colonies benefited from British export subsidies that lowered their price to American consumers. Britain also permitted the colonies to import certain products directly from the British West Indies and southern Europe, such as salt for curing fish and Madeira wine. However, most non-British imports, whether from Europe or Asia, first had to be shipped through Britain. About 20 percent of the colonies' imports from Britain consisted of foreign goods that originally came from Asia, mainly tea and pepper, or from Europe. This artificial routing through Britain involved extra fees, commissions, warehouse rents, and transportation costs and is estimated to have raised the costs of imports of European and Asian goods by about 20 percent.[8]

In a pioneering calculation, Lawrence Harper (1939) tallied up the costs and benefits to the colonies from these trade restrictions for the year 1773. He estimated the total cost to be $3.3 million, only about 2 percent of colonial income. The enumeration of tobacco was by far the largest component, accounting for three-quarters of the total cost. Thomas (1965) revised Harper's calculation down to $2.7 million, but also took into account the benefits to the colonies from being part of the British Empire. These benefits were estimated to be $1.8 million and arose in part from the lower insurance rates on shipping due to the protection provided by the Royal Navy. In this broader calculation, the net cost to the colonies came to just $0.9 million, a slight 0.6 percent of colonial income.[9] As McCusker and Menard (1985, 354) conclude, "Whatever the costs of membership in the British Empire, they were largely offset by the benefits: naval protection; access to a large free-trading area; easy credit and cheap manufactures; and restricted foreign competition."

The fact that the aggregate burden of Britain's commercial policies on the colonies was small, however, does not mean that these restrictions were unimportant in spurring demands for independence. Only a minority of the colonial population is believed to have actively supported independence in 1776, and this vocal and politically powerful minority may have been precisely those most affected by Britain's trade policies. In fact, about 90 percent of the economic burden of the Navigation Acts is believed to have fallen upon the southern colonies, particularly tobacco planters in Maryland and Virginia, and might have reduced the region's income by as much as 2.5 percent in 1770.[10]

It was not a coincidence that these planters strongly supported independence. Virginians believed, apparently with good reason, that freeing the tobacco trade from Britain's commercial regulations would make the crop much more profitable. Indeed, in the 1640s, Virginia's House of Burgesses petitioned for a "free export of their Tobacco to foreign Markets directly," but their request was rejected by the British Privy Council. In 1774, in a draft of instructions to its delegates to the Continental Congress, the Virginia legislature declared that "the exercise of a free trade with all parts of the world, possessed by the American colonists as of natural right, and which no law of their own had taken away or abridged" was a subject of "unjust incroachment" by the British authorities.[11]

Another group that held grievances against British policy were urban merchants in Boston, New York, and Philadelphia. These merchants were also dismayed by British commercial regulations that restricted their freedom to trade with other regions of the world. "The merchants of revolutionary America made up but a very small part of the population, but they wielded economic and political power within most of the Colonies far out of proportion to their numbers," Jensen (1969, 109) notes. Meanwhile, farmers who made up the bulk of the population "did not share the economic grievances of either merchants and tradesmen of the coastal cities or of the tobacco growing planters of Virginia and Maryland" and only later supported the movement toward independence.[12]

In sum, the colonies were not impoverished and exploited victims of British rule. The costs of British mercantilist trade regulations were roughly offset by the benefits of protection within the British Empire. In fact, the colonies had conducted their business under the Navigation Acts without complaint for more than a century and had flourished as a result. "The dispute between Britain and the colonies was not over Parliament's right to regulate this or that trade, to tax a particular activity, or to pursue a specific policy," McCusker and Menard (1985, 357) conclude. "The conflict centered on the issue of power over the long haul, on the shape of things to come, on who would determine the future of the British Empire in the Americas."[13] In a comprehensive review of contemporary writings, Dickerson (1951) could not find any evidence that the Navigation Acts or Britain's commercial policies were a major source of complaint in the colonial assemblies. At the same time, such trade regulations did adversely affect certain groups, particularly tobacco farmers. They and others were to become among the most vocal proponents of independence and played a catalytic role in the drive for national sovereignty.

With the colonies generally prospering under British rule, something must have changed to bring about the resistance that ultimately led to revolution. That change began after the end of the Seven Years War in 1763, when Britain attempted to institute new policies that the colonists believed would threaten their comfortable state. After 1763, British policy aimed to extract revenue from the colonies to pay for the defense costs incurred on their behalf during the war. This policy shift implied a major increase in the tax burden on the colonies. While most colonists accepted Britain's long-standing regulation of America's trade, they resisted British attempts to put more of the financial burden of supporting the colonies onto the colonists themselves. By discounting the benefits of protection within the British Empire, the colonists saw the new taxes and regulations as a threat to their prosperity and future well-being. The colonies were in a position of economic strength, not weakness, and this gave them the confidence to confront their overseas rulers.

SHIFTING THE TAX BURDEN

The Seven Years War in 1763, known as the French and Indian War in the United States, was undertaken in large part to protect the colonies from neighboring threats. The war proved to be very expensive, increasing the British government's debt from less than £80 million in 1757 to £134 million in 1764. The annual interest on this debt amounted to nearly £5 million at a time when the government's annual revenue was only about £9 million.[14]

In addition to the fiscal challenge of financing this debt, the British government had to pay the considerable ongoing cost of protecting the newly enlarged North American territories. As a result of its victory, Britain acquired a huge amount of land—not just most of North America east of the Mississippi River, but Canada and parts of the West Indies as well—and it all needed to be defended. The cost of maintaining a standing army of ten thousand soldiers in North America amounted to nearly 4 percent of the British government's budget.[15] With the external threat of the French and Indians having been removed, Americans failed to appreciate the substantial costs that Britain incurred in defending the colonies.

Given the economic size of the colonies and the fact that expenses had been and were being incurred on their behalf, British officials naturally thought that the colonists should contribute more to the costs of defense and the servicing of debts. Therefore, successive British administrations sought to raise additional revenues from what they viewed as the wealthy and undertaxed American colonies. To the dismay of the British authorities, most of the measures they enacted were met with stiff resistance.

In the Sugar Act of 1764, Parliament required that the colonies pay a three-shilling duty on sugar and molasses imported from places other than the British West'Indies. This was actually half of the official duty that dated back to 1733, but that tax had been routinely ignored by American merchants and British customs officials. The customs service was also reinvigorated to better enforce existing laws to reduce smuggling and increase revenue. These measures generated grumbles in the colonies, but no outright opposition.

The Stamp Act of 1765 levied duties on public documents and printed materials, such as legal documents, newspapers, property deeds, and playing cards. Although such taxes were common in Britain, these new internal taxes provoked sharp protests in the colonies. Residents of the commercial colonies, principally Massachusetts and New York, argued that they had not been properly represented in Parliament for such internal taxation to be accepted. They took the position that Britain had the authority to regulate the foreign trade of the colonies, but could not impose internal taxes without their consent. British officials rejected the distinction between external and internal taxes and asserted that they had the power to impose any taxes they chose.

Aside from harassing the local officials responsible for enforcing the Stamp Act, colonial opponents of the measure searched for a way of eliminating the tax altogether. The Stamp Act Congress, the first joint meeting of representatives of all the colonies initiated on their own, sought to formulate a unified response to the British action. In October 1765, colonial delegates adopted a Declaration of Rights, which complained that "the duties imposed by several late acts of Parliament, from the peculiar circumstances of these colonies, will be extremely burthensome and grievous, and, from the scarcity of specie, the payment of them absolutely impracticable." The Congress also stated that taxes should not be imposed without their consent and noted that "the restrictions imposed . . . on the trade of these colonies will render them unable to purchase the manufactures of Great Britain." The colonies also agreed to try to force Britain to repeal the Stamp Act through commercial pressure in the form of non-importation agreements.[16]

The non-importation movement began as a private initiative. In late October, two hundred leading merchants in New York vowed to stop importing British goods starting in January 1766. Philadelphia and Boston merchants soon followed. The leaders of the boycott thought that the lost sales would force British exporters to lobby on their behalf in London. In November 1765, General Thomas Gage, the British commander in Boston, described the strategy this way:

> Their first plan of clamor, in terrifying the stamp officers, and even threats of rebellion to prevent the stamps being issued, has been completed throughout. And in order to gain the merchants in Great Britain to their interest, the American merchants have wrote that no dry goods may be sent out to them, unless the Stamp Act is repealed, and some go as far as to say they will not pay their debts but upon that condition; and they flatter themselves, from all these circumstances that the Parliament will be prevailed upon to repeal the act.[17]

The colonial merchants were not simply acting out of principle. They were also taking advantage of the opportunity to reduce their large inventories, which had accumulated during the recession that followed the initial boom at the end of the French and Indian War, at much higher prices than would otherwise be possible.

The impact of the colonial boycott of British goods is uncertain, because non-importation lasted just a few months and coincided with a general economic slowdown. The volume of America's imports from Britain fell 7 percent in 1766, after having fallen 14 percent in 1765, making it hard to disentangle the impact of non-importation from the recession in reducing trade.[18] The falloff in North American orders was keenly felt in Britain, which was also experiencing an economic downturn, and British merchants flooded Parliament with petitions describing the hardship and loss of employment arising from the cancellation of American orders for their goods.[19]

Even if the economic impact of non-importation was modest compared to the recession, the political impact was large enough that the protesters achieved their objective: pressure from British manufacturers was an important factor in Parliament's decision to repeal the Stamp Act. Recognizing that the Stamp Act and sugar duties were generating little revenue and much ill will, Parliament repealed both measures in March 1766. The non-importation movement quickly collapsed once word of the repeal arrived in the colonies.

However, along with the repeal, Parliament also passed the Declaratory Act, which asserted its full power and authority to make laws and govern the colonies and reiterated its legal right to tax both external and internal commerce. With Britain still desperate to tap into the colonial economy as a source of revenue, the new chancellor of the exchequer, Charles Townshend, proposed establishing customs commissioners in the major colonial port cities to strengthen the enforcement of the customs laws and ensure the collection of import duties. Townshend also proposed a new set of low duties on many different commodities—initially on tea, glass, paper, lead, and painting materials, and later on other items—to discourage smuggling and the evasion of duties. Townshend was careful to ensure that these duties were imposed on external trade and did not include the objectionable internal taxes.

Yet the Townshend measures, which included the controversial policy of quartering soldiers in private homes, provoked even greater colonial resistance than the Sugar Act had. Once again, it triggered a trade boycott. This time, as opposition to Townshend's policies brewed during 1768, civic leaders, rather than city merchants, orchestrated the movement for the non-importation or non-consumption of British goods. Debate over the duties festered for two years before merchants could be persuaded to enact effective non-importation agreements. As before, some merchants initially supported non-importation as an opportunity to unload inventories at higher prices, but now business was generally good, and there was little desire among merchants to stop trade. They depended upon commerce for their livelihoods and did not wish to see non-importation carried on beyond a short period of time. By contrast, local artisans and craftsmen enthusiastically embraced non-importation. These self-employed shoemakers, blacksmiths, soap and candle producers, furniture makers, ropemakers, and the like, produced goods that competed against British imports. They wanted boycotts not only to put pressure on Britain, but to help reduce foreign competition and promote local manufacturing.[20]

Thus, this second non-importation movement only emerged gradually and unequally across the colonies. By the spring of 1769, the merchants of three major port cities—Philadelphia, New York, and Boston—had implemented non-importation agreements. By the summer of 1769, the non-importation movement had spread to the southern colonies. Imports in

Carolina and Georgia declined in 1770, but they did not fall at all in Maryland and Virginia, where tobacco planters had large debts to service. Still, the overall volume of imports from Britain dropped 38 percent in 1769.

By this time, yet another British ministry was taking yet another look at customs duties imposed in America. Lord North's administration saw once again that the duties were failing to raise much revenue but had stoked popular resentment. North proposed undoing the taxes of his predecessor, and in April 1770 Parliament repealed the Townshend duties, with the exception of the one on tea, which had raised three-quarters of the revenue. Unlike the Stamp Act repeal, this action was not the result of political pressures from British merchants adversely affected by nonimportation. Unfortunately for the leaders of the non-importation movement, the colonial boycott occurred at a time when the orders of British manufacturers were running strong. The rising demand for woolen exports in Europe due to the Russo-Turkish war and a bountiful domestic harvest all served to cushion the British economy from the decline in trade with America.[21] Although trade fell even more with this non-importation effort than during the Stamp Act protest, the effort failed to inflict serious damage on British mercantile interests, and they were not instrumental in achieving repeal of the duties. However, the timing of events gave many colonists the impression that the British government had capitulated a second time to their demands.

The leaders of the American non-importation movement strenuously argued that the boycott should continue until the duty on tea was abolished as well. But merchants could not resist taking advantage of the British repeal as an excuse to resume trade, and the non-importation movement quickly collapsed. Trade recovered somewhat in 1770, and then shot up dramatically in 1771, the first full year in which trade was restored.

By this time, a pattern had been established: when new British taxes were imposed, a non-importation movement would begin, and British policymakers would retreat. The colonists drew the conclusion—correctly in the case of the Stamp Act but incorrectly in the case of the Townshend duties—that British policy could be manipulated with American trade embargos. The colonists took from this experience an exaggerated impression of their ability to coerce British policy through economic means. In fact, non-importation only had a significant impact when it coincided with an economic downturn in Britain; the colonies could have only a modest influence on the country, because just 15 percent of British exports were destined for America in 1765.[22] Yet the impression stuck that America possessed great commercial leverage. Later, Thomas Jefferson and James Madison would attempt to use commercial coercion—boycotts, embargoes, and non-importation—against Britain and were repeatedly surprised and frustrated by the ineffectiveness of these actions in bringing about desired changes in Britain's policy.

From 1770 until early 1773, trans-Atlantic relations were eerily calm. During this period, the colonial grievances festered, but the British government did not undertake any new actions that might become a rallying cry for protest. Then an economic crisis hit Virginia, while a new tea act inflamed Massachusetts. In the South, Virginia planters, already weighed down by heavy debts and resentful of the control of their trade by Scottish agents, faced a devastating collapse in tobacco prices in 1772 and 1773. The trigger was a financial crisis in Britain that was quickly transmitted to the colonies. Tobacco prices dropped by half and credit extended to Virginia and Maryland planters was curtailed. The debt burden of tidewater planters soared, leading to a wave of foreclosures and imprisonment. The catastrophe intensified anti-British sentiment, and Chesapeake planters imagined that their financial prospects would be brighter if only they were free to sell their produce to the world market directly instead of through Britain, as the Navigation laws required.[23]

The Tea Act, passed by Parliament in early 1773, also put the colonies back in confrontation with Britain. This legislation aimed to help bail out the financially troubled East India Company by giving it a monopoly on tea sales in the colonies. The British government also sought to undercut smugglers—two-thirds of the tea consumed in America was believed to have been smuggled to avoid paying any duty—by slashing the import duty on tea and allowing the company to transport cargo directly to North America without stopping in Britain. The revenue implications of bringing the smuggled tea into legal channels of trade and taxing it were enormous.[24]

Even though Britain was actually reducing the price of legal tea imports, colonial merchants—many of whom were probably complicit in the illegal smuggling—protested the granting of a monopoly privilege to the East India Company and the payment of duty. They succeeded in riling up other colonists against the British action and, in the fall of 1773, American ports began turning away East India ships loaded with tea. In Boston, several ships landed but were not permitted to unload. At the instigation of local merchants who profited from smuggled tea, crowds gathered near the docks on December 16, 1773. About one hundred fifty people stormed an East India Company ship and dumped 342 chests of tea (about

90,000 pounds) into the harbor. Thus, the famous Boston Tea Party was
not a protest about an unfair tax increase, since the duty was actually being reduced, but about a British attempt to make the smuggling of tea unprofitable so that the East India Company could gain control of the trade.[25]

Outraged by these events, British officials passed the Coercive Acts
(known as the Intolerable Acts in America) in the spring of 1774. These
measures closed the port of Boston until the destroyed tea had been paid
for, gave the royal governor direct authority over the local government,
and required the colonies to provide housing and provisions for British soldiers. Britain and the thirteen North America colonies were now on a collision course.

The colonies banded together in the First Continental Congress, which
convened in September–October 1774. The Congress denied Parliament's
jurisdiction over the domestic affairs of the colonies, except as it pertained
to the regulation of foreign trade, and pointedly rejected internal taxation
without representation. The Congress issued the Declaration of Rights and
Grievances, which explained that the colonists "cheerfully consent to the
operation of such acts of the British parliament, as are bona fide restrained
to the regulation of our external commerce, for the purpose of securing
the commercial advantages of the whole empire to the mother country,"
but excluded "every idea of taxation, internal or external, for raising a revenue on the subjects in America without their consent." Furthermore, the
declaration continued, the colonists were "entitled to life, liberty, & property, and they have never ceded to any sovereign power whatever, a right to
dispose of either without their consent."[26]

The colonies essentially wanted a return to Britain's pre-1763 benign
neglect with regard to their internal affairs. They also requested the repeal
of many laws enacted after 1763, but not the Tea Act, which it accepted as
part of the Navigation Acts. The Congress called for the non-importation
of all goods from Britain, Ireland, and the British West Indies starting in
December 1774 until the Coercive Acts had been repealed. After issuing
these demands, the representatives adjourned until May 1775 and awaited
the British response.

Britain opted for a military solution. In early 1775, the government declared Massachusetts to be in a state of rebellion and sent its armed forces
to occupy Boston, leading to the clashes at Lexington and Concord. In
May, Congress decided to augment non-importation with non-exportation:
a ban on all exports to Britain and the West Indies starting a year later. The
delay in enforcing the export ban was a concession to the South, whose

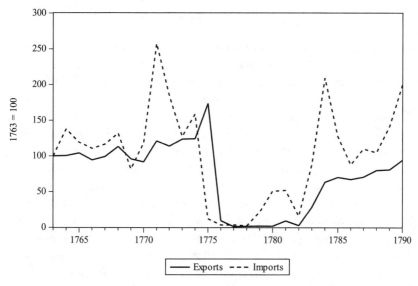

Figure 1.1. Value of exports and imports—American colonies and England and Scotland, 1763–1790. (US Bureau of the Census 1975, series Z-213–14, Z-227–28.)

representative protested that an immediate ban would impose a huge and unfair burden on the planters because crops for sale during the current year had already been planted.

The national embargo on trade with Britain had a much more pronounced effect on commerce than the previous non-importation movement. Imports from Britain simply evaporated in 1775, as figure 1.1 shows. Exports rose in 1775 as American farmers and planters strained to make as many last shipments to Britain as possible, but then disappeared the following year. By this time, fighting had broken out between British and colonial forces in Massachusetts, and the colonies began to move toward independence.

Many of the political pamphlets of this period asserted colonial rights under the English constitution and argued for American sovereignty, but the underlying grievance was also economic in nature. "The commercial dispute preceded the constitutional, not just once but again and again in these years," Lynd and Waldstreicher (2011, 609) note. "It is important that colonists melded economic and constitutional arguments under the category of sovereignty—but not so important that we should ignore the originating nature of economic forces."

TRADE AND INDEPENDENCE

Parliament responded to the American embargo in early 1775 by restricting the trade of the thirteen colonies to Britain alone. The British government raised the stakes later that year by enacting the Prohibitory Act,
which banned all trade with the colonies. In retaliation for colonial resistance and in the hopes of ending the rebellion, Britain sought to isolate
the American states by completely cutting off their foreign trade. British authorities especially wanted to prevent the colonies from importing
military supplies, such as gunpowder, muskets, bayonets, and ammunition, from other countries. The complete stoppage of all foreign commerce
caused consternation in Congress. In October 1775, John Adams wrote,
"Can our own People bear a total Cessation of Commerce? Will not Such
Numbers be thrown out of Employment, and deprived of their Bread, as to
make a large discontented Party? Will not the Burthen of supporting these
Numbers, be too heavy upon the other Part of the Community? Shall We
be able to maintain the War, wholly without Trade? Can We support the
Credit of our Currency, without it?"[27]

In early 1776, the Second Continental Congress debated what to do
next. On April 6, 1776, in defiance of Britain, Congress declared that
the colonies were no longer bound by British mercantile regulations and
that American ports were open to trade with all countries except Britain.
Whereas Congress asserted in October 1774 that Parliament had no authority over the colonies except for the regulation of its external trade,
now it denied even this. Adams believed that the April proclamation was
America's true declaration of independence. Now, Adams thought, "the
utmost encouragement must be given to trade—and therefore We must
levy no Duties at present upon Exports and Imports—nor attempt to con-
fine our Trade to our own Bottoms, or our own seamen."[28]

In July 1776, the Continental Congress formally declared independence
from Britain. Among the many grievances cited in the Declaration of Independence, Congress complained about Britain's "cutting off our trade with
all parts of the world" and "imposing taxes on us without our consent." By
this time, trade between the two countries had completely collapsed. This
had less to do with Britain's enforcement of the coastal blockade than its
military strategy of controlling the major cities, which were also the major seaports. British military forces occupied Boston (1775–76), New York
(1776–83), and Philadelphia (1777–78) along with other key commercial cities at various times during the war. These ports had been America's main
gateways to the rest of the world, and this occupation choked off foreign

trade more than the blockade itself. The ports of other coastal towns were simply not equipped to handle large volumes of trade.

The states tried to make up for the lost trade with Britain by promoting commerce with France and other European countries. Congress appointed a committee led by John Adams that came up with the "treaty plan of 1776."[29] Adams and his colleagues drafted a template commercial treaty that the diplomats could use to negotiate with foreign powers. Under the plan, the United States would seek "national treatment" from other nations, meaning that US merchants and ships (if not goods) would receive the same standing in foreign countries as their own domestic merchants and ships. This audacious request was far more demanding than the standard most-favored-nation (MFN) treatment. Under MFN, US goods and ships would be treated the same as the most-favored foreign nation in the country's market. Under MFN, the United States could not be discriminated against compared to other foreign nations, but a country still might tax foreign goods and ships.

The treaty plan bore little fruit and had virtually no effect on trade because of the wartime conditions. Still the first trade agreement the United States concluded was an important one: the Treaty of Amity and Commerce with France in February 1778. Although the treaty did not have a significant impact on bilateral trade during the war, the agreement symbolized the informal alliance between the two nations.[30] Despite British efforts to cut off the trade of the colonies, the French navy helped keep some North Atlantic sea routes open, and shipments of French military supplies aided the American war effort.

The agreement also contained the "conditional" MFN clause. This meant that if either party granted another country better treatment for its goods or vessels, that treatment would not automatically be extended to the other; new concessions would have to be negotiated.[31] Although the conditional MFN requirement came at the request of French negotiators, the United States persisted in using it until adopting an unconditional MFN policy in 1923. Under unconditional MFN, a tariff reduction granted to one country would automatically be extended to other countries with whom it had MFN agreements.

Data on the volume of US trade during the Revolutionary War are scant. The fragmentary statistical evidence suggests that it was a fraction of its prewar levels. Although trade began to recover after 1778, when British troops withdrew from Boston and Philadelphia, it still remained at low levels. The total tonnage of ships passing through Philadelphia in 1780, for example, was just a third of the tonnage in 1770.[32] Commerce with other countries failed to make up for the loss of trade with Britain, and the Royal Navy made it difficult to get gunpowder and other supplies into the country.

The American economy suffered grievously as a result of the damage caused by the Revolution and the disruption to foreign commerce. "The foreign sector was simply too central to the performance of the entire economy for its disruption to be suffered lightly," McCusker and Menard (1985, 367) note. One indication of the economic damage caused by the Revolution is the sharp decline in real per capita income, nearly as severe as the reduction during the Great Depression of the early 1930s. McCusker (2000, 156) estimates that real per capita income fell 15 percent between 1774 and 1781, whereas Lindert and Williamson (2013, 741) estimate that it fell 20 percent between 1774 and 1800. Since the latter figure takes into account the economic recovery in the 1790s, Lindert and Williamson conclude that "the Revolutionary disaster and the Confederation turmoil could have been America's greatest income slump ever, in percentage terms" (741). Whatever the precise amount, Americans paid a very high economic price to achieve their independence.

Eventually, with some crucial military assistance from France, America won the war for independence at the Battle of Yorktown in October 1781. A provisional peace agreement with Britain was reached late the following year, and Britain legalized trade with the United States in May 1783. Great Britain formally ended the hostilities and recognized the thirteen colonies as free and sovereign states with the Treaty of Paris, signed in September 1783.

After seven years of severely limited international trade, Americans anticipated a great economic revival with the reopening of commerce. Rather naively, they assumed that political independence would not prevent the resumption of close economic ties with Britain and that Britain would allow America to resume its previous commercial position in the British Empire. Early indications supported this assumption: the Earl of Shelburne, the British minister in charge of the peace negotiations and a disciple of Adam Smith, was inclined to be magnanimous with the renegade colonies. An October 1782 draft of the peace treaty included liberal provisions for commercial reciprocity. In negotiating the treaty with Britain, Benjamin Franklin had the audacity to ask for the freedom of American vessels to trade within the British Empire, and it appeared he might succeed. In March 1783, Chancellor of the Exchequer William Pitt introduced a bill in Parliament that would have granted the United States virtually all of its former trade privileges, even allowing American ships to enter British colonial ports on the same terms as British ships.[33] This liberal approach was also met strong opposition. Shipping interests wanted to preserve their exclusive control of British trade in the West Indies and elsewhere without competition from American ships. Tory nationalists were in no mood to be conciliatory to the rebellious Americans and wanted strict navigation laws to strengthen Britain's maritime security.

America's hopes for regaining its previous commercial access to the British Empire fell apart when the government collapsed and a new coalition, led by Lord North and Charles James Fox, took over in April 1783. The Fox-North ministry was determined to increase Britain's naval strength and was not inclined to grant commercial concessions to the United States. Instead, the Privy Council banned American ships in the British West Indies, a temporary exclusion that was made permanent five years later. In addition, some American goods were banned from the West Indies, while others would face stiff duties that they did not have to face before. Even if the shipping ban and high duties could be partially evaded, they were a heavy blow to New England's economy.

Still, the legalization of Britain's trade with America in May 1783 led to a surge in bilateral trade and a brief economic boom in the United States. Having been deprived of most foreign goods for eight years, American consumers gorged themselves on British products, and imports soared, as figure 1.1 shows. Exports to Britain jumped as well, but only to half of their prewar level. Of course, exports to Britain were expected to be lower after the war because the country's trade was no longer bound by British commercial regulations; hence American goods did not need to be shipped to Britain for reexport elsewhere. Although the United States had won its freedom from the Navigation Acts, it had lost its privileged access to the markets of the British Empire, a loss that was not offset by new export opportunities elsewhere. Although statistical data for the period are scant, the available evidence suggests that, overall, US exports were significantly lower than before the war.[34]

The immediate result was a severe trade deficit. At least with respect to Britain, the United States imported £7.6 million but only exported £2.5 million over the three years 1784–1786.[35] Prior to the revolution, America's trade surplus with the West Indies helped finance trade deficits with Britain. Now, thanks to Britain's restrictive policies, the United States did not have the export earnings from the West Indies to pay for British imports, so it had to make payment in specie. The United States is estimated to have lost £1.26 million in gold and silver over these three years. The outflow of specie produced a sharp deflation: consumer prices dropped more than 12 percent in 1783, the first year in which trade with Britain was restored, and fell in every subsequent year until 1790. Between 1783 and 1790, domestic prices declined a cumulative 27 percent.[36]

This monetary contraction led to a severe recession starting in 1784 that prolonged the economic distress of the revolutionary war period. Many economic indicators did not return to their prewar levels until the end of the 1780s. New England suffered far more than other regions. The shipbuilding industry was decimated by the ban on carrying goods to the West Indies; Britain also kept in place a ban imposed in 1776 on the purchase or repair of ships in the United States. The fishing and whaling industry suffered from the loss of British markets as well: in 1786, the cod fisheries were operating at just 80 percent of the prewar level.[37]

Southern crop producers also had difficulty recovering from the economic dislocations of the war. Britain confiscated an estimated thirty thousand slaves from Virginia during the war and imposed stiff import duties on tobacco after the war. As a result, Virginia's tobacco production was nearly 20 percent lower in 1783–84 than it had been in 1774. Rice exports, now also subject to high duties in Britain, were in 1783–86 less than half of what they had been in 1770–73.[38]

Although the United States was now free to trade with the rest of the world, commerce with other countries remained limited. Americans hoped that trade with France would pick up the slack from Britain, but it remained disappointingly low. "Americans had been accustomed to British merchants, who shared their culture, offered comparatively high-quality merchandise at bargain prices, and provided them with long-term credit," Buel (1998, 69) observes. "French merchants were ignorant of American customs, offered high-priced but inferior merchandise, and proved reluctant to extend any credit." France's navigation policies also put obstacles in the way of American ships in the French West Indies, while the French tobacco monopoly continued to restrict purchase from Virginia.

The only bright point in the postwar trade situation was a considerable improvement in the terms of trade, partly because exports were no longer hindered by the Navigation Acts. The price of tobacco rose from its prewar level, and the price of non-British imports fell because they no longer had to be shipped through Britain. Unfortunately, this good news was short-lived. After rebounding immediately after the end of the war, the terms of trade slid during the rest of the 1780s. And with the lower volume of trade, the gains from trade were probably a fraction of what they had been prior to the war.

Thus, the American economy was mired in a terrible state throughout the 1780s. Exports were crippled by the lack of access to markets in the British Empire, and the monetary drain resulted in persistent deflation. As James Madison lamented in 1785, "The Revolution has robbed us of our trade with the West Indies, the only one which yielded us a favorable balance, without opening any other channels to compensate for it. . . . In every point of view, the trade of this country is in a deplorable condition."[39]

THE COMMERCIAL NEGOTIATIONS OF 1784–86

The solution to the country's faltering economy, it was widely believed, was to persuade Britain to lift the Privy Council's restrictive Orders in Council. That would stimulate America's shipping and export sectors and help close the trade deficit, thereby reducing the drain of specie and ending the deflation of prices. To accomplish this, Americans pinned their hopes on a trade agreement with Britain that would restore the commercial benefits that they previously enjoyed as a part of the British Empire. New England merchants, in particular, pleaded with Congress to address in some way Britain's restrictive policies.

In 1784, with the goal of export expansion in mind, Congress initiated a plan to secure commercial agreements with other countries and open up the blocked paths of American ships and goods in foreign markets. Trade agreements had been concluded with the Netherlands and Sweden in the early 1780s, but Congress aimed to reach accords with the two most important powers, Britain and France, as well as Prussia, Denmark, Tuscany, Portugal, Russia, and others. John Adams, Thomas Jefferson, and John Jay were each given a two-year commission to negotiate such trade agreements. Adams was sent to London and Jefferson to Paris, while Secretary of Foreign Affairs John Jay remained in New York and used diplomatic channels to explore other possible agreements.

In London, Adams tried to persuade British officials that the obstacles they placed on America's trade were counterproductive. He proposed that the nations give each other "national treatment" in terms of shipping in their ports. He quickly discovered that the British were completely uninterested in any serious negotiations. Their officials had been influenced by Lord Sheffield's *Observations on the Commerce of the American States with Europe and the West Indies*, a 1783 pamphlet which made a strong case that the country should keep its restrictions on American commerce in place. Sheffield shrewdly observed that the new American Congress could not regulate the trade of the states, and therefore it was powerless to retaliate against Britain. Furthermore, he argued, Britain should have little interest in a commercial agreement, because it would maintain its access to the US market without any discrimination even in the absence of a treaty. Therefore, Britain could protect its own commercial interests and make no concession at all with the assurance that it would suffer no reprisals from the United States.

Sheffield's pamphlet caused a sensation on both sides of the Atlantic because it correctly identified a key weakness in the American system of government. The Articles of Confederation, drafted in 1777 and implemented in 1781, set out the legal framework for the national government and severely limited its powers. Under the Articles, the United States was essentially a league of thirteen independent states rather than a single unified nation. As article 2 stated, "Each state retains its sovereignty, freedom, and independence, and every power, jurisdiction, and right, which is not by this Confederation expressly delegated to the United States, in Congress assembled." Because so few powers were expressly delegated to Congress, political authority was highly decentralized: the states were sovereign, and the national government was extremely weak.

Furthermore, article 9 of the Articles of Confederation explicitly stated that "no treaty of commerce shall be made whereby the legislative power of the respective States shall be restrained from imposing such imposts and duties on foreigners, as their own people are subjected to, or from prohibiting the exportation or importation of any species of goods or commodities whatsoever." Thus, the government lacked any capacity to respond to British commercial regulations. There could be no national trade policy because there were thirteen state trade policies.

Adams wrote that "the United States are willing to throw wide open every port in their dominions to British ships and merchants and merchandise, and I am ready, in their behalf to pledge their faith in a treaty to this effect, upon the reciprocal stipulation of this nation, that her ports will be equally open to our ships, merchants, and products."[40] When asked by British diplomats what the United States could offer in exchange for better commercial treatment, he could make no reply. As a result, British officials ignored his offer. Adams bristled at the lack of diplomatic respect shown for him and his country, but Sheffield was right: the United States had a very weak bargaining position, because it already had an open market, and the government had no ability to close it. The British government's position was simple: having chosen to be independent, the United States was not entitled to enjoy the privileges of colonial status and therefore it gave up any inherent right to trade within the British Empire.

Recognizing the futility of his mission, Adams fired dispatch after dispatch to Congress explaining that the threat of retaliation was the only way to persuade Britain to reach a commercial agreement. Adams insisted that action be taken:

> Patience, under all the unequal burthens they impose upon our commerce, will do us no good; it will contribute in no degree to preserve the peace with this country. On the contrary, nothing but retaliations, reciprocal prohibitions, and imposts, and putting ourselves in a posture of defense, will have any effect. . . . Confining our exports to our own ships, and laying on heavy duties upon all foreign luxuries, and encouraging our own manufactures, appear to me to be our only resource, although I am very sensible to the many difficulties on the way.[41]

Such retaliation, of course, could only take place if the states acted in concert with one another. That in turn could be achieved only if the states granted Congress the power to regulate the nation's commerce. Adams sent Congress a copy of Sheffield's pamphlet and lamented its influence: "A system which has in it so little respect for us and is so obviously calculated to give a blow to our nurseries of ships and seamen, could never have been adopted but from the opinion that we had no common legislature for the government of commerce."[42]

Adams' frustration grew over time. The United States was offering open trade on liberal terms, but Britain and France remained committed to retaining their exclusive privileges in the colonial trade. In 1785, Adams wrote: "The United States of America have done more than all the economists of France toward propagating in the world this magnanimous sentiment" of liberty of commerce, but "that liberty is not universally and reciprocally admitted." A prolific correspondent, Adams warned his colleagues back home of his difficult negotiating situation and argued that it was time to get tough: "We have hitherto been the bubbles of our own philosophical and equitable liberality; and, instead of meeting correspondent sentiments, both France and England have shown a constant disposition to take a selfish and partial advantage of us because of them, nay, to turn them to the diminution or destruction of our own means of trade and strength. I hope we shall be the dupes no longer than we must. I would venture upon monopolies and exclusions, if they were found to be the only arms of defence against monopolies and exclusions."[43]

Jefferson had an equally difficult time negotiating with the French government in seeking to open the French West Indies to American ships and goods. Jefferson found little interest among the French in changing their policy or in persuading the national tobacco monopoly to purchase more from the United States and help his home state of Virginia. Similarly, John Jay had little success in convincing other European countries to enter into friendly commercial arrangements. Writing to Jefferson, Adams said, "We must not, my Friend, be the Bubbles of our own Liberal Sentiments. If We cannot obtain reciprocal Liberality, We must adopt reciprocal Prohibitions, Exclusions, Monopolies, and Imposts—our offers have been fair—more than fair. If they are rejected, We must not be the Dupes."[44]

Adams and Jefferson exchanged many letters discussing the situation and proposing ways around the Articles of Confederation. Yet even if the diplomats had had a credible threat of reprisals, they still might not have been able to negotiate satisfactory commercial agreements. The United States was demanding much more than improved bilateral trade: it wanted access to the indirect trade of the European powers with their overseas colonies, mainly in the West Indies, and direct access for American ships and goods in the home country as well. The United States was essentially asking the European powers to end mercantilism and put all trade on an open, non-discriminatory basis. Of course, Britain and nearly every other European country wanted to keep a monopoly on its colonial trade. The United States was an outsider, a non-colonial power that was demanding entry into an exclusive colonial trade network. The new nation was simply asking for too much and had too little to offer in return. "The really important fact is that the United States was demanding special consideration, privileges such as no European country had ever granted to another," Setser (1937, 74) notes. Foreign governments "refused to alter their established policies at the demand of a new nation which had little to offer in return."

The two-year diplomatic commissions expired in May 1786 without any success. The prospects for restoring economic prosperity through trade expansion had dimmed considerably.

FLOUNDERING UNDER THE ARTICLES OF CONFEDERATION

The problem with the Articles of Confederation was not simply that Congress did not have powers over trade policy that would give government officials the credibility to negotiate treaties of commerce with other countries. Since Congress was not permitted to impose import duties, the national government could not raise revenue to fund its operations, finance the national debt, or pay for national defense. These closely intertwined problems had long been recognized. In 1782, Alexander Hamilton wrote that "the vesting of Congress with the power of regulating trade ought to have been a principal object of the Confederation for a variety of reasons," adding that "it is as necessary for the purposes of commerce as of revenue."[45]

The inability to raise any revenue left Congress entirely dependent on the requisitions of funds from the states. Even here, it lacked the ability to compel the states to pay, and they proved increasingly reluctant to respond to Congress's funding requests. In October 1781, just after the victory at Yorktown, Congress requested $8 million from the states for 1782. By January 1783, Congress had received only $420,000 of that amount. By March 1787, states had paid two-thirds of the October 1781 and April 1784 requisitions, one-fifth of the September 1785 requisition, and just 2 percent of the August 1786 requisition.[46] "By the end of 1786, Congress literally was receiving no money from the states for current federal needs and expenses," Brown (1993, 25) notes.

Furthermore, without a reliable source of revenue, Congress could not borrow on credit markets. An attempt to float a loan in October 1786 failed without having attracted a single subscriber. As James Madison concluded, "Experience has sufficiently demonstrated that a punctual and unfailing compliance by 13 separate and independent Governments with periodical demands of money from Congress, can never be reckoned upon with the certainty requisite to satisfy our present creditors, or to tempt others to become our creditors in future."[47]

The consequences were dire. The national government was essentially broke and without credit. Not only did Congress lack the funds to pay the interest on the government's domestic and foreign debts, but it even considered disbanding because it could not pay its own members, officers, and staff. Congress could not finance an army to address the country's new foreign-policy challenges, such as the continued British occupation of western forts in violation of the Treaty of Paris. Writing in 1787, Madison observed that

> the present System neither has nor deserves advocates; and if some very strong props are not applied will quickly tumble to the ground. No money is paid into the public Treasury; no respect is paid to the federal authority. Not a single State complies with the requisitions, several pass over them in silence, and some positively reject them. The payments ever since the peace have been decreasing, and of late fall short even of the pittance necessary for the Civil list of the Confed-

eracy. It is not possible that a Government can last long under these circumstances.[48]

In terms of taxing imports, there was no national trade policy, but rather thirteen state trade policies. Eleven of the thirteen colonies enacted their own tariff laws during the 1780s. (New Jersey and Delaware, the only two states that did not pass tariff legislation, lacked the large seaports of their neighbors and wanted to provide every encouragement to trade that they could.) Most of these state tariffs were relatively low, about 5 percent, and the structure of duties was quite similar.[49] They were mainly designed to raise revenue, although some duties imposed by Massachusetts and Pennsylvania aimed to protect domestic manufactures.

This decentralized system had problems, but trade wars between the states were not among them. With rare exceptions, most of the products of one state were given duty-free treatment in the others. States also did not usually discriminate against the shipping of other states. The main problem was not trade relations between the states, but rather trade relations between the United States and the rest of the world.[50]

Attempts to modify the Articles of Confederation and remedy these two shortcomings failed repeatedly during the 1780s. In February 1781, Congress requested that the states amend the Articles and empower it to levy an import duty of 5 percent. The tariff's proceeds would be devoted exclusively to paying the interest and principal on the national debt, with nothing devoted to the operating expenses of the national government, and the duties would be abolished when the debt had been retired. This modest proposal addressed the fear that an excessively powerful central government would threaten state sovereignty. However, amendments to the Articles required the unanimous consent of the states. At first, enactment of the measure looked promising: it was approved by eleven states within a year, but then the proposal stalled in the Rhode Island legislature. In November 1782, the Rhode Island legislature unanimously rejected the proposal, choosing to finance its own expenditures with its own import duties rather than ceding that power to the national government and having to impose direct taxes instead. Shortly thereafter, Virginia repealed its previous ratification of the amendment.

Madison proposed a similar revenue plan in early 1783 that called for a twenty-five-year authorization for Congress to impose specific duties on enumerated items and a 5 percent duty on all other imports. Congress approved the measure in April 1784, but once again the unanimous approval of the states proved to be out of reach. Rhode Island agreed to it this time, but Connecticut rejected it twice until finally accepting it in early 1784. By July 1786, every state had approved the proposal except for New York. The state had rejected the revenue plan in 1785, after upstate agricultural interests realized that their taxes would increase if the state gave up its claim on the import duties collected in New York City. Then New York passed it in 1786 with the requirement that it administer the import duties, determine how much would be given to the national government, and be able to make payments to Congress in New York currency. Congress found these conditions unacceptable because it needed gold and silver coin to repay foreign creditors, thus leaving the matter unresolved.

Aside from revenue, another problem with having thirteen state trade policies was the inability to formulate a credible national response to Britain's discrimination against American commerce. As we have seen, the attempts to negotiate commercial agreements had failed. Some states tried to retaliate against the Orders in Council that blocked US trade with the British West Indies. For example, in 1785, in response to the Orders, Massachusetts prohibited British ships from loading American goods in its ports. But when Connecticut refused to follow this example, British ships merely shifted their destination from Boston to New Haven, and Massachusetts was forced to suspend its action a year later.[51] Indeed, the neighboring states of New York and New Jersey, as well as Pennsylvania and Delaware, could not enact anti-British shipping legislation unilaterally without simply deflecting trade to their neighbor. Some states were persistent: in 1787, New York put duties on imported goods coming from Connecticut and New Jersey to punish them for not levying additional duties on British goods or tonnage. That effort failed, and the duties were soon abolished, because no other state cared to join New York's effort: smaller states tended to free ride off of the retaliatory actions of larger states and thus undermine any attempted reprisal. The British easily evaded the differing state-by-state policies on navigation by simply landing at the most welcoming ports.

The national government had no power to solve this collective-action problem, and British authorities recognized this. As a British magazine reported, "By the latest letters from the American States, the restraint laid upon their trade with the British West Indies has thrown them into the utmost perplexity; and by way of retaliation they are passing laws inimical to their own interest; and what is still worse, inconsistent with each other. . . . Hence the dissensions that universally prevail throughout what may be called the thirteen Dis-United States." Speaking before Parliament in 1787, Lord Grenville defended the government's policy, noting with respect to the United States that "we do not know whether they are under one head, directed by many, or whether they have any head at all."[52] Many in Britain believed that the United States would simply collapse as a nation and break up into its constituent parts.

The nation's political leaders increasingly worried that foreign countries would not take the United States seriously if they remained thirteen independent states. Jefferson believed that, as long as the regulation of commerce remained "in the hands of thirteen Legislatures, they [Britain] need not fear a union in their proceedings."[53] Madison concurred: "If it be necessary to regulate trade at all, it surely is necessary to lodge the power, where trade can be regulated with effect, and experience has confirmed what reason foresaw, that it can never be so regulated by the States acting in their separate capacities."[54]

With the failure of Adams and Jefferson to secure commercial treaties, Congress considered measures to establish a national trade policy. In December 1784, Congress appointed a committee to amend article 9 of the Articles of Confederation and give it "the powers to regulate the commercial intercourse of the States with other powers." Led by James Monroe, the committee recommended in early 1785 that Congress have the "sole and exclusive" authority of "regulating the trade of the States, as well with foreign nations, as with each other, and of laying such imposts and duties upon imports and exports as might be necessary for the purpose."[55]

But Congress failed to act. By June 1785, Monroe reported to Jefferson that nothing had been done with the committee's report: "The importance of the subject and the deep and radical change it will create in the bond of the union, together with the conviction that something must be done, seems to create an aversion or rather a fear of acting on it. . . . Some gentleman have inveterate prejudices against all attempts to increase the powers of Congress; others see the necessity but fear the consequences."[56]

The inaction was due to sectional dissention on the matter. While New England was desperate to give Congress the power to deal with the trade situation, and the Mid-Atlantic states were in general agreement, the South was reluctant to move forward. The South was less adversely affected by British shipping regulations in the West Indies and still had close ties to Britain for the sale of tobacco and other crops. It was wary of granting more extensive powers to the national government, fearing that they would be used to exclude British shipping, reduce competition for transportation services, and put exporters and importers at the mercy of New England merchants. Richard Henry Lee, a Virginian who served as president of Congress, feared that giving Congress the power to regulate commerce would create "a monopoly of the carrying business . . . in favor of the northern states."[57] He and others dreaded the "intrigue and coalition" of the New England states, which "might fix a ruinous monopoly upon the trade & productions of the [southern] Staple States."[58] This would reduce competition for shipping services, leading to higher transportation costs and lower prices for staples. Although Madison, Monroe, and Jefferson were prominent Virginians who wanted to give Congress greater authority over commerce, their views were not shared by many in the state.

New England merchants and politicians were dismayed by the South's unwillingness to act. New England was the region most affected by the British restrictions on the West India trade and believed the South was refusing to consider the national interest or acknowledge the economic distress in other parts of the country. They wanted to give some preferences for American shipping, such as a tax on goods coming or going on British vessels, to strengthen the American shipbuilding and shipping industries, but they recognized that the South disagreed: "They may get their goods to market cheaper if our ships have nothing to do," one New England politician complained.[59] Boston merchants demanded that Congress act and tried to organize a boycott of British goods. The failure of this effort led to a growing frustration over the South's intransigence, and even talk of secession if the South would not allow the situation to be remedied.

In August 1785, when Madison heard reports that New England states might break away and form a subconfederation if the South continued to block commercial reforms, he reported to Jefferson as follows:

The machinations of G.B. [Great Britain] with regard to Commerce have produced much distress and noise in the Northern States, particularly in Boston, from whence the alarm has spread to New York and Philada. . . . the sufferers are every where calling for such augmentation of the power of Congress as may effect relief. . . . If any thing should reconcile Virga. to the idea of giving Congress a power over her trade, it will be that this power is likely to annoy G.B. against whom the animosities of our Citizens are still strong. They seem to have less sensibility to their commercial interests; which they very little understand, and which the mercantile class here have not the same motives if they had the same capacity to lay open to the public, as that class have in the States North of us. The [high] price of our Staple since the peace is another cause of inattention in the planters to the dark side of our commercial affairs. Should these or any other causes prevail in frustrating the scheme of the Eastern and Middle States of a general retaliation on G.B., I tremble for the event. A majority of the States deprived of a regular remedy for the distresses by the want of a federal spirit in the minority must feel the strongest motives to some irregular experiments. The danger of such a crisis makes me surmise that the policy of Great Britain results as much from the hope of effecting a breach in our confederacy as of monopolising our trade.[60]

Madison argued that the Articles had to be amended lest dissention over the issue threaten the union itself:

I conceive it to be of great importance that the defects of the federal system should be amended, not only because such amendments will make it better answer the purpose for which it was instituted, but because I apprehend danger to its very existence from a continuance of defects which expose a part if not the whole of the empire to severe distress. The suffering part, even when the minor part, cannot long respect a Government which is too feeble to protect their interest; but when the suffering part come to be the majority part, and the despair of seeing a protecting energy given to the General Government, from what motives is their allegiance to be any longer expected? Should G. B. persist in the machinations which distress us; and seven or eight of the States be hindered by the others from obtaining relief by federal means, I own, I tremble at the anti-federal expedience into which the former may be tempted.[61]

At first, some advocates of a stronger national government believed that Britain's uncompromising attitude on its commercial restrictions could be a blessing in disguise if it aroused patriotic sentiments and promoted domestic political change. Gouverneur Morris thought that Britain's intransigence would do "more political good than commercial mischief" by stoking American resentment and thereby fostering demands to reform the Articles.[62] Merchants, farmers, shipbuilders, fishermen—nearly everyone who suffered from the struggling economy—advocated giving Congress powers over foreign commerce. But this alternative theory was proving wrong; as the decade progressed, states became more self-interested and less unified, more sectional and less national in their thinking.

One example of the sectional divide came when an envoy from Spain promised a commercial treaty if the United States relinquished its rights to navigate the Mississippi River. (Spain had closed the Mississippi to American commerce in 1784.) New England and Mid-Atlantic states were happy to give up these rights to obtain better access to the markets of Spain and its colonies. The South was appalled that its claim to use the Mississippi might be bargained away and attacked the North for ignoring the river's commercial importance to the region. But the South was outvoted in Congress by seven to five, and John Jay's negotiating instructions allowed him to give up US interests in the Mississippi River for not more than twenty years. Southern leaders were horrified by this decision, although no such agreement was concluded.

By the mid-1780s, there was a growing consensus among political leaders that the system of government under the Articles of Confederation was unworkable. The government's dysfunction in the face of a floundering economy was creating strong sectional tensions that threatened the union itself. As Madison wrote to Jefferson, "Most of our political evils may be traced to our commercial ones."[63] Congress's inability to raise revenue through import duties or to regulate foreign commerce were among the primary considerations that led to the movement to revise the Articles of Confederation and strengthen the national government. The Virginia legislature called for state representatives to meet in Annapolis in September 1786 to consider solutions to the country's commercial problems. Ironically, Madison opposed the convention on the grounds that it was "liable to objection and will probably miscarry," but he was willing to give it a try. "Yet I despair so much of its accomplishment at the present crisis that I do not extend my views much beyond a Commercial Reform," he wrote. "To speak the truth, I almost despair even of this."[64]

Madison's pessimism about the prospects for such a meeting seemed justified because the sectional forces that divided Congress would also be present in any meeting of state representatives. While the idea of such a meeting had been floating around for some time, it was also met with great suspicion by those concerned about state sovereignty. As it happened, the Annapolis Convention was poorly attended and was not in a position to propose giving new commercial powers to the national government. Instead, the Annapolis delegates called for another convention that would discuss not just commerce but the entire structure of the federal system. This set the stage for the Constitutional Convention in Philadelphia in May 1787.

FOREIGN COMMERCE AND
THE CONSTITUTION OF 1787

The country's dismal experience under the Articles of Confederation gave political leaders a compelling economic and foreign-policy rationale for creating a stronger national government. Indeed, the desire to give Congress the power to collect revenue so that it could pay debts and provide for the national defense, as well as regulate foreign commerce so that it could credibly negotiate with other nations over navigation rights and market access, was a major factor behind the movement to hold the constitutional convention. As Madison recalled much later in life, "It was well known that the incapacity [of the States to regulate foreign commerce separately] gave a primary and powerful impulse to the transfer of the power to a common authority capable of exercising it with effect. . . . . In expounding the Constitution and deducing the intention of its framers, it should never be forgotten, that the great object of the Convention was to provide, by a new Constitution, a remedy for the defects of the existing one; that among these defects was that of a power to regulate foreign commerce."[65]

From May to September 1787, representatives from the thirteen states met in closed sessions in Philadelphia to draft a new constitution. "The whole community is big with expectation," Madison wrote as the convention began. "And there can be no doubt that the result will in some way or other have a powerful effect on our destiny."[66] The convention began with a critical decision that greatly facilitated the proceedings: the provisions of the proposed constitution would be approved by majority voting by state. Had unanimity been required, the convention would likely have been deadlocked.[67]

The delegates had no difficulty in agreeing to give Congress the power to impose import duties. Article 1, section 8, clause 1 of the new Constitution contained the key provision relating to trade policy: "The Congress shall have power to lay and collect taxes, duties, imposts and excises, to pay the debts and provide for the common defense and general welfare of the United States; but all duties, imposts and excises shall be uniform throughout the United States." This uncontroversial passage was adopted without significant debate or apparent dissent. Few could disagree with John Rutledge's observation that "taxes on imports [were] the only sure source of revenue" for the government. Everyone expected, as Gouverneur Morris noted, that revenue would be drawn "as much as possible from trade."[68] A more controversial provision made these powers the exclusive prerogative of Congress, not the states. According to article 1, section 10, clause 2: "No state shall, without the consent of the Congress, lay any imposts or duties on imports or exports, except what may be absolutely necessary for executing its inspection laws." This provision passed by the narrow margin of 6–5.[69]

The proposal to grant Congress the general power to regulate foreign commerce—meaning regulations other than import duties, such as shipping policy—was highly contested. This proposal became bound up with the slave trade and formed part of the "dirty compromise" that played out over a few days in late August.[70] The shipping states of New England desperately wanted to give the federal government the authority to regulate commerce so that preferences for American ships in US ports could be enacted. In their view, such preferences, through differential tonnage duties, would not only promote the merchant marine, but would put the government in a better position to negotiate the elimination of foreign regulations that blocked the access of US exporters in foreign markets. Speaking for his state, Nathaniel Gorham of Massachusetts argued that "the eastern states had no motive to union but a commercial one."[71]

As we have seen, southern states feared giving Congress the power to regulate commerce. With their economy dependent upon large exports of agricultural staples, they wanted unfettered competition to ensure inexpensive shipping services. If British ships were handicapped by extra tonnage duties in US ports, the South believed that it would be exploited by New England shipping interests and charged exorbitant freight rates that would reduce its exports. As Richard Henry Lee wrote to Madison, "It seems clearly beyond a doubt to me that giving the Congress the power to legislate over the trade of the union would be dangerous in the extreme to the five Southern or staple States whose want of ships & seamen would expose their freightage & their produce to a most pernicious and destructive monopoly."[72] If it could not deny Congress the power to regulate commerce, the South wanted a super-majority (two-thirds) vote to enact such regulations so that it could potentially block such legislation.

How could the opposing views of the North and South be reconciled? The essence of the "dirty compromise," as Finkelman (1987, 214) observes, was that "the South Carolina delegation would support the commerce clause if New England would support protection for the slave trade and a prohibition on export taxes." This inter-regional bargain allowed the convention to get around these vexing issues, but each element of the compromise was controversial.

First, the South demanded a ban on export taxes to protect the interests of the staple-exporting states. A constitutional ban on export taxes was a bitter pill for most northern delegates, who felt that Congress should have the authority to tax exports as well as imports. Gouverneur Morris of Pennsylvania argued that "local considerations ought not to impede the general interest" and questioned whether "it would not in some cases be equitable to tax imports without taxing exports; and that taxes on exports would be often the most easy and proper of the two." Alone among the southerners at the convention, James Madison and George Washington also opposed the ban on export taxes. Madison thought that such taxes "might with particular advantage be exercised with regard to articles in which America was not rivalled in foreign markets," such as tobacco, and speculated that the burden of such a tax would be paid by foreign consumers.[73]

But most southern delegates strongly opposed giving Congress the authority to tax exports. Once again, the South believed that Congress could not be trusted with such power, fearing that it would be used as an instrument of oppression by the North to destroy its staple exports of tobacco, indigo, and rice. George Mason of Virginia "hoped the Northern states could not deny the Southern this security" against having the products of his region singled out for taxation. Mason argued that taxes on exports and imports were different because consumption of the nation's imports was equally distributed across the states, whereas production of the nation's exports was highly concentrated in just a few states. A delegate from South Carolina "was strenuously opposed to a [taxing] power over exports; as unjust and alarming to the staple States." Another thought that export taxes would be "partial and unjust" because they would mainly hit southern staples and would therefore "engender incurable jealousies."[74]

As a compromise, Madison proposed that export taxes be implemented only with the approval of a two-thirds majority of each chamber of Congress. This motion was defeated by a 6–5 vote, with all southern states voting against. The complete ban on export taxes then passed by a vote of 7–4, with the South voting as a bloc in favor (Maryland, Virginia, North Carolina, South Carolina, and Georgia, joined by Massachusetts and Connecticut), with New Hampshire, New Jersey, Pennsylvania, and Delaware opposed. As a result, article 1, section 9, of the Constitution states that "no tax or duty shall be laid on articles exported from any state."

The next issue, whether the slave trade should be allowed to continue or should be taxed or banned, was the subject of an even more fractious debate. Although northern shipping interests profited from the traffic in slaves, most delegates from the North abhorred the slave trade. They viewed slavery as morally repugnant and sought to end the trade, particularly as the three-fifths clause gave the South the ability to increase its seats in the House of Representatives by expanding its slave population. The South was divided: Maryland and Virginia already prohibited the importation of slaves because slave owners there wanted to preserve the high value of their current holdings, whereas South Carolina and Georgia wanted to continue importing slaves to help expand agricultural production. For these two states, a constitutional ban on the slave trade was a deal breaker. Charles Pinckney of South Carolina reported "his firm opinion" that if the constitution outlawed the slave trade, then even if he and "all his colleagues were to sign the Constitution & use their personal influence, it would be of no avail toward obtaining the assent of their constituents. S. Carolina & Georgia cannot do without slaves. . . . [He] should consider a rejection of the clause [protecting the slave trade] as an exclusion of S. Carol. from the union."[75]

To break this impasse, Gouverneur Morris suggested that "the whole subject be committed [to a special committee] including the clauses relating to taxes on exports & to a navigation act," in the hope that "these things may form a bargain among the Northern & Southern States." Oliver Ellsworth of Connecticut agreed, stating that "this widening of opinion has a threatening aspect. If we do not agree on this middle & moderate ground he was afraid we should lose two States, with such others as may be disposed to stand aloof, should fly into a variety of shapes and directions, and most probably into several confederations and not without bloodshed."[76] The Committee of Eleven, as the select committee was called, soon reported a compromise whereby Congress could only impose a modest fee on imported slaves and would be forbidden from prohibiting the slave trade until the year 1800. Madison criticized the slave trade provision as "dishonorable to the national character," but after changing the date to 1808, twenty years after the Constitution would be ratified, the provision was adopted by a 7–4 vote. The affirmative votes coming from three New England states, Maryland, and three Deep South states.

The final element of the "dirty compromise" was the commerce clause. The Committee of Eleven proposed dropping any requirement of a supermajority to approve regulations of trade. Delegates from the North insisted upon a simple majority rule to enact such regulations. George Clymer from Pennsylvania argued that the "Northern & middle States will be ruined, if not enabled to defend themselves against foreign regulations." Nathaniel Gorham from Massachusetts asked, "If the Government is to be so fettered as to be unable to relieve the [commercial distress of the] Eastern States what motive can they have to join in it, and thereby tie their own hands from measures which they could otherwise take for themselves?"[77] Madison also supported a majority vote so that the country could more easily retaliate against foreign commercial restrictions, but most southern delegates were strongly opposed. They insisted that the commerce clause should be exercised by a super-majority vote of two-thirds.

This dispute threatened the dirty compromise. To preserve it, Charles Pinckney from South Carolina announced that "it was the true interest of the S. States to have no regulation of commerce; but considering the loss brought on the commerce of the Eastern States by the revolution, their liberal conduct towards the views of South Carolina, and the interest the weak Southn. States had in being united with the strong Eastern States, he thought it proper that no fetters should be imposed on the power of making commercial regulations; and that his constituents though prejudiced against the Eastern States, would be reconciled to this liberality."[78] Therefore, Pinckney and the South Carolina delegation decided to support a simple majority rule as proposed by the Committee of Eleven. According to Madison's notes, the "liberal conduct" that Pinckney referred to was "the permission to import slaves." As Madison explained, "An understanding on the two subjects of *navigation* and *slavery*, had taken place between those parts of the Union, which explains the vote on the Motion depending, as well as the language of Genl. Pinckney and others." In essence, some New England states supported delaying the prohibition on the slave trade in exchange for South Carolina's support for giving Congress the power to regulate commerce.[79]

As a result, the motion to require a two-thirds majority in Congress to pass regulations of commerce was defeated by a vote of 7–4, with South Carolina alone among southern states in voting against it. The commerce clause was then adopted without recorded opposition. According to clause 3 of article 1, section 8 of the Constitution, Congress was given the specific power to "regulate commerce with foreign nations, and among the several states, and with the Indian tribes."

The last trade-related provision of the Constitution was the requirement that all treaties with foreign countries have the approval of two-thirds of the Senate (article 2, section 2, clause 2). This created a large political obstacle to any commercial agreement that might affect import duties. The explanation for this provision relates to the South's desire for a two-thirds vote on regulations of commerce and, in particular, the recent memory that the northern states had considered bargaining away the rights to navigate the Mississippi River, something deeply prejudicial to southern interests.[80] In essence, a two-thirds majority was included to protect regional interests in any treaty that the president might reach.

The convention adjourned in September 1787 and sent the proposed Constitution to the states for ratification. Alexander Hamilton, James Madison, and John Jay collaborated on a series of newspaper articles, later collected as *The Federalist Papers*, to persuade the people of New York to support the Constitution. Several of the essays discussed the advantages of the proposed Constitution from the standpoint of revenue and the regulation of trade. In *Federalist 11*, Hamilton emphasized the bargaining advantages of giving the federal government powers over commerce:

> By prohibitory regulations, extending, at the same time, throughout the States, we may oblige foreign countries to bid against each other, for the privileges of our markets. . . . Suppose, for instance, we had a government in America, capable of excluding Great Britain (with whom we have at present no treaty of commerce) from all our ports; what would be the probable operation of this step upon her politics? Would it not enable us to negotiate, with the fairest prospect of success, for commercial privileges of the most valuable and extensive kind, in the dominions of that kingdom?[81]

Hamilton held out the hope that American navigation laws would "produce a relaxation in [Britain's] system" and enable the United States to engage in commerce with the West Indies once again.

In June 1788, New Hampshire became the ninth state to ratify the Constitution, thereby bringing it into effect. By the fall, plans for the transition to the new government were being put in place. George Washington was elected president and launched the new government after taking the oath of office in New York on April 30, 1789. The new Congress sat on March 1789 and almost immediately began considering a law that would impose a tariff on imports. A new era in US trade policy had begun.

CHAPTER TWO

Trade Policy for the New Nation, 1789–1815

One of the first goals of the new federal government was to put the nation's fiscal and trade policies in order. Using the powers granted to it by the new Constitution, Congress began to impose duties on imports and regulate foreign commerce. The need to raise revenue through duties on imports was undisputed, although some members of Congress also thought it was necessary to protect manufacturing industries from foreign competition. The most controversial trade issue involved commercial relations with Britain, particularly after American shipping became entangled in the war between Britain and France in 1793. The debate over the appropriate American response divided the nation's leadership. While the Federalist administrations of George Washington and John Adams pursued a policy of commercial peace in the 1790s, the Republican administrations of Thomas Jefferson and James Madison engaged in protracted commercial conflict in the 1800s. These disputes culminated in the War of 1812, which dramatically reshaped the American economy and soon gave rise to protective tariffs.

THE TRADE-POLICY PHILOSOPHY
OF THE FOUNDING FATHERS

Under the new constitution, the nation's political leaders had the opportunity to shape US trade policy for the first time. What general principles informed their policy views and guided their thinking? As students of the Enlightenment and opponents of British mercantilism, the Founding Fathers favored free and open commerce among nations and the abolition of all restraints and preferences that inhibited trade.[1] "It is perhaps an erroneous opinion," Benjamin Franklin wrote in 1781, "but I find myself rather inclined to adopt that modern one, which supposes it is best for every country to leave its trade entirely free from all encumbrances."[2] Thomas Jefferson also extolled the benefits of free commerce. "I think all the world would gain by setting commerce at perfect liberty," he wrote in 1785. In his *Notes on the State of Virginia,* Jefferson argued that "our interest will be to throw open the doors of commerce, and to knock off all its shackles, giving perfect freedom to all persons for the vent of whatever they may choose to bring into our ports, and asking the same in theirs."[3] They also believed that trade restrictions were imposed at the behest of private interests, not the public interest. As Franklin wrote, "Most of the restraints put upon it in different countries seem to have been the projects of particulars for their private interest, under the pretense of public good."[4]

During this period, the term *free trade* did not mean zero tariffs and the absence of any government restrictions on trade. It was generally understood that governments would need to tax trade for revenue purposes. Instead, free trade meant the freedom of a country's merchants to trade anywhere they wanted without encountering discriminatory prohibitions or colonial preferences as long as they paid the required duties. Free trade could be more accurately characterized as open trade in which countries could impose import duties and regulate shipping but did so in a nondiscriminatory manner.

The Founding Fathers were acquainted with Adam Smith's *The Wealth of Nations* (1776), one of the most influential books of the period.[5] Smith attacked British mercantilist policies and advocated the "obvious and simple system of natural liberty," in which individuals would be free to pursue their own economic interests within the legal framework established by government. In this system of economic liberty, trade between countries was not a zero-sum game in which one country gained at the expense of another, as mercantilist doctrine seemed to suggest. Rather, Smith contended, trade should be left free and open because all countries could benefit from imports of goods that were relatively abundant elsewhere in exchange for exporting goods that were relatively abundant at home. As Smith (1976, 457) put it,

> What is prudence in the conduct of every family can scarce be folly in that of a great kingdom. If a foreign country can supply us with a commodity cheaper than we ourselves can make it, better buy it of them with some part of the produce of our own industry, employed in a way in which we have some advantage. The general industry of the country . . . will not thereby be diminished . . . but only left to find out the

way in which it can be employed with the greatest advantage. It is certainly not employed to the greatest advantage, when it is thus directed
towards an object which it can buy cheaper than it can make.

Most Americans embraced the view that commerce was naturally beneficial and required no central direction, in part because they did not want
to create an overly powerful national government that might play favorites with certain producers. For example, in one of the first Congressional
debates over import tariffs in 1789, James Madison echoed Smith in stating that

> I own myself the friend to a very free system of commerce, and hold it
> as a truth, that commercial shackles are generally unjust, oppressive
> and impolitic—it is also a truth, that if industry and labor are left to
> take their own course, they will generally be directed to those objects
> which are the most productive, and this in a more certain and direct
> manner than the wisdom of the most enlightened legislature could
> point out. Nor do I think that the national interest is more promoted
> by such restrictions, than that the interest of individuals would be pro-
> moted by legislative interference directing the particular application of
> its industry.[6]

Most of the founding fathers would have agreed with this sentiment,
although some, notably Alexander Hamilton, envisioned a more active
role for the government in trade. Writing in 1782, Hamilton considered the
idea that trade could be left to itself without government encouragements
or restraints as "one of those wild speculative paradoxes, which have
grown into credit among us, contrary to the uniform practice and sense
of the most enlightened nations." In Hamilton's view, since this particular maxim was "contradicted by the numerous institutions and laws that
exist everywhere for the benefit of trade, by the pains taken to cultivate
particular branches and to discourage others, by the known advantages derived from those measures, and by the palpable evils that would attend
their discontinuance, it must be rejected by every man acquainted with
commercial history."[7]

However, Adam Smith also discussed several exceptions to the general principle of free trade, and America's leaders found these exceptions
to be particularly relevant to the nation's circumstances. For example,
Smith (1976, 463–65) argued that it might be necessary to protect domestic
industries essential for national defense; in fact he defended the Naviga-

tion Laws on the grounds that defense "is of much more importance than opulence." Smith also held that "it may sometimes be a matter of deliberation how far it is proper to continue the free importation of certain foreign goods. . . . when some foreign nation restrains by high duties or prohibitions the importation of some of our manufactures into their country" (467). In such a case, a policy of reciprocity, or retaliating against foreign trade barriers by restricting imports from that country, might be appropriate, depending on the probability of the retaliation successfully removing the foreign barriers. Although Smith questioned whether nations should respond this way in every case, he clearly believed that retaliation could play a constructive role in keeping trade open.[8]

While supporting the goal of free and open trade, America's political leaders knew that both of Smith's qualifications—defense and reciprocity—were highly relevant to their situation. The problems caused by the country's dependence on crucial imported supplies during the Revolution, such as gunpowder and clothing, were still firmly etched in memory. And the inability of the states to coordinate a collective response to Britain's commercial restrictions in the 1780s had been an important reason for the establishment of the new constitution. Hence, the nation's policymakers faced two critical questions: Should the United States enact its own navigation laws to favor American shipping over foreign carriers? And should the United States respond in kind to foreign trade barriers and discriminatory policies that adversely affected its own exports and shipping? Most believed the answer to both questions was an unqualified yes, although there was a spirited debate about how such policies should be designed. Thus, while the founding fathers favored free and open trade in principle, they were also deeply concerned about national defense and foreign discrimination against American commerce.

With respect to shipping, nearly everyone agreed that the United States should have its own navigation laws in the form of preferences for American shipping. As Jefferson wrote, "As a branch of industry, it is valuable, but as a resource of defense, essential."[9] More controversial was the American response to foreign prohibitions, duties, and regulations, regardless of whether they were specifically aimed at the United States. In fact, the most important qualification to the founding fathers' support for free trade was the question of whether it had to be reciprocated by other countries for the United States to adopt it as well. If other countries protected their markets, the United States might be forced to do the same. In 1785, Thomas Jefferson wanted to start by "throwing open all the doors of commerce and knocking off all its shackles. But as this cannot be done for others, unless they do it for us, and there is no probability that Europe will do this, I suppose we may be obliged to adopt a system which may shackle them in our ports, as they do us in theirs"[10] And Madison wrote, "Much indeed is it to be wished, as I conceive, that no regulations of trade—that is to say, no restriction or imposts whatever—were necessary." "A perfect freedom is the System which would be my choice." But, he continued, "before such a system will be eligible perhaps for the U.S., they must be out of debt; before it will be attainable, all other nations must concur in it."[11]

Much of the early debate over government's role in foreign trade also reflected different views of the nation's economic future. Alexander Hamilton and the Federalists saw the United States as emulating Britain and becoming a commercial power with large cities, a strong financial system, and a flourishing foreign commerce. The economy would be balanced, with manufacturing industries operating alongside agricultural production, and would continue to have close ties to Britain. By contrast, Jefferson and James Madison saw the United States as remaining a largely rural country, primarily devoted to agriculture. Jefferson famously held that "those who labour the earth are the chosen people of God" and were the most virtuous, the most wedded to liberty, and the one's whose interests were most bound to that of their country. They were suspicious of merchants, who lacked loyalty and virtue, and wanted to avoid manufacturing, which gave rise to workers living in impoverished urban slums where republican virtues would fail to take hold.

As a result, Jefferson and Madison were pro-French and anti-British, pro-agriculture and pro-farmer, and anti-finance and anti-large-scale manufacturing. They viewed the great commercial and manufacturing powers of the Old World, with Britain at the head, as corrupt and degenerate. To maintain its republican virtue, America would have to avoid this path of development. Jefferson wanted the United States to remain an agrarian nation, exchanging its surplus produce for the manufactures produced far away: "While we have land to labour then, let us never wish to see our citizens occupied at a work-bench, or twirling a distaff. Carpenters, masons, smiths, are wanting in husbandry: but, for the general operations of manufacture, let our work-shops remain in Europe."[12] At times, Jefferson and his compatriots even seemed to want Americans to withdraw from world trade completely.[13] Their ambivalence about trade reflected the era's undercurrent of disgust (at least among some elites) with the corrupting effects of commerce, with its unseemly focus on the consumption of trifles and luxuries. This attitude had to be weighed against their reluctance to impose government restraints upon individual freedom.

In the end, however, such philosophical debates had little relevance for the policy choices faced by the nation's political leaders. The decisions they made were based on a pragmatic assessment of the country's circumstances. As George Washington stated, "It has long been a speculative question among Philosophers and wise men whether foreign Commerce is of real advantage to any Country—that is, whether the luxury, effeminacy, & corruption which are introduced by it, are counterbalanced by the conveniences and wealth of which it is productive." But, Washington added, the answer is of "very little importance to us" because "the spirit for Trade which pervades these States is not to be restrained."[14] This reality forced Jefferson, with some reluctance, to conclude that "our people have a decided taste for navigation and commerce. They take this from their mother country, and their servants are in duty bound to calculate all their measures on this datum."[15]

THE FIRST TARIFF ACT

The first order of business for the new Congress was raising revenue to finance the federal government's operations and service the public debt.[16] The wisdom of imposing duties on imports to generate revenue for the government was uncontested: import tariffs were convenient to administer, and direct taxes were highly unpopular.

On April 8, 1789, two days after Congress first achieved a quorum, James Madison introduced a bill in the House of Representatives to levy duties on imports. Citing the government's urgent revenue requirements, Madison argued that a tariff should be imposed without delay so that the spring importations from Europe could be taxed. As a temporary expedient, he recommended adopting the tariff structure approved by the Continental Congress in 1783, which called for a 5 percent ad valorem tax on all imports and higher specific duties on such commodities as alcohol, tea, and coffee. Madison stated that a more permanent tariff schedule could be crafted at a later date, but that Congress should act quickly to avoid missing the spring imports and to get revenue flowing into the Treasury's coffers as soon as possible: "The deficiency in our Treasury has been too notorious to make it necessary for me to animadvert upon that subject. . . . Let us content ourselves with endeavoring to remedy the evil. To do this a national revenue must be obtained; but the system must be such a one that, while it secures the object of revenue, it shall not be oppressive to our constituents."[17]

Madison's proposal sparked a debate as to whether revenue should be the sole objective of the import duties. Several members argued that, in addition to raising revenue, tariffs should be levied to promote domestic manufactures. As Thomas Hartley of Pennsylvania put it, "No argument . . . can operate to discourage the committee from taking such measures as will tend to protect and promote our domestic manufactures . . . I think it both politic and just that the fostering hand of the General Government should extend to all those manufactures which will tend to national utility."[18]

This was just the sort of debate that Madison wanted postponed to a later date. "From what has been suggested by the gentleman who have spoken on the subject before us, I am led to apprehend that we shall be under the necessity of traveling further into an investigation of principles than what I supposed necessary," he replied. "It was my view to restrain the first essay on this subject principally to the object of revenue, and make this rather a temporary expedient than anything permanent." Any delay in imposing duties to investigate the conditions of manufacturing or to debate the proper degree of protection for manufacturers would only mean foregoing valuable revenue, jeopardizing the nation's finances: "If the committee [were to] delay levying and collecting an impost, until a system of protecting duties shall be perfected, there will be no importations of any consequence, on which the law is to operate, because, by that time all the spring vessels will have arrived." Madison reiterated his view that Congress should impose a tariff immediately and then consider government policy toward manufacturing at a later date: "However much we may be disposed to promote domestic manufactures, we ought to pay some regard to the present policy of obtaining revenue."[19]

Yet, forced into a debate over principles, Madison decided to make his own clear. He was a "friend to a very free system of commerce" and regarded "commercial shackles as unjust, oppressive, and impolitic." At the same time, he was not a dogmatic advocate of commercial freedom, because he recognized "that exceptions exist to this general rule, important in themselves, and claiming the particular attention of this committee." Madison identified three such exceptions. The first was revenue, which could be "more conveniently and certainly raised by [tariffs] than any other method without injury to the community." On this point, there was no dissent.[20]

The second exception concerned navigation. "If America were to leave her ports perfectly free, and to make no discrimination between vessels owned by citizens and those owned by foreigners, while other nations make such discrimination, such a policy would go to exclude American shipping from foreign ports, and we should be materially affected in one of our most important interests." Because this outcome would be detrimental to American interests, Madison believed that the United States should impose higher tonnage charges on foreign ships entering US ports than on American ships.[21]

The third exception concerned national defense. Madison agreed in principle with the long-standing argument that "each nation should have within itself, the means of defense independent of foreign supplies." Yet he was skeptical of the principle's applicability: "There is good reason to believe that when it becomes necessary, we may obtain supplies from abroad as readily as any other nation whatsoever," particularly now that the nation had achieved independence. However, Madison was open to the idea of helping infant industries.[22]

As this exchange demonstrates, within just a few days of the opening of Congress, the great debate over trade policy was joined. That perennial debate revolves around the proper objective of import duties: to raise revenue, to restrict imports in order to protect domestic manufacturers, or to achieve reciprocity—or some combination of the three.

Despite his hope that Congress would expedite the tariff bill to start raising revenue as quickly as possible, Madison could not prevent members from arguing about the appropriate duty on various goods, often requesting special treatment for particular items. A representative from Massachusetts supported placing a specific duty on imported nails; another from Pennsylvania urged protection for iron goods, paper, and glass; and another from Virginia advocated duties on hemp and coal. Representatives from New England objected to hemp duties as detrimental to manufacturers of rope needed for ships, while those from the South objected to a duty on nails as unfair to consumers in the region. New England argued for high duties on rum and low duties on molasses to protect distilleries at the expense of sugarcane producers and refiners, while the South sought the opposite.

These clashing members rarely appealed to general principles. More often, "the arguments were based largely on local interests rather than doctrinal conviction regarding free trade or protection," Elkins and McKitrick (1993, 66–67) note. "Although the principle of protection was certainly discernible in the act which finally emerged, it was balanced throughout by the primary consideration of revenue and of what the government in any given case might reasonably hope to collect" (ibid.). Still, by the standards of later experience, the debate over the first tariff bill was not very divisive. The bill included some protective duties but consisted mainly of a low 5 percent tax on most manufactured imports. Although no final vote on the bill was recorded, the measure passed the House on June 1, 1789.

The Senate debate provided a preview of the sectional tariff debate that would continue for the next half century. South Carolina's Pierce Butler railed against the tariff as an unfair exaction on his region, which was heavily dependent on exports. As Senator William Maclay (1988, 73) of Pennsylvania noted in his diary, "Butler flamed away and threatened a dissolution of the Union with regard to his State—*as sure as God was in the firmament*. He scattered his remarks over the whole Impost bill, calling it partial, oppressive, &ca. and solely calculated to oppress S. Carolina and Yet ever and anon declaring how clear of local Views how candid and dispassionate he was. He degenerated into one declamation His State would live and die glorious &ca. &ca."

South Carolina would have violent objections to the tariff for many decades to come, but Butler's inflamed rhetoric was not just ineffective in persuading his Senate colleagues, but downright offensive. As Maclay (1988, 72) noted, "Butler's party had conducted themselves with so little deecorum, that any effect their Arguments might have had, was lost by their Manner." Maclay observed that other states took a more productive stance, but the whole issue was fraught with controversy: "The Senators from Jersey Pennsylvania Delaware and Maryland, in every Act seemed desirous of making the impost productive, both as to revenue, and effective for the encouragement of Manufactures. . . . But the Members both from the north and more particularly from the South, were ever in a flame, When any Articles were brought forward that were in any considerable Use among them" (74).

By mid-June, the Senate passed an amended House bill. The House rejected nearly all the Senate amendments, but the Senate refused to agree to the House version. Maclay (1988, 84) thought that "this really seems like playing at cross purposes—or differing for the sake of Sport." Within its first three months, and not for the last time, Congress appeared deadlocked. Beyond the usual sectional divisions, many suspected that mercantile interests were responsible for the delay, so that goods could be imported before the new duties took effect. As Maclay (1988, 69) noted, "It now seems evident, that a merchantile influence is exerted to delay the impost, untill they get-in all their Summer goods—this is a detestable . . . but I have not a name for it. I wish we were out of this base, bad place." By the end of June, however, the House finally accepted most of the Senate amendments, and the bill cleared Congress. President George Washington signed the tariff bill on July 4, 1789, making it the second law enacted by the new federal government. The duties went into effect on August 1, 1789. By later standards, Congress had acted quickly, but not as fast as Madison had wanted to get revenue from the spring importation.

The preamble of the new law stated that import duties were necessary "for the support of government, for the discharge of the debts of the United States, and the encouragement and protection of manufactures." The first tariff schedule of the United States consisted of three parts: specific duties on select products, ad valorem duties on most other goods, and duty-free treatment for a small number of items. Specific duties were imposed on thirty-six commodities, such as molasses and coffee (two and a half cents per gallon and per pound, respectively), distilled spirits (ten cents per gallon), salt (six cents per bushel), and nails (one cent per pound). Most of these specific duties were designed as revenue taxes on alcohol or luxury taxes on goods consumed mainly by the wealthy. At the same time, some of these duties provided incidental protection for some producers; although domestic spirits were subject to an excise tax, for example, the rate was much lower than the import tax. Other specific duties were imposed explicitly for the benefit of domestic producers, such as those on boots and shoes, nails and spikes, fish, and hemp.

Most imports were subject to ad valorem duties at one of four levels: 15 percent on carriages and parts, 10 percent on china, stone, and glassware, among other goods, 7.5 percent on cotton and woolen clothing, hats, hammered or rolled iron and other metal manufactures, and leather manufactures, among others, and 5 percent on all other articles not specified. Seventeen goods were placed on the duty-free list, including saltpetre, brass, tinplates, iron and brass wire, cotton and wool, hides, furs, and skins. Finally, the law established drawbacks, a provision for the rebate of import duties paid on goods that were subsequently reexported to another destination.

As the first Treasury secretary, Alexander Hamilton performed the vital task of setting up the customs service at the major US ports and overseeing its administration. By all accounts, he managed the customs service with efficiency and great attention to detail, ensuring that it operated smoothly and free of corruption. In fact, the revenue collected from customs duties increased sharply after the federal government took over responsibility for the customs service. The revenue from the ports of New York, Philadelphia, Baltimore, and Charleston jumped from almost $2 million in 1785–88 to nearly $12 million in 1792–95. The greater revenue was mostly due to the revival of foreign trade that occurred after the adoption of the Constitution, but also to an increase in the rates of duty and an improvement in the efficiency of the customs service in collecting them.[23] This was a significant achievement, given the almost complete dependence of the federal government on customs for its revenue. In 1792, for example, customs duties (both on imported merchandise and shipping tonnage) accounted for $3.4 million of the $3.7 million of total government receipts. In that year government spending, including debt service, amounted to about $5.1 million, meaning that there was still a substantial budget deficit.

Levying taxes on imports proved to be an economically and politically efficient method of raising revenue. They were economically efficient because foreign goods arrived at just a few large seaports, and therefore very few government employees were needed to collect the taxes on them. The administrative cost of enforcing import duties was just 4 percent of the gross revenue collected, while the cost of collecting domestic excise taxes involved many more tax collectors scattered around the country and cost 20 percent of gross revenue.[24]

Equally important, import duties were a politically efficient way of raising revenue. Tariffs were automatically built into the domestic price of imported goods and avoided the "political minefield" of domestic taxes.[25] Hamilton's fiscal program brought about a welcome shift in the nation's tax system away from direct taxes (poll and land) imposed by states toward customs duties imposed by the federal government. By assuming state debts, Hamilton's program enabled states to reduce direct taxes by as much as 75 percent in some cases.[26] In shifting the nation's revenue system from direct taxes to import taxes, the tax burden as perceived by most people fell sharply. The frequent protests over state taxes in the 1780s largely disappeared in the 1790s. And since customs duties were less intrusive than other forms of taxation, the federal government avoided sparking a debate about its legitimacy.

At the same time, Hamilton sought to supplement and diversify the government's revenue sources away from customs duties, which fluctuated depending on the level of imports, to more dependable forms of internal revenue, such as excise taxes. Hamilton worried that complete dependence on tariff revenue would be risky in time of war and might put the nation's finances in jeopardy at just the wrong time. Yet domestic taxes were highly unpopular, and Congress was reluctant to enact them. In the aftermath of the fight over the Constitution and the uncertain public support for the new federal government, Hamilton was cautious about proposing new domestic taxes, for fear that they might trigger a domestic political backlash, as they did with the Whiskey Rebellion in 1794. As a result, Hamilton managed to diversify the source of government revenue only to a minor extent.

Despite the growth in customs revenues that came with expanding trade, the fiscal position of the federal government remained precarious in the early 1790s. In 1792, the interest alone on US debt soaked up 87 percent of total revenue. The United States covered its deficit only through a large loan from the Netherlands, which helped pay off previous foreign loans and allowed for the redemption of significant amounts of domestic debt.[27] Still, this refinancing meant that the nominal value of the national debt did not fall during the 1790. (It was not until 1796 that the government's tax revenue would cover its current expenditures and interest on the debt.) This left Hamilton open to charges that he was not serious about paying down the debt, but political constraints prevented further increases in either import duties or excise taxes. As Edling (2007, 306) points out, "Faced with a choice between raising taxes to pay off the debt rapidly or accepting indebtedness for at least the foreseeable future, Hamilton opted for the latter alternative."

These revenue constraints made Hamilton extremely sensitive to the government's fiscal position. He worked to husband the government's meager financial resources and maintain the country's creditworthiness. As we will see, he desperately wanted the United States to remain neutral in any European military conflict, fearing that American involvement would ruin the nation's finances. Becoming entangled in a war for which it was unprepared would cause government expenditures to soar and its revenues to collapse. As we will see, this fear of fiscal dislocation deeply colored Hamilton's approach to the issue of trade reciprocity.

Recognizing the government's fragile fiscal position, Hamilton sought to generate additional revenue by boosting the specific duties in the tariff schedule. In January 1790, in his first report to Congress as Treasury secretary, Hamilton proposed increasing the duty on Madeira wine from 18 cents to 20 cents, on Hyson tea from 20 cents to 40 cents per pound, on coffee from 2.5 cents to 5 cents per pound, and on chinaware from 10 percent to 12.5 percent, among many other adjustments. Congress enacted most of these recommendations in August 1790. Still more increases followed. Acting again on Hamilton's advice, Congress increased the duties on spirits in March 1791. At this point, Hamilton believed that "the duties on the great mass of imported articles have reached a point, which it would not be expedient to exceed" for fear of discouraging trade.[28]

And yet the government's revenue requirements continued to grow. In

1792, in order to finance new expenditures to protect the western frontier, Congress raised ad valorem duties by 2.5 percentage points, pushing the base rate from 5 percent to 7.5 percent. The schedule was hiked another 2.5 percentage points in 1794, bringing the base rate to 10 percent, while duties on sugar and wine were also increased to retire the public debt at a faster pace. In 1797, Congress increased the base rate yet again, to 12.5 percent, and imposed higher specific duties on sugar, molasses, tea, cocoa, and other products. In each of these cases, the primary purpose of the adjustment was to raise revenue to finance government operations and service the national debt. Thus, although the average tariff was initially around 12 percent in 1790 and 1791, subsequent revisions quickly brought it up to about 20 percent by the mid-1790s, as Figure I.1 showed.[29]

HAMILTON'S REPORT ON MANUFACTURES

In constructing the first tariff, Congress largely sidestepped the issue of protecting fledgling manufactures from foreign competition, but it could not avoid such a discussion for long. In his first annual message to Congress in January 1790, President Washington noted that the safety and interest of a free people "require that they should promote such manufactories as tend to render them independent of others for essential, particularly military, supplies." Seven days later, the House of Representatives requested that the secretary of the Treasury "prepare and report to the House, a proper plan or plans, conformable to the recommendations of the President . . . for the encouragement and promotion of such manufactories as will tend to render the United States independent of other nations for essential, especially military, supplies."[30] Nearly two years after this request, in December 1791, Hamilton delivered his famous *Report on the Subject of Manufactures*.

This brilliant report ranks among the most important and influential policy documents in US history.[31] Hamilton made a broad-ranging and powerful case for government promotion of domestic manufacturing, providing not only theoretical justifications for such a policy but specific proposals for government action as well. In a clear reference to Adam Smith, Hamilton conceded that "if the system of perfect liberty to industry and commerce were the prevailing system of nations, the arguments which dissuade a country in the predicament of the United States from the zealous pursuits of manufactures would doubtless have great force." In such a case, the United States could freely exports its staples in exchange for imports of manufactures produced in Europe. But that system "is far from characterizing the general policy of nations," and the United States was precluded from engaging in such unobstructed exchange. While it could easily import manufactured goods, the United States could not "exchange with Europe on equal terms" because it faced "numerous and very injurious impediments to the emission and vent of their own commodities."[32] To Hamilton, this meant that the country should consider developing its own domestic supply of manufactures, particularly those needed for national defense.

Hamilton next turned to the contention, also associated with Adam Smith, that such government support was unnecessary because "industry if left to itself, will naturally find its way to the most useful and profitable employment: whence it is inferred, that manufactures without the aid of government will grow up as soon and as fast, as the natural state of things and the interest of the community may require."[33] Hamilton had long dissented from this view, which he thought ignored the lessons of history and experience that governments almost invariably seek to regulate trade for the benefit of their own merchants and producers.[34]

Thus, Hamilton argued that the United States had a national interest in fostering domestic manufacturing and maintained that "the incitement and patronage of government" was required to overcome the inhibitions that prevented them from becoming established. These impediments included "the strong influence of habit and the spirit of imitation—the fear of want of success in untried enterprises—the intrinsic difficulties incident to first essays toward a competition with those who have previously attained to perfection in the business to be attempted—the bounties, premiums and other artificial encouragements, with which foreign nations second the exertions of their own Citizens in the branches, in which they are to be rivaled."[35]

In Hamilton's view, this last factor—the artificial encouragements in other countries—constituted the greatest obstacle. This meant that domestic manufacturers not only had to contend with the "natural disadvantages of a new undertaking" but also "the gratuities and remunerations which other governments bestow" on their own producers. "To maintain between the recent establishments of one country and the long matured establishments of another country, a competition upon equal terms, both as to quality and price, is in most cases impracticable," he declared. "The disparity in the one, or in the other, or in both, must necessarily be so considerable as to forbid a successful rivalship, without the extraordinary aid and protection of government."[36]

After discussing other difficulties in establishing manufacturing in the United States, such as the high price of labor and the scarcity of capital, Hamilton examined the means by which government could promote domestic manufacturers. These included import duties, pecuniary bounties (subsidies), patents, and other measures. Hamilton rated bounties as "one of the most efficacious means of encouraging manufactures, and it is in some views, the best. . . . though it is less favored by public opinion than other modes." He gave three reasons for preferring subsidies over tariffs as a means of promoting manufacturers. First, subsidies have a "more immediate tendency to stimulate and uphold new enterprises, increasing the chances of profit, and diminishing the risks of loss, in the first attempts." Second, "bounties have not, like high protecting duties, a tendency to produce scarcity." Third, bounties promote exports and enlarge the size of the potential market for domestic producers.[37]

In essence, subsidies were a more direct and positive encouragement that, unlike import tariffs, did not create scarcity and artificially raise domestic prices. For this reason, Hamilton believed that subsidies could conciliate the agricultural and manufacturing interests of the country, which might otherwise clash over tariff restrictions. Of course, Hamilton was also well aware of the public's strong prejudice against bounties, candidly admitting that "there is a degree of prejudice against bounties from an appearance of giving away the public money."[38]

Although Hamilton favored direct, targeted subsidies as the best way to promote manufacturing, he was less enthusiastic about, but not opposed to, moderate duties that gave domestic producers a competitive advantage over foreign producers, provided that those duties did not compromise revenue and efficiency. Hamilton was skeptical of protective tariffs because they sheltered efficient and inefficient producers alike, resulting in higher prices for consumers, at least temporarily, and encouraged tariff-evasion and smuggling, which cut into government revenue.

Hamilton concluded his report by making specific policy recommendations with respect to a long list of itemized products. He proposed an increase in tariff rates on twenty-one products, a reduction in tariff rates on five raw materials used in manufacturing, and government subsidies to five industries. Most of the proposed tariff increases would raise the existing duties by a very small amount, from 5 to 10 percent. The tariff reductions on raw materials—raw wood, raw copper, raw cotton, raw silk, and sulfur (for gunpowder)—entailed the elimination of a 5 percent duty. Despite the stress placed on subsidies in the report, Hamilton proposed them only for domestic producers of coal, raw wool, sail cloth, cotton manufactures, and glass (window and bottles). Perhaps this list was short because Hamilton recognized the political reality that funds for bounties were scarce, and Congressional support for them was weak.

After receiving Hamilton's report in December 1791, Congress apparently tabled it with no clear indication of when it would be taken up for debate. Whenever that debate was to take place, however, Madison (in the House) and Jefferson (as Secretary of State) were prepared to fight it. They believed that bounties were unconstitutional and, if enacted, would set a dangerous precedent. Less than a month after Hamilton's report was issued, Madison complained that it "broaches a new constitutional doctrine of vast consequence . . . I consider it myself as subverting the fundamental and characteristic principle of the Government, as contrary to the true & fair, as well as the received construction, and as bidding defiance to the sense in which the Constitution is known to have been proposed, advocated and adopted. If Congress can do whatever in their *discretion* can be *done by money*, and will promote the *general welfare*, the Government is no longer a limited one possessing enumerated powers, but an indefinite one subject to particular exceptions."[39] Hamilton anticipated this particular objection in his report, noting that Congress had the express authority under the Constitution to impose taxes "to pay the debts and provide for the common defence and general welfare." In his view, the phrase "general welfare" was "as comprehensive as any that could have been used" and "necessarily embraces a vast variety of particulars."[40]

Jefferson also plotted against the report using a similar line of constitutional argument. Jefferson noted that import duties were the traditional means of promoting manufactures and that the use of bounties "has been found almost inseparable from abuse."[41] Later that month, in a meeting with President Washington, Jefferson attacked "the Report on manufactures which, under colour of giving *bounties* for the encouragement of particular manufactures, meant to establish the doctrine that the power given by the Constitution to collect taxes to provide for the *general welfare* of the US permitted Congress to take every thing under their management which *they* should deem for the *public welfare*, and which is susceptible of the application of money." The conversation ended there, without any apparent reaction from Washington, according to Jefferson's notes.[42] In July 1792, Jefferson reminded himself to "condemn [the] report on manufactures." He did so in a letter to Washington in September 1792, writing that Hamilton's system "flowed from principles adverse to liberty, and was calculated to undermine and demolish the republic." The system was a threat to the Constitution because "in a Report on the subject of manufactures, (still to be acted upon) it was expressly assumed that the general government has a right to exercise all powers which may be for the *general welfare*."[43]

Although the *Report on Manufactures* was never presented as a single legislative package, and hence there was no opportunity for a congressional debate on its proposals, it probably would have faced a firestorm of opposition from Madison and his allies from the South. Congress's resistance to appropriating public funds to help particular industries became evident in a divisive debate over compensation to cod fisheries in New England for the duty on imported salt used to cure fish. In the course of that debate, so much hostility was directed at the term "bounties" that any attempt to get Congress to approve a general program of subsidies was sure to be met with strong resistance.[44]

Although bounties were a political nonstarter, Hamilton succeeded in persuading Congress to enact the tariff proposals in the *Report on Manufactures* within six months of its publication. Hamilton was handed an opportunity to shape new tariff legislation shortly after the humiliating defeat of American military forces by western Indians in November 1791. In March 1792, Congress asked for the Treasury's advice on how to raise additional revenues in order to finance increased expenditures for the protection of the frontier.[45] Hamilton wasted no time in taking advantage of this request, forwarding his recommendations just ten days later. Hamilton's brief report presented three methods of raising the $526,000 required to finance the additional military expenditures: selling the government's stake in the Bank of the United States, borrowing the funds from creditors, or raising taxes. Hamilton ruled out the first two options as imprudent and recommended higher import duties, even though he recognized that "taxes are never welcome to a community." One advantage of the tariffs, he argued, was that because "a spirit of manufactures prevails at this time, in a greater degree, than it has done at any antecedent period; and, as far as an increase of duties shall tend to second and aid this spirit, they will serve to promote essentially the industry, the wealth, the strength, the independence, and the substantial prosperity of the country."[46]

With this, Hamilton proposed a temporary increase in the base rate on imports from 5 percent to 7.5 percent, in addition to permanent changes in the specific and ad valorem duties on a host of specified goods. Most of the recommended changes in ad valorem duties were taken straight from the *Report on Manufactures*. Few specific duties were mentioned in the report, because few manufactured goods were subject to them, and Hamilton did not propose any bounties, because he had been asked by Congress to suggest ways of raising money, not spending it.

Congress's debate over the revenue bill was brief, but several representatives objected to what they considered to be its false pretext. For example, John Page of Virginia announced his intention of voting against the measure, arguing that "it is not a bill for the protection of the frontiers, but for the encouragement of certain manufactures. . . . It is a bill very different from what it ought to be." John Mercer of Maryland asked whether "the submission of a provision to defend the frontier authorize [sic] a system for the encouragement of manufactures? . . . Independent of the constitutional question of the right of Congress, why should we be compelled to consider the extensive range and delicate refinement of encouraging manufactures by extensive duties operating as indirect bounties, under the pressure of providing for an Indian war?"[47]

When the votes were cast, the tariff passed by the comfortable margin of 37–20. This was one of the first recorded votes on tariffs in the House and revealed a sharp division between the North and the South, one that would persist for almost two centuries. Representatives from New England and the Mid-Atlantic states voted 20–7 in favor of the bill, while those from the South voted 13–7 against. The vote suggested that the tariff increase did not have overwhelming political support and passed only because it was tied to increased military expenditures to protect the frontier. "Had circumstances been different, it is extremely doubtful that this tariff proposal would have stood much chance in Congress," Clarfield (1975, 459) concludes. "By linking military appropriations to the impost, however, Hamilton managed to neutralize a good deal of the opposition."

Therefore, Hamilton's tariff proposals in the *Report on Manufactures* in December 1791 formed the basis for his recommendations to the House in March 1792 and were largely accepted by the Congress in May 1792. In the report, Hamilton proposed twenty-one tariff increases and five decreases, most of which were repeated in the 1792 report. In the end, Congress enacted eighteen of the increases and three of the reductions.[48] Thus, Congress adopted almost all of Hamilton's proposals for higher tariffs on manufactured goods, although a program of bounties was never proposed or seriously entertained. For this reason, nine months after the *Report* had been issued and four months after the tariff vote, Jefferson believed the report was "still to be acted upon." And yet Congress had done all it was going to do with the report—namely, implement its tariff proposals without touching the bounty or other recommendations.

The *Report on Manufactures* would influence the public debate over trade policy and government's role in promoting manufactures for many decades to come. The report was frequently cited to justify high tariffs to protect domestic manufacturers from foreign competition. Yet Hamilton was much less of an advocate of "protectionism" than he was later made out to be.[49] Because revenue considerations were absolutely paramount to him, Hamilton preferred modest duties on imports, not excessively high duties. Moderate duties would keep imports flowing into the country, providing the essential tax base that would produce a reliable stream of revenue to fund government expenditures and establish the public credit. "Experience has shown that moderate duties are more productive [of revenue] than high ones," Hamilton observed in 1782.[50]

Indeed, Hamilton was skeptical of high protective tariffs because they sheltered both inefficient and efficient producers, led to higher prices for consumers, and gave rise to smuggling, which cut into government revenue. In *Federalist 35*, Hamilton noted,

> There are persons who imagine that [high import duties] can never be carried to too great a length; since the higher they are, the more it is alleged they will tend to discourage an extravagant consumption, to produce a favourable balance of trade, and to promote domestic manufactures. But all extremes are pernicious in various ways. Exorbitant duties on imported articles would beget a general spirit of smuggling; which is always prejudicial to the fair trader, and eventually to the revenue itself: They tend to render other classes of the community tributary in an improper degree to the manufacturing classes to whom they give a premature monopoly of the markets: They sometimes force industry out of its more natural channels into others in which it flows with less advantage. And in the last place they oppress the merchant, who is often obliged to pay them himself without any retribution from the consumer.[51]

Partly for these reasons, Hamilton preferred bounties to tariffs. Yet even here, Hamilton cautioned that "the continuance of bounties on manufacturers long established must always be of questionable policy. . . . But in new undertakings, they are as justifiable, as they are oftentimes necessary."[52] Thus, Hamilton might well have opposed the high import duties for established industries that were imposed after the Civil War, because his primary concern was with launching and establishing new industries, not supporting existing ones. As Clarfield (1975, 459) has noted, "The key word in Hamilton's conception was *encouragement*, not *protection*" for manufacturers.

In his own day, manufacturing interests were not wholly aligned behind Hamilton. His proposed tariff levels were quite modest compared to what domestic manufacturers would have liked and were later imposed, although at the time domestic producers were protected by relatively high transportation costs. Moderate duties served the interests of merchants engaged in commerce, such as those in New York and Massachusetts, but fell short of meeting the demands of manufacturers who preferred shutting out most imports of foreign goods. Hamilton's reluctance to endorse protectionist duties disappointed these manufacturers, who had hoped for greater government support but discovered that their petitions for higher tariffs went unanswered. His failure to back protective duties eventually had political repercussions. "By the end of 1793, Hamilton's pro-importer political economy was driving manufacturers from Boston to Charleston into opposition to the Federalists," Nelson (1979, 977) observes.[53] "In 1794 New York's General Society of Mechanics and Tradesmen shifted their support from the Federalists to nascent Republican organizations. It was becoming apparent to many American manufacturers that Hamilton's policies contravened their interests" (977).

At first, it seems puzzling that import-competing manufacturers would seek political refuge with the Jeffersonian Republicans. Jefferson and Madison had long been on record as praising the virtues of an agrarian-based economy, fearing the consequences of large-scale manufacturing, and opposing most government interference in the economy. But even as they resisted the more activist government policies that Hamilton envisioned, Jefferson and Madison were willing to consider much more draconian restrictions on trade than Hamilton's revenue-based policy would ever allow. Their hostility to Britain's policies led them to call for a policy of aggressive reciprocity and trade sanctions to punish Britain for its restrictions on American commerce.

Hamilton vigorously opposed these efforts for fear that they would start a trade war that would reduce imports from Britain, thereby shrinking the tax base on which his plans to fund the public debt hinged. This would ruin America's standing on credit markets. As a result, when the Washington administration under Hamilton's guidance sought political accommodation with Britain, Tench Coxe, a Treasury official who penned a first draft of the *Report on Manufactures* for Hamilton, shifted his allegiance to the Jeffersonian Republicans in the belief that their trade policies were better suited to promoting domestic industries.

THE RECIPROCITY DEBATE

Although the first tariff act had been passed with minimal rancor, and a divisive debate over the *Report on Manufactures* had been avoided, a sharp conflict was brewing deep within the Washington administration over trade policy. Already on such issues as the public debt and a national bank, a rift had developed that pitted Hamilton against Jefferson and Madison. This divergence of views led to the emergence of two opposing political factions, the Federalists, led by Washington and Hamilton, and the Republicans, led by Jefferson and Madison. (In the 1830s, the Jeffersonian Republicans became known as the Democrats and the Federalists had become the Whigs and then the Republicans in the 1850s.)

The chief dispute between the Federalists and Republicans on trade related to America's ties to Britain and France. The Federalists, drawing their support from the commercial states of New York and New England, wanted to maintain friendly commercial relations with Britain. While frustrated about the restrictions on American access to its domestic and colonial markets, they still believed that Britain was the best source of supply and the best foreign market for US goods. The Federalists did not want to disrupt that commercial relationship and opposed discriminatory trade and shipping policies that might offend Britain and spark retaliatory action against the United States.

As already noted, Hamilton put a priority on the fiscal solvency of the federal government and on ensuring a large and steady stream of customs revenue to finance its operations, pay down its debts, and establish the nation's creditworthiness. Any trade war with Britain would disrupt imports and the flow of revenue from import duties, undermining the country's finances and ability to borrow on credit markets. Given the fragility of the nation's finances, Hamilton's overriding goal was to ensure that the government could finance the public debt: "Nothing can more interest the National Credit and prosperity, than a constant and systematic attention to husband all means previously possessed for extinguishing the present debt, and to avoid, as much as possible, the incurring of any new debt."[54]

Given this fragility, Hamilton believed that the United States had to avoid any significant drop in imports and loss of the customs revenues they generated, while also avoiding any sudden, unexpected rise in spending. Becoming embroiled in a war was the quickest way to bring about a collapse in revenue and a surge in expenditures. Nothing, in his view, could more quickly destroy the nation's finances and ruin its creditworthiness. Therefore, despite the public resentment against Britain, Hamilton vigorously opposed discriminating against the country out of fear that a trade war would jeopardize his entire fiscal program. Hamilton thought that America was in a much weaker position than Britain and had much more to lose as a result of a conflict.

By contrast, the Jeffersonian Republicans despised Britain for its mercantilist policies, especially the exclusion of American ships and goods from the British West Indies. Those policies harmed southern exporters and interfered with the natural course of the country's commerce. Republicans believed that the nation's political independence could not be fully realized unless the country had its economic independence as well. Madison complained that Britain "has bound us in commercial manacles, and very nearly defeated the object of our independence."[55] In Jefferson's view, "dependence begets subservience and venality, suffocates the germ of virtue, and prepares fit tools for the designs of ambition." Jefferson and Madison demanded that strong action be taken. In particular, they wanted to give trade preferences to France as a way of cultivating an alternative to the British market and putting pressure on Britain to change its policies.[56] Of course, there was an inconsistency in the Jeffersonian argument: If discrimination succeeded in changing Britain's policy, which they anticipated happening, it would expand trade between the two countries and reinforce US "commercial dependence" on Britain.

In April 1789, as Madison unveiled his plan to impose tariffs on merchandise imports, he also proposed to levy duties on the tonnage of ships entering American ports. Under Madison's scheme, the tonnage duties would have three categories: one rate for American vessels, a higher rate for foreign vessels from countries that had a treaty of commerce with the United States, and the highest rate for foreign vessels from countries without such a treaty. Establishing tonnage duties that favored American ships was not controversial: there was broad support for giving some preference to domestic shipping in the handling of US foreign trade to encourage the development of the merchant marine. But Madison's real objective was to discriminate against Britain in favor of France, because the United States had a commercial treaty with France but not with Britain. Madison believed that it was unacceptable for the United States to impose relatively light duties on British manufactures, while major US exports, such as flour and wheat, fish and salted provisions, were highly restricted, if not banned, in British markets. The discriminatory tonnage duties would reduce America's commercial dependence on Britain and shift trade toward France, its wartime ally.

Madison was even confident that the United States possessed the economic power to force Britain to relax its commercial restrictions. Speaking in the House, Madison contended that the country was in a position "to wage a commercial warfare," because it exported foodstuffs and raw materials that were essential to Britain, while it imported manufactured goods and other trifles that it could do without. In a trade war, Britain's commercial interests would be "wounded almost mortally, while ours are invulnerable." "If we were disposed to hazard the experiment of interdicting the intercourse between us and the powers not in alliance, we should have overtures of the most advantageous kind tendered by those nations," Madison contended. "We possess natural advantages which no other nation does; we can, therefore, with justice, stipulate for a reciprocity in commerce." "We must make the other nation feel our power to induce her to grant us reciprocal advantages," he concluded. "I have, therefore, no fears of entering into a commercial warfare with that nation; if fears are to be entertained, they lie on the other side."[57]

In May 1789, the House passed Madison's bill to impose duties on ships entering American ports. The schedule was six cents per ton on American ships, thirty cents per ton on those from nations "in alliance" with the United States, and fifty cents per ton on all other foreign ships. But a month later, the Senate rejected this measure in favor of a uniform fifty-cent duty on all foreign tonnage. Opposition to Madison's discrimination scheme was spearheaded by the mercantile community in New York and New England.

President Washington regretted the Senate's action as "adverse to my ideas of justice and policy."[58] He was apparently unaware that Hamilton (not yet his Treasury secretary) had worked with senators to defeat tonnage discrimination against Britain. Hamilton later revealed that he had been "decidedly opposed to those discriminating clauses" in Madison's bill on the grounds that a provocation could start a trade war and jeopardize his planned fiscal program.[59] Madison and the House initially rejected the Senate version, but finally accepted it to avoid further delays in collecting revenue.

Madison reintroduced tonnage discrimination in the spring of 1790, but this time the proposal died in the House. The issue returned again in early 1791 when France insisted that it should be exempt from the higher foreign tonnage duty because of the 1778 commercial treaty. Although Jefferson disagreed with the French interpretation of the treaty, he wanted to give France the preference as a gesture of good will. Hamilton opposed this idea because there was "a want of reciprocity in the thing itself"; that is, French ships would be treated as American ships were in US ports, but US ships would only get equal treatment with other foreign ships in French ports. Hamilton also believed that granting a unilateral concession would set a bad precedent; instead, he recommended negotiating a new treaty of commerce with France which "would perhaps be less likely than apparently gratuitous and voluntary exemptions to beget discontents elsewhere."

Hamilton then summarized his position for Jefferson: "My commercial system turns very much on giving a free course to Trade and cultivating good humour with all the world. And I feel a particular reluctance to hazard anything in the present state of our affairs which may lead to commercial warfare with any power."[60] As a final point, Hamilton noted that the revenues from the tonnage duties were earmarked for paying down the public debt: "I do not mention this as an insuperable objection but it would be essential that the same act which should destroy this source of revenue should provide an equivalent. This I consider as a rule which ought to be sacred, as it affects public credit."[61]

Hamilton's response dismayed Jefferson, who wrote that "our treasury still thinks that these new encroachments of Gt. Brit. on our carrying trade must be met with passive obedience and non-resistance, lest any misunderstanding with them should *affect our credit, or the prices of our public paper*." Jefferson later took his complaint to the president. "My system was to give some satisfactory distinctions to the French, of little cost to us, in return for the solid advantages yielded us by them; and to have met the English with some restrictions, which might induce them to abate their severities against our commerce," he explained. "I have always supposed this coincided with your sentiments; yet the Secretary of the Treasury, by his cabals with members of the legislature and by high-toned declamations on other occasions, has forced his own system, which was exactly the reverse."[62] Washington listened to Jefferson but did not overrule Hamilton.

American policy received another jolt when France declared war on Britain in February 1793. The European war represented both an opportunity and a threat to the new nation. America's shipping exports received a tremendous boost from the conflict, but the expansion of the reexport or carrying trade to Europe also put the United States in a hazardous situation of navigating between the two belligerents.

The economic impact of the conflict on the United States was generally favorable. As British and French merchant shipping was diverted into military service, American merchants stood ready to take over the lucrative commercial routes. US reexports—foreign-produced goods that landed in the United States before being shipped to other destinations—soared in the early 1790s. In almost every year between 1797 and 1807, exports of foreign products exceeded exports of domestic products. Shipping earnings surged as well. The European war rendered moot the Congressional debate over tonnage discrimination. When Madison first proposed the discriminatory duties, the tonnage of domestic and foreign ships engaged in US foreign trade was roughly equal; by the mid-1790s, American ships carried more than 90 percent of US foreign commerce.

The reexport boom of the 1790s had a modest but positive impact on the economy and perhaps contributed 2–3 percent to national income.[63] Of course, the prosperity of the period was also artificial in that it depended upon continued conflict between Britain and France. The benefits of the expansion in the foreign trade sector were felt mainly in commercial shipping, which was concentrated in the port cities of New York, Boston, Philadelphia, and Baltimore. After having languished since the mid-1770s, American shipbuilding also experienced a sharp expansion during the 1790s.[64]

Other parts of the economy did not necessarily share in the prosperity. Although the war kept prices for wheat and flour high, other exports suffered because of the conflict. The rise in shipping earnings was largely the result of an increase in freight rates, which raised the cost of exporting other domestic goods. Indeed, exports of domestic merchandise were crowded out by the reexport boom and grew only slightly in volume during the 1790s. Southern states, such as Virginia and South Carolina, not only failed to benefit from the growth in reexports, but their commodity exports were impeded by the higher shipping costs. The share of total exports from the South fell during the decade, causing much local resentment. John Randolph of Virginia disparaged the reexport trade as "this mushroom, this fungus of war" that harmed the South's economy.[65] Thus, the benefits of the reexport trade must be set against the loss of domestic exports and the direct and indirect costs of undertaking commerce during a period of war.[66]

The European war reignited the policy debate in the Washington administration about how to approach the situation. Jefferson and Madison favored supporting France, while Hamilton wanted to avoid becoming embroiled in the conflict. In April 1793, President Washington issued the "Neutrality Proclamation" that declared the United States would not take sides and would continue to engage in shipping and commerce wherever it could.

Despite this declaration, navigating an even course between the two

European belligerents proved to be the nation's major foreign policy challenge over the next twenty years. The British government began to crack down on US trade with France after issuing Orders in Council in June 1793 that allowed its navy to seize all foodstuffs being shipped to any port controlled by France or its colonies. The government rejected US claims that "free ships mean free goods." Under this doctrine, if American merchants possessed the right to navigate in an area, they also had a right to ship goods free from confiscation or outside interference. However, Britain was serious about enforcing the Orders and disrupted America's trade and shipping in the West Indies, quickly seizing three hundred US ships and either jailing the crews or impressing them into the British navy.

This gave Jefferson the opportunity to release his long-anticipated report to Congress on "privileges and restrictions on the commerce of the United States in foreign countries."[67] Issued in December 1793, Jefferson's *Report on Commercial Restrictions* began by extolling the benefits of free trade: "Instead of embarrassing commerce under piles of regulating laws, duties and prohibitions, could it be relieved from all its shackles in all parts of the world, could every country be employed in producing that which nature has best fitted it to produce, and each be free to exchange with others mutual surpluses for mutual wants, the greatest mass possible would then be produced of those things which contribute to human life and human happiness; the numbers of mankind would be increased and their condition bettered."[68] However, Jefferson's report documented the numerous barriers placed on American goods and ships in foreign markets, such as Britain's near prohibitory duties on foodstuffs and the navigation policy of many European countries that prevented American ships from carrying foreign goods to their market.

Jefferson's preferred course of action was "friendly arrangements" with other countries to remove such barriers to trade. "Would even a single nation begin with the United States this system of free commerce, it would be advisable to begin it with that nation," Jefferson wrote. "Some nations, not yet ripe for free commerce in all its extent, might still be willing to mollify its restrictions and regulations for us, in proportion to the advantages which an intercourse with us might offer." But, he insisted, trade had to be free on both sides. Jefferson argued that "should any nation, contrary to our wishes, suppose it may better find its advantage by continuing its system of prohibitions, duties, and regulations, it behooves us to protect our citizens, their commerce, and navigation, by counter prohibitions, duties, and regulations, also. Free commerce and navigation are not to be given in exchange for restrictions and vexations, nor are they likely to produce a relaxation of them."[69] Thus, what Jefferson had called "my system" involved a far-reaching policy of reciprocity: high duties and prohibitions abroad would be met with high duties and prohibitions at home, all with the objective of freeing trade from such barriers. "Where a nation imposed high duties on our productions, or prohibits them altogether, it may be proper for us to do the same by theirs."

Jefferson conceded that such a policy might prove costly, but if the United States did nothing, while others imposed duties and prohibitions on its commerce and navigation, he thought that would simply encourage the adoption of similarly illiberal policies elsewhere:

> It is true, we must expect some inconvenience in practice from the establishment of discriminating duties. But in this, as in so many other cases, we are left to choose between two evils. These inconveniences are nothing, when weighted against the loss of wealth and loss of force, which will follow our perseverance in the plan of indiscrimination. When once it shall be perceived that we are either in the system or in the habit of giving equal advantages to those who extinguish our commerce and navigation by duties or prohibitions, as to those who treat both with liberality and justice, liberality and justice will be converted by all, into duties and prohibitions. It is not to the moderation and justice of others we are to trust for fair and equal access to market with our productions, or for our due share in the transportation of them; but to our own means of independence, and the firm will to use them.[70]

To implement a policy of reciprocity, Jefferson suggested adopting a two-column tariff schedule, one set of duties for goods from preferred countries and another set of higher duties for goods from nonpreferred countries. Somewhat surprisingly, given his previous views, Jefferson mentioned that such discriminatory duties would provide "indirect encouragement to domestic manufactures of the same kind, may induce the [foreign] manufacturer to come himself into these States, where cheaper subsistence, equal laws, and a vent of his wares, free of duty, may ensure him the highest profits from his skill and industry."[71]

The publication of Jefferson's report prompted Madison to move that Congress take immediate action to implement a policy of reciprocity. In January 1794, Madison proposed that countries without a commercial treaty with the United States (meaning Britain) should face higher tariffs on merchandise and duties on shipping. Hamilton worked feverishly to defeat these proposals and head off a confrontation with Britain.[72] Hamilton argued that it was completely unrealistic to expect British policy to change as a result of such actions and that setting up new trade barriers would hurt the United States more than Britain. "The folly is too great to be seriously entertained by the discerning part of those who affect to believe the position—that Great Britain . . . will submit to our demands urged with the face of coercion and preceded by acts of reprisal. . . . It is morally certain that she will not do it." His allies in Congress spoke out strongly against any reciprocity measure that involved discriminating against Britain.[73] In a speech largely written by Hamilton, William Loughton Smith of South Carolina condemned the report as promoting "a false estimate of the comparative condition of our commerce" with France and Britain. Smith urged the country to temper its resentment and warned of

> the impracticability and Quixotism of an attempt by violence, on the part of this young country, to break through the fetters which the universal policy of nations imposes on their intercourse with each other. . . . The main argument for the chance of success, is, that our supplies to Great Britain are more important to her than hers to us. But this is a position which our self-love gives more credit to than facts will altogether authorize; . . . while a commercial warfare with Great Britain would disturb the course of about one-sixth of her trade, it would disturb the course of more than one-half ours.

Smith concluded by asking, "Why should this young country throw down the gauntlet in favor of free trade against the world? There may be spirit in it, but there would certainly not be prudence."[74]

A heated House debate over Madison's reciprocity proposal consumed much of January 1794, but Madison repeatedly postponed a vote on it, recognizing that it probably would be defeated. With the American economy enjoying a revival after 1789, few wanted to jeopardize the recent gains in an attempt to inflict wounds on Britain. Then, in March, news arrived of strict new Orders in Council which instructed the British navy to blockade the entire French West Indies to all foreign commerce. Americans were outraged that Britain, after having excluded US ships from the British West Indies, was now seizing more ships and telling the United States that it could not trade with the French West Indies either. This deepened the crisis in Anglo-American relations and put the two countries on a collision course. After President Washington reported on the hardships faced by the detained American crews, a defiant Congress declared a thirty-day embargo (later extended for another thirty days) on all shipping to foreign ports. For this, France retaliated by intercepting American ships bound for Britain, harassing the crews, and seizing their cargo. The situation was quickly unraveling and putting the nation on the brink of war with both powers.

Hamilton urgently warned Washington against declaring war or taking commercial reprisals against Britain. He rejected Madison's claim that the United States possessed great commercial strength: "Tis as great an error for a nation to overrate as to underrate itself. . . . Tis our error to overrate ourselves and to underrate Great Britain. We forget how little we can annoy [and] how much we may be annoyed. . . . To precipitate a great conflict of any sort is utterly unsuited to our condition to our strength or to our resources." He argued that a trade war would inflict more harm on the United States than it would on Britain. If the United States cut off bilateral commerce, Britain would simply divert its purchases of food and materials to other suppliers, whereas such an action "deprives us of a supply for which no substitute can be found elsewhere—a supply, necessary to us in peace, and more necessary to us if we are to go to war."[75]

Which faction had a more accurate appraisal of the situation? In terms of economic leverage, the figures on bilateral trade seem to confirm Hamilton's view. While Britain sent nearly 20 percent of its exports to the United States, only 6 percent of its imports came from the United States. On the other hand, about 90 percent of US imports and 25 percent of exports were with Britain.[76] Madison would argue that these percentages were misleading: the United States exported essential food and materials to Britain, whereas it imported trifles. Yet Britain also had alternative sources of supply for most of the goods that it purchased from the United States.

In April, Congress considered sequestering payments to British creditors and prohibiting trade. Hamilton wrote to Washington that these actions "cannot but have a malignant influence upon our public and mercantile credit. . . . Every gust that arises in the political sky is the signal for measures tending to destroy [our] ability to pay or to obstruct the course of payment." In particular, continuing the embargo would lead to the "derangement of our revenue and credit." Such a precipitous act would "give a sudden and violent blow to our revenue which cannot easily if at all be repaired from other sources. It will give so great an interruption to commerce as may very possibly interfere with the payment of the duties which have heretofore accrued and bring the Treasury to an absolute stoppage of payment—an event which would cut up credit by the roots."[77]

Meanwhile, Madison proposed ending all commerce with Britain in six months. This measure was far too extreme for southern planters, who were dependent upon exports, and so instead it was decided to suspend all importations from Britain. In late April 1794, the House passed this revised proposal by a vote of 58–38, but the Senate vote was tied, and Vice President John Adams cast the deciding vote to defeat it.

Having avoided retaliation, Washington accepted Hamilton's advice to seek a negotiated settlement. The president sent Chief Justice John Jay to Britain to reach a diplomatic understanding about the treatment of neutral commerce. Jay recognized that "no man could frame a treaty with Great Britain without making himself unpopular and odious."[78] Nonetheless, in late 1794 Jay concluded an agreement in which Britain agreed to evacuate the North American frontier posts that it had agreed but failed to vacate after the revolution, to pay for damages caused by the Orders in Council, and to open the British West Indies to small US ships. In exchange, Jay was forced to make many concessions that affected the United States as a neutral carrier of merchandise. The United States gave up the "free ships make free goods" doctrine and accepted Britain's right to seize enemy goods from neutral ships, thus failing to protect American sailors from possible impressment. In addition, under the terms of the Jay treaty, the United States agreed to give Britain most-favored-nation status and not discriminate against it in terms of duties on goods and tonnage.

The terms of the treaty were so embarrassing that Washington delayed forwarding it to the Senate and sought to keep its provisions secret. When the treaty was leaked, it created an uproar. Jefferson thought it "execrable," Madison declared it "a ruinous bargain," and their fellow Republicans branded Jay a traitor for having sold out American interests.[79] One of the most controversial foreign-policy agreements in American history, the Jay treaty set up a major political battle between the Federalists and the Republicans. The debate revealed a sharp political division over whether America possessed enough economic power so that commercial pressure on Britain would liberalize its trade and shipping policies. Eventually, in June 1795, the Senate approved the agreement by the closest possible vote of 20–10, exactly the two-thirds majority required, and Washington signed it the next month.

The Jay treaty put the issue of commercial discrimination to rest for a decade. Hamilton won the policy battle and secured his fiscal system for an extended period. Indeed, in his Farewell Address, drafted by Hamilton, President Washington stated that the United States should avoid permanent alliances with any portion of the world: "The great rule of conduct for us in regard to foreign nations is in extending our commercial relations, to have with them as little political connection as possible." Washington argued for commercial neutrality and nondiscrimination:

> Harmony, liberal intercourse with all nations are recommended by policy, humanity, and interest. But even our commercial policy should hold an equal and impartial hand; neither seeking nor granting exclusive favors or preferences; consulting the natural course of things; diffusing and diversifying by gentle means the streams of commerce, but forcing nothing, . . . [while] constantly keeping in view that it is folly in one nation to look for disinterested favors from another; that it must pay with a portion of its independence for whatever it may accept under that character; that, by such acceptance, it may place itself in the condition of having given equivalents for nominal favors, and yet of being reproached with ingratitude for not giving more.[80]

Although the Jay treaty succeeded in reducing tensions with Britain, commercial relations with France deteriorated sharply. France accused the United States of abandoning its previous pledge of neutrality by signing the treaty. In retaliation, the French navy and privateers declared open season on American shipping, patrolling the Caribbean and even the eastern seaboard and harassing American merchants. The French government issued a series of decrees closing its ports to neutral ships and allowing it to confiscate any neutral vessel that had visited a British port or carried British goods. In the year after June 1786, France seized 316 American ships and, over the next three years, inflicted $20 million in shipping losses on merchants.[81] The small US navy tried to protect American shipping in the Caribbean to little avail. In June 1798, Congress banned all commerce with France and its colonies in a "quasi-war" that lasted more than two years.

Just as Washington had resisted Republican calls for war against Britain in 1794, President John Adams now resisted Federalist calls for war against France. Like Washington, Adams sent an envoy to reach a negotiated settlement. In an agreement concluded in September 1800, the United States agreed to drop its claim over shipping losses in exchange for an end to the hostilities. Like the Jay treaty, the agreement fell far short of meeting all US objectives, but it resolved a conflict that had put the country precariously close to war. Thus, the incoming Jefferson administration would inherit commercial peace with both Britain and France.

JEFFERSON'S TRADE EMBARGO

The historic election of 1800 shifted political power from the Federalists to the Republicans as Thomas Jefferson became president and his Republican party gained control of Congress. In his inaugural address, Jefferson stated that "we are all Republicans, we are all Federalists," but soothing rhetoric would not suppress the fierce partisan divisions that arose over the next fifteen years, particularly over trade policy.[82]

Despite the Republican criticisms of Hamilton's fiscal program, the Jefferson administration made few changes to the system in place. Jefferson abolished internal excises to reduce the tax burden, but this made the federal government entirely dependent upon import duties, a revenue source that was liable to disruption during times of conflict. Although they wanted to take a more aggressive stance against Britain's commercial policies, the Republicans also reduced defense spending that could have protected the nation's shipping industry. These economies in the nation's finances permitted a more rapid reduction in government debt, which had grown after the Louisiana Purchase in 1803. The acquisition of Louisiana roughly doubled the size of the United States and secured the use of New Orleans as a port for western products.

The international scene was relatively quiet when Jefferson began his presidency. The Jay treaty of 1796 and the Franco-American convention of 1800 established orderly commercial relations with Britain and France and largely ended the harassment of American shipping. A temporary truce between Britain and France in 1801 also contributed to more peaceful conditions as the new century began. When the European conflict abated between 1801 and 1803, reexports collapsed as American shipping had to compete once again with the British and the French merchant marine for the carrying trade. Jefferson was also forced to defend America's trade interests in the Mediterranean when the Barbary Coast states of North Africa demanded tributes be paid to them to stop acts of piracy against American shipping. To finance this action, Congress increased the ad valorem tariff schedule another 2.5 percentage points in 1804, bringing the base rate on imports to 15 percent and the top rate to 22.5 percent.[83]

In May 1803, however, France resumed its military campaign against Britain. This time the conflict lasted for twelve years and was carried out with even greater ferocity than before, making it difficult for the United States to avoid getting tangled in the struggle. As before, the war created huge demands for American shipping services, and reexports surged again, more than quadrupling between 1803 and 1806. Under international law, Britain and France were supposed to respect neutral ships as carrying neutral goods. Initially, Britain and France did not intercept American shipping, but as the conflict intensified, each side was driven to take extreme measures to defeat the enemy. The belligerents sought to strangle each other's economy by destroying its foreign trade and depriving it of essential foodstuffs and raw materials. Britain gained control of the seas in 1805 with the Battle of Trafalgar and declared a blockade of the entire coast of Europe in 1806. France countered with the Continental System that aimed to squeeze Britain's exports to Western Europe and eliminate an important source of its specie earnings.[84] The United States was caught in the middle of this potentially explosive situation: if it obeyed Britain, it would run afoul of France; if it followed France, it would alienate Britain.

Once again, Britain and France began harassing American shipping across the Atlantic, but Britain bore the brunt of America's complaints because of the greater reach of its navy and its draconian impressment policies. Various Orders in Council instructed the Royal Navy to intercept neutral shipping to prevent contraband from reaching France or any port that France controlled. To enforce the order, British naval vessels began patrolling the east coast of the United States, conducting searches of American vessels to determine a ship's cargo and destination, and to check on the nationality of its crew members. Ships suspected of aiding France were detained and sent to Halifax, Nova Scotia, to face prosecution under British law. Even if a ship's goods were not confiscated, the resulting delays could be very costly. But what most upset Americans was the impressment of as many as ten thousand US citizens into the British navy because of the arbitrary rules for determining a person's nationality on the high seas.

Jefferson objected to the British and French attacks on American shipping, but beyond issuing diplomatic protests it was not clear what could be done about the situation. The United States continued to insist that "free ships make free goods" and that, as a neutral party, the United States was free to trade wherever it wanted without interference. But these claims were simply ignored in the brutal struggle between the European powers.

In 1805, the Republican Congress responded to the attacks on American shipping and the impressment of sailors by passing a partial nonimportation measure, which banned the importation of selected manufactured goods from Britain and its dependencies. Congress postponed implementing this measure when Jefferson dispatched James Monroe and William Pinkney to London to seek a diplomatic solution. Although British officials refused to give a formal commitment to end impressment, informally they pledged to avoid holding American citizens and made some concessions with respect to the West Indies trade. In return, the United States would be barred from enacting retaliatory commercial legislation against Britain for a decade.

Like the Jay treaty, the Monroe-Pinkney agreement fell far short of US negotiating objectives, although in some respects it was more generous than its predecessor. It would have given greater security to merchant shipping in the West Indies, provided clearer definitions of contraband, and stopped impressments and seizures within five miles of the US coast. The United States would have had to concede little in return except the promise to remain neutral and not impose any discriminatory measures against Britain.[85] But unlike Washington, who accepted the imperfect Jay treaty, Jefferson was unsatisfied with the British concessions in the Monroe-Pinkney agreement. Jefferson insisted that any deal should explicitly end impressment and impose no constraint on American policy: "We will never tie our hands by treaty from the right of passing a nonimportation or non-intercourse act," he insisted, because the United States needed to have the power "to make it in [Britain's] interest to become just."[86] Jefferson refused to submit the agreement for Senate ratification for fear it might pass, according to some. "To tell you the truth," he reportedly said, "I do not wish any treaty with Great Britain."[87]

Thus, by allowing the Jay treaty to expire in 1803 and rejecting the Monroe-Pinkney agreement as its successor, the United States was left without a framework for commercial relations with Britain. More importantly, by rejecting the compromise, Jefferson took the middle road of accommodation off the table. The remaining options—acquiescing to British policy, imposing trade sanctions, or declaring war to defend the country's commercial rights—were either unacceptable or dangerous. As Hickey (1989, 16) concludes, "By rejecting this treaty, the United States missed an opportunity to reforge the Anglo-American accord of the 1790s and to substitute peace and prosperity for commercial restrictions and war."

Without an agreement in place, a clash between the two sides was almost inevitable. In June 1807, the British navy fired on the US warship Chesapeake off the coast of Norfolk, Virginia, killing several American sailors. The British boarded the vessel and captured four men alleged to be deserters from the Royal Navy. The public was outraged, and Republicans demanded retaliation. Jefferson insisted that Britain take responsibility for the incident and make amends, but Britain was unrepentant and tightened its impressment policies even further.

Determined to avoid a military conflict, Jefferson settled upon a trade embargo as a form of "peaceable coercion." An embargo would avoid the bloodshed of war and would force British concessions, it was hoped, by depriving the country of essential supplies. Secretary of State James Madison had long advocated an embargo, writing to Jefferson in 1805 that "the efficacy of an embargo also cannot be doubted. Indeed, if a commercial weapon can be properly shaped for the Executive hand, it is more and more apparent to me that it can force all the nations having colonies in this quarter of the globe to respect our rights."[88] By contrast, Treasury Secretary Albert Gallatin (1879, 1: 368) thought that it was "entirely groundless" to hope that trade sanctions would win concessions from Britain: "In every point of view, privations, sufferings, revenue, effect on enemy, politics at home, &c., I prefer war to a permanent embargo. Governmental prohibitions do always more mischief than had been calculated and it is not without much hesitation that a statesman should hazard to regulate the concerns of individuals as if he could do it better than themselves."

In the end, Jefferson believed that he had little choice but to opt for an embargo. "The alternative was between [the embargo] and war, and, in fact, it is the last card we have to play, short of war."[89] On December 18, 1807, Jefferson called on Congress to ban all American ships from departing to foreign ports.[90] In effect, the president was calling for a stop to all foreign trade. The ostensible reason for doing so was to protect the country's ships and sailors from British and French encroachments and deprive the belligerents of American goods, forcing them to change their policies. The decision to impose a trade embargo had its roots in the belief—which, as we saw in chapter 1, was only partially true—that the non-importation movement in the 1760s and 1770s had succeeded in changing British policy toward America. As they had in the early 1790s, Jefferson and Madison continued to believe that the United States possessed sufficient economic leverage to influence British policies.

The Senate acted immediately, passing the shipping ban by a 22–6 vote on the same day it received the president's message. Three days later, without recorded debate, the House approved the measure by 82–45, as table 2.1A shows. The vote was highly partisan: Republicans supported the measure by 82–19, while Federalists opposed it 26–0. Although strenuously opposed, Federalists could not really claim that the embargo was unconstitutional, because they themselves had enacted one for a brief period in 1794. Jefferson signed the measure on December 22, and the shipping ban took effect at the end of the month.

The embargo was the most dramatic, self-imposed shock to US trade in its history.[91] The legislation prohibited all American ships from sailing

TABLE 2.1. Voting in the House of Representatives on the embargo

A. The imposition of the embargo, December 21, 1807

	Republicans		Federalists		Total	
Region[a]	Yea	Nay	Yea	Nay	Yea	Nay
New England	19	0	0	15	19	15
Mid-Atlantic	27	7	0	9	27	16
South	28	10	0	2	28	12
West	8	2	0	0	8	2
Total	82	19	0	26	82	45

B. The retention of the embargo, February 24, 1809

	Republicans		Federalists		Total	
Region[a]	Yea	Nay	Yea	Nay	Yea	Nay
New England	1	13	0	15	1	28
Mid-Atlantic	10	27	0	6	10	33
South	18	16	0	2	18	18
West	4	3	0	0	4	3
Total	33	59	0	23	33	82

Source: https://www.govtrack.us/congress/votes/10-1/h30 and https://www.govtrack.us/congress/votes/10-2/h199.

Note: This vote is on an amendment to eliminate all passages from a bill that would repeal the embargo. A vote in favor is thus a vote to retain the embargo. The final bill that actually repealed the embargo replaced it with non-intercourse restrictions on trade and was passed in a partisan vote, with Federalists opposing the continuation of any restrictions on trade.

[a] Classification: New England includes Maine, New Hampshire, Vermont, Massachusetts, Rhode Island, and Connecticut. Mid-Atlantic includes New York, Pennsylvania, New Jersey, Delaware, and Maryland. South includes Virginia, North Carolina, South Carolina, and Georgia. West includes Ohio, Kentucky, and Tennessee.

to foreign ports and all foreign ships from taking on cargo in the United States. Although foreign ships were permitted to bring goods to the United States, few did so, because they would have had to return empty.

The embargo brought America's foreign commerce to a grinding halt in the spring and summer of 1808. The embargo's impact can be seen in figure 2.1. The timing of the embargo meant that exports fell more than imports in 1808. After December 1807, no American ship was allowed to leave the United States for a foreign destination. As a result, exports fell immediately upon the imposition of the embargo (there could be no spring exports) and remained low throughout the year. Very few American

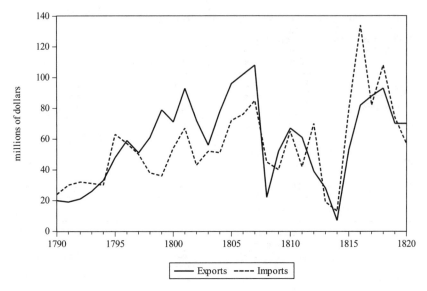

Figure 2.1. US merchandise trade, 1790–1820. (US Bureau
of the Census 1975, series U-190, 194.)

vessels appeared in European ports in 1808. Exports of domestic produce fell more than 80 percent in 1808 from the previous year, and reexports dropped almost as much. These figures understate the impact of the embargo, however, because the government's statistics were collected for the fiscal year, not the calendar year. Therefore, the figures for 1808 refer to the period from October 1, 1807 to September 30, 1808, and thus include three months in which the embargo was not in effect.[92]

Meanwhile, Congress wanted to encourage the many American vessels that spent the winter months in European ports to return home. Therefore, US ships returning from Europe in the spring and summer of 1808 were permitted to unload their cargoes, after which they had to remain in port and not return to sea. As a result, imports for domestic consumption declined only 50 percent in fiscal year 1808. Of course, by mid-summer, the number of American ships with foreign cargo arriving into port had slowed to a trickle.

The embargo had a dramatic impact on prices in the United States, driving down the prices of exported goods and driving up the prices of imported goods. Figure 2.2A presents the monthly domestic prices of the four leading commodity exports—cotton, flour, tobacco, and rice—that accounted for about two-thirds of domestic exports in 1807. Export prices

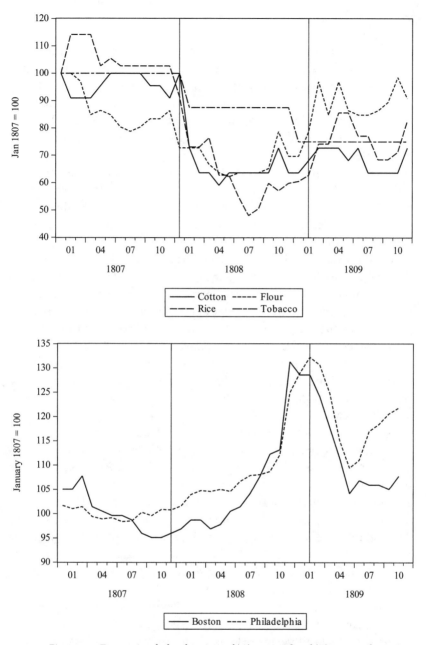

Figure 2.2. Domestic wholesale prices of (A) exported and (B) imported commodities, monthly, 1807–1809. (For exported goods: Cole 1938. Prices are of Georgia upland cotton at New York, superfine flour at New York, tobacco at New York, and rice at Philadelphia. For imported goods: Smith and Cole 1935, 147, and Bezanson, Gray, and Hussey 1936, 353. The Boston index is a weighted average of prices on eighteen imported commodities. The Philadelphia index is a weighted average of prices of fifty-nine imported commodities.)

dropped sharply in early 1808, demonstrating the embargo's immediate impact once it was known that farmers would be denied access to foreign markets. The export-weighted average of the prices fell 27 percent between December 1807 and June 1808.[93] Prices bottomed out in the summer of 1808 but began to recover toward the end of the year, evidence that merchants were willing to violate the embargo as time went on and the fall harvest began to appear. According to Heaton (1941, 189), there was "little effort to indulge in large-scale defiance of the Embargo, at least until the end of 1808, when patience was becoming exhausted and repeal seemed inevitable." Indeed, by late 1808, the embargo was increasingly disregarded and some ships left port in violation of the law, although the precise number is unknown.

Unlike exports, which were concentrated in a few key commodities, imports were a highly diversified set of goods. Figure 2.2B presents monthly price indexes for imported commodities in Boston and Philadelphia. Both series indicate that prices of imported goods did not rise immediately in the spring of 1808 because imports continued to arrive in the port cities. However, prices escalated quickly by the fall of 1808 as the number of returning ships dwindled, and imports became increasingly scarce. The wholesale prices of imported commodities rose about 33 percent in both cities during the embargo, but fell sharply once the embargo was lifted in March 1809.

The embargo had an immense impact on the US economy. Exports of domestic merchandise were about 8 percent of GDP in 1807, and the dramatic changes in export and import prices and volumes rippled through the entire economy. Irwin (2005b) suggests that the welfare loss associated with the reduction of trade was about 5 percent of GDP. The year has been called a "depression" by Thorp (1926, 116), who gives it the following description based on contemporary newspaper accounts: "Rigid embargo causes paralysis on coast, gradually spreading inland; severe distress in New England; further sharp decline in commodity prices to low point, third quarter; foreign trade completely checked."

The embargo generated heated opposition in the commercial states of New England and New York. Massachusetts, which handled a third of the nation's tonnage in foreign trade, saw large protests against the measure, and even grumbles about secession. The harbors that usually bustled with activity fell silent with the absence of commerce, and seafaring communities suffered from high unemployment due to the loss of trade. A New Hampshire Federalist penned this verse:

Our ships all in motion, once whiten'd the ocean;
They sail'd and return'd with a Cargo;
Now doom'd to decay, they are fallen a prey,
To Jefferson, worms, and EMBARGO.[94]

With imports of British manufactures no longer coming into the country, however, small textile mills began sprouting up in Rhode Island and Massachusetts.[95] While nascent manufacturers benefited from the elimination of imports, Strum (1994, 59) reports that "this industrial growth did not compensate for the considerable distress that the embargo caused," not just in coastal cities but among farmers who marketed their crops.

The South also suffered enormously from the loss of commodity exports, although many of its staples could be stored, and cultivators held out hopes that their goods could be exported later in the year or in 1809. Despite the hardship, the South supported the embargo as a necessary burden. One South Carolinian noted that it is "difficult to imagine the pecuniary effect and the individual distress, occasioned by the embargo. . . . Yet, notwithstanding this distress, . . . there is everywhere an acquiescence in the measure proceeding from a confidence in the government."[96] The South still deeply resented Britain and remained loyal to Jefferson and the Republicans. Unlike New England, there were virtually no anti-embargo meetings or protests from Virginia to Georgia, although planters hoped the embargo would work and be lifted quickly.

There was also strong support for the embargo in Kentucky, Tennessee, and the Mississippi Valley. While farmers from this region did not care much about the impressment of sailors, they attributed declining commodity prices (tobacco, hemp, and cotton) to the loss of markets in the West Indies, not the embargo. Even Jefferson conceded that the lower price of staples was due to the embargo, but popular opinion west of the Appalachians chose to blame Britain instead.

The Philadelphia region was one part of the country that apparently did not suffer greatly from the embargo.[97] The scarcity of imported manufactured goods gave rise to domestic production of substitute products, such as iron works. Yet even in the Mid-Atlantic, the losses to merchants and the farming community, in terms of foregone income due to lower commodity prices, vastly exceeded the gains accruing to newly established manufacturing firms.

In cutting off the nation's trade, the Jefferson administration also deprived the government of customs revenue to fund its operations. Although a revenue shortfall was not felt in 1808 because of the American vessels that returned to ports in the spring, customs revenue fell more than half in 1809. Treasury Secretary Gallatin confronted a fiscal deficit for the first time, but the Treasury could absorb the shortfall, because it had built up large balances from previous fiscal surpluses, and the price of government debt was surprisingly unaffected by the embargo.[98]

Given the enormous incentives for merchants to evade the embargo, enforcement was a critical issue from the start. The longer the embargo was in place, the less the public was willing to tolerate it, and the more merchants were willing to violate it. In March 1808, Congress tightened the embargo by forbidding any exports over land to prevent American goods from reaching Britain via Canada. Federalists protested that this was not something that could be justified as protecting shipping and sailors. Congress soon passed additional legislation to strengthen the embargo's enforcement. All ships engaged in the coastal trade had to post a bond worth twice the value of the ship and cargo as security that it would not depart to a foreign destination; fishing vessels were prohibited from taking on any cargo and had to post a bond four times the value of the ship. Those found violating the embargo were subject to fines, forfeitures, and seizures.

These supplementary measures were necessary because violations of the embargo became a growing problem in 1808. Reports of smuggling across the Canadian border in upstate Vermont and New York were common, and customs agents were occasionally attacked for trying to interfere. There were also many illicit exchanges of goods with British ships anchored off the Atlantic coast. Therefore, customs officials began inspecting and detaining ships engaged in the domestic coastal trade on suspicion of exporting goods to Newfoundland or to British ships patrolling along the coast.

To ensure the embargo's success, Jefferson strongly supported these enforcement measures: "It is important to crush every example of forcible opposition to the law," he instructed Gallatin.[99] In May 1808, Jefferson wrote to Gallatin:

> The numerous and bold evasions of the several embargo laws threatened altogether to defeat the great and interesting objects for which they were adopted, and principally under cover of the coasting trade. Congress, therefore, finding insufficient all attempts to bind unprincipled adventurers by general rules, at length gave a discretionary power to detain absolutely all vessels suspected of intentions to evade

the embargo laws, wheresoever found. In order to give to this law the effect it intended, we find it necessary to consider every vessel suspicious which has on board any articles of domestic produce in demand in foreign markets, and most especially provisions.[100]

The innumerable enforcement problems were left to Gallatin to solve, as the president remained aloof from the administration of the embargo.[101]

As the nation's economic distress increased through 1808, so did the political opposition to the embargo, and pressures mounted for its abolition. Federalists attacked it for destroying the nation's prosperity and debilitating the government's finances, arguing that the measure was futile and would ultimately fail to coerce Britain into changing its policies. Because of the embargo's adverse impact on numerous interests—New England shipping, southern planters, and government revenue—the Jefferson administration did not have much time to prove its efficacy before domestic political pressures would succeed in terminating it.

By the summer of 1808, Gallatin (1879, 1:401) informed Jefferson that even more "odious and arbitrary" enforcement policies would be needed to make the embargo work. The Treasury secretary declined to endorse the draconian measures that would be required to make it effective, and he was dismayed at having to enforce a policy that he did not fully support. Furthermore, Gallatin was upset with the president's detached view of the problems the embargo had created and hinted that it could not continue indefinitely without a growing number of people beginning to ignore it.

In frustration, Gallatin (1879, 1:398) wrote to Jefferson:

If the embargo must be persisted in any longer, two principles must necessarily be adopted in order to make it sufficient: 1st, that not a single vessel shall be permitted to move without the special permission of the Executive; 2d, that the collectors be invested with a general power of seizing property anywhere, and taking the rudders or otherwise effectually preventing the departure of all vessels in harbor; . . . I am sensible that such arbitrary powers are equally dangerous and odious. But a restrictive measure of the nature of the embargo applied to a nation under such circumstances as the United States cannot be enforced without the assistance of means as strong as the measure itself. I mean generally to express an opinion founded on the experience of this summer, that Congress must either invest the Executive with the most arbitrary powers and sufficient force to carry the embargo into effect, or give it up altogether.

In late summer, Gallatin (1879, 1:401) reported that "the embargo is now defeated . . . by open violations, by vessels sailing without any clearances whatever, an evil which, under the existing law, we cannot oppose in any way but by cruisers." He also warned Jefferson that the embargo was having an "inconsiderable effect" on Britain but was a growing political disaster for the Republicans, who had an eye to the upcoming presidential election.

The harsh enforcement of the embargo might be considered unusual for a president who championed limited government and civil liberties. But Jefferson did not refrain from seeking even greater executive powers to strengthen the embargo, and he blamed merchants for making such measures necessary. Jefferson could not understand why Americans would violate the law and was dumbfounded that some could put their own private interests above what he believed to be the national interest. He concluded that merchants were simply treasonous and therefore even stricter enforcement was required. He replied to Gallatin: "This embargo law is certainly the most embarrassing one we have ever had to execute. I did not expect a crop of so sudden & rank growth of fraud & open opposition by force could have grown up in the U.S. I am satisfied with you that if orders & decrees are not repealed, and a continuation of the embargo is preferred to war, (which sentiment is universal here), Congress must legalize all *means* which may be necessary to obtain its *end*."[102]

He continued to believe the embargo was a useful test of the effectiveness of trade coercion: "I place immense value in the experiment being fully made, how far an embargo may be an effectual weapon in future as well as on this occasion." Jefferson was prepared to call out the militia for the purpose of "preventing or suppressing armed or riotous assemblages of persons resisting the custom-house officers in the exercise of their duties, or opposing or violating the embargo laws."[103] Army regulars were called out to enforce routine laws as the Jefferson administration declared war against smugglers.[104]

The embargo was certainly felt in Britain and drew some complaints, but it failed to inflict much harm. It was imposed when the British economy was relatively strong, and Britain withstood the loss of US trade without much disruption.[105] Britain's manufacturers softened the embargo's impact by shifting their exports to Latin America and began to purchase many of the goods previously imported from the United States from Spain and other countries. As a result, Britain rejected an American offer to terminate the embargo in exchange for repealing the Orders. Thus, by the late summer of 1808, Jefferson's experiment with "peaceful coercion" was widely considered to be unsuccessful. As the US envoy to France reported to Madison, "We have somewhat overrated our means of coercing the two great belligerents to a course of justice. The embargo is a measure calculated above any other, to keep us whole and keep us in peace; but, beyond this, you must not count upon it. Here it is not felt and in England . . . it is forgotten" [106]

With the November election approaching, Gallatin warned Jefferson that the Republicans would suffer losses if the embargo was not lifted. Gallatin suggested that only Virginia, South Carolina, and Georgia were firmly behind the administration, while the Federalists had gained strength in New England. Despite the controversy over the embargo, the Federalist party was still weak, however, and the Republicans emerged relatively unscathed in the election. The Republican majority in the House was cut in half, but they remained firmly in control of Congress, and Madison easily defeated his Federalist rival to become president.

The election outcome strengthened Jefferson's resolve to continue with the policy. He viewed the embargo as "a temporary evil, and a necessary one to save us from greater and more permanent evils—the loss of property and the surrender of rights."[107] When Congress reconvened in November 1808 after a six-month summer recess, the debate about the wisdom of the embargo and its future began. While Federalists demanded an immediate end to the embargo, Jefferson indicated that he was committed to seeing it through, because the alternatives, submission or war, were worse.

By this point, the embargo had been in effect for almost a year with no clear sense of when it might end. With Jefferson's term in office coming to a close, Madison and Gallatin implored him for guidance about future policy, but he declined to advise them, allowing the new administration to decide for itself the proper course of action. Thus, Madison and Gallatin began discussions with the outgoing Congress about policy during the transition period from November 1808 to March 1809.[108] If the outgoing Congress did not act, the embargo would remain in effect at least until the fall of 1809, when the new Congress was scheduled to convene.

Madison himself favored "an invigoration of the embargo, a prohibition of imports, *permanent* duties for encouraging manufactures, and a *permanent* navigation act: with an extension of preparations and arrangements for the event of war," as well as non-intercourse with France.[109] In January 1809, Congress enacted yet another enforcement act, which gave the authorities sweeping power to seize cargoes and ships suspected of violating the embargo. Merchants were required to post large bonds for domestic coastal voyages, and the loading or departure of any ship for domestic destinations now required official clearance. The authorities could even seize goods in a wagon or cart heading toward the seacoast and hold it until bond had been posted in order to guarantee that the goods would not be taken out of the country. Stiff penalties and even confiscations were imposed for violations, and state militias were put at the disposal of federal officials in enforcing the law.

The Republicans succeeded in passing the enforcement law, but only after an acrimonious debate. Outraged Federalists complained that the enforcement bill amounted to military despotism at a time of peace and denounced it as unjust, oppressive, and unconstitutional. (Some of the provisions may have violated the search-and-seizure provisions of the Fourth Amendment of the Constitution.) The draconian enforcement of the embargo, with no indication of when it might end, pushed Federalist New England into greater opposition. In response to a remark in Congress that the economy was not really suffering from the embargo, Josiah Quincy of Massachusetts was dumbfounded: "But has my honorable colleague traveled on the seaboard? Has he witnessed the state of our cities? Has he seen our ships rotting at our wharves; our wharves deserted, our stores tenantless, our streets bereft of active business; industry forsaking her beloved haunts, and hope fled from places where she had from earliest time been accustomed to make and fulfill her most precious promises?" He warned that New England could not tolerate the embargo much longer: "You cannot lay a man upon the rack and crack his muscles by slow torment, and call patriotism to soothe the sufferer."[110] Even before the new enforcement act had passed, the Massachusetts and Connecticut legislatures called existing compliance measures "unconstitutional" and protested against the destruction of commerce, implicitly threatening to no longer enforce the embargo.

New England's hostility toward the embargo and revulsion at its enforcement began to erode political support for the embargo; even Republicans from New England began to question the wisdom of continuing it. Violations began to escalate, and an increasing number of ships left port illegally. The first crack in the Republican political support for the embargo appeared shortly after Congress had strengthened its enforcement. A Virginia Republican offered a resolution that would terminate the embargo at an unspecified future date, initially suggested to be June 1. Jefferson later wrote that this unleashed a "sudden and unaccountable revolution of opinion" that "resembled a kind of panic" among New England and New York Republicans in favor of an early lifting of the embargo.[111] Orchard

Cook, a Massachusetts Republican, remarked that "The South say[s] embargo or war, and the North and East say, no embargo, no war. . . . I lament that this difference of opinion exists; yet, as it does exist, we must take things as they are, and legislate accordingly. The genius and duty of Republican government is to make laws to suit the people, and not attempt to make the people suit the laws."[112] Even Madison came to see that "the Eastern seaboard is become so impatient under privations of activity and gain . . . that it becomes necessary for the sake of the Union that the spirit not be too much opposed."[113]

Republican unity on the embargo collapsed, and the date for its termination was moved up to March 4, when Madison would be inaugurated. As a compromise with the hardliners, the lifting of the embargo was coupled with continued non-importation measures against Britain and France. This compromise won the support of the House on February 27, the Senate the next day, and was reluctantly signed by Jefferson on March 1. Table 2.1B shows the House vote on whether to retain the embargo. Federalists who unanimously opposed the embargo were now joined by many Republicans, particularly from New England and the Mid-Atlantic states. Surprisingly, although the South continued to have an economic interest in lifting the embargo, the region still showed strong support for maintaining it.

Why did Republican support for the embargo dissolve so quickly in January-February 1809? Jefferson blamed two House Republicans from Massachusetts, Joseph Story and Ezekiel Bacon, and especially Story, whom he called a "pseudo-Republican," for fomenting panic about the strength of the New England opposition to the embargo.[114] While admitting that "considerable discontent was certainly excited in Massachusetts, . . . its extent was magnified infinitely beyond its reality, an intrigue (I believe) not more than two or three members, reputed republicans, excited in Congress a belief that we were under the alternative of civil war, or a repeal of the embargo," Jefferson wrote with dismay. "Thus were we driven by treason among ourselves from the high & wise ground we had taken, and which, had it been held, would have either restored us our free trade, or have established manufactures among us."[115]

Many years later, Jefferson suggested that he voluntarily decided to end the embargo to preserve national unity.[116] However, Joseph Story insisted that Jefferson fought stubbornly to keep it in place. Story said that he always thought the embargo was "a doubtful policy" but initially supported it as a "fair experiment." As Story (1852, 184–85) recalled:

A year passed away, and the evils, which it inflicted upon ourselves, were daily increasing in magnitude and extent. . . . Alive to the sufferings of my fellow-citizens, and perceiving that their necessities were driving them on to the most violent resistance of the measure— and, indeed, to a degree which threatened the very existence of the Union—I became convinced of the necessity of abandoning it, and as soon as I arrived at Washington I held free conversations with many distinguished members of the Republican party on the subject, which were soon followed up by consultations of a more public nature. I found that as a measure of retaliation the system had not only failed, but that Mr. Jefferson from pride of opinion, as well as from that visionary course of speculation, which often misled his judgment, was resolutely bent upon maintaining it at all hazards. He professed a firm belief that Great Britain would abandon her orders in council, if we persisted in the embargo; and having no other scheme to offer in case of the failure of this, he maintained in private conversation the indispensable necessity of closing the session of Congress without any attempt to limit the duration of the system. The consequence of this would be an aggravation for another year of all the evils which then were breaking down New England. I felt that my duty to my country called on me for a strenuous effort to prevent such calamities.

Story knew the embargo would collapse if it was continued through 1809, and he sought to impress upon fellow Republicans the necessity of abandoning it. According to Story, the Jefferson administration attempted to persuade him to end his opposition to the embargo. "The whole influence of the Administration was directly brought to bear upon Mr. Ezekiel Bacon and myself, to seduce us from what we considered a great duty to our country, and especially New England. We were scolded, privately consulted, and argued with, by the Administration and its friends, on that occasion" (Story 1852, 187). These discussions led Story to believe that Jefferson

was determined on protracting the embargo for an indefinite period, even for years. I was well satisfied, that such a course would not and could not be borne by New England, and would bring on a direct rebellion. It would be ruin to the whole country. Yet Mr. Jefferson, with his usual visionary obstinacy, was determined to maintain it; and the New England Republicans were to be made the instruments. Mr. Bacon and myself resisted, and measures were concerted by us, with the aid of Pennsylvania, to compel him to abandon his mad scheme. For this he never forgave me. (187)[117]

Story explicitly rejected Jefferson's version of events: "It is not a little remarkable, that many years afterwards, Mr. Jefferson took great credit to himself for yielding up, *suâ sponte*, this favorite measure, to preserve, as he intimates, New England from open rebellion. What to me was almost a crime, became, it seems in him an extraordinary virtue. The truth is, that if the measure had not been abandoned when it was, it would have overturned the Administration itself, and the Republican party would have been driven from power by the indignation of the people, goaded on to madness by their suffering" (1852, 185).

Jefferson's embargo led to a virtual shutdown of foreign commerce and was therefore one of the most dramatic trade policy experiments in history. What are we to make of this attempt at "peaceable coercion"? The embargo must be considered a failure: it imposed large costs on the economy but failed to achieve any of its objectives. Although the United States managed to avoid a war and save ships and sailors from further encroachments, the embargo severely disrupted commerce and inflicted large economic losses on farmers, fishermen, merchants, and ship owners, all of which greatly aggravated sectional tensions. Had the administration persisted with the embargo, its enforcement would have led to a national crisis.

Yet Jefferson steadfastly maintained that economic pressure on Britain could have succeeded if it had been given more time. Shortly after leaving office, Jefferson held that the embargo "would have saved us had it been honestly executed a few weeks longer." In 1815, Jefferson insisted that "a continuance of the embargo for two months longer would have prevented our war" of 1812. And just months before his death, Jefferson referred to the embargo as "a measure which persevered in a little longer . . . would have effected its object completely." Yet there is no evidence to support these views.[118]

Alexander Hamilton, although no longer alive, was one person who almost perfectly anticipated the trade and revenue effects of the embargo, and even its domestic political repercussions. In 1794, Hamilton argued against any embargo against Britain and predicted: "The consequences of so great and so sudden a disturbance of our Trade which must affect our exports as well as our Imports are not to be calculated. An excessive rise in the price of foreign commodities—a proportional decrease of price and demand for our own commodities—the derangement of our revenue and

credit—these circumstances united may occasion the most dangerous dissatisfaction & disorders in the community and may drive the government
to a disgraceful retreat—independent of foreign causes."[119] With the except
for the derangement of credit, which was more firmly established in 1808
than it had been in 1794, each one of Hamilton's predictions came true.

TRADE DISRUPTIONS AND THE WAR OF 1812

Although Congress repealed the embargo in March 1809, trade remained
depressed over the next six years, first because of a series of legislative
measures that restricted imports from Britain and France, and then because of the War of 1812. With the lifting of the embargo, exports and imports jumped immediately as hundreds of American ships took to the seas
once again (see figure 2.1). But trade did not return to its previous levels,
because the non-intercourse law banned all trade with Britain, France,
and their colonies. At least officially, American ships could sail anywhere
except to ports controlled by the British and French, and US ports were
closed to British and French ships and goods. However, the impact of this
measure was diminished by a presidential error. Believing that an agreement had been reached with a British representative in Washington to lift
the non-intercourse measure in exchange for a change in British policy,
President Madison opened trade with Britain in April 1809 on the assumption that the deal would be approved in London. It turned out that the
diplomat had exceeded his official instructions; the British government
did not approve the agreement, and Madison was forced to reimpose non-
intercourse four months later.

The non-intercourse measure was due to expire in early 1810. Madison
deferred to Congress, but he wanted to reimpose an embargo, something
legislators were unwilling to consider. Frustrated that Congress was unwilling to take a hard line, Madison complained that the Federalist party
"prefers submission of our trade to British regulation" while the Republican party "confesses the impossibility of resisting it."[120] In May 1810,
after an extensive debate, Congress passed Macon's Bill No. 2 that restored
open trade with both Britain and France, but with an unusual provision: If
either Britain or France repudiated its policy of harassing American shipping, the United States would resume non-importation against the other
country. This led to another diplomatic stumble by Madison. When France
hinted that a change in policy might be forthcoming, he reinstated non-
importation against Britain in March 1811. However, the president soon
learned that France had actually not decided to change its policy toward

American shipping. Yet Madison kept non-importation against Britain in effect, whereby American goods could be exported to Britain but imports of British merchandise were prohibited.

The Republican policy of allowing exports but banning imports had practical and political problems. The practical issue was that an export restriction actually might have exerted more influence over British policy than non-importation. Due to a poor European harvest and trade disruptions elsewhere, the British army in Spain was now heavily dependent upon imports of American grain. Some observers believed that the Orders in Council would be repealed if the United States now imposed an export embargo, but opposition from grain producers in the Mid-Atlantic region prevented Madison from exploiting this new British vulnerability.[121]

The unequal treatment of exports and imports also created a political problem in exacerbating sectional tensions. Non-importation was detrimental to the New England shipping industry and New York merchants in the Federalist Northeast. Permitting exports served the interests of Mid-Atlantic grain and flour producers and southern staples producers and enabled them to be relatively unaffected by the trade sanctions. Republicans from the South and Mid-Atlantic generally supported the trade measures, but a minority joined with Federalists in opposing them. One Republican opponent, John Randolph of Virginia, called the restrictive system "a series of the most impolitic and ruinous measures, utterly incomprehensible to every rational, sober-minded man."[122] The Federalists, drawing their support mainly from New England and New York, voted almost unanimously against every proposed restriction of commerce between 1806 and 1812. Federalists complained that such measures did more damage to the United States than it inflicted on other countries in depriving them of American goods. The trade restrictions hit particularly hard in New England, where secessionist sentiments reappeared.[123]

If Madison privately complained that Congress was unwilling to strike back against Britain, he could have no such complaints about the Twelfth Congress that opened in December 1811. The new Congress was filled with a new generation of younger Republicans, including Henry Clay of Kentucky and John Calhoun of South Carolina. Led by Clay, these "War Hawks" were fed up with the economic stalemate and wanted to take decisive military action against Britain. Their speeches were filled with fervent patriotic rhetoric about redeeming the nation's honor, asserting the country's independence, and regaining national respectability. "The outrages in impressing American seamen exceed all manner of description," a Virginia writer explained in April 1812. "Indeed the whole system of aggression now is such that the real question between G. Britain and the U. States has ceased to be a question merely relating to certain rights of commerce. . . . it is now clearly, positively, and decidedly a *question of independence*, that is to say, whether the U. States are really an independent nation."[124]

The United States had to fight for "free trade and sailors' rights" because the country's honor was at stake, the War Hawks believed.[125] But as Clay noted, even "if pecuniary considerations alone are to govern, there is sufficient motive for the war."[126] The War Hawks were less upset about the interference with shipping, which was New England's problem, than with the low price of southern staples. This was blamed on the obstructions that Britain placed on American commerce. Felix Grundy of Tennessee argued that "It is not the carrying trade, properly so called, about which this nation and Great Britain are at present contending. Were this the only question now under consideration, I should feel great unwillingness . . . to involve the nation in war. . . . The true question in controversy, is of a very different character; it involves the interest of the whole nation. It is the right of exporting productions of our own soil and industry to foreign markets."[127] "We were but yesterday contending for the indirect trade— the right to export to Europe the coffee and sugar of the West Indies," Clay explained. "Today we are asserting our claim to the direct trade—the right to export our cotton, tobacco, and other domestic produce to market." Calhoun saw "the hand of foreign injustice" as the explanation for the low prices of southern staples.[128]

A deeper source of the confrontational attitude was the growing nationalism in the United States, especially in the frontier states and deep South. British support for Indians on the frontier was one source of anti-British feeling. Another was the growing interest in territorial expansion. The expansionist impulse put attention on Canada and Florida. The South wanted to wrest Florida from Spanish control, while many constituencies wanted to absorb Canada, which seemed ripe for the taking, since Britain was engaged in fighting France. Conquering Canada would push Britain out of North America once and for all and solve multiple problems: it would stop British support for Indians on the frontier, end their control of fishing off the coast of Newfoundland, and impede their ability to interfere with the West Indies trade. Henry Clay claimed that "Canada was not the end but the means, the object of the war being the redress of injuries, and Canada being the instrument by which that redress was to be obtained."[129] But John Randolph, one of the few Republicans from Virginia who opposed this aggressive stance, argued that the War Hawks wanted a land grab, "a scuffle and scramble for plunder."[130] Federalists and antiwar Republicans repeatedly argued that starting a war would not improve the prices of hemp, tobacco, or cotton, but simply make matters worse. However, they were a minority in Congress.

Thus, a variety of motives led to the War of 1812. As Hickey (1989, 28) explains, "Many Republicans had concluded that there were compelling diplomatic, ideological, and political reason for going to war against England. If all went well, the Republicans could expect to win concessions from the British, vindicate American independence, preserve republican institutions, maintain power, unify their party, and silence the Federalists." In April 1812, in preparation for war, Congress enacted a ninety-day total embargo on trade as a defensive measure to get American ships out of harm's way.

As the United States moved toward war, Britain was showing the first signs of weakening. Unlike Jefferson's embargo three years earlier, the non-importation policy starting in March 1811 coincided with an economic slump in Britain. Although the extent to which the ban on imports exacerbated the recession is uncertain, British manufacturers believed that ending non-importation would increase demand for their goods. Unemployed workers in Manchester, Liverpool, Birmingham, and other industrial cities sent dozens of petitions to Parliament demanding repeal of the Orders in Council so that the United States would end its non-importation policy.[131] Already suffering under heavy taxes due to the war against France, Britain did not welcome the prospect of another war in North America. The weak economy and pressure from labor and industry helped persuade the British government to relax its policy toward neutral shipping. On June 23, 1812, Foreign Secretary Lord Castlereagh announced the suspension of the Orders in Council that had been an irritant to Anglo-American relations for so long. As Castlereagh conceded in his diary, "One does not like to own that we are forced to give way to our manufacturers."[132] The apparent vindication of the Republican policy of commercial pressure was an illusion, to some extent, because the policy worked only when it coincided with a recession in Britain that was not itself the result of US trade policies.[133]

Unfortunately, word of this suspension did not reach the United States until August, well after political developments in Washington had pushed the country toward military action. In June 1812, Madison asked Congress to declare war against Britain. In his message, the president cited several grievances: the continued impressment of sailors, the unlawful seizures of ships and cargo, the Orders in Council, and the arming of Indians in the West. Federalists were dumbfounded that the country was rashly starting a war for which it was ill-prepared. And they were incredulous that the country would take the side of a French despot bent on military conquest (Napoleon) against a country with constitutional government that happened to be an important customer for American goods. Even in the South, some questioned whether John Calhoun's aggressive stance was not a "delusive hope" that some good would come from a military conflict.[134] A divided House quickly voted to declare war on Britain. The decision was highly sectional: most of the support for the war came from the South and West, while Republicans in seaport towns and Federalists from northern commercial states were strongly opposed. The Senate soon followed in a similarly divided vote.

Thus, on June 19, 1812, just two days after the British government announced that it was suspending the Orders in Council, the United States formally declared war on Britain. Later that month, somewhere in the north Atlantic, the ship from Britain bringing news of the Orders in Council suspension passed the ship from the United States bringing news of the declaration of war. Had there been more rapid means of communication, the conflict might have been averted. "Madison later indicated that the declaration of war 'would have been stayed' if he had known about the repeal of the Orders," Hickey (1989, 42) writes. "But without a [transatlantic] cable, it took weeks for the news to reach America, and by then the die was cast."

The war went poorly for the United States. Plans for a quick seizure of Canada went awry, and by the end of the year, Congress was already showing an interest in ending the conflict. Britain proved strong enough to fight France in Europe and the United States in North America simultaneously. As a result, the war dragged on for more than two years.

In terms of trade policy, the war prompted Congress in July 1812 to double all import duties until one year after hostilities ceased. In addition, a 10 percent surcharge was imposed on goods arriving on foreign ships, and the tonnage duties on foreign ships were quadrupled. Non-importation of British goods continued and was reinforced by restrictions on exports to Canada to prevent supplies from reaching the enemy. Later, in December 1813, a complete embargo on foreign trade required that all American ships remain in port, thereby bringing exports to any foreign destination to a halt. Meanwhile, the Royal Navy blockaded the East Coast to interfere with trade, except the smuggling of contraband to its forces. The blockade stretched from Long Island to New Orleans and deliberately exempted New England in the hopes that sympathetic merchants would provide them with supplies in violation of US law.[135]

The combination of war, non-importation, and blockade squeezed US trade to the lowest levels in recorded history, with the possible exception of the Revolutionary war, a period for which good statistical data do not exist. Figure 2.1 shows that exports dropped almost 90 percent, while imports shrank more than 80 percent between 1811 and 1814. As a result, customs revenue shriveled up, and the federal debt tripled between 1812 and 1816.

The wartime embargo proved to be very short-lived. In April 1814, following the initial British victory against Napoleon, European ports were reopened to US shipping. A large majority in Congress voted to repeal both the embargo and non-importation, but this made little difference to trade. With Napoleon no longer a threat, Britain shifted its military forces across the Atlantic to confront the United States. The Royal Navy tightened its blockade, extended it to New England ports as well, and managed to sail up the Potomac River and burn the White House and Capitol building.

By this time, neither side had an interest in prolonging the conflict. From the American standpoint, the war was a disaster and failed to achieve any of its objectives. The economy suffered grievously from the war and loss of trade. "Unlike most American wars," Hickey (1989, 305) notes, "this one did not generate a general economic boom. . . . Although people in the middle and western states prospered, those in New England and the South did not. Manufacturing thrived because of the absence of British competition, but whatever gains were made in this sector of the economy were dwarfed by heavy losses in fishing and commerce."

In December 1814, the United States and Britain concluded a formal peace agreement with the Treaty of Ghent. The peace treaty restored the *status quo ante bellum* and did not mention impressment or neutral shipping rights, the ostensible reasons for the war. The Senate approved the treaty in February 1815, paving the way for the resumption of normal peacetime trade for the first time in many years.

THE BIRTH OF INFANT INDUSTRIES

In 1796, after touring the country, the French diplomat Talleyrand observed that America "is but in her infancy with regard to manufactures: a few iron works, several glass houses, some tan yards, a considerable number of trifling and imperfect manufactories of kerseymere [a course kind of knitting] and, in some places, of cotton . . . point out the feeble efforts that have hitherto been made [to] furnish the country with manufactured articles of daily consumption."[136]

The seven-year disruption of America's imports, from 1808 through 1814 due to embargoes, non-importation, blockades, and war, dramatically changed this situation. The suppression of imports gave rise to domestic production of manufactured goods and began a structural shift in the economy. While the promotion of domestic manufacturing was not the primary intention of Jefferson and Madison, their trade policies restricted imports so severely that enterprising entrepreneurs started producing manufactured goods to replace those formerly imported. Although he had no desire to see large-scale factories appear on America's shores, Jefferson anticipated that the embargo would provide "indirect encouragement" to small domestic manufacturers. In contrast to his earlier views, he welcomed this development as a way of achieving economic independence. "Our embargo, which has been a very trying measure, has produced one very happy & permanent effect," Jefferson wrote after leaving office in 1809. "It has set us all on domestic manufacture, & will I verily believe reduce our future demands on England fully one half."[137]

Similarly, in his November 1809 message to Congress, Madison praised non-importation for promoting the growth of domestic manufacturing: "In the midst of the wrongs and vexations experienced from external causes there is much room for congratulation on the prosperity and happiness flowing from our situation at home. . . . The face of our country everywhere presents evidence of laudable enterprise, of extensive capital, and of durable improvement. In a cultivation of the materials and the extension of useful manufactures, more especially in the general application to household fabrics, we behold a rapid diminution of our dependence on foreign supplies."[138]

This marked a distinct change from the attitude of Republicans in the early 1790s, when they opposed Hamilton's efforts to promote manufacturing and encourage industrialization. By the time of Jefferson's embargo, "the Republican press was without a doubt far more open to a new manufacturing economy than the Federalists," who remained wedded to commerce, Peskin (2002, 251) notes. Indeed, the Republican policy of commercial warfare promoted the growth of domestic manufacturing much more than the Federalist policy of keeping the channels of trade relatively open and free. As Merrill Peterson (1970, 515) observed, "Ironically, the factories and workshops [Jefferson] had preferred to keep in Europe would the more likely result from his commercial system than from Hamilton's fiscal system."

As a result, manufacturing interests swung behind the Republicans. "By the first decade of the nineteenth century, manufacturing supporters were at least as likely to be Republicans as Federalists," Peskin (2002, 242–43, 235) notes. The "parties appeared almost to switch positions on the issue of manufacturing and the role of the federal government in the economy. . . . A British traveler to Philadelphia at this time observed that the Federalist and Republican parties were respectively 'merely other terms for importers and manufacturers.'" A June 1809 vote in the House of Representatives illustrates this remarkable political change. A Republican congressman from Massachusetts introduced a resolution asking the secretary of the Treasury to prepare a report on the status of manufacturing in the country and to recommend measures "for the purpose of protecting and fostering the manufactures of the United States." More than 80 percent of Republicans favored this request, while Federalists were divided.

This resolution led to Treasury Secretary Gallatin's *Report on Manufactures* in April 1810. Because data on the state of manufacturing were incomplete, Gallatin concluded that he did not have enough information to recommend a plan "best calculated to protect and promote American manufactures," but he noted three ways of doing so: bounties, import duties, and government loans. Gallatin argued that bounties were most appropriate for exported goods and that high tariffs were "liable to the treble objection of destroying competition, of taxing the consumer, and of diverting capital and industry into channels generally less profitable to the nation." Therefore, since "the comparative want of capital, is the principal obstacle to the introduction and advancement of manufactures in America, it seems that the most efficient, and most obvious remedy would consisting in supplying that capital." Arguing that the nation's banks would be too short-sighted to fund such new ventures, Gallatin proposed that the government create a circulating stock of between $5 million and $20 million that could be used for loans for new manufactures.[139] This proposal for government-sponsored venture capital loans went nowhere in Congress, but it is ironic that less than twenty years after Madison sought to scuttle Hamilton's *Report on Manufactures*, his own Treasury secretary issued one with strikingly similar conclusions.

Although Gallatin did not recommend higher tariffs, Madison proposed them as the means of supporting new industries. In his annual message to Congress in December 1810, he applauded the growth of manufacturing that was occurring because of disrupted trade with Britain: "Such indeed is the experience of economy as well as of policy in these substitutes for supplies heretofore obtained by foreign commerce that in a national view the change is justly regarded as of itself more than a recompense for those privations and losses resulting from foreign injustice which furnished the general impulse required for its accomplishment. How far it may be expedient to guard the infancy of this improvement in the distribution of labor by regulations of the commercial tariff is a subject which cannot fail to suggest itself to your patriotic reflections."[140]

Of course, the trade disruptions were a mixed blessing for American industry. Production by import-substituting manufacturers increased, but export-oriented manufacturing, most importantly shipbuilding, suffered. Production by commercial industries collapsed in 1808 due to the embargo and contracted even more during the War of 1812. For import-competing manufacturers, production spiked during the war, but the gain in output was largely reversed after trade resumed in 1815.[141]

Thus, the tumultuous experience of dealing with British trade policies after independence had transformed Thomas Jefferson and his fellow Republicans. In 1785, Jefferson lauded farmers as the chosen people of God and pleaded, "Let our workshops remain in Europe." In 1813, Jefferson now wrote that "out of the evils of impressment and of the orders in council, a great blessing for us will grow. I have not formerly been an advocate for great manufactories. I doubted whether our labor, employed in agriculture, and aided by the spontaneous energies of the earth, would not procure us more than we could make ourselves of other necessaries. But other considerations entering into the question, have settled my doubts."[142] Three years later, Jefferson was even more enthusiastic: "Within the thirty years that have elapsed [since the publication of *Notes on Virginia*], how are circumstances changed! To be independent for the comforts of life we must fabricate them ourselves. We must now place the manufacturer by the side of a agriculturalist. . . . . Experience has taught me that manufactures are now as necessary to our independence as to our comfort."[143]

The manufacturers that had arisen during the period of disrupted trade marked the beginning of a new era in US trade policy. Now commerce and agriculture were joined by a third economic interest, manufacturing, as the key sectors that would shape the politics of trade policy. Madison and the Republican Congress did not want the new industries to disappear as a result of renewed competition from Britain. Therefore, as we shall see in chapter 3, the Madison administration helped give rise to the first truly protective tariff in US history, leading to many trade-policy battles in the decades to come.

CHAPTER THREE

Sectional Conflict and Crisis, 1816–1833

The end of the War of 1812 marked the beginning of a new era in US trade policy. The dominant problem of the post-independence period, securing neutral trading rights from Britain and France, disappeared as the reexport trade shrank to a fraction of its former importance. Instead, the trade-policy debate shifted to whether import duties, in addition to raising revenue for the government, should be used to protect domestic producers from foreign competition. Those in Congress who favored doing so quickly pushed the average tariff on dutiable imports up to its highest level in US history, an average of 62 percent in 1830. This generated strong political opposition and led to a dangerous predicament when South Carolina decided to nullify the 1828 "Tariff of Abominations." Thus, a sectional dispute over tariff policy put the United States on the brink of one of its worst political crises since independence.

PROTECTIONISM EMERGES

The Treaty of Ghent, which ended the war between the United States and Britain, was signed in December 1814 and ratified by the Senate in February 1815. The return of peace meant the resumption of overseas commerce after many years of disruption. The opening of trade in the spring of 1815 provided welcome relief for export-oriented agricultural producers. The prices of major export crops, including cotton, tobacco, and rice, rose sharply as access to foreign markets was restored. As happened after the Revolutionary war, the increase in exports could not keep pace with an even greater surge in imports. As figure 2.1 shows, exports increased sharply in 1815 and 1816, but not nearly as much as imports. Imports in 1815 and the first half of 1816 were subject to the high wartime duties; the average tariff on dutiable imports was about 49 percent in 1815. But these duties, double those in the previous tariff act of 1804, did not restrain the enormous pent-up demand for British manufactured goods.

The surge of imports helped the government collect enough customs revenue to start paying down the debts incurred during the war. But the imports were an unwelcome shock for fledgling domestic industries that had begun operation and expanded production when competing imports had been kept out of the market, a period dating back to Jefferson's trade embargo in 1808. The influx of low-priced foreign goods threatened to destroy many of the new manufacturers and had a particularly devastating impact on producers of iron, cotton, and woolen goods. These young and inexperienced producers were simply too small and inefficient to withstand the onslaught of foreign competition that came with a return to normal trading conditions. As the price of imports fell 28 percent from 1814 to 1816, industrial production declined 7 percent in 1816 as vulnerable firms went bankrupt and shut down.[1]

British manufacturers were immediately accused of "dumping" their goods in a deliberate attempt to destroy the infant industries. In a famous speech in the House of Commons in April 1816, Henry Brougham stated that "it was well worthwhile to incur a loss upon the first exportation, in order, by the glut, to stifle in the cradle those rising manufacturers in the United States which the war had forced into existence contrary to the natural course of things."[2] This remark has often been quoted to prove that British producers were deliberately cutting their prices to destroy the new American entrants, but Brougham actually argued that the substantial losses incurred by British merchants in 1816 were not intentional but the result of a mad rush to sell in the market when commerce was reopened.[3]

Of course, everyone expected that many of the new manufacturing establishments would face severe difficulties once trade resumed. In submitting the peace treaty to Congress in February 1815, President James Madison requested that Congress consider the "means to preserve and promote the manufactures which have sprung into existence, and attained an unparalleled maturity throughout the United States, during the period of the European wars."[4] This was a critical issue facing Congress after the war. Neither the Madison administration nor Congress wanted to see the new industries destroyed with the return of foreign competition. America's military weakness had been so embarrassingly evident during the war, and patriotic sentiment had developed to such an extent, that many in Congress were determined to support the new manufacturers and ensure that the country achieved economic independence from foreign sources of supply. This task was made easier by the disappearance of the Federalist party from national politics after the war, leaving Congress without an organized political party in favor of low tariffs and open commerce.

With the high wartime duties scheduled to remain in effect until early 1816, Congress did not act on the issue in 1815. In his December 1815 annual message to Congress, Madison reiterated his long-held belief that "however wise the theory may be which leaves to the sagacity and interest of individuals the application of their industry and resources, there are in this as in other cases exceptions to the general rule." For one, the United States could only adopt a liberal trade policy if it was reciprocated by other countries. Furthermore, "experience teaches that so many circumstances must concur in introducing and maturing manufacturing establishments, especially of the more complicated kinds, that a country may remain long without them, although sufficiently advanced and in some respects even peculiarly fitted for carrying them on with success." Therefore, because the war gave a "powerful impulse to manufacturing industry," there was now good reason for believing that, if they were given "a protection not more than is due to the enterprising citizens whose interests are now at stake," domestic manufactures would not only be safe "against occasional competitions from abroad, but a source of domestic wealth and even of external commerce."[5]

In February 1816, at the request of Congress, Treasury Secretary Alexander Dallas delivered a report proposing a new schedule of import duties. Dallas focused on two issues: raising enough revenue to pay the government's expenses, especially the debts incurred during the war, and satisfying the country's three main economic interests—agriculture, industry, and commerce. This was a difficult balancing act because the interests of agriculture and commerce were not the same as those of industry. Farmers and planters wanted easy access to foreign markets to sell their goods and purchase various articles of consumption, while merchants and shipping interests benefited from an expanding volume of both exports and imports. However, manufacturers facing competition from British producers had an interest in restricting imports as much as possible.

Dallas noted that the government had regarded the establishment of domestic manufactures as important ever since Hamilton's *Report on Manufactures* in 1790, but policy measures to achieve that objective had never really been undertaken. The country was almost wholly cut off from foreign supplies of weapons and munitions of war, clothing, and other goods during the war, and Dallas pointed out that "from these circumstances of suffering and mortification have sprung . . . the means of future safety and independence" with the emergence of domestic producers of such goods. With the resumption of trade, Dallas concluded, "the preservation of the manufactures . . . becomes a consideration of general policy, to be resolved, by a recollection of past embarrassments, by the certainty of an increased difficulty of reinstating, upon any emergency, the manufactures which shall be allowed to perish and pass away, and by a just sense of the influence of domestic manufactures upon the wealth, power, and independence of the Government."

Dallas then placed domestic industries into one of three categories. First, there were "firmly and permanently established" manufactures, such as cabinets, hats, iron castings and muskets, window glass, leather manufactures and paper. Second, there were industries "recently or partially established . . . but which, with proper cultivation, are capable of being matured to the whole extent of demand," including cotton and woolen goods of the coarser kind, plated wares, iron manufactures (such as shovels, axes, and nails), and beer and spirits. Finally, there were goods "which are so slightly cultivated as to leave the demand of the country wholly . . . dependent upon foreign sources for supply," including finer cottons and linens, silk and woolens such as carpets and blankets, chinaware, other glass products.[6]

Curiously, Dallas proposed duties inversely related to the requirements of the industry, that is, high duties for those able to withstand foreign competition and low duties for those least able to compete. Dallas proposed imposing the highest tariffs (35 percent) on the goods in the first category for which domestic production was secure because, for these well-established industries, prohibitive duties could be imposed "without endangering a scarcity of supply, while the competition among the domestic manufacturers alone would sufficiently protect the consumer from exorbitant prices." The "slightly cultivated" industries in the third category (mainly luxury goods) deserved no support at all because "the present policy of the Government is directed to protect, not to create manufactures." For the "recently or partially established" infant industries in the second category, Dallas recommended government support in the form of import duties that "will enable the manufacturer to meet the importer in the American market upon equal terms of profit and loss." These duties were more modest, ranging from 33–1/3 percent on cotton textiles, 30 percent on earthenware and glass, 28 percent on woolen manufactures, 22 percent on iron goods, 20 percent on linens, and so forth. Dallas concluded that "it is respectfully thought to be in the power of the Legislature, by a well-timed and well-directed patronage, to place them, within a limited period, upon the footing on which the manufacturers included in the first class have been so happily placed. . . . Although some indulgence will always be required, for any attempt so to realize the national independence in the department of manufactures, the sacrifice cannot be either great or lasting. The inconveniences of the day will be amply compensated by future advantages."[7]

Congress promptly took up the administration's proposals. For the first time since the nation's founding, the tariff debate focused more on protecting industries from foreign competition than raising revenue. The tariff should be set "as would give the necessary and proper protection and support to the agriculture, manufactures, and commerce of the country," Henry Clay of Kentucky asserted. "The revenue was only an incidental consideration, and ought not to have any influence in the decision upon the proposition before the committee."[8]

Flooded with petitions from many interested parties, particularly manufacturers requesting tariff increases and commercial interests urging tariff reductions, the House instructed the Ways and Means Committee to craft a bill consistent with Dallas's proposal. However, in March 1816, the chairman of the committee, William Lowndes of South Carolina, reported a bill that reflected his southern preferences and shaved down many of the suggested duties. For example, the 35 percent duty on paper and leather was reduced to 30 percent, the 33–1/3 percent duty on cotton textiles was cut to 25 percent (and scheduled to be reduced to 20 percent in 1819), the 22 percent duty on iron goods was marked down to 20 percent, and so on, although the 15 percent duty on unenumerated goods was retained. Most of the discussion centered on a few key commodities, particularly iron goods and sugar, with special attention to cotton textiles.

The Congressional debate exposed two opposing factions that would clash repeatedly in coming decades: a high-tariff group of Mid-Atlantic states and a low-tariff group of southern states. At this point, New England was divided because it had a mix of commercial and manufacturing interests, but it would soon join the Mid-Atlantic in supporting protection when manufacturers became a larger economic force in the region. The leader of the high-tariff faction was Henry Clay. He wanted "thorough and decided protection by ample duties" for home manufacturers with the objective of encouraging industrial growth by displacing imports from the domestic market. The country's national security depended on ending foreign dependence on critical supplies, such as boots and clothing, arms and munitions, Clay insisted, but he also touted the broader economic benefits from encouraging domestic production of manufactures.

The South resisted the effort to enact higher tariffs. Their representatives complained that the tariff increased the price of imported goods
that the South consumed, reducing their standard of living. Furthermore,
by reducing imports, higher tariffs would translate into lower foreign demand for exports, most of which came from the South. Therefore, high
import tariffs would put a heavy economic burden on the South by reducing its exports and increasing the price of the imports it consumed. The
mercurial John Randolph of Virginia denounced tariffs as an artificial way
of promoting northern industry at the expense of southern agriculture. He
suggested that the issue came down to this:

> whether you, as a planter will consent to be taxed, in order to hire an-
> other man to go to work in a shoemaker's shop, or to set up a spinning
> jenny. For my part I will not agree to it, . . . I will not agree to lay a
> duty on the cultivators of the soil to encourage exotic manufactures;
> because, after all, we should only get much worse things at a much
> higher price. . . . Why pay a man much more than the value for it, to
> work up our own cotton into clothing, when, by selling my raw mate-
> rial, I can get my clothing much better and cheaper from Dacca [In-
> dia]. . . . I am convinced that it would be impolitic, as well as unjust,
> to aggravate the burdens of the people for the purpose of favoring the
> manufacturers.[9]

But after the tumultuous experience of the past decade, even southern
representatives could not oppose a moderately protective tariff. This acceptance did not reflect any warm feelings for northern manufacturers,
but arose from a strong sense of nationalism and concern for the country's
defense. The lack of domestic supplies of important materiel had hampered the recent war effort. John Calhoun of South Carolina, later a fierce
tariff critic, supported the 1816 tariff bill because the issue of protection
was "connected with the security of the country."[10]

The House passed the bill in April 1816 by a vote of 88–54. The Senate quickly followed, and Madison signed the measure later in the month.
Most of New England's representatives voted in favor of the higher duties;
with small cotton textile firms having sprouted up in the region, it was
no longer dominated by merchant and shipping interests, as it had been a
decade earlier. The Mid-Atlantic states, led by Pennsylvania, strongly supported the bill because many iron and glass producers were located there
and faced competition from imports. The South was split but slightly more
unfavorable to the legislation. It did not favor the higher tariffs as a general

matter and had supported failed amendments to reduce the tariff on cotton and woolen manufactures to 20 percent. At the same time, anti-British sentiment was very strong in the South, and the fear of another war convinced members from the region that the protection of new manufacturers was necessary. These concerns about national defense were decisive in ensuring support for the tariff in the South, whose votes were critical for the legislation's passage. In a sign of the battles to come, however, representatives from the South also made clear their opposition to any additional protection to industry.[11]

The Tariff of 1816 was the first "protectionist" tariff of the United States in the sense that it was mainly designed to provide assistance to domestic manufacturers facing foreign competition. Given Madison's opposition to Hamilton's *Report on Manufactures* in the 1790s, it is ironic that his administration helped institutionalize government support for manufacturing by imposing high duties on imports.[12] However, the federal government never had a conscious policy of starting "infant industries." Rather, those industries emerged as a by-product of the trade interruptions and then pressured Congress to protect them from foreign competition. The direction of causality is important: Congress did not deliberately create the infant industries through policy measures; the industries emerged and then compelled Congress to enact higher tariffs for their benefit. In other words, Congress was not farsighted in shaping the future path of the economy but simply reacted to the political pressures that it faced.

THE GROWTH OF THE COTTON TEXTILE INDUSTRY

The period after the War of 1812 saw the emergence of two important sectors of the economy: cotton in the South and cotton textiles in the North. While cotton producers were dependent on exports, the cotton textile industry faced competition from imports. As a result, the two regions of the country developed strongly opposing interests with respect to trade. The coming battles over US trade policy would pit manufacturers in the North against agricultural exporters in the South for many decades to come.

In 1793, Eli Whitney introduced a new invention, the cotton gin, which led to an astonishing improvement in productivity. It used to take a farmhand one day to remove seed from one pound of cotton fiber, but with the cotton gin the same person could separate the seed from three hundred pounds of cotton fiber per day. In 1793, the United States produced 10,000 bales of cotton, just 1 percent of world production. By 1830, the country produced 732,000 bales of cotton, about half of the world's production.[13] As a result, the growth in cotton exports was explosive. In 1792, the year before the introduction of the cotton gin, the United States exported 138,328 pounds of raw cotton. Just two years later, cotton exports were 1.6 million pounds. By 1800, the United States exported 17.8 million pounds. By 1821, cotton alone comprised almost half of total exports. Cotton was the largest single commodity export of the United States throughout the nineteenth century and remained so as late as 1929, when it alone comprised 18 percent of total exports. The expansion of cotton production reinforced the South's position as an export-oriented region and strengthened its opposition to high tariffs. The cotton gin also entrenched the South's attachment to the "peculiar institution" of slavery, because harvesting cotton was so labor-intensive.

Meanwhile, the New England cotton textile industry was the most striking new industry to have arisen during the period of disrupted trade. From the tariff of 1816 to the present day, the textile and apparel industry has been at the center of trade-policy debates. The first cotton mill in the United States was set up in Rhode Island in 1790 using the Arkwright technology. This spinning technology was brought to the country by Samuel Slater, a superintendent of an early Lancashire mill. Slater memorized blueprints of the equipment used before he sailed to America because Britain banned the export of textile machinery, and officials would have searched his possessions for descriptions of the technology as he left the country. The technology gradually spread through Massachusetts and Rhode Island, and by 1807, the United States had about fifteen cotton mills working eight thousand spindles, according to Gallatin's *Report on Manufactures*. The spinning mills simply converted raw cotton into thread, which was then woven into fabric by artisans working outside the mill.

The embargo changed everything. Domestic textile production became enormously profitable: the price of textiles shot up with the drop in imports, while the price of cotton plummeted with the inability to export. This wider gap between the price of textiles and the cost of cotton spurred the rapid entry of many small spinning factories, as figure 3.1 shows. The number of textile mills jumped from about 15 before the embargo to 87 in 1809, and Gallatin estimated that 112 would be in operation by the start of 1811. Gallatin wrote that "the injurious violations of the neutral commerce of the United States, by forcing industry and capital into other channels, have broken inveterate habits, and given a general impulse, to which must be ascribed the greatest increase in manufactures during the last two years."[14]

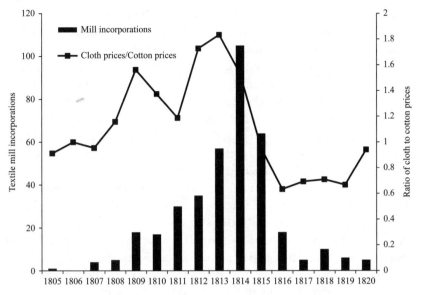

Figure 3.1. Textile mill incorporations and relative cloth/
cotton prices, 1805–1820. (Lebergott 1984, 128.)

Domestic manufacturers were unprepared for the flood of imports that
poured into the country in 1815 and 1816 when trade resumed. Although
still protected by 35 percent wartime duties, most small mills were inefficient and simply could not compete against the cheaper goods produced by
the larger and more advanced British producers. The profitability of American mills was squeezed as imports drove down the price of textiles while
exports pushed up the price of cotton. As figure 3.1 shows, entry into the
industry ceased, and business failures multiplied; about half the spindles
around Providence, Rhode Island, were said to be idle during 1816.

The technology that helped ensure the industry's survival was the
power loom, which allowed factories to weave yarn into cloth (instead of
sending thread out to be spun by individual artisans) and then made into
apparel. The power loom enabled spinning and weaving to be done under
one roof in larger enterprises. By integrating these operations, the power
loom allowed cloth to be mass produced and reduced its cost by half.[15] The
technology diffused rapidly through New England: by 1820, there were
1,667 power looms in use by eighty-six firms. According to the Census
of 1820, about 100,000 spindles were involved in spinning, but more than
225,000 in both spinning and weaving.

The power loom was also based on pirated British technology brought over in the minds of enterprising individuals. Francis Cabot Lowell, who personally observed the introduction of the power loom in Lancashire around 1810, returned to the United States and helped organize the Boston Manufacturing Company with his business partner, Nathan Appleton, a Boston merchant. Located in Waltham, Massachusetts, the firm started producing sturdy, inexpensive coarse cloth in 1815 and became fully operational in 1816. The Boston Manufacturing Co. was so successful that, despite the struggling economy, it declared a dividend of 17 percent in October 1817 and invested in another mill in 1818. From 1817 to 1826, its average annual dividend was nearly 19 percent.[16]

The success of the New England industry was not so much due to the tariff as to the transfer of new technology from Britain and the ability of American entrepreneurs and skilled artisans to improve the technology and apply it to local conditions. Lowell introduced the power loom not because tariff protection was in place but because the technology had just become available in Britain, was easily transferable to the United States, and sharply reduced production costs and therefore was highly profitable. The power loom was a critical cost-saving innovation whose adoption was a necessity because lower textile and higher cotton prices made efficiency an imperative after the war. The power loom revolutionized the industry and produced a huge shakeout among existing firms: the sales of firms that adopted the new technology grew rapidly, while many of the old spinning mills in Rhode Island and around Philadelphia were driven out of business.

Although the power loom was more important to the survival of the industry than the 1816 tariff, Lowell was instrumental in shaping the duties on imported cotton textiles to his benefit. As Appleton (1858, 13) recounted, "The Rhode Island manufacturers were clamorous for a very high specific duty. Mr. Lowell was at Washington, for a considerable time, during the session of Congress [in 1816]. His views on the tariff were much more moderate, and he finally brought Mr. Lowndes and Mr. Calhoun to support the minimum 6 1/4 cents the square yard, which was carried." In other words, Lowell helped establish a "minimum valuation" provision that was applied to imported textiles. The minimum valuation provision meant that anything priced at less than 25 cents per yard would have to pay a duty of 6.25 cents a yard. This provision was regressive because it put a heavy burden on cheap cloth imports and a lighter burden on expensive cloth imports.

The Lowell compromise was politically savvy in that it proposed a tariff structure that balanced the interest of southern cotton exporters and

New England textile manufactures facing foreign competition. The tariff was designed to be high enough to keep out inexpensive Indian fabrics that did not use American cotton but competed with domestic producers, but not so high as to keep out higher-priced, higher-quality British goods that used American cotton, something southern export interests would have found objectionable.

The larger textile firms were not fearful of British imports, because the two countries tended to produce different types of products. The New England power looms produced mass quantities of plain weaves, such as sheeting and shirting, with lower-count yarns than British products. British imports tended to be high-quality fabrics with high yarn counts, such as ginghams and pattern weaves that power looms were not able to produce. Since there were no imports of low-count, plain-woven goods from either Britain or India after 1816, the minimum valuation was a binding constraint on imports from India but not on Britain until 1819, when deflation lowered their price.[17]

The cotton textile industry grew steadily throughout this period. In 1826, one of the first years in which data are available on domestic production and imports, the shares of the market are about equal. By 1830, however, domestic production far exceeded imports (as discussed in chapter 4). Thus, it appears that if the cotton textile industry was an "infant," it matured quickly. While trade disruptions led to the establishment of small spinning mills, the adoption of the power loom led to the success of large, mass-production enterprises, which were able to supply most of the growing demand for cloth. Economic historians have been skeptical that protective duties were essential to the industry's growth. Zevin (1971, 128) concluded that "while the tariff may have had demand augmenting effects which contributed to the cyclical recovery from the postwar depression, the tariff made no significant contribution to the secular growth of American demand for New England mill products over the period from 1815 to 1833." In Taussig's (1931, 60) view, the early progress of the cotton textile industry, "though perhaps somewhat promoted by the minimum duty of 1816, would hardly have been much retarded in the absence of protective duties."[18]

THE OUTBREAK OF TARIFF CONFLICT

The 1820s saw some of the fiercest political battles ever waged over trade policy in the nation's history. A powerful coalition in Congress representing northern manufacturers and western raw materials producers pushed relentlessly for higher tariffs in 1820, 1824, 1827, and 1828. While the effort to increase duties failed in 1820 and 1827, the coalition's successes in 1824 and 1828 infuriated southern politicians who represented export-dependent crop producers. The South vigorously opposed every bid to raise tariffs, but its minority position in Congress left it unable to stop it. This failure pushed South Carolina to the brink of secession. How did import duties become one of the most divisive issues in American politics during this time?

The source of the emergent protectionist sentiment was a severe recession in 1818–19. If the dislocations of the war and the adjustments to peacetime commerce were not wrenching enough, America's financial system was in chaos. The Madison administration closed the Bank of the United States in 1811, and the government had to finance the war without a central bank. Although the Second Bank of the United States was chartered in 1816, it sought to build up its reserves of specie in order to service the debts arising from the Louisiana Purchase. To do so, the bank tightened credit in the summer of 1818. Meanwhile, state banks had become vastly overextended, partly as a result of lending to land speculators. This created an excess of paper currency that came to a painful end as banks began to demand repayment in specie, which led to the Panic of 1819. The panic and subsequent financial contraction led to plummeting land prices and a rash of bank failures. The economy suffered through a severe deflation and recession. Consumer prices dropped 11 percent between 1819 and 1821, and the price of cotton fell almost 60 percent over the same period.

Not surprisingly, the downturn led to demands for higher tariffs.[19] As the economic suffering intensified, producer groups and merchant associations, towns and state legislatures, mainly from the North, sent messages to Congress pleading for higher duties to alleviate the economic distress and reduce widespread unemployment. They requested higher tariffs to secure the home market for domestic producers, to encourage raw materials to be processed at home rather than being exported for processing abroad, and thus end the nation's dependence on imports. The petitioners were not looking for temporary relief, but a permanent tariff system that would secure their position in the domestic market.

The campaign for higher import duties was strong because it was well organized and benefited from nationwide publicity. A Philadelphia printer named Mathew Carey helped establish the Philadelphia Society for the Promotion of National Industry that joined other groups in sending memorials and petitions to Congress asking for greater protection for domestic industries. Carey played a key role in spreading the agitation for a higher tariff outside of Pennsylvania to the nation at large.[20] Carey's argument was simple: free trade led to a drain in specie, the decay of industry, and the rise in unemployment, while tariffs would secure the home market for industries and their workers and thereby strengthen the economy. Hezekiah Niles, the editor of the influential *Weekly Register*, also published an endless stream of editorials extolling the benefits of higher tariffs in protecting domestic industries from foreign competition.

Although the recession originated in the nation's troubled financial sector, manufacturers blamed foreign competition for the weak economy.[21] Yet higher duties were proposed as a potential remedy because the government had no other policy instruments with which to address the slump. The government did not have a discretionary monetary policy, and there was no fiscal policy, because federal spending was a tiny part of the overall economy. Therefore, producers facing competition from imports had no alternative but to demand that the only available policy tool, import tariffs, be raised to cushion them from the sharp economic downturn.

The financial crisis hit agricultural producers just as hard, if not harder, than manufacturers because of the collapse in commodity prices. Although the government could protect import-competing manufacturers through higher tariffs, it had no readily available means of helping exporters, because Congress was not prepared to enact export subsidies or price supports for any commodity.[22] Southern planters resented the demands that Congress consider higher tariffs to help manufacturing while doing nothing to help agriculture. Memorials and remonstrations from the South dismissed the idea that low tariffs were a cause of the depression, arguing that higher tariffs would only worsen the situation.

At this time, presidents were neither expected nor encouraged to meddle with the legislative process, which was considered to be strictly Congress's business. But President James Monroe gently nudged Congress in the direction of increasing the tariff. In his annual message to Congress in November 1818, he offered this modest suggestion: "The strict execution of the revenue laws . . . has, it is presumed, secured to domestic manufactures all the relief that can be derived from the duties which have been imposed upon foreign merchandise for their protection. Under the influence of this relief several branches of this important national interest have assumed greater activity, and although it is hoped that others will gradually revive and ultimately triumph over every obstacle, yet the expediency of granting further protection is submitted to your consideration."[23]

A year later, Monroe accused other countries of dumping their goods in the United States and dropped another hint: "It is deemed of great importance to give encouragement to our domestic manufacturers. In what manner the evils which have been adverted to may be remedied, and how far it may be practicable in other respects to afford to them further encouragement, paying due regard to the other great interests of the nation, is submitted to the wisdom of Congress."[24] These presidential invitations set the stage for the next trade battle in Congress.

As a new Congress convened in December 1819, the new speaker of the House, Henry Clay, took authority over tariff legislation away from the Ways and Means Committee and gave it to the rival Committee of Manufactures, which he had packed with supporters of protection. In March 1820, the committee chairman, Henry Baldwin of Pennsylvania, reported a bill to increase import duties across the board. Baldwin promised that a higher tariff would improve the unfavorable balance of trade, end the drain of specie, and increase employment, while ensuring an expanding home market for domestic agricultural producers.[25]

Baldwin also criticized Lowndes for having scaled down the duties recommended by Dallas in 1816. Baldwin argued that the poor economy was indisputable proof that the 1816 duties had been set too low. In response, Lowndes defended the tariff of 1816 and sharply questioned the need for higher rates. The issue was not whether manufactures are useful or whether the government should assist manufacturers, he insisted, for that question had been answered affirmatively. But manufacturers were already supported with considerable duties on imported goods, and the "encouragement already afforded was as great as could reasonably be granted." Lowndes argued that high tariffs were not a remedy for the poor economy because carriage makers and others were suffering from a want of employment and yet did not face any competition from imports. "It is a distress from which our tariff can give no relief," he insisted, and yet, by raising prices, higher tariffs would reduce the real incomes of consumers.[26]

Other southern members of Congress joined in the attack. Higher tariffs would constitute an unjust subsidy to industry at a time when the vast majority of citizens were employed in agriculture, they complained. Southern agriculture was suffering just as much as northern manufacturing, but high tariffs that would help the latter would only harm the former. The troubles faced by manufacturers were due to the nation's financial problems, not foreign competition, and therefore higher import duties were an inappropriate remedy, particularly when other regions were suffering more than the North. The purpose of the tariff was to raise revenue, they argued, not to protect certain industries at the expense of others. As John Randolph of Virginia stated, "It is not consonant with the principles of a wise policy to lay duties not for the purpose of raising revenue to the government, but to operate as a bounty on any particular species of labor at the expense of the community in general on whom taxes are laid."[27] The encouragement of trade through low duties, he and others insisted, would help revive the economy.

Clay countered that the United States could not follow a policy of free trade (although that was not really the alternative) unless it was reciprocated by other countries. As he put it,

> All other countries but our own exclude, by high duties, or absolute prohibitions, whatever they can respectively produce within themselves. The truth is, and it was in vain to disguise it, that we are a sort of independent colonies of England—politically free, commercially slaves. Gentlemen tell us of the advantage of a free exchange of the produce of the world. But they tell us of what never has existed, does not exist, and perhaps never will exist. They invoke us to give perfect freedom on our side, whilst, in the ports of every other nation, we are met with a code of odious restrictions, shutting out entirely a great part of our produce, and letting in only so much as they cannot possibly do without. . . . At present I will only say, that I am too a friend of free trade, but it must be a free trade of perfect reciprocity.[28]

Whatever the merits of the case, it would have been very difficult for Congress to do nothing in response to the strong constituent pressures. Indeed, the Baldwin bill "represented the culmination of a sustained and concerted lobbying campaign that singled out the moderate Tariff of 1816 as the principal cause of the nation's economic distress."[29] In April 1820, the Baldwin bill passed the House by a vote of 91–78. The Mid-Atlantic region strongly supported the bill; the South was overwhelmingly opposed, while New England was split owing to the coexistence of merchant shipping and manufacturing interests. But a month later, in the Senate, where the political power of the North and South was more equally balanced, the bill was defeated by a single vote. Unlike its 1816 position, the South now unanimously opposed the bid to increase tariffs. The South voted 14–0 to table the bill, while other regions voted 21–8 to keep it alive. The South's support for the Tariff of 1816 had depended on three factors: the need for additional revenue, the continuing threat of war with Britain, and the surge of manufactured imports. All three factors were absent in 1820.

The sectional pattern of the 1820 vote would be repeated for many decades to come. The South had little hope of stopping tariff legislation in the House, where it was outnumbered because representation was based on population. Therefore, the South aimed to defeat tariff bills in the Senate, where its power was more evenly matched with that of the North. Given the North-South standoff, the rapidly growing Midwest would soon be a critical swing region in the sectional division over tariff legislation.

One issue on which all members of Congress could agree was that statistical data on foreign trade was woefully incomplete. Up to this point, the annual Treasury publications on foreign trade reported only the quantity of goods imported subject to specific duties and the total value of goods charged with ad valorem duties, but failed to enumerate the quantity and value of imported goods. In 1820, Congress authorized the collection of more detailed data on exports and imports. Consequently, US trade statistics improve beginning in 1821, but it was not until after the Civil War that more comprehensive data become available.

CLAY'S AMERICAN SYSTEM

The early 1820s have been described as the "Era of Good Feelings" for the absence of partisan conflict, but good feelings about the tariff were in short supply. The question of using import duties to protect domestic manufacturers from foreign competition became a controversial and divisive issue, sharpening existing sectional divisions.

Even as the economy recovered after the Panic of 1819 and government finances improved, President Monroe continued to suggest that Congress increase import duties. For example, in his annual report to Congress in December 1822, Monroe gave an optimistic assessment of the nation's trade, noting that the government's finances were strong and that "our commercial differences with France and Great Britain have been placed in a train of amicable arrangement on conditions fair and honorable in both instances to each party." The previous disputes with Britain about shipping rights simply vanished. American shipping was no longer harassed, the West Indies was no longer a significant part of US trade, and the British market gradually became more open to US products.[30]

The president also reported that manufacturing industries were now doing well but deserved further support. Yet he warned that "the interest of every part of our Union, even of those most benefitted by manufactures, requires that this subject should be touched with the greatest caution, and a critical knowledge of the effect to be produced by the slightest change." Still, he concluded that "I am persuaded that a further augmentation may now be made of the duties on certain foreign articles in favor of our own and without affecting injuriously any other interest."[31]

Congress did not act on the president's suggestion. Philip Barbour of Virginia used his position as the new House speaker for the Seventeenth Congress (1821–23) to prevent the introduction of any new tariff bills. Supporters of protection never gave up hope of enacting higher duties, but had to wait until they controlled the key leadership positions on Congress. That came in December 1823 with the convening of the Eighteenth Congress, the first elected under the new apportionment of seats based on the 1820 census. The census found that population, and hence political power, had shifted to states in the North: Whereas the South gained only two House seats, Pennsylvania and New York picked up ten seats, Ohio eight seats, and other border states (such as Kentucky and Tennessee) another eight seats. Although the North-South balance of power remained even in the Senate, these apportionment changes, along with the election of Henry Clay as the speaker once again, made it much easier to get tariff legislation through the House.

When the new Congress convened, President Monroe repeated his call for a tariff revision. As in 1820, Clay referred the matter to the Committee on Manufactures, which reported a bill in January 1824. The committee again held that the Tariff of 1816 had been inadequate and that higher duties were needed to help manufacturers in particular and the economy more generally.

Speaking before the House over two days in March 1824, Clay gave an important address that proposed something called the "American System." He opened by describing the nation's weak economy and the "general distress that pervades the whole country," attributing the economic woes to the fact that "we have shaped our industry, our navigation, and our commerce in reference to an extraordinary war in Europe, and to a foreign market, which no longer exists."[32] While there may have been a large foreign market for US goods and services during the exceptional wartime period, those markets had long since vanished. Excessive reliance on overseas markets made farmers and planters dependent on an unreliable source of demand and put domestic industries at the mercy of strong overseas competitors.

To counter this overdependence on foreign markets, Clay suggested that the United States concentrate on developing its own market.

> We have seen that an exclusive dependence upon the foreign market must lead to still severer distress, to impoverishment, to ruin. We

must then change somewhat our course. We must give a new direction to some portion of our industry. We must speedily adopt a genuine
American policy. Still cherishing a foreign market, let us create also a
home market, to give further scope to the consumption of the produce
of American industry. Let us counteract the policy of foreigners, and
withdraw the support which we now give to their industry, and stimulate that of our own country.[33]

As he put it,

It is most desirable that there should be both a home and a foreign market. But with respect to their relative superiority, I cannot entertain
a doubt. The home market is first in order, and paramount in importance. The object of the bill under consideration is to create this home
market and lay the foundations of a genuine American policy. It is
opposed; and it is incumbent upon the partisans of the foreign policy
(terms which I shall use without any invidious intent) to demonstrate
that the foreign market is an adequate vent for the surplus produce of
our labor.[34]

The remedy for the nation's economic problem, he concluded, "consists in
modifying our foreign policy, and in adopting a genuine American System.
We must naturalize the arts in our country by the only means which the
wisdom of nations has yet discovered to be effectual—by adequate protection against the otherwise overwhelming influence of foreigners. This is
only to be accomplished by the establishment of a tariff."[35]

Clay proposed that Congress adopt a tariff structure similar to the
failed Baldwin bill of 1820, which would increase the tariff on cotton and
woolen manufactures from 25 percent to 33-1/3 percent. Congressional inaction, he warned, "will complete the work of destruction of our domestic
industry" and such a "fatal policy" would lead to "impoverishment and
ruin."[36]

Clay's "American System" address was a landmark in US trade policy. The vision set out in the speech was much greater than the particular
duties he proposed. Clay was an economic nationalist who believed that
the federal government should take an active role in strengthening the
economy by promoting manufacturing industries, establishing a national
banking system, and financing internal improvements to create a transportation network of roads, bridges, and canals that would bind the nation
together. In terms of trade policy, the American System involved reducing

the nation's dependence on foreign markets and creating a strong home market through high protective tariffs. Rather than exporting the country's raw materials to Britain for manufacture, they should be shipped to the North for processing into final goods which would then be sent back to the South for consumption. This arrangement would employ American labor, not foreign labor, to make the manufactures that were consumed at home. This would diversify the nation's employment and strengthen the economy, but it would not happen naturally: the government had to undertake measures to ensure that this would happen.

Clay knew that changing the direction of the economy through protective tariffs would be controversial, so he tried to ease the worries of potential opponents: "And what is this tariff? It seems to have been regarded as a sort of a monster, huge and deformed—a wild beast, endowed with tremendous powers of destruction, about to be let loose among our people, if not to devour them, at least to consume their substance. But let us calm our passions, and deliberately survey this alarming, this terrific being. The sole object of the tariff is to tax the produce of foreign industry with the view of promoting American industry."[37]

Anticipating criticism from the South, Clay denied that higher tariffs would promote manufacturing industries at the expense of other sectors of the economy. Instead, he argued, tariffs would produce a balanced, self-sufficient economy with strong demand for all producers. It was not just industries in the North that would flourish under the tariff, Clay maintained, but agricultural and raw materials producers in the South and West as well. He was confident that the factories in New England could provide a stronger and more stable source of demand for southern cotton and could eventually supply the South with cotton goods that would be cheaper and better than those imported from Britain. In fact, he maintained that protective tariffs would not diminish British demand for southern cotton because it was the most competitive source of supply in the world and would create new demand for cotton at home that would more than make up for any lost exports.[38] The American System was not a sectional piece of legislation, he concluded, but one that would bring the country together and work to the advantage of all interests and all regions.[39]

Despite Clay's rhetorical efforts, many of his colleagues were unpersuaded. Daniel Webster of Massachusetts rose immediately to "dissent entirely" from the picture of distress painted by Clay. The economic troubles caused by the Panic of 1819 had passed, he noted, and the nation's prosperity was increasing. This growth was built on free enterprise without limits on trade that would depress trade-dependent industries such as the commercial and shipping interests of New England. The issue was not an "American" as opposed to a "foreign" economic policy, he countered. Rather, there were three great interests in the country—agricultural, commercial, and industrial—and any proposed legislation that operated to the benefit of one without considering the consequences for the other two was "dangerous." The adoption of an American System would eventually lead to the prohibition of imports, Webster feared, which would impose an incalculable cost on shipbuilders and merchant interests.[40]

Webster's polite but firm rejection of Clay's proposal contrasted with the bitter denunciation and scorn issued by southern Congressmen. They fervently denied that higher import tariffs would benefit all sections of the country, viewing it instead as a sectional proposal that would simply reward politically powerful special interests in the North at the expense of the South. As James Hamilton of South Carolina complained, "All sorts of pilgrims had traveled to the room of the Committee on Manufactures, from the sturdy ironmaster down to the poor manufacturer of whetstones, all equally clamorous for the protection 'of a parental, of an American policy.'"[41] Christopher Rankin of Mississippi sneered that "the idea of a home market for either our produce or manufactures . . . is most fallacious; it has no foundation in reason or truth, but is calculated to delude and deceive the people."[42] Robert Hayne of South Carolina denounced "this scheme of promoting certain employments at the expense of others as unequal, oppressive, and unjust, viewing prohibition as the means and the destruction of all foreign commerce the end of this policy." Hayne complained about the incoherence in the bill: "There are duties on the manufactured articles, and duties on the raw material; . . . the whole bill is a tissue of inconsistencies. In attempting to gratify the wishes of interested individuals, we are legislating in the dark, distributing the national funds by a species of State lottery—scatting abroad bounties and premiums of unknown amount; and all this, without the rational prospect of producing any effect, except that of sowing the seeds of dissension among the people. . . . We are opening a Pandora's box of political evils."[43] Adding to the hyperbole was John Randolph of Roanoke, who attacked the tariff as "an attempt to reduce the country south of Mason and Dixon's line, and east of the Allegheny Mountains, to a state worse than colonial bondage; a state to which the domination of Great Britain was, in my judgment, far preferable."[44]

Stripping away the heated rhetoric, the South made two key objections to Clay's system. First, higher import duties would discourage exports, and the sale of exportable goods (cotton and tobacco) at home could not possibly make up for the loss of foreign markets. Second, higher tariffs would harm consumers by raising the price of manufactured goods. Thus, southern income would receive a double blow: the prices of the goods it sold would fall and the prices of the goods it bought would rise. To the South, the American System was merely a scheme to enrich the North at the expense of the South. The South, particularly South Carolina, a major cotton-producing state, objected so passionately that Robert Hayne issued this warning:

> I take this occasion to declare that we [the South] shall feel ourselves justified in embracing the very first opportunity of repealing all such laws as may be passed for the promotion of these objects. Whatever interests may grow up under this bill, and whatever capital may be invested, I wish it to be distinctly understood that we will not hold ourselves bound to maintain the system; and if capitalists will, in the face of our protests and in defiance of our solemn warnings, invest their fortunes in pursuits made profitable at our expense, on their own heads be the consequences of their folly![45]

In April 1824, after intense debate, the House passed the tariff bill by the slim margin of 107–102. The strongest support came from the Mid-Atlantic states, while the South was completely opposed. In the Senate, some of the rates were reduced, but the bill passed a month later by the narrow vote of 25–21; fourteen nay votes from the South were nearly offset by eleven yea votes from the Midwest. President Monroe signed the bill shortly thereafter.

The Tariff of 1824 helped raise the average tariff on dutiable imports from about 38 percent in 1823 to about 42 percent in 1825. Import duties on cotton and woolen manufactures were increased from 25 percent to 33-1/3 percent. The act also pushed up the tariff on raw wool from 15 percent to 30 percent and hiked duties on iron, hemp, and most other goods as well. However, the circumstances of its passage were quite different from those affecting the Tariff of 1816, which passed with the benefit of a national consensus that manufacturers, particularly those related to national defense, deserved some protection after the War of 1812. They even differed from those surrounding the failed tariff of 1820, which was considered in the midst of a major recession. Instead, the Tariff of 1824 was enacted when the national economy was doing reasonably well, giving the appearance that government policy was being used to promote one section of the county at the expense of another. These different circumstances marked a clear shift in the political coalition driving US trade policy. Even

Thomas Jefferson, who, as we have seen, had come to favor protecting domestic industries, viewed Congress's actions with a skeptical eye.[46]

Clay's "American System" speech attempted to provide an overarching
rationale for protective tariffs without getting bogged down in the details
of specific tariff rates, although invariably those became the subjects of
the debate. Clay's remarks started a long and acrimonious wrangle over
the appropriate and just rates of duty in the tariff code. Each state had its
own particular producer interests that its representatives sought to protect: iron and glass in Pennsylvania, hemp in Kentucky, flax in Tennessee,
sugar in Louisiana, wool in Ohio and Vermont, and cotton and woolen
manufactures in Massachusetts. Protecting these producers from foreign
competition put them at odds with the export-oriented interests of cotton
in South Carolina, tobacco in Virginia, merchants in New York, and shipping in Massachusetts.

Tariff legislation was also becoming more complex. As the American
economy began producing a growing range of products, and the linkages
between the production of various goods became more intricate, Congress
also faced sharper trade-offs in dealing with import duties on a case-by-
case basis. The conflict was not just between export-oriented and import-
competing industries, but between producing and consuming industries,
particularly raw materials producers and final goods producers. For example, by the 1820s, the iron industry had separated into two distinct
branches, each with different trade interests. In the past, iron producers
had used their furnaces and forges to produce basic products (pig and bar
iron) as well as final consumer goods (such as pots and stoves, wire and
nails, rails and machinery). As the industry evolved, firms began to specialize in either the production of the primary raw materials or the secondary finished goods. For the pig and bar iron producers, no amount of
protection from foreign competition was too much. But manufacturers
of iron products wanted inexpensive raw materials and asked for low tariffs on basic iron goods and high tariffs on the final products that they
produced.[47]

Similarly, whalers in Massachusetts called for high duties on imported
tallow, but Boston tallow chandlers and soap boilers called for low duties
to reduce their production costs; both industries claimed that they were
depressed and deserved legislative support. There were also conflicts between hemp producers (used for making rope) and the shipping industry
(consumers of rope), and between those supporting high molasses duties
and rum producers, who wanted low duties, to mention just a few. The
tariff was becoming a "tedious disagreeable subject," as Daniel Webster

put it, because it involved so many conflicting interests and trade-offs that satisfying all interested parties in any piece of tariff legislation was simply impossible.

The producers most unsatisfied by the 1824 tariff were the woolens manufacturers. Envious of the protection received by cotton textile producers, they believed that the 1824 tariff discriminated against them by increasing the duty on raw wool (from 15 percent to 30 percent) proportionately more than it increased the duty on woolen goods (from 25 percent to 33–1/3 percent). In early 1827, the House voted to remedy this matter, but the Senate vote was tied, allowing Vice President John Calhoun of South Carolina to cast the decisive vote against it. Thus, the woolens bill of 1827 suffered the same fate as the Baldwin tariff in 1820, which passed the House but was defeated in the Senate by a single vote.

This failure convinced woolens manufacturers that they had to strengthen their political position by joining with other producers of raw materials in demanding greater protection from imports. They helped organize the Harrisburg Convention in August 1827, which was attended by manufacturers, newspaper editors, politicians, and pamphleteers who supported protective tariffs.[48] The Harrisburg convention received nationwide publicity and marked the high point of the antebellum protectionist movement. In particular, this meeting enabled wool producers and woolens manufacturers to come together and arrive at a mutually agreed upon set of duties. In a public statement written by Hezekiah Niles, the convention called for greater protection for all industrial products, such as glass and iron, but with primary attention to woolens, for which they advocated a 50 percent tariff along with a minimum valuation. The convention also proposed higher duties on such raw materials as sugar, hemp, flax, lead, and wool.

This pressure for higher duties came at the start of a presidential election year and set the stage for a new tariff bill in early 1828. This legislation became known as the "Tariff of Abominations" and helped raise the average tariff on dutiable imports to the highest level in history. But it also brought sectional tensions to their highest state since the nation's founding and led to the Nullification Crisis of 1833.

THE TARIFF OF ABOMINATIONS

The Tariff of 1828 was the result of bizarre political machinations that are imperfectly understood even today. Called "a mere farrago of political tricks and undisguised appetites," the Tariff of 1828 is said to have "resulted not from a conspiracy of one section against another but from an irresponsible bit of political chicanery in which all the sections shared."[49]

The disputed presidential election of 1824 served as a political backdrop to these events. A four-way race for the presidency prevented any candidate from receiving an outright majority in the Electoral College, although Andrew Jackson of Tennessee received a large plurality in the popular vote, with John Quincy Adams of Massachusetts far behind. For the first time, under the procedures set out in the Constitution, the House of Representatives would determine the next president. Although Jackson had the strongest claim to the office, Adams secured the presidency after Clay and Webster threw their support behind him in the House. Adams then appointed Clay as secretary of state, a position then seen as a stepping stone to the presidency, while Jackson supporters denounced the whole affair as a "corrupt bargain."

The 1828 presidential election was a rematch between Adams and Jackson. Adams championed the American System of protective tariffs and internal improvements, and drew his support from the North. Jackson stood for limited government and states' rights, and drew his support from the South. Yet the tariff was one issue on which Jackson did not necessarily agree with his southern allies. As a former general, Jackson supported a strong national defense. As a senator, Jackson voted for the Tariff of 1824 and against amendments that would have reduced some of its rates. When asked about his position on the tariff during the 1824 election campaign, Jackson said he was in favor of a "judicious examination and revision of it; and so far as the Tariff before us embraces the design of fostering, protecting, and preserving within ourselves the means of national defense and independence, particularly in a state of war, I would advocate and support it. The experience of our late war ought to teach us a lesson; and one never to be forgotten." This vague statement led Clay to snort that he was in favor of an "*in*judicious" tariff.[50]

However, in light of the strong southern opposition to high tariffs, which was part of the growing political backlash against Adams' proposed expansion of federal power, Jackson was viewed as being much less supportive of high protective duties than either Adams or Clay. The South supported Jackson as their best alternative and hoped that they could persuade him to join the cause of lower tariffs.

In the 1828 election, Jackson's political base was in the South, while Adams had a lock on New England. The crucial swing states were in the Mid-Atlantic and Midwest. Led by Senator Martin Van Buren of New York, Jackson's supporters sought to exploit the protectionist sentiment aroused by the Harrisburg Convention to gain political support for Jackson in those pivotal states. Van Buren apparently believed that Jackson's allies in the new Congress should push for a tariff bill that would raise import duties on the raw materials produced in states that Jackson needed to win the presidency, such as Pennsylvania (iron), Kentucky (hemp), and Ohio (wool), thereby proving that they were sympathetic to their interests. Although higher tariffs on raw materials would harm the industrial users of those materials in New England, those states were voting for Adams anyway. Whatever the outcome, Van Buren's too-clever-by-half strategy was supposedly designed to help Jackson: if the bill passed, the Jackson allies could claim the credit; if the bill was vetoed by Adams or defeated by his supporters, they could claim that the president was no friend of the Mid-Atlantic and Midwest.[51]

The strategy unfolded at the opening of the Twentieth Congress in December 1827. Jackson's supporters controlled the Committee on Manufactures after the speaker of the House (from Virginia) appointed five supporters of Jackson and two supporters of Adams to serve on it. For the first time, the committee held open hearings on the prospective tariff legislation. A total of twenty-eight individuals, including nine members of Congress, appeared before the committee, representing iron and steel, wool and woolens, hemp, flax, glass, and paper interests.[52] In March 1828, the committee reported a highly skewed bill that significantly increased duties on raw materials but provided no compensatory tariff adjustments for manufacturers using those products. Most glaringly, instead of addressing the concerns of New England woolen manufacturers, as the Harrisburg Convention had demanded, the bill proposed increasing the tariff on raw wool from 30 percent to 50 percent, along with a specific duty, without adjusting the duty on woolen manufactures.

As an Adams supporter, the chairman of the Committee on Manufactures, Rollin Mallary of Vermont, disowned the committee's bill and blamed it on other members. The various sides were at loggerheads. The House debate was dreary. "Day after day passes without any sensible advance in the public business," John Taylor of Virginia complained. "One dull prosing speech after another & arguments for the fiftieth time repeated are hashed up & dished in new covers."[53] States that produced raw materials favored the measure, while representatives from Pennsylvania and New England were incredulous that such a bizarre tariff structure was even being considered. John Barney of Maryland asked: "While it proposed to increase the duties on the raw materials, wool, hemp, and flax, in a ratio almost equivalent to prohibition, it refuses to extend corresponding protection to the manufacture; thus annihilating the manufactories themselves. What avail is it to the grower of these articles that foreign competition is excluded, if, at the same time, you destroy the home market? The manufacturer asks for bread—we give him a stone."[54]

Samuel Smith of Maryland, who supported higher tariffs for manufacturers, dubbed the measure a "bill of abominations," and the label stuck.[55] The bill was so lopsided that many began to suspect that it was designed to be defeated by the New England delegation or elicit a presidential veto. Yet throughout the House debate, the South had been uncharacteristically silent. "The Jackson party are playing a game of brag on the subject of the tariff," Clay complained. "They do not really desire the passage of their own measure; and it may happen, in the sequel, that what is desired by *neither party* commands the support of both."[56] Under the House's rules, the reported bill was not amendable on the floor, and so it quickly went to a vote. In April 1828, the bill passed by a margin of 105–94. Figure 3.2 shows the North-South voting division.

What was the South's view of this turn of events? Their representatives had been largely silent during the debate, apparently having been assured by Van Buren and the northern Jackson supporters that the bill would either fail in the Senate, like the 1827 woolens bill but this time due to opposition from Massachusetts, or be vetoed by President Adams. To kill the bill, all the South had to do was to keep the duties on raw materials high enough to force senators from New England to vote against it, or so it was thought. As Niles' *Weekly Register* reported, "It would be too much to say—and we shall not say it—that the committee reported a bill with a coldly calculated design that it should not pass; but it is as clear as that the sun shines at mid-day, that all the open and well known anti-tariff members, every one of them, believed that the bill was so drawn as to contain within itself the elements of its own destruction. It is impossible that they could have supported it on any other principle, unless we suppose that they are all fools, which cannot be admitted."[57]

In May, the bill was reported to the Senate, where the real battle was to take place. "Its fate rests on our ability to preserve the bill in its present shape," confided John Tyler of Virginia, adding that "if we can do so, it will be rejected."[58] However, unlike in the House, the bill could be amended on the Senate floor. Confident that the bill was structured to be defeated, the South resisted every effort to change it. Although several proposed amendments to reduce the duties on raw materials and to raise those on finished manufactures were rejected, things soon began to unravel: seven of fourteen amendments making the bill more amenable to New England were

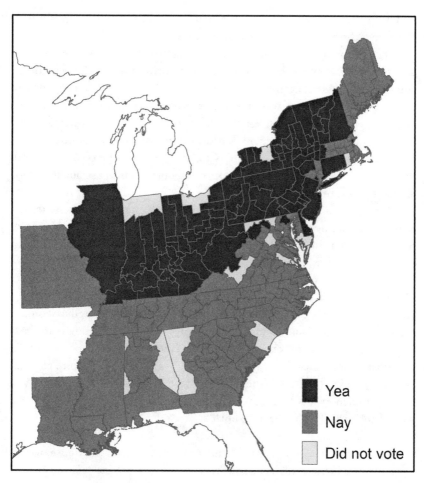

Figure 3.2. House vote on the Tariff of Abominations, April 22, 1828. (Map courtesy of Citrin GIS/Applied Spatial Analysis Lab, Dartmouth College.)

passed. In particular, the South was outmaneuvered on one critical vote in which the Senate voted 24–22 to raise the tariff on woolen manufactures from 33–1/3 percent to 45 percent (and then to 50 percent the following year) along with a minimum valuation provision. This went a long way to satisfying New England's problems with the measure, yet the South was stunned to see Van Buren vote for the amendment. Indeed, Van Buren's vote allowed the amendment to be carried; had he voted against it, the vote would have been tied, and Vice President John Calhoun would have blocked it, thereby making passage of the whole bill unlikely. This vote tipped Van Buren's hand: contrary to what representatives from the South had been led to believe, he and other northern Jackson supporters actually supported the bill and genuinely wanted it to pass.

The change in the tariff on woolen manufactures persuaded enough senators from New England to support the entire bill and thus ensure its final passage. After agonizing over his vote, Daniel Webster decided to support it, although he was in an awkward position, given his previous stance against most tariffs. The Senate passed the bill by a vote of 26–21. Two days later, after the reconciliation in the conference committee, the House accepted the higher woolens tariff by a vote of 115–67, with Adams forces strongly in favor and Jackson supporters split. President Adams signed the bill into law in May 1828.[59]

Having been duped into playing along with the tariff schemers, the South was stunned by this unexpected turn of events. Robert Hayne of South Carolina thundered that "there is not a provision [in the bill] that holds out a shadow of benefit to us. . . . In this business, from beginning to end, the interests of the South have been sacrificed, shamefully sacrificed! Her feelings have been disregarded, her wishes slighted, her honest pride insulted! I say that this system of protective duties has created discordant feelings, strife, jealousy, and heart-burnings, which never ought to exist between the different sections of the same country."[60]

Most of the invective was aimed at Clay and Adams, despite the fact that they had not initiated the bill. The South was also infuriated at Van Buren's treachery. As Calhoun recalled many years later, the Senate had passed the tariff "by a breach of faith":

Relying on the assurance on which our friends acted in the House, we anticipated with confidence and joy that the bill would be defeated and the whole system overthrown by shock. Our hopes were soon blasted. A certain individual [Martin Van Buren], then a senator, but recently elected to the highest office in the Union, was observed to assume a mysterious air in relation to the bill, very little in accordance with what, there was every reason to believe, would have been his course. The mystery was explained when the bill came up to be acted upon. I will not give in detail his course. It is sufficient to say, that, instead of resisting amendments, which we had a right to expect, he voted for all which were necessary to assure the votes of New England; particularly the amendments to raise the duties on woolens which were known to be essential for that purpose. All these amendments, with one or two exceptions, were carried by his votes. Why such a course, which good faith, as well as the public interest, so obviously dictated, was avoided, and the opposite pursued, has never been explained.[61]

Nearly two decades later, George McDuffie of South Carolina explained his votes on the amendments to keep high duties in the Tariff of 1828: "We saw this system of protection was about to assume gigantic proportions, and to devour the substance of the country, and we determined to put such ingredients in the chalice as would poison the monster and commend it to his own lips. This is what is sometimes called 'fighting the devil with fire,' a policy which, though I did not altogether approve, I adopted in deference to the opinions of those with whom I acted."[62]

Representatives from the South were not the only ones upset with the outcome. Hezekiah Niles and Mathew Carey did not consider it a fair application of the protective tariff doctrine because it made little economic sense to raise the cost of raw materials to manufacturers. And the legislative process had been so overtly political and disreputable that it gave Congressional tariff-making a very bad name. After the House passage, someone suggested adding "for the encouragement of domestic manufacturers" in the title of the bill, to which John Randolph of Virginia replied "the bill referred to manufactures of no sort or kind, but the manufacture of a President of the United States."[63] Looking back, Calhoun later described the 1828 tariff as "a combined measure, originating with the politicians and manufacturers, and intended as much to bear upon the presidential election as to protect manufacturers." In retrospect, Calhoun said that he "was amazed at the folly and infatuation of that period. So completely absorbed was Congress in the game of ambition and avarice, from the double impulse of the manufacturers and politicians, that none but a few appeared to anticipate the present crisis, at which all are now alarmed, but which is the inevitable result of what was then done."[64]

Few members of Congress could be proud of the Tariff of 1828, let alone all the complex political machinations behind its passage. "Harmony and concord among the friends of the American System can only be preserved by the adherence to what has been done, although some if it has been ill done," Clay conceded after the fact.[65] Even President Adams, a strong supporter of the American System, regretted the legislation: "The tariff of the last session was in its details not acceptable to the great interests of any portion of the Union, not even to the interest which it was specially intended to subserve."[66]

Jackson's reputation was untarnished by Congress's action, and he easily beat Adams in the election of 1828, but it is doubtful that the tariff played any role in this outcome. The most important consequence of the legislation was that South Carolina, deeply upset that the Tariff of Abominations had followed so closely on the heels of the Tariff of 1824 and tired of complaining about the inequity of high protective tariffs, abandoned hope of obtaining a legislative remedy for its grievances. Instead, it began to consider alternative measures, such as nullification, that would soon threaten the Union. In the summer of 1828, Calhoun wrote that he had never seen such universal excitement in the South over the tariff: "There is but one impression, that it is unjust, unconstitutional, and oppressive." While South Carolina was strongly attached to the Union, he warned that "I am compelled, by a regard to truth, to say, that the sense of injustice has a strong tendency to weaken it and if long continued may finally wholly estrange this [state] from the other sections."[67]

TARIFF POLITICS AND SOUTHERN DISCONTENTS

The average tariff on dutiable imports climbed steadily during the 1820s, rising from about 25 percent in 1820 to reach 62 percent in 1830, the highest level in US history. What underlying political forces explain this movement toward higher tariffs? And why did it generate such deep hostility in the South?

In part, the tariff laws of 1824 and 1828 were much more controversial than previous ones because they did not reflect the government's need for additional revenue. The government ran fiscal surpluses after 1822, and by the end of the decade, the national debt was close to being extinguished. Furthermore, the tariffs did not reflect the demands of producers suffering in the midst of a general economic downturn. While the attempt to pass tariff legislation in 1820 was understandable, given the economic slump that followed the Panic of 1819, the tariffs of 1824 and 1828 were not a response to widespread economic distress. Instead, they simply reflected forceful moves by domestic producer interests to protect themselves as much as possible from foreign competition, or by politicians seeking to gain political advantage in promoting those interests.

The tariff debates of the 1820s exposed a sharp cleavage between two competing positions: those who favored a tariff for revenue only, and those who favored a tariff for the protection of domestic industries. The revenue-tariff proponents came mainly from the South and wanted a small and frugal government with limited powers. They recognized that import duties were an essential source of finance for the federal government and could not be abolished completely, but they did not want the government favoring certain industries with high duties. They proposed that all imports be subject to a single uniform duty set at a modest rate, somewhere between 10 and 20 percent.[68]

By contrast, supporters of protective tariffs agreed with Henry Clay that "the sole object of the tariff is to tax the produce of foreign industry with the view of promoting American industry." In general, these advocates came from the North and Midwest and wanted different duties imposed on different goods, depending upon their perceived importance to the national economy. In general, they wanted low duties on the raw materials used in the production of manufactured goods and high duties on final goods. Their objective was to use domestic raw materials to produce final goods at home rather than to export them for processing abroad and then import the final product. The duties on imports of final goods should be high enough to assure that domestic producers competing against foreign firms could stay in business. They also wanted tariffs in the form of specific duties instead of ad valorem duties. They believed that ad valorem duties gave importers an incentive to understate the value of their goods to avoid paying the tax; specific duties would prevent such fraudulent under-invoicing of foreign goods. In addition, if import prices were to fall, the ad valorem equivalent of a specific duty would automatically rise, giving the domestic industry greater protection from the lower prices. Specific duties also obfuscated the degree to which imports were taxed: if the specific duty on iron was set at $10 per ton, there would be no way of knowing whether this was a high or a low rate without information about the price of imported iron.

Despite the controversy about import duties in the 1820s, political changes made protective tariffs easier to enact in Congress. The American economy consisted of three principal sectors—agriculture, industry, and commerce—each concentrated in a different part of the country with a distinctive, trade-related economic interest. Prior to the War of 1812, average tariffs were relatively modest, because the agricultural exporting interests of the South and the commercial shipping interests of New England worked together to keep them low. Industrial interests in the Mid-Atlantic states, such as Pennsylvania, were a minority in Congress and lacked the political power to enact higher protective duties.

After the War of 1812, the balance of political power between these sectors and regions had shifted. The commercial shipping interests of New England had been overtaken by local manufacturing interests, particularly cotton textiles. The growth of manufacturing and relative decline of shipping and shipbuilding in New England helped turn the region from one supporting open trade to one supporting protective tariffs, although its representatives were often divided depending on their particular constituency. In 1825, for example, the Boston firm of W. & S. Lawrence shifted its business from importing and merchandising foreign goods to manufacturing goods itself, sharply changing its economic interests. Politicians followed this rebalancing of economic power and altered their voting patterns, the classic example being Daniel Webster, who opposed tariffs up to 1824 but began supporting them after that.[69]

The Mid-Atlantic states provided the greatest political support for protectionist legislation because they were the location of other domestic manufacturers, such as the iron and glass industries. Although the mercantile community in New York had shipping interests that favored low taxes on imports, most other Mid-Atlantic states firmly supported higher tariffs. Pennsylvania was a major political force for higher tariffs because many of the earliest manufacturers were located around Philadelphia. As early as 1810, Pennsylvania accounted for about 20 percent of the country's manufacturing production and more than 40 percent of iron production.[70] Pennsylvania was also one of the nation's most populous states and therefore had a large group of representatives in the House who fought for higher tariffs.

The South was an implacable opponent of protective duties throughout the antebellum period. The region still produced staple crops, particularly cotton and tobacco, which were heavily dependent on exports to foreign markets. The South vigorously denounced high tariffs as sectional legislation that helped manufacturing industries in the North at the expense of agriculture in the South. High tariffs were said to impose a ruinous burden on the South by depressing the prices of exported staple crops and inflating the prices of imported manufactured goods that it consumed. The South voted almost uniformly against any tariff increase, except for Louisiana, which favored protective duties for its sugar interests.[71]

The Midwest had mixed interests with respect to trade in the 1820s. Kentucky was a leading producer of hemp (used for making ropes and cotton bagging), and Ohio was a leading producer of wool; both raw materials faced some competition from imports, and therefore representatives tended to support higher import duties. Illinois and Indiana produced wheat and flour, for which there was potentially a large foreign market, but high transport costs and British duties prevented these goods from reaching overseas consumers. Overall, the Midwest's trade-related economic interests were less sharply defined than those of the North or the

South because its geographic position kept it largely isolated from foreign commerce, although reductions in transportation costs would change this in the 1840s.

The Midwest's relative isolation gave it a unique position in American trade politics. With neither the North nor the South holding an absolute majority of seats in Congress, the Midwest held the crucial swing votes. The North controlled less than half the seats in the Senate, and although it had a slight majority of seats in the House, this was often divided between different political interests (or political parties after the mid-1830s). The South held less than 40 percent of the House and Senate. Hence, both the North and the South needed support from the Midwest to enact their legislative agendas. Furthermore, as figure I.6 showed, the Midwest gained political strength over the antebellum period, largely at the expense of the North. By 1850, the Midwest controlled more than a quarter of the seats in Congress. The Midwest became the pivotal player in the political system due to its intermediate position between the opposing interests of the North and South on many issues—not just the tariff but also slavery.

The Senate was the key battleground for the fierce trade debates of the period. In 1824 and 1828, the Senate vote was virtually identical: about two-thirds of senators from the North supported the higher tariffs, while the South was almost unanimously opposed. Senators from the Midwest broke in favor of the legislation, and this support was critical to its passage. Had it not been for the votes of the Midwest, the South would have stopped the effort to increase tariffs.

How were the pro-tariff forces in the North able to persuade representatives from the Midwest to vote for tariff legislation that was not directly tied to their economic interest? One reason is that the Midwest had something to gain on an issue of even greater importance to them: internal improvements.[72] The Midwest strongly supported federal spending on canals, roads, and other transportation improvements as a way of reducing the region's economic isolation and attracting labor and capital from the East. The Mid-Atlantic also encouraged such expenditures because its geographic position made it the logical place for transportation outlets from those regions; it therefore stood to gain a disproportionate share of federal spending. New York (since it already had the Erie Canal) and New England (which was geographically separated from the Midwest) were less enthusiastic about such spending, but northern states were generally willing to spend the surplus revenues generated by high tariffs on internal improvement projects in order to win votes in Congress from the Midwest.

Henry Clay, of course, was the politician most responsible for creat-

ing the "American System" coalition that combined support for protective tariffs and internal improvements.[73] In essence, high tariffs that
would benefit the North would raise the revenue needed to finance internal improvements that would benefit the Midwest. The tariff debates in
Congress reveal many veiled and not-so-veiled references to this North-
Midwest coalition.[74] Writing to Webster in 1827, Clay noted that he was
"most anxious . . . that they [internal improvements] should be supported
in New England, and that the West and Pennsa. should be made sensible
of that support. . . . You have your equivalents in other forms. . . . We
must keep the two interests of D[omestic] M[anufactures] & I[nternal]
I[mprovements] allied."[75]

The great failure of American System advocates was their inability to
enact a comprehensive plan for either internal improvements or the encouragement of manufactures. Instead, internal improvement projects
proceeded in a piecemeal fashion, in which politicians got to pick and
choose which canal or road proposal to support. The result was an ad hoc
process in which Congress set about "advancing pet projects with increasingly dubious claims of national significance and indulging in ever more
bitter attacks on each other."[76] Proponents also failed to develop a comprehensive plan for protecting domestic industries with import duties. As
seen in the debates regarding the Tariff of Abominations, the process by
which Congress set import duties was deeply political rather than based
on some rational design. Congress struggled over the conflicting interests
of raw materials producers in the Midwest and those of industrial goods
producers in the North. The most difficult problem of this sort was adjusting the tariff schedule to satisfy both wool producers and manufacturers
of woolen goods.

Thus, the North-Midwest coalition seemed to be an interlocking system of trading votes for tariffs for votes for internal improvements, but it
was potentially unstable if tariffs were ever to become delinked from internal improvements. The South was aware of this potential weakness and
tried to split the coalition by separating the two issues. As Senator William Smith of South Carolina astutely observed, "Destroy the tariff and
you will leave no means of carrying on internal improvements; destroy
internal improvements and you leave no motive for the tariff."[77]

Indeed, the South failed to see how it could gain from any aspect of the
American System. It bitterly opposed both high tariffs and spending on
internal improvements: such spending was a justification for keeping tariffs high, and high tariffs generated excess revenue that was unnecessary
unless spent on internal improvements. The South objected to protective

tariffs because they encouraged industries that were almost exclusively located in the North. These tariffs were directly contrary to the South's economic interests as a producer of exported goods. The South also objected
to internal improvements because it was not geographically positioned to
benefit from any federal spending on such projects. The region was unsuited for canals running from west to east, and it already had easy access
on the eastern seaboard for its cotton and tobacco, while the Mississippi
River and New Orleans served as outlets for inland crops.

In sum, the South viewed import duties as a tax on the South for the
benefit of the North and an important cause of the South's economic troubles. John Tyler, a Virginia senator who later became president, succinctly
summarized the region's perspective: "The protective tariff is the cause
of our calamities and our decay. We buy dear, and sell cheap. That is the
simple secret. The tariff raises the price of all that we buy, and diminishes
the demands for our products abroad by diminishing the power of foreign
nations to buy them."[78]

John Calhoun produced a powerful summary of the South's complaints
in "Exposition and Protest," which he drafted for the South Carolina legislature in late 1828. The key problem with protective tariffs was that their
"burdens are exclusively on one side, and the benefits on the other." As
described by Calhoun, the North and South were hopelessly divided over
this fundamental issue. "On the great and vital point, the industry of the
country, two great sections of the Union are opposed. We want free trade;
they, restrictions. We want moderate taxes, frugality in the government,
economy, accountability, and a rigid application of the public money to the
payment of the public debt, and the objects authorized by the Constitution; in all these particulars, if we may judge by experience, their view[s]
of their interest are the opposite."[79]

In fact, the tariff reduced the price of what the South sold because
"a duty, whether it be laid on imports or exports, must fall upon this exchange, and . . . must in reality be paid by the American producer of the articles exchanged," Calhoun explained. Hence, "there is little or no difference between an export and import duty." "Our very complaint is, that we
are not permitted to consume the fruits of our labour, but that through an
artful and complex system, in violation of every principle of justice they
are transferred from us to others."[80]

Thus, southerners dismissed the claims of American System advocates that high tariffs served the "general welfare" of the country; instead,
they believed that the tariff siphoned off the South's wealth and sent it to
other sections of the country. The tariff was simply viewed as "a means by

which a few northern industrialists became rich by legislative favoritism
at the expense of southern agriculture" or, in the words of one southerner,
as "a miserable, mean, unprincipled rascally 'pick-pocket' scheme to steal
and defraud from one portion of the people their property for the exclusive
benefit of another."[81] Even worse, Calhoun argued that tariffs destroyed
more income in the South than it transferred to the North, thus reducing
overall national income. As he put it, "If all we lose be gained by other
citizens of the other section, we would at least have the satisfaction of
thinking, that however unjust and oppressive, it was but a transfer of property, without diminishing the wealth of the community. Such, however, is
not the fact, and to its other mischievous consequences, we must add, that
it destroys much more than it transfers. . . . The exact amount of loss, from
such intermeddling, may be difficult to ascertain, but it is not therefore
less certain."[82]

The pressure for higher tariffs by the North and for more spending on
internal improvements by the Midwest led the South to look with dismay
at the degraded state of the nation's politics: "The government is rapidly
degenerating into a struggle among the parts to squeeze as much out of
one another as they possibly can," Calhoun complained. "The South being
the least, and I may add less avaricious than the other, is destined to suffer
severely in this odious struggle."[83]

As the decade went on, and the South seemingly lost battle after battle, its anti-tariff rhetoric became more inflamed and impassioned. The
South's insistence that it was being oppressed and exploited by the other
sections became shriller. South Carolina went far beyond any other southern state in expressing its fears about the direction of national policy. If
Pennsylvania was the bastion of protectionist support in the North, South
Carolina was the citadel of low-tariff agitation in the South. A confluence
of these various factors made South Carolina more extreme than other
southern states. The depressed economic condition of the Carolina cotton
economy in the 1820s was one factor behind the state's prickly sensitivity. Although the collapse of cotton prices in 1819 and again in 1825 affected all cotton producers, planters in South Carolina were particularly
hard-hit. The second collapse coincided with increasing soil exhaustion
on upcountry plantations and greater domestic competition, as cotton cultivation moved to more fertile lands in the southwest, such as Alabama
and Mississippi.

As the prosperity of the North grew in relation to the South, the high
tariff became a standard explanation for the economic difficulties of
southern planters. What could the South do about the situation? As a mi-

nority in Congress, the South simply did not have enough votes to determine policy. And they recognized that it was fruitless to try to persuade members of Congress from manufacturing states to adopt their views on tariff policy. Recognizing that it was fighting a losing political battle in Congress, the South for a time made the argument that protectionist tariffs were unconstitutional because they had not been imposed for the "general welfare." This argument was easily dismissed. Clay replied that the critics had "entirely mistaken the clause of the Constitution on which we rely." It was not the first clause of article 1, section 8, which mentions debts and general welfare, but clause 3, which gives Congress the power to regulate commerce with foreign nations. Under this article, "the grant is plenary, without any limitation whatever," Clay noted.[84]

Even the aging James Madison, who was sympathetic to the view that protective tariffs had been pushed too far, agreed that there was nothing unconstitutional about the policy. After the Virginia legislature passed a resolution declaring that import duties for the protection of domestic manufactures were unconstitutional, Madison wrote a detailed letter explaining why such duties were permitted.[85] Furthermore, Madison believed that the tariff issue had been completely overblown by southern politicians:

> With respect to the existing tariff, however justly it may be complained of in several respects, I cannot but view the evils charged on it as greatly exaggerated. . . . I cannot but believe, whatever well-founded complaints may be agst. the tariff, that, as a cause of the general sufferings of the country, it has been vastly overrated; that if wholly repealed, the limited relief would be a matter of surprise; and that if the portion only having not revenue, but manufactures for its object, were struck off, the general relief would be little felt.[86]

Thus, as a minority in Congress with little hope of changing the constellation of political forces that had led to higher tariffs, and with the constitutional argument failing to compel any reconsideration of the policy, the South saw its only alternatives as submission or resistance. Submission would lead to federal despotism, which was viewed as intolerable. This gave rise to the idea that the South should consider leaving the union. If the exploitation of the South through high tariffs continued, Thomas Cooper argued, "we shall 'ere long be compelled to calculate the value of our union; and to enquire of what use to us is this most unequal alliance? By which the south has always been the loser and north always the gainer? Is it worth our while to continue this union of states, where the north demand to be our masters and we are required to be their tributaries?"[87]

An underlying factor in this discontent was that the North was over-taking the South in wealth and income. In 1774, the South was well ahead of the North in terms of income and wealth; by the 1840s, it was well behind.[88] The relative decline in economic status gnawed at the South, which feared that its political power was shrinking as well. In losing the tariff battles of the 1820s, the South saw the loss of its economic and po-litical position in the Union and feared that it had become a permanent and besieged minority in Congress. In fact, many in the South may have been concerned less about the harm the tariff was doing to it and more about the benefits received by the North, which was growing in popula-tion and wealth.

Of course, something else was lurking behind the South's extreme re-action to tariffs in the 1820s. Many southerners believed that the tariff was merely the first skirmish in a struggle that would determine if the federal government would have the power to abolish slavery. Therefore, the South resisted higher tariffs as a first line in the defense of their peculiar institu-tion. James Hamilton of South Carolina called the tariff fracas "a battle at the outposts, by which, if we succeeded in repulsing the enemy, *the citadel would be safe*," the citadel being slavery.[89] He and his colleagues reasoned that a high tariff that created a stronger national government would be in a better position to meddle with slavery. In fighting against the tariff, the South was really fighting for limited government that would preserve states' rights against unlimited government power that eventu-ally could be used to eliminate slavery. William Smith intoned that the "paragraph of the Constitution which authorizes Congress to provide for the 'general welfare' . . . has given you a Tariff, by which you are taxed to support manufacturers that are wallowing in wealth. And it will, as soon as the Northern States . . . have finished internal improvements, rend your government asunder, or make your slaves your masters."[90] John Randolph warned that a Congress that could build roads wherever it wanted could also "emancipate every slave in the United States."[91]

For this reason, John Calhoun concluded in 1830,

> I consider the Tariff, but as the occasion, rather than the real cause of the present unhappy state of things. The truth can no longer be dis-guised, that the peculiar domestic institution of the Southern States, and the consequent direction, which that of her soil and climate have given to her industry, has placed them in regard to taxation and appro-

priation in opposite relation to the majority of the Union; against the danger of which, if there be no protective power in the reserved rights of the states, they must in the end be forced to rebel, or submit to have their permanent interests sacrificed, their domestic institutions subverted by colonization and other schemes, and themselves and [their] children reduced to wretchedness.[92]

The South's enormous economic stake in slavery far outweighed the impact of protective tariffs on its income. In 1860, the aggregate value of slaves as property was $3 billion, nearly 20 percent of the nation's wealth. The value of slaves was more than 50 percent greater than the capital invested in railroads and manufacturing combined, a calculation that excludes the value of land in southern plantations. Slavery generated a stream of income that enabled overall white per capita income in the South to approximate that of northern whites. In the seven cotton states, nearly a third of white income came from slave labor. Thus, slavery was essential to the prosperity and standard of living of many southern whites.[93]

The only real threat to this way of life came from the North. The growing strength of the abolitionist movement posed a direct challenge to the position of wealthy Southern whites. Once again, South Carolina was particularly sensitive to this danger. Blacks far outnumbered whites in the state and there were constant fears of a slave rebellion. Without a commitment by the federal government to respect states' rights, Southerners feared that its expanding powers might affect the status quo. Calhoun believed that "there is a deep, and, if not removed in time, a fatal disease lurking in the system," the disease being an overly powerful national government dominated by a northern majority that could dictate policy to the South.[94] As William Freehling (1965, 255) stated, "Put in simple terms, the nullification crusade was produced by two acute problems: protective tariffs and slavery agitation; and to most nullifiers, the separate issues had long since intermeshed in a single pattern of majority tyranny."

Meanwhile, the North had no sympathy for the South's position and became increasingly fed up with what it saw as the South's hysterical complaints about the tyranny of the tariff. Advocates of the American System professed to believe that all sections of the country would benefit from protective duties, and they could not understand what the fuss was all about. Protective tariffs would simply shift demand for cotton from British to American factories without any diminution in overall demand, they contended, ignoring the fact that British textiles were exported throughout the world rather than just sold in the American market. Senator Asher

Robbins of Rhode Island issued this taunt: "Show me, I again ask it, the connection between the [tariff] as the cause, and your distress as the effect. . . . Your complaints—what are they? One is, that your lands are worn down and that your crops are unprofitable. Pray, is the [tariff] the cause of that sterility?"[95] Others criticized the South for blaming the tariff for all its troubles but never mentioning the instability of the currency or the growing production of cotton in the Southwest.

As the South's criticisms of the tariff became increasingly strident, the North became equally resentful as well. Congressmen from the North began equating free trade with "slave power" and denouncing lazy Southern plantation owners for earning riches off the hard labor of their slaves while selfishly denying the security that tariffs gave to employment of northern free labor and the capital invested in industry by entrepreneurs. They asked why one fifth of the country should dictate to the rest of the country what the nation's tariff policy should be. And they turned the South's arguments against them: it was the South, rather than the North, that was being narrow and selfish. Why should national policy be dictated by slave owners, leaving the majority hostage to the slave-holding minority? Henry Clay said that the general welfare was not defined as the South's welfare and that for the North to sacrifice its own interests to the South "would be to make us the slaves of slaves."[96] To the charge that protective tariffs supported rich capital-owners in the North, Clay responded sharply: "But is there more tendency to aristocracy in a manufactory, supporting hundreds of freemen, or in a cotton plantation, with its not less numerous slaves, sustaining perhaps only two white families—that of the master and the overseer?"[97]

In retirement, James Madison watched the nasty tariff debate with growing dismay. "Were the tariff, whatever be the degree in which it has added to the other causes of depression, to be removed so far as it has protective operation, the other causes remaining the same, the relief would be but little felt." Madison noted that more tobacco was now exported from New Orleans than from Virginia. "The more the question of the tariff is brought to the test of facts, the more it will be found that the public discontents have proceeded more from the *inequality* than from the *weight* of its pressure, and more from the exaggerations of both than from the reality, whatever it may have been, of either."[98] Madison attributed the declining value of land and the lower prices of staples in the South mainly to the cheap and fertile land in Mississippi and Alabama.

While the South had strongly objected to the 1824 tariff, it found the

1828 tariff intolerable. North-South relations deteriorated rapidly after its passage. Two political factors also facilitated the tariff hikes of 1824 and 1828 and hence contributed to the impending crisis. First, Congress as an institution failed to manage and control the issue well. The competition between the Ways and Means Committee and the Committee on Manufactures over the authority to report tariff legislation to the House floor was a microcosm of the larger sectional conflict. The Ways and Means Committee, a standing committee since 1802, traditionally had the prerogative to report tariff bills as revenue measures. But in 1819, House Speaker Henry Clay established a separate Committee on Manufactures, packed it with supporters of high tariffs, and began referring tariff matters to it, thus bypassing the more moderate Ways and Means Committee. The Committee on Manufactures reported the controversial tariff bills of 1820, 1824, 1827, 1828, 1830, and 1832, but, as we will see in chapter 4, it was the Ways and Means Committee that ultimately forged the Compromise of 1833. This reestablished the committee's authority over trade policy. Given its more moderate approach, the loss of control by Ways and Means over the issue during the 1820s allowed extremely divisive sectional politics to get out of hand.

Second, presidential leadership was notably lacking throughout this period. Of course, presidents were not expected to play an active role in formulating legislation at this time, but they could help manage conflict by signaling their position in their annual message to Congress. As we shall see, Andrew Jackson might have eased sectional tensions earlier if he had been more engaged on the issue. Certainly Calhoun believed that the president was the only person who could calm the discontent in the South.[99] Unfortunately, Jackson's failure to act decisively during the tariff controversy in his first term gave South Carolina nullifiers their strongest arguments against opponents who hoped for redress from the federal government.

THE NULLIFICATION CRISIS

In July 1828, shortly after the passage of the Tariff of Abominations, Calhoun wrote that he had never seen such universal excitement in the South over the tariff. "There is but one impression," he noted, "that it is unjust, unconstitutional, and oppressive." Crowds in South Carolina burned Adams and Clay in effigy, but they did not blame Jackson's supporters for the debacle. Calhoun feared that, while his constituents were strongly attached to the Union, "I am compelled, by a regard to truth, to say, that the sense of injustice has a strong tendency to weaken it and if long continued may finally wholly estrange this [state] from the other sections."[100]

At the request of the state legislature, Calhoun secretly drafted his "Exposition," which set out South Carolina's objections to the protective tariffs enacted during the 1820s. Published in December 1828, the "Exposition" declared "that the Act of Congress of the last session, with the whole system of legislation imposing duties on imports, not for revenue, but for the protection of one branch of industry, at the expense of others, is unconstitutional, unequal and oppressive; calculated to corrupt the public morals, and to destroy the liberty of the country." Calhoun argued that "the Constitution authorizes Congress to lay and collect an import duty, but it is granted for the sole purpose of revenue—a power in its nature essentially different from that of imposing protective or prohibitory duties." Now, that "power is abused by being converted into an instrument of rearing up the industry of one section of the country, on the ruins of another."[101] Calhoun then set out the doctrine of nullification, in which the states had the right to strike down a federal law that it found to be unjust or unconstitutional. The South never tested this proposition in federal court, probably because it knew that it would lose.

The election of Andrew Jackson as president over John Quincy Adams in 1828 gave the South a ray of hope. Jackson supported states' rights, a strict construction of the Constitution, and limited government, and he was expected to champion the South's cause when it came to tariff policy as well. But Jackson took a middle ground, refusing to adopt a strong anti-tariff stance that would alienate his northern supporters. Indeed, in his March 1829 inaugural address, Jackson revealed little about his position when he stated that "it would seem to me that the spirit of equity, caution, and compromise in which the Constitution was formed requires that the great interests of agriculture, commerce, and manufactures should be equally favored; . . . that perhaps the only exception to this rule should consist in the peculiar encouragement of any products of either of them, that may be found essential to our national independence."[102] This was hardly the clarion call for the tariff reductions that the South desperately wanted to hear, but Southerners remained optimistic that the president would ultimately come around to their side, because he was certainly no friend of Henry Clay and his American System.

The South also took comfort from the fact that Jackson began to split the North-Midwest coalition by delinking the issues of the tariff and internal improvements. Jackson's veto of the Maysville Road Bill in May

1830 was the first blow to the coalition. Congress had helped finance road improvements in the past, and there was nothing particularly unusual about this bill. But in vetoing it, Jackson raised constitutional questions about federal support for internal improvements by noting that the road was wholly within Kentucky and was therefore a local project, not a national one. Three days later Jackson vetoed another turnpike bill on similar grounds. "It is the only thing that can allay the jealousies arising between the different sections of the Union, and prevent that flagitious *log-rolling legislation*, which must, in the end, destroy everything like harmony, if not the Union itself," Jackson explained.[103]

The vetoes helped change the dynamic in Congress that had tied higher tariffs to spending on internal improvements. Senator Thomas Benton (1854, 1:167) later wrote that the Maysville veto was "a killing blow" to a national system of internal improvements, and Martin Van Buren recalled it as "the entering wedge to the course of action by which that powerful combination known as the Internal Improvement party was broken asunder and finally annihilated."[104] By splintering the North-Midwest alliance, the veto helped stop the momentum toward ever-higher import duties.

But the South was not content with simply preventing further tariff increases; it wanted a significant reduction in rates. Here another factor came into play: as the government began recording large fiscal surpluses, the political tide began to turn toward a moderation of import duties. Still, appeasing the South would not be easy: northern supporters of protection refused to acknowledge any harm to the South and were prepared to defend the existing level of duties.

In his first annual message to Congress in December 1829, President Jackson suggested that, in view of the recent fiscal surpluses and decline in national debt, some duties on goods not produced in the United States, notably tea and coffee, could be reduced. In 1830, competing House committees proposed different bills. Ways and Means Committee Chair George McDuffie of South Carolina recommended repealing the duties in the 1824 and 1828 tariffs and going back to the 1816 rates, whereas Committee on Manufactures Chair (and former president) John Quincy Adams of Massachusetts recommended no change to existing duties. But the general sentiment in the House was that tariff adjustments along the lines suggested by the president should be made. "Thereupon ensued one of the most tedious and fruitless debates in the history of Congress," Stanwood (1903, 1:362) reports, with set speeches "of interminable length and quite devoid of fresh arguments and novel illustrations."

Eventually, Congress agreed to reduce duties on imported tea, coffee, cocoa, and even on some protected articles such as salt and molasses. The North mistakenly believed this concession would appease the South, but the reductions were simply designed to reduce revenue and did not address the protected articles—cottons, woolens, and iron—that were the South's main concern. The South dismissed the legislation as "nothing but sugar plums to pacify children" and rejected it as failing to address the protectionist system that they had been complaining about.[105]

In his December 1830 annual message to Congress, Jackson conceded that the reduction in revenue duties left the tariff controversy unresolved: "I am well aware that this is a subject of so much delicacy, on account of the extended interests it involves, as to require that it should be touched with the utmost caution, and that while an abandonment of the policy in which it originated—a policy coeval with our Government, and pursued through successive Administrations—is neither to be expected or desired, the people have a right to demand, and have demanded, that it be so modified as to correct abuses and obviate injustice." If protective tariffs had been imposed on their merits, Jackson stated, the system would command support and "the branches of industry which deserve protection would be saved from the prejudice excited against them when that protection forms part of a system by which portions of the country feel or conceive themselves to be oppressed." Furthermore, "the vital principle of our system—that principle which requires acquiescence in the will of the majority—would be secure from the discredit and danger to which it is exposed by the acts of majorities founded not on identity of conviction, but on combinations of small minorities entered into for the purpose of mutual assistance in measures which, resting solely on their own merits, could never be carried." Jackson asked Congress to carefully consider its next step: "To make this great question, which unhappily so much divides and excites the public mind, subservient to the short-sighted views of faction, must destroy all hope of settling it satisfactorily to the great body of the people and for the general interest."[106]

Although Congress did nothing during 1831, the political pressure for tariff adjustments continued to build. Many observers feared that if the new session of Congress did not make real reforms, then South Carolina would nullify the tariff and secede from the nation, perhaps bringing other southern states along with it. Furthermore, groups in favor of moderate duties began to assert themselves. Among the dozens of petitions, statements, and memorials that Congress received was one from a Free Trade

Convention that met in Philadelphia in the fall of 1831. The convention statement, drafted by former Treasury Secretary Albert Gallatin, called for a uniform tariff of 20–25 percent on all imports to avoid giving special preference to any particular article. The statement maintained that the protective system that forced industry into

> unprofitable pursuits which cannot be sustained without exaggerated duties paid by the consumer, and a corresponding national loss, does not open new channels of productive industry, but diverts it from profitable to unprofitable pursuits to the community. It is truly remarkable that the advocates of the restrictive system should pretend to consider your memorialists as wild theorists, when there cannot be a plainer matter of fact than that if a man pays two dollars more for his coat, his plough, or the implements of his trade, it is a loss to him, which he must pay out of the proceeds of his industry, and that the aggregate of those individual losses is an actual national loss.

The statement argued that the United States had achieved unparalleled economic growth because of robust domestic competition and the freedom of individuals to pursue employment for which their labor and capital were best suited: "To ascribe that unexampled and uninterrupted prosperity, which even legislative errors cannot arrest, to a tariff is one of the most strange delusions by which intelligent men have ever suffered themselves to be deceived."[107]

The growing economy and burgeoning fiscal surplus, along with the fear that further delay might trigger some extreme action by South Carolina, created another opportunity for resolving the impasse. In his December 1831 annual message, President Jackson held out the possibility of further tariff reductions once the public debt was extinguished within just a few short years. "The confidence with which the extinguishment of the public debt may be anticipated presents an opportunity for carrying into effect more fully the policy in relation to import duties which has been recommended in my former messages." The tariff should be slashed to reduce revenue "with a view to equal justice in relation to all our national interests" and "is deemed to be one of the principal objects which demand the consideration of the present Congress."[108]

In the House, competing proposals once again came from McDuffie's Ways and Means Committee and Adams's Committee on Manufactures. Ways and Means issued a sweeping condemnation of existing policy: "the protecting system is utterly ruinous to the planting states, injurious to the Western states, and exclusively beneficial to the manufacturing states, and ought to be abandoned with all convenience and practicable dispatch, upon every principle of justice, patriotism, and sound policy."[109] The committee advocated abolishing all protective tariffs and adopting a uniform tariff set at 25 percent in the first year, 18.75 percent in the second year, and 12.5 percent in the third year. Although the South enthusiastically supported this proposal, the House rejected it as too extreme.

This gave the Committee on Manufactures the opportunity to craft a bill. Adams sought to appease the South without sacrificing too much protection for industry, but Clay rejected any accommodation. In Clay's view, "the discontents were almost all, if not entirely, imaginary or fictitious, and in almost all the Southern States had, in a great measure, subsided." "Here is one great error of Mr. Clay," Adams wrote in his diary, because in fact the discontent was not fictitious and had not subsided. Adams noted that Clay forcefully exclaimed, in private consultation, that he would "defy the South, defy the President, and the devil" to preserve and strengthen the American System.[110] Clay feared that if there was "any attempt to repeal any existing duty, laid for protection, no matter on what article, the seeds of fatal division will be sown" and the entire system would be destroyed.[111] Adams judged Clay's position to be "exceedingly peremptory and dogmatical."[112]

Clay proposed abolishing or cutting the revenue duties on tea, coffee, spices, indigo, and even alcohol in order to save the critical duties that protected manufacturers. Adams retorted that such a bill would be rejected by the South and would not pass. Instead, working with Secretary Louis McLane, Adams crafted a more balanced measure that would reduce tariffs on cotton and woolen textiles somewhat, but slash duties on coarse woolens (used to clothe slaves) to 5 percent. Clay rejected this compromise and, in a spirited address over three days in early February 1832, gave a robust defense of protective tariffs. He argued that the Tariff of 1824 had transformed the country from "gloom and distress to brightness and prosperity." This happy outcome was "mainly the work of American legislation, fostering American industry, instead of allowing it to be controlled by foreign legislation, cherishing foreign industry." Abandoning protection now would lead to the destruction of iron foundries, woolen, cotton, and hemp manufactories, and sugar plantations, and "lead to the sacrifice of immense capital, the ruin of many thousands of our fellow citizens, and incalculable loss to the whole community." Furthermore, when gentlemen have succeeded in their design of an immediate or gradual destruction of the American system, what is their substitute? Free trade! Free trade! The call for free trade is . . . unavailing . . . It never has existed, it never will exist. . . . To be free, it should be fair, equal, and reciprocal . . . Gentlemen deceive themselves. It is not free trade that they are recommending to our acceptance. It is, in effect, the British colonial system that we are invited to adopt; and, if their policy prevail, it will lead substantially to the recolonization of these States, under the commercial dominion of Great Britain.[113]

He went so far as to attack the Swiss-born Albert Gallatin as an "alien" who, in participating in the Free Trade Convention, did not have the country's best interests at heart.

The South was sickened by Clay's hard line. John Tyler of Virginia responded, "The South seeks to lay no rude or violent hand on existing [manufacturing] establishments, but it has a right to expect an amelioration of its burdens. The proposition of the Senator from Kentucky yields nothing to her complaints. The taxes which he proposed to repeal have never been complained of, and have existed from the foundation of the Government."[114]

The South was also skeptical of the Adams-McLane compromise, which had the support of moderates in Congress and had gone some way to address the South's objections. That compromise would essentially repeal the Tariff of Abominations and move duties back down to those in the 1824 tariff, but it was viewed with suspicion by Calhoun and his allies because it seemed to satisfy Hezekiah Niles and Mathew Carey.

Although the Southern delegation in the House was wary of the Adams-McLean compromise, enough saw it as a move in the right direction, and the South split over the bill. In June 1832, the House passed the bill by a 132–65 margin; average rates were reduced, but protective rates on cotton, woolen, and iron manufactures were retained. The Senate soon followed by a vote of 32–16, with the South largely opposed, and Jackson signed the measure. Because it passed with some southern support in the House, the president was led to believe that the legislation would end conflict on the matter: "The people must now see that all their grievances are removed, and oppression only exists in the distempered brains of disappointed ambitious men."[115] But Clay quietly claimed victory, assuring Niles that "every principle for which I contended at the commencement of the Session [has] been substantially adopted," particularly by maintaining protective duties (except on cotton bagging "where it was voluntarily abandoned") and reducing revenue duties.[116]

In fact, the outcome failed to placate the South. As John Tyler of Virginia warned his colleagues,

> I invoke honorable Senators to pause, long to pause ere they decide that this grinding system shall receive no abatement. Its oppression, if that were the only circumstance, would be as nothing in comparison with the alienation of feeling which it has produced. What can compensate for the loss of that affection on the part of even a single state in this union? Flatter not yourselves that this is, exclusively, a South Carolina question. No, sir, it is a Southern question. Every state on the other side of the Potomac feels alike interested in it. . . . Do you seek to give perpetuity to the Union, practice not injustice, for, as certain as fate itself, they who sow injustice will reap iniquity.[117]

South Carolina was upset that the legislation did not challenge the principle of protection and failed to reduce duties on the "exchangeable products" of cotton, woolens, and iron, which they insisted should be immediately cut to 15 percent.

Calhoun thought that the 1832 bill was dangerous because, "while it diminished the amount of burden, [it] distributed that burden more unequally than even the obnoxious act of 1828: reversing the principle adopted by the bill of 1816, of laying higher duties on the unprotected than the protected articles, by repealing almost entirely the duties laid upon the former, and imposing the burden almost entirely on the latter." Furthermore, the bill was supposed "to be a *permanent* adjustment" of the tariff, but it failed at that, and now "all hope of relief through the action of the General Government" was shattered. Therefore, South Carolina was "compelled to choose between absolute acquiescence in a ruinous system of oppression, or resort to her reserved powers" of nullification to end "the flood of political corruption which threatens to sweep away our Constitution and our liberty." In Calhoun's view, the issue "involves no longer the mere question of free trade, but of liberty & despotism."[118]

Action then shifted to the South Carolina state legislature. The state was divided between the radical nullifiers, who argued that it was futile to depend on Congress for relief because the northern majority was bent on permanently repressing the South, and the more moderate unionists, who held out hope that a better compromise could be reached. The problem for the extreme nullifiers was that, given the limited concessions of 1830 and 1832, one could not rule out further concessions in the future. This is where Jackson's first-term inaction proved costly; as long as John Quincy Adams had been president, moderate forces in South Carolina believed that a change in policy would come with a new administration. When Jackson did little more than accept the limited reform offered by Congress, the nullifiers lost hope for change.

The debate in South Carolina centered on whether the state should oppose the North's legislative "oppression" by working within the federal system or by asserting state sovereignty through nullification. The nullifiers thought the unionist cause was hopeless and labeled their opponents "submissionists." Unionists believed that nullification was unconstitutional and dangerous, but their apathy allowed the nullifiers to gain political strength between 1829 and 1833. Although the nullifiers narrowly lost their bid for a majority in the South Carolina state legislature in 1830, they regrouped and gained control of the state legislature in the October 1832 election. The nullifiers won about 60 percent of the vote and captured about two-thirds of the seats in an electrifying campaign that saw huge turnout.[119]

Events then moved swiftly. The state legislature immediately called for a special convention to consider nullification. In late November 1832, the convention issued the Nullification Ordinance, which contended that

> the Congress of the United States, by various acts purporting to be acts laying duties and imposts on foreign imports, but in reality intended for the protection of domestic manufactures and the giving of bounties to classes and individuals engaged in particular employments, at the expense and to the injury and oppression of other classes and individuals, and by wholly exempting from taxation certain foreign commodities, such as are not produced or manufactured in the United States, to afford a pretext for imposing higher and excessive duties on articles similar to those intended to be protected, has exceeded its just powers under the Constitution, which confers on it no authority to afford such protection, and has violated the true meaning and intent of the Constitution, which provides for equality in imposing the burdens of taxation upon the several states and portions of the confederacy.[120]

The Ordinance declared that the tariffs acts of 1824 and 1828 were "unauthorized by the constitution of the United States, and violate the true meaning and intent thereof, and are null, void, and not law, nor binding upon this State, its officers or citizens." Therefore, "it is further ordained, that it shall not be lawful for any of the constituted authorities, whether of this State or of the United States, to enforce the payment of duties imposed by the said acts within the limits of this State" starting in February 1833. Any attempt by the federal government to force the state to comply with the tariff would be "inconsistent" with South Carolina remaining part of the union. A subcommittee of the convention set out the terms of a compromise that would satisfy South Carolina: a uniform tariff not exceeding 12 percent on all imports.[121]

President Jackson was furious with South Carolina's decision. In December 1832, Jackson issued the Nullification Proclamation, which denounced the refusal by any state to enforce federal law as "incompatible with the existence of the Union, contradicted expressly by the letter of the Constitution, unauthorized by its spirit, inconsistent with every principle on which it was founded, and destructive of the great object for which it was formed." He declared that it was an "impractical absurdity" for any one state to pass judgment on and refuse to enforce a federal law. As commander in chief, the president warned South Carolina that "disunion by armed force is treason."[122]

Jackson also ridiculed the supposed economic rationale for South Carolina's action:

> You are deluded by men who are either deceived themselves or wish to deceive you. Mark under what pretenses you have been led on to the brink of insurrection and treason on which you stand! First a diminution of the value of our staple commodity, lowered by over-production in other quarters and the consequent diminution in the value of your lands, were the sole effect of the tariff laws. The effect of those laws was confessedly injurious, but the evil was greatly exaggerated by the unfounded theory you were taught to believe, that its burdens were in proportion to your exports, not to your consumption of imported articles.[123]

The enraged Jackson remarked privately that the nullifiers were "in a state of insanity" and that "the wickedness, madness and folly" of the state's leaders "has not its parallel in the history of the world." He called nullification "this abominable doctrine that strikes at the root of our Government and the social compact, and reduces everything to anarchy," and he wrote to a general vowing to "crush the monster [of disunion] in its cradle before it matures to manhood."[124]

The conflict over tariff policy brought the United States to its most dangerous crisis since independence.[125] The stakes were high because the structure of power in the federal system was now in question. By endorsing nullification, South Carolina chose a risky strategy that changed the fundamental issue from the injustice of the tariff to the power of a state to defy the federal government. While several southern states supported it on the tariff question, few defended its extreme position on states' rights. Georgia showed some support, but other southern states were horrified by South Carolina's decision. The question looming over the country was whether a political compromise might be reached before the dispute erupted into armed conflict.

CHAPTER FOUR

Tariff Peace and Civil War, 1833–1865

The Nullification Crisis was defused by the Compromise of 1833, which ushered in a quarter-century of gradually declining tariffs. From its peak of 62 percent in 1830, the average tariff fell to less than 20 percent by 1859. With one brief exception, there was no strong movement to push them back up again, belying the notion that tariffs were a cause of the Civil War. However, the stability of this policy depended on the dominance of the Democrats in national politics. The Republican electoral sweep in 1860 and the outbreak of the Civil War brought about a major shift in US trade policy. The war made high taxes on imports a fiscal necessity, and the Republicans began to construct a powerful political coalition to ensure that import duties would remain high for the rest of the century.

THE COMPROMISE OF 1833

As we saw in chapter 3, the passage of the 1828 Tariff of Abominations, and the subsequent failure to modify it, sparked a furious backlash in the South. In 1832, South Carolina passed the Nullification Ordinance, in which it declared the tariff unconstitutional and threatened not to enforce it. In effect, a dispute over trade policy had become an unprecedented constitutional crisis. However, while southern states opposed high protective tariffs, South Carolina's extreme reaction only served to isolate it from the others. No other southern state was facing the economic problems related to cotton that South Carolina was, and none were willing to go as far as Carolina nullifiers. Other southern states supported President Andrew Jackson and denounced the South Carolina radicals for not exhausting all means of negotiations and compromise. South Carolina's action also changed the debate from one over whether the tariff was excessive to one about the right of states to veto federal legislation.

Meanwhile, Jackson was firmly resolved that nullification would not stand and was quite prepared to use force to settle the matter. The administration immediately sponsored a Force Bill in Congress that would authorize the president to use the armed forces if necessary to collect tariff revenues from federal customs houses.

Yet the president also sought to defuse the crisis by trying to address South Carolina's complaints. Ten days after issuing the Nullification Proclamation, Jackson struck a conciliatory note in his December 1832 annual message to Congress. While agreeing that protection was necessary to secure a domestic supply of essential goods, Jackson noted that experience "makes it doubtful whether the advantages of this system are not counter-balanced by many evils, and whether it does not tend to beget in the minds of a large portion of our country-men a spirit of discontent and jealousy dangerous to the stability of the Union."[1] Although the southern complaints were exaggerated, the president said, the tariff should be adjusted so that no region of the country could have reason for complaint.

Thus, Jackson retreated from his earlier position that the 1832 tariff reform had been adequate, now suggesting that protective tariffs should be reduced as well. "Large interests have grown up under the implied pledge of our national legislation, which it would seem a violation of public faith suddenly to abandon," he stated. "But those who have vested their capital in manufacturing establishments cannot expect that the people will continue permanently to pay high taxes for their benefit, when the money is not required for any legitimate purpose in the administration of the Government." Therefore, a gradual tariff reduction was called for: "If upon investigation it shall be found, as it is believed it will be, that the legislative protection granted to any particular interest is greater than is indispensably requisite for these objects, I recommend that it be gradually diminished, and that as far as may be consistent with these objects the whole scheme of duties be reduced to the revenue standard as soon as a just regard to the faith of the Government and to the preservation of the large capital invested in establishments of domestic industry will permit."[2]

Congress was also anxious to avoid a military confrontation with South Carolina and immediately began considering another tariff revision. In January 1833, Rep. Gulian Verplanck of New York introduced a bill that would reduce most protective tariffs to 20 percent within two years. These reductions ran into the stiff opposition from advocates of protection, who claimed that such radical cuts would paralyze industry. Henry Clay and his allies resisted accommodating South Carolina, arguing that the state's intransigence should not be rewarded with concessions. Even John Quincy Adams, who brokered the failed tariff compromise in 1832, was appalled by South Carolina's response, viewing its politicians as a bunch of bullies who were simply trying to blackmail the country into adopting its preferred tariff policy.

As a result, despite the urgency of the situation, the House acted slowly. By mid-February, no progress had been made in moving the legislation forward. As Senator Thomas Benton (1854, 1:309) recalled, "A prompt passage of the bill might have been expected; on the contrary, it lingered in the House, under interminable debates on systems and theories, in which ominous signs of conjunction were seen between the two extremes which had been lately pitted against each other, for and against the protective system. The immediate friends of the administration seemed to be the only ones hearty in the support of the bill; but they were no match, in numbers, for those who acted in concert against it—spinning out the time in sterile and vagrant debate."

As time slipped away, the risk of a military showdown increased. Congress had overwhelmingly passed a Force Bill allowing the president to use the armed forces in the execution of federal tariff laws. Jackson ordered the relocation of the customs house from the city of Charleston to a federal fort in the harbor and authorized it to collect import duties there. Now, South Carolina would have to attack a federal installation in order to nullify the tariff. Although South Carolina delayed implementing nullification to see how Congress would respond, time was running out for a peaceful resolution to the stalemate.

Alarmed at the House's dithering, the Senate took the initiative. Sensing danger to his system of protective tariffs, Henry Clay, the champion of the American System, took to the floor on February 12 and proposed a compromise measure. In his address, Clay stated,

> I am compelled to express the opinion . . . that, whether rightfully or wrongly, the tariff stands in imminent danger. If it should even be preserved during this session, it must fall at the next session. . . . The fall of that policy, sir, would be productive of consequences calamitous indeed. When I look to the variety of interests which are involved, to the number of individuals interested, the amount of capital invested, the value of the buildings erected, and the whole arrangement of the business for the prosecution of the various branches of the manufacturing art which have sprung up under the fostering care of this government, I

cannot contemplate any evil equal to the sudden overthrow of all those interests. . . . I believe the American system to be in the greatest danger; and I believe it can be placed on a better and safer foundation at this session than at the next. . . . Let us not deceive ourselves. Now it's the time to adjust the question in a manner satisfactory to both parties. Put it off until the next session, and the alternative may, and probably then would be, a speedy and ruinous reduction of the tariff, or a civil war with the entire South.[3]

Clay reluctantly agreed to the tariff level being considered in the House, about 20 percent, but with a much longer transition period, stretched over nine years instead of the two years in the Verplanck bill.

The context for Clay's shocking announcement was the election of 1832. Not only had Jackson soundly defeated Clay for the presidency, but the incoming Congress was going to be overrun with Jackson supporters. The next Congress promised to be much more hostile to the American System than the outgoing one. If the current Congress postponed dealing with the issue, not only would it risk a military confrontation in South Carolina, but the tariff policy would be put into the hands of those who were likely to reduce protection significantly. As Clay wrote a few days before his address, "My belief is, that the Tariff is marked by the present administration for destruction, and that its object will be accomplished if some means are not soon devised to avert it, at the next Session."[4] By acting now, Clay hoped to defuse the crisis and buy some time for the policy of protective tariffs. With South Carolina on the brink of revolt, the federal government recording large fiscal surpluses, a popular president now supporting a reduction in protective tariffs, and a new Congress poised to challenge the American System, Clay concluded that maintaining the status quo would be impossible.[5]

After Clay spoke, John Calhoun of South Carolina rose to announce that he would also support the compromise out of a "desire to see this agitating question brought to a termination."[6] The *Register of Debates* records that Calhoun's brief remarks were followed by "a tumultuous approbation in the galleries." If Clay and Calhoun could agree, then the resolution of the crisis was at hand.

Benton (1854, 1:342) later gave the "secret history" of the compromise, which he largely attributed to Rep. Robert Letcher of Kentucky, a supporter of the American System who proposed it to Clay (who is said to have received it coolly at first) and to Webster (who rejected any compromise whatsoever). Letcher worked as an intermediary between Clay and

Calhoun (who were not on speaking terms) because Calhoun's support was necessary to give the compromise legitimacy. In the outside view, "Mr. Calhoun and Mr. Clay appear as master spirits, appeasing the storm which they had raised; on the inside view they appear as subaltern agents dominated by the necessity of their condition, and providing for themselves instead of their country—Mr. Clay, in saving the protective policy, and preserving the support of the manufacturers; and Mr. Calhoun, in saving himself from the perils of his condition."

The compromise was a true one in that no faction was completely satisfied with the outcome, but at the same time both sides could claim victory. Daniel Webster—who, ironically, had opposed Clay's American System in 1824—had not been consulted in the backroom deal-making and bitterly accused Clay of abandoning the cause of protection. Northerners resented Clay for bowing to southern pressure. Making an allusion to slavery, John Davis of Massachusetts complained: "You propose to bind us, hand and foot, to pour out our blood upon the altar, and sacrifice us as a burnt offering, to appease the unnatural and unfounded discontent of the South; a discontent, I fear, having deeper root than the tariff, and will continue when that is forgotten."[7] Rufus Choate of Massachusetts reprimanded his colleagues: "South Carolina has nullified your tariffs, and therefore you repeal them."[8]

To his critics, Clay responded, "I have been represented as the father of this [American] system, and I am charged with an unnatural abandonment of my own offspring. . . . But in what condition do I find this child? It is in the hands of the Philistines, who would strangle it. I fly to its rescue, to snatch it from the custody, and to place it on a bed of security and repose for nine years, where it may grow and strengthen, and become acceptable to the whole people."[9] By and large, manufacturing interests also supported the compromise. "The manufacturers flocked in crowds in Washington City—leaving home to stop the bill—arriving at Washington to promote it," Benton (1854, 1:316) recalled. "Those practical men soon saw that they had gained a reprieve of nine years and a half in the benefits of protection, with a certainty of the re-establishment of the system at the end of that time."

The compromise tariff gave South Carolina less than it had demanded, but it succeeded for the first time in putting the protective duties on cotton goods, woolens, and iron on a downward trajectory. In light of the urgent situation, and with both Clay and Calhoun lending their support to the compromise, the Senate appeared to accept the gradual phaseout as a reasonable outcome.

Once the compromise appeared workable in the Senate, Robert Letcher of Kentucky (and a Clay ally) introduced the bill in the House on February 25, which passed it the next day by a vote of 119–85. On March 2, the Senate passed it by a vote of 29–16, and it was signed by Jackson the next day. In the Senate, the South unanimously approved the compromise, while the North and West were split. The defection of the West did not go unnoticed by American System proponents. As the compromise was being debated, George Briggs of Massachusetts observed that "We are now soon to know, Mr. Chairman, whether this [protective] system, in which New England is so vitally interested, against her remonstrance, is to be overthrown by a combination of Southern votes with the votes of the Western and Middle States"[10] The North's split increased the credibility of the reform in the eyes of the South and, in Clay's opinion, helped "to reconcile the south more strongly to a measure, in which it has gained a nominal triumph, whilst all the substantial advantages have been secured to the tariff states." Clay was pleased with the outcome and wrote, "My friends flatter me, with my having completely triumphed."[11]

The compromise provided that all duties above 20 percent would be reduced by one-tenth of the excess above 20 percent starting in January 1834, with another one-tenth deducted in January 1836, another in January 1838, and another in January 1840, summing to a 40 percent reduction in the excess over 20 percent. In 1842, the remaining 60 percent excess over 20 percent would be removed, three-tenths in January 1842 and another three-tenths in July 1842. At the end of the transition period, in which the largest tariff cuts would come, the United States would have a fairly uniform 20 percent tariff on all dutiable imports. The compromise required that, from July 1842, import duties would "be laid for the purpose of raising such revenue as may be necessary to an economical administration of the government." Thus, Congress agreed to abandon protective tariffs and adopt a revenue standard for import duties.

The South Carolina nullifiers endorsed the compromise, and a state convention ended the crisis by repealing the Nullification Ordinance. As with any agreement, however, it was one thing to pass a compromise measure and yet another to ensure that it would be enforced. The South bore much of the risk in the compromise, because the low duties it sought would arrive only after a period of nine years. The South remained wary because, as Thomas Foster of Georgia accurately noted, the current Congress "had no power to bind our successors."[12] The South rightly feared that Congress could renege at any time on its intention either to reduce duties during the transition period or to maintain them after 1842. In presenting the compromise, Clay tried to assure the South that it would not be tampered with. If the bill passed with the consent of all, he "had no doubt the rate of duties guarantied would be continued after the expiration of the term, if the country continued at peace."[13]

For its part, the North feared that the compromise would prevent future Congresses from protecting manufacturing industries, even if economic circumstances were to change. To answer these charges, Clay admitted that "the bill contains no obligatory pledges—it could make none, none are attempted. . . . The next Congress, and every succeeding Congress, will undoubtedly have the power to repeal the law whenever they may think proper. . . . The measure is what it professes to be, a compromise; but it imposes, and could impose, no restriction upon the will or power of a future Congress."[14] Thus, while agreeing that the compromise could not bind the actions of future legislators, Clay believed that subsequent Congresses would avoid tampering with it. As it turned out, Clay was largely correct, but not necessarily for the reasons he gave.

AFTERMATH OF COMPROMISE: THE WALKER TARIFF OF 1846

The Compromise of 1833 succeeded in removing tariff policy from national politics for almost a decade. From 1833 until 1842, as provided under the compromise, the phased-in tariff reductions took effect without interference from Congress. Why was no attempt made to deviate from the compromise? It was certainly described in solemn terms, as "sacred" and as "the great bond of peace to this Union." But the main reason the compromise was untouched prior to 1842 was political: the Jacksonian Democrats, who were largely from the South and strongly supported the compromise, had unified control of government in every year from 1833 until 1841. Since they remained in power, others preferring higher tariffs—namely, the Whig party that included Henry Clay and Daniel Webster—did not have the opportunity to change the nation's trade policy.

The emergence of the Second Party System in the mid-1830s meant the return of partisan conflict over government policy. Just as Hamilton's Federalists and Jefferson's Republicans had clashed in the early years of the republic, now Whigs and Democrats fought over economic policy. But there were few disputes about tariff policy in the four years after the Compromise of 1833, during which time the economy was strong, demands for protection remained in check, and the government's fiscal surpluses (due in part to the sale of public land) allowed government debt to be paid down. While Clay vowed to fight any tariff reductions beyond those called for in the compromise, he did not attempt to subvert it by proposing higher import duties. Even Daniel Webster admitted that Congress "should not be disposed to interfere with it [the tariff] until a case of clear necessity should arise."[15]

However, the Compromise of 1833 was tested after the financial panic of 1837 and especially during the Crisis of 1839, which led to four years of severe deflation and an economic depression. As in previous cases, the downturn had its origins in the financial system. After the Second Bank of the United States was abolished in 1836, state governments began borrowing huge sums of money. The collapse of internal improvement projects in the Midwest and South in the summer of 1839 contributed to a wave of bank failures throughout the region, which produced a 22 percent contraction in the money supply.[16] Without a central bank to act as a lender of last resort or to offset the monetary shock, the federal government was unable to address the slump.

As a result, political pressures for trade protection grew stronger, and the stage was set for renewed political conflict over tariff policy. The North-South sectional dispute over tariffs did not disappear, but was increasingly played out through two political parties, the Democrats and the Whigs. Drawing their political support from the South and from poorer farming communities in the North, Democrats advocated limited government, which meant a strict construction of the Constitution, states rights, and a tariff for revenue only. Drawing their political strength from the North, particularly from more commercial and manufacturing communities, the Whigs wanted an activist federal government with a national bank, federally financed internal improvements, and protective tariffs for domestic industries. The underlying economic interest of each region largely, but not entirely, explained which party was consistently chosen to represent the region in Congress.[17]

The struggling economy enabled the Whigs to sweep into office against the incumbent Democrats in the election of 1840. Although the Whigs supported higher tariffs, their plans to revisit the issue were stymied by Vice President John Tyler, who unexpectedly became president after William Harrison died shortly after his inauguration. Tyler was a Virginia Democrat who had been chosen only to win support for the Whigs in the South in the expectation that he would never become president. Tyler immediately alienated the Whigs by twice vetoing legislation to create a national bank and blocking efforts to increase tariffs. The Whigs were anxious to raise tariffs, in part because the federal government's fiscal position had weakened considerably: the government ran a $10 million budget deficit in fiscal year 1841 and was expected to lose another $5 million per year as a result of the last and largest tariff cuts from the Compromise of 1833 that were due to take effect in 1842. Yet despite the economic downturn and growing fiscal deficit, Tyler stunned Whigs by saying that "the compromise act should not be altered except under urgent necessities which are not believed at this time to exist."[18]

The question of adjusting import duties to raise revenue also became intertwined with provisions of the Land Act of 1841. Under that act, which regulated the distribution of revenue from public land sales, any increase in import duties above the 20 percent limit mandated in the Compromise of 1833 would result in a sequester of the revenue from land sales. In his annual message to Congress in December 1841, Tyler reaffirmed that "it might be esteemed desirable that no such augmentation of the taxes should take place as would have the effect of annulling the land-proceeds distribution act of the last session, which act is declared to be inoperative the moment the duties are increased beyond 20 per cent, the maximum rate established by the compromise act."[19] But the president did not offer a way out of the government's fiscal difficulties.

In June 1842, the final reduction in import duties under the compromise took effect, cutting government revenue even more. Additional revenue was needed to close the fiscal gap, so the Whigs passed two bills imposing higher tariff rates (similar to those found in the 1832 legislation) in July and August 1842. (Of course, they were not strictly revenue measures since they kept coffee and tea on the duty-free list and mainly imposed higher tariffs on imported manufactured goods.) Tyler vetoed both on the grounds that adhering to the terms of the compromise was the "highest moral obligation," and they would stop the distribution of revenue from public land sales at a time when the federal government desperately needed those funds. In late August, Congress passed the tariff bill without the distribution provision. This legislation squeaked through the House by a vote of 104–103 and the Senate by a vote of 24–23. Tyler reluctantly signed the bill, which helped increase the average tariff from 26 percent in 1842 to 37 percent in 1844.

The Tariff of 1842 reintroduced differential duties across imported goods and doubled protective duties. The fact that the final low tariffs envisioned by the Compromise of 1833 were in effect for just two months, July and August, before Congress had overturned them, rekindled old animosities. Southern politicians complained of a violated contract and a breach of faith. John Calhoun summed up the region's complaints:

We have patiently waited the nine years of slow reduction, and resisted every attempt to make changes against the manufacturing interest, even when they would have operated in our favor, and for which we have received the thanks of those who represented it on this floor. And now, when the time has arrived, when it is our turn to enjoy its benefits, they who called on us to adhere to the act, when the interest of the manufactures was at stake, and commended us for our fidelity to the compromise, turn round, when it suits their interest, and coolly and openly violate every provision in our favor.[20]

John Jones of Virginia argued that for nine years, "while the South had to bear the burdens of the arrangements, it tamely and quietly submitted to the consequences. . . . Now, when we are to reap the advantages of the compromise act, what is the spectacle which we see exhibited? The very party who enacted the law have come forward and declared that they will not execute the promises nor discharge the obligations there imposed."[21] Yet the South was powerless to stop the enactment of the new tariff.

Although the American System had been moribund for nearly a decade, and support for it had waned even in Clay's home state of Kentucky, the weak economy gave the Whigs an opportunity to resurrect the policy. But turmoil within the Whig party—they were forced to expel Tyler from their ranks because of policy feuding—allowed the Democrats to recapture the House in the midterm election of 1842. The Ways and Means Committee quickly reported a bill that would put tariff rates somewhere between the 20 percent called for in the Compromise of 1833 and the higher rates in the Tariff of 1842. This proposal split the party: Southern Democrats thought the rates too excessive, while Northern Democrats were concerned about the potential harm to their industrial constituencies. In May 1844, the House tabled the bill by just six votes; the Whigs joined with enough Northern Democrats to spike the measure. In any event, the measure would have died in the Senate, where the Whigs retained control.

The presidential election of 1844, which pitted Democrat James Polk against Whig Henry Clay, was the first in which the political parties issued platform statements that outlined their policy positions. The Whig platform endorsed "a tariff for revenue to defray the necessary expenses of the government, and discriminating with special reference to the protection of the domestic labor of the country." The Democrats supported a tariff for revenue only ("no more revenue ought to be raised than is required to defray the necessary expenses of government") and rejected protective duties because "justice and sound policy forbid the Federal Government to foster one branch of industry to the detriment of another, or to cherish the interests of one portion to the injury of another portion of our common country."[22]

Given the recent electoral strength of the Whigs, Polk and the Democrats had to manage the issue of protective tariffs carefully as they took on Clay, the aging champion of the American System. Public opinion seemed to view the tariff favorably and attribute the economic recovery after the Crisis of 1839 to the higher duties enacted in 1842. Sen. Robert Walker (D-MS) informed Polk that political support for "the tariff is much stronger now through the Union, than it ever was before, & in Pennsylvania, New York, Connecticut & New Jersey, it is irresistible. In Pennsylvania, the last legislature, nearly two thirds of whom were democrats, passed resolutions of instruction *unanimously* in favor of the tariff, & the entire democratic press of the state has assumed the same ground. Many new manufactories are springing up throughout the state, & the old establishments are all again in successful operation. No man now attempts in that state to oppose tariff policy."[23]

To finesse the issue, Walker suggested that Polk call for a revenue tariff with some incidental protection to allow domestic industries to reap reasonable profits while still ensuring effective competition, arguing that this position was not as doctrinaire as the "tariff for revenue only" stance. Polk took this advice and wrote a letter in June 1844, which soon became public, stating that he was "opposed to a tariff for protection *merely*." Polk (1969, 7:267) described his position as follows: "In adjusting the details of a revenue tariff, I have heretofore sanctioned such moderate discriminating duties, as would produce the amount of revenue needed, and at the same time afford reasonable incidental protection to our home industry." That compromise language—a revenue tariff with incidental protection— served Democratic interests well by allowing them to emphasize the "revenue tariff" part in the South and the "incidental protection" part in the North. The position was not a complete evasion, because it explicitly used the key words "incidental protection" and "discrimination" in favor of domestic industries. The letter helped reassure voters in Pennsylvania, which ultimately went for the Democrats, although questions were raised in South Carolina about Polk's fidelity to the cause of low tariffs.

The 1844 election hinged more on the annexation of Texas than on tariff policy and proved to be a clean sweep for the Democrats. They secured both houses of Congress with large majorities and the presidency with the narrow election of Polk. This victory paved the way for a reversal of the Tariff of 1842 and a radical overhaul of the tariff structure.

In his inaugural address, President Polk adhered to the spirit of his campaign letter by endorsing a low-revenue tariff with incidental protection.[24] In his diary, he stated his belief that a tariff reduction was "the most important domestic measure of my administration."[25] To manage that, he appointed Robert Walker as his Treasury secretary. In November 1845, Walker presented to the cabinet a far-reaching proposal to reduce tariff rates and restructure the tariff schedule. Despite some opposition from those who believed the proposed reductions were extreme, Polk supported Walker, though he privately admitted that his Treasury secretary was "speculative and perhaps too highly wrought."[26]

In his December 1845 annual message to Congress, Polk set the stage for Walker's proposal. The president argued that the Tariff of 1842 violated the principles of a revenue tariff and tended more to prohibition than to incidental protection. In recommending lower duties, Polk insisted that "I am far from entertaining opinions unfriendly to the manufacturers. On the contrary, I desire to see them prosperous as far as they can be so without imposing unequal burdens on other interests." Polk also called for "the abolition of the minimum principle, or assumed, arbitrary, and false values, and of specific duties, and the substitution in their place of ad valorem duties as the fairest and most equitable indirect tax which can be imposed."[27]

Just days later, in the annual report of the Treasury Department, Walker unveiled his tariff proposal. He attacked the Tariff of 1842 as "unjust, unequal, as well in its details as in the principles upon which it is founded." He argued that protective tariffs discriminated in favor of the manufacturer against the farmer, mechanic, merchant, and shipping industry, and thereby increased the profits of capital while doing nothing for the wages of labor. He rejected the argument that protective tariffs made goods cheaper by explaining that "the occasional fall in price of some articles after a tariff is no proof that this was the effect of the tariff." He rejected the argument that the United States should retaliate against foreign trade barriers: "that agriculture, commerce, and navigation are injured by foreign restrictions constitutes no reason why they would be subject to still severer treatment, by additional restrictions and countervailing tariffs, at home." In fact, he contended, "by countervailing restrictions, we injure our own fellow-citizens much more than the foreign nations at whom we propose to aim their force." Higher tariffs at home would not lead to lower tariffs abroad, he argued, but would merely encourage and perpetuate existing foreign trade barriers.[28]

Walker then proposed a new tariff based on Democratic principles, which included converting all specific duties to ad valorem duties (so the rate of taxation was completely transparent) and creating a tariff schedule with just a few different rates of duty. Walker rejected having a single uniform duty, such as 20 percent, arguing that luxuries deserved to be taxed at higher rates and that some limited discrimination in rates across goods should be made. All imported goods would be assigned one of nine tariff categories. Schedule A consisted of alcoholic beverages, such as brandy and other spirits, and would be taxed at 100 percent. Schedule B comprised various spices and imported foods (fruit and meat), tobacco products, and wine, and would be taxed at 40 percent. Schedule C goods included a long list of items such as ready-made clothing; earthenware; manufactures of metal, silk, wool, and glass; and raw materials such as sugar and tobacco: these would be taxed at 30 percent. Schedule D goods, most notably cotton textiles, would be taxed at 25 percent. Schedule E goods included chemicals, nails and spikes, and manufactures of hemp and flax, all of which would be taxed at 20 percent. Four remaining schedules—F (15 percent), G (10 percent), H (5 percent) and I (duty-free)—rounded out the tariff schedule.

Walker's report was one of the few instances in the nineteenth century when the executive branch provided a detailed tariff plan for Congress's consideration. In April 1846, the Ways and Means Committee reported a tariff bill that largely reflected Walker's proposal. With Democrats firmly in control of the House, the bill's passage was a foregone conclusion, although some details were the subject of contention. Representatives from Ohio demanded that coffee and tea be put on the free list to help consumers; Walker objected to the loss of revenue but was forced to compromise. In July 1846, the House passed the Walker tariff by a partisan and sectional vote of 114–95. Democrats voted 113–18 in favor of the bill, with all of the nay votes coming from the North, principally Pennsylvania. With their stronghold in New England and the Mid-Atlantic, Whigs voted 71–1 against the measure.

Senate passage promised to be more difficult because Democrats had only a slim majority, and those from Connecticut and Pennsylvania were prepared to vote against the bill. Polk (1910, 2:53) noted in his diary that "the city is swarming with manufacturers who are making tremendous exertions to defeat it." Although the party had difficulty maintaining unity, the president and his allies put enormous pressure on Northern Democrats to support the administration. (One senator was intercepted at the Baltimore and Ohio railway station as he was going home and brought directly to the president, who persuaded him to stay in town and vote for the bill.) The Senate debate was intense. Clay fiercely attacked the bill: "We should not have subverted a patriotic system of domestic protection . . . for the visionary promises of an alien policy of free trade, fostering the industry of foreign people and the interests of foreign countries, which has brought in its train disaster and ruin to every nation that has had the temerity to try it."[29]

The Senate vote was expected to be close, perhaps even a tie, which would force Vice President George Dallas to break the stalemate. Dallas was a Democrat from Pennsylvania who favored protection, even voting against Clay's compromise in 1833, but he was also bound by his party's platform. Not knowing whether to choose between his party or his state, Dallas desperately wanted to avoid casting the deciding vote. When the dreaded moment came, however, Dallas made the painful decision to vote in favor of the bill. Although he did not approve of all its provisions, he stated, most Americans wanted a reduction in import duties, and majority opinion in the House was clear. At the last minute, however, Spencer Jarnagin, a Tennessee Whig who favored protection but had been instructed by the state legislature to vote for the bill and had previously abstained, changed his vote to yea. This pushed it over the top by a 29–28 margin, and the vice president's vote was unnecessary.

The House quickly concurred in one Senate amendment, and the president signed the bill. In his diary, Polk (1910, 2:55) wrote that the legislation had given

rise to an immense struggle between the two great political parties of the country. The capitalists and monopolists have not surrendered the immense advantages which they possessed, and the enormous profits which they derived under the tariff of 1842, until after a fierce and mighty struggle. This city has swarmed with them for weeks. They have spared no effort within their power to sway and control Congress, but all has been proved to be unavailing and they have been at length vanquished. Their effort will probably now be to raise a panic (such as they have already attempted) by means of their combined wealth, so as to induce a repeal of the act.

The Walker tariff brought about the most far-reaching reduction in import duties to date. The average tariff on dutiable imports fell sharply, from 34 percent in 1845 to 26 percent in 1848. Unlike the Compromise of 1833, the tariff reduction was not phased in over time and took effect immediately.

The tariff also involved some tacit coordination with Britain. At the time, British policy was moving away from mercantilism and toward free trade; in fact, Parliament was on the cusp of repealing the Corn Laws, which severely limited imports of wheat. Walker and the Democrats hoped that, if the United States reduced its tariffs on manufactures, Britain might be encouraged to open up its agricultural markets. Indeed, Walker had closed his report with this statement: "Let our commerce be as free as our political institutions. Let us, with revenue duties only, open our ports to all the world, and nation after nation will soon follow our example. If we reduce our tariff, the party opposed to the corn laws of England would soon prevail, and admit all our agricultural products at all times freely into her ports."[30] The House delayed passage of the Walker tariff to see if Britain was actually going to repeal the Corn Laws, which it did in May 1846.[31] Although the British response to the Walker tariff was a minor consideration in its passage, this was one of the few instances in which Congress was considering what other countries might do when it changed the tariff schedule.

The Walker tariff remained in effect for eleven years, the second longest span of any tariff legislation passed by Congress. Although tariffs were not quite as low or as uniform as many in South Carolina wanted, the South as a whole strongly supported the Walker tariff. In fact, the South had clearly won the battle for establishing and maintaining a low "revenue" tariff with incidental protection. As figure 4.1 shows, with the

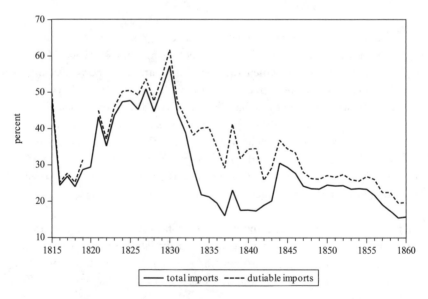

Figure 4.1. Average tariff: Total and dutiable imports, 1815–1860. *Note*: There was no observation for dutiable imports in 1820. (US Bureau of the Census 1975, series U-211–12.)

exception of the 1842–46 period, tariffs had fallen continuously since the Compromise of 1833. Indeed, the tariff was not again a major political issue until the late 1850s.

What political and economic factors account for the persistence of low tariffs after 1846? The main reason that tariff policy remained unchallenged from 1846 until the Civil War is that no party except the Democrats ever had unified control of government. During this period, the Whigs and later the Republicans, who were more favorable to protective tariffs, would sometimes capture the House or the Senate or the presidency, but the Democrats always retained control of the other parts of government and therefore had the power to block any effort to increase tariffs.

For example, in 1848, Zachary Taylor, a Whig, was elected president and appointed a staunch protectionist from Pennsylvania as his Treasury secretary. In his first message to Congress in December 1849, Taylor called for a revision of the tariff and the reinstitution of specific duties "at rates high enough to afford substantial and sufficient encouragement to our industry, and at the same time so adjusted as to insure stability."[32] The Democratic Congress simply ignored this suggestion and made no move to change policy. His successor, Millard Fillmore, also a Whig, repeatedly called for higher duties. For example, in his annual message of December 1850, Fillmore conceded that an excessive tariff would be a cause of dissatisfaction, but argued for a modest tariff increase. With the Democrats firmly in control of Congress, this plea fell on deaf ears. In his messages for 1851 and 1852, Fillmore again called Congress's attention to the problems with ad valorem duties, the supposedly languishing state of manufacturers under the Walker tariff, and the unsatisfactory structure of duties that sometimes protected raw materials at the expense of manufacturers. Each time, Democrats in Congress took no notice.

The lack of unified government, except under the Democrats, was the proximate reason for the continuity of tariff policy from 1846 until 1860. This begs the question of why low-tariff forces were so well represented in Congress when they had been so weak just two decades earlier. The growing economic interest of the Midwest in open trade was critical to this development. The Midwest had always produced potentially exportable goods, such as wheat, other grains, and animal products, but prior to the 1840s, high transportation costs prevented them from gaining access to world markets. As transportation costs fell, foreign markets became a small but growing part of the demand for Midwestern agricultural products.

The expansion of agricultural production further west, and the perception that domestic demand was limited, gave the region hope that it could

someday emerge as the "granary of the world." In his tariff report, Walker
(1845, 13) explicitly sought to rally the support of the region in favor of
lower tariffs. He observed that the great fertile lands of the Midwest were
producing an abundance of agricultural produce for which "the home market, in itself, is wholly inadequate." As he put it, "the States of Ohio, Indiana, and Illinois, if cultivated to their fullest extent, could of themselves
raise more than sufficient food to supply the entire home market. . . . They
must have the foreign market, or a large surplus, accompanied by great
depression in price, must be the result." Because import tariffs were effectively a tax on agricultural exports, Walker noted that the Midwest "must
be the greatest sufferers by the tariff, in depriving them of the foreign
market."

In fact, the Midwest provided decisive support for the Senate passage
of the Walker tariff. The Senate passed the bill by a single vote, 28–27, and
senators from the Midwest voted in favor 14–4. Without those votes, the
South would not have been able achieve victory. This change in position
did not go unnoticed. "How is it that some of the States which built up
this [protective] system by the votes of their Representatives and Senators
now desert it?" asked Senator James Morehead (W-KY). "Why have Ohio
and other States changed, which used to vote unanimously for the protective policy, now that this great policy embraces an interest of three hundred millions of dollars?" Sidney Breese (D-IL) immediately replied: "If
the manufacturing interests embrace a capital of four hundred millions,
the agricultural interests amount to a thousand millions. Illinois wants
a market for her agricultural products; she wants the market of the world.
Ten counties of that State could supply all the home market. We want a
foreign market for our produce, which is now rotting in our granaries."[33]

Several factors helped Midwestern farmers achieve greater access to
foreign markets and thereby increase their export orientation. The dramatic decline in transportation costs due to internal improvements, particularly the rapid expansion of railroad networks in the 1850s, helped fuel
exports from the Midwest. The repeal of the Corn Laws by Britain in 1846
and the Crimean War in the early 1850s also boosted foreign demand for
American grains. As a result, the Midwest's hopes of selling more to foreign markets were fulfilled as wheat and flour exports surged, increasing
from 6 percent of total exports in the late 1830s to 11 percent in the late
1850s. Thus, the Midwest's latent economic interest in exporting became
operative during this period.[34]

As the region was becoming more closely tied to foreign markets,
its political weight was also growing. From 1820 to 1850, as figure I.4

showed, the Midwest gained Congressional seats almost entirely at the expense of the North, not the South. The states that joined the union between the tariff votes in 1828 and 1846—Arkansas, Florida, Michigan, and Texas—added eight new votes in the Senate, seven of which were in favor of the Walker tariff. Together the South and Midwest controlled two-thirds of the Senate by 1850. Thus, the old export-oriented economic interests of the South were joined by new ones in the Midwest, and both sought low tariffs to promote foreign commerce. As cotton and tobacco producers in the South had long recognized, farmers in the Midwest now embraced lower import duties to increase imports and therefore the exports required to pay for them. As a result, the combined political strength of the South and Midwest checked the North's ability to enact protective tariffs. The North had little hope of overturning this coalition, and modest tariffs might have persisted for decades had the Civil War not intervened.

ANTEBELLUM TRADE AND PROTECTION

While politicians debated the details and purposes of import duties, the size and structure of the American economy changed significantly during the antebellum period. Between 1820 and 1860, the population of the United States grew from 9.6 million to 31.4 million. Although agriculture was still by far the most important economic activity, the share of the labor force employed in industry (mining, manufacturing, and construction) rose from 8 percent in 1810 to 20 percent in 1860.[35]

Despite this gradual shift in the economy, the composition of America's foreign trade was largely unchanged. About 85 percent of exports were raw materials (mainly cotton) and food (wheat and flour). About two-thirds of imports consisted of manufactured goods, principally from Britain, with the remainder being food and beverages, such as wine and spirits, coffee and tea, most of which did not compete with American products. Customs receipts still accounted for roughly 90 percent of federal government revenue throughout the antebellum period.

Of course, the tariff was controversial not because it raised revenue, but because protective duties affected resource allocation across different sections of the country. Three key economic questions about US trade policy in the antebellum period can be posed: (1) Was there a national economic gain or loss from the tariff? (2) Did the tariff redistribute income from the South to the North, and if so, by how much? (3) Did import tariffs play a significant role in promoting industrialization?

The first question is whether import tariffs were beneficial or costly to the nation as a whole. All taxes create what economists call a "dead-weight loss," a measure of the inefficiency caused by the tax in changing the incentives for production and consumption. The deadweight loss from the duties imposed in 1859 was tiny, only about 0.2 percent of GDP, both because the average tariff on total imports was low (about 15 percent), and because the ratio of imports to GDP was small (less than 8 percent). Put differently, federal spending was only 1.6 percent of GDP, and customs revenue was about 1.2 percent of GDP, so import duties could not possibly generate a very large deadweight loss. However, when the Tariff of Abominations of 1828 pushed the average tariff to more than 60 percent, the deadweight loss of the tariff might have been as high as 2.5 percent of GDP.[36]

This deadweight loss could have been offset by other gains. The most plausible gain would have been an improvement in the country's terms of trade. The terms of trade, the price of a country's exports relative to the price of its imports, are closely related to the gains from trade. The terms of trade are said to improve when a country's export prices increase or its import prices decrease; in either case a country would give up fewer exports in exchange for more imports. The more favorable the terms of trade, the more a country benefits from trade, other things being equal. Many countries cannot influence their terms of trade. However, as the world's largest cotton producer, accounting for about 80 percent of world production in the antebellum period, the United States could affect the world price of cotton. A policy to restrict exports of cotton might have improved the terms of trade by increasing the price that the world had to pay for American cotton, enabling the United States to enjoy a higher real income at the expense of the rest of the world.[37]

An export tax would directly reduce cotton exports and increase the world price. Of course, export taxes were unconstitutional precisely because the South had feared that they might be used against its exports, but it is still instructive to consider their hypothetical impact. An optimal export tax would maximize national income by balancing the benefits of improved terms of trade against the cost of deadweight losses. Two different methods have been used to calculate the optimal export tax and its welfare consequences: simulation via a computable general equilibrium model and estimation to determine the elasticity of export demand facing the United States. Both methods yield similar conclusions: Harley's (1992) simulation indicates that the optimal export tax on cotton would have been around 60 percent and the welfare gain would have been close to 1 percent of GDP, while Irwin's (2003c) estimation of the elasticity of export demand for US cotton implies an optimal export tax of about 45–55 percent and a welfare gain of about 0.3 percent of GDP. Had such a policy been implemented, the nation as a whole would have benefited a slight amount, but large losses would have been inflicted on southern cotton producers, unless the proceeds of the tax were rebated to them. Still, despite the huge US market share in cotton, the potential economic gains from an optimal export tax would probably have been very modest.

An import tariff might have achieved a similar outcome, because exports and imports are closely related to one another. As discussed in the introduction, the Lerner Symmetry Theorem holds that an import tariff is equivalent to an export tax. By reducing imports, an import tariff would indirectly reduce cotton exports and thereby improve the terms of trade. However, this sequence of events requires that the tariffs not simply reduce all exports, but cotton exports in particular. Harley's (1992) simulations suggest that import tariffs failed to do this. The United States exported many goods besides cotton: wheat, flour, and packing-house products (salted beef and pork, tallow, and lard) accounted for a significant share of exports. These exports, not cotton, were the marginal ones that adjusted to changes in the overall level of trade. In other words, to the extent that import tariffs reduced exports, they reduced marginal exports (food) and not the infra-marginal exports in which the United States possessed some monopoly power (cotton). As a result, import tariffs would have slashed food exports while leaving cotton exports largely unaffected, thus failing to improve the terms of trade.

The second question is whether the South was harmed by import tariffs, as southern politicians insisted, and if so to what extent. Harley (1992) examines how the welfare of three main factors of production—land, labor, and capital—would have been affected by removing the 20 percent tariff on imports in 1859, when imports were about 6 percent of GDP. According to his results, landowners stood to gain the most from eliminating the tariff (about a 10 percent increase in welfare), because agricultural production would expand. Labor would gain slightly (just 1 percent of its welfare), and capital would lose slightly (roughly 4 percent of its welfare). In a somewhat different view of the workforce, laborers in manufacturing would be worse off by 6–15 percent for those employed in the cotton textile industry, while farmers and planters would gain by 3–9 percent, depending upon the particular modeling assumptions made. In terms of aggregate regional income, the North would lose an imperceptible amount (0.1 percent) from an elimination of the tariff, because it produced both agricultural and manufactured goods. The welfare of the agrarian Midwest would increase about 1 percent and that of the South about 2 percent from eliminating the tariff.

Thus, in terms of its distributional effects, the tariff brought about a higher return to capital in the North and a lower value of land throughout the country, with labor not significantly affected. The South lost a small amount, in the aggregate, from import duties, but those losses were probably concentrated on a few politically influential landowners who orchestrated the heated political reaction against tariffs. As these results make clear, however, there was a clear economic rationale for capital-owners in the North to support the tariff and for planters in the South to oppose it. Furthermore, the redistribution of national income as a result of the tariff was probably significantly higher in the 1820s, when the tariff was much higher, than in 1859.

The third issue is the relationship between the tariff and early industrialization. The United States experienced rapid industrialization during the antebellum period. Even though protective tariffs declined after 1833, the nation continued the shift toward industry between 1840 and 1860, perhaps at an even faster pace than before. Between 1839 and 1859, the manufacturing sector expanded from about 15 percent of GDP to 21 percent of GDP.[38] There are many explanations for the growth of manufacturing during this time, including the expansion of the domestic market and the stable political environment that encouraged investment and capital accumulation.[39] Protective tariffs were just one of many factors in promoting the early growth of industry, but their role is controversial even today. Some have contended that the United States would have remained an agrarian economy with little domestic industry were it not for the tariffs, while others have argued that industrialization would have proceeded more or less as it did even without the tariffs.

In considering the relationship between foreign competition, tariff protection, and domestic manufacturing, several points must be kept in mind. First, many manufacturing industries were not affected by imports at all. These include the leather, wood, and food-processing industries, some of which were even successful at exporting. In fact, almost 17 percent of exports in 1859 consisted of semifinished and finished manufactured goods (excluding food manufactures), a surprisingly large proportion given the nation's huge resource advantage in producing agricultural goods. While these industries were often based on local natural resources, some manufacturing activities clearly would have taken place even without the tariff. Second, even if all protective duties had been abolished, the ability of the United States to import manufactured goods was limited by its capacity to export goods in return. The United States was a rapidly growing country with a large population. For it to have imported all of the manufactured goods that it desired to consume, the country's capacity to export cotton, wheat, and other agricultural products would have had to expand enormously: any increase in imports would have to be matched by an increase in exports to pay for them. (Similarly, foreign manufacturing capacity would have had to expand significantly as well.) Given the large size of the economy and its increasing demand for manufactured goods, it is implausible that the growing US economy would have remained entirely dependent on imported manufactured goods without any significant increase in domestic production.

In fact, as table 4.1 shows, almost all of the manufactured goods that Americans consumed were produced at home. For example, in 1859, after many years of relatively low protective tariffs, imports of manufactured goods were only about 9 percent of domestic consumption of manufactured goods, about the same as in 1839. This was down from 23 percent in 1810. Thus, by the 1840s, abolishing all import duties would have had a significant impact on certain industries, but would likely have had only a modest effect on manufacturing production overall.

As a result, many economic historians have argued that protective tariffs did not play a crucial role in America's industrialization. "In the main,

TABLE 4.1. Selected data on trade and production of manufactured goods, 1810–1859 (in millions of current dollars)

Year	Imports of manufactured goods	Exports of manufactured goods	Net exports of manufactured goods	Value of domestic production of manufactured goods	Imports as a share of domestic consumption
1810	≈49	6	− 43	173	23%
1839	55	16	− 39	547	9%
1849	121	23	− 98	1,019	11%
1859	191	46	− 145	1,886	9%

Sources: Imports and exports of manufactured goods, US Bureau of the Census 1975, series U-223-224, semi-manufactures and finished manufactures; excludes manufactured foodstuffs. Figure for imports of manufactures in 1810: assumed 75 percent of the $65 million in imports in that year were manufactured; comparable percentage in 1821 was 65 percent. Exports of manufactured goods in 1810: assumed 15 percent of $42 million in exports; same percentage as in 1820. Value of domestic production: for 1810, from Tench Coxe's estimate in *Statement of the Arts and Manufactures of the United States of America: For the Year 1810* (Philadelphia: A. Cornman, 1814), page li; for 1839, projected from Gallman's value added in manufactures for that year (Gallman 1960, 43) using a factor of 2.3, which is ratio of value of manufactured products to value added in manufacturing, average of 1849 and 1859; for 1849 and 1859, from Census data, as reported in *Statistical Abstract of the United States* (1913, 666). Imports as a share of domestic consumption calculated as imports divided by production minus exports.

the changes in duties have had much less effect on the protected industries than is generally supposed," Taussig (1931, 152) concluded. "Their growth had been steady and continuous, and seems to have been little stimulated by the high duties of 1842, and little checked by the more moderate duties of 1846 and 1857." Industrial production grew steadily and consistently throughout the antebellum period, regardless of the ups and downs of the tariff, according to Davis's (2004) data.

Most of the debate centers on the cotton, woolen, and iron industries, which were protected by relatively high tariffs. How much output would have been lost in these manufacturing industries had the protective duties been substantially reduced? The impact depends crucially on the elasticity of substitution between imported and domestic products—that is, the degree to which consumers shift their purchases between domestic and foreign goods when the prices of imported goods change. A low elasticity of substitution implies that domestic and foreign goods are different products and imperfect substitutes for one another, indicating that a tariff reduction would have a small effect on the domestic industry. A high elasticity of substitution implies that domestic and foreign goods are similar products or close substitutes for one another, indicating that a tariff reduction would have a large effect on the domestic industry. Unfortunately, there are few empirical estimates of this important parameter for the antebellum period.

Harley's (1992) model provides a benchmark for thinking about this issue. He distinguishes between the cotton textile industry, which he views as vulnerable to foreign competition and hence dependent on the tariff, and other manufacturing industries that were more firmly established. These included the leather industry (shoes and boots), which competed successfully against British products in Canada; and the food-processing, tobacco, and wood products industries, which were also untouched by foreign competition or even successful at exporting. Harley assumes the elasticity of substitution between domestic and imported goods is ten in the case of cotton textiles, a high number that implies domestic and foreign textile products were close substitutes for one another, and five in the case of other manufactured goods. In simulating the removal of the 20 percent tariff in 1859, he finds that overall manufacturing output falls by 17 percent. However, the effects differ significantly across industries. In the case of cotton textiles, domestic production falls 35 percent because of the high elasticity of substitution; in the case of other manufactured goods, domestic production falls 14 percent. To pay for the increase in imports, farm exports nearly triple, while cotton exports rise less than 10 percent.

However, these simulation results probably represent an extreme case, because they are based on the large elasticity of substitution, the value of which was assumed rather than estimated. Others have concluded that the tariff was not essential to the cotton textile industry, even as early as the 1820s, because American and British producers specialized in different varieties of cotton goods, implying a much lower elasticity of substitution between them. As Zevin (1971, 126–27) noted, "imports from Britain and the products of New England mills tended to fall into quite distinct product classifications. . . . The imports were largely ginghams, woven in intricate patterns to which the power looms had not yet been adopted. New England power looms were supplying plain weaves—sheeting, shirting, and, somewhat later, twills—usually made of lower count yarns than the British cloths." In other words, Britain concentrated on finer cotton goods, while America specialized in making heavier, standard cloths. As a result, domestic producers may have been insulated from foreign competition by the different characteristics of their products, and any growth in imports would not necessarily come at the expense of domestic production.[40]

This view is supported by the fact that the sharp reduction in the cotton textile tariff in 1846 had surprisingly little impact on the domestic industry. The Walker tariff of 1846 pulled the rug out from under domestic producers when it eliminated the minimum valuation and replaced the nearly 60 percent ad valorem equivalent then in effect with a simple 25 percent ad valorem duty. Imports soared by a factor of three and doubled their share of the market to 15 percent, but, as figure 4.2 shows, there was no decline in domestic output. This implies that there were limited opportunities to substitute foreign products for domestic ones in consumption and therefore suggests that the tariff was not critical to the growth of the industry.[41]

By contrast, the iron industry faced more direct competition from imports. Bar and pig iron were relatively homogeneous products, and imports were a close substitute for domestic production. As a result, the elasticity of substitution between domestic and foreign iron was relatively high, and domestic production very sensitive to fluctuations in import prices. The American iron industry was not as firmly established as the textile industry and suffered under a variety of handicaps that impaired its competitive position, such as limited capitalization and small furnaces, as well as the lack of anthracite coal for smelting.[42] About 40 percent of domestic iron output was dependent upon tariff protection for its existence, according to Davis and Irwin (2008). Of course, the tariff on imported iron harmed other domestic industries, particularly iron-using industries, and raised

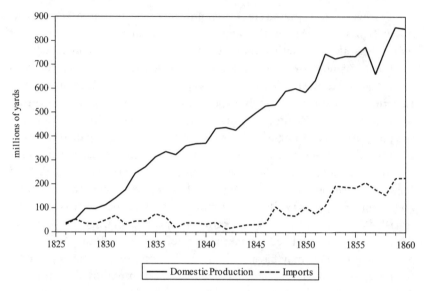

Figure 4.2. Domestic production and imports of cotton
textiles, 1826–1860. (Irwin and Temin 2001, 782.)

the cost of bridges and other infrastructure projects, farm implements, and railroad construction. As noted earlier, the iron industry was divided between pig and bar iron producers and those producing final goods using iron, such as farm equipment. Bar and pig iron producers wanted high levels of protection for their products, but that would have increased the production costs of other industries, harming their competitive position against other foreign producers.

While most manufacturing industries grew steadily throughout the antebellum period, the tariff certainly affected the level of production in some trade-sensitive sectors. "We often hear it said that any considerable reduction from the scale of duties in the present tariff . . . would bring about the disappearance of manufacturing industries, or at least a disastrous check to their development," Taussig (1931, 153) observed. "But the experience of the period before 1860 shows that predictions of this sort have little warrant." The Harley estimate that 17 percent of domestic manufacturing was dependent upon the tariff may be an upper bound if the estimated sensitivity of cotton textile manufactures to imports is too high. Taussig (1931, 61) concluded that, although the conditions for infant industry protection were present in the antebellum period, "little, if anything, was gained by the protection which the United States maintained." In his view, the "ingenuity and inventiveness" of American mechanics and the large and growing domestic market were much more responsible for the expansion of manufacturing during this period than protective tariffs.

In fact, domestic manufacturers complained more about the volatility of prices, which added to the uncertainty of their investment plans, than about the level of imports.[43] Most producers would have preferred stable demand and stable prices rather than simply higher tariffs by themselves, but they sought such tariffs as an imperfect way of stabilizing the market. For example, as figure 4.3 shows, the antebellum iron industry was buffeted by severe shocks, most of which were tied to economic developments in Britain, the leading source of iron imports. The British railway boom in the mid-1840s led to a significant increase in iron prices in both countries and enabled domestic production to double. A commercial crisis in Britain in late 1847 ended the boom, leading to excess capacity and a sharp drop in British export prices. Consequently, imports surged and domestic production fell by nearly half.[44] Domestic producers blamed the Walker tariff reduction and British "dumping" for their distress.

Yet tariffs were incapable of assuring such stability or smoothing import-price fluctuations when large demand and supply shocks in Britain were transmitted to the United States. A higher tariff would increase the domestic price and allow smaller, less efficient producers to survive in the

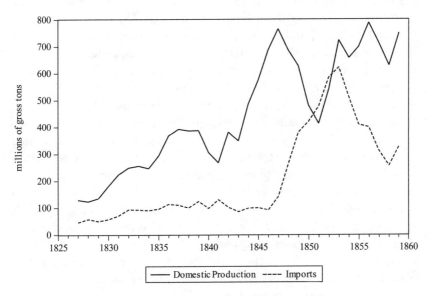

Figure 4.3. Domestic production and imports of pig
iron, 1827–1859. (Davis and Irwin 2008.)

market, but such a tariff would not necessarily stabilize that higher price or insulate producers from macroeconomic fluctuations in general.

Another hotly debated question was whether economic fluctuations were driven by or could be mitigated by import duties. Henry Carey, Hezekiah Niles, and other tariff advocates blamed every economic slump on "free trade" and credited every economic expansion to "protection." Yet most economic downturns were the result of financial corrections after credit markets engaged in excessive lending. The Panic of 1819, the Crisis of 1839, and the Panic of 1857 all had their origins in land speculation fueled by cheap credit. Higher tariffs could do little to protect producers from such boom-bust cycles.

The timing of tariff changes and economic fluctuations made it seem that the two were closely linked, with a lag. The tariff reduction in 1833 was followed by the Crisis of 1839, and the tariff reduction of 1857 coincided with the Panic of 1857 (as we shall see). This pattern seemed to validate those who warned against cutting import duties, but the relationship was different than they suggested. A domestic economic boom would give rise to a large fiscal surplus, which allowed Congress to reduce import duties, but the inevitable end of the boom would result in a recession and a fiscal deficit, putting pressure on Congress to increase import duties to protect manufacturers and generate revenue. Thus, the Panic of 1819 led to the Tariff of 1824, the Crisis of 1839 led to the Tariff of 1842, and the Panic of 1857 led to the Morrill Tariff of 1861. Given the lag between the downturn and the legislation, the economy had usually begun recovering from the downturn by the time the higher tariff had taken effect. This pattern created the illusion of a causal relationship: a lower tariff would lead to hard times, and a high tariff would be followed by good times.

In each case, however, the legislated change in import duties was responding to—not driving—the swings in the economy. The political pressure to respond to a downturn manifested itself in the demand for high protective tariffs because the federal government did not have the ability to stabilize the monetary or financial system, and in fact sometimes destabilized it. By contrast, the Walker tariff of 1846 significantly reduced duties, but was followed by an economic boom, not a recession. While free-trade advocates argued that the lower duties caused the expansion, they were as mistaken as their protectionist counterparts in attributing macroeconomic developments to changes in import duties rather than other causes, monetary and real. In this case, the boom came largely as a result of the California gold rush of 1849 and other factors.

TARIFFS ON THE EVE OF THE CIVIL WAR

After the enactment of the Walker tariff in 1846, the tariff issue faded from the national political debate. From 1845 to 1860, the Democrats controlled at least two of the three institutions—the House, the Senate, and the presidency—responsible for tariff legislation. The Democrats supported the status quo under the Walker tariff and could block any move to change policy. The Whigs never achieved a unified government during this period, and hence they never had the opportunity to raise tariffs.

The nation's strong economic growth during these years was the basis for maintaining existing policies. A wave of economic prosperity followed the Mexican War in 1847 and the California gold rush in 1849 and enabled the government to record large fiscal surpluses, eliminating the need for a higher tariff for revenue purposes and muting demands by import-competing producers for protection. In his memoirs, James Blaine (1884, 196), a leading Republican, recalled, "After 1852 the Democrats had almost undisputed control of the government, and had gradually become a free-trade party. The principles embodied in the tariff of 1846 seemed for the time to be so entirely vindicated and approved that resistance to it ceased, not only among the people but among the protective economists, and even among the manufacturers to a large extent. So general was this acquiescence that in 1856 a protective tariff was not suggested or even hinted by any one of the three parties which presented Presidential candidates."

Having largely defeated the movement for protective tariffs, Democrats reestablished the idea of a "tariff for revenue only" as the guiding principle of trade policy. For example, in December 1854, Democratic President Franklin Pierce declared that a tariff for "revenue, and not protection, may now be regarded as the settled policy of the country."[45] Under this standard, import duties were to be imposed only to raise funds for economical government expenditures; any tariff rates above 20–30 percent were considered excessive, and any significant budget surplus called for a reduction in duties. Because import duties raised almost all of the government's revenue, there was little scope for alternative commercial policies, such as reciprocity agreements with other countries. Indeed, Congress did not encourage the president to undertake negotiations that might lead to such agreements.[46]

As the political debate over tariffs subsided, the divisive issue of slavery came to dominate national politics. Fearing a sectional split over the matter, the Democrats had long suppressed slavery as a topic of political discussion. From 1836 to 1844, a gag rule in the House prevented any debate on the issue, as Democrats voted to table hundreds of antislavery petitions. This containment strategy succeeded until the acquisition of Texas raised the prospect of extending slavery into newly acquired territories. This strained the Missouri Compromise of 1820, which prohibited slavery north of 36° 30′ latitude. President Tyler's invitation to California and New Mexico to enter the union as free states outraged the South, which wanted to maintain a balance between free and slave states in the Senate so that it could have veto power over antislavery legislation. To resolve the standoff, Henry Clay brokered the Compromise of 1850, but this merely postponed the conflict.

Democrats then tried to grant statehood to the Kansas and Nebraska territories. In a concession to the Southern wing of the party, however, the Democrats passed the Kansas-Nebraska Act of 1854, which repealed the Missouri Compromise and allowed the territories to enter with slavery if determined by popular sovereignty. This proved to be a huge political blunder, as its architects underestimated the hostile reaction of the antislavery forces among Northern "free-soil" Democrats and many Whigs. The Kansas-Nebraska Act threw American politics into turmoil, splintering the Democrats, destroying the Whig party, and giving rise to the antislavery Republican party, comprised of old Whigs and abolitionist Northern Democrats. Although the Republicans would later adopt many of the activist government policies advocated by the Whigs, such as a national banking system and protective tariff, they were more of an antislavery coalition without a strong position on trade policy at this stage. Indeed, the Republicans, who managed to capture the House in the midterm election of 1854, made no mention of tariff policy in their 1856 election platform.

Meanwhile, the continued strength of the economy gave the government large fiscal surpluses and allowed the outstanding public debt to be reduced by half. The Walker tariff came under some criticism for having set duties on raw materials too high and thereby harming the manufacturers who used them in production. These two factors led to growing pressure to reduce import duties once again. In December 1853, President Franklin Pierce proposed lower tariffs to reduce government revenue and to allow all raw materials used in manufacturing to enter duty-free. With Congress focused on the controversy over slavery, Pierce repeated his proposal in his annual message of December 1855, noting that "the conspicuous fact that the annual revenue from all sources exceeds by many millions of dollars the amount needed for a prudent and economical administration of public affairs cannot fail to suggest the propriety of an early revision and reduction of the tariff of duties on imports."[47]

In control of the House, the Republican ranks included a large number of former Northern Democrats who opposed the Democrats on slavery but continued to support limited government and lower tariffs. In view of the president's message, the Ways and Means Committee reported a bill in August 1856 that would cut existing rates of duty by about 20 percent, on average. However, the House was unable to act on the bill before adjourning prior to the fall election.

The 1856 election saw the Democrats regain unified control of government, with James Buchanan elected president. The combination of a unified Democratic government and a large fiscal surplus seemed to assure the passage of new tariff legislation. Once the House took up a tariff bill in January 1857, however, members still struggled to focus on import duties because of the raging controversy over slavery. When the House finally turned to tariff policy, the debate focused primarily on the extent to which duties on raw materials should be reduced. Aware that there was no possibility of increasing tariffs on final goods, northern manufacturers supported efforts to cut or eliminate duties on raw materials to reduce their costs of production. Wool manufacturers wanted free wool, and railroad interests demanded free iron. Indeed, the tenor of the debate demonstrated how much advocates of protection had lost political power. "The tone of the discussion was vastly different from that of thirty years before when the bill of 1828 was under consideration," as Stanwood (1903, 2:99) notes. "Protectionists put forward their opinions in the most timid manner; the free traders were bold and radical in the expression of views."

In February 1857, the House approved the bill and sent it to the Senate, which made some minor modifications and passed it just six days later. A conference committee quickly resolved the minor differences between the House and Senate versions, and the bill was signed by Pierce on March 3, 1857, his last day in office.

The Tariff of 1857 allowed the average tariff on dutiable imports to slide from 26 percent in 1856 to less than 20 percent in 1860, about a 20 percent reduction in rates, bringing it to its lowest level in the nineteenth century. The average tariff on total imports fell from 22 percent to 16 percent over the same period. Blaine (1884, 197) later recalled that the legislation did not spark a huge debate and was "well received by the people, and was indeed concurred in by a considerable proportion of the Republican party. . . . Some prominent Republicans, however, remained true to their old Whig traditions, opposed the reduction in duties."

However, the nation's rapid economic growth, which had given rise to large fiscal surpluses and hence the tariff revision, soon came to an end. The new tariff law took effect in July 1857, the peak of the business cycle. In August 1857, the Ohio Life Insurance & Trust Co. collapsed, and the Panic of 1857 had begun. The Panic was attributed to the aggressive financing of western railroads and to land speculation by eastern financial institutions and the sudden collapse in value of those investments. The United States fell into a recession, industrial production dropped nearly 7 percent, and the fiscal surplus quickly turned into a large deficit.[48]

Although the Treasury now recommended increasing tariff rates to raise more revenue, President James Buchanan rejected such a move. In his first annual message to Congress in December 1857, Buchanan stated that the new tariff "has been in operation for so short a period of time and under circumstances so unfavorable to a just development of its results as a revenue measure that I should regard it as inexpedient, at least for the present, to undertake its revision."[49] Taking this cue from the president, the Democratic Congress did not act in 1858.

By the end of 1858, as the deficit continued to grow and federal borrowing continued to increase, the president changed course. Denying that the tariff of 1857 had anything to do with the nation's financial troubles, Buchanan conceded that "it would be ruinous to continue to borrow" to finance the deficits and therefore import duties should be increased. In addition to raising revenue, this would "to some extent increase the confidence of the manufacturing interests and give a fresh impulse to our reviving business." Buchanan also advocated replacing the ad valorem duties with specific duties, which were a "more reliable" source of revenue that would give the American manufacturer "incidental advantages to which he is fairly entitled under a revenue tariff."[50]

This concession marked the return of tariff politics to the nation's capital and gave advocates of protective tariffs a fresh opportunity to reverse the recent reduction in duties. The economic downturn helped the Republicans capture the House in the mid-term election of 1858, and the party, sensing political opportunity, became much more sympathetic to a policy of protection. The tariff was a particularly important issue in Pennsylvania, a key swing state. The tariff on iron goods and coal had been reduced from 30 percent to 24 percent in the Tariff of 1857, a relatively small change, but many people blamed it for the state's deep recession. Henry Carey crowed about the nation's economy being in a "terrific free-trade crisis."[51]

Meanwhile, the Democrats were divided. Southern Democrats resisted any increase in tariffs and preferred to have the government borrow its way through the budgetary shortfall. Northern Democrats, led by those from Pennsylvania who had lost their seats in the 1858 election but returned to complete their term, blocked legislation authorizing additional government borrowing because they wanted to force an upward tariff revision. With Congress locked in stalemate during 1859, Buchanan renewed his plea for higher duties on imports in his December 1859 annual message.

When the new Thirty-seventh Congress open in March 1860, the Republicans had control of the House and came up with their own revenue proposal. Justin Morrill of Vermont presented a bill that substituted specific duties for ad valorem duties and supposedly set them about equal to the rates in the 1846 Walker tariff. Although Morrill rejected the "stale argument of free trade," he insisted that "there are no duties proposed on any article for the simple purpose of protection" and "the average rates of duty upon manufactured articles are not higher, but lower, than they are now." The minority Democrats were powerless to stop the House Republicans from passing the measure that spring. The motivation for the House action was chiefly revenue; indeed, Morrill himself stated that the act "was not asked for, and but rather coldly received by manufacturers, who always and justly fear instability."[52] In the Senate debate, John Sherman noted that when a colleague stated that "the manufacturers are urging and pressing this bill, he says what he must certainly know is not correct. The manufacturers have asked over and over again that they should be let alone"[53] Of course, even if the demands of industrial interests were not the motivating force behind the legislation, they still sought to influence Congress's decisions about the different rates in the bill. Yet, having been cut out of tariff policymaking since the early 1840s, manufacturers were no longer as politically influential as they had once been.[54]

Because Democrats still controlled the Senate, House Republicans had no expectation that the bill would become law. Indeed, Finance Committee Chairman Robert Hunter of Virginia declared the bill "the most monstrous piece of financial legislation that I have ever seen."[55] He did not deny the government's need for revenue, but attacked the bill for reintroducing protective duties. The Democrats narrowly succeeded in tabling the measure until the next session of Congress in December 1860. This may have been a strategic error on their part; had Democrats shown more flexibility, they might have agreed to a temporary return of the 1846 duties to address the government's fiscal deficit in exchange for a return to the 1857 rates after the downturn had passed. As Huston (1987, 265) put it, "Democrats actually had a marvelous opportunity to undermine the

Republican economic appeal and to demonstrate their concern for the material welfare of the northerners." In refusing to consider a return to the 1846 duties to generate revenue, Huston observes, Democrats could have "gutted the Republican charge of the Slave Power conspiracy. . . . Instead the southern Democrats allowed the Republicans to picture southerners as men whose only concern was to guard the economic and social welfare of the peculiar institution" (207). But Southern Democrats strongly opposed any tariff adjustment, and this intransigence gave the Republicans an electoral advantage going into the 1860 election.

Given that the Republican party was still a coalition of Whigs and free-soil Democrats, the Republican platform of 1860 broached the issue of protective tariffs with care, stating that, "while providing revenue for the support of the general government by duties upon imports, sound policy requires such an adjustment of these imports as to encourage the development of the industrial interests of the whole country."[56] Abraham Lincoln, the party's presidential nominee, recognized the political sensitivities of the tariff issue within his party. In October 1859, he described himself to a correspondent from Pennsylvania as "an old Henry Clay tariff Whig," but added that

> I have not changed my views. I believe yet, if we could have a moderate, carefully adjusted, protective tariff, so far acquiesced in, as to not be a perpetual subject of political strife, squabbles, charges, and uncertainties, it would be better for us. Still it is my opinion that, just now, the revival of that question will not advance the cause itself, or the man who revives it. I have not thought much on the subject recently, but my general impression is that the necessity for a protective tariff will ere long force its old opponents to take it up; and then its old friends can join in and establish it on a more firm and durable basis. We, the Old Whigs, have been entirely beaten out on the tariff question; and we shall not be able to re-establish the policy, until the absence of it, shall have demonstrated the necessity for it, in the minds of men heretofore opposed to it.[57]

Thus, Lincoln sought to downplay the tariff in the campaign and did not even want a party plank on the matter. As he wrote in May 1860, "The tariff question ought not to be agitated in the Chicago [Republican] convention" because Republicans were still a fragile coalition of pro-tariff Whigs and anti-tariff Democrats.[58]

Although slavery dominated the 1860 election campaign, Lincoln's supporters highlighted his tariff views in the key swing states of Pennsylvania, Illinois, Indiana, and New Jersey. In particular, Pennsylvania proved to be the "keystone state" because of its large number of electoral votes, second only to New York. And here, Huston (1987, 267) notes, "the economic issue of protectionism was absolutely essential in transforming Pennsylvania from a Democratic to a Republican state." James Blaine (1884, 207) attributed Lincoln's victory to his position on the tariff: "Had the Republicans failed to carry Pennsylvania, there can be no doubt that Mr. Lincoln would have been defeated. . . . The tariff therefore had a controlling influence not only in decoding the contest for political supremacy but in that more momentous struggle which was to involve the fate of the Union." The Panic of 1857 renewed the salience of economic issues that had been of minor importance during the sectional controversy of the 1850s, giving the Republicans an electoral boost.

Meanwhile, deeply divided between Northern and Southern factions over slavery, the Democrats had two candidates running for president. Although the combined popular vote for the Democrats was greater than for Lincoln, the split allowed the Republicans to take the White House. Just as in 1856, when the Whig/Republican split allowed a Democrat to be elected with a plurality of the vote, the Democratic split in 1860 allowed a Republican to be elected by a plurality. Lincoln received less than 40 percent of the national vote, but won a comfortable majority in the Electoral College.

Because of Lincoln's position on slavery, his victory immediately led South Carolina to secede from the Union, followed by several other states in the lower South. Even though the Democrats retained control of the Senate until the new Congress convened in the fall of 1861, Southern senators did not return to Washington when the old Congress reconvened in December 1860. The loss of a dozen Democrats put the chamber in the hands of the Republicans and Northern Democrats, thus paving the way for the passage of the Morrill tariff. The Northern Democrats favored a tariff increase and dominated a select committee appointed to consider the legislation. In February 1861, after amending the House bill extensively, the Senate passed the measure by a vote of 25–14. The House agreed to all but one of the 156 amendments, and the Senate concurred, whereupon President Buchanan, a Democrat, signed it on March 2, just two days before Lincoln's inauguration.[59] The circumstances of its passage undermine the claim that the tariff rather than slavery was the real cause of the Civil War: The South did not secede because of the Morrill tariff; the Morrill tariff was enacted because the South seceded. In addition, the bill was signed by Democrat James Buchanan, not Republican Abraham Lincoln.

At the same time, the Morrill tariff went well beyond its supposed purpose of restoring the duties of the Walker tariff. Many of the specific duties were set significantly higher than the equivalent ad valorem duties under the old tariff. By one calculation, the average tariff on dutiable imports rose from 19 percent under the Tariff of 1857 to 27 percent under the Morrill tariff.[60] In addition, the failure to tax coffee or tea meant that it was not really conceived as a revenue measure. Some Republicans claimed that the tariff was not high enough, while Northern Democrats thought it was much too high. Thaddeus Stevens (R-PA) complained that the House bill had been changed in the Senate and "it is no longer a protective tariff," while William Cullen Bryant, the Republican editor of the *New York Evening Post*, wrote that "the new Tariff bill effects a complete revolution in our commercial system, returning by one huge step, backward to the old doctrine of protection."[61]

While Lincoln clearly wanted more revenue to address the budget deficit, imposing high protective tariffs was not his primary concern. In February 1861, as he traveled to Washington for the inauguration, Lincoln stated, "The condition of the Treasury at this time would seem to render an early revision of the tariff indispensable. The Morrill tariff bill now pending before Congress may or may not become a law. I am not posted as to its particular provisions, but if they are generally satisfactory, and the bill shall now pass, there will be an end of the matter for the present."[62] The president-elect also professed to be open-minded about tariff policy: "I do not understand this subject in all its multiform bearings, but I promise you that I will give it my closest attention, and endeavor to comprehend it more fully."[63] Much to the consternation of Henry Carey and other tariff proponents, Lincoln appointed Salmon Chase, a former Democrat who had favored low tariffs throughout his career, as Treasury secretary. Of course, the new president entered office confronting more serious matters than whether import duties should be raised or lowered by some modest amount. The nation was in the midst of an unprecedented crisis.

THE CIVIL WAR

On April 12, 1861, just eleven days after the Morrill tariff took effect, Confederate forces bombarded Fort Sumter, a federal installation in Charleston, South Carolina. This marked the beginning of the Civil War. Although historians still debate the various factors driving the South's decision to leave the Union, the sectional tensions arising from tariff policy, as we have seen, had diminished considerably in the quarter-century before 1860. With the Compromise of 1833, the South had essentially won the antebellum battle over tariffs. In 1860, the average tariff on dutiable imports was less than 20 percent, and northern manufacturers had largely given up hope of enacting much higher ones. The Morrill tariff of 1861, partly a fiscal adjustment to the Panic of 1857, was enacted only because the South had left Congress. For these reasons, one cannot conclude that the South broke away because of a dispute over tariff policy.

Instead, as historians have made clear, the Civil War was about slavery. The election of the Republicans posed an immediate—or at least a perceived—threat to the existence of slavery. For the South, the economic stake in slavery was enormous, far exceeding that of import duties. By 1860, the economic value of slave holdings was about $2.7 billion, much greater than the combined value of capital invested in railroads and manufacturing. In the seven leading cotton states, nearly a third of the income of whites was derived from slave labor. The only real danger to this system came from the North and the growing political strength of the abolitionist movement, which sought to change existing property rights by defining slaves as free people rather than property.[64]

The Civil War was the nation's bloodiest and most destructive conflict. The economic cost of the war amounted to $6.6 billion (in 1860 dollars), or nearly 150 percent of 1860's GDP.[65] The casualties were horrific: roughly 625,000 killed and another 400,000 wounded. Naturally, the conflict severely disrupted foreign trade. Exports, which mostly came from the South, collapsed from about 7 percent of GDP in 1860 to less than 2 percent in 1865. Imports also fell sharply during the war.

The financial requirements of the war put huge demands on the revenue system of the federal government. The Morrill tariff was not designed to raise enough money to fight a major war. Once the staggering costs of the conflict became apparent, Treasury Secretary Chase reluctantly recommended further increases in import duties to raise revenue. In July 1861, the Ways and Means Committee reported a new tariff bill that added coffee and tea to the dutiable list and increased taxes on luxuries, such as sugar. With little debate, the Republican Congress passed the bill in August. With the government's budgetary shortfall growing by the day, Congress increased these duties yet again in December. These measures helped boost the average tariff on dutiable imports from 19 percent in 1861 to 36 percent in 1862.

Despite these tariff increases, it quickly became apparent that import duties could not even come close to financing the North's enormous wartime expenditures. As a result, the Internal Revenue Act of 1862 imposed a wide array of new domestic taxes, including an income tax, an inheritance tax, and high taxes on domestic production of goods and services, such as railroads and telegraphs. James Blaine (1884, 1:433) described the Internal Revenue Act of 1862 as

> one of the most searching, thorough, comprehensive systems of taxation ever devised by any Government. Spirituous and malt liquors and tobacco were relied upon for a very large share of revenue. . . . Manufactures of cotton, wool, flax, hemp, iron, steel, wood, stone, earth, and every other material were taxed three percent. Banks, insurance and railroad companies, telegraph companies, and all other corporations were made to pay tribute. The butcher paid thirty cents for every beef slaughtered, ten cents for every hog, five cents for every sheep. Carriages, billiard-tables, yachts, gold and silver plate, and all other articles of luxury were levied upon heavily. Every profession and every calling, except the ministry of religion, was included within the far-reaching provisions of the law and subjected to tax for license. Bankers and pawn-brokers, lawyers and horse-dealers, physicians and confectioners, commercial brokers and peddlers, proprietors of theaters and jugglers on the street, were indiscriminately summoned to aid the National Treasury."

At the same time as it imposed these domestic taxes, Congress also undertook a major upward revision of the duties in the tariff schedule. The main purpose of this revision was to equalize the tax burden on imports and domestic producers; since the latter were now being directly taxed, the former had to be taxed as well so that there would be no discrimination in favor of foreign producers. In supporting the bill, Justin Morrill (R-VT) stated, "It will be indispensable for us to revise the tariff on foreign imports, so far as it may be seriously disturbed by any internal duties—on some things the tax proposed is more than the present tariff— and to make proper reparation, otherwise we shall destroy the goose that lays the golden egg. . . . If we bleed manufacturers, we must see to it that the proper tonic is administered at the same time."[66] Thaddeus Stevens (R-PA) simply stated, "We intend to impose an additional duty on imports equal to articles. It was done by way of compensation to domestic manufacturers against foreign importers."[67]

The bill, which reduced the number of items on the free list and raised duties on most imports, was rushed through Congress with little debate.

Supporters of the measure, sometimes called the second Morrill tariff, argued that this "war tariff" would be temporary. In July 1862, the large Republican majorities in the House easily passed it by a vote of 69–36. The Senate followed and, after a brief conference committee to resolve the differences, President Lincoln signed the act later in the month.

As expenditures continued to grow and the fiscal deficit continued to expand, Congress was forced to enact additional revenue measures in June 1864, including an enormous increase in internal taxation, another large hike in import duties, and the authorization for further federal borrowing. Once again, Morrill argued that an increase in tariff rates was needed to compensate domestic producers for the heavy burden of domestic taxes levied upon them:

> Its primary object is to increase the revenue upon importations from abroad, and at the same time to shelter and nurse our domestic products, from which we draw much the largest amount of revenue, so that the aggregate amount shall not be diminished through the substitution of foreign articles for those which we have been accustomed to find at home. . . . When we impose a tax of 5 per cent upon our manufactures and increase the tariff to the same extent upon foreign manufactures, we leave them upon the same relative footing they were at the start, and neither has cause of complaint.[68]

Once again, the legislation was passed quickly, with little debate. As Stanwood (1903, 2:129) reports: "The objects of the measure were so well understood, the methods of accomplishing what was desired were so fully agreed upon, and the majority of the dominant party was so large, that the debates upon it were quite uninteresting and almost as brief as a discussion of a private pension bill." The House and Senate discussed the tariff bill for two days each and passed it with overwhelming majorities. Another smaller increase in selected import duties, on goods ranging from cotton textiles to liquors, was enacted in April 1865. The 1864 and 1865 legislation helped push the average tariff on dutiable imports up to 48 percent in 1865.

These wartime tariff increases were enacted with little opposition. Although some Northern Democrats griped about the high level of taxation—the burden on consumers and merchants, and the "crude and defective" approach taken in the hastily drafted legislation—the necessity for additional revenue was so obvious, and the Republicans so dominated

Congress, that opposition was pointless. In Taussig's view (1931, 166), Congress had "neither the time nor disposition to inquire critically in the meaning and effect of any proposed scheme of rates. The easiest and quickest plan was to impose the duties which the domestic producers suggested as necessary for their protection. Not only during the war, but for several years after it, all feeling of opposition to high import duties almost entirely disappeared."

Despite these heavy tax increases, the revenue they raised covered only one-fifth of total federal expenditures during the war; most of the spending was financed by borrowing. Consequently, the need to service the enormous public debt would make it very difficult to reduce tariffs and other domestic taxes after the war. In fact, the import duties enacted in 1864 essentially remained in place until 1883. As we shall see, the government's pressing revenue requirements and Congress's reluctance to dispense with a program favored by vested interests, contributed to the maintenance of high import duties for many decades after the war. Another consequence of the Civil War was that the federal government was never again as dependent upon import duties as it had been in the antebellum period. Before the war, about 90 percent of federal income came from customs revenue; after the war, the scope of domestic taxation, particularly excise taxes on alcohol and tobacco, had expanded so much that only about half of federal revenue came from customs duties.

What were President Lincoln's views on the tariff during this time? Although he is often portrayed as a strong supporter of protective tariffs, Lincoln's presidential papers show that he had virtually no interest in tariffs other than as a way of paying for the war. "After he reached Washington to assume the presidency in 1861, Lincoln rarely considered the tariff other than as a method to raise money," Luthin (1944, 629) observes.[69] Lincoln did not care about the indiscriminate protection enacted during this period as a way of encouraging industry; for him, the tariff was simply a means to an end, a way of mobilizing the financial resources necessary to win the war. Henry Carey, "who had repeated consultations with Lincoln during the war, was keenly disappointed at the lack of attention manifested toward the [tariff] question by the President, who was always so deeply absorbed in the political and military aspects of the war," Luthin (1944, 629) notes. Indeed, in early 1865, Carey bitterly wrote, "Protection made Mr. Lincoln president. Protection has given him all the success he has achieved, yet has he never, so far as I can recollect, bestowed upon her a single word of thanks."

NORTH-SOUTH TRADE WARFARE

With the formation of the Confederacy, the South was now free to choose its own tariff schedule. The Confederate Constitution, adopted in March 1861, mandated an explicit "tariff for revenue only" policy. The Constitution gave the Confederate Congress the power "To lay and collect taxes, duties, and imposts and excises, for revenue necessary to pay the debts, provide for the common defense, and carry on the Government of the Confederate States; but no bounties shall be granted from the treasury; nor shall any duties or taxes on importations from foreign nations be laid to promote or foster any branch of industry, and all duties, imposts, and excises shall be uniform throughout the Confederate States." Ironically, unlike the US Constitution, the Confederate Constitution permitted export taxes if passed with a two-thirds majority.[70]

The first Confederate tariff schedule was simply the one that was in effect for the United States in November 1860, which was the Tariff of 1857. The Confederacy did not set its own duties until May 1861, when it modeled its tariff code after the Walker tariff of 1846, but with a maximum of 25 percent duties in Schedule A, 20 percent duties in Schedule B, and so on, dropping five percentage points in each classification. The tariff on key manufactured goods (iron, textiles, and shoes) was set at 15 percent, and most imported products were assessed with duties of 10 or 15 percent. Low duties were imposed on war materiel, such as arms, ammunition, and gunpowder. The duties also applied to goods coming from the North, although the South permitted duty-free imports of breadstuffs from the Midwest to temper the region's dismay at the South's secession.

Free-trade sentiment was still very strong in the South. In fact, the Confederate House voted to abolish the tariff completely by a vote of 67–16 in May 1862, but the proposal died in the Senate.[71] Having broken away from the Union, however, many Southerners now began to see the benefits of protecting local manufacturers and establishing the industries necessary to fight the war and preserve its independence.[72] Thus, the South could not avoid having a debate about its own protective tariff strategy. Fearing that the war would end quickly and their businesses would be ruined once northern and foreign competition returned, Southern manufacturers were reluctant to make significant investments in production facilities. While the Confederate House considered a proposal to use import duties to encourage investment in iron production, it did not pursue the matter.

The Confederacy faced much graver financial problems than the North because its economy was much smaller and more dependent upon foreign commerce, giving it a limited domestic tax base on which to finance wartime expenditures. In his first report, Confederate Treasury Secretary Christopher Memminger expected that a 12.5 percent average import duty would raise $25 million in revenue annually. In fact, the Confederacy raised just $3.4 million in customs duties over the entire war. During the war, the Confederate government collected only $258 million in taxes and loans but spent $1.5 billion, resorting to monetary inflation to make up the difference.[73]

The South's one economic advantage was Britain's dependence on its cotton, but Southern leaders were uncertain about how to exploit this. Some thought that the South should exercise its economic leverage and restrict cotton exports, forcing Britain to support the Confederate cause. Others believed that cotton exports should be encouraged to maximize export earnings and allow the Confederacy to import critical supplies from abroad. Whatever the merits of these alternatives, the Confederate authorities never settled on a consistent strategy. At first, the Confederacy sought to restrict exports of cotton to put pressure on Britain to provide military support. But cotton planters resisted any mandatory scheme to cut production, and so it was left to state governments and private citizens to enforce an informal embargo on cotton exports. This was a remarkable success: cotton exports shrank from 3.6 million bales in 1860 to just 10,129 bales in 1861, even though domestic production remained high. Yet the embargo was completely ineffective in influencing British policy: Lancashire textile producers, long concerned about their excessive dependence on US cotton, had been able to diversify their sources of supply to India, Egypt, and Brazil. The South's embargo also came at a time when there was a glut of cotton on the world market.[74]

Having played a large part in driving the South toward secession, cotton planters failed to support the Confederate government with the resources it needed to fight the North. Plantation owners rejected any reduction in the production or export of cotton as part of the war effort, insisting "on their right to grow unlimited amounts of cotton; to retain it for sale whenever they chose; and to sell it whenever, and to whomever, they chose."[75] For example, the taxation of exports was an obvious source of revenue, an option left open by the Confederate Constitution. In February 1861, the South imposed an export tax of one-eighth of a cent per pound on raw cotton in the hope that it would raise tens of millions of dollars. But this minuscule tax amounted to just 1.5 percent of the specie value of cotton. The tax was so widely ignored and so easily evaded that it was only collected on 5 percent of cotton exports and yielded just $28,000 to the Confederate treasury.[76]

The Confederate government also considered creating a marketing board that would buy the entire cotton harvest and negotiate foreign sales itself, but this option was ruled out as being too expensive. Planters also refuse to link Confederate bonds to cotton sales abroad and resisted attempts to divert slaves from the cotton fields into other uses, such as food production or military service. Instead, they simply continued to produce cotton.[77]

Thus, all efforts by the South to restrict cotton exports were opposed or would likely have failed for domestic political reasons. Plantation owners liked to boast about the economic power of "King Cotton," but they were afraid of actually exercising that power. They feared that any export restraint would promote the cultivation of cotton in other regions of the world, undermining the sale of American cotton after the war. Producers hoped that the mere threat of withholding southern cotton supplies would scare Britain into providing support, but it failed to do so.

The North's naval blockade was another key reason for the South's failure to benefit from any export leverage. In April 1861, President Lincoln announced that southern ports would be blockaded from Virginia to Texas. Of course, the blockade was never perfectly enforced: the capture rate on in-bound and out-bound vessels was only about 35 percent during 1862–65, higher for sailing ships and lower for steam ships. Although the blockade was porous, the effort significantly raised the cost of foreign trade to the South despite the efforts of blockade runners, who did their best to evade the Union navy. Over the course of the Civil War, the South is estimated to have exported only 0.5 million bales of cotton to Europe, despite producing 6.8 million bales. Nearly a million bales were smuggled, captured, or sold to the North, another half a million used in the South, and nearly two million kept as inventory and sold after the war. Still, the high price of cotton in Britain made for large profits for those who successfully evaded the blockade; more than 90 percent of steam powered vessels that ran the blockade attempted a second voyage.[78]

Of course, the war was a disaster for the South. By 1865, its economy lay in ruins. The destruction of wealth and income was enormous. In 1860, the South's per capita income was 72 percent of the national average; in 1880 it was 51 percent of the national average. The South took nearly a century to recover its prewar economic position relative to the North.[79]

While the Civil War had a temporary impact on foreign trade, the impact on US trade policy was long-lasting. The "temporary" duties that were imposed during the war became the new status quo. Not only had special interests arisen that wanted to maintain those tariffs, but the South was now a much weakened force in American politics and lost the influence that it previously had over the country's tariff policy. As a result, the wartime tariffs would remain in place for many decades to come.

PART II

Restriction

CHAPTER FIVE

The Failure of Tariff Reform, 1865–1890

The Civil War marked a major shift in US trade policy. With import duties having been pushed up to high levels during the war, the Republicans succeeded in constructing a powerful coalition that made it extremely difficult to reduce them after the war. While Democrats advocated tariff reforms, they were often politically divided and failed to gain unified control of the government for nearly thirty years. This chapter examines how the high-tariff regime became entrenched after the Civil War and explores some of the economic consequences of the protection given to import-competing industries.

THE STRUGGLE FOR POST-WAR TARIFF REFORM

The postwar Congress was overwhelmed by the enormously complex problems surrounding reconstruction, particularly the military occupation of the South and the reintegration of the Confederacy into the Union. Although the high tariffs imposed during the war had been widespread and indiscriminate, legislators had little time or inclination to consider comprehensive tax reform. Furthermore, the Civil War left the federal government with enormous debts to pay. The outstanding public debt rose from $65 million in 1860 to nearly $2.7 billion in 1865, about 30 percent of GDP.[1] The servicing of this debt precluded any immediate tariff changes that would significantly reduce customs revenue.

Still, with military expenditures having fallen sharply after the war, the federal government was able to run large budget surpluses through the 1870s and 1880s. These fiscal surpluses permitted the rapid retirement of debt and kept the idea of tariff reductions on the agenda. With time, this would put Congress under pressure to ease the tax burden on producers and consumers. The Republicans planned to reduce internal taxes first and then address import duties. Reform of internal taxes was achieved gradually in various pieces of legislation stretching from 1866 to 1872, when the income tax was finally abolished. Because import duties had been imposed to compensate for domestic taxes on producers, the prolonged phase out of domestic taxes meant that tariff adjustments were also postponed.

By leaving high import duties untouched for so long, manufacturers received an unprecedented degree of nominal protection. For example, in 1864, Congress raised the tariff on imported pig iron from $6 per ton to $9 per ton, in part to compensate for the domestic production tax of $2 per ton. Although the production tax was eliminated in 1866, the $9 duty remained in place. The postwar deflation of decline in prices also boosted the ad valorem equivalent of specific duties. About 60 percent of the 815 dutiable items in the tariff schedule were covered by specific or compound duties. Import prices fell about 16 percent from 1867 to 1870, resulting in higher ad valorem equivalents of these duties.[2] Consequently, the average tariff on dutiable imports rose from 36 percent in 1864 to 47 percent by 1870, about where it remained for the next forty years.

Many domestic producers, having been built up behind this tariff wall, feared the return of foreign competition and stood ready to oppose any significant reduction in the protection they were receiving. Many industries grew as a result of military contracts and had "become accustom[ed] to large and easy profits even when [their production] methods were inefficient," as Beale (1930, 277) writes. These producers not only wanted to keep existing duties in place, but wanted to increase them to compensate for the reduction in federal procurement spending.

Given the difficulty of scaling back the Civil War tax system while also providing enough revenue to finance the debt, Congress created a special commission in March 1865 to give advice on revenue collection, tax reform, and debt management. In its January 1866 report, the commission recommended keeping the income tax and import tariffs in place while abolishing all direct taxes on manufacturing production. Congress soon began reducing many direct taxes as suggested by the commission's report. But instead of simply maintaining import duties, Justin Morrill (R-VT) reported a bill in June 1866 that would increase some of them, particularly for wool. This sparked the first contentious debate on postwar tariff policy and produced a replay of the antebellum debate over protective versus revenue duties. Northern Republicans lined up in support of protection. Rufus Spaulding (R-OH) announced, "I wish to say I am in favor now and at all times in this House of the highest rate of protection to

American industry in every shape in which you may bring it forward."[3] "I am willing and anxious to go for the very highest duties that are necessary to protect every branch of our industry," Samuel McKee (R-KY) concurred. "We need protective duties not for revenue alone but in order that we may build up on our own soil manufacturing establishments by which we may manufacture everything that is necessary for our use, so that our own people may not be dependent upon foreign countries for their supplies."[4]

Meanwhile, Democrats and liberal Republicans attacked the bill as contrary to the goal of relieving the burden of heavy taxation and reducing the "temporary" wartime duties. "You are trying to inaugurate a protective system," Francis Le Blond (D-OH) complained. "Years ago the people of the United States settled this question, and they settled it in favor of a tariff for revenue alone."[5] John Kasson (R-IA) agreed and warned that if Congress shifted from a tariff for revenue to a tariff for protection, special interests would come to have a disproportionate influence on policy: "I know very well that the iron interest, the cotton interest, the glass interest, and many others, can send gentleman here to advocate their interests, and that they may be heard before the committee and may fill our lobbies; but the great interest of the consumers of the country is not organized into a system of mutual protective associations. That interest must be heard by members on this floor who seek to protect it. It must be heard here as much as these organizations of capital."[6]

Given the solid Republican control of Congress, the Democratic opposition was largely irrelevant. The South was still not represented in Congress, and Northern Democrats were weak and discredited because of their antiwar stance and sympathy for the South. In July 1866, the House passed the controversial Morrill proposal by a vote of 94–53; Republicans voted 87–28 in favor, and Democrats voted 25–7 against. Two days later, the Senate engaged in a spirited debate over the bill. Because of the late session, the Republicans were split over whether to stay and act on the bill or postpone consideration until after the fall election. With the support of Democrats, the Senate voted to table the measure until the next session. Although the bid to raise rates failed, the episode demonstrated that reducing import duties would be a difficult task.

Recognizing that it could benefit from further advice on postwar financial matters, Congress created the position of the special commissioner of the revenue in 1866. David A. Wells, the chairman of the earlier revenue commission, was appointed to a four-year term. Although tariff policy was viewed as the most politically sensitive postwar economic issue, Republicans believed that Wells—a well-known supporter of protection and a friend of the tariff activist Henry Carey—was a safe appointment. However, after having spent time in Washington, Wells was shocked to see that powerful special interests operating behind the scenes were having an inordinate influence on government policy. He was further surprised by the fact that politicians served those interests for what he saw as selfish political reasons and not for the best interests of the country. In July 1866, in private correspondence, Wells remarked, "I have changed my ideas respecting tariffs and protection very much since coming to Washington. . . . I am utterly disgusted with the rapacity and selfishness which I have seen displayed by Penn[sylvania] people, and some from other sections on this subject."[7]

In his first report as special commissioner, Wells (1867, 8) argued that "looking at the tariff solely and exclusively from a revenue point of view, few or no reasons can be adduced in support of a demand for any extensive changes in its existing rates and provisions." But he believed that the structure of the tariff was "exceedingly complicated and difficult of comprehension" and required revision due to the many haphazard changes made during the war. Wells recommended reducing duties on raw materials and maintaining existing duties on final goods. In his view, the provision of inexpensive raw materials was "essential to the prosperity of the manufacturing industry of the United States" and yet that principle was "almost entirely disregarded under the existing tariff" (34).

He then entered into dangerous political territory by criticizing the "excessive" duties of the recent House bill. Wells (1867, 42) argued that the bill would have reduced imports "to a point beyond what it would be either safe or expedient" and that it was "exorbitant in its rates, tending to further inflation of prices, destructive of revenue and of what little of foreign commerce yet remains, and prejudicial to the general interests of the country." He added that "admissions have been made to him by representatives of many of the producing interests of the country likely to be affected by this bill, that the rates of duty imposed by it are higher than are necessary for the adequate protection of their interests."

Wells (1867, 40–41) tried to anticipate the objections of Republicans by insisting that the issue confronting the country "is not one legitimately involving any discussion of the principles of either protection or free trade." On that question, the policy of the nation was "definitely settled. . . . With a tariff averaging nearly fifty per cent in its rates, free trade in any form is simply an impossibility." Instead, trying to frame the issue as one of restoring normal business conditions and stimulating the economy, Wells made two observations: "First, that the present tariff rates are already of an extreme character, and that any legislation in the same direction must necessarily soon reach a limit, unless the country is prepared to adopt the policy of entire prohibition and commercial non-intercourse; and, secondly, that if a tariff whose average rates (nearly fifty per cent) are higher than have ever been levied by the United States, or by any other civilized nation in modern times, fails to be reasonably protective, the remedy should be sought in remov[ing] the causes which have neutralized its protection, rather than by increasing the average of the duties."

To head off another bid to increase import duties, Wells and Treasury Secretary Hugh McCulloch collaborated in drafting a new schedule of tariff rates for Congress's consideration. They proposed modifying the House bill that was then before the Senate by reducing import duties toward their prewar levels. In particular, they aimed to provide tax relief for final-goods producers by slashing duties on raw materials they used, such as scrap iron, coal, lumber, hemp and flax, while maintaining the high existing duties on final products.[8]

In January 1867, the Senate accepted this proposal without much controversy, and it easily passed. However, the revision stumbled in the House. As the lame-duck session was drawing to a close, Morrill tried to rally support for it, arguing that it was better than no change at all. Although a majority supported the bill, a super-majority vote to suspend the rules and bring the bill to the House floor failed just short of the two-thirds needed, and the bill died. This proved to be a crucial missed opportunity for postwar tariff revision.

Wells was not just disheartened but radicalized by these events. "I have been intending to write you for some time past and tell you confidentially of the change which my recent intimate connection with tariff legislation has produced in my opinions, in respect to free-trade and protection," he confided to a friend. "Frankly, I have become thoroughly disgusted with the extreme views, which I once, and as you know quite recently, thought it heresy to disbelieve."[9] Now dismayed by what he saw as gross inequities in the tariff system, Wells kept his views to himself and was not yet prepared to publicly renounce his previous support of protection. Aware that his report had raised questions about his commitment to that policy, he tried to reassure Henry Carey by complaining of "a most persistent and determined effort on the part of some to draw me in with the ranks of the free traders. . . . You may be assured . . . that I have not turned a free trader."[10]

After Congress's failure to reform the tariff in 1867, Wells largely avoided the issue in his second report, which focused on internal taxes.

In his third report, published in January 1869, Wells (1869a, 23) bluntly observed that the matter of tariffs "involves more of prejudice and of opinion founded on private self-interest than almost any other policy issue facing the government." He continued, "It is important to recognize the fact that under the existing financial condition of the country, the old-time issues between the advocates of free trade on the one hand, and protection on the other, have ceased to be of any real practical importance—inasmuch as in the arrangement of a tariff with a view to revenue, the requirements of the government must certainly, for the present, necessitate so high an average of duties as to afford all that can be reasonably asked for on the grounds of protection."

But Wells (1869a, 46) insisted that there was considerable scope for tariff reductions, singling out salt, pig iron, and lumber as striking illustrations in which "a duty originally levied for revenue and protection, or as an offset to internal taxes, has been continued long after its object has been fully attained, for the interest of the few, but to the detriment of the many." Wells contended that the higher duties on pig iron simply padded the profits of domestic producers: "The manufacturers of pig iron have, to the detriment of the rolling-mill interest, and to the expense of every consumer of iron from a rail to a ploughshare, and from a boiler plate to a tenpenny nail, realized continued profits which have hardly any parallel in the history of legitimate industry." In his view, a tariff reduction would reduce prices paid by consumers and profits received by protected businesses without diminishing domestic production.

The main theme of Wells's critique was that tariffs on intermediate goods reduced the protection afforded to producers of final goods. Wells (1869a, 35) faulted the existing tariff for trying to provide "indiscriminate and universal protection" across all industries, arguing that universal protection was impossible because the finished product of one industry was the raw material of another. As he explained, "coal is the finished product of the miner, but the raw material for the manufacture of pig iron; pig iron, in turn, becomes the raw material for the manufacturer of bar iron; bar iron for machinery, machinery for textile fabrics, textile fabrics for clothing, and clothing for the laborer, whose efforts in the single department of agriculture determine the national prosperity." Thus, an import tax imposed on a raw material was "equivalent to a reduction in protection to the produce which results from its manufacture." Unless the entire impact of a tariff was fully examined, Wells (1869a, 36) noted, "It never can be known, whether the benefit that may follow from the imposition or increase of a particular duty will not be more than counterbalanced by the injury that the same duty may inflict indirectly."

Wells was essentially taking sides, trying to help producers of final goods as opposed to producers of raw materials and intermediate goods. Wells (1869a, 34) went on to make a scathing charge:

> In carrying out the idea of protection, but one rule for guidance would appear to have been adopted for legislation, viz, the assumption that whatever rate of duty could be shown to be for the advantage of any private interest, the same would prove equally advantageous to the interests of the whole country. The result has been a tariff based upon small issues rather than upon any great national principle; a tariff which is unjust and unequal; which needlessly enhances prices; which takes far more, indirectly, from the people than is received into the Treasury; which renders an exchange of domestic for foreign commodities nearly impossible; which necessitates the continual exportation of obligations of national indebtedness and of the precious metals; and which, while professing to protect American industry, really, in many cases, discriminates against it.

Wells (1869a, 49) again denied that he was attacking the system of protection or advocating free trade. "The question of tariff revision has nothing whatever to do with either the theory or the practice of free trade or protection," although he could not help adding that "protection implies help and defense to the weak; but in the instances cited the help has been given to the strong at the expense of the weak." Wells (1869a, 80) concluded that the current tariff system "is in many respects injurious and destructive, and does not afford to American industry that stimulus and protection which is claimed as its chief merit."

This provocative report sparked an outcry in Congress and a firestorm among tariff advocates. Henry Carey compared him to Judas and insinuated that Wells had been bought by British capitalists after visiting the country in 1867. Some members of Congress tried to stop publication of his report and terminate payment of his salary. The House Committee on Manufactures launched an investigation and complained that "they do not conceive the promulgation of special theories to have been part of the duty imposed upon the commissioner." The Republican majority accused him of using "fallacious and unreliable" statistics on the cost of pig iron production and therefore reaching conclusions that were "grievously in error" and would "subvert the protective policy of our country."[11] William D. Kelley (R-PA), known as "Pig Iron Kelley" for his staunch support of iron and steel interests, repeatedly attacked Wells and charged that his statistics had been "culled and marshaled . . . [so] as to lead to conclusions false, delusive, and damaging to our country."[12]

In his final report of December 1869, Wells (1869b, 71–72) responded by noting that "it has hitherto been impossible for anyone to suggest any reduction or modification [in import duties] whatever, looking to the abatement of prices artificially maintained in the interest of special industries, without being immediately assailed with accusations of corrupt and unpatriotic motives." The goal of such slander was to "prevent discussion and . . . divert the attention of the people from the real and true issues." It was "unquestionably true" that the American people supported tariffs that protected established industries employing large numbers of workers. But "when it can be proved that any tax thus laid upon the community *is not necessary* to maintain a protected industry in a moderate degree of prosperity," he argued, "if it be one which yields its profits mainly to the capitalist, instead of dividing the returns equitably among large classes of skilled or ordinary operative[s]; and especially if it be one whose product is to become in turn the raw material of other and still more extensive industries, so that the enhancement of price at the bottom is repeated through the several successive stages, and thus becomes a tax not only on the final consumer but on each intermediate producer," then the tariff schedule should be reexamined.

Wells (1869b, 72) asserted that the prevailing tariff reflected "the will of highly organized and aggressive associations of capitalists." He again singled out pig iron as "a conspicuous example" of where "excessive and unnecessary duties have been imposed and maintained, with a view of enhancing the costs of articles indispensable to many other branches of production." Wells (1869b, 83) speculated that lower pig iron prices would enable the shipbuilding industry to sell an additional six hundred iron ships, requiring the employment of thirty thousand workers, "more than two and a half times as many [as] are at present directly engaged in the manufacture of pig iron."

Wells's outspoken reports sparked a national debate but had no immediate impact on legislation. After the failure of the Wells proposal in 1867, various tariff bills floundered in Congress in 1868 and 1869. But stalwart protectionists, such as "Pig Iron" Kelley and Gen. Robert Schenck from Ohio, objected to any reduction in protective duties, convincing the presi-

dent to abolish Wells's position and thereby stop the publication of troublesome and politically inconvenient reports. Yet the renewed controversy
about the tariff led to growing concerns among Republicans. Although the
new Republican president, Ulysses S. Grant, initially advised Congress to
postpone any action on the tariff, party members felt pressure to reduce
some duties as a concession to those demanding tax relief for consumers.
In particular, Midwestern Republicans still had some residual anti-tariff
views from the antebellum period, and moderates, such as James Garfield
of Ohio and William Allison of Iowa, wanted lower duties to safeguard the
protective system against its political opponents.

In early 1870, the Republican Congress finally undertook major tax
reform by abolishing inheritance taxes, phasing out the income tax, and
considering changes to the tariff. The motivation was more political than
economic: they feared that a failure to address the issue would give a political advantage to Democrats, who would make much more drastic tariff
cuts if they regained power. Proposing a 20 percent reduction of duties on
protected goods, Allison stated, "I warn those who insist so pertinaciously
upon a retention of these high duties upon necessary articles of consumption that they only hasten the time when a more radical change will be
made in our tariff laws."[13] Garfield supported this view: "The demand is
now made from many parts of the country, and not without reason, that
the war tariff shall also be adjusted to the conditions of peace."[14] Just as
Henry Clay had tried in 1832, the Republican leadership attempted to
head off a more drastic revision of the tariff by cutting revenue duties on
consumer items, such as coffee, tea, sugar, and alcoholic beverages, while
maintaining most protective duties on raw materials and manufactured
goods. Advocates of protective duties were also desperate to abolish the
income tax, without which Congress would have to keep import duties
at higher levels to raise revenue. In early 1870, the Ways and Means Committee reported a bill doing all this. Although moderate Republicans were
not convinced the measure went far enough, the House overwhelmingly
passed it in June 1870. The Senate followed, and President Grant signed
it in July 1870. As a result, the average tariff on dutiable imports fell from
47 percent in 1869 to 42 percent in 1871.

However, this action failed to relieve the pressure on Republicans to
enact more extensive tariff reforms. When Southern states officially rejoined the Union in 1868 and 1870, Democrats gained a large number of
seats in Congress. In the election of 1870, the Republican majority in the
House fell sharply as Democrats attacked the Grant administration for

corruption. With Democrats now posing a greater threat to their political power, Republicans decided to appease popular opinion by scaling back import tariffs even more.

In his annual message to Congress in December 1870, President Grant stated that further revenue reform "has my hearty support," proposing that "all duty should be removed from coffee, tea and other articles of universal use not produced by ourselves."[15] The House quickly responded by providing a "free breakfast table," as it was called. The Senate failed to act until 1872, when it added a 10 percent reduction in protective duties on cotton and woolens, iron and steel, and other sensitive manufactured products. "We cannot deny the fact that the duties on wools and woolens are on average from seventy to seventy-five percent," John Sherman (R-OH) noted. "To say that this industry, the manufacture of wool, which can easily be raised in this country, into woolen cloth, a simple manufacture, requires a duty of seventy per cent ad valorem, it seems to me is carrying the doctrine too far; . . . in my deliberate judgment it is better for the protected industries in this country that this slight modification of duties should be made, rather than invite a contest which will endanger the whole system."[16]

Despite opposition from "Pig Iron" Kelley and other staunch protectionists, the House followed the Senate's lead. Many Republicans believed it was an act of political necessity to save the system of protection; even Morrill conceded that "the great error of those who favor a protective tariff is that they sometimes ask too much."[17] The House passed it by an overwhelming margin, and the Senate followed just days later. President Grant signed the bill in June 1872, the first postwar reduction in the key protective duties on cottons, woolens, metals, paper, glass, and leather. Although the 10 percent reduction in rates was slight, it was about as much as the Republicans would yield to the pressure for a downward revision.

Congress's action blunted the ability of Democrats to use the tariff issue in the 1872 presidential election. Despite the informal alliance between Democrats and liberal Republicans, who opposed the corruption of the Grant administration and the harsh reconstruction measures imposed on the South, the two groups ensured their defeat by nominating an unpredictable political amateur, Horace Greeley, the publisher of the *New York Tribune,* as their presidential candidate. Greeley united the two sides in their disgust of political corruption and support for civil service reform, but he strongly supported protective tariffs, whereas most of his supporters demanded tariff reform. The Democratic platform conceded that "there are in our midst honest but irreconcilable differences of opinion with regard to the respective systems of Protection and Free Trade," and the party split meant that the issue would not be contested in the election.[18]

The disarray among the Democrats allowed the establishment Republicans to retain unified control of government with the reelection of President Grant. Furthermore, even the modest reduction in the Tariff of 1872 proved to be short-lived. Like the Tariff of 1857 before it, the legislation was passed at a peak in the business cycle. In September 1872, Jay Cooke & Co., the country's preeminent investment bank, closed its doors after becoming overextended in financing the Northern Pacific Railroad. This triggered the Panic of 1873, and the economy plunged into a recession. The downturn enabled the Democrats to capture the House in the midterm election of 1874, their first major political success since the Civil War. Although the Democratic House would be unable to change the tariff by itself, it could now block Republican legislation.

However, the old Congress was still scheduled to meet early in 1875 before the newly elected one was to convene later that year. In light of the decline in government revenues due to the slump, President Grant suggested "the propriety of readjusting the tariff so as to increase the revenue."[19] Taking the hint, the outgoing Republican Congress swiftly but narrowly repealed the 10 percent reduction in protective duties and raised duties on tobacco and spirits, sugar and molasses before the Democrats took over the House. Thus, in a move that Stanwood (1903, 2:191) described as a "bold, even audacious, defiance of the opposing party," the Republicans undid their previous, incremental tariff reform, which had been in effect for only three years.

This marked the end of any immediate postwar tariff reform. Although the Democrats controlled the House for six of the next eight years, Republicans held the Senate and ensured that no important tariff legislation would be passed during that period.

THE TARIFF COMMISSION AND
THE MONGREL TARIFF OF 1883

Despite the debate over import duties in the early 1870s, the tariff was still not a major issue in presidential politics. In 1876, tariff policy merited only a brief mention in the election platforms of both parties. The Republican platform simply stated that the tariff "should be so adjusted as to promote the interests of American labor and advance the prosperity of the whole country." The Democratic platform emphasized civil service and expenditure reform, and denounced the existing tariff "as a masterpiece of injustice, inequality and false pretense" that "has impoverished many industries to subsidize a few." They demanded a tariff "only for revenue," not for the protection of special interests.[20]

The election of 1876 stands out as one of the most disreputable in American history. Democrat Samuel Tilden won 51.0 percent of the vote to Republican Rutherford B. Hayes's 47.9 percent, but lost the Electoral College by a single vote. The Democrats disputed the close election returns in three Southern states still controlled by Republicans under postwar reconstruction. (Officials in South Carolina, Florida, and Louisiana were accused of awarding their combined twenty electoral votes to Hayes when the popular vote actually supported Tilden.) Congress appointed a special Election Commission to investigate the matter, but the commission voted along party lines to award all twenty electoral votes to Hayes. After Southern Democrats planned to filibuster the commission's report, Congress reached the Compromise of 1877, wherein the South would accept Hayes as president if remaining federal troops were removed from the region. This brought the reconstruction period to an end.

By the time of Hayes's inauguration in March 1877, the economy had recovered from the Panic of 1873, and the government's budget was once again in surplus. President Hayes suggested that Congress repeal all internal taxes (except on alcohol) and rely mainly on import duties on tea and coffee for revenue, but he was cautious and made no attempt to prod Congress into considering such tariff changes. As he wrote privately, "The practical question and the theoretical may be and usually are very different. My leanings are to the free trade side. But in this country the protective policy was adopted in the first legislation of Congress in Washington's time, and has been generally adhered to ever since. Large investments of capital, and the employment of a great number of people depend upon it. We cannot, and probably ought not to suddenly abandon it."[21]

The Democrats made further political gains in the 1878 election, capturing the Senate for the first time since the late 1850s. Republicans feared the public was tiring of their rule and worried that the pro-reform message of their opponents might gain further in popularity. After the Compromise of 1877, Republicans could no longer win elections by "waving the bloody shirt" and reminding the electorate of the Democrats' disloyalty to the Union in supporting the South. As the 1880 election approached, James Blaine of Maine advised his fellow Republicans to "fold up the bloody shirt and lay it away. It's of no use to us. You want to shift the main issue to protection."[22]

Thus, the fading of Reconstruction as a political issue set the stage for intensified partisan conflict over the tariff, but that did not happen in the election of 1880. Once again, the Democrats did not help their cause by nominating a political novice—this time General Winfield Scott Hancock—as their presidential candidate. The befuddled general could not hide his ignorance of tariff policy and was roundly ridiculed for making the empty statement that "the tariff question is a local question." The political cartoonist Thomas Nast brilliantly skewered Hancock by depicting him as whispering to someone: "Who is Tariff, and why is he for revenue only?"[23]

An economic revival enabled the Republicans to regain control of both houses of Congress and retain the presidency with Chester Arthur taking over in 1881. But as the government's fiscal surplus began to swell to unprecedented proportions, Republicans found it harder to avoid the issue of tariff reform. In fiscal years 1882 and 1883, revenues exceeded expenditures by more than 50 percent, and increased public awareness of political corruption and the lobbying of producer interests in Washington put unwanted attention on the special interests supporting high duties.

Once again, moderate Republicans feared the political consequences of inaction. As John Sherman (1895, 2:844) wrote in mid-1882, after the Senate failed to reduce import duties, "If this Congress shall adjourn, whether the weather be hot or cold, without a reduction of the taxes now imposed upon the people, it will have been derelict in its highest duty. There is no sentiment in this country stronger now than that Congress has neglected its duty thus far in not repealing taxes that are obnoxious to the people and unnecessary for the public uses; and if we should still neglect that duty, we should be properly held responsible by our constituents."

In his first annual message to Congress in December 1881, President Arthur endorsed the creation of a commission to investigate the problem of excessive revenue, agreeing that the tariff needed careful revision, with a due regard being "paid to the conflicting interests of our citizens."[24] Congress accepted this recommendation and appointed a Tariff Commission in May 1882. Fearful of repeating the Wells fiasco, however, the Republican majority made sure to pack the commission with safe appointments. Chaired by John Hayes, the secretary of the National Association of Wool Manufacturers, the commission had eight other members: an iron manufacturer, a wool grower (the president of the National Association of Wool Growers), a sugar grower, an officer of the New York Customs House, a statistician from the Census Office, and three former members of Congress. The commission's mandate was "to take into consideration and to thoroughly investigate all the various questions relating to the agricultural, commercial, mercantile, manufacturing, mining, and industrial interests of the United States, so far as the same may be necessary to the establishment of a judicious tariff, or a revision of the existing tariff, upon a scale of justice to all interests."[25]

The commission held hearings in twenty-nine cities over nearly three months, producing 2,625 pages of testimony from 604 witnesses, mostly manufacturers advocating the maintenance of existing tariffs on imports that affected their business. Based on its composition, the commission was expected to propose few changes to the existing system. Instead, it stunned everyone by proposing an enlargement of the duty-free list and a reduction of about 20–25 percent in protective duties. The Tariff Commission (1882, 5) report began as follows:

> Early in its deliberations the Commission became convinced that a substantial reduction of tariff duties is demanded, not by a mere indiscriminate popular clamor, but by the best conservative opinion of the country, including that which has in former times been most strenuous for the preservation of our national industrial defenses. Such a reduction of the existing tariff the Commission regards not only as a due recognition of public sentiment and a measure of justice to consumers, but one conducive to the general industrial prosperity, and which, though it may be temporarily inconvenient, will be ultimately beneficial to the special interests affected by such reduction.

Echoing Wells's earlier reports, the commission (1882, 16) cited many instances of excessive protection that were "positively injurious to the interest which they are supposed to benefit" and "numerous inconsistencies" in the tariff code, such as "the anomaly of finished articles bearing half the duty levied on the material out of which it is made." The commission argued that "excessive duties generally, or exceptionally high duties in particular cases, discredit our whole national economic system and furnish plausible arguments for its complete subversion."

Like the aim of the short-lived 10 percent tariff reduction in 1872, the commission's main objective was to make enough concessions to head off a more serious attack on protective duties. As the chairman of the commission, John Hayes, later wrote, "Reduction in itself was by no means desirable to us; it was a concession to public sentiment, a bending of the top and branches to the wind of public opinion to save the trunk of the protective system. In a word, the object was *protection through reduction*.

We were willing to concede only to save the essentials both of the wool and woolen tariff. . . . We wanted the tariff to be made by our friends."[26]

The Tariff Commission transmitted its report to Congress in December 1882, the same month as the president's annual message to Congress. Arthur used this opportunity to make tariff reform a priority. Calling attention to the ballooning fiscal surplus, the president warned that "such rapid extinguishment of the national indebtedness as is now taking place is by no means a cause for congratulation; it is a cause rather for serious apprehension." The problem was that "either the surplus must lie idle in the Treasury or the Government will be forced to buy at market rates its bonds not then redeemable, and which under such circumstances cannot fail to command an enormous premium, or the swollen revenues will be devoted to extravagant expenditure, which, as experience has taught, is ever the bane of an overflowing treasury." But Arthur went further: "The present tariff system is in many respects unjust. It makes unequal distributions both of its burdens and its benefits."[27]

Congressional Republicans resented the president's intrusion into what they believed was a matter for the legislature alone, but in light of public sentiment, they also viewed it as dangerous to be seen as doing nothing. Adding to the pressure for reform was the Democratic capture of the House of Representatives in the 1882 election. Believing that the unpopularity of high tariffs was partly responsible for their electoral defeat, Republicans sought to enact a more moderate tariff before they lost their majority. As before, they preferred to shape the tariff reduction to their own liking, rather than lose control of the issue and have the Democrats do it for them.

Just prior to the election, during the summer of 1882, the House passed a measure that reduced domestic sales taxes. After the election results became clear, the Senate picked up the bill, added significant tariff cuts based on the commission's recommendation, and passed it in February 1883. Although the House Republican leadership wanted to enact the legislation before the new Congress came to power, they also wanted much higher tariffs than the Senate had proposed. They were also annoyed by the Senate because the Constitution required that all revenue measures start in the House. Racing to beat the deadline of March 4, 1883, when Congress was due to adjourn, and after which the Democrats would take control, Republicans engaged in a highly complicated legislative maneuver involving an unorthodox manipulation of the rules to move the Senate proposal immediately to a conference committee.[28] Amid acrimony, the committee revised the bill by raising tariff rates above those in the Senate version, even though the House had not even debated or voted on any tariffs. In effect, the conference committee eliminated any significant downward revisions from the measure.

The House and Senate rushed to pass the bill in early March, whereupon it was signed by President Arthur. The bill earned the moniker the "Mongrel Tariff" because of the haste with which it had been thrown together and passed. While sales taxes on tobacco and alcohol were reduced, the tariff schedule was adjusted only slightly, reducing rates on noncompeting imports and maintaining them on protected products without much effect on the overall level of duties. The Republicans recognized that public sentiment favored lower duties, but they were determined to preserve the high protective duties. At the same time, they were under no great pressure to enact large changes, given the political weakness of the Democrats.

The Mongrel Tariff of 1883 was another missed opportunity to revise the tariff code after the Civil War. "If the committee had embodied . . . the recommendations of the tariff commission, including the schedules without amendment or change, the tariff would have been settled for many years," John Sherman (1895, 2:851) later wrote. "Unfortunately this was not done, but the schedules prescribing the rates of duty and their classification were so radically changed by the committee that the scheme of the tariff commission was practically defeated." Instead, the conference committee "restored nearly all the inequalities and incongruities of the old tariff, and yielded to local demands and local interests to an extent that destroyed all symmetry or harmony." In Sherman's view (1895, 2:854–55), the Tariff of 1883 simply postponed the battle for another day and "laid the foundations of all the complications since that time."

THE REPUBLICAN COALITION FOR PROTECTION

What underlying political factors account for the failure to achieve any meaningful tariff changes in the decades after the Civil War? As in the late antebellum period, unified government was the key to producing any change in America's tariff policy. Simply put, unified government under the Democrats was necessary to enact or maintain lower tariffs, and unified government under the Republicans was necessary to enact or maintain higher tariffs, while divided government kept the status quo intact.

For the first decade after the war, Republicans held unified control of government, enabling them to prevent any significant reductions in the tariff schedule. In Congress, the party was dominated by stalwarts who resisted any change in protective duties. Republican presidents, such as James Garfield, Rutherford Hayes, and Chester Arthur, were much more moderate. They were willing to support modest tariff reductions to provide tax relief for consumers and defuse political tensions over the issue, but they had a limited impact on policy because Congressional leaders controlled the legislative process.

The Republican political position was secure for several years after 1865 because the South was excluded from Congress. Six former Confederate states were readmitted in 1868 and another four in 1870. Republicans sought to delay this process because they "realized that a return of the South to Congress meant a union of South and West which would deprive the growing business interests of the country of the favors that radical rule would insure to them," Beale (1930, 276) notes. In the meantime, they diluted the South's strength in Congress by admitting several Republican-leaning states to the union, including Kansas (1861), West Virginia (1863), Nevada (1864), and Nebraska (1867). With their small populations, these states did not alter the balance of political power in the House, but they significantly diminished the South's position in the Senate.

Although Republicans were politically dominant in the late 1860s and early 1870s, American politics was very competitive over the next twenty years and the two parties were roughly equal in strength at the national level. From 1875–89, government was mostly divided, ensuring that no major policy changes would be made. Democrats controlled the House in six of the seven Congresses between 1875 and 1889, while Republicans controlled the Senate in six of the seven Congresses. The Republicans held the presidency until the election of a Democrat in 1884. The pattern led to an entrenchment of the status quo, since unified control of government was so rare. As the discussion in chapter 6 shows, the Democrats did not win unified control of government until the election of 1892, but they only held this position for one Congress (two years) during which time they squandered the opportunity to undertake a serious tariff revision.

In addition, partisan differences on the issue were less sharply defined after the Civil War than they had been before the war. The South's opposition to protective duties had weakened, while Northern Democrats had come to support existing duties. George Atkinson (R-WV) summarized the position of the two parties in saying that "the Democratic doctrine is a tariff for revenue with incidental protection, while the Republicans advocate a tariff protection with incidental revenue."[29]

The geographic distribution and intensity of trade-related economic

interests was the primary source of Republican political strength and
Democratic weakness. Exports were fairly concentrated in cotton, wheat,
and provisions (bacon and ham) that came from the South and the Midwest. Cotton was still the nation's single largest export, accounting for
a quarter of all exports. More than two-thirds of the cotton crop was exported, giving the South a continued strong interest in low tariffs. Although Midwestern farm products also constituted a sizeable share of exports, only a small share of domestic production was exported, meaning
that farmers in the region were not very dependent on foreign markets.

Meanwhile, imports were highly diversified and competed against a
wide range of industries spread across the manufacturing belt of the Northeast and upper Midwest. The core of the Republican coalition was located
in the North. The production of iron and steel was highly concentrated in
Pennsylvania and Ohio, and the production of cotton and woolen manufactures was highly concentrated in New England; these manufacturing
industries were among the chief beneficiaries of protective tariffs. These
densely populated regions gave these interests great political strength in
the House. Other elements of the Republican coalition cut across several
different parts of the country, including sheep farmers (wool), sugarcane
and beet growers, and others. These groups did not overlap much in terms
of geography, which gave the party broad appeal across the northern half
of the country.[30] The Republicans used this economic geography to build a
powerful coalition in support of high protective tariffs.

Economic interests were also stronger after the Civil War, because the
process by which they exerted political influence changed. In the antebellum period, special-interest lobbying was done informally; politicians
certainly heard from interested constituent groups through petitions and
memorials, but lobbying tended to be done at a distance. During the war,
the federal government began spending millions of dollars in procurement
and became a political machine for dispensing lucrative contracts, land
grants, and other privileges. As a result, Washington became a magnet for
lobbyists and special-interest groups. The growth of the federal government led to the formation of business and labor organizations that opened
offices in the nation's Capital or regularly sent agents there to ensure
that their interests were represented. Producer interests began forming
national organizations, in part to influence Congress's decisions about
import duties. These groups—such as the National Association of Wool
Growers, the National Association of Wool Manufacturers, and the American Iron and Steel Association, among many others—made campaign

contributions, distributed informational literature, pressured congressional committees, and the like.

One of the most effective interest groups of the period was the American Iron and Steel Association, formed in 1864 under the leadership of the staunch protectionist James Swank. "Protection in this country is only another name for Patriotism," Swank wrote. "It means our country before any other country; the employment of American labor in preference to the employment of the labor of other countries."[31] Swank's AISA "made and unmade Congressmen, controlled Republican State committees, and lobbied in the halls of national conventions, while its spectacular success in retiring [low-tariff advocate Congressman William] Morrison had added greatly to its prestige," Allan Nevins (1932, 418) observed. "Its purse was almost bottomless, for every iron master knew that the existing tariff schedules placed millions if not tens of millions annually in the pockets of the mill-owners."

The Mongrel Tariff of 1883 created a tariff schedule with fourteen main classifications of goods, at least six of which were covered by a single trade association (metals, chemicals, paper, wool, silk, flax and hemp). As Josephson (1938, 330) wrote with respect to the Mongrel Tariff of 1883: "Lobbyists descended like a flock of buzzards upon Washington, crowding all the hotels that winter, pulling, tugging at the statesmen in the name of all the diverse, conflicting interests that employed them, . . . as committeemen in both chambers wrestled with long schedules and with the unblushing and unending demands of lobbies for sugar, iron, wool, glass, marble, and a hundred other trades." Sometimes a single member of Congress was powerful enough to ensure that constituent interests were reflected in legislation. William "Pig Iron" Kelley, the Pennsylvania Republican, resisted any change in Schedule C, the metals schedule. One member of Congress said that Kelley "thinks tariff, talks tariff, and writes tariff every hour of the day . . . a roommate of his tells me that he mumbles it over in his dreams during the night."[32] Similarly, representatives from Louisiana kept a vigilant eye on Schedule E (sugar), Massachusetts and Rhode Island concentrated on Schedule I (cotton goods), Ohio and Massachusetts focused on Schedule K (wool and manufactures), and so on.

The close relationship between business interests and government policymakers led to charges of corruption, especially during the Grant administration. Although the term *lobbying* predates this period, it supposedly refers the fact that President Grant often enjoyed a cigar and brandy in the Willard Hotel near the White House, prompting political wheelers and dealers to mill around the hotel lobby on the chance of getting a brief word with the president.[33] After leaving office, Rutherford B. Hayes complained in his diary about "the rottenness of the present system" because of the influence of special-interest money. "This is a government of the people, by the people, and for the people no longer," he wrote. "It is a government by the corporations, of the corporations, and for the corporations."[34] Stanwood (1903, 2:52) wrote that "Washington had come to be filled with as fine a band of plunderers as ever besieged a National Congress: tax swindlers, smugglers, speculators in land grants, railroad lobbyists, agents of ship companies, mingled with the representatives of industries seeking protection, until it seemed as if Congress was little more than a Relief Bureau."

A high-tariff policy could not survive politically if it just served the interests of a few industries in the North. With the addition of new states shifting the political weight of the country westward, Republicans sought to broaden political support for protectionism beyond eastern industries to include Midwestern producers of raw materials (such as wool, hemp, hides, and flaxseed). They did so by advocating the same structure of protection as the Whigs had proposed in the antebellum period: a combination of moderate tariffs on raw materials produced in the Midwest and higher tariffs on manufactured goods produced in the East. By bringing raw materials producers under the umbrella of the protectionist policy, the Republicans hoped to head off antiprotectionist agrarianism in the Midwest. "In adjusting the details of the tariff," Justin Morrill explained, "I would treat agriculture, manufactures, mining, and commerce, as I would our whole people—as members of one family, all entitled to equal favor, and no one to be made the beast of burden to carry the packs of the others."[35]

Republicans recognized that protection for raw materials producers and final-goods producers would stand or fall together. The Democrats tried to split the two interests by proposing moderate tariff protection for final-goods producers along with duty-free raw materials, which would reduce the production costs of final goods. Republicans recognized the danger that this sort of division posed to the whole system of protection. "The dogma of some manufacturers, that raw materials should be admitted free of duty, is far more dangerous to the protective policy than the opposition of free traders," John Sherman (1895, 1:191) warned. As he put it, "A denial of protection on coal, iron, wool, and other so-called raw materials will lead to the denial of protection to machinery, to textiles, to pottery and other industries. The labor of one class must not be sacrificed to secure the protection for another class."

Ironically, despite the fact that the party never received much support from industrial regions of the country, the Democratic tariff proposals of the period were actually designed to help manufacturers by putting raw materials on the duty-free list and thereby reduce their production costs. Democrats especially pushed this idea with respect to wool, arguing that free wool would improve the competitive position of domestic wool manufacturers. While this may have been a cynical ploy to undermine the political alliance between wool producers and wool manufacturers, such a policy may have helped manufacturers more than the Republican tariff structure. The Democrats used this line of reasoning to argue that import duties on steel should be reduced so that the cost of building railroads would fall and thereby accelerate transportation improvements. Samuel Cox (D-NY) added, "The protectionists know that it stands on shaky ground. They would postpone its modification, because one link in the common bond which binds its selfish enactments and mutual aggrandizement once severed the whole chain falls to pieces."[36]

Final-goods producers may have been tempted by the Democratic program of having duty-free raw materials, but they could never be sure that the Democrats might not slash tariffs on their products as well. These industrial interests recognized the importance of coalition-building across potentially conflicting constituencies to maintain the existing system of protection. These groups tried to come together and present Congress with a unified front, as opposed to squabbling with each other so that disputes had to be resolved by politicians. Therefore, raw materials producers in the Midwest and final-goods producers in the East—such as hide producers in Ohio and shoe manufacturers in Massachusetts; sugarcane and sugar beet growers in Louisiana and Michigan, and sugar refiners in New York; iron ore mining interests in Michigan and Minnesota, and iron and steel manufacturers in Pennsylvania and Ohio—tended to cooperate rather than oppose one another. To the extent that they had conflicting interests with respect to tariffs, they preferred to reach a compromise among themselves rather than have politicians make arbitrary decisions for them.

Of these various interests, wool producers and wool manufacturers took on special importance. John Hayes, the Secretary of the National Association of Wool Manufacturers, recognized that his organization could not obtain higher duties from Congress without the cooperation of wool growers in the Midwest. Sheep raisers who were spread across Ohio, Michigan, and elsewhere had long vowed to oppose efforts by wool manufacturers to obtain higher duties if those manufacturers sought to reduce the duty on raw wool imports. In the view of the wool growers, if the manufacturers were not their friends then they were enemies. Therefore, Hayes organized a meeting of the manufacturers and growers in December 1865 to hammer out an agreement for higher duties on both goods. This proposal was presented to Congress as stand-alone legislation for the wool industry, unattached to other tariff legislation, and became the Wool and Woolens Act of 1867.[37]

As a result, the Democratic policy of low or no tariffs on raw materials and moderate duties on final goods failed to win over industrial interests. Those interests apparently preferred the security under the Republicans of having high tariffs all around. Republicans sidestepped the fact that lower raw materials prices would improve the position of downstream industries. They did not structure the tariff code to favor manufacturing in particular; rather, they wanted all sectors of the economy—from raw materials to final manufactures—protected with high tariffs and insulated from foreign competition, even if this was sometimes detrimental to final-goods producers.

However, as in the antebellum period, the Northeast-Midwest alliance was never completely secure. On balance, the Midwest's interests with respect to trade were mixed: some raw material producers demanded protection (wool and beet sugar); others had a weak interest in exporting to foreign markets (grain and meat). The Midwest never viewed protection as a singular benefit to the region and viewed with suspicion the industrialists in the Northeast. At the same time, it was willing to trade away its votes on tariff legislation in exchange for policies that would more directly serve the region's interests, such as a more liberal land policy, a more inflationary monetary policy, or greater regulation of railroads and monopolies.[38]

Republicans not only appealed to producer interests affected by imports, but pitched their message to workers in those sectors as well. By the 1880s, about a quarter of the labor force was employed in manufacturing. The Republicans argued that protective tariffs were needed to safeguard the high wages of American labor from the competition of low-wage foreign workers. Republicans would often attack Democratic proposals to cut tariffs as "bills to reduce American wages." "Reduce the tariff, and labor is the first to suffer," William McKinley (R-OH) argued.[39] This argument was not wholly accepted by organized labor. Only some industrial workers saw their jobs at risk from foreign competition, while many others worried about the impact of the tariff on their cost of living. Industries were divided in terms of their exposure to import competition. For example, the Knights of Labor was so split over trade policy that it declared itself neutral on the issue. At its first convention in 1881, the Federation of Organized Trades and Labor Unions, the precursor of the American Federation of Labor (AFL), found that one faction wanted to endorse protection, while another wanted to endorse free trade; the next year the delegates voted to take no position on the subject. In 1906, Samuel Gompers stated that the AFL's neutrality on the issue had served the organization well and therefore would remain its policy.[40]

Perhaps the greatest political threat to the high-tariff system was the government's large fiscal surplus. The Republicans sought to increase government spending as a way of reducing the surplus and maintaining political support for protective tariffs. Before the Civil War, the Whigs disposed of surplus revenue by devoting large sums to internal improvements. After the Civil War, federal expenditures on pensions for veterans of the Union army served the same purpose. The Republicans first introduced a disability pension program for veterans and their dependents in 1862. This proved to be a brilliant political strategy for both eliminating the surplus revenue and tying large numbers of voters (Union soldiers and their dependents) to the Republican party.

As a result, the federal government spent staggering sums on military pensions in the decades after the Civil War. The Grand Army of the Union became a major political force for the Republican party and encouraged the growth of transfer payments for its members. With the Arrears of Pension Act of 1879, the Republicans expanded the program to cover not only combat injuries and deaths, but also disability and old-age benefits. This encouraged applicants with "newly discovered Civil War related disabilities," and new claims rose from 1,600 per month to 10,000 per month, putting thousands of new beneficiaries on the dole. Federal expenditures nearly doubled in one year when lump-sum payments were made to all the newly eligible veterans for the retroactive benefits. The Republicans then enacted the Dependent Pension Act of 1890, which severed the link between war-related injuries and government pensions. This produced another sharp rise in the number of pensioners and the cost of disbursements. At its peak, in the early 1890s, pensions accounted for nearly 40 percent of federal spending, although it subsequently declined as the Civil War generation passed from the scene.[41]

Democrats attacked the pension system as "a shrewd scheme by which the protected interests proposed to use up the surplus and prevent a revision of the tariff." In the words of James Beck (D-KT), "They want to save the soldiers from going to the poorhouse by absorbing all the surplus revenue, when in fact they are really seeking to save the tariff in order to enrich a few men that are making princely fortunes out of it at the expense of the great mass of the people."[42] Abuse of the government program was rampant: after the 1879 expansion in benefits, about a quarter of all pensions were thought to have been based on fraudulent claims. The Pension Bureau became viewed as "a graft-ridden political machine identified with and controlled by the Republican party," Bensel (1984, 63) notes. This compelled Democrats, under the leadership of President Grover Cleveland, elected in 1884, to enact administrative and civil service reform. Although Democrats sought to base pension eligibility on proof of veteran status and an objective assessment of injury or disability, they were largely unsuccessful in taking on the entrenched interests that fought to preserve the generous benefits.

While formidable political forces stood in defense of high tariffs, those that favored a significant tariff reduction were ineffective and divided. The core of the Democratic party was still in the South, which continued to believe that it was subjected to a double injury: its exports were being implicitly taxed by the high import duties, and the revenue was being spent in the North (this time on pensions, not internal improvements). But a North-South split over tariffs repeatedly undermined attempts to achieve party unity on the matter. Southern Democrats favored returning to the rates of duty in the Walker tariff of 1846; Northern Democrats, many of whom came from industrial constituencies, wanted to maintain existing tariffs. This split was candidly acknowledged in the Democratic platform in 1872, which stated, "There are in our midst honest but irreconcilable differences of opinion with regard to the respective systems of protection and free trade."

The individual most responsible for the intra-party split was Samuel Randall, a Pennsylvania Democrat and House speaker from 1875–80. An ardent supporter of protection, Randall consistently enlisted twenty or more Northern Democrats to block any action by his party to reduce tariffs. Like "Pig Iron" Kelley, Randall was considered "immoveable" on the subject of high tariffs. "I am an American, and therefore I am a protectionist," he reasoned.[43] As speaker, Randall used his power to ensure that the Ways and Means Committee, even under the Democrats, would slow any bid to reduce tariffs. Randall met fierce resistance from the party's rank-and-file in the South and Midwest. The Democrats achieved greater unity on the issue after a party caucus denied Randall the speakership in 1883, but even then the party still had difficulty forming a united front to tackle tariff reform.

Democrats also faced rhetorical disadvantages in attacking existing policy. Republicans argued that high tariffs were the foundation of the nation's industrial prosperity. By contrast, the Democratic position—"a tariff for revenue only"—was hardly an inspiring rallying cry. The bland pitch worked in the late antebellum period, when tariffs were already low, and Democrats wanted to signal their commitment to small government. Now that import tariffs were substantially higher, Democrats had to confront voters' fears that a reduction in import duties would severely disrupt the economy. Unfortunately for the Democrats, the logic of the protectionist catechism—that tariffs increased output in protected industries, which increased the demand for labor and led to higher wages—seemed more persuasive to the public than trying to explain its flawed logic. As William Morrison (D-IL) put it, "The trouble with the tariff question is that the Republicans have the advantage on catch words, and the people as a rule do not understand the question, and it is too hard a study for them."[44]

Democrats argued that tariff reform meant tax relief. As Roger Mills (D-TX) put it, "Enormous taxation upon the necessaries of life has been a constant drain upon the people—taxation not only to support all the expenditures of Government, but taxation so contrived as to fill the pockets of a privileged class, and taking from the people $5 for private purposes for every dollar that it carries to the public Treasury." The Democrats maintained that tariffs increased the cost of living and reduced the purchasing power of wages. "The benefits of the tariff all go one way," as Mills asserted, "from the consumer to the manufacturer, but not from the manufacturer to the consumer."[45]

Democrats had some success in portraying the system as corrupt. Samuel Cox of New York, one of the more colorful orators in Congress, argued that the tariff was nothing less than the odd collection of individual tariffs and amounted to "petty larceny" as every interest tried to exact some income at the expense of others. As he put it, "Let us be to each other instruments of reciprocal rapine. Michigan steals on copper; Maine on lumber; Pennsylvania on iron; North Carolina on peanuts; Massachusetts on cotton goods; Connecticut on hair pins; New Jersey on spool thread; Louisiana on sugar, and so on. Why not let the gentleman from Maryland steal coal from them? True, but a comparative few get the benefit, and it comes out of the body of the people. True, it tends to high prices, but does not stealing encourage industry?"[46]

As much as Democrats were dismayed by the corrupt politics behind tariffs, they ran up against a simple problem: the policy delivered tangible benefits to important constituencies, which in turn gave their political support to the Republicans. Democrats floundered in their attempts to find a way to break the Republican's deep political support for maintaining the existing policy. They particularly suffered from the fact that the "tariff reform" movement had no organizational basis to counterbalance such producer lobbies as the American Iron and Steel Association and the National Association of Wool Manufacturers. Indeed, no major industrial or agricultural producer association advocated significant tariff reductions. "Compared with the realistic business men on the Republican side, the reformers who aided the Democrats seemed amateurs," Nevins (1932, 420–21) observed. "The American Free Trade League, with David A. Wells as president, distributed tariff reform documents, but its activities were feeble beside those of the Iron and Steel Association." Indeed, the League "was all facade, for it did nothing to raise campaign funds, sent out a few pamphlets, and aroused little attention." Although Southern exporters of cotton and tobacco were well represented by southern Democrats in Congress, they were not formally organized and were largely discredited because of their association with the Confederate South.

In Congressional debates, Republicans and Democrats brought out the same arguments about trade policy again and again, year after year, decade after decade. Republicans asserted that high tariffs protected domestic industries from foreign competition and ensured that workers had employment at high wages. Democrats maintained that tariffs were taxes that imposed a heavy burden on consumers and farmers, while also impeding exports. For every argument on one side, there was a counter-argument on the other. Republicans saw protective tariffs as helping all producers facing foreign competition and ultimately strengthening the economy as a whole, whereas the Democrats saw those policies as redistributing income to one group at the expense of another. For Republicans, protective tariffs led to general economic progress. For Democrats, such protection gave special interests a privileged position at the expense of the general welfare. Republicans saw a harmony of interests with a strong and growing manufacturing sector as a benefit to farmers and landowners. Democrats saw societal conflicts that pitted capital against labor, big business against the consumer, industry against agriculture, bankers and railroads against small farmers, urban manufacturers against rural farmers and planters. For Republicans, protective tariffs made the country stronger and more powerful. For Democrats, protection led to political corruption and a growing concentration of wealth.

Not only did the two parties have different visions about how tariff policy affected the nation's polity, they disagreed about its specific consequences. For example, the two parties disputed whether tariffs would increase or decrease domestic prices. Democrats contended that taxes on imported goods raised domestic prices and hurt consumers. Republicans conceded that tariffs might increase prices in the short run, but argued that protection would stimulate more domestic production that would eventually reduce prices and benefit consumers. As Binger Hermann (R-OR) put it, "Protection begets production, production begets competition, and competition begets cheap prices."[47] Because the late nineteenth century was one of deflation, Republicans could always point to the falling price level as evidence in favor of their assertion. Of course, the country's monetary policy under the gold standard, not the tariff, was responsible for the deflation of this period.

Conversely, Republicans held that a tariff reduction would leave the United States at the mercy of foreign monopolists who would exploit American consumers. Lower tariffs would not reduce consumer prices, they reasoned, because foreign producers would simply exploit their market power and raise their prices. "The day the telegraph announces that we have reduced the duty on pig and railroad iron will be the day on which the price of British iron will go up," Kelley stated.[48] Yet this contention created a contradiction for the protectionist position: if a lower tariff simply allowed foreign exporters to raise their prices, then domestic producers would not be harmed by the tariff reduction because prices would not fall. And there was no evidence that British iron and steel exporters or other producers behaved this way; they appear to have been highly competitive with one another and with other producers in Germany, Belgium, and elsewhere. Lower tariffs did lead to lower prices and greater imports, which is precisely why domestic producers facing foreign competition feared the prospect of tariff reductions.

Finally, Republicans branded all opponents of protective tariffs or advocates of tariff reform as "free traders" who represented foreign interests that only wanted to weaken the United States. Anglophobia figured prominently in late nineteenth-century American politics. Advocates of lower tariffs, such as David Wells, were often smeared as being foreign agents conspiring to open up the American market on behalf of British monopolies. Those unpatriotic enough to believe in "free trade" were simply part of a British plot to destroy the nation's industries and compromise its economic independence.[49]

Advocates of protective tariffs and proponents of tariff reform both looked to intellectuals to provide a justification for their position. The leading figure for protective tariffs was Henry Carey. The son of Mathew Carey, a leading proponent of the American System in the antebellum period, Carey believed in free trade until the economic recovery that oc-

curred after the Tariff of 1842 persuaded him of the merits of protectionism. In his book *Harmony of Interests* (1851), Carey denied that agriculture and manufacturing were opposing interests, contending instead that
there was a "harmony of interests" between them: when one flourished,
all would benefit. In his view, international trade disrupted this domestic harmony and ought to be discouraged. Carey held that the home market should be developed at the expense of the world market to create a
web of economic association that would bring farmers and manufacturers together. Carey also attacked merchants for the wasteful activity of
transporting goods between markets. His three volume *Principles of Social Science* (1858) became the principal text of the Philadelphia School of
Political Economy that embraced protectionism as its key doctrine.[50]

Despite being the leading thinker for the protectionist cause, Carey
was a turgid writer whose arguments were often convoluted.[51] Yet Carey's
energetic efforts gave him an international reputation and even gave protectionism a veneer of intellectual respectability. The era's leading economist, John Stuart Mill, took Carey seriously as "the only writer, of any
reputation as a political economist, who now [1865] adheres to the Protectionist doctrine." But Mill pointed out basic errors in Carey's analysis and
concluded that his argument for protection was "totally invalid"; privately,
Mill wrote that Carey's *Principles* was "about the worst book on political
economy I ever read."[52] The hostility was apparently mutual: one contemporary remarked that Carey was "a man of plain speech, and swears like a
bargeman whenever Mill's name is mentioned."[53]

Meanwhile, tariff reformers looked to David Wells, who founded the
American Free Trade League after his government service, for intellectual
leadership. Academic economists were also largely in favor of free trade,
and some wrote popular books on the subject.[54] For the most part, however,
the economists received little attention in Washington, and their views
were usually dismissed by politicians. James Garfield, who was sympathetic to their views, noted, "As an abstract theory of political economy,
free trade has many advocates and much can be said in its favor; nor will
it be denied that the scholarship of modern times is largely on that side;
that a large majority of the great thinkers of the present day are leading in
the direction of what is called free trade." Despite this, "there is a strong
and deep conviction in the minds of a great majority of our people in favor of protecting American industry."[55] More frequently, academic opinion
was bitterly attacked and ridiculed in Congress. Republicans rejected the
theory of comparative advantage as the "refinement of reasoning to cheat
common sense" and accused economists of poisoning the minds of the na-

tion's youth with "academic theories."[56] As Speaker of the House Thomas Reed (D-ME) stated, "Every boy who graduated from college graduated a free trader, and . . . everyone one of them who afterwards became a producer or distributor of our goods became also a protectionist."[57]

ECONOMIC EFFECTS OF TRADE PROTECTION

Despite the impressive expansion of the US economy in the three decades after the Civil War, the nation's foreign trade showed surprisingly little change. Exports and imports slowly recovered from the war and stabilized at around 6 percent of GDP. Cotton and other agricultural products continued to dominate exports, while imports consisted of a diversified mix of consumer goods, raw materials, and manufactured products.

The average tariff was also stable during this period. Between 1860 and 1900, the average tariff on dutiable imports was about 40–45 percent. As figure I.1 showed, it never fell below 38 percent nor rose above 52 percent. The distinction between dutiable and nondutiable imports became important after 1872, when coffee and tea were put on the duty-free list. From this point, about a third of imports entered the country duty-free.

A key question regarding trade policy during this period is how much domestic producers competing against imports benefited from the protection they received and how much of a burden this protection put on other sectors of the economy. This straightforward question is actually very difficult to answer. The rate of import duty listed in the tariff schedule is known as the "nominal" rate of protection, which is often taken to indicate the implicit subsidy given to domestic producers. For example, if there is a 30 percent tariff on imported goods that pushes the domestic price of those goods above the world price by that amount, then domestic producers of similar goods implicitly receive a 30 percent subsidy as a result of the tariff. However, this conclusion is not entirely accurate: If imported goods are imperfect substitutes for domestic goods, or the world price falls as a result of the tariff, then the implicit subsidy to domestic producers would be less than 30 percent.

More importantly, nominal rates of protection are a misleading indicator of the assistance given to domestic producers because they ignore the structure of duties across different goods. For example, if pig iron is subject to high import duties, while machinery built with iron is subject to low import duties, the machinery industry would suffer rather than benefit from the tariffs in place. The "effective" rate of protection, defined as the percentage change in value added in an activity as a result of the tariff structure, takes into account the duties on intermediate and final goods in determining the degree to which producers of final goods are protected from foreign competition.[58] One implication of low tariffs on intermediate goods and high tariffs on final goods, which was the general tendency of tariff code in the nineteenth century, is that the effective rate of protection for final goods is much higher than indicated by the nominal rate. Of course, the effective rate of protection can also be lower than the nominal rate of protection—or even negative, meaning that the final-goods industry is being taxed, not subsidized, by the tariff system. As David Wells always stressed, many protected goods were intermediate products used in the production of other final goods. High tariffs on these materials raised the production costs of final-goods producers, reducing the demand for their products and harming their competitive position vis-à-vis foreign competitors. For example, the high price of steel rails significantly raised the cost of laying railroad tracks, thereby reducing railroad investment.

Unfortunately, the nominal and effective rates of protection do not reveal anything about the incidence of the tariff. In other words, did the burden of the tariff fall primarily on consumers in the form of higher prices, or exporters in terms of reduced foreign sales? The "net" rate of protection, defined by Sjaastad (1980) as the proportionate change in the domestic price of importable and exportable goods relative to non-traded goods, helps determine the degree of assistance given to import-competing producers and the burden placed upon exporters. In this framework, the imposition of an import tariff raises the domestic price of importable goods relative to exportable goods and, initially, relative to non-traded goods as well. But the expansion of the import-competing sector creates greater demand for non-traded goods and drives up their price as well. The higher price of non-tradeable goods reduces the protection given to domestic producers competing against imports and puts an additional burden on exporters because the price of exportables declines relative to the price of non-tradeables. (An alternative adjustment to a higher tariff would be a nominal exchange-rate appreciation, which would also lower the relative price of tradeable goods, but this was not possible under the gold standard.)

Thus, a higher tariff increases the price of non-traded goods and inflates the cost structure of the economy. In the late nineteenth century United States, Irwin (2007) found that a 10 percent increase in the price of imported goods would raise the price of non-traded goods by 6 percent. In this case, a 30 percent average tariff on total imports would push up the price of non-traded goods by 18 percent. As a result, the net subsidy to import-competing manufacturers would be 10 percent (measured as the increase in the price of importable relative to non-traded goods), and the net tax on agricultural exporters would be 15 percent (measured by the decline in the price of exportables relative to non-tradeables).[59] Thus, import-competing producers captured only about a third of the benefits of the tariff, while export-oriented producers faced a tax amounting to about half the tariff rate. This means that a relatively high nominal rate of protection did not necessarily translate into a high degree of net protection to import-competing industries.

This framework can also be used to reveal the income transfers associated with the incidence of protection. Table 5.1 presents a matrix that records the implied income transfers among five domestic groups: import-competing producers, exporters, consumers, taxpayers, and the government. According to these results, the 30 percent average tariff on imports was responsible for reshuffling about 9 percent of GDP between various agents in the economy. The implicit export tax cost exporters 4.3 percent of GDP and forced consumers to pay 3.1 percent of GDP in terms of higher prices for importable goods, 2.5 percent going to import-competing producers and 0.5 percent going to the government in revenue. In terms of the beneficiaries, import-competing producers gained 2.5 percent of GDP from consumers, while consumers gained the equivalent of 3.2 percent of GDP at the expense of exporters by virtue of the lower prices of exportable goods. The government collected 1.6 percent of GDP in customs revenue, much of which was paid to Civil War veterans. Thus, the redistribution of domestic income brought about by the high-tariff policy was sizeable and justified its status as one of the most controversial issues in national politics during this period.

A key question is whether American consumers (households) gained or lost from high tariffs. Republicans claimed that protection created jobs in

TABLE 5.1. Intersectoral transfers as a result of tariff protection, c. 1885

From \ To	Import-competing industries	Consumers	Taxpayers	Government	Total
Exporters	0.0	3.2	0.0	1.1	4.3
Consumers	2.5	—	0.0	0.5	3.1
Government	0.0	0.0	1.6	—	1.6
Total	2.5	3.2	1.6	1.6	8.9

Source: Irwin 2007.

Note: As a percentage of GDP, figures may not sum to totals due to rounding.

protected industries and kept the real wages of workers higher than they would be otherwise. Democrats claimed that protection increased the cost of living and reduced real wages. Of course, protective tariffs were not the primary reason that wages in the United States exceeded those in Europe and elsewhere: America's high ratio of land per worker was the primary reason for the higher wages. (High wages were not unique to the United States but were found in other countries, such as Australia and Canada, that had a similarly large endowment of land per worker.)[60] But even though trade protection was not responsible for the country's high wages, the question is whether protection increased or decreased the real income of workers. Import duties almost certainly increased nominal wages by increasing the general price level, but whether real wages were higher or lower as a result of the tariff is an open question.

Unfortunately, economic theory does not lead to precise conclusions about the impact of protection on real wages. The famous Stolper-Samuelson (1941) theorem holds that the factor of production that is scarce (in comparison to other countries) benefits unambiguously from protection, but this result assumes that there are just two factors of production. This assumption is inappropriate, because the United States at this time is more accurately characterized as having three primary factors: land, labor, and capital. In a standard "specific factors" trade model, where land is a specific factor in the agricultural sector, capital is a specific factor in manufacturing, and labor is a mobile factor of production used in both sectors, the effect of protection on real wages is ambiguous: consumers gain from the lower price of exportables but lose from the higher price of importables. This "neoclassical ambiguity" of the specific-factors framework means that the change in real wages depends upon the weights of goods in the consumption bundle.[61] If consumer spending was concentrated on imported goods, then protection would reduce real wages; if consumer spending was concentrated on exported goods, whose relative price fell with protection, then real wages would rise.

The available evidence indicates that consumer spending was skewed toward expenditures on exportable rather than importable goods. Food, which accounted for more than half of exports in the mid-1880s, accounted for about 40 percent of an average household's consumption expenditures. Only about 15–20 percent of consumer expenditures went to clothing, the major importable good in the consumption bundle.[62] Table 5.1 suggests that consumers roughly broke even as a result of protection, paying about 3 percent of GDP to import-competing producers and the government but gaining about 3 percent of GDP at the expense of exporters. If consumers' gains and losses from protection were roughly equal, and the revenue from import duties was redistributed to specific groups, such as Union veterans, this implies that northern consumers who received a disproportionate share of the tariff revenue may have gained from the policy, while southern consumers may have lost.

High taxes on imports not only redistributed income, but distorted production and consumption decisions, resulting in an inefficiency known as the deadweight loss. Immediately after the Civil War, because of the higher duties imposed on all imports, the deadweight loss from the taxation of imports was relatively high: about 1–1.5 percent of GDP in the late 1860s and early 1870s.[63] After coffee and tea were put on the duty-free list in 1872, however, the deadweight loss fell to less than 1 percent of GDP and continued to fall until World War I. By contrast, the static deadweight loss of tariffs was only about 0.25 percent of GDP in 1859. Of course, all taxes create deadweight losses, and it is not clear that another form of taxation during this period would have been more efficient.[64]

These deadweight losses would be smaller still if the tariff improved the terms of trade, either reducing the price of imports or increasing the price of exports. Unlike the antebellum period, the postbellum period has seen little consideration given to the possibility that import tariffs improved the terms of trade during that time. In terms of export market power, the United States lost much of its ability to influence the world price of cotton after the Civil War because of the rise of other foreign suppliers. In addition, when the McKinley tariff abolished the sugar duty in 1891, taking the average tariff from about 70 percent to zero overnight, the tariff reduction was passed through completely to consumer prices with no impact on the world price, although subsequent increases in the sugar tariff reduced the world price somewhat.[65] Therefore, the evidence casts doubt on the idea that the tariff had a significant impact on the terms of trade.

How much would a tariff reduction have affected domestic manufacturers competing against imports? Unlike the antebellum period, which saw the large 1846 Walker tariff reduction, in the postbellum period import duties were not significantly changed. Therefore, we do not observe what would have happened to imports and domestic production if tariff policy had been significantly different. As a result, economists have used counterfactual simulations to speculate about the possible impact of a large reduction in tariffs. The magnitude of the impact depends critically on the elasticity of substitution between domestic and imported products. If imported and domestically produced goods are nearly perfect substitutes for one another, meaning the elasticity of substitution is very large, then a tariff reduction that reduces the domestic price of imported goods will have a big impact on the domestic industry. If imported and domestically produced goods are imperfect substitutes for one another, meaning the elasticity of substitution is small, then a tariff reduction will have a small impact on the domestic industry.

In the case of pig iron, a relatively homogeneous product, the elasticity of substitution was relatively high. One simulation by Irwin (2000a) indicates that, had the 1869 Wells proposal for cutting the tariff on imported pig iron from 60 percent to 20 percent been implemented, domestic pig iron production would have fallen by about 7 percent, and the import market share would have risen from about 7 percent to about 18 percent. What is striking about this result is that even a large tariff change and a large elasticity of substitution had a relatively muted impact on the domestic industry, suggesting that most of the pig iron industry would have survived even a fairly steep tariff reduction. Why is the impact so modest? Even though the tariff is reduced by two-thirds, from 60 percent to 20 percent, the domestic price of imports at most falls by 25 percent.[66] Although the volume of imports would rise by 200 percent, imports of pig iron were quite small in comparison to domestic production.

It is also hard to make the case that tariffs were of decisive importance for other industries. As noted in chapter 3, the cotton textile industry was firmly established well before the Civil War. Economic historians have suggested that the role of the tariff in helping the wool and woolens industry was greatly exaggerated in the political debate over trade policy.[67] Leather manufactures, such as shoes, were resilient industries that were not very dependent on protection from foreign competition and were even exporting successfully. By the late nineteenth century, imports of manufactured goods were only about 3 percent of domestic production of manufactured goods (see table 5.2). And the United States was a leader in many food-manufacturing industries, particularly with the rise of the meat-packing industry. Nearly 20 percent of US exports consisted of manufactured goods, suggesting that some industries would have continued to succeed even if protective tariffs had been reduced. The question of whether the tariff increased the rate of economic growth is considered in chapter 6.

THE GREAT TARIFF DEBATE OF 1888

A quarter-century after the Civil War, Congress had still not significantly altered the tariff schedule as set during the war. In fact, tariffs had crept

TABLE 5.2. Selected data on trade and production of manufactured goods, 1859–1899 (in millions of current dollars)

Year	Imports of manufac- tured goods	Exports of manufac- tured goods	Net exports of manufac- tured goods	Value of domes- tic production of manufac- tured goods	Imports as a share of domestic consumption
1859	191	46	−145	1,886	9%
1869	220	61	−159	4,232	5%
1879	180	133	−47	5,370	3%
1889	327	166	−161	9,372	3%
1899	262	381	119	13,014	2%

Sources: Imports and exports of manufactured goods, US Bureau of the Census 1975, series U-223–224; semi-manufactures and finished manufactures (excludes manufactured foodstuffs). Value of domestic production, US Bureau of the Census, Census Reports, 1900, *Manufacturing, United States by Industries*, vol. 7, Part I, xlvii (Washington, DC: Government Printing Office, 1902). Imports as a share of domestic consumption calculated as imports divided by production minus exports plus imports.

up because of the post–Civil War deflation that lasted until the mid-1890s. The average tariff on dutiable imports, which stood at 38 percent in 1873, reached about 47 percent by the late 1880s, partly because of the slow but steady decline in prices.[68]

Furthermore, despite the reduction in many internal taxes and the rise in government spending on veterans, fiscal surpluses continued to swell to unprecedented proportions. During the 1880s, the federal government took in $1.40 for every dollar it spent. In fiscal year 1888, for example, the federal government ran a budget surplus of $111 million above that year's $268 million in expenditures, which included debt-service payments and contributions to the sinking fund. Callable debt was completely retired by 1887, forcing the government to purchase noncallable debt in the open market at premiums as high as 29 percent above par. The Treasury spent $45 million in such premiums to bondholders between 1888 and 1890.[69] Democrats were appalled that the import duties and internal taxes paid by consumers, laborers, and farmers were not only funding generous pensions for veterans and their families, but providing large, unearned windfalls to wealthy investors in New York as well.

The enormous fiscal surplus was viewed as a major economic problem in the 1880s. Some forecast that if the surpluses continued, they would extinguish the national debt, resulting in the accumulation of assets in the Treasury, thus draining liquidity from the financial system and dis-rupting the nation's economy. At one point, nearly a third of the nation's circulating money stock was sitting dormant in the vaults of the Treasury Department. The budget surplus energized advocates of tax cuts and tariff reductions to press their case.

Both Democrats and Republicans agreed on the goal of reducing government revenue, but they disagreed about how to accomplish it. The Democrats maintained that cutting tariff rates would reduce customs revenue while giving consumers a well-deserved tax cut on the goods they purchased. Republicans countered that lower tariffs would simply encourage more imports and thereby increase customs revenue; instead, they advocated higher tariffs to squeeze imports and reduce the revenue collected. In fact, it is not obvious which position was correct, because the revenue impact of a change in tariff rates depends on the elasticity of import demand. If import demand is elastic, then higher duties will reduce tariff revenue; if import demand is inelastic, then higher duties will increase tariff revenue. Irwin (1998b) estimated the revenue-maximizing tariff rate was, on average, more than 60 percent during this period, suggesting that the Democratic position, that tariff revenue would fall with a reduction in the tariff rate, was correct.

Having recaptured the House in the 1882 congressional elections, the Democrats were poised to take advantage of the growing public sentiment in favor of lower taxes. Though they did not have unified control of government, the Democrats were prepared to score some political points by passing a tariff reduction that the Republicans would be forced to defeat in the Senate. In March 1884, William Morrison (D-IL), chairman of the Ways and Means Committee, reported a bill that proposed a 20 percent across-the-board reduction of all duties (except those on liquors and silk) and put some raw materials on the duty-free list. The reduction was proposed "as a measure of partial relief to the people from unnecessary taxes, as a measure of justice to consumers, and conducive to the general industrial prosperity."[70] Despite having a majority of nearly eighty, House Democrats were unable to pass the bill because an internal split undermined party unity: Samuel Randall of Pennsylvania led a band of Northern Democrats who represented industrial constituencies and staunchly opposed any crack in the tariff wall. To the dismay of the party leadership, Randall managed to find forty Democrats, mainly from the northeast, to strike the enabling clause from the bill by a vote of 159–155.

In the presidential election campaign of 1884, the Democrats attacked Republicans for their failure to reform the tariff along the lines suggested by the Tariff Commission. In their platform, they "pledged to revise the tariff in a spirit of fairness to all interests" and "denounce[d] the abuses of the existing tariff" that "impoverished many to subsidize a few." However, the Democrats weakened their position considerably by conceding that "the necessary reduction in taxation can and must be effected without depriving American labor of the ability to compete successfully with foreign labor, and without imposing lower rates of duty than will be ample to cover any increased cost of production which may exist in consequence of the higher rate of wages prevailing in this country."[71] Republicans responded by vowing to correct the inequities in the tariff and reduce the budget surplus, "not by the vicious and indiscriminate process of horizontal reduction, but by such methods as will relieve the taxpayer without injuring the laborer or the great productive interests of the country." Under a Republican administration, they insisted, "the imposition of duties on foreign imports shall be made, not 'for revenue only,' but . . . to afford security to our diversified industries and protection to the rights and wages of the laborer."[72]

The 1884 election gave the country its first Democratic president, Grover Cleveland, since the Civil War. The Democrats retained control of the House, but fell short of capturing the Senate, thereby depriving them of unified government and thus dooming the chance for tariff reform. Cleveland himself did not enter office well informed about the issue. Shortly after the election, the president-elect asked one of his supporters,

> what big questions he ought to take up when he got into the White House. I told him I thought he ought to take up the tariff. I shall never forget what then happened. The man bent forward and buried his face in his hands on the table before him. After two or three minutes he straightened up and, with the same directness, said to me: "I am ashamed to say it, but the truth is I know nothing about the tariff . . . Will you tell me now how to go about it to learn?"[73]

Initially, the Cleveland administration did not propose any tariff changes, choosing instead to concentrate on administrative and civil service reform, and ending corruption in the pension system.[74] Although his Treasury secretary criticized the tariff code as "chaos rather than a system," President Cleveland, in his first annual message to Congress, sounded a cautious note:

> The proposition with which we have to deal is the reduction of the revenue received by the government, and indirectly paid by the people, from customs duties. The question of free trade is not involved, nor is

there now any occasion for a discussion of the wisdom or expediency of
a protective system. Justice and fairness dictate that in any modification of our present laws relating to revenue, the industries and interests
which have been encouraged by such laws, and in which our citizens
have large investments, should not be ruthlessly injured or destroyed.[75]

Stung by their legislative failure in 1884, House Democrats were reluctant
to resurrect the issue because they could count on opposition from the
Randall renegades. But pressure from party activists encouraged the Ways
and Means Committee to try again, which it did. Once again, however,
Randall enlisted the votes of enough Democrats, mainly from New Jersey,
New York, and Pennsylvania, to join with Republicans in killing the bill,
frustrating the party's efforts.

Outraged by this obstruction, the president and his congressional allies set out to outmaneuver the high-tariff Democrats in the House. The
party leadership denounced Randall and packed the Ways and Means
Committee with southern Democrats, while the president stepped up his
rhetoric against the existing system. In his annual message of December
1886, Cleveland called the fiscal surplus "a perversion of the relations between the people and their Government and a dangerous departure from
the rules which limit the right of Federal taxation." The tariff should be
modified, the president insisted, to allow for a more equitable distribution of income. While farmers were forced to sell in competitive markets
and pay stiff taxes on their purchases, manufacturers piled up fortunes because their market was protected from foreign competition.[76] Like the two
previous attempts, this one also failed: Although Democratic opposition
to a tariff reduction was weaker, Republicans could still count on enough
of them to help block any new legislation.

In September 1887, just before the start of a new session of Congress,
Cleveland met with Speaker John Carlisle (D-PA) and the new Ways and
Means Committee chair Roger Q. Mills (D-TX). They agreed to try to destroy the party's tariff dissidents. As Cleveland (1933, 158) wrote, "From
my standpoint, there is but one policy to be pursued: we have got to take
Mr. Randall by a flank movement, and if possible draw his supports from
him one by one."

In December 1887, Cleveland took the unusual step of devoting his entire annual message to Congress to the issue of tariff reform. The president delivered a brisk statement that blasted the tariff as an "indefensible extortion and a culpable betrayal of American fairness and justice."[77]

Warning of the danger to the financial system from the enormous fiscal surplus, the president insisted that

> our present tariff laws, the vicious, inequitable, and illogical source of unnecessary taxation, ought to be at once revised and amended. These laws, as their primary and plain effect, raise the price to consumers of all articles imported and subject to duty by precisely the sum paid for such duties. Thus the amount of the duty measures the tax paid by those who purchase for use these imported articles. Many of these things, however, are raised or manufactured in our own country, and the duties now levied upon foreign goods and products are called protection to these home manufactures, because they render it possible for those of our people who are manufacturers to make these taxed articles and sell them for a price equal to that demanded for the imported goods that have paid customs duty. So it happens that while comparatively a few use the imported articles, millions of our people, who never used and never saw any of the foreign products, purchase and use things of the same kind made in this country, and pay therefor nearly or quite the same enhanced price which the duty adds to the imported articles. Those who buy imports pay the duty charged thereon into the public Treasury, but the great majority of our citizens, who buy domestic articles of the same class, pay a sum at least approximately equal to this duty to the home manufacturer. This reference to the operation of our tariff laws is not made by way of instruction, but in order that we may be constantly reminded of the manner in which they impose a burden upon those who consume domestic products as well as those who consume imported articles, and thus create a tax upon all our people.[78]

Although tariff reductions should be undertaken without "imperiling the existence of our manufacturing interests," Cleveland continued, this "should not mean a condition which, without regard to the public welfare or a national exigency, must always insure the realization of immense profits instead of moderately profitable returns." Indeed, he ridiculed the notion that American manufacturers were still infants that required extensive support through high tariffs: "It suits the purposes of advocacy to call our manufacturers infant industries still needing the highest and greatest degree of favor and fostering care that can be wrung from Federal legislation," but that did not reflect the reality that American producers had a strong and entrenched position in the domestic market.[79] As he pointed out, only 2.6 million workers were employed in industries protected by the tariff, with 14.8 million employed elsewhere, so a vast majority of workers was being taxed for the benefit of a small minority.[80]

Recognizing that Congress would face political difficulties in attempting yet another tariff revision, Cleveland asked the legislature to take a "broad and national contemplation of the subject and a patriotic disregard of such local and selfish claims as are unreasonable and reckless of the welfare of the entire country." Cleveland denied that his proposals had anything to do with the theoretical principles of free trade and protection, but were based simply on the situation confronting the country: "It is a *condition* which confronts us, not a theory. . . . The question of free trade is absolutely irrelevant, and the persistent claim made in certain quarters that all the efforts to relieve the people from unjust and unnecessary taxation are schemes of so-called free traders is mischievous and far removed from any consideration of the public good."[81]

Cleveland's powerful message ensured that tariff policy would be at the top of the nation's political agenda in 1888, a presidential election year. Following the president's message, the Democratic majority on the Ways and Means Committee once again began to formulate new tariff legislation. To expedite matters, no hearings were held; instead, Mills simply crafted a bill to reduce the average tariff on dutiable imports from 54 percent to 33 percent by once again moving raw materials to the duty-free list and reducing the protective tariffs on final goods.

Led by William McKinley of Ohio, the Republican minority vigorously attacked what they described as "a radical reversal" of government policy and "a direct attempt to fasten upon this country the British policy of free foreign trade." They contended that any reduction in protective duties would also slash wages and destroy domestic industries. They particularly attacked the idea of putting raw wool on the free list because that would expose "our flocks and fleeces to merciless competition from abroad" and would "break down one of the most valuable industries of the country." They even objected on fiscal grounds, arguing that a tariff reduction would encourage more imports and hence swell the government coffers with even more revenue.[82]

In the spring of 1888, with an eye to the fall presidential election, the House engaged in a heated debate over the Mills bill. "As long as our government shall endure, it shall be known as 'the Great Tariff Debate of 1888,'" William Springer (D-IL) declared.[83] Mills gave the opening speech for the Democrats and argued that the protective tariffs should be reformed because they taxed the consumption of the great masses of people instead of the income of the wealthy few, created trusts and monopolies that exploited consumers, and generated excessive revenues at a time when the budget surplus needed to be reduced. Acknowledging that the fiscal surplus was excessive, William "Pig Iron" Kelley responded that all internal taxes on alcohol should be lowered but protective tariffs be preserved because otherwise American industry would shrivel up, creating massive unemployment, if left undefended against "overwhelming foreign assaults." He denied that high tariffs led to higher prices for consumers, because, rather than creating trusts and monopolies, they spurred domestic competition that actually reduced prices. Finally, using a now-dated emotional appeal, Kelley waved the "bloody shirt" and tied the Democrats to free trade, slavery, and the Civil War.

The standard Democratic and Republican arguments were repeated by other members in one hundred fifty speeches—described as "dry and flavorless" by Stanwood (1903, 1:234)—that took more than a hundred hours. The stakes were high: "It is the entire system which is on trial," McKinley warned. Seeing "each industry . . . as a pillar in its structure," one member of Congress warned that if the country "let some free trade Samson pull down one of these pillars, . . . the whole temple of American industry must fall."[84] In July 1888, the House passed the Mills bill by a partisan vote of 162–149. The Democratic leadership finally succeeded in overcoming the Randall renegades, and only four Democrats voted against the bill.

Of course, the House's action was largely symbolic because the Mills bill was dead on arrival in the Republican-controlled Senate. The Republican leadership met to decide whether to ignore what the House had done or to fashion their own legislation. The party caucus, led by William Allison of Iowa and Nelson Aldrich of Rhode Island, decided to go on the offensive and prepare a bill that would raise tariff rates instead. The Allison bill would preserve high protective duties while cutting internal taxes on whiskey and tobacco. Although reported from the Finance Committee in October, the bill never came to a vote. Congress adjourned in the final weeks of the fall election campaign without taking action on the bill.

The Congressional tariff battle set the stage for the presidential election campaign of 1888. In their election platform, the Democrats declared, "Upon this great issue of tariff reform, so closely concerning every phase of our national life, and upon every question involved in the problem of good government, the Democratic party submits its principles and professions to the intelligent suffrages of the American people." The party emphasized the need for frugality in public expenditure, maintaining that "all unnecessary taxation is unjust taxation" and stressing the inequity of protection: "The interests of the people are betrayed, when, by unnecessary taxation, trusts and combinations are permitted and fostered, which, while unduly enriching the few that combine, rob the body of our citizens by depriving them of the benefits of natural competition." They called for the support of farmers (since "the price of nearly everything they buy is increased by the favoritism of an unequal system of tax legislation") and sought to reassure established industries that they "should not, and need not, be endangered by a reduction and correction of the burdens of taxation."[85]

Meanwhile, the Republicans stood their ground. In the 1884 campaign, they had reluctantly conceded that tariff reform was necessary; now, with the unified Democrats posing a strong and credible threat to the policy, the Republicans felt compelled not just to defend the existing system but to promise its extension. In their platform they announced, "We are uncompromisingly in favor of the American system of protection; we protest against its destruction as proposed by the President and his party. They serve the interests of Europe; we will support the interests of America. . . . We denounce the Mills bill as destructive to the general business, the labor, and the farming interests of the country." The protective system "must be maintained" because "its abandonment has always been followed by general disaster to all interests." To deal with the fiscal surpluses, Republicans promised to abolish all domestic taxes on tobacco and spirits: "We favor the entire repeal of internal taxes rather than the surrender of any part of our protective system at the joint behests of the whiskey trusts and the agents of foreign manufacturers."[86]

The election of 1888 was a national referendum on the country's tariff policy.[87] Although the issue was as much one of excessive taxation as excessive trade protection, the outcome would determine the fate of tariff reform and the protective system. Republicans tried to paint the president and his party as "free traders," something Cleveland (1933, 189) dismissed as a "pure unadulterated fabrication." Still, despite their recent political gains, the Democrats lacked the aggressiveness and resourcefulness of the well-organized Republicans. The election is also considered to be one of the most corrupt in American history, with reports of vote-buying and other irregularities, particularly in the pivotal swing states of New York and Indiana.[88]

When the final votes had been tallied, Cleveland outpolled his Republican opponent, Benjamin Harrison, by the slim margin of 90,000 votes, earning 48.6 percent of the vote to Harrison's 47.8 percent. But the result was a bitter blow to the Democrats: Harrison captured enough votes in the populous northern states to win the Electoral College decisively by 233 to 168. Not surprisingly, the electoral map showed a sharp North-South division: the South voted overwhelmingly for the Democrats, while the Republicans captured every state in the North and Midwest. Even worse for the Democrats, the Republicans regained control of the House by a slim margin and retained control of the Senate.[89]

Although the electorate had been closely divided, the campaign for tariff reform suffered an enormous setback. The country seemed to have endorsed Republican protectionism, or at least failed to embrace Democratic tariff reform. This allowed Republicans to weave the system of protection even further into the nation's political and economic fabric. Of course, the election was so close that the issue would not disappear from the political scene. In December 1888, Cleveland delivered a parting shot in his annual message to Congress, arguing that "to the extent that the mass of our citizens are inordinately burdened beyond any useful public purpose and for the benefit of a favored few, the Government, under pretext of an exercise of its taxing power, enters gratuitously into partnership with these favorites, to their advantage and to the injury of a vast majority of our people." Cleveland viewed the situation as "injurious to the health of our entire body politic" because it was based on "selfish greed and grasping avarice."[90]

THE MCKINLEY TARIFF OF 1890

The Republican electoral triumph in 1888 restored unified government for the first time in six years. The Republicans consolidated their hold on power by admitting six western states—Washington, Idaho, Montana, Wyoming, North Dakota, and South Dakota—to the union in 1889 and 1890. Just as they had done during the Civil War, the Republicans admitted territories that favored their party and denied statehood to more heavily populated but Democratic-leaning territories, in this case Arizona and New Mexico.[91] The addition of twelve new Republicans to the Senate further diluted Democratic strength in the chamber, but did not significantly affect the balance of power in the House.

However, admitting these states also created some problems for the Republicans. The new states shifted the geographic distribution of political power to the West and heightened existing tensions within the party between western producers of raw materials and eastern producers of final goods. In addition, tariff politics became entwined with, and even overshadowed by, monetary politics that contributed to the sectional tensions. The United States experienced many years of deflation after joining the gold standard in 1873, and Midwestern farmers and Western mining interests pressed for the coinage of silver. Agrarian populists believed that the federal purchase and minting of silver would increase farm prices and stop the deflation that raised the cost of servicing farm mortgages and other debts. Thus, farmers wanted rising prices to reduce their debts, while mining states simply wanted higher prices for their minerals. The coinage of silver would accomplish both objectives. This brought agrarian and mining regions together, but put them at odds with eastern Republicans, who opposed a bimetallic monetary standard and favored a strict adherence to the gold standard.

After his election victory, President Benjamin Harrison called on the new Republican Congress to revise the tariff code to ensure the "just and reasonable protection of our home industries." In his December 1889 message to Congress, he stated, "The preparation of a new schedule of customs duties is a matter of great delicacy because of its direct effect upon the business of the country, and of great difficulty by reason of the wide divergence of opinion as to the objects that may properly be promoted by such legislation. . . . The inequalities of the law should be adjusted, but the protective principle should be maintained and fairly applied to the products of our farms as well as of our shops."[92]

This message opened the contentious Fifty-first Congress, led by House Speaker Thomas Reed (R-ME). This Congress dealt with a wide range of controversial issues, from tariffs and the trusts to veteran pensions and silver purchases. To advance their policy agenda in the Senate, however, the Republicans needed the cooperation of the West. This meant that silver had to be a part of the legislative package. As Senator William Stewart of Nevada flatly stated, "There will be no tariff legislation this session unless a silver bill is passed."[93] Addressing the National Silver Convention in 1889, another Nevada Republican described the region's perspective:

> Protection is not a great moral principle in whose behalf men can be expected to sacrifice their personal interests. It is a coalition in which results should be mutual, and thus far the wheat and silver States have not received their share. In all Nevada there is neither a spindle nor a loom, and the prairies of the Dakotas stretch for hundreds of miles unlit by furnace fire. How can Massachusetts expect that the people of the Northwest will continue to vote for a high protective tariff to sustain New England factories when both political parties in Massa-

chusetts openly avow hostility to the great exporting industries of the Northwest? . . . Free coinage would, as you know, not only restore silver to its former value, but it would . . . add 35 percent to the present prices of wheat, of cotton, and of farm produce, and it would increase the wages of the laborer and add to his opportunities for obtaining employment.[94]

If eastern interests wanted to enact a higher tariff, they would have to compromise with western silver interests. John Sherman of Ohio was the key Republican legislator who orchestrated the passage of the silver and antitrust legislation in 1890 to help secure the passage of a new tariff act. In essence, eastern Republicans voted for the silver purchase act in exchange for western Republican votes on the tariff. The Sherman Silver Purchase Act of 1890 required the government to buy 4.5 million ounces of silver a month using paper money and to keep the price of silver at parity with gold.

At the same time, the Republicans moved quickly in preparing new tariff legislation. Having criticized the secret drafting of the Mills bill by Democrats, the Republican Ways and Means Committee decided to hold open hearings on the tariff revision. Dozens of industry representatives appeared before the committee, generating fourteen hundred pages of testimony. Of course, the hearings were mainly a public relations exercise. Interested parties could speak on the issue, and those testifying almost invariably favored higher rates, but, as before, the real drafting of the bill was done in secret session by the Republican majority.

In April 1890, Ways and Means Chairman William McKinley reported a bill that proposed a significant increase in import duties on protected items. "We do not conceal the purpose of this bill—we want our own countrymen and all mankind to know it," McKinley proclaimed. "It is to increase production here, diversify our productive enterprises, enlarge the field, and increase the demand for American workmen. What American can oppose these worthy and patriotic objects?"[95] Julius Burrows (R-MI) proudly noted that the bill was "to be a measure of protection from its enacting clause to its closing paragraph."[96] The bill proposed to raise the average tariff on dutiable imports from about 41 percent to 52 percent, increasing most rates on raw materials, such as wool, and final goods, such as metals, with the exception of sugar (for reasons discussed below). The goal was both to reduce customs revenue and "to enlarge our own manufacturing plants and check those supplies from abroad which can be profitably produced at home. . . . We have not been so much concerned about the prices of the articles we consume as we have been to encourage a system of home production which shall give fair remuneration to domestic producers and fair wages to American workmen."[97]

The McKinley tariff had four novel features: a full tariff schedule for agricultural goods; the placement of sugar on the duty-free list, with a subsidy to domestic sugar producers as compensation; a new tariff on imported tinplate to create a new domestic industry; and a provision for reciprocity agreements (to be discussed in chapter 6).

First, even though imports of commodities such as wheat, corn, and barley were negligible, Republicans began imposing duties on agricultural goods in an attempt to bring Midwestern farm states into the protectionist coalition. Given that the United States was a major net exporter of these products, imposing import duties on them was largely a symbolic gesture to give the appearance of tariff equality between agriculture and industry, and supposedly balance eastern and western interests. The duties would have a marginal effect in reducing imports from Canada of barley, eggs, meat, potatoes, and butter to benefit some farmers, mainly in Minnesota and North Dakota near the border, but most producers of these crops would be unaffected by them.

Second, the McKinley tariff put sugar on the free list to slash the fiscal surplus. Sugar duties alone accounted for nearly a quarter of all customs revenue. The move harmed sugarcane growers in Louisiana, a Democratic state, but helped sugar refiners in the Northeast. To cut the fiscal surplus even further, as well as offset the harm to western sugar beet farmers, domestic growers were granted a bounty of two cents per pound, equivalent to the previous import duty. The sugar duty yielded $55 million in government revenue, and the sugar subsidy cost about $7 million in additional spending, so the change in sugar policy resulted in a budgetary swing of more than $60 million. McKinley proclaimed, "We have thus given the people free and cheap sugar, and at the same time we have given to our producers, with their invested capital, absolute and complete protection against the cheaper sugar produced by cheaper labor of other countries."[98]

Third, the McKinley bill imposed a higher duty on imported tinplate, a thin sheet of iron or steel coated with tin and used to make cans to preserve food, drums to store and ship petroleum, sheets for roofing, and various household utensils. At the time, there was no domestic production of tinplate, and the United States was entirely dependent upon imports from Britain. McKinley represented the district in eastern Ohio where potential tinplate producers were located and ensured that the provision, specifically designed to create a domestic tinplate industry by making foreign tinplate prohibitively expensive, was included in the bill. However, tinplate consumers—the Standard Oil Company, the food-canning industry, and the roofing industry, all of which used tinplate extensively—were well organized and opposed the increased duty. This made it difficult even for Republicans to muster political support for the higher tariff, and the House approved the increase by only a single vote. Democrats took a dim view of the action, saying that it "involved a new and distinct perversion of the Federal taxing power by making present, tangible, and profitable industries the sport and prey of prospective, conjectural, and speculative adventures."[99] (The next section of this chapter discusses whether tinplate was an infant industry and whether the policy worked.)

In May 1890, McKinley opened the House debate with a ringing endorsement of protection. The Republican majority and Speaker Reed's rules limited the floor debate over the bill, with no possibilities for amendments, ensuring that the outcome was no surprise. The House quickly passed the bill in a partisan vote of 164–142; Republicans voted 163–2 in favor of the bill, while Democrats voted 140–1 against it.[100] Figure 5.1 shows the House vote. As in the antebellum period, the North-South division stands out, although now the upper Midwest was also strongly in the Republican camp.

The bill was then sent to the Senate, where the chair of the Finance Committee, Nelson Aldrich (R-RI), took responsibility for ushering it

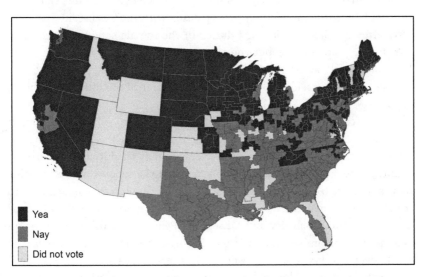

Figure 5.1. House vote on the McKinley tariff, May 21, 1890. (Map courtesy of Citrin GIS/Applied Spatial Analysis Lab, Dartmouth College.)

through the chamber. The bill was reported from the committee in mid-June, but was held up by demands from western Republicans and Democrats for the coinage of silver. This is when John Sherman stepped in with a compromise to satisfy the western silver interests—the Sherman Silver Purchase Act—which allowed the tariff bill to move forward.

In July and August, in dozens of roll-call votes on individual commodities, the Senate made 496 amendments to the House bill. The higher tinplate duty was one of the more controversial provisions, and tinplate-using industries—such as the Standard Oil Company, which purchased oil drums, and food processors who purchased cans made from tinplate—opposed the new tariff on the grounds that it would raise their costs. To allay the fear that the duty would burden tinplate-consuming industries without fostering any domestic production, William Spooner (R-WI) introduced an unusual provision in which the tinplate duty would expire in six years unless domestic production reached one-third of imports. This is the only instance in which Congress made tariff protection contingent on the performance of the domestic industry.

After prolonged debate, the Senate passed the bill in September 1890 in a straight party-line vote of 40–29. A House-Senate conference committee worked for ten days going through the four thousand items in the tariff code and accepted 272 of the 496 Senate amendments. "I have been hard at work for a week or more on this tariff conference committee," Sherman sighed. "I trust I will not live long enough to have any connection with another." McKinley was not entirely pleased with the final result, particularly after the Senate cut some duties in the metals schedule: "Many of the changes I do not like, but you see there is no time to specify. I scarcely know what will be the end of it."[101] After both chambers approved the conference version, President Benjamin Harrison signed the bill on October 1, 1890.

The McKinley tariff was the first major overhaul of the entire tariff schedule since the Civil War. Of course, the revision was not designed to reduce duties; in fact, it raised the average tariff on dutiable imports by about 4 percentage points. It sharply reduced the federal budget surplus by making sugar duty-free, which was part of the Republican strategy to insulate protective tariffs from any major reduction. The Republicans also passed the Disability and Dependent Pension Act to extend pension benefits to noncombatants and their children as another way of reducing the budget surplus. Enacted twenty-five years after the end of the Civil War, this legislation doubled government spending on military pensions between 1889 and 1893. Consequently, the Fifty-first Congress became known as the "Billion Dollar Congress" for its lavish spending on veterans' benefits, silver purchases, and sugar bounties. If the fiscal surpluses of the 1880s were viewed as a problem, the Republicans solved it. The fiscal surplus soon disappeared completely when a severe economic downturn struck in 1893 and pushed the federal budget into a large deficit.

Republicans had chosen to increase tariffs at a time when public sentiment, as revealed in the presidential election of 1888, was closely split over whether to reduce them or not. If the electorate had been uneasy about Cleveland's proposal to cut tariffs in 1888, it had not necessarily endorsed a significant increase. Some Republicans worried about the public's reaction to their work. James Blaine (R-ME) warned that the tariff hike was "injudicious from beginning to end. . . . Such movements as this for protection will protect the Republican party only into speedy retirement."[102] Even McKinley seemed to distance himself from the tariff that bore his name. When asked why he approved of such high rates in the House proposal, McKinley replied, "for the best reason in the world, to get my bill passed. My idea was to get the act through Congress, and to make necessary reductions later. I realized that some things were too high, but I couldn't get my bill through without it. . . . No tariff bill was ever framed that was not largely made up by compromises."[103]

The bill also had international ramifications in rattling the British Empire. The tariffs shut out Canadian agricultural products and, by blocking imports of British woolen goods, also reduced demand for Australian wool. The United States was by now the world's largest economy, and its actions had repercussions around the globe. The McKinley bill contributed to a rise in protectionist sentiment in Britain and its dominions, leading to calls to establish a trade bloc with tariff preferences within the British Empire. While some Americans thought high tariffs against its goods would "starve Canada into annexation" and force Canada to join the United States, Canada was instead pushed into closer ties with Britain.[104] Members of Congress did not fully appreciate that the United States had become a global economic power and that its trade policies were increasingly felt in other countries.

DID TARIFFS PROMOTE INFANT INDUSTRIES?

One reason that Republicans gave for supporting protective tariffs is that they would help nurture "infant industries" by protecting them against their more established (usually British) rivals. The idea behind infant industry protection is that new firms suffer from an initial cost disadvantage that prevents them from starting production in an industry already dominated by foreign producers. If new firms were given the chance to gain production experience, it was thought, they could reduce their costs and compete effectively against their more established foreign rivals. Without temporary protection from foreign competition giving them time to mature, some domestic industries, it was feared, would never arise.[105] For the protection of an infant industry to improve welfare, however, the industry must at some point be able to survive without government assistance and generate some long-term economic benefits that exceed the costs to consumers from the higher prices that they paid when imports were restricted. If it fails to reduce its costs and is unable to survive on its own, the infant industry will remain an inefficient, high-cost industry that burdens the economy.[106] Unfortunately, infant industry policies are very difficult to assess: *ex ante*, it is almost impossible to know whether an industry is an "infant" that has the chance of growing up to be successful, and *ex post*, it is difficult to determine if import protection (as opposed to other factors) was required to allow it to develop.

The debate over infant industries centered on three issues: whether tariff protection would (1) create new wealth and capital or merely divert it from other more profitable activities; (2) stimulate domestic producers to acquire new technology and reduce costs, or inhibit competition and stifle the incentive for such improvements; and (3) generate long-term net benefits for the economy or simply give rise to inefficient industries that would require ongoing government support and forever burden consumers with high prices. Of course, the two political parties took opposing positions on the desirability of protecting infant industries. To Republicans, any protected industry that started or increased domestic production was beneficial, even if it never became competitive on world markets and even if the policy harmed consumers and downstream user industries. Their goal was simply to keep the domestic market for domestic firms and eliminate imports. Meanwhile, Democrats rejected this view as unfair government interference in the economy that helped some industries at the expense of others, harmed agriculture and export-oriented producers, reduced competition, and forced consumers to pay high prices.

The United States never really had an infant industry policy in the sense of deliberately identifying and targeting assistance to specific industries. Instead, the post–Civil War tariff code provided across-the-board protection to every industry facing foreign competition, whether it produced raw materials, capital goods, or final goods. And surprisingly few

candidates have been put forward as good examples of infant industry protection. Cotton and woolen manufactures were, by this time, mature industries that had been protected for decades. The silk industry was sometimes mentioned as having successfully matured under protection, but it
remained vulnerable to foreign competition and required substantial, ongoing protection.

The iron and steel industry is more frequently cited as illustrating the
benefits of protective tariffs. Although the industry was well established
before the Civil War, it received significant protection after the war and
grew to an enormous size, eventually proving to be competitive on world
markets (see the discussion in chapter 6).[107] The question has always been
whether the industry grew rapidly after the Civil War because of protection from foreign competition, or whether America's abundance of natural
resources—particularly iron ore and coal in western Pennsylvania—would
have allowed it to develop even without the need for tariffs. In their study,
Berglund and Wright (1929, 134) concluded that "whatever had been our
policy with respect to the tariff, the United States would have developed a
great iron and steel industry," although they conceded that "without the
tariff, the initial steps might have been delayed, and the growth might
have been slower."[108]

Figure 5.2 gives a sense of proportion for the threat posed by foreign

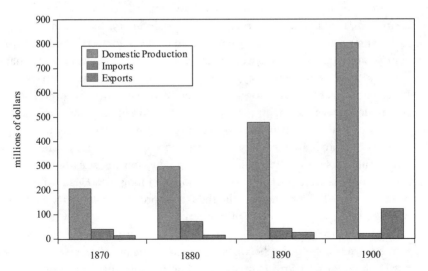

Figure 5.2. Iron and steel manufactures, value of domestic production, imports,
and exports, 1870–1900. (*Statistical Abstract of the United States* 1913, 665.)

competition by showing the value of domestic production of iron and steel manufactures, along with imports and exports. Even in the 1870s, imports comprised a relatively small percentage of domestic consumption. By 1890, the United States produced more pig iron than Britain. Even if the United States had completely abolished its tariff, Britain simply did not have the production capacity to supply the entire American market, except at significantly higher prices. Over the whole period, Berglund and Wright (1929, 116–17) "find it hard to believe that foreign competition is a matter of any great concern to the domestic industry as a whole" because imports were so small in relation to domestic production and "neither the general trend nor the annual fluctuations [in domestic production] appear to be perceptibly influenced by downward changes in the tariff."

A more plausible case of a successful infant industry policy may be steel rails, which were the backbone of the country's rapidly expanding railroad network. The United States imposed a 45 percent tariff on imported rails until 1870, when a specific duty of $28 per ton was imposed. The sharp decline in steel rail prices meant that the ad valorem equivalent reached more than 100 percent, an enormous burden on railroad construction but a tremendous stimulus to steel rail production. Imports were completely squeezed out of the market, and the United States began exporting rails after the turn of the century. Despite this train of events, Taussig (1915, 154) believed that factors such as technological improvements and new iron ore discoveries "were much more important than the protective tariffs" in accounting for the growth of the industry. By contrast, Head (1994) suggested that protection could have enabled domestic producers to gain production experience, resulting in declining production costs that eventually allowed the industry to become competitive on world markets. In a counterfactual simulation, Head found that country-specific learning by doing was so important to the steel rail industry that, under free trade, domestic production would not have begun until 1913. By blocking imports, the tariff allowed domestic firms to acquire the production experience that was critical to reducing their production costs. Although steel rail consumers were hurt in both the short and long run, Head finds that overall welfare (which includes the industry's profits) was slightly positive over the long run as a result of protection.

However, this simulation model assumes that the benefits of production experience spill over between domestic firms but not between countries—that is, that learning-by-doing is country-specific. The assumption of no international spillovers of learning-based knowledge implies that subsequent entrants cannot adapt or build upon the production experience of the British leaders. This ensures that the first producers in an industry have an entrenched and virtually insurmountable advantage over subsequent rivals. If there are international spillovers of production knowledge, due to labor mobility or other reasons, the case for infant industry policies is weakened considerably. In that case, experienced producers no longer have an entrenched advantage over potential entrants who can take advantage of existing knowledge generated by other producers. In fact, US producers were able to borrow from and adopt British technological advances, including those arising from learning by doing.[109]

Another supposedly successful case of infant industry protection was the tinplate industry. Unlike many manufacturing industries, tinplate failed to receive significant tariff protection because of a mistaken interpretation of the tariff code in 1864 by the secretary of the Treasury, who erroneously moved a comma in the tariff act by just two words. Instead of receiving a tariff of more than 50 percent, as implied by the 1864 act, imported tinplate was construed as falling under a different section of the tariff code and received a duty of only 15 percent.[110] The Treasury's decision meant there was almost no domestic production in the 1870s and 1880s, and the United States was entirely dependent on imports from Britain.

Congress remedied the error in 1890, as we have seen, but made protection contingent on the successful growth of the industry. The experiment appeared to succeed: the McKinley tariff sharply increased duties; many firms entered the industry, and domestic production soared after 1891, matching the quantity of imports by 1896 and capturing nearly 90 percent of the domestic market by 1899. To evaluate whether the tinplate industry was truly an infant industry, however, requires answering the question: Was protection necessary for the establishment of the industry, or would it have happened at some point anyway?

The two obstacles preventing the establishment of domestic tinplate production were the high cost of raw materials and the lack of production experience. The iron and steel sheets that were to be coated with tin accounted for nearly three-quarters of the cost of producing tinplate. On this score, British producers had a significant cost advantage, because the price of iron and steel inputs were roughly 50 percent higher in the United States. As a result, domestic iron- and steel-using industries paid a significant premium for their inputs, compared with their foreign counterparts, leading to negative effective protection.[111] This premium declined rapidly in the early 1890s, for reasons to be discussed in chapter 6, and the prices of iron and steel raw materials were roughly equivalent in the two countries by the turn of the century. This is the basis for the belief that domestic tinplate producers would eventually have entered the industry even without the aid of the tariff.

Another obstacle to the establishment of domestic tinplate production was the lack of previous production experience. But because there were international spillovers of knowledge, the obstacles to entrants who lacked production experience were less severe because they could learn from the experience of other established producers. The tinplate industry appears to have been characterized by both domestic and international technological and learning-based knowledge spillovers. The international spillovers arose from the migration of skilled tinplate workers from Wales to the United States, partly as a result of the tariff.[112] Indeed, the early US plants were partly owned or managed by Welsh immigrants who carried with them the technical knowledge of tinplate production. They essentially transplanted Welsh production methods into the United States.

Taussig (1915, 178) was skeptical that the tinplate industry was really an infant industry, arguing that its growth after 1890 "was due chiefly to the cheapening of the fundamental raw material," namely rolled iron and steel sheets. Irwin (2000) confirmed Taussig's view: the benefits of cheaper iron to the industry were much greater than the effect of greater production experience in lowering production costs. This analysis suggested the tinplate industry would have developed in the United States around 1901, instead of 1891, in the absence of the McKinley tariff, as the domestic price of basic iron and steel converged to the British price. In other words, the high domestic price of iron and steel raw materials was the primary reason why the domestic tinplate industry failed to develop sooner: the tariff accelerated the development of the industry but did not ultimately account for its success. The McKinley tariff also failed to improve economic welfare: the initial large losses of consumers were not offset by the stream of profits received by domestic producers, because tinplate production was a low-margin business in which entry was relatively easy.

Judging the impact of tariffs in promoting infant industries has always been controversial. Taussig (1915, 153) concluded that "there is a *prima facie* case for the protectionist, again an apparent confirmation of the validity of the young [infant] industries argument, from the nature and extent of the industrial development during the last two decades of the nineteenth century." And yet, he continued, "the same doubt may be expressed: would not all this growth have taken place in any case?" In fact, there are many reasons to entertain doubts: after the Civil War, most manufacturing industries were no longer "infants."

In sum, protective tariffs were maintained after the Civil War because of the strong political coalition that stood behind them. However, that did not leave the policy immune from criticism. In fact, objections to the tariff would only increase in the early twentieth century.

CHAPTER SIX

Protectionism Entrenched, 1890–1912

The enactment of the McKinley tariff after the Great Tariff Debate of 1888 once again postponed any significant change in the post–Civil War import duties. The system of protection through high tariffs seemed politically secure and firmly entrenched. Those duties were sometimes defended on the grounds that they helped the United States to become an industrial nation, a claim that is examined in this chapter. However, the turn of the century brought a significant new development that had the potential to alter the course of US trade policy: for the first time in its history, the United States became a net exporter of manufactured goods. This dramatic shift in the pattern of trade gave many large industries an interest in promoting exports through reciprocity agreements rather than being sheltered behind high protective tariffs. Yet this ultimately failed to bring about any changes in policy: import duties remained high, Democrats squandered their one opportunity to enact lower tariffs, Congress rejected reciprocity agreements, and the partisan battle between Republicans and Democrats over trade policy continued unabated.

PROTECTIONISM AND AMERICA'S INDUSTRIAL EXPANSION

The decades after the Civil War were a period of uniformly high protective tariffs and unprecedented economic expansion and growth in manufacturing production. One of the most controversial questions in the history of US trade policy is the relationship between the two: Were high tariffs responsible for the strong economic growth of the late nineteenth century and the emergence of the United States as an industrial power?

The basic facts of the country's expansion after the Civil War are astounding. Between 1860 and 1900, the US population doubled, railroad track mileage grew from about 31,000 miles to 258,000 miles, pig iron output increased by a factor of sixteen, and coal production grew by a factor of twenty-three. In 1870, the United States accounted for 23 percent of the world's production of manufactured goods; by 1913, that share had risen to 36 percent, largely at the expense of Britain, whose share fell from 32 percent to 14 percent.[1] By the turn of the century, the United States was the world's leading manufacturing producer.

The United States also became the world's largest economy, with one of the highest per capita incomes in the world. In 1870, the US economy was about the same size as Britain's; by the turn of the century, its GDP was twice as large. The relative standing of the two countries in terms of per capita income in 1870 is disputed—some calculations suggest that US per capita income was about 20 percent below Britain's around 1870, while others suggest that it was 20 percent above it. But there is a consensus that by 1910 US per capita income exceeded that in Britain by a substantial margin: one calculation has per capita income 26 percent higher and per worker GDP 38 percent higher in that year.[2]

Were high tariffs responsible, at least in part, for the extensive growth experienced during this period? Contemporary proponents of protection certainly thought so. In 1890, William McKinley of Ohio triumphantly stated, "We lead all nations in agriculture, we lead all nations in mining, and we lead all nations in manufacturing. These are the trophies which we bring after twenty-nine years of a protective tariff. Can any other system furnish such evidences of prosperity?"[3] If protective tariffs accelerated economic growth or promoted the country's economic development, it would be difficult to argue that protection was a costly policy or that free trade would have been a better policy.[4]

And yet most economic historians have been skeptical about whether America's rapid growth in the late nineteenth century can be attributed to protective tariffs. They note that there were many other factors driving the huge economic expansion, not least of which was that the North American continent was packed with an abundance of land and other natural resources, with few barriers to their exploitation. Congress did not carefully design the tariff schedule with industrial expansion in mind. Instead, import duties were set without much regard to the economic importance of the protected industry, because they were imposed for political reasons rather than to achieve some specific economic purpose.[5] Douglass North (1960b, 199) concludes that "on balance, it is doubtful if the tariff promoted American industrialization much more rapidly than would have occurred in its absence, and it is even more doubtful that it resulted in any net addition to national income over this period." In part, this is because "the tariff indiscriminately blanketed protection on many raw materials and manufactures, aiding and abetting those which represented a poor use of resources as well as some in which we were efficient." Nevertheless, there are several channels through which trade policy might have promoted growth during this period, and each deserves some consideration.

Of course, to say that the US economy grew rapidly in the late nineteenth century is to make a comparative statement. A common point of reference is Britain, the leading industrial nation that pursued a policy of free trade during this period. Table 6.1 compares the economic performance of the two economies from 1870–1913, based on data compiled by Angus Maddison. Over this period, real GDP grew nearly 4 percent per year in the United States, compared to about 2 percent in Britain. In terms of the underlying sources of growth, America's economic expansion was partly due to a rapid increase in population. Between 1870 and 1913, the US population more than doubled, growing from 40 million to 97 million, while Britain's population only rose from 31 million to 45 million.

Yet per capita GDP also grew more rapidly in the United States, at about 1.8 percent per year compared with 1.0 percent in Britain. The faster growth of per capita income was fueled by more rapid capital accumulation. After accounting for growth in the labor force and capital stock, the total-factor productivity "residual" appears to have been roughly comparable in the two economies. In other words, the United States grew faster than Britain in the late nineteenth century because of labor-force growth and capital accumulation, not because of increases in productive efficiency. The growth in per capita income was mainly the result of capital deepening, arising from high rates of saving and investment, rather than greater productivity.

TABLE 6.1. Comparative growth performance: United States and United Kingdom, 1870–1913 (annual average percentage growth)

	United States	United Kingdom
Real GDP	3.94	1.90
Population	2.09	1.21
GDP per capita	1.81	1.01
Non-residential capital stock	5.53	1.73
Total factor productivity	0.33	0.31

Source: Maddison 1995, 255.

Although growth accounting tells us where to look for the sources of growth, it does not tell us anything about the role of trade policy specifically. To say that the United States experienced strong economic growth because its labor force and capital stock grew rapidly raises the question of why this happened and whether high tariffs encouraged or discouraged these developments. In fact, the United States had an unusual policy mix: while it blocked the importation of some foreign goods, it offered virtually unimpeded entry to people, capital, and ideas into the country from abroad. In this sense, the United States was a very open economy in the nineteenth century.

In terms of the growth of the labor force, tariff policy is unlikely to have influenced fertility decisions or death rates, so it probably did not affect the natural rate of population increase or the labor force participation ratio (the percent of the work-age population employed). Nearly one-third of the population increase from 1870 to 1900 was due to immigration from abroad, and it is plausible that some of this immigration was induced by high tariffs.[6] A theorem by Robert Mundell (1957) holds that international trade in goods and the international movement of factors of production (such as labor and capital) are substitutes for one another. To the extent that the United States discouraged imports by imposing high barriers on foreign goods, it might have encouraged greater immigration by foreign nationals. Yet tariffs were probably a small factor in promoting immigration overall, except in a few cases discussed below.[7]

In terms of capital accumulation, the share of capital formation in GDP increased significantly around the time of the Civil War; net investment rose from about 10 percent of GDP before the war to nearly 20 percent of GDP after. But it is unlikely that high tariffs played much of a role in this capital-deepening. Economic historians have concluded that capital accumulation was a savings-driven rather than an investment-driven phenomenon: the relative price of capital goods and real interest rates declined sharply during this period, suggesting that a shift in the supply of savings due to the development of financial markets dominated any shift in investment demand.[8] The growth in savings was facilitated by the National Banking Acts of 1863 and 1864, which helped stabilize the financial system and encourage the entry of more than seven hundred banks during the Civil War era. These banks, spread largely across Ohio and the upper Midwest, were a major factor in promoting the growth of manufacturing in the region and the rapid increase in the nation's capital stock.[9] In addition, the biggest rise in the capital-output ratio occurred in the services sector, such as railroads and urban housing, with only a modest change in manufacturing. Furthermore, high tariffs on imported capital goods may have impeded (rather than promoted) capital investments and have been shown in other contexts to be particularly damaging to a country's growth prospects.[10]

Of course, consistent with Mundell's theorem, protective tariffs could have promoted capital investment from abroad. Since tariffs prevented foreign producers from exporting directly to the US market, they might have made foreign direct investments in the United States to serve consumers inside the tariff wall. Yet the contribution of foreign investment to total capital accumulation in the post–Civil War period was very small: foreign capital inflows financed only 6 percent of net capital formation from 1869–1914. Thus, almost all of domestic investment was financed by domestic savings. In addition, few multinational corporations were capable of making sizeable foreign investments in the United States prior to World War I.[11]

If the links between protective tariffs and the expansion of the labor force or the accumulation of capital are weak, their relationship to aggregate productivity growth is equally tenuous. Table 6.1 indicated that aggregate productivity growth was no more rapid in the United States than in Britain during this period. Table 6.2 presents total-factor productivity growth by sector and shows that productivity growth in non-traded sectors (such as transportation, services, utilities, and communications) was much more rapid than in agriculture or manufacturing, the sectors most affected by trade. Productivity growth in the service sector is usually explained by particular technological innovations—such as railroads, electrification, the telegraph—none of which depended on protective tariffs. And yet the service sector was key to US economic performance during

TABLE 6.2. US total factor productivity growth by sector (average annual percentage change)

	1869–1909	1879–1909	1889–1909
Agriculture	0.8	0.6	0.4
Manufacturing	1.2	1.1	0.9
Mining	—	1.5	1.0
Transportation	2.8	2.6	2.1
Utilities and communications	2.0	2.3	3.0
National	1.5	0.6	1.3

Source: Kendrick 1961, 331, 362, 396, 464, 540, 580.

this period. As Broadberry (1998) has shown, output per worker in the United States grew relative to that in Britain because US labor productivity in services converged to the higher level in Britain.

If protective tariffs did not directly affect labor-force growth, capital accumulation, or total-factor productivity, they might have increased economic growth by shifting resources out of agriculture and into manufacturing. Table 6.3 presents the contributions of three main sectors of the economy—agriculture, industry, and services—to national income and the allocation of the labor force across those sectors. Over the late nineteenth century, the share of agriculture in total output and employment declined, while the share of industry and services increased. Such a structural shift was an important feature of late nineteenth-century economic growth, because output per worker was much higher in industry and services than in agriculture.

TABLE 6.3. Structural change in the US economy, 1840–1900

A. Percentage distribution of national income

	Agriculture	Industry	Services
1840	47	16	37
1850	40	22	38
1860	38	22	40
1870	36	25	39
1880	31	25	44
1890	21	30	49
1900	19	31	50

B. Percentage distribution of US labor force

	Agriculture	Industry	Services
1840	67	9	24
1850	60	16	24
1860	56	15	29
1870	50	21	29
1880	48	21	31
1890	40	21	39
1900	36	23	41

Source: US Bureau of the Census 1975, series F-238-249, D-167-181.

Note: Agriculture includes agriculture, forestry, and fisheries; industry includes mining and manufacturing; services include construction and all other sectors.

The shift of resources from agriculture to industry could be due to the "push" of resources out of agriculture (due to productivity growth in the sector) or the "pull" of resources into industry and services (as a result of greater demand for these sectors, including tariffs that reduced imports).[12] In terms of the former, rising agricultural productivity is almost always a key part of the industrialization process. Productivity growth in agriculture allows the farm sector to release labor that can be employed in other parts of the economy where output per worker is higher. The improvement in agricultural productivity was an important factor in US economic development: output per worker in agriculture changed very little between 1800 and 1850, but then increased significantly from 1850 to 1870 and continued to grow for the rest of the century.[13] This mid-century burst in agricultural productivity is associated with the increase in American industrialization after 1850.

Trade policy can either promote or retard this structural change, in which resources are shifted from agriculture to industry. Since the United States was a large exporter of agricultural goods, international trade may have slowed the movement of resources from agriculture to industry. By contrast, protective duties might have encouraged the shift of labor and capital from agriculture to industry, a policy known as import substitution, and thereby might have increased real income.

Yet structural change—the shift of resources from agriculture to industry—accounts for only a modest portion of America's overall growth in output per worker during this period. More than three-quarters of aggregate productivity growth was due to the increase in labor productivity within each sector, not the result of shifting resources between sectors. With about half of the labor force still employed in agriculture as late as 1880, overall growth in output per worker simply could not have been very high without strong labor productivity growth in agriculture. While such growth decompositions do not have a causal interpretation, this result suggests that the role of protective duties in promoting output per worker was not large. And, of course, such structural change had been occurring in the decades before the Civil War, when the average tariff was much lower.

Most arguments that emphasize the contribution of protective tariffs to economic growth put special emphasis on expanding the size of the manufacturing sector. But the role of manufacturing is often overstated. As Broadberry (1998, 400) observes, "The United States caught up with and overtook Britain in terms of aggregate labor productivity largely by shifting resources out of agriculture and improving their relative productivity position in services rather than by improving their position in manufacturing. The key role attributed by many economic historians and growth economists to developments within manufacturing as the major factor driving convergence or divergence of productivity needs to be seriously qualified, and attention needs to be shifted to developments within services."

As noted in chapter 4, the United States had a fairly large manufacturing sector before the Civil War, one that had even flourished under low protective tariffs after 1846.[14] Table 5.2 showed that imports of manufactured goods were just 9 percent of domestic consumption of manufactured goods in 1859, prior to the war, and just 3 percent after the Civil War. Even a large increase in imports would have a limited impact on the overall size of the manufacturing sector and a minor impact on the overall economy.

Consider the following calculation based on data for 1869, when manufacturing was arguably the most vulnerable to foreign competition in the post–Civil War period. In that year the United States imported $220 million of non-food manufactured goods, while producing $3,385 million worth of manufactured goods with 2.053 million workers (or $1,648 per worker in manufacturing).[15] Abolishing the 40 percent average tariff on manufactured imports would have reduced the relative price of imports by 29 percent. If the elasticity of import demand was–2.6, as estimated by Irwin (1998b), this would increase manufactured imports by 75 percent, or $163 million. If these additional imports reduced domestic production of manufactured goods on a one-for-one basis—which overstates the impact, because most imports were imperfect substitutes for domestic goods— that would have displaced 99,119 workers in manufacturing. This was about 4.8 percent of manufacturing employment, or about 1.6 percent of the total labor force, and would have reduced manufacturing employment from 2.47 million to 2.37 million.

Such a shift would have limited consequences for the overall economy. If 1.6 percent of the labor force were shifted from manufacturing, where total-factor productivity was growing 1.2 percent a year, to agriculture, where it was growing 0.8 percent a year, economy-wide productivity growth would have fallen from 1.50 percent to 1.49 percent a year. The cumulative effect starting in 1870 would have been to reduce the level of GDP in 1913 by a slight 0.2 percent. When considered this way, the impact of tariff protection on the level of national income and on aggregate productivity, in terms of shifting of labor from agriculture into industry, appears to be small.

This discussion has been based on the premise that the tariff made a positive contribution to America's economic growth. There are other reasons to believe that import duties may have detracted from US economic performance. As already noted, tariffs on capital goods made investment spending more costly and less efficient. The high cost of basic iron and steel hampered the development of downstream industries, such as tinplate (considered in chapter 5), and raised the cost of construction and transportation projects. In addition, protection tended to encourage the survival of smaller, less efficient firms in a given industry rather than larger, more efficient enterprises, thereby reducing an industry's average productivity. Unfortunately, there has been little economic research to quantify these factors.

In sum, it is difficult to make the case that high import tariffs were an important factor driving late nineteenth-century US economic growth. The reallocation of labor brought about by the tariff was relatively modest, and the productivity consequences were small as well. The service sector, which was not directly affected by import duties, generated much of the growth in employment and productivity, and played a key role in increasing the US lead over Britain in per capita income in the late nineteenth century. And agriculture laid the foundation for the farm equipment and machinery industry, an important part of the manufacturing economy. Indeed, the United States became a net exporter of agricultural implements as John Deere, American Harvester, and other producers sold large quantities to the world market. Thus, it appears that trade-related factors were not critical to the overall growth and expansion of the American economy.[16]

At the same time, it is difficult to argue that the high-tariff policy was costly and inefficient. As already noted, the static deadweight loss of the tariff was small, amounting to about 0.5 percent of GDP around the mid-1870s. Protection did not breed many inefficient industries that were far behind the technological frontier, because new firms with access to the best technology in the world could freely enter the market. This ensured that domestic competition remained robust. Falling transportation costs made the United States a large, integrated national market, and the rise of large business enterprises meant that smaller, less-efficient firms found it difficult to survive, even if foreign competition was limited by import duties.[17]

If protective tariffs were not responsible for America's economic growth, what was? The United States was an enormous continental market with an abundance of resources waiting to be filled with people. Much of the growth was extensive—adding more labor, cultivating more land, digging more mines, investing more capital—rather than intensive—improving the productivity of the currently employed resources. The nation had free internal trade and the free movement of labor and capital across states, an abundance of agricultural land and untapped mineral resources, and the enforcement of contracts and protection of property rights through a non-politicized judicial system. The size and scale of the market, knitted together with railroads and other transportation improvements, led to efficient large-scale businesses and innovative organizational structures that encouraged industry specialization and ensured robust domestic competition.[18] The federal government did not interfere with the process of creative destruction and limit competition or artificially prop up inefficient industries. The country had a well-functioning capital market that facilitated high investment rates, access to the world's best industrial technology from Britain and elsewhere, and an expanding system of high schools that ensured high levels of literacy among the general population. In short, the country was well situated for both extensive and intensive growth, regardless of the trade policy it chose.

More than any other country in the world at this time, the United States had an extraordinarily diversified economy with an abundance of prime agricultural land, a large endowment of raw materials, and growing technical expertise in manufacturing. At this point, international trade was not critical to the prosperity of the country. "Even if every port of the United States were blockaded today, and remained so for ten years, the people of the United States would suffer only some inconveniences and disturbances in values [i.e., prices]," the steel magnate Andrew Carnegie (1890, 64–65) opined. "No one desires the closing of our ports as the country is prospering too well to welcome any changes; but it is well for us to know, and for other nations to understand, that it would only be disturbing and inconvenient, not serious, nor in any way dangerous to the life and prosperity of this world within itself." Conversely, even if the United States had abolished all tariffs, foreign trade still would have been a relatively small part of the continental-sized American economy. The share of merchandise trade in GDP was just 5–6 percent during this period; setting the tariff to zero might have increased the share to 7–8 percent.

The most underrated international factor behind America's industrialization was the work done by unskilled immigrants who labored in the manufacturing industries and by skilled immigrants who facilitated the absorption of new technology. The influx of unskilled migrants transformed the workforce between 1880 and 1920. Immigrants and their children, who were willing to accept lower wages than native-born citizens, comprised more than half of manufacturing workers in 1920. The availability of these workers is thought to have accelerated the pace and scale of manufacturing in the United States by a modest amount.[19]

The migration of skilled artisans was also important during this period. A country that is behind the technological frontier can improve its productivity by adopting the world's best technology, usually by importing new capital goods or receiving foreign direct investment. For the United States, a leading conduit for technology transfer from abroad was the immigration of skilled workers. A significant number of British immigrants were craftsmen who had experience with industrial technology. "British immigrants to industrial America directly transfused the skills and experience of the premier industrial nation of the early twentieth century into the veins of the rising giant of the twentieth," Berthoff (1953, 28–29) points out. The close cultural relationship between the two countries allowed technology to diffuse rapidly across the Atlantic. The United States had the good fortune to be the former colony of the country that experienced the first Industrial Revolution. With the bond of a common history, language, and culture, the United States could easily assimilate new ideas, machinery, and other technology from the country then at the world's technological frontier, although skilled immigrants from Germany also made important contributions to the nation's technology.

For example, in metallurgy, the United States quickly copied many new technologies developed in Britain. Just a few years after Bessemer steel technology proved commercially successful in Britain, patent agreements allowed it to spread quickly throughout the United States. Even better, American engineers often improved upon the imported technology.[20] Immigrants not only started their own firms in the iron and steel industry, but the American woolen industry was founded largely on English experience. British thread, lace, and silk manufacturers from Nottingham came to set up branch mills in America, while foreign textile operatives often rose through the ranks of overseers and superintendents and eventually established their own factories. In some cases, there is a direct link between tariffs that reduced British exports and the subsequent emigration of skilled workers to the United States. "Nearly the whole English silk industry migrated to America after the Civil War," Berthoff (1953, 41) observes, when tariffs increased, and "owners of British factories crated their machinery and left for [Paterson] New Jersey with their workmen." In these cases, where import duties prompted the migration of British citizens with technical knowledge, the tariff may have increased the pace at which technology moved between the two countries.

Because the United States industrialized under a regime of high tariffs, some observers have tried to draw lessons from America's experience in the late nineteenth century that would apply to developing countries today. Unfortunately, the vast differences between the United States then and developing countries today invalidate any such comparison. The United States has never really been a developing country in the modern sense of the term: it has always been a high-wage country, not a low-wage country, and has never had difficulty attracting skilled and unskilled immigrants from abroad. In the nineteenth century, the United States had a relatively small and unobtrusive government, an enormous domestic market, and close economic and cultural ties to the country at the world's technological frontier from which it could easily adopt new innovations. Many developing countries today have large, intrusive, and often corrupt governments, relatively small domestic markets, and create barriers to foreign investment and technology transfer. These differences mean that the US experience has few policy lessons for developing countries today.

TRADE POLITICS IN THE 1890S

In the wake of the Great Tariff Debate of 1888, as we saw in chapter 5, the Republicans raised import duties in the McKinley tariff of 1890. At a time when the public debate was about how to reduce the tariff and the fiscal surplus, this response seemed out of line with public sentiment. In fact, the "Billion Dollar Congress" had miscalculated, and electoral retribution was swift. The Democrats made big gains in the 1890 midterm elections. Although Republicans narrowly retained the Senate, the House flipped from a Republican majority of seven to a Democratic majority of one hundred forty seven. Even McKinley lost his bid for reelection after being gerrymandered out of his Ohio seat by the Democratic state legislature. Although the tariff was not entirely responsible for the Republican electoral disaster, many observers at the time believed that to be the case. In the opinion of Theodore Roosevelt, a rising Republican politician, "The overwhelming nature of the disaster is due entirely to the McKinley bill."[21] In fact, House Speaker Joseph Cannon later conjectured that any revision of the tariff would harm the incumbent party at the next election, an idea for which there is empirical support.[22]

The 1892 presidential election saw a rematch between Grover Cleveland and Benjamin Harrison. Although the tariff was again an important election issue, monetary politics—particularly the coinage of silver—dominated the campaign. Despite the apparent unpopularity of the McKinley

tariff, Republicans reaffirmed their commitment to "the American doctrine of protection." The party's platform stated that "all articles which
cannot be produced in the United States, except luxuries, should be admitted free of duty, and that on all imports coming into competition with
the products of American labor, there should be levied duties equal to the
difference between wages abroad and at home."[23] Meanwhile, the Democrats denounced "Republican protection as a fraud, a robbery of the great
majority of the American people for the benefit of the few." The McKinley
tariff was "the culminating atrocity of class legislation" and they vowed
to repeal it. The Democratic platform repeated the party's belief that the
federal government had "no constitutional power to impose and collect
tariff duties, except for the purpose of revenue only."[24]

The continued unpopularity of the Billion Dollar Congress hurt Republicans and allowed Democrats to sweep into office in 1892 as the
Democrats retained the House, captured the Senate, and Cleveland won
the presidency. For the first time since 1858, Democrats secured unified
control of government. In his inaugural address, President Cleveland proclaimed that his party finally had a mandate to introduce major changes
in tariff policy:

> The people of the United States have decreed that on this day the con-
> trol of their Government in its legislative and executive branches shall
> be given to a political party pledged in the most positive terms to the
> accomplishment of tariff reform. They have thus determined in favor
> of a more just and equitable system of Federal taxation. The agents
> they have chosen to carry out their purposes are bound by their prom-
> ises not less than by the command of their masters to devote them-
> selves unremittingly to this service.[25]

With their first unified government in nearly forty years, Democrats
seemed poised to carry out this pledge, and expectations of major policy
change ran high among reformers within the party.

Yet the Democratic victory was inauspiciously timed. In late 1892, the
failure of Baring Brothers, a major investment house in London, precipitated an outflow of gold from the United States and with it a sharp monetary contraction. The drain on the Treasury's gold reserves contributed
to a financial panic that began in the closing days of the Harrison administration and led to widespread bank failures. Fears that silver agitators
might force the United States off the gold standard also led to a run on
the Treasury's reserves and accelerated the financial contraction.[26] Two

months before Cleveland's inauguration, the stock market had collapsed, and the nation's gold reserves had dwindled to precariously low levels.

Cleveland returned to office just as this economic disaster was unfolding, ruining his chance for tariff reform. Cleveland reluctantly gave priority to the country's financial situation and called for a special session of Congress to repeal the Sherman Silver Purchase Act. Unlike most Democrats, Cleveland had conservative monetary views (he was pro-gold and anti-silver) and had to ally himself with conservative Democrats and eastern Republicans to repeal the silver act. Given the pro-silver views of most Democrats, Cleveland's position fractured party unity and alienated the very allies he would need to reform the tariff.

Although Cleveland succeeded in repealing the silver act, thereby strengthening the country's commitment to the gold standard, this failed to stimulate the economy, and the United States fell into a severe depression. The year 1893 was marked by a wave of bank runs, bankruptcies, and foreclosures. Industrial production fell 17 percent from a peak in May 1892 to the trough of February 1894, with the sharpest drop from April 1893 to February 1894. The unemployment rate jumped from less than 4 percent in 1892 to more than 12 percent in 1894.[27]

With the economy still contracting, Cleveland turned to tariff reform in his December 1893 annual message to Congress. The president noted that "after a hard struggle, tariff reform is directly before us," and "nothing should intervene to distract our attention or disturb our effort until this reform is accomplished by wise and careful legislation." The duties imposed on the necessaries of life should be reduced because "the benefits of such a reduction would be palpable and substantial, seen and felt by thousands who would be better fed and better clothed and better sheltered." Given the weakening economy, Cleveland recognized that getting genuine tariff reform through Congress would be difficult. "In my great desire for the success of this measure, I cannot restrain the suggestion that its success can only be attained by means of unselfish counsel on the part of the friends of tariff reform and as a result of their willingness to subordinate personal desires and ambitions to the general good," he urged. "The local interests affected by the proposed reform are so numerous and so varied that if all are insisted upon, the legislation embodying the reform must inevitably fail."[28]

Yet cracks in party unity appeared almost immediately when some Democrats argued that tariff legislation should be postponed until the economy was recovering. But with the president pushing Congress to act, the new Ways and Means Committee chairman, William L. Wilson of

West Virginia, a staunch supporter of tariff reform, made the decision to go forward. Thus, in the fall of 1893, the Ways and Means Committee held hearings, described by a Wilson confidant as the "customary rubbish," on a new tariff.[29] In December, Wilson reported a bill that moved many raw materials (wool, coal, lumber, iron, and copper) onto the free list, while making moderate reductions in duties on final goods, thereby posing little threat to cotton textile and steel producers.[30]

The House debate opened in January 1894, but it unexpectedly morphed into a discussion about an income tax.[31] Populist Democrats from the Midwest had long supported an income tax as a way of shifting the tax burden from consumers of imported goods to rich industrialists, such as the Vanderbilts, Rockefellers, and Carnegies. An income tax would also generate revenue for the government and allow tariffs to be reduced. Although support for such a tax had been growing among Democrats, the idea faced many political hurdles. Cleveland supported a corporate income tax, but he and Democratic leaders feared a personal income tax would split the party, because Tammany Hall Democrats in New York strongly opposed the idea. Wilson believed the income tax was a distraction from tariff reform and might defeat his bill if attached to it. Meanwhile, Republicans denounced the income tax as "rank class legislation" that would lead to socialism, complaining that it was a sectional measure designed to extract money from only a few, high-income states, such as New York and Connecticut.

Early in the debate, Benton McMillin (D-TN) proposed amending the Wilson bill to impose a 2 percent tax on incomes above $4,000. Although strongly opposed by eastern Republicans, the McMillin amendment had broad support in the South and West and was adopted by a vote of 175–56. This cleared the way for the House vote on the tariff. Republicans were outraged. Thomas Reed (R-ME) proclaimed that "after thirty years of protection, undisturbed by any serious menace of free trade, . . . this country was the greatest and most flourishing nation on the face of this earth. . . . Those who will vote against this bill will do so because it opens our markets to the destructive competition of foreigners."[32] In reply, House Speaker Charles Crisp (D-GA) maintained that consumers paid the import tax, not foreigners, as Republicans alleged, and that consumers deserved relief from a system that favored the wealthy Eastern elites: "Whilst there may be here and there some monopolists or gentlemen of large wealth who will criticize and condemn us, yet all over the country, in the homes of the farmers, in the homes of the workers, and in the homes of the men employed in every industry in the United States, there will be rejoicing and happiness."[33]

In a rousing speech, Wilson rallied Democrats by declaring, "This is not a battle over percentages, over this or that tariff schedule; it is a battle for human freedom."[34] In February 1894, the House passed the bill in a partisan vote of 204–140; Democrats voted 191–17 in favor, while Republicans voted 122–0 against. The margin was unexpectedly large because as many as forty Democrats had been expected to vote against the measure.[35]

The Wilson bill then moved to the closely divided Senate. To expedite the legislation, Senate Democrats decided not to hold public hearings, but also stated that they would not feel bound by the House version. Senators from the Northeast immediately sought to strip the income tax provision from the bill, but they were outnumbered by those from the South and West. Then eight high-tariff Democrats under the leadership of Arthur Gorman of Maryland joined with Republicans to reinstate many of the protective duties. The Senate made a total of 634 amendments to the House version. The principle of free raw materials was watered down with the reimposition of duties on iron ore, coal, and sugar, although salt, lumber, and wool remained duty-free. Specific duties were reintroduced, and higher duties on cotton, woolens, and glass manufactures were also imposed. Matt Quay (R-PA) laboriously made the case for higher duties on dozens of goods in an address that stretched over twelve days and filled 235 pages of the *Congressional Record*. The Senate struggled over the measure until it finally passed in early July 1894 by a vote of 39–34.

House Democrats were deeply dismayed by the Senate's changes. Wilson stated that his bill was "based upon two clear and intelligent principles": that tariffs should be imposed on final goods, not raw materials, and that duties should be ad valorem, not specific. Yet in the Senate version, "these two great fundamental principles of just taxation and these two great fundamental principles of Democratic policy [were] in a large measure overridden and neglected."[36] The conference committee was deadlocked. The inability of Democrats to address the severe recession had already generated much public criticism. Now they were demonstrating that they lacked a strong commitment to reducing the tariff, aside from moving some raw materials to the duty-free list while avoiding significant rate reductions that would affect political powerful industries. Some Democrats suggested abandoning the effort, which would allow them to blame the economic slump on the McKinley duties, and then regroup for another attempt at tariff reform in 1896. But after having stressed the importance of tariff reform for so many decades, the party would have been ashamed to pass up an opportunity to do so under its first unified government in nearly forty years.

The Senate's actions also prompted Cleveland, whose relations with Congress had always been cool, to end his silence. The frustrated president blasted the Senate Democrats for abandoning the cause of tariff reform. Cleveland (1933, 365–66) insisted on "the necessity of free raw materials as the foundation of logical and sensible tariff reform" in any Democratic bill. In his view, it was simply inexcusable to put a farmer's wool on the free list while protecting a corporation's iron ore and coal with import duties. As Cleveland (1933, 365–66) explained,

> When we give to our manufacturers free raw materials we unshackle American enterprise and ingenuity, and these will open the doors of foreign markets to the reception of our wares and give opportunity for the continuous and remunerative employment of American labor. With materials cheapened by their freedom from tariff charges, the cost of their product must be correspondingly cheapened. Thereupon justice and fairness to the consumer would demand that the manufacturers be obliged to submit to such a readjustment and modification of the tariff upon their finished goods as would secure to the people the benefit of the reduced cost of their manufacture, and shield the consumer against the exaction of inordinate profits.

The president then committed a political blunder. In a letter that Wilson read on the floor of the House in July 1894, Cleveland wrote, "Every true Democrat and every sincere tariff reformer knows that this bill in its present form . . . falls far short of the consummation for which we have long labored, for which we have suffered defeat without discouragement, which, in its anticipation, gave us a rallying cry in our day of triumph, and which, in its promise of accomplishment, is so interwoven with Democratic pledges and Democratic success that our abandonment of the cause of the principles upon which it rests means party perfidy and party dishonor."[37]

Instead of trying to win Senate Democrats over to his side, the president alienated them even further by calling them, in effect, traitors to the cause of tariff reform. They viewed Cleveland's statement as a personal attack on their integrity. Arthur Gorman (R-MD) called the message "the most extraordinary, the most uncalled for, and the most unwise communication that was ever penned by a president of the United States. . . . Never in the course of my life . . . have I thought the provocation was sufficient, the abuse and misrepresentation violent enough, or the aspersion of character sufficient to induce me to talk of private matters in public."[38] He then gave his account of the Senate's deliberations, maintaining that no principles had been compromised and arguing that his fellow Democrats had done the best they could under the circumstances.

If the president hoped that Senate Democrats would be chastened and fall in line, he was sorely mistaken; his attack only hardened their views. Even the House speaker was miffed at Cleveland's insult, and the party caucus instructed Wilson, to his dismay, to accept the Senate amendments. In the end, the House leadership largely accepted the Senate version and shoved it through by limiting debate to two hours, allocating one-tenth of a second for discussion of each Senate amendment, according to one member's calculation.

Cleveland now faced the decision of whether to sign the bill or not. In a letter to Wilson, Cleveland (1933, 363) wrote, "I found myself questioning whether or not our party is a tariff-reform party." To another representative, the president complained, "Senators have stolen and worn the livery of Democratic tariff reform in the service of Republican protection." In the end, Cleveland could not bring himself to endorse the measure, but neither could he veto it, because that would simply preserve the existing McKinley tariff rates. Thus, in August 1894, the Wilson-Gorman tariff bill became law without the president's signature. In explaining why he declined to sign the bill, Cleveland stated, "There are provisions in this bill which are not in line with honest tariff reform, and it contains inconsistencies and crudities which ought not to appear in tariff laws or laws of any kind. Besides, there were . . . incidents accompanying the passage of the bill through the Congress, which made every sincere tariff reformer unhappy, while influences surrounded it in its latter stages and interfered with its final construction, which ought not to be recognized or tolerated in Democratic tariff-reform counsels."[39]

Despite Cleveland's disappointment, the Wilson-Gorman tariff of 1894 made a reasonable dent in the average tariff on dutiable imports, which was cut from 50 percent to 39 percent, a reduction of 11 percentage points, or about 20 percent. The episode reflected badly on the Democrats, however, who had squandered their first opportunity to reform the tariff since the Civil War. While making great claims to support tariff reform, the party appeared to stand for just watered-down protectionism.

Republicans were gleeful at the Democratic infighting. Two months later, in the midterm election of 1894, the Republicans captured both houses of Congress, bringing the brief period of Democratic rule to an end. Although the Republican victory was mainly due to the depressed economy, the Democrats' mishandling of the tariff issue did not put them in good light. Even the income tax passed by the Democrats proved to be a failure. In January 1895, the Supreme Court struck down the law, holding that the income tax was a direct tax and therefore unconstitutional because it was not apportioned according to population.[40]

Meanwhile, the economy continued to suffer. After briefly stabilizing in 1894, the economy slipped back into a severe recession that lasted until mid-1897. For five consecutive years, from 1894 through 1898, the unemployment rate stood at more than 11 percent. Hammered by falling commodity prices, farmers were forced into widespread foreclosures. Urban areas saw violent labor unrest, with strikes, pickets, and lockouts. Confronting large fiscal deficits, the federal government lacked the political will to provide much assistance to relieve the distress. But the root cause of the nation's economic problems was a contractionary monetary policy, as the gold standard ensured tight credit and continuing deflation.

The ongoing economic disaster made monetary policy and silver coinage the nation's dominant political issue once again. The recession fueled agrarian hostility to the gold standard and enabled populist free silver supporters, led by William Jennings Bryan, to gain control of the Democratic party. Many farmers believed that a silver standard, a bimetal standard, or even a paper (greenback) standard would lift prices and ease the heavy burden of debt that grew as prices fell. A more expansionary monetary policy, which would have required that the United States leave the gold standard, would have ended the deflation or even have led to inflation. It would have also resulted in a fall in the value of the dollar against other currencies, which would have discouraged imports (like a tariff) but also boost exports (unlike a tariff).

When the Republicans won control of Congress in the 1894 midterm election, divided government ensured that there would be few legislative accomplishments for the next two years. This set the stage for the presidential election of 1896 that pitted Democrat William Jennings Bryan against Republican William McKinley. Given the party's bungling of tariff reform, Bryan downplayed the tariff issue during the campaign and focused instead on silver and monetary policy. The Democratic platform stated that "until the money question is settled we are opposed to any agitation for further changes in our tariff laws."[41] Meanwhile, as a supporter of the gold standard and tariff protection, McKinley sought to unite Eastern hard-money interests with Midwestern protectionist interests. With the American economy suffering, Republicans were only too happy to "renew and emphasize our allegiance to the policy of protection, as the bulwark of American industrial independence, and the foundation of

American development and prosperity." The platform stated bluntly, "The ruling and uncompromising principle is the protection and development of American labor and industries," making all the usual claims about supporting the true American policy of taxing foreign products and encouraging home industry in order to uphold the American standard of wages for the workingman.[42]

McKinley tried to make the election a referendum on tariff policy, where he was confident of victory, but Bryan kept the campaign focused on monetary policy. The Republicans managed to defuse that issue by pledging to reach an international agreement on the monetization of silver. In the event, McKinley won the popular vote by 51.0 percent to Bryant's 46.7 percent. As usual, Republicans ran strong in the industrial North and Midwest, while Democrats continued to hold their base in the South and West. Historians debate whether the 1896 election resulted in a political realignment, but the election did usher in a sixteen-year period of Republican political dominance.[43]

Having recaptured unified control of government, the Republicans' first order of business was to reverse the Democratic tariff reduction in 1894. In his inaugural address, President McKinley stressed the need to reduce the fiscal deficit and strengthen tariff protection for American industry. As he stated, "The controlling principle in the raising of revenue from duties on imports is zealous care for American interests and American labor. The people have declared that such legislation should be had as will give ample protection and encouragement to the industries and the development of our country."[44] McKinley argued that the inadequate revenues received by the government under the Wilson-Gorman tariff made it difficult to maintain the nation's gold reserves. Higher tariffs would improve the fiscal balance and reverse the outflow of gold, helping to restore the nation's prosperity, as well as give industry further protection from foreign competition. He called for a special session of Congress on the grounds that the ailing economy urgently required higher import duties.

Even before the new president took office, House Republicans began preparing new tariff legislation. On the day Congress convened, Ways and Means Committee chairman Nelson Dingley (R-ME) reported a tariff bill to restore the rates of the 1890 McKinley tariff. Western silver interests demanded protection for raw materials, so imports of wool, hides, iron ore, and lumber were moved off the free list and once again made subject to duties. Duties on most final goods were increased, although those on cotton goods and basic iron and steel products remained unchanged. Given their minority position, Democrats only put up modest rhetorical opposition to the bill, although they insisted that silver coinage held out greater hope for promoting economic recovery than higher taxes on consumers. In March 1897, after four days of debate, the House passed the bill by a partisan vote of 205–122; Republicans voted 198–0 in favor and Democrats voted 118–5 against.

In the Senate, Nelson Aldrich (R-RI) and the Finance Committee completely rewrote the bill to increase duties even further. They acted because the House bill had "free-trade tendencies" that would "cripple or destroy numerous industries." They substituted specific duties for ad valorem duties "to protect honest importers and domestic producers from the disastrous consequences resulting from fraudulent undervaluations of imported merchandise." On the floor, senators went over the bill laboriously, schedule by schedule, in the spring and early summer of 1897, with dozens of roll call votes on specific commodities. A total of 872 amendments were made to the bill, most of which pushed tariffs higher. The majority leadership resisted these increases, which they regarded as excessive. Aldrich began to look like a moderate when he stated that "industrial conditions in this country with a very few exceptions do not demand a return to the rates imposed by the act of 1890."[45] The president's close associate, Mark Hanna (R-OH), scolded the chamber: "Mr. McKinley stands for protection, not exclusion," and he privately remarked that manufacturers were "squatting behind the tariff like a lot of God damn rabbits."[46]

The Senate passed its version by a vote of 38–28; Republicans voted 35–0 in favor and Democrats voted 25–1 against. The conference committee quickly adopted nearly all of the Senate's amendments, allowing McKinley to sign the measure into law in late July 1897. The legislation took just four months of Congress's time, almost all of which was in the Senate.

Stanwood (1903, 2:364) called the Dingley tariff "the most universally and comprehensively protective tariff ever enacted" to date. It remained in effect for thirteen years, until 1909, making it the longest-lasting piece of tariff legislation in US history. Although the stated goal was to restore the same nominal specific rates of duty in the 1890 tariff, the fall in the price level meant that those duties had a higher ad valorem equivalent. Indeed, the average tariff rose from 42 percent in 1897 (before the enactment of the Dingley tariff) to 52 percent in 1899, slightly higher than the 47 percent in 1891 after the McKinley tariff was enacted.

Around the same time, the world supply of gold began to grow more rapidly with increased supplies coming from Australia, South Africa, and Alaska. The easing of global monetary conditions fostered a strong economic recovery, and world prices began to rise again. As in the past, this timing gave rise to the popular perception that the McKinley tariff was responsible for the economic resurgence.

With the new Republican tariff in place and the economy finally growing, the issue of tariff policy fell off the nation's political agenda once again. McKinley was happy to put the matter to rest: "We have quit discussing the tariff and have turned our attention to getting trade wherever it can be found."[47] Indeed, policymakers began to shift their focus away from closing the market to imports to opening foreign markets for exports. This new attention to exports was driven by new developments, to be discussed shortly, but proved to be controversial. Some Republicans were willing to seek greater market access abroad, while others feared that agreements to do so might require a reduction in protective duties. Meanwhile, Democrats worried that government efforts to take advantage of commercial opportunities might lead the United States into becoming a colonial power like European countries.[48] As William Howard (D-GA) stated, "I am in favor of the extension of commerce, but I do not regard commercial extension of our commerce as synonymous with territorial aggrandizement."[49]

The case of sugar illustrates how America's commercial expansion came with new foreign policy entanglements. In 1876, the United States signed a limited reciprocity treaty with Hawaii (for political not commercial reasons) that gave preferential access to its sugar in the United States in exchange for Hawaiian preferences for selected American products. Bilateral trade soared after the treaty and transformed Hawaiian politics, enriching the islands' planter class, which had made large investments in sugar production. The McKinley tariff of 1890, however, granted duty-free access to all imported sugar. Having lost its preferential access to the US market, Hawaii plunged into a deep recession. This led to political instability, and a group of Americans on the island overthrew the Hawaiian monarch in 1893. A few years later the United States annexed the territory.[50]

Meanwhile, Cuba benefited from having been granted duty-free access for its sugar under the McKinley tariff. But when Congress reimposed duties on imported sugar (except from Hawaii) in 1894, Cuba's sugar production plummeted. The collapse of the Cuban economy led to an insurrection against Spanish rule in 1895, which Spain brutally suppressed. Eventually this led to US military intervention in the Spanish-American War of 1898.[51] Thus, the tariff on just one commodity—sugar—deeply embroiled the United States in the domestic politics of two island territories.

The United States was just beginning to learn that its tariff policies could have significant international consequences. But contrary to the suggestions of some revisionist historians, the United States was not bent on establishing a commercial empire and had no grand imperial designs regarding trade.[52] As Palen (2015, 185) notes, "Republican imperialism of economic nationalism encountered strong opposition from both stalwart home-market protectionists and American free traders." In general, American business interests were only somewhat interested in seeking foreign markets as an outlet for their surplus products and were not interested in the acquisition of foreign territory.

AMERICA'S EXPORT BOOM IN MANUFACTURED GOODS

Despite the steady expansion of US industry in the late nineteenth century, the commodity composition of foreign trade remained remarkably stable. Exports continued to be dominated by agricultural goods, particularly raw cotton, grains (wheat and corn), and meat products, which together accounted for nearly two-thirds of total exports in 1890. Manufactured goods comprised about 20 percent of total exports, a figure that had been stable for many decades. Meanwhile, America's imports consisted of a wide variety of consumer products (coffee, tea, and sugar), raw materials (tin and silk), and manufactured goods, imported primarily from Britain but increasingly from Germany and other European countries. Throughout this period, the overall growth in trade was slow: export volume crept up only 30 percent in the fifteen years between 1880 and 1895.[53]

In the mid-1890s, however, US trade underwent a remarkable transformation. Exports of manufactured goods surged, jumping to 35 percent of total exports by 1900 and reaching nearly 50 percent by 1913. As figure 6.1 shows, after having been a large net importer of manufactured goods since the colonial period, the United States quickly became a large net exporter around the turn of the century. Between 1890 and 1910, the United States reversed a century-old trade pattern based on exporting agricultural products and importing manufactured goods.

The export surge began in the early 1890s. Exports of manufactured goods doubled in value between 1895 and 1900, increasing their share of total exports from 26 percent to 35 percent. In this five-year period, the volume of manufactured exports rose an astounding 90 percent, partly due to a worldwide economic boom. Growth in manufactured exports paused before surging again between 1908 and 1913, bringing their share of total

Figure 6.1. Trade in finished manufactured goods, 1870–1930: Share of total exports/imports. (US Bureau of the Census 1975, series U-213–224.)

exports to nearly 50 percent. World War I pushed the net export position in manufactured goods to even higher levels that were maintained in the 1920s, but the key transition for this development was the decade after 1895.[54]

European observers dubbed the dramatic change the "American Commercial Invasion." The US share of world manufactured exports jumped from 4 percent in 1890 to 11 percent in 1913, reaching 18 percent by 1929. This reflected an enormous increase in domestic production: in 1913, the United States accounted for 36 percent of the world's manufacturing production, up from 23 percent in 1870. The fraction of manufacturing output that was exported, by contrast, was relatively small and stable over this period. For example, in 1914, manufactured exports were about 6 percent of manufacturing production, about the same as they had been in 1879. The share of domestic production exported was much higher in certain sectors, such as petroleum, chemicals, and manufactured foods, but it never reached more than 10 percent in most industries.[55]

What accounts for the abrupt change in the structure of exports? Why were the 1890s a transitional decade for US trade rather than some earlier or later period? A shift in comparative advantage toward manufactured goods could result from changes in factor endowments or technology relative to other countries. Yet these explanations seem unable to explain the change: capital per worker and total-factor productivity in manufacturing did not grow unusually fast in 1890s, nor did agricultural exports experience a noticeable collapse. Instead, the leading explanation for America's export success in manufactured goods is the country's improved ability to exploit its abundance of raw materials. While commodity exports before the Civil War were primarily agricultural, exports after the war shifted toward raw materials, particularly minerals. The newly emergent comparative advantage in certain manufactured goods resulted from the growing abundance of such primary resources as iron ore, copper, and petroleum used in the production of these manufactured goods.[56]

Although all manufactured exports grew rapidly during this period, the rapid growth of iron and steel exports was the main driving force behind the dramatic change in the composition of exports. Iron and steel products rose from 4 percent of total exports to 9 percent between 1895 and 1900 as export volume soared. The largest single category was machinery, which included engines, electrical machines, farm equipment, sewing machines, cash registers, and printing presses. Other key products included steel rails, pipes and fittings, wire, tools, locks and hinges, billets, and structural iron and steel. Exports of innovative new goods–such as automobiles, phonographs, office equipment (typewriters), and electrical products—surged as well, but started from such a small base that they constituted a tiny part of overall export growth prior to World War I.

Why did iron and steel products suddenly became competitive on world markets after 1895? Here is where the link between the exploitation of natural resources and manufactured exports can be seen. The surge of iron and steel exports can be traced to the bountiful supply of iron ore that appeared once the Mesabi range in Minnesota was opened in 1892. The commercial development of these enormous mineral deposits had dramatic consequences: Minnesota's share of the country's iron ore production jumped from 6 percent in 1890 to 24 percent in 1895, and then to 51 percent in 1905.[57] The domestic price of iron ore plunged by half when the Mesabi shipments hit the market. Because iron ore accounted for more than half the materials costs of producing blast furnace products, the steep fall in the price of iron ore significantly reduced the cost of producing pig iron and thus final iron and steel products. This price reduction significantly improved the competitive position of domestic producers vis-à-vis British producers, which were then the leading exporters of iron and steel goods.[58] Having an abundance of natural resources at home, particularly iron ore and coal, gave domestic producers access to cheap raw materials and allowed supply to expand without encountering resource constraints. By 1900, the United States accounted for 34 percent of the world's pig iron production and 37 percent of the world's steel output.[59]

The second largest category of manufactured exports was copper, also a minerals-based product. Exports of copper manufactures rose from 0.3 percent of exports in 1890 to 6 percent of exports in 1913, as electrification generated a huge demand for copper wire and other copper-based products. Massive copper extraction in the West allowed this growth to occur. Another large category of manufactured exports was petroleum, which became an article of export only after the oil discoveries in the 1860s. Although refined in the United States, petroleum was the least processed of these new natural resource–based exports.

Despite its abundance of natural resources, the United States never exported its minerals in their raw state; the country was even a small net importer of both iron ore and copper throughout this period. Instead, the United States exported the final, processed goods that used those minerals. There were two reasons for this. First, large domestic producers were vertically integrated and kept the cost advantage of raw material abundance within the firm. For example, US Steel owned the major iron ore mines, and Standard Oil of New Jersey owned the major oil fields. Second, many of these minerals were not easily traded, which had major implications for trade flows. If the world market for iron ore was perfectly integrated, the abundance of natural resources would not necessarily favor domestic producers, because those resources would be available to producers in all countries at the world price. But the Lake Superior iron ores were not an internationally traded commodity, because of high transportation costs; the St. Lawrence Seaway linking the Great Lakes to the Atlantic Ocean was not yet open. Hence, the price impact of the Mesabi Range was not transmitted to the world market except through the price of final iron and steel goods produced in the United States.

The contrast with raw cotton is instructive. Cotton was also a raw material, but one that was easily transportable and hence exported in huge quantities.[60] One reason the United States never developed an internationally competitive, export-oriented textile or apparel industry was that cotton was available to foreign producers at roughly the same price as domestic producers. The enormous production of cotton in the South did not give a particular cost advantage to the domestic textile industry: US firms had the same raw materials costs and technology as their British rivals, but had to pay higher wages.

Another important feature of the export surge was that it was driven almost entirely by the largest firms in an industry. US Steel Corporation by itself accounted for 90 percent of the country's iron and steel exports in 1909.[61] Similarly, International Harvester dominated exports of farm equipment, Standard Oil dominated exports of petroleum, Westinghouse dominated exports of electrical machinery, and Armour dominated exports of processed food. Because the export surge was concentrated in just a few large firms in a few industries, it had a limited impact on US trade policy. While the increase in exports was substantial, it still amounted to a modest share of the total production of those firms. The exports were not broadly based and did not create a large constituency in favor of major policy changes.

Yet the export boom did bring some subtle changes to American trade politics. Iron and steel producers, who had been at the center of political battles over tariff policy since before the Civil War, began to lose interest in protection. Instead, they began to focus on the importance of export markets, which in turn gave rise to increased interest in reciprocity as an alternative to protectionism. Some exporting firms began organizing in support of promoting exports through a policy of reciprocity. The National Association of Manufacturers (NAM) was formed in 1894 by small and medium-sized businesses that were interested in selling in foreign markets. Other smaller groups formed as well, such as industry-specific export groups or broader entities, such the National Reciprocity League (1902) and the American Export Association (1909). But these interest groups had virtually no impact on policy. Although large firms no longer needed protective tariffs, such duties still had enormous value for smaller producers that did not export and remained vulnerable to residual competition from imports, and who were therefore prepared to lobby vigorously to limit foreign competition. Most small businesses remained vulnerable to competition from imports and feared a reduction in tariffs. Consequently, NAM proposed reciprocity trade agreements "only where it can be done without injury to any of our home interests."[62]

Finally, we should note that the export expansion occurred without any significant government support. The federal government did not play a direct role in bringing about the change in the composition of exports and was almost entirely passive when it came to promoting exports. As Becker (1982, xiv) notes, "The expansion of the exports of American manufactured goods between 1893 and 1921 is remarkable more for the lack of close government cooperation than for closer ties between business and government in the making of these sales."

THE RECIPROCITY MOVEMENT

The growth in manufactured exports was too recent a development to have influenced the congressional debate over the Dingley Tariff of 1897. Yet the increasing exports of manufactured goods brought into question the necessity of high protective tariffs to restrict imports and strengthened the hand of domestic producers with a stake in opening foreign markets for exports. This gave rise to the idea of reciprocity as a new approach to trade policy.

The reciprocity movement was spearheaded by the influential Republican James Blaine, who had served as speaker of the House and was twice secretary of state. Once an ardent protectionist, Blaine became an enthusiastic proponent of promoting exports through reciprocity agreements, particularly with Latin America. Blaine's idea was to offer tariff reductions on tropical goods that did not compete with domestic producers, in exchange for lower foreign tariffs on manufactured and agricultural goods produced by the United States. Blaine saw several advantages to this approach. First, reciprocity agreements would strengthen the economy by expanding manufactured exports without exposing domestic industries to foreign competition. Second, by reducing some import duties, reciprocity would quell the Democratic attacks against high tariffs and thereby bolster domestic political support for protective duties. If the advocates of protection did not act to moderate the system, Blaine feared that Democrats might destroy it completely if they regained power. "The enactment of reciprocity . . . is the safeguard of protection," he argued. "The defeat of reciprocity is the opportunity of free trade."[63] Third, reciprocity agreements would strengthen ties with Latin America and serve American foreign policy interests in the region. Blaine's advocacy of reciprocity gained a foothold among a minority of Republicans, but was generally viewed with suspicion by the party's establishment, which did not want to see any deviation from existing policy.

Blaine first advocated reciprocity in 1881, when he served as secretary of state in the Garfield administration. Blaine observed that Latin American countries sold their raw materials to the United States but purchased most of their manufactured goods from Europe. Blaine saw an opportunity to displace Europe as Latin America's main supplier of manufactured goods by offering concessions on the tariffs the United States imposed on its imports from the region. Blaine hoped to strengthen regional trade cooperation, but his short tenure in office did not allow much to be accomplished.

Blaine resumed his efforts to promote closer ties with Latin America in 1890, when he returned as secretary of state in the Harrison administration. He convinced the president that the pending McKinley tariff bill should include a reciprocity provision. Such a provision, as he saw it, would allow the executive branch to negotiate agreements reducing foreign barriers to US exports in exchange for concessions on noncompeting imports. Blaine was particularly adamant that the tariff bill not put sugar on the duty-free list, because it was a valuable bargaining chip whose duty could be reduced in such negotiations. "The charge against the protective policy which has injured us most is that its benefits go wholly to the manufacturer and the capitalist, and not at all to the farmer," Blaine noted. "Here is an opportunity where the farmer may be benefited—primarily, undeniably, richly benefited. Here is an opportunity for a Republican Congress to open the markets of forty million of people to the products of American farmers," but "there is not a section or line in the entire [McKinley] bill that will open a market for another bushel of wheat or another barrel of pork."[64]

Blaine failed to convince the Ways and Means Committee about the merits of his proposal. Most Republicans were too attached to existing policy and too jealous of Congress's constitutional authority to give the executive branch the ability to reduce duties in negotiated agreements. However, President Harrison supported Blaine and forwarded to Congress a report from him about a Pan American conference in which great interest had been expressed in closer commercial ties with the United States.[65] Harrison noted that almost 90 percent of imports from Latin America already entered the United States free of duty, making it difficult to offer concessions that would persuade those countries to reduce their barriers against American exports. If Congress decided that it could not offer concessions on dutiable imports from Latin America, Harrison suggested imposing penalty duties on countries that did not give fair market access to American goods.

The Senate Finance Committee accepted this recommendation. While keeping coffee, tea, hides, sugar, and molasses on the free list, it amended the House bill to allow the president to suspend duty-free treatment of imports from countries imposing "unequal or unreasonable" duties on US exports. This provision was accepted by the conference committee. Thus, Congress adopted a punitive form of reciprocity: the United States did not offer tariff concessions to other countries, but demanded better treatment for its exports under the threat of penalties and retaliatory duties.

This provision enabled Blaine, assisted by John W. Foster, a State Department aide, to undertake negotiations with Central and South American countries to secure better access for US products. If they did not cooperate, the countries would risk having higher tariffs imposed on their exports of sugar and other commodities to the United States. In 1891–92, Blaine reached ten agreements, all but two of which were with countries in the Western Hemisphere. For example, Brazil eliminated its duties on US wheat, flour, pork, and farm equipment, and reduced its tariffs on other American goods so that it would continue receiving duty-free access in the United States for its hides, sugar, and coffee. Three countries—Colombia, Venezuela, and Haiti—failed to respond satisfactorily and were slapped with penalty duties, although duties were not imposed on Argentina or Mexico, despite their reluctance to conclude agreements. The US Tariff Commission (1919, 28) later concluded that this provision of the McKinley tariff had been "moderately effective both as a measure of retaliation and as a means of securing tariff favors."

Meanwhile, Democrats opposed the reciprocity provision on the grounds that it avoided any change in protective duties on goods that competed with domestic producers. They believed it merely fiddled with a tariff system that needed a thorough overhaul. Charles Crisp of Georgia argued that "no amount of juggling, no amount of sophistry, no amount of theory will prevent them from understanding really what this protective system is; that its effect is to take from one class to give to another, to take from the masses to give to a class."[66] In their 1892 election platform, Democrats denounced "the sham reciprocity which juggles with the people's desire for enlarged foreign markets and freer exchanges" by maintaining protective duties.[67] Consequently, the Democratic electoral victory in 1892 ended the Republican reciprocity experiment. The Wilson-Gorman Act of 1894 reimposed uniform duties on sugar and terminated the Blaine program. This quick reversal of American policy outraged Latin American countries; they complained bitterly about the abrogation of the reciprocity agreements and retaliated by imposing higher duties on American goods.

Yet the idea of reciprocity did not disappear. The depression of 1893–96 gave rise to the mistaken view that the nation's economic difficulties were caused by "overproduction" and that therefore exports were the only way of dealing with excess production. The hope that the country could export its way out of the slump helped shift the domestic debate away from using high tariffs to reduce imports toward expanding foreign markets for exports. The rapid expansion of manufactured exports after 1895 demonstrated the potential for foreign consumers to be an important source of demand for US goods, as long as producers had access to those markets.

Foreign discrimination against US exports also became more pro-nounced in the 1890s, adding to concerns about whether American goods were treated fairly in foreign markets. Over that decade, Germany con-cluded many bilateral trade agreements that included tariff concessions that were not extended to the United States. France's Meline tariff in 1892 created a two-tiered, maximum-minimum schedule of import duties; US goods were subject to the maximum duties because the two countries did not have a trade agreement. And countries of the British Empire began granting preferences to one another. In 1897, for example, Canada gave a 25 percent tariff preference to British goods, a margin that increased to 33 percent three years later. The discrimination against the United States by a large, neighboring market held back the growth of exports. More gen-erally, colonial trade networks expanded and had become more exclusive by the end of the nineteenth century. Competition between colonial pow-ers for territorial control in Africa and Asia meant that European coun-tries could establish dominant positions in certain regions of the world, guaranteeing export markets for themselves or, equally troubling, gaining preferential access to raw materials.

These problems made American officials increasingly concerned about ensuring equal access to markets around the world. For example, in 1899, Secretary of State John Hay issued the "Open Door" notes with respect to China, which European powers had carved into different spheres of influ-ence. Hay sought assurances that Europe would respect China's territorial integrity and guarantee "the benefits of equality of treatment of all foreign trade throughout China." Although it had its own preferential trade ar-rangements with Hawaii (and soon with Cuba and the Philippines after the Spanish-American War), the United States wanted to guarantee that all countries "shall enjoy perfect equality of treatment for their commerce and navigation within such spheres."[68] The Open Door notes reaffirmed the American interest in establishing equality of treatment as a funda-mental principle guiding trade policy, but involved no concrete actions on the part of the United States.

Many believed that the only way the United States could combat the spread of these exclusionary policies was by adopting some form of reci-procity and taking a more active role in negotiating trade agreements with other countries. Yet reciprocity was a minor issue in the 1896 election. Having disposed of Blaine's reciprocity provision in the 1894 Wilson-Gorman tariff, the Democratic platform was silent about the matter. The Republican platform attacked the elimination of reciprocity as "a National calamity," arguing that "Protection and Reciprocity are twin measures of

American policy and go hand-in-hand."[69] Furthermore, the incoming Republican president, William McKinley, had become a convert to the cause of reciprocity. In 1890, as chairman of the Ways and Means Committee, McKinley had been cool to the idea, but Blaine gradually convinced him of its merits. By 1895, McKinley favored the policy on the condition that it not compromise protection for domestic industries. As he put it, "We want a reciprocity which will give us foreign markets for our surplus products and in turn that will open our markets to foreigners for those products which they produce and we do not."[70]

The Dingley tariff of 1897 experimented once again with reciprocity. Section 3 of the act authorized the president to reduce duties by a limited amount on a specified list of commodities—including argol (crude tartar), wine, brandy, champagne, and paintings—for countries that made "reciprocal and equivalent concessions" for US goods. The section also reintroduced the penalty duties of the McKinley tariff, giving the president the discretion to withdraw duty-free treatment for imports of coffee, tea, and vanilla beans from any country deemed to be "reciprocally unequal and unreasonable" in its trade policy. In addition, section 4 authorized, for the first time, the president to reduce import duties (within two years, by no more than 20 percent, in agreements lasting no more than five years) on a limited number of articles (that were "natural products of such foreign country . . . and not of the United States") for countries giving equivalent tariff concessions to the United States. Although the section did not grant any real authority beyond the president's existing treaty-making power, Congress's invitation to negotiate trade agreements with other countries marked a break from the past and implied that it would favorably receive them. But the invitation was also carefully circumscribed, as the many qualifications suggest.

In October 1897, President McKinley appointed John Kasson, a former congressman and veteran diplomat, to head a special State Department reciprocity division that would be responsible for negotiating the agreements.[71] Under section 3, the United States concluded argol agreements (as they were called) with Germany, France, Italy, Portugal, and Switzerland. For example, Germany removed restrictions on American meat exports and applied its conventional tariff to most American goods. Under the broader section 4 authority, Kasson concluded agreements with eleven countries, mainly small Central American nations but also France and Argentina. In December 1899, the president submitted most of these agreements to the Senate for approval.

Though they covered just a few commodities, the Kasson treaties encountered stiff opposition. Sheep farmers vehemently opposed the Argentine agreement, which would have cut duties on Argentine wool by 20 percent. An agreement with France would have allowed most US exports to enter under the country's minimum tariff schedule rather than the maximum, while the United States would have to reduce duties on 126 goods by between 5 and 20 percent. But the proposed reduction in duties on French undergarments provoked enough resistance from the hosiery industry to scuttle the entire deal. Export interests that would benefit from the improved market access abroad were not engaged in the political fight because the economic stakes for them were too small.[72]

As a result, the Kasson treaties languished in the Senate Foreign Relations Committee, never to be voted upon. In his annual message of December 1900, McKinley urged Congress to approve them: "The policy of reciprocity so manifestly rests upon the principles of international equity and has been so repeatedly approved by the people of the United States that there ought to be no hesitation in either branch of the Congress in giving to it full effect." Yet the president did not force the issue, because he worried about splitting his party before the presidential election.[73] After his reelection, McKinley used his inaugural address in March 1901 to press for ratification of the agreements once again. Because the nation's production was "increasing in such unprecedented volume," the country had to seek foreign markets as an outlet for its products. Therefore, the president said, "reciprocal trade arrangements with other nations should in liberal spirit be carefully cultivated and promoted."[74]

But the Republican leadership in Congress was too attuned to domestic political opposition to move the treaties forward. As a result, these and other reciprocity treaties failed to gain support throughout the nineteenth century, as table 6.4 shows. In fact, these piecemeal treaties, which would only affect a small amount of trade with just a few countries, had little appeal for either party. While Republicans did not want to remove the few trade barriers protecting small- and medium-sized firms in various industries, Democrats dismissed the proposed reductions as a sham because they were mainly limited to noncompeting tropical goods and failed to address the core protective duties for cotton, woolen, and iron and steel manufacturers. Secretary of State John Hay lamented to Kasson, "What a lot of fine things we could do if it were not for the Senate," because there had never been "a period in our history so pregnant with opportunity."[75] Dismayed by the Senate's inaction and McKinley's lukewarm support, Kasson resigned in March 1901.

By this time, with America's export boom in full swing, McKinley

TABLE 6.4. The fate of reciprocity treaties, 1840–1911

Year	Country	Outcome	In effect
1844	Germany	Senate rejects	
1854	Canada	Senate approves	1855–1866
1855	Hawaii	Senate rejects	
1856	Mexico	Senate rejects	
1867	Hawaii	Senate rejects	
1871	Canada	Senate rejects	
1875	Hawaii	Senate approves	1876–1900
1883	Mexico	Senate ratifies treaty, rejects authorizing legislation	
1884	Dominican Republic	Negotiated by President Arthur, withdrawn by President Cleveland	
1888	Canada	Senate rejects	
1890	Great Britain	Great Britain rejects	
1899	France	Senate withholds vote	
1899	Argentina	Senate withholds vote	
1899	Ecuador	Senate withholds vote	
1899	Nicaragua	Senate withholds vote	
1899	Great Britain	Senate withholds vote	
1901	Russia	Senate rejects	
1902	Great Britain	Senate amendments unacceptable to Britain	
1902	Cuba	Senate approves	1902–1934
1909	Canada	Senate approves, Canada rejects in 1911	

Source: Compiled from US Tariff Commission 1919.

had decided to endorse the idea of reciprocity more forcefully. Speaking at the Pan American Exposition in Buffalo on September 5, 1901, McKinley declared that economic "isolation is no longer possible or desirable." He noted that "our capacity to produce has developed so enormously and our products have so multiplied that the problem of more markets requires our urgent and immediate attention. . . . We must not repose in fancied security that we can forever sell everything and buy little or nothing." Instead, policymakers would have to build on the phenomenal growth in manufactured exports over the preceding decade and start cultivating foreign markets for American goods. As the president argued,

Reciprocity is the natural outgrowth of our wonderful industrial development under the domestic policy now firmly established. . . . The period of exclusiveness is past. The expansion of our trade and commerce
is the pressing problem. Commercial wars are unprofitable. A policy
of good will and friendly trade relations will prevent reprisals. Reciprocity treaties are in harmony with the spirit of the times, measures
of retaliation are not. If perchance some of our tariffs are no longer
needed, for revenue or to encourage and protect our industries at home,
why should they not be employed to extend and promote our markets
abroad?[76]

In short, McKinley proposed a fundamental shift in US trade policy.
Of course, his success would depend upon having the political courage to
take on congressional Republicans who were strongly opposed to such a
change. We will never know if McKinley could have been successful, because, just a day after delivering the address in Buffalo, he was shot by
an assassin and died shortly thereafter. Yet it is unlikely that McKinley
would have succeeded in making reciprocity a cornerstone of US trade policy. To judge by the difficulties that his successors had, even determined
presidential leadership would have failed to convince the conservative Republican leadership in Congress to deviate from the status quo.

NEW ARGUMENTS AGAINST PROTECTIVE TARIFFS

The political support underlying the Republican policy of high protective tariffs had been very stable since the Civil War. But as the economy
grew and changed shape, old coalitions began to fracture. Big industrial
firms, especially in the iron and steel industry, were now exporting to the
world and no longer needed protection from foreign competition. Civil
War veterans were passing from the scene, making pension expenditures
a less compelling justification for high tariffs. And within the Republican
party, progressive "insurgents" from Midwestern agricultural states began sharply criticizing the tariffs that favored manufacturing industries.
Progressive Republicans supported a protective tariff in principle, but believed the structure of duties was biased in favor of big business in eastern
states that did not need government assistance. They wanted to reduce the
burden of tariffs on consumers and farmers by cutting rates on industrial
goods while raising rates on agricultural goods and raw materials. Thus,
cracks started to emerge in the Republican Northeast-Midwest protectionist coalition.

The progressive movement arose out of the social upheavals that accompanied the nation's industrialization and gained political strength around the turn of the century. Dismayed by government favoritism and the political power of big business, progressives wanted to take policy decisions out of the hands of corrupt politicians in Congress and give them to impartial experts working in independent government agencies. These agencies, it was thought, could establish regulations to protect labor (working hours and conditions) and consumers (railroad rates and food and product safety), free from the influence of business interests and party politics. The progressive insurgents originally arose within the Republican party, which favored a larger and more active economic role for the government than Democrats did at the time.

The progressives succeeded in shifting the debate over tariff policy. Led by such figures as William Borah of Idaho and Robert LaFollette of Wisconsin, the insurgents complained that the existing tariff schedule was unfair: tariffs were far too high on eastern manufactured goods and not high enough on agricultural goods and raw materials produced in the Midwest. They argued that this promoted industrial monopolies that exploited farmers and consumers. As a result, Republican insurgents from the corn and wheat belt across the upper Midwest began to oppose Republican stalwarts from urban, industrial constituencies in the East. As Sarasohn (1989, 67) notes, however, "the [progressive] insurgents were not opposed to protection, but to excessive protection, a term that they seemed to define anew with each vote."

The regional split within the party occurred not just on tariff policy, but over other issues as well, such as the income tax. The Old Guard Republican establishment from the East opposed the income tax because it would fall heavily on their constituents and would weaken the justification for high import duties. Progressive Midwestern Republicans supported an income tax for precisely those reasons. Although there were few progressive Republicans in the House, there were enough of them in the Senate, where the Republican majority was relatively slim, so that a shift of three to five votes to the Democratic side could have a decisive impact.

While Democrats praised the efforts to reduce tariffs on industrial goods, the Republican insurgents did not return the compliment. While insurgents were often at odds with the Republican leadership, they were not about to align themselves with low-tariff Democrats. Although they sometimes voted together, the insurgents were generally hostile to Democrats; it was not an alliance but an occasional marriage of convenience. While Democrats professed to believe in low tariffs in general, progressive Republicans were half-hearted and inconsistent in their opposition to excessive duties, maintaining their support for a "reformed" protective tariff. For example, Borah used standard arguments about the benefits of protection to justify a high duty on imported barley.

Of course, while the East-West Republican split on tariff policy was emerging as a relatively new phenomenon, the Democrats had always been seriously divided over the issue, only on a North-South basis. Northern Democrats representing industrial constituencies had always resisted tariff reductions, while southern Democrats representing more rural districts wanted extensive tariff cuts. As we have seen, the party's difficulties with this division went back to the 1870s when Samuel Randall of Pennsylvania thwarted several Democratic attempts to reduce duties.

With the United States having become a net exporter of manufactured goods, and the idea of progressive reform emerging as a growing force in American politics, the tariff seemed ripe for renewed political conflict. Unless the Republicans could come up with new justification for maintaining existing levels of protection, these new developments promised to benefit the Democrats, who had been associated with the idea of tariff reform for many decades.

Furthermore, by the turn of the century a new generation of tariff critics was making two main arguments against protective tariffs: that they were responsible for the high cost of living and put an unfair tax burden on workers, and that they were distorting the American economy by promoting monopolies and increasing industrial concentration. Although these criticisms were largely inaccurate, the arguments gained wide currency and fed the public's growing misgivings about high tariffs while putting Old Guard advocates of protection on the defensive.

Regarding the cost of living, tariffs clearly increased the domestic price of imported goods above what they would have been without the tariffs.[77] Ida Tarbell, the muckraking journalist, was the person most responsible for driving this message home. In a six-part series entitled "The Tariff in Our Times," published in the periodical *The American* in 1906–7 and later as a book, Tarbell sought to expose the corrupt politics and special interests that operated behind the scenes and influenced Congress in setting the tariff. In 1909, Tarbell published two widely noted articles—"Where Every Penny Counts" and "Where the Shoe Is Pinched"—in which she popularized the notion that protection inflated the profits of manufacturers while raising the cost of living and reducing the standard of living of working families. For the working class, "every penny added to the cost of food, of coal, of common articles of clothing means simply less food, less warmth, less covering." She noted that the buying and mending of shoes accounted for a quarter of consumer spending on clothing. "It was hard enough for the poor to buy shoes ten years ago before the Dingley tariff, but with every year since it has been harder," she complained. The high cost of shoes was based on the duties on imported leather and thread, which benefited the beef trust and the leather trust, let alone the even higher tariff on shoes, which benefited the United Shoe Company. All of these added costs were borne by the consumer. "At a time when wealth is rolling up as never before, a vast number of hard-working people in this country are really having a more difficult time making ends meet than they have ever had before," she concluded.[78]

Reformers also charged that duties on consumer goods were regressive and hit poor households with higher prices for basic consumer goods while increasing profits for rich industrialists. While this story was plausible, there is almost no empirical evidence on the distributional burden of taxation during this period. As we saw in chapter 5, the tariff may have been broadly neutral with respect to consumers overall, although the tariff was almost certainly more regressive than an income tax. This argument helped resurrect the idea that an income tax would be a more equitable way of raising government revenue.

Critics sometimes took the argument about the cost of living further and blamed the tariff for rising prices. After decades of deflation following the Civil War, the consumer price index rose nearly 20 percent between 1899 and 1913. Of course, the tariff was not responsible for this development. As already noted, the United States was on the gold standard, and the overall price level was determined by global monetary conditions. Inflation appeared in the late 1890s because new gold discoveries increased the worldwide supply of gold. That the tariff was not responsible for the rising price level is evident from the fact that every country on the gold standard, even those that practiced free trade, such as Britain, also experienced rising prices. (And, of course, high tariffs had not prevented deflation from occurring during 1873–96.) Still, the argument that tariffs were responsible for the higher cost of living resonated with the general public.[79]

Finally, tariff critics complained that, by protecting domestic firms from foreign competition, high tariffs gave rise to monopolies that earned large profits at the expense of consumers and farmers. A brief but frenzied merger wave—which started in 1896, peaked in 1899, and subsided by 1903—led to the consolidation of many industries and transformed the landscape of American business. The most dramatic example was the creation of the US Steel Corporation in 1901, which at one point accounted for about 90 percent of domestic iron and steel production. Other large industrial firms also emerged, such as American Tobacco, Diamond Match, International Harvester, and Standard Oil. These corporations dominated the domestic market, absorbing smaller firms or driving them out of business.[80]

Critics had long complained that import duties reduced competition and encouraged monopolies. As Benton McMillin (D-TN) argued, "While the Government has thrown up its tariff walls without, monopolists have joined hands within for the purpose of putting up prices and plundering the people through the devices known as trusts, pools, and combines."[81] Republicans vigorously denied any connection between the tariff and the growth of big business. In 1902, President Theodore Roosevelt maintained that "the cases in which the tariff can produce a monopoly are so few as to constitute an inconsiderable factor in the question. The question of regulation of the trusts stands apart from the question of tariff revision. The only relation of the tariff to big corporations as a whole is that the tariff makes manufactures profitable. . . . To remove the tariff as a punitive measure directed against trusts would inevitably result in ruin to the weaker competitors who are struggling against them."[82]

The fact that the Dingley tariff of 1897 was immediately followed by a huge wave of industrial consolidations lent credibility to the accusation that the tariff encouraged monopolization. In 1899, testifying before Congress on the trust movement, Harry Havemeyer, the president of the American Sugar Refining Company (the sugar trust), famously pronounced that "the mother of all trusts is the customs tariff bill." Havemayer's widely publicized statement became the populist rallying cry that "the tariff is the mother of the trust," but he was widely misinterpreted. He did not mean that the tariff gave rise to the trust movement, but rather that the tariff gave much greater security to domestic firms than did monopolization, which was always being disciplined by the entry of new competitors.[83]

Did protective tariffs promote the monopolization of the domestic market? In theory, an import quota might reduce foreign competition in a way that facilitates collusion among domestic firms, but import quotas were not used at this time. A nonprohibitive import tariff simply raises the price of imports and enables domestic firms to capture a larger share of the market, but does not necessarily promote industry consolidation or facilitate collusion. Import tariffs might even have reduced domestic concentration by allowing smaller, less efficient firms to survive.

Economic historians have been skeptical about whether protective tariffs led to the rise of big business during this period. High tariffs had been in place for many decades prior to the merger wave of the late 1890s. Furthermore, business consolidations also occurred in sectors that were dependent on exports, not just those protected from imports. American Tobacco, International Harvester, the meat-packing trust, the Standard Oil Company, as well as US Steel were exporters and did not fear imports. Trusts were also created in industries that were completely unaffected by international trade.[84]

So what led to the great merger wave from 1897 to 1903, if not the tariff? Ironically enough, the antitrust laws may have been a contributing factor. In 1890, Congress passed the Sherman Antitrust Act prohibiting contracts or combinations in restraint of trade. Three key Supreme Court decisions in the late 1890s ruled that cartels, or horizontal agreements to fix prices, were illegal, but mergers that accomplished the same result were legal. By making informal business cartels illegal, the Sherman Antitrust Act may have triggered the mergers that resulted in legal consolidations.[85]

While protective tariffs were not a major factor behind the consolidation, tariffs on raw materials and intermediate goods may have promoted some firms to become vertically integrated. As McCraw (1986, 53) notes, "If a steelmaker located on the Atlantic Coast had to pay a protected market price for pig iron and coking coal from Western Pennsylvania, rather than importing it cheaply by ship from Canada, he would more likely integrate backward and acquire these inputs at their unprotected cost." Beyond this, there were more important technological factors and market incentives to create larger corporations.[86]

In sum, economists have been skeptical about the argument that protective tariffs were responsible for the rising cost of living or the increase in industrial concentration, while granting that duties were regressive in comparison to an income tax. Yet all of these arguments gave Democrats and progressive Republicans political ammunition that they could use to attack the Old Guard Republicans. The Old Guard denied that high tariffs were protecting special interests, arguing that protective duties helped maintain high wages for workers and promoted the growth and stability of the economy. They refused to repudiate the Dingley tariff: House Speaker Joseph Cannon (R-IL) drew fire for calling it, "all things considered, the most perfect and just customs law ever enacted."[87] Unable to put forward fresh arguments to justify existing duties, the Republican establishment exploited the ever-present fear that reducing tariffs would expose large segments of the economy to a flood of imports, driving firms out of business, workers out of jobs, and wages down to lower levels.

Unfortunately for them, this argument had lost credibility at a time when American manufacturing was increasingly dominated by large, firmly established corporations that were now exporting to the world. Aside from exaggerating the importance of protection for the manufacturing sector, it also exaggerated its impact on labor income. As we have seen, wages had always been much higher in the United States than in Europe because of its large per capita endowment of land.[88] And the steady growth of real wages was tied to the growth of labor productivity; between 1890 and 1913, real wages increased roughly 30 percent because labor productivity increased by about 30 percent.[89]

With the tremendous strides that American manufacturers were making in world markets, the argument that high tariffs were needed to save jobs and protect high wages was becoming less credible over time. By the turn of the century, the American economy was populated by large corporations that were many times bigger than their European counterparts. And they were highly efficient because they were forced to compete in the large, integrated, and highly competitive American market, unlike European producers, who still faced trade barriers within the continent that kept the size of markets much smaller.[90] As a result, many large manufacturers had become uninterested in the tariff. Indeed, political support for the tariff was found not so much among big businesses but among the many small manufacturers who were the most vulnerable to foreign competition.

The loss of the iron and steel industry as a major source of protectionist agitation was symbolic of how the old Republican coalition was changing. In 1908, the steel magnate Andrew Carnegie publicly stated that the tariff on imported iron and steel could be safely eliminated without any significant effect on domestic production. He argued that the iron and steel industry was well past the point of being an infant industry, and the industry could fend for itself without fear of foreign competition. Steel producers no longer needed protection "because steel is now produced cheaper here than anywhere else, notwithstanding the higher wages paid per man," Carnegie (1908, 202) argued. "That there is a cult who regard [the doctrine of protection] as sacrosanct and everlasting, none knows better than the writer; but its members are few and not likely to increase, since our country has admittedly developed and gained, and is to continue gaining, manufacturing supremacy in one department after another until it reaches a position where free trade in manufactures would be desirable for it, all the markets of the world open to her, and hers to the world," he continued. "Our difficulty will then be to get other nations to agree to free trade."

Carnegie's widely publicized remarks enraged Old Guard Republicans, who subpoenaed him to appear before Congress. Republicans were prepared to grill him over his heretical and inconvenient views on protection, but Carnegie turned the table on them. He proceeded "to alternately mystify, baffle, bamboozle, and infuriate committee members by ridiculing their attempts to understand the steel industry, disputing the figures they had gathered, and assuring them they were in over their heads when it came to business," Nasaw (2006, 705) writes. With a sharp wit and incomparable command of business details, Carnegie humiliated his inquisitors and made them seem like ignorant, misinformed fools who were way out of their league in arguing that American industry still needed protection.

All of these factors put Republicans under increasing pressure to rethink their support for old-fashioned, high-tariff protectionism. With the death of President McKinley, the question was whether his successor, Theodore Roosevelt, a promising young reformer associated with the progressive wing of the party, would take on the party establishment and propose tariff reforms.

TARIFF STANDPATTERS: ROOSEVELT AND TAFT

Although President Roosevelt was a passionate progressive reformer in many areas, tariff policy was not one of them. Roosevelt began his career sympathetic to the idea of free trade, but changed his position to advance in the party. By the time he became president, Roosevelt adhered to the mainstream Republican position on protection.[91] More accurately, and perhaps uncharacteristically, he was indifferent to the whole issue. In 1894, he described himself as not "very keen about the tariff business myself, having, as you know, a tinge of economic agnosticism in me." Roosevelt often remarked that tariff policy was simply a matter of political expediency, not of principle. "My feeling about this tariff question is . . . that it is one of expediency and not morality," he once noted. "There is nothing any more intrinsically right or wrong in a 40 percent tariff than in a 60 percent tariff."[92] Roosevelt (1924, 8:51) argued that tariff policy "should be decided solely on grounds of expediency. Political economists have pretty generally agreed that protection is vicious in theory and harmful in practice, but if the majority of the people in interest wish it, and it affects only themselves, there is no earthly reason why they should not be allowed to try the experiment to their heart's content."

Roosevelt came into the presidency wary of proposing any tariff changes, because he knew the issue was a political minefield. "There is no question that there is dynamite in it," he observed. "There is a widespread feeling that [the tariff] should be altered, but there is equally widespread difference as to what the alterations should be, and there is no doubt whatever that if they are too extensive, or if anything in the nature of a general revision takes place, there will be a panic or something approaching to it, with consequent disaster to the business community and incidentally to the Republican party. Personally I think it of very much less consequence what tariff we have than it is to have continuity of tariff policy."[93]

Roosevelt's term in office, from 1901–09, was one of general economic prosperity and a period of unified Republican government. With economic growth strong and the budget in surplus, the conservative Republican Congress, led by Speaker Joseph Cannon of Illinois, had no compelling reason to revise the tariff code. Roosevelt fought the Old Guard Republicans over business regulation, conservation, and naval expansion, but he was unwilling to take them on over tariffs. "On the interstate commerce business, which I regard as a matter of principle, I shall fight," Roosevelt vowed. "On the tariff, which I regard as a matter of expediency, I shall endeavor to get the best results I can, but I shall not break with my party."[94]

In his first annual message to Congress in December 1901, Roosevelt signaled that he would not push Congress for a change in tariff policy in deference to the party's Old Guard "standpatters" who opposed any change. There was, he said, a "general acquiescence in our present tariff system as a national policy." Although he put in a kind word about reciprocity, he qualified it by adding that "reciprocity must be treated as the handmaiden of protection."[95] Roosevelt considered asking for the passage of the Kasson reciprocity treaties, but Senator Nelson Aldrich of Rhode Island, a powerful Old Guard Republican, advised him against it. Roosevelt backed down and said that he would simply call the Senate's attention to them. With such a lackluster endorsement, the treaties died a quiet death in the Senate. By postponing action on reciprocity in 1902, Roosevelt effectively deferred any action on tariffs for years to come.[96]

Roosevelt dismissed public criticism of protection as "irrational" and held that "ninety-five percent of the complaints about the tariff had no basis whatever."[97] "The country has acquiesced in the wisdom of the protective-tariff principle," he reiterated in 1902. "It is exceedingly undesirable that this system should be destroyed or that there should be violent and radical changes therein." Despite his reputation as a reformer, Roosevelt put his reform efforts elsewhere. Having repeatedly stated that the tariff "should be decided solely on grounds of expediency," he found it expedient to do nothing.

After his landslide victory in the 1904 presidential election, however, Roosevelt began to think that some tariff revision might be necessary to appease public opinion. "In my judgment," he wrote shortly after the election,

> "if we do not amend or revise the tariff, . . . we will be putting a formidable weapon in the hands of our opponents. I am aware that there are dangers in the attempt to revise it, but I am convinced that there are more dangers if we do not attempt to revise it. You cannot be aware of how many Republicans bitterly resent the proposition that there should be no change in the tariff. . . . I am convinced that the mere standpatters, if they have their way, will come pretty near to smashing the whole Republican party; . . . it will be the greatest mistake, from the standpoint of the protectionists, if the protectionists refuse to have the tariff amended."[98]

Still, he approached the issue without enthusiasm. He did not think "it at all a vital matter to reduce [tariffs], so far as the welfare of the people is concerned"; he wanted simply "to meet the expectation of people that we shall consider the tariff question. . . . I am going to make every effort to get something of what I desire in the way of an amendment to the present tariff law; but I shall not split with my party on the matter, for it would be absurd to do so."[99]

In November 1904, Roosevelt sent a letter to Speaker Cannon with some draft language for discussing the tariff issue in his annual message to Congress. Roosevelt proposed saying that, although doing away with tariffs "would be a ruinous calamity" for the nation, the time had come for Congress to reconsider the tariff schedule, "not radically to revise or alter it, but to see if there are not points where it can with advantage be amended."[100] Cannon and Aldrich insisted that the president remove any mention of the tariff from his message or they would block the expansion of the Interstate Commerce Commission's power to regulate the railroads, something the president desperately wanted.[101] Mark Hanna, a powerful Republican senator from Ohio, explicitly warned the president, "As long as I remain in the Senate and can raise a hand to stop you, you will never touch a schedule of the tariff act."[102] Without the support of Republican leaders in Congress, Roosevelt abandoned the idea of modifying the tariff: "At present the party is so far from being a unit in favor of amendment or reduction of the present tariff that there is a strong majority against it—a majority due partly to self-interest, partly to inertia, partly to timidity, partly to genuine conviction—these motives operating differently in different States or with different individuals."[103]

Roosevelt's unwillingness to challenge the status quo did not end the demands in some quarters for tariff reform. In 1906, looking toward the next presidential election, Roosevelt privately predicted that "the tariff is of course what will cause us the most trouble. . . . The demand for its immediate revision is entirely irrational; but this does not alter the fact that there is a strong demand; and as Cannon and the Congressional leaders will not—and I believe really cannot—say that there will be an immediate revision, I should not be surprised to see this issue used to defeat us."[104]

Sensing the shift in public sentiment, William Howard Taft, the Republican candidate in the 1908 presidential election, signaled his willingness to take on the party's inflexible position on tariffs. As Roosevelt's secretary of war, Taft went against the grain of his party by talking up tariff reform and allying himself with those who favored a downward revision of duties. The Republican platform even pledged that the party was "unequivocally for a revision of the tariff by a special session of Congress immediately following the inauguration of the next President," but did not explicitly endorse a downward revision and explicitly denied that protective duties would be abandoned. The purpose of the Republican policy was "not only to preserve, without excessive duties, that security against foreign competition to which American manufacturers, farmers and producers are entitled, but also to maintain the high standard of living of the wage-earners of this country, who are the most direct beneficiaries of the protective system."[105]

So on what basis would tariff rates be revised? According to the platform, "The true principle of protection is best maintained by the imposition of such duties as will equal the difference between the cost of production at home and abroad, together with a reasonable profit to American industries." This became the new credo for the Republicans: the tariff should be set to "equalize the differences in the cost of production between domestic and foreign producers." This standard gave the appearance of being an objective and "scientific" way to set tariffs, thus ruling out special favors or excessive protection to politically influential industries. As we shall see in chapter 7, however, the principle was largely meaningless and impossible to implement.

Taft endorsed this idea, even as he supported the idea of tariff reform. "The Republican party has in times past laid down the rule that the amount of protection which should be allowed is that which represents the difference between the conditions prevailing in Europe and those which prevail in this country, [and] the time has come for a readjustment," he wrote to Roosevelt in 1907. "There are individual instances known to me and known to everyone in which the amount of the tariff is greatly in excess of this difference. . . . These inequalities ought to be remedied."[106]

Given his experience with the obstructionist Congress, Roosevelt warned Taft to "move with great caution" on the tariff issue. This did not stop Taft from announcing during the campaign, "It is my judgment that a revision of the tariff in accordance with the pledge of the Republican platform will be, on the whole, a substantial revision downward." Roosevelt later recalled telling Taft "that he was making pretty drastic promises, and that there might be difficulty in having them kept, . . . but [Taft] was perfectly breezy and cheerful, and declined to consider the possibility of trouble ahead."[107]

In their 1908 election platform, the Democrats welcomed "the belated promise of tariff reform now offered by the Republican party in tardy recognition of the righteousness of the Democratic position on this question; but the people cannot safely entrust the execution of this important work to a party which is so deeply obligated to the highly protected interests as is the Republican party."[108] The Democrats advocated giving duty-free treatment to imports of all goods that competed with the products of "trust-controlled" industries, something known as the "Iowa idea" for its Midwest origins. The party also pledged to reduce the cost of living by slashing tariffs on the necessities of life.

Just as they had in the three previous presidential elections, the Republicans cruised to victory in 1908. Taft easily defeated his Democratic opponent, William Jennings Bryan, who lost his third presidential election, and the Republicans retained control of Congress. In his March 1909 inaugural address, Taft called for a special session of Congress to expedite the revision. The new tariff schedule "should secure an adequate revenue and adjust the duties in such a manner as to afford to labor and to all industries in this country, whether of the farm, mine or factory, protection by tariff equal to the difference between the cost of production abroad and the cost of production here," the president stated. "It is thought that there has been such a change in conditions since the enactment of the Dingley Act, drafted on a similarly protective principle, that the measure of the tariff above stated will permit the reduction of rates in certain schedules and will require the advancement of few, if any."[109]

Whatever hope that Taft had for a downward tariff revision should have been tempered after considering the Republican leadership in Congress. The speaker and the chairmen of the key committees were Old Guard conservatives and no friends of tariff reform. Speaker Cannon had no patience for progressives and opposed regulation and reform for fear that it would muddy the Republican message, but he also recognized the advantages of allowing the passage of a bill that would appear to satisfy the public sentiment for a tariff adjustment.

Just days after Taft's inaugural, Ways and Means Committee Chair Sereno Payne (R-NY) reported a bill that the committee had been working on since the election. The majority report conceded that "there has been a popular demand, more or less widespread, for the general cutting of rates."[110] The bill's approach was like the old Democratic approach: to reduce rates on raw materials while keeping high duties on final manufactured goods. As a result, coal, iron ore, wood pulp, and hides were put on the duty-free list, and tariffs on pig iron, steel, and lumber were cut by about one half. Duties on wool and woolens, cotton goods, and refined sugar were left largely intact, while those on fabrics, gloves, hosiery, and glass were increased. In general, the bill reshuffled rather than reduced most duties and thus proposed only modest changes overall.[111] The Republicans wanted to dispense with the matter quickly without fundamentally revising the protective duties. "I do not think it worthwhile at this time to engage upon any academic discussions of the tariff question," Payne said. "The country is overwhelmingly in favor of a protective tariff."[112]

The minority Democrats dismissed the bill as a failure, charging that "most of the changes in a downward direction are more apparent than real" and that it would do nothing to reduce the cost of living for consumers and workers. They argued that the Republican bill could not "be defended on any ground whatsoever, even by a standpatter. In all, the reductions, both apparent and real, fall far short of the substantial relief which the people were led to expect."[113] Hopelessly outnumbered in the House, Democrats had no chance of blocking the bill, and their opposition was perfunctory. In April 1909, the House approved the Payne bill by a partisan vote of 217–161; Republicans supported passage 213–1 while Democrats opposed it 160–4.

As always, the Senate's response was less predictable. By now the Senate had gained a reputation as "the graveyard of tariff reform" for its ability to block all reductions. A key reason for the lack of any significant tariff changes after the Civil War is that the Republicans controlled the Senate for twenty-one of twenty-three sessions from 1867 to 1913. And sure enough, the tariff bill came under the control of Nelson Aldrich, chairman of the Finance Committee and the Republican majority leader, an Old Guard stalwart of old-fashioned protectionism. The powerful Rhode

Island senator viewed the purpose of the revision differently than the president. Certainly the Republican platform promised tariff changes, Aldrich admitted, but "where did we ever make the statement that we would revise the tariff downward?"[114] In the spring and summer of 1909, producer lobbyists had ready access to Aldrich and the Finance Committee, which operated in closed sessions. The committee made 847 amendments to the Payne bill, including about 600 rate hikes that reversed many of the cuts made by the House.

Aldrich tried to push the legislation through the Senate without debate, but that proved impossible. Instead, a bitter floor fight broke out between the Old Guard Republicans from the East and the progressive insurgents from the Midwest. For two months, the progressive insurgents, led by Robert LaFollette (R-WI), Albert Cummins (R-IA), and William Borah (R-ID), delivered withering criticisms of the bill, which they were not allowed to help frame, as it was debated schedule by schedule. The insurgents blamed the high cost of living on the tariffs that protected big businesses from foreign competition. They repeatedly attacked Schedule K, the wool and woolens schedule, which had changed little since 1867. Jonathan Dolliver (R-IA) dismissed the bill as a "petty swindle on the American public" and "a rank interchange of political larcenies." According to Dolliver,

> I stand here to defend the people against exactions of avarice and to defend the good name of [the] protective tariff against those who are using it as a mere asset in the operation of financing conspiracies in restraint of trade. . . . The protective tariff doctrine is sound. It fails only through the inequalities with which it is applied to our affairs. It fails only when avarice and greed, anxious to make more money, have such influence with Congress as to rewrite tariff laws, not in the interest of the people, not in the interest of the unnumbered millions of our people, but in the narrow, naked, personal interest of a few men scattered here and there in various sections of our beloved country.[115]

Joseph Bristow (R-KS) argued that the protective system was "being contorted into a synonym for graft and plunder."[116] The insurgents attacked tariff "jokers," little tricks written into the legislation, such as obscure classifications of goods devised by domestic producers for their own particular products. For example, cotton cloth could be considered "colored," and therefore subject to a higher rate, even if it had just a single non-white thread in it. While a tariff would be reduced on one type of good that was no longer imported, it would be increased on another that was, giving the impression that the overall level was unchanged. Insurgents blasted the Old Guard as "reactionary tools of the trusts and eastern corporations."[117]

Even as they railed with indignation against the inequities of the tariff and special-interest politics, the insurgents made it clear that they were not opposed to protection. Rather, they envisioned a revision that would reduce duties on industrial goods (iron, machinery, cotton and woolen textiles) and increase duties on agricultural products and raw materials (barley, hides, wool, paper, coal, and iron ore).[118] Francis Newlands (R-NV) favored an "equitable" tariff revision: "I am not willing that it should be revised entirely in the interests of Eastern manufacturers at the expense of Western products, and if there is to be a protective tariff, I shall endeavor to see that the West gets its fair share of protection."[119] The Republican insurgents attacked the party leadership for favoring Eastern industries, but since they favored equal protection for raw materials producers in the West, they did not ally themselves with Democrats, whom they viewed as wanting lower tariffs all around.

The Old Guard mounted a fierce defense of the existing system. The attack on Schedule K, the wool and woolens schedule, outraged Aldrich, who called it "the crucial schedule of this bill":

> There is no Senator sitting upon this side of the Chamber, there is no person who is acquainted with the tariffs of this or any other country, who does not know that an assault upon the wool and woolen schedule of this bill is an attack upon the very citadel of protection and the lines of defense for American industries and American labor. If the Senate destroys the relations in that schedule or destroys the schedule itself, you demoralize the whole protective system; and you destroy every line of defense which the people of the country have who believe in the protective policy.[120]

Despite this defensiveness, the Old Guard far outnumbered the insurgents and therefore could be completely dismissive of them, often walking out on their speeches.

The Senate held dozens of roll-call votes on individual lines of the tariff bill, from the duties on blankets, lumber, hides, boots and shoes, petroleum, textbooks, and tea, among many others. "It has been tariff, tariff, tariff, all the time, literally morning, noon, and night," Henry Cabot Lodge (R-MA) complained. "I have never been so worked in my life."[121] The Democrats largely held back and allowed the Republican factions to attack one another. Yet these votes also exposed a weakness in the Democratic position, as party unity in favor of lowering duties often evaporated when it came to votes on specific commodities of local interest. For example, Democrats voted against putting lumber on the free list and reducing duties on hides and barley.

An even more important development occurred in the course of debating the tariff when Congress began considering an income tax. Democrats proposed an income tax in part to compensate for the lost revenue from lower import duties. Taft and other progressives also supported an income tax and worked to build support for it. The Old Guard may have been able to block significant tariff reforms, but they had more difficulty controlling the groundswell of support for an income tax. Speaker Cannon killed the introduction of an income tax in the House, and Chairman Aldrich spiked it in the Senate Finance Committee, but they could not prevent the proposal from coming up on the Senate floor. Joseph Bailey (D-TX) proposed a tax of 3 percent on net income of individuals and corporations, while progressive Albert Cummins (R-IA) proposed a graduated income tax on individuals. The Bailey-Cummins amendments quickly gained bipartisan support, but were strongly opposed by the Old Guard, who saw them as an indirect attack on protective tariffs.[122]

Aldrich struggled to separate the income tax from the tariff and thereby buy time for the policy of protection. To quell the uprising, the Republican leadership insisted that a constitutional amendment was necessary to ensure that the Supreme Court would not strike down the law, as it had in 1895. President Taft supported this approach, adding that he had "become convinced that a great majority of people of the country are in favor of vesting the National Government with power to levy an income tax, and that they will secure the adoption of the amendment in the States, if proposed to them."[123]

Despite his role in instigating the tariff revision, Taft remained on the sidelines throughout Congress's deliberations.[124] The president admitted that he was "bewildered by the intricacies of the tariff measure," but encouraged the insurgents to "go ahead, criticize the bill, amend it, cut down the duties—go after it hard. I will keep track of your amendments. I will read every word of the speeches you make, and when they lay that bill before me, unless it complies with the platform, I will veto it."[125] Aldrich also worked closely with the president: he knew the insurgents could not stop the bill, but the president could. He reassured Taft that the bill would merit his support, and pledged his cooperation on other legislative matters.

Finally, in early July 1909, the Senate passed the tariff bill by a vote of 45–34; Republicans voted 44–10 in favor, with the no votes coming from progressives, while Democrats voted 24–1 against the bill. Speaker Cannon and Majority Leader Aldrich stacked the conference committee appointed to reconcile the House and Senate versions with Old Guard protectionists. With the bill in conference, Taft finally became engaged and began pushing the conferees to adopt the House bill, which was closer to the downward revision he wanted. The conference spent an inordinate amount of time on the tariff on hides, which the House put on the free list but the Senate kept at the existing duty of 15 percent. The president sent an ultimatum to the Congress, insisting that he would not sign a bill that did not have the free raw materials included in the House bill (opposed by Senator Aldrich) and the Senate reductions in the tariff on gloves and hosiery (opposed by Speaker Cannon). The veto threat was credible and forced the conferees to agree. Still, despite some success in shading tariffs lower somewhat, as in the House bill, Taft's late attempt to intervene limited his impact on the bill. And the president managed to alienate both the proponents of high tariffs and the insurgents: the former objected to his insistence on reductions, while the latter were disappointed that he did not demand more cuts in rates on industrial goods.

Despite the controversy, Taft signed the Payne-Aldrich bill in August 1909, saying that "I believe it to be the result of a sincere effort on the part of the Republican party to make a downward revision and to comply with the promises of the platform."[126] The public reaction was mixed, because the rates in the tariff schedule simply tinkered with duties in the Dingley tariff of 1897. The new act lowered duties on 650 items, raised them on 220, and left 1,150 untouched. The average tariff on dutiable imports fell slightly, from 46 to 41 percent, but the measure failed to live up to the promises that Taft had made.

The Payne-Aldrich tariff contained some innovations. It introduced to a two-column tariff schedule of minimum and maximum duties. The minimum duties were the standard ones, while the maximum duties, set 25 percent higher, were scheduled to go into effect against all goods coming from countries which "unduly discriminate" against US exports. To assist him in this task, the act authorized the president to create a Tariff Board to look into the trade policies of other governments.[127] The maximum duties were never put into effect, because the Board found no significant foreign discrimination against US exports. However, Taft soon began to use the Tariff Board to investigate the differences in the cost of production between domestic and foreign producers in various industries. Democrats adamantly opposed the creation of any such government body on the grounds that it would entrench the system around a bad principle, that of setting tariffs to equalize differences in the costs of production of domestic and foreign producers. Therefore, they terminated the board when they regained control of Congress in 1912.

The Senate also passed a proposed amendment to the Constitution allowing an income tax. The amendment required the approval of three-fourths of the state legislatures, a significant enough hurdle that Old Guard Republicans were confident that its passage could be blocked. Indeed, the strongest opposition to the income tax came from the wealthiest, industrialized, urban states in the Northeast, such as Connecticut, Rhode Island, and Pennsylvania, where the Republican party was strong.

But there was more immediate political fallout from the Payne-Aldrich tariff. Speaking in Winona, Minnesota, the heart of insurgent country, in the fall of 1909, Taft argued that the new tariff was "a substantial achievement in the direction of lower tariffs and downward revision." He added, "On the whole, I am bound to say that I think the Payne Tariff Bill is the best tariff bill that the Republican party ever passed and therefore the best tariff bill that has been passed at all. I do not feel that I could have reconciled any other course to my conscience than that of signing the bill." These remarks created an uproar among already alienated Republican voters in the Midwest. He later admitted that, in describing the bill, the "comparative would have been a better description than the superlative."[128]

The Payne-Aldrich tariff had other reverberations as well. As in the aftermath of the McKinley tariff, Republicans paid a high price for the Payne-Aldrich tariff when it lost control of the House in the 1910 midterm elections. Although Republicans retained control of the Senate, Democrats and progressive Republicans could combine forces to move legislation through the chamber.

When the new Congress convened, the new speaker, Champ Clark of Missouri, declared that the first priority of Democrats was "an honest, intelligent revision of the tariff downward to give every American citizen an equal chance in the race of life, and to pamper none by special favor or special privilege; to reduce the cost of living by eradicating the enormities and cruelties of the present tariff bill."[129] In August 1911, Democrats in the House and a coalition of Democrats and progressive Republicans in the Senate passed three bills to reduce duties on raw wool and wool and cotton manufactures. Taft vetoed each bill, ostensibly on the grounds that the Tariff Board had not completed a cost-of-production investigation. "It is on account of my ignorance of the question of the tariff that I am going to veto these bills," Taft reportedly confessed to a senator. "That is a very honest statement to make, Mr. President, but it would be a ruinous one to make public," came the reply.[130] In one veto message, Taft stated he could not permit Congress to "blindly enact a law which may seriously injure any industries involved and the business of the country in general" without a study of the matter.[131] Old Guard Republicans were relieved by the president's veto, but progressives castigated him for abandoning the cause of tariff reform.

Taft alienated progressive Republicans even more by negotiating a reciprocity agreement with Canada. In 1866, the United States had abrogated the Reciprocity Treaty of 1854. Ever since then, Canada had protected its market and sought preferences for its exports in the markets of the British Empire, but it still had an interest in a trade agreement with the United States. In 1909, bilateral discussions began, and a new accord was reached. In exchange for reducing its duties on manufactured goods, Canada would gain better access for its livestock, grain, timber, meat, and dairy products (but not wool) in the United States. What Taft thought would be a great achievement of his administration seemed once again to prove his political ineptitude and further estranged him from progressive Republicans. They viewed a trade agreement with Canada as another example of the government keeping protective duties on manufactured goods high while reducing duties on precisely those goods produced in the Midwest's farm belt. The agreement reinforced the perception that farmers would get no help from the Washington establishment. The pact also alienated the Republican Old Guard, who viewed it as a threat to the alliance between raw materials and final-goods producers that provided the core support for the protective system. Furthermore, it violated the Republican pledge that the tariff should be set to equalize the costs of production; if that was the ostensible principle guiding the party's trade policy, then how could it be arbitrarily bargained away?

Even though it meant more competition for wheat farmers, cattle ranchers, and other producers of primary products, the accord was broadly popular because it would help manufacturers in a neighboring market. Newspapers wanted cheaper access to Canada's paper and pulp and used their editorial pages to help drum up support for the agreement. Taft worked hard for its approval and the agreement passed in February 1911 without debate in the House by a vote of 221–92; Democrats supported the bill 143–5, but the Republicans were split 78–87. The Senate failed to act before the end of the congressional session, so the bill was passed again by the House in April and then by the Senate in July by a vote of 53–27; Democrats voted 32–3 in favor and Republicans voted 24–21 against. However, in a September 1911 referendum, Canadian voters rejected the agreement, and it never went into effect.[132]

Thus, despite the fact that the United States had become a net exporter of manufactured goods, American trade politics did not change significantly in the last decade of the nineteenth century or the first decade of the twentieth. Although divided, Republicans remained committed to high tariffs, while Democrats struggled to gain political power and overcome party divisions of their own. Both parties professed an interest in promoting exports, but a policy of reciprocity was never seriously considered. Any significant reduction in protective duties would inflict too high a political price on the party that sought to gain greater market access abroad for exporters. As a result, trade policy remained fixed in the long-standing status quo.

CHAPTER SEVEN

Policy Reversals and Drift, 1912–1928

Although the United States emerged as the world's leading industrial power and became a net exporter of manufactured goods in the 1890s, these developments failed to change the course of US trade policy. Instead, import duties remained high, a brief flirtation with reciprocity sputtered out, and the partisan stalemate over trade policy continued unabated. Despite a brief period of lower tariffs under the Democrats (1913–1922), Republicans reverted to economic isolationism after World War I by raising import duties in 1922 and again in 1930. However, the goal of trade policy slowly began to shift from protecting manufacturing industries against imports to protecting agricultural producers from low prices, something import duties were ineffective in doing.

THE DEMOCRATIC TRIUMPH OF 1912

Despite significant changes in the US economy in the first decade of the twentieth century, no major changes were made to US trade policy. Republicans controlled seven consecutive Congresses after 1896, leaving Democrats demoralized and protective tariffs intact. At the same time, high protective tariffs were under attack for promoting the growth of monopoly trusts and the high cost of living, keeping Old Guard Republicans on the defensive. The party's failure to address these issues in the 1909 Payne-Aldrich tariff left them vulnerable in the 1910 and 1912 elections. Indeed, the Democratic and progressive Republican gains in the 1910 midterm elections were widely viewed as a repudiation of the Republican establishment.

In the 1912 election, President William Howard Taft ran for reelection on a platform that reaffirmed the party's support for protection. The platform stated that the high tariff policy "has been of the greatest benefit to the country, developing our resources, diversifying our industries, and protecting our workmen against competition with cheaper labor abroad, thus establishing for our wage-earners the American standard of living. The protective tariff is so woven into the fabric of our industrial and agricultural life that to substitute for it a tariff for revenue only would destroy many industries and throw millions of our people out of employment."[1]

Republicans denied that the tariff was responsible for rising prices, pointing out that countries with low tariffs were experiencing the same inflation of consumer prices. Yet "some of the existing import duties are too high, and should be reduced," they conceded. "Readjustment should be made from time to time to conform to changing conditions and to reduce excessive rates, but without injury to any American industry." To do this "requires closer study and more scientific methods than ever before" and therefore the Republicans proposed the creation of an expert commission much like the Tariff Board.[2]

The Democrats nominated Woodrow Wilson, the Governor of New Jersey and a former professor and president of Princeton University, as their presidential candidate. A student of government and politics, Wilson had a long and deep interest in tariff policy. Having grown up in the South, Wilson was a lifelong opponent of protection and a determined advocate of tariff reform. As a young man, he testified against high tariffs before the 1882 Tariff Commission, and a year later he helped organize the Atlanta branch of the Free Trade Club of New York.[3] In a scathing article, "The Tariff Make-Believe," Wilson (1909, 543) argued that tariffs were simply a way for politicians to dispense the largess of the government to special interests in exchange for political favors. He dismissed the pleas from industry for protection—the "pitiful tales, hard-luck stories, petition for another chance"—as "an act very unpalatable to American pride, and yet very frequently indulged in with no appearance of shame." In his view, "If any particular industry has been given its opportunity to establish itself and get its normal development, under cover of the customs, and is still unable to meet the foreign competition which is the standard of efficiency, it is unjust to tax to people of the country any further to support it."

Wilson (1909, 538) criticized the Payne-Aldrich tariff as "miscellaneously wrong in detail and radically wrong in principle." He attacked the so-called "jokers" in the tariff bills, "clauses whose meaning did not lie upon the surface, whose language was meant not to disclose its meaning." For example, the Payne-Aldrich legislation changed the tariff on imports of electric carbons from ninety cents per hundred weight to seventy cents per hundred feet, an apparent reduction but one that actually doubled the duty. Wilson condemned the process by which Congress drew up the tariff code. Congress never asked "what part of the protective system still benefits the country and is in the general interest; what part is unnecessary; what part is pure favoritism and the basis of dangerous and demoralizing special privilege?" Instead, he observed, in all tariff legislation "the committees of the House and Senate, when making up the several schedules of duties they were to propose, have asked, not what will be good for the country, but what will be good for the industries affected . . . what rates of duty will assure them abundant profits?"[4]

Wilson insisted that tariff reform and antitrust policy be put at the top of the Democratic agenda. Even though the party had opposed the Payne-Aldrich duties, they had lost credibility on the issue and were even accused of hypocrisy when some members lobbied for higher duties on products of interest to their own constituents, sometimes even asking for duties higher than those proposed by Republicans.[5] But Wilson was determined to force the party to live up to its past pronouncements. As a result, the Democratic platform declared "it to be a fundamental principle of the Democratic party that the Federal government, under the Constitution, has no right or power to impose or collect tariff duties, except for the purpose of revenue, and we demand that the collection of such taxes shall be limited to the necessities of government honestly and economically administered." It blasted high Republican tariffs as

> the principal cause of the unequal distribution of wealth; it is a system of taxation which makes the rich richer and the poor poorer; under its operations the American farmer and laboring man are the chief sufferers; it raises the cost of the necessaries of life to them, but does not protect their product or wages. The farmer sells largely in free markets and buys almost entirely in the protected markets. In the most highly protected industries, such as cotton and wool, steel and iron, the wages of the laborers are the lowest paid in any of our industries. We denounce the Republican pretense on that subject and assert that American wages are established by competitive conditions, and not by the tariff.

The party endorsed "the immediate downward revision of the existing high and in many cases prohibitive tariff duties, insisting that material reductions be speedily made upon the necessaries of life" and argued that "articles entering into competition with trust-controlled products and articles of American manufacture which are sold abroad more cheaply than at home should be put upon the free list."[6]

If Republicans were in a vulnerable position going into the election, party divisions ensured their demise. Dismayed by Taft's performance in office, former president Theodore Roosevelt entered the presidential race as a candidate for the Progressive "Bull Moose" Party, which demanded more government regulation of business. On the tariff, Progressives were ambivalent, advocating "a protective tariff which shall equalize conditions of competition between the United States and foreign countries, both for the farmer and the manufacturer, and which shall maintain for labor an adequate standard of living." They condemned Republicans for enacting the "unjust" Payne-Aldrich tariff and Democrats for wanting to destroy protection, which "would inevitably produce widespread industrial and commercial disaster." They supported the creation of a non-partisan Tariff Commission, but did not state what its mission should be. They professed to want lower tariffs, but opposed the reciprocity agreement with Canada because it could harm some northern farmers.[7]

In the presidential election of 1912, Roosevelt siphoned off enough Republican votes from Taft to hand the election to the Democrats. The election was scarcely a mandate for Wilson, who earned just 44.5 percent of the popular vote, while the combined total for Taft and Roosevelt was 53.7 percent. Regardless, the Republican split allowed the Democrats to secure unified control of government for the first time since 1894, making Wilson only the second Democratic president since the Civil War and the first of southern birth since before the Civil War. In addition, the Congressional seniority system meant that long-standing members of Congress—meaning Southern Democrats—assumed key leadership positions in the House and Senate. These Southern Democrats favored lower tariffs and were prepared to go along with Wilson.

In his inaugural address in March 1913, Wilson outlined an ambitious legislative program: a substantial reduction in the tariff, sweeping banking and currency reform, and new regulations on corporations. Tariff reform was given top billing because the existing policy "cuts us off from our proper part in the commerce of the world, violates the just principles of taxation, and makes the Government a facile instrument in the hand of private interests." He immediately called for a special session of Congress to reduce tariffs.[8]

Unlike previous presidents, Wilson viewed himself as the leader of his party and as having responsibility for overseeing the bill's passage through Congress. Wilson took an active interest in the details of the tariff schedule and worked closely with the Democratic leadership to en-sure that the legislation was done to his satisfaction. Even before he took office, Wilson met with Ways and Means Committee chair Oscar Under-wood (D-AL) to lay out his expectations about the provisions of the leg-islation.[9] Wilson pressed Underwood to shift many raw materials to the free list and to reduce duties on both industrial and farm goods.[10] Keenly aware of past failures to reform the tariff because of party divisions, Wil-son and Underwood sought to ensure maximum party unity on the issue. They prepared to fight with Democrats representing a variety of special interests—whether it be shoes from Massachusetts, sugar beets from Colo-rado, textiles from North Carolina, wool from Ohio, or cane sugar from Louisiana—who might hold out for higher duties. Therefore, before pro-ceeding, the House Democrats agreed to a binding party caucus in which they pledged to support any measure accepted by a two-thirds vote of the caucus.

The Ways and Means Committee held public hearings on the proposed revision, but business representatives who testified in favor of maintain-ing or increasing rates received a cool reception. A young Democratic con-gressman from Tennessee, Cordell Hull (1948, 72), later recalled, "For the first time in many years the beneficiaries of high-tariff privilege found themselves confronting an unfriendly committee which would not permit them virtually to write their own rates. This seemed very disconcerting to many of their representatives who appeared before the committee. . . . Many of them called on all of us who were engaged in preparing the bill. We would receive and hear them courteously, but after that our courses diverged."

Yet the committee's bill also made concessions for Democrats from the South and West by imposing duties on farm products, retaining protection for leather goods and sugar, and levying a 15 percent duty on wool. Before the bill was reported, Wilson intervened to stop this attempt at limiting the reform. The president threatened to veto any bill that did not put food, sugar, leather, and wool on the free list, compromising only by allowing a three-year phase out of the sugar duty. In particular, Wilson insisted that reducing the wool and woolens duties was a fundamental component of any tariff reform.[11] The committee took the president's threat seriously and changed the bill accordingly.

To demonstrate his commitment to tariff reform, Wilson took the un-usual step of addressing a joint session of Congress on April 8, 1913. No president had appeared before Congress since John Adams in November 1800. The joint session was a spectacular event: every seat in the House chamber was taken, and a huge crowd gathered outside the Capitol. Wilson spoke only briefly but made it clear that he would not tolerate a repeat of the party's failed efforts at tariff reform in 1894. Because of changed economic circumstances, Wilson argued that the country was in desperate need of a tariff revision:

> We long ago passed beyond the modest notion of "protecting" the industries of the country and moved boldly forward to the idea that they were entitled to the direct patronage of the Government. For a long time—a time so long that the men now active in public policy hardly remember the conditions that preceded it—we have sought in our tariff schedules to give each group of manufacturers or producers what they themselves thought that they needed in order to maintain a practically exclusive market as against the rest of the world. Consciously or unconsciously, we have built up a set of privileges and exemptions from competition behind which it was easy by any, even the crudest, forms of combination to organize monopoly; until at last nothing is normal, nothing is obliged to stand the tests of efficiency and economy, in our world of big business, but everything thrives by concerted arrangement.

The time had come, Wilson maintained, to change this:

> We must abolish everything that bears even the semblance of privilege or of any kind of artificial advantage, and put our business men and producers under the stimulation of a constant necessity to be efficient, economical, and enterprising, masters of competitive supremacy, better workers and merchants than any in the world. Aside from the duties laid upon articles which we do not, and probably cannot, produce, therefore, and the duties laid upon luxuries and merely for the sake of the revenues they yield, the object of the tariff duties henceforth laid must be effective competition, the whetting of American wits by contest with the wits of the rest of the world.

Wilson announced that he was withholding all other legislation from Congress so that nothing would "divert our energies from that clearly defined duty" of enacting a tariff bill.[12]

The burden was now clearly on the Democratic leadership in Congress to follow through. They controlled both chambers of Congress for the first time in eighteen years. Just a few weeks later, the Ways and Means Committee reported a bill that replaced complex specific duties with simple ad valorem duties, while reducing the average tariff from 40 percent to 30 percent, a 26 percent reduction, on average. The notion that tariffs should be set to equalize the costs of production was "absolutely rejected as a guide to tariff making"; instead, the party offered what it called a "competitive tariff."[13] Of course, the Republican minority objected to the "complete reversal of the economic policy of the government" that over time, it said, had built up industry and helped farmers prosper. Republicans complained that the Democratic proposal was a free-trade bill that would put American industry and workers at grave risk. They also reminded Democrats of their marginal election victory: "The party proposing it is in power, not by the grace of majority of the American people, but by a division in the ranks of the majority on other questions than that of protection."[14]

In May 1913, the House opened debate on the bill. Sam Rayburn (D-TX) set the tone: "The system of protective tariff built up under the Republican misrule has worked to make the rich richer and the poor poorer. The protective tariff has been justly called the mother of the trusts. It takes from the pockets of those least able to pay and puts into the pockets of those most able to pay."[15] The binding caucus held firm, and the bill was pushed through by a vote of 281–139. Democrats voted 274–5 in favor (four of the five dissents came from Louisiana because of sugar) and Republicans voted 127–5 against, while other parties, including the Progressives, voted 7–2 against. Figure 7.1 shows the geography of the House vote. As in

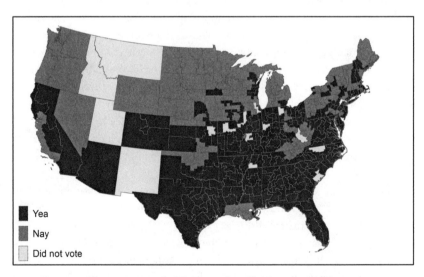

Figure 7.1. House vote on the Underwood tariff, May 8, 1913. (Map courtesy Citrin GIS/Applied Spatial Analysis Lab, Dartmouth College.)

previous tariff votes, the division was between Northern Republicans and Southern Democrats, with Democratic support even creeping into Ohio, Illinois, and Indiana.

The bill then moved to the Senate, still known as the "graveyard of tariff reform," where the larger representation of western states made it difficult to pass tariff reductions on raw materials and agricultural goods. True to form, the Finance Committee reported a bill that made 676 amendments to the House version, most of which were increases in rates. Fearing that the House bill could unravel in the Senate, Wilson took the offensive. The president went to Capitol Hill and directly confronted Senate Democrats, urging them not to break ranks. He refused to compromise with western members who wanted higher duties on wool and sugar. He warned the public that Washington had been invaded by scores of "pestiferous" lobbyists who were pressing for higher duties on raw materials: "I think that the public ought to know the extraordinary exertions being made by the lobby in Washington to gain recognition for certain alterations of the tariff bill."[16]

The president's statements prompted a progressive Republican from Iowa to propose an investigation into special-interest lobbying over the tariff. Although this motion caught Democrats off guard, they could not oppose it, and so Congress launched a sweeping investigation into industry contacts with senators on tariff matters and the financial holdings of senators in relation to protected industries. To almost everyone's surprise, the investigation revealed that there had been virtually no corrupt lobbying over tariffs. Furthermore, no trusts were involved, except the Federal Sugar Refining Company, which actually supported Wilson's proposal for duty-free sugar, something rejected by cane and beet farmers, who had spent large sums to keep the duties in place.[17] The investigation concluded that old-fashioned influence peddling or outright corruption had given way to industries exerting their political strength simply through constituent pressure. In addition, small- and medium-sized businesses were the key opponents of the tariff reductions, not big business or large trusts, because they were most vulnerable to foreign competition. The trusts and other large industrial concerns were now largely silent on tariffs because they were indifferent to them.

Unlike Grover Cleveland's clumsy attempt to shame the Senate in 1894, Wilson succeeded in generating a strong public reaction against the special interests that were trying to shape the bill: angry constituents wrote their congressmen and demanded that the Senate not weaken the House's attempt at tariff reform. As a result, Senate Democrats were united enough to pass the bill in September by a partisan vote of 54–37. Only two progressive Republicans, Robert LaFollette of Wisconsin and Miles Poindexter of Washington, voted in favor of the Democratic legislation. The other progressives remained aligned with mainstream Republicans and voted to keep the high duties in place, although this position caused them some discomfort.[18] After both chambers approved the conference version, Wilson signed the bill on October 3, 1913.

Thus, a combination of presidential leadership and a disciplined Congress controlled by southern Democrats led to the largest downward adjustment in import duties since the Walker tariff of 1846, which was also the product of southern Democrats. Under the new schedule, the average tariff on dutiable imports would fall from 40 percent to 27 percent, a cut of about one-third. The Underwood-Simmons tariff, as it was called, made a substantial across-the-board reduction of about 25 percent in duties on manufactured goods and put a large number of products on the duty-free list, including wool, iron, coal, lumber, meat, dairy products, leather boots and shoes, wood pulp and paper, wheat, and agricultural supplies; the duty on sugar was to be abolished gradually over three years. The share of duty-free imports rose from 54 percent of total imports in 1912 to 69 percent in 1916. Confronting the infamous Schedule K on the wool and woolen duties, Democrats succeeded in putting raw wool on the free list (the existing tariff had been about 44 percent) and cutting the tariff on woolen manufactures by one-third to one-half. This was an unlikely political achievement, given that Colorado, Montana, and Ohio were major wool-growing states. Ad valorem duties replaced specific duties, and the structure of the tariff was altered to keep rates high on luxury goods while reducing them on consumer goods.

Democrats were elated at their success. Wilson's Secretary of Agriculture, David Houston, exclaimed, "Think of it—a tariff revision downward at all—not dictated by the manufacturers; lower in the Senate than in the House—one which will not be made in the conference committee room!! A progressive income tax!! I did not think we would live to see these things!!"[19]

As Houston mentioned, the 1913 tariff bill also contained an income tax. As we saw in chapter 6, the Senate approved a constitutional amendment allowing an income tax during the debate over the Payne-Aldrich tariff of 1909. The amendment required approval by three-fourths of the state legislatures. Southern states quickly endorsed it, but Republicans from New York and Connecticut objected to the "sectional character" of the income tax and complained that they would be "plundered" by income and corporate taxes.[20] However, the political debate about the income tax was now much less contentious than it had been in the 1890s. The fact that many states had adopted an income tax on their own helped pave the way for national ratification. The support of New York was key, and when Tammany Hall Democrats decided to endorse it, the income tax amendment was certain to succeed. The Sixteenth Amendment to the Constitution was certified in February 1913, just in time for the tariff deliberations.[21] The 1913 tariff act imposed a 1 percent federal tax on incomes of couples exceeding $4,000, as well as those of single persons earning $3,000 or more, in order to compensate for the lost revenue from the reduction of tariff rates. The income tax was proposed partly on grounds of national security, out of fear that the government needed a reliable source of revenue in times of war when imports were likely to be disrupted.

This monumental change in the tax system severed the already tenuous link between protective import duties and the revenue requirements of the government. The income tax ended the dependence of the federal government on import duties for a substantial fraction of its revenues. In fiscal year 1913, customs receipts accounted for 45 percent of federal revenue. In fiscal year 1916, this had fallen to 28 percent. After World War I, the share was less than 5 percent.[22] Because the nation's personal and corporate income constituted a significantly larger tax base than just imports, the federal government now had access to a potentially enormous source of revenue. This set the stage for large increases in government expenditures in the future.

WORLD WAR I AND THE REVENUE ACT OF 1916

Unfortunately, the economic impact of the Underwood-Simmons tariff, the most significant tariff reduction since the Civil War, will never be known. In the summer of 1914, less than a year after the new tariff took effect, World War I broke out in Europe, severely disrupting world trade. Because of the war, American exports surged to record levels, while imports dropped off, making it impossible to know how domestic industries would have fared under the lower duties in normal times.

The outbreak of the war initially triggered a short recession in the second half of 1914. As political tensions escalated that summer, the United States experienced a significant loss in gold reserves as Europeans investors sold their dollar securities to bring their assets back home.[23] Monetary conditions tightened until the end of the year, and the economy began to slump. Industrial production fell 12 percent from its July peak to its November trough, although it regained its previous level by June 1915.[24] The downturn clearly stemmed from the capital outflows as a consequence of the war, but Republicans blamed it on the reduced tariff rates because it occurred so soon after the 1913 tariff act. The weaker economy had electoral consequences as well: Democrats saw their House majority cut significantly in the 1914 midterm election.

As it did during the Napoleonic Wars a century earlier, the United States became a neutral carrier of goods to Europe early in the conflict. The volume of exports nearly doubled between 1914 and 1916, while those of finished manufactured goods nearly tripled. Overall imports remained unchanged, and imports of manufactured goods fell significantly. Consequently, America's merchandise trade surplus soared from $471 million in 1914 to more than $4 billion in 1919. The decline in imports gave rise to domestic production to replace the formerly imported goods, giving these industries "protection more effective than any tariff legislation" could provide, Taussig (1931, 448) suggested.

A more immediate policy concern was the decline in customs receipts, which fell by about a third during the five-year period of reduced imports. Meanwhile, federal expenditures soared from $742 million in 1916 to $18.9 billion in 1919 after the United States entered the war. There was no way import duties could have financed this massive increase in expenditures, and the president refused to borrow all the money needed to make up the difference. Faced with an enormous fiscal deficit, the Wilson administration proposed higher income taxes.

The Revenue Act of 1916 was primarily designed to address the shortfall in government revenue, although it also had important trade-policy provisions.[25] The legislation increased taxes on personal and corporate income, canceled the transfer of sugar to the free list, hiked import duties on chemicals and dyes to protect American producers from German dumping, and created an independent Tariff Commission. Political factors explain part of this adjustment of trade policy by the Wilson administration. In late 1915, with the next year's presidential election clearly in sight, Treasury Secretary William McAdoo reported to the president that Republicans were going to make the tariff an issue in the 1916 election. During an extensive tour of the Midwest, McAdoo found "a carefully cultivated sentiment, amounting to a genuine fear, on the part of manufacturers and many business men, that this country is in jeopardy from a possible invasion of its markets by manufacturers and merchants of Europe after peace is restored."[26]

Wilson's cabinet considered how to address the growing public fears about dumping after the war so that the low tariffs they had enacted could be preserved.[27] Commerce Secretary William Redfield supported legislation that would allow higher duties to be imposed on any imported products found to have been dumped in the US market. McAdoo opposed this idea as "an entering wedge for reopening the entire tariff subject."[28] As an alternative to antidumping legislation, McAdoo and Agriculture Secretary David Houston proposed creating an independent Tariff Commission. Progressives had long advocated using nonpartisan experts, insulated from political pressure, to "take the tariff out of politics" and improve the quality of information on trade policy that reached members of Congress.[29] Yet most Democrats were skeptical: they opposed the idea of a Tariff Board in 1909, fearing that it would be stacked with protectionists or given an objectionable mandate, such as setting tariffs to equalize the costs of production between domestic and foreign producers. Wilson also opposed the creation of such an agency for precisely these reasons. As late as mid-1915, the president vowed to "explode the nonsense" of Republicans who kept arguing for an independent commission.[30]

But now the administration was under pressure to counter Republican attacks on the issue. Houston contacted his former Harvard economics professor, Frank Taussig, to ask his advice about the wisdom of creating a Tariff Commission. In a memo laying out his views, Taussig argued that such a commission would not be able to forecast the impact of postwar trade flows on American industry, but could still provide useful and impartial information for policymakers. Congress, relying solely on public hearings and private lobbying for facts and analysis, had no independent source of information about the conditions of trade and domestic production, but a commission could play that role.[31]

Taussig's memo persuaded members of the cabinet about the merits of creating an independent, nonpartisan, fact-finding agency devoted to trade and tariff policy. McAdoo and Houston helped convince Wilson that such a body could provide useful information on trade conditions at home and abroad, particularly given the wartime disruptions to commerce, and would be a good political move, neutralizing Republican attacks and bolstering progressive support.[32] As he warmed to the idea, Wilson told fellow Democrats that Republicans "are desperately clinging to the one issue of the tariff, and nobody on either side of the house can prove anything about the tariff now. . . . Anyone who stands up and says that he can predict what is going to follow this war sufficiently to suggest what tariff policy should be is talking in ignorance."[33]

In January 1916, Wilson announced that he had changed his mind and now supported an independent commission to provide information on such matters as the impact of import duties on domestic industries, methods of handling unfair foreign competition or dumping, and other issues.[34] The reason Wilson gave was that "all the circumstances of the world have changed, and it seems to me that in view of the extraordinary and far-reaching changes which the European war has brought about, it is absolutely necessary that we should have a competent instrument of inquiry along the whole line of the many questions which affect our foreign commerce." Wilson reassured members of Congress that his change of mind on the commission reflected no "change in attitude toward the so-called protection question. That is neither here nor there." He simply believed that impartial information could be useful for government officials in shaping trade policy in the future. The political question of determining the level of import duties or other features of the country's trade policy was completely separate from the proposal; Congress was not asked to delegate any policymaking authority to the body, which would only have the authority to conduct fact-finding investigations and provide information to assist Congress.[35]

Despite Wilson's conversion, Democratic leaders in Congress opposed creating such an agency, fearing that it would be a threat to the low tariffs they had enacted and be captured by protectionist interests. But they could not deny the political case for such an entity so that Democrats could respond to Republican attacks. Other groups also weighed in: the American Protective Tariff League viewed a Tariff Commission as "dangerous and expensive," while the Chamber of Commerce, the American Federation of Labor, and the National Grange supported it. At the president's request, therefore, Congress included provision for a Tariff Commission in the Revenue Act of 1916.

The Tariff Commission was to be composed of six members, not more than three of whom could come from the same political party in order to preserve its nonpartisan standing. (The political representation requirement had no impact on the commission's view because there were many high-tariff Democrats that could be chosen by Republicans and many progressive, low-tariff Republicans who could be selected by Democrats.) Wilson appointed three Democrats and three progressive Republicans to twelve-year terms on the commission and made Frank Taussig its first chairman. The Tariff Commission began operation in April 1917 and started studying government finance during the war. During its first five years in operation, the Tariff Commission produced several industry studies and reports on such issues as the competitive position of Japan, free trade zones, antidumping policy, and customs administration. It made recommendations on mundane administrative details, such as improving the tariff classification schedule, but one of its early reports also led to the adoption of the unconditional most-favored-nation clause (to be discussed later).

The Revenue Act of 1916 also included a provision to prevent foreign "dumping" in the United States. The law made it illegal to dump goods "with the intent of destroying or injuring an industry in the United States." The remedy was not higher import duties, which McAdoo and Houston wanted to avoid, but rather fines (triple damages) and possible imprisonment for those found guilty; that is, the 1916 antidumping law was a criminal statute with criminal punishments. The law was rarely invoked, because proving that an exporter had a "predatory intent" with the goal of limiting or restraining competition was extremely difficult. Another controversial provision in the Revenue Act of 1916 was the imposition of new import duties on various chemicals—imported dyestuffs, medicines, and synthetics—to protect American producers from German competition after the war.

SLIDING BACK TO PROTECTION

The closely fought presidential election of 1916 hinged on America's role in World War I. Wilson narrowly defeated his Republican rival, marking the first time that a Democratic president had been reelected for consecutive terms since Andrew Jackson in 1832. The Democrats barely retained their control of Congress as well, making the party's hold on power fragile.

Although tariffs played a minor role in the campaign, the Republicans branded the Underwood-Simmons tariff "a complete failure in every respect" and called the 1916 antidumping provision an inadequate substitute for permanent protection. "The Republican party stands now, as always, in the fullest sense for the policy of tariff protection to American industries and American labor," the Republican platform stated. Meanwhile, the Democratic platform reaffirmed the party's belief "in the doctrine of a tariff for the purpose of providing sufficient revenue for the operation of the government economically administered, and unreservedly endorse the Underwood tariff law as truly exemplifying that doctrine."[36]

Having campaigned on a pledge to keep the country out of war, Wilson found himself asking Congress for a declaration of war in April 1917, just a month after his inauguration. This move came after Germany announced a campaign of unrestricted submarine warfare on all ships in a declared war zone. The German gamble was designed to break the battlefield stalemate, but it also threatened American exports.[37] This development, along with the Zimmerman telegram that hinted at a possible German alliance with Mexico, led the United States into the war. The nation quickly mobilized and tipped the military balance of power in favor of the Allies. America's formal participation in World War I was brief. In November 1918, the Allies and Germany signed an armistice that brought the conflict to an end.

Tariff policy was hardly discussed during the war, but the end of the conflict brought a whole new set of economic challenges. The entire world economy had been uprooted by the conflict, and international trade and finance remained disrupted for an extended period. The volume of world trade did not recover to its prewar level until 1924. British production had shifted away from export markets and toward wartime production; because it could not quickly readjust after the war, American manufacturers were able to continue their domination of world markets into the postwar period. Germany's economy was also damaged by the conflict; in addition to suffering a devastating hyperinflation in 1922–23, the country faced the prospect of paying large reparations for an extended period. The Communist revolution in Russia disrupted that country's exports of grain, to the benefit of American farmers seeking foreign sales. As a result, the United States emerged from the war in a much stronger economic position. The US share of world manufacturing production rose from 36 percent in 1913 to 42 percent in 1926/29, while that of every major European country fell.[38] The United States also emerged as a financial power and became a large creditor to the rest of the world.

In January 1918, President Wilson delivered his famous "Fourteen Points" address before a joint session of Congress. Wilson set out his vision of how the United States could help establish a new postwar world based on national self-determination and international cooperation, bringing secret diplomacy to an end and making World War I "the war to end all wars." The centerpiece of his proposal was the creation of a League of Nations that would guarantee political independence and territorial integrity, thereby preventing future military conflicts. Wilson's second and third points related to trade policy. The second called for absolute freedom of navigation on the seas. The third proposed "the removal, so far as possible, of all economic barriers and the establishment of an equality of trade conditions among all the nations consenting to the peace and associating themselves for its maintenance."[39] In effect, Wilson was calling for international cooperation to reduce trade barriers and ensure that non-discrimination was the basis for commercial relations around the world.

Along with the League of Nations, these ideas generated much consternation in Congress, even among some Democrats, as potentially compromising American sovereignty. Wilson clarified his remarks in an October 1918 letter to a senator. His third point, he explained, did not threaten national sovereignty, because every country remained free to impose whatever trade barriers it wanted. Rather, he was merely suggesting that, whatever tariffs or other measures that a country chose to impose, those policies should be applied in a non-discriminatory manner to establish "equality of trade conditions."[40] Not only did this make economic sense, Wilson argued, but it would reduce international commercial tensions that bred political frictions that could lead to war: "The experiences of the past among nations have taught us that the attempt by one nation to punish another by exclusive and discriminatory trade agreements has been a prolific breeder of that kind of antagonism which oftentimes results in war, and that if a permanent peace is to be established among nations, every obstacle that has stood in the way of international friendship should be cast aside." He denied that he wanted to interfere with the ability of a country to enact whatever level of tariff it wanted: "To pervert this great principle [of non-discrimination] for partisan purposes, and to inject the bogy of free-trade, which is not involved at all, is to attempt to divert the mind of the nation from the broad and humane principle of a durable peace by introducing an internal question of quite another kind."[41]

Thus, in Wilson's view, the United States had an opportunity to reassert its long-standing interest in having non-discrimination as a principle of world trade. Such a principle would not only serve the interests of American exporters, who faced barriers in foreign markets, especially the colonial markets of European powers, but would weaken the economic nationalism that led to international friction and contributed to World War I.

While determined to create the League of Nations, the president did not have a concrete plan for the postwar economic order. As he departed for the Paris Peace Conference in December 1918, Wilson told his negotiating team that he was "not much interested in the economic subjects" that might be raised, adding that "I do not think that international trade questions will be directly broached by the Peace Conference."[42]

Even if there had been big plans for postwar trade policies, domestic political developments would have put them in jeopardy. The Republicans gained control of Congress in the 1918 midterm elections, producing a two-year standoff between the president and Congress. Republicans were not only prepared to thwart any plans for League efforts to reduce trade barriers, which was viewed as a threat to Congress's authority over trade policy, but they were also anxious to enact higher tariffs if given the chance.

The partisan divide focused mainly on the League of Nations. The president engaged in an intensive public campaign in late 1919 to win support for the League. Republican skeptics ranged from those with mild reservations to hard-core isolationists who were irreconcilably opposed to participation in the League. Henry Cabot Lodge (R-MA), the chairman of the Senate Foreign Relations Committee, sought to include fourteen reservations to the charter, most notably rejecting any commitment to preserve the territorial integrity of other states, but also asserting Congress's authority over tariff policy. However, Wilson stubbornly refused to consider any changes to the charter or its application to the United States. In November 1919, when the Senate finally prepared to vote on the matter, Wilson demanded that Democrats reject all reservations to the treaty. This unwillingness to compromise ensured the League's defeat, and the Senate failed to ratify the Treaty of Versailles or join the League of Nations.

It is unlikely that American participation in the League would have made a significant difference to its trade policy. The United States was not alone in wanting to maintain its own tariff system and preserve its domestic policy autonomy. As a result, the League's Covenant made no mention of reducing barriers to trade. Article 23(e) of the League of Nations charter merely stated, "Subject to and in accordance with the provisions of international conventions existing or hereafter to be agreed upon, the Members of the League . . . will make provision to secure and maintain freedom of communications and of transit and equitable treatment for the commerce of all Members of the League." Thus, only equitable—and not even equal—treatment was called for, and this only with respect to members of the League. Indeed, while the Allies were allowed to discriminate against the trade of the defeated Central Powers, the Treaty of Versailles mandated that Germany give preferential access to goods from the Allied and Associated Powers. In effect, the Versailles conference deferred substantive discussion of sensitive economic questions to a later date.[43] The League sponsored the World Economic Conference of 1927, which discussed many aspects of international trade policy, but even then no concrete steps were taken.

The bitter fight between the Democratic president and the Republican Congress over the League carried over to tariff policy as well. Although protectionist pressures were dormant during the war, Republicans were clearly waiting for an opportunity to reverse the Underwood-Simmons tariff reduction in 1913.[44] During the war, the average tariff on dutiable imports dropped from 40 percent in 1913 to just 16 percent in 1920, its lowest level since 1792. This reduction was partly due to the 1913 tariff legislation but mostly due to wartime inflation, which reduced the ad valorem equivalent of the many specific duties in the tariff code. Republicans feared that this decline would leave the nation's industries exposed to foreign competition after the war and allow the country to become the dumping ground for the world. Democrats dismissed such fears, pointing to the large US trade surplus and the fact that American manufacturers were exporting large quantities of goods to other markets. As long as Europe was struggling to recover from the war, they observed, any fear that a flood of foreign goods would destroy domestic industries was an illusion. Indeed, although exports of manufactures fell off somewhat after the war, imports of manufactures were unchanged in 1919 but then jumped in 1920, albeit from artificially low levels. Furthermore, Democrats argued, the United States was now a creditor nation and should keep its market open to enable other countries to earn the dollars they needed to pay their debts.

Divided government left immediate postwar trade policy in limbo. With Wilson still in office, the Republican Congress did not bother to take up a tariff revision in 1919 or 1920, knowing that any bill they passed would be vetoed. In a message to a special session of Congress in May 1919, Wilson reminded Congress that "there is, fortunately, no occasion for undertaking in the immediate future any general revision of our system of import duties. No serious danger of foreign competition now threatens American industry. Our country has emerged from the war less disturbed and less weakened than any of the European countries which are our competitors in manufacture."[45]

Calling attention to the nation's large trade surplus and the need to export to foreign markets, Wilson reiterated his view that the tariff should be kept at existing low levels in his annual message to Congress in December 1919.

The prejudice and passions engendered by decades of controversy between two schools of political and economic thought, the one believers in protection of American industries, the other believers in tariff for revenue only, must be subordinated to the single consideration of the public interest in the light of utterly changed conditions. . . . The

productivity of the country, greatly stimulated by the war, must find
an outlet by exports to foreign countries, and any measures taken to
prevent imports will inevitably curtail exports, force curtailment of
production, load the banking machinery of the country with credits
to carry unsold products and produce industrial stagnation and unemployment. If we want to sell, we must be prepared to buy.

Wilson also rejected isolationism on political as well as economic grounds,
saying that the United States had a great opportunity to shape the world
economic system for the betterment of all: "No policy of isolation will
satisfy the growing needs and opportunities of America. The provincial
standards and policies of the past, which have held American business as
if in a strait-jacket, must yield and give way to the needs and exigencies
of the new day in which we live."[46] Republicans greeted these words with
skepticism.

The presidential election of 1920 would determine the fate of the
nation's postwar trade policy.[47] The Democratic platform reaffirmed
the party's traditional policy "in favor of a tariff for revenue only and
confirm[ed] the policy of basing tariff revisions upon the intelligent research of a non-partisan commission, rather than upon the demands of
selfish interests." The Republican platform reiterated the party's "belief
in the protective principles" and promised to revise the tariff "as soon as
conditions shall make it necessary for the preservation of the home market for American labor, agriculture and industry."[48] The election was not
much of a contest, as the Republicans, aided by a sharp recession, swept
back into office.

THE RETURN OF REPUBLICAN PROTECTIONISM

A severe economic downturn after the war boosted the Republican electoral fortunes and fueled demands for higher import duties. During the
war, the nation's new central bank, the Federal Reserve, which had been
created in 1913, banned the export of gold and agreed to purchase Treasury
securities to help finance the war. The consequent monetary expansion
resulted in a rise in domestic inflation, which reached nearly 20 percent
by 1918.[49] When the country went back on the gold standard and lifted the
embargo on gold exports in mid-1919, the United States experienced a large
loss of gold reserves, and the Federal Reserve responded by sharply tightening monetary policy in early 1920.

By mid-1920, prices, output, and employment were all plummeting.

The United States experienced one of the most intense deflations in its history: wholesale prices dropped 26 percent between June and December 1920; by June 1921, wholesale prices were 42 percent below where they had been a year earlier, and farm prices had fallen even more. Real output also declined sharply: farm production dropped 14 percent in 1921, and industrial production fell 26 percent in the year after June 1920. The unemployment rate jumped from 2 percent in 1919 to 11 percent in 1921.[50]

As in previous cases, the economic downturn was driven by monetary conditions, not factors related to trade. As the economy contracted, the volume of imports also fell sharply—by 16 percent in 1920. And there had been no postwar surge in imports: the volume of imports increased just 28 percent in the two years after 1918, as European economies struggled to recover from the war.

These painful economic conditions helped produce a landslide victory for the Republicans in the 1920 election, returning the party to the political dominance it had enjoyed prior to 1912. Warren Harding was elected president with just over 60 percent of the popular vote, and the Republicans gained huge majorities in the House and Senate. The outgoing Republican Congress immediately began considering new tariff legislation to address the postwar recession and alleviate the economic distress of farmers in particular. The underlying problems facing agriculture included the overexpansion of production and the rise in indebtedness due to the war, the severe deflationary monetary shock, and the decline in agricultural exports after the war. But all of this was beyond Congress's immediate control. Having no policies other than import duties at their disposal, Congress sought higher tariffs on agricultural imports as a way of protecting farmers from declining prices.

Shortly after the election, Joseph Fordney (R-MI), the chairman of the Ways and Means Committee, introduced emergency tariff legislation that would increase duties for a period of ten months on selected agricultural commodities, including wheat, corn, beans, potatoes, onions, peanuts, rice, lemons, peanut and cottonseed oil, cattle and sheep, and cotton and raw wool. The committee's report noted that "prevailing prices in many instances are far below the farmers' production costs. . . . Conditions are steadily growing worse, and unless remedial legislation is enacted at an early date, the inevitable result will be the abandonment of many farms and the slaughtering of the livestock thereon and irreparable injury to the agricultural resources of the country."[51]

The bill was rushed through the Ways and Means Committee over the objections of some Democrats who thought that its hastily prepared prohibitory rates would not help agriculture and would only trigger foreign retaliation against the country's farm exports. Because many Democrats represented agricultural states that were suffering, however, it was difficult for them to oppose a measure ostensibly designed to help their constituents. In December 1920, after devoting virtually no time for hearings or debate on the matter, the House passed the bill by a vote of 194–85; 92 percent of Republican supported the bill, while just 63 percent of Democrats opposed it. The Senate quickly followed.

The outgoing Republican Congress had passed the legislation so quickly that it landed on Woodrow Wilson's desk before he left office. On his last full day as president, Wilson vetoed the bill and excoriated the Republicans for passing it. In a blistering veto message, Wilson faulted the legislation for pretending to help farmers because the United States was a large exporter of many of the commodities on the list, except for sugar and wool. For example, while imports of wheat jumped from 5 million bushels in 1920 to 57 million bushels in 1921, exports of wheat also increased from 220 million bushels to 366 million in 1921. Because the country was a large exporter of such commodities, the prices that farmers received were those prevailing on the world market; import tariffs could not increase domestic prices to any significant degree. "Very little reflection would lead anyone to conclude that the measure would not furnish in any substantial degree the relief sought by the producers of most of the staple commodities which it covers," the president argued, because the decline in commodity prices was a worldwide phenomenon. The problem facing farmers was deflation, not rising imports, and reducing imports was no cure for falling prices. Wilson also warned Congress against imposing higher tariffs on manufactured goods: "If there ever was a time when America had anything to fear from foreign competition, that time has passed. I cannot believe that American producers, who in most respects are the most effective in the world, can have any dread of competition when they view the fact that their country has come through the great struggle of the last few years, relatively speaking, untouched, while their principal competitors are in varying degrees sadly stricken and laboring under adverse conditions from which they will not recover for many years." He concluded his veto message by saying that there was no justification for "a policy of legislation for selfish interests which will foster monopoly and increase the disposition to look upon the Government as an instrument for private gain instead of an instrument for the promotion of the general well-being."[52]

Although House Republicans failed to override the president's veto, they quickly prepared new legislation for the incoming Republican president, Warren Harding. Harding subscribed to the party's traditional views on the tariff, but he admitted to being "very much at sea" in trying to understand matters of trade policy.[53] In his inaugural address, Harding rejected the Democratic position: "It has been proved again and again that we cannot, while throwing our markets open to the world, maintain American standards of living and opportunity, and hold our industrial eminence in such unequal competition. There is a luring fallacy in the theory of banished barriers of trade, but preserved American standards require our higher production costs to be reflected in our tariffs on imports."[54]

Addressing Congress a month later, Harding called on legislators to enact higher import duties: "The urgency of an instant tariff enactment, emergency in character, . . . cannot be too much emphasized. I believe in the protection of American industry, and it is our purpose to prosper America first. . . . One who values American prosperity and maintained American standards of wage and living can have no sympathy with the proposal that easy entry and the flood of imports will cheapen our cost of living. It is more likely to destroy our capacity to buy."[55]

The Republican Congress responded by passing the Emergency Tariff of 1921, which was essentially the same bill that Wilson had just vetoed. The legislation covered just a few agricultural commodities and was set to last just six months (later extended) until a more comprehensive tariff revision could be formulated. In May 1921, Harding signed the measure. The goal of the Emergency Tariff was to increase domestic farm prices by reducing imports of agricultural goods, but the legislation came too late: farm prices had stopped falling five months prior to the bill taking effect. In fact, a subsequent Tariff Commission study found that prices had stabilized for all agricultural products regardless of whether they were affected by the higher duties or not.[56]

Of course, Republicans were also anxious to replace the 1913 Underwood-Simmons duties with higher rates of protection for all industries facing foreign competition. Although there was no postwar surge in imports, and in fact the volume of imports fell sharply due to the recession during this period, the economic slump provided the Republicans with another rationale for increasing import duties. Nationalist sentiment also strengthened support for isolationist policies after the war. These factors not only reinforced the traditional Republican support for protectionism, but antiforeign sentiment brought to an end to what had been a relatively open immigration policy when quotas were imposed on the number of immigrants from abroad.[57]

In January 1921, with domestic objectives firmly in mind, the Ways and Means Committee began hearings to revise the entire tariff code. This began a twenty-month Congressional journey to determine the postwar tariff schedule. As small- and medium-sized businesses lined up with complaints about foreign competition and requests for higher tariffs, Joseph Fordney (R-MI), chairman of the committee, stated that it was their duty to "give the boys what they wanted."[58]

Reporting a bill in July 1921, the Republican majority on the Ways and Means Committee called the existing tariff "wholly inadequate" and said, "This industrial depression is the inevitable result of the offering of foreign goods upon the American market at less than the American cost of production."[59] Many raw materials that had been put on the free list in 1913, such as hides and wool, were put back on the dutiable list, and specific duties replaced ad valorem duties. Although the 1909 tariff was the basis for the revision, tariffs on industrial products, such as chemicals, cutlery, clocks and toys, minerals, and agricultural goods, were increased from the 1909 level, while the iron and steel schedule was hardly touched, because the industry was not threatened by imports. Finally, the bill included a controversial American valuation provision. This provision required that the tariff on certain imported goods be based on the US price of the good, not the foreign export price. This would raise the valuation of the imported good and hence increase the applied tariff as well. This provision was adopted to address fears of the under-invoicing of merchandise by foreign suppliers or importers.

The Democratic minority called the bill a "monstrosity," the product of corrupt dealings that was "in keeping with the intrigue, secrecy, and jobbery which inspired its covert subtleties, its concealed indirections; framed its newly invented schedules, cast its complex and compounded rates, and fixed its unascertainable and incalculable duties, with the trickery which has transformed schedules, hidden jokers, transplanted items, changed nomenclature, and made it impossible to compare it with any of its predecessors." Democrats attacked the goal of trying to "equalize cost of production" between domestic and foreign producers, a "crude, brutal system that will impose the same duty upon a country of high-cost production as it will upon a country of low-cost production; that we are to impose the same duty upon the intelligent, high-cost production of Canada that we are to impose upon the coolie labor of India, China, and Japan."[60] Finally, they rejected the need for the revision based on the unwarranted fear of an import surge. They pointed out that the war had been over for nearly two and a half years and no import surge had ever materialized.

The House debate was unexceptional, with both sides repeating familiar arguments. For the Republican majority, Fordney argued that the bill would protect farmers from imports, create more jobs for workers, and safeguard industry against the revival of European competitors. "To those who believe in flooding our markets with cheap foreign goods, closing our mills, throwing our labor out of employment and mortgaging our farms, while the foreign mills run overtime, the foreign farms thrive, and labor prospers, this act is, as proclaimed by them, 'infamous' and 'outrageous,' but to those who believe in American prosperity, in American institutions and American labor, this act is salvation," Fordney declared. Without protection, he contended, domestic wages would fall: "Free trade here could have but one result, and that is that it would bring our laboring people to the low standard of life and living endured by the low-paid labor of foreign countries.[61]

Meanwhile, Democrats attacked the bill as a tax on every working family and ridiculed the notion that higher tariffs would relieve farmers from low agricultural prices. Higher agriculture duties "represent an attempt to fool the farmers and swindle the stockmen into the belief that they will get enough benefit out of this bill to fully compensate them for the higher prices that they must pay for all the manufactured goods upon which high protective or even prohibitive duties are levied in this measure," as Carl Hayden (D-AZ) put it. "Time will soon disclose the utter futility of attempting by a tariff to boost the price of wheat or corn or short-staple cotton and the numerous other farm and range products where importations are negligible and the surplus must be sold abroad."[62] Given the large Republican majority, the bill's passage was a foregone conclusion. In July 1921, the House passed the bill by a partisan vote of 289–127; Republicans voted 283–6 in favor, while Democrats voted 119–5 against.

The Senate Finance Committee began hearings immediately after the House action. Once again, public testimony was dominated by representatives from small- and medium-sized firms that demanded greater protection. With manufactured exports propelled to new high levels during and after the war, however, many representatives of big businesses actually testified in favor of lower rates. As David Walsh (D-MA) noted, the hearings revealed "for the first time in American history [that] the representatives of great big business are here asking for the lowering of rates and the representatives of small business . . . are asking for excessively high rates."[63] The large producers feared foreign countries would impose retaliatory tariffs against their exports, while bankers and financiers pointed out that the United States was now a creditor nation and should therefore keep its market open to allow European countries to repay their dollar-denominated debts.

However, pressing tax legislation and the death of the Finance Committee's chairman delayed consideration of the bill for more than a year. This, in itself, is remarkable: that tariff legislation was set aside to give priority to other matters indicated that it was no longer as important a policy matter as it once had been. Tariff legislation lacked the urgency of the past and had fallen in the hierarchy of congressional priorities. Congress now had other domestic policies, such as the income tax and federal regulations, that had a much greater impact on the economy than changes in import duties. The Senate held hearings on the bill in July–August 1921; the legislation was then set aside, and hearings resumed from November 1921–January 1922. In his December 1921 annual message to Congress, President Harding urged Congress to act more quickly: "I cannot too strongly urge in early completion of this necessary legislation." While acknowledging that there was always "a storm of conflicting opinion about any tariff revision," the president believed that "We cannot go far wrong when we base our tariffs on the policy of preserving the productive activities which enhance employment and add to our national prosperity."[64]

During the Senate delay, the proposed tariff bill provoked heated public debate at home and abroad. The most controversial changes were the American valuation provision and the embargo on imported dye, which was supported by the chemical industry but opposed by the textile industry. When the Finance Committee finally reported the bill in April 1922, it had made 2,436 amendments to the House version. Although it raised many of the rates in the House bill, the Senate dropped the American valuation provision and imposed a one-year embargo on imported dyes instead of the five years requested by the chemical industry. Opening the Senate debate, the Finance Committee chair, Porter McCumber (R-ND), declared, "Of all times in the history of the country, this is the time in which a protective tariff is most needed to sustain our American industries and our millions of people dependent upon them." The underlying issue was "protecting the American standard of wages and the American standard of living through the protection of our American markets."[65]

In contrast to the strict party discipline in the House, the sectional fight in the Senate was more intense. Once again, the divide between raw material and agricultural producers in the West and Midwest and the industrial interests in the East was exposed. The Senate debate became a free-for-all as representatives from the West denounced high duties on cotton, woolen, and silk manufactures but supported higher duties on manganese, tungsten ores, and other metals. They insisted that barbed wire be put on the free list, but proposed higher duties on high-grade manganese ore, against the objections of iron and steel producers. While Western ranching interests wanted high duties on cattle and hides, shoe manufacturers from Massachusetts wanted to keep hides on the duty-free list to hold down the cost of leather shoes.[66]

The endless conflicts led to dozens of floor votes on amendments, which further delayed the bill's passage. The Senate debated and voted on rate changes for innumerable obscure products: crude magnesite, burned and grain magnesite, caustic calcined magnesite, shelled almonds, unshelled almonds, shelled walnuts, unshelled walnuts, pork, lamb, wheat, cream, paddy rice, milled rice, cotton yarn, cotton waste, cotton cloth, cotton quilts, cotton underwear, and dozens of other products. By May 1922, the Senate was seriously bogged down and began marathon sessions, starting at 11:00 a.m. and ending at 10:30 p.m., to expedite matters. Even longer hours failed to speed the bill's progress, as individual Senators had a stake in specific lines of the tariff schedule, forcing consideration of nearly every item on the dutiable list.[67]

Democrats denounced the "excessive rates" in the Republican bill, but did not strongly defend the tariff they had passed almost a decade earlier. The Democrats no longer had an effective slogan to represent their position on tariffs. With the income tax in place, calls for "a tariff for revenue only" were obsolete. The partisan debate had shifted from "protective" versus "revenue" tariffs to "high" versus "moderate" tariffs—"with a not-too-great emphasis upon the word *moderate*," Berglund (1923, 28) adds. The difference in position was a matter of degree, not principle, as the Wilsonian reformers were no longer in command of the Democratic party.

Even the commitment of the South to low tariffs was weakening. The South was not uniformly against all protective tariffs because of various local interests, such as sugar in Louisiana, graphite in Alabama, and ferroalloys in Tennessee. In fact, as the Southern economy began diversifying and attracting unskilled, labor-intensive industries from the North, notably textiles and apparel in the Carolinas, more constituents in the region began to see the merits of high tariffs against foreign competition. While representatives from the South voted against the bill on the final roll call, in terms of the roll-call votes on particular commodities, they were no longer as implacably opposed to higher tariffs as they had been in the past.[68]

After four months of laborious floor debate, the Senate passed the bill

in August 1922 by a partisan vote of 48–25; Republicans voted 45–1 in favor, Democrats voted 24–3 against. Another month was taken in conference to reconcile the differences between the House and Senate versions.
The conferees accepted the higher agricultural duties introduced in the
Senate, weakened the American valuation proposal (now enforced at the
discretion of the president), and dropped the dye embargo. In late September, President Harding signed the Fordney-McCumber tariff of 1922.

The 130-page bill had taken twenty months to work its way through
Congress. The Fordney-McCumber tariff helped increase the average levy
on dutiable imports sharply, from 16.4 percent in 1920 to 36.2 percent in
1922. However, because of the impact of falling prices on the specific duties, only about half of this increase was actually due to the higher rates in
the legislation. The tariff revision came much too late to take any credit
for the brisk economic recovery: the recession ended in July 1921, but the
new tariff law was not enacted until September 1922, fourteen months after the economic trough.

FLEXIBLE TARIFFS, ANTIDUMPING,
AND UNCONDITIONAL MFN

The Fordney-McCumber tariff marked a return to the traditional Republican policy of protection, but it also contained three important administrative innovations: a new flexible tariff provision, a new antidumping
procedure, and the unconditional most-favored-nation (MFN) clause. The
flexible tariff provision gave the president the authority to adjust a tariff
rate on a particular good by as much as 50 percent (up or down) if the Tariff
Commission concluded that such an adjustment was necessary to equalize the costs of production between domestic and foreign producers. The
driving force behind this unprecedented grant of authority was William
Culbertson, an entrepreneurial, moderate Republican on the Tariff Commission. In October 1921, while the tariff bill lay dormant in the Senate
Finance Committee, Culbertson wrote a memorandum to President Harding proposing the idea.[69] The inability of Congress to adjust tariff rates
in a timely way in light of rapidly changing circumstances had generated
growing concern in the business community and among policymakers.
After the war, prices had been volatile, and the pattern of trade was highly
uncertain, leaving many to fear that tariffs might be inappropriately set
across a range of goods. Culbertson argued that this problem could be addressed if Congress allowed the president, with the guidance of experts at
the Tariff Commission, to adjust import duties as economic conditions

demanded. He also wanted the flexible tariff authority to be used to moderate the excessive duties in the tariff schedule that arose because of political deal-making in Congress.[70]

Culbertson persuaded the president about the merits of this idea. In his annual message to Congress in 1921, Harding expressed the hope that "a way will be found to make for flexibility and elasticity [in the tariff], so that rates may be adjusted to meet unusual and changing conditions which cannot be accurately anticipated" and proposed that the Tariff Commission be involved in this process.[71] Culbertson worked closely with Secretary of State Charles Evans Hughes and Reed Smoot (R-UT) of the Senate Finance Committee to draft an acceptable provision.[72] Section 315 of the Fordney-McCumber tariff act gave the president the authority to investigate differences in the cost of production and adjust tariffs to ensure that those costs were equalized. In signing the legislation, Harding stated that "if we succeed in making effective the elastic provisions of the measure, it will make the greatest contribution to tariff-making in the nation's history."[73] Although the constitutionality of this provision was quickly challenged, the Supreme Court upheld the delegation of tariff-setting authority to the president in 1928.[74]

A controversial aspect of the flexible tariff provision was using the tariff to equalize the costs of production between domestic and foreign producers. Advocates argued that this was an objective and measurable standard for setting tariffs in a scientific and nonpolitical way. They believed that this approach would provide adequate protection for domestic industries yet also "take the tariff out of politics." Of course, this doctrine had many problems, including the fact that international differences in the costs of production were the very basis for international trade. Setting that point aside, every tariff rate in the 1922 act would, in principle, have to be adjusted after a Tariff Commission investigation, since none of them had been formulated on that basis. But could government officials really calculate the "cost of production"? Culbertson (1923, 262) was confident of the Tariff Commission's ability to use modern accounting techniques to determine such costs and believed that any criticism of the doctrine "results either from ignorance or from a design to defeat scientific tariff methods."

But most experts, including Frank Taussig, the former chairman of the Tariff Commission, argued that it was impossible to determine an industry's costs of production, because different firms had different costs. Whose costs of production should be measured, Taussig asked, those of large producers or small producers? Which costs should be measured, marginal costs or average costs? Should transportation costs be included or excluded? Should one think of the cost of producing coffee in Maine or in California? Should one calculate the cost of producing a small number of automobiles or a large number when there are economies of scale? How should capital costs be allocated in multiproduct firms? What about seasonal variation in costs? What about joint costs, such as cotton and cottonseed oil, where the latter is a by-product of the former? If government officials asked firms about their costs to determine the tariff, would this not give the firms an incentive to inflate their figures in the hope of obtaining a higher tariff? If average costs across all firms in an industry were used, then the tariff would not protect the least-efficient, highest-cost producers, while it would pad the profits of the lowest-cost, most efficient producers—was this an equitable outcome? And what about foreign costs: would they not be different for goods coming from Germany as opposed to Japan? Since different countries had different costs, let alone different firms, would each country require its own product-specific tariff in order to "equalize costs" of production?

Taussig and other economists concluded that the whole exercise of arriving at a single number that represented "the cost of production" was meaningless, that it would be impossible for government officials to undertake the task without bias and prejudice, and that the results would inevitably be arbitrary and lack any "scientific" basis.[75] Because of these complications, Taussig (1920, 134–35) spoke for most economists in rejecting the cost-of-production approach as one that gave the "appearance of fairness" but was ultimately "worthless" as a solution to the problem of setting tariffs in a political environment. And this conclusion was reached without raising a more fundamental objection that international differences in the cost of production were the basis for trade in the first place.

Regardless of these conceptual difficulties, Congress recognized that the executive branch could react more quickly to changing economic circumstances than the legislative branch could through legislation, and therefore it adopted the provision. There was also the general expectation that it would be used to reduce rates. As Smoot stated, "If the President is given this power, I think there will be many, many more occasions when he will exercise it in lowering rates than in increasing them; in fact, if the conditions become normal, I expect the President of the United States to lower . . . the majority of rates."[76]

In practice, the flexible tariff provision had very little effect on import duties, partly because each proposed change required a time-consuming investigation by the Tariff Commission. During the period 1922–1929,

more than 600 applications for rate changes on 375 commodities were received by the commission, and yet it was only able to complete 47 investigations on 55 commodities.[77] Furthermore, the provision was used to raise
rates more than reduce them. From 1922–29, the Tariff Commission issued 41 reports recommending changes in duties, and the president made
37 proclamations adjusting duties. In 32 cases, duties were increased—
often by the full 50 percent—on 16 types of chemicals, wheat flour, butter,
straw hats, print rollers, and pig iron, as well as on narrowly defined goods
such as taximeters, men's sewed straw hats, sodium nitrate, precipitated
barium carbonate, and onions. The 5 reductions were on minor and obscure products: mill feed, bobwhite quail, paintbrush handles, phenol, and
cresylic acid.[78]

The use of section 315 was also overshadowed by a political storm concerning the independence of the Tariff Commission in these deliberations.
Critics charged that the Harding and Coolidge appointees were biased and
undermined the goal of having an independent, nonpartisan expert body.
For example, Harding's first three appointees to the Tariff Commission
were the editor of a protectionist magazine and secretary of the Home
Market Club of Boston (Thomas O. Marvin), a lobbyist for the pottery industry (William Burgess), and a high-tariff Democrat with ties to Louisiana sugar interests (Henry H. Glassie).

Even worse, open warfare broke out at the Tariff Commission about
a sugar report in 1924.[79] The controversy centered on one of the commissioners, Henry Glassie, whose wife held major sugar investments. The
Wilson-appointed commissioners challenged Glassie's right to participate
in the sugar investigation. Glassie refused to recuse himself from the case
on the grounds that it was a fact-finding investigation, not a judicial one.
Although President Calvin Coolidge supported Glassie, Congress passed
a law denying salary to any member of the commission taking part in
an investigation in which family members had a financial interest. With
Glassie disqualified, the Wilson appointees outnumbered the Harding appointees by three to two. Fearful that the sugar report would recommend
lower duties, the White House tried to influence the commission's vote by
putting pressure on some of the Wilson appointees. One Wilson appointee
was denied reappointment, while Culbertson was offered a position at the
Federal Trade Commission, which he turned down. Coolidge asked Culbertson to delay the sugar report; after he demurred, Culbertson found
himself accused of malfeasance for having accepted compensation for lec-
turing at Georgetown University.

When the report was finally issued in August 1924, the Tariff Commission was indeed split. The three Wilson appointees recommended reducing the sugar tariff from 1.76 cents per pound to 1.23 cents, while the two Harding appointees opposed this recommendation. Coolidge delayed making a decision for many months, during which time further pressure was put on the Wilson appointees to change their vote. Finally, in June 1925, nearly a year after the report had been released, the president decided not to adjust the sugar tariff, citing the divergent conclusions from the commission. Edward Costigan, one of the original commissioners appointed by Wilson, was outraged: "Thus, a major report of the commission was ignored and a commission investigation of the first order, which had engaged the services of an expert staff for nearly two years and cost the Government many thousands of dollars, was thrown overboard, following an unprecedented series of lobbying drives and political maneuvers, in some of which the White House actively shared."[80] Costigan resigned in protest and publicly declared the Republican appointees unfit for service, while Culbertson quit to take a diplomatic position in Romania.[81]

With the Tariff Commission's reputation for impartiality tarnished, Democrats and progressive Republicans created a select congressional committee in March 1926 to investigate the matter. Culbertson testified that "to stay on the Tariff Commission was worse than futile: it was to continue to lend my name as a sanction to a situation which for me had become intolerable." The Select Committee's report was divided as well, with three of five Senators (two Democrats, one insurgent Republican) recommending that the flexible tariff provision be repealed. The majority reported that the provision took up a huge amount of the commission's time "with no substantial result of general importance to the public." They found "controversies of such acute character arose in the commission that certain of its members became suspicious of the good faith of others, and bitter disputes, sometimes personal occurred, resulting about the time this select committee was created in a partial breakdown and a threatened complete breakdown of the Tariff Commission." They concluded that "the commission as a body was not functioning in an impartial or quasi-judicial manner, as we believe it was the intention of Congress that it should function."[82]

Progressives were sorely disappointed that the flexible tariff provision had failed to "take the tariff out of politics" and had been used to increase duties more than to reduce them. The insurgent George Norris (R-NE) wanted to abolish the commission because it had "fallen into hands of reactionaries and no longer served the purposes for which [it was] created."[83] Even David Houston, who as agriculture secretary helped convince President Wilson to create a commission, expressed disappointment with its performance. Recalling Wilson's reluctance to embrace the idea, Houston (1926, 187) admitted, "I am now inclined to think that his first view was right and that I was wrong. The conception was a good one, and the law was well conceived; but it has been pretty well demonstrated that the Commission cannot get the facts to the public for its education and that Congress will pay little attention to its economic findings." Houston concluded that the flexible tariff provision had been a "mistake" because it "radically changed [the Tariff Commission's] status from a fact-finding body to a piece of political machinery." He viewed the flexible provision as "a futile conception" because Republican administrations would simply adjust tariffs upward and Democratic administrations would adjust them downward.

Republicans also became suspicious of the flexible tariff provision because it posed a threat to Congress's authority. They even began to lose faith in the idea that the costs of production could be measured and provide a scientific basis for setting tariffs. "The theory that tariff rates should be determined by the difference in domestic and foreign costs of production has proved well-nigh impractical, since it is difficult in many instances to ascertain foreign costs of production," Smoot admitted. "Practically the only thing an American manufacturer is interested in is the actual competition he is compelled to meet in the American market."[84]

The second new feature of the tariff law allowed import duties to be adjusted to prevent foreign dumping in the US market. As we have seen, the Antidumping Act of 1916 made it illegal to sell imported goods at prices substantially lower than the market value in the exporting country "with the intent of destroying or injuring an industry in the United States," but proving predatory intent on the part of foreign exporters was almost impossible. In addition, the statute was enforced through the court system, which meant lengthy delays, and the remedy included fines and possible imprisonment, as did the antitrust laws. All of these factors left the statute unused.

The Antidumping Act of 1921, part of the Emergency Tariff Act of that year, changed matters considerably. This new antidumping law allowed the Treasury secretary to impose duties on imports if an investigation determined that imports "at less than [their] fair value" were injuring or were likely to injure a domestic industry.[85] The "fair value" was considered to be the price charged by an exporter in its home market. Thus, a foreign exporter charging a lower price on its sales in the United States than in its own home market could be found guilty of dumping. The Treasury Department was to administer the law and could impose import duties equal in magnitude to the dumping margin as the remedy. Antidumping duties did not become an important part of US trade policy until the 1970s and 1980s, as is discussed in later chapters. From 1921 to 1934, there were just fifty-four findings of dumping—about four per year. From 1934 to 1954, there were only seven findings of dumping.[86] Despite its infrequent use, the antidumping law was another step in the delegation by Congress of some tariff-setting authority to the executive branch. Congress simply could not afford the time to overhaul all the hundreds of rates in the tariff schedule every few years, nor could it update individual tariffs on a regular basis.

The third new aspect of trade policy in the early 1920s was the adoption of the unconditional most-favored-nation (MFN) clause in commercial agreements. As with the flexible tariff provision, William Culbertson was the driving force behind this policy shift. Although barely noticed at the time, the adoption of the unconditional MFN clause ultimately had far-reaching consequences for US trade policy by making it possible for the United States to participate more easily in international agreements to reduce trade barriers.

The background to this change was the spread of discriminatory trade policies by European countries in the decades prior to World War I. France, Germany, and other countries had adopted maximum-minimum tariff schedules, and the United States was often ineligible for the lower tariff rates if it lacked any trade agreement with those countries. The United States also faced widespread discrimination against its trade as a result of colonial trade networks. Furthermore, the United States found itself getting embroiled in an increasing number of tariff disputes and conflicts over the treatment of its goods in foreign markets, although the stake in each case was usually small. As a country with inflexible tariff rates determined by Congress, the United States found itself at a disadvantage in global trade, because the executive branch could not effectively negotiate with other countries to secure equal treatment in foreign markets.

In 1919, in a report entitled *Reciprocity and Commercial Treaties*, the Tariff Commission addressed this growing problem. Completed under the guidance of Frank Taussig, then the commission's chairman, the report proved to be one of the most influential government documents on trade since Alexander Hamilton's *Report on Manufactures*. The report noted that, to the extent that the United States sought to eliminate discrimination by other countries through bilateral negotiations, it was handicapped by its long-standing use of the conditional interpretation of the MFN clause, a policy that dated back to the Treaty of Amity and Commerce with France in 1778. Under conditional MFN, a concession granted to one country would not be given automatically to other countries unless they also granted new concessions. If taken seriously, this meant that if the United States agreed to reduce its tariff on some goods to secure equal treatment for its exports in another country, those tariff reductions would not be extended to other countries unless they also granted some new concessions. This would create a new disadvantage for other countries, many of whom might already be treating American goods quite favorably. If those countries were harmed by the new disadvantages they faced, they might even retaliate against the United States. Thus, an active trade policy based on conditional MFN could produce a tariff schedule that was riddled with discriminatory provisions and exceptions across many countries. At the very least, conditional MFN deeply complicated the process of international bargaining to achieve equal market access.[87]

The Tariff Commission argued that the old conditional MFN policy no longer served the nation's interests. The United States could not realistically have a country-by-country trade policy because, as the commission's report stated, "The separate and individual treatment of each case tends to create misunderstandings and friction with countries which, though supposed to be not concerned, yet are in reality much concerned." Therefore, the commission concluded,

> A great gain would be secured, now that the United States is committed to wide participation in world politics, if a clear and simple policy could be adopted and followed. The guiding principle might well be that of equality of treatment—a principle in accord with American ideas of the past and of the present. Equality of treatment should mean that the United States treat all countries on the same terms, and in turn require equal treatment from every other country. So far as concerns general industrial policy and general tariff legislation, each country—the United States as well as others—should be left free to enact such measures as it deems expedient for its own welfare. But the measures adopted, whatever they be, should be carried out with the same terms and the same treatment for all nations. (US Tariff Commission 1919, 10)

Of course, if it offered equal treatment to all countries unconditionally, the United States might lose bargaining leverage against other countries. Such leverage could be restored either by giving special concessions to countries that gave equal treatment to American goods or by imposing penalty duties on countries that did not. The commission argued that penalty duties imposed at the discretion of the president—"not for the purpose of securing discrimination in its favor, but to prevent discrimination to its disadvantage"—was the better option. Although the commission did not make a specific policy recommendation, it strongly implied that unconditional MFN with penalty duties for countries discriminating against the United States would be the best approach.

President Wilson drew attention to the commission's report in a message to Congress in May 1919.[88] Congress did not act upon the matter until considering the tariff revision in early 1921. At the same time that he was encouraging senators to adopt the flexible tariff provision, Culbertson was also working to convince them about the merits of unconditional MFN with penalty duties. As a result, section 317 of the Fordney-McCumber tariff allowed the president to proclaim new or additional duties, not exceeding 50 percent, upon imports of any or all products of a country found to impose "any unreasonable charge . . . which is not equally enforced upon the like articles of every foreign country" or to discriminate "in such a manner as to place the commerce of the United States at a disadvantage compared with the commerce of any foreign country." As Senator Smoot argued,

> We would base the commercial policy of the United States upon the twin ideas of granting equal treatment to all nations in the market of the United States, and of exacting equal treatment for the commerce of the United States in foreign markets. We do not believe that the United States should pursue a general policy of special bargains and special reciprocity treaties. . . . We stand for a simple, straightforward, friendly policy of equal treatment for all, with no discriminations against any country except as that country has first discriminated against us.[89]

This provision sparked virtually no debate in Congress, which was preoccupied with setting the many duties in the tariff schedule. The phrasing of section 317 appeared to endorse unconditional MFN, although it did not explicitly mandate it.

Just days after President Harding signed the Fordney-McCumber tariff in September 1922, Culbertson wrote to Secretary of State Charles Evans Hughes, drawing his attention to section 317 and its implicit endorsement of unconditional MFN. Hughes acknowledged the significance of section 317—"the importance of this policy can hardly be overestimated"—and suggested that Culbertson write up a memorandum explaining his view. That memo made a powerful case for equality of treatment and unconditional MFN.[90] The conditional approach "affords us no security against discriminations in foreign countries, and in this period of reconstruction, when many countries are revising their treaties and reconsidering their grants of most-favored-nation treatment, the conditional most-favored-nation principle is liable to be applied against us." Culbertson concluded with the following recommendation: "Now that Congress has taken a definite stand for the policy of equality of treatment, it would seem to follow logically that in the revision of our commercial treaties we should adopt the unconditional form of the most-favored-nation clause."[91]

Hughes sent the memorandum to Henry Cabot Lodge (R-MA), the chairman of the Senate Foreign Relations Committee. Lodge found it "very convincing and very well put, and I think that Mr. Culbertson makes a very strong case."[92] Having received Lodge's tacit approval, Hughes then forwarded the Culbertson and Lodge correspondence to the president and expressed the view that "there is an opinion among many that for the future the United States should adopt the unconditional form of most-favored-nation clause in its treaties of commerce and navigation." In February 1923, President Harding wrote to Hughes, "I have gone over your letter and the argument of Mr. Culbertson with some considerable deliberation, and I am pretty well persuaded that the negotiation of the unconditional provision is the wise course to pursue." Harding gave permission to proceed with the negotiation of unconditional MFN agreements with other countries.[93] With that, the United States adopted the unconditional MFN clause.[94]

The new unconditional MFN policy was unveiled in a new commercial treaty with Germany in 1924. The treaty did not alter any import duties, but required that each country extend unconditional MFN benefits to each other in the application of its tariff and other commercial benefits. Thus, there was no change in the US tariff schedule, but the United States obtained assurances that it would continue to receive equal treatment in Germany's market even if Germany reached new trade agreements with other countries.

The decision to adopt unconditional MFN went relatively unnoticed at the time. The implications were not fully appreciated by contemporary observers, because no immediate policy changes were evident.[95] But if the United States ever decided to undertake tariff negotiations with other countries, something that was not foreseen at the time, unconditional MFN would greatly facilitate the conclusion of such agreements. In particular, it would minimize the difficulties for third parties, preventing them from having grounds for retaliating against the United States.

THE TARIFF AND AGRICULTURE IN THE 1920S

Once the economy emerged from the short but severe recession in 1920–21, Republicans enjoyed the electoral benefits of a strong economy during the 1920s. With progressives in disarray and Democrats weak and divided, Republicans secured easy victories in the presidential elections of 1924 and 1928 and retained uninterrupted control of Congress. This ensured the Fordney-McCumber duties against the threat of any downward revision. In his 1923 annual message to Congress, President Coolidge argued that the Fordney-McCumber tariff had accomplished its dual objectives of raising revenue and restoring prosperity. No further tariffs changes were necessary because "a constant revision of the tariff by the Congress is disturbing and harmful."[96] A year later, Coolidge praised protective tariffs for securing "the American market for the products of the American workmen" and enabling "our people to live according to a better standard and receive a better rate of compensation than any people, anytime, anywhere on earth, ever enjoyed."[97] In his 1926 annual message, Coolidge again hailed the strength of the economy as "predicated on the foundation of a protective tariff."[98] He rejected the view that America's creditor status implied that it should open its market to foreign goods; in his view, one year's worth of strong economic growth would create more demand for foreign goods, and thus help foreign countries earn dollars to repay their debts, than lower tariffs.

Meanwhile, to the discouragement of those desiring lower tariffs, Democrats were largely vanquished as a political force. As Senator Cordell Hull (1948, 1:124) of Tennessee lamented, "I had become one of the voices whose notes, pleading for lower tariffs, international cooperation, and better national financing, shattered against a stone wall. . . . I became progressively more discouraged until in 1929 I almost decided to retire from Congress." The 1924 Democratic platform denounced the Fordney-McCumber tariff as "the most unjust, unscientific and dishonest tariff tax measure ever enacted in our history. It is class legislation which defrauds the people for the benefit of a few; it heavily increases the cost of living, penalizes agriculture, corrupts the government, fosters paternalism and, in the long run, does not benefit the very interests for which it was intended."[99] But with the economy growing steadily, there was little apparent public discontent with the Republican tariff policy. After the war, the public cared little about the issue, and most of the popular resentment about protective duties, so evident around the turn of the century, had dissipated.

Of course, tariff policy did not completely fade away as a political issue. The one segment of the American economy that was not doing well during the 1920s was agriculture. The nation's farmers suffered from high levels of indebtedness after wide price fluctuations buffeted the sector during and after World War I. Agricultural prices doubled during the war as foreign demand for crops soared. This triggered a wave of land speculation and large investments in machinery and buildings, all of which pushed farm indebtedness to high levels. When farm prices did not collapse as expected after the war, another wave of land speculation took place. Then the tightening of monetary conditions in 1920–21 led to a sharp fall in commodity prices, putting heavily indebted farmers under enormous financial pressure.[100] Although manufacturing industries were also slammed by the recession, they snapped back, and industrial production grew steadily for the remainder of the decade. By contrast, agriculture remained in a prolonged slump. Farm income did not regain its prewar level until 1925 and was flat for the remainder of the decade. As the real burden of mortgage and other debt rose sharply due to falling prices, farms began to fail in increasing numbers. Foreclosures rose from 3 percent of farms in 1913–20 to 11 percent over 1921–25, and reached an astounding 18 percent of farms from 1926–29.[101] The divergent paths of prosperous industry and struggling farms once again bred agrarian resentment in the Midwest against the industrial and commercial wealth of the East.

With nearly a quarter of the American labor force still employed in agriculture, Congress could not ignore the farm sector's severe distress, as evidenced by falling farmland values, mortgage foreclosures, and rural bank failures. With manufacturers already protected by import tariffs, Congress considered numerous proposals during the 1920s for government policies that would give more assistance to farmers.[102] In an influential book entitled *Equality for Agriculture*, George N. Peek and Hugh S. Johnson, president and vice president of the Moline Plow Company, suggested that farm relief should be provided by boosting farm prices to their prewar level. They developed the idea of a "parity price" for farmers that would guarantee the purchasing power of farm products based on the price level in 1910–14.[103]

The question was how to achieve the objective of higher farm prices. One way this could be done was supposed to be through "tariff equality," in which the agricultural products that farmers sold would be protected as much as the manufactured products that they purchased. While the average tariff on manufactured goods was about 45 percent, the average tariff on agricultural products was only about 22 percent. Therefore, tariff equality could mean either increasing duties on agricultural imports or decreasing duties on manufactured imports. Farm groups had no desire to attack the principle of protection or to take on industrial interests in a fight to slash their tariffs, so the consensus seemed to be that higher tariffs on agricultural imports were desirable.[104]

The problem with higher import tariffs as the solution to agriculture's difficulties was that the United States remained a large net exporter of the crops that most farmers produced, particularly grains (wheat and corn) and traditional staples (cotton and tobacco). The prices of these commodities were determined by the world market. Higher duties on agricultural imports would give most farmers little, if any, relief from low prices. In the debate over the Fordney-McCumber tariff, Senator Carl Hayden (D-AZ) said that including higher tariff rates on agricultural goods "can be explained in no other way than that they represent an attempt to fool the farmers and swindle the stockmen into the belief that they will get enough benefit out of this bill to fully compensate them for the higher prices that they must pay for all the manufactured goods upon which high protective or even prohibitive duties are levied in this measure. . . . Time will soon disclose the utter futility of attempting by a tariff to boost the price of wheat or corn or short-staple cotton and the numerous other farm and range products where the importations are negligible and the surplus must be sold abroad."[105]

The failure of the Emergency Tariff of 1921 and the Fordney-McCumber tariff of 1922 to provide much assistance to agricultural producers led to legislative proposals to increase farm prices directly, through programs ranging from federal loans and cooperative marketing arrangements to government purchases of farm surpluses at guaranteed prices and export subsidies. The most noteworthy of these schemes was developed by Senator Charles McNary (R-OR) and Representative Gilbert Haugen (R-IA). The McNary-Haugen plan, first introduced in 1924 and considered repeatedly over the rest of the decade, combined domestic price supports with an export subsidy as a way of implementing the price parity concept advocated by Peek and Johnson.[106] Under the plan, the government would create an export corporation that would buy enough domestic output of a particular commodity to raise the price to a target set by the government and tied to the general price index. Imports would be restricted to prevent them from coming in at prices below the target. The government would then dispose of any surplus it held by exporting it at the lower world market price. The financial loss arising from purchasing the commodities at high domestic prices and selling the surplus at low world prices would be financed by an "equalization fee" on domestic sales. The plan could not feasibly include all agricultural produce, so it was limited to basic commodities, such as wheat, wool, cattle, and swine.

While farm organizations, from the National Grange to the American Farm Bureau Federation, supported the scheme, opponents attacked the McNary-Haugen bill as unconstitutional, sectional, and unworkable.[107] In 1924, the House defeated it; the greatest support came from the Midwest, but almost all states in the East and South opposed it. Recognizing the need to cultivate additional political support, representatives from the Midwest reintroduced the bill and included cotton in the program. The combination of cotton- and corn-belt support led to its passage by Congress in 1927.

Although Midwestern Republicans supported the measure, the party's eastern establishment did not, because farmers were not traditionally part of their political base.[108] Indeed, Coolidge vetoed the bill, arguing that government price-fixing would be difficult to administer and would distort markets, and that the equalization fee was unconstitutional. The president also maintained that the bill was sectional and selective because it helped farmers who produced wheat, corn, and cotton and raised hogs, but not those who produced oats, barley, and vegetables, in addition to ignoring beef and poultry producers.

Despite the president's opposition, farm supporters continued to insist that something be done to relieve the financial distress in agriculture. In early 1928, Congress passed another McNary-Haugen bill, this time by a wider margin than before, and tried to address the president's objections by covering all commodities. Once again, Coolidge vetoed the bill on the grounds that it would "poison the wellsprings of our national spirit."[109] In his sharply worded veto message, Coolidge once again faulted the scheme for being an unwise price-fixing measure that would assist some farmers at the expense of others and be impossibly complex to administer.

Frustrated by their failure to secure agricultural relief, the Midwestern Republican insurgents were determined to do something to help their agricultural constituents. With price supports having been blocked, they began to lash out against high tariffs for industrial producers. In December 1927, Senator William McMaster (R-SD) proposed an immediate, downward revision of the tariff, aiming primarily at machinery and equipment used by farmers. Denouncing agricultural tariffs as a fraud, McMaster started attacking protection for industry:

The only way agriculture can win relief is by arousing the industrial East. I want to see the industrial group placed on the defensive just as agriculture has been on the defensive for the last seven years. The West must strike industry where it hurts to get any necessary relief. I know no better way to bring the East to its senses than to tamper with the tariff. The farmer is determined in this. They must either get the benefits of the tariff or they must be relieved of the burdens of the tariff.[110]

Senate Finance Committee chairman Reed Smoot (R-UT) condemned the McMaster proposal: "It is difficult for me to measure the disastrous effect of adopting this resolution. It is an attack in the dark without a redeeming feature."[111] Smoot and the Old Guard Republicans insisted that no tariff revision was needed for at least two years. Yet the Republican leadership was overwhelmed by insurgent Republicans from the Midwest and low-tariff Democrats from the South who came together to pass the McMaster resolution.

In the House, where Eastern interests had greater representation, the proposal was tabled, but only by a surprisingly narrow margin. Once again, a battle between the agricultural Midwest and the industrial East was postponed. But the agrarian demands for tariff reform and new tariff legislation would force Congress to revisit the issue sooner than the Republican leadership had expected or desired. The insurgents demanded a revision that would reduce tariffs on industrial products and increase them on agricultural goods, thereby supposedly providing relief for America's ailing farmers. It is ironic that the seeds of the Hawley-Smoot tariff were laid not by greedy industrial lobbyists or the Republican leadership, but by progressive Republicans from the Midwest.

CHAPTER EIGHT

The Hawley-Smoot Tariff and the Great Depression, 1928–1932

In the 1920s, the focus of trade policy shifted from protecting manufacturing to protecting agriculture. Congress struggled to find the right way to assist farmers and relieve farm distress, turning to a tariff revision after President Coolidge vetoed price-support legislation. The resulting Hawley-Smoot tariff of 1930 proved to be the most controversial piece of trade legislation since the Tariff of Abominations in 1828. The subject of heated debate during its difficult passage through Congress, the legislation helped push the average tariff on dutiable imports to near-record levels just as the economy was sliding into the Great Depression. The early 1930s saw an unprecedented contraction of world trade, during which time many other countries retaliated against the United States and significantly increased their own trade barriers. The Hawley-Smoot tariff had far-reaching consequences and it marked the last time that Congress ever set duties in the entire tariff schedule.

THE ORIGINS OF THE HAWLEY-SMOOT TARIFF

As we saw in chapter 7, Congress began paying more attention to agriculture than manufacturing in the 1920s. While the manufacturing sector had been the primary concern of policymakers in the nineteenth century, American industry now dominated world markets, and policymakers shifted their focus to the nation's troubled farm sector. Farmers came under enormous financial difficulty after commodity prices plummeted in 1920–21, which led to a decade of economic hardship. Although Congress tried to establish price supports for certain commodities, President Coolidge twice vetoed such legislation.

The plight of agriculture was an important backdrop to the presidential election of 1928. Both parties pledged to help the ailing farm sector, although they were vague as to precisely what they would do. Democrats promised measures "to establish and maintain the purchasing power of farm products and the complete economic equality of agriculture" through government credit and marketing assistance. Republicans promised to "place the agricultural interests of America on a basis of economic equality with other industries to insure its prosperity and success" and stressed the need for further protection for farmers against foreign competition.[1]

In terms of trade policy, the differences between the parties in 1928 were perhaps as slight as they had ever been. The Democratic presidential candidate, Alfred E. Smith of New York, came from the party's conservative, high-tariff wing. His nomination reflected the growing power of the party's urban North, which wanted to adopt positions closer to those of the Republicans in order to attract the support of business. This northern wing had few complaints about the existing tariff and sought to reassure industry that the party would not slash import duties, as had been done during the Wilson administration. Therefore, while attacking the excessive tariffs for big business, the platform declared that a Democratic tariff would ensure the "maintenance of legitimate business and a high standard of wages for American labor" and the "equitable distribution of the benefits and burdens of the tariff among all." The platform even endorsed the old Republican standard for the tariff, that the "difference between the cost of production at home and abroad, with adequate safeguard for the wage of the American laborer, must be the extreme measure of every tariff rate."[2]

Thus, Democrats no longer put forth tariff reform as a defining issue for the party.[3] During the campaign, Al Smith vowed that his party, "if entrusted with power, will be opposed to any general tariff bill. . . . No revision of any specific schedule will have the approval of the Democratic party which in any way interferes with the American standard of living and level of wages."[4] Party leaders believed that tariff reform was not a winning issue in the North, leaving only the party's Southern wing still devoted to the possibility of lower tariffs.

Meanwhile, the Republican platform reaffirmed the protective tariff as "a fundamental and essential principle of the economic life of this nation" and as "essential for the continued prosperity of the country." The party argued that it was "as vital to American agriculture as it is to American manufacturing." However, the platform continued, "certain provisions of the present law require revision in the light of changes in the world competitive situation. . . . We realize that there are certain industries which cannot now successfully compete with foreign producers because of lower foreign wages and a lower cost of living abroad, and we pledge the next Republican Congress to an examination and, where necessary, a revision of these schedules to the end that American labor in these industries may again command the home market, may maintain its standard of living, and may count upon steady employment in its accustomed field."[5]

While the Republican presidential candidate, Herbert Hoover, acknowledged that foreign trade was important for the country's economy, he warned that lower tariffs would lead to more imports and lower wages. In accepting the party's nomination, Hoover declared that "the most urgent economic problem in our nation today is in agriculture. It must be solved if we are to bring prosperity and contentment to one-third of our people directly and all of our people indirectly." He insisted that an "adequate tariff is the foundation of farm relief" and pledged to "use my office and influence to give the farmer the full benefit of our historical tariff policy."[6]

The general economic prosperity of the 1920s, apart from agriculture, allowed the Republicans to crush the Democrats once again in the 1928 election. The Republicans retained control of the presidency and increased their majorities in Congress. House Republicans immediately set to work on a tariff bill even before Hoover's inauguration. In some sense, it was unusual for the Republicans to take up the tariff at this time: the economy was generally doing well, imports were not flooding into the country, and businesses were not agitating for higher tariffs. Yet just as Republicans had modified their 1897 tariff in 1909 to appease progressive reformers, they were now revising their 1922 tariff to appease agricultural interests represented by progressive insurgents from the Midwest. In particular, Senator William Borah (R-ID) had been pressuring party leaders to work toward "tariff equality" for agricultural goods.

THE CONTENTIOUS REVISION OF THE TARIFF

In December 1928, Willis C. Hawley (R-OR), the chairman of the Ways and Means Committee, issued a public notice that hearings on the tariff would be held shortly. In January 1929, the committee began forty-three days and five nights of hearings on the tariff revision. The committee heard statements from 1,100 individuals in what amounted to 10,684 pages of testimony published in eighteen volumes. The tariff was examined paragraph by paragraph, schedule by schedule: chemicals; earthenware; metals; wood; sugar; tobacco; agricultural products; beverages; cotton manufac-

tures; flax, hemp, and jute; wool; silk; rayon; paper and books; and sun-
dries. Often working well into the evening, the committee listened to and
questioned producers from around the country who had a stake in each
of the nearly three thousand enumerated goods. As in previous revisions,
testimony was received primarily from small- and medium-sized producers, almost all of whom argued for maintaining or increasing duties on
imports. After the public hearings ended in late February, the majority
members of the committee proceeded, as was standard practice, to draft
the tariff schedule in private, without consulting the minority members.

In March 1929, President Hoover delivered his inaugural address and
called for a special session of Congress to act upon "agricultural relief
and limited changes in the tariff."[7] House Speaker Nicholas Longworth
(R-OH) expressed the hope that Congress could complete farm relief and
tariff legislation within a month or so. With the Democrats having relaxed
their traditional anti-tariff position during the election, Longworth remarked that "the line of cleavage between the two great political parties
would seem to have crumbled in the past few years almost to questions of
detail." Noting that minority leader John Garner (D-TX) was sympathetic
to protective tariffs, Longworth anticipated that "we will hear resounding
from his party no clarion call that the American consumer shall be permitted to buy in the cheapest market."[8]

In proposing the session, Hoover called for "an effective tariff upon
agricultural products that will compensate the farmer's higher costs and
higher standards of living." Hoover subsequently sent Congress a message describing his views on the forthcoming legislation. The president
and party leaders did not believe that Congress should rewrite the entire
1922 tariff act, but merely raise rates on agricultural goods and adjust a
few other duties for goods where "there has been a substantial slackening
of activity in the industry during the past few years, and a consequent
decrease of employment." Finally, Hoover noted, "In determining changes
in our tariff we must not fail to take into account the broad interests of
the country as a whole, and such interests include our trade relations
with other countries. It is obviously unwise protection which sacrifices
a greater amount of employment in exports to gain a less [sic] amount of
employment from imports."[9]

Of course, by the time this message was sent, the Ways and Means
Committee had nearly completed its work on the tariff bill. In early May
1929, Hawley presented the results to the House. In the majority committee report, Republicans stated that the existing tariff "has fully justified
its existence in restoring confidence and rehabilitating industry" and "for

the great majority of the articles for which it provided protection, it is still efficient and sufficient." However, conditions had changed for some industries, and the legislation was necessary "in order to make the tariff meet modern conditions." Therefore, the bill increased 845 rates and decreased 82 rates in the existing tariff. "The Republican members believe that the readjustments are justified by existing differences in competitive conditions, and necessary for the welfare of all interested in the changes made, and that they will maintain and promote the general welfare." Although the report contended that "the average rate on dutiable imports will not be materially changed" as a result of the readjustment, the Tariff Commission calculated that the average rate on imports would rise from 34.6 percent to 43.1 percent in the House bill. Finally, acknowledging that foreign countries were concerned about the upward tariff revision, the majority stated that "our first duty was to our own people and to maintenance of their prosperity."[10]

In presenting the bill on the House floor, Hawley maintained that "we all enjoy the American standard of living which has been created and is maintained by the protective tariff." When asked what underlying principle guided the rate changes, Hawley replied, "Wherever the evidence indicates and from our information proves that American industry was suffering from a competitive condition to its disadvantage in competition with the foreign producer or with foreign imports, we adjusted that rate to meet the competitive conditions." This meant that, for domestic industries, "whatever rate was necessary for their protection should be written." "There is no intention to prohibit any importations," Hawley insisted. "The intention is that they should not come in to the disadvantage of American producers and laborers."[11]

The committee's minority report, written by Cordell Hull of Tennessee, criticized the excessive or prohibitive tariffs in the Republican approach because they ensured that "the old and worst type of log-rolling and political pressure of conflicting interests will be continued."[12] Hull emphasized that import tariffs would not help the majority of American farmers who depended on export markets: "There is now at least tacit confession by all candid persons that only the minor specialities of agriculture can secure any material tariff benefits."[13] And he attacked the bill, arguing that "existing prohibitive tariffs injure the American farmer first, by increasing his production costs; second, his living costs; third, his transportation costs; fourth, by decreasing his foreign markets and exports; and fifth, by decreasing his property values due to surplus congestion."

Despite the Republican leadership's insistence that the primary goal was to help agriculture, the bill increased duties on manufactured goods as much as it increased duties on agricultural goods. Midwestern Republicans were even more disappointed that the bill did not include an export debenture program. Developed as an alternative to the McNary-Haugen price-support plan, discussed in chapter 7, the debenture scheme was a subsidy designed to help the many export-oriented farmers for whom an import tariff would be meaningless.[14] The Republican leadership strongly opposed the export debenture, which exacerbated sectional tensions within the party. Eastern Republicans supported higher tariffs on industrial goods but believed that imports of raw materials and foodstuffs were harmful because they raised the costs of production for producers and the cost of living for households. For example, Fiorello H. LaGuardia (R-NY) strongly supported tariffs to "protect American labor" but opposed higher tariffs on sugar and butter and denounced a higher duty on potatoes as "nothing but downright larceny."[15] In contrast, insurgents from the Midwest supported "tariff equality" for agriculture—meaning lower tariffs on manufactured products and higher tariffs on agricultural goods—along with an export subsidy for farm goods.

Dissatisfied with the bill, Hoover met with House Republicans to demand that they increase agricultural tariffs and reduce industrial tariffs in line with his campaign pledge. The president also insisted that the bill include the "flexible tariff" authority that would allow him to adjust duties after a Tariff Commission report. As Hoover (1951–52, 1:292–93) wrote in his memoirs,

> I believed that the only way to get the tariff out of Congressional logrolling was through empowering this bipartisan commission to adjust the different rates on dutiable goods upon the basis of differences in cost of production at home and abroad, and to make these readjustments after objective examination and public hearings. . . . Any tariff passed by the logrolling process, inevitable in the Congress, is bound to be very bad in spots. The object of the flexible tariff was to secure, in addition to more equitable rates, a hope that Congressional tariff making could be ended.

The meeting was unsuccessful in that the president's intervention had little apparent effect on the House bill.

Southern Democrats, such as Hull, argued that "this bill sharply raises the question of whether a tariff rate can ever be made too high, and also the question of whether this Government would ever, under any circumstances, reduce any particular number of tariff rates."[16] But the opposition of most Democrats was not based on a demand for lower tariffs, and the old slogan of "a tariff for revenue only" was obsolete. Rather, they wanted a different distribution of the benefits of the tariff. "I believe in the principle of protection," Garner stated. "But I believe protection should be equally distributed; that the farmers of the South and West are as much entitled to the benefits of tariff protection as the manufacturers of New England and Pennsylvania." He complained that "every effort to lower industrial rates to a point of parity with agricultural rates has met the opposition of that small coterie of Republican leaders who have controlled the destinies of this bill" and that "defeat of the export debenture killed the last hope of over 80 percent of American farmers to secure any substantial relief through the tariff."[17]

Democrats complained about the measure, but they did not have the votes to affect the outcome. Given the large Republican majority, House passage of the bill was a foregone conclusion. On May 28, 1929, the House approved the Hawley bill by a vote of 264–147. "Whether it was because of the heat of the day or weariness superinduced by long hours of discussion, the enthusiasm that usually marks the conclusion of labors on a big party measure was lacking in the House chamber on this occasion," the *New York Times* reported. "There was only a feeble cheer on the Republican side as Speaker Longworth announced the passage of the bill, while the Democrats, overwhelmed by superior numbers, moved sullenly in their seats."[18] As usual, the vote ran along party lines: Republicans voted 244–12 in favor, and Democrats voted 134–20 against (along with 1 Farmer-Laborer).

As figure 8.1 shows, the North-South geographic divide that had existed for so long was still readily apparent. Republicans from the Northeast, industrial Midwest, and the far West supported the bill, with only a few "corn belt" and "wheat belt" insurgents from Minnesota, Iowa, South Dakota, and Nebraska dissenting. Democrats from the South uniformly opposed the measure, except those from Louisiana and Florida, where sugar interests were strong. That said, more northern Democrats voted for the bill than Midwestern Republicans voted against it—a revealing indicator of the relative strength of dissent in the two parties.[19]

The bill was then referred to the Senate Finance Committee, chaired by Reed Smoot of Utah. Smoot was widely recognized as an exceptionally capable and indefatigable legislator who was unquestionably the most knowledgeable member of Congress about the details of the tariff schedule. He was also a committed protectionist who, as a matter of principle,

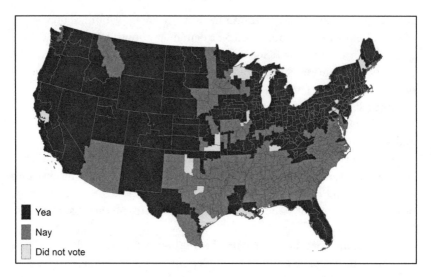

Figure 8.1. House voting on the Hawley tariff bill, May 28, 1930. (Map courtesy
Citrin GIS/Applied Spatial Analysis Lab, Dartmouth College.)

opposed almost any reduction in tariff rates.[20] A leader in the Mormon
church, Smoot was known as the "apostle of protection" and "the sugar
senator" because of his staunch defense of Utah's sugar beet industry. As
one senator put it, "Of course the Senator from Utah would say that in
some instances the rates are not high enough. I can state the rate which he
has in mind, and even if it were double the rate now provided in the bill, it
would not be high enough for him. He dreams of sugar, he tastes sugar, he
sees sugar morning, evening, and night."[21]

As past experience had demonstrated, the Senate's consideration of the
bill promised to be more contentious because of the greater strength of
western interests and the inability of the Republican leadership to control the bill once it reached the floor. Angered that the House raised tariffs on industrial goods more than on farm goods, a bipartisan coalition
of Midwestern Republicans and Southern Democrats complained that it
was contrary to the president's expressed desire for a limited tariff revision that would primarily benefit farmers. Even before the Finance Committee had begun deliberations, senators from the Midwest (representing
agricultural interests) and West (representing mining and cattle interests)
made their displeasure known. Republican William E. Borah of Idaho proposed that the Finance Committee only be allowed to revise the agricultural schedules, thereby keeping tariffs on industrial goods at their cur-

rent rates. "The real fight here is between the agricultural interests and the industrial interests," Borah explained. "We feel that we are fighting for equality; that that equality is constantly removed by the fact that duties are substantially increased upon the things we have to buy, even though they may be increased to some extent upon the things we have to sell."[22] The Borah resolution failed by a single vote, with Republicans voting 32–13 against, and Democrats voting 25–7 in favor, but the vote demonstrated the strength of the insurgent agricultural coalition in the Senate and foreshadowed the difficult fight to come.

The Finance Committee then began laborious hearings that lasted from May until September 1929. The committee heard from 1,004 witnesses in testimony that ran 8,618 printed pages in eighteen volumes. (One volume was devoted to protests from foreign countries, an issue that will be considered later.) Once again, representatives of numerous producer interests appeared before the committee to request that higher tariffs be imposed on competing imports. In early September, the committee reported the bill, which increased 177 rates and decreased 254 rates of duty from the House version. In presenting the bill to the Senate, Smoot knew that a big battle was brewing. "The people elected a Republican President and Congress in order that a readjustment of the tariff might be in the hands of the friends of protection," he warned. "If that mandate is rejected and defeated by a group or section of that country, the people will know where to place the blame." He accused Democrats of being "aided by sectional forces boding no good to the country" and "abetted by groups of internationalists who are willing to betray American interest and surrender the spirit of nationalism."[23]

Senator Furnifold Simmons (D-NC) led the Democratic attack, calling the tariff bill "indefensible" and a violation of the campaign pledge to help farmers. "Instead of removing, as promised, the tariff discriminations against agriculture, it greatly increases and extends those discriminations, and . . . for every dollar it gives to the farmer, it takes from him several dollars in the increased cost of his purchases," he exclaimed. Simmons rejected the bill as "unsatisfactory" to farmers because duties were being imposed either in cases where imports were negligible or where producers depended on exports to the world market and imports were irrelevant: "The only way the farmer can secure or hope to secure even approximate equality through tariff legislation is by imposing such duties on his products as will or can be effective and by drastic reduction in the duties imposed upon such industrial products as he does not produce and must of necessity buy for farm, home, and family," Simmons argued.[24]

The Senate then began the long and complicated process of revising the bill. From September 1929 until February 1930, the Senate considered the bill in the "committee of the whole." Unlike the House Ways and Means Committee, the Finance Committee could not control the floor debate on the bill or limit amendments to it. The "committee of the whole" procedure permitted open-ended discussion in which any Senator could offer amendments and request votes on tariffs for specific goods.

The Senate debated the administrative clauses of the tariff bill for several weeks before moving on to the tariff schedules. At this point what came to be called "the coalition"—Democrats and the few insurgent Republicans who broke ranks with their party in the Borah vote—succeeded in reshaping the bill. From late October through mid-November 1929, in a series of roll-call votes, the coalition succeeded in slashing industrial tariffs, often restoring them to the 1922 level. They not only added an export debenture program, but they also eliminated the flexible tariff provision sought by the president and the Republican leadership.

The Old Guard Senators from eastern industrial states watched with dismay as the coalition took control. George Moses (R-NH) blasted Borah and his supporters as the "sons of the wild jackass," an epithet that stuck and became a badge of honor for the insurgents. After a vote to reduce the tariff on pig iron from $1.50 to $0.75 per ton, David Reed (R-PA) attacked the coalition for doing "damage to the stability and the structure of American industry." Reed sighed with exasperation, "The coalition has made up its mind to knock out every increase in the industrial rates, and we might as well go ahead and have done with it. Then the bill will go to conference, and the House and the Senate will never agree, but we will at least be rid of it and can go on with our routine business." Reed also attacked the insurgents for their hostility toward industrial interests: "The attitude of the Western states, the Middle Western states in particular, the corn belt so called, is one of extreme ill-will toward the industrial states of the East, particularly ours [Pennsylvania]. You might almost think that we were at war with each other."[25] Western Senators responded that Reed would have been quite happy to put manganese ore on the free list to help the steel industry without considering the problems it would have caused for mining states.

The uncertainty surrounding the Senate's deliberations was a moment for presidential leadership. No one had any idea what the White House thought of the insurgent campaign. Did Hoover want the revision confined to the agricultural schedule, or did he approve of the higher rates on industrial goods as well? Yet Hoover never seemed to care about the tariff rates themselves and refused to provide any guidance to Congress, not that his advice would have been welcomed. A White House statement released in late October 1929 read simply, "The President has declined to interfere or express any opinion on the details of rates or any compromise thereof, as it is obvious that, if for no other reason, he could not pretend to have the necessary information in respect to many thousands of commodities which such determination requires."[26]

Then, in early November, Smoot shocked the Senate by conceding defeat. Admitting that his committee had lost control of the bill, he offered to hand it over to the coalition and recess for ten days to allow them to rewrite it as they pleased. To expedite the process, he proposed that the Senate then vote on the coalition's bill without debate, something he could in no way guarantee. He may have been trying to call the coalition's bluff, and in fact Borah and Simmons rejected the offer. The members of the coalition were critics of the proposed legislation, but they did not have a common position on what would constitute a better schedule of duties.[27]

With its work on the tariff unfinished, the Senate adjourned for the year in late November, just weeks after a major crash in the stock market. The Federal Reserve had started raising interest rates in January 1929 in an effort to reign in surging stock prices. This tightening of monetary policy began to slow the economy and eventually produced a sharp fall in asset prices. The stock market collapse in late October signaled uncertainty about the nation's economic outlook. Some observers have linked the stock market crash to Congress's consideration of the tariff, but it is highly unlikely that the congressional debate had any significant impact on financial markets.[28] In fact, the run-up and subsequent crash in stock prices was not broadly based but almost entirely concentrated in public utilities companies, which came from a sector of the economy least affected by import duties. In addition, the Senate's work on the bill was far from over, and no conclusions could be reached about the final outcome.

When Congress reconvened in January 1930, the Senate—still acting as a committee of the whole but now considering the overall bill, not just Finance Committee amendments to the House bill—took further actions to moderate the proposed tariffs. Week after week, the Senate was preoccupied with the laborious process of voting on tariffs for such goods as crude and scrap aluminum, shoes, coal tar dyes, woven silk fabrics, calcium carbide, glass rods, and milk cans. After six days of wearisome debate over sugar, the Senate reduced the tariff on raw sugar from $2.20 per hundredweight, as proposed by the Finance Committee, to the 1922 Fordney-McCumber rate of $1.75 per hundredweight, in contrast to the

House rate of $2.40. The voting margin on many commodities was quite close, indicating the instability of factions seeking support for higher or lower duties on particular goods, yet the insurgent coalition still seemed to have the upper hand.

Finally, in early March 1930, nearly a year after the House had passed the bill, the Senate completed consideration of the bill in a committee of the whole. Whereas the House bill had increased 845 rates and reduce 82 rates from the 1922 tariff, the Senate bill now left 620 rates higher and 202 lower. The legislation then shifted to the Senate proper for further debate before final passage. On the floor, senators could once again offer amendments and request new votes on specific tariff rates, even if precisely the same issue had just been considered and voted on during the committee of the whole. There was no substantive difference between the Senate considering the bill as a committee of the whole and as the Senate proper, but—with a gloomier economic outlook—opponents of the reductions in the industrial tariffs had time to regroup and propose new amendments. A different voting coalition emerged, one based not on agricultural versus industrial interests but on classic vote-trading among unrelated goods.

This new logrolling coalition succeeded in reversing many of the tariff reductions that had been voted upon in the committee of the whole. For example, on March 5, the day after it took the bill from the committee of the whole, the Senate reconsidered the sugar duties. Less than two months after the Senate had voted to restore the 1922 rate on imported sugar, Smoot succeeded in pushing the rate up to $2.50 per hundredweight. Similarly, the Senate reversed previous votes on cement, softwood lumber, and other goods as the insurgent coalition unraveled. In this final stage, the Senate increased 75 duties (on imports valued at $355 million) and decreased 31 duties (on $34 million of imports) from the committee of the whole version.

The March 1930 reversals of the previous actions to moderate the tariff rates gave rise to accusations of vote-trading based on backroom deals and special-interest lobbying. Robert LaFollette (R-WI) characterized the Senate bill as "the product of a series of deals, conceived in secret, but executed in public with a brazen effrontery that is without parallel in the annals of the Senate. . . . it seems to me that a vote for this bill condones the vote-trading deals by which some of the most unjustifiable rates in the bill were obtained. . . . this Congress has demonstrated how tariff legislation should not be made."[29] Statements on the Senate floor pointed to several commodities—sugar, lumber, concrete, and others—as ones that were likely to have been involved in logrolling. Just prior to the vote reconsidering the duty on lumber, for example, David Walsh (D-MA) stated,

> I cannot help but say that things have been happening here in recent weeks that have somewhat shaken my confidence in the judgment of the Senate always being reflected upon conscientious conviction. If logrolling, which is the trading of votes, is not here, then some other invisible influence has brought about a shifting of votes and reversals of judgment that is unparalleled in the history of legislation. There have been some very suspicious circumstances connected with the shifting of votes on many of these items. Indeed, it has been admitted privately that votes have been and will be exchanged on all important items.[30]

The insurgent Republicans were dismayed by these reversals. "The farmer has been betrayed by this bill," LaFollette thundered. "The farmer's back has been made the springboard from which the industrial lobbyists have leaped to new and higher tariff rate levels for the benefit of the special industrial interests they represent. The agricultural tariff granted the farmer, in many instances ineffective, carries with it the obligation to pay higher prices upon almost every article that is used upon the farm." Branding it "the worst tariff bill" in the nation's history, LaFollette argued that the legislation would cost consumers $1 billion in higher prices.[31]

A widely cited study by University of Wisconsin economists John R. Commons, Benjamin H. Hibbard, and Selig Perlman found that many agricultural tariffs would be ineffective in assisting domestic producers. They calculated that the sugar duty cost the American public $289 million in 1928, and the Hawley-Smoot duties would increase this to $384 million per year.[32] Smoot rejected the report, saying that the "eminent economists" had made some "idiotic errors" and that "if they missed the mark half so widely as they missed the mark in sugar, every line of the tract is verbal rubbish." Smoot said that Congress was being asked to accept the advice of the economists "in a matter of which they have not the slightest practical knowledge" whereas "practical sugar men . . . have appeared before the Senate Finance Committee to tell of the absolute necessity of a higher rate on sugar. They have assured us that a higher rate is no threat to the consumer, and that it is no threat to the welfare of Cuba."[33]

On March 24, 1930, ten months after the House passage, the Senate completed its deliberations and passed the bill by a vote of 53–31; Republicans voted 46–5 in favor and Democrats voted 26–7 against.[34] The Senate made 1,253 amendments, either technical or rate changes, to the House version. The floor debate that occurred from September 1929 to February 1930, it was later calculated, took 527 hours and filled 2,638 pages of the *Congressional Record* at a printing cost of $131,000.[35] Several lengthy speeches were given, including Henry Ashurst's (D-AZ) 15 pages on tomatoes and Gerald Nye's (R-ND) 35 pages on lumber.

In April 1930, a House-Senate conference committee began resolving the differences between the two bills. The conference committee generally adopted the higher rates in the original House bill, but differences arose over other provisions. The House included a weak flexible tariff provision but rejected an export debenture. The Senate rejected the flexible tariff provision but included an export debenture. Now President Hoover, who had been largely silent during the Senate consideration of the bill, threatened to veto the bill unless it included a stronger flexible tariff provision and dropped the export debenture; he was apparently uninterested in the height or structure of the tariff rates themselves.[36] The Senate capitulated, dropping the export debenture by the narrow vote of 43–41 and adding the flexible tariff provision after the vice president broke a tie.

On June 13, 1930, the Senate approved the conference report by a vote of 44–42, with Republicans voting 39–11 in favor and Democrats voting 30–5 against. The close margin reflected the loss of support by Republicans from agricultural states who were dismayed that the conference bill contained higher industrial rates than those passed by the Senate. However, the votes of five Democrats were critical to the passage, and specific commodities convinced these Democrats to support the measure: sugar in Louisiana, wool in Wyoming, and fruit in Florida. Although the insurgents got eleven of fifty Republicans to vote against the final bill, they were bitterly dismayed at their failure to have a greater influence on the final legislation.

The next day the House passed the conference bill with few defections from either party. In urging its passage, Hawley stated, "If this bill is enacted into law . . . we will have a renewed era of prosperity such as followed the enactment of every Republican tariff bill, in which all of the people of the United States in every occupation, every industry, and every employment will share as they have always shared, which will increase our wealth, our employment, our comfort, the means of supplying our necessities, that will promote our trade abroad, and keep the name of the United States still before the world as the premier nation of solid finance, fairness, and justice to all the people, and one which for all time intends to provide for its own."[37]

Few members of Congress rejoiced at the passage of the bill. Democrats and insurgent Republicans ramped up their attack as the legislation approached final passage. Senator George Norris (R-NE) called the outcome

> protection run perfectly mad. . . . It is conceived and written in the interest of victorious business organizations who are using their power, which they obtained by the practice, in my judgment, of many unfair and deceitful means, to put through the Congress one of the most selfish and indefensible tariff measures that has ever been considered by the American people. In my judgment, those who are behind it will see that they have used their own power to bring about their own destruction, because, after all, in the long run . . . a tariff bill which builds up a part of our people to the damage and injury of other parts of our people will bring its own ruin."[38]

House Minority leader John Garner lambasted the bill as "violating every precept of common sense, justice, and sound economics. Under the guise of protecting the products of agriculture, the Republican majority in both Houses has inflicted upon the country industrial rates that are indefensible; rates that can only serve to add to the burden the farmers and consumers have carried for years; rates that will tend to reduce, and in fact eliminate, the foreign markets for many of our products, both industrial and agricultural." Garner continued,

> Every attempt to give agriculture the advantage of equal protection has been defeated. Every effort to lower industrial rates to a point of parity with agricultural rates has met with the opposition of that small coterie of Republican leaders who have controlled the destinies of this bill. Those leaders raised a smoke screen under cover of which they manipulated the industrial rates to the highest point in the history of tariff making. They endeavored to camouflage this action by increasing rates on agricultural products of which a surplus is produced and upon which any tariff is inoperative. They flatly refused to accept the export debenture which would have made the tariff operative upon these surplus products of agriculture, and yet they have the audacity to refer to this bill as a measure designed for the relief of agriculture.[39]

Finally, Garner concluded, "The Hawley-Smoot tariff is not the result of the application of economic facts derived from research and investigation. It is not the result of the application of scientific deduction or findings. It is the result of political subserviency to a small but powerful group, financially able to maintain in Washington a large and efficient corps of lob-byists and to control to a great extent the financial affairs as well as the policies of the Republican party."[40]

The bill then went to the White House for the president's approval. Hoover (1951–52, 1:296) later wrote that he was "deluged with a mass of recommendations as to approval or veto from representatives of a diver-sity of interests." Manufacturers offered tepid support for the legislation, at least for finally resolving uncertainty about Congress's action, if not for the actual outcome. Farm organizations were skeptical of, if not outright hostile to, the bill. Organized labor was largely neutral, although individ-ual unions were not.[41]

But the overall public reaction to Congress's long, drawn-out tariff-making process was largely negative. The president's correspondence sec-retary informed him that "there has seldom been in this country such a rising tide of protest as has been aroused by the tariff bill."[42] Opposition to the bill was much more vocal than it had been with previous tariff acts, either because the economic rationale for raising tariffs was so weak or because the public saw the blatant role played by special-interest politics during the poorly disguised congressional logrolling. The spectacle of the Senate voting multiple times on tariffs for the same goods, with the outcome shifting depending upon which coalition had the upper hand or which votes were traded among which senators, was widely ridiculed.

A survey of editorial opinion revealed that 238 out of 324 newspapers did not believe that the Hawley-Smoot tariff was in the nation's best inter-est.[43] Walter Lippmann, the preeminent columnist of the day, criticized the tariff bill as "a wretched and mischievous product of stupidity and greed."[44] Executives of banks and financial institutions reminded Hoover that the United States was now a creditor nation and that high tariffs pre-vented other countries from earning the dollars needed to service their war debts. Thomas Lamont of J. P. Morgan, an advisor to Hoover, later re-called, "I almost went down on my knees to beg Herbert Hoover to veto the asinine Hawley-Smoot Tariff. That Act intensified nationalism all over the world."[45] Secretary of State Henry Stimson is said to have "fought like mad" for two days in an attempt to persuade Hoover to veto the measure.[46] Hoover would later be attacked for his lack of leadership on the matter.[47]

One notable response to the tariff bill was a statement signed by 1,028 economists and prominently featured on the front page of the *New York Times* on May 5, 1930. The economists called the higher tariffs "a mis-take" and argued that American manufacturers did not need greater tariff protection: "Already our factories supply our people with over 96 percent of the manufactured goods which they consume, and our producers look to foreign markets to absorb the increasing output of their machines. Further barriers to trade will serve them not well, but ill." Higher import barriers would increase the prices paid by consumers, leading to greater profits for low-cost firms and encouraging inefficient production by high-cost firms, and would harm the many workers who did not produce goods that could be protected by tariffs. Exports would suffer because "countries cannot permanently buy from us unless they are permitted to sell to us, and the more we restrict importation of goods from them by means of even higher tariffs, the more we reduce the possibility of exporting to them." Finally, higher tariffs would "inevitably inject . . . bitterness" into international economic relations and "plainly invite other nations to compete with us in raising further barriers to trade."[48]

Despite these criticisms, the president was not predisposed to reject his own party's measure. Given that a Republican Congress had delivered tariff legislation that he had requested, including the flexible tariff provision and dropping the export debenture, it would have been almost impossible for him to justify vetoing the bill. As Hoover described the bill,

> It contains many compromises between sectional interests and between different industries. No tariff bill has ever been enacted or ever will be enacted under the present system that will be perfect. A large portion of the items are always adjusted with good judgment, but it is bound to contain some inequalities and inequitable compromises. There are items upon which duties will prove too high and others upon which duties will prove to be too low. Certainly no President, with his other duties, can pretend to make that exhaustive determination of the complex facts which surround each of those 3,300 items, and which has required the attention of hundreds of men in Congress for nearly a year and a third.[49]

Hoover hailed the flexible tariff provision which could be used to "remedy inequalities" in the tariff and "gives great hope of taking the tariff away from politics, lobbying, and logrolling." But Hoover was anxious to dispose of the whole matter: "It is urgent that the uncertainties in the business world which have been added to by the long-extended debate of the measure should be ended. . . . As I have said, I do not assume the rate structure in this or any other tariff bill is perfect, but I am convinced that the disposal of the whole question is urgent. . . . Nothing would so retard business recovery as continued agitation over the tariff."[50] With that, at 12:59 p.m. on June 17, 1930, Hoover signed the Tariff Act of 1930, and it took effect the next day. With hindsight, Hoover (1951–52, 1:299) wrote that "raising the tariff from its sleep was a political liability despite the virtues of its reform."

THE HAWLEY-SMOOT TARIFF IN PERSPECTIVE

The Hawley-Smoot tariff of 1930 has achieved eternal notoriety as an ill-timed piece of legislation that reflected special-interest logrolling run amok.[51] Although not completely out of the ordinary, the Hawley-Smoot tariff was unusual on several dimensions. The political rationale behind the Fordney-McCumber tariff of 1922 is easy to understand: control of government had shifted to the Republicans, who wanted to reverse the existing low-tariff policy of the Democrats, and the economy was in turmoil from postwar monetary and financial readjustments. The political rationale behind the Hawley-Smoot tariff of 1930 is not as easy to understand because none of these factors was present. The Republicans had been firmly in control of government for many years, and work on the new tariff began prior to the business-cycle peak in August 1929, when the unemployment rate was only about 3 percent. There had been no sudden rise in imports or sharp fall in import prices when plans for the tariff revision were first made. The stock market crash and recession only came well into the Senate's consideration of the bill.

At almost two hundred pages, the Hawley-Smoot bill was also lengthier and more complicated than its predecessors. Figure 8.2 shows how tariff legislation had been getting progressively longer over time, which reflected the increasing complexity of the tariff schedule. The bill specified rates of duty on almost 3,300 enumerated items. The level of detail in the tariff code was mind-numbing. For example, in the final legislation, paragraph 390 of Schedule 3 (Metals, and manufactures of) read: "Bottle caps of metal, collapsible tubes, and sprinkler tops, if not decorated, colored, waxed, lacquered, enameled, lithographed, electroplated, or embossed in color, 30 per centum ad valorem; if decorated, colored, waxed, lacquered, enameled, lithographed, electroplated, or embossed in color, 45 per centum ad valorem." Paragraph 8 of Schedule 1 (Chemicals, oil, and paints) read: "Antimony: Oxide, 2 cents per pound; tartar emetic or potassium-antimony tartrate, 6 cents per pound; sulphides and other antimony salts and compounds, not specifically provided for, 1 cent per pound and 25 per centum ad valorem."[52] The tariff law consisted of nearly two hundred pages of such detail. "The existing minuteness with respect to rates is

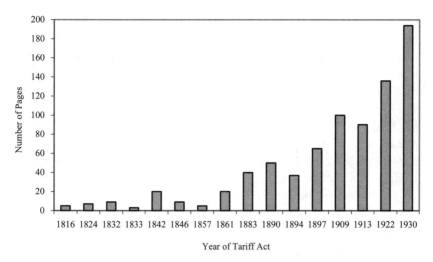

Figure 8.2. Length of tariff legislation, 1816–1930. (Schattschneider 1935, 23.)

partly an absurdity and partly a partisan fraud to cover up what the tariff really is—namely, a mass of private legislation," Senator David Walsh (D-MA) complained.[53]

Out of the 3,295 dutiable items in the tariff code, the final bill made 890 increases, 235 decreases, and left 2,170 duties unchanged from the existing schedule. The changes in the tariff rates bore little relationship to the one-time objective of setting the tariff to equalize the costs of production. Whereas the Tariff Commission purported to show that a 31 percent duty on imported canned tomatoes would equalize the cost of production, Congress put the duty at 50 percent. When the commission found that a duty of 56 cents per bushel on flaxseed would equalize costs, Congress set the tariff at 65 cents.[54] "Despite a pretense in the debates that there was some objective test of national welfare," Fetter (1933, 418) dryly noted, "the record of voting on individual items furnishes much evidence in support of the cynical proposition that sound protection was that which raised the prices of things produced by one's constituents, and unsound protection that which raised the prices of things made by someone's else constituents."

The legislation did not increase duties by an unusually large amount. Using 1928 imports as a base, the Tariff Commission calculated that the average tariff on dutiable imports was 41.14 percent, using the 1930 rates, up from 35.65 percent, using the 1922 rates.[55] Thus, the legislation raised the average tariff on dutiable imports by about six percentage points, about a 15 percent increase in rates. Of course, this is an average; because most of the duties were left unchanged and only a few reduced, those that increased did so much more than this figure suggests. In historical context, however, the Hawley-Smoot increase was not necessarily extreme. The McKinley tariff of 1890 increased tariffs on dutiable imports by about 4 percentage points, a 10 percent increase. It was significantly less than the Fordney-McCumber tariff of 1922, which pushed up the average tariff rate by more than 13 percentage points, a 64 percent increase. Nevertheless, it marked a further addition that came on top of the already high Fordney-McCumber duties.

The legislated increase in import duties in 1930 was only partly responsible for the higher tariff during this period. As figure 8.3 shows, the average tariff on dutiable imports increased in 1930, but then rose further in 1931 and again in 1932, when it peaked at 59.1 percent, the second-highest recorded value in history.[56] The severe deflation in import prices accounts for the rise of the average tariff on dutiable imports in 1931 and 1932 because about two-thirds of dutiable imports were subject to specific duties. Import prices fell 18 percent in 1930, 22 percent in 1931, and another 22 percent in 1932 for a cumulative decline of 49 percent after 1929.[57] The impact of deflation on specific duties allowed the average tariff on du-

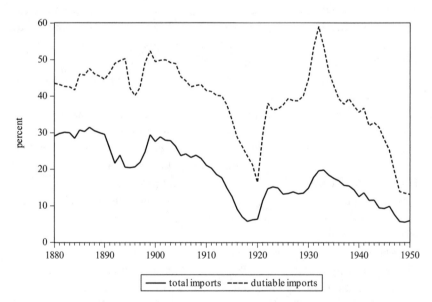

Figure 8.3. Average tariff on imports, total and dutiable, 1880–1950. (US Department of Commerce 1975, series U-211–12.)

tiable imports to creep up to 53 percent in 1931 and to 59 percent in 1932. This deflation-induced increase in the tariff was unrelated to congressional legislation: it began in 1929 and was driven by monetary factors that almost certainly would have occurred even if the bill had not passed.

Looking at the whole period, the combined impact of the higher legislated rates and deflation increased the average tariff on dutiable imports from 40 percent in 1929 to 59 percent in 1932, an increase of 19 percentage points, or about 47 percent. The legislation raised the average tariff by 15 percent, and deflation raised the average tariff by another 30 percent. Thus, about one-third of the increase in the average tariff during this period was because of the legislation and two-thirds because of the deflation.[58]

The complexity of the bill made it unwieldy for Congress to manage, particularly in the Senate, which was widely ridiculed for holding multiple roll-call votes on the rates of duty on dozens of individual commodities and products. It also meant that the legislation took a long time—eighteen months, from January 1929 to June 1930—to work its way from hearings in the House through the Senate and conference committee to the president's desk. The Underwood tariff of 1913 took just eight months of Congress's time, a little bit longer than most tariff legislation in the nineteenth century. But the Fordney-McCumber tariff of 1922 took twenty-one months of Congress's time, indicating the legislation was absorbing more and more of Congress's time. Although logrolling had always been a part of tariff legislation, that seemed to be a growing problem too.

The legislative ordeal generated immense frustration among members of both parties. Congressmen were well aware that the time-consuming process kept them spending day after day debating such arcane matters as the appropriate duty on clothes pins, cordage, silk hats, glass rods, hempseed oil, paper board, and zinc-bearing ores, when they could have been working on other pressing matters. The tortuous path of the legislation made members of Congress painfully aware of the absurdities involved in revising the tariff schedule. As Thaddeus Caraway (D-AR) complained: "The trouble is the system. The instances are many where protection is accorded to those industries that least need it, while others, really deserving, are passed or else not given the protection to which they are entitled. Just look at the schedules in the bill now before the Senate. The rates in that bill bear no appreciable relation to imports, and very frequently they bear little, if any, relation to the earning capacity of the individuals or the corporations seeking higher duties."[59]

Furthermore, the final outcome drew widespread public criticism and satisfied very few of the interested parties. One of the ironies of the Hawley-Smoot tariff is that it did not originate as a result of pressure from manufacturers. Instead, it originated from progressive Republicans who thought a tariff adjustment—in the vain hope of achieving "tariff equality"—would help its agricultural constituents. The tariff revision was offered by politicians rather than demanded by interest groups. However, once the door was open to changing the tariff for some groups, others—namely, small and medium-sized businesses in manufacturing, even if not suffering from increased foreign competition—were only too happy to take advantage of the situation for themselves. The episode illustrates how politicians can use economic interests for their own purposes, not just the other way around.

The pretense of the legislation was that it was designed to help farmers. Yet the problems facing most farmers—low prices and high debts—could not be remedied through higher taxes on imports.[60] Most farmers received few benefits from import restrictions, because the United States was a net exporter of most agricultural goods, aside from wool and sugar. Midwestern farmers produced grains and meat, while Southern farmers produced cotton and tobacco; the country sold half of its cotton, a third of its tobacco, and a fifth of its wheat and flour to foreign markets. "The contention of the supporters of this bill that it is an agricultural measure is ridiculous," insisted John Garner of Texas. "With few exceptions the increases upon agricultural products are inoperative, and practically every increase upon the products of manufactures is operative."[61] By contrast, most agricultural imports were in categories of goods for which there was either no domestic production, such as coffee and tea, or very limited domestic production, such as various tropical fruits. For example, one agricultural producer advocated a tariff of 75 cents per bunch on imported bananas—not because the United States produced bananas but because "the enormous imports of cheap bananas into the United States tend to curtail the domestic consumption of fresh fruits produced in the United States," particularly apples.[62]

Subsequent studies have sought to determine the underlying political and economic factors behind the passage of the Hawley-Smoot bill. In a classic 1935 study, *Politics, Pressures, and the Tariff*, political scientist E. E. Schattschneider attributed the act not to party politics or an ideological attachment to protection, but to the absence of any force that would stop producer groups from demanding and Congress from providing higher duties. Focusing primarily on the public hearings that Congress held, Schattschneider (1935, 285) expected that the economic interests supporting and opposing the tariff would be approximately equal, but found instead that the pressures exerted upon Congress were "extremely unbalanced. . . . The pressures supporting the tariff are made overwhelming by the fact that the opposition is negligible." Schattschneider (1935, 109) described the highly skewed forces confronting Congress this way: "The primary, positive, offensive activity of domestic producers seeking increased duties almost completely dominated the whole process of legislation. The pressures from this quarter were more aggressive, more powerful, and more fruitful by a wide margin of difference than all of the others combined." Opposition to higher tariffs by consumer groups or importers was "usually inconsequential," Schattschneider (114, 141) noted, and "opposition to duties based on a dissent from the philosophy of protection was extremely rare."

Schattschneider (1935, 127–28) explained the imbalance between the forces in favor of higher tariffs and those opposed on the grounds that the "benefits are concentrated while costs are distributed." As he noted, "The benefits of the legislation to an individual producer are obvious while many of the costs are obscure. The benefits, moreover, are directly associated with a single duty, or at most, a few duties, while costs tend to rise from multitudes of them." This explained why Congress heard almost exclusively from businesses, with little participation by labor, consumers, or the broader community in the legislative process.[63] Furthermore, the practice of "reciprocal non-interference" meant that producers would not oppose higher duties for other producers; the unspoken rule was that it is "proper for each to seek duties for himself but improper and unfair to oppose duties sought by others." Schattschneider (283) concluded that protective tariffs were "politically invincible" and that tariff policy was "a dubious economic policy turned into a great political success. The policy has been firmly established in public favor, . . . and nearly all important opposition has, for the time being, disappeared."

Yet because he focused almost exclusively on the public hearings, Schattschneider painted an incomplete—indeed, a misleading—picture of the whole legislative process. It is certainly true that Congress received a very selective view of the range of economic interests affected by tariff legislation at committee hearings, because only a small number of producer interests tended to participate in that venue. But by choosing to focus on the committee hearings and not the debates on the House and Senate floor, he neglected to examine the opposition to the measure by most Democrats in both chambers and by Republicans representing agricultural states. Furthermore, Schattschneider gave the impression that Congress was simply responding to producer interests, whereas, as pointed out earlier, industry had not been clamoring for higher duties in 1928 and 1929. Rather, Republican politicians were offering higher duties to placate agricultural interests and lost control of the process.

THE GREAT DEPRESSION AND
THE COLLAPSE OF US TRADE

The United States reached a business-cycle peak in the summer of 1929 as the Senate was holding hearings on the bill. Over the next three and a half years, the United States experienced an unrelenting economic contraction that became known as the Great Depression. Although the economic decline began well before the implementation of the new tariff in June 1930, many observers have linked the Hawley-Smoot tariff to the economic catastrophe that followed in its wake. What is the relationship between the Hawley-Smoot tariff, the collapse of US trade, and the Great Depression more generally?

Between 1929 and 1932, the United States experienced one of the worst peacetime collapses of its trade in history, excluding the embargo of 1808–09. During this period, the value of exports and imports fell nearly 70 percent, partly due to falling prices. In quantity terms, the volume of exports fell 49 percent, and the volume of imports fell 40 percent over those three years. The drop in trade was much greater than the decline in real GDP, which fell 25 percent over that period. By 1932, exports had shrunk to just 2.7 percent of GDP from 5.0 percent in 1929, while imports fell to 2.0 percent of GDP from 3.8 percent of GDP in 1929.[64]

How much did the Hawley-Smoot tariff contribute to this unprecedented decline in trade? As we have seen, the Hawley-Smoot act raised the average tariff rate on dutiable imports by about six percentage points, or 15 percent. There are two reasons why a tariff increase of this magnitude would have a modest effect on imports. First, a 15 percent increase in the price of dutiable imports, in which the average tariff rises from 40 percent to 46 percent, does not translate into a 15 percent increase in the domestic price of imports. An imported good that costs $1 would sell for $1.40 before and $1.46 after the new tariff, an increase of about 4 percent in the price paid by consumers. Second, only one-third of imports in 1929 were subject to duty, partly because high tariffs already discouraged such imports. Still, two-thirds of imports (usually raw materials, such as silk, coffee, and rubber) entered the United States free of duty before the Hawley-Smoot duties took effect.

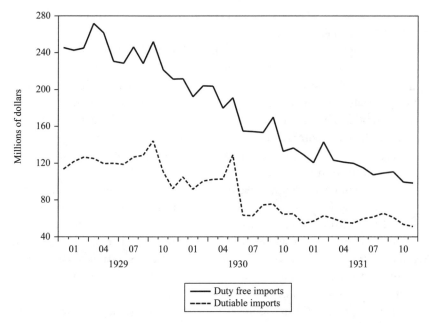

Figure 8.4. Value of imports, dutiable and duty-free, by month, 1929–1931. (*Monthly Summary of Foreign Commerce*, December 1930 and December 1931.)

The impact of the higher duties on imports can be seen in figure 8.4, which presents monthly data on imports of dutiable goods and duty-free goods. A sharp drop in the value of dutiable imports is clearly evident in July 1930. Dutiable imports fell 34 percent in the three months after its imposition compared to the three months prior to its imposition (excluding June when imports surged as merchants sought to clear goods through customs before the higher tariffs took effect). Duty-free imports fell 14 percent over the same period. Taking duty-free imports as a control group, this comparison suggests that the Hawley-Smoot act reduced dutiable imports by about 20 percent. Since dutiable imports comprised one-third of total imports, this would imply that total imports fell about 7 percent as a result of the higher tariffs.[65] Thus, the tariff had a substantial impact on dutiable imports but a modest effect on overall imports.

This decline is relatively small in comparison to the subsequent collapse in trade. The volume of imports fell 41 percent between the second quarter of 1930 and its trough in the third quarter of 1932. The most important factor behind this collapse was the steady decline in real GDP, which fell 30 percent on a quarterly basis during this period.[66] Indeed, the volume of imports had already fallen 15 percent in the year prior to the imposition of the Hawley-Smoot tariff (1929:Q2–1930:Q2), a period when real GDP declined 7 percent.

As a rough calculation, higher tariffs account for about half the 41 percent decline in import volume from 1929–32. Depending on the assumption about the elasticity of import demand, the higher Hawley-Smoot duties probably accounted for about 7 percentage points of the decline, and the deflation-induced increase in duties accounted for about 15 percentage points. Thus, the combined impact of the higher tariff rates and deflation-induced increase in duties explains a significant part of the decline in imports, but far from the entire collapse.

What about the even greater drop in exports between 1929 and 1932? The declining foreign demand for US goods was due to several factors, including declining foreign incomes due to the Great Depression abroad; higher foreign tariffs, trade preferences, and other trade restrictions aimed directly or indirectly at the United States; the depreciation of the British pound against the dollar in late 1931 until early 1933; and other factors that are difficult to quantify with precision.

Turning to the Great Depression more generally, there is little doubt that it was one of the greatest economic calamities in US history. The period from mid-1929 until early 1933 was marked by severe deflation, falling output, and rising unemployment. From August 1929 to March 1933, industrial production fell 55 percent, the wholesale price index slid 37 percent, and farm prices plunged 64 percent. On a quarterly basis, real GDP declined 36 percent between the business-cycle peak in the third quarter of 1929 and its trough in the first quarter of 1933; on an annual basis, real GDP fell 25 percent between 1929 and 1932. The unemployment rate is estimated to have reached 24.9 percent in 1932, up from 4.6 percent in 1929. Even after the economy turned the corner in 1933 and began to grow, the recovery was incomplete and sputtered at various times; for example, the economy suffered another severe recession in 1937–38. As late as 1939 the unemployment rate was still more than 17 percent, or 12 percent if those working in temporary government relief programs are included.[67]

As we have seen, the Hawley-Smoot tariff itself was not a response to the Great Depression. Preparation for tariff revision began in late 1928, well before the stock market crash, the slide in industrial production, and the increase in unemployment. Although the economic decline following the business-cycle peak in August 1929 probably made the Senate more favorable to the tariff legislation in early 1930, the recession was still relatively mild at this point. The slump intensified after a banking panic in late 1930, a tightening of monetary and financial conditions in late 1931, and a continued economic slide through much of 1932, and it culminated in a severe banking crisis in early 1933.

Because the Depression followed so closely on the heels of the tariff increase, many people at the time believed that the Hawley-Smoot tariff was responsible for the economic disaster. However, as in the case of previous downturns, the consensus among economic historians is that monetary and financial factors were the dominant cause of the Great Depression. Friedman and Schwartz (1963) contend that a banking panic in October 1930 led to a large, unanticipated fall in the money supply that turned what had been a fairly normal recession into the Great Depression. The panic led the public to withdraw currency from the banking system because there was no deposit insurance; if a bank failed, depositors would lose all of their money. The loss of deposits forced banks to curtail lending, which reduced investment spending, and contributed to the decline in the money supply, which led to deflation and reinforced all these problems. With deflation, real interest rates soared, and investment collapsed. Falling prices also increased the real burden of debt, making it harder for borrowers to repay banks, which in turn increased the fragility of the financial system. Many economists blame the Federal Reserve for not taking more aggressive action to stop the bank failures and the decline in the money supply, actions that could have prevented the Depression.[68]

At the global level, most countries were on the gold standard at this time, which was another source of deflationary pressure. An increase in the demand for gold by central banks in the late 1920s, with no commensurate increase in the supply, produced a tightening of monetary conditions that reduce the world price level.[69] The gold standard linked the world's leading economies through a regime of fixed exchange rates, which enabled the rapid transmission of monetary shocks and financial disturbances from one country to another. For example, after Britain abandoned the gold standard in September 1931, the United States rapidly began to lose gold reserves. The Federal Reserve responded by sharply raising interest rates to prevent the gold outflow and maintain the value of the dollar against other currencies. In doing so, the Federal Reserve chose to maintain the gold peg rather than help the domestic economy, tightening monetary policy when the economy was very weak. This led to more deflation and bank failures and simply intensified the Depression.

Given the overriding importance of monetary and financial factors in bringing about the Great Depression, the Hawley-Smoot tariff almost surely played a relatively small role in the economic crisis. In 1929, dutiable imports constituted just 1.4 percent of GDP. It is hard to believe that an increase in the average tariff from 40 percent to 46 percent on those imports could lead to an economic collapse on the scale of the Great Depression. As we have seen in earlier chapters, there are no strong theoretical or empirical grounds for concluding that higher tariffs are driving factors in business-cycle fluctuations. For example, the much larger Fordney-McCumber tariff increase in 1922 was followed by an economic recovery, itself the result of other factors.

And yet there are several channels by which the tariff might have ameliorated or exacerbated the Depression. Dornbusch and Fischer (1986, 468–69) suggest that a tariff might have helped the economy, because "from either a Keynesian or a monetarist perspective, the tariff by itself would have been an expansionary impulse in the absence of retaliation. In the Keynesian view, the reduction in imports diverts demand to domestic goods; in the monetarist view the gold inflow increases the domestic money stock if not sterilized."

From a Keynesian perspective, a tariff shifts domestic expenditure from foreign goods to domestic goods. If the tariff reduces spending on imports, without adversely affecting exports, then net exports increase and expand aggregate demand for domestic goods.[70] However, there is no evidence that the Keynesian mechanism was operative at this time. If it had been, imports would have declined more than exports, and real net exports would have contributed to economic growth. In fact, the opposite was the case: exports fell even more than imports, and real net exports were a drag on the economy, providing no stimulus to aggregate demand.[71]

From a monetarist perspective, an increase in the tariff could lead to a larger surplus in the balance of trade, because imports would fall with no immediate change in exports. The incipient trade surplus would generate an inflow of gold and an expansion of the money supply, unless the central bank sterilizes the gold inflow by taking offsetting policy actions to leave monetary conditions unchanged. This monetary expansion would give the economy a short-run boost but eventually lead to higher prices and return the balance of trade to its original position. However, in the two months immediately following the imposition of the Hawley-Smoot tariff, the United States actually exported large amounts of gold. This gold outflow was sterilized by the Federal Reserve so that it had no effect on monetary conditions. Subsequent gold inflows were relatively small, yet the money supply declined due to the onset of the first banking crisis, which sharply reduced the ratio of deposits to currency. Even if the Hawley-Smoot tariff led to some gold inflows after it was imposed, which is not clear, that would have been completely swamped by other factors.

Furthermore, the Federal Reserve's policy of sterilizing gold inflows and outflows meant that any such gold inflows would not have led to monetary expansion.[72] Thus, neither the Keynesian nor the monetarist channels through which the tariff might have provided a short-run stimulus to the economy was operational during this period. Even if they had worked, their effects would have been an extremely small offset to the enormous monetary and financial shocks of the period.

There are other mechanisms by which the Hawley-Smoot tariff might have exacerbated the Great Depression. In a standard trade framework, the higher tariff would have reduced America's real income by eliminating some of the static gains from trade. Yet the static welfare losses associated with Hawley-Smoot tariff were probably very small, certainly in comparison to the magnitude of the Depression.[73] Crucini and Kahn (1996; 2007) argue that the adverse macroeconomic effects of trade policy can be much larger once one allows for trade in intermediate inputs and takes into account the dynamics of capital accumulation and labor supply that result from a permanent change in the tariff, as well as foreign retaliation. In their simulation, the higher tariff could have brought about a 2 percent decline in GDP, which is significant but still very far from the observed 25 percent decline in real GDP.

Of course, some economists believe the Hawley-Smoot tariff played a significant role in the onset of the Depression. Meltzer (1976, 469–70) contends that it "worked to convert a sizeable recession into a severe depression" by attracting gold from other countries, thereby contributing to the deflationary impulse sent around the world. Meltzer also suggests that the Hawley-Smoot tariff and foreign retaliation were particularly detrimental to agricultural exports, thereby reducing farm prices and leading to bank failures in farm states in 1930 and 1931. Yet farm prices started falling a year before the enactment of the tariff, and their downward trend seemed unaffected by it. The rate of farm foreclosure was no higher in 1930 or 1931 than it had been in the late 1920s; only as the severity of the Depression intensified in 1932 and 1933 did it reach the incredible rates of 28 and 39 percent.[74] And although the banking panics were concentrated in agricultural regions, such as the Midwest farm states and the cotton South, historians have shown that these banking problems were due to bad management practices and not declining exports. Finally, there was another factor at work: a severe drought in the late summer of 1930 that devastated the south-central United States.

The Hawley-Smoot tariff might have adversely affected the economy in other ways during this period. One contention is that Congress's lengthy consideration of the tariff bill contributed to business uncertainty, thereby leading to the postponement of investment and the slide into recession. While the collapse in investment was a major contributor to the economic decline in the early 1930s, the resolution of uncertainty about the tariff after June 1930 does not appear to have helped the economy at all.[75] Another argument is that, by restricting the exports of European and Latin American countries to the United States, the tariff made it more difficult for those countries to earn dollars and service their debts. This may have disrupted the international financial system and might have forced foreign countries to default on their World War I loans, but any such effects were extremely small.[76]

In sum, the consensus among most economists is that the Hawley-Smoot tariff played a relatively small role in either exacerbating or ameliorating the Great Depression. The effect of the tariff was almost certainly minimal in comparison to the powerful deflationary forces at work through the monetary and financial system. When compared to a decline in the money supply by one-third, even a substantial change in tariff policy is unlikely to have had any significant macroeconomic effects, particularly when dutiable imports were just 1.4 percent of GDP.

FOREIGN RETALIATION AND THE DESTRUCTION OF THE WORLD TRADING SYSTEM

While it was not responsible for the Great Depression, the Hawley-Smoot tariff contributed to the severe deterioration in trade relations in the early 1930s. The tariff hike came at a critical moment for the world economy and helped undermine fragile multilateral efforts to limit the spread of trade barriers. After the World Economic Conference of 1927, the League of Nations sought to hold regular meetings to encourage the expansion of trade and limit the use of protectionist measures. The League tried to negotiate a tariff truce in 1930 and 1931, but the US action and other policy developments helped discourage these efforts. Even though it was not a member of the League, the United States may have made it easier for other countries to raise their own import duties and impose their own trade restrictions. "The Hawley-Smoot tariff in the United States was the signal for an outburst of tariff-making activity in other countries, partly at least by way of reprisals," the League of Nations (1932, 193) reported at the time. "Extensive increases in duties were made almost immediately by Canada, Cuba, Mexico, France, Italy, [and] Spain."

As the Hawley-Smoot bill was being debated in Congress, foreign governments warned that it would have adverse consequences for world trade, and US trade in particular, should it be enacted. Near the end of its consideration of the bill, the Senate passed a resolution (with the votes of Democrats and progressive Republicans) requesting that the Hoover administration report all of the foreign protests filed with the State Department. As of September 1929, there were fifty-nine protests from twenty-three countries, mainly in Western Europe. Another forty-two foreign governments filed protests after that date.[77]

In ushering the tariff legislation through Congress, the Republican leadership never seriously acknowledged the possibility that foreign governments might take action against US exports. Smoot and other Republicans believed that "the tariff is a domestic matter, and an American tariff must be framed and put into force by the American Congress and administration. No foreign country has a right to interfere."[78] While true enough, that missed the point: other countries were not interfering in the legislative process, but simply warning that they might take countermeasures if the legislation were enacted. Although eastern Republicans voted against an export debenture for agricultural goods on the grounds that foreign countries would simply negate the subsidy with countervailing duties, they seemed to ignore the possibility that foreign countries would retaliate against the higher tariffs by raising their duties on American exports. While there are twenty pages of debate in the *Congressional Record* on the duty to be imposed on imported tomatoes, there is very little consideration of the international response to the higher tariffs. Any mention by Democrats of possible foreign retaliation was dismissed by Republicans as hypothetical.

In fact, several countries did retaliate. Canada's reaction was by far the most significant. Canada was the most important foreign market for US goods, taking nearly 20 percent of US exports in 1929. About 43 percent of Canada's exports were sent to the United States; this dependence made it quite sensitive to changes in its access to the US market. The Liberal government of Prime Minister Mackenzie King, which traditionally had pursued pro-American, low-tariff policies, expressed its concern to the Hoover administration about the pending tariff legislation on several occasions as the bill worked its way through Congress.

After the tariff passed, the King government immediately reduced duties on 270 goods imported from the British Empire and imposed countervailing duties on sixteen American products that comprised nearly a third of US exports to Canada. These goods included potatoes, soups, livestock, fresh meats, butter and eggs, wheat and wheat flour, oats and oatmeal, and cast iron pipe—most of them agricultural products that the new US tariff was supposedly designed to help. Cordell Hull (1948, 1:355) used a simple example to illustrate how the Hawley-Smoot tariff backfired against the United States. After the US tariff on imported eggs rose from 8 cents to 10 cents a dozen, Canada followed by raising its tariff on imported eggs from 3 cents to 10 cents a dozen to match the US rate. While US imports of eggs from Canada fell from 13,299 dozen in 1929 to 7,939 dozen in 1932, American exports of eggs to Canada dropped from 919,543 dozen to 13,662 dozen over the same period.

Of even greater significance, Canadian backlash against the Hawley-Smoot duties contributed to the election of the pro-British, high-tariff Conservative party in the general election of July 1930. The opposition Conservatives had attacked the initial retaliation as inadequate and hoped to capitalize on the Canadian electorate's anger about the US action, particularly in regions producing goods exported to the United States. The anti-American message found fertile ground. "By arousing nationalistic sentiments and contempt for the United States in Canada," Kottman (1975, 633) observed, "the Smoot-Hawley Tariff provided a climate in which the [Conservatives'] ultra-protectionist rhetoric had greater appeal than the [Liberals'] endorsement of expanded imperial trade." The Conservatives won the election, and swing votes in Quebec and the Prairie Provinces, whose exports were particularly harmed by the US tariff, influenced the outcome.[79]

In September 1930, the new Conservative government passed an emergency tariff that substantially increased import duties on goods such as textiles, agricultural implements, electrical equipment, meats, and many others, most of which came from the United States. Officials did not use the word *retaliation* to describe the action, but the message was clear. "Despite Canadian denials of reciprocal action aimed at the United States in the new Dominion tariff schedules," the *New York Times* reported, "the impression appeared to be rather general tonight that Canada had made the only answer possible to the American tariff bill, and in a form which might affect an international trade situation that has already shown alarming symptoms."[80] One estimate suggests that US exports to Canada fell 21 percent as a result of the higher Canadian tariffs, enough to wipe out 4 percent of total exports.[81] As reported earlier, the Hawley-Smoot tariff reduced total imports by about 7 percent, but if exports fell by 4 percent as a result of Canada's reaction alone, the retaliatory offset to exports almost matches half the impact of the tariff on imports. And if other countries retaliated as well, it is easy to see why exports declined as much as imports after 1930.

In Europe, the reaction to the American tariff "was disapproval—immediate, undisguised, and unanimous," as Bidwell (1930, 130) reported. The European press and public opinion, industry and agricultural groups, government officials, and business leaders were appalled by the action. In their view, the world's largest creditor nation, with a substantial trade surplus, was needlessly restricting the exports of countries that were desperately trying to pay off their burdensome World War I debts. The world's leading economic power—a country that had enjoyed robust economic growth through the 1920s while Europe struggled with postwar reconstruction—had just significantly increased its tariffs for no justifiable reason after having already raised duties in 1922. And the United States had not only refused to join the League of Nations, but it was now undermining the League's efforts to negotiate a multilateral tariff truce.[82] These were some of the reasons behind the European resentment that greeted the US action.

Although the new tariff was a diplomatic affront, the overall economic effect of the duties on Europe was limited, because only 6 percent of European exports were destined for the United States. Still, this figure grossly understates the potential impact. In economic terms, European exports to the United States were crucial in earning the scarce dollars that Europe needed to pay debts and finance imports. These exports often consisted of highly specialized manufactured goods in key industries. Because American manufacturers were so efficient at mass production and protected by high tariffs, European exporters faced significant obstacles in selling in the United States. Only European producers of high-priced specialty goods could overcome the high import duties and maintain a position in the market. Yet in some cases, the new duties were designed to squeeze out even these goods, which were minor from the standpoint of the American economy but critical for European manufacturers.

Unlike Canada, however, Britain, France, Germany, and other European countries generally refrained from retaliating directly against the United States. Often they were prevented from doing so by commercial treaties that guaranteed MFN treatment for American goods, although there were many subtle ways of discriminating against US goods. However, several smaller European countries took direct action against the United States, including Spain, Italy, Switzerland, and Portugal. Spain passed a new tariff in July 1930 that withdrew MFN treatment for American goods, allowing it to discriminate against the United States. It took aim at several leading US exports to the country, notably automobiles, sewing machines, and razor blades. American car exports to Spain dropped 94 percent in three years, while British, German, and Canadian vehicles were unaffected by the duties and saw their sales surge.[83] Italy also targeted imports of automobiles, farm equipment, and radios, all goods imported from the United States. Outraged by the higher tariff on watches, various groups in Switzerland organized a boycott of American goods. Still, the combined impact of these measures against US exports was probably slight.

The Hawley-Smoot tariff had ramifications in other countries. The higher tariff on imported sugar had a devastating impact on Cuba, whose economy was largely driven by sugar exports to the United States. Dye and Sicotte (2003) estimate that one-third to one-half of the decline in Cuba's export earnings after 1930 was caused by the new duties. According to their calculations, the sugar tariff erased 10 percent of Cuba's national income between 1929 and 1933, amounting to more than a third of the overall decline in Cuba's GDP over that period. Cubans felt betrayed by the higher duties, and the country's severe economic problems led to the overthrow of the pro-American government in the revolution of 1933. The revolution fundamentally changed the country's politics, and the country began to distance itself from the United States.

Of course, as the Great Depression spread around the world, purely domestic considerations probably would have led to higher tariffs in other countries even if Congress had not passed the Hawley-Smoot tariff. However, because the United States was one of the first to raise its tariffs as the Depression intensified, it signaled a breakdown in policy discipline and a wave of tariff increases in other countries soon followed, even if they were not directed specifically against the United States.

The Hawley-Smoot tariff was a damaging development from the standpoint of the world economy and contributed to the global rise in protectionist sentiment in the early 1930s. However, the real collapse of the world trading system began with the failure of a major Austrian bank in June 1931. While this banking crisis was more a symptom rather than a cause of the difficulties in the world economy, which had already suffered from nearly two years of recession and deflation, it sparked a chain reaction that had enormous consequences for trade policy. The Austrian bank failure produced a financial panic and a currency crisis that spread to neighboring countries. The crisis forced Germany to impose exchange controls in July 1931 to prevent the outflow of gold and stop the downward pressure on the mark in foreign exchange markets. Facing a rapid loss of gold and foreign exchange reserves, other central European countries followed Germany by imposing strict controls on foreign exchange transactions that impeded trade and capital flows alike.

Financial pressure then spread to Britain. After intervening to support the pound on foreign exchange markets, Britain relented in September 1931 by abandoning the gold standard and allowing the pound to depreciate against other currencies. The depreciation of sterling meant that British exports were significantly more price-competitive on world markets, while imports were more expensive. Other countries whose currency was tied to the pound sterling, including Denmark, Finland, India, Norway, and Sweden, also left the gold standard and allowed their currencies to depreciate. Japan followed in December 1931.

While there were sound reasons for Britain's decision, it also contributed to the breakdown of international trade relations. First, the British action triggered a defensive reaction by countries that remained on the gold standard. These countries responded by imposing higher trade barriers against countries whose currency had depreciated. A month after the British decision, France imposed a 15 percent surcharge on British goods to offset the depreciation of sterling. In early 1932, the Netherlands, which traditionally had a policy of free trade, increased duties by 25 percent, partly to offset the competitive advantage gained by sterling area producers. Second, the British move stopped the speculative attack on the pound but put other countries under financial pressure and led them to impose exchange controls. In September–October 1931, Uruguay, Colombia, Greece, Czechoslovakia, Iceland, Boliva, Yugoslavia, Austria, Argentina, Belgium, Norway, and Denmark all imposed exchange controls to prevent a loss of gold and foreign exchange reserves.[84] Many countries that remained on the gold standard also imposed import quotas; by 1936, nearly two-thirds of French imports were covered by quantitative restrictions.

Exchange controls turned out to be among the most restrictive trade practices of the 1930s. Governments began regulating access to foreign exchange not only to prevent capital flight but also to curtail spending on imports. In essence, governments determined what and how much would be imported. Exchange controls enabled government officials to slash spending on imports: imports in exchange-control countries were 23 percent lower than in non–exchange control countries, conditional on the change in their GDP in the early 1930s.[85] Foreign exchange controls were supplemented with higher tariffs and quotas to further limit spending on imports and reduce the drain on the balance of payments.

As a result, the multilateral system of world trade began to implode as

countries with balance-of-payments problems resorted to bilateral clearing arrangements, exchange controls, import quotas, licensing systems,
and much higher tariffs in a fruitless attempt to insulate their economies
from the worldwide economic collapse. Indeed, the disintegration of the
gold standard in late 1931 created many more problems for trade policy
around the world than the Hawley-Smoot tariff had in mid-1930. As the
League of Nations (1933, 16–17) reported,

> In the sixteen months after September 1, 1931, general tariff increases
> had been imposed in twenty-three countries, in three of them twice
> during the period—with only one case of a general tariff reduction.
> Customs duties had been increased on individual items or groups of
> commodities by fifty countries. . . . Import quotas, prohibitions, licens-
> ing systems and similar quantitative restrictions, with even more fre-
> quent changes in several important cases, had been imposed by thirty-
> two countries. . . . This bare list is utterly inadequate to portray the
> harassing complexity of the emergency restrictions that were superim-
> posed upon an already fettered world trade after the period of exchange
> instability was inaugurated by the abandonment of the gold standard
> by the United Kingdom in September 1931. By the middle of 1932, it
> was obvious that the international trading mechanism was in real dan-
> ger of being smashed as completely as the international monetary sys-
> tem had [been].

As other countries sank deeper into the Depression, they imposed more
restrictions on imports in an effort to stimulate their domestic economies.
As more countries raised trade barriers, they provided an excuse for others to follow. Because a reduction in one country's imports amounted to a
reduction in another country's exports, these "beggar thy neighbor" policies were a futile attempt to stimulate growth. No country could insulate
itself from the effects of the depression via increased trade barriers.

To compound these problems, Britain followed the devaluation of the
pound by abandoning its traditional policy of free trade. A month after
Britain left the gold standard, a general election returned a National Government dominated by the Conservative party, which had traditionally
favored protection and imperial preferences. In November 1931, the new
Parliament enacted the Abnormal Importations Act, which gave the Board
of Trade administrative discretion to increase tariffs by up to 100 percent
on goods it deemed fit. In February 1932, Parliament approved the Import
Duties Act of 1932, which imposed a general tariff of 10 percent on all im-

ports. This marked an end to Britain's long-standing policy of open trade. Whereas 70 percent of US exports entered Britain duty-free in 1930, only 20 percent did by the end of 1931.[86]

Even worse, from the US perspective, Britain began to retreat into an imperial economic bloc by establishing tariff preferences for trade among the former British colonies, principally Australia, Canada, New Zealand, and South Africa. These countries had long sought preferential access for their exports of agricultural goods and raw materials in Britain, offering preferences for British manufactures in exchange. Britain was never previously in a position to offer tariff preferences to others because since the mid-nineteenth century it had generally adhered to a policy of non-discriminatory free trade. But now, having imposed a 10 percent general tariff, the country was in a position to do so.

At a conference in Ottawa in July–August 1932, Britain agreed to establish such imperial preferences. Although this trade bloc was not created in direct retaliation against the United States, it was a product of the international climate that the Hawley-Smoot tariff helped foster. "Unquestionably the American Congress had precipitated the tariff responses in both Canada and the United Kingdom," Kottman (1968, 37) concluded. "Shortly before the Ottawa Conference, the American chargé in the Canadian capital reported a 'quiet but definite undercurrent of antagonism and bitterness towards the United States trade policy' whenever comments were made of the impending gathering." Furthermore, this official noted, "most of the people I have talked to have not failed to refer to our tariff and to accuse it of starting the world movement toward restriction of trade." Indeed, Canada's prime minister defended the Ottawa agreements before Parliament by stating that the country needed to secure preferences on its exports to Britain to make up for the lost markets in the United States.

These preferences discriminated against the United States in two of its largest export markets, Canada and Britain, which together took more than a third of US exports. By 1937, about half of British exports to and imports from the Commonwealth enjoyed preferences of about 20 percent, on average. This put American exporters at a significant competitive disadvantage in selling into these markets and led to a decline in the US share of Canadian and British imports.[87] As we will see, the United States spent the next two decades trying to dismantle this discriminatory trade bloc that put its exporters at such a significant disadvantage in major foreign markets.

The British imperial system was not the only preferential trade bloc that emerged at this time that was detrimental to American commercial interests. In 1931, Germany began licensing imports and sought preferential trade agreements with countries in south Eastern Europe. In Asia, Japan created what it called the "Great East Asia Co-Prosperity Sphere" in which it used its political and military influence for economic gain, such as the exclusive control of raw materials and natural resources.

Thus, the entire multilateral system of world trade was shattered by events of the early 1930s. Trade was burdened not just with higher tariffs, but a proliferation of import-licensing requirements, quotas and quantitative restrictions, foreign exchange controls, bilateral and preferential trade agreements, bulk trading and barter arrangements, and so on.[88] These policies severely impeded world trade, the volume of which fell by 26 percent between 1929 and 1933. Nearly half of this decline was due to higher tariffs and non-tariff barriers, according to Madsen (2001), many of which discriminated against the United States.

As a result, the trade policy environment around the world was dramatically different in 1932 than it had been just three years earlier. The problem was not just increased worldwide protectionism and discrimination aimed at the United States in particular, but that these trade barriers and preferential policies were not relaxed when the economic recovery finally came later in the decade. Most of the trade restrictions remained in place; thus, despite the recovery of world production by the late 1930s, world trade had failed to reach its 1929 peak by the end of the decade.

The Hoover administration never responded to these developments. The president blamed the Depression on Europe, not on domestic monetary policy or financial instability, and insisted that high tariffs were needed to protect the American economy from imports. Congressional Republicans expressed no regrets about having enacted higher duties on imports, which they said were needed now more than ever. Smoot (1931, 173–74) insisted that "in this hour of national distress protection is imperative." Without the tariff, "America would have become a dumping ground for all the surplus products of the world." Smoot denied that the United States started the worldwide movement toward higher trade barriers: "It is difficult to understand why anyone should try to fasten responsibility for the general movement toward higher protective duties upon the United States. Many nations revised their tariffs before Congress passed the Smoot-Hawley bill in June 1930, and many have increased their duties since. Each country has been prompted by economic considerations of its own."

Although Republicans tried to defend their policies against Democratic attacks, the economic slump diminished the electoral prospects of incumbents. Not surprisingly, Democrats won control of the House in the midterm election in 1930. With the aid of progressive Republicans, Democrats also achieved a working majority in the Senate on trade issues. With Hoover still in the White House, however, divided government from 1931 until 1933 ensured that there would be no major policy changes.

The widespread perception that the Hawley-Smoot tariff was at least partly responsible for the economic disaster of the period helped rejuvenate the dormant low-tariff wing of the Democratic party. In August 1931, Sen. Kenneth McKellar (D-TN) proposed repealing the Hawley-Smoot tariff and enacting an immediate, across-the-board tariff cut of 25 percent. Although most Democrats thought that the tariff increase had been unwise, this idea was a political nonstarter. Even they could not muster any political support for a unilateral tariff reduction when the country was experiencing rising unemployment and falling output.

Instead, Democrats and progressive Republicans sought a different approach. Disillusioned by the way the "flexible tariff" provision had been employed to raise tariffs during the 1920s, they rallied behind a proposal from James Collier (D-MS), the chairman of the Ways and Means Committee, to wrest from the president the ability to adjust tariff rates and give Congress that authority instead. The bill would also create an office of consumers' council, so that consumer interests, and not just those of producers, would be represented when tariff changes were contemplated. Finally, in view of the deterioration in international trade relations, the bill invited the president to confer with other countries to improve the trade situation, although it did not authorize the reduction of any tariffs in such negotiations.[89]

Congress passed the Collier bill in early 1932, but the president vetoed it. In his veto message, Hoover objected to the elimination of presidential authority over the flexible tariff, arguing that the provision was "the proper way to eliminate excessive duties and any injustices in the tariff and to provide flexibility to changed economic conditions." Because of the depreciation of foreign currencies and lower foreign prices, Hoover argued that "there never has been a time in the history of the United States when tariff protection was more essential to the welfare of the American people than at present" and that it was "imperative that the American protective policy be maintained."

Hoover also dismissed the call for international negotiations, arguing that tariff policy was "solely a domestic question." He worried that such a conference "would surrender our own control of an important part of our domestic affairs to the influence of other nations or alternatively would lead us into futilities in international negotiations." Instead, he offered this challenge: "If the Congress proposes to make such a radical change in our historic policies by international negotiation affecting the whole of American tariffs, then it is the duty of the Congress to state so frankly and indicate the extent to which it is prepared to go."[90] As the United States approached the 1932 presidential election, the economy remained stuck in the Depression and the future of trade policy was highly uncertain.

PART III

Reciprocity

CHAPTER NINE

The New Deal and Reciprocal Trade Agreements, 1932–1943

The Great Depression produced a major political realignment in favor of the Democrats, who brought about a historic transformation in US trade policy. In 1934, at the request of the Roosevelt administration, Congress enacted the Reciprocal Trade Agreements Act (RTAA) which authorized the president to reduce import duties in trade agreements negotiated with other countries. In making an unprecedented grant of power to the executive, the RTAA changed the process of trade policymaking and put import duties on a downward path. This chapter explains how such a radical change was possible just a few years after Congress enacted high duties in the Hawley-Smoot tariff of 1930.

TRADE POLICY AND THE NEW DEAL

The central issue in the presidential election of 1932 was President Herbert Hoover's handling of the Great Depression.[1] Despite some government efforts, including limited public works spending, new federal relief programs, and loans from the Reconstruction Finance Corporation, Hoover's policies failed to ameliorate the nation's economic crisis. The monetary contraction continued through the first quarter of 1933, with production continuing to slide and unemployment continuing to increase.

Because of the lingering controversy over the Hawley-Smoot tariff and its contribution to the world's economic disaster, the election campaign paid some attention to the trade policy differences between the two parties. Hoover and the Republicans defended the recent tariff increase and, in light of the country's bleak economic situation, strongly opposed any reduction in import duties. They even suggested that further tariff hikes might be necessary to offset the depreciation of foreign currencies against the dollar, particularly after Britain and sterling bloc countries left the gold standard in September 1931. The Republican platform affirmed that the party "has always been the staunch supporter of the American system of a protective tariff. It believes that the home market, built up under that policy, the greatest and richest market in the world, belongs first to American agriculture, industry and labor. No pretext can justify the surrender of that market to such competition as would destroy our farms, mines, and factories, and lower the standard of living which we have established for our workers."[2]

Meanwhile, the Democrats were again divided into high-tariff and low-tariff factions based largely on geography. The northern faction, led by the 1928 presidential nominee, Al Smith, and party chair John Jakob Raskob, controlled the Democratic National Committee and tried to write a high-tariff plank into the party's platform. Raskob's apparent acceptance of the status quo and suggestion that the party should not reduce tariffs that could harm industrial producers dismayed the party's southern base, which strongly objected to the Hawley-Smoot tariff.[3] Led by its senior statesman, Cordell Hull of Tennessee, the party's southern wing still championed Woodrow Wilson's goal of reducing tariffs, particularly if it could undo the damage to US exports. This group insisted that the party take a stand because "there must be more than mere hair-splitting differences between the two political parties on tariff and commercial policy"[4]

The Democratic presidential candidate, Franklin Roosevelt, did not have a clearly articulated view on trade policy, but he rejected the Smith-Raskob attempt to fix the party's platform in a way that would alienate the southern wing of the party. As a result, the Democratic platform stated, "We condemn the Hawley-Smoot Tariff Law, the prohibitive rates of which have resulted in retaliatory action by more than forty countries, created international economic hostility, destroyed international trade, driven our factories into foreign countries, robbed the American farmer of his foreign markets, and increased the cost of production." But the compromise plank also fell short of calling for tariff reductions, proposing instead "a competitive tariff for revenue with a fact-finding tariff commission free from executive interference, reciprocal tariff agreements with other nations, and an international economic conference designed to restore international trade and facilitate exchange."[5]

In formulating his position, Roosevelt received a wide range of advice. Raymond Moley, one of Roosevelt's close advisers and a member of his so-called brain trust, was responsible for drafting the main campaign speech on the tariff. "No speech in the campaign was such a headache as this,"

Moley (1939, 50, 47) recalled, because tariff policy was "an apple of discord that had disrupted the Democratic party for a generation." The speech-writing process was one of "clash and compromise" within the Roosevelt camp as the candidate and his advisors attempted to satisfy various constituencies within the party.

Roosevelt first received a proposed draft from Charles Taussig, the president of the American Molasses Co., a nephew of Frank Taussig, and an intermediary between Cordell Hull and the Roosevelt campaign. The Hull-Taussig draft blamed the economic slump on high tariffs and advocated a 10 percent reduction in duties. Other advisers thought that such a move would be politically impossible in the midst of the depression. Hugh Johnson, who had championed the concept of a parity price for agriculture in the 1920s, argued that there was no assurance that a unilateral tariff reduction would have a favorable impact on trade or improve the economy because trade restrictions had spread around the world. Instead, Johnson prepared an alternative draft that advocated bilateral tariff negotiations with foreign countries to gradually reopen the channels of world commerce. "What is here proposed is that we sit down with each great commercial nation separately and independently and negotiate with it alone," Johnson wrote, "for the purpose of reopening markets of these countries to our agricultural and industrial surpluses."[6]

At this point, Edward Costigan, a Democratic senator from Colorado and former member of the Tariff Commission, suggested that the Hull-Taussig and Johnson drafts be combined with enough equivocation to leave room for maximal flexibility.[7] Taking this advice, Roosevelt instructed Moley in September 1932 to "weave the two together." Moley was left speechless, because the two drafts seemed completely incompatible: one called for unilateral tariff cuts, while the other called for negotiations with trading partners. His difficulties were soon compounded when word reached the campaign that "the reaction to a horizontal tariff proposal in the West and Middle West would be immediate and devastating." As Moley (1939, 49) learned, "there was a strong sentiment there for tariff *increases* on certain commodities!" Roosevelt then sought the advice of pro-tariff Congressmen from western states. Rep. Thomas Walsh (D-MT) took over the process, discarded the draft based on Hull's ideas, and began editing Johnson's draft that proposed tariff bargaining. According to Moley (1939, 50–51):

We showed Roosevelt the finished product. He rearranged it somewhat, made a few additions, and, when he had sent away the stenographer, smiled at me gayly, 'There! You see? It wasn't as hard as you thought it was going to be.' I allowed that I wouldn't have thought it would be hard at all had I known he was going to ignore the Hulls of the party, substantially, and merely throw them a couple of sops in the form of statements that some of the 'outrageously excessive' rates of the Hawley-Smoot tariff would have to come down. 'But you don't understand,' he said. 'This speech is a compromise between the free traders and the protectionists.' And he meant it too!

Moley concluded that Roosevelt had effectively endorsed the Smith-Raskob view in favor of the status quo while giving up the traditional Democratic stance in favor of a "tariff for revenue only," opting instead for a "tariff for negotiation." As Moley (1939, 52) concluded, "So began seven years of evasion and cross-purposes on the tariff. But for the student of statesmanship the process was instructive." Rexford Tugwell (1968, 478), another member of the brain trust, took more benign view of Roosevelt's equivocation, thinking that it was "doubtless regarded by Roosevelt as no more than a necessary means of avoiding an issue on which he preferred not to take a stand during the campaign—something which, as I have noted, seemed to be the rule about other issues as well."

Roosevelt gave his tariff speech in Sioux City, Iowa, in September 1932. He condemned the Hawley-Smoot tariff of 1930 for destroying America's foreign trade, insisting that its "outrageously excessive rates" of duty "must come down." Roosevelt argued that import duties were a meaningless form of farm relief, given the export position of most American farmers, and one that led to foreign retaliation that diminished the foreign market for the country's farm surplus. He proposed holding an international conference to reduce tariffs around the world through "Yankee horse trading." As Roosevelt (1933, 702) put it, "The Democratic tariff policy consists, in large measure, of negotiating agreements with individual countries permitting them to sell goods to us in return for which they will let us sell to them goods and crops which we produce."[8] In the process, he promised not to bring harm to any American industry.

Meanwhile, President Hoover continued to defend high tariffs and suggest that the United States had imported the depression from Europe. If the Hawley-Smoot duties were reduced, he warned, "the grass will grow in the streets of a hundred cities, a thousand towns; the weeds will overrun the fields of a million farms. . . . Their churches, their hospitals and schoolhouses will decay."[9] The president challenged Roosevelt to name which of the "outrageously excessive" rates he would cut. To reassure

Western and Midwestern voters, Roosevelt responded by saying that there were no excessively high duties on farm products. He was then challenged by those in the East to specify the excessive duties on industrial products. At this point, Roosevelt fully retreated, stating: "I favor—and do not let the false statements of my opponents deceive you—continued protection for American agriculture as well as American industry."[10]

Of course, the Great Depression crushed any hope that the Republicans could retain the presidency. Roosevelt won in a landslide, and the Democrats captured both houses of Congress with large majorities.[11] Because of their seniority within the party, many southern Democrats rose to positions of leadership on important committees. Robert Doughton of North Carolina had taken over the House Ways and Means Committee in 1931, and Pat Harrison of Mississippi became chairman of the Senate Finance Committee in 1933. This ensured that the key committees were led by Southern Democrats who were very sympathetic to the reduction of import duties. In addition, Roosevelt appointed Cordell Hull as his secretary of state, ensuring that at least one senior administration official would also favor that policy.

The new president immediately made it clear that measures to promote domestic economic recovery would take priority over foreign trade policy. In his inaugural address in March 1933, Roosevelt stated that "our international trade relations, though vastly important, are in point of time and necessity secondary to the establishment of a sound national economy. I favor as a practical policy the putting of first things first. I shall spare no effort to restore world trade by international economic readjustment, but the emergency at home cannot wait on that accomplishment."[12]

In fact, when Roosevelt took office, the country was in the midst of a major banking crisis. The president immediately declared a bank holiday to restore confidence in the nation's financial system. In April, Roosevelt prohibited the export of gold and suspended the convertibility of the dollar into gold, which effectively took the country off the gold standard. Both actions helped improve monetary and financial conditions. The bank holiday succeeded in restoring confidence in the financial system, and monetary reflation was made possible now that gold reserves were officially no longer a factor in setting monetary policy.

The abandonment of the gold standard had an immediate, positive effect on the economy and started the recovery process. The policy change allowed the Federal Reserve to set monetary policy in line with domestic economic conditions, not simply to defend the dollar's gold parity. The shift to a more expansionary monetary policy, which allowed the money supply to grow instead of shrink, ended four years of continuous deflation and started the economic recovery. For example, industrial production soared in the four months after March 1933, fell back, and then started rising again, ending the year 28 percent higher than when Roosevelt took office—with virtually no consumer price inflation. More than any other element of the New Deal, the abandonment of the gold standard and the freeing of monetary policy was critical to the subsequent economic expansion.[13]

Freed from the gold parity, the dollar began to depreciate on foreign exchange markets; by July it had declined 13 percent against the Canadian dollar and roughly 30–45 percent against other major currencies. The impact on trade was quickly felt: the volume of exports rose 40 percent between the first and fourth quarters of 1933, while the volume of imports increased 23 percent over the same period with the economic revival.[14]

Roosevelt had also promised to negotiate with other countries to reduce trade barriers and help expand foreign commerce. In April 1933, Roosevelt announced his intention to request authority from Congress to begin discussion with other countries to reach agreements that would reduce tariffs. However, as we shall see shortly, he soon postponed this request to ensure that Congress would pass the National Industrial Recovery Act and the Agricultural Adjustment Act. Roosevelt's political advisors feared that adding trade legislation to the agenda for the first one hundred days might overload Congress and jeopardize the timely passage of the other domestic components of the New Deal.

The delay, along with Roosevelt's equivocations during the campaign, raised questions about the administration's commitment to a more liberal approach to trade policy. Indeed, it was not clear what sort of trade policies would emerge from the new administration. As State Department economic adviser Herbert Feis (1966, 262) recalled, there was "chaos and conflict within the government about the nature and direction of our commercial policy during the first year of Roosevelt's presidency." One State Department official wrote in late 1933 that "every department, especially the Tariff Commission, was in a fog as to the foreign trade policy to be pursued."[15]

The problem was that economic policymakers within the Roosevelt administration were split between New Deal nationalists and Wilsonian internationalists. On one side, the brain trust, led by Columbia University professors Raymond Moley and Rexford Tugwell, were economic nationalists who believed that domestic controls and planning were necessary to restore economic growth and achieve full employment. The New Dealers had little regard for open trade policies and, furthermore, believed that domestic policies to promote economic recovery and foreign trade agreements to liberalize imports were fundamentally incompatible. The New Deal policies they championed sought to raise domestic prices for agricultural and industrial goods by reducing domestic supply; it was thought that this would restore business profitability and thereby reduce unemployment. For example, the National Recovery Administration (NRA) promoted codes of "fair competition" that permitted cartels and business associations in the hope that they would reduce output and increase prices and profits. Of course, the premise behind this approach was erroneous: the previous decline in prices had not been due to overproduction but to the decline in the money supply.[16]

Yet there was a tension between reducing domestic supply (in an effort to raise prices) and lowering trade barriers. If the supply-reduction policies succeeded and domestic prices rose, consumers might simply shift their purchases to imports and thereby reduce demand for domestic goods. To prevent this from happening, many New Deal policies allowed the president to impose import restrictions to ensure that higher domestic prices would not be undermined by imports. For example, section 3(e) of the National Industrial Recovery Act gave broad powers to the president to use import quotas or fees to regulate any imports that would "render ineffective or seriously endanger the maintenance of any code or agreement." (The Supreme Court declared the NIRA unconstitutional in 1935.)

The same conflict applied with even greater force in agriculture. New Deal policy was again based on the idea that overproduction of agricultural goods had produced a glut of commodities that depressed prices. The Agricultural Adjustment Act (AAA) encouraged production cutbacks and acreage restrictions to reduce supply and thereby increase the price of farm goods; farmers who reduced their acreage under production would be compensated with the revenue from a tax on processors. A 1935 amendment to the AAA gave the president the authority to impose import quotas that would reduce imports by as much as 50 percent from their 1928–33 level if imports were rendering ineffective or materially interfering with its programs.

The primary purpose of these provisions was not to protect domestic producers by reducing the share of imports in the domestic market. Rather, the goal was to prevent additional imports from undercutting government price supports designed to help manufacturers and farmers. At the same time, there was nothing in the statute that would prevent the president from using the authority in a protectionist manner. While some in the administration wanted to employ the authority for that purpose, import quotas were rarely imposed during the 1930s, covering only about 8 percent of imports in 1936, almost entirely sugar.[17] However, the introduction and use of import quotas marked a departure from the traditional US opposition to them.[18]

In contrast to the illiberal approach to trade of the New Dealers, the new secretary of state, Cordell Hull, represented traditional low-tariff southern Democrats. During the administration's first year, when there was tremendous uncertainty about its trade policy, Hull was a determined advocate of reducing trade barriers through negotiations. Ultimately he was successful, making Hull a pivotal figure in the history of US trade policy. Indeed, of all the people who have left a mark on US policy, none has had a greater or more lasting impact than Cordell Hull. Hull's lifelong project, the reciprocal trade agreements program, fundamentally changed the direction of US trade policy over the course of the 1930s and 1940s. His success demonstrates that individuals, not just impersonal economic and political forces acting through Congress, can shape policy at critical moments.

Trained as a lawyer, Hull represented Tennessee in Congress when Roosevelt asked him to become secretary of state. Personifying the long-standing southern opposition to high tariffs, Hull believed that excessive import duties discouraged exports, harmed consumers and workers by increasing the cost of living, promoted the growth of monopolies and trusts, and redistributed income from poor farmers in the South and Midwest to rich industrialists in the North.[19]

World War I opened Hull's eyes to the international implications of trade policies. The war marked "a milestone in my political thinking," he recalled in his memoirs. "When the war came in 1914, I was very soon impressed with two points," Hull (1948, 81) wrote. "I saw that you could not separate the idea of commerce from the idea of war and peace" and that "wars were often largely caused by economic rivalry conducted unfairly." In Hull's view, the quest of the European powers to gain access to foreign markets, particularly the competitive rivalry to establish colonial empires and secure preferential access to the world's raw materials, was a factor behind the international tensions that eventually led to military conflict. Hull "came to believe that if we could eliminate this bitter economic rivalry, if we could increase commercial exchanges among nations over lowered trade and tariff barriers and remove unnatural obstructions to trade, we would go a long way toward eliminating war itself."[20] Having fought for lower tariffs solely for domestic reasons in the past, Hull (1948,

84) found that "for the first time openly I enlarged my views on trade and tariffs from the national to the international theater."

Therefore, Hull (1948, 81) recalled,

> Toward 1916 I embraced the philosophy that I carried throughout my twelve years as Secretary of State. . . . From then on, to me, unhampered trade dovetailed with peace; high tariffs, trade barriers, and unfair economic competition, with war. Though realizing that many other factors were involved, I reasoned that, if we could get a freer flow of trade—freer in the sense of fewer discriminations and obstructions—so that one country would not be deadly jealous of another and the living standards of all countries might rise, thereby eliminating the economic dissatisfaction that breeds war, we might have a reasonable chance for lasting peace.

Consequently, Hull (1948, 84) decided to devote all his political energy to reducing trade barriers: "After long and careful deliberation, I decided to announce and work for a broad policy of removing or lowering all excessive barriers to international trade, exchange and finance of whatsoever kind, and to adopt commercial policies that would make possible the development of vastly increased trade among nations. This part of my proposal was based on a conviction that such liberal commercial policies and the development of the volume of commerce would constitute an essential foundation of any peace structure that civilized nations might erect following the war."

Hull watched with frustration the failure of international economic conferences during the 1920s, became an outspoken critic of the Hawley-Smoot tariff, and was horrified by the rise of protectionism and fascism around the world as a result of the Great Depression. The spread of illiberal trade policies and the rise of international tensions in the early 1930s seemed only to confirm the lessons he had learned from World War I. Although the prospects for change were dim, Hull never gave up hope that international cooperation on trade policy might make the world a safer and more prosperous place. As Hull (1937, 14) later affirmed, "I have never faltered, and I will never falter, in my belief that the enduring peace and welfare of nations are indissolubly connected with friendliness, fairness, equality, and the maximum practicable degree of freedom in international economic relations."

In his first address as secretary of state, Hull declared that "most modern military conflicts and other serious international controversies are rooted in economic conditions, and that economic rivalries are in most modern instances the prelude to the actual wars that have occurred." Easing global political tensions required "fair, friendly, and normal trade relations." The time had come for the United States to exercise its leadership and establish world trade policies on an open, non-discriminatory basis. "Many years of disastrous experience, resulting in colossal and incalculable losses and injuries, utterly discredit the narrow and blind policy of extreme economic isolation," he continued. "In my judgment, the destiny of history points to the United States for leadership in the existing grave crisis."[21]

Hull was highly respected across the political spectrum for his experience and integrity.[22] But his insistence that economic rivalry was the cause and not the consequence of international friction was debatable, to say the least. Many of his contemporaries thought that he was naive and completely exaggerated the likelihood that freer trade would promote peace. Several of his Senate colleagues warned Roosevelt that, as much as they liked and admired Hull, he was unsuited to be secretary of state. While not directly critical of Hull himself, most members of Congress were skeptical that increased trade would solve the political problems of the world. The isolationist Senator Hiram Johnson (R-CA) described him as a man with "more delusions concerning the world than a dog has fleas."[23] Hull was so focused on trade relations in the 1930s that he seemed oblivious to the broader conflicts that were moving the world toward another war. Although he inspired loyalty among those in the State Department, many in the Roosevelt administration viewed Hull as an idealist who chose to believe certain things rather than understand the world as it was. Roosevelt excluded him from most high-level foreign policy decisions.

Yet Hull persevered within the administration and outlasted his critics. The reciprocal trade agreements program was his pet project, and it eventually changed the direction of US trade policy. As Butler (1998, ix) writes, "Cordell Hull's determination, persistence, and legislative experience were determining factors at every stage of the conception, passage, and implementation of the Trade Agreements Act." Dean Acheson (1969, 9–10), who was at the State Department at this time and later served as secretary of state, recalled,

> The Secretary—slow, circuitous, cautious—concentrated on a central political purpose, the freeing of international trade from tariff and other restrictions as the prerequisite to peace and economic development. With almost fanatical single-mindedness, he devoted himself

to getting legislative authority, and then acting upon it, to negotiate 'mutually beneficial reciprocal trade agreements to reduce tariffs' on the basis of equal application to all nations, a thoroughly Jeffersonian policy. . . . Mr. Hull's amazing success with this important undertaking, a reversal of a hundred years of American policy, was due both to his stubborn persistence and to his great authority in the House of Representative and the Senate.[24]

TOWARD A NEW TRADE POLICY

Had they came to power under ordinary circumstances, the Democrats might simply have reduced import duties through legislation, as they had done in 1894 and 1913. But the domestic and foreign economic situation in the early 1930s conspired to change the situation. First, a unilateral tariff reduction was politically impossible in the midst of the Depression with the unemployment rate so high. Though he had originally proposed a 10 percent reduction in tariffs during the election campaign, Hull (1948, 358) later admitted that "it would have been folly to go to Congress and ask that the Smoot-Hawley Act be repealed or its rates reduced by Congress."

Furthermore, foreign trade barriers—in the form of higher tariffs, import quotas, and exchange controls—had increased sharply in the early 1930s. Even more problematic, American goods suffered from discrimination in foreign markets. The Ottawa agreements of 1932 created a system of imperial preferences aimed at keeping US goods out of major export markets, such as Canada and Britain. Germany also established preferential trade arrangements with southeastern Europe, while Japan set up the so-called "Greater East Asia Co-Prosperity Sphere." Standing outside of these trade blocs, the United States saw its share of world trade shrink. While Hawley-Smoot may have spawned some of these barriers, its unilateral repeal was not going to eliminate them. Many officials feared that abolishing the Hawley-Smoot duties would accomplish little unless opportunities were created for increasing exports as well.[25]

The World Economic Conference in London in June 1933 presented the new administration with its first opportunity to depart from Republican isolationism and cooperate with other countries in establishing better economic relations. Although the major topic of discussion was international monetary coordination and exchange-rate stability, Hull was determined to propose a multilateral effort to reduce tariffs. He departed for the London conference with the expectation that the administration would soon request trade-negotiating authority from Congress, as the White House had indicated it would, enabling him to make substantive proposals on trade.[26] While sailing across the Atlantic, however, Hull was stunned to learn that Roosevelt had decided to postpone such a request. The president cabled Hull to say that trade-negotiating authority was "not only highly inadvisable, but impossible of achievement" at the moment, although the true reason was that trade policy was secondary to securing congressional passage of other New Deal legislation.[27]

Hull (1948, 251) was devastated—"the message was a terrific blow"— and he considered resigning, but Roosevelt assured him that he would support trade reforms in the near future. In any event, Hull found no support for a multilateral effort to reduce tariffs among the countries participating in the London conference. As Hull (1948, 356) recalled,

> In earlier years I had been in favor of any action or agreement that would lower tariff barriers, whether the agreement was multilateral . . . regional . . . [or] bilateral. . . . But during and after the London Conference it was manifest that public support in no country, especially our own, would at that time support a worth-while multilateral undertaking. My associates and I therefore agreed that we should try to secure the enactment of the next best method of reducing trade barriers, that is, by bilateral trade agreements which embraced the most-favored-nation policy in its unconditional form—meaning a policy of nondiscrimination and equality of treatment.

Despite the failure of the meeting, Hull received high marks for his performance, which strengthened his hand within the administration. Hull also benefitted from his success at a Pan American conference in Uruguay in December 1933, in which delegates expressed their support for American-led efforts to open up trade. "The President, still pursuing the theory of retaining full discretionary authority to fix tariff rates at any height deemed necessary for the successful operation of the AAA and NRA, was slow to embrace my liberal trade proposal at Montevideo," Hull (1948, 353) wrote. "But the success it achieved among the Latin American countries and in the press at home made him more friendly toward it." Shortly after the December conference, Roosevelt announced his intention to request trade-negotiating authority from Congress.

In March 1934, after consulting with key congressional leaders, the president formally requested authority from Congress to undertake trade negotiations with other countries and, "within carefully guarded limits, to modify existing duties and import restrictions in such a way as will benefit American agriculture and industry." In submitting the proposed legislation, Roosevelt stated that "it is part of an emergency program necessitated by the economic crisis through which we are passing." As he explained, "a full and permanent domestic recovery depends in part upon a revived and strengthened international trade, and . . . American exports cannot be permanently increased without a corresponding increase in imports." Noting that "other governments are to an ever-increasing extent winning their share of international trade by negotiating reciprocal trade agreements," Roosevelt argued that "if American agricultural and industrial interests are to retain their deserved place in this trade, the American government must be in a position to bargain for that place with other governments by rapid and decisive negotiation. . . . If [the government] is not in a position at a given moment rapidly to alter the terms on which it is willing to deal with other countries, it cannot adequately protect its trade against discriminations and against bargains injurious to its interests." However, in using the proposed authority, the president wished to "give assurance that no sound and important American interests will be injuriously disturbed. The adjustment of our foreign trade relations must rest on the premise of undertaking to benefit and not to injure such interests."[28]

The administration's draft legislation was just three pages long.[29] Under the proposal, the Roosevelt administration would have the authority to reduce import duties by up to 50 percent in trade agreements with other countries. These tariff reductions could be implemented by executive order and would not need congressional approval. In addition, the tariff reductions would apply to imports from all countries through the unconditional most-favored-nation (MFN) clause, as adopted by the Harding administration in 1923. This was much more sweeping authority than Congress had ever granted any previous president. The Roosevelt administration justified the unprecedented request on the grounds that the foreign trade situation constituted an "emergency" and that decisive executive action to promote trade was desperately needed.

The administration's bill was introduced by Robert Doughton (D-NC), the chairman of the Ways and Means Committee. The committee's hearings were a sharp contrast to its consideration of the Hawley-Smoot tariff just five years earlier. In 1929, the committee heard from 1,131 witnesses (none from the executive branch) over forty-three days, generating 11,200 pages of published testimony (plus index) in 18 volumes. In 1934, the committee heard from just 17 witnesses (7 from the executive branch) over five days in testimony amounting to 479 published pages in one volume. While the 173-page Hawley-Smoot bill took eighteen months to work its way through Congress, the 3-page Reciprocal Trade Agreement Act took just four months to be enacted.[30]

Several key administration officials testified before the committee and argued that executive action was necessary to revitalize world trade for the benefit of the American economy. Hull argued that "the primary object of this new proposal is both to reopen the old and seek new outlets for our surplus production, through the gradual moderation of the excessive and more extreme impediments to the admission of American products into foreign markets." He stressed that the negotiating authority was emergency legislation designed to stimulate foreign trade in response to "unprecedented economic conditions."[31]

The Democratic majority on the Ways and Means Committee endorsed the administration's request and favorably reported the bill. The Republican minority report objected that the legislation "contemplates the abandonment of the principle of protection for domestic industry, agriculture, and labor by allowing duties to be modified without reference to the difference in cost of production of domestic and foreign articles." Republicans complained that the bill gave the president "the absolute power of life and death over every existing domestic industry dependent upon tariff protection, and permits the sacrifice of such industries in what will undoubtedly be a futile attempt to expand the export trade of other industries," thus risking "serious possibilities of disastrous consequences." They also charged that the bill was an unconstitutional delegation of Congress's power to levy taxes and that any negotiated trade agreement had to be approved by Congress.[32]

To allay some Democratic concerns about the unprecedented grant of authority, Doughton introduced a key amendment on the House floor that would ensure ongoing congressional influence over trade policy.[33] While the administration had proposed (with the concurrence of the Ways and Means Committee) that the negotiating authority have no time limit, the House agreed to limit it to just three years, after which it would terminate unless renewed by Congress. This proved to be an important means by which Congress could oversee the program, because the threat of not renewing the negotiating authority would keep the executive branch accountable to the legislature and sensitive to its concerns. Had the time limit not been added, a two-thirds majority of both houses of Congress would have been required to override a presidential veto of any bill stripping away the negotiating authority.[34]

House Democrats rallied behind the president's proposal. The Roosevelt administration had enormous political authority in its first few years, and the Democratic Congress was willing to grant it extraordinary powers over the economy. Although giving the president the ability to reduce tariffs would have been unthinkable in ordinary times, the badly handled Hawley-Smoot revision in 1929–30 and the ensuing economic collapse helped persuade Democrats that such discretionary authority was necessary. As Charles Faddis (D-PA) put it, tariff policy

> is not a matter which can be satisfactorily disposed of in Congress. . . . It is a matter for slow and careful consideration. It must be gone into cautiously, step by step, with the idea of a general plan. Congress cannot do this, for in this country the tariff is to each Member of Congress a local issue. The tariff has always been a logrolling issue. Such an issue can have no general plan, and without a general plan the issue can never be settled. We must have a national tariff policy. At the present time we can have it no other way except by giving the authority to formulate it to the President.[35]

Republicans strenuously objected to giving the president the ability to reduce tariffs, arguing that the delegation of such authority was unconstitutional and would erode the protection given to key industries. These criticisms would be repeated for more than a decade. But like the claim during the 1820s that protective tariffs were unconstitutional, the claim that the RTAA was unconstitutional had no force. One problem with the argument was that Republicans themselves had delegated "flexible tariff" authority to the president in 1922 and 1930, which the Supreme Court had ruled as constitutional. Of course, objecting to the constitutionality of the RTAA was just a political maneuver to prevent tariffs from being reduced. When asked why he had supported President Hoover's bid for a flexible tariff provision but now opposed Roosevelt's similar request, Harold Knutson (R-MN) replied: "Frankly, I know the purpose of this legislation is to lower rates. If I thought for a minute that it was proposed to raise rates to meet the present conditions, I would vote for this legislation and be glad of the opportunity to do so."[36]

Given the large Democratic majority, the House passage of the bill was a foregone conclusion. On March 29, 1934, the House passed the RTAA by a vote of 274–111, with Democrats voting 269–11 in favor, Republicans voting 99–2 against, and Farmer-Laborer voting 3–1 in favor. Western Democrats had the most difficulty supporting the bill because that region was hit hardest by the Depression, and many wanted price supports and tariff protection for their crops and commodities.

But could Democrats hold together and get the bill through the Senate? As seen in the past, party control was much weaker in the Senate, and the West had greater representation. Almost all tariff legislation had encountered difficulties in the Senate, and the minority Republicans still had hopes that they could derail the administration's plans. They attacked the legislation, arguing that reducing tariffs in the midst of a depression was economic suicide. Arthur Vandenberg (R-MI) called the bill a "dangerous measure" that gave "autocratic Presidential power in connection with the tariff." Republicans went so far as to say that the RTAA would create a "fascist dictatorship in respect to tariffs" and warned that there were "no shackles upon the use of this extraordinary, tyrannical, dictatorial power over the life and death of the American economy."[37] Even progressive Republicans who opposed the Hawley-Smoot tariff fell in line with their party and objected to the bill. William Borah (R-ID) worried that the trade authority would be used to exchange lower US duties on imported raw materials for lower foreign duties on US manufactured goods, thereby helping the East at the expense of the West.

The Senate Finance Committee amended the House bill to include a requirement that the administration give public notice of its intent to negotiate an agreement and allow interested parties to have a voice in the process. Otherwise, the committee moved quickly, reporting the bill less than a month after the House passage. On the Senate floor, the Democratic leadership defeated a series of proposed amendments, mainly from Republicans, ranging from an exemption of wool and other agricultural commodities from any tariff reduction to a requirement that Congress approve any trade agreement and a ban on any agreement with countries whose wages were less than 80 percent of those in the United States. Democrats held together and fought these proposed changes to the legislation. "If we are going to destroy the ability of the President to act promptly we might as well quit wasting our time in debating the bill at all," Alben Barkley (D-KY) argued.[38]

On June 4, 1934, the Senate approved the RTAA by a vote of 57–33, with Democrats voting 51–5 in favor and Republicans voting 28–5 against. The House concurred with the Senate changes and sent the bill to the president for his signature. Hull (1948, 357) later recalled the moment: "At 9:15 on the night of June 12 I watched the President sign our bill in the White House. Each stroke of the pen seemed to write a message of gladness on my heart. My fight of many long years for the reciprocal trade policy and the lowering of trade barriers was won. To say I was delighted is a bald understatement."

Hull (1948, 357) later contended that "in both House and Senate we were aided by the severe reaction of public opinion against the Smoot-Hawley Act." In fact, the passage of the RTAA simply reflected the massive change in the partisan composition of Congress, with Democrats replacing Republicans. After examining the votes of all members of Congress who voted on both Hawley-Smoot and the RTAA, Schnietz (2000) clearly shows that Congress did not "change its mind" about the wisdom of the Hawley-Smoot tariff. That would imply that members who voted for Hawley-Smoot later regretted its consequences and voted for the RTAA. Of the ninety-five members of Congress who voted in favor of Hawley-Smoot, only nine voted in favor of the RTAA. Of those nine, seven were Democrats; only two of eighty-six Republicans changed their view.

One of the two Republicans, Arthur Capper of Kansas, may have changed his mind due to the events that followed the passage of Hawley-Smoot. "I am a firm believer in the protective tariff," Capper stated. "But it has seemed to me ever since we enacted the latest tariff act . . . that the United States has a Gordian knot to undo in the matter of interference with world trade by tariffs, quotas, embargos, and similar trade restrictions." In Capper's view, if the United States wanted to restore world trade, it had few options other than to seek reciprocal trade agreements.

> But if reciprocal trade agreements are to be negotiated, it does not look as if Congress, from the practical viewpoint, is qualified, or even able, to undertake the task. . . . . our experience in writing tariff legislation, particularly in the postwar era, has been discouraging. Trading between groups and sections is inevitable. Log-rolling is inevitable, and in its most pernicious form. We do not write a national tariff law. We jam together, through various unholy alliances and combinations, a potpourri or hodgepodge of section and local tariff rates, which often add to our troubles and increase world misery. For myself, I see no reason to believe that another attempt would result in a more happy ending.[39]

One remarkable aspect of the RTAA was the utter lack of interest by the industry groups that usually tried to influence Congress's setting of tariff rates. The Ways and Means Committee received only sixty-three pieces of RTAA-related correspondence, fifty-nine of which opposed the bill. Unlike the Hawley-Smoot tariff, the RTAA attracted very little support or opposition by interest groups, even export associations who stood to benefit from it.[40] One reason for the almost complete lack of interest, according to Haggard (1988, 112), is that in contrast to 1930 "when interest groups were the main protagonists and specific tariff rates the issue, the most important issues at stake in 1934 were institutional, centering on the transfer of authority from Congress to the executive." The RTAA was simply enabling legislation, and no one knew how the authority would be used, how successful the negotiations would be, how extensive any agreements might be, or which interests might be most affected. When the RTAA was passed, Congress and trade-affected economic interests could not anticipate how important the legislation would become, or even whether it would be sustained by future Congresses.

Thus, the RTAA did not arise because of the demands of interest groups, but because Cordell Hull and other southern Democrats had long championed a significant reduction in tariffs and the promotion of exports. The Great Depression prevented a unilateral tariff reduction and presented policymakers with the need to address the many foreign trade barriers that had arisen against US exports. The policy change was not driven by interest groups; instead, administration officials took the lead in changing policy, and interest groups later followed. Similarly, it is interesting to recall that the Hawley-Smoot tariff was also largely initiated by politicians as a way of appeasing agricultural interests; it was not something that industry demanded or that farmers believed would help them in any significant way. This suggests that politicians can sometime use economic interests to achieve their political goals and that a country's tariff policy is not just the result of economic interests manipulating politicians for their own self-interested ends.

THE RECIPROCAL TRADE AGREEMENTS ACT OF 1934

According to its preamble, the RTAA was enacted "for the purpose of expanding foreign markets for the products of the United States . . . as a means of assisting in the present emergency in restoring the American standard of living." The president could proclaim lower duties on foreign goods entering the United States "in accordance with the characteristics and needs of various branches of American production."[41] The RTAA, which was technically an amendment to the Tariff Act of 1930, allowed the president to enter into trade agreements with foreign countries provided "reasonable" public notice of the intention to negotiate an agreement was given to allow interested parties to present their views. This authority would expire in three years. As a result of such agreements, the president could issue an executive order increasing or decreasing import duties on particular goods by no more than 50 percent, but could not transfer any article between the dutiable and duty-free lists. The duties would apply to imports from all countries on an unconditional MFN basis.

Because of its importance for US trade policy, the RTAA has long attracted the interest of scholars studying regime change.[42] Some studies have interpreted the RTAA as a cleverly designed institutional mechanism to lock in the Democrats' preferred tariff level. With hindsight, this interpretation seems true, but the RTAA's success was not guaranteed from the outset. There was absolutely no assurance that other countries would be willing to negotiate with the United States or that any such agreements would reduce tariffs in any significant degree. The Democratic Congress and the Roosevelt administration could not commit future policymakers to continue the reciprocal trade agreements approach. The RTAA could easily have been reversed by the Republicans when they returned to power, and until the early 1940s they explicitly vowed to abolish the RTAA and even reverse any tariff changes that it brought about. While the reputational costs to American foreign policy of reversing the tariff reduction by withdrawing from a trade agreement were higher than a reversal of a unilateral tariff reduction, those costs were not prohibitive. A bipartisan consensus in favor of the RTAA did not emerge until after World War II (as discussed in chapter 10).

Rather than a far-sighted Democratic ploy to introduce irreversible tariff changes, the RTAA was a pragmatic response to the circumstances of the day: The Great Depression prevented any serious consideration of a unilateral tariff reduction, and the proliferation of new foreign trade barriers that so impeded US exports demanded a response. Of course, the RTAA also tipped the political balance of power in favor of lower tariffs. First, Congress essentially gave up the ability to legislate duties on specific goods when it delegated tariff-negotiating power to the executive. If the president was successful in concluding trade agreements, Congress would no longer have to set import duties and go through the process of vote-trading to help different import-competing interests. Once tariffs were bound in a trade agreement, it would be more difficult for Congress to start changing them in legislation. Furthermore, Congressional votes on trade policy were now framed simply in terms of whether to continue the RTAA program or not, and if so under what conditions.

The RTAA also reduced the threshold of political support needed for members of Congress to approve tariff reductions by means of executive agreements as opposed to treaties. The renewal of the RTAA required a simple majority in Congress, whereas any treaty negotiated by the president prior to the RTAA had to be approved by two-thirds of the Senate. This reduced the number of legislators needed to pass agreements that reduced import duties and conversely increased the number of legislators needed to block such agreements under the RTAA.

In addition, the RTAA delegated powers over trade policy to the executive branch, which was more likely to favor moderate tariffs than the Congress. The president had a national electoral base and was more likely to favor policies that would benefit the nation as a whole than were members of Congress, who represented specific geographic regions. The president was also more likely than Congress to take into account a broader set of factors in setting trade policy, including exporter and consumer interests, as well as foreign policy and national security considerations.

Finally, the RTAA helped boost the bargaining position and lobbying strength of exporters in the political process. Previously, import-competing domestic producers were the main lobby group on Capitol Hill in relation to trade legislation, since they reaped the benefits of high tariffs. Such tariffs harmed exporters, but only indirectly: The cost to any exporter of any particular import duty was miniscule, and therefore exporters failed to organize an effective political opposition. By directly tying lower foreign tariffs to lower domestic tariffs, the RTAA fostered the development of exporters as an organized group opposed to high tariffs and supporting trade agreements. The lower tariffs negotiated under the RTAA also increased the size of the export sector and thereby strengthened political support for continuing the program.

Of course, the RTAA did not end lobbying by industries facing foreign competition. As Francis B. Sayre (1939, 96), an assistant secretary of state responsible for overseeing the trade agreements program, stated, "Every time it is proposed to lower a tariff, the lobbyists and the politicians descend upon Washington, and intense pressures are brought to bear upon those responsible for decisions." Although this did not change, the RTAA diverted such political pressure away from a relatively sympathetic Congress toward the less sympathetic executive branch. The State Department was much less responsive to producer interests than members of Congress who faced reelection by these constituents. The State Department was also able to balance pressure from import-competing interests with export interests, as well as to consider the broader diplomatic and economic benefits of trade agreements. For this reason, Vandenberg complained that negotiated tariff reductions represented "the cloistered and wishful guesses of bureaucrats with free-trade inclinations"[43]

Of course, the RTAA did not make a shift toward freer trade inevitable, because sustaining the program required the ongoing support of the president and a majority in Congress. The RTAA passed easily in 1934 because the Democrats had large majorities in Congress. As long as those majorities were maintained, the RTAA was likely to be continued, but the program would have been in serious jeopardy had the Republicans regained control of Congress in the 1930s.

THE TRADE AGREEMENTS PROGRAM IN OPERATION

Less than three months after the enactment of the RTAA, the State Department signed a trade agreement with Cuba and announced its intention to negotiate with eleven other countries. Yet the trade agreements program got off to a slow start because of intense conflict with the Roosevelt administration. As Hull (1948, 370) recalled, "The greatest threat to the trade agreements program [in its first year] came not from foreign countries, not from the Republicans, not from certain manufacturers or growers, but from within the Roosevelt administration itself, in the person of George N. Peek." This bureaucratic infighting nearly destroyed the entire program.

Within the administration, George Peek was not alone in his belief that lower tariffs would conflict with New Deal programs that sought to raise domestic prices. In March 1934, Roosevelt appointed Peek to be his foreign trade adviser, operating outside the State Department. Hull (1948, 370) was dumbfounded: "If Mr. Roosevelt had hit me between the eyes with a sledgehammer he could not have stunned me more than by this appointment." Despite his help in drafting the RTAA legislation, Peek branded agreements to reduce tariffs as "unilateral economic disarmament" and scorned the unconditional MFN clause as "un-American." Taking high tariffs, exchange controls, and import quotas as a fixed part of the global trade environment, Peek favored government-brokered bilateral trade deals to dispose of America's surplus agricultural production. Peek proposed to negotiate barter arrangements, deal by deal, making the government a commercial agent for the nation's exports and imports. "Under an emergency short-time approach every effort should be made to effect trade 'deals' between this and other countries that are mutually advantageous," Peek (1936, 178) wrote. "We should explore, for example, the possibilities of selling wheat to China, pork to Russia, and the like. Direct barter, to obviate exchange difficulties, in some cases may be possible."

Hull abhorred the idea that the government should become the broker for American farmers and manufacturers, cutting deals and making

trade bargains with other countries. If the United States adopted this approach, and other countries followed, it could find itself on the losing end
of managed trade arrangements. Hull wanted to eliminate special trade
deals entirely and make equality of treatment the cornerstone of trade relations. Government should get out of directing trade flows and ensure
that private enterprise had an opportunity to compete in an open and non-
discriminatory world market, free from government interference and trade
preferences. Peek thought Hull was naive and impractical for trying to return the world economy to non-discriminatory, market-driven trade.

These fundamentally different visions for trade policy led to inter-
necine battles in the Roosevelt administration. As Peek jockeyed with
other agencies for influence over trade policy, Hull and the State Department were forced to spend much of 1934 and early 1935 fighting off his
efforts to gain control of trade policy. When Peek was also appointed to
head the Export-Import Bank, a new government agency designed to finance exports through concessional loans to foreign purchasers, he was
positioned to broker specific trade deals.[44] For example, in December 1934,
Peek arranged for the Bank to sell eight hundred thousand bales of cotton
to Germany for a certain amount of money, one-quarter of which would
be paid in dollars and the remainder in German marks, with a premium.
The marks would then be sold by the Export-Import Bank at a discount to
American importers of German goods.

Hull and his assistant Francis Sayre argued strenuously against such
preferential deal-making. In their view, Peek failed to recognize that economic nationalism through government-brokered transactions would not
help American commerce flourish in the long-run. That strategy risked a
further carving up of world trade on the basis of political deals and, to the
extent that the United States was successful, made it vulnerable to the
threat of foreign retaliation. Indeed, Brazil threatened to cut off trade negotiations with the United States and retaliate, because its cotton exports
were going to be displaced as a result of Peek's deal with Germany. After
the State Department intervened, Roosevelt withdrew support for Peek's
plan; that this arrangement had been made with Nazi Germany did not
help Peek's cause. Thereafter, Peek's influence began to wane. He became
an increasingly strident internal critic of the administration, and Roosevelt accepted his resignation in November 1935. Out of office, Peek wrote
a blistering attack on the RTAA in his 1936 book *Why Quit Our Own?*

With Peek's departure, the State Department consolidated its control
over trade policy and began to move forward with trade negotiations. The
organizational structure is shown in figure 9.1 The trade agreements pro-

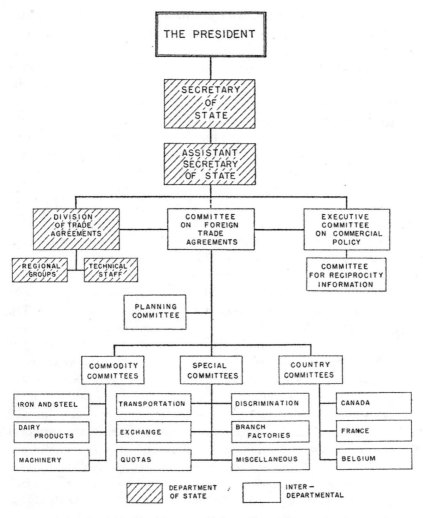

Figure 9.1. The administration of the Trade Agreements Program.

gram was overseen by the Executive Committee on Commercial Policy, administered by the interdepartmental Trade Agreements Committee, and assisted by the Committee on Reciprocity Information. Each of these committees included representatives from the Departments of Agriculture, Commerce, and Treasury, as well as the Tariff Commission, but the State Department coordinated and dominated the process.

The trade agreements process worked as follows. The assistant secretary of state would first explore whether certain countries were interested

in negotiating a trade agreement with the United States. If the country
was agreeable in principle to reducing tariffs, the interdepartmental committee would announce the government's intent to negotiate with the
country. Time was set aside for public comment, usually from exporters
hoping that particular foreign tariffs would be reduced and from domestic
producers opposed to tariff reductions on certain commodities imported
from the prospective partner country. These comments were received by
the Committee for Reciprocity Information. "Often the outcry at public
hearings over the expected ruinous effects of proposed tariff cuts would
be based on fear rather than fact," Sayre (1957, 170) recalled. Yet, he continued, "the hearings were real, never superficial. We always were ready
to modify our original ideas as a result of these hearings. We were bent on
doing an honest and sound piece of work."

Then the Trade Agreements Committee would begin the bilateral
negotiations. The United States would not offer an across-the-board tariff reduction; instead, it would offer tariff cuts on a selective, product-by-
product basis "in accordance with the characteristics and needs of the
various branches of American production," as required by the RTAA. The
selective approach had two purposes. First, certain politically important,
import-sensitive sectors could be exempted from the reduction and thus
not have to face greater foreign competition. Second, tariffs would be reduced only on goods of which the partner country was a "principal supplier." This would give other countries an incentive to negotiate with the
United States, since their exporters would benefit the most, in addition to
mitigating the problem of other countries free riding on the unconditional
MFN nature of the tariff reductions. If an agreement was concluded, the
changes in the tariff rates would take effect by executive order.

As the State Department built up negotiating experience, it developed
a template for reciprocal trade agreements with a set of provisions that
could be modified to reflect the particulars of each country. The first section of the agreement related to trade in general and included articles on
the most-favored-nation clause, internal taxes, quotas and exchange controls, and monopolies and government purchases. The second section contained provisions relating to the tariff concessions, such as the changes
in import duties by each country and the conditions governing the withdrawal or modification of those concessions. (Of course, the exact changes
in duties were determined in the negotiations.) The final section dealt
with matters such as territorial application, exceptions to MFN treatment,
general reservations, consultations on technical matters (such as sanitary

regulations of trade), and the provisional application, duration, and possible termination of the agreement.[45]

The trade agreements process meant that the State Department and other executive branch officials began to play a more important role in the formation of trade policy than the committee chairs in Congress who traditionally dominated the process. Although Secretary Hull was rarely involved in the details of the trade negotiations himself, his strong support for the program made it a central part of the State Department's activities during the 1930s. Given his passionate interest in reducing trade barriers and his long tenure as Secretary of State, Hull gave the State Department a lasting purpose and direction that shaped its approach to trade policy long after his departure.[46]

At the start of the RTAA, Assistant Secretary of State Francis Sayre, a Harvard law professor and son-in-law of Woodrow Wilson, and Herbert Feis, a State Department official and an economist, were responsible for implementing and overseeing the program. Although Sayre and Feis had other responsibilities, both "would play very important roles in drafting the trade legislation, lobbying for its passage through Congress, ensuring that the State Department oversaw its implementation after passage, and negotiating individual agreements with the United States' trading partners."[47] Another economist, Henry Grady, headed the Trade Agreements Committee from 1934 to 1936. He was succeeded by Harry Hawkins, also an economist, who ran the Department's Trade Agreements Division from 1936 until 1944. By all accounts, Hawkins was the key individual responsible for the success of the program. He was highly respected and handled the negotiations and the interdepartmental process with great diplomatic skill. In his memoirs, Hull (1948, 366) singled out Hawkins for unusually high praise: "No one in the entire economic service of the Government, in my opinion, rendered more valuable service than he. Hawkins was a tower of strength to the department throughout the development of the trade agreements, and especially in our negotiation with other countries, which at times were exceedingly difficult."[48]

The trade agreements program got off to a slow start not just because of the Hull-Peek dispute but because other countries were reluctant to reduce trade barriers when their economies were still far from full employment and weak from the Depression. As a result, the United States had mixed success in concluding trade agreements during the 1930s and even less success in negotiating sizeable reductions in import duties. By 1936, agreements had been reached with only three of the nine largest US export markets: Canada, France, and the Netherlands. Germany had requested negotiations, but the United States refused because of its discriminatory trade policies, particularly its privileged barter arrangements with southeastern Europe. Japan, Argentina, and Australia expressed no interest in negotiating with the United States, and talks with Italy broke down. Many of the agreements were with Latin American countries, whose raw material exports did not pose a threat to domestic industries.[49]

Hull keenly wanted a trade agreement with Britain, the second largest US export market. As we saw in chapter 8, Britain adopted a system of imperial preferences that gave special treatment to goods from the British Empire. The State Department was particularly keen to reduce the preference margins in the Ottawa agreements that discriminated against American goods in Britain and Canada, America's two most important foreign markets.[50] Testifying before Congress in 1940, Hull called imperial preferences "the greatest injury, in a commercial way, that has been inflicted on this country since I have been in public life."[51]

After the midterm election of 1936, Hull pressed Britain to open trade negotiations, but British officials were reluctant. The United States took just 6 percent of British exports, and Britain did not want to jeopardize its preferential access to markets where it had a much larger commercial stake. As the risk of a European war increased, Britain began to recognize the diplomatic advantages of reaching an agreement with the United States. Britain eventually decided to pursue it to solidify Anglo-American cooperation. Prime Minister Neville Chamberlain agreed to move forward because "it would help to educate American opinion to act more and more with us, and because I felt sure it would frighten the totalitarians. Coming at this moment, it looks just like an answer to the Berlin-Rome-Tokyo axis."[52] Because the United States was formally a neutral power, however, the State Department had to downplay the foreign policy implications of the agreement "in deference to the widespread isolationist sentiment here," Hull (1948, 529) recalled. "We could stress our belief that liberal commercial policy, epitomized by the trade agreements, tended to promote peace, but we had to be careful to emphasize that an agreement with Britain on trade comported no agreement whatever in the nature of a mutual political or defense policy."

In January 1938, both countries formally announced their intention to start negotiations, which began the following month. The discussions were difficult on both sides: the United States was in the midst of the severe 1937–38 recession, which made officials reluctant to expose manufacturing industries to more competition from imports, while Britain was reluctant to reduce its imperial preferences and wanted more concessions from the United States, on the grounds that its tariffs were, on average, much higher than Britain's. The result was "a limited and unspectacular treaty, produced by difficult and protracted negotiations."[53] The extent of the tariff reductions was exceedingly modest, and little progress was made in reducing the margins of preference that discriminated against American exports. At the same time, public opinion supported the effort. In a March 1938 poll, nearly three-quarters of respondents thought that the United States should reduce its tariffs on British goods if Britain did the same for American goods; only one-quarter opposed such a policy, and there was no significant partisan difference in the result.[54]

However, the agreement was in effect for less than a year before Britain entered World War II in September 1939. The agreement was rendered inoperative because Britain was forced to adopt severe trade controls as part of the war effort. Still, the agreement marked the beginning of closer political and economic ties between the two nations.

By the end of the 1930s, the RTAA could be considered a modest success. By 1940, the United States had signed agreements with twenty-one nations that accounted for nearly two-thirds of US trade. Table 9.1 lists the countries that signed trade agreements with the United States during this period. The State Department publicized the fact that exports to agreement countries rose 63 percent between 1934–35 and 1938–39, while exports to non–agreement countries rose only 32 percent. Meanwhile, imports from agreement countries rose 22 percent, while imports from non–agreement countries rose 13 percent over the same period.[55] Furthermore, the United States seemed to be making progress in regaining its previous share of world trade. The United States accounted for 61 percent of Canada's imports in 1932, when imperial preferences were introduced. That share fell to 57 percent in 1936, but rose to 63 percent by 1939.[56] How much of this recovery can be attributed to the RTAA is open to question, but the general trend seemed to support the view that the trade agreements made a positive contribution in expanding the US share in some foreign markets.

The trade agreements had a relatively modest effect in reducing US import duties. Figure 9.2 shows a scatterplot of the average tariff rate by schedule in 1880 and in 1939. This figure reveals that the basic structure of import duties was little changed from the late nineteenth century, another indication of the lasting stability of policy over this period. In addition, tariff rates had come down only slightly. The Tariff Commission found that the first thirteen agreements implemented by 1936 reduced the average tariff on dutiable imports from 46.7 percent to 40.7 percent, a six-

TABLE 9.1. Trade agreements, 1934–1944

Country	Signed	Effective
Cuba	Aug. 24, 1934	Sept. 3, 1934
Brazil	Feb. 2, 1935	Jan. 1, 1936
Belgium (and Luxembourg)	Feb. 27, 1935	May 1, 1935
Haiti	March 28, 1935	June 3, 1935
Sweden	May 25, 1935	Aug. 5, 1935
Colombia	Sept. 13, 1935	May 20, 1936
Canada	Nov. 15, 1935	Jan. 1, 1936
Honduras	Dec. 18, 1935	Mar. 2, 1936
The Netherlands	Dec. 20, 1935	Feb. 1, 1936
Switzerland	Jan. 9, 1936	Feb. 15, 1936
Nicaragua	Mar. 11, 1936	Oct. 1, 1936
Guatemala	Apr. 24, 1936	June 15, 1936
France	May 6, 1936	June 15, 1936
Finland	May 18, 1936	Nov. 2, 1936
Costa Rica	Nov 28, 1936	Aug. 2, 1937
El Salvador	Feb. 19, 1937	May 31, 1937
Czechoslovakia	Mar. 7, 1938	April 16, 1938
Ecuador	Aug. 6, 1938	Oct. 23, 1938
United Kingdom	Nov. 17, 1938	Jan. 1, 1939
Canada (second agreement)	Nov. 17, 1938	Jan. 1, 1939
Turkey	Apr. 1, 1939	May 5, 1939
Venezuela	Nov. 6, 1939	Dec. 16, 1939
Cuba (first supplementary agreement)	Dec. 18, 1939	Dec. 23, 1939
Canada (supplementary fox-fur agreement)	Dec. 13, 1940	Dec. 20, 1940
Argentina	Oct. 14, 1941	Nov. 15, 1941
Cuba (second supplementary agreement)	Dec. 23, 1941	Jan. 5, 1942
Peru	May 7, 1942	July 29, 1942
Uruguay	July 21, 1942	Jan. 1, 1943
Mexico	Dec. 23, 1942	Jan. 30, 1943
Iran	Apr. 8, 1943	Jun. 28, 1944
Iceland	Aug. 27, 1943	Nov. 19, 1943

Source: US Tariff Commission 1948.

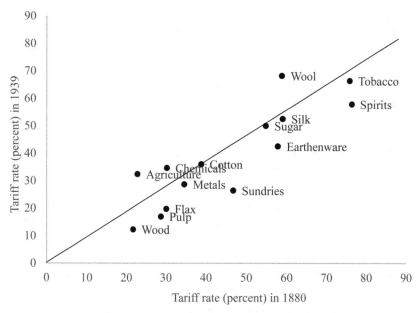

Figure 9.2. Average tariff rate by schedule, 1880 and 1939. (*Statistical Abstract of the United States* 1885, 13–4; 1942, 572–74).

percentage-point drop. This would bring the average tariff back to where it had been prior to the enactment of the Hawley-Smoot duties.[57] Thus it could be said that the tariff reductions negotiated under the RTAA effectively reversed the Hawley-Smoot increase with the added advantage of having foreign countries reduce their tariffs on US exports as well.

More broadly, the average tariff on dutiable imports fell from 46.7 percent in 1934 to 37.3 percent in 1939, putting it just below the pre-Hawley-Smoot level of 40.1 percent in 1929. Some of this decline was the result of an 11 percent increase in import prices between 1934 and 1939, which reduced the ad valorem equivalent of the specific duties that had been nominally set in 1930. These higher import prices knocked about 3.3 percentage points off the average tariff. Therefore, of the actual decline in the tariff of 9.4 percentage points, 6.1 percentage points were due to trade agreements, and 3.3 percentage points were due to import price inflation.[58]

What was the impact of this tariff reduction on America's foreign trade? The impact on exports is very difficult to determine because information is not available on the extent to which other countries reduced their tariffs. Regarding imports, if the lower tariffs were fully passed through to import prices, the tariff reduction attributable to the RTAA would have reduced the average price of dutiable imports by about 4 percent. This would have a limited impact on total imports, the growth of which was driven more by the economic recovery. The volume of imports only rose 23 percent between 1933 and 1939, a number kept down because of the severe 1937–38 recession, while export volume rose 60 percent over that period.[59] While there are no conclusive studies on the matter, the RTAA may have made a small contribution to the economic recovery after 1933 by promoting export growth.

The impact on imports, although distorted by the recession, was modest by design. Hull instructed his department to undertake the tariff reductions with vigor but "gradually and with due care at every stage."[60] Hull was very cautious and did not want to offend powerful domestic interests that might trigger congressional opposition to the program. Hull and his deputies went to great lengths to avoid harming domestic producers by reducing tariffs more on imports that did not compete with domestic production. He consistently maintained that the program was designed to reduce excessive tariffs, not introduce free trade. As Sayre (1957, 170) recalled, "Our whole program was based upon finding places in the tariff wall where reductions could be made without substantial injury to American producers." (One could read "without substantial injury" as meaning "without arousing political opposition.") "The trade agreements program is not in any sense a free trade program," Grady (1936, 295) held. "It is merely an attempt . . . to restore . . . to American enterprise its natural markets abroad and at the same time [provide] reasonable protection for domestic industry."

The extent of the tariff reductions varied considerably across commodities because the State Department negotiators had discretion in choosing where to make the cuts, avoiding politically sensitive industries wherever possible. Hull insisted that the president be briefed on the concessions in every prospective trade agreement to ensure that the State Department had political cover for any trade agreement that it reached. Roosevelt usually approved the agreements put before him and was much more willing than Hull to take political risks. As Francis Sayre (1957, 170) recalled, "Occasionally, however, a proposed cut might do local hurt, and I would say to the President: 'Here we must make a tariff cut which might harm you politically. You may hear about this.' Almost always he would reply, 'Well, Frank, if it's necessary, go ahead, go ahead.' He had confidence in us and did not hesitate to follow through with our program."[61]

The Roosevelt administration highlighted its cautious approach when it appealed to Congress to renew the program in 1937. In a letter to the

Ways and Means Committee, the president stated, "In the process of obtaining improvement in our export position the interests of our producers in the domestic market have been scrupulously safeguarded."[62] Testifying before Congress in 1940, Hull argued,

> No evidence of serious injury has been adduced in the assertions and allegations which have been put forward by the opponents and critics of the trade-agreements program. Naturally, in some individual cases, producers have had to make adjustments to the new rates. Generally speaking, because of the moderate, painstakingly considered, and carefully safeguarded nature of the duty reduction made in the trade agreements, such adjustments have not occasioned serious difficulty. . . . I invite any person to show a single instance of general tariff readjustment either upward or downward, in the entire fiscal history of the Nation, wherein there has been exercised as much impartiality, care, and accuracy as to facts as has uniformly characterized the negotiation of our 33 agreements—or any more solicitude for the welfare of agriculture, labor, business, and the population of the country in its entirety.[63]

In fact, even the American Tariff League conceded that the trade agreements program had been run fairly.[64]

Despite the modest overall reduction in duties over the 1930s, the program remained controversial. Many politically active, import-sensitive interests were frustrated in having to deal with the State Department instead of their elected representatives on Capitol Hill. Unlike members of Congress, State Department officials generally resisted pressure from industry groups who wanted exemptions from possible tariff reductions.[65] Indeed, these interests had significantly less influence on the executive branch than they had with Congress.[66] To administration supporters, this was a good thing: as Senator Harry Truman (D-MO) argued, the administration had "placed the adjustment of tariff duties in the hands of the most competent men available for the purpose, men beyond the reach of political logrolling and tariff lobbying at the expense of national welfare."[67] The RTAA was beginning to change the process of trade policymaking even more than it was changing the schedule of import duties themselves.

RENEWING THE RTAA IN 1937

Republicans voted overwhelmingly against the RTAA in 1934 and continued this opposition in the 1936 presidential election campaign. The

Republican platform vowed to "repeal the present reciprocal trade agreement law," deeming it "destructive" for "flooding our markets with foreign commodities" and "dangerous" for entailing secret negotiations
without legislative approval.[68] The Democratic election platform simply
stated, "We shall continue to foster the increase in our foreign trade which
has been achieved by this administration; to seek by mutual agreement
the lowering of those tariff barriers, quotas and embargoes which have
been raised against our exports of agricultural and industrial products;
but continue as in the past to give adequate protection to our farmers and
manufacturers against unfair competition or the dumping on our shores of
commodities and goods produced abroad by cheap labor or subsidized by
foreign governments."[69]

After the Democrats won another landslide victory in the 1936 election, Hull focused on renewing the RTAA, which was due to expire in
June 1937. In a letter requesting the renewal of the tariff-reduction authority, Roosevelt wrote to Ways and Means Committee Chairman Doughton, "Our vigorous initiative in the field of liberalization of commercial
policies has been an important factor in arresting the world trend toward
national economic isolation, which seemed almost irresistible 3 years
ago. . . . But while accomplishment has been substantial and gratifying,
the task is by no means completed. In international trade relations, emergency conditions still exist. Barriers operating against our trade are still
excessive. Their reduction continues to be an essential requirement of a
full and balanced economic recovery for our country."[70]

Roosevelt wanted the negotiating authority to be made permanent, but
Hull doubted that Congress would agree, and he was right.[71] Testifying before Congress, Assistant Secretary of State Sayre emphasized the care with
which duties had been and would be reduced:

> To open up trade channels, trade barriers must naturally be reduced on
> both sides. This does not mean free trade. It does not mean throwing
> open the flood gates so as to allow the importation of great quantities of
> foreign goods which are highly competitive with our own. It does not
> mean, as some would have you believe, lessened home production in
> return for increased production in American export industries. What it
> does mean is reducing on both sides such barriers as have no economic
> justification and cause injury rather than benefit to our Nation as a
> whole. If by the judicious and careful lowering of an unjustifiable trade
> barrier, we can increase our national trade without substantial injury
> to efficient domestic producers, both countries gain.[72]

The hearings allowed many opponents of the RTAA to voice their objections, including the National Grange, the National Cooperative Milk
Producers Federation, the American Mining Congress, and the National
Wool Growers Association, among others. Unlike 1934, when the RTAA
was merely prospective legislation, now it had been used to make actual
tariff changes, and this gave rise to greater opposition. Although few of
these groups could point to dire consequences that had befallen them
as a result of the trade agreements, they warned that lower tariffs might
threaten their survival in the future by leaving them dangerously exposed
to greater foreign competition. They feared that they would not be able
to obtain relief from imports should the need arise, because the administration's procedures were rigid, and State Department officials seemed
indifferent to their fate. A few large export groups supported the RTAA for
opening up foreign markets to US goods, including the American Cotton
Shippers Association, the Chamber of Commerce, the Automobile Manufacturers Association, and others.

As expected, the Ways and Means Committee favorably reported the
bill, but the minority Republicans changed the tone of their opposition to
the RTAA: "It has been generally assumed that because we have consistently opposed the methods of administration of the present trade agreements program, we do not favor any reciprocal negotiations whatsoever
with foreign countries." They insisted that this was not the case, even
though the "pseudo-reciprocity" of the RTAA was "open to many serious
objections." Still, they repeated the charge that the RTAA was an unconstitutional delegation of power to the president, that Congress should have
an opportunity to approve the agreements, and that it ignored the principle of protection by permitting tariff rate changes without reference to
the difference in the cost of production.[73]

Given the Democratic majority and the lack of much opposition to the
few trade agreements reached over the previous three years, the House easily passed the renewal in February 1937 by a vote of 285–101. The vote was
typically partisan: Democrats supported the renewal by 277–11, and Republicans and other parties opposed it by 90–8.

Not unexpectedly, the Senate fight was more difficult. Republican
opponents claimed that lower tariffs could allow a surge of imports that
would damage the economy. They accused the State Department of running a "star chamber" in determining which domestic producer interests
would be sacrificed in the negotiations. Arthur Vandenberg (R-MI) said
that he did not object to the idea of reciprocity, but declared "this particular kind of reciprocity is unfortunate, ill-advised, unwarranted and in

direct violation of the Constitution of the United States."[74] They feared the unraveling of protective tariffs and complained that further moves to reduce them would jeopardize the recovery from the Depression.

Senators of both parties from the West strongly opposed the renewal.[75] The West had been hard hit by low commodity prices, and the recovery from the Depression had been slow. Opposition was particularly strong among Senators representing cattle, wool, and copper interests in Colorado, Wyoming, and Nevada. Other farmers in the region were not deeply involved in trade; they were simply trying to hold onto the domestic market and had little hope of exporting more, but they feared the RTAA might undercut their tenuous position by letting in more imports. On top of these economic objections, isolationist sentiment among senators such as Gerald Nye (R-ND) held that open trade was part of an internationalist agenda by the Eastern establishment that catered to the interests of big business at the expense of the West. As a result, western Senators proposed amendments to effectively kill the legislation. Key Pittman (D-NV) asked that a two-thirds Senate vote be required to approve trade agreements, a motion that was narrowly defeated but which still received significant Democratic support. Another amendment offered by Claude Pepper (D-FL) would have prohibited a reduction in duties on agricultural goods below the level necessary to equalize the costs of production. The amendment passed, but the Democratic leadership forced a reconsideration of the vote and succeeded in reversing it.

Despite these threats, the Senate comfortably passed the renewal just days after the House by a vote of 58–24. Democrats supported the measure by 54–9 while Republicans opposed it 14–0 (with other parties 4–1 in favor). One reason the Roosevelt administration was able to maintain Democratic support for renewal was that the trade agreements seemed to be of little significance. The tariff reductions were modest, dutiable imports were only about 2 percent of GDP, and the downside of continuing the program appeared minimal. Furthermore, after a flurry of agreements were reached in 1935 and 1936, few were concluded after that: aside from the British accord, agreements were reached only with Czechoslovakia and Ecuador in 1938 and Turkey and Venezuela in 1939.

By the end of 1930s, Hull had outlasted his critics within the administration and had managed to establish the reciprocal trade agreements program as the key feature of US trade policy. As the decade progressed, however, the justification for the program began to shift from promoting the economic recovery to countering the growing threats to world peace. Of course, Hull had long believed that liberalized trade would promote peace.

In 1934, he wrote that "trade between nations is the greatest peace-maker and civilizer within human experience." The trade agreements program is "the first step in a broad movement to increase world trade. Upon this program rests largely my hope of insured peace and the fullest measure of prosperity."[76]

But as Europe moved toward war, Hull's single-minded obsession with reducing trade barriers seemed completely misplaced. Roosevelt's advisor, Harold Ickes (1953–54, 2:218–19), complained in his diary that "All [Hull] ever tried to do, in addition to his futile protests at continued encroachment by the dictators, was to negotiate reciprocal trade agreements. These were all right so far as they went; they might have led to something in ordinary times when peace was the principal preoccupation of the nations of the world, but as I remarked to the President on one occasion, with the world in turmoil, they were like hunting an elephant in the jungle with a fly swatter."

Roosevelt shared this skepticism. After a cabinet meeting in January 1939, Ickes (1953–54, 2:568) noted, "The president spoke rather contemptuously of the reciprocal trade agreements in an emergency such as this, although I do not think that he had any intention to hurt Hull's feelings. He remarked how futile it was to think that we could be doing ourselves any good, or the world any good, by making it possible to sell a few more barrels of apples here and a couple of automobiles there."

As Roosevelt remarked to Treasury Secretary Henry Morgenthau, "Trade treaties are just too goddamned slow. The world is marching too fast."[77] At best, members of Congress believed that Hull exaggerated the links between trade and peace and the importance of trade agreements in world politics. At worst, they viewed him as completely out of touch with the darkening reality of the world. That said, Hull conceded in private that "only five percent [of the trade agreements program] is economic, while the other 95 percent is more or less political or psychological."[78]

WORLD WAR II AND US TRADE

The outbreak of war in Europe in September 1939 first affected American trade politics during the congressional battle over renewing the RTAA in 1940. Although the war effectively ended further trade negotiations, Hull believed that the worldwide conflict gave the RTAA a new and stronger rationale. In late 1939, Hull (1948, 746–47) delivered a widely noted address in which he stated that "the trade agreements program should be retained intact to serve as a cornerstone around which the nations could rebuild their commerce on liberal lines when the war ended." As he argued: "If there is anything certain in this world, it is that, after the present hostilities come to an end, there will be an even more desperate need than there was in recent years for vigorous action designed to restore and promote healthy and mutually beneficial trade among nations." The trade agreements program "offers a solid basis for the hope that, with peace regained, there will be a good opportunity for completing the work of trade restoration. That precious opportunity would be lost if we, who have in the recent past taken a position of world leadership in this vital work, should now reverse our own policy and turn our face straight back toward suicidal economic nationalism, with its Hawley-Smoot embargoes."

Roosevelt was impressed with Hull's speech and commended it to his cabinet. "For the first time since 1933," Hull (1948, 747) wrote, "I had the feeling that the President was really behind me on trade agreements." But Roosevelt also feared that Hull was fighting a losing battle. Political sentiment was now running against renewal. Even more than in 1937, import-sensitive interests, particularly in the West, were increasingly vocal about their opposition to renewal. As Roosevelt told Ickes (1953–54, 3:68), "Hull is all wrapped up in this idea of reciprocal trade agreements. It is the one thing that he is interested in. But public sentiment is against them and I wish that Hull would not press the matter. He will be defeated, I think, and it will break his heart."

Despite misgivings in Congress about the trade agreements program, public opinion was not hostile to the idea: a Gallup poll in January 1940 revealed that only 10 percent of those surveyed understood the term *reciprocal trade*, but 71 percent of those who did supported Hull's program, and just 29 percent opposed it.[79]

In January 1940, President Roosevelt requested a second three-year renewal of the RTAA from Congress, arguing that it "should be extended as an indispensable part of the foundation of any stable and durable peace." The rationale for the program had clearly shifted from expanding trade to promote recovery from the Depression to expanding trade to promote peace after the war. Testifying before Congress, Hull stated that the negotiating authority would help pave the way for postwar cooperation on trade policy: "Even a temporary abandonment of the program now would be construed everywhere as its permanent abandonment. Unless we continue to maintain our position of leadership in the promotion of liberal trade policies, unless we continue to urge upon others the need for adopting such policies as the basis of post-war economic reconstruction, the future will be dark indeed. The triumph or defeat of liberal trade policies after the war will, in large measure, be determined by the commitments which the nations will assume between now and the peace conference"[80]

Raising the issue of trade policy in an election year was always risky, but public opinion was broadly in support of the trade agreements program.[81] Large Democratic majorities in Congress seemed to assure the RTAA's renewal, as well as the knowledge that the program would be effectively on hold during the war. Of course, the Roosevelt administration worked diligently behind the scenes to ensure its passage through the House.[82] The Democrats managed to defeat a Republican amendment to recommit the bill and require Congressional approval of all trade agreements and secure additional protection for domestic producers against foreign competition. In February 1940, the House passed the renewal (by a vote of 218–168) in partisan fashion: Democrats voted 212–20 in favor, and Republicans voted 146–5 against.

The Senate battle was more contentious than in 1937, once again because of opposition among the Democrats. Southern Democrats remained solidly behind the act, but western Democrats opposed it with greater tenacity than before. Key Pittman (D-NV), the chairman of the Senate Foreign Affairs Committee, who represented western mining and agricultural interests, led the opposition. He and his allies complained that tariff reductions had allowed a "flood" of imported minerals and farm goods to swamp the domestic market. Prior to the renewal battle, this faction had prevented the State Department from offering any reduction in the copper and beef tariffs in prospective trade agreements with Chile and Argentina; as a result, copper was taken out of the Chilean agreement, and Argentina broke off negotiations. Joseph O'Mahoney (D-WY) feared that "tariffs protecting agricultural items may be reduced in order to secure concessions from foreign countries for manufactured goods."[83] So many Senate Democrats were opposed to the renewal that Vandenberg and the Republicans decided to back off and "let them do the fighting" to kill the bill.[84]

The Senate Finance Committee came close to not reporting the bill; only the efforts of committee chair Pat Harrison of Mississippi saved the renewal from defeat at this point and later as well.[85] On the Senate floor, Pittman proposed an amendment requiring Senate approval (by a two-thirds majority) of all trade agreements, which would effectively kill the program. The night before the vote, Pittman was confident that he had enough support to pass it, but the amendment was defeated by just three votes, 44–41, after the administration made an intense effort to persuade western Senators to oppose it.[86] Other amendments to dilute the president's power or restrict the program also failed by close margins.

In April 1940, the Roosevelt administration managed to squeak out a narrow victory—by just five votes—on the final Senate passage. Democrats were deeply split, voting 38–18 in favor, while Republicans voted 17–3 against. The fact that more Democrats than Republicans voted against the renewal indicated the fragile political support behind the RTAA. This heartened RTAA opponents such as Hiram Johnson (R-CA), who wrote, "The White House had to break its neck to put them over this time, and did it then by a very scant majority. Old Hull is a 'nut' and he had gathered about him some superannuated free traders, and some young men who have adopted that as a philosophy of government. Each time we have been getting closer to whipping him, so I don't feel particularly badly about the present extension."[87] Of course, the fierce political battle was disproportionate to the underlying stakes because, with Europe now embroiled in war, the trade agreements program was effectively on hold. At the same time, a failure to renew the authority would have been a blow to the administration.

The changing world scene also brought a subtle change to the Republican position. Although the party voted overwhelmingly against the renewal, the party platform for the 1940 election indicated a softening in their stance. The platform reiterated the long-standing belief that tariff protection was "essential to our American standard of living," but the Republicans did not call for a repeal of the RTAA, as they did in 1936. Instead, they criticized the implementation of the program: "We condemn the manner in which the so-called reciprocal trade agreements of the New Deal have been put into effect without adequate hearings, with undue haste, without proper consideration of our domestic producers, and without Congressional approval. These defects we shall correct."[88]

America's entry into the war after Japan's attack on Pearl Harbor in December 1941 led to many new developments. Republican isolationists were discredited, trade agreements were all but forgotten on Capitol Hill, and the war brought far-reaching changes to the American economy. World War II disrupted foreign trade much more severely than World War I had. With Britain and other allies in desperate need of food supplies and war materiel, the United States became the farm and factory for the Allies. The federal government began mobilizing resources for the war effort, industrial and agricultural production surged, and unemployment vanished. Exports jumped from $3 billion in 1939 to nearly $13 billion in 1943, while imports were virtually unchanged. As it did during World War I, the United States ran an enormous trade surplus. In 1943, merchandise exports stood at 6.5 percent of GDP, while imports fell to just 1.5 percent of GDP.

The counterpart to American trade surpluses were the large trade deficits on the part of Britain and the allies. The only way that they could afford to run such large trade deficits was through financial assistance. Having shifted its domestic production toward the war effort and away from goods for exports, Britain no longer had the export earnings that would enable it to purchase American goods. As a result, it quickly ran down its stock of gold and dollar reserves. In March 1941, the United States stepped in with the Lend-Lease program. Under Lend-Lease, the president was authorized to sell, transfer, exchange, or lend equipment to any country defending itself against the Axis powers and to accept repayment "in kind or property, or any other direct or indirect benefit which the President deems satisfactory." From March 1941 until December 1945, the United States sent nearly $50 billion in goods and services overseas through the Lend-Lease program, accounting for more than 80 percent of merchandise exports during the war. In effect, Lend-Lease was a massive export subsidy in which the federal government purchased agricultural goods, aircraft, tanks and other vehicles, ordnance, and supplies, and shipped them to the Allies to prevent their military collapse.[89]

The war effectively put the trade agreements program on hold in 1941 and 1942. When Cordell Hull made the case for renewing the program in 1943, he looked again to the future, emphasizing the long-term goal of promoting international economic cooperation after the war. Such cooperation was necessary, Hull argued, if the United States was to contribute to economic recovery and world peace:

> A revival of world trade was an essential element in the maintenance of world peace. By this I do not mean, of course, that flourishing international commerce is of itself a guaranty of peaceful international relations. But I do mean that without prosperous trade among nations any foundation for enduring peace becomes precarious and is ultimately destroyed. . . . . Repudiation of the trade-agreements program, or the curtailment of it in scope or time by amendment, would be taken as a clear indication that this country, which in war is bearing its full share of responsibility, will not do so in peace.[90]

However, Hull rejected asking for the authority to reduce tariffs even further, instead choosing just to request a three-year extension of the existing authority that allowed tariffs to be reduced by up to 50 percent from their 1934 level.[91]

This appeal did not convince Republicans like Eugene Millikin (R-CO), who attacked "the new propaganda to surrender our home market" for "illusory internationalist goals."[92] But the war had persuaded many Republicans to shed the isolationist views that they held in the 1930s. This marked a major shift in US foreign policy, as bipartisan support for greater American participation in world affairs after the war began to emerge. Mindful of the refusal to join in the League of Nations after World War I, congressional leaders did not want to jeopardize the chances for international cooperation and peace after World War II.

The signs of change were best illustrated in the intellectual evolution of Senator Arthur Vandenberg of Michigan, the key Republican spokesman on foreign-policy issues, who had been an isolationist in the 1930s but gradually modified his views. As he began shedding his past isolationism, Vandenberg (1952, 34) insisted that America "must not fumble the peace" after the war.[93] Vandenberg had opposed the RTAA in 1934, 1937, and 1940, but in 1943 announced, "I favor extension of the Trade Agreements Act for the duration of the war because I am opposed to any needless interruptions in our inter-allied relationships while we are still engaged in the military pursuit of total victory." However, Vandenberg insisted that the administration should not have complete discretion over the settlement of postwar trade issues:

> There have always been deep-seated convictions in Congress and the country (1) against the constitutionality of this delegated trade-agreements power, and (2) against the economic wisdom of permitting the State Department, which is essentially a political rather than an economic arm of government, to make unchecked decisions which may spell life or death for various sectors of industry, agriculture, and labor within our own United States. These convictions—having nothing to do with so-called isolationism—long antedated the issues of this war, and will continue to postdate them as long as the Republic lives.[94]

The discrediting of isolationism muted Republicans' opposition to the 1943 renewal of the RTAA, but wartime bipartisanship did not make them full-fledged supporters of the act. Republican opinions on foreign policy still ranged widely, from the stalwart isolationism of Hiram Johnson of California to the fervent internationalism of Joseph Ball of Minnesota. Republicans wanted to cooperate with the Roosevelt administration during the war without giving it a blank check to set policy after the war. Their objections focused less on the substance of lower tariffs, because the RTAA's impact had been modest, than on the administration's decision-making process. They complained that the executive branch was too secretive about its plans for postwar trade negotiations and insisted that all trade agreements be brought back to Congress for approval.

With some Republicans supporting the RTAA as part of a bipartisan foreign policy during the war, Congress was expected to renew the legislation much more easily in 1943 than three years earlier. The main question was whether the renewal would pass without debilitating amendments; as Jere Cooper (D-TN) noted, "It is apparent that the main effort to kill this measure is by way of amendment."[95] Noting that a majority of House members believed that the extension should only last until the end of the war, so that Congress could influence postwar trade arrangements, Milton West (D-TX) proposed limiting the president's negotiating authority to just two years, instead of the three requested. This would give Congress the opportunity to review the whole trade agreements program after the war was expected to be over. The House Democratic leadership and the Roosevelt administration opposed the amendment, but it passed by a vote of 196–153.[96]

The success of this amendment prompted a flurry of others to undercut the authority in the renewal. One would require Senate approval of trade agreements, another would prevent trade agreements from allowing agricultural imports at prices below US production costs. Before things got out of control, House Speaker Sam Rayburn stepped down from his chair to address the chamber from the floor. Rayburn warned that "it is necessary for us to think just a little before we act favorably on this amendment and other amendments that will be offered. We have reached a test now in the House of Representatives as to whether or not we are for the reciprocal trade program. We will have none if amendments like the pending amendment, as well as others that may be proposed, are adopted."

Rayburn argued that the trade agreements program had been beneficial to the country and that "crippling amendments" should be rejected. Looking ahead to the end of the war, the Speaker warned,

> I do not want anything to happen in the House of Representatives of the United States of America that will make the people of the world feel that when this war is over we are coming back to the shores of America, stick our heads in the sand, and not do a man's part in the world's great work. . . . My plea to you today is for the duration, at least

for two years and much preferably three, we go along with this program and not be misunderstood, not disappoint the hope of the world.
We are not only going to help the democracies of the earth win this
war, but we are going to do a man's part in trying to keep the peace of
the world after this war is over.[97]

After this plea, the House voted down all remaining amendments and
passed the two-year renewal in an overwhelming bipartisan vote of 343–65.

As usual, the fight was more difficult in the Senate than in the House,
mainly in beating back complicating amendments, but the vote still
proved easier than in 1940. The Senate concurred in a bipartisan vote of
59–23; Democrats voted 41–8 in favor, and Republicans voted 18–13 in favor. This vote did not guarantee Republican support for the trade agreements program after the war, but it demonstrated that the party's blanket
opposition was slowly easing.

There was an impending sense that big changes would be coming in
US trade policy after the war. World War II had fundamentally altered
America's role in the world. As the Ways and Means Committee report on
the 1943 renewal noted, "The issue before us involves much more than the
narrow and sterile tariff debates of the past. . . . The broad question before
us today is not whether a particular tariff rate is a little too high or a little
too low but rather whether we as a Congress shall establish a policy which
will best serve the major interests of the country as a whole and authorize
a practical procedure for making such a policy effective."[98]

Similarly, in justifying the 1943 renewal of the RTAA, the State Department described the stakes involved: "The general objectives of the program are to substitute economic cooperation for economic warfare in our
relations with other countries; to give economic substance to our good-
neighbor policy; and to create the kind of international economic relations
upon which a structure of durable peace can be erected."[99] At this time,
the State Department had not yet given serious consideration to postwar
economic policy. However, American officials were about to hold informal
discussions with their British counterparts about the possibility of a multilateral agreement on commercial policy after the war. These discussions
began the conception of something more ambitious than ever envisioned
by the supporters of the original RTAA in 1934.

CHAPTER TEN

Creating a Multilateral Trading System, 1943–1950

Although Congress delegated trade-negotiating powers to the executive branch through the Reciprocal Trade Agreement Act of 1934, the bilateral agreements reached during the 1930s had only a modest effect in reducing import duties. During World War II, the State Department began making ambitious plans for a multilateral agreement to reduce trade barriers and eliminate discriminatory trade policies around the world. The result was the negotiation of the General Agreement on Tariffs and Trade in 1947. Despite some concerns about this executive action, Congress recognized that a system of open world trade broadly served the nation's economic and foreign-policy interests, although lack of Congressional support ended the attempt to establish an International Trade Organization.

A NEW ORDER FOR WORLD TRADE

Shortly after winning reelection in November 1940, President Franklin Roosevelt started to move away from a policy of neutrality and began helping Britain in the war against Nazi Germany. Britain did not have the financial resources to pay for military and civilian supplies, but the president was determined to provide some form of assistance. The idea of making loans to Britain, as had been done during World War I, was rejected on the grounds that debt repayments had contributed to the instability of the interwar world economy.[1] In December 1940, the president unveiled Lend-Lease, a program of economic and military assistance for Britain and others fighting the Axis powers. Under Lend-Lease, the US government would purchase military supplies and provide them to the Allies under the fiction that they would be "returned" after the war, thereby eliminating the need for repayment. After intense debate, Congress approved the Lend-Lease program in March 1941.

Although recipient countries were not expected to pay for the goods, the United States was not prepared simply to give them away without getting something in return. The legislation required the recipients to provide a "direct or indirect benefit which the president deems satisfactory" as compensation for the assistance.[2] This unspecified benefit became known as "the consideration" and was the price that Britain, in particular, would have to pay for American support.

The decision to supply Lend-Lease goods without providing loans or asking for payment meant that the State Department, rather than the Treasury Department, was given responsibility for handling the consideration.[3] While the Treasury Department would have primary authority for dealing with postwar monetary and financial issues, the State Department would take the lead in most other postwar arrangements. At the top of the State Department's list of priorities was the reconstruction of the world trading system. Secretary of State Cordell Hull and his followers believed that efforts to promote growing world trade were needed to help lay the groundwork for a lasting peace.

In a radio address in May 1941, Hull set out his vision of the postwar world, stating that it was "none too early to lay down at least some of the principles by which policies must be guided at the conclusion of the war." The overarching goal for the postwar period was "the task of creating ultimate conditions of peace with justice." This would require "a broad program of world economic reconstruction" in which "the main principles, as proven by experience, are few and simple." Among these principles were that "non-discrimination in international commercial relations must be the rule, so that international trade may grow and prosper" and "raw materials must be available to all nations without discrimination." Furthermore, "extreme nationalism must not again be permitted to express itself in excessive trade restrictions." Hull concluded by saying that, "in the final reckoning, the problem becomes one of establishing the foundation of an international order in which interdependent nations cooperate freely with each another for their mutual gain."[4]

The outbreak of another war in Europe convinced almost everyone that America's failure to provide leadership after World War I had contributed to the outbreak of World War II, and government officials were determined not to repeat the mistakes of the past. A key goal was simply to free world trade from the destructive trade policies that had arisen during the 1930s and help the world economy flourish once again. As the dominant world power, the United States was in a strong position to help put world trade on an open and non-discriminatory basis. American officials saw an "unparalleled opportunity to obtain a large and world-wide reduction of trade barriers" after the war and believed that "every possible measure should be explored to take advantage of the present unique opportunity to preserve and strengthen the free-enterprise basis of world trade."[5] In addition to reducing tariffs, eliminating quotas, and dismantling discriminatory trading blocs, American policymakers were deeply concerned about how state trading and state-owned industries had begun to crowd out private US firms in world trade. In such a world, the United States, with its largely private enterprise economy, would operate at a competitive disadvantage in foreign markets.

In May 1941, State Department officials began drafting a formal Mutual Aid Agreement. In exchange for Lend-Lease assistance, State Department officials believed that Britain should cooperate with the United States in establishing an open, multilateral trading system, the cornerstone of which would be non-discrimination. Britain's participation was critical to the success of this endeavor. Although its global power was severely diminished, Britain still played a leading role in international trade and finance, and led a large number of Commonwealth countries, including Australia, Canada, India, South Africa, New Zealand, and Ceylon. If it rejected the American proposals, Britain could create its own formidable trade bloc based on the preferential tariffs in the Ottawa agreements and the sterling-centered payments system, leaving the United States outside that important sphere. As a result, the State Department under Hull wanted to abolish imperial preferences and significantly reduce other trade barriers. Because Britain now desperately needed American assistance, the State Department was in a much stronger position to make demands on Britain than it had been in 1938, when a reciprocal trade agreement failed to accomplish much.[6]

In June 1941, the British government dispatched John Maynard Keynes, the brilliant economist and influential adviser to the UK Treasury, to Washington to discuss the terms and conditions of the mutual aid agreement. Keynes was the famous author of the *General Theory of Employment, Interest, and Money* (1936), which made a case for activist government policies to maintain economic stability and ensure full employment. At this point, Keynes believed that economic planning would be needed to ensure full employment after the war. Such planning, in his view, would involve controls on international trade, including import quotas and state trading. Keynes was also pessimistic about the prospects for a postwar agreement to ensure open world trade and worried that his country would face severe balance of payments problems after the war. Therefore, he went into the negotiations convinced that Britain would long be dependent upon its privileged bilateral trade relationships within the sterling bloc to conduct its foreign trade.

When Keynes was sent to Washington, Britain's main objective was simply to postpone any specific commitments on postwar economic policy.[7] But American officials were not easily diverted from their goal, and Assistant Secretary of State Dean Acheson presented Keynes with a draft aid agreement in July 1941. In exchange for assistance, article 7 of the draft stated that postwar arrangements "shall be such as to not burden commerce between the two countries but to promote mutually advantageous economic relations between them and the betterment of world-wide economic relations; they shall provide against discrimination in either the United States or the United Kingdom against the importation of any product originating in the other country; and they shall provide for the formulation of measures for the achievement of these ends."[8] Keynes asked whether this implied that imperial preferences, exchange controls, and other trade measures would be restricted in the postwar period. Acheson replied that it did, but assured Keynes that "the article was drawn so as not to impose unilateral obligations, but rather to require the two countries in the final settlement to review all such questions and to work out to the best of their ability provisions which would obviate discriminatory and nationalistic practices and would lead instead to cooperative action to prevent such practices."[9]

This exchange produced a long outburst from Keynes, who was dismayed at what he perceived to be an attempt to force unilateral obligations on Britain when it wanted to keep imperial preferences and might need various trade controls to survive in the postwar world.[10] Keynes made no promises and told Acheson that the British government was divided over postwar trade policy; some wanted a return to free trade, another group (including Keynes) believed in the use of import controls, and a third group wanted to preserve imperial preferences.[11]

In fact, Keynes was shocked by the State Department proposals and privately dismissed the draft of article 7 as the "lunatic proposals of Mr. Hull."[12] To him, the Americans seemed to believe in an outdated ideology of limited government intervention that ignored the new reality that governments would need extensive trade controls to ensure economic stability. Keynes (1980, 239) rejected one State Department memo on trade as "a dogmatic statement of the virtues of laissez-faire in international trade along the lines familiar forty years ago, much of which is true, but without any attempt to state theoretically or to tackle practically the difficulties which both the theory and the history of the last twenty years [have] impressed on most modern minds."[13]

The clash between Keynes and Acheson over imperial preferences would be repeated at nearly every bilateral meeting over the next six years. For example, a few weeks later, in August 1941, President Roosevelt and Prime Minister Winston Churchill met off the coast of Newfoundland, Canada, to issue a joint declaration on the purposes of the war against fascism and the guiding principles to be followed after the war. Churchill presented a first draft of what became known as the Atlantic Charter, which included a pledge that the two countries would "strive to bring about a fair and equitable distribution of essential produce around the world."[14] Undersecretary of State Sumner Welles tried to introduce tougher language that called for the "elimination of any discrimination." Roosevelt softened this to say that mutual economic relations would be conducted "without discrimination," but Churchill insisted that discrimination could be eliminated only "with due respect for existing obligations."[15]

Over the strong objections of Welles, Roosevelt accepted this compromise language. As a result, the final version of the Atlantic Charter stated that the countries "will endeavor, with due respect for their existing obligations, to further the enjoyment by all States, great or small, victor or vanquished, of access, on equal terms, to the trade and to the raw materials of the world which are needed for their economic prosperity." Hull (1948, 975–6) was "keenly disappointed" with this language because the "with due respect" qualification "deprived the article of virtually all significance since it meant that Britain would continue to retain her Empire tariff preferences against which I had been fighting for eight years." Hull's State Department would not give up its attack on imperial preferences, which in their view "combined the twin evils of discrimination and politicization of foreign trade."[16]

At the same time, Roosevelt urged Churchill to conclude the mutual aid agreement soon, telling him that there was no specific obligation to eliminate imperial preferences, just a commitment to negotiate in good faith over the issue.[17] This assurance helped Churchill to persuade his Cabinet to approve the Mutual Aid Agreement, which was signed in Washington in February 1942. Article 7 stated that, in exchange for American assistance, the countries agreed "not to burden commerce between the two countries, but to promote mutually advantageous economic relations between them and the betterment of world-wide economic relations," and they also agreed to action, "open to participation by all other countries of like mind, directed to the expansion, by appropriate international and domestic measures, of production, employment, and the exchange and consumption of goods, which are the material foundations of the liberty and welfare of all peoples; to the elimination of all forms of discriminatory treatment in international commerce, and to the reduction of tariffs and other trade barriers." Unfortunately, article 7 continued to be interpreted differently by American and British officials. The State Department viewed it as an implicit promise to abolish imperial preferences, whereas the British government viewed it merely as a pledge to discuss the issue.[18]

The signing of the Mutual Aid Agreement allowed both sides to focus on bringing the article 7 obligation into effect. British policymakers wanted to come up with their own trade-policy proposals before American officials became wedded to their own plan. In July 1942, James Meade, an economist with the Economic Section of the War Cabinet Secretariat, wrote a short memorandum entitled "Proposal for an International Commercial Union."[19] Meade proposed a multilateral trade convention with three key features: (1) open membership to all states willing to carry out the obligations of membership, (2) no preferences or discrimination (with an exception for imperial preference) among the participants, and (3) a commitment to "remove altogether certain protective devices against the commerce of other members of the Union and to reduce to a defined maximum the degree of protection which they would afford to their own home producers against the produce of other members of the Union." Meade's proposal circulated in the British government and generally received approval, with the reservation that Britain would retain the right to impose import quotas if it faced balance of payments difficulties. Meade's proposal formed the basis for the country's negotiating position with respect to article 7.[20]

Meanwhile, US proposals for the implementation of article 7 were delayed through 1942 because of America's entry into the war after the attack on Pearl Harbor. The delay continued into 1943, when the State Department was focused on getting Congress to renew the RTAA (discussed in chapter 9). Finally, in September 1943, a British delegation arrived in Washington to meet with their American counterparts to discuss trade matters. Officials from the UK Board of Trade and the War Cabinet's Economic Section, including economists James Meade and Lionel Robbins, met with Harry Hawkins of the State Department and officials from other federal agencies on commercial policy issues. In parallel discussions, John Maynard Keynes and other UK Treasury officials met with Harry Dexter

White of the Treasury Department on postwar financial and exchange rate issues.[21] These officials represented the staff level, not the political level, of their governments, meaning that these were exploratory discussions to prepare the ground for higher-level negotiations.

The main issues in the commercial policy discussions were tariffs and preferences, quantitative restrictions, investment, employment policy, cartels, commodity agreements, and state trading. With respect to tariffs and preferences, the United States favored bilateral negotiations to reduce duties on a selective, product-by-product basis, in order to avoid reductions on sensitive products, as had been the practice under the RTAA. Britain strongly favored multilateral tariff reductions on an across-the-board basis in order to free up international trade to the fullest extent possible. British officials thought that the more cautious American approach, coupled with the insistence on safeguards and escape clauses, would limit the potential for tariff reductions to expand international trade. As the discussions progressed, the British representatives began to persuade their counterparts about the merits of a broader multilateral approach. US officials did not rule out such an approach, and Hawkins himself seemed to favor it, but it ran counter to the traditional bilateral negotiations that had been pursued under the RTAA.[22] The two sides had a wider gap on preferences and matters such as quantitative restrictions: the United States opposed them, but Britain wanted the option of using them for balance of payments purposes.

Still, the discussions were fruitful, and both sides agreed that they had a solid basis for moving forward. As a result, the interagency Special Committee on Relaxation of Trade Barriers issued an interim report in December 1943 that began with a succinct statement of the prevailing view among American officials:

> A great expansion in the volume of international trade after the war will be essential to the attainment of full and effective employment in the United States and elsewhere, to the preservation of private enterprise, and to the success of an international security system to prevent future wars. In order to create conditions favorable to the fullest possible expansion of international trade, on a non-discriminatory basis, it will be necessary for nations to turn away from the trade-restricting and trade-diverting practices of the inter-war period and to cooperate in bringing about a reduction of the barriers to trade erected by governments during that period. International trade cannot be developed to an adequate extent unless excessive tariffs, quantitative restrictions on imports and exports, exchange controls, and other government devices

to limit trade are substantially reduced or eliminated. Moreover, if this is not done, there may be a further strengthening of the tendency, already strong in many countries before the war, to eliminate private enterprise from international trade in favor of rigid control by the state.[23]

The report stated that "the most promising means of reducing, eliminating, or regulating these various types of trade restrictions, on a worldwide basis, is the negotiation among as many countries as possible of a multilateral convention on commercial policy" and noted that the United States was the only country that could lead the world in this direction. It proposed "a substantial reduction of protective tariffs in all countries"; the abolition of import quotas, which "are among the devices most destructive of international trade and least conformable to a system of private enterprise"; "the elimination of all forms of discriminatory treatment in international trade," particularly imperial preferences; the establishment of principles for state trading; the elimination of export subsidies; and the creation of an international commercial policy organization as "essential to the successful operation of the proposed convention."

However, plans for postwar trade arrangements materialized slowly, because priority was given to establishing the United Nations (at Dumbarton Oaks, Washington, DC) and the international monetary system (at Bretton Woods, New Hampshire). Only by October 1944 was a sketch of a multilateral commercial convention circulating within the government. The draft suggested that the United States propose a 50 percent horizontal tariff reduction, subject to a 10 percent floor, and the elimination of tariff preferences and import quotas, with some exceptions. The proposed convention would also deal with foreign exchange controls, state trading (ensuring equality of treatment), and subsidies (both export and domestic subsidies would be phased out, with some exceptions). President Roosevelt himself specifically instructed Hull to include provisions on restrictive business practices.[24]

To this point, Congress and the public were largely unaware of the ambitious plans that the Roosevelt administration had been developing with respect to postwar trade policy. In November 1944, Acheson testified before Congress in one of the first public discussions of the administration's postwar commercial policy proposals. Acheson (1944, 660) began by warning that "the pre-war network of trade barriers and trade discrimination, if allowed to come back into operation after this war, would greatly restrict the opportunities to revive and expand international trade. Most of these barriers and discriminations are the result of government action. Action

by governments, working together to reduce these barriers and to eliminate these discriminations, is needed to pave the way for the increase in
trade after the war, which we must have if we are to attain our goal of full
employment." With the approaching transition from war to peace, he continued, the world was "presented with a unique opportunity for constructive action in cooperation with other countries. . . . We therefore propose
to seek an early understanding with the leading trading nations, indeed
with as many nations as possible, for the effective and substantial reduction of all kinds of barriers to trade."

Acheson described the US objectives as the elimination of discriminatory treatment in trade, the abolition of import quotas and prohibitions,
the reduction of tariffs, and the establishment of rules with respect to
government monopolies and state trading. In addition, he anticipated the
creation of an international organization to study world trade problems
and recommend solutions. "We propose, in other words, that this Government go on with the work which it has been doing during the last 10 years,
even more vigorously, with more countries, and in a more fundamental
and substantial way," Acheson (1944, 660) concluded. Even though no specific policy actions were imminent, Acheson set the stage for the renewal
of the RTAA in 1945: "In order to achieve this, we need to continue and to
extend the efforts that we have made, through the reciprocal trade agreements program, to encourage an expansion of private foreign trade on a
non-discriminatory basis."

THE 1945 RENEWAL OF THE RTAA

By the presidential election of 1944, the end of World War II was in sight,
and political attention shifted away from the military campaign and toward postwar foreign policy. The Democratic platform stated that "world
peace is of transcendent importance" and pledged to "extend the trade
policies initiated by the present administration," but provided no specifics.[25] The Republican platform revealed a further, if highly qualified, step
toward accepting the trade agreements program and the possibility of further tariff reductions negotiated by the president:

> If the postwar world is to be properly organized, a great extension of
> world trade will be necessary to repair the wastes of war and build an
> enduring peace. The Republican Party, always remembering that its
> primary obligation . . . is to our own workers, our own farmers and
> our own industry, pledges that it will join with others in leadership in

> every co-operative effort to remove unnecessary and destructive barri-
> ers to international trade. We will always bear in mind that the domes-
> tic market is America's greatest market and that tariffs which protect
> it against foreign competition should be modified only by reciprocal
> bilateral trade agreements approved by Congress.

This suggested that the Republicans accepted the idea of reciprocity but
still rejected the unconstrained delegation of authority to the president.
If this caveat was not enough to hamper the program, however, the party
also pledged to "maintain a fair protective tariff on competitive products
so that the standard of living of our people shall not be impaired through
the importation of commodities produced abroad by labor of producers
functioning upon lower standards than our own."[26]

The 1944 election kept the Democrats in control of Congress and Roosevelt as president. With the election settled, the State Department began
preparing for the renewal of trade-negotiating authority under the RTAA,
which was due to expire in June 1945. For the first time, this renewal
would take place without Cordell Hull. After serving as Secretary of State
for eleven years, Hull retired from public life in November 1944. Hull had
championed the reciprocal trade agreements program from its inception,
and this transition could have marked a setback for the program within
the State Department and administration. Yet Hull's immediate successors continued to believe that the program served the national economic
interest and furthered the country's foreign-policy goals. In fact, the new
assistant secretary of state for economic affairs, Will Clayton, embraced
the cause of non-discriminatory trade liberalization with even greater zeal
than Hull. A successful cotton broker, Clayton came from the Southern
Democratic tradition in favor of freer trade. As Clayton (1963, 501) later
put it, "I have always believed that tariffs and other impediments to international trade were set up for the short-term, special benefit of politically
powerful minority groups and were against the national and international
interest." In December 1944, Clayton wrote to the retired Hull, "The first
letter I sign on State Department stationary is to you. I want to assure you
that your foreign policy is so thoroughly ingrained in my system that I
shall always work and fight for it."[27]

The political conditions for the 1945 renewal were favorable: Roosevelt
had just won an unprecedented fourth term as president, the Democrats
still controlled Congress with large majorities, and public opinion favored
America's global leadership to ensure a lasting peace. A Gallup poll found
that 75 percent of those questioned supported continuing the trade agree-

ments program, and just 7 percent were opposed, with 18 percent expressing no opinion. When asked if the program should be used for further tariff
reductions, 57 percent answered yes, 20 percent no, and 23 percent had no
opinion.[28]

Yet the 1945 renewal of the RTAA was unlike any previous one because it would provide the statutory basis for postwar tariff negotiations.
There were two sensitive features to the administration's proposal: the
magnitude of the tariff reduction allowed and the method of tariff reduction permitted. The State Department decided to ask for authority to reduce import duties by up to 50 percent from their 1945 rates, not from the
1934 rates, as in previous renewals. This new tariff-cutting authority was
sought because the 50 percent maximum reduction in tariffs specified in
the original 1934 act had been made on about 42 percent of dutiable imports in previous reciprocal trade agreements, leaving little room for additional tariff cuts under the old authority.[29]

State Department officials also debated whether to stick with reducing
tariffs on a selective, product-by-product basis or to propose reducing tariffs on a horizontal (across-the-board) basis. The selective basis granted in
previous RTAA renewals had been designed to avoid reductions that might
harm certain politically powerful, import-sensitive industries. As a result
of discussions with Britain and Canada, however, officials had been persuaded that a horizontal tariff reduction would be a more efficient method
of reducing import duties. This approach was written into the draft RTAA
renewal legislation that the administration circulated for congressional
consideration.

In early March 1945, senior State Department officials conferred with
key Democratic leaders on Capitol Hill. The initial reaction of House
Speaker Sam Rayburn, Ways and Means Committee Chairman Robert
Doughton, and others was reported to be "very discouraging." While the
Democratic leadership saw no problem with a three-year renewal of the
negotiating authority under section 1 of the draft legislation, or even with
the new 50 percent tariff reduction authority in section 2, they regarded
section 3, permitting a horizontal as opposed to selective tariff reductions,
as problematic. While congressional leaders "seemed to like the objective
of the section," a State Department memo reported, "they were fearful
that its inclusion would complicate and prolong Congressional consideration" of the new 50 percent authority and "make it very difficult, if not
impossible, to get section 2 unqualified by some form of Congressional
approval." The congressional leaders "did not close the door to section 3
but Departmental officers who met with them came away with the feeling

that the leaders felt very strongly that it should be dropped."[30] This left administration officials pondering whether to seek authority to reduce tariffs by up to 50 percent on a selective basis, or to reduce them by a smaller amount on a horizontal basis. State Department staff who had worked on trade matters during the war pressed to keep both, but given the reaction on Capitol Hill, Acheson and Clayton decided to ask for the authority to reduce tariffs by up to 50 percent on a selective basis only.[31]

Late that month, Roosevelt formally requested the renewal of the RTAA for three years. In making the request, the president stated that "we cannot succeed in building a peaceful world unless we build an economically healthy world" and that "trade is fundamental to the prosperity of nations." Therefore, he continued,

> The reciprocal trade agreement program represented a sustained effort to reduce the barriers which the Nations of the world maintained against each other's trade. If the economic foundations of the peace are to be as secure as the political foundations, it is clear that this effort must be continued, vigorously and effectively. . . . The purpose of the whole effort is to eliminate economic warfare, to make practical international cooperation effective on as many fronts as possible, and so to lay the economic basis for the secure and peaceful world we all desire.[32]

Roosevelt died a month later, making this his last statement on trade policy. But his death did little to change US policy, because his successor, Harry Truman, assured continuity. As a Democratic Senator from Missouri, Truman had always faithfully supported the RTAA. In his first press conference as president, just days after taking office, Truman affirmed, "I am for the reciprocal trade agreements program. Always have been for it. I think you will find in the record where I stood before, when it was up in the Senate before, and I haven't changed." At the same time, Truman did not understand all the details of the negotiations or even the issues at stake. After Clayton briefed him on the status of the postwar plans for commercial policy, Truman sighed, "I don't know anything about these things. I certainly don't know what I'm doing about them. I need help."[33]

The stakes in the 1945 RTAA renewal were much greater than in any previous renewal. The Ways and Means Committee began hearings in mid-April and heard from eighty-nine witnesses, thirty-three of whom favored the renewal (seven were administration officials). Clayton testified that without American leadership, an open multilateral trading system would likely be supplanted by economic blocs and government barter arrangements, both of which distorted trade and were "contrary to our deepest convictions about the kind of economic order which is most conducive to the preservation of peace."[34] Among the groups that testified in favor were the American Farm Bureau Federation, the Congress of Industrial Organizations (United Automobile and Aircraft Workers), and the Chamber of Commerce, groups that saw the advantages of larger export markets in the postwar world. The witnesses against the bill included representatives from some labor groups and small- and medium-sized producers from specific industries, such as glass and pottery, wool growing and processing, textiles and shoes, lumber, cattle, and sugar.

In favorably reporting the bill, the Democratic majority stressed the opportunity to create a new system for postwar world trade. The Republican minority denied that they were economic isolationists but worried about imports harming domestic industries. They accused the Democrats of having "bowed to the demands of the State Department" and claimed that they had "been overreached by the soft talk of world planners and globocrats who, we believe, would put the American worker, the American farmer, and the American businessman on the international auction block."[35]

Robert Doughton (D-NC), who had been the Ways and Means chairman in 1934 when the original RTAA had been passed, began the debate on the House floor by stating that "the whole idea of the Reciprocal Trade Agreements Act is to find a better market for our surplus products in a world freer from economic barriers, which means fuller employment, larger profits, and a higher standard of living." He argued that "opponents of the bill admitted that they had not been hurt by the reductions in tariff rates already made, but expressed fear that sometime in the distant and uncertain future they might suffer because of duties lowered under trade agreements. Fear was the text, the sermon and the song of the opposition."[36]

Some Republicans stated that they would support a renewal, but only if the new tariff-cutting authority allowed for in section 2 was removed. Leading the opposition, Harold Knutson (R-MN) warned against deep tariff cuts on employment grounds: "The chairman spoke eloquently about wanting to provide jobs for the returning veterans. Please tell me how you are going to provide jobs if you transfer our payrolls to Czechoslovakia, France, the United Kingdom, China, Germany, Russia, and India?" Charles Plumley (R-VT) said, "I feel very strongly that now more than ever the United States needs reasonable barriers in the nature of protective tariffs against the flood of goods from destitute and devastated areas, manufactured and produced at starvation wages supporting a standard of living we will not tolerate and with which we cannot compete." He added, "America can best help the world by being prosperous and strong, and we can remain neither if we surrender our home market to the pauperized labor of all the world."[37]

Dean Acheson was unimpressed by the Congressional debate, which speculated more about the potential impact of imports on domestic industries than it focused on the foreign-policy goal of strengthening the free world through cooperative measures to expand trade. Acheson (1969, 107) wrote that he found it "a dreary and wholly unrealistic debate. Few of the claimed virtues of the bill were really true and none of the fancied dangers. The true facts lay in a different field from that where the shells from both sides were landing." On the third day of the debate, Acheson (1969, 107) wrote, "I have had a day of frenzied lobbying on the Hill. We are in real trouble and may or may not come through tomorrow. We are trying to get a letter from the president in which he lays his political head on the block with ours. It will be interesting to see if he signs it."

On the final day of the House debate, Knutson proposed deleting all of section 2 of the proposed bill, the new 50 percent tariff-cutting authority, which was "the crux of the whole fight."[38] Anticipating this motion, House Speaker Sam Rayburn took the unusual step of addressing the House from the floor, warning that "there is a big chance here to make a big mistake." Rayburn argued that the trade agreements program had to be strengthened to ensure postwar cooperation on economic matters. He then read a letter from President Truman pledging that American industry and labor would not be sold out in any trade agreement. The president wrote,

> I assume there is no doubt that the act will be renewed. The real question is whether the renewal is to be in such a form as to make the act effective. For that purpose the enlargement of authority provided by section 2 of the pending bill is essential. I have had drawn to my attention statements to the effect that this increased authority might be used in such a way as to endanger or "trade out'" segments of American industry, American agriculture, or American labor. No such action was taken under President Roosevelt and Cordell Hull, and no such action will take place under my presidency.[39]

The proposed amendment to eliminate section 2 was narrowly rejected by a vote of 197–174. A swing of just twelve members of the House could have reversed the outcome of this crucial vote and brought down the plans for significant trade liberalization after the war. Galvanized by the president's appeal, the Democratic leadership helped defeat the remaining amendments that would have given Congress veto power over any agreement, reduced or eliminated the new authority, or otherwise eviscerated the bill, with close but somewhat larger majorities.

At about 6:30 p.m., on May 26, 1945, the House voted 239–153 to renew the RTAA for three years. As usual, the final vote was largely along party lines: Democrats voted 203–12 in favor, and Republicans voted 139–33 against. Although the final margin was comfortable, Acheson (1969, 107) noted that "this does not tell the true story. It was very close on the critical amendments which would have killed the bill. Our toughest one was an amendment to strike out the additional authority given the President to reduce tariffs." Figure 10.1 shows the House vote, with support mainly coming from the Democratic South, as usual, but with some new support also coming from the Northeast, where manufacturing industries hoped to benefit from expanding postwar exports.

The renewal then moved to the Senate, where it faced more dangers. In the Finance Committee, Democrats defeated Republican amendments to reduce the authority to two years and require congressional approval of trade agreements, but Robert Taft (R-OH) persuaded the committee, in a 10–9 vote, to eliminate section 2 of the bill, and three of eleven Democrats voted against the president. Acting Secretary of State Joseph Grew criti-

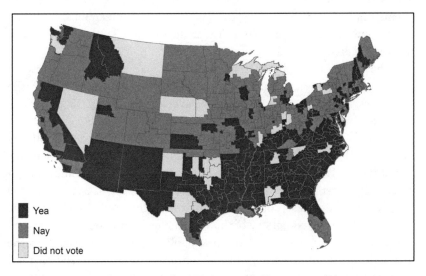

Figure 10.1. House voting on the RTAA renewal, May 26, 1945. (Map courtesy Citrin GIS/Applied Spatial Analysis Lab, Dartmouth College.)

cized the committee's action and told the press that, without section 2, the renewal would be "an empty symbol of our hopes for cooperation with the rest of the world in an economic field."[40]

On the Senate floor, the Democratic leadership insisted that unless the new 50 percent negotiating authority were reinstated, the renewal would be meaningless. Taft said that he agreed that the Smoot-Hawley rates were too high and supported the trade agreements program, but opposed the authority to reduce tariffs by an additional 50 percent because the existing tariff cuts had not been tried under normal conditions. "If we reduce the rates by 50 percent, . . . the country will be hurt," he worried. "We have the responsibility of doing all we can to prevent our people being driven out of work."[41] The Democratic majority managed to save section 2 of the bill by a 47–33 vote and then defeated another six hostile amendments, including a requirement that the Senate ratify all trade agreements, a prohibition on any cuts in duties on agricultural commodities, and the imposition of import quotas on textiles.

On June 20, 1945, "after what seemed like a millennium of talk" in Acheson's (1969, 108) view, the Senate approved the extension by a 54–21 vote. Democrats voted 38–5 in favor, along with one Progressive, while Republicans voted 16–15 against. Thus, at this critical juncture, 15 of 31 (48 percent) Senate Republicans broke ranks and supported the renewal, even though some had voted for the limiting amendments. As Edward Johnson (R-CO) said, "I don't know how it happens, but somehow it always seems that a day or two before you come to voting on reciprocal trade you always have enough votes to beat it, but then when you vote somehow all your votes disappear and it passes."[42]

The Republican split on trade policy in 1945 was driven largely by a swing of Northern Republicans behind the RTAA, particularly in the northeast, whose states had an above-average concentration of export-oriented producers.[43] A simple comparison of Senate Republican voting in 1934 and 1945 makes this point. The propensity of Midwest Republicans to vote for the RTAA was unchanged: six of fourteen Midwest Republicans voted for the RTAA in 1934 (the only Republicans to do so) and eight of twenty Midwest Republicans voted for the renewal in 1945. However, the propensity of northeastern Republicans to support the RTAA increased dramatically: in 1934, not one of the fifteen Northern Republicans favored the RTAA, but six of nine Northern Republicans did so in 1945. With the Republicans dropping their pledge to repeal the RTAA and ending their attacks on its constitutionality, some cross-party support for the program was beginning to emerge, at least in the Senate. Indeed, if the RTAA was to survive, it would need some cross-party appeal at some point, because eventually the Republicans would return to power.

Harry Hawkins later wrote that the 1945 renewal "marks the high point in the legislative basis of the trade-agreements program."[44] However, he noted, "this enactment took place when the war was drawing to a close—at a time when there was a shortage of goods rather than serious market competition, when the creation of a permanent peace was still widely regarded as an attainable goal, and when peaceful trade among nations was widely recognized as an important foundation for international peace." These unique circumstances facilitated its passage. Even so, securing Congress's support for the RTAA had not been easy, and changing conditions would only make its renewal more difficult in the future.

TOWARD A MULTILATERAL TRADE AGREEMENT

Just days after Congress renewed the RTAA, Hawkins, now posted at the US Embassy in London, informed his British counterparts that Congress had approved legislative authority to undertake significant tariff reductions, but only on a selective basis, with no horizontal tariff cuts. Therefore, the United States proposed going ahead with a "multilateral-bilateral" approach, wherein countries would negotiate bilaterally on a product-by-product basis with the principal supplier of a good in question and then generalize the resulting tariff reductions to other participating countries via the unconditional MFN clause.[45] British officials were sorely disappointed at this news, which was a blow to their hopes for a large, across-the-board multilateral tariff reduction. The British were also pessimistic about the length of time it would take to negotiate bilaterally, citing the protracted 1938 trade negotiations between the two countries.

The United States also briefed Canadian officials on this development. Norman Robertson, Canada's Undersecretary of State for External Affairs and a staunch supporter of an open, multilateral trading system, was "deeply disappointed and dismayed" by the news that a horizontal tariff reduction would be impossible. Selective tariff reductions, the Canadians emphasized, would "emphasize the sanctity of protectionism" and make countries "adopt the same careful and cautious attitude toward the reduction or removal of tariffs" and "obscure the truth that trade barrier reduction is also of benefit to the country doing the reducing."[46]

Yet Canadian officials also made a suggestion that soon took on enormous consequence. If the multilateral-bilateral approach had to be taken, they thought it would be undesirable to have many countries at the bargaining table. In Canada's view, "a general conference of all countries might be dangerous, since the views of the many small countries might unduly weaken the bolder measures which the large trading nations might find it possible to agree upon. . . . judging from past experience, the presence at a general international conference of the less important, and for the most part protectionist-minded, countries, would inevitably result in a watering-down of the commitment which a smaller number of the major trading nations might find it possible to enter into."[47] Therefore, Canadian officials suggested that a small "nuclear" group of eight to twelve countries that were deeply committed to reducing trade barriers be convened first. Until Canada's suggestion, the State Department had envisioned a single, large multilateral gathering that would negotiate tariff reductions, establish rules about trade policy, and create an International Trade Organization (ITO). Canada proposed moving in two steps: a smaller group would negotiate a reduction in trade barriers first, and then a larger group would finalize the text of an agreement creating an ITO.

This idea had an immediate impact on American policy. In July 1945, the Executive Committee on Economic Foreign Policy recommended abandoning the multilateral-bilateral approach and adopting instead a "selective nuclear multilateral-bilateral" approach.[48] Under this approach, about a dozen countries would negotiate bilateral agreements for selective tariff reductions and reach informal agreement on rules dealing with tariff and non-tariff barriers to trade. This agreement would then be presented to a larger international conference that would create the ITO. Thus, by July 1945, the United States had a rough conception of the process by which it could move from draft proposals to negotiated agreements through a two-track procedure that would lead to a General Agreement on Tariffs and Trade as distinct from an International Trade Organization.

Despite protesting the limitations on US negotiating authority, Britain was still a reluctant partner, especially as a new Labour government confronted the country's severe economic problems. What rekindled the stalled discussions between the two countries was President Truman's abrupt decision in August 1945, after Japan's surrender ended World War II, to terminate Lend-Lease aid to Britain and the allies. The decision stunned the British government, which still lacked the ability to pay for critical imports of food, fuel, and raw materials. Keynes (1979, 410) warned that, without financial assistance, Britain was facing a "financial Dunkirk." He was immediately dispatched to the United States to secure a loan that would help finance Britain's balance of payments shortfall.

The British loan negotiations took place in Washington in September–

November 1945, with parallel discussions over article 4 and commercial policy. The US trade negotiators handled the contentious issue of imperial preferences clumsily. Assistant Secretary of State Clayton implied that Britain had agreed to abolish imperial preferences in the Mutual Aid agreement, which was not the case, and implicitly threatened to deny Britain financial assistance if it did not eliminate them, a stand the British viewed as blackmail. When Britain resisted, American officials backed down and accepted the position that elimination of preferences was not a condition for financial assistance.

Despite this friction, these Anglo-American commercial policy discussions proved to be a critical breakthrough that ended two years of inaction. By November, the two sides issued a joint statement that "action for the elimination of preferences will be taken in conjunction with adequate measures for the substantial reduction in barriers to world trade on a broad scale" and that existing commitments would not stand in the way of actions to reduce preferences.[49] More importantly, the two sides agreed on the outline of a trade-policy charter that would be presented to other governments for consideration.

In December 1945, the State Department published its "Proposals for Expansion of World Trade and Employment," the first public disclosure of the administration's plans. The proposals sought to address the four factors held responsible for the diminished volume of world trade: government trade restrictions, private trade restrictions (cartels and combinations), disorderly markets for primary commodities, and irregularity in domestic production and employment. Regarding the first factor, the proposals stated that "barriers of this sort are imposed because they serve or seem to serve some purpose other than the expansion of world trade. Within limits they cannot be forbidden. But when they grow too high, and especially when they discriminate between countries or interrupt previous business connections, they create bad feeling and destroy prosperity. The objective of international action should be to reduce them all and to state fair rules within which those that remain should be confined."[50] The proposals called for an international conference on tariffs to be held "not later than the summer of 1946" and noted that "no government is ready to embrace 'free trade' in any absolute sense. Nevertheless, much can usefully be done by international agreement toward reduction of governmental barriers to trade."

The United States then did two things. First, the State Department invited fifteen countries to participate in a meeting of "nuclear" countries that would negotiate tariff reductions. However, domestic politics intruded. In April 1946, Truman was asked to sign off on the list of items contemplated for duty reduction, while also being warned that "experience has shown that once this list is published, minority interests will put strong pressure on the Administration for commitments that particular tariff rates will not be cut."[51] This request triggered alarm bells at the White House and higher levels of the State Department because of the upcoming midterm elections. As a result, Truman and Secretary of State James Byrnes decided to postpone the negotiations among the "nuclear" countries until early 1947. The rationale was that the administration wanted Congress to pass the British loan before the State Department gave the required ninety-day public notice about the tariff items that would be subject to negotiation. If Congress approved the loan in mid-1946, as anticipated, then the public notice and public hearings on the potential tariff reductions would come uncomfortably close to the congressional elections. To avoid stirring up political controversy over the trade proposals, Truman and Byrnes decided to issue the public notice immediately after the election, meaning that the negotiations could not begin until early 1947. Clayton sent an impassioned memo asking to adhere to the original schedule; he wanted to accelerate the process, supposedly quipping that "we need to act before the vested interests get their vests on."[52] However, the decision had been made, and this plea failed.

Second, in February 1946, the United States proposed convening a general United Nations conference on trade and employment. The goal of the conference was not to engage in tariff negotiations, but to prepare a charter for an International Trade Organization, although the committee drafting an agenda would work in concert with the smaller nuclear group that was exchanging tariff concessions. The first meeting of the UN Preparatory Committee for the International Conference on Trade and Employment convened at Church House in London during October–November 1946.[53] This preparatory meeting was the first one in which other countries (including Australia, India, China, Ceylon, Lebanon, Brazil, Chile, and several others) could help shape the multilateral convention on commercial policy. The main goal of the developing countries was to ensure that the rules did not prevent them from using import quotas to promote objectives related to employment and economic development. As a result, new chapters of the draft ITO charter were included on both issues.

At the landmark London meeting, the participants agreed on most of the provisions of a draft charter for an ITO, although the draft was not yet binding on governments. The participants agreed to limit the use of quantitative restrictions, exchange controls, and export subsidies, except under specific circumstances. Other chapters set out broad rules regarding state trading, economic development, restrictive business practices, intergovernmental commodity agreements, and the structure of the ITO. The Preparatory Committee recommended a process to implement "certain provisions of the charter of the International Trade Organization by means of a general agreement on tariffs and trade" among a smaller group of countries, perhaps the first mention of a general agreement separate from the ITO.[54]

In November 1946, shortly after the midterm elections, President Truman approved the plans for the meeting to negotiate tariff reductions, signing off on the publication of the list of goods on which the United States was prepared to offer concessions. The State Department announced that the tariff negotiations would take place in Geneva in April 1947, with at least eighteen countries participating. The public hearings on the proposed tariff reductions were not nearly as contentious as officials had feared. But the outcome of the November election was stunning: a Republican sweep gave them control of Congress for the first time since 1932, temporarily ending a long era of Democratic political dominance. Given the past Republican support for protective tariffs and hostility toward the RTAA, this electoral shift threatened the impending Geneva negotiations. Although the Republicans could not revoke the negotiating authority granted in 1945 (they could not override a presidential veto of such a measure), the new majority in Congress could severely complicate the negotiations.

Indeed, conservative Republicans immediately called for postponing the April meeting and repealing the RTAA in the future. In December 1946, Senator Hugh Butler (R-NE) wrote a forceful letter to Clayton arguing that the voters had repudiated the administration's tariff-reduction program, and therefore the Geneva negotiations should "be temporarily suspended until the new Congress shall have an opportunity to write a new foreign trade policy." As Butler put it, "The attempt to use the authority of the Trade Agreements Act, previously wrested from a Democratic Congress, to destroy our system of tariff protection, seems to me a direct affront to the popular will expressed last month."[55]

Clayton refused to postpone the Geneva meeting and countered every point in Butler's letter, maintaining that

far from intending "to destroy our system of tariff protection," our Government is entering into the projected trade negotiations for the purpose of insuring that tariffs, rather than discriminatory import quotas, exchange controls, and bilateral barter deals, shall be the ac-

cepted method by which nations regulate their foreign trade. If it were
not for the initiative which our Government has taken in this matter,
the world would be headed straight toward the deliberate strangula-
tion of its commerce through the imposition of detailed administrative
controls. I need hardly tell you that such a development would be seriously prejudicial to the essential interests of the United States.

Clayton also shot back, "We are fighting for the preservation of the sort
of world in which Americans want to live—a world which holds out some
promise for the future of private enterprise, of economic freedom, of rising standards of living, of international cooperation, of security and peace.
The trade agreements program is an instrument whose aid we need if we
are to achieve these ends."[56]

In January 1947, Thomas Jenkins (R-OH) introduced a resolution to
postpone the Geneva negotiations until the Tariff Commission could
report on the impact of lower tariffs on domestic industries. Given the
length of time it would take the commission to undertake such a study,
the Jenkins resolution would delay the Geneva conference indefinitely. To
prevent a serious rift from developing between Congress and the administration, Senators Arthur Vandenberg (R-MI) and Eugene Millikin (R-CO),
chairmen of the Foreign Relations and Finance Committees, respectively,
met with Acheson and Clayton. A former isolationist who had become a
strong proponent of a bipartisan foreign policy, Vandenberg had opposed
the RTAA in the 1930s but now supported multilateral cooperation to reduce trade barriers.[57] However, he feared that the State Department put too
much weight on foreign-policy considerations and discounted the potential harm to domestic producer interests when it negotiated tariff reductions. The Senate leaders wanted to limit the executive's authority over
tariff matters without jeopardizing the entire trade agreements program.

These discussions produced a compromise that allowed the Geneva
conference to go forward. In February 1947, Vandenberg and Millikin issued a statement arguing that it would be "undesirable" to postpone the
April conference in view of the extensive preparations for it. They also
suggested that legislative changes to the RTAA would be "made more
appropriately" in 1948 when it was up for renewal. However, they noted
"considerable sentiment for procedural improvements leading to more certain assurance that our domestic economy will not be imperiled by tariff
reductions and concessions." In particular, they requested five procedural
changes to address the fear that a "tariff adequate to safeguard our domestic economy may be subordinated to extraneous and overvalued dip-

lomatic objectives."[58] These included allowing the Tariff Commission to determine the point beyond which import duties should not be reduced for fear of harming a domestic industry, something that became known as "peril points." More importantly, Vandenberg and Millikin wanted the mandatory inclusion of an escape-clause procedure that would make it easier for domestic industries to receive temporary protection if they were faced with injury as a result of imports.

A few weeks later, President Truman issued an executive order embracing most of these recommendations. The order established an administrative process for considering and acting upon complaints from domestic firms about the harmful impact of foreign competition as a result of negotiated tariff reductions. It required that, in all future trade agreements, the United States could withdraw or modify concessions "if, as a result of unforeseen developments and of the concession granted by the United States on any article in the trade agreement, such article is being imported in such increased quantities and under such conditions as to cause, or threaten, serious injury to domestic producers of like or similar articles."[59] The process would work as follows. Any domestic producer that felt harmed by foreign competition could petition the government for relief from imports. The Tariff Commission would investigate the complaint and make a recommendation to the president "for his consideration in light of the public interest." If the Tariff Commission found grounds for restricting imports to prevent injury, the president had the option of restricting imports or doing nothing.

In announcing the new procedures, Truman insisted that "the provisions of the order do not deviate from the traditional Cordell Hull principles," but "simply make assurance doubly sure that American interests will be properly safeguarded." The executive order did not incorporate all of the senators' suggestions, in particular one in which the Tariff Commission would recommend tariff limits (or "peril points") below which a negotiated reduction should not go. While Butler rejected the president's action as inadequate, Vandenberg and Millikin welcomed it as "a substantial advance in the legitimate and essential domestic protections which should be part of an equally essential foreign trade program."[60]

The compromise was one of several critical moments in the process of forging a bipartisan consensus in favor of creating a system of open trade after World War II. The agreement avoided a repeat of the conflict between a Democratic president and a Republican Congress that occurred after World War I. This particular compromise established an important component of US trade policy—the "escape clause"—which provided that

domestic interests could be safeguarded against the possible adverse effects of trade liberalization.[61] Such a safeguard was essential in addressing
the concerns of some Republicans about the trade agreements program and
helped win their acquiescence to the Geneva conference, though not necessarily their support for it.[62] It also proved to be a politically useful device
for Congress to channel protectionist pressures away from the legislature.

In March 1947, Truman threw his support behind the upcoming Geneva meeting in a speech at Baylor University in Texas. The president
stressed the importance of reaching an international agreement on trade
policy:

> If the nations can agree to observe a code of good conduct in interna-
> tional trade, they will cooperate more readily in other international af-
> fairs. Such agreement will prevent the bitterness that is engendered by
> an economic war. It will provide an atmosphere congenial to the pres-
> ervation of peace. As a part of this program we have asked the other na-
> tions of the world to join with us in reducing barriers to trade. We have
> not asked them to remove all barriers. Nor have we ourselves offered to
> do so. But we have proposed negotiations directed toward the reduction
> of tariffs, here and abroad, toward the elimination of other restrictive
> measures and the abandonment of discrimination. These negotia-
> tions are to be undertaken at the meeting which opens in Geneva next
> month. The success of this program is essential to the establishment of
> the International Trade Organization [and] to the strength of the whole
> United Nations structure of cooperation in economic and political af-
> fairs. . . . The negotiations at Geneva must not fail.[63]

A month later, Dean Acheson, Will Clayton, and Winthrop Brown (chairman of the Committee on Trade Agreements) met with the president to review the tariff concessions that the State Department was prepared to offer at Geneva and discuss the political sensitivities involved, particularly
in the case of zinc, woolen goods, and cotton textiles. When told that he
could expect strong political protests from some special interests, Truman
replied "I am ready for it" and approved the recommendations.[64]

THE GENERAL AGREEMENT ON TARIFFS AND TRADE

In April 1947, at the Palais des Nations in Geneva, Switzerland, representatives from eighteen countries met to conclude an agreement on the principles for the conduct of trade policy and to negotiate tariff reductions.

The United States was anxious to reduce tariffs, ban import quotas, and modify or eliminate imperial preferences. Meanwhile, Western European countries were facing huge balance of payments deficits and wanted the maximum tariff concessions from the United States so that they could increase their exports and earn the precious dollars they needed to purchase the imports. These imports were vital for their economic reconstruction, but they also wanted to retain the right to use trade controls to limit spending on imports because of their balance of payments difficulties.

The negotiation of the proposed General Agreement on Tariffs and Trade (GATT) proceeded smoothly due to extensive preparatory work.[65] The preamble to the agreement stated that trade relations "should be conducted with a view to raising standards of living, ensuring full employment and a large and steadily growing volume of real income and effective demand." These objectives could be achieved in part "by entering into reciprocal and mutually advantageous arrangements directed to the substantial reduction of tariffs and other barriers to trade and to the elimination of discriminatory treatment in international commerce."[66]

Many provisions of the GATT were taken from the reciprocal trade agreements of the 1930s. Article 1 set forth the unconditional most-favored-nation (MFN) clause, which stated that "any advantage, favour, privilege or immunity granted by any contracting party to any product originating in or destined for any other country shall be accorded immediately and unconditionally to the like product originating in or destined for the territories of all other contracting parties." Exceptions were granted for preexisting preferences, such as imperial preferences and the special trading relationship between the United States and Cuba. Article 2 was the (annexed) schedule of tariff concessions produced by the Geneva negotiations. Article 3 called for national treatment (non-discrimination) in internal taxes and regulations by declaring that they "should not be applied to imported or domestic products so as to afford protection to domestic production." Article 11 introduced a general ban on import quotas, with exceptions for countries experiencing balance of payments difficulties or when agricultural imports interfered with domestic measures (article 12).

Other provisions in the GATT allowed countries to rcimpose trade barriers otherwise prohibited by articles 2 and 11 of the agreement. Article 6 concerned dumping, defined as the selling of goods at "less than the normal value," and set out procedures for imposing antidumping duties in cases where the dumping "causes or threatens material injury to an established industry . . . or materially retards the establishment of a domestic industry." Article 19 adopted the US language regarding the escape clause. Other articles contained further qualifications to the principle of non-discrimination and the objective of reducing trade barriers. Article 18 permitted developing countries to impose trade restrictions to foster economic development. Article 20 allowed trade interventions to safeguard public health and safety. Article 21 covered action to protect national security. Many other articles dealt with mundane issues such as marks of origin, customs valuation, goods in transit, the publication and administration of trade regulations, state trading enterprises, and governmental assistance for economic development.

Along with finalizing these rules, the participating countries also negotiated tariff reductions on a bilateral, product-by-product basis. The tariff negotiations were much more contentious than finalizing the text of the general agreement had been. Going into the conference, State Department officials faced the choice of revealing all of the tariff reductions authorized by the president, showing the maximum degree to which the US delegation could reduce duties and thereby minimizing strategic bargaining, or holding some concessions back in the hopes of striking a better deal. As an act of good faith, Clayton decided to put all of the American offers on the table from the start. Other countries professed not to be impressed, held back their offers, and the stalemate began.[67]

One commodity, wool, took on critical importance. Owing to domestic political sensitivities, the US delegation had no authorization to reduce the wool tariff. As the Geneva conference began, the new Republican Congress was even in the process of enacting legislation that would further tighten restrictions on imported wool in an effort to support domestic prices.[68] The House passed the measure in May 1947 by the sizable majority of 151–65, with many Democrats voting in favor. The Senate had already passed similar legislation and, despite strong objections from the administration, the conference committee not only kept the import fee but allowed the president to impose import quotas as well. Though they accounted for just 1 percent of total farm income, wool producers had historically been one of the most politically powerful agricultural groups in Congress.[69]

The wool legislation could have jeopardized the entire Geneva negotiation. Australia was a major wool exporter, and it was the main commodity on which they sought a US tariff reduction. Outraged that the United States was unwilling to make any concessions on wool and might even restrict imports further, the Australian delegation threatened to walk out of the conference, taking other members of the British Commonwealth with them. This threat was viewed as credible. Clayton flew back to Washington to intervene at the highest political levels. The president granted Clayton and Secretary of Agriculture Clinton Anderson, who supported the bill, fifteen minutes each to make their case. Clayton urged the president to veto the bill, arguing that it would wreck the ongoing negotiations. Anderson urged the president to sign the bill, saying that the Geneva meeting was doomed to failure, and the legislation would help rural farmers. Clayton apparently had the better argument: Truman vetoed the bill on the grounds that it "contains features which would have an adverse effect on our international relations and which are not necessarily for the support of our domestic wool growers."[70]

Truman did more than just veto the legislation. He immediately gave Clayton the authority to reduce the wool tariff by 25 percent. The president's approval of a significant reduction in the wool tariff after Congress had just approved an increase was "the greatest act of political courage that I have ever witnessed," Clayton (1963, 499) later said. Although Australia grumbled about the small size of the tariff reduction, Truman and Clayton saved the conference with their quick and decisive action. Once the authorization to reduce the wool tariff was made official in August, the stalemate over tariff reductions was broken, and more offers were forthcoming.

With the wool problem resolved, the Geneva negotiations turned to address the largest obstacle to a successful agreement: Britain's imperial preferences. The elimination of these discriminatory preferences had been a key US objective since the Ottawa Agreements were reached in 1932. Yet the Geneva conference began on an inauspicious note. At an opening press conference, when asked if a 50 percent US tariff reduction would be sufficient incentive to eliminate imperial preferences, the lead British negotiator, Stafford Cripps, replied with a terse "no."[71] Cripps stubbornly defended imperial preferences, partly due to the extreme economic difficulties that Britain faced after the war. He also gave a speech that harshly criticized the United States and disparaged the importance of tariff negotiations and the ITO charter.

The sour British attitude cast a pall over the whole conference.[72] In a key meeting in July 1947, Clayton and Cripps clashed over preferences. Clayton insisted that the time had come for Britain to eliminate them, a demand Cripps dismissed out of hand. A US cable described Cripps as "marked by complete indifference bordering on open hostility toward the objectives of the Geneva conference" and that the "vested interests that have been built up under the preferential system are strong, and the United Kingdom has shown no willingness to take the political risks involved in reducing or removing the protection afforded them by the preferences which they enjoy."[73] Clayton was furious over Cripps's "callous disregard of their commitment on preferences," and the American team was flabbergasted when Cripps suggested that the United States should withdraw some of its offers if it believed it had not received adequate concessions.[74]

Fears about the foreign-policy ramifications of a breakdown in the Geneva negotiations, and concerns about Britain's evident economic weakness, played a key role the negotiation's end-game. In late August, with the GATT text finalized but the tariff negotiations still deadlocked, Clayton cabled Undersecretary of State Robert A. Lovett in Washington and outlined four options: (1) conclude an agreement without a substantial elimination of preferences; (2) conclude an agreement without a substantial elimination of preferences by withdrawing some US offers on tariff reductions, as twice suggested by Cripps; (3) discontinue negotiations with Britain and seek to conclude agreements with others on multilateral basis; (4) adjourn the tariff negotiations indefinitely.[75] Clayton was so upset with the British negotiating stance that he recommended the third option, although his staff strongly disagreed.

Lovett discussed the alternatives with Truman in the Oval Office. The president rejected options 1 and 4 and favored option 2 over 3, and the two agreed that option 2 was the lesser of two evils. In explaining the decision, Lovett made it clear to Clayton that foreign-policy considerations were paramount. In particular, the president and senior State Department officials were worried that a failure at the conference would further weaken Britain's economic and political position and strengthen that of the Soviet Union.[76] The president's decision, overriding Clayton's advice to abandon an agreement with Britain because of imperial preferences, brought the Geneva negotiations to a conclusion. To Clayton's disappointment, Britain's imperial preferences remained largely intact, as margins were unchanged on 70 percent of Britain exports to the Commonwealth, but he accepted the "practical necessity" of compromise.[77]

On October 29, 1947, President Truman welcomed the conclusion of the Geneva conference as "a landmark in the history of international economic relations. Never before have so many nations combined in such a sustained effort to lower barriers to trade. Never before have nations agreed upon action, on tariffs and preferences, so extensive in its coverage and so far-reaching in its effects, . . . [and] it confirms the general acceptance of an expanding multilateral trading system as the goal of national policies."[78] Other world leaders also hailed the result. Max Suetens of Belgium, the chairman of the Geneva meeting, praised the meeting as "the most comprehensive, the most significant, and the most far-reaching negotiations ever undertaken in the history of world trade."[79] In Canada, Prime Minister Mackenzie King praised the result as "the widest measure of agreement on trading practices and for tariff reductions that the nations of the world have ever witnessed. . . . For Canada, the importance of the general agreement can scarcely be exaggerated. The freeing of world trade on a broad multilateral basis is of fundamental importance for our entire national welfare."[80] By contrast, British officials were muted in noting the conclusion of the conference.

In the United States, the retired Cordell Hull issued a statement noting his "profound gratification" at the conclusion of the Geneva conference, stating that "the nations which participated in the negotiations have made a long stride toward the goal of economic betterment and world peace."[81] The public also seemed to be pleased with the agreement. At the conclusion of the Geneva negotiations, Gallup (1972, 1:695) reported that only 34 percent of those surveyed had heard of the GATT; of those who had heard, 63 percent approved of the agreement, 12 percent opposed, and 25 percent expressed no opinion.

However, Republicans in Congress were critical of the outcome and made it clear that they would soon attempt to restrict the president's future authority over trade policy. Millikin worried about the future consequences of the tariff reductions: "In anything resembling normal times, some of the cuts would be catastrophic. For example, they made substantial reductions in the raw material productions of the West which would not be borne in normal times. Copper, livestock, livestock products such as hides and wool, numerous metals, agricultural products—all of these things can be produced cheaper abroad than here."[82] He predicted that Congress would seek to implement the "peril points" provision that Truman had rejected earlier in the year. And Harold Knutson (R-MN), the chairman of the Ways and Means Committee, attacked the Geneva agreement and complained about "the do-gooders who have traded us off for very dubious and nebulous trade concessions that may never be realized."[83]

The GATT was an achievement of the State Department and White House, but would not have been possible without the tacit support of key Republicans, particularly Arthur Vandenberg. The GATT also put into practice three long-standing Republican ideas: the notion of reciprocity, the unconditional MFN policy, and the opposition to quantitative restrictions on trade. The RTAA had started the process of trade agreements and tariff reductions; the GATT was a more formal multilateral mechanism that bound import tariffs at lower levels (for three years, later extended indefinitely) and raised the political costs of any attempt to raise them. But what really ensured the preservation of the lower tariffs into the future was that enough Republicans, even after having won control of Congress in the 1946 election, now accepted the trade agreements program and allowed the Geneva negotiations to proceed. Of course, the GATT was neither a treaty nor an organization, but simply a trade agreement put into effect by executive order. As a result, participants were "contracting parties" (not "members"), and the agreement was an interim arrangement to be applied provisionally until Congress approved the ITO Charter.

THE DECLINE IN US TARIFFS

During World War II, the average tariff on dutiable imports was largely unchanged, standing at 33 percent in 1944. Just six years later, it had fallen to almost 13 percent, a decline of 60 percent, as figure 10.2 shows. What accounts for this enormous drop? How was it politically possible for Congress to have allowed tariffs to fall to their lowest level since 1791?

The obvious explanation for the decline in tariffs is the 1947 Geneva negotiation. In fact, however, these negotiated reductions in tariff rates were responsible for only a fraction of the decline. The main reason for

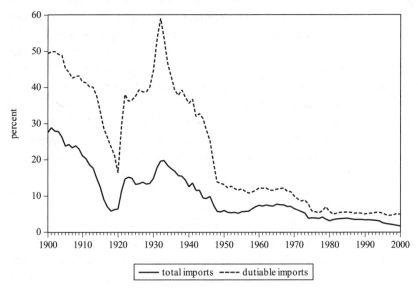

Figure 10.2. Average tariffs of the United States, 1900–1970.
(US Bureau of the Census 1975, series U-211–12.)

the postwar decline was the sharp increase in import prices after the war. About two-thirds of the tariffs were specific duties, and rising import prices reduced the ad valorem equivalent of those duties, just as deflation increased the ad valorem equivalent during the Great Depression. In this case, import prices rose 41 percent between 1944 and 1947, and this increase was largely responsible for the sharp decline in the average tariff in the immediate postwar period.[84]

Which was more responsible for the lower tariff: the negotiated reductions in 1947 or higher import prices? The Geneva negotiations reduced the average tariff about 21 percent, while the higher import prices reduced the tariff by about 40 percent.[85] Thus, in the crucial postwar period, the six years after 1944 when the average tariff fell from 33 percent to 13 percent, about two-thirds of the reduction was due to higher import prices and one-third to negotiated tariff cuts. In fact, in 1948 alone, the year that the Geneva tariff reductions took effect, higher import prices accounted for one-third of the tariff reduction.[86]

The Tariff Commission (1948, 19–20) also sought to determine the relative importance of reciprocal trade agreements and higher import prices in reducing the average tariff over the longer horizon from the early 1930s to 1948. They concluded that "it seems probable that they have been not far from equal in their effects."[87] Over a slightly longer period from the early 1930s until the early 1950s, the cumulative impact of higher import prices dominated the sporadic, negotiated rate reductions in bringing about a lower tariff. Between 1932 and 1954, the average tariff on dutiable imports fell from 59 percent to 12 percent. About two-thirds of this reduction can be attributed to higher import prices and one-third to the reciprocal trade agreements and the Geneva negotiation. Over the postwar period from 1945 to 1967, about three-quarters of the tariff reduction can be attributed to higher import prices.

Neither Congress nor import-sensitive interests anticipated the inflation-driven reduction in tariffs. In fact, it was widely believed that the deflation of the early 1930s could return after the war because previous wars—the War of 1812, the Civil War, and World War I—all had been followed by deflation. The Tariff Commission (1948, 20) thought it "impossible to forecast, even roughly, the prices of imported goods a few years hence." Yet import prices rose 56 percent in the five years after 1945, making the lower average tariffs an accomplished fact by 1950. While the Truman administration's handling of the Geneva tariff negotiations generated some controversy, no one seemed to notice the quiet but gradual erosion of specific duties that made up most of the tariff schedule.

Still, the Geneva negotiations were critical in establishing the GATT and demonstrating that international cooperation to reduce trade barriers was possible. In this first multilateral round, the twenty-three participating countries made no fewer than 123 agreements to reduce duties on 45,000 tariff items constituting about one-half of the value of world trade.[88] In the case of the United States, about half of dutiable imports were subject to tariff reductions, and the average reduction was 35 percent. Since many duties were not cut, the average reduction in all tariffs was 21 percent. Table 10.1 shows the negotiated reductions by tariff schedule, which were not symmetric across products or countries. These tariff reductions became effective on January 1, 1948, by executive order and did not require congressional approval. If they had, they would have encountered opposition by special interests in Congress, and the Republican Congress might not have approved them.

The degree to which foreign countries reduced their tariffs in this negotiation is difficult to know because foreign tariff data is not readily available. The GATT did not report any calculation of the reduction, and the Tariff Commission only reported the value of foreign imports that were affected by the tariff concessions, with no indication about the depth of the reduction in duties. The average tariff on dutiable imports for core European countries (Germany, France, and Britain) was about 22 percent prior to the 1947 Geneva conference. If these countries had reduced their tariffs as much as the United States did in the negotiation, their average tariff would have fallen to about 17 percent.[89]

The immediate impact of these tariff reductions on trade flows was almost surely limited, given the dislocations of the war and the widespread use of foreign exchange controls, but they promised to be greater in the future as normal economic conditions returned. Yet some studies point to the success of the GATT agreement in stimulating world trade, even at this early stage. Goldstein, Rivers, and Tomz (2007) found that bilateral trade among GATT participants increased by 136 percent, on average, in the first two years of the agreement's existence, compared to trade among nonparticipants. Other studies also indicate that the GATT promoted the postwar expansion of world trade that helped foster economic recovery around the world.[90]

While the multilateral tariff reductions gave some stimulus to world trade starting in 1948, import tariffs were not the most important constraint on trade at the time. European currencies were not freely convertible into dollars, and official exchange controls gave governments enormous discretion in how they allocated foreign exchange. Britain and

TABLE 10.1. Imports of commodities subject to rates of duty reduced by trade agreements, by tariff schedule (based on reductions in effect Jan. 1, 1948)

Tariff schedule	Value of dutiable imports, 1939 (millions)	Proportion subject to reduced rates Equivalent ad valorem on imports subject to reduced rates			Average reduction in rates		
		Pre-agreement rates	As of 1947 (pre-Geneva)	As of Jan. 1, 1948 (post-Geneva)	Pre-agreement to pre-Geneva	Pre-agreement to post-Geneva	Pre-Geneva to post-Geneva
1. Chemicals, oils, and paints	$56.6	37.2	31.5	30.4	15	18	3
2. Earths, earthenware, and glassware	$25.4	43.0	40.3	34.9	6	19	13
3. Metals and manufactures of	$89.7	40.3	27.7	21.4	31	47	23
4. Wood and manufactures of	$17.0	16.8	10.6	7.0	37	58	34
5. Sugar, molasses, and manufactures of	$90.5	69.4	35.2	24.4	49	65	31
6. Tobacco and manufactures of	$36.0	77.5	58.6	55.2	24	29	6
7. Agricultural products and provisions	$173.8	36.8	23.1	21.3	37	42	8

(continued)

TABLE 10.1. (Continued)

Tariff schedule	Value of dutiable imports, 1939 (millions)	Proportion subject to reduced rates Equivalent ad valorem on imports subject to reduced rates			Average reduction in rates		
		Pre-agreement rates	As of 1947 (pre-Geneva)	As of Jan. 1, 1948 (post-Geneva)	Pre-agreement to pre-Geneva	Pre-agreement to post-Geneva	Pre-Geneva to post-Geneva
8. Spirits, wines, and other beverages	$59.1	109.8	56.0	34.7	49	68	38
9. Cotton manufactures	$27.3	38.3	33.8	28.9	12	25	14
10. Flax, hemp, jute, and manufactures of	$54.8	24.7	18.5	9.8	25	60	47
11. Wool manufactures	$49.3	76.3	60.8	47.7	20	37	22
12 & 13. Silk manufactures and rayon and synthetics	$15.5	37.6	35.2	28.5	6	24	19
14. Paper and books	$11.50	21.8	17.3	14.3	21	34	17
15. Sundries	$133.3	28.8	24.3	19.2	16	33	21
Free list subject to excise tax on importation	$38.1	31.3	21.1	16.7	33	47	21
Total	$877.7	48.2	32.2	25.4	33	47	21

Source: US Tariff Commission, *Operation of the Trade Agreements Program, June 1934–April 1948*, part 3. Trade-Agreement Concessions Granted by the United States, Report No. 160. Washington, DC: GPO, 1948, 37.

Western European countries were running large trade deficits with the United States and sought to conserve their scarce dollar resources. The "dollar shortage" prompted Britain and its sterling-area partners to use various administrative mechanisms, such as import licensing, to divert imports away from the United States, because dollar reserves were so valuable. With these foreign exchange restrictions, tariff reductions as a result of the Geneva negotiation did not immediately translate into much additional access to European markets for US exporters.

This led to some complaints in Congress that the negotiations were a one-sided giveaway by the United States. "The notion that we are operating a trade system governed by true reciprocity is fantastically erroneous," Eugene Millikin argued. "While under the guise of reciprocity, we have opened our markets to the world's exports, in many instances at close to free trade levels, the foreign nation beneficiaries have circumvented their concessions by various devices, such as state trading, import quotas, bilateral agreements, preference systems, import licenses, and exchange restrictions."[91] At the same time, Britain and Europe were more comfortable making tariff reductions knowing that import controls were in place to guard against excessive imports from the United States.[92] Once the convertibility of European currencies into dollars was fully established in 1958, trans-Atlantic trade could take place more freely with the lower European tariffs in effect.

Surprisingly, given how much anxiety it had caused US negotiators, the dispute over imperial preferences largely disappeared after the Geneva conference. They were never again a major issue, removing what had been a major problem in Anglo-American commercial relations. The tariff preferences of the Ottawa agreements, which had been made in specific rather than ad valorem duties, were eroded by inflation. With about half of Britain's exports and imports covered by preferences, the average margin of preference on trade between Britain and the Commonwealth had been about 11 percent in 1937, but dropped to 6 percent by 1953.[93] The preferences were phased out when Britain joined the European Economic Community in 1973, and they were completely abolished in 1977.

EXPLAINING THE SHIFT IN US TRADE POLICY

The early postwar period brought about the most momentous shift in US trade policy since the nation's founding. The objective of US trade policy shifted from restriction to reciprocity, from using protective tariffs to shield domestic industries from foreign competition to using trade agreements to reduce trade barriers around the world. The early postwar period witnessed one of those rare first-order changes in which the basic goals of trade policy were altered. A unique conjunction of factors account for this radical change.

This regime shift in US trade policy was initiated by the executive branch with the acquiescence of Congress. Scholars have debated whether the RTAA by itself was responsible for this discontinuity in policy. The RTAA was clearly an important institutional change that altered the process of trade policymaking, but the RTAA did not have a large, immediate impact on trade-policy outcomes. As we have seen, average import duties only declined modestly during the 1930s. And the political foundation of the RTAA during this period was not secure. Even by the end of the 1930s, it was not obvious that the RTAA would be a permanent feature of US trade policy: the Republicans were no closer to supporting it in 1940 than they had been in 1934, and even many Democrats voted against the renewal in that year. Of course, the RTAA was a necessary ingredient to the changes that occurred in the late 1940s. As such, it proved to be an important and lasting institutional change, but only after the unique circumstances after World War II made it a vital part of US foreign economic policy.

The change in the Republican party's position after the war was critical to the survival of the RTAA and to making the shift to reciprocity politically secure. In 1936 the Republicans vowed to repeal the RTAA. In 1948, the party's election platform announced their conditional support for it: "At all times safeguarding our own industry and agriculture, and under efficient administrative procedures for the legitimate consideration of domestic needs, we shall support the system of reciprocal trade and encourage international commerce."[94] There was always some risk that the Republicans would abolish the act after the war, but this would have been more difficult than it appeared. The Republican Congress elected in 1946 could not strip President Truman of his negotiating authority, because it could not override a presidential veto of such legislation. The key development was the softening of the Republican opposition to the RTAA. The Republican party had become split on the matter between the eastern industrial and financial interests that supported it and the western interests that still clung to protectionism.[95]

Although some Republicans still complained that Congress had lost its constitutionally granted authority over tariffs by delegating too much power to the executive branch, few members of Congress wanted to resume direct responsibility for setting tariff rates again. As Arthur Vandenberg reminded his colleagues, "Tariff-rate making in Congress is atrocious. It lacks any element of economic science or validity. I suspect the 10 members of the Senate, including myself, who struggled through the 11 months it took to write the last congressional tariff act, would join me in resigning before they would be willing to tackle another general congressional tariff revision."[96]

Even Robert Taft (2003, 228–29), the influential Republican senator from Ohio who opposed the reciprocal trade agreements extension in 1945, wrote, "I was not in favor of returning to the fixing of tariff rates by Congress, which inevitably brought about a serious logrolling procedure, but I favored a tariff board authorized to fix tariffs according to some standard prescribed by Congress having some relation to difference in the cost of production in the United States and abroad." Thus, most Republicans were disinclined to scrap the whole system, but were unlikely to pursue trade agreements with the enthusiasm of Democratic administrations and wanted more checks on the process.

By getting itself out of the business of setting individual tariff rates and putting it in the hands of the executive branch, Congress took a more limited role in determining trade policy. This delegation of authority clearly made a difference to trade-policy outcomes. Given its past sensitivity to import-competing interests that opposed significant tariff reductions under any circumstances, it is almost impossible to believe that Congress would have voted to slash tariffs by 80 percent on its own initiative. Yet Congress took no action to offset the decline in the average tariff on dutiable imports from 59 percent in 1932 to 12 percent twenty years later. This dramatic reduction, which would have been unthinkable in previous decades, took place without much political controversy. There is little evidence of any Congressional concern that inflation was eroding the ad valorem equivalents of specific duties, as might be suggested by proposals to convert specific duties into ad valorem duties or increase the specific duties themselves. The erosion in tariffs was permitted to run its course without any Congressional interference.

This raises the question: had there been no import-price inflation, would the United States have arrived at the same low-tariff point by doubling or tripling the size of its tariff reduction in the GATT negotiations? Given the strong political resistance in Congress to granting further unconditional trade-negotiating powers to the president after 1947, it is clear that there were binding political constraints on the depth of negotiated tariff cuts. The sharp reduction in actual tariffs was to some degree a historical accident brought about by import-price inflation and the prevalence of specific duties.

Why did Congress stand by and allow tariffs to decline by such a large amount? The most important reason is that the lower tariffs had almost no immediate impact on imports and had almost no adverse consequences for domestic industries. There was no import surge after World War II, just as there had been none after World War I. After 1945, imports rose slowly from about 2 percent of GDP to about 3 percent of GDP, where they remained for most of the 1950s. This was unusually low: even during the high tariff period of the 1920s, imports amounted to about 4–5 percent of GDP.

The import share was low not because of high US trade barriers, but because of the destruction of production capacity in the rest of the world as a result of the war. This economic dislocation meant that Western European and East Asian countries simply could not produce enough goods for export. Hence, import competition was not significant enough to displace many American workers from their jobs, and thus falling tariffs had few political costs for members of Congress. Millikin grumbled that the GATT negotiations had cut tariffs to an extent that "in anything resembling normal times would be catastrophic," but the times were anything but normal. The lower tariffs came at a unique period in history when foreign countries were unable to export a large volume of goods; hence, changes in import policy generated virtually no constituent pressures to which politicians would have to respond. With few complaints from import-competing industries, Congress did not have a "trade problem" that it was forced to address.

The counterpart to the low level of imports was the high level of exports. The Truman administration had a strong interest in preserving a high level of employment through a continued high level of exports into the postwar period. The nation emerged from World War II as the world's dominant economic power, the only major industrial nation with its production capacity not only intact but enlarged as a result of the conflict. The US share of world trade in manufactured goods was 17 percent in 1937 and stood at 26 percent in 1954.[97] With the European economy in ruins, the United States ran large export surpluses in every major industrial group—machinery and equipment, motor vehicles, chemicals, and miscellaneous manufactures—except metals. Some key sectors were more dependent on exports than they had been before the war. In 1947, for example, the United States exported 32 percent of its wheat output (versus 10 percent in 1938), 11 percent of its coal output (3 percent in 1937), 39 percent of its machine tools (23 percent in 1937), 21 percent of its agricultural machinery and implements (14 percent in 1937).[98]

Behind these exports were jobs. The export surplus directly accounted for 1.33 million jobs in 1946 and 1.97 million jobs in 1947.[99] Although this was a small fraction of total civilian employment, which was about 58 million, this growth in export-related employment accounted for almost half of private-sector employment gains in those two years. At a time when many Americans feared the return of double-digit unemployment rates and another depression after the war, the creation of jobs through exports was welcomed. Maintaining a high level of exports was a way of keeping America's enormous productive capacity in use.

One way of sustaining these exports was for the United States to increase its imports, which would enable foreign countries to earn the dollars they needed to buy American goods. And reducing US import restrictions was one way of increasing imports. Large manufacturers, farm representatives, and labor unions supported the Truman administration's efforts to reduce import tariffs as a way of promoting exports. These business groups included the Chamber of Commerce, the American Farm Bureau, and the American Bankers Association. (The president of Ford Motor Co., Henry C. Ford II, even called for eliminating the tariff on imported automobiles.) They were joined by major labor groups, such as the Congress of Industrial Organizations (representing more than 6 million workers), the United Automobile and Aircraft Workers, the Textile Workers' Union of America, and the Amalgamated Clothing Workers of America, all of whom supported the 1945 RTAA extension. The official policy of major unions, such as the American Federation of Labor and the Congress of Industrial Organizations, was to support trade liberalization, except in cases where a member union felt threatened and only with the qualification that it desired trade "in accordance with fair labor standards."[100]

Most Americans were not well informed about the trade agreements program—a Gallup poll in 1945 found that only one in ten people surveyed was familiar with it—but three-quarters of those who knew about it supported it.[101] Virtually all public opinion surveys in the late 1940s and early 1950s showed a clear majority in favor of lower tariffs in the context of the reciprocal trade agreements program. A large majority of all newspaper editorials also supported the policy.[102]

This favorable sentiment would have been almost completely missed if one only studied the testimony given at congressional hearings. Such hearings were dominated by small- and medium-sized business interests that generally sold in the domestic market alone and had little or nothing to gain from access to foreign markets. The industries most actively opposed to tariff reductions were glassware, pottery and tiles, textiles and apparel, bicycles, watches, paper and pulp, cutlery, coal, ball bearings, copper, lead and zinc, milk, mushroom, umbrellas, and wool.[103] Despite their complaints about imports, few industries sought relief through the escape clause. From 1947 to 1951, only twenty-one applications for import relief were received, most of which were dismissed after a preliminary investigation by the Tariff Commission. President Truman only faced three escape-clause decisions: he accepted the commission's recommendation for higher tariffs on women's fur felt hats and hat bodies and on hatters' fur, while rejecting relief for watches.[104]

Congress still proved to be sensitive to the complaints of these import-competing interests. Empirical studies of congressional voting behavior in the early postwar period, such as those by Fordham (1998a; 1998b), show that these interests influenced votes against freer trade but that export-oriented interests do not explain many of the votes in favor of open trade. Either export production was not geographically concentrated enough, or support for open trade was so widespread that this producer influence could not be detected. This is consistent with other factors, such as foreign-policy considerations, influencing congressional votes in favor of open trade.

This asymmetry in political influence between specific import-competing interests and diffuse export interests became known as the "birdcage" phenomenon. This referred to the example of New York's fifteenth district, which included Staten Island and the shipping piers in New York City. Despite the fact that billions of dollars in exports and imports passed through his district every year, supporting the employment of thousands of longshoremen, Rep. John Ray (R-NY) voted against trade-negotiating authority because a birdcage factory employing fifty workers in his district felt threatened by imports. The congressman defended his decision by stating that he had heard from almost every one of those fifty workers, whereas he had not heard from any workers whose jobs depended on trade. Therefore, he felt obligated to vote against the RTAA.[105] As Senator Paul H. Douglas (D-IL) put it, "It is not the intelligence of the House and the Senate which I doubt; it is their ability to withstand the concentrated pressure of industries demanding protection, in view of the fact that the general interest is imperfectly represented, is diffused, and is, thereby, relatively weak."[106]

And yet the relationship between small domestic producers and their congressional representatives had changed as a result of the RTAA. Members of Congress were now in a better position to ignore import-competing interests in voting for reciprocal trade agreements. There were export, employment, and foreign-policy reasons for doing so. Drawing on Lowi's (1964) notion that trade policy had been transformed from a "distributive" issue to a "regulatory" issue, Nelson (1989, 90) notes that trade policy in Congress was no longer about the "accommodation of discrete, individual interests" through tariff logrolling, but instead focused on "the determination of two general rules: one regulating the degree of tariff-cutting authority available to the executive; and the other regulating the ease of access to an administered protection mechanism and the conditions necessary for accommodation within that mechanism." Rather than lobbying Congress over the rate of duty in a specific line in the tariff schedule of interest to a few specific producers, those domestic industries that were sensitive to imports had to lobby over the generic set of legislative guidelines governing administrative procedure (such as the escape clause) for the imposition of higher tariffs. This diluted the incentive for such firms to make demands on Congress, since their efforts could no longer directly impact the import duty in the specific line of the tariff schedule of interest to them.

In sum, with imports at artificially depressed levels and causing no problems for domestic producers, with American producers exporting vast amounts of agricultural produce and manufactured goods to other countries, and with public opinion broadly supporting existing policies, the trade agreements program was able to survive into the postwar period.

This favorable domestic economic context was strongly reinforced by foreign-policy concerns. Indeed, foreign policy was arguably a crucial factor behind the political support for the postwar trade agreements program. After the war, the dominant US foreign-policy objectives were promoting economic recovery in Europe and containing the spread of Soviet Communism—two goals that were closely linked. As the Central Intelligence Agency concluded in mid-1947, "The greatest danger to the security of the United States is the possibility of economic collapse in Western Europe and the consequent accession to power of Communist elements."[107] This meant that administration officials and members of Congress did not view trade policy in isolation, but in the context of a dangerous foreign-policy situation. This context significantly weakened the influence of those seeking to preserve the country's old policy of high tariffs.[108] We have already seen the interplay between economic policy decisions and foreign-policy concerns at the conclusion of the Geneva tariff negotiations in 1947. Economic reconstruction in Western Europe was viewed as a necessary part of the defense against Communism, a factor that weighed heavily on the minds of US officials.

In this regard, the immediate economic problem confronting American policymakers after the war was the enormous foreign demand for US goods and the insufficient capacity of foreign countries to pay for those goods. The United States supplied food and manufactured goods that were essential to feed Europe's people and resurrect its industry, but Europe was unable to produce sufficient exports to pay for these critical imports. Having also depleted their gold and foreign-exchange reserves, European countries faced enormous difficulty in financing their imports. The "dollar gap"—the difference between the hard currency dollars that Europe earned on its exports and had to pay to keep up its imports—ran in the billions of dollars.

There were three ways of addressing the situation. The first option would be for the United States to continue offering loans, grants, and assistance in dollars that would enable Europe to continue buying American goods. This was not a long-run solution, because Congress was not going to appropriate billions in foreign aid indefinitely. (The Marshall Plan was a particular response to a specific European crisis that had national security overtones.)

The second option would be for Europe to slash its spending on imported goods. In fact, most European countries already imposed strict exchange controls and quantitative restrictions to conserve dollar resources and shift purchases toward countries but did not require dollar payment, such as the sterling area in the case of Britain. But slashing spending on imports was unattractive to both Europe and the United States. From the US perspective, that would mean lower exports and hence lower employment on the farm and in the factory at a time when officials wanted to keep exports at a high level. From Europe's perspective, they desperately needed large imports of food to avoid starvation, fuel to heat houses and provide power for industry, and capital goods to rebuild infrastructure.[109] If austerity forced these countries to reduce their imports even more, it would exacerbate existing shortages and further hamper the process of recovery and reconstruction, creating fertile ground for leftist political parties.

The third option would be for the United States to open its market to foreign goods and allow European countries to earn more dollars by expanding their exports. By keeping its market open to imported goods, and by helping to reduce trade barriers around the world through tariff negotiations, the United States could promote Europe's economic recovery and enhance its own national security. This policy of restoring world trade at high levels seemed like the most sensible long-run solution to the "dollar shortage" problem and economic reconstruction.

The trade-offs among these options were well understood at the time. Not surprisingly, the Truman administration chose financial assistance (the British loan and Marshall Plan) in the short run and open trade (through GATT negotiations) in the long run. "If a severe shrinkage in the flow of dollars abroad occurred, it would not only reduce our exports now, but would also force other countries to try to save dollars by making discriminatory trading arrangements that would adversely affect the long-run future of our foreign trade," Truman warned. "Moreover, it would set back recovery and reconstruction abroad, and might precipitate developments which would have serious consequences for world political stability"[110]

Critical decisions about America's foreign economic policy had to be made shortly after the end of the war. As noted earlier, Britain faced severe balance of payments problems with the abrupt termination of Lend-Lease in 1945, and Congress reluctantly approved a loan in 1946. The next year was one of crisis. Although the European recovery had begun, the brutally cold winter of 1946–47 exhausted coal supplies, reduced export earnings, and diverted precious foreign exchange to the purchase of imported fuel. This was followed by a long, dry summer in 1947 that curtailed agricultural production throughout Europe. These ongoing shortages and austerity measures generated social unrest in France and elsewhere.[111]

In May of that year, while traveling in Europe during the GATT negotiations, Will Clayton reported to Washington, "It is now obvious that we grossly under-estimated the destruction of the European economy by the war; . . . without further prompt and substantial aid, . . . economic, social, and political disintegration will overwhelm Europe."[112] In response to Clayton's gloomy report from Western Europe, Secretary of State George C. Marshall proposed new economic aid to the region in what became known as the Marshall Plan. A majority of the Marshall Plan funds were spent on food, fuel, and raw materials that relieved the resource constraints at the time, not on investment or infrastructure.[113] In Clayton's view, the Marshall Plan made the Geneva trade negotiations "more important than ever because without [a] sound permanent program of reciprocal multilateral trade, no temporary emergency program could possibly have any permanent worthwhile results."[114]

These economic problems coincided with the onset of the Cold War and the fear of Communist expansion in Western Europe. A sense of crisis and urgency pervaded the Truman administration in the spring of 1947.

Government officials believed that unless quick action was taken, the European recovery might unravel, generating popular unrest, political turmoil, and the possible election of a leftist or authoritarian regime. The economic difficulties had enormous implications for national security.

The 1947 Geneva negotiations took place with this backdrop. American officials wanted to assist Europe's ability to import from the United States not simply because it would help maintain exports, but because anything that jeopardized the European recovery and risked economic collapse, political chaos, and possible Communist takeovers would be detrimental to America's national security. The national security consequences of allowing the European economy to continue to flounder seemed frightening. As Clayton warned, "If the countries of Western Europe must resist Communism in conditions of cold and hunger and economic frustration, they will almost certainly lose the battle."[115]

Thus, promoting a system of freer world trade seemed to serve US economic, foreign-policy, and national security interests all at the same time. For the first time, Cordell Hull's belief that flourishing international trade was a necessary part of a durable peace actually seemed to resonate with policymakers and the public. The United States did not fight World War II against fascism, it was commonly said, to see a Communist takeover of Western Europe. As late as 1958, Deputy Undersecretary of State C. Douglas Dillon said, "When the free world is menaced as never before by an over-all economic, political and military threat from international communism, it is essential that this process of opening up the channels of trade which link the free world should not grind to a halt."[116] This is one reason why Republicans abandoned their attempts to terminate the trade agreements program: they opposed Communism more than they feared growing imports, and they were not willing to take actions that might jeopardize the weak European recovery and risk pushing some countries into the Communist bloc.

World War I and World War II were similar for the United States in that they increased exports and diminished imports, and turned the country into a major creditor nation. Yet the outcomes for trade policy were different: the country opted for economic isolationism after World War I and economic openness after World War II. One reason for the difference is that the Democrats were in power after World War II, whereas Republicans were in power after World War I. Congressional Democrats broadly supported the foreign-policy objectives of the Roosevelt and Truman administrations, whereas congressional Republicans were skeptical about the Wilson administration's plans for the postwar order. Because World War II had been much more devastating than World War I had been, there were almost no fears about a surge of imports after the war, and the United States was expected to have large trade surpluses for many years to come. Furthermore, the decade of the 1930s and the outbreak of World War II undermined the credibility of those advocating isolationism. Just as isolationism in foreign policy had been thoroughly discredited as a result of the interwar experience, isolationism in economic policy had been similarly discredited. It was even now viewed as dangerous.

Policymakers and the public were very conscious of the similarities between the end of World War I and World War II. In reporting the bill to renew the RTAA in 1945, the Ways and Means Committee wrote,

> The committee is struck with the parallel which exists between the situation in which we find ourselves now and the situation at the end of the last war. Then, as now, we had an opportunity to embrace liberal commercial policies, which we rejected with disastrous consequences known to all. . . . Unless the United States gives an unequivocal indication that its tremendous economic power and prestige will be thrown in the balance on the side of liberal and enlightened trade policies there will be no other country capable of offering effective leadership in the conditions of economic disorganization and uncertainty which will prevail. In failing to provide such leadership, this country would not escape any of the dangers implicit in the uncertain state of the post-war world. Rather, by such failure, we would merely make it doubly certain that all our worst fears would become realities. By serving notice that the United States will press forward with its established policy of trade liberalization and expansion, this country can take a long step toward eliminating in advance many of the most disturbing uncertainties of the coming period of reconstruction and readjustment.[117]

For administration officials and most members of Congress, these enormous foreign-policy concerns overshadowed the seemingly trivial concerns about a handful of import-competing industries.

Despite all of these factors, the shift to a new trade policy after 1947 was not easily accomplished. It would be erroneous to conclude that Congress, by delegating trade authority to the president, abdicated any role in trade policy. While Congress never again revised the duties in the tariff schedule, it continued to influence trade policy by limiting the president's

authority and enacting various procedural escape clauses that were expanded over the postwar period. It also refused to support a new international trade organization.

THE RTAA FLOUNDERS, THE ITO FADES AWAY

Having completed the GATT in October 1947, the Truman administration's next goal was to conclude the negotiation of the ITO charter and
secure its ratification by Congress. Attended by representatives from more
than fifty countries, the United Nations Conference on Trade and Employment met in Havana, Cuba, from November 1947 to March 1948 to finalize the charter and create a new international organization. (There were
no tariff negotiations at the Havana meeting.) The charter had grown considerably in length from its inception as the "Proposals" released by the
State Department in December 1945. It was now a large document that
went well beyond the GATT, having 106 articles covering a wide range of
issues, such as employment, economic development, restrictive business
practices, commodity agreements, and foreign investment, as well as commercial policy.[118]

The Havana meeting did not begin well. As Clair Wilcox (1949, 47),
who led the US negotiating delegation, recalled, "The conference opened
with a chorus of denunciation in which the representatives of thirty
underdeveloped nations presented variations on a single theme: the Geneva draft was one-sided; it served the interests of the great industrial
powers; it held out no hope for the development of backward states. Some
eight hundred amendments were presented, among them as many as two
hundred that would have destroyed the very foundations of the enterprise.
Almost every specific commitment in the document was challenged."

Latin American countries, many of which did not participate in the
1947 Geneva conference, now had their chance to react to the proposed
charter. They demanded sweeping exceptions to the rules limiting tariff
preferences and quantitative restrictions, and insisted on being able to
restrict production and trade in primary commodities. They argued that
governments should have broad discretion to impose import quotas and
other trade restrictions to protect infant industries, promote economic development, and safeguard the balance of payments.[119]

Because the conference included many different countries at many different stages of economic development with many conflicting views on
policy, the amended Havana charter became enormously complex. Many
of the articles were written so broadly as to be devoid of content, while

others with substance were loaded with exceptions. The US attempted to include a chapter that would protect investors from expropriation and confiscation, but developing countries equated foreign investment with economic imperialism and wanted to be able to regulate it without constraint.

By December 1947, Wilcox was downcast and believed that "it is unlikely that we will be able to get wide agreement on a Charter which is close enough to the Geneva draft to satisfy us." In January 1948, the US delegation had to decide whether (1) to press for an acceptable charter with the support of a majority of countries (rather than unanimity), or (2) to get agreement on major issues and adjourn to resolve the differences at a later time, or (3) to agree on a purely consultative ITO without substantive commitments. Clayton decided to press on and do the best they could, although Wilcox thought this was unwise.[120]

Finally, in March 1948, the Havana charter was completed and signed by the United States and representatives of fifty-two other countries. Unlike previous trade agreements authorized by the RTAA that took effect by executive order, the ITO charter would establish an international organization and had to be approved by Congress. That same month, the Republican majority on the Ways and Means Committee passed a resolution saying that the signing of the charter should not be "construed as a commitment by the United States to accept all or any of the provisions of the proposed charter."[121] With the Republicans in control of Congress, the Truman administration chose not to submit the charter to Congress until after the 1948 election, which they hoped would return the Democrats to power and significantly improving the chance of getting the ITO approved.

In the meantime, the State Department focused on renewing the RTAA, which was due to expire in June 1948. President Truman requested a three-year renewal without new tariff-cutting authority beyond the 50 percent granted in 1945. Truman called the RTAA "an essential element of United States foreign policy" and said it was needed to negotiate with other countries seeking to join the GATT.[122] This would be the first time that the Republicans controlled the RTAA's fate. Many Republicans did not want to renew the program and preferred to see it expire quietly. They were skeptical of the administration's intentions and especially suspicious of the State Department, which they believed had harmed domestic industries in the pursuit of overrated diplomatic objectives.[123]

At the same time, the Republican leadership did not want the party to be labeled as "isolationist." Vandenberg and other party leaders ruled out terminating the program, so they prepared a one-year renewal rather than the three years requested by the president. They also introduced the "peril point" provision that required the president to submit the list of goods that might be subject to tariff reductions to the Tariff Commission in advance of trade negotiations. The commission would then report on the maximum allowable reduction that could be made without inflicting serious harm on domestic producers in the industry. The House version would have prohibited any tariff reduction until the commission issued a report, for which there was no deadline. While the law did not prevent any tariff from being reduced below the "peril point," the president would have to notify Congress and justify any decision to do so. Congress would then have the opportunity to override any reduction beyond the peril point if it disapproved. At a minimum, the peril point provision would severely hamper the negotiating process by introducing delays and uncertainties into the mix. Democrats called the proposed bill "a sham and typical protectionist device" and accused Republicans of trying to sabotage the RTAA.[124] In May 1948, the House approved the one-year renewal in a partisan vote.

In the Senate, both Vandenberg and Taft agreed that the peril point provision should be included, but did not think that its application should be mandatory or subject to a congressional veto. They modified the bill extensively, establishing a four-month time limit for the Tariff Commission report, dropping the congressional veto, and giving the president the discretion to reduce tariffs below the peril point (but still requiring a statement to Congress in such a case). The Senate bill passed overwhelmingly, with Republicans voting 47–1 and Democrats split 23–17 in favor. The conference committee adopted the Senate's less-restrictive version.

Truman was dismayed by the one-year renewal and the "complicated, time-consuming, and unnecessary" peril point provision. Despite these "serious defects," the president signed the bill in the belief that it was "essential that the reciprocal trade agreements program should not lapse." Although the one-year renewal was not a major constraint on policy because no major trade negotiations were planned, Truman wished that the "defects contained in this year's extension would be corrected in order that the act be restored as a fully effective instrument of permanent US policy."[125]

The Democrats succeeded in recapturing Congress in the 1948 election, which (along with Truman's unexpected reelection) restored unified government. In 1949, the Democrats enacted a new three-year (retroactive) extension of negotiating authority without any peril point provision.[126] Surprisingly, the renewal easily passed the House with a bipartisan vote of 319–69; Democrats voted 234–6 in favor, as did Republicans 84–63. The renewal also easily passed in the Senate. The 1949 legislation showed that the Republicans were split: the extension of negotiating authority without peril points gained the support of 57 percent of House Republicans and 45 percent of Senate Republicans. The 1948 and 1949 votes demonstrated that about half of House and Senate Republicans would vote for a three-year extension without any restrictive provisions, while all of them would vote for a reciprocal trade agreements program that included the peril point requirement. Since the Republicans giving unconditional support to the RTAA could also depend upon the support of most Democrats, a bipartisan coalition to sustain it was in place.

However, this did not mean the ITO would be welcome on Capitol Hill. In April 1949, nearly a year after the ITO charter had been completed, Truman submitted it to Congress and stated, "The Charter is the most comprehensive international economic agreement in history. It goes beyond vague generalities and deals with the real nature of the problems confronting us in the present world situation. While it does not include every detail desired by this Nation's representatives, it does provide a practical, realistic method for progressive action toward the goal of expanding world trade."[127]

In fact, the charter was in deep trouble. The basic problem was that business support for the ITO was nonexistent, even among those groups that had supported the 1945 RTAA renewal. As early as May 1948, the Chamber of Commerce decided to withhold its support for the charter. The Chamber stressed the importance of supporting free enterprise and market competition in world trade and argued that "the present charter is not consistent with these principles, and the United States should withhold acceptance and seek renegotiation."[128] This was a huge blow to the administration's hopes for enlisting private-sector support for the charter. The Chamber of Commerce had been a strong advocate of the reciprocal trade agreements program, and its failure to endorse the ITO was guaranteed to cause problems in Congress.

Other usually pro-trade groups joined in the growing chorus against the ITO. The US Council of the International Chamber of Commerce called it "a dangerous document because it accepts practically all of the policies of economic nationalism; because it jeopardizes the free enterprise system by giving priority to centralized national governmental planning of foreign trade; because it leaves a wide scope to discrimination, accepts the principles of economic insulation and in effect commits all members of the ITO to state planning for full employment."[129] Coming from an organization that strongly supported America's economic involvement in the world economy, the National Foreign Trade Council's rejection was particularly damaging. It argued that the employment provision "would operate inexorably to transform the free enterprise system of this country into a system of planned economy, with consequent initiative-destroying regimentation, reduction in productive output and standards of living, and threat to the free institutions and liberties of the American people."[130] They were joined by the National Association of Manufacturers and the American Farm Bureau Federation.

Hearings before the House Foreign Affairs Committee in the spring of 1949 revealed that the charter had few supporters.[131] For rather different reasons than the chambers of commerce, but with equal force, the American Tariff League and small industries that wanted protection— including chemicals, dairy producers, livestock, glassware producers, woolen manufacturers, the paper and pulp industry—opposed the charter on the grounds that it might lead to more trade. The American Bar Association raised questions about whether it would compromise US sovereignty. Thus, the charter failed to receive any significant political support among key interest groups.

The ITO even seemed to be a low priority for the Truman administration. The political environment in Washington in 1949 was markedly different from what it had been just a few years earlier. Clayton and Wilcox had left the government, and the State Department's commitment to the charter now seemed half-hearted. The heady optimism of the early postwar period, with its promise of making the world anew, had given way to the Cold War. The 1945 RTAA renewal was a distant memory, and the ITO already appeared to be a relic from a bygone era. As early as January 1948, British officials reported that "Clayton admitted very frankly that he had found considerable difficulty in getting United States authorities at Washington to take any concerted interest in the Charter, their attention being almost entirely directed to Marshall Aid. This was one of the reasons why he was, he said, most apprehensive lest [the] Charter would be crowded out unless completed very shortly."[132]

Clayton's sense turned out to be correct. Far more pressing foreign-policy concerns and national security issues—the Marshall Plan, the Berlin airlift, the creation of the North Atlantic Treaty Organization (NATO), the Communist takeover of China—pushed the ITO off the administration's policy agenda. Citing the pressure of other business, the Foreign Affairs Committee never reported the charter to the House floor in 1949. Truman reminded Congress of the pending ITO Charter in his

State of the Union message in January 1950. But the outbreak of the Korean War in June 1950 provided another excuse for the House to postpone any action.

In November 1950, with the RTAA due to expire in seven months, State Department staff anticipated that "there will be strong opposition" to renewal and "a real possibility of defeat. We cannot overcome this opposition and avoid defeat unless we make it clear that the trade program is an essential, indispensable part of our foreign policy." They feared that "reintroduction of the ITO will engage us in fruitless argument and end in almost certain defeat or indefinite delay."[133] In other words, pushing for the ITO might jeopardize the renewal of the RTAA. As a result, Secretary of State Dean Acheson informed Truman that "the ITO is no longer a practical possibility." He recommended that "in order to move our trade program forward in a positive way, . . . we should drop the ITO and instead we should seek from Congress, in connection with the renewal of the Trade Agreements Act, authority to participate in the establishment of an appropriate international organization under the General Agreement on Tariffs and Trade."[134] The president accepted this recommendation.

Thus, the Truman administration bowed to political reality. The State Department issued a press release in December 1950 stating that "the interested agencies have recommended, and the President has agreed, that, while the proposed Charter for an International Trade Organization should not be resubmitted to the Congress, Congress be asked to consider legislation which will make American participation in the General Agreement more effective."[135] With other countries waiting for the United States before approving the ITO Charter, since it would be meaningless without American participation, the organization was dead. The opposition of the private sector, the reluctance of the Democratic leadership to embrace the charter, and the perception within the Truman administration that the ITO was not worth the fight combined to kill the ITO.[136]

What accounts for this failure? The biggest problem for the ITO was the charter itself. The charter was a sprawling document with provisions to stabilize raw material prices and agricultural markets, end restrictive business practices, and promote full employment. It was too comprehensive in areas where there was little national, let alone international, consensus, and exceptions were built in everywhere to make the details acceptable to everyone. The business community thought that the ITO did not go far enough in removing foreign trade barriers and might even provide legal cover to foreign governments to strengthen those barriers. Business groups also decided that the exceptions and escape clauses were too numerous, that too many concessions were made to state-owned industries, that exchange controls could be retained indefinitely, and that the charter was too soft on quantitative restrictions and too permissive toward government interventions ostensibly imposed in the name of "full employment," which some viewed as a code term for government planning and state control.[137]

The fact that all of the major domestic interests that supported the RTAA renewals and the GATT now lined up to oppose the ITO was damning. No Congress was going to embrace the charter when so many groups across the political spectrum were actively opposed to it. In retrospect, the ITO may not have been able to make much of a contribution to freeing global commerce from trade barriers, and perhaps even have sanctioned continued interference in trade by governments. The ITO Charter was a complex agreement creating a potentially large and unwieldy organization—like the United Nations Conference on Trade and Development (UNCTAD), established in 1964—and its diverse membership might have hindered its effectiveness. By contrast, the GATT was a relatively simple agreement focused on a few key principles and a few simple rules for merchandise trade alone. It imposed some loose constraints on the policies of the participating countries, but also gave them enough flexibility in using discretionary trade policies to encourage further liberalization.

Although it was not a formal international organization, the GATT continued to function as a small secretariat in Geneva to facilitate further trade negotiations and resolve trade disputes. Negotiations at Annecy, France, in 1949 allowed the accession of eleven countries as new contracting parties to the GATT. The original twenty-three countries did not exchange new tariff concessions with one another, but they did negotiate with the new participants. At Torquay, United Kingdom, in 1950–51, the original contracting parties exchanged new tariff concessions with each other, and seven countries, most importantly West Germany, joined the agreement. The tariff reductions at Annecy and Torquay were slight, as table 10.2 shows. Still, by 1952, the GATT had thirty-four contracting parties accounting for more than 80 percent of world trade and had clearly become the main forum for international discussion of trade policy.

Thus, the immediate postwar period was an enormously eventful one for US trade policy. The main objective of policy had shifted decisively from restriction to reciprocity. A bipartisan consensus had emerged to support efforts to take gradual steps to free world trade from government-imposed trade barriers. The domestic debate was less about whether tariffs

TABLE 10.2. United States tariff reductions in GATT negotiations

	Percentage of dutiable imports subject to tariff reduction	Average reduction of tariffs that were reduced (percent)	Weighted average reduction of all duties (percent)
First round, Geneva, April–October 1947	54	35	19
Second round, Annecy, April–August 1949	6	35	2
Third round, Torquay, 1950–51	12	26	3
Fourth round, Geneva, 1955–56	16	15	2
Fifth round, Geneva, 1961–62	20	20	4
Sixth round, Geneva 1964–67	64	35	22

Source: Evans 1971, 12, 281–82.

should be reduced in concert with other countries, but about the particular ways of helping a few import-competing industries cope with foreign competition. Furthermore, the US-led efforts to reduce trade restrictions around the world had borne fruit. Although the ITO had failed, the GATT largely established non-discrimination and unconditional MFN as benchmarks for trade policy among a core set of countries. The GATT signaled that the developed countries were not going to revert to interwar protectionism but would instead promote the expansion of world trade in the years to come.

In light of the future difficulties that some industries would have with competition from imports, Alfred Eckes (1995) suggested that the United States sacrificed its economic interests for foreign-policy or national security objectives in the early postwar period. But as Richard Cooper (2000, 148) responded, "It is difficult to sustain that any such economic sacrifice was either consciously decided or in fact made. The broad trade liberalization that has taken place over the past half century has strongly served US economic (as well as security) interests, in the decisive sense that it has increased US standards of living far more than would have been the case if world trade had remained restricted by policies such as those in place in 1945, or 1950, or 1960." The US economy also flourished in the decades after World War II, and the reduction in trade barriers helped promote a more rapid economic recovery from the war in Europe and Japan than would otherwise have been possible. The worldwide economic boom after World War II stands in marked contrast to the dismal two decades after World War I. While many factors account for the different outcomes over the two postwar periods, many economists believe that US leadership in helping reduce trade barriers and create the GATT contributed to the economic growth that followed World War II.

CHAPTER ELEVEN

New Order and New Stresses, 1950–1979

Although average tariffs fell sharply during and after World War II, the economic destruction in Europe and Asia due to the war meant that most domestic firms were not threatened by foreign competition. By the mid-1960s, however, Western Europe and Japan had rebuilt their industries to the point where they could pose a challenge to American producers. By the 1970s, other countries in Asia, such as Taiwan and South Korea, had begun to export labor-intensive manufactured goods as well. These developments ushered in a difficult and prolonged period of adjustment for American manufacturers and sparked a widespread backlash against imports, although multilateral negotiations to reduce tariffs continued in the 1960s and 1970s. The growing pressures of foreign competition strained and even reversed old partisan divisions over trade: many Democratic constituencies were now harmed by imports, while Republican constituencies stood to benefit from expanding exports.

TRADE POLICY BECALMED IN THE 1950S

After an intense period of activity from 1945 to 1947, the political energy devoted to trade policy dissipated over the next decade. The International Trade Organization, as we have seen, generated no enthusiasm at home and died in 1950. The remainder of the decade saw few new trade-policy initiatives being undertaken. Under largely divided government, Congress repeatedly but grudgingly renewed the RTAA.

The lull in trade policy cannot be attributed only to divided government itself, which in the past had been responsible for political gridlock. Rather, even when the government was unified under the Democrats (1951–52) or the Republicans (1953–54), Congress proved more reluctant to grant trade-negotiating powers than in the past. Furthermore, the president and executive branch officials did not make a compelling case for further efforts to reduce trade barriers.[1]

The trade policy stalemate of the 1950s owed less to differences between the parties than to dissension within each party. The Republicans were divided between internationalists like President Dwight Eisenhower, who supported increased world trade, and conservative economic nationalists in Congress, who were concerned about the potential harm to domestic industries. The once-united Democrats also became increasingly divided over trade policy as the long-standing position of southern Democrats in favor of lower tariffs weakened. As a result, trade policy fell into a holding pattern with no major effort to break out of the status quo.[2]

For example, President Truman requested a three-year renewal of the RTAA in 1951. The Democrats controlled Congress, and passage of the extension should have presented no problem. On the House floor, Richard Simpson (R-PA) reintroduced the peril point provision, as might be expected from a Pennsylvania Republican. But unlike the result in 1949, when the Democrats easily defeated a similar amendment, the House approved it by a vote of 225–168; Republicans voted 184–5 for the amendment, and Democrats voted 162–41 against, but so many Democrats broke ranks that the peril points provision was kept in the renewal. The defectors were led by southerners, comprising twenty-seven of the forty-one Democrats who voted with the Republicans.

The Senate Finance Committee dealt a further blow to the president's request by retaining the House's peril points provision and voting for a two-year extension instead of three. In signing the RTAA renewal, Truman lamented the inclusion of the "cumbersome and superfluous" peril points provision, this time inserted by his own party. He also warned that the "danger of reverting to product-by-product legislation in the field of tariffs is obvious," a reference to the attempt to insert special provisions for particular industries.[3] As Wilkinson (1960, 65–66) concluded, "If the legislation of 1945 represented the zenith of the Trade Agreements Program, the Extension Act of 1951 was certainly the nadir."

The 1951 vote signaled a historic shift in the political economy of US trade policy. For nearly two centuries, the South had been the bedrock of the low-tariff, anti-protectionist force in Congress. This was no longer the case, because the export-oriented interests of cotton and tobacco had weakened, while the import-competing interests of cotton textiles had strengthened.

As late as 1929, cotton was still the largest single export, accounting for 15 percent of total US exports. But the introduction of agricultural price supports in the 1930s ensured that farmers would receive a guaranteed price, regardless of how much they exported. The price support was set so high that domestic cotton was often priced out of the world market, and exports fell off considerably. As a result, cotton producers looked to Washington, not to world markets, for the income they would receive for their crops. "We no longer farm in Mississippi cotton-fields," the novelist William Faulkner put it. "We farm now in Washington corridors and Congressional committee-rooms."[4] Severing the link between cotton production and the world market made cotton producers less interested in promoting exports by reducing import tariffs.

As government stockpiles of cotton grew, the Agriculture Department introduced an export subsidy to dispose of the surplus. The subsidy created an even greater gap between the domestic and world price of cotton. Somewhat perversely, the United States had to impose an import quota to support the high domestic price and prevent cotton purchasers (textile and apparel firms) from importing cotton—sometimes the very US cotton that had been exported because of the subsidy—at the lower world price.[5] The Agricultural Adjustment Act of 1948 extended price supports to other commodities, such as milk, peanuts, and potatoes, and soon import quotas on those goods were necessary as well. Thus, agricultural price supports not only weakened an important, export-oriented lobby group, but created new demands to limit imports.

A second important factor in changing the trade-policy views of southern members of Congress was the migration of cotton textile production from New England to the South.[6] The spread of electricity meant that textile mills no longer needed to be located near waterways to generate power, freeing the industry from its original sites near rivers in New England. Because wages for unskilled workers were much lower than elsewhere in the country, the South began to attract investment in textiles and apparel and other unskilled, labor-intensive industries. Prior to World War I, about two-thirds of textile production was located in the North. By 1947, as figure 11.1 shows, more than three-quarters of textile production was in the South. Of course, unskilled, labor-intensive industries were precisely the ones in the United States that were vulnerable to foreign competition. The textile and apparel industry had never been a major exporter and had always faced competition from imports, originally from Britain in the nineteenth century and now increasingly from low-wage countries in East Asia, such as Japan.

These developments eroded the long-standing support of southern

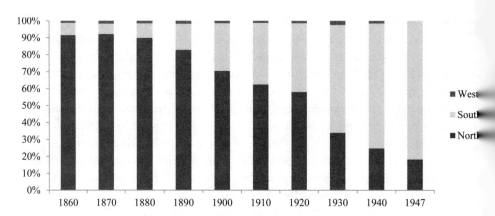

Figure 11.1. Distribution of cotton textile production, by region.
(US Bureau of the Census, *Census of Manufactures*, various years.)

Democrats for lower tariffs and gave representatives from the region a much greater stake in protecting the industry from imports. In 1955, Senator Strom Thurmond (D-SC) argued that Congress should no longer consider legislation that might result in further tariff reductions, a remarkable statement coming from a representative of a state that once almost seceded from the Union because of protective tariffs. The change in the South's interests made votes on trade bills much more difficult for the Democrats. Northern Democrats continued to be as sensitive to import-competing industries as they had been in the past, including coal from Pennsylvania, textiles, paper, and watches from New England, and chemicals from New Jersey. Meanwhile, Republicans from the North and West remained split between the Old Guard economic nationalists and the new internationalists, who rejected protectionism and isolationism. As a result of these intra-party splits, the traditional partisan divisions over trade policy became blurred in the 1950s.

Domestic political factors were also important in the 1951 vote. With the economies of Western Europe on the road to recovery and the threat of Communism having receded, the foreign-policy rationale for a more liberal trade policy was not nearly as strong in the early 1950s as it had been in the late 1940s. This is not to say that trade policy had become delinked from foreign policy; national security continued to significantly affect congressional voting on trade throughout the 1950s.[7] Had there been no foreign-policy case for maintaining open trade policies, a gradual slide back to more protected markets for certain commodities might have become more pronounced. But as foreign economic policy became less of an urgent priority, purely domestic factors once again began intruding on trade policy: support for open trade policies became more tentative, and extensions of presidential negotiating authority included more conditions and additional safeguards for import-competing producers.

The election of 1952 gave the Republicans unified control of government for the first time since the Hoover administration. Had the Republican party not adjusted its position on the RTAA in the 1940s, this political swing could have marked a big reversal on trade policy. The party's official position was now one of accepting the RTAA, but pressing harder for "the elimination of discriminatory practices against our exports" and providing more safeguards for domestic industries.[8] Of course, the party was split between conservatives who were dismayed by the loss of protection under the trade agreements program and internationalists who supported open trade and feared the spread of Communism in Europe.[9] In his memoirs, President Dwight Eisenhower (1963, 195) recalled that some congressional Republicans, including Senate Majority Leader Robert Taft (R-OH) and Senate Finance Committee Chair Eugene Millikin (R-CO), "were unhappy with the Trade Agreements Act, and a few even hoped we could restore the Smoot-Hawley Tariff Act, a move which I knew would be ruinous." Coming from the more liberal, internationalist wing of the party, Eisenhower wanted to continue promoting trade, in opposition to the more conservative members of his party. The party split prevented any new initiatives from being launched, but also ruled out any reversal of the tariff reductions that had taken place.[10]

Even before Eisenhower had a chance to make any proposals regarding trade policy, congressional Republicans moved ahead with legislation of their own. Robert Simpson (R-PA) introduced a measure to increase tariffs, impose new import quotas, and give greater powers to the Tariff Commission. To head off the bill, the president had little choice but to delay and compromise. In early 1953, Eisenhower requested a one-year renewal of the RTAA as an interim step, "pending completion of a thorough and comprehensive reexamination of the economic foreign policy of the United States."[11] Despite the lobbying efforts by coal, lead, zinc, and other import-sensitive sectors, Congress defeated the Simpson bill and extended negotiating authority for a single year in exchange for Eisenhower's pledge not to negotiate any new trade agreements. Although neither party seriously considered terminating the trade agreements program or reversing the existing tariff reductions, most Republicans in Congress were content to keep trade policy in an extended hiatus.

As promised, the Eisenhower administration established the Commission on Foreign Economic Policy to make recommendations about the future of US trade policy. In its February 1954 report, the Randall Commission, as it was known, failed to reach any startling conclusions. The report called for the swift termination of grant-based economic aid, a further increase in two-way trade with Europe to close the remaining "dollar gap," and the rapid convertibility of European currencies into dollars. The report stated that "the nations of the free world would be stronger and more cohesive if many of the existing barriers to the exchange of their goods were reduced, if unnecessary uncertainties and delays caused by such barriers were eliminated, and if adequate international arrangements for discussing and finding solutions to their common trade problems were developed and maintained."[12] The commission called for giving the president new authority to renegotiate the GATT and seek its eventual approval by Congress.

However, the commission was also divided and could not speak with one voice. Three conservative Republicans—Eugene Millikin of Colorado, Daniel Reed of New York, and Richard Simpson of Pennsylvania—dissented from many of the report's recommendations. They argued that the RTAA, if extended at all, should be continued for just two more years, with strengthened administrative procedures to allow any industry harmed by imports to receive an upward tariff adjustment.

In March 1954, a month after the commission issued its report, Eisenhower requested a three-year renewal of the RTAA, complete with peril points and the escape clause, as well as added authority to cut tariffs on specific items by up to 15 percent. The president argued that this would help achieve four interrelated objectives: "aid, which we wish to curtail; investment, which we wish to encourage; convertibility, which we wish to facilitate; and trade, which we wish to expand."[13] The Republican Congress balked at this request, citing other pressing business and, for the second year in a row, approved just a one-year extension of the RTAA as an interim measure.

Eisenhower had only slightly better luck in obtaining trade authority in 1955, because the 1954 midterm elections gave the Democrats a majority in Congress. At least on trade matters, the Republican president had more success working with the Democratic Congress from 1955–60 than with the Republican Congress in 1953–54. The Democratic leadership supported Eisenhower's request for negotiating authority for three years. The House leadership tried to ensure its passage with a closed rule to prevent any amendments, but so many members wanted the chance to slip special-interest provisions into the bill that the closure rule was voted down. This prompted Speaker Sam Rayburn (D-TX), as he had done at critical moments in the past, to leave his chair and speak from the floor. He warned that "The House on this last vote has done a most unusual thing and under the circumstances a very dangerous thing."[14] With further arm-twisting by the speaker and majority whip, the House reconsidered its action and endorsed by a single vote a closed rule that would limit debate and prohibit amendments from the floor.

The precarious nature of Congress's support for further executive actions on trade policy was exposed again by the narrow defeat of Reed's motion to recommit the House bill by the slim margin of 206–199, with splits in both parties. Democrats voted 140–80 to consider the bill, while Republicans voted 119–66 to send it back to committee. The vote revealed that the House battle was between bipartisan supporters of trade expansion and a group of conservative Republicans and southern Democrats who were opposed.[15]

In the end, Congress approved the 1955 RTAA extension. The negotiating authority allowed the president to reduce tariffs by 15 percent (in three annual installments of 5 percent, thus introducing the idea of phased-in tariff reductions) and to bring down very high tariffs to 50 percent. At the same time, it included statutory language to make the Tariff Commission more inclined to recommend protection in escape-clause cases. The commission only had to find that imports "contribute materially" to the threat of serious injury to recommend tariff remedies to the president, and it was also given authority to block imports that "threaten to impair the national security."

This negotiating authority was put to use in the fourth round of multilateral GATT negotiations in Geneva (1955–56). The Geneva conference resulted in some additional tariff reductions and added several new contracting parties, most importantly Japan.[16] This was controversial because Japan was known to be a potential export powerhouse. Western European countries resisted admitting Japan, fearing the impact of its exports of labor-intensive goods on domestic producers, while the United States insisted on strengthening a key ally in Asia and integrating it into the trade system.[17]

Of course, Japan's accession also generated fears within the US textile and apparel industry. Although overall import penetration was no greater in textiles than for other manufacturing industries in the 1950s, Japan had a tendency to achieve rapid growth in exports of narrow categories of goods, creating problems for certain producers. In the specific case of cotton textiles, for example, imports as a percent of domestic production rose from less than 3 percent in 1939 to 22 percent by 1958. Prompted by southern Democrats, Congress repeatedly considered legislation or amendments to the RTAA that would protect to the textile and apparel industry. In 1955, the Senate came within two votes of mandating import quotas to assist domestic producers. The Eisenhower administration opposed this effort, but in 1957 Japan agreed to a five-year plan to restrict its exports of cotton textiles. Yet, with a growing number of alternative sources of world supply, country-specific trade restrictions were rendered ineffective: as the share of US cotton textile imports from Japan fell from 63 percent in 1958 to 26 percent in 1960, the share from Hong Kong increased from 14 percent to 28 percent.[18]

At the Geneva meeting, the United States also received a waiver from its GATT obligations regarding its agricultural price supports. The GATT already allowed countries to restrict agricultural imports when they had policies in place to reduce domestic production; the 1955 waiver allowed the United States to restrict imports even when the production or marketing of domestic crops was not being restricted. Other countries followed the United States in obtaining such a waiver, which effectively took agriculture policy outside of GATT disciplines.[19]

The United States missed an opportunity arising from the 1955 Geneva conference to strengthen the institutional foundations of the GATT. The GATT was an executive agreement, not a formal international organization, since it was expected to be superseded by the International Trade Organization. In fact, Congress took pains to signal that it did not necessarily approve of it. Every renewal of negotiating authority during the 1950s—1951, 1953, 1954, 1955, and 1958—included the following disclaimer: "The enactment of this Act shall not be construed to determine or indicate the approval or disapproval by the Congress of the Executive Agreement known as the General Agreement on Tariffs and Trade."[20]

In March 1955, the contracting parties agreed to set up the Organization for Trade Cooperation (OTC) to administer GATT rules and sponsor international trade negotiations, although it would have no powers over the trade policies of member countries. The next month, President Eisenhower submitted a bill on the OTC to Congress, arguing that "failure to assume membership in the Organization for Trade Cooperation would be interpreted throughout the free world as a lack of genuine interest on the part of this country in the efforts to expand trade." If the United States did not act to strengthen this institution, the world trading system might erode. "Such developments would play directly into the hands of the Communists," the president warned. But Congress was wary of the OTC for the same reason that it did not want to endorse the GATT: it was still skeptical of any executive agreement that might diminish its authority over trade policy. Citing other pressing business, Congress deferred hearings on the bill and then never acted on it.[21]

As multilateral negotiations to further reduce trade barriers were on hold through much of the 1950s, some domestic interests attempted to carve out special pockets of protection with the support of Congress, much as farmers had done with price supports. For example, the petroleum industry repeatedly sought and eventually received government help against imports. The United States had been a net exporter of petroleum before World War II, but expanding production in the Middle East and North Africa depressed the world price, and the United States became a net importer after the war. By the mid-1950s, net imports accounted for more than 10 percent of domestic consumption.[22] The major petroleum producers, such as Standard Oil, Texaco, and Shell, owned vast foreign reserves and had no interest in restricting imports. But small, independent producers in Texas, Oklahoma, and California were not so diversified and suffered from high production costs and idle capacity. They demanded a quota on imports on the grounds that dependence on foreign oil threatened national security.

With the support of coal producers and coal miners in Pennsylvania, Richard Simpson led the charge for an oil-import quota. As gasoline and home heating oil began displacing coal as a source of energy, the National Coal Association and United Mine Workers sought to prop up demand for coal by restricting imports of oil. Thus, the coal states of Kentucky, Pennsylvania, and West Virginia joined with the oil states of Oklahoma, Louisiana, and Texas to support the bid for a quota. Despite his opposition to protection, Eisenhower announced a "voluntary" program of import quotas on oil in 1955 which, not surprisingly, failed. Meanwhile, the Suez Crisis of 1956 disrupted the flow of oil from the Middle East and demonstrated the plausibility of a national-security rationale for standby domestic production capacity. This led to the establishment of a Mandatory Oil Import Quota Program (MOIP) in 1959 that restricted imports of crude oil and refined products to about 12 percent of US production.[23]

The import quota, which was in effect until 1973, had a very important unintended consequence that struck the United States about twenty years later. The MOIP gave preferential treatment to oil imports from Mexico and Canada, but discriminated against imports from Venezuela and the Middle East. These countries responded by forming the Organization of Petroleum Exporting Countries (OPEC) in 1960. Controlling some 80 percent of the oil sold on world markets, OPEC sought to restrict production and hence increase the world price, which they succeeded in doing in the early 1970s. Thus, the oil-import quota not only led to a more rapid depletion of domestic supply, but helped to spawn the creation of OPEC, thereby contributing to the energy crisis of the 1970s.[24]

The labor movement also began wavering in its support for open trade in the 1950s. After World War II, the sense among major labor unions was that exports sustained more jobs than imports threatened them. The American Federation of Labor and the Congress of Industrial Organizations, which merged in 1955 to become the AFL-CIO, declared their support for gradually lowering trade barriers, provided that adversely affected workers were given adjustment assistance and international fair labor standards were negotiated.[25] By the end of the decade, as imports began to displace workers in the apparel industry (ladies' garment workers, men's clothing workers, textile workers, hatters, and leather goods workers in particular), some unions began to rethink their support for lower tariffs.

Still, with imports stable at less than 3 percent of GDP, protectionist pressures were generally muted through the decade, and new instances of trade protection were rare. The peril points never proved to be much of a hindrance, because multilateral trade negotiations were sporadic and never promised significant changes to existing policy.[26] The escape clause, the main channel for protection, was rarely invoked. From 1947–62, the Tariff Commission conducted 135 escape-clause investigations relating to 106 products. No injury was found in 72 of the 113 completed cases. In the 33 cases in which injury was found, the president accepted 15 and rejected 26.[27] In most instances presidents decided that foreign policy or other interests took priority over stopping injury to the domestic industry, as when President Truman rejected restrictions on garlic imports from Italy. Imports of dried figs, clover seed, women's fur felt hats, watches, bicycles, linen toweling, spring clothespins, safety pins, stainless steel table flatware, lead and zinc, and carpets and rugs were restricted in escape-clause cases, but these goods constituted a tiny fraction of total imports.[28]

Despite the lack of enthusiasm for further trade liberalization in Congress, the political forces in favor of open trade easily sustained the status quo in the 1950s. Although export-oriented interests still influenced votes in favor of liberal trade, the RTAA survived partly due to the linkage of trade policy to foreign policy and national security.[29] Even if members of Congress did not have many strong, export-oriented interests in their constituencies, most were satisfied with existing policy for those broader reasons. In particular, Republicans were sympathetic to the view that freer world trade was an important part of the fight against Communism. As

Eisenhower put it in his 1955 State of the Union message, "We must expand international trade and investment and assist friendly nations whose own best efforts are still insufficient to provide the strength essential to the security of the free world."[30] In a study of Congressional voting patterns in the 1950s, Bailey (2003) reported evidence "consistent with the view that the American people cared deeply about the Soviet threat and were willing to support politicians who pursued even difficult aid and trade policies that furthered national security goals." If public opinion had not been so favorable to supporting foreign allies, the RTAA renewals in 1955 and 1958 would have failed to pass, according to his findings.

THE CHALLENGE OF THE EUROPEAN ECONOMIC COMMUNITY

As a forum for negotiating the reduction of trade barriers, the GATT was relatively quiet during the 1950s. Congress's reluctance to allow the president to undertake new negotiations was matched by Europe's reluctance to reduce trade barriers when it was still struggling to cope with economic dislocations after the war. The United States strongly encouraged efforts by Western European nations to expand trade with each other in order to promote their economic recovery and wean them off foreign aid. In 1949, looking to the eventual end of financial assistance, the US administrator of the Marshall Plan insisted on the integration of the Western European economy.[31]

To this end, Western European governments worked out programs to restore the multilateral payments system and move toward freer trade in Europe. The European Payments Union was formed to end bilateral trade balancing and help finance trade flows across Europe, a step toward full currency convertibility (in which European currencies could be freely bought and sold for purposes of trade). The members of the Organization for European Economic Cooperation (a forerunner of the Organization for Economic Cooperation and Development, or OECD) agreed to a Code of Trade Liberalization under which increasing shares of their imports would be freed from quantitative restrictions and foreign-exchange controls. Having survived the economic difficulties of the immediate postwar years, Western Europe was soon rapidly recovering from the war, and import quotas and other policies that discriminated against dollar imports were quickly dismantled in 1955 and 1956. In 1958, remaining exchange controls were lifted, and European currencies became freely convertible into dollars for current account transactions.

The capstone of these efforts was the Treaty of Rome, signed in 1957 by six countries: Belgium, France, West Germany, Italy, Luxembourg, and the Netherlands. They agreed to form the European Economic Community (EEC) and create a Common Market. The EEC was a customs union, whereby member countries abolished all tariffs on trade between them and maintained a common external tariff on goods from nonmembers. In addition, seven other nations—Britain, Sweden, Norway, Denmark, Switzerland, Austria, and Portugal—established the European Free Trade Association (EFTA), wherein member countries abolished all tariffs on trade between them but kept their own independent tariffs on goods from nonmembers. The EEC and EFTA were cooperative, not competing, trade arrangements with the potential to create a large free-trade zone within Europe.

The formation of the EEC and EFTA posed a dilemma for US policymakers. The United States supported European economic cooperation in the belief that trade expansion would promote economic growth, foster political stability, and check Soviet expansionism. As much as it desired these outcomes, however, the United States did not want Western Europe to form a separate trade bloc that would have an adverse effect on its exports. For example, since West Germany's goods would receive duty-free treatment in France, while US goods would be subject to the EEC tariff, the level of the external tariff would determine the degree of discrimination against American goods.

Concerns about the adverse impact of the EEC on US exports made the 1958 renewal of the RTAA much easier than in previous years. Eisenhower requested a five-year renewal of trade-negotiating authority and the ability to reduce tariffs by 25 percent from their current levels. Given the difficulties that trade legislation had earlier in the decade, Speaker Sam Rayburn thought it would take "blood, sweat, and tears" to get the package through Congress, but he was wrong. The business community was energized by the formation of the EEC and demanded government action against European preferences, and members of Congress responded. Although the negotiating authority was extended for four years, not the five requested, it was still the longest extension ever. And although the tariff-cutting authority was pared back from 25 percent to 20 percent, larger reductions in duties greater than 50 percent were permitted. In contrast to previous years, the administration was successful in its request because the negotiating authority had a clear and distinct purpose: helping to minimize the impact on US exports when tariffs on trade within Western Europe were eliminated.

The 1958 RTAA renewal put the United States in a strong position to bargain for a reduction in the EEC's tariff. The first stage of the negotiations (1960–61) addressed the conformity of the EEC with the provisions of the GATT and the level of its proposed external tariff. A customs union invariably departs from the most-favored nation (MFN) treatment established in article 1 of the GATT because it discriminates in the tariff treatment of imports from member and nonmember states. But article 23 of the GATT permitted customs unions if two requirements were met. First, import duties and other restrictive regulations of commerce must be "eliminated with respect to substantially all trade between the constituent territories of the union." Second, the external tariff "shall not on the whole be higher or more restrictive than the general incidence of the duties and regulations of commerce applicable in the constituent territories prior to the formation of such union."[32] On the basis of the second condition, the United States insisted that the EEC establish a low tariff, but the EEC countered that any concessions given on its tariff had to be reciprocated by other countries.

In the second phase of the negotiations, from 1961–62, known as the Dillon Round, the United States and Europe discussed tariff reductions.[33] The EEC offered to cut its tariffs on industrial goods by 20 percent, although it refused to consider agricultural duties while it was formulating a Common Agricultural Policy. But the United States was unable to respond effectively to this offer. Negotiators could not match the 20 percent offer for fear of violating the peril points provision; although that provision constituted no real legislative constraint, there would be a political cost to going beyond it. In addition, the State Department was still required to negotiate on a selective, product-by-product basis and was not authorized to undertake across-the-board tariff reductions.

The Dillon Round ended shortly before the president's trade-negotiating authority expired in June 1962. The tariff reductions amounted to only a 4 percent weighted average cut, insufficient to reduce the margin of preference given to European goods and thereby leaving the problem for American exporters unresolved.

THE TRADE EXPANSION ACT OF 1962

The election of John F. Kennedy as president in 1960 restored unified government under the Democrats. Coming from Massachusetts, with its declining textile industry, Kennedy was not naturally predisposed to promote further trade liberalization. In fact, he made a campaign promise to help protect industries troubled by imports. At the same time, the new president was firmly committed to strengthening ties with Western Europe and preventing any disintegration of the Atlantic alliance.[34] Furthermore, policymakers and exporters continued to worry about trade diversion resulting from the formation of the EEC. They also worried about investment diversion: if American businesses found it more difficult to export to Europe, they might shift some of their investment spending from the United States to Europe in order to reach consumers behind the EEC's tariff. Thus, the Kennedy administration united the foreign-policy objective of strengthening the Atlantic alliance with the economic objective of minimizing Europe's discrimination against American exports in pressing forward with a revitalized trade program.

With trade-negotiating authority expiring in mid-1962, the new administration had the option of choosing a simple renewal of the RTAA or proposing something bolder. At the urging of Undersecretary of State George Ball, Kennedy decided to revise the trade agreements program in light of the disappointing Dillon Round. The RTAA "must not simply be renewed, it must be replaced," the president was to argue.

In January 1962, Kennedy unveiled his administration's proposal to revamp the trade agreements program. The primary rationale for the Trade Expansion Act was to promote the strength and unity of the Western alliance. "The two great Atlantic markets will either grow together or they will grow apart," the president said, and "that decision will either mark the beginning of a new chapter in the alliance of these nations—or a threat to the growth of Western unity." Kennedy argued that the new legislation was critical for five reasons: to respond to the challenge of the EEC, to reverse the deterioration in the balance of payments, to boost economic growth, to counter Communist efforts at capturing a greater share of world trade, and to promote the integration of Japan and other developing countries into the world trading system. The president emphasized that congressional support should be bipartisan: "This philosophy of the free market—the wider economic choice for men and nations—is as old as freedom itself. It is not a partisan philosophy. For many years our trade legislation has enjoyed bipartisan backing from those members of both parties who recognized how essential trade is to our basic security abroad and our economic health at home. This is even more true today. The Trade Expansion Act of 1962 is designed as the expression of a nation, not of any single faction, not of any single faction or section."[35]

The Kennedy administration's proposal built on past practice but was new on several dimensions. The president requested the authority to make across-the-board tariff reductions of up to 50 percent, thereby abandoning the bilateral product-by-product negotiating approach that had been used since 1934. In addition, peril points were to be scrapped, and the Tariff Commission was required simply to advise the president on the broader economic effects of tariff reductions, clearing the way for more significant cuts.

The administration also proposed a new way of helping workers harmed by imports. Rather than limit imports through the escape clause, direct government aid in the form of trade adjustment assistance (TAA) would be provided to workers and communities adversely affected by imports. TAA included income support, relocation benefits, training assistance, and other financial compensation for displaced workers. The program helped win the support of George Meany, the president of the AFL-CIO, for the legislation.[36] Kennedy also proposed tightening the eligibility requirements in escape-clause cases; now a prolonged shutdown of production facilities or unemployment caused by imports had to affect an entire industry, not just one product in an industry.

These features marked a bold change from the traditional RTAA approach. The original goal of the RTAA was to eliminate the excessive tariffs in the Hawley-Smoot schedule in exchange for tariff concessions by other countries. In this incarnation, the RTAA aimed to reduce tariffs on a selective basis and thereby avoid harm to domestic interests, although the escape clause was included to allow tariffs to be raised temporarily when "unforeseen developments" resulted in injury to an industry. With the abandonment of the selective approach, the proposed legislation explicitly recognized that some domestic interests would be harmed by tariff reductions and that the remedy should not be import restrictions but direct government assistance. This assistance was designed to promote the adjustment of labor and capital to the new competitive conditions and to help workers find employment in other sectors of the economy. As Undersecretary of State Ball put it, "The concept that we must protect every American industry against the adjustments required by competition is alien to the spirit of our economy."[37] The end of peril points also signaled a recognition that figuring out which particular tariff level might bring "harm" to an industry was impossible to determine.

The Kennedy administration was so politically shrewd in selling this package to Congress that its legislative proposal passed largely intact. The administration organized a nationwide campaign to enlist business support with the rallying cry "trade or fade." As in the past, a number of broad coalitions (both industry and labor groups) testified before Congressional committees in favor of the new negotiating authority, while many smaller business interests spoke against it. Stimulated by the emergence of the EEC, a large number of corporate executives and exporter groups testified in favor of negotiations in 1958 and 1962, many more than in the early and mid-1950s. The National Association of Manufacturers, American Farm Bureau Federation, and other umbrella organizations supported the bill because their constituents were worried about European discrimination against their products.[38]

The Kennedy administration also managed to neutralize the opposition of import-sensitive industries so that they would not campaign against the legislation. For example, the biggest obstacle to the legislation was expected to be the textile bloc of roughly one hundred members from the Northeast and South who would fight any proposal that might harm the textile and apparel industry. To win votes in the South during the 1960 election campaign, Kennedy promised to help textile producers. Shortly after taking office, Kennedy announced a seven-point program to assist the industry, including a conference of textile importing and exporting countries to discuss managing trade in textile products.[39]

Responsibility for negotiating the agreement fell to Undersecretary of State George Ball. It was not a task that he and other liberals relished. As Ball (1982, 188) recalled, "During his Presidential campaign, [Kennedy] had committed himself to taking care of textile import problems, and the industry promptly demanded that he redeem his promise. The President turned the problem over to me. It caused me more personal anguish than any other task I undertook during my total of twelve years in different branches of the government." Ball fundamentally opposed protecting the industry and could not understand why domestic producers did not invest abroad to take advantage of lower wages in Asia: "Rather than concentrating 1.3 percent of our labor force on the production of textiles, our country might have shifted more rapidly to the capital-intensive and knowledge-intensive industries and services that befitted a nation with an advanced economy" (188).

Despite his personal views, Ball carried out the president's wishes and thereby prevented the industry from opposing the administration's trade plan. In July 1961, the State Department helped conclude the Short-Term Arrangement (STA) on cotton textiles with other importers (the EEC, Britain, and Canada) and exporters (Japan, Hong Kong, India). The exporters agreed to set quantitative limits (in essence, export quotas) on their textile shipments for one year. In February 1962, a five-year Long-Term Arrangement (LTA) was concluded. The LTA capped the rate of growth of exports of cotton textiles and expanded the number of products covered to include wool, man-made fibers, and silk products as well. The LTA involved nineteen countries and stipulated a minimum annual growth in quotas of 5 percent. It also introduced the concept of "market disruption," in which a sharp increase in imports would be enough to trigger additional limits on imports, even if injury was not proven, as would be required in an escape-clause case. The LTA was renewed in 1967 and expanded to include many other exporters and products.

Advocates of a liberal trade policy, including Ball, viewed the textile quotas—which, alongside import quotas on agricultural goods, was the most glaring retreat from the principles of the trade agreements program since its inception—as a very high price to pay for the passage of the Trade Expansion Act. Still, the quotas served a political purpose. The LTA was so successful in satisfying the demands of the textile and apparel industry that it actually won the support of the American Cotton Manufacturers Institute (ACMI) for the bill. At its annual meeting, the directors of the AMCI expressed their thanks to the Kennedy administration for its "unprecedented degree of thoughtful consideration" and stated, "We believe that the authority to deal with foreign nations proposed by the President will be wisely exercised and should be granted by the Congress."[40]

To build further support for (or prevent opposition to) the bill, Kennedy made implicit promises to help the lumber and oil industries. In March 1962, the president accepted the Tariff Commission's recommendation for relief in two escape-clause cases, significantly increasing import duties on woven carpets and flat glass. This decision was perfectly timed to coincide with the Ways and Means Committee hearings on the Trade Expansion Act (TEA). Although the legislative package proposed by the Kennedy administration was initially greeted with skepticism by the committee's chairman, Wilbur Mills (D-AR), the escape-clause action helped win his support.

As if to demonstrate the need for a new trade agreement with Europe, several trans-Atlantic trade disputes broke out at this time, the most famous being the "chicken war."[41] In July 1962, the EEC introduced a variable import levy on foreign poultry as part of its new Common Agricultural Policy. The levy roughly doubled the previous duty of about 15 percent and reduced US poultry exports by two-thirds within a few weeks. After eighteen months of fruitless negotiation, the United States retaliated by imposing higher duties (technically, withdrawing tariff concessions from previous GATT negotiations) on potato starch, dextrin, brandy, and light trucks that were imported primarily from Western Europe. The higher tariffs on the first three goods were eventually lifted, but the 25 percent tariff on light trucks has persisted to this day. All of this showed to policy-makers at the time the dangers of a retaliatory trade war if countries began to impose trade restrictions and depart from GATT principles.

The mobilization of business support, the pacification of potential opponents, and the growing risk of a trade war with Europe greatly eased the bill's passage through Congress, although Finger and Harrison (1996, 217) note that "Kennedy was criticized by members of his own party for the mercenary way in which he put together the votes needed to pass the TEA." Public opinion was also broadly supportive of the legislation. A March 1962 Gallup poll suggested that, of those who had heard of the Kennedy plan, 38 percent favored lower tariffs, 15 percent favored higher tariffs, 18 percent wanted them kept about the same, and 29 percent expressed no opinion. However, just 13 percent of those questioned were familiar with the details of the legislation.[42]

Of course, legislators adjusted the bill somewhat to their own liking. The Ways and Means Committee stripped control of the trade negotiations from the State Department and created the ambassador-ranked position of Special Trade Representative in the Executive Office of the President to conduct foreign trade negotiations. This reflected Congress's growing belief that trade policy and foreign policy should be undertaken by separate entities. Legislators had long-standing concerns that the State Department was too focused on diplomatic objectives and therefore too weak in representing the country's commercial interests. Even strong supporters of lower trade barriers, such as Paul Douglas, a Democratic Senator from Illinois and former economics professor at the University of Chicago who had co-organized the economists' petition against the Hawley-Smoot tariff in 1930, wanted the change. Douglas was appalled at the State Department's indifference to foreign discrimination against American exports, particularly through the use of non-tariff barriers.[43] Douglas advocated taking a stronger stand against countries that so brazenly blocked American exports.[44]

In June 1962, the House passed the Trade Expansion Act by an overwhelming margin, 298–125. Democrats voted 218–35 in favor, while Republicans voted 90–80 against. The Republican split was due largely to its traditional concerns about the potential harm to import-competing industries and the substitution of trade adjustment assistance for trade remedies such as peril points and the escape clause. In September, the Senate easily passed the legislation by the margin of 78–8; Democrats voted 56–1, and Republicans voted 22–2 in favor.

This Senate vote marked a major shift in how Congress passed trade legislation. At least since the Civil War, the majority leadership in the House was able to enforce rules restricting amendments and limiting the floor debate so that a party-line vote—usually with strict party discipline and few defectors—was the outcome. As a result, the House vote was usually a predictable win for the majority party. The problem always came in the Senate, where party discipline was weak, and members could propose amendment after amendment to hold up passage. For this reason, the Senate became known as the "graveyard" of tariff reform for Democrats and the source of the logrolling problem for Republicans, as demonstrated in 1929–30. Now, starting in 1962, party discipline in the House was weakening, as the rank-and-file members felt they could disregard the party's whips if a particular vote might harm their chances for reelection. The result was more party defections and increased difficulty in passing controversial trade legislation. Meanwhile, Senate votes on trade issues were becoming more bipartisan and more internationalist because fears about reelection were less pressing. The ease with which the Senate was able to pass controversial trade legislation became particularly evident from the 1970s onward: the hard, close trade votes were now in the House, not the Senate, where support for trade agreements and negotiating authority became much more predictable.

In signing the bill in October 1962, Kennedy hailed the legislation: "We cannot protect our economy by stagnating behind tariff walls, but . . . the best protection possible is a mutual lowering of tariff barriers among friendly nations so that all may benefit from a free flow of goods. Increased economic activity resulting from increased trade will provide more job opportunities for our workers." He also emphasized the foreign-policy rationale for the bill: "A vital expanding economy in the free world is a strong counter to the threat of the world Communist movement," and trade expansion is "an important new weapon to advance the cause of freedom."[45] Over the next half century, presidents of both parties would consistently invoke these two themes—creating jobs at home and fostering a freer world abroad—in pushing for new trade agreements.

The Trade Expansion Act ended the trade-policy drift of the 1950s and paved the way for the Kennedy Round of GATT negotiations. "By permitting the reduction of American tariffs to very low levels and making possible the Kennedy Round, [the Trade Expansion Act] marked a major turn away from a course that was otherwise coming close to stopping the process of American trade liberalization altogether," Diebold (1999, 268) observed. "And that would have been tantamount to setting back the liberalization of the global trading system as well."

THE KENNEDY ROUND AND
CONGRESSIONAL BACKLASH

The sixth round of multilateral trade negotiations among the contract-ing parties of the GATT got off to a slow start. After months of prepara-tory work, the Kennedy Round negotiations finally began in Geneva in May 1964 with the participation of forty-six countries. The main goal of the United States was to reduce the EEC's external tariff in order to cut the margin of preference given to European firms and against American firms selling in the Common Market. The main goal of the EEC was to address the high spikes in the US tariff schedule, but also modify various objectionable policies, such as the American Selling Price (which applied the US price in assessing duties on imported goods), the Buy America Act (which gave preferences to domestic firms in government procurement contracts), and the escape clause (which they feared would close the mar-ket to their goods).

Compared with previous multilateral negotiations, the Kennedy Round was prolonged and difficult, taking three years before finally concluding in June 1967. About half of 1965 was lost when the EEC was unable to par-ticipate due to a dispute between France and its partners about negotiating objectives. By early 1966, little progress had been made. The talks might have continued indefinitely had the president's negotiating authority not been due to expire in 1967. In addition, the number of participants in the negotiation had grown. The number of contracting parties to the GATT had risen from the original twenty-three to more than seventy by the con-clusion of the Kennedy Round. However, the negotiations were still pri-marily between the United States and the EEC, with Japan and Britain also playing an important role; developing countries did not participate in the tariff negotiations.

The first battle concerned the precise formulae to be used for reducing tariffs. When the United States proposed a uniform 50 percent reduction in tariffs, with limited exceptions, the EEC objected, arguing that some peaks would remain very high in the US tariff schedule, while its own would be at a uniformly low rate. The EEC suggested lowering tariffs to some target level, such as 10 percent for manufactures, 5 percent for semi-manufactures, and zero for raw materials. In the end, the EEC accepted the US position that all parties attempt to reduce tariffs uniformly, with some exceptions.

The United States also insisted that agricultural goods be subject to the same liberalization as industrial goods, but the EEC refused to agree.

"Because of the powerful agricultural protectionism in the Common Market, it was obvious that we would not get all the concessions we wanted for American agriculture," President Lyndon Johnson (1971, 312) recalled in his memoirs. "The question was whether we should accept what we could get, plus a major liberalization of trade in industrial products, or abandon the effort."[46]

In May 1967, after reviewing the final package item by item in the Cabinet Room, Johnson's advisers unanimously endorsed the agreement, and the president agreed. Top officials in the Johnson administration then briefed the congressional leadership and reported that "the questioning was keen and specific, but the general results favorable." As Johnson (1971, 313) noted,

> As expected, members of Congress paid closest attention to items of concern to their own states and districts. Speaker McCormack, whose home state of Massachusetts manufactures shoes, asked about increased shoe imports under the new agreement. Senator Robert Byrd of West Virginia asked about glass imports. Senator Herman Talmadge of Georgia worried about textiles and farm products. Senator George Aiken of Vermont wondered whether maple sugar sales to Canada would be affected. One sweeping question was in many minds, and it was eventually asked by Senator John Patore of Rhode Island: Had we lost our shirt in our eagerness to make the Kennedy Round a success?

Johnson (1971, 314) believed that "we had bargained hard and patiently," but recognized that members of Congress "would soon hear complaints from nervous special-interest groups back home, though they probably would hear little from the vast majority of constituents who would benefit from the trade agreement."

On June 30, 1967, just a few hours before the president's negotiating power was due to expire, Ambassador Michael Blumenthal, the deputy trade representative, signed the Kennedy Round agreement for the United States. The primary accomplishment of the round was the reduction of tariffs on industrial products by about 35 percent, on average. Table 11.1 shows the average tariff rates in the United States, EEC, United Kingdom, and Japan before and after the round. The largest cuts were in machinery, transportation equipment, and chemicals, with smaller cuts in iron and steel. The duties on textiles and woolen goods were largely exempt from any reduction. The lower duties went into effect by executive order and were phased in over five years, starting in 1968 and finishing in 1972.

TABLE 11.1. Average tariff on dutiable imports: Pre- and post-Kennedy Round (non-agricultural, dutiable imports, other than mineral fuels), percentage

	Before Kennedy Round	After Kennedy Round
United States	13.5	9.6
EEC	12.8	8.1
United Kingdom	16.6	10.6
Japan	15.5	9.5

Source: Preeg 1970, 208–11.

In addition, the Kennedy Round negotiations reached several "codes" on non-tariff barriers to trade. The United States agreed to abolish the American Selling Price (ASP), which was a way of raising the effective tariff (mainly on chemicals) by using the domestic price rather than the foreign price as the way of valuing imports. A new antidumping code required a change in US law: dumped imports had to be the "principal cause" of material injury, whereas the existing US law had no injury requirement.

Despite its support for the Trade Expansion Act, Congress did not welcome the results of the negotiation. A major complaint about the Kennedy Round was its failure to deal with agriculture, particularly the adverse effects of the EEC's Common Agricultural Policy on US farm exports. The negotiation was also believed to have inadequately addressed non-tariff barriers against American exports while further opening up the US market to imports. In 1966, before the round had been completed, Sen. Everett Dirksen (R-IL) complained that "the United States appears intent upon concluding an agreement which will not repair the damage to our farmers, while inflicting new damage upon manufacturing. . . . It looks very much as though we are offering to give them [other countries] our shirt in exchange for a handkerchief."[47] Congress was also dismayed by the drafting of codes that would standardize antidumping regulations and abolish the ASP. Thus, within the executive branch, Evans (1971, 299) notes, "The euphoria generated by the successful conclusion of the Kennedy Round in the summer of 1967 was short-lived, and was soon replaced by serious doubts that the agreement could withstand the forces being mobilized against it."

Although the Kennedy Round tariff reductions went into effect by executive order, Congress needed to approve other elements of the deal. In the spring of 1968, President Johnson requested that Congress abolish the ASP, approve the antidumping agreement, and grant new tariff-cutting authority, which had expired in late 1967. The Ways and Means Committee hearings on this proposal went poorly: rather than endorsing the administration's request, representatives of the textile, footwear, steel, and oil industries called for import quotas. With a presidential election on the horizon, Congress ignored Johnson's request and did not act on the ASP and antidumping codes. This was a harbinger of difficult years ahead for trade policy. Although the strong economy and a low rate of unemployment had kept trade politics in abeyance during most of the 1950s and 1960s, higher inflation and unemployment, along with growing balance of payments problems, were around the corner. Indeed, America's position in the world economy was about to change in a way that would put existing policies under enormous stress.[48]

The presidential election campaign of 1968 was dominated by a debate over domestic affairs and the Vietnam War, but trade policy was not entirely neglected. The Democrats pledged to build upon the Trade Expansion Act "in order to achieve greater trade cooperation and progress toward freer international trade."[49] By contrast, the Republicans promised a tougher approach, including "hard-headed bargaining to lower the nontariff barriers against American exports." While offering "to work toward freer trade among all nations of the free world," Republicans also underscored the problems caused by imports:

A sudden influx of imports can endanger many industries. These problems, differing in each industry, must be considered case by case. Our guideline will be fairness for both producers and workers, without foreclosing imports. Thousands of jobs have been lost to foreign producers because of discriminatory and unfair trade practices. The State Department must give closest attention to the development of agreements with exporting nations to bring about fair competition. Imports should not be permitted to capture excessive portions of the American market but should, through international agreements, be able to participate in the growth of consumption. Should such efforts fail, specific counter-measures will have to be applied until fair competition is re-established.[50]

The Republican platform was widely interpreted as endorsing "fair trade" as an objective of trade policy. The statement was prescient in describing the major concerns of US trade policy over the next two decades.

Just as Kennedy had in 1960, the new Republican president, Richard

Nixon, was willing to use trade policy for electoral purposes. During the campaign, Nixon openly courted import-affected workers in an attempt to win the endorsement of organized labor in the North and textile workers in the South. When campaigning in the Carolinas, Nixon promised to reinforce the Kennedy administration's limits on textile imports to cover woolen and synthetic fabrics in addition to cotton products.[51]

After winning the election, Nixon made good on his pledge by seeking to expand restrictions on Japan's textile exports to include the rapidly growing category of man-made fibers, such as polyesters, acrylics, and nylons. Even though imports of man-made fibers constituted less than 4 percent of domestic production, domestic producers strongly supported further limits on imports.[52] In November 1969, Nixon and Japan's prime minister reached a secret agreement whereby the United States would return the island of Okinawa in exchange for tighter limits on textile exports. Believing it had solved the textile problem, the Nixon administration submitted a bill to Congress asking for a four-year authorization to reduce import tariffs up to 20 percent from 1967 levels, including the power to eliminate the ASP. It also proposed strengthening executive powers to retaliate against foreign unfair trade practices and expanding government aid to industries and workers harmed by trade by easing the statutory requirements for import relief and adjustment assistance.

In taking up the administration's proposals in early 1970, the chairman of the House Ways and Means Committee, Wilbur Mills (D-AR), took the unusual step of adding a provision to impose quotas on imported textiles and shoes. Though Mills favored free trade in principle, he thought this provision would improve his own political fortunes as well as give the Nixon administration negotiating leverage to secure a more effective textile agreement with Japan. In fact, by early 1970, it was clear that Japan's prime minister could not persuade other government officials or industry executives to enforce the new export restraints.[53] And Mills's strategy did not work: Japan refused to make further concessions, and Nixon threatened to veto the measure if it imposed limits on imports other than textiles, such as shoes.

Mills also lost control of the bill. The Ways and Means Committee added a provision imposing quotas on every imported good whose share of the US market exceeded 15 percent. Although this provision was later dropped, the House passed the bill in November 1970 with quotas on textiles, apparel, and footwear that would limit imports by category and country of origin to their average level of 1967–69, allowing no more than a 5 percent annual increase thereafter.[54] The Mills bill passed by a 215–165 vote, with both parties split over the measure. Democrats were divided geographically: Southern Democrats strongly supported it by 70–11, while Northern Democrats went 72–67 against it. Meanwhile, Republicans were narrowly opposed by 82–78. The vote marked an important change: for the first time, Democrats were supporting greater protection for domestic industry, and Republicans were opposed. In addition, the old North-South division over trade that held from the early nineteenth century until at least the 1930s had dissolved. As figure 11.2 shows, a new geographic pattern was evident in which the South and Northeast were largely in favor of import restrictions, and the West was largely opposed.

The Mills bill died when Congress adjourned before the Senate could act on the measure. This marked the end of an extreme trade measure that would have imposed significant trade barriers for manufacturing industries affected by imports, something not seen since the days of the Hawley-Smoot tariff. Although it almost certainly would have drawn a presidential veto, the unexpected popularity of the Mills bill was an indicator of growing protectionist pressures. After forty years of Congressional support for open trade policies, the ground was shifting in US trade politics.

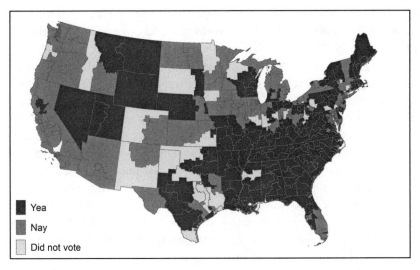

Figure 11.2. House vote on Mills bill, November 19, 1970. (Map courtesy Citrin GIS/Applied Spatial Analysis Lab, Dartmouth College.)

A NEW WORLD FOR US TRADE POLICY

What was happening to make Congress adopt a more protectionist out-look? Ever since the Reciprocal Trade Agreements Act in 1934, Congress had taken a step back from active control over trade policy. Although it refused to endorse the International Trade Organization in the 1940s and other trade initiatives in the 1950s, Congress had accepted most executive branch actions on trade policy. The Mills bill of 1970 represented a reas-sertion of congressional authority to regulate trade and threatened a sig-nificant departure from the trade policies established after World War II. This change reflected an important new development: some domestic in-dustries were now facing much greater foreign competition than they had seen in many decades, if ever. Trade politics was about to become much more difficult simply because imports were starting to play a much larger role in the economy. After World War II, imports were less than 3 percent of GDP, an unusually low level in historical terms. Because the economic recovery of Western Europe and Japan from the war had taken so long, im-ports as a share of GDP were no higher in 1965 than they had been in 1950. Starting in the mid-1960s, however, imports began to rise while exports remained at about the same proportion of GDP.

The rise in imports might have been anticipated as other countries recovered from the war, but it nonetheless came as a surprise to indus-try leaders and policymakers. In 1950, the United States accounted for 27 percent of world GDP and 23 percent of world exports. By 1973, the US share of world GDP had fallen to 22 percent, and its share of world trade to 16 percent.[55] The US share of world exports of manufactured goods declined from 25 percent in 1960 to 19 percent in 1972. Thanks to their strong economic recovery, Europe and Japan began to make their presence felt in world markets, which was interpreted by many as a worrisome de-cline in US competitiveness. In reality, this was simply a return to nor-mal conditions of competition. The immediate postwar position of the US economy as the world's sole industrial power was unsustainable. That the growing economic strength of Europe and Asia was not only inevitable but desirable did not make the experience any less painful for some domestic producers. Having grown accustomed to operating in a world without se-rious foreign competition, many industries and their workers were now forced to adapt to a new situation.

Aside from the postwar economic boom, another factor behind the expansion in world trade was the container revolution. Introduced in the mid-1960s, the container streamlined the process of loading and unloading cargo and dramatically reduced the costs of shipping goods. "Before containerization, international trade was extremely expensive: crating, insuring, transporting, loading, unloading, and storing goods being exported often cost 25 percent or more of the value of goods," Levinson (2006b, 49–50) notes. "By making goods transportation drastically cheaper, containerization allowed manufacturers, wholesalers, and retailers to stretch their supply chains around the world with little concern for the expense of transporting inputs and finished products." One study found that, starting in the early 1970s, containerization increased trade among developed countries by about 17 percent and, with a 10–15 year lag, increased trade among all countries (including developing) by about 14 percent.[56]

The impact of the container on New York City was particularly striking. The share of containers in shipping entering the port of New York rose from 6 percent in 1960 to 31 percent in 1970. The use of containers led to a huge improvement in port efficiency and a steep decline in port-related employment. The container played a key role in the dramatic collapse of the industrial base around New York City between 1967 and 1975, when the city lost a quarter of its factories and a third of its manufacturing jobs, particularly in garments and apparel.[57]

Yet another factor behind the growth in imports was that tariffs were relatively low and still falling. For nearly twenty years, from the early 1950s until the late 1960s, the average tariff on dutiable imports was roughly unchanged at about 12 percent. As a result of the Kennedy Round and import-price inflation, the average tariff was cut in half to about 6 percent by 1975.[58] While this decline in tariffs certainly encouraged more imports, it was not the primary factor behind the growth of imports. Regardless of any changes in US policy, the enormous expansion of production in Europe and Asia and improvements in transportation efficiency were responsible for bringing more imports into the domestic market.

To many observers, the most visible manifestation of the country's loss of international competitiveness was the erosion of the US trade surplus during the 1960s. The merchandise trade surplus shrank over the decade, and in 1971, the United States was poised to run its first trade deficit since the 1930s. The export surplus of the immediate postwar period, which policymakers said needed to be maintained to support jobs and also justified reducing trade barriers, had disappeared. Government support for exports had also shrunk over this period. In 1960, about 13 percent of US exports received government financing through loans and grants, foreign agricultural assistance under Public Law 480, and military grant aid; by 1977, that figure had shrunk to just 1.5 percent.[59]

Which sectors of the economy were the most vulnerable to foreign competition? Compared to other countries, the United States had always been a high-wage economy, and therefore it was no surprise that unskilled, labor-intensive industries were among the first segments of American manufacturing to feel the pain of greater foreign competition. The textile and apparel industry was particularly vulnerable because production was very labor-intensive and based on standardized technology. The share of imports in domestic consumption rose steadily over the postwar period. The industry had tremendous political clout: it employed 2.3 million workers in 1967, almost 12 percent of total manufacturing employment, most of which was concentrated in the South. The textile and apparel industry had successfully persuaded the Eisenhower and Kennedy administrations to force Japan into limiting its clothing exports when this competition emerged in the mid-1950s. The footwear industry was in a similar situation, facing intensified foreign competition, but it failed in repeated attempts to get similar trade restrictions because it employed fewer workers and was less regionally concentrated.

Labor-intensive industries were not the only segments of manufacturing that began to have problems with imports. Highly concentrated, capital-intensive industries, often with strong labor unions, also ran into difficulties. The steel industry was first on this list. As we have seen in earlier chapters, the steel industry had been a powerful force for protective tariffs in the nineteenth century, but had become internationally competitive around the turn of the century. However, domestic production was highly concentrated among a small number of imperfectly competitive producers. They had the power to set prices, accommodate union demands for higher wages, and pass those costs onto consumers with little fear of foreign competition.[60]

The steel industry's trade problems began at the end of the 1950s. In July 1959, the United Steel Workers shut down domestic production for 116 days, the longest industrial strike in the nation's history. During the strike, steel-consuming industries, such as construction and automobiles, desperately sought alternative sources of supply and turned to imported steel. In 1959, for the first time in the twentieth century, imports of steel exceeded exports. Imports jumped from 1.5 percent of domestic consumption in 1957 to 6.1 percent in 1959.

The lesson that management took from the costly shutdown was that labor peace had to be purchased with generous wage concessions in order to keep factories running and prevent consumers from buying foreign steel. By the mid-1970s, average wages in the steel industry were more than 70 percent higher than the average wage in manufacturing; by the early 1980s, this premium had risen to 95 percent.[61] While the generous wage settlements pacified the steel workers, it also saddled the firms with high labor costs that did not reflect underlying improvements in labor productivity. While the steel industry was able to pass along higher wages to steel consumers in the absence of foreign competition, this was no longer feasible when consumers had access to a growing number of foreign suppliers.

Meanwhile, steel production capacity steadily grew in Japan and Germany. The United States accounted for 53 percent of world steel production in 1950, but just 21 percent in 1970. In itself, this decline did not indicate any failure by the industry, because maintaining such a high share of world production would have been unrealistic; the earlier share reflected the artificial distribution of production capacity immediately after the war. But the rise of foreign competition exposed the lack of robust domestic competition that allowed high-cost firms to survive, as well as poor choices in technology.

Burdened with inflated costs, domestic producers began to price themselves out of the market and lose market share to foreign steel. Import penetration rose from less than 5 percent in 1960 to about 15 percent in 1970, as shown in figure 11.3. The steel industry and its workers had a huge stake in arresting this growth in imports. Management wanted to prevent foreign competition from undermining profitability, while workers wanted to preserve their high wages and current employment levels. As a result, the industry demanded protection from imports. In late 1967, Senator Vance Hartke (D-IN) introduced legislation to limit steel imports to 9.6 percent of the domestic market. To discourage such legislation, the Johnson administration welcomed an offer from Japan and Germany to cap their steel exports. In the resulting voluntary restraint agreements (VRAs), Japan and the EEC agreed to hold their steel exports to 5.8 million tons each, down from 7.5 million tons for Japan and 7.3 million tons for the EEC, with 5 percent growth each subsequent year. The VRAs were in effect for three years (from 1969 to 1971) and were later renewed for another three years (until 1974). Though the volume of steel imports fell, foreign producers upgraded the quality of their exports to higher value stainless and alloy steel products, so the overall value of imports did not fall. Furthermore, Japan believed that some categories of steel (fabricated structural steel and cold finished bars) were not covered by the agreement and those exports were not restricted.

This steel action, preceded by the Long-Term Arrangement on trade in

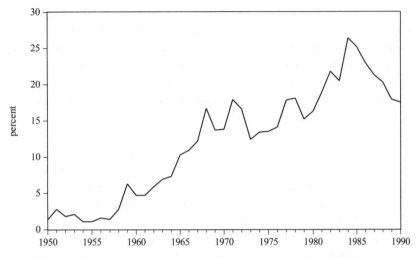

Figure 11.3. Imports as a share of domestic consumption: Steel,
1950–1990. (American Iron and Steel Institute, *Annual Statistical
Report*, various years; measured by volume [net tons].)

cotton textiles negotiated by the Kennedy administration in 1962, was just
the tip of the growing protectionist iceberg that was developed over the
next two decades. For the next twenty years, the same scenario would repeat itself time and again: as import penetration would rise, producers and
workers would complain, Congress would consider legislation mandating
a sharp cutback in imports, and the executive branch would negotiate "voluntary" export restrictions with other countries to manage the situation.

As policymakers in the executive branch and Congress sought to understand and cope with the new global environment, the early 1970s became a period of trade-policy turmoil. The sense that America's position
in the world economy was under threat was reflected in a report by the
president's Commission on International Trade and Investment Policy (the
Williams Commission) released in July 1971. The report (1971, 1–3) began
by stating, "The world has changed radically from the one we knew after
World War II. At the conclusion of World War II, the United States emerged,
alone among the major industrial countries, with its production capacity
and technological base not only intact, but strengthened. We did not have
to worry about our competitive position in the world. The main limitation on our exports was the 'dollar shortage' of our trading partners." As a
result, the United States took a leadership role and assumed responsibility
for the economic support and defense of the non-Communist world.

Now, however, there was "new mood" in the United States and a "developing crisis of confidence in the system." The report noted that this was reflected in

> mounting pressures in the United States for import restrictions as foreign-made textiles, clothing, shoes, steel, electronic products, and automobiles penetrate our market; growing demands for retaliation against foreign measures which place American agricultural and other products at a disadvantage in markets abroad; a growing concern in this country that the United States has not received full value for the tariff concessions made over the years because foreign countries have found other ways, besides tariffs, of impeding our access to their markets; labor's contention that our corporations, through their operations abroad, are 'exporting jobs' by giving away the competitive advantage the United States should derive from its superior technology and efficiency; a sense of frustration with our persistent balance-of-payments deficit and a feeling the other countries are not doing their fair share in making the international monetary system work; an increasing concern that the foreign economic policy of our government has given insufficient weight to our economic interests and too much weight to our foreign policy relations, that it is still influenced by a 'Marshall Plan psychology' appropriate to an earlier period.[62]

The Williams Commission called for a "new realism" in trade policy. The American market was generally more open to foreign goods than were the markets of other countries, because the United States supposedly had lower tariffs and maintained fewer non-tariff barriers than its trading partners. Therefore, the report argued, the United States should be more aggressive in demanding that Western Europe and Japan share the responsibility for maintaining the system of open world trade.

The Williams Commission report was released in the midst of a tumultuous year for trade policy. In that year, 1971, the United States recorded its first merchandise trade deficit since 1935. By later standards, the trade deficit was small, and import penetration was miniscule, but this was a new development, and the news triggered alarms about the country's deteriorating competitiveness. In April 1971, Treasury Secretary John Connally stated that the United States was "in bad shape" in world trade, that trade policy needed "a radical change." The country would reach "a point of decision fairly soon on how we are going to proceed in this decade and hereafter," he asserted. "The standard of living in the United States is at stake—no less than that."[63]

The appearance of a trade deficit was far from the only concern as the economy began to falter and the unemployment rate ticked up from 3.5 percent in 1969 to 5.9 percent in 1971. These developments fanned protectionist pressures, and Congress was soon awash with new proposals to limit imports. The most controversial one was the Burke-Hartke bill, named for its legislative sponsors, Rep. James Burke (D-MA) and Sen. Vance Hartke (D-IL). Introduced in late 1971, and like the Mills bill before it, the Burke-Hartke proposal would have created a huge system of government-managed trade on a product-by-product, country-by-country basis. Under the bill, the quantity of imports, by product category and by country, would not be allowed to exceed the average quantity of imports during 1965–69. This would effectively roll back the volume of imports in 1972 by one-third. By one calculation, the reduction in trade would be equivalent to increasing the average tariff on dutiable imports from 6.8 percent to 19.6 percent.[64] Once trade had been cut back to 1965–69 levels, the ratio of imports to domestic production would not have been allowed to grow, effectively freezing import penetration on a product and country basis. A new government agency would be set up to administer the quotas and grant exemptions, as well as tighten the restrictions if imports were "inhibiting" domestic production. The agency would also have the authority to restrict foreign investment and oversee antidumping and escape-clause actions.

The change in view of the principal sponsor of the legislation, James Burke of Massachusetts, reflected the broader political shift on trade. A Democrat, Burke had voted for the Trade Expansion Act of 1962, arguing that trade would create "more jobs, more business and a stronger all-around economy."[65] Less than a decade later, Burke was in an entirely different camp. This was true for many other Northern Democrats from the manufacturing belt. "Our international trade policies have collapsed, American industries are injured, and six million Americans are unemployed," Hartke complained. "Yet this administration has no policy to meet this crisis."[66]

The simultaneous appearance of higher unemployment and a trade deficit led many to attribute job losses to foreign competition. An AFL-CIO report stated that, as a result of growing imports and lagging exports, "between 1966 and 1969 US foreign trade produced the equivalent of a net loss of half a million American jobs."[67] This widely publicized job-loss figure shifted the trade debate away from foreign-policy goals and improving foreign market access to the counting of domestic jobs gained or lost as a result of trade. A Bureau of Labor Statistics official responded that "the relationships between domestic employment and import levels are complex" and that "these figures (on jobs and imports) are so hypothetical that any conclusions drawn from them can be misleading or erroneous," but the union analysis resonated with the public and members of Congress.[68] Later studies showed that job losses were much more closely tied to rising labor productivity and shifts in domestic demand than to declining exports or rising imports. For example, studying nineteen industries from 1963–71, Frank (1977) found that, of the four sectors that experienced declining employment (textiles, apparel, leather products, and fabricated metal products), the rise in net imports was a dominant factor in only one sector (leather products).

At this point, organized labor was more opposed to foreign investment by American companies than to imports. Starting in the late 1960s, companies began shifting labor-intensive assembly operations in the United States to other countries—particularly final stages of the production of apparel and consumer electronics—in order to reduce production costs. For example, in the case of televisions, electronic components would be fabricated in the United States, shipped to Mexico for assembly, and then returned to the United States for final sale. This was encouraged under sections 806.30 and 807 of the US tariff code, which allowed for the duty-free entry of US components sent abroad for further processing or assembly. This provision affected only a small amount of imports, but the offshore assembly provision was an important factor in the overseas relocation of the apparel and electronics industries.

Although it was widely recognized that the off-shoring of labor-intensive assembly operations could reduce costs enough to prevent all production in those industries from moving abroad, organized labor opposed any loss of jobs associated with the multinational relocation of production and assembly.[69] Consequently, it sought in Burke-Hartke the legislative means not just to regulate imports, but also to prevent the relocation of production abroad.[70] It was no secret that organized labor, especially the AFL-CIO, was behind the Burke-Hartke legislation.[71] As a member of the Williams Commission exclaimed, "Labor wants to dismantle the whole goddamned system of international commerce!"[72] Although the labor movement complained more about foreign investment than imports, it was easier to implement policies to reduce imports than to stop foreign investment.

The Burke-Hartke bill was a radical piece of legislation that would have restricted imports based on mandated quantities. It would have completely undermined the postwar trading system based on market competition and GATT rules on using tariffs instead of quotas. Of course, the Burke-Hartke bill had little chance of being enacted: it was never reported from committee and never came to a vote in the House; it would probably have encountered strong resistance in the Senate, and almost surely would have been vetoed by the president. Still, it was a signal of some of the trade pressures building in the political system.

THE NIXON SHOCK

One source of the country's growing trade difficulties was the increasing overvaluation of the dollar relative to other foreign currencies. The misalignment of the dollar made US products more expensive relative to foreign products at home and abroad, and reflected structural problems with the fixed exchange-rate system that originated with the Bretton Woods agreement of 1944. The Bretton Woods system formalized the dollar, ostensibly backed by gold reserves, as the world's key reserve currency. The exchange rates between foreign currencies and the dollar were fixed but adjustable with the permission of the International Monetary Fund (IMF).

As we have seen, Europe faced a shortage of dollars after World War II, but by the 1960s the dollar shortage had become a dollar glut. The growing supply of dollars meant that, by the late 1960s, foreign holdings of dollars (nearly $50 billion) far outstripped US gold reserves (about $10 billion). The United States could never meet its obligation to exchange gold for dollars if foreign central banks started demanding gold for their dollar reserves.[73]

The United States itself had limited policy options to deal with the situation. Because the dollar was the world's reserve currency and the anchor of the international monetary system, other countries could revalue or devalue their currencies against the dollar, but the United States could not unilaterally devalue the dollar against other currencies. As the US balance of payments position shifted from surplus to deficit, foreign central banks were obligated to purchase excess dollars to maintain the fixed exchange rate and prevent the dollar from depreciating, which partly explains the increase in their official holdings of dollar reserves. European countries and Japan became increasingly concerned about the inflationary impact of their growing dollar reserves. At the same time, they were reluctant to revalue their currencies against the dollar for fear of reducing the growth of their exports, but some began to consider exchanging some of their dollar reserves for American gold.

The Nixon administration viewed the refusal of other countries to revalue their currencies as a betrayal. In its view, the United States had made enormous efforts to promote the economic recovery of Western Europe and Japan after the war, and now those countries were unwilling to adjust their exchange rates and help the United States because it might jeopardize the competitive position of their export industries. This attitude only reinforced the administration's predilection to "get tough" with foreign allies. As Treasury Secretary John Connally put it, "My philosophy is that the foreigners are out to screw us. Our job is to screw them first."[74]

The United States did not have an exchange-rate problem with all countries. The British pound and French franc were both chronically weak and had been devalued against the dollar in the late 1960s; the United States continued to run trade surpluses with those countries, and their exports did not contribute significantly to protectionist pressures at home. Nor was West Germany viewed as a major problem, because its government, fearing the spillover of inflation from the United States, had revalued the Deutsche mark against the dollar in late 1969. In May 1971, Germany abandoned the fixed rate and allowed the mark to appreciate against the dollar. However, Japan firmly opposed any change in its exchange rate, which had been established at 360 yen per dollar in 1949 and had remained there ever since. The Japanese government was extremely reluctant to do anything that might impede the country's ability to export to the United States. Therefore, from the US perspective, Japan was considered the major obstacle to achieving an appropriate adjustment of the dollar.[75]

Given the protectionist pressures in Congress and the mounting imbalance between US gold reserves and the foreign accumulation of dollars, the Nixon administration began preparing for changes in the international monetary system in 1971. Connally wanted to end the "benign neglect" of the deteriorating balance of payments situation and take control of events to avoid facing a sudden run on US gold reserves by foreign central banks. Connally wanted to close the gold window—that is, suspend the ability of foreign central banks to convert their dollars into gold—at a time of his own choosing rather than being put in the embarrassing position of having to deny foreign official requests for gold. Paul Volcker, the Undersecretary of Treasury for Monetary Affairs, headed an interagency planning group to prepare for this eventuality.

The "Nixon Shock" of August 1971 focused mainly on new domestic policies, particularly the imposition of wage and price controls to reduce inflation, but also international policy due to several events that summer.[76] In May, a Treasury Department study concluded that the dollar was overvalued by 10–15 percent and that a foreign exchange crisis was inevitable.[77] In July, the Williams Commission published its report and proposed that "if our balance of payments problem persists, and if other countries find a further accumulation of dollars objectionable, the United States should indicate its readiness to adopt a temporary uniform import tax and export subsidy" to force other countries to revalue their currencies.[78] New data was also released that month showing that the United States ran an unexpectedly large trade deficit in June and was on track to have its first annual trade deficit since World War II. These data convinced Treasury officials that the existing dollar parities could not be maintained for much longer.

On Friday, August 6, a report by the Joint Economic Committee of Congress reached the "inescapable conclusion" that "the dollar is overvalued." (Ironically, the report was entitled "Action Now to Strengthen the US Dollar.") The report stated that "dollar overvaluation leads to the perpetuation of US [trade] deficits and thus increases the risk of an international monetary crisis that would break the system apart."[79] That same day, the Treasury also announced that it would sell about $200 million in gold to France and use nearly $800 million of foreign exchange to buy back dollars from Belgium and the Netherlands.

These developments contributed to strong selling pressure on the dollar on Monday, August 9. Over the course of that week, foreign central banks intervened massively to support the dollar, buying about $3.7 billion to prevent their currencies from appreciating. Meeting with the president, Connally proposed closing the gold window and imposing a 10 percent import surcharge. The purpose of the surcharge would be to compel Japan and other countries to revalue their currencies, since they were reluctant to do so voluntarily. The president liked this idea—"the import duty delights me," he said—because it was a way of striking back against other countries and extracting concessions from them.[80]

On Friday afternoon, August 13, Nixon brought a small number of economic advisers and aides to Camp David for a secret meeting to decide what to do. Although Federal Reserve chairman Arthur Burns strongly opposed closing the gold window, everyone else thought that this step was necessary. Connally argued that simply closing the gold window by itself would not necessarily get other countries (Japan) to revalue their currencies and insisted upon the 10 percent import surcharge as a way of forcing them into doing so.[81] He argued that it would be politically popular at home and should remain in effect until new exchange-rate parities were negotiated.[82] The president endorsed the idea, saying that "the border tax is not too damned aggressive, just aggressive enough."[83] When the president asked if other countries could retaliate against the surcharge, he was told that they could not retaliate under GATT rules if it was imposed for balance of payments purposes, which seemed to clinch the case.

On the evening of Sunday, August 15, President Nixon announced the new policies in a nationally televised speech. Most of the address focused on the domestic economic situation, particularly the decision to impose a ninety-day wage and price freeze and other emergency measures to control inflation. The decision to close the gold window was not described as leading to a devaluation of the dollar, but as a way of improving the competitive position of US manufacturing in the global market. The surcharge was not the main focus of the speech, but was mentioned:

> I am taking one further step to protect the dollar, to improve our balance of payments, and to increase jobs for Americans. As a temporary measure, I am today imposing an additional tax of 10 percent on goods imported into the United States. This is a better solution for international trade than direct controls on the amount of imports. This import tax is a temporary action. It isn't directed against any other country. It is an action to make certain that American products will not be at a disadvantage because of unfair exchange rates. When the unfair treatment is ended, the import tax will end as well. As a result of these actions, the product of American labor will be more competitive, and the unfair edge that some of our foreign competition has will be removed. This is a major reason why our trade balance has eroded over the past 15 years[84]

Nixon and Connally were correct in thinking that the import surcharge would be popular: 71 percent of Americans surveyed approved it, while 14 percent disapproved, and 15 percent were unsure, according to one poll.[85]

Having shocked the world with these moves, the Nixon administration insisted that other countries revalue their currencies in exchange for the removal of the surcharge. Connally's opening bid was for a 24 percent revaluation of the yen and an 18 percent revaluation of the mark. This was not a problem for Germany, which had already allowed the mark to appreciate, but Japan resisted the demand.[86] The Nixon shock unleashed massive selling of the dollar on foreign exchange markets, forcing Japan's central bank to intervene massively to prevent the yen from appreciating. On Monday and Tuesday, August 16–17, Japan bought $1.3 billion to support the dollar and keep the yen at the old rate of ¥360. The volume of trading on foreign-exchange markets eventually proved stronger than the government's willingness to buy dollars and prevent the appreciation of its currency. By the end of August, Japan's Finance Minister announced that the government would allow the yen to float, although there would be continued government intervention to slow its appreciation.[87]

Although foreign-exchange markets were forcing currencies to deviate from their official parities, foreign governments were still reluctant to agree to a formal change in exchange-rate parities. The surcharge also became an increasing source of international tension. While it had been aimed principally at Japan, the 10 percent surcharge applied to dutiable imports from all countries, including those running trade deficits with the United States. The EEC filed a complaint against the United States in the GATT, and other countries hinted that they might retaliate. By September, there was growing dissention within the Nixon administration, led by National Security adviser Henry Kissinger, about continuing the surcharge.[88] By late November, with Kissinger constantly reminding him of the foreign-policy difficulties caused by the unresolved exchange-rate issue, Nixon began to worry about the political costs of the stalemate and signaled to Connally that he should settle the matter as soon as possible.

The new exchange-rate parities were finally established at a meeting at the Smithsonian Institution in Washington in December. On the first day of the negotiations, the United States asked for 19.2 percent revaluation of the yen and 14 percent for the mark. Germany agreed to a 13.57 percent revaluation of the mark, which put pressure on Japan, because German officials insisted that the yen be revalued by at least 4 percentage points more than the mark, or at least 17.57 percent. Japan's finance minister insisted that the number had to be less than 17 percent, telling the story of the finance minister who was assassinated in 1930 when he revalued the yen by that amount after Japan went back on the gold standard. Connally settled for a 16.9 percent revaluation of the yen. (The finance minister later revealed that he had received permission from the prime minister to revalue the yen by as much as 20 percent.)[89]

President Nixon hailed the Smithsonian agreement as "the most significant monetary agreement in the history of the world."[90] The trade-weighted depreciation of the dollar against major currencies was slightly less than 8 percent, or 12 percent excluding Canada. However, the new parities merely formalized what foreign exchange markets had already established. Two days later the president signed an executive order removing the 10 percent surcharge, which had been in effect for four months. The surcharge only applied to about half of US imports, because it did not apply to duty-free imports (about one-third of total imports) or imports subject

to quantitative restrictions (about 17 percent of dutiable imports, including petroleum, sugar, meat, dairy products, other agricultural imports, and
cotton textiles that were covered by the Long-Term Arrangement on textiles). Still, the surcharge is estimated to have reduced affected imports by
6–8 percent, enough to get the attention of other countries.[91]

Despite Nixon's grandiose statement about the Smithsonian agreement, the new exchange rate parities only lasted about a year. In March
1973, more pressure from foreign exchange markets forced governments to
give up responsibility for maintaining fixed exchange rates and allow currencies to fluctuate in value, marking the formal end of the Bretton Woods
exchange-rate system. The collapse of the fixed exchange-rate regime had
important implications for trade policy. In the short run, the depreciation
of the dollar against other currencies helped reverse the trade deficit, and
the United States recorded merchandise trade surpluses in 1973 and 1975.
The depreciation of the dollar also helped ease the protectionist pressures
that had been building up in Congress, as reflected in the Mills bill of 1970
and the Burke-Hartke bill of 1971. Volcker (1978–79, 7) later stated, "The
conclusion reached by some that the United States shrugged off responsibilities for the dollar and for leadership in preserving an open world order
does seem to me a misinterpretation of the facts. . . . The devaluation itself
was the strongest argument we had to repel protectionism. The operating
premise throughout was that a necessary realignment of exchange rates
and other measures consistent with more open trade and open capital markets could accomplish the necessary balance-of-payments adjustment."[92]
Indeed, the exchange-rate adjustment helped ensure that Burke-Hartke-
type legislation was not reintroduced, and Congress even began considering new legislation to reduce trade barriers.

In the longer run, the ending of the system of fixed exchange rates
and the adoption of floating rates permitted countries to relax the controls they maintained on international capital movements. Such controls
helped ensure that exchange rates remained fixed, but now they were no
longer necessary. The dismantling of capital controls led to an enormous
rise in international capital flows and would enable countries to run large
current account imbalances in coming years. This led to large exchange-
rate movements that would have significant repercussions for trade policy,
particularly in the 1980s, as will be seen in chapter 12.

Despite the exchange-rate agreement, Japan continued to be the major
focus of trade policymakers. After more than two years of wrangling, the
long-standing textile dispute with Japan was finally resolved. The Nixon
administration ratcheted up the pressure in September 1971 with an ulti-

matum: either agree to further restraints on textile exports on US terms, or import quotas would be imposed under the emergency authority in the Trading with the Enemy Act of 1917. The threat of using that particular statute to instigate a trade action against an ally was a huge diplomatic slap and persuaded Japan to adopt export restraints on non-cotton goods, such as wool and man-made fibers.[93] Ironically, the export quotas adopted by Japan were never binding, because the country's wages were rising so rapidly due to its strong economic growth that textile production was moving to other lower-wage Asian countries.

The US restrictions on imported textiles had global ramifications. As Asian producers diverted some of their textile exports from the United States to Europe, the EEC sought to protect its own industry from increased imports. American officials welcomed the EEC's participation in the textile agreements, because it seemed to legitimize its own restrictions. In 1974, these countries created a general framework for managing trade in textiles and apparel known as the Multifiber Arrangement (MFA). The MFA constituted a multilateral system of bilateral restraints on trade in textiles and apparel involving eighteen countries and covering about three-fourths of world imports of cotton, wool, and man-made fibers. Informal agreements ("understandings") were reached with ten other exporting countries that restraints might be imposed if their exports grew too rapidly and caused problems for domestic producers. The entire arrangement depended on compromises by both exporters and importers. The importing countries were able to limit foreign exports of man-made and wool fibers (in addition to cotton), while exporters were given fairly high annual growth rates in the bilateral quotas (not less than 6 percent, as opposed to 5 percent in the original LTA with Japan). In addition, exporters benefited from some flexibility in being able to shift exports between years and product categories, so they could carry over unused quotas from the past or borrow from the future.

Thus, what had begun as a "short-term" deal in 1957 between the United States and Japan to regulate trade in cotton textiles had metastasized into an enormously complex, multilateral arrangement covering dozens of countries and many types of fabrics. Of course, the whole managed-trade arrangement was a blatant violation of GATT provisions, since the measures were discriminatory in their application and used quotas and not tariffs to intervene in trade. (Ironically, the MFA was monitored by the Textile Surveillance Body in the GATT.)

The steel industry also got its protection renewed in 1972 when Japan and the EEC agreed to a three-year extension of the VRAs through 1974.

The extension cut export volumes, specified tonnage limits on different categories of steel, and reduced the annual allowable growth rate in those exports. The continuation of limits on imported steel was not tied to any improvement in performance by the domestic industry. Critics charged that the VRAs fostered complacency by domestic producers and allowed workers to bargain for higher wages and benefits.[94]

Although the depreciation of the dollar, the reappearance of a trade surplus in 1973, and the decline in the unemployment rate helped alleviate the sour mood on Capitol Hill regarding trade, the country's sense of vulnerability was shaken with the oil price shock in late 1973. The Organization of Petroleum Exporting Countries (OPEC), formed after the United States imposed an import quota on oil in the late 1950s, imposed an oil embargo on the United States for its support of Israel in the 1973 Arab-Israeli war. The shock severely disrupted the world economy and tipped the United States back into recession. It also had a huge effect on trade: Petroleum imports more than tripled in value in 1974, accounting for a quarter of all imports. While imports doubled as a share of GDP, exports kept pace with the rising imports because of the depreciation of the dollar and rising commodity prices for agricultural exports.

THE TRADE ACT OF 1974

The exchange-rate adjustments of the early 1970s, as well as the import limits on textiles, apparel, and steel, helped ease protectionist pressures on Congress. It also gave the Nixon administration the opportunity to approach Congress, cautiously, about renewing the president's trade-negotiating authority, which had lapsed in 1967. In April 1973, Nixon requested a renewal of trade-negotiating authority for five years, with permission to reduce tariffs by up to 60 percent in reductions staged over ten years and to eliminate tariffs under 5 percent. The main justification for the new authority was the desire to address foreign subsidies and nontariff barriers that impeded exports to Europe and elsewhere, including the expansion of the EEC to include Britain, Denmark, and Ireland. Drawing on the 1971 Williams report, the administration also proposed extensive changes to the trade laws governing import remedies and adjustment assistance.

Labor unions immediately attacked the administration proposal on the grounds that a further reduction in trade barriers would damage the economy. AFL-CIO President George Meany declared that "the proposals provide no specific machinery to regulate the flood of imports and, indeed, some would increase the amount of damage to American employment and industrial production."[95] Import-sensitive industries lined up to oppose the administration's request, including textiles and apparel, chemicals, shoes, stone products, iron and steel, cutlery, hardware, and watches.

Others favored the president's request, including producers of paper, machinery, trucks and tractors, and aerospace products. These export-oriented industries complained about foreign non-tariff barriers that inhibited their sales and saw new negotiations as a way of addressing them. With world commodity prices at record highs in the early 1970s, farmers and agricultural groups also took a new interest in global markets and supported the administration's proposal. Stung by the EEC's Common Agricultural Policy, which impeded farm exports, these groups also wanted Europe's agricultural subsidies cut and its import quotas on farm goods eliminated.

There was still bipartisan support for negotiations to sweep away foreign trade barriers in other countries. Most members of Congress argued that American firms could successfully compete in world markets as long as they had a "level playing field": that is, if foreign markets were genuinely open, and unfair trade practices were eliminated. Congress was "tired of the United States being the 'least favored nation' in a world which is full of discrimination," Senator Russell B. Long (D-LA) said. "We can no longer expose our market, while the rest of the world hides behind variables levies, export subsidies, import equalization fees, border taxes, cartels, government procurement practices, dumping, import quotas, and a host of other practices which effectively bar our products."[96] Members of Congress believed that the US market was much more open to imports than those of other countries, and therefore the United States had little to lose and much to gain in seeking to open foreign markets for US exports. In fact, for the year 1966, a greater share of US imports (36 percent, mainly textiles and apparel) were impeded by non-tariff barriers than the EEC's imports (21 percent, mainly agricultural) or Japan's imports (31 percent, mainly agriculture).[97]

The bill also included a new provision called "fast track" to facilitate congressional consideration of any negotiated agreement. In the past, trade negotiations had only dealt with import tariffs, and the president could simply issue an executive order to implement the lower import duties that resulted from an agreement. In the Kennedy Round, however, negotiators came up with agreements on non-tariff barriers to trade that required Congress to approve changes in domestic law. Yet, as we have seen, Congress refused to consider any of the codes negotiated during the Kennedy Round.

With tariffs on industrial products already fairly low, new trade agreements would have to focus on non-tariff barriers to open trade further. But the EEC and other trading partners were reluctant to engage in negotiations if Congress was unlikely to approve the outcome.

To get around this problem, Congress agreed to set up a "fast-track" procedure. Under fast track, Congress agreed to vote either up or down, without any opportunity for amendment, on any trade agreement reached by the president within ninety days of submission. Since any agreement dealing with non-tariff barriers necessarily involved changes in domestic law, both the House and Senate would have to approve the legislation implementing an agreement. With the fast-track process, Congress also pledged not to alter the agreement itself or delay making a decision about whether or not it should be approved.[98] Support for fast track was bipartisan, because everyone recognized that some new congressional procedure would be required to conclude any trade agreement that went beyond simply cutting tariff rates. It also made the executive branch cooperate more closely with members of Congress before finalizing any agreement to ensure their eventual support of it.

The administration's proposal moved slowly through the House in 1973. The Ways and Means Committee rejected a proposal for mandatory import quotas in cases where the foreign-market share exceeded 15 percent, an idea that received some support from Democrats, another indication of how much the party's support for open trade had slipped. In December 1973, the House passed the bill by a vote of 272–140. While the minority Republicans voted heavily in favor by 160–19, the Democratic majority split over the bill. Northern Democrats voted 101–52 against the bill, led by those from states producing steel (Pennsylvania and Ohio) and footwear (Maine and Massachusetts). Southern Democrats voted 60–20 in favor, because the opposition of the textile and apparel industry had been neutralized by the recently concluded MFA.[99]

Senate action on the bill was delayed for most of 1974 by debate over an amendment sponsored by Charles Vanik (D-OH) and Henry Jackson (D-WA) that tied the granting of MFN status to the Soviet Union to the freedom of Soviet Jews to emigrate.[100] The Nixon administration wanted the president to have the unqualified power to grant MFN status to Communist countries, but Congress refused. In December 1974, the Senate passed the bill by an overwhelming margin, and remaining differences with the House version were quickly resolved in a conference committee.

By then, Nixon had resigned over the Watergate scandal, and Gerald Ford had become president. In a trip to Japan just three months after tak-

ing office, Ford (1979, 210–11) assured the prime minister that he "had always been a proponent of free trade and that [he] wasn't about to alter those
convictions despite obvious political pressures to which [he] would be subjected during a period of high unemployment at home." However, as he
recalled in his memoirs, Ford was unhappy with the trade bill. Although
it was "the most significant trade legislation in the past forty years," Ford
(1979, 224–25) "was concerned by its inclusion of language that could only
be viewed as objectionable and discriminatory by other nations, primarily
the Jackson-Vanik Amendment." However, he "decided reluctantly to sign
the measure into law" because he believed "a veto would have been overridden by an overwhelming majority" in Congress. In January 1975, Ford
signed the Trade Act of 1974.

The Trade Act of 1974 granted the president negotiating authority over
tariffs and non-tariff barriers, allowing the United States to participate
more actively in the Tokyo Round of GATT negotiations that had begun in
November 1973 (to be discussed shortly). The president was permitted to
reduce import duties by as much as 60 percent and eliminate those under
5 percent. The fast-track procedure was established to expedite Congress's
approval (or disapproval) of any agreement covering non-tariff barriers that
required legislative changes to domestic law. Congress also agreed to give
the president the authority to give duty-free access to selected goods from
qualified developing countries under a program called the Generalized
System of Preferences (GSP).

The Trade Act of 1974 demonstrated that Congress was interested in
opening markets to more trade and the negotiation of rules on non-tariff
barriers, not just in protecting import-competing industries. At the same
time, it made it easier for industries affected by imports to receive protection and workers to receive adjustment assistance. By this time, it was
generally recognized that the attempt in the Trade Expansion Act of 1962
to shift government support away from escape-clause protection and toward trade adjustment assistance had failed. The 1962 legislation certainly
made it more difficult for industries to receive escape-clause protection: in
the twenty-nine investigations from 1962 to 1969, the Tariff Commission
ruled affirmatively in only three cases.[101] But trade adjustment assistance
proved equally difficult to obtain: over that same period, the Tariff Commission did not accept a single petition for assistance. From 1969 to 1973,
the commission approved just four cases—earthenware, marble, pianos,
and sheet glass—covering only 3,180 workers.

The Trade Act of 1974 eased the requirements to receive escape-clause protection and adjustment assistance without attempting to substitute one for the other. Section 201 set out the new statutory requirements governing escape-clause actions. The 1962 requirement that injury must be "a result in major part of concessions granted under trade agreements" was dropped; section 201 simply required that imports be a "substantial cause of serious injury," allowing any increase in imports, even those unrelated to previous tariff concessions, to be grounds for receiving protection. This vastly increased the number of cases in which industries could seek temporary relief from imports.

The legislation also specified a strict timetable for the disposition of escape-clause cases. The Tariff Commission was renamed the International Trade Commission (ITC) and now had to make an injury determination within six months of receiving the petition. If the injury was found, then the president would have sixty days to decide whether or not to grant the relief proposed by the ITC. Congress also tried to shift the default outcome to the granting of relief by mandating that the president "shall" provide the trade relief recommended by the ITC "unless he determines that provision of such relief is not in the national economic interest of the United States." The temporary import relief could last up to five years, with the possibility of being renewed for an additional two years, and could take various forms, usually tariffs (declining each year) but also import quotas, orderly marketing arrangements, or other measures. The import duties had to be applied on a non-discriminatory basis to imports from all countries.

The Trade Act of 1974 also strengthened trade adjustment assistance. As already noted, the statutory criteria governing adjustment assistance were so strict that the Tariff Commission approved only four applications in more than a decade. The difficulty in obtaining adjustment assistance turned organized labor, which had strongly supported it in 1962, against it. The head of the AFL-CIO dismissed it as "burial insurance" and bluntly stated that "adjustment assistance cannot solve modern trade problems."[102] To address this problem, the legislation eased the certification requirements and shifted authority over the program from the Tariff Commission to the Department of Labor.

The new law also made it easier for firms to obtain relief from dumping. Previously, dumping meant a foreign producer was selling its exports at a price below the exporter's home-market price. The 1974 act made exporting at "less than average cost" another actionable form of dumping, a definition that accounted for the possibility that the home market price might be artificially depressed along with the export price. The legislation also imposed strict time limits on the administrative process, which had been known to drag on for years.

Finally, section 301 of the Trade Act of 1974 strengthened presidential authority to deal with "unjustifiable, unreasonable, and discriminatory" foreign trade practices found to burden or restrict US commerce.[103] Section 301 allowed a US exporter to petition the Special Trade Representative about objectionable foreign policies or practices that discriminated against US producers. The trade representative could then decide whether to initiate an investigation and seek a negotiated settlement to end the practice. If a solution was not forthcoming, the president was authorized to impose retaliatory duties on the exports of the offending country. Seven of the first ten section 301 actions were aimed at the EEC and focused on various discriminatory policies, such as its levy on egg imports; minimum import prices for canned fruits, juices, and vegetables; export subsidies on malt and wheat exports; a feed-mixing requirement for livestock; and preferential tariffs on oranges and grapefruit juice.

Finally, the Trade Act of 1974 made several institutional changes. Congress formally established the position of the Special Representative for Trade Negotiations, which previously existed only by executive order, and provided for greater congressional involvement in trade negotiations, in addition to creating private-sector advisory groups.[104] Thus, the Office of the US Trade Representative (USTR) became the negotiating arm of the executive branch. Congress also changed the name of the Tariff Commission to the International Trade Commission (ITC), as already noted, and made it an independent agency, not part of the executive branch. As an independent agency, the ITC had to submit its proposed budget directly to Congress, giving it greater leverage over the agency's activities.[105]

In sum, the Trade Act of 1974 was a key piece of trade legislation. After the outburst of protectionist pressures in the early 1970s, Congress sought to create a system that would shift political pressure for import relief away from legislative remedies and toward administrative ones by opening legal avenues for more escape-clause cases and antidumping actions. The bill contained an odd mixture of trade liberalization and trade protection. On the one hand, it gave the president the authority to liberalize trade further, expanding both exports and imports, and gave developing countries duty-free access to the US market through the Generalized System of Preferences (GSP). At the same time, it gave import-competing firms and workers greater access to government assistance through temporary tariffs or additional unemployment insurance.

The passage of the Trade Act of 1974 also confirmed that partisan divisions over trade policy had become blurred. The new divisions were based on changing constituency characteristics. On the whole, Democrats found it more difficult to support open trade policies because of their ties to labor unions, which feared job losses, especially in the industrial northeast and Midwest. Meanwhile, Republicans still had concerns about reducing trade barriers and ensuring that market access was reciprocal, but they were also much more willing to oppose protectionist measures that might indirectly harm exports than they had been in previous decades.

THE TOKYO ROUND

As early as 1972, the United States, the EEC, and Japan declared their intention to start a new round of multilateral trade negotiations, the seventh such round since the original 1947 GATT conference in Geneva. The Tokyo Round began in November 1973 with the hope that Congress would soon give the president negotiating authority. Although the world economy was reeling from a recession and high inflation, the Tokyo Round sought to reduce tariff levels further and restrict the use of non-tariff barriers.[106] In the negotiations, the United States, the EEC, and Japan agreed to cut tariffs by 34 percent, on average, although average tariffs were already fairly low at this point, as Table 11.2 shows. As in the Kennedy Round, tariffs were reduced by formula, such that higher duties were cut proportionately more than lower ones, rather than by the old method of bilateral bargaining over particular rates.

With tariffs having fallen to relatively low levels, the negotiation put

TABLE 11.2. Average tariff levels pre– and post–Tokyo Round, in percentages

	All industrial products		Raw materials		Semi-finished articles		Finished manufactures	
	Pre–Tokyo Round	Post–Tokyo Round	Pre–Tokyo Round	Post–Tokyo Round	Pre–Tokyo Round	Post–Tokyo Round	Pre–Tokyo Round	Post–Tokyo Round
United States	6.5	4.4	0.9	0.2	4.5	3.0	8.0	5.7
European Community	6.6	4.7	0.2	0.2	5.1	4.2	9.7	6.9
Japan	5.5	2.8	1.5	0.5	6.6	4.6	12.5	6.0
Canada	13.6	7.9	1.0	0.5	14.8	8.3	13.8	8.3

Source: Congressional Budget Office 1987, 32.

some emphasis on regulating the use of non-tariff barriers. (The lowering of tariffs was likened to the "draining a swamp" that "revealed all the snags and stumps of non-tariff barriers that still have to be cleared away."[107]) The Tokyo Round addressed non-tariff barriers through six codes covering government procurement, technical barriers to trade, subsidies and countervailing duties, customs valuation, import licensing procedures, and antidumping.[108] Given the difficulty in defining and regulating such barriers, these codes were largely procedural in content and contained few specific obligations. The codes spelled out broad and general rules, such as requiring transparency and national treatment, but the negotiating countries were not obligated to sign them, and thus participation was optional. Still, the codes represented an initial attempt to extend the disciplines of GATT rules to different regulatory impediments to trade.

The negotiations also addressed subsidies and countervailing duties. The EEC employed subsidies to a much greater extent than the United States: in 1978, the share of manufactured exports supported by official export credits was 56 percent in the United Kingdom, 34 percent in Japan, 30 percent in France, and just 11 percent in Germany and the United States.[109] A key US negotiating objective was to restrict such subsidies on the grounds that they distorted resource allocation and impaired the functioning of markets to the detriment of the United States. By contrast, the EEC only wanted such subsidies penalized if they caused injury to another country's industry. In the compromise outcome, the EEC agreed to limit domestic subsidies that affected trade, and the United States agreed to a material injury test in countervailing duty cases. In other words, subsidized exports had to be causing harm to a domestic industry for countervailing duties to be imposed; previously, the United States did not have such a requirement. The antidumping code was also adjusted to the less demanding US standard in which dumped imports had to cause material injury, and not necessarily be a "principal" cause of injury, in order to be countered by duties.

The Tokyo Round was the first in which developing countries began playing a more active role in the GATT. That role was still quite limited, because developing countries received "special and differential treatment," meaning that they did not have to reduce their own tariffs in order to receive the benefits of tariff reductions by developed countries. The poorest developing countries also benefited from various tariff preference schemes, such as the Generalized System of Preferences, which technically violated the MFN clause.

Like previous negotiations, the Tokyo Round failed to deal with agricultural trade. The EEC refused to reduce the level of subsidies or liberalize the trade barriers in the Common Agricultural Policy, despite US insistence that something be done. Negotiators also failed to reach an agreement on the question of whether safeguards could be discriminatory in their application. Article 19 of the GATT required that safeguards, such as the section 201 escape clause, be applied in a non-discriminatory way against imports from all sources. The GATT had no provision for selective and discriminatory arrangements such as voluntary export restraints and orderly marketing arrangements, which had been introduced and would proliferate over the next decade.

The Tokyo Round generated relatively little domestic controversy. One group that feared the outcome was the textile and apparel industry. In a show of political strength, the industry and its workers persuaded Congress to pass a bill in late 1978 that would prohibit trade negotiators from reducing tariffs on textile and apparel. Senator Ernest Hollings (D-SC) argued that the industry was in dire straits, explaining that "when a man is hemorrhaging, you don't cut another vein."[110] Representatives from the South backed the legislation and appealed to President Jimmy Carter, who was from Georgia, to sign the measure. The president's advisers were strongly opposed, on the grounds that it would constitute a bad precedent that would lead other industries to seek similar exemptions. It would also jeopardize the ongoing negotiations and prompt other countries to withdraw their offers of tariff reductions affecting US exports. With inflation running at high levels, they argued, the country did not need a policy that would further increase prices. Other interests groups, particularly retailers and some manufacturers, also weighed in against the bill.

In November 1978, Carter vetoed the bill on the grounds that it would "not address the real causes of the industry's difficulties." The benefits to the industry would be "transient" but "would prompt our trading partners to retaliate by withdrawing offers in areas where our need for export markets is the greatest—products such as tobacco, grains, citrus, raw cotton, paper, machinery, poultry, and textile-related areas such as mill products and fashion clothing." The president concluded that "the loss of these export areas is too high a price for our Nation to pay."[111]

The Tokyo Round concluded in April 1979. Overall, its achievements were mixed. While import tariffs in advanced countries were cut to even lower levels, developing countries were not expected to reciprocate. The codes on non-tariff barriers were vague, and their adoption was optional—and agricultural trade remained unaddressed. Two months later, the Carter administration submitted the Tokyo Round implementing legislation to Congress for approval. Congress had to move quickly because the fast-track provision in the Trade Act of 1974 required an up or down vote without amendment within sixty days. US Trade Representative Robert Strauss, a skilled Democratic operator, had made great efforts to keep Congress and interested private-sector groups informed during the negotiations. This helped ensure that major constituencies were not surprised by, and would broadly support, the outcome. As Strauss (1987, vii) later recalled, "I spent as much time negotiating with domestic constituents (both industry and labor) and members of the US Congress as I did negotiating with our foreign trading partners." For instance, Senator Russell Long (D-LA) and the Senate Finance Committee staff insisted that they participate in the drafting the implementing legislation to ensure that Congress would support it. As a result of this legislative-executive cooperation, the Trade Agreements Act of 1979 sailed through Congress, passing in the House by 395–7 and the Senate by 90–4.[112] The overwhelming margin of support reflected Strauss's exceptional political acumen and demonstrated that no domestic groups felt seriously threatened by the results of the negotiation.[113]

However, Congress made the passage of the Trade Agreements Act of 1979 contingent on further administrative changes to trade policy, in particular, an executive order by the president shifting authority over the antidumping process from Treasury Department to the Commerce Department. Congress had long complained that Treasury did not take dumping petitions seriously and was responsible for long procedural delays due to its reluctance to impose duties. For example, when Zenith filed an antidumping complaint about imports of black-and-white television sets in 1971, the Tariff Commission ruled that the industry had suffered injury, but Treasury did not act on the finding until 1978, when it rejected it.[114] Congress clearly wanted more zealous enforcement of the antidumping law, and the Commerce Department, an agency whose constituency group was American business, was more likely to welcome such petitions than Treasury.

In addition, the Office of the US Trade Representative (USTR) was formally created and given primary responsibility for formulating and coordinating trade policy in the executive branch. USTR had principal responsibility for negotiating trade agreements, but in doing so it had to reflect a balanced perspective from many government agencies, including those representing foreign-policy interests (State Department), business interests (Commerce Department), farm interests (Agricultural Department), worker interests (Labor Department), competition concerns (Justice Department), and consumers and economic efficiency interests (Council of Economic Advisers). Thus, USTR led an extensive, interagency consultative process that guided the formulation of US trade policy.

CREEPING PROTECTIONISM

America's participation in world trade deepened significantly in the 1970s. Merchandise exports and imports as a share of GDP doubled over the decade, rising from nearly 4 percent of GDP in 1970 to roughly 8 percent in 1979. While merchandise trade surpluses gave way to merchandise trade deficits after 1976, they were initially driven by large imports of petroleum after the oil shock of 1973. The United States continued to have trade surpluses on agricultural and manufactured goods, as well as services. In addition, a growing share of trade was conducted with Asia: about 40 percent of US imports in the 1980s came from that region, up from 17 percent in the 1950s. This reflected the rapid economic development of several East Asian countries, particularly Japan, Hong Kong, Taiwan, and South Korea. As a result, policymakers began shifting their attention away from Europe and toward newly industrializing countries across the Pacific.

Overall, the manufacturing sector held its own during the 1970s, but important structural changes were occurring within manufacturing which led to many painful adjustments. Exports were shifting toward newer, more advanced goods, where America's technological superiority over other countries was the greatest, such as machinery and aerospace, where skilled workers earned relatively high wages. Meanwhile, the United States began importing more labor-intensive manufactured goods, such as textiles and apparel, as more and more East Asian countries industrialized. In standardized, capital-intensive goods, such as basic steel products and even automobiles, foreign production capacity had increased significantly, which led to greater competition at home and abroad. Thus, while advanced industries in high technology and machinery performed well, older industries experienced protracted difficulties. This process of adjustment entailed the reallocation of labor and capital away from older, established industries (textiles, apparel, footwear, and steel) and toward newer industries (electrical machinery, aerospace, semiconductors, computers, and telecommunications equipment).

Despite the growing trade surplus in manufactured goods during the 1970s, the industries suffering from import competition inevitably attracted most of the attention. The restructuring process gave rise to the perception that manufacturing as a whole was suffering. Although manufacturing production rose 36 percent during the 1970s, the story was different with respect to employment. Manufacturing employment rose by almost four million in the 1960s, but manufacturing ceased to be a source of net job creation over the 1970s. Instead, the number of workers in manufacturing fluctuated around nineteen and twenty million over that decade, although this leveling off masked significant declines in some labor-intensive industries and increases in other industries. In the industries where employment fell, most studies indicated that the major factors were changes in demand and productivity growth, not imports.[115]

As we have seen, Congress recognized that legislating industry assistance on a case-by-case basis was time-consuming and controversial. Therefore, it modified the laws governing trade remedies in the Trade Act of 1974 to allow firms and workers harmed by imports to obtain temporary relief more easily in the form of higher tariffs. Although these provisions had been in place for decades, the rising foreign penetration of the domestic market helped unleash a spurt of new import-relief cases in the late 1970s. The main legal avenues by which firms could petition the government for higher duties on imports were the escape clause, antidumping duties, and countervailing duties. The escape clause was supposed to be the principal avenue by which industries harmed by imports could receive temporary protection from imports. Under section 201 of the Trade Act of 1974, if the ITC found that imports were "a substantial cause of serious injury," it could recommend imposing a higher tariff (declining over five years) on imports from all sources. The president had complete discretion about whether to grant import relief or not.

In fact, the escape clause failed to provide much help for petitioning industries. From 1975 to 1980, forty-four section 201 cases were filed, but only nine resulted in tariffs being imposed. In seventeen of the forty-four cases, the ITC ruled that the petition did not meet the statutory requirements for import relief. In the other twenty-seven cases, the ITC ruled that imports were a cause of injury and recommended higher tariffs in twenty-four cases and adjustment assistance in three others.[116] In most cases, however, Presidents Ford and Carter denied relief on the grounds that it would be contrary to the national economic interest, because trade barriers would put a significant burden on consumers, add to inflationary pressures, damage relations with foreign countries, and bring a windfall to the prosperous firms in the industry while offering little help to those most harmed by imports.[117]

The escape clause had another problem: the higher duties had to be applied to imports from all sources and not selectively on the imports causing the problem for the domestic industry. Thus, all foreign export-ers would be subject to the trade restrictions, even if just one country was responsible for a sharp increase in imports. This was one reason why presi-dents were reluctant to grant relief: they did not want to inflict needless harm on Canada and Western Europe if imports from Japan and South Ko-rea were the main source of competition for domestic producers. Thus, presidents faced a difficult choice. If the president granted escape-clause relief, it might satisfy the domestic industry, but it would anger foreign countries whose exports were not a source of the problem. If the president denied import relief, the domestic industry would be upset and might turn to Congress for a remedy.

The compromise outcome that satisfied almost everyone was a negoti-ated settlement involving a voluntary export restraint (VER) or an orderly marketing arrangement (OMA), in which only the country (or countries) whose exports were harming domestic producers would agree to limit its sales in the United States. To the extent that those exports were re-stricted, the domestic industry would be satisfied. The foreign exporters were relieved that they were not being hit by higher tariffs, as would hap-pen if escape-clause or antidumping measures were imposed. Even better for them, exporters who restricted their sales often found that the higher price they were able to charge in the United States would more than com-pensate for the lower quantity sold, possibly increasing their profits. The higher revenue earned by the constrained exporters was called a "quota rent." Some foreign firms even approached American officials and asked that a VER or OMA be arranged, even if no US industry had complained about imports, because they were seeking such rents for themselves.

The exporters in countries that were not part of the VER or OMA were also happy with these arrangements, because they were free to increase their exports and fill the gap left by the constrained exporters. This often left the import relief so porous that the domestic industry found it of little value. For example, in an escape-clause case involving non-rubber foot-wear, President Carter decided to negotiate OMAs with Taiwan and South Korea rather than impose higher tariffs, as recommended by the ITC. The OMAs were in effect from 1977 to 1981 and only limited the exports of these two countries. As a result, the decline in exports from Taiwan and Korea was quickly offset by a rise in exports from Hong Kong and the Phil-ippines. The Carter administration then came under pressure to extend the import restrictions to cover these new suppliers. The administration responded in 1978 by requiring certificates of origin from Hong Kong's footwear exports, since many suspected that Taiwan and Korea were simply reshipping their goods via Hong Kong to avoid the export restraint. In addition, Taiwanese and Korean firms started changing the types of goods they sold to avoid the OMA restrictions. South Korean producers reduced the leather content of their athletic shoes, adding more rubber and fabric so that they were not "non-rubber footwear" as defined under the agreement and therefore did not fall under the export limits.[118] In the end, the OMAs failed to slow imports of footwear and hence did not prevent the continued decline of the domestic shoe industry.

An OMA covering imports of color televisions also failed to help the domestic industry. After imports surged from 1.1 million sets in 1975 to 2.9 million in 1976, a group of labor unions and smaller firms filed a section 201 petition. The ITC ruled that imports were a substantial cause of serious injury and proposed imposing tariffs starting at 25 percent and declining to 10 percent over five years. Instead, President Carter negotiated a three-year OMA with Japan to reduce the number of imported television sets to 1.56 million. While television imports from Japan fell, imports from South Korea increased by a factor of nine (from 97,000 units to 437,000 units), and imports from Taiwan doubled (322,000 units to 624,000 units) in a single year. Despite the OMA, the number of imported color television sets was about the same in 1978 as it had been in 1977.[119]

The administration then forced Korea and Taiwan into the OMA in 1979, capping their exports at 526,000 units each. In response, the product mix changed: imports of assembled televisions fell off, but imports of unassembled televisions rose from virtually zero in 1976 to nearly 3 million by 1980. These examples illustrated the limits of trade remedies as a way of helping domestic industries overcome foreign competition. The globalization of manufacturing production meant that country-specific trade restraints were easily evaded, because foreign supplies could come now from any number of countries. Because the OMAs were so easily circumvented, they were largely ineffective in helping domestic producers maintain their share of the market.

Politically influential industries, such as textiles and apparel and steel, also received special trade protection, sometimes supplemented with antidumping and countervailing duties. The textile and apparel industry continued to be protected by the Multifiber Arrangement (MFA), which had become institutionalized as part of US trade policy. In December 1977, during the Tokyo Round negotiations, twenty-one countries finalized a second Multifiber Arrangement (MFA-II) that updated restrictions on exports from developing countries of cotton, wool, and man-made fiber clothing products. This time the EEC, rather than the United States, was behind the effort to tighten the MFA quotas by reducing the annual growth rates, constraining the ability of exporters to shift supplies across years and product categories, and allowing "reasonable departures" from the quotas (meaning tighter limits) if import surges caused injury to domestic producers. This patchwork of export-restraint agreements remained in force from 1978 until 1981, when it was updated once again.[120]

The second round of VRAs on steel expired in 1974, a time when the world steel market was booming. But steel producers in Europe and Japan added production capacity during this period, which led to significant overcapacity once world demand began to weaken. Even worse, from the standpoint of domestic steel producers, European governments often subsidized their firms to prevent plant closings and minimize unemployment, thereby prolonging the adjustment process by keeping capacity operational that otherwise would have been shut down.[121] To some degree, the US industry was a victim of the subsidized excess capacity abroad that kept world production higher and world prices lower than would otherwise have been the case. At the same time, the domestic steel industry failed to improve productivity enough to make its products competitive in the market and suffered from high costs that arose from the substantial wage premium paid to unionized workers.

When steel demand softened in 1977, domestic producers resumed their efforts to get new import restrictions. The Carter administration sought to reach OMAs with foreign suppliers: Japan agreed to such an arrangement, while the EEC did not. Consequently, the steel industry filed numerous antidumping petitions against European producers. Concerned that the antidumping duties might create insurmountable barriers to imports, the Carter administration proposed a "trigger-price mechanism" (TPM): the government would monitor prices and accelerate an antidumping investigation if imports arrived at prices below the specified triggers. The "fair value" reference prices for imports were based on estimated Japanese production costs, profit margins, and other expenses. The TPM increased the likelihood of duties being imposed, and the price floors applied to all imports, so that there could be no supply diversion. Once accepted by the US and European steel industries, the trigger-price mechanism was put in place in January 1978.

Almost immediately the domestic industry complained that the trigger prices were set too low. Because the trigger prices were based on Japanese costs, higher-cost European producers were still permitted to "dump" steel and increase their share of the market. In March 1980, US Steel filed antidumping and countervailing duty petitions against European producers, prompting the Carter administration to suspend the price floors. The trigger-price mechanism was reinstated several months later at a 12 percent higher price level in exchange for a withdrawal of the petitions.[122]

All of these trade actions were relatively mild, however, compared to what was to come over the next few years. The 1970s was a decade of transition. The United States no longer dominated world manufacturing, and many industries now faced competition from imports. In addition, the emergence of large capital flows between countries, something that had not been a feature of the Bretton Woods system, meant that trade flows were now much more likely to be affected by exchange-rate movements. A confluence of factors meant that even stronger political pressures to restrict imports would emerge in the 1980s.

CHAPTER TWELVE

Trade Shocks and Response, 1979–1992

The 1980s were one of the most difficult periods in the history of US trade policy. The combination of two powerful macroeconomic forces—a severe recession from 1979 to 1982 and the significant appreciation of the dollar against other currencies from 1980 to 1985—squeezed domestic producers of traded goods, particularly in manufacturing. The United States also began running large trade deficits, which became a symbol of the country's troubles with trade. The intensification of foreign competition meant that the political pressures for import restrictions increased dramatically.[1] The Reagan administration responded by limiting imports in many sectors, but also resisted congressional pressure to do more, particularly with respect to Japan. The economic recovery starting in 1983 and the fall in the value of the dollar starting in 1985 eventually helped relieve the pressure on producers of traded goods and enabled the import restraints to be removed by the early 1990s. This period also saw the continued reversal of the historic partisan divisions over trade policy, as many Democratic constituencies were now hurt by imports, while Republicans constituencies stood to benefit from open trade.

DOUBLE TROUBLE: DEEP RECESSION AND STRONG DOLLAR

The macroeconomic forces driving trade policy originated with a shift in monetary policy designed to stop inflation. In 1979, with consumer prices rising at about 12 percent a year, Federal Reserve Board chairman Paul Volcker started tightening monetary policy. This policy succeeded in reducing inflation, but also drove up real interest rates and produced the most severe recession since the Great Depression. The manufacturing sector was particularly hard hit: employment dropped 12 percent from 1979 to 1983, with massive layoffs in large, trade-sensitive industries such as automobiles and steel. The full force of the Federal Reserve's policy was felt in 1982, when industrial production fell more than 7 percent, and the unemployment rate peaked at almost 11 percent by year's end.[2]

The new administration of President Ronald Reagan also pursued an expansionary fiscal policy, cutting tax rates and ramping up defense spending. The combination of a tight monetary policy and a loose fiscal policy led to a growing fiscal deficit, high real interest rates, and a steady appreciation of the dollar on foreign-exchange markets. Between 1980 and 1985, the dollar rose about 40 percent against other currencies on a real, trade-weighted basis. The dollar's appreciation dealt a crushing blow to the competitive position of domestic producers of traded goods. The strong dollar undermined exports by making American goods more expensive to foreign consumers and gave imports a significant edge in the domestic market by making foreign goods less expensive to consumers. Consequently, the merchandise trade deficit grew to reach nearly 3.5 percent of GDP in 1987. Only after the dollar began to depreciate in 1985 did the trade deficit eventually begin to subside.

Why did such large trade deficits, which were completely outside the range of previous historical experience, suddenly appear at this time? A fundamental change in the international financial system, discussed in chapter 11, now made large, sustained trade imbalances possible. In previous decades, trade imbalances had been small because the Bretton Woods system of fixed exchange rates involved government restrictions on the international movement of capital. When countries could only buy and sell goods with each other, exports and imports had to be roughly balanced. When the fixed exchange-rate system finally collapsed in 1973, and countries adopted floating exchange rates, these capital controls were no longer necessary. As governments began to permit greater international capital movements, investors in different countries were able to buy one another's assets as well. Consequently, financial flows between countries increased enormously.[3] The increase in capital movements between countries allowed large trade imbalances to emerge. In the US case, other countries wanted to use the dollars they earned exporting to the United States to buy US assets rather than American-made goods. As a result, the dollar appreciated in value and exports began to fall short of imports as foreign investment in the United States surged.

Changes in Japan's policy were particularly important. Japan had long been a country with a high savings rate and low interest rates. In December

1980, Japan liberalized capital outflows and allowed Japanese investors to purchase assets in the United States, a country with a low savings rate and relatively high interest rates. As a result, Japanese financial institutions began selling yen to buy dollars, so that they could purchase higher-yield, dollar-denominated assets.[4] This drove up the value of the dollar in terms of yen on foreign-exchange markets. The appreciation of the dollar (or, conversely, the depreciation of the yen) made Japanese goods more price-competitive and American goods less price-competitive in world markets.

Both the severe recession and the strong dollar put export-dependent and import-competing sectors of the economy under enormous pressure. In the early 1980s, as figure 12.1 shows, exports fell sharply as a share of GDP, while imports were roughly unchanged. Yet this figure is misleading in suggesting that imports were not of growing importance in the domestic market. The value of imports relative to GDP did not increase much in part because the price of imports was lower due to the strong dollar, even as the volume of imports rose significantly. Over the period 1982–85, the volume of imports of semi-finished and finished manufactured goods grew 50 percent and 72 percent, respectively. Meanwhile, the volume of exports of semi-finished and finished manufactures grew only 9 percent and 1 percent, respectively.[5]

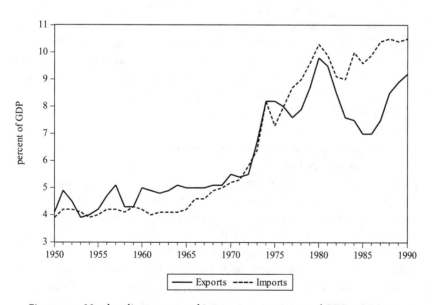

Figure 12.1. Merchandise exports and imports as a percentage of GDP, 1950–1990.
(US Department of Commerce, Bureau of Economic Analysis, www.bea.gov/.)

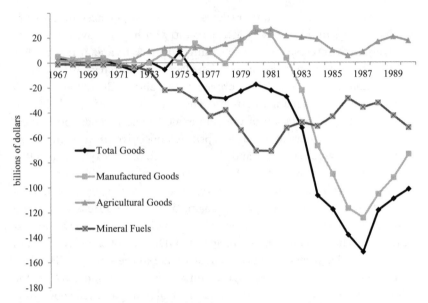

Figure 12.2. US balance of trade, by category, 1967–1990. (US Department
of Commerce, *Highlights of U.S. Trade*, various issues.)

The strength of the dollar against other currencies also contributed
to a significant change in the structure of the trade balance. During the
1970s, the overall trade deficit was driven by net imports of mineral fuels
(petroleum) that slightly exceeded net exports of manufactured and agricultural goods. During the 1980s, as figure 12.2 shows, the trade surplus
in agricultural goods continued, and the deficit in mineral fuels stabilized,
but the trade balance in manufactured goods fell sharply into deficit.
Starting in 1983, the United States became a large net importer of manufactured goods.

These developments led to an ongoing debate about the health of the
manufacturing sector. Much of the concern focused on jobs. After rising
by nearly 4 million during the 1960s, manufacturing employment oscil-
lated between 18.5 and 21.0 million workers during the 1970s and 1980s.
Large declines in manufacturing employment were seen in 1968–70, 1973–
74, and 1979–82. In the first two periods, the declines were almost entirely
cyclical, coinciding with recessions and largely unrelated to trade. But in
1981–82, when manufacturing employment fell 12 percent, a loss of nearly
3 million jobs, about a third of the employment decline was due to trade—
the fall in manufactured exports and rise in imports—and the other two-
thirds were due to the recession.[6]

Over the longer period from 1979–94, however, trade actually contributed to higher employment in manufacturing. Although manufacturing employment fell 13 percent during this period, Kletzer (2002) calculates that if exports and imports had been frozen at their 1979 level, manufacturing employment would have declined 16 percent. The reason is that both exports and imports of manufactured goods grew during this period, but exports are more tightly linked to job creation than imports are linked to job destruction. In particular, not all imports of manufactured goods are direct substitutes for domestic production: imports may be so different from domestically produced goods that they do not really compete with one another.[7]

Aside from these cyclical fluctuations, the economy was also undergoing long-term structural changes that resulted in significant employment shifts between industries. While some manufacturing industries were expanding employment, others were experiencing large, permanent declines in employment. Between 1977 and 1987, the number of production workers in the primary metals industry (blast furnaces and basic steel products) fell by 390,000, and employment in textiles and apparel fell by nearly 600,000. For these sectors, production cutbacks and plant closures led to mass layoffs of blue-collar workers. The term "deindustrialization" came into use, and images of shuttered factories across the Rust Belt, as the industrial Midwest came to be known, became etched in popular memory. On the other hand, employment in the transportation and electronics industries rose 350,000 over this period, and increased by 430,000 in printing and publishing.[8]

Despite the difficulties for workers, overall manufacturing output continued to grow through most of this period. Even during the severe recession of 1979–82 when manufacturing employment fell 12 percent, manufacturing production fell just 4 percent. Conversely, in the 1983–89 expansion, manufacturing production grew 36 percent, but employment rose only 4 percent. Production and employment were no longer coupled with one another: productivity improvements enabled output to grow without new workers being hired. This was due to changes in the composition of manufacturing output (the expansion of technology and capital-intensive industries, and the relative decline of labor-intensive industries), as well as the general improvement in labor productivity due to new technology and equipment.

Manufacturing also declined as a share of the economy during this period: between 1970 and 1990, manufacturing's share of GDP fell from 24 percent to 18 percent. In view of the growing trade deficit, foreign competition was often blamed for the 6 percentage-point decline. But manufacturing's share still would have fallen five percentage points over that period even if trade in manufactured goods had been balanced, as Krugman and Lawrence (1994) note. In other words, the overwhelming proportion of the declining share of manufacturing in the economy was due to non-trade factors, such as the shift in consumer demand from goods to services and the decline in the relative price of manufactured goods owing to rapid productivity growth. (Furthermore, manufacturing's share of economic output was stable in real terms, suggesting that much of its declining share of nominal GDP was due to the falling relative price of manufactured goods due to productivity growth.)

However, the experiences of the 1970s and 1980s were different. In the 1970s, the United States had a growing trade surplus in manufactured goods. Trade expanded manufacturing's share of the economy because exports of skill-intensive goods (aircraft and machinery) more than offset imports of labor-intensive goods (apparel and footwear). The story was different in the 1980s. During that decade, manufacturing's contribution to GDP fell 3.1 percentage points, almost the same magnitude as in the 1970s, but manufacturing's share would have fallen just 1.7 percentage points if trade had been balanced. Thus, more than half of the decline in manufacturing's share of GDP in the 1980s can be attributed to the trade deficit.

The real issue confronting the manufacturing sector was an intensification of competition, driven as much by developments in technology as by foreign competition, which forced restructuring in almost every industry. Domestic firms responded to greater competition by trying to become more efficient, closing inefficient production facilities, and finding ways of maintaining production with fewer workers in order to reduce costs. Competition forced all domestic firms to reduce production costs, upgrade the quality of their products, or move into new lines of business in order to survive. Firms struggled to reduce costs and increase efficiency by adopting new technology, trimming the workforce, and reorganizing production. Of course, different industries adjusted in different ways. The automobile industry was driven to improve product quality and produce smaller, more fuel-efficient cars. The steel industry began to rationalize production by shutting down excess capacity. Labor-intensive industries modernized by substituting capital (machinery) for labor. In industries where capital or technology could not be substituted for labor, such as the assembly of consumer electronics or the manufacture of shoes, domestic production was likely to be sent abroad to take advantage of cheaper labor.

Consequently, the labor-intensive assembly stage of production in many industries moved to other countries.

This restructuring across industries occurred regardless of its exposure to international competition: trade was only slightly related to cross-industry variation in worker displacement rates. Although industries with high displacement rates were often import-sensitive, not all import-sensitive industries had high displacement rates.[9] Restructuring was usually achieved by reducing the number of workers employed rather than by cutting the wages of existing workers.[10] Regardless of whether they lost their jobs because of changes in imports, improvements in technology, shifts in consumer demand, the displacement of workers from their jobs was a hard blow for those affected. The earnings of displaced workers often fell significantly when they lost their jobs. In particular, older, unionized workers received a substantial wage premium above the average worker in manufacturing and earned substantially less if employed elsewhere in the economy.[11] On the other hand, workers in the labor-intensive sectors that were most vulnerable to competition from imports—such as footwear, leather products, and textiles and apparel—tended to be women and minorities with few skills. If displaced from their jobs, these workers often found employment at comparable wages elsewhere in the economy, because they were already among the lowest paid workers in the labor force.[12]

While unemployment rose sharply in the 1979–82 recession, the unemployment rate fell back down to 5 percent by the end of the decade. While trade did not affect total employment, it did affect the composition of employment across different sectors of the economy. Imports destroyed jobs in low-wage manufacturing industries (apparel, footwear, leather) and in some high-wage unionized sectors (autos and steel), while exports created jobs in high-wage industries (aerospace, machinery, pharmaceuticals). Unfortunately, the strong dollar prevented exports from keeping pace with imports in the early and mid-1980s, and both exporters and import-competing industries were squeezed. This pressure shifted employment out of the production of tradable goods and into the production of non-tradables, such as services.

Even in the absence of this pressure, the United States was increasingly becoming a service economy. As incomes rose, American consumers demanded more services, ranging from health care, education, and finance to recreation and leisure. Because labor-productivity growth in services was slower than in other sectors of the economy, the share of the labor force devoted to the production of services also had to increase to accommodate this demand. Just as workers in previous generations had transitioned from agriculture to manufacturing, the growing share of the labor force employed in services—which rose from 67 percent in 1970 to 77 percent in 1990—was part of a long-run trend. While the total number of workers in manufacturing was about the same in 1970 and 1990, their share in total employment fell from 27 percent to 17 percent. This development had little to do with trade: productivity improvements in manufacturing, due to the substitution of capital for labor in production and the advance of new technology, were far more important in explaining the declining share of employment in manufacturing than increased imports. Even if trade had been balanced, manufacturing's employment share would have been only one percentage point higher than it was—18 percent instead of 17 percent—given the rapid growth in labor productivity in manufacturing.[13]

The confluence of these many different factors in the early 1980s led to concerns about the "competitiveness" of US manufacturing and fears about the "deindustrialization" of America. To be sure, some industries had fallen behind their foreign competitors in productive efficiency and product quality, and competition was forcing domestic firms to improve both or go out of business. However, the main problem facing manufacturers was not some deep-rooted structural issue, but an exchange rate that posed an enormous obstacle to its ability to compete in domestic and foreign markets. The 40 percent real appreciation of the dollar against other currencies over 1979–85 made it extremely difficult for both export-oriented and import-competing producers to remain price-competitive against foreign producers. The dollar's appreciation reduced manufacturing employment in trade-impacted industries about 4–8 percent, on average.[14] That domestic producers did not suffer from a structural "competitiveness" problem was demonstrated by the resurgence in manufactured exports and the pickup in factory employment once the dollar started depreciating in 1985.

In sum, increased imports were just one of many challenges facing the manufacturing sector in the early 1980s. Unlike a sharp decline in domestic demand, increases in productivity growth, intensified competition and technological change, and shifts in consumer demand, all of which significantly affected employment in manufacturing but were beyond the immediate reach of policymakers, restricting imports was an action that policymakers could take in order to help import-competing industries. Consequently, there was a sharp increase in protectionist pressures.

EMERGENCE OF PROTECTIONISM

The nation's struggling economy was a key issue in the 1980 presidential election. While trade was not yet a major concern, the Republican nominee, Ronald Reagan, held out the prospect of import relief to drum up political support, particularly in the South. Reagan pledged to protect the textiles and apparel industry from further market disruption.[15] Regarding automobiles, Reagan initially disavowed import quotas, saying that the industry's problems stemmed from excessive regulation rather than Japanese imports, but campaign advisers floated the idea that Japan might "voluntarily" restrain its exports. While Reagan did not make an explicit pledge to reduce steel imports, he promised tax and regulatory relief for the industry and criticized the Carter administration's decision to suspend the trigger-price mechanism, saying that trade had to be "fair."

Reagan won the 1980 election on a platform of reducing government's role in the economy. In their public pronouncements, the president and his administration appeared strongly committed to free trade.[16] The administration's July 1981 Statement on Trade Policy declared that free trade, a term that previous administrations had never explicitly endorsed, was critical to ensuring a strong economy. It vowed to "strongly resist protectionism," yet warned that "the United States is increasingly challenged not only by the ability of other countries to produce highly competitive products, but also by the growing intervention in economic affairs on the part of governments in many such countries. We should be prepared to accept the competitive challenge, and strongly oppose trade-distorting interventions by government."[17]

In fact, the Reagan administration was sharply divided over trade policy. Officials in some agencies (the Treasury and State Departments, the Office of Management and Budget, the Council of Economic Advisers) wanted to uphold free-market principles and reduce government intervention in the economy. Elsewhere, officials in the Commerce and Labor Departments representing the business community and labor wanted the government to help firms and workers struggling with foreign competition. Reagan himself was often conflicted between his strong belief in free enterprise and limited government and his desire to help out American industries and their workers.[18]

As a result, despite its free-trade rhetoric but in light of the tremendous shocks affecting traded-goods industries, the Reagan administration often accommodated domestic industries seeking relief from foreign competition.[19] At critical junctures, the administration either made a political calculation about the electoral benefits of protecting large industries from imports, or restricted imports to forestall congressional legislation. Consequently, the share of imports covered by some form of trade restriction, after rising from 8 percent in 1975 to 12 percent in 1980, jumped to 21 percent in 1984.[20] "For the first time since World War II, the United States added more trade restraints than it removed," noted William Niskanen (1988, 137), a former economic adviser in the administration. He described policy in this period as "a strategic retreat," in that the outcome, while not desirable in itself, was better than the most likely alternative, which was believed to be import quotas imposed by Congress. The administration's strategy, he said, was "to build a five-foot trade wall in order to deter a ten-foot wall [that would have been] established by Congress." This pattern can be seen by looking at trade policy with respect to automobiles, steel, textiles and apparel, and other goods.[21]

Automobiles

The automobile industry was the last major manufacturing industry to be affected by the intensification of foreign competition that began for most industries in the late 1960s. It was also the first to receive protection from the Reagan administration. The automobile industry was structurally similar to the steel industry: a few firms dominated the market (the Big Three: General Motors, Ford, and Chrysler), production was regionally concentrated (in the industrial Midwest), and a powerful union represented labor (the United Auto Workers). As in other industries, imports were not a major concern in the decades after World War II. In the 1960s, the foreign share of the domestic market was stable and less than 7 percent, mostly imports from Germany. As late as 1968, Japan's market share was only about 1 percent. The Big Three ceded the low-margin, small-car segment of the market to foreign producers and concentrated their product line on the more profitable mid-size and large-car segment of the market.

This strategy was upended when the oil price shock of 1973 shifted consumer demand to smaller, less expensive, more fuel-efficient cars. Caught without a deep product line in this category of vehicles, the Big Three saw the foreign share of the domestic auto market nearly double between 1975 and 1980, as figure 12.3 shows, particularly from Japan.

As Japan's share of the market grew, the views of labor and management began to change. Unlike other unions, the United Auto Workers (UAW) had opposed the Burke-Hartke bill of 1971, but soon it was demanding that

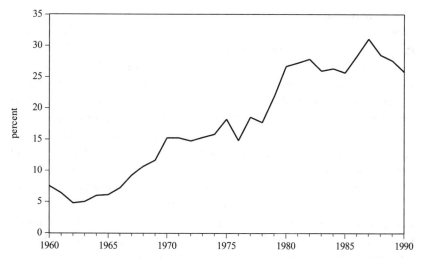

Figure 12.3. Foreign automobiles as a share of US car registrations, 1960–1990.
(*Ward's Automotive Yearbook* [Detroit: Ward's Reports], various issues.)

import quotas be imposed and that Japanese firms begin building cars in the United States. At this point, GM, Ford, and Chrysler did not want to restrict imports because they themselves had begun importing foreign-produced cars under their own nameplate. In 1975, the UAW charged twenty-eight foreign auto manufacturers in eight countries with dumping, but domestic producers did not support the petition because 40 percent of imported cars came from their subsidiaries, especially in Canada. The Treasury Department dropped the antidumping investigation after receiving assurances of corrective action from foreign manufacturers.[22]

A second oil price shock in 1979 combined with the severe recession of the early 1980s inflicted far more damage on domestic producers. The Big Three suffered enormous financial losses and cut back production, throwing about three hundred thousand auto workers out of work, while a greater number of workers in supplying industries lost their jobs as well. Chrysler was on the verge of bankruptcy until it received government-backed loan guarantees.

In the summer of 1980, Ford and the UAW filed a section 201 escape-clause petition for import relief. General Motors and Chrysler did not support the petition: GM imported small cars from Japan under its nameplate, while Chrysler did not want to alienate the Carter administration, which had given it financial assistance and was on record as opposing import restrictions. In November 1980, just days before the presidential election, the International Trade Commission (ITC) voted unanimously that the automobile industry had suffered serious injury as a result of imports, but in a 3–2 vote ruled that imports were not a "substantial cause" of serious injury and therefore the industry was not entitled to relief. This finding appeared to hinge on a technicality: under the Trade Act of 1974, a substantial cause is "a cause which is important, and not less important than any other cause," meaning that imports had to be the most important cause of injury for relief to be granted. But the ITC determined that the growing demand for compact cars and the declining demand for large cars was a greater source of injury than foreign competition and, on this basis, the petition was rejected. Following that decision, both presidential candidates promised some form of aid for the automobile industry. The House also passed a resolution authorizing the president to negotiate limits on Japanese exports, and Senator John Danforth (R-MO) introduced a bill restricting the number of cars imported from Japan to 1.6 million per year.

In March 1981, shortly after President Reagan took office, Transportation Secretary Drew Lewis urged the president to "keep faith with our campaign pledge" and restrict auto imports from Japan. Budget director David Stockman (1986, 154) was appalled: "This preposterous idea was so philosophically inimical to what I thought we stood for that for a few moments I just sat back, concussed . . . here was a cabinet officer talking protectionism in the White House, not two months into the administration." Reagan's advisers were divided: Lewis, Commerce Secretary Malcolm Baldrige, and Trade Representative William Brock favored restricting automobile imports, while Stockman, Treasury Secretary Don Regan, and Council of Economic Advisers Chair Murray Weidenbaum were opposed. The split between the business advocates and the free-market proponents reflected a tension that was present throughout the Reagan administration.

The president was undecided but clearly sympathetic to the auto producers, noting that government regulation was part of the industry's problem. He refused to threaten a veto of the Danforth bill, a clear signal to Japan that something was going to be done to limit imports if it did not restrain its exports. When presented with various options, Reagan favored the idea of asking Japan to "voluntarily" limit its exports of automobiles, and so this approach was taken.[23] Stockman (1986, 158) remarked bitterly: "And so the essence of the Reagan administration's trade policy became clear: Espouse free trade, but find an excuse on every occasion to embrace the opposite. As time passed, we would find occasions aplenty." After being pressured by the administration, Japan soon announced that it would limit its auto exports to the United States to 1.68 million cars per year, a reduction of nearly 8 percent from the quantity exported in 1980. The voluntary export restraint would be in effect for three years, from April 1981 to March 1984, although the export limit could increase over this time.

The voluntary export restraint (VER) was not a new trade-policy instrument, particularly for Japan. More than any other country, Japan seemed to increase its exports in narrow product categories rapidly, causing problems for producers in importing countries. When cotton textile producers complained about excessive imports from Japan in the 1930s, Japanese producers decided to limit their own exports rather than face import restrictions imposed by the United States. In the 1950s, Japan adopted a number of VERs on products ranging from tuna to cotton textiles and stainless steel flatware.[24] As noted in chapter 11, exporting countries generally favored VERs rather than having to face a tariff or quota imposed by the importing country. With a VER, exporters would profit from a quota-rent, the extra revenue that they received from charging a higher price in the protected market for their limited exports.

The auto VER was probably not binding on Japan's exports in 1981 and 1982, when the severe recession depressed the demand for automobiles. As a result, the export restraint initially failed to provide much help for domestic producers. The UAW continued to demand that Japanese firms build production facilities in the United States to create more jobs at home. Congress also began considering domestic content legislation that would require all cars sold to contain a certain proportion (up to 90 percent) of US-made parts and labor or else face import quotas. In December 1982 and again in December 1983, the House passed a domestic-content bill with Democratic votes and Republican opposition, although in each case the Senate failed to take it up. While it was widely recognized that the president would veto the domestic-content bill, the House votes sent a signal to Japan about the domestic political problems caused by its exports.

The 1984 election played a role in Reagan's decision to ask Japan to renew the VER, because he did not wish to alienate large numbers of voters in the industrial Midwest by lifting the restriction. As the economy recovered and automobiles sales rebounded, the VER became a binding constraint on Japanese auto sales in 1984 and 1985, though set at the higher level of 1.85 million vehicles. The economic effects of the VER are considered later in the chapter, but the export restraint and the opening of Japanese production facilities in the United States stabilized the import share of the market by the end of the decade.

STEEL

The steel industry was also hit hard by the recession in the early 1980s. The large, integrated producers, including US Steel and Bethlehem, suffered enormous financial losses that forced them to reduce output and lay off hundreds of thousands of workers. Although steel imports declined with the collapse in demand, domestic production fell more rapidly. As figure 11.3 showed, the share of imports in domestic consumption rose from 15 percent in 1979 to nearly 22 percent in 1982.[25]

In January 1982, major steel firms filed 155 antidumping and countervailing duty petitions against forty-one different suppliers of nine different products from eleven countries, but aimed primarily at the EEC.[26] The ITC ruled affirmatively in about half of these cases, but the prospect of long-lasting and severe tariff penalties on European producers, as well as highly varied antidumping duties being imposed across a range of countries and producers, was unattractive to all parties. To persuade the firms to withdraw their petitions, the Reagan administration brokered a new voluntary restraint agreement (VRA) that limited EEC exports to 5.5 percent of the US market in eleven product categories. European producers preferred the quantitative restrictions, because those would allow them to avoid steep antidumping or import tariffs and enable them to charge higher prices. The domestic steel industry also preferred this outcome, because it fixed the volume of imports (unlike the trigger-price mechanism or antidumping and countervailing duties, which affected the price) and applied to all EEC countries. Japan continued to restrict its steel exports by agreement, limiting them to 5–6.5 percent of the US market, depending upon the product.

The restraint agreements failed to provide as much help as the domestic steel industry had hoped, because imports grew from countries whose exports were not constrained by the VRA. The share of the market held by producers outside of Japan, the EEC, and Canada rose from 5 percent to 10 percent between 1982 and 1984. Thus, the overall foreign market share continued to climb, reaching 26 percent in 1984. Steel producers sought to plug the holes in this leaky system by filing more than two hundred antidumping petitions against imports from countries not party to the VRAs, such as South Korea, Spain, Brazil, Mexico, Poland, and South Africa.

In a further effort to block imports, Bethlehem Steel and the United Steel Workers filed a section 201 escape-clause petition in 1984. The ITC concluded that imports were a substantial cause of serious injury in five product categories, but found no injury in four others. The petition had been timed so that the president would have to make a decision about the

ITC recommendations just eight weeks before the 1984 presidential election. The president was put in a difficult position: with about half of steel capacity located in Pennsylvania, Ohio, Indiana, and West Virginia, many potential votes were at stake. The Congressional Steel Caucus pressed for a mandatory five-year quota limiting imports to 15 percent of domestic consumption. Reagan's Democratic opponent in the election, former Vice President Walter Mondale, proposed capping the foreign market share at 17 percent.

Reagan rejected the ITC's proposed tariff on the grounds that it was "not in the national economic interest to take actions which put at risk thousands of jobs in steel fabricating and other consuming industries or in the other sectors of the US economy that might be affected by compensation or retaliation measures to which our trading partners would be entitled" in an escape-clause action. Instead, he directed USTR to negotiate "surge control" arrangements or understandings with countries "whose exports to the United States have increased significantly in recent years due to an unfair surge in imports—unfair because of dumping subsidization, or diversion from other importing countries who have restricted access to their markets"—with the goal of "a more normal level of steel imports, or approximately 18.5 percent, excluding semi-finished steel."[27] Thus, the president went well beyond the section 201 case in promising to secure export-restraint agreements covering all segments of industry considered in the petition, even those the ITC turned down, against all major foreign suppliers of steel.

Of course, the restraint agreements still had to be negotiated. Steel imports surged in late 1984 and early 1985 before the market-share quotas could be finalized, prompting additional dumping and subsidy complaints against various European and Latin American countries. By August 1985, the product- and country-specific quotas of the VRAs were in place and covered fifteen countries accounting for 80 percent of steel imports. The VRAs were scheduled to expire in December 1989.

TEXTILES AND APPAREL

As Reagan had promised in the 1980 election campaign, the Multifiber Arrangement (MFA) was renewed for a third time in 1981. In effect from 1982–86, MFA-III reduced the annual growth of textile and apparel exports from developing countries from 6 percent to 2 percent and included tighter country-of-origin requirements and anti-surge and market-disruption provisions to limit export growth in sensitive categories. Over the course of the 1980s, the restraints were expanded to include other countries. By 1985, the MFA covered imports of textile and apparel goods from thirty-one countries in 650 separate product categories.

Like its predecessors, however, MFA-III failed to stem the rapid growth in apparel imports. This growth occurred because the quota allocations had grown over time, and some product categories were vastly underutilized. There was ample room for foreign exporters to expand their shipments by shifting products between categories and years: apparel from countries with filled quotas could ship their products to countries with unfilled quotas for some minor processing and then be exported to the United States. (For example, if a country's exports of shirts hit the limit, it could export sleeveless shirts to another country with an unfilled export quota for final stitching.) Foreign producers could also alter their production mix, upgrading their products to take advantage of different limits in different categories. As a result, the protection provided by the MFA was a "screen rather than a solid wall," as Cline (1990, 169) put it. The porous nature of the MFA allowed imports to surge in 1983 and 1984, fueled by the economic recovery and the strong dollar, and import penetration increased sharply, as figure 12.4 shows.

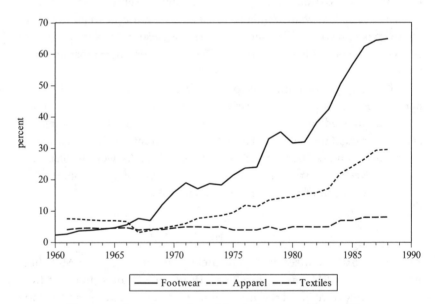

Figure 12.4. Imports as a share of domestic consumption, textiles and apparel, 1960–1988. *Note:* Textile mill products (SIC 22), apparel and other mill products (SIC 23), and non-rubber footwear (SIC 314). (US Department of Commerce, *Industrial Outlook,* various issues.)

Figure 12.4 also shows that import penetration was quite different for the textile and apparel industries. While the two were often lumped together, they were actually quite distinct. The textile industry produced fabrics and found it relatively easy to substitute capital machinery for labor and thereby improve productivity. Textile mills manufactured yarn, thread, carpets, and upholstery in highly automated mills located mainly in Georgia and the Carolinas. By adopting advanced technology, the industry shed workers but remained competitive: the import share was neither high nor rising, and some segments of the industry were able to export.

By contrast, the apparel industry produced clothing and garments. This involved cutting textile fabric and sewing and assembly operations—including pressing, dyeing, washing, and packaging—to convert it into clothing and other finished goods. This was a labor-intensive process that employed mainly unskilled women and minorities in plants spread out across Pennsylvania, the South, and southern California. Because production was necessarily labor-intensive, domestic firms found it difficult to innovate, keep costs low, and remain competitive against foreign producers who had access to low-wage labor. As a result, the share of the market taken by imports was rising rapidly and a much larger share of the job losses in the industry was due to foreign competition. Meanwhile, import penetration in the non-rubber footwear market, which was not protected after the failure of the OMAs in the late 1970s, surged as domestic shoe production plummeted.[28]

The MFA's failure to stop apparel imports explains why apparel producers and allied textile firms, and particularly labor unions, made enormous political efforts to secure legislation that would tighten the restrictions on imports and slow the decline in employment. The textile and apparel industries remained one of the country's largest employers in manufacturing, with nearly two million workers in the mid-1980s. Industry representatives argued that tighter import restrictions were needed to save jobs and that domestic production was critical for national defense. It succeeded in getting Congress to approve import limits in 1985–86, 1987–88, and again in 1990, only to have each bill vetoed by the president.

The first battle was over the Textile and Apparel Trade Enforcement Act of 1985, introduced by Rep. Ed Jenkins (D-GA). In pleading the industry's case, Jenkins stated, "I know of no other industry or group of workers that has suffered more hardships than has the textile industry, as a direct result of cheap foreign imports."[29] The legislation would have reduced textile and apparel imports from 10 billion yards to 7 billion yards from twelve countries, mainly in Asia. The bill had more than 260 House cosponsors, and support came not just from the South, but also Pennsylvania (the home to many small mills) and even New England (although mills were fast dying out there).

This campaign ran up against widespread opposition. Some apparel manufacturers, such as Levi Strauss, had become importers and wanted the freedom to source from abroad. Retailers, such as Gap, JC Penney, and Kmart, opposed import limits and stressed the consumer interest in inexpensive clothing. Agricultural producers, represented by the American Farm Bureau Federation and other groups, feared foreign retaliation against their exports if the bill passed. Administration officials also rejected new import restrictions as a protectionist move that would jeopardize US negotiating goals in the next GATT round. The industry also suffered from bad press. The media portrayed the industry as an uncompetitive one that employed low-wage, unskilled workers who could get jobs in other sectors of the economy. The implication was that the shrinkage of the industry was inevitable and that the United States could do without domestic apparel production if it wanted to compete in high-technology sectors in the twenty-first century. Many members of Congress saw it as a low-wage, sunset industry of the past, not a sunrise, high-technology industry of the future.

Still, the House passed the Jenkins bill in November 1985 by a vote of 262–159; Democrats voted 187–62 in favor, while Republicans split 79–75 in opposing it.[30] A month later, the Senate passed a less stringent version by a vote of 60–39, which the House accepted to avoid a protracted reconciliation process. To no one's surprise, Reagan vetoed the bill. While he was "well aware of the difficulties" facing the industry and "deeply sympathetic about the job layoffs and plant closings that have affected many workers in these industries," the president concluded, "It is my firm conviction that the economic and human costs of such a bill run far too high—costs in foreign retaliation against US exports, loss of American jobs, losses to American businesses, and damage to the world trading system upon which our prosperity depends."[31]

Supporters of the bill delayed an override vote until the upcoming midterm election, hoping to force the administration to strengthen the expiring MFA. In July 1986, the Reagan administration announced a new, five-year MFA that included export limits on new fibers such as ramie, linen, and silk blends, new bilateral agreements with Hong Kong, South Korea, and Taiwan, the countries targeted in the Jenkins bill, and new safeguards to stop import surges. This was not enough to satisfy the labor unions, however, and the prospect of a close congressional override vote led the president to spend time phoning members of the House and asking for their support. In the end, the House failed to override the veto.[32] In 1987, the industry and its workers again tried to get Congress to enact legislation that would cap overall textile and apparel imports at 1986 levels. The House passed the bill in late 1987 and the Senate followed a year later, but once again it was vetoed by President Reagan.

What explains the failure of the apparel industry and its workers to receive protection through legislation beyond that given in the MFA negotiated by the executive? Despite the efforts of the congressional Textile Caucus, the industry and its workers did not have as much political strength as might appear from the number of workers in the industry. Textile and apparel firms were divided about the merits of trade protection; textile firms were embracing new technology that enabled them to remain competitive, while apparel firms were increasingly sourcing their production from other countries. Advocates of import relief also encountered unexpectedly strong opposition from retailers, who put up a strong fight on behalf of consumers. Finally, the industry was already the beneficiary of the MFA, and its decline was not due to "unfair trade practices" by foreign governments. Import restraints were seen, at best, as a costly way of slowing the inevitable contraction of the industry.

AGRICULTURE

Agricultural producers were also affected by the economic hardship caused by the recession and strong dollar. While farmers prospered during the commodity-price boom of the 1970s, they suffered when commodity prices collapsed in the early 1980s. Net farm income dropped by a third between 1979 and 1982, pushing farm indebtedness to record levels. Lower prices meant that it was more attractive for farmers to sell their crops to the government at the fixed price support than to sell them at the prevailing market price. As a result, the cost of federal farm programs escalated rapidly.

As government outlays to purchase and hold surplus crops grew, the Agriculture Department attempted to boost farm prices by reducing domestic production. This was done through acreage set-asides, in which farmers were paid to keep land idle. In addition, export subsidies were sometimes used to dispose of the government-held commodity stocks. These export subsidies put the United States on a collision course with the EEC, which had long been doing the same thing. One commodity, wheat, took on particular importance. Formerly a net importer, the EEC became a net exporter of wheat in the 1980s after it set domestic target prices so high that large production surpluses appeared. These surpluses were dumped on the world market using export subsidies. That policy, as well as the strong dollar, led to a sharp decline in foreign demand for American wheat. In 1983, the Reagan administration debated using selective export subsidies to reduce wheat stocks and punish the Europeans for distorting the world wheat market. The 1985 farm bill created the Export Enhancement Program to combat the EEC's subsidies by providing for targeted export assistance to help American farmers increase sales in foreign markets.[33] In one case, the United States displaced French exports by selling wheat to Egypt at $100 a ton when the US market price was $225 ton. Taxpayers were left to make up the difference.[34]

The United States was not alone in intervening in agricultural markets. The increasing use of domestic price supports, import restrictions, export subsidies, and other policies led to massive distortions in world agricultural markets. The Organization for Economic Cooperation and Development (OECD) documented the extensive support that governments gave to agricultural producers: in 1986, about 23 percent of US farm income, 39 percent of EEC farm income, and 65 percent of Japanese farm income came from policy measures.[35] Interventions in one country led to spillover problems in other countries. For example, the Common Agricultural Policy enabled the EEC to increase its share of world food exports from 8 percent in 1976 to 18 percent in 1981.[36] This depressed world prices, which led to more import restrictions and more costly price supports in other countries. The agricultural subsidy wars of the early 1980s made farm reform a major US negotiating priority in the next GATT round.

With most American farmers trying to export their produce to world markets, the demand to cut agricultural imports was not strong, with the exception of sugar.[37] In the 1970s, raw sugar was protected only by a modest import tariff. The 1981 farm bill established a new domestic price support program for sugar at a time when world prices were relatively high, but mandated that it involve no federal outlays. In 1981–82, the falling price of sugar exposed the contradiction of having a government price support program that did not allow for any budgetary expenditures. The only way to keep the domestic price high and avoid government payments was to restrict imports in a bid to keep the domestic price at the government's target price.

To do so, the Department of Agriculture imposed emergency quotas on imported sugar in May 1982. This slashed sugar imports from 5 million tons in 1981 to 3 million tons in 1982. To comply with GATT provisions about non-discrimination, the quotas were allocated to countries based on their share of imports in 1975–81, when a non-discriminatory tariff was in place. As sugar prices kept falling, officials reduced the import quotas six times over the next two years, resulting in a 75 percent reduction in the sugar imports allowed from Caribbean and Central American countries.

The government's attempt to restrict sugar imports to balance supply and demand at the target price sometimes pushed the domestic price of sugar to more than five times the world price. This enormous price gap made it profitable to import refined sugar products that were not covered by the quotas—including packets of iced tea and cocoa, boxes of cake mix, tins of maple sugar, and other high-sugar content products—and then extract the sugar for sale at the high domestic price. In 1983, the Reagan administration banned imports of certain blends and mixtures of sugar and other ingredients in bulk containers on the grounds that they interfered with the price support program. Foreign exporters of processed foods, particularly in Canada and the EEC, vehemently protested the move.

The high domestic price of sugar also accelerated the substitution of high-fructose corn syrup for sugar in food manufacturing. In 1984, Coca Cola and Pepsi announced that they would use corn syrup instead of sugar as the sweetener in their soft drinks. This sharply reduced domestic demand for sugar and required the Agriculture Department to slash the import quota by another 20 percent for all exporting countries. The high domestic price of sugar meant that sugar-using industries faced higher production costs in comparison to their foreign competitors, driving many candy and confectionary producers to other countries and reducing domestic employment in the food-manufacturing industry.

Finally, the sharp reduction in sugar imports led to foreign-policy problems. The quotas reduced the export earnings and damaged the economies of Caribbean and Central American countries at a time when many of them were struggling with the global debt crisis and even fighting Communist-backed insurgencies. The US move hurt relations with those countries, and so the United States tried to help them with other trade preferences, such as the Caribbean Basin Initiative of 1983. The sugar quotas also led farmers in the region to stop producing sugar and start cultivating illegal narcotics that were smuggled into the United States, starting a war with drug traffickers.

The United States compounded all of these problems in August 1986 when it decided to subsidize the sale of the entire accumulated stock of 136,000 tons of sugar to China. The government took an enormous loss; sugar had been purchased at 18 cents per pound but was then sold at just under 5 cents per pound. Within two days of the sale, the world price of sugar dropped more than 20 percent, from 6.3 cents to 5.0 cents per pound, to the outrage of sugar-exporting countries.[38]

THE RISE OF ADMINISTERED PROTECTION

As we have seen, three large and politically powerful industries—automobiles, steel, and apparel—all benefited from executive-negotiated agreements with foreign countries to limit their exports. For their part, farmers relied on government price supports to insulate them from fluctuations in world commodity prices. But what about the many smaller, less politically influential industries that also felt the pain of the recession and increased foreign competition? What could they do to obtain government relief from imports? Since these producers could not command the attention of Congress or the executive branch, they fell back upon the system of trade laws that allowed domestic firms to petition the government for temporary duties on imports.[39]

As we saw in chapter 11, the main legal avenues by which domestic firms could request trade protection were the escape clause, antidumping duties, and countervailing duties. The escape clause, based on section 201 of the Trade Act of 1974, was supposed to be the principal means by which industries harmed by imports could receive temporary relief from foreign competition. If imports of a particular good were found to be "a substantial cause of serious injury," the ITC would recommend that the president impose a higher tariff, phased out over five years, on imports from all sources. The president had complete discretion about whether to grant import relief or not.

However, we also saw that, in most escape-clause cases, either the ITC failed to find that imports were a substantial cause of serious injury, or the president rejected the provision of any relief. After the auto petition was turned down in 1980, the ITC dismissed petitions on fishing rods in 1981, tubeless tire valves in 1982, stainless steel table flatware and non-rubber footwear in 1983, canned tuna and potassium permanganate in 1984, and electric shavers, metal castings, and apple juice in 1985. President Reagan did grant escape-clause protection to heavyweight motorcycles, some steel products, and wood shakes and shingles, but turned down relief for unwrought copper and another non-rubber footwear case that the ITC had approved. Given this record, domestic firms knew that they were unlikely to obtain much assistance using the escape clause and therefore few both-

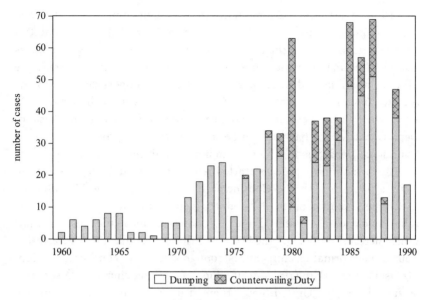

Figure 12.5. Number of trade-remedy cases initiated,
1960–1990. (Baldwin 1998, tables 11.1–4.)

ered to initiate cases. As Senator Fritz Hollings (D-SC) put it, "going the 201 route is for suckers."[40]

Consequently, domestic producers turned to antidumping and countervailing duties. Figure 12.5 presents the number of antidumping and countervailing duty petitions filed from 1960 to 1990 and shows that the demand for trade remedies increased significantly in the 1980s. From 1980–93, 682 AD cases and 358 CVD cases were filed. Many of them (38 percent of AD and 55 percent of CVD cases) were filed by the steel industry as a way of forcing the president to negotiate VRAs with foreign exporters (after which the petitions were withdrawn) or as a way of closing the market to countries or products not covered by the VRAs.[41] Regarding countervailing duties, petitioning firms had a significant burden of proof in having to demonstrate that the foreign exports were subsidized and a cause of material injury. The difficulty in proving the existence of subsidies meant that relatively few CVD cases were filed, except by the steel and chemical industries. Just 21 percent of the CVD cases resulted in duties being imposed, because they were often terminated or suspended when replaced by VRAs.[42]

By default, the antidumping law became the principal means by which small industries received some relief from foreign competition. The low burden of proof needed to find dumping and the high likelihood that duties would be imposed were the main attraction to potential filings. Congress also changed many of the provisions in the trade laws to encourage the filing of petitions and increase the probability of import duties as being the final outcome. Perhaps the most important procedural change came in 1979, when authority over dumping cases was shifted from the Treasury Department (which had little interest in the enforcing the statute) to the Commerce Department (which championed producer interests).

The antidumping process started with a firm or industry association filing a petition with the Commerce Department and the ITC alleging that imports from a particular country were being sold at "less than fair value" and causing "material injury." Commerce made the "less than fair value" determination, and the ITC made the "material injury" determination. Under normal circumstances, foreign sales were considered "dumping" (sold at less than fair value) if a foreign exporter charged a lower price on its sales in the United States than in its home market.[43] Commerce almost always ruled that dumping occurred: from 1980–92, dumping was found in 93 percent of all cases. Commerce often found large dumping margins: the average antidumping duty was 26 percent in the period 1980–84 and 41 percent from 1985–89. The average antidumping duty in effect in 1992 was 46 percent in non-steel cases and 27 percent in steel cases.[44]

Meanwhile, the ITC would determine if the petitioning industry had suffered from or was threatened with "material injury"—defined as "harm which is not inconsequential, immaterial, or unimportant"—as a result of the dumped imports. In making the injury determination, the ITC looked at such factors as changes in the industry's output, employment, and capacity utilization. (Under the law, only the harm to domestic producers was considered, not the harm or injury to consumers or other domestic industries that might result from the imposition of additional duties.) The ITC made an affirmative injury finding in two-thirds of cases from 1980 to 1992, and about 40 percent of antidumping cases filed resulted in duties being imposed.[45] In the 1980s, antidumping duties covered a wide array of products such as staples from Sweden, color television sets from Korea and Taiwan, raspberries from Canada, pistachios from Iran, candles from China, cut flowers from Colombia, and frozen orange juice from Brazil. However, because the goods subject to antidumping duties were narrowly defined products, the total share of US imports covered by such duties was less than 1 percent.

From the standpoint of domestic petitioners, the antidumping process had several advantages over the escape clause. First, the "material injury" standard in a dumping case was much less stringent than the "serious injury" requirement in an escape-clause case, making it more likely that the ITC would make an affirmative injury finding. The antidumping process also did not involve any presidential discretion: if Commerce and the ITC ruled in favor of the petitioner, antidumping duties went into effect automatically without further review. And unlike escape-clause relief, which was usually phased out over five years, antidumping duties could remain in place for an indefinite period. In the early 1990s, the mean duration of an antidumping duty was seven years, and about a fifth of such duties had been in place for ten or more years.[46]

However, unlike escape-clause duties, which applied to imports from all sources, antidumping duties only applied to imports coming from countries named in the petition. In other words, antidumping duties were selective and did not prevent other suppliers from expanding their exports when the targeted countries were hit. Such supply diversion made antidumping duties a leaky form of protection. For example, after antidumping duties were imposed on semiconductors from Japan, imports from Japan plummeted and production shifted to Taiwan. As Taiwanese semiconductor exports surged, they too were hit with antidumping duties. Then production shifted to Korea, where the same pattern repeated itself. Eventually, firms learned to file multiple petitions to cover imports from many different potential sources of supply.

As antidumping actions were increasingly used against imports, they came under criticism from economists. The administrative system strongly favored domestic petitioners and did not consider the interests of consumers, either downstream user industries or households, when such duties were imposed. Finger (1993, 13) argued that "antidumping is ordinary protection, albeit with a good public relations program" because it was based on the allegation of "unfair" foreign competition. The welfare cost of US antidumping and countervailing duty actions amounted to $4 billion in 1993—a considerable sum.[47] Although US exports were adversely affected by the spread of antidumping to other countries, Congress favored the existing system so much that it refused to allow changes in the process to be negotiated at the multilateral level.

ASSESSING THE PROTECTIONISM OF THE 1980S

Three questions can be posed about the new import restrictions imposed in the 1980s: What explains the type of policy instruments used? What were the economic effects of the import barriers? Did protection helped revitalize the protected industries?

The main policy instruments used to protect domestic firms from foreign competition were tariffs (antidumping, countervailing duties, or escape-clause actions) or quotas (export restraints). Generally speaking, the largest and most politically influential industries were protected from foreign competition through negotiated export-restraint agreements—textiles and apparel with the MFA, automobiles with the VER, and steel with the VRAs—whereas smaller, less politically influential industries had to file petitions for other trade remedies. Domestic producers liked the certainty that came with a specific quantitative limit on imports; foreign exporters also preferred an export quota because they could charge a higher price in the US market and earn a valuable "quota rent."

The main difference between an import tariff and an export restraint is that a tariff generates revenue for the government while an export restraint generates a quota rent for exporting firms. Thus, an import tariff redistributed income from domestic consumers to domestic producers and the government, whereas an export restraint redistributed income from domestic consumers to domestic and foreign producers. Not surprisingly, foreign firms strongly preferred an export restraint to an import tariff, but the welfare consequences for the importing country were very different in the two cases. With a tariff, the losses to consumers exceeded the gains to domestic producers and the government by a deadweight loss that arose from the distortion of production and consumption. With a foreign export restraint or import quota, the losses included the deadweight loss and the much larger quota rent captured by foreign exporters. Furthermore, export quotas gave foreign firms an incentive to upgrade the quality of their products. This meant that they could move into the production of new, higher-end products and compete more directly with American producers.

In the 1980s, economists began producing quantitative estimates of the impact of various trade restrictions. For the first time, policymakers were confronted with an explicit calculation of the costs and benefits of trade protection. In almost every case, the costs of such restrictions to consumers and downstream industries exceeded the gains reaped by the protected domestic industry.[48] For example, De Melo and Tarr (1992, 199) concluded that all major US trade restrictions in 1984 resulted in a net welfare loss of $26 billion, about 0.7 percent of GDP—about the same welfare loss that would have been generated by a 49 percent across-the-board tariff. Almost all of this loss—$21 billion of the $26 billion—was due to foreign export restraints in textiles and apparel, automobiles, and steel. About 70 percent of the $26 billion was due to the transfer of quota rents from domestic consumers to foreign producers; the remainder was due to the deadweight losses. Such findings suggested that the economic loss could have been significantly lower if tariffs had been used to protect domestic industries instead of export restraints or import quotas (or if the government had auctioned off the rights to import under the quota).[49] Of course, foreign countries would have strongly objected if tariffs had been imposed, possibly even retaliating against them, whereas the quota rents compensated their exporters to some extent for accepting restrictions on their exports.

The Multifiber Arrangement (MFA) protecting the textile and apparel industry was the single most costly trade intervention of this period. De Melo and Tarr (1992) calculated that the welfare loss amounted to $10.4 billion in 1984, of which $6 billion was due to the transfer of the quota rent to foreign exporters.[50] The MFA losses were large because of the high implicit barriers, the large volume of restricted imports, and the sizeable quota rents generated by the policy.[51] The main purpose of the MFA, as with other import restrictions, was to slow the loss of jobs in the industry. Most estimates suggested that the MFA kept domestic employment in the textile and apparel industry higher than it otherwise would have been by about two hundred and fifty thousand jobs—about 10–15 percent of industry employment.[52] Import restrictions could not stop the loss of jobs due to technological change; indeed, most of the fall in employment during this period was due to productivity improvements and the shift to more capital-intensive production methods, not declining output due to rising imports.[53] The problem was that import restrictions were a costly and inefficient way of saving some jobs in the industry. The import restrictions were being used to save very poor jobs: average hourly earnings in the apparel and non-rubber footwear industries were among the lowest in all of manufacturing. The consumer cost of protection per job saved, which measured the total loss to consumers divided by the number of jobs saved in the protected industry, was more than $100,000 for industries in which the average worker earned perhaps $12,000 annually.[54]

By quantifying the consumer cost per job saved as a result of restricting imports, these studies put advocates of protectionist policies on the defensive. While some members of Congress were willing to have consumers pay this price with the hope that it would ensure the continued employment of their constituents, most policy analysts were less sympathetic. They pointed out that trade protection preserved jobs in relatively low-wage industries at the expense of high-wage jobs in export industries. Some analysts explicitly stated that these jobs were simply not worth keeping at that price. After studying the matter in relation to the textile, apparel, and non-rubber footwear industries, the Congressional Budget Office (1991, xi–xii) bluntly concluded that because "the estimated consumer costs are all higher than the average annual earnings of the workers. . . . it would generally be more efficient for government to allow the jobs to disappear and compensate any displaced workers who cannot find equivalent work."

The second most costly trade restriction in the 1980s was Japan's auto VER. If the VER had been removed in 1984, De Melo and Tarr (1992) calculate that the welfare gain would have been $10 billion, of which $8 billion was the quota rent transferred to Japanese producers. The restraint allowed Japanese exporters to increase their price by about $1,000 per car.[55] The jobs saved in this industry were high-wage union jobs, but some analysts questioned the fairness of forcing consumers with lower average incomes than unionized workers to pay more for their cars to save the jobs of highly-paid auto workers. Others noted that export restrictions might ultimately hurt domestic producers because they gave foreign producers an incentive to upgrade the quality of products so that they could charge the highest possible markup on their constrained exports. For example, Japanese automobile producers, which had specialized in producing small, inexpensive, fuel-efficient cars, began producing larger, higher-quality vehicles that competed more directly with American brands after the VER was imposed.

Studies such as these provided greater information about the economic effects of trade restrictions, something that had been absent in previous discussions of trade policy. The findings of various studies bred widespread skepticism in policy circles about the wisdom and rationale for those restraints, giving members of Congress reason to pause before endorsing them. For example, in 1984 the Congressional Budget Office (CBO) was asked to evaluate the economic consequences of proposed legislation that would impose a five-year quota on imported steel that would cap the foreign market share at 15 percent. The CBO (1984) estimated that the quotas would raise the price of imported steel by 24–34 percent, increase domestic production by 6 percent, and boost steel-industry employment by 6–8 percent. However, by increasing the average price of steel by 10 percent (both domestic and imported), the quotas would reduce domestic steel consumption by 4–5 percent and lead to employment losses in steel-consuming industries that would roughly offset the employment gains in the steel industry. The fact that trade protection would not result in a net gain in employment (since it was an intermediate good used by other industries) was a strike against it. Furthermore, the CBO (1984, xv) argued that "there is little prospect that the quota would reverse the secular decline in the industry, since it does not address the underlying factors that have conditioned this decline."

There was also little evidence that temporary trade protection helped protected industries adapt to the new world of global competition. In a report entitled "Has Trade Protection Revitalized Domestic Industries?" the CBO (1986, 101) concluded that "trade restraints have failed to achieve their primary objective of increasing the international competitiveness of the relevant industries." Similarly, another study of the escape clause found that most industries receiving such protection were undergoing long, secular declines that limits on imports could not reverse. Looking back, the International Trade Commission (1982b, 86) concluded, "One observes how relatively little effect escape-clause relief had on firm adjustment either because so much of the firm's injury was caused by non-import-related factors, or because the decline of imports following relief was small."

These reports, among many others, identified two reasons for the failure of import restrictions to help struggling domestic industries. First, the restrictions were not very effective in reducing imports. The MFA was a porous sieve, Japan's auto VER was not binding in its first two years and was then circumvented by foreign investment in the United States, and the steel VRAs and antidumping/countervailing duties could not prevent supply diversion. Indeed, most country-specific or product-specific trade restrictions were ineffective because of growing imports from new sources of supply or from new types of products. Despite an orderly marketing arrangement, machine tool imports were 10 percent higher in 1988 than in 1986 due to increased shipments from unconstrained suppliers.

Second, import barriers could slow but not stop the competitive pressures that were forcing producers to improve their efficiency. Like all labor-intensive industries, the textiles and apparel industry was modernizing and reducing employment only partly because of imports. In the textile industry, for example, the ITC report found that domestic producers of tufted carpets drove existing Wilton and velvet carpet producers out of business. The auto and steel industries also faced competitive pressure to increase productivity and improve product quality. By the late 1980s, an increasing number of Japanese auto producers had production facilities in the United States, meaning that import restrictions could no longer significantly diminish foreign competition. Similarly, the large, integrated steel producers had to fend off the rapidly rising market share of the small but efficient domestic mini-mills. The mini-mills had much lower costs than the integrated producers because they could process scrap metal instead of forging it from raw materials. By the early 1980s, mini-mills had captured about 20 percent of the steel market. The mini-mills were also responsible for the dramatic increase in the steel industry's productivity in the 1980s and 1990s. While the industry lost about 75 percent of its workforce between 1962 and 2005, about four hundred thousand workers, shipments of steel were roughly the same in the two years, meaning that output per worker rose by a factor of five.[56] Thus, steel producers would have faced massive restructuring even in the absence of foreign competition.

All of these cases illustrated what Robert Baldwin (1982) called the "inefficacy of trade policy" in helping struggling domestic industries.[57] A classic example of the limitations of import restrictions was the celebrated Harley-Davidson motorcycle case, often heralded as the import-relief success story of the decade. As conventionally told, Harley-Davidson was pushed to the brink of bankruptcy by Japanese competition, but the company recovered quickly after it received temporary import relief in 1983 in an escape-clause case. In fact, import relief had little to do with Harley-Davidson's turnaround. The early 1980s recession, rather than imports, had been the primary cause of the steep decline in demand for Harley's products. The company's resurgence came with the general economic recovery that began in 1983. Furthermore, Harley-Davidson mainly produced "heavyweight" motorcycles with piston displacements of more than 1000 cc, which were not imported because Honda and Kawasaki already produced them in the United States. Japanese producers mainly exported medium-weight bikes of 700–850 cc piston displacement, but Suzuki and Yamaha simply evaded the tariff by producing a 699 cc version that was not subject to the duty (initially set at 45 percent). Thus, protection had almost no impact on Harley-Davidson because Honda and Kawasaki were already manufacturing heavyweight motorcycles in the United States and other Japanese producers easily evaded the escape-clause tariffs on medium-weight bikes.[58]

If import barriers were so ineffective, why were they so often used? They arose as a second-best response to the inability or unwillingness of the president or Congress to adjust the underlying macroeconomic policies that were responsible for the strong dollar and the large trade deficit. The reality was that trade policies alone could do little to make the adjustment process less painful as long as the dollar continued to strengthen. Trade protection may have bought some firms more time to adjust, but ultimately it did not prevent large employment losses in labor-intensive industries. The main reason that most trade-sensitive industries began to perform better was that the economy began to recover in 1983, and the dollar began to depreciate in 1985. Trade protection played a very limited role in helping these industries, but it often imposed large costs on consumers.

CONGRESS THREATENS ACTION

While the Reagan administration protected several large American industries—automobiles, steel, and textiles and apparel—from foreign competition, it was still doing far too little to address the trade situation in the eyes of many in Congress. Legislators were frustrated by the administration's apparent indifference to the growing trade deficit and the problems of struggling industries. In response, some administration officials argued that the trade deficit reflected the strength of the American economy and that the strong dollar reflected international confidence in the nation's economy. To members of Congress, particularly those from regions struggling to cope with the recession and strong dollar, this benign interpretation showed a callous disregard for the difficult situation facing industries in their states and the lost jobs of their constituents. The pressure in Congress to "do something" about the trade situation came most strongly from the Midwest and the South Atlantic, where half of all import-sensitive employment was located, as table 12.1 shows. Both areas

TABLE 12.1. Distribution of employment in trade-sensitive manufacturing industries, by region, 1990

| Region | All manufacturing | Industries sensitive to | | | Factory workers receiving trade adjustment assistance (1987–92) |
		Imports only	Exports only	Both imports and exports	
Employment (thousands)	19,143.3	1,391.9	2,117.6	412.9	314.9
Percent	100.0	100.0	100.0	100.0	100.0
New England	6.4	8.2	8.7	11.7	8.0
Mid-Atlantic	14.3	19.7	10.9	18.4	21.3
South	23.9	26.0	14.2	15.8	28.0
Mid-West	29.5	24.4	22.3	41.5	25.5
Oil States	8.2	6.5	12.1	4.6	9.4
West	17.8	15.3	32.0	8.1	4.8

Source: Shelburne and Bednarzik 1993, 6–8.
Note: As a percentage of GDP, figures may not sum to totals due to rounding.

of the country saw large numbers of plant closings and the layoff of thousands of workers in the early and mid-1980s.

The nation's old manufacturing belt, which stretched from upstate New York through Pennsylvania and Ohio and into Illinois, was particularly hard hit. This region, shown in figure 12.6, was the location of heavy industry production, particularly automobiles and steel. It became known as the "Rust Belt" because it was where most of the nation's "deindustrialization" was occurring. While national manufacturing employment rose 1.4 percent between 1969 and 1996, manufacturing employment in the Rust Belt fell by a third.[59] The manufacturing jobs lost in this region did not come back even after the recession had ended and the dollar had

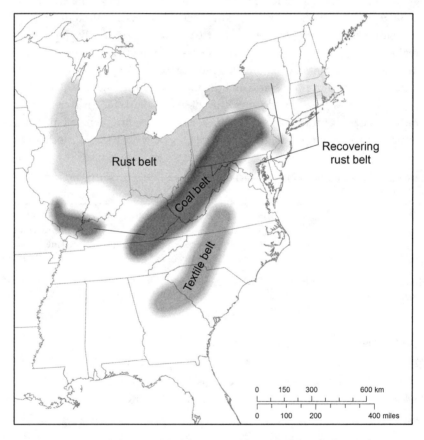

Figure 12.6. The Rust Belt. (Map courtesy Citrin GIS/Applied Spatial Analysis Lab, Dartmouth College; based on work by Brendan Jennings 2010, Benjamin F. Lemert 1933, and John Tully 1996.)

declined in value, leaving the Rust Belt region depressed. Although unemployment rates in the Rust Belt returned to the national average within five years of the massive job losses experienced in the early 1980s, this adjustment took place almost entirely through the out-migration of people rather than in-migration of jobs or a change in labor force participation.[60] Of course, the United States remained a large exporter of manufactured goods, so the Midwest had significant export-sensitive employment as well, but these industries also suffered under the strength of the dollar.

The South Atlantic, the location of more than two-thirds of the nation's production of textile mill products, also suffered from shuttered mills and mass layoffs. The apparel industry alone accounted for more than half of the trade adjustment assistance certifications granted during 1987–92. However, the South was able to absorb this blow more easily than the industrial Midwest. The South was attracting manufacturing investment from the Midwest and from foreign countries because of its favorable business climate.

Not surprisingly, representatives from the industrial Midwest and the textile South demanded that Congress and the administration take action to stop further employment losses. These regions were largely Democratic constituencies, and leaders such as Richard Gephardt from Missouri, John Dingell from Michigan, and Ernest "Fritz" Hollings from South Carolina were among the most vocal members of Congress advocating that policies be enacted to reduce foreign competition. The industrial Midwest was deeply scarred by the economic trauma of the early 1980s, and the region's congressional representatives remained hostile to agreements that would reduce trade barriers well into the twenty-first century. Labor unions in the Midwest strongly pushed Democratic lawmakers into supporting import restrictions. The party became much more skeptical of trade, marking a major change from its traditional position.

Other regions of the country also suffered in the early 1980s but did not support import restrictions. The nation's grain belt—the agricultural states of Kansas, Nebraska, Iowa, South Dakota, and Minnesota—still depended on exports. Farmers were slammed by high interest rates and falling commodity prices. On top of that, the strong dollar priced American agricultural goods out of world markets. But farm groups opposed new import restraints out of fear that their agricultural exports would be the first target of foreign retaliation: if the United States began limiting imports of clothing or steel, for example, other countries could easily shift their wheat or soybean purchases from the United States to Canada or other foreign suppliers. Consequently, Republicans from the agricultural Midwest, such as Robert Dole of Kansas, not only wanted to open foreign markets for agricultural exports through GATT negotiations, but fought efforts to close the domestic market to imports. If anything, they wanted export subsidies, lower interest rates, and a weaker dollar, much like the Midwest Populists in earlier decades.

The West was less affected by the trade difficulties of the early 1980s. As table 12.1 indicated, the West accounted for 18 percent of the nation's manufacturing employment but 32 percent of the nation's export-sensitive employment, with fewer industries facing direct competition from imports. California and Washington, in particular, were largely export-oriented, with a high concentration of production of high-technology goods, such as electrical equipment and aircraft, electronics and computers, as well as traditional exports of lumber and wood products. Although concerned about the strong dollar, representatives from the West, such as Robert Matsui of California, also tended to oppose protectionist measures sponsored by the industrial Midwest and textile South.

Because the industrial Midwest and the textile South were hardest hit by the trade shocks of the period, a new voting pattern began to be seen in Congress, one that first became evident in the 1970 vote over the Mills bill (shown in figure 11.2). In essence, the North-South division over trade policy seen throughout American history was reconfigured into a rough East-West pattern.[61] In addition, the traditional partisan division over trade, in which Democrats favored open trade, and Republicans favored protectionist policies, began to flip. Now, many Democratic constituencies were harmed by imports while Republican constituencies tended to benefit from open trade.

Because Congress was divided, it was unlikely to pass protectionist legislation. (The auto VER, the steel VRA, and the apparel MFA were all negotiated by the executive branch with some pressure but little direct involvement from Congress.) In fact, somewhat surprisingly, given the growing pressure to address the trade situation, Congress enacted a moderate trade bill in 1984. The Trade and Tariff Act of 1984 contained no major innovations: it withheld from the president trade-negotiating authority and relaxed the statutory criteria for providing import relief, and it combined a popular idea (authority to reach a free-trade agreement with Israel) with a less popular program (the renewal of trade preferences for developing countries).[62] The Reagan administration worked hard to remove any provision that might lead to special import restrictions for specific industries, such as for wine, copper, footwear, and dairy producers.[63] The most controversial proposal was a reciprocity amendment sponsored by Senator John

Danforth (R-MO) that would have set up an administrative mechanism to restrict imports from countries that did not provide the United States with the equivalent degree of market access, a provision clearly aimed at Japan. After Reagan threatened to veto the measure, the Danforth amendment was dropped, and the bill was passed with an overwhelming bipartisan majority in the House and unanimously in the Senate.

But this legislation was a misleading indicator of congressional sentiments on trade. Although a strong economic recovery began in 1983, Congress watched with growing alarm as the dollar continued to appreciate, and the trade deficit continued to grow. Members of Congress, particularly Democrats, complained that the Reagan administration was doing nothing to ease the pain of traded-goods industries. "President Reagan seems willing to preside over the de-industrialization of America," House Speaker Thomas P. O'Neill (D-MA) complained. "We in Congress are not."[64]

Of course, the basic problem was the strength of the dollar on foreign exchange markets. As Danforth put it, "No trade agreements, however sound, no trade laws, however enforced, will give Americans a fair chance to compete in the international marketplace if an overvalued dollar has the same effect as a 25–50 percent [foreign] tariff. To say this is not to belittle trade agreements. Rather it is to state the absolute necessity of dealing effectively with the exchange rate issue."[65] And yet the exchange rate was outside of Congress's direct control. The appreciation of the dollar was the consequence of large capital inflows, due in part to the country's monetary and fiscal policy. Congress could not directly influence monetary policy, which was the preserve of the Federal Reserve, and it was reluctant to adjust fiscal policy (i.e., cut the budget deficit) to reduce foreign capital inflows.

In 1984, as the trade deficit surged past $100 billion, an enormous figure at the time, trade pressures peaked with more than six hundred trade bills introduced in Congress. These bills proposed everything from the creation of a Department of International Trade and Industry (to mimic Japan) to sectoral reciprocity requirements, industry protection, and easier requirements in antidumping and countervailing duty cases.[66] The proposal that received the most attention came from Rep. Richard Gephardt (D-MO) and would require countries running "excessive" trade surpluses with the United States—namely Japan, Taiwan, South Korea, and Brazil—to reduce their surpluses or faced a 25 percent surcharge on their imports.

Although the Democratic leadership endorsed the Gephardt amendment, this support may have been a strategic way of pushing the Reagan

administration out of its benign neglect of the trade problems. Several decisions by the administration in 1984–85 fueled the perception that it was
indifferent to the trade pressures being felt by members of Congress. In
March 1985, with the presidential election of 1984 safely behind him, the
president stated that Japan would not be asked to renew the auto export
restraint. Although Japan announced that it would continue to enforce the
limit for a fifth year, this time at the higher level of 2.3 million vehicles,
members of Congress were upset that the administration let Japan off the
hook. Reagan's decision prompted the Senate to pass, by a vote of 92–0, a
nonbinding resolution denouncing "unfair Japanese trade practices" and
urging the president to retaliate against Japan unless it opened its market
and started importing more goods to offset the additional auto exports.[67]
"We are in a trade war, and we are losing it," Senator Lloyd Bentsen (D-TX)
complained.[68]

President Reagan also earned the ire of Congress for rejecting section
201 escape-clause petitions in which the ITC had found injury to domestic
producers of copper and non-rubber footwear. The president justified these
decisions on the grounds that import restrictions would impose a costly
and unjustifiable burden on consumers, risk foreign retaliation against
US exports, slow the industry from making necessary competitive adjustments, and only temporarily save jobs. Even so, his decisions frustrated
many in Congress. As Destler (1995, 124) pointed out, Reagan's actions
were undertaken "without any apparent recognition that denying relief
through established channels to an industry that was clearly damaged by
imports was bound to increase pressure for statutory solutions"—that is,
that constituent pressure would be diverted to members of Congress.

The only overtly protectionist legislation that passed Congress in 1985
was a bill to restrict imports of textiles and apparel. The Textile and Apparel Trade Enforcement Act of 1985 sought to address the failure of the
MFA to stem the growth of imports, which had risen from 4.9 million
square yards in 1980 to 10.2 million in 1984. As noted earlier, the MFA
was a particularly porous form of protection, because restricted imports
could shift between countries and between product types. As discussed
earlier in the chapter, the Jenkins bill (named for its sponsor, Representative Ed Jenkins, a Georgia Democrat) mandated a 36 percent reduction in
textile imports and a 20 percent reduction in apparel imports from existing levels. The bill would roll back imports from principal suppliers (Taiwan, South Korea, and Hong Kong) by establishing country- and product-
specific export quotas and new limits on silk, linen, and ramie fiber goods.
The bill would replace the bilateral arrangements in the MFA with com-

prehensive import quotas imposed unilaterally by the United States. It also included a provision to help the footwear and copper industries that had been denied import relief by the president. Imports of footwear would be capped at 60 percent of the domestic market for eight years, and the president was instructed to negotiate a five-year VRA with foreign copper exporters.

Although the House and Senate passed the Jenkins bill in late 1985, members of Congress knew this action was largely symbolic, because Reagan announced that he would veto it, which he did. In fact, most Democrats were not enthusiastic about enacting import restraints. Despite pressures from the industrial Midwest and textile South, the party's leadership believed that such blatant protectionism was not good policy: it would violate GATT rules and lead to retaliation against US exports. As Ways and Means Committee Chair Dan Rostenkowski (D-IL) argued, "Don't be dissuaded [from opposing the bill] by those who tell you that is a great political issue. Bad economics doesn't make for good politics."[69]

Recognizing that embracing protectionism was not necessarily a winning political strategy or an attractive policy option, Congress flirted with other fads. Some Democrats believed that an "industrial policy," a national strategy of government support for investment in manufacturing, should be adopted, although the details of such a policy remained vague.[70] Others pushed for an across-the-board surcharge on imports or something like the Gephardt proposal for higher tariffs on countries running large trade surpluses with the United States. Of course, none of these ideas was likely to become policy: it was extremely difficult to move legislation through Congress that would satisfy all regions of the country, let alone get the approval of the president.

These proposals reflected Congress's searching for some means of relieving the trade pressures, given its inability to do anything directly about the strong dollar. Most members recognized that restricting imports would be a costly and ineffective way of addressing the trade deficit or reducing foreign competition. Even Gephardt conceded that only a small fraction of the trade deficit was due to foreign trade policies. Though sympathetic to those industries harmed by imports, Congress generally shied away from embracing outright protectionism, which was still far from being viewed as a desirable policy. As Rep. Don Bonker (D-WA) noted, "We [Democrats] have the stigma of protectionism, which comes by way of our closeness to labor and sponsorship of the domestic content bill."[71]

Thus, Congress did not "go protectionist," as Destler (1995, 66) points out. As Destler (1991, 277) put it, "Legislators became publicly engaged.

They went on record in all sorts of ways; they forced the administration into a more aggressive international bargaining posture. But they did not—in the end—change American trade policy more than very slightly along its most important dimension, the openness of the US market to imports. And they did not themselves impose specific trade restraints on behalf of specific clients." Rep. Don Pease (D-OH) explained, "We are trying to propose a respectable course between the Reagan policy of free trade at any cost and outright protectionism."[72] Or, as Rep. Thomas Downey (D-NY) stated, "Just because Reagan has no trade policy doesn't mean we should have a bad one."[73]

RECIPROCITY AND JAPAN

As it searched for a solution to the trade pressures, Congress tried to put some of the burden on other countries by focusing on foreign "unfair" trade policies. The "trade hawks," led by Gephardt, attacked other countries for engaging in unfair trade practices and keeping their markets closed. In this effort, Japan was singled out for special attention.[74] Japan was an economic success story, a country that lay devastated after World War II but grew rapidly in the postwar period and eventually became the world's second largest economy. Japan's exports to the United States soared in the 1970s and 1980s and were highly concentrated in particular industries, leading to growing trade friction between the two countries. As Japan became an export powerhouse, the composition of its exports shifted from labor-intensive goods to more sophisticated and technologically advanced products. Industry after industry seemed to fall prey to Japanese competition, from cotton textiles and apparel in the 1950s to transistor radios, record players, and sporting goods in the 1960s; television sets, consumer electronics, and steel in the 1970s; and finally automobiles, semiconductors, and office equipment in the 1980s.

Americans were both awed by Japan's technological prowess and fearful of its industrial dominance. Japan's success was sometimes attributed to its Ministry of International Trade and Industry (MITI), which crafted targeted industrial policies—ranging from research and development subsidies to administrative guidance—to promote certain sectors of the economy. Some in this debate portrayed American producers as competing on an uneven playing field in facing government-supported Japanese firms, while others countered that American producers were careless about quality and slow to modernize. They also contended that MITI's influence was exaggerated and that Japanese firms were successful because they were fiercely competitive at home and provided quality products at reasonable prices. For example, administrative guidance and industrial policy did not seem to account for the success of Japan's automobile and consumer electronics industries, since neither was singled out for government assistance.[75]

The large bilateral trade imbalance symbolized the trade "problem" with Japan. From the US perspective, the issue was simple: Japan exported too much and imported too little. Under US pressure, Japan was sometimes willing to restrict its exports, so the question turned to getting it to import more. Unlike almost every other advanced economy, Japan's imports of manufactured goods were strikingly small and failed to increase much in the 1960s and 1970s. In 1985, imports of manufactured goods as a share of manufacturing GDP was 32 percent in the United States but just 9 percent in Japan.[76] Of course, this did not prove that Japan's market was closed to foreign goods. Japan's distinctive factor endowments may have been largely responsible: Japan lacked domestic supplies of food, fuel, and raw materials, so its imports of primary goods squeezed out imports of manufactured goods.[77] Furthermore, Japan did not have many formal trade barriers: its tariff levels were comparable to those of the United States, and most import quotas had been abolished by the early 1980s.

And yet, as US Trade Representative William Brock acknowledged in 1983, "The perception, and indeed the reality, has been that the American market place has been much more open to Japanese goods than has the Japanese market to American ones."[78] Foreign businesses confronted a host of non-tariff barriers in selling to Japan, including arcane product standards and testing-certification requirements that affected imports of pharmaceuticals and agricultural products, as well as product-safety requirements that deterred imports of electrical goods, motor vehicles, and sporting equipment. There were frequent complaints about burdensome customs procedures, insufficient intellectual property protection, discriminatory government procurement practices, targeted administrative guidance, and collusive business practices, among other informal means of keeping foreign goods out of the market. Japan's vertically integrated market structure, dominated by large, bank-centered industrial groups (keiretsu), as well as the country's complex retail distribution system, created additional hurdles for foreign firms. As a result, foreign participation in Japan's economy remained very low.

To address the complaints about market access in Japan, the Reagan administration initiated the Market-Oriented Sector-Selective (MOSS) negotiations in 1985. The MOSS talks focused on four sectors—telecommunications, electronics, forestry products, and medical equipment and pharmaceuticals—and concentrated on testing and certification requirements, government procurement rules, and other regulations and private practices that created obstacles to foreign producers in Japan.[79] While Japan resisted any changes, arguing that foreign firms needed to improve the quality of their goods and redouble their efforts to sell in the market, it also made concessions in opening its market. And yet questions remained about whether these concessions had any real effect in promoting trade. Exporters were frustrated by the fact that their sales did not always increase when Japan's trade barriers were reformed or removed. Indeed, subsequent analysis suggested the negotiations were a limited success. Only a small minority of the sectoral agreements—six out of twenty-seven—had a positive impact on trade, and even this was sometimes the result of diverting trade away from other partners rather than trade creation.[80]

The limited impact that such bilateral trade negotiations had on US exports led some to argue that the United States needed to adopt a "results-oriented" trade policy. The focus should not be on reducing trade barriers in principle, it was said, but on achieving a measurable increase in foreign sales. The Reagan administration had sharp internal debates about whether this was the right approach to take with Japan. On one side were the hard-liners (the black hats) of the Commerce Department and USTR, who wanted tough negotiations under the threat of retaliation to produce demonstrable results in terms of higher exports. On the other side were the soft-liners (white hats) of the Justice Department, the Office of Management and Budget, and the Council of Economic Advisers, who feared that results-oriented trade deals with fixed market shares would result in the cartelization of markets. The former group was accused of "Japan-bashing," while the latter group was accused of being "soft" on foreign competitors.[81]

The failure of agreements with Japan to put a significant dent in its large trade surplus should not have been unexpected: opening up particular markets on a piecemeal basis might help some exporters sell more in Japan, but the bilateral trade deficit did not exist because Japan imported "too little" in protected sectors. Rather, it existed because Japan was experiencing large capital outflows, a matter entirely outside the scope of trade negotiations.

THE 1985 TRADE-POLICY SHIFT

After President Reagan won reelection in 1984, key personnel changes dramatically transformed the administration's approach to trade policy. In particular, White House Chief of Staff James Baker and Treasury Secretary Donald Regan switched jobs. At Treasury, Regan had maintained a policy of benign neglect with respect to the dollar, regarding its strength as a vote of confidence for the administration's policies. But Baker, much like fellow Texan John Connally, Treasury secretary in the early 1970s, was concerned that the strong dollar was causing protectionist pressures to build in Congress. When he took over as Treasury secretary, Baker (2006, 427) recalled, "We confronted an overvalued dollar, measured against other currencies, and a trade imbalance that favored the Japanese, Germans, and other trading partners at the expense of US manufacturers and exporters. These two economic problems, in turn, had created a big political problem—a protectionist fever in Congress that grew hotter each time Honda or Mercedes won another customer from the Big Three or another pop economist wrote about the inevitable triumph of Japan, Inc." Like Connally before him, Baker sought to relieve the pressures by helping to engineer a decline in the value of the dollar against other currencies.[82]

After convincing the president and Federal Reserve Board Chairman Paul Volcker of the need to adopt a new exchange-rate policy, Baker sought international agreement to bring about an orderly decline in the value of the dollar.[83] Other countries resisted the call to strengthen their currencies, just as they had in 1971, but as Baker (2006, 429–30) noted, "Our leverage with them was that if we didn't act first, the protectionists in Congress would throw up trade barriers. Auto makers and other industries were pounding the desks at the White House, Treasury, and Congress, demanding that something be done to save them from foreign competition, and Congress was listening. By late summer [1985], top foreign economic officials had begun to see that we were serious."

The result was the Plaza Accord, named for the famous New York hotel where the September 1985 meeting was held. At the meeting, Japanese and European officials agreed to undertake measures that would lift the value of their currencies against the dollar, including coordinated central bank intervention in foreign exchange markets.[84] Although the dollar had actually begun to depreciate in February 1985, it continued to fall against other major currencies over the next four years. Because exchange-rate changes have a lagged effect on trade flows, however, the trade deficit continued to grow for another two years before finally receding.

In addition to taking action on the dollar, Baker and US Trade Representative Clayton Yeutter came up with a new trade agenda to defuse protectionist pressure in Congress. The administration began taking a more aggressive stance against foreign unfair trade practices and attempted to revive bilateral and multilateral negotiations to reduce trade barriers. The package was designed to impress Capitol Hill, serve as a warning to key trading partners, and shift the debate from closing the US market to opening foreign markets.

On September 23, 1985, the day after the Plaza Accord was announced, President Reagan unveiled this new strategy. The president portrayed the United States as the victim of other countries' trade policies and spoke of the responsibilities that they had in maintaining an open trading system. As he put it,

> to make the international trading system work, all must abide by the rules. All must work to guarantee open markets. Above all else, free trade is, by definition, fair trade. When domestic markets are closed to the exports of others, it is no longer free trade. When governments subsidize their manufacturers and farmers so that they can dump goods in other markets, it is no longer free trade. When governments permit counterfeiting or copying of American products, it is stealing our future, and it is no longer free trade. When governments assist their exporters in ways that violate international laws, then the playing field is no longer level, and there is no longer free trade. When governments subsidize industries for commercial advantage and underwrite costs, placing an unfair burden on competitors, that is not free trade.

Therefore, the president continued,

> we will take all the action that is necessary to pursue our rights and interests in international commerce under our laws and the GATT to see that other nations live up to their obligations and their trade agreements with us. I believe that if trade is not fair for all, then trade is free in name only. I will not stand by and watch American businesses fail because of unfair trading practices abroad. I will not stand by and watch American workers lose their jobs because other nations do not play by the rules.[85]

The new strategy involved a more aggressive use of section 301 of the Trade Act of 1974, until now a relatively neglected part of US trade law.

Under section 301, USTR had the authority to investigate and respond to any foreign government acts, policies, or practices that were "unreasonable, unjustifiable, or discriminatory" and "burden or restrict US commerce."[86] Such an investigation usually started with a firm or industry association filing a petition with USTR, which had complete discretion to accept or reject the case. In any such investigation, USTR sought to resolve the problem by consulting with the foreign government whose policies were under scrutiny. If the consultations did not resolve the matter, a range of remedial enforcement actions could be taken, most importantly retaliation in the form of higher tariffs against the country's exports.

Reagan announced that USTR would initiate several section 301 cases involving South Korea's restrictions on foreign insurance firms, Brazil's obstruction of trade in informatics (computer hardware and software), and Japan's barriers on the sale of foreign tobacco products. The president set a short deadline for resolving existing cases on Japan's market for leather and non-leather footwear and the EEC's subsidies for canned fruit before moving to retaliation. USTR also began to look into whether Japan's telecom procurement policies excluded foreign producers from the market.

A high-profile case involving Japanese semiconductors exemplified this new strategy of more aggressively defending US producer interests and attacking foreign trade barriers.[87] US domination of semiconductor production was threatened, as were other industries, by Japan's rapid penetration of global markets in the 1980s. In 1978, American firms accounted for 55 percent of worldwide industry revenues, and Japanese firms accounted for 28 percent; by 1986, Japan's share had risen to 46 percent, while the US share had fallen to 40 percent. The relative decline of the semiconductor industry seemed to symbolize the country's loss of technological leadership and was partly due, it was commonly thought, to industrial targeting by the Japanese government.

In June 1985, the Semiconductor Industry Association (SIA) filed a section 301 petition alleging that Japan's semiconductor market was closed to foreign producers due to structural barriers in Japan. These structural barriers—including anticompetitive business practices among its firms condoned by the government and supported by official regulations—denied "fair and equitable market opportunities" to American firms in Japan's market and therefore were deemed "unreasonable" under the meaning of section 301.

The semiconductor case was complex, because it also involved a dumping case. Although the US economy was in a strong recovery, the semiconductor industry suffered a severe cyclical slump in 1984–85 due to a slowdown in computer production. The plummeting price of semiconductors led to large losses for all producers in the industry. However, while American firms were pushed to the brink of bankruptcy and reduced output sharply, Japanese firms continued to produce because they had ongoing access to credit due to their close ties to large banks. Japanese competition forced almost every American producer of one particular device, dynamic random-access memories (DRAMs), out of the market. In general, the SIA did not want the Commerce Department to impose antidumping duties: they did not want to create obstacles to the shipment of various devices across borders, because the production of semiconductors was worldwide; even the electronic workers' union feared the off-shoring of semiconductor production if import barriers were increased. Furthermore, the industry's problem was not dumping in the United States in particular but the worldwide depression of prices in general. Antidumping duties would not solve that problem, but instead make the country a "high price island" to the detriment of semiconductor-using industries such as computer manufacturers and telecommunications equipment producers. At the same time, given the size of the US market, denying Japanese firms access to American consumers would be a way of forcing Japan to resolve the issue.

Despite the SIA's opposition to tariffs, one small DRAM producer (Micron Technology) filed an antidumping complaint against four Japanese exporters of 64K DRAMs. Micron contended that the home market sales of the Japanese producers were below their costs of production. This opened a floodgate. Micron's June 1985 petition was followed in September by an antidumping petition from three major semiconductor producers (Intel, Advanced Micro Devices, and National Semiconductor) concerning another device, Erasable Programmable Read-Only Memories (EPROMs). The Commerce Department then, for the first time, initiated its own dumping case against Japan on 256K and future generations of DRAMs.[88]

The fact that the US government initiated a dumping case and gave strong backing to the section 301 case put Japan under enormous pressure to resolve the conflict. If it did not find a way to end the dispute before the statutory deadlines facing USTR and the ITC, Japan would face antidumping duties on its semiconductor exports and retaliatory tariffs on its other exports. As a result, in July 1986, the United States and Japan reached a five-year agreement to end dumping and open up Japan's market, allowing the dumping and section 301 cases to be suspended. Japan's government agreed to enforce export price floors (adjusted quarterly) on semiconductors sold in world markets and to encourage its businesses to purchase foreign semiconductors. In a secret side letter to the agreement,

Japan accepted that the foreign share of its semiconductor market should increase to 20 percent from the existing level of about 8 percent.[89]

The market share target, which was generally acknowledged to exist, was controversial in both countries. In the United States, proponents argued that it provided "affirmative action" for foreign producers in a market that was difficult to penetrate. The 20 percent target was held up as an example of a "results-oriented" approach that some thought should be employed more generally, since previous efforts to open up Japan's market had proven disappointing. But critics argued that the target constituted "managed trade," in which the commercial outcome was determined by government deals without regard to market competition and productive efficiency. In Japan, businesses resented their government's meddling with the prices they could charge and the sources from which they could buy. They feared that if this was done in the case of semiconductors, other industries would be next. The agreement sparked a nationalist backlash among some in Japan who urged the government to say "no" to foreign demands.

In fact, Japan's government had difficulty in getting local firms to comply with the terms of the agreement. Government officials could not easily prevent "dumping" in third markets or persuade Japan's industrial buyers to increase their purchases of foreign semiconductors. The SIA soon complained that Japan was failing to live up to both the dumping and the market-access provisions of the agreement. With trade pressures at a peak in Congress, the Reagan administration could not back down and risk another "failed" trade agreement with Japan.

In January 1987, just six months after the semiconductor agreement was signed, USTR gave Japan sixty days to demonstrate that it was enforcing the agreement. The administration wanted concrete signs that third-market dumping had ceased and foreign sales of semiconductors in Japan were increasing. In April, the United States stunned Japan by declaring it in non-compliance with the agreement and retaliated by imposing 100 percent tariffs on $300 million of computers, televisions, and power tools imported from the country. This unilateral action, one of the largest retaliations of the postwar period and the first such action against Japan, dramatized the seriousness with which the administration viewed the semiconductor agreement and the trade problem with Japan. The retaliatory tariffs were partially lifted later in the year after Commerce determined that dumping had ceased. (Semiconductor production migrated to Taiwan and South Korea to avoid the antidumping measures, but those countries were also later charged with dumping.) The remainder were eliminated in 1991 when the foreign share of Japan's semiconductor market reached 20 percent.

The United States began taking a hard-line stance against the EEC as well. In 1985, higher duties were imposed on imports of European pasta in retaliation for the EEC's restrictions on imports of citrus products. In 1986, Spain and Portugal joined the EEC and had to adopt its common external tariff. Although their tariffs on manufactured goods would fall, Spain and Portugal now had to restrict imports of agricultural goods as part of the Common Agricultural Policy. With American exports of feed grains to those countries expected to drop by $1 billion, USTR threatened the EEC with retaliation unless compensation was given for the lost sales. In December 1986, after Europe failed to act, the Reagan administration announced that it would impose 200 percent duties on $400 million worth of European exports to the United States. A month later, the two sides reached an agreement whereby the EEC would guarantee that Spain would import a certain amount of American corn and sorghum for the next four years and reduce its duties on other goods.[90]

The Reagan administration took other trade actions in 1986 to head off protectionist trade legislation on Capitol Hill. Section 232 of the Trade Expansion Act of 1962, which gave the president the authority to restrict imports on grounds of national security, was invoked to persuade Japan, West Germany, Taiwan, and Switzerland to reduce their exports of machine tools to the United States. The administration imposed a 35 percent countervailing duty on red cedar shakes and shingles from Canada. USTR also continued to press the EEC over its ban on beef that had been treated with growth hormones and Brazil over its restrictions on information technology products and pharmaceuticals, and pursued other cases as well.

Between the Plaza Accord and the new section 301 policy, September 1985 marked a dramatic shift in US trade policy. Did these policies work? With time, the depreciation of the dollar helped reduce the trade deficit and relieve protectionist pressures. And section 301, Bayard and Elliott (1994, 64) conclude, "appears to have been a reasonably effective tool" in opening up foreign markets. At least initially, however, these actions did little to reduce the trade pressures coming from Congress. The trade deficit continued to grow in 1986 and 1987, and Congress continued to demand that the administration address the trade situation, including providing more relief for domestic industries competing against imports. As Rep. John Dingell (D-MI) complained, "While our trading partners have relentlessly pursued their economic self-interest in determining import and export policies, this country has been hamstrung by a free-trade ideology that ignores the reality of the world trading system."[91] Treasury Secretary Baker conceded in 1987 that the administration had been "a little late" in addressing the trade deficit, but insisted that "for the last several years, no administration has worked harder than we have against subsidized imports and trade barriers abroad." Responding to critics who complained that the administration was too wedded to a free-trade philosophy, Baker replied that the president had "granted more import relief to United States industry than any of his predecessors in more than half a century."[92]

Meanwhile, Democrats in Congress continued to work on trade legislation. In May 1986, the House passed a bill that included the controversial Gephardt provision that would require countries with "excessive and unwarranted" trade surpluses with the United States (Japan, Germany, and Taiwan) be given six months to change their policies and start reducing their surpluses by 10 percent annually. If they did not comply, the president would have no option but to retaliate against them. The bill also expanded the avenues for firms and workers to obtain relief from foreign competition; for example, import relief under the escape clause would be allowed if imports were an "important" cause of injury rather than a "significant" cause. The House passed the bill by a 295–115 vote, with Democrats voting 236–4 in favor and Republicans voting against 111–59. Although Democrats took the harder line, many Republicans also voted for the bill. "Republicans are displaying the same kind of protectionist urges that Democrats are showing because their constituents are showing it," William Frenzel (R-MN), a leading free trade advocate in Congress, admitted. "They are reflecting what their constituents feel."[93]

But the president was unpersuaded. "This anti-trade bill isn't protectionism, it's destructionism," Reagan responded. The president said that the legislation was not an "omnibus trade bill" but an "ominous anti-trade bill," adding that "this bill is so potentially destructive that even many of those who voted for it did so in the expectation that it would be vetoed. . . . Well, if it comes to that, I assure them they'll get their wish."[94] Speaker O'Neill countered, "We don't believe we are protectionists. We believe we are patsies for the rest of the world, and we want to be fair-traders."[95]

The Republican Senate adjourned before acting on the bill, but the Democrats captured the Senate in the November 1986 midterm election. This gave the Democrats unified control of Congress and paved the way for the passage of a trade bill that would reach the president's desk. In January 1987, the new House Speaker Jim Wright (D-TX) declared that "the first imperative in the 100th Congress will be to come to grips with the steady decline in American competitiveness and the corollary increase in the trade deficit."[96] Recognizing that a new trade bill could have some desirable features, such as trade-negotiating authority, administration officials began working more closely with Congress in order to strip out objectionable provisions, such as the "procedural protectionism" that limited executive discretion in trade cases, and make the bill acceptable to the White House. In early 1987, the new House passed a bill similar to the previous one. On the House floor, Gephardt introduced a watered-down version of his provision requiring that countries running large trade surpluses with the United States be threatened with retaliation. The Gephardt amendment narrowly passed by a vote of 218–214, which, in view of the administration's opposition to it, ensured that it would not survive in a conference committee. The Senate soon passed its own trade bill by 71–27, but the October 1987 stock market crash prevented the completion of the reconciliation process before Congress adjourned.

The bill's prolonged path through Congress was finally completed in 1988, but not until after more last-minute wrangling. In April 1988, the conference committee dropped the Gephardt amendment, and both chambers passed the bill, but the president vetoed it because of a plant-closing provision. Congress passed the bill again without the provision, and finally, after three years of work, the Omnibus Trade and Competitiveness Act of 1988 was completed in a form that the president could approve.[97]

At more than a thousand pages, the wide-ranging legislation made many incremental changes to the nation's trade laws. It reduced presidential discretion and expanded avenues for firms and workers to receive relief from imports in administrative trade cases. More importantly, the president was granted new negotiating authority, which allowed the executive to reduce tariffs by up to 50 percent in trade agreements reached within five years. The authority also ensured that Congress would give "fast-track" consideration to any agreements that required changes in domestic legislation, meaning that it would have sixty days to approve or disapprove of an agreement without amendment, after the president submitted it to Congress. These provisions were needed to conclude the Uruguay Round of trade negotiations that had been launched in 1986 and will be discussed in chapter 13.

The bill also included a controversial "Super 301" provision. Under Super 301, USTR was required to identify priority countries in 1989 and 1990 and negotiate the elimination of barriers to key US exports within a fixed time period. Another "Special 301" provision called on USTR to examine the failure of other countries to respect intellectual property rights, particularly as it affected the high-technology (software and semiconductors), entertainment (movies and music recordings), and pharmaceutical industries.

The Omnibus Trade and Competitiveness Act of 1988 capped a long struggle to formulate a trade bill that would be acceptable to the Reagan administration. To avoid a presidential veto, the legislation did not come with special protection for any specific industries. However, the textile and apparel industry was still unsatisfied with the MFA. In September 1987, the House passed a bill to impose import quotas on 185 categories of textiles and apparel and 15 categories of non-rubber footwear, but the vote fell short of the two-thirds majority needed to override a veto. The Senate did not pass the bill until September 1988. As expected, Reagan vetoed it— the second textile quota bill that had been sent to him.

By this time, however, the enormous political pressures over trade that had marked the early- and mid-1980s had eased considerably. By 1987, the dollar had fallen back to its 1980 level, and exports were finally accelerating, as figure 12.1 showed. The growth in exports and moderation of imports, combined with the long economic expansion that brought down the unemployment rate, relieved much of the pressure on traded-goods industries. As a result, pressures in Congress to address trade problems also began to dissipate.

THE MULTILATERAL SYSTEM IN DISARRAY

So far, this chapter has said little about the multilateral trading system. In fact, the value of the GATT was severely questioned during the trade-policy turmoil of the early 1980s. Previous multilateral trade agreements, such as the Kennedy Round in the 1960s and the Tokyo Round in the 1970s, had cut and bound tariffs on manufactured goods at low levels for developed countries. While tariffs remained in check, the GATT failed to stem the spread of non-tariff barriers to trade around the world. This left trade-policy observers concerned that the postwar system of open and non-discriminatory trade was being eroded and could even fall apart.

The trade barriers that had proliferated since the 1970s included variable import levies (in the case of European agricultural imports), anti-dumping and countervailing duties, voluntary export restraints, orderly market arrangements, and other forms of managed trade. Between 1966 and 1986, the share of imports covered by non-tariff barriers rose from 36 percent to 45 percent in the United States, from 25 percent to 54 percent in the EEC, and from 31 percent to 43 percent in Japan.[98] The increase was particularly large in the case of the EEC due to the expansion of the

Common Agricultural Policy, but non-tariff barriers were applied to an increasing share of manufactured goods as well. The spread of voluntary export restraints was particularly striking. In 1989, the GATT reported that 236 export-restraint agreements were in effect, 67 involving exports to the United States and 127 involving exports to the EEC. Most of these originated in the 1980s and operated outside GATT rules or disciplines.[99]

Considered either as an institution or as a set of rules, the GATT failed to contain the ever-changing forms of protectionism that spread during this period. This raised the question of whether the GATT should be taken seriously if its rules were so widely ignored and its provisions so easily circumvented. In a 1978 article "The Crumbling Institutions of the Liberal Trade System," University of Michigan law professor John Jackson argued that "almost every rule of GATT is inadequate to the present problems of world trade," sometimes because of evasion but often due to lack of enforcement. Trade rules were violated because there was no effective dispute-settlement mechanism to hold countries accountable if they restricted trade. "The tragedy is that a defective rule system tends to punish those who abide and reward the transgressors," which only encourages "further erosion of rules." All of this contributed to the deterioration in the world trading system.[100] "The real danger to the GATT is not that a trade war will break out, but that the major signatories to the GATT will simply pretend that the General Agreement is not there," Arthur Dunkel, the director-general of the GATT, remarked in 1982. He believed that "this would effectively end the GATT" and the rules-based system of trade. The only thing holding the system together, he argued, was a "sort of a balance of terror" in which countries feared imposing too many protectionist measures only because they might bring retaliation.[101]

After the conclusion of the Tokyo Round in 1979, officials at USTR began planning for the next round of multilateral trade negotiations. The agenda consisted of old issues (agriculture and safeguards) and new ones (services and high-technology products). The United States started pressuring other countries to endorse the agenda and start negotiations, but the moment was inauspicious because of the world economic slump. A GATT ministerial meeting in November 1982, in which the United States pushed to launch a new trade round, collapsed amid acrimony and dissension. As Richardson (1994, 641) put it, "The European Community was especially resistant to agricultural liberalization, India and other developing countries were dead set against services liberalization, and all accused the United States of ramming its agenda onto the table without adequate documentation, interpretation, persuasion, or quid pro quo." At the same time, participants worried about mounting protectionism. The ministerial declaration warned that the multilateral trading system "is seriously endangered" because protectionist pressures had multiplied, and governments were disregarding GATT rules. The ministers called for a "standstill and rollback" on trade barriers—an immediate halt to the introduction of new trade barriers and the start of their removal—but these words went largely unheeded.[102] American officials left Geneva disheartened that other countries had rejected opening new trade negotiations. Frustrated with the GATT process, they began to consider seriously, for the first time in the postwar period, alternatives to the multilateral approach to reducing trade barriers.[103]

Although it only became apparent with hindsight, the outcome of the 1982 GATT ministerial meeting played an important role in persuading US trade officials to consider alternative methods of reducing trade barriers. If GATT participants were not willing to strengthen the enforcement of existing rules and patch holes in the legal framework, the United States was prepared to bypass the multilateral process by undertaking unilateral actions to enforce trade rules and address foreign trade barriers, as well as starting bilateral and regional discussions to open trade further. In 1985, President Reagan again called for the start of a new multilateral trade round, but warned that "if these negotiations are not initiated or if insignificant progress is made, I'm instructing our trade negotiators to explore regional and bilateral agreements with other nations."[104] In fact, disenchantment with the GATT was one reason that Trade Representative William Brock argued that the Trade and Tariff Act of 1984 should include authority to reach a bilateral trade agreement with Israel. Concluded the next year, the trade agreement phased out all tariffs on bilateral trade over ten years. Because Israel was a popular ally, the agreement encountered no opposition in Congress.[105]

While the agreement with Israel was more of a foreign-policy gesture and hardly signaled a major change in trade policy, the possibility of a free-trade agreement with Canada soon appeared. Canada had long been concerned about maintaining its access to the US market, particularly in light of trade actions that had damaged its economy: Canadian exports had not been exempt from the 10 percent import surcharge in 1971, and its other exports were routinely harassed with antidumping and countervailing duties, which caused protracted problems for the bilateral relationship in the 1980s. Canadian producers often found themselves at the mercy of the Commerce Department and the ITC where an unfavorable ruling could disrupt their exports for an extended period. Canadian officials also feared that business investment suffered because its access to the US market could not be guaranteed.

At the same time, Canada had long worried about being dominated by its giant neighbor and losing its sovereignty and unique culture. These domestic sensitivities left Canadian officials quite ambivalent about whether to seek a closer economic relationship with the United States. Of course, while the United States could announce its willingness to explore a bilateral trade agreement, the initiative had to come from Canada; any such proposal from the United States would have aroused fears among Canadian nationalists that it was plotting to take the country's resources and control its economy.[106]

A 1985 report by a Royal Commission on Canada's economic future served as the catalyst for moving forward. Like the United States, Canada had growing concerns about its productivity performance and the competitive position of its exports in world markets. The report urged Canadian officials to embrace policies that would lead to a more flexible and dynamic economy, less sheltered from foreign competition and fragmented across provinces. To this end, the report urged a "leap of faith" with the negotiation of a free-trade agreement with the United States. Such an agreement would not only expose the Canadian economy to greater competition, thereby forcing producers to improve their efficiency, but also lock in Canada's access to the US market and leave the country much less vulnerable to unpredictable changes in American policy. In October 1985, after much debate within the government, Conservative Prime Minister Brian Mulroney, who earlier in his career had opposed the idea of free trade with the United States, wrote to President Reagan and requested the negotiation of a free-trade agreement.

The economic stakes in such an agreement were much higher for Canada than for the United States. In 1985, nearly three-quarters of Canadian exports (about 20 percent of its GDP) were destined for the United States, whereas 20 percent of US exports (1 percent of its GDP) was sent to Canada. On average, Canadian tariffs were higher on American products (about 9 percent) than US tariffs were on Canadian products (about 4 percent). About 80 percent of Canada's exports to the United States and 65 percent of US exports to Canada were already duty-free due to a special 1965 agreement that eliminated tariffs on bilateral trade in automobiles and auto parts. Yet the United States had something to gain beyond lower tariffs: Canada maintained many restrictions on foreign investment (particularly in financial services, energy, and natural resources) and subsidized many producers (the source of complaints from American firms).

Not surprisingly, given the imbalance in economic size between the two countries, Canada took the negotiations far more seriously than the United States.[107] Neither the Congress nor the Reagan administration seemed to realize that the Canadian government had taken a huge political step in proposing a deal. Negotiations began in early 1986 and did not start well.[108] Canadian negotiators were constantly frustrated at the lack of high-level attention given to the negotiations by the Americans. The lead USTR negotiator, Peter Murphy, was not in a position to provide leadership; he was a staff-level official who lacked the political authority to conclude a deal.[109]

The two countries also had different conceptions of the agreement. The United States wanted a simple accord to eliminate tariffs, reduce Canadian subsidies, and open up the country to foreign investment. Canada sought a broader agreement that would rein in the use of trade remedies, which routinely harassed Canadian exporters. It proposed harmonizing antidumping and countervailing duty rules, which USTR ruled out as something Congress would never agree to do.

Unable to get any change in US trade laws, Canadian negotiators proposed creating a binding, impartial system to settle disputes over the implementation of those laws. By mid-September 1987, Canadian officials were frustrated by the failure of American negotiators to take the idea seriously. (Two influential Senators, Lloyd Bentsen and John Danforth, said that it was out of the question.) Believing that no agreement was better than a bad or limited agreement, the Canadians were prepared to declare the negotiations a failure. The deadline for concluding the talks was coming up rapidly: Congress had to be notified by midnight October 3, 1987, for the agreement to be eligible for "fast-track" consideration. In late September, Canadian negotiators said the talks were on the brink of failure and that dispute settlement was a make-or-break issue, all of which came as a surprise to higher-level Reagan administration officials.

Alerted to an imminent breakdown, Treasury Secretary James Baker took over the negotiations and eventually saved the deal. Sam Gibbons (D-FL), the chair of the trade subcommittee of the Ways and Means Committee, called Canadian ambassador Allan Gotlieb and suggested that, since joint rules on antidumping and countervailing duties were unacceptable to Congress, a tribunal be set up to review the application of the existing trade laws of each country in the case of a dispute.[110] Although Canadians were worried that the United States could later simply strengthen its antidumping and countervailing duty laws, the idea of an impartial tribunal was a concession. The Canadians encouraged Senator

Bill Bradley (D-NJ) and a few other strong congressional supporters of an agreement to call Baker and show their support for this idea. Despite the opposition of USTR, and after his initial skepticism, Baker came around to the proposal. He began building support in Congress for an independent review system, while extracting further concessions from the Canadians on banking services and cross-border investment.[111]

After receiving assurances that a deal was looking good, the Canadians returned to the bargaining table but found that nothing had changed. On the night that Congress had to be notified that an agreement had been reached, the Canadians were prepared to declare the negotiation a failure. Around 9:00 p.m., Baker burst into the negotiating room, flung down a piece of paper, and exclaimed, "All right you can have your goddamn dispute settlement mechanism."[112] Ten minutes before midnight, the agreement was finalized and a messenger dispatched to Capitol Hill, where the president's notice was delivered one minute before the deadline. As Ambassador Gotlieb (2006, 493) later stated: "If it were not for Baker, there would be no agreement."

President Reagan and Prime Minister Mulroney signed the accord in January 1988, but it was not formally submitted to Congress until July 1988 after extensive hearings. (The administration had been negligent in not consulting very much with members of Congress about the negotiations, a mistake that would not be repeated with the North American Free Trade Agreement.) In a bipartisan vote that summer, Congress overwhelmingly approved the agreement, the House by 366–40 and the Senate by 83–9.[113] By contrast, Canada had an intense public debate over the issue, and the 1988 election hinged on the issue. The Conservatives won the election, the House of Commons approved the agreement, and it took effect in January 1989.

The US-Canada free trade agreement was a historic achievement that cemented economic ties and reduced trade friction between the neighboring countries. The 250-page text had twenty-one chapters and annexes, and included a ten-year phase-out of all tariffs on bilateral trade, an agreement on trade in services, a cautious opening of investment and financial services, an impartial panel to settle disputes over trade remedies, special protection for Canadian culture that restricted foreign investment in media and film, and various other provisions. However, because bilateral trade was already fairly free, the agreement had a limited impact on the overall US economy.

Although this was a major step in the direction of bilateral trade agreements, the United States did not give up on the multilateral system. In

1986, it managed to lead other countries in the GATT to start the Uruguay Round of trade negotiations. These negotiations were concluded in 1993 and are discussed in chapter 13.

THE PROTECTIONIST TIDE RECEDES

The continued depreciation of the dollar against other currencies after the Plaza Accord in September 1985 eventually succeeded in providing relief for industries competing against imports and exporters selling on the world market. From its February 1985 peak to the April 1988 trough, the real trade-weighted value of the dollar fell nearly 30 percent. As a result, export growth picked up, and import growth moderated. In fact, export-related industries accounted for half of the increase in manufacturing employment in 1987–88 before the economy slowed in 1989.[114] The merchandise trade deficit peaked at $159 billion in 1987 and then fell over the next three years. With continued economic growth, these developments greatly eased protectionist pressures. As figure 12.5 showed, the number of antidumping petitions filed by domestic firms fell sharply after 1987. Of course, many of the recently imposed import restrictions remained in place: nearly a third of Japan's exports to the United States were still restricted in some way.

This environment gave the new administration of President George H. W. Bush, and his trade representative Carla Hills, the opportunity to roll back some of the protectionist measures that had accumulated during the 1980s. The three big protected sectors were automobiles, steel, and textiles and apparel, and the special protection given to each soon came to an end. First, Japan's voluntary export restraint in automobiles faded away. Japan had repeatedly renewed the VER after 1981, but eventually it was no longer binding because major Japanese auto producers established production facilities in the United States that replaced exports from Japan. By 1991, Japanese firms accounted for 15 percent of domestic production of cars and light trucks. As a result, the VER was no longer needed: the export limit was 2.3 million vehicles that year, but the country shipped only 1.73 million from Japan. In 1992, Japan reduced the export cap to 1.65 million vehicles, but over the next year Japan exported only 1.4 million vehicles, well under the limit.

In early 1994, Japan announced that it would no longer enforce the export restraint. Union officials and automobile executives in the United States grumbled about the decision, but they were not in a strong position to demand that it be continued. The automobile industry had recovered from the dark days of the early 1980s in terms of profitability and production, if not employment. Furthermore, Japanese firms had done what both the industry and union had asked: namely, to "make cars where they sell them." And having taken investment stakes in some Japanese producers, the Big Three were now among the leading importers of cars from Japan.

The steel industry posed a more difficult challenge. The comprehensive VRAs won by the steel industry in 1984 were set to expire in 1989, shortly after the 1988 presidential election. Like the automobile industry, the steel industry was in much better shape than it had been a few years earlier: capacity utilization had increased considerably, financial losses had turned into profits, and imports had receded as the weaker dollar helped bolster the competitive position of the industry. In addition, the large steel firms had gradually rationalized production by shutting down inefficient plants and modernizing production facilities to increase productivity and reduce labor costs.

However, in running for president in the 1988 election, Vice President George H. W. Bush responded to weak poll numbers in Ohio and Pennsylvania by pledging to renew the import restraints, although he did not make any specific promises. The prospect of renewing the VRAs sparked a fierce debate that now included opposition from steel-consuming firms, such as the heavy earth-moving equipment producer Caterpillar and other major steel consumers. They complained that steel protection raised their production costs and harmed their competitive position against foreign rivals. Noting that they employed many more workers than the steel industry itself, the steel users argued that these jobs were jeopardized by steel shortages and higher prices caused by import restrictions.

This put the integrated steel producers in the unusual position of defending the VRAs, at a time when they were earning large profits, against the opposition of another major group of manufacturers. With the steel industry demanding a five-year extension of the VRAs, and steel users insisting that they be abolished, the Congressional steel caucus had to mediate between the two groups. Congress itself was divided. (Sam Gibbons quipped that the 1989 congressional reauthorization of the administration's authority to conclude agreements limiting steel imports was "the only bill I ever introduced that nobody liked and everybody agreed to vote for.")[115] The Bush administration proposed a compromise that would extend the import restraints for a transition period of two and a half years, after which they would be eliminated. To help steel consumers during this period, the VRAs would be relaxed if steel was in short supply. The administration also argued that the ongoing GATT negotiations, rather than export restraints, were the proper way to deal with global excess capacity and trade-distorting practices in the steel market.

The integrated steel producers and the United Steel Workers were disappointed with this decision. Both had benefited from import restraints since 1967, and losing the VRAs reflected the industry's diminished political clout. When the VRAs expired in early 1992, the steel industry immediately swamped the Commerce Department and ITC with more than eighty antidumping and countervailing duty petitions. Although Commerce found dumping and subsidy margins as high as 109 percent, the ITC made an affirmative injury determination in only thirty-two cases; most were dismissed because imports were often selling at higher prices than domestic steel. The rejection of these cases was another blow to the industry's hopes for continued protection.

The textile and apparel industry also saw its special protection taken away. By 1991, the MFA's export quotas involved 41 countries and covered 69 percent of textile and 88 percent of apparel imports.[116] However, as we have seen, the MFA was a sieve rather than a wall in keeping out imports, and domestic producers constantly fought to get the restrictions tightened. Hoping that the Bush administration would be more sympathetic than its predecessor, the industry made yet another attempt to get comprehensive trade protection from Congress. In April 1990, the Congressional Textile Caucus introduced the third major textile and apparel bill in five years. Like the 1988 legislation, the bill would set an overall cap on imports by product (rather than by country) and limited their growth to one percent per year. To defuse opposition to the bill from Midwestern farm states, which had previously opposed such legislation out of fear that foreign countries would retaliate against its agricultural exports, the bill included a provision that would allow a country's textile quota to increase if it increased its imports of US agricultural goods. The bill also included a provision to freeze imports of non-rubber footwear at their 1989 level in order to win extra votes from members of Congress with shoe producers in their districts. Despite these efforts to broaden the bill's appeal, the textile and apparel industry was still in a weak political position: the American Apparel Manufacturers Association did not support the measure, because many of its members had already moved plants overseas or imported goods from foreign garment makers.

Congress passed the bill without enthusiasm, because President Bush had already announced that he would veto it. The president called it "highly protectionist" legislation that would damage the economy, increase already high costs of clothing to consumers, and violate the rules of the GATT.[117] All of this would occur, the president noted, without eliminating any unfair trade practices or opening any closed markets abroad. This veto cleared the ground for the complete abolition of the MFA in the Uruguay Round, as discussed in chapter 13.

Other trade issues of the 1980s also faded away during the Bush administration. When the 1986 US-Japan semiconductor agreement came up for renewal in 1991, opposition from domestic computer producers (consumers of semiconductors) helped end the antidumping provisions of the agreement. The orderly marketing arrangement for machine tools expired, and other trade restraints lapsed. As a result, the share of imports covered by special protection measures receded from 21.5 percent in 1984 to 10.4 percent in 1990.[118] The trade protection of the 1980s proved to be a temporary and not a permanent part of US policy.

After the intense trade pressures of the 1980s, what explains the relatively easy reversal of protectionism in the early 1990s? The unwinding of import restrictions was largely due to three factors: changed circumstances, economic adjustments, and increased domestic opposition.

The changed circumstances included the economic recovery that began in 1983 and continued through most of the 1980s: the growth in domestic demand revived the manufacturing sector and reduced unemployment. The depreciation of the dollar against other currencies, which helped both import-competing producers in the domestic market and exporters in the world market, was also critical in relieving protectionist pressures and allowing existing measures to disappear.

The economic adjustments included the response of domestic firms to deal with the intensification of competition. Although many of these adjustments were painful, including the closing of less efficient, higher-cost production facilities and the layoff of many workers, the results were lower costs and greater efficiency. Many firms had to change their product mix, usually by upgrading product quality, such as the semiconductor industry's shift from producing commodity memory chips to focusing on specialized devices and sophisticated microprocessors. In addition, many industries became globally diversified with investments in overseas production, which reduced their interest in erecting trade barriers around the US market. Many foreign firms also established production facilities in the United States, which further diminished the value of restricting imports to domestic firms.

Finally, domestic opposition to protectionist measures had strengthened. Firms that purchased imported intermediate goods to produce final goods became much more active in objecting to import restrictions on their inputs. Unlike previous decades, steel purchasers strongly opposed the steel industry's demands for import limits, and the same was true for semiconductors. In the case of apparel, retailers spoke for domestic house-holds in trying to keep the price of clothing low. Consumers of imported goods thus became politically active, not household consumers but busi-ness consumers whose profitability was at stake. This opposition dramati-cally changed the politics of trade policy: instead of just being presented with the view of import-competing producers and their workers, members of Congress and administration officials were now forced to confront and reconcile the conflicting views of different constituencies.

Another trade issue left over from the 1980s was the use of section 301 to attack foreign unfair trade practices. The use of this tool to open up foreign markets also began to fade with time, although initially it did not appear that way. As mentioned earlier, the Omnibus Trade and Competi-tiveness Act of 1988 included a "Super 301" provision in which USTR had to identify trade barriers and policy distortions in "priority countries" and retaliate if the practices were not eliminated within three years. This was Congress's way of pushing the executive to use high-pressure tactics to open foreign markets, particularly in Japan.[119]

Bush administration officials were divided about how much to make demands on allies, such as Japan. In her confirmation hearings, USTR Carla Hills promised to take a tough line in addressing unfair trade prac-tices and gave assurances that new negotiations, unlike those in the past, would get results. (Using the analogy of taking a crowbar to pry open for-eign markets to American goods, Hills became known as "crowbar Carla.") At the same time, administration officials did not want a results-oriented trade policy to degenerate into "managed trade," in which explicit market-share targets would be set, as in the 1986 semiconductor agreement.

In May 1989, USTR named Japan, Brazil, and India as "priority coun-tries" under Super 301. Japan was cited for discriminatory procurement policies with respect to supercomputers and satellites and for technical barriers in forestry products; Brazil was cited for various quantitative im-port restrictions; and India was cited for barriers on trade-related foreign investment and in services trade, particularly insurance. (South Korea and Taiwan offered enough concessions to stay off the priority list, and the EEC also went unnamed.) A year later, Hills announced that the nego-tiations with Japan had successfully opened up the market for American supercomputers and forestry products, which were of interest to Senator Max Baucus, an influential Democrat from Montana.

But then Super 301 faded away. To the frustration of Japan critics,

USTR did not name it as a priority country in 1990. Instead, the Bush administration launched the Structural Impediments Initiative (SII) to address the market-access problems with Japan without the pressure arising from Super 301.[120] In 1990, only India was named as a priority country, but it refused to negotiate with the United States. Recognizing the futility of the situation, the United States did not press the matter by retaliating. After that, Super 301 expired and was not renewed. Bayard and Elliott (1994, 313) concluded that Super 301 was "no more likely to produce results than regular section 301," but was "unnecessarily inflammatory" in provoking confrontations with other countries.

By the early 1990s, concern about foreign unfair trade practices had diminished. Japan became yesterday's problem when it entered a prolonged economic slump; in the face of a stronger yen and a weaker economy, Japanese producers were no longer the competitive threat they had been a decade earlier. Yet the new administration of President Bill Clinton initially sought to reinvigorate the push for a "results-oriented" trade policy.[121] In March 1993 Japan announced that the foreign share of its semiconductor market had reached 20 percent, although it insisted that figure was neither a target nor a promise. The Clinton administration viewed the semiconductor agreement as a potential model for other sectors. Meeting with Japan's prime minister that year, President Clinton called for a "focus on specific sectors and specific structures with a view towards getting results" on market access.[122] The experience with the semiconductor agreement—namely, the difficulty in getting domestic producers to agree to purchase foreign products—made Japanese officials strongly opposed to ever again accepting numerical benchmarks for imports.[123] While the Clinton administration struggled to come up with a framework for the bilateral trade relationship, Japan successfully avoided making any more commitments regarding imports. By 1995, the matter was dropped.

Thus, by the early 1990s, the political and economic environment for trade policy was much calmer than it had been in the early 1970s or the 1980s. The system of open trade had been put under enormous stress during those years, resulting in the proliferation of export-restraint agreements and other forms of trade protectionism. While the pressure to impose new trade barriers had been strong, there was no reversion to the high tariffs seen prior to 1934. Furthermore, the groundwork was laid for further liberalization. As the trade measures of the 1980s began to expire, the United States stood on the brink of a new era of trade expansion.

CHAPTER THIRTEEN

From Globalization to Polarization, 1992–2017

If the 1980s saw the imposition of many temporary import restrictions to protect domestic producers from foreign competition, the 1990s saw the opposite: major initiatives to roll back trade barriers and deepen America's integration into the world economy. These included the conclusion of the North American Free Trade Agreement (NAFTA), the completion of the Uruguay Round, which created the World Trade Organization (WTO), and the establishment of Permanent Normal Trade Relations (PNTR) with China. Along with market-opening reforms in developing countries, these measures led to an enormous increase in world trade. These policy actions, however, generated increasing political controversy and eroded the bipartisan consensus in favor of freer trade. Although several bilateral agreements were concluded in the 2000s, the fight over trade policy had become sharply partisan by this time, and the prospects for further trade agreements diminished. As the country's political and economic polarization increased, US trade policy became more contentious than at any time in the post–World War II period.

THE NORTH AMERICAN FREE TRADE AGREEMENT

If trade friction with Japan was the defining feature of US trade policy in the 1980s, NAFTA was the defining trade-policy battle of the 1990s. The political scars from that battle were still evident in American trade politics more than a quarter of a century later. As we saw in chapter 12, the shift toward bilateral and regional trade agreements began in the mid-1980s and grew out of a frustration with the reluctance of major trading partners to reduce trade barriers, scale back intervention in agricultural and other markets, and strengthen the enforcement of GATT rules. In

1985, President Reagan laid down this challenge: "If these [proposed multilateral trade] negotiations are not initiated or if insignificant progress is
made, I'm instructing our trade negotiators to explore regional and bilateral agreements with other nations."[1] Of course, while the United States
could announce its willingness to start regional or bilateral negotiations,
other countries had to embrace the idea for anything to be accomplished.

After the free-trade agreement with Canada was concluded, the United
States offered the same opportunity to others in the Western Hemisphere.
In his 1988 State of the Union message, Reagan stated that "our goal must
be the day when the free flow of trade, from the tip of Tierra del Fuego to
the Arctic Circle, unites the people of the Western Hemisphere in a bond
of mutually beneficial exchange." Given the lack of enthusiasm that many
Latin America countries had for reducing trade barriers, this invitation
was likely to be ignored.[2]

But a major political development intervened. The unexpected fall of
the Berlin Wall in November 1989, the collapse of Communism in Eastern Europe and later the Soviet Union, and the end of the Cold War not
only shook up world politics, but had ramifications for economic policy
as well. Socialism was no longer an economic model for most developing
countries, and many of them embarked on policy reforms that included
opening up to international trade. In January 1990, Mexican President
Carlos Salinas de Gotari went to Davos, Switzerland, to attend the World
Economic Forum, an international meeting of government officials and
business leaders. The Salinas government had been seeking to modernize
the Mexican economy by undertaking domestic reforms to improve productivity and make its producers more competitive in the world market.[3]
Without major changes in policy, it was believed, the country's standard of
living would only fall further behind that of other countries. In attending
the meeting, Salinas hoped to draw attention to Mexico's reforms with the
hope of attracting foreign investment.

Yet international investors were unimpressed by the modest Mexican
initiatives; instead, the world's business community was transfixed by the
new opportunities in Eastern Europe. The failure to get the world's attention convinced Salinas that Mexico had to do something big, like seek a
free-trade agreement with the United States.[4] Mexico could only attract
foreign investment, he and his advisers reasoned, if it became an export
platform to the United States. And this could only happen if it had guaranteed access to the US market.

Officials at USTR were initially hesitant about starting negotiations
with Mexico. They worried that the Mexican overture might not be se-

rious and wanted to stay focused on completing the ongoing Uruguay Round (to be discussed shortly). To demonstrate the Salinas government's interest, Mexican officials approached James Baker, now secretary of state and the most influential cabinet member in the George H. W. Bush administration. The president and other senior administration officials saw the Mexican proposal as a historic opportunity. The United States had a history of troubled relations with Mexico, and a trade agreement would improve economic cooperation and deepen commercial ties with an important neighbor.[5] In June 1990, Bush and Salinas met in Washington and announced that the two governments would start preparatory work on a free-trade agreement. After initially demurring, Canada soon asked to join the negotiations.[6] In February 1991, the three countries announced their intention to start formal negotiations.

These initial steps would lead to one of the most contentious and divisive trade-policy debates in US history. The debate brought business interests, labor unions, and grass-roots political groups, most of which were opposed to any such agreement, into the policy arena. At issue was fear about what the agreement would mean for the country. This was the first time that the United States was negotiating a major bilateral trade agreement with a developing country. Although Mexico's economy was small compared to that of the United States, and most of its exports already entered duty-free under the Generalized System of Preferences (GSP), Mexican wages were considerably lower than those in the United States. The prospect of a free-trade agreement with such a country sparked fears about job losses from increased imports.

Before Mexico was willing to start the negotiations, the Bush administration had to renew its fast-track negotiating authority, which was due to expire in 1991. The 1988 Omnibus Trade Act had granted fast-track authority for three years with the possibility of a two-year extension, taking it to 1993, unless either the House or Senate objected. Under normal circumstances, the extension would be a routine matter, particularly because Congress strongly supported the ongoing GATT negotiations. But to almost everyone's surprise, the renewal sparked stiff opposition. Critics of the prospective agreement with Mexico were determined to defeat fast track in order to stop it even before any negotiations had begun. (As discussed in chapter 12, fast track was a procedure set out in the Trade Act of 1974 to accelerate congressional consideration of trade agreements reached by the executive branch.) Furious about the prospect of expanded trade with Mexico, labor unions led the opposition. By allowing Mexican goods to freely enter the United States, they believed the agreement would encourage American firms to move production or assembly operations to Mexico and take advantage of its low wages.[7] They saw the agreement as guaranteeing that its members would lose their jobs. As the AFL-CIO put it, "The proposed US-Mexico free trade agreement would be a disaster for workers in both countries. It would destroy jobs in the United States, while perpetuating exploitation of workers and inflicting widespread damage on the environment in Mexico. The beneficiaries would be multinational corporations and large banks."[8]

The prospective North American Free Trade Agreement (NAFTA) also drew the opposition of some domestic producers who felt threatened by Mexican competition, such as fruit and vegetable producers. But unlike previous trade battles, NAFTA elicited broad public disapproval that went well beyond producer and labor interests. Critics complained about the agreement's impact on the environment, working conditions, human rights, illegal drug trafficking, and immigration. Environmental groups feared that NAFTA would allow businesses to take advantage of Mexico's weak regulations and exacerbate pollution along the US-Mexico border. They also worried that it might lead to the relaxation of domestic environmental standards in order to keep industries located in the United States. Human rights activists worried about poor working conditions in Mexico and whether expanded trade would mean more exploitation and intensified poverty among rural farmers.

However, failure to grant the two-year extension of fast track would also jeopardize the conclusion of the ongoing Uruguay Round of GATT negotiations, which had broad political support. Even NAFTA skeptics in Congress did not want to put obstacles in the way of a new multilateral trade agreement. For this reason, Rep. Richard Gephardt (D-MO) announced that he would support fast track without necessarily endorsing any particular trade agreement. Most Democrats opposed killing fast track, but they allowed the question to be debated and brought to a vote. In May 1991, the House voted 231–192 against the resolution to stop fast track. The next day, the Senate rejected a similar resolution by a vote of 59–36. While the effort to stop fast track was defeated, these procedural votes demonstrated the political strength of NAFTA opponents.[9] The battle over fast track in 1991 was a prelude to the fight over NAFTA two years later.

The unexpected controversy over fast track was the first indication that trade politics was going to be different in the post–Cold War era. During the Cold War, expanding trade was seen as an important way of solidifying economic relations within the Western alliance, thereby promoting national security and countering the threat of Communism. With that threat gone, the foreign-policy rationale for rejecting the demands of domestic constituencies opposed to trade had diminished considerably. At the same time, the economic importance of labor-intensive industries most vulnerable to foreign competition, such as apparel, was shrinking rapidly, weakening their political clout. Now, more vocal opposition to freer trade came from a much broader group consisting of national labor unions, environmental groups, and human rights activists. The movement was spearheaded by organized labor, which was in the best position to make large financial contributions to members of Congress. The reciprocal trade agreements program had never been threatened by such public activism in the past, and this new opposition caught pro-trade business groups off guard.[10]

The renewal of fast track allowed the formal negotiation of NAFTA to begin in June 1991. The negotiating groups contended with many issues, including market access, rules of origin, agriculture, financial services, investment, and dispute settlement. The negotiations followed the template of the US-Canada FTA, but went beyond it in covering new areas such as intellectual property and transportation. By the time the NAFTA negotiations concluded fourteen months later, in August 1992, the agreement ran to more than two thousand pages in twenty-two chapters with numerous annexes.

The market-access provisions were the cornerstone of the agreement. On average, applied tariffs were 5 percent in the United States, 8 percent in Canada, and 12 percent in Mexico. However, non-tariff barriers raised the tariff equivalent to 9 percent in the United States, 12 percent in Canada, and 31 percent in Mexico.[11] Because its trade barriers were substantially higher, Mexico would have to do most of the liberalization, creating significant opportunities for US exporters. The agreement called for the gradual phaseout of all tariffs on North American trade in blocks of five, ten, or fifteen years, although some duties were abolished immediately. The United States requested a lengthy transition period for labor-intensive goods, such as footwear and garments, glassware, and brooms. In agriculture, import quotas were converted to equivalent tariff barriers and then phased out, with some exceptions for sensitive sectors (sugar and orange juice for the United States, corn and beans for Mexico). The United States also insisted on protection against import surges on agricultural goods, such as citrus fruits, tomatoes, onions, and watermelons.

A key issue was determining what constituted a "North American" product—that is, which products were eligible for duty-free treatment among the three countries. With each country continuing to apply their existing tariffs on imports from other countries, the different tariff levels across the three countries could give rise to "transshipment," in which goods would be imported into a low-tariff country and then shipped into a high-tariff country to evade those duties. For example, because the United States imposed a 25 percent tariff on imported trucks, other countries (such as Japan) might try to export trucks to Canada or Mexico and then ship them across the border into the United States to avoid paying the higher US duty. To prevent transshipment and ensure that only "Mexican" or "Canadian" goods received duty-free treatment in the United States, NAFTA established rules of origin. These rules mandated the minimal amount of North American content that any given product had to contain in order to qualify for duty-free status.

Rules of origin were particularly important in the case of automobiles. The US auto industry wanted high North American content rules to ensure that Mexico did not become an export platform for Japanese or other foreign producers who would simply send parts to Mexico for assembly and then ship the vehicles into the United States. In the US-Canada FTA, the domestic content rule was that 50 percent of the value of an automobile had to be of US or Canadian origin for it to qualify for duty-free treatment. For NAFTA, the United Auto Workers pushed for an 80 percent rule, Ford and Chrysler 70 percent, and General Motors 60 percent. Mexico and Canada wanted to keep the 50 percent requirement in the US-Canada FTA, but reluctantly accepted 60 percent. US negotiators had promised auto producers a number higher than 60 percent to prevent their opposition. While they were able to persuade Mexico to go to 65 percent, Canada remained firm at 60 percent and so the negotiators split the difference and arrived at a 62.5 percent rule.[12]

Rules of origin were also an issue for textiles and apparel, where US negotiators tried to ensure that US-made fabric would be used for all apparel made in Mexico. The agreement had a "yarn-forward" rule and "triple transformation test," in which eligible goods had to be cut and sewn in a NAFTA country from fabric woven in a NAFTA country from yarn made in a NAFTA country. These complicated regulations aimed to keep duty-free trade within North America.

On investment, NAFTA prohibited investment-related performance requirements, such as local content provisions and export performance mandates.[13] It also protected foreign investors against discriminatory treatment in the event of an expropriation or significant policy change affecting the value of their investments by requiring that governments pay compensation at fair market value. NAFTA's controversial chapter 11 allowed private investors to bring complaints about a possible breech of these obligations to a special arbitration body which would adjudicate any dispute. Foreign investment in the energy sector was a sensitive issue for Mexico, as it had been for Canada. The United States had to accept a provision in Mexico's constitution that banned foreign ownership in its oil and gas sector, although it persuaded Mexico to liberalize the procurement rules for the state oil monopoly.

In services, national treatment and most-favored-nation (MFN) standing were required as general principles, with special exceptions applying in case of telecommunications, financial services, and transportation. Canada insisted on preserving its cultural exemption that limited foreign media participation, including television and radio, magazines and newspapers. Other provisions of NAFTA dealt with intellectual property, government procurement, competition policy, and dispute settlement.

When the NAFTA negotiations concluded in August 1992, the United States was in the midst of the presidential election campaign, which only served to draw more critical attention to it. Furthermore, the economy was just emerging from a brief recession in 1990–91. Although the downturn was mild compared to the early 1980s, the sluggish recovery of employment made voters sensitive to the argument that NAFTA would cost American jobs. Conservative commentator Pat Buchanan, a candidate in the Republican primary, stoked up fears by warning that NAFTA would devastate the middle class and harm blue-collar workers. In the Democratic primary, several candidates argued that the agreement would damage the economy and destroy jobs. The wild card in the election was Ross Perot, a Texas billionaire with a surprisingly strong third-party candidacy. Perot warned that if NAFTA was enacted, "you are going to hear a giant sucking sound of jobs being pulled out of this country."[14] The phrase "a giant sucking sound" became the most memorable sound-bite of the entire NAFTA debate and summed up the country's fears about expanding trade with its low-wage neighbor. Perot went on to capture 19 percent of the popular vote in the election, an astonishingly large share for a third-party candidate, and became the public face of the anti-NAFTA campaign after the election.

While President Bush strongly supported the agreement, his Democratic challenger approached NAFTA with caution. A Southern Democrat from Arkansas, Bill Clinton was a "New Democrat" who advocated centrist economic policies that rejected the protectionist approach of labor unions and Northern Democrats from the Rust Belt.[15] Clinton was favorably disposed to NAFTA, but the anti-NAFTA states of Ohio and Michigan were critical to winning the election. For much of the campaign, he hedged his position, supporting the idea of a trade agreement in principle but uncommitted about the agreement in hand. Finally, in a campaign speech in October 1992, Clinton announced his support for the agreement, provided it protected labor and the environment. "The issue is not whether we should support free trade or open markets. Of course we should," he said. "The real question is whether or not we will have a national economic strategy to make sure we reap its benefits."[16]

Clinton defeated Bush in the 1992 election, and thus NAFTA's fate hinged on a Democratic president who had not negotiated it. In his memoirs, Clinton (2004, 432) recalled, "I was a free-trader at heart, and I thought I had to support Mexico's economic growth to ensure long-run stability in our hemisphere." He viewed the agreement as marking a historic break from the mutual suspicion and lack of cooperation that had characterized the bilateral relationship for so long. Clinton and his economic advisers supported freer trade, but his political advisers opposed fighting for a trade agreement that would divide the party and offend many Democratic constituencies.

In February 1993, just weeks after taking office, President Clinton delivered a major address that acknowledged America's "mixed feelings" about globalization. Clinton explained that rapid changes in the world economy would inevitably affect the United States and bring with it uncertainty about the future. But the country had no choice but to adapt to this new environment, he insisted, because "open and competitive commerce will enrich us as a nation." Therefore, "in the face of all the pressures to do the reverse, we must compete, not retreat." The United States must "seek to open other nations' markets and to establish clear and enforceable rules on which to expand trade."[17] Going beyond economics, he pointed to the larger implications of the new global economy: "American jobs and prosperity are reason enough for us to be working at mastering the essentials of the global economy. But far more is at stake, for this new fabric of commerce will also shape global prosperity or the lack of it, and with it, the prospects of people around the world for democracy, freedom, and peace."[18]

Following the president's campaign pledge, US Trade Representative Mickey Kantor began negotiating side agreements to NAFTA concerning labor and the environment. (The text of NAFTA itself was not open for renegotiation, since it had been signed by President Bush in December 1992.) These negotiations took from April to August 1993. The side agreements had both a substantive and a political purpose. The substantive purpose was to strengthen the agreement by setting up tri-national commissions to deal with labor and environmental disputes. The political purpose was to weaken the opposition to NAFTA by giving undecided members of Congress the political cover they needed to support it.[19]

The anti-NAFTA movement was large and well organized for the looming battle in Congress. The AFL-CIO strongly opposed the agreement and led dozens of other unions in the fight. The major theme of the anti-NAFTA campaign was that it would cost American jobs. NAFTA "would be a disaster for millions of working people in the United States, Canada and Mexico," the head of the AFL-CIO maintained, because it is based "solely on exploitation. It would destroy jobs and depress wages in the US and Canada. . . . It should be rejected and renegotiated to advance the overall public interest."[20] "This agreement is not about free trade," it was argued, but "about guaranteeing the ability of US investors to move plants to Mexico to take advantage of cheap wages and poor working conditions in producing goods for export to the US market."[21] This opposition was not difficult to understand: manufacturing workers had been hard-hit in the 1980s, and membership in labor unions had fallen from 22.2 million in 1975 to 16.6 million in 1991.[22] NAFTA was a major test of the labor movement's strength within the Democratic party.

While the labor side agreement did nothing to reduce union opposition to NAFTA, the environmental side agreement split the conservation movement. The World Wildlife Fund, the National Wildlife Federation, the Audubon Society, and the Environmental Defense Fund came to see NAFTA as helping to achieve environmental objectives. If NAFTA modernized the Mexican economy and made it more prosperous, it was argued, the country would have the ability to adopt newer, cleaner production technology and have the resources to clean up the environment. Other organizations, including the Sierra Club, Friends of the Earth, and Greenpeace, strongly opposed NAFTA, believing that the side agreement was a sham and that uncontrolled economic growth would simply lead to further environmental degradation.

A wide range of other groups—the Americans for Democratic Action, the Evangelical Lutheran Church in America, lay Catholic organizations, the Congressional Black Caucus, and the American Federation of State, County, and Municipal Employees (AFSCME)—also opposed the agreement. The civil rights activist Jesse Jackson said "NAFTA is a shafta, shifting our jobs out of the country."[23] Public Citizen, an advocacy group founded by the consumer advocate Ralph Nader, argued that NAFTA was undemocratic. As he put it, "From its morbidly secretive conception by corporate lobbyists and their Bush administration allies, to the fast-track procedural straitjacket that prohibits amendments to NAFTA, to the decisions by the inaccessible international tribunals that are alien to this country's jurisprudential practices, NAFTA diminishes US democracy."[24] Public Citizen contended that the agreement would only benefit multinational corporations and harm marginalized minority groups such as the poor, although Hispanics tended to favor the agreement. Anti-NAFTA activists also capitalized on Mexico's poor image in the United States, where many viewed the country as dirty, corrupt, and run by drug lords and political elites.

Former presidential candidate Ross Perot, who coined the memorable phrase "giant sucking sound" referring to jobs being lost to Mexico, also mounted a formidable grass-roots campaign against NAFTA. Perot's book, *Save Your Job, Save Our Country: Why NAFTA Must Be Stopped*, portrayed NAFTA as a conspiracy of big business and foreign agents that would enrich multinational companies at the expense of the average worker. Its main message was that NAFTA "will pit American workers against Mexican workers in a race to the bottom. In this race, millions of Americans will lose their jobs." Perot also hammered away at the idea that the agreement would "radically reduce" the nation's sovereignty and complained that foreign lobbying for NAFTA was distorting the American political process. (USTR issued a seventy-four-page rebuttal attacking the book's "false and misleading" claims.)

The loud voices in the public debate against NAFTA drowned out the quiet but powerful producer interests that supported NAFTA. The National Association of Manufacturers and the Chamber of Commerce supported the agreement. The Chamber argued that the agreement would "create more jobs, lower prices for consumer goods, and strengthen competitiveness for American firms at home and abroad."[25] Midwestern farmers also saw tremendous opportunity for increased agricultural exports to Mexico, although citrus growers in Florida, vegetable farmers in California, and sugar producers in Florida feared imports from Mexico.[26]

The textile and apparel industry was divided over NAFTA. The textile industry believed it might gain from NAFTA because the rules of origin required that any clothing imported from Canada or Mexico had to be made from North American yarn and fabric to receive duty-free treatment. The textile producers hoped that these rules would allow them to become the main supplier of fabric for apparel producers in Mexico. Of course, the labor unions in the textile and apparel industry remained adamantly opposed. The industry's divisions and inability to speak with one voice effectively neutralized it as an anti-NAFTA force.

The intense hostility directed against NAFTA seemed out of proportion to the economic stakes involved. The Mexican economy was just 4 percent of the size of the US economy. Nearly half of US imports from Mexico already entered duty-free under the Generalized System of Preferences (GSP) or at reduced rates under the *maquiladora* production-sharing arrangement. The remainder of Mexico's exports to the United States faced an average tariff of about 4 percent, although it was higher on most labor-intensive goods. Even without NAFTA, there was nothing stopping American firms from moving their production to Mexico. Meanwhile, Mexican barriers against US exports were significantly higher than US barriers against Mexican exports, so proponents of NAFTA could legitimately argue that the agreement would help "level the playing field" in terms of market access.

For these reasons, the International Trade Commission's study of NAFTA concluded that it would benefit the economy but that the overall gains were likely to be small. NAFTA was projected to increase US real GDP by 0.5 percent or less, the ITC (1993, 2/3–4) suggested; such a small number was "to be expected due to the vast difference in size between the Mexican and US economies as well as the initial low level of US trade barriers." While an agreement would significantly affect bilateral trade in certain goods, the change in trade would likely have a negligible impact on production levels in most industries. Furthermore, the ITC concluded that NAFTA "is likely to have little or no effect on employment levels in the United States, but it could cause some shift in employment among occupations" with sizeable job losses in only a few industries, such as apparel, household appliances, sugar and ceramics, offset by job gains in export industries. The report predicted that average wages would rise a negligible amount, but noted that "the preponderance of evidence indicates an almost indiscernible effect on US wage rates for both low-skilled and high-skilled groups."

Economists generally agreed with these conclusions and supported NAFTA. More than three hundred economists of all political stripes, including several Nobel laureates, signed a petition endorsing the agreement. Paul Krugman (1993) summarized NAFTA in five simple propositions: (1) that it would have no effect on the number of jobs in the United States; (2) that it would not hurt and might help the environment; (3) that it would produce a small gain in real income for the United States; (4) that it would probably lead to a slight fall in real wages of unskilled American workers; and (5) that NAFTA was really a foreign-policy issue rather than an economic issue. Along with most economists, Krugman (1993, 13) believed that "the intensity of this debate cannot be understood in terms of the real content or likely consequences of the agreement, nor is the debate's outcome likely to turn on any serious examination of the evidence." Instead, he argued, "the hard-core opposition to NAFTA is rooted in a modern populism that desperately wants to defend industrial America against the forces that are transforming us into a service economy. International trade in general and trade with Mexico in particular have little to do with those forces; clinging to the four percent average tariff the United States currently levies on imports of manufactures from Mexico might save a few low-wage industrial jobs for a little while, but it would do almost nothing to stop or even slow the long-run trends that are the real concern of NAFTA's opponents."

Other economists viewed the agreement more positively. In a widely cited study by the Institute for International Economics, Hufbauer and Schott (1993, 14) concluded that "NAFTA will exert a modest but positive effect on the US labor market." They projected that NAFTA would create 171,000 net new jobs in the United States within five years on the assumption that exports to Mexico would continue to grow more rapidly than imports from Mexico. NAFTA opponents countered that the economic impact would be large and negative, not small and positive. A study sponsored by the AFL-CIO predicted job losses of 550,000 due to greater imports from Mexico, based on the assumption of "investment diversion" that US firms would invest less at home and more in Mexico as a result of NAFTA.[27]

With both sides trying to undercut the others' arguments, the acrimonious debate made it difficult for the American public to understand the potential impact of the agreement. Claims that NAFTA would destroy jobs, reduce wages, increase immigration, and harm the environment were met with counterclaims that NAFTA would create jobs, increase wages, decrease immigration, and improve the environment. While NAFTA opponents argued that the agreement would have a big, negative impact, most standard analyses pointed to a small, positive impact overall, even if some unskilled workers stood to lose. Nevertheless, the fears resonated with the public at large: "A belief that NAFTA would destroy hundreds of thousands of jobs, devastate the environment, undermine democracy, or threaten American society certainly is more compelling [to the public] than a belief that NAFTA would have only modest effects," Mayer (1998, 270) noted. Consequently, in the political debate, some of the small, positive impacts were gradually exaggerated to become larger impacts, because few politicians would be willing to fight for something where the gains were small, but the opposition was fierce. "The anti-NAFTA people are telling malicious whoppers," Krugman observed, while "the pro-NAFTA side is telling little white lies."[28]

By the summer of 1993, the prospect that Congress would approve NAFTA looked bleak. The anti-NAFTA groups had been working hard for months to convince the public to oppose it, pounding away with the argument that NAFTA would destroy jobs and hurt workers. "The domestic grassroots opposition to NAFTA was based less on what NAFTA *was* and more on what it *symbolized*," Mayer (1998, 257, 266) observed. "NAFTA stood for all that had happened to American workers in the 1980s and all they feared for the future."[29] During the August congressional recess, members of Congress went back to their districts and only heard bad things about the agreement from their constituents. When Congress reconvened in September 1993, most political observers believed that NAFTA was dead. Key Democratic leaders in the House, including Majority Leader Richard Gephardt (D-MO) and Chief Whip David Bonior (D-MI), opposed the agreement.[30] Rank-and-file Democrats feared electoral retribution from labor unions if they supported it.

Meanwhile, the proponents were largely silent. The administration had only completed the side agreements in August and had yet to focus on making the public case for NAFTA. The president supported NAFTA but was prone to indecision. As late as mid-summer, a fierce debate still raged within the administration about whether he should make an all-out push for NAFTA, knowing that it would divide the party, or focus on another issue (such as health care) around which Democrats could unite. The president's political advisers opposed investing much time and effort in fighting what they thought would be a losing battle for NAFTA, while his economic advisers, including Treasury Secretary Lloyd Bentsen (a former senator from Texas), were strong supporters. According to Harris (2005, 95), "It was Bentsen who had the decisive voice in answering the political team's objections—and Clinton's anguished doubts. At a cabinet meeting, he slammed his fist down on the table for emphasis in front of the president. The gesture stilled the room. NAFTA was not merely good policy, he argued, it was shaping into a critical test of the president's own principles. Did he have the nerve to fight for them?" Shortly after that, Clinton (2004, 540) decided that he was "ready to go all out to pass NAFTA in the Congress."[31]

The Clinton administration faced a major uphill battle and had only two months to energize the business community and build congressional support for NAFTA before the scheduled vote in mid-November. The magic number of votes required for the House to approve NAFTA was 218. About 120 Republicans were expected to support it, meaning that 100 House Democratic votes were also needed. The administration was far short of that mark: Democrats opposed to the agreement far outnumbered those in support, and public opinion was running strongly against the agreement, making it extremely difficult for the many undeclared members to announce their support.

In mid-September 1993, Clinton kicked off the campaign to win congressional and public support for NAFTA by signing the labor and environmental side agreements. He was joined at the White House by three former presidents, who offered their strong support. The president argued that "this debate about NAFTA is a debate about whether we will embrace these changes [in the global economy] and create the jobs of tomorrow, or try to resist these changes, hoping we can preserve the economic structures of yesterday." Clinton acknowledged the public's fear of change and said,

> It is clear that most of the people that oppose this pact are rooted in the fears and insecurities that are legitimately gripping the great American middle class. It is no use to deny that these fears and insecurities exist. It is no use denying that many of our people have lost in the battle for change. But it is a great mistake to think that NAFTA will make it worse. Every single solitary thing you hear people talk about, that they're worried about, can happen whether this trade agreement passes or not, and most of them will be made worse if it fails.[32]

He also highlighted the foreign-policy implications of the agreement: "For decades, we have preached and preached and preached greater democracy, greater respect for human rights, and more open markets to Latin America." NAFTA, he said, finally gave the United States an opportunity to advance these goals.[33]

Thus began a massive campaign to push NAFTA through Congress. The administration tried to shift the debate from how much more the United States would import from Mexico to how much more it would export to Mexico. NAFTA would give the United States preferential access to Mexico's market, giving its firms a competitive advantage over exporters from Europe and Japan. Officials argued that NAFTA, by reducing trade barriers in Mexico, would create an export boom, creating two hundred thousand jobs over two years and up to a million jobs over five years. More trade and investment would help raise Mexican wages and standards of living, thereby reducing immigration into the United States. The administration repeatedly argued that a rejection of NAFTA was a validation of the status quo, which no one found acceptable. All of the problems that the United States had with Mexico, ranging from weak labor and environmental standards to immigration and drug trafficking, existed without NAFTA and would not change if it was defeated. No one promised that NAFTA would be a panacea, supporters argued, but the agreement was potentially part of the solution to these problems, or at least a step in the right direction.

While the president and his team were mainly worried about securing Democratic support for NAFTA, they had to keep Republicans on board as well. In mid-October, Minority Whip Newt Gingrich (R-GA) complained that Clinton's efforts on behalf of the agreement had been "pathetic." Gingrich warned the president that unless he got personally involved and went all-out to ensure the support of 100 House Democrats, the 120 House Republican votes needed to win could not be guaranteed. This criticism spurred Clinton to become more directly engaged in the political battle. Recognizing that NAFTA was a significant test for his presidency, Clinton and top administration officials spoke personally with about two hundred members of Congress. "I courted some of these congressmen longer than I courted my wife," Treasury Secretary Bentsen quipped.[34] James Robinson, the CEO of American Express and head of the Business Roundtable, urged other business leaders to call at least three members of Congress every day and encourage them to support NAFTA.

Undecided members faced intense pressure from both sides to declare their voting intentions. In September, surveys indicated that House members opposed the pact by 43 percent to 38 percent, with 19 percent taking no position. By November, the president's efforts began to pay off: nearly three-quarters of the 83 undecided members decided to support the agreement, and some even moved from declared opposition to declared support. Many members of Congress recognized that NAFTA was, in the long run, a good idea, but they feared the political consequences of supporting the agreement in the face of public opposition. To give undecided members the political cover they needed to support NAFTA, the administration unveiled a special trade adjustment assistance program to cushion the blow to displaced workers.

As the administration stepped up its efforts to get NAFTA through Congress, labor unions also got more aggressive in their opposition.

Unions threatened to withhold campaign contributions from Democrats who voted for NAFTA, one leader warning those who did so, "We're gonna whip your ass and throw you out of office." The president infuriated labor leaders by accusing them of using "roughshod, muscle-bound tactics." "We're not threatening anybody," replied a high-ranking AFL-CIO official, but "if you vote to ship jobs of our members out of this country, we're not going to support you anymore." The bitter recriminations strained relations among the traditional Democratic allies.[35]

Two weeks before the scheduled vote, the prospects for NAFTA's passage still looked bleak. House leaders David Bonior and Richard Gephardt went to the White House and offered to postpone the vote so that the president could avoid a humiliating defeat, but Clinton refused. Eight days before the House vote, Vice President Al Gore and Ross Perot debated NAFTA on CNN's "Larry King Live." By all accounts, the well-prepared Gore trounced Perot, who came across as testy and unfocused. (As one newspaper headline put it, "Ross Gets Gored.") Gore emphasized that improved access to the Mexican market would increase exports and create jobs in the United States. Reminding viewers that the United States was already open to imports from Mexico, he stressed that NAFTA would help level the playing field for US exports by reducing Mexican trade barriers. He pressed Perot to describe how he would change the agreement or what his alternative to NAFTA would be, but Perot could not give a good answer. Perot lost significant credibility as a result of his poor performance. One poll found that 59 percent of viewers said that Gore had the better argument, while only 22 percent thought Perot did.[36]

These efforts on behalf of NAFTA even began to shift public opinion in its favor. In September, one poll found that 25 percent of Americans favored NAFTA, and 36 percent opposed it; by mid-November, the same poll found 36 percent favored NAFTA, and 31 percent opposed it.[37] While some minds were being changed, more significant was the fact that undecided voters, like undecided members of Congress, were breaking in favor of the agreement. The administration and business supporters succeeded in countering the opponents on the economic implications of the agreement, even on the sensitive issue of jobs. They were also clearly winning the argument on the foreign-policy dimensions of the agreement by asking the broader question: What would it say about the character of the United States if it rejected an agreement that would strengthen ties with an important neighboring country?

In the final days before the scheduled House vote, the administration pulled out all the stops in order to win the support of 218 representatives.

Many undeclared members delayed announcing their voting intention until the last possible minute either to avoid political attacks on themselves or to extract further concessions from the administration.[38] A large block of undecided House members from Florida and Louisiana held out for concessions on sugar, citrus fruits, and winter vegetables (such as tomatoes). The administration vowed to use price supports to help vegetable growers if imports caused domestic prices to fall and pressured Mexico into modest changes that would make it more difficult for them to export sugar. (Mexican officials, who were counting the House vote as well, had little choice but to agree.) As a result, the Florida Fruit and Vegetable Association, Gulf Citrus Growers, and others dropped their opposition to NAFTA, and the administration picked up about twenty-five votes. An additional five Midwestern votes were won on promises to investigate Canadian wheat subsidies, while four southern votes were secured by promising to protect apparel manufacturers from cheap imports in the Uruguay Round.[39] Ross Perot complained that "no votes were changing until the pork started flowing."[40]

On November 17, 1993, the House prepared to vote on NAFTA. The floor debate took eleven hours, and 240 members gave speeches. David Bonior (D-MI) gave a rousing and emotional address in which he attacked NAFTA as "a bad deal" that would "drive down our standard of living" and "lock in place a Mexican system that exploits its own people and denies them the most basic political and economic rights." He continued, "The working people who stand against this treaty don't have degrees from Harvard. They don't study economic models. And most of them have never heard of Adam Smith. But they know when the deck is stacked against them. They know it's not fair to ask American workers to compete against Mexican workers who earn $1 an hour. The work of America is still done by people who pack a lunch, punch a clock and pour their heart and soul into every paycheck. And we can't afford to leave them behind."[41]

Minority Leader Robert Michel (R-IL) gave a spirited defense of the agreement, pleading with his colleagues, "Do not sacrifice the jobs of tomorrow to the fears of today." He drew laughter for his description of "the three most famous non-elected opponents of NAFTA: Ross Perot, Pat Buchanan, and Ralph Nader—the Groucho, Chico, and Harpo of the NAFTA opposition" (a reference to the Marx Brothers comedy trio) whose "only response to the challenges of global competition is to retreat, whine and whimper."[42]

At 10:26pm that evening, the most epic trade-policy battle in Congress since the end of World War II concluded when the House approved NAFTA by a vote of 234–200, a wider margin than expected. The Clinton administration had organized an impressive come-from-behind victory. House Speaker Thomas Foley (D-WA) called NAFTA "the Lazarus Act" because it had been miraculously raised from the dead.[43] The anti-NAFTA activists, who had invested so much time and energy into defeating the agreement, suffered a crushing defeat.[44]

By its own admission, the administration could not have won without the support of Republicans, who voted 132–43 in favor. Democrats voted 156–102 against the agreement (along with one independent), with Northern Democrats voting 124–49 against, and Southern Democrats voting 53–32 in favor. Clinton later "speculated that NAFTA would be at least thirty votes closer to a majority if Congress had a secret ballot," but in his view "the substance of NAFTA consistently lost to raw politics, with heavy pressure especially from trade unions."[45]

The geography of the House vote on NAFTA is shown in figure 13.1. Most of the support came from west of the Mississippi River, particularly the Southwest, while the East was divided. A number of subsequent studies have tried to explain the reasons for the votes of individual members.[46] According to Magee (2010), the chances of NAFTA passing would have been significantly lower had Republican George H. W. Bush been reelected in 1992, because that would have reduced Democratic support for the agreement. In contrast to the ferocious battle in the House, the Senate eas-

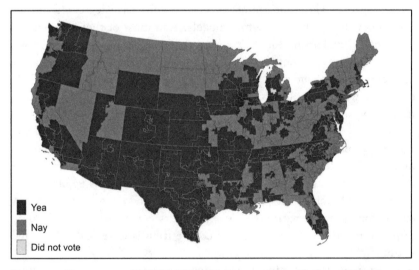

Figure 13.1. House vote on NAFTA, November 17, 1993. *Note*: Alaska and Hawaii voted nay. (Map courtesy Citrin GIS/Applied Spatial Analysis Lab, Dartmouth College.)

ily approved NAFTA three days later by a vote of 61–38; Republicans voted 34–10 in favor and Democrats split 28–27 against. NAFTA took effect on January 1, 1994, although tariffs were phased out over a decade.

What was the economic impact of NAFTA? For all the fears about a "giant sucking sound," the United States experienced an exceptionally strong labor market in the mid- to late-1990s. The unemployment rate fell to less than 4 percent by late 2000, manufacturing employment held steady, and wages rose even for less-skilled workers. Imports did not cause a pronounced increase in worker displacement. While NAFTA accelerated the decline in apparel employment, studies showed that the agreement did not have a major impact on either net employment or gross job flows in other trade-affected industries.[47]

Later studies found that NAFTA had a substantial impact on trade but modest effects on prices and welfare.[48] NAFTA promoted rapid growth in bilateral trade, and the North American economy became more integrated. While critics focused on the growth of imports from Mexico, about 40 percent of the value of those imports consisted of US-made intermediate goods and components, although this suggested the loss of some labor-intensive assembly jobs. In all, NAFTA did not exacerbate or ameliorate many of the existing problems facing the two economies. In retrospect, Hufbauer and Schott (2005, 4) point out that "much of what was promised from NAFTA could never be achieved solely through a free trade deal; much of what has occurred since NAFTA was ratified cannot be attributed to policy changes that the trade pact mandated."

However, the US bilateral trade surplus quickly turned to deficit when Mexico was struck by a financial crisis in late 1994. The crisis plunged Mexico into a severe recession, and the peso plummeted against the dollar. Because some forecasts of net job creation as a result of NAFTA hinged on the continued growth of the trade surplus, critics pointed to the sudden appearance of a trade deficit to claim that jobs had been lost as a result of the agreement. While NAFTA itself had nothing to do with the Mexican financial crisis, which had been brewing for several years, this turn of events bred skepticism about claims that trade agreements would lead to domestic employment gains.

Mexico's economic crisis made it difficult to isolate the immediate impact of NAFTA, although the country's economic performance eventually began to improve. NAFTA's biggest impact may have been political: it contributed to the modernization drive that helped diminish the power of the Institutional Revolutionary Party (PRI) that had ruled the country for decades and move the country toward multiparty democracy. As Preston and Dillon (2004, 226) note, NAFTA "forced Mexicans to rethink the defensive, self-isolating nationalism that was a key article of the PRI revolutionary doctrine. Whereas the traditional PRI regarded the United States as an imperialist bully, NAFTA called on Mexicans to see their neighbor as a partner, even a friend." Beyond the economic effects of the agreement, NAFTA had a lasting impact on American trade politics. The bitter divisions among Democrats over NAFTA were still felt a quarter of a century later.

THE URUGUAY ROUND

On December 15, 1993, less than a month after Congress approved NAFTA, representatives from 117 countries concluded the Uruguay Round of multilateral trade negotiations. After seven years of negotiation, the Uruguay Round produced sweeping agreements that would reshape world trade and trade policy into the twenty-first century. President Clinton hailed the outcome as "the largest, most comprehensive set of trade agreements in history."[49] Among other things, the participants abolished the Multifiber Arrangement (MFA), reformed agricultural trade policies, extended rules to new areas (e.g., services), protected trade-related intellectual property rights, created a more effective dispute-settlement system, and established the World Trade Organization.

To appreciate the significance of the Uruguay Round, we must recall the trade-policy environment of the early 1980s, when the United States struggled to get other countries to agree to launch a new round of trade negotiations. As chapter 12 recounted, the GATT seemed increasingly irrelevant by the end of the 1970s. GATT provisions were often ignored as export-restraint agreements proliferated and agricultural subsidies grew. The United States, of course, was far from blameless for this situation, but it was virtually alone in wanting to do something about it.

US officials believed that the GATT did not address the realities of modern trade and were anxious to repair the holes in its framework. Agricultural policies highly distorted world markets through a complex array of production subsidies, export subsidies, and import controls, all of which had been untouched by previous negotiations. GATT rules did not restrict the use of export-restraint agreements, export and domestic subsidies, and other non-tariff barriers, all of which were becoming increasingly widespread. Noncompliance with its rules was a growing problem because the GATT lacked an effective enforcement mechanism. In addition, new trade issues had arisen that existing rules did not address. The GATT had no provisions for trade in services—banking and financial services, maritime and transportation services, construction and legal services, and so forth —that were of growing importance in world trade. The United States was also concerned about the proliferation of counterfeit goods and the infringement of copyrights, trademarks, and patents in many countries. The violation of intellectual property protection had become a major issue for high-technology, entertainment, and pharmaceutical industries.

A new GATT round was also believed to be necessary because the landscape of world trade had changed significantly since the Tokyo Round of the 1970s. Back then, just a few developed countries—the United States, the EEC, Japan, Canada, and some others—were involved in the negotiations to reduce tariffs and establish rules and disciplines on policy measures. Developing countries accounted for a small share of world trade and did not participate. By the late 1970s, East Asian countries were a rapidly growing part of world trade and wanted to reduce the barriers that hindered their exports of labor-intensive goods, particularly textiles and apparel. In addition, developing countries were now a rapidly growing market for exports from developed countries. The United States maintained that developing countries could no longer "free ride" on the tariff cuts made by developed countries. The US position was that the rules of the GATT should apply to everyone and that developing countries should be required to participate in the reduction of trade barriers.

In his 1985 State of the Union message, President Reagan repeated the call for a new round of multilateral trade negotiations and followed up at a G-7 meeting of world leaders. In September 1986, at Punta del Este, Uruguay, representatives from more than a hundred countries agreed to start the Uruguay Round, the seventh round of negotiations under the auspices of the GATT. The round was scheduled to end in December 1990, but actually continued for another three years.[50]

The Uruguay Round had a wide-ranging agenda. Most previous rounds had focused almost exclusively on tariffs on industrial goods, although the Tokyo Round also addressed non-tariff barriers, subsidies, and government procurement. In the Uruguay Round, separate negotiating groups dealt with tariffs, non-tariff measures, tropical products, natural resource products, textiles and clothing, agriculture, GATT articles, safeguards, most-favored-nation agreements, subsidies and countervailing measures, dispute settlement, trade-related investment measures, trade-related intellectual property rights, and the functioning of the GATT system. Congress set out the US negotiating objectives in the Omnibus Trade and Competitiveness Act of 1988, which were to achieve "(1) more open, equitable, and reciprocal market access; (2) the reduction or elimination of barriers and other trade-distorting policies and practices; and (3) a more effective system of international trading disciplines." The United States was largely responsible for ensuring that the negotiations covered new issues, such as agriculture, services, trade-related intellectual property (TRIPs), and trade-related investment measures (TRIMs).

The United States insisted that agriculture be part of the negotiating agenda because it wanted to reduce or eliminate trade-distorting farm-support programs, particularly the EEC's Common Agricultural Policy (CAP). The CAP not only closed the European market to agricultural imports, but high subsidies shifted Europe from being a net purchaser of many commodities to having large surplus production. This surplus production was often dumped onto world markets with large export subsidies. As we saw in chapter 12, the United States responded by creating the Export Enhancement Program (EEP) to subsidize its own wheat exports and later other crops, such as cotton. The US-EEC subsidy war drove down world grain prices and harmed agricultural exporting nations that did not employ subsidies. These countries, including Australia, Canada, New Zealand, Argentina, Brazil, and Uruguay, among others, formed the Cairns group to demand the elimination of all export subsidies and the opening of agricultural markets.

Research by the Organization for Economic Cooperation and Development (OECD) also drew attention to the market distortions and financial costs of existing agricultural policies. The OECD found that government subsidies for agriculture cost billions of dollars and took a variety of forms, usually price supports backed by export subsidies. The OECD calculated that producer subsidy equivalents—the percentage of farm income derived from government subsidies—amounted to 22 percent for the United States, 39 percent for the European Community, and 64 percent for Japan in 1986–88.[51]

The United States proposed the elimination of all trade-distorting agricultural subsidies by the year 2000. At the very least, the United States wanted income support for farmers "decoupled" from production decisions to reduce the incentives for overproduction that so distorted world markets. The United States and the Cairns group put European negotiators, whose mandate was to preserve the CAP with minimal reforms, on the defensive. The United States made repeated threats to retaliate against Europe if no agreement was reached.

The United States was also interested in extending existing GATT rules, such as nondiscrimination and national treatment, to trade in services. Services included a wide range of activities, including financial services (banks, insurance, and accounting), professional services (legal, educational, and medical), and business services (advertising, consulting, construction, and design). The United States had a substantial export surplus in services and was well positioned to capitalize on this growing area of trade. At the same time, the United States wanted some services (air and maritime transport and some financial services) off the negotiating table.

The United States also sought an agreement on trade-related investment measures (TRIMs) so that American companies operating abroad would receive the same "national treatment" as local companies and not face discriminatory barriers. Developing countries resisted US demands to eliminate local-content and export-performance requirements as conditions for foreign direct investment. However, the TRIMs negotiations lacked a focused agenda and were generally considered to be the "most frustrating and least productive" part of the round.[52]

The United States was initially alone in pushing trade-related intellectual property (TRIPs) onto the agenda.[53] American firms had long complained about the need to protect their products against foreign counterfeit goods in such industries as apparel (brand names and designer wear), entertainment (music and motion pictures), and high technology (semiconductors and software). In all of these industries, illegal reproduction, design theft, and counterfeiting were growing problems. Since most countries could not condone stealing, at least publicly, the US objective did not raise much opposition in principle, but coming up with specific rules and enforcing them was another matter. In fact, many developing countries recognized that they would need to provide greater intellectual property protection if they were to attract foreign investment and promote local innovation. However, the US desire to obtain stronger patent protection for the pharmaceutical industry was particularly controversial. This raised the sensitive issue of the pricing of medicines in developing countries, which had an interest in obtaining inexpensive generic drugs.

Since the protection of intellectual property was given such a high priority by the United States, other countries recognized that some agreement had to be included in any final deal.[54] The unspoken threat that hung over the negotiations was that, if other countries did not agree to establish rules in this area, the United States would determine by itself what constituted proper protection of intellectual property and use trade sanctions through section 301 and Super 301 to enforce its interpretation. Because other countries strongly objected to such unilateral actions by the United

States, they were willing to agree to an accord on TRIPs and to establish binding rules on dispute settlement.

The negotiations also reduced tariffs and eliminated major trade barriers, particularly export-restraint agreements. India, Pakistan, Indonesia, and other developing countries believed that the Multifiber Arrangement (MFA) held back their textile and apparel exports and should be dismantled without delay. They viewed the abolition of the MFA as an obligation, not a concession, on the part of developed countries. The United States initially resisted the elimination of the MFA, proposing instead a system of global export quotas (instead of country-by-country quotas), a position shared only by Canada. After President Bush vetoed a bill calling for tighter import quotas, however, the administration backed the gradual phaseout of the MFA to facilitate an agreement on TRIPs.

The United States also wanted to eliminate other managed trade arrangements, such as voluntary export restraints, orderly marketing arrangements, and so forth. This would mean abolishing the more than two hundred export-restraint agreements that had sprung up in the 1970s and 1980s.[55] If a country wanted to protect domestic producers from foreign competition, it would have to invoke the escape clause or apply antidumping and countervailing duties rather than seek export restraints. At the same time, the United States was reluctant to modify its antidumping and countervailing duty laws, which other countries thought were abused for purely protectionist purposes.[56]

The negotiating group on the Functioning of the GATT System sought to address other weaknesses in the existing framework. There was a consensus that an effective dispute-settlement system should be established and integrated across the different Uruguay Round agreements. Countries wanted to have a dispute-settlement system "both as a means of defending their interests in specific disputes, and as a broad guarantee of their existing rights and of the value of the new commitments they were hoping to negotiate in the Uruguay Round."[57] The United States was virtually alone in having the power to enforce agreements for itself through section 301 and the threat of retaliation; smaller countries were unable to do so because other countries would not take their threats of retaliation seriously. Smaller countries were determined to address this power imbalance by establishing an impartial process for settling disputes that would be equally available to all countries. This would end the unilateral enforcement of US claims of trade rights and allow other countries to hold the United States accountable for its own trade policies as well. Despite the bitter foreign complaints about section 301, the director-general of the GATT, Arthur Dunkel, suggested that its aggressive use in the late 1980s was one of the best things the United States ever did for the GATT: instead of undermining the rules-based multilateral trading system, the US deployment of section 301 helped unite the world behind the idea of strengthening that system.[58]

Making the GATT a formal international organization was also discussed. Ever since 1947, the GATT had "provisional status" on the assumption that it would be superseded by the International Trade Organization (ITO), which never came into being for lack of congressional support, as discussed in chapter 10. The GATT had a small secretariat, but it had little formal standing compared to the International Monetary Fund and the World Bank. In 1990, John Jackson, a University of Michigan law professor, suggested that a permanent international trade organization be created.[59] Canada took up this idea and proposed that a World Trade Organization fill this role. The European Community (EC) agreed but wanted it called the Multilateral Trade Organization (MTO), while the United States was "frankly hostile" to the plan.[60] The American position was that it was premature to focus on the institutional structure before agreeing on the substantive rules. As US Trade Representative Carla Hills put it, "You need to have the rules before you build the courthouse."[61]

The first years of the Uruguay Round negotiations were slow as the work program was established, but steady progress was made after a midterm review in 1989. The negotiations moved forward when President Bush vetoed a textile quota in 1990 and agreed to abolish the MFA gradually. In agreeing to do so, the United States met a key demand of developing countries and was able to win concessions in other areas, such as intellectual property and investment.

The effective deadline for the conclusion of the round was December 1990 so that Congress would have enough time to review and vote on any agreement before fast track expired in mid-1991. Although much of the agreement was settled by this time, agriculture remained unresolved. Negotiators had decided to categorize different types of subsidies as either permissible or impermissible, but there was still no consensus on how much subsidies and agricultural trade barriers should be reduced. In October 1990, to put pressure on Europe, Congress reauthorized the Export Enhancement Program that subsidized agricultural exports and included a "GATT trigger" that would expand the program if no agreement was reached.

A GATT ministerial meeting in Brussels in December 1990 sought to finalize details on agricultural subsidy levels and conclude the round.

The United States had backed away from the zero option, proposing instead a 75 percent reduction in domestic (price and income) support and a 90 percent reduction in export subsidies. The EC's counteroffer was a 15 percent reduction in domestic support and no commitments on export subsidies.[62] The differences were far too wide, and the meeting ended in failure, with many participants attributing it to Europe's unwillingness to compromise.[63]

Although the impasse on agriculture remained, the Uruguay Round negotiations were by no means dead.[64] The United States kept alive the hopes of reaching an agreement by extending fast track for another two years while ratcheting up pressure on Europe to reach a deal on agriculture. In a speech to American farmers, President Bush said that "sooner or later, the EC must stop hiding behind its own Iron Curtain of [agricultural] protectionism."[65] The United States also demonstrated that a failure to reach an agreement on agricultural subsidies meant that it would resort to unilateral trade sanctions. In early 1992, the Bush administration announced that it would retaliate against the EC's subsidies for oilseed producers by imposing high tariffs against $1 billion of European exports. When a GATT panel supported the US position, the administration imposed duties of 200 percent on $300 million worth of white wine and other agricultural goods from Europe.

The threat of a trade war led to a November 1992 negotiating breakthrough on domestic support levels, export subsidies, and market access in agriculture. The Blair House agreement, named for the house across the street from the White House where American and European negotiators met, called for a 21 percent reduction in export subsidies over six years, albeit from a higher subsidy base (1990–91 rather than 1986–87). This agreement was the last major trade accomplishment of the Bush administration, as the president was defeated in that month's election.

The Blair House agreement resolved a major stumbling block but did not quite mark the end of the round. Key changes in the negotiating personnel led to a pause in the negotiations: Bill Clinton replaced George Bush as president, Mickey Kantor replaced Carla Hills as US Trade Representative, and Peter Sutherland replaced Arthur Dunkel as director-general of the GATT. Despite this turnover, negotiating positions did not change significantly. The GATT negotiations were rejoined in July 1993, and the remaining details, such as the exchange of tariff concessions and the specific texts of the agreements, were finalized.

One unresolved issue was whether a new international trade organization should be created. The Bush administration never endorsed the idea, fearing that Congress would have reservations about it, but plans for such an organization were included in the draft agreement. On December 15, 1993, the last day of the negotiations, Kantor agreed to a new institution but wanted the name changed from the Multilateral Trade Organization to the World Trade Organization, the name originally proposed three years earlier. Although the new institution had no direct power over the trade policies of member countries, the WTO formalized the status of the GATT Secretariat and made the application of the commitments in the agreements definitive rather than provisional. With that decision, Director-General Peter Sutherland gaveled the negotiations to a close. In April 1994, the final Uruguay Round agreement was formally signed by 117 nations in Marrakesh, Morocco, and scheduled to take effect in January 1995.

The Uruguay Round was the most ambitious and far-reaching multilateral trade negotiation since the establishment of the GATT in 1947. The MFA was to be phased out over ten years. Agricultural subsidies were to be reduced and constrained. Export-restraint agreements were abolished, forcing countries to use safeguards, antidumping or countervailing duties to provide domestic producers with relief from imports. A dispute-settlement procedure was established. Countries agreed to cut import duties by about one-third. A General Agreement on Trade in Services (GATS) was reached, along with agreements on Trade-Related Intellectual Property (TRIPs), Trade-Related Investment Measures (TRIMs), safeguards, subsidies, dispute settlement, and technical issues in trade (such as sanitary and phyto-sanitary measures against imports).

The United States was largely responsible for initiating the round and for pushing new areas of trade onto the agenda.[66] It was able to do so because of two implicit threats. If an agreement was not reached, other countries feared that United States would (1) walk away from the multilateral trading system and undertake bilateral and regional trade initiatives that would exclude (and thus discriminate against) countries that did not participate, and (2) unilaterally enforce its own trade rights through section 301 and the threat of retaliation. While the United States wanted to constrain the policies of other countries through new WTO rules, the rest of the world also wanted to constrain the United States from what it saw as abuses of power.

Of course, the Uruguay Round agreements had to be approved by Congress before US participation was assured. The Clinton administration spent the spring and summer of 1994 drafting the Uruguay Round implementing legislation, which was not sent to Congress until a few weeks before it adjourned for the midterm elections.[67]

The congressional debate on the Uruguay Round was entirely different from the debate over NAFTA just a year earlier. Passage was virtually assured, because the agreement involved substantial commitments by
the rest of the world—on agriculture, intellectual property, and dispute
settlement—that would favor American exports. Major businesses—especially large firms, ranging from Boeing and General Electric to American
Express and Procter and Gamble—were strongly in favor. Other key constituencies supported the agreement for its provisions on agriculture and
intellectual property: Midwestern farm states welcomed the reduction in
European agricultural subsidies, and California's entertainment and high-
technology industries welcomed the intellectual property commitments.
Even trade hawks such as Richard Gephardt announced that they would
support the Uruguay Round agreement. In addition, opposition from labor and environmental groups was much weaker than with NAFTA; these
groups were critical but not very active. Only in the case of textiles and
apparel was there much alarm about the domestic impact of the deal.
Therefore, members of Congress faced significant political pressure to approve, and only light pressure to reject, the Uruguay Round agreements.

On November 30, 1994, after a four-hour debate described as "routine
and one-sided," the House approved the Uruguay Round legislation by a
bipartisan vote of 288–146; two-thirds of both Democrats and Republicans
supported it. Unlike what happened with NAFTA, twice as many Democrats supported the Uruguay Round as opposed it, while fewer Republicans
supported the Uruguay Round than had supported NAFTA.[68] The Senate
also easily approved the agreement in a bipartisan vote of 76–24, and President Clinton signed an executive order putting the Uruguay Round agreement into effect on January 1, 1995.

What was the economic impact of the Uruguay Round? As with most
trade agreements, it is impossible to know precisely how much it expanded world trade, let alone its broader economic consequences. Average
applied tariffs were cut by a third. In developed countries, tariffs on industrial products were low, while those on labor-intensive manufactured
goods were higher, as table 13.1 shows. Meanwhile, even after the Uruguay Round reductions, tariffs in developing countries remained relatively
high.[69]

The termination of the MFA, the scaling back of agricultural subsidies,
and the elimination of voluntary export restraints were the areas where
most of the efficiency gains were expected. The abolition of the MFA was
probably the most significant reform in the package. By 1994, the United
States had agreements with forty countries that specified export limits

TABLE 13.1. Post–Uruguay Round average applied tariffs for selected countries

	Industrial tariffs	Agricultural tariffs	Textile and clothing
Developed countries			
United States	3.1	2.2	14.8
European Union	2.9	3.7	8.7
Japan	1.4	10.5	7.2
Canada	2.6	1.5	14.2
Australia	9.7	3.3	21.6
Developing countries			
Argentina	10.6	4.9	12.1
India	29.0	60.1	42.4
Korea	7.6	11.6	13.0
Thailand	26.8	26.5	28.9

Source: Finger, Ingco, and Reincke 1996.

on as many as 105 categories of products covering about half of US imports of textiles and apparel. The export quotas of the MFA acted like an export tax; the implicit tax on clothing exports from China was 40 percent in 1992.[70] Because the ten-year phaseout was back-loaded, only about 20 percent of the liberalization had occurred by 2004, meaning that the import shock was large when the quotas were finally abolished on January 1, 2005. In fact, the 18 percent of China's apparel exports that were restricted by MFA quotas in 2004 (the share was so small precisely because they were restricted) jumped 450 percent in 2005 when they were no longer constrained, whereas China's unconstrained apparel exports increased 50 percent that year. The price of the previously constrained exports fell 38 percent in 2005, to the benefit of consumers.[71] Harrigan and Barrows (2009) calculate that the MFA quotas cost US consumers $7 billion per year, or roughly $63 per household (approximately 4.5 percent of the average household's apparel budget). The abolition of the MFA also reshuffled market shares across countries: the share of US clothing imports from China jumped from 21 percent to 28 percent between 2004 and 2005. The share from South Asian exporters, such as India, Pakistan, and Bangladesh, increased by a smaller amount, while apparel imports from Mexico (which had previously benefited from NAFTA) dropped 7 percent.

The agreement on agriculture resolved the long-standing US-EC conflict over subsidies, but delivered significantly less market opening than originally hoped. In the process of converting the complicated array of existing trade barriers into tariffs, countries imposed new duties that were higher than the equivalent existing combination of non-tariff restrictions—a practice known as "dirty tariffication."[72] Despite the failure to improve market access significantly, government support for agriculture in OECD countries fell considerably after 1995. The producer subsidy equivalent (PSE) across all OECD countries declined from 37 percent in 1986–88 to 30 percent in 1995–97 before the Uruguay Round agreement really took effect, but then slid to 18 percent in 2011–13. The nominal protection coefficient (NPC) indicated that OECD farmers received, on average, prices almost 50 percent higher than world prices in 1986–88, but just 10 percent more by 2011–13. This reduction was largely driven by European reforms that occurred for reasons other than the Uruguay Round agreement, including budgetary constraints and higher commodity prices. Still, international pressure to decouple transfer payments from production decisions and adopt other policy reforms facilitated the process.[73]

Many of the Uruguay Round agreements established new rules and practices whose impact on world trade was difficult to quantify. For example, the GATS agreement may have increased trade in services, but it is not clear how much liberalization, and therefore additional trade, took place because of the agreement itself. The Agreement on Safeguards effectively ended export-restraint agreements and forced countries to use standard trade remedies, but the aggregate trade effects were hard to determine.

Although the new dispute-settlement system largely formalized existing practices, it transformed the way countries dealt with trade conflicts. Under the new system, countries could file complaints about possible violations of WTO agreements. If consultations failed to resolve the matter, the WTO would appoint a three-member panel to determine whether an agreement had been violated. (The panel decision could be appealed to an Appellate Body, which would rule on matters of law and legal interpretation in the panel report.) Unlike the standard practice under the GATT, the new system prevented countries from blocking the establishment of a panel or the adoption of a panel report. It also set specific time requirements to expedite cases. If the panel found that a violation had occurred, the defendant country was obligated to bring its policy into conformity with the rules. Of course, the WTO had no authority to force any country to change its policy, but if a country failed to comply with a ruling, the complainant could seek permission from the WTO to retaliate against the noncompliant country. In practice, most countries accepted the panel ruling, and there were few retaliations. Because it was costly and time-consuming to bring a case, only strong cases were taken to the WTO: plaintiffs almost always won, and defendants almost always lost. Thus, the United States tended to win the cases it brought and lose the cases brought against it.

The system worked well enough that it effectively ended the unilateral approach previously taken by the United States. After 1995, section 301 cases were superseded by cases being brought into the WTO's dispute-settlement system, which proved to be effective in enforcing the many WTO agreements. Despite the fears that the WTO would infringe on the sovereignty of the United States, particularly in cases involving environmental standards or health and safety regulations, most cases were fairly mundane and dealt with narrow technicalities.[74] At the same time, the legalistic approach to trade disputes made it less adept at handling highly political trade disputes, such as the conflict between the United States and the Europe over subsidies to aircraft producers (Airbus and Boeing) and food regulations (hormones in beef and genetically modified crops). These cases still required a negotiated and not a legal solution.

However, the Uruguay Round agreement proved to be the last major substantive agreement reached by the WTO members. In 1995, the WTO had 128 member countries; by 2015, this had grown to more than 160. This expansion created a problem for the institution as a trade-liberalizing body. The WTO is often called a "member-driven" organization because the institution has no real independent power outside of what the member states want to achieve through it. The WTO also operated on the basis of a consensus among its members in negotiating the rules and agreeing on the reduction of trade barriers. Of course, reaching such a consensus is extremely difficult, and the larger the membership, the more difficult this proved to be. In particular, the more active participation of developing countries such as India and Brazil, which had long been reluctant to reduce trade barriers, made the next round of trade negotiations much more problematic.

POST-NAFTA TRADE POLITICS

In its first two years, the Clinton administration secured congressional passage of two landmark trade agreements, NAFTA and the Uruguay Round, although NAFTA and most of the Uruguay Round agreements had been negotiated by the previous administration. President Clinton also presided over a period (1993–2001) when the country's economic performance was remarkably strong. By the end of the 1990s, the unemployment rate had fallen to just 4 percent, reaching 3.8 percent in April 2000, a rate not seen for three decades. Despite fears that NAFTA would cost jobs, manufacturing employment remained stable, and real wages grew at a strong pace, with notable gains for low-wage workers. Productivity growth accelerated with advances in information technology. The federal budget deficit briefly turned to a surplus and, although the trade deficit began to swell again, the strong economy meant that, unlike in the 1980s, there were few complaints about foreign competition.

The economy of the 1990s would later be looked back upon with envy. Yet, "paradoxically, as economic performance improved, the political environment [for trade policy] deteriorated," Lawrence (2002, 279) observed. Although protectionist pressures were subdued, and there were no proposals to reverse existing trade agreements, "the political consensus in support of trade agreements in the United States was severely eroded," and the trade agenda stalled. In large part, the continuing controversy over NAFTA was responsible for this development. NAFTA exposed bitter divisions within the Democratic party and poisoned the political atmosphere for trade policy for decades, making it difficult (but not impossible) for any president to move forward with new initiatives. Members of Congress did not want to go through such a tumultuous and divisive debate again. They were keenly aware of the public's sensitivity to trade and wished to avoid the subject altogether.

American politics also became much more partisan in the 1990s than it had been in previous decades. In a stunning development, Republicans captured the House in the 1994 midterm elections, gaining control of the chamber for the first time in forty years.[75] While having more Republicans in Congress might have strengthened the hand of a pro-trade Democratic president, as demonstrated by their cooperation over NAFTA, the two sides began fighting with each other on many issues, making it difficult to cooperate on trade matters.

The Democratic split on trade and the new partisanship were on display in the 1997–98 battle over fast track. Two years after getting the Uruguay Round through Congress, President Clinton proposed renewing fast track, which had expired in 1994. The president argued that the country should not be left behind as developing countries were beginning to open their markets and reduce state control of their economies. "We've worked hard to tear down trade barriers abroad so that we can create good jobs at home," he said. "Now we must act to expand our exports, especially to Asia and Latin America, two of the fastest-growing regions on earth, or be left behind as these emerging economies forge new ties with other nations." But, Clinton continued, "this is about more than economics. By expanding trade, we can advance the cause of freedom and democracy around the world."[76]

Yet the political environment was not ripe for a renewal of fast track. Still smarting over the passage of NAFTA, labor unions were determined to defeat the president's bid. Once again, House Minority Leader Richard Gephardt and Minority Whip David Bonior led the Democratic opposition. And as a stand-alone measure, without being embedded in a larger trade bill and with no tangible trade agreement in hand or on the horizon, fast track was vulnerable to defeat.[77] Sensing trouble, the Clinton administration asked Congress to delay any vote until the fall of 1997. Once again, the number of House votes needed to gain passage was 218. Republicans were expected to deliver 150 votes, but getting even 70 of 206 Democratic votes was thought to be extremely difficult. Just days before the vote, only 112 Republicans and 42 Democrats had announced their support. At 1:15 a.m. on the morning of November 10, 1997, the day of the scheduled vote, President Clinton called House Speaker Newt Gingrich and asked him to postpone it. AFL-CIO President John Sweeney called the defeat of fast track "the first bit of blue sky working Americans have seen in US trade policy in many years."[78]

If Democratic discord was not problem enough for fast track, partisanship intruded the following year. Against the opposition of the Clinton administration, Speaker Gingrich brought a vote on fast track to the House floor. Republicans knew that the vote would fail and simply sought to expose Democratic divisions and hand the president a defeat just before the 1998 midterm election. Even pro-trade Democrats were dismayed by the Republican move. "Today's exercise on this legislation soils our national trade policy with the mud of partisan politics," complained Robert Matsui (D-CA).[79] Fast track was easily defeated by a vote of 243–180.

What had changed to make the political environment for trade policy so contentious? Aside from the anger still felt by NAFTA opponents, a broader phenomenon was becoming apparent: the United States was entering into a new era of partisanship and political division. This was true not just on trade policy, but on most political issues coming before Congress, making it difficult for a Republican Congress to cooperate with a Democratic president. This new era of partisanship was not an aberration, however, but a return to a historical norm. The period from the late 1940s through the 1980s was the unusual period in Congress for the degree of bipartisanship shown.[80]

Figure 13.2 illustrates the increased partisan voting in Congress by showing House votes, by party, on important trade legislation from 1890 to 2015. The vertical axis measures the share of each party voting for lower tariffs or against higher tariffs. Every trade vote, from the McKinley tariff of 1890 through the second extension of the RTAA in 1940, was almost a straight party-line vote: Republicans voted for higher tariffs and against lower tariffs, while Democrats voted for lower tariffs and against higher tariffs. This pattern began to break down in the 1950s when Republicans started supporting trade agreements. For several decades, trade votes were largely bipartisan. This bipartisan pattern was driven in large part by foreign-policy concerns, discussed in chapter 11, until the end of the Cold War in 1989. It continued until the Democrats lost their base in the South and began drawing most of their support from the North, particularly the Rust Belt. Although Democrats sponsored some of the protectionist legislation of the 1970s and 1980s, they supported the trade bills in 1984, 1988, as well as the Uruguay Round. However, NAFTA was a turning point: after NAFTA, Democratic support for trade legislation weakened considerably. Indeed, Congress's vote on NAFTA looked almost bipartisan in comparison with the wrangling over trade policy in the late 1990s and into the 2000s.

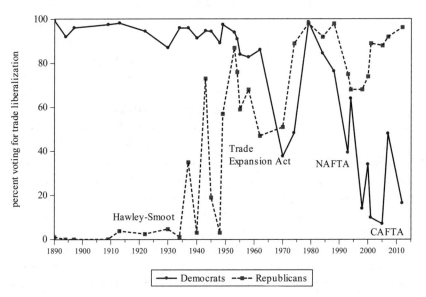

Figure 13.2. House voting on trade legislation, by party,
1890–2015. (Compiled by the author.)

One important political change was the demise of Southern Democrats and their replacement by Southern Republicans. From the Civil War until the Great Depression, Southern Democrats dominated the party, outnumbering Northern Democrats from the manufacturing belt, who tended to support protective tariffs. After Franklin Roosevelt and the New Deal solidified the party's hold in northern urban constituencies in the 1930s, the Democrats were geographically diversified, but there was little intra-party feuding on trade during the calm period of the 1950s and 1960s, when foreign competition was in abeyance. The import shocks of the 1970s pushed Northern Democrats (representing the industrial belt) into opposing freer trade, while Southern Democrats (representing the textile belt) continued to support it because the MFA was in place to protect the textile and apparel industry. The demise of Southern Democrats weakened the party's support for freer trade. As the number of Southern Democrats declined, a trend that accelerated in the early 1990s, Northern Democrats came to dominate the party and determine its position on trade issues. Northern Democrats from the Rust Belt were attuned to the interests of labor unions and the loss of jobs in manufacturing. They did not want President Clinton or his successors to negotiate further trade agreements that would arouse the opposition of labor unions and other constituents.[81]

While this geographic shift changed the complexion of the Democratic party, Southern Republicans were more ideologically in favor of free trade. The replacement of Democrats by Republicans in the South diminished the clout of the textile and apparel industry and of their unionized workers. In South Carolina, for example, Democrat Ernest "Fritz" Hollings, a firm advocate of import limits, was replaced by Republican Jim DeMint, a strong free trader, in the Senate. Rather than saving old textile jobs, the Republicans focused on attracting new, non-union, manufacturing jobs to the region. Southern apparel producers were rapidly declining in economic strength and influence as the region became more internationalist in outlook and sought to attract domestic and foreign investment in other manufacturing industries.

Democrats from the Rust Belt (depicted in figure 12.7) complained that trade agreements such as NAFTA served the interests of big business but not workers. "Our trade policy serves the needs of nominally American multinational corporations whose business visions and plans are global in scope and which maintain no national allegiances," Marcy Kaptur (D-OH) protested. "Free trade advocates want the American people to believe that those of us who oppose fast track are ignorant of the new international economy and are pursuing an 'America-last' strategy," William Lipinski

(D-IL) added. "They think we are protectionists, as if it were some kind of dirty word. Well, if trying to protect American jobs, the American standard of living, and American working families makes me a protectionist, then I will gladly wear that label."[82]

At the same time, Democrats in other regions of the country, particularly the West, represented states with export-oriented industries, such as high technology and aerospace. They clung to the party's traditional position in favor of open trade. The geographic division among Democrats became less North-South than between those states with strong ties to organized labor and those without.[83]

While opposition to trade grew stronger among the Democrats, however, the party also grew weaker in national politics. Republicans captured the House in 1994 and held it until the 2006 election, when they lost it briefly before recapturing it again in 2010. Shifts in the country's political geography also weakened the strength of old manufacturing regions in Congress. The five largest Rust Belt states—New York, Pennsylvania, Ohio, Michigan, and Illinois—lost eleven seats in the reapportionment of the House after the 1990 census and another seven seats after the 2000 census. Meanwhile, California, Texas, Florida, and Arizona picked up fifteen new House seats after the 1990 census and another seven after the 2000 census. Furthermore, farm states in the Midwest—including Iowa, Kansas, South Dakota, and Nebraska—continued to support export-oriented policies as agricultural producers and to see foreign markets as opportunities for expanding sales. Wheat, soybeans, corn, meat, and animal hides still ranked high in terms of exports. As the political weight of the country shifted away from the industrial North and Midwest and toward the South and West, opponents of trade agreements were put in a weaker political position. These shifts in regional political strength meant that members of Congress representing old manufacturing interests could try to block new trade agreements, but they would never be strong enough to roll back those agreements.

In addition, the United States had become a service economy, in which the agricultural and manufacturing sectors were no longer as important as they had been in previous decades. A majority of workers were not directly affected by the problems that labor-intensive or unionized manufacturing industries had in dealing with foreign competition. Manufacturing's share of total employment had fallen from more than 25 percent in 1970 to less than 15 percent by 2000. The share of unionized workers in private-sector employment also fell from 20 percent in 1983 to 11 percent in 2014.[84] With that shrinkage came diminished political power.

These political and economic factors, as well as the new WTO rule against export-restraint agreements, made it difficult for industries facing competition from imports to get protection the way that they did in the 1970s and 1980s. For example, the Asian financial crisis of 1997–98 led to a huge diversion of steel shipments to the United States. Steel imports soared, driving down prices and contributing in part to the layoff of roughly 170,000 steel workers as firms cut back production or went bankrupt. This unleashed a flood of antidumping and countervailing duty petitions, but legislative aid was not forthcoming. Although the House passed a bill in March 1999 by a wide margin calling for import quotas, everyone knew the effort would fail: the president had already issued a veto threat, and the Senate did not even bother to take the measure up.[85] The inability of the steel industry to receive much of a hearing during this cyclical crisis illustrated how much industry trade politics had changed. In the 1970s and 1980s, Congress would have been quick to demand action, and the executive would have negotiated export-restraint agreements with foreign countries. Now neither Congress nor the president was willing to act on the industry's behalf, and WTO rules no longer permitted export-restraint agreements, leaving the industry to take its chances with administrative trade remedies.[86]

Although it did not come close to passing any new import restrictions, Congress also did not encourage the president to seek new trade agreements. In fact, there was little immediate prospect of accomplishing anything in multilateral or regional trade discussions. The Clinton administration was interested in building on the Uruguay Round by pressing forward with new negotiations to discuss e-commerce, agriculture, and services, but global sentiment was not favorable to new trade talks. The European Union (EU) and Japan did not want further discussions about their agricultural policies, and developing countries were still absorbing their Uruguay Round commitments, leaving most WTO members unenthusiastic about starting new negotiations.

The WTO was proving valuable in resolving trade disputes, but its membership was reluctant to move forward with new trade negotiations. The multilateral system no longer consisted mainly of the United States, Western Europe, and Japan, as in past negotiating rounds. Developing countries were now fully in the mix, which made reaching a consensus on the agenda much more difficult. For example, the Clinton administration and congressional Democrats wanted to ensure that labor standards and environmental provisions were included in all new trade agreements, but developing countries were strongly opposed. They were suspicious of having enforceable provisions on worker rights in trade agreements out of fear that developed countries might use such provisions to block their exports of labor-intensive manufactured goods. At the first WTO ministerial meeting in Singapore in 1996, developing countries rebuffed an American attempt to put labor standards onto the trade agenda.

The next WTO ministerial meeting, in Seattle in 1999, was more eventful. The gathering attracted huge public protests as a wide range of groups, including labor unions, environmental groups, human rights activists, religious organizations, and others, voiced a multitude of complaints about the trading system. These groups feared that the new WTO agreements would infringe on national sovereignty and undermine domestic regulations to protect the environment and working conditions, although these fears were never realized. Among the protesters were fringe groups—dismissed as "recreational revolutionaries" by some trade officials—including anarchists, some of whom smashed storefront windows in downtown Seattle. This violence brought out the riot police, leading to confrontations involving tear gas and mass arrests. These skirmishes were called "The Battle in Seattle" and were later depicted in a movie of that name.

While the rambunctious protests outside the convention center got most of the media attention, the ministerial meeting broke down over a lack of consensus among WTO members about the parameters of a new negotiating round. A key issue was labor standards, which developing countries thought had been tabled at Singapore. Yet President Clinton raised the issue again and perhaps inadvertently scuttled the meeting by stating, "ultimately I would favor a system in which sanctions would come for violating" an agreement on labor standards. This statement "stunned delegates, and even his own negotiators" and confirmed the worst fears of developing countries.[87] The meeting ended with no decision to start new negotiations but with greater suspicion among developing countries about the content of a new trade agenda.

Other regional trade initiatives that the United States was involved in, including the Free Trade Area of the Americas (FTAA) and the Asia-Pacific Economic Cooperation (APEC) discussions, failed to advance as well.[88] Yet the Clinton administration succeeded in persuading Congress to pass the African Growth and Opportunity Act of 2000, which gave duty-free treatment to select goods from sub-Saharan Africa, but not without a fight with labor unions once again. More significantly, the administration oversaw the accession of China to the WTO.

CHINA AND THE EXPANSION OF GLOBAL TRADE

The collapse of Communism in 1989 allowed Eastern Europe and later the former Soviet Union to become integrated into the world economy, although their impact on global trade was modest. A more important consequence of the collapse was the discrediting of the socialist planning model, involving high trade barriers and state-led industrialization policies, that had been embraced by many developing countries. After seeing the success of export-oriented growth policies in Taiwan and South Korea in the 1960s and 1970s, developing countries began adopting pro-market reforms, particularly the relaxation of state economic controls, which included opening their markets to international trade. Even without any changes in US policy, economic reforms around the world in the late 1980s and early 1990s would increase the participation of developing countries in world trade and have significant ramifications for the US economy.

The biggest change occurred in China. In the 1970s, China was one of the poorest countries in the world, with a population of about a billion people, and it had virtually no presence in world markets. In 1978, China's premier, Deng Xiaoping, began to open what had been a closed economy, moving it away from rigid state control and central planning toward a market-oriented system with limited private enterprise. Agricultural collectives were phased out, and private farming was introduced; the state monopoly on foreign trade was abolished; foreign investment was gradually permitted; and trade barriers were reduced in stages.

These policy reforms led to a dramatic acceleration in China's economic growth and sparked a rapid expansion in its foreign trade. With hundreds of millions of unskilled workers migrating from the rural areas to coastal manufacturing centers, China soon became the world's largest exporter of labor-intensive goods, particularly apparel, footwear, toys, and sporting goods. China also became the assembly location for the world's consumer electronics. Within two decades, China made an enormous impact on world markets and trade flows. China's share of world exports rose from miniscule proportions in 1980 to 5 percent in 2000, reaching 12 percent in 2014.[89]

The United States had little contact with the country after China's Communist revolution in 1949, until President Nixon's famous trip to Beijing in 1972. In 1980, President Carter opened trade with China by allowing its goods to be given MFN status instead of being subject to the much higher non-MFN duties that were still in effect from the Hawley-

Smoot tariff of 1930. The Trade Act of 1974 gave the president the authority to grant Communist countries MFN status on an annual basis, provided Congress did not vote to disapprove. The renewal continued without controversy until China's brutal crackdown on protesters in Tiananmen Square in 1989. Thereafter, Congress sought to link China's MFN status to improvements in human rights, but subordinating growing commercial interests to human rights concerns proved difficult. Throughout the 1990s, President Clinton argued that political and economic engagement with China would serve American foreign-policy goals, including human rights objectives, better than withdrawing MFN status, which would essentially cut off bilateral trade.[90]

In the 1990s, the United States began discussing the terms under which China could join the GATT. Once it did so, China would be required to adhere to its rules, and the United States would be obligated to grant MFN status without annual review. For the United States to allow its admission, China would have to commit to a wide-ranging package of tariff reductions and market-access commitments. By 1995, China also had to agree to the Uruguay Round agreements. While other countries were willing to accept China as a new member of the WTO, the United States delayed and sought to wring as many concessions from China as possible.

In November 1999, during the WTO ministerial meeting in Seattle, US Trade Representative Charlene Barshefsky announced that an agreement had been reached and that the United States would support China's admission. China agreed to substantial tariff reductions, with rates dropping from an average of 25 percent to 9 percent, a phaseout of import quotas and licensing requirements, and a commitment to open up services and adhere to agreements on trade-related investment and intellectual property.[91] The United States did not get many commitments on reforming state-owned enterprises and government procurement, but was allowed to invoke a special China safeguard to protect against import surges and use a special methodology relating to nonmarket economies in dumping and subsidy cases for an extended period.

For the agreement to take effect, Congress had to approve "Permanent Normal Trade Relations" (PNTR) with China. Since this issue came up so soon after the battles over NAFTA and fast track, Democrats were not pleased with the administration's decision to bring a vote on China's trade status before Congress in an election year. "The president has thrown an apple of discord within the Democratic Party at a time when we are trying to win the House of Representatives," Rep. Nancy Pelosi (D-CA) grumbled.[92] Democrats wished to avoid a NAFTA-style debate about whether another low-wage, undemocratic country should be given permanent access to the US market. Since it had a much larger labor force and much lower wages than Mexico, China could potentially have a much bigger impact on the US economy than Mexico.

Businesses and agricultural producers strongly favored granting PNTR to China. American multinationals that had investments in China, or had contracting arrangements with Chinese firms, wanted the assurance that they could ship goods made or assembled there back to the United States at the low MFN rates. These firms also saw the potential to sell more goods to China if government barriers were swept aside and trade rules were established and enforced. In addition, dozens of agricultural groups, representing farmers, producers, and processers, urged passage of the bill because they saw China as a large and growing market for soybeans and other products. These groups also feared that if Congress rejected PNTR, they would lose sales to European or Asian competitors whose governments had already given China MFN status. In addition, many foreign-policy specialists argued that increased trade and integration of China would lead to more bilateral engagement and strengthen regional security. It was even hoped that such engagement would promote the rule of law, improve the human rights situation, and perhaps even encourage a movement toward democracy.

The opponents of PNTR emphasized the potential problems associated with increased trade with China: the threat of large job losses and a growing trade deficit, the unresolved question of human rights, and the lack of adequate labor and environmental standards. The range of opposition to PNTR was greater than in the case of NAFTA because labor and environmental groups were joined by human rights activists and even some groups on the political right. These included social conservatives, religious groups, and national security hawks who opposed anything that might strengthen a Communist country and potential adversary. Many conservatives feared that the transfer of advanced technology to China would threaten America's national security. These groups believed that the annual review of MFN gave the United States leverage over China and was the only way to keep it on good behavior. Consequently, Republican support for PNTR was weaker than for previous trade initiatives.

The PNTR debate repeated many features of the NAFTA debate. Minority Leader Richard Gephardt and Minority Whip David Bonior led the Democratic opposition in the House; the White House invited former presidents back to Washington to help make the case for trade with China; and members of Congress delayed announcing how they would vote until the last minute.[93] Even though the economy was close to a business-cycle peak, and the unemployment rate was below 4 percent, the House vote still posed a challenge because of the continued political sensitivity of trade. A week before the vote, about a hundred members of the House were formally uncommitted. In May 2000, after extensive debate, the House passed PNTR by a vote of 237–197. Republicans voted 164–57 in favor, and Democrats (along with two independents) voted 140–73 against.[94] The Senate easily passed the legislation by a vote of 87–13 later that year. President Clinton signed the bill, paving the way for China's accession to the WTO.

Since the United States had been giving China MFN status since 1980, the tariffs applied to China's goods did not change as a result of PNTR. Yet, as figure 13.3 shows, over the next eight years, imports from China soared. This import shock was significantly larger in magnitude than Japan's in the 1980s or Mexico's in the 1990s. What accounts for this surge and what was its impact on the US economy and trade politics?

The main explanation for the rapid growth in imports from China in the 1990s and 2000s was the large size and rapid growth of the Chinese economy. For nearly three decades, China's real GDP grew at more than 10 percent per year and China became the world's second largest economy in the early 2000s. This economic expansion was a massive shock

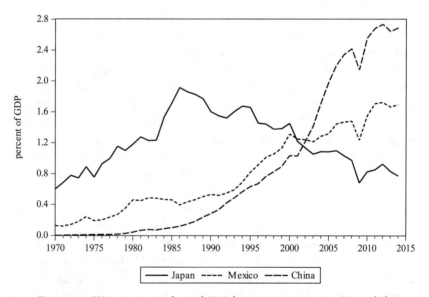

Figure 13.3. US imports as a share of GDP, by country, 1970–2015. (Compiled by the author, based on data from the US Bureau of the Census.)

to world markets, both on the supply side (in terms of the production of labor-intensive manufactured goods that China exported) and on the demand side (in terms of the raw materials and commodities that China imported). The passage of PNTR accounts for some of the rapid growth in US imports after 2001, since it resolved uncertainty about whether China's exports would continue to receive favorable tariff treatment in the United States.[95] Had China ever lost its MFN status, the average tariff on its goods would have risen from 4 percent to 37 percent, and as high as 70 percent on some items. The threat that these duties might be reimposed if relations between the two countries deteriorated discouraged some trade and investment.

The import surge partly explains the unusually large loss of manufacturing jobs between 2001 and 2003. Although the United States suffered a short recession in 2001, the 17 percent drop in manufacturing employment during this period seemed wholly disproportionate to the mild downturn.[96] Beyond the narrow window of 2001–3, the surge of imports from China is estimated to have had a considerable effect on US employment in certain import-competing industries during the 1990s and 2000s. According to Autor, Dorn, and Hanson (2013), imports from China explained 21 percent of the decline in US manufacturing employment over the period 1990 to 2007—a loss of 1.5 million jobs. Their results indicate that imports from China led to the loss of 548,000 US manufacturing jobs between 1990 and 2000 and another 982,000 jobs between 2000 and 2007. Many of these workers did not have the skills or education to find reemployment either in export sectors or other manufacturing industries, and they also lacked the geographic mobility to move to regions of the country that were creating jobs. Instead, they were often forced to take jobs in the service sector, or they dropped out of the labor force altogether and went on government disability programs.

Furthermore, because of the industry mix that was hit by the imports —low-skill, labor-intensive manufactures, such as apparel and furniture— the adverse impact was geographically concentrated in states such as Tennessee, Missouri, Arkansas, Mississippi, Alabama, Georgia, North Carolina, and Indiana.[97] The impact was particularly large in apparel, where China's economic rise coincided with the phaseout of the MFA. The combination of the two dealt a major blow to domestic apparel production: output and employment underwent a stunning decline in the 1990s and 2000s, even though the economy as a whole was expanding. The apparel industry lost about half a million jobs between 1995 and 2005 as mills and factories, often in poor, rural counties, closed. In some cases, textile and apparel plants were simply shut down, and the equipment was dismantled and shipped to China and South Asia to be used for production there.

Although the China import shock was large, the job losses did not receive much attention at the time because the impact was masked by other factors working at the national level. In the 1990s, the labor market was strong and other opportunities for displaced workers were created. Since workers in the textile and apparel industry were paid much less than the average worker in manufacturing, those that later found employment were likely to earn the same or even higher wages than they had before.[98] In the 2000s, the job losses did not get more attention because a housing boom was creating new jobs in construction.[99] In fact, the national unemployment rate was falling from 2002 through 2006 as imports from China were surging. Yet, in general, the outcome for displaced workers was much worse in this period because the labor market was not as strong, and those workers had fewer employment options. Still, these job losses should be put in perspective: imports from China may have resulted in the involuntary displacement of 97,000 manufacturing workers per year (on average, adjusted to account for voluntary separations), but that is less than one-fifth of total involuntary job loss in manufacturing and less than 5 percent of all involuntary job losses over the same period.[100]

Imports from China were also far from being the most important factor in the decline in manufacturing employment at this time. The production of manufactured goods was going through a revolution in which new technology and capital equipment, employing just a few skilled workers (such as engineers), were able to produce more and more goods with less and less labor. For example, in the 1980s it took 10 labor hours to produce a ton of steel; by 2015 that figure was down to 2 labor hours. One study attributed 87 percent of job loss in manufacturing between 2000 and 2010 to improved productivity and only 13 percent to trade. However, there were two outliers in which job losses due to trade were much higher: 40 percent in the case of furniture and 44 percent in the case of apparel and leather, both unskilled, labor-intensive industries.[101]

Imports from China and other developing countries also had a surprisingly small impact on income inequality in the United States during this period. Wage inequality—measured by the relative wages of college graduates to high-school graduates, or the relative wage of non-production (white collar) workers to production (blue-collar) workers—began increasing in the 1980s, around the time when the growth in world trade accelerated. It was commonly believed that increased trade, particularly with labor-abundant developing countries, was responsible for depressing the wages of unskilled, blue-collar worker relative to skilled, white-collar workers. Yet economists generally found that growing imports from developing countries were not responsible for much of the increased inequality. One estimate puts the contribution of trade with low-wage countries at something shy of 10 percent of the overall rise in the college wage premium from 1980 to 2006.[102] Lawrence (2008, 37) found that "without the impact on wage inequality between 1981 and 2006, the wages of blue-collar workers would have been 1.4 percent higher than they were in 2006 and that almost all of this took place before 2000." Furthermore, the timing of the increase in trade and the increase in wage inequality did not match up: inequality grew rapidly in the 1980s when trade with developing countries was growing slowly, whereas inequality leveled off when imports from low-wage countries started accelerating in the 1990s and 2000s.[103] As a result, "the recent increase in US inequality has little to do with global forces that might be expected to especially affect unskilled workers—namely, immigration and expanded trade with developing countries," Lawrence (2008, 73) concluded. "Instead, the sources of increased inequality have been the rising share of the super rich—a development in which trade is likely to have played only a small role—and the increased share of profits in income, much of which could be cyclical."

China's export surge of 2001–7 had an important macroeconomic dimension as well. The overall US current account deficit reached a record 6 percent of GDP in 2007, although it did not generate as much alarm as the smaller deficits had in the 1980s. Meanwhile, China's current account surplus ballooned to 10 percent of GDP in 2007, a magnitude far outside the normal range of experience for a rapidly growing developing country.[104] US exports to China failed to grow at anything close to the pace of imports from China, and the bilateral trade deficit with China grew from $83 billion in 2000 to nearly $260 billion in 2007.

The bilateral trade imbalance did not go unnoticed. Just as in the 1980s with Japan, attention was put on the exchange rate. Whereas Japan's trade surplus had been driven by private outward capital flows, China's trade surplus was related to government intervention in the foreign exchange market. Starting in the mid-1990s, China fixed the value of its currency (the renminbi) against the dollar. China's foreign exchange reserves rapidly accumulated, growing from less than $200 million in 2000 to $1.6 trillion by 2007, and later peaking at nearly $4 trillion in 2014. This reserve accumulation indicated that China's central bank was buying dollars and selling renminbi, which kept its currency undervalued and boosted exports.[105]

As China's exports began to surge, some US producers started complaining that its currency policies were giving the country an unfair advantage in trade. This got the attention of members of Congress. Starting in 2003, Senators Charles Schumer (D-NY) and Lindsay Graham (R-SC) introduced legislation to impose a 27.5 percent tariff on goods from China until it revalued its exchange rate. (That number was a simple average of 15 and 40, which were two contemporary estimates of the renminbi's undervaluation.) More than one hundred similar bills were subsequently introduced, but all died in committee.

President George W. Bush's administration did little to challenge China's currency policy, at least in public. The Omnibus Trade and Competitiveness Act of 1988 required the secretary of the Treasury to provide semiannual reports on the exchange-rate policies of the major trading partners and consider "whether countries manipulate the rate of exchange between their currency and the United States dollar for purposes of preventing effective balance of payments adjustment or gaining unfair competitive advantage in international trade." The Treasury Department never named China as a "currency manipulator," but officials quietly pushed for a change in policy.[106] In July 2005, China began to allow the renminbi to appreciate steadily against the dollar.

The situation changed as a result of the financial crisis of 2008, when US imports plunged, slashing the current account deficit. The crisis also saw China's current account surplus drop to about 3 percent of its GDP, a more sustainable level that eased bilateral trade tensions. Still, after this correction had taken place, the House passed a bill in 2010 that would have allowed the Commerce Department to define an undervalued currency as an export subsidy in countervailing duty cases, but the Senate did not take the measure up.

Because the import surge from China was concentrated in certain goods, legislators from districts producing similar goods were swayed to vote against further trade agreements. For example, Howard Coble, a conservative Republican from the Sixth District of North Carolina, voted in favor of NAFTA in 1993. After imports of kitchen cabinets and yarn and thread from China had threatened workers in his district, he began voting against trade agreements in the 2000s. He was not alone: several representatives from districts adversely affected by Chinese imports voted against trade agreements in the 2000s, but not enough of them to block those agreements (to be discussed shortly).[107]

Unlike the import shock from Japan in the 1980s, very few protection-ist policies were put in place in response to the import shock from China in the 2000s. To be sure, China became the target of antidumping and countervailing duty petitions, just as Japan had been forced to adopt ex-port restrictions on automobiles, steel, semiconductors, and many other goods. But the political pressure to restrict imports from China was con-siderably less than in the case of Japan, partly because the foreign busi-ness presence in China was much greater than it had been with Japan.[108] Whereas Japan was perceived to have a closed market, both to foreign goods and foreign investment, China was relatively open to foreign brands and to foreign investment. While Japanese exports were products made in Japan by Japanese producers (Toyota, Honda, Panasonic, Sony) that com-peted directly with American producers, Chinese exports were sourced by American firms themselves and consisted of American name brands (foot-wear by Nike, apparel sold by Walmart, electronic devices by Apple). Few American consumers could name more than one or two Chinese brand names, as they could for Japanese brands.

China's leading exports to the United States include consumer elec-tronics, sporting goods and toys, apparel and footwear, and furniture, sec-tors which had already experienced a secular decline in the United States and goods that were already largely imported from other countries in Asia. Furthermore, China's large share of the world's consumer electronics ex-ports did not reflect the country's technological sophistication as much as its low labor costs, which made it the world's most cost-effective place for large-scale, labor-intensive assembly operations. In fact, only about half the value of China's exports to the United States was actually due to con-tent that was "made in China." Many of its exports were processed goods or assembled from foreign-made components, meaning that much of their value was in the intermediate components purchased from such countries as Japan, Korea, Germany, and the United States.[109]

As a result, there were many fewer advocates in the early 2000s of pro-tecting domestic producers from imports from China than there had been in the 1980s with respect to Japan.[110] Restricting imports was no longer considered a serious policy option. Large, globalized firms had a strong interest in keeping trade open. Many domestic firms benefited from hav-ing access to a wide array of intermediate goods on the world market. And the domestic firms that faced direct competition from China lacked much political clout in Congress, as indicated by the decline of the apparel and furniture industries. The WTO ruled out export-restraint agreements, and domestic firms could only file antidumping and countervailing duty

petitions. Such selective duties on China would not stimulate more production in the United States but only divert imports from China to other
Asian suppliers. If consumer electronics, sporting goods and toys, apparel
and footwear, and furniture were not imported from China, those goods
were likely to be imported from other Asian countries. Indeed, some of the
growth in China's exports to the United States was simply a displacement
of the exports of other suppliers in Asia and elsewhere.[111]

BUSH'S BILATERALISM

In securing congressional passage of NAFTA and the Uruguay Round, and
ushering China into the world trading system, the Clinton administration
dramatically changed the trade-policy landscape and accelerated the process of globalization. President Clinton's emphasis on the inevitability of
economic change, however, was always tempered by an acknowledgement
of the public's fears about trade. By contrast, his Republican successor,
George W. Bush, spoke with more conviction about free trade than Clinton
had, but overlooked the qualms felt by many Americans, despite presiding
over a weaker economy. The Bush administration pushed eight bilateral
trade agreements through Congress, but did so over increasing Democratic
opposition.

During the 2000 election campaign, Bush made strong statements
in favor of the economic, political, and moral benefits of free trade.[112] He
pledged to secure trade-negotiating authority, complete the proposed Free
Trade Area of the Americas (FTAA), and initiate new multilateral and
bilateral trade negotiations. And yet, like most presidential candidates,
electoral politics was paramount. The steel industry was still recovering
from the 1997–98 import surge, and Ohio, Pennsylvania, and West Virginia were key states in the election. Campaigning at a West Virginia steel
mill, Bush's vice presidential running mate, Richard Cheney, promised aid
to the steel industry. "If our trading partners violate our trade laws, we
will respond swiftly and firmly," Cheney told workers. "There should be
no more looking the other way so that politics can triumph over principles."[113] This pledge was nothing out of the ordinary, since every administration since Lyndon Johnson had given trade protection to the steel industry, with the exception of the Clinton administration.

After the election, the promise on steel came due. The United Steel
Workers and Congressional Steel Caucus said their support for new trade-
negotiating authority was contingent on the administration taking action
against steel imports. In June 2001, to preempt the filing of antidumping

petitions, the Bush administration took the unusual step of initiating a section 201 escape-clause case on behalf of the steel industry, the first time that had ever been done. Of course, the ITC still had to rule that imports were "a substantial cause of serious injury" to steel producers. Although steel imports jumped during the Asian financial crisis of 1997–98, they fell back considerably in 1999–2000, raising the question of whether escape-clause tariffs could be imposed in 2002 for an import surge that had occurred three or four years earlier. The WTO safeguard agreement required that there be an absolute increase in imports for higher tariffs to be imposed, which was not true after 1999. Yet the ITC determined that the steel industry had been injured by increased imports in many but not all categories of goods.

In March 2002, after some debate within the administration, the president accepted the ITC recommendation and imposed tariffs of up to 30 percent on selected categories of imported steel.[114] In this particular case, the protection was designed to be porous. About 37 percent of the steel imports covered by the decision were exempt from the safeguard duties, including imports from countries with free-trade agreements with the United States and those from small developing countries. In addition, the administration imposed the safeguard duties for a period of three years and one day. Under WTO rules, any safeguards scheduled to be in place for more than three years require a midterm review, which meant that the administration could revisit the issue and modify or remove the duties after just a year and a half.[115]

Meanwhile, the European Union and several other countries immediately challenged the steel action through the WTO's dispute-settlement system. In 2003, a WTO panel found that the ITC decision was inconsistent with the safeguard agreement, a decision reaffirmed by the Appellate Body.[116] The administration then faced the choice of rescinding the steel tariffs, keeping the tariffs in place and accepting retaliation against US exports by the complainants, or offering compensation in the form of tariff reductions on other goods. This decision was perfectly timed with the mandatory midterm review. At this point, the Bush administration announced that the safeguard tariffs had achieved their purpose and therefore would be lifted. This decision was not difficult, because the steel measures had received unfavorable press in the United States and around the world, had been in effect through the 2002 midterm elections and had thus served their political purpose, and had coincided with a recovery in domestic steel prices that boosted industry profitability.

The Bush administration's main focus was on getting negotiating authority from Congress and concluding new trade agreements. Prior to the election, Robert Zoellick, who became Bush's first trade representative, outlined a policy known as "competitive liberalization."[117] In the past, the United States had mainly focused on multilateral trade liberalization through the GATT, while occasionally signing bilateral and regional trade agreements (such as NAFTA) when the opportunity arose. The Bush administration planned to pursue bilateral and regional negotiations more aggressively as a way of putting pressure on other countries who, out of their reluctance to reduce trade barriers, were holding up multilateral negotiations. Once in office, Zoellick energetically took up this agenda by asking Congress to pass "trade-promotion authority" (TPA), the new term for fast track. "In the absence of this authority, other countries have been moving forward with trade agreements while America has stalled," Zoellick stated. "We cannot afford to stand still—or be mired in partisan division—while other nations seize the mantle of leadership of trade from the United States."[118] Even though Republicans controlled the House, Congress was reluctant to embrace such an ambitious trade agenda. In the spring and summer of 2001, Speaker Dennis Hastert (R-IL) was forced to postpone three scheduled votes on TPA due to lack of support. Public sensitivity about trade was still high: less than two years had passed since the "Battle in Seattle" and the PNTR controversy, and the economy was now suffering from a mild recession.

Zoellick hoped to use the WTO ministerial meeting, scheduled for November in Doha, Qatar, to launch a new round of multilateral trade negotiations and persuade Congress to pass TPA. Of course, the previous WTO ministerial meeting in Seattle in 1999 had been a disaster, and few expected the Doha ministerial, which promised to be equally fractious, to succeed. But the terrorist attacks of September 11, 2001, temporarily changed the international climate. In a show of support, other countries rallied around the United States, and the WTO membership agreed to launch a new round.[119] Even so, many developing countries were reluctant to do so. The obligations they had undertaken in the Uruguay Round, particularly in terms of intellectual property, were increasingly viewed as excessive, and the market access they were promised in agriculture and clothing either never materialized or was erased by China's domination of the market. Developing countries insisted that the Uruguay Round outcome be rebalanced if they were to start a new round. Hence, the negotiations were named the Doha Development Round with the pledge that they would focus on the economic benefits for developing countries.

The prospect of a new multilateral trade round helped the Bush administration get Congress to support TPA.[120] Previous presidents in divided governments needed a bipartisan coalition to advance their trade agendas: Ronald Reagan and George H. W. Bush worked with Democratic Congresses, while Bill Clinton needed Republican votes because of insufficient Democratic support. But George W. Bush had a Republican majority in Congress and did not need Democratic votes as long as the party stuck together. As a result, trade voting became sharply partisan. Convinced that Democrats would not cooperate with them, Republicans made little effort to win bipartisan support for new trade initiatives. Instead, the administration and Republican leadership focused on using its majority to pass trade bills without labor and environment provisions, which they viewed as burdensome regulations that might limit trade, even though such provisions might have won some Democratic support.

In December 2001, the House passed the Bipartisan Trade Promotion Authority Act of 2001 by the very partisan vote of 215–214, with Republicans voting 194–24 in favor and Democrats voting 188–20 against. The administration and the House leadership put enormous pressure on Republicans not to stray from the party line and undermine the president in a time of war.[121] Congress was able to pass TPA in 2001, after having failed to do so in 1998, because there were more Republican members of the House (adding thirteen more votes in favor) and more Republicans switched from no to yes than Democrats switched from yes to no (adding sixteen more votes in favor).[122] However, the partisan nature of the vote indicated that Republicans had a small margin of error, since even some of their members had reservations about trade.[123] Rep. Sander Levin (D-MI) warned, "This is not the type of authority which facilitates a broadly bipartisan trade policy. Another narrow vote will not be a victory for US trade policy, but instead will mean trouble for each new trade agreement because all the same issues and debates will be repeated."[124]

In any event, the Doha Round quickly became deadlocked as the United States could not convince the EU to compromise on agricultural subsidies nor the developing countries to embrace more trade reforms. Indeed, the compromise reached at Doha to label the negotiations a "development" round may have sowed the seeds of discord.[125] Not long after the start of the round, it was evident that having so many countries with such diverse interests at the negotiating table was making it extremely difficult to reach agreement. Yet enough progress had been made on the agricultural and nonagricultural market-access negotiations that ministers in

2008 hoped to resolve the remaining issues and bring the negotiations to a close. However, a dispute between the United States and India over the extent to which developing countries could raise tariffs on agricultural goods in the event of an import surge created a deadlock. Both sides refused to compromise, and the meeting ended in failure. Instead of simply being a problem that negotiators could revisit later, the 2008 impasse seemed to mark the collapse of the Doha Round in its entirety. The round limped on for a few more years without any serious effort to make a breakthrough. At the December 2015 WTO ministerial meeting in Nairobi, Kenya, the members failed to reaffirm the Doha agenda and effectively put the round to rest. This was the first time that GATT participants had failed to conclude a trade-negotiating round.

Of course, long before the problems in the Doha Round were fully evident, Zoellick had already indicated that the administration would pursue a strategy of "competitive liberalization," wherein bilateral and regional trade agreements would be used to put pressure on reluctant reformers. Therefore, the Bush administration moved quickly to reach trade agreements with willing partners. Up to this point, the United States had signed just four FTAs: with Israel in 1985, Canada in 1988, followed by NAFTA in 1993, and then Jordan in 2001 (signed by Bush but initiated by the Clinton administration). Zoellick quickly expanded the number of bilateral trade negotiations. In the six-year period 2002–7, the United States concluded agreements with Singapore, Chile, Australia, Morocco, Bahrain, Oman, Peru, Korea, Colombia, Panama, and five Central American countries (the Central American Free Trade Agreement and the Dominican Republic, or CAFTA-DR). Other negotiations—with five nations in southern Africa as well as with Malaysia, Thailand, and the United Arab Emirates—were unsuccessful. The plans for the Free Trade Area in the Americas and the Middle Eastern free-trade agreement also failed to make headway.

From the US perspective, free-trade agreements were pursued mostly for foreign-policy reasons, because the commercial benefits promised to be tiny. Why did other countries want to sign a free-trade agreement with the United States? Many developing countries wanted to lock in domestic economic reforms, including lower trade barriers, and hoped that guaranteed access to the US market would attract foreign investment. For example, nearly all of Peru's exports to the United States were given duty-free status under the GSP, but the eligible quantities were restricted, which in turn limited investment in those sectors. Peru wanted to remove the remaining obstacles facing its exports to the United States and receive the same market access as Mexico and other countries had.

The initial free-trade agreements (FTAs) were relatively uncontroversial and easily passed in the Republican-controlled Congress, as shown on table 13.2. In 2003, Congress approved the Chile and Singapore agreements by comfortable margins, the first FTAs with countries in South America and Asia. Negotiations with Chile had been intermittent since the early 1990s, while the Singapore agreement dealt mainly with services, since the country did little manufacturing. In 2004, Congress also passed agreements with Australia and Morocco, two allies in the war in Iraq and Afghanistan. None of these agreements aroused any significant opposition on economic grounds, because the bilateral trade flows were small. Neither country produced labor-intensive manufactured goods that were so politically sensitive, and in cases where they exported goods that threatened a domestic industry, such as sugar from Australia, the agreement had long phaseouts of trade barriers or no liberalization at all.

The Central America Free Trade Agreement, which included Costa Rica, El Salvador, Guatemala, Honduras, and Nicaragua, along with the Dominican Republic, was much more controversial. The CAFTA-DR debate in 2005 was a repeat of the NAFTA debate—a decade later but on a much smaller scale. Although these economies were tiny in comparison to that of the United States, and the trade flows very small, opponents portrayed CAFTA-DR as a major expansion of NAFTA and therefore a threat to the United States. Once again, opponents argued, the United States was opening up its market to imports from low-wage developing countries. Once again, opponents contended, workers would be hurt, jobs would be lost, and wages would be reduced, with all the benefits going to multinational corporations. As expected, labor unions adamantly opposed the agreement, but despite the difficulties they suffered, textile mill owners were split over whether to oppose it; by this point, many firms had embraced globalization.[126]

As in the NAFTA debate, the political rhetoric exaggerated the potential economic consequences of the agreement, because the CAFTA economies were just 2 percent of the size of the US economy.[127] Although the stakes for the United States were small, the political effort required to push the agreement through Congress was considerable. The day of the House vote (July 27, 2005) was tense because the outcome was uncertain. "This is not a major trade vote," Ways and Means Committee Chair Bill Thomas (R-CA) argued. "It is a major political vote, and it was made a political vote by Democrats."[128] The House vote was expected to be so close that the president made a rare appearance on Capitol Hill to rally Republican members, urging them to set aside parochial concerns and support the

TABLE 13.2. US regional and bilateral trade agreements

Country or region	House vote	Senate vote
Israel	422–0 (D: 241–0, R: 181–0) 5/7/1985	Voice vote 5/23/1985
Canada	366–40 (D: 215–30, R: 151–10) 8/9/1988	83–9 (D: 43–7, R: 40–2) 9/19/1988
North American Free Trade Agreement (NAFTA)	234–200 (D: 102–157, R: 132–43) 11/17/1993	61–38 (D: 27–28, R: 34–10) 11/20/1993
Jordan	Voice vote 7/31/2001	Voice vote 9/24/2001
Chile	270–156 (D: 75–129, R: 195–27) 7/24/2003	65–32 (D: 22–25, R: 43–7) 7/31/2003
Singapore	272–155 (D: 75–128, R: 197–27) 7/24/2003	66–32 (D: 22–25, R: 44–7) 7/31/2003
Australia	314–109 (D: 116–85, R: 198–24) 7/24/2004	80–16 (D: 32–14, R: 48–2) 7/15/2004
Morocco	323–99 (D: 120–81, R: 203–18) 7/22/2004	85–13 (D: 39–8, R: 46–5) 7/21/2004
Central American Free Trade Agreement & Dominican Republic (CAFTA-DR)	217–215 (D: 15–188, R: 202–27) 7/28/2005	54–45 (D: 11–33, R: 43–12) 6/30/2005
Bahrain	327–95 (D: 115–82, R: 212–13) 12/7/2005	Voice vote 12/13/2005
Oman	221–205 (D: 22–177, R: 199–28) 6/20/2006	62–32 (D: 13–27, R: 49–5) 9/19/2006
Peru	285–132 (D: 109–116, R: 176–16) 11/8/2007	77–18 (D: 30–17, R: 47–1) 12/4/2007
Panama	300–129 (D: 66–123, R: 234–6) 10/12/2011	77–22 (D: 30–21, R: 47–1) 10/12/2011
Colombia	262–167 (D: 31–158, R: 231–9) 10/12/2011	66–33 (D: 21–30, R: 45–3) 10/12/2011
Republic of Korea	278–151 (D: 59–130, R: 219–21) 10/12/2011	83–15 (D: 37–14, R: 46–1) 10/12/2011

Source: *Congressional Quarterly Almanac*, various years.

administration. Mark Foley (R-FL) called it "a gut-wrenching night" as the White House and House leadership, having written off any support from Democrats, pressured Republican members for their votes. Yet Republican opposition from textile states like North and South Carolina, sugar states like Louisiana and Idaho, and old manufacturing states like Ohio and Pennsylvania made it difficult to win full party backing.

The vote took place at 11 p.m. and was scheduled to last fifteen minutes, but thirty minutes later the vote was frozen at 214–211 in favor, with 8 Republicans yet to vote. The vote was held up for about an hour while the Republican leadership figured out which members could vote against CAFTA while still ensuring the bill's passage.[129] In the end, CAFTA was approved by the narrow vote of 217–215; Republicans voted 202–27 in favor, while Democrats voted 187–15 against.[130] The Senate followed in September by a vote of 54–45.[131]

While using the Republican majority to get trade legislation passed by one or two votes was in some ways a clever political strategy, it was not the way to build a strong bipartisan consensus on trade policy, if it was still possible to have one. Trade was clearly becoming an uncomfortable issue even for Republican members of Congress, none of whom wanted to vote regularly on such controversial matters. The decision not to seek bipartisan support, either because the Democratic opposition was implacable or because Democrats would insist on labor and environment provisions that would make the agreements unpalatable to Republicans, made it difficult to squeeze the votes through Congress.

In 2006, Congress approved a free-trade agreement with Bahrain, but a similar agreement with Oman encountered unexpectedly stiff resistance and almost went down to defeat. Once again, the House vote was held open beyond the time limit as the Republican leadership scrambled to round up support. The bill passed by 221–205, but the Oman vote was a bad omen for future trade agreements, since the country posed no threat to any domestic producers. Agreements with small countries meant the economic benefits to the United States were tiny, but the political costs of defending one's vote against hostile critics were large, and even Republican legislators came to view these votes as a nuisance.

The Bush administration's political strategy on trade policy could succeed only as long as Republicans had a working majority in Congress. That majority was lost when Democrats captured the House and the Senate in the 2006 midterm elections. The election dashed administration hopes that TPA would be renewed when it expired in 2007. And if the administration put more trade agreements before Congress, it would have to compromise to win the support of pro-trade Democrats. Shortly after the election, in early 2007, the Bush administration bowed to political reality and reached an understanding with Democrats—the so-called May Tenth Agreement—that labor and environmental provisions would be included in pending and future trade agreements. This paved the way for Congress to consider the recently concluded agreements with Colombia, Panama, Peru, and Korea. The labor and environmental provisions of the Peru FTA were revised to ensure that it would receive some Democratic approval. Consequently, the House passed the Peru agreement in November 2007 in a comfortable bipartisan vote of 285–132. Republicans voted 176–16 in favor, and Democrats voted 116–109 against it, but the Democratic split was a vast change over its near unanimous vote against CAFTA-DR.

By this time, however, the working relationship between the parties had become so contentious on other issues that compromises on trade were becoming nearly impossible to reach. TPA expired in June 2007, and the Democratic Congress gave no signal that it would be renewed. This was followed by a complete breakdown in cooperation on trade in April 2008. With his term in office nearly over, President Bush was anxious for Congress to pass the trade agreement with Colombia. House Speaker Nancy Pelosi (D-CA) recommended that the president delay submitting the implementing legislation for the FTA with Colombia, which was particularly controversial because of concerns over human rights violations and the suppression of organized labor. The president went ahead and submitted it anyway. Outraged that the president would send the agreement to Congress in an election year without first securing the support of Congressional leaders, Pelosi and House Democrats retaliated by voting to remove it from the fast-track timetable, thereby allowing Congress to postpone consideration of the agreement indefinitely.[132] Bush expressed his frustration at the "unprecedented and unfortunate action" taken by the House, which he accused of taking "a shortsighted and partisan path" at "the expense of our economy and our national security."[133]

The president's action and the House's reaction represented a serious breakdown in executive-legislative cooperation on trade policy. The commitment that Congress would give timely consideration to any trade agreement reached by the president, that is, consider it within ninety days of submission in an up or down vote, was gone. Now the House had demonstrated that it could change the rules under which it considered trade agreements anytime it wanted, and therefore fast track was not really a commitment. The impasse left the Colombia, Korea, and Panama FTAs in limbo for five years.

The Bush administration spent enormous energy negotiating bilateral trade agreements and large amounts of political capital in forcing Congress to vote repeatedly on trade agreements that were, for the most part, of modest economic importance. The countries with whom the United States enacted trade agreements between 2001 and 2008 accounted for less than 5 percent of US trade. In 2012, according to an International Trade Commission study (2016, 21), existing bilateral and regional trade agreements—from Israel in 1984 to Korea, Colombia, and Panama in 2011—increased total US exports by 3.6 percent and US imports by 2.3 percent, real GDP by 0.2 percent, and real wages by 0.3 percent. Despite the political attacks made on them, the economic effects were positive but small.

Yet, in pushing the later (and smaller) agreements through Congress, the Bush administration increased the fragility of what remained of the postwar bipartisan consensus on trade policy. Although Democrats had not been cooperative, the vote on Peru showed that agreements could be passed with bipartisan support if they included provisions regarding labor and the environment. The consequences of many small FTAs were small economic gains at a large political cost, which meant that congressional Democrats were even less likely to support trade initiatives when they swept into power in the 2008 election.

OBAMA'S HESITANCE

The election of Barack Obama as president in 2008 gave the Democrats unified control of government for the first time in more than a decade. In line with House Democrats, the Obama administration recognized that trade was a divisive issue within the party and among constituents and therefore should be raised as little as possible. While the administration did not embrace new measures to restrict imports (with one exception), neither did it push for many new trade agreements until its second term.

Obama entered office without great enthusiasm for trade agreements. In contrast to southern Democrats such as Bill Clinton, who had a long tradition of supporting freer trade, Obama was a northern Democrat with a constituency that was deeply suspicious of—if not outright hostile to—trade agreements such as NAFTA. In his memoir The Audacity of Hope, published when he was a senator from Illinois, Obama recounted his struggle about how to vote on CAFTA in 2005. Obama (2006, 172) conceded that the "agreement posed little threat to American workers—the combined economies of Central American countries involved were roughly the same as that of New Haven, Connecticut," and he concluded that "overall, CAFTA was probably a net plus for the US economy." Yet labor leaders viewed it as a large threat and reminded him of their view that NAFTA had cost thousands of workers their jobs. When President Bush asked for his support, Obama (2006, 176) replied "that resistance to CAFTA had less to do with the specifics of the agreement and more to do with the growing insecurities of the American worker. Unless we found strategies to allay those fears, and sent a strong signal to American workers that the federal government was on their side, protectionist sentiment would only grow." Obama voted against CAFTA, admitting that "my vote gave me no satisfaction, but I felt it was the only way to register a protest against what I considered to be the White House's inattention to the losers from free trade."

In the 2008 election campaign, Obama blamed NAFTA for the loss of a million jobs and argued that it should be renegotiated, adding, "I don't think NAFTA has been good for America, and I never have." He later backed off these statements and said that the campaign rhetoric was "overheated and amplified," but he insisted that "we can't keep passing unfair trade deals like NAFTA that put special interests over workers' interests."[134] While one of his economic advisers reassured alarmed Canadians that this was just campaign talk, the incident revealed Obama's ambivalence about trade.

As president, Obama had many reasons not to have an ambitious trade agenda. Aside from his own qualms about the matter, he had no desire to focus on an issue that would divide his party. More importantly, Obama entered office facing the worst economic crisis since the Great Depression. After a collapse in housing prices, many overleveraged banks and households were pushed into insolvency. In this fragile environment, the investment bank Lehman Brothers declared bankruptcy in September 2008, and financial markets temporarily ceased to function. By early 2009, the United States was in a severe recession. Industrial production fell 17 percent between December 2007 and June 2009, and the unemployment rate reached 10 percent in October 2009. As a result, Obama spent his first year in office persuading Congress to enact a fiscal stimulus and new financial regulations.

Fortunately, the president could afford to neglect trade policy because the economic crisis did not translate into a trade-policy crisis. As it initially unfolded, the financial collapse and economic slump reminded many commentators of the early 1930s, generating fears that protectionism and beggar-thy-neighbor policies would reappear. World trade received a huge jolt: the volume of world trade fell 12 percent in 2009, according to the WTO, the largest drop recorded in the postwar period.

To the surprise of many observers, however, the financial crisis and global recession did not lead to an outbreak of protectionism around the world. Only a tiny fraction of the decline in world trade could be traced to higher trade barriers.[135] In the United States, the main reason the Great Recession of 2008–9 did not lead to protectionist pressures is that imports fell sharply. Real imports of goods were an astounding 22 percent lower in the second quarter of 2009 than a year earlier. Since no major industry faced a surge of imports, domestic producers could not blame foreign competition for their problems. There was no jump in the filing of anti-dumping petitions, the current account deficit narrowed sharply, and protectionist pressures in Congress were largely absent.

There are several other reasons why the severe recession did not lead to the protectionism of the 1930s. First, countries had many more policy instruments for addressing the economic crisis than they did during the Depression. As discussed in chapter 8, countries resorted to draconian import restrictions in the 1930s because they lacked other macroeconomic policy tools—principally monetary policy, which was constrained by the gold standard—to stabilize the financial system and prevent deflation. Now, in 2008 and 2009, central banks acted swiftly to provide liquidity to financial markets and shore up the banking system, thereby preventing a prolonged downturn.

Second, in the 1930s countries could impose higher trade barriers without violating any international trade agreements, whereas now WTO agreements prevented the arbitrary imposition of trade restrictions. Of course, countries were free to violate those agreements, but if they did so they would have no illusion that they could escape retaliation by other countries. In fact, there was no jump in WTO disputes during or after the crisis.[136]

Third, in comparison to the 1930s, foreign investment had transformed the world economy and reduced the economic benefits of import restrictions for domestic firms. The largest firms in the United States, Europe, and Asia were multinational in their production operations and supply chains so that they no longer had a vested interest in pushing for higher trade barriers. For example, auto producers did not ask for trade protection, as they did in the early 1980s, because it would not solve any of their problems; they were diversified into other markets with equity stakes in foreign producers, and foreign firms already operated production facilities in the United States, making border protection irrelevant.

The Obama administration did not face much pressure to impose new trade barriers, but in September 2009 it used a special safeguard provision to levy new duties on car and truck tires imported from China.[137] That this minor case involving Chinese tires was the only one in which the White House intervened to limit imports indicated just how insignificant the demands for protection had become. (The case was the result of a petition filed by a labor union, not a domestic firm.) As past experience suggested, the safeguard action failed to provide much help to domestic tire producers. First, the United States imported cheaper, lower-quality tires that were very different from the higher-quality, more expensive ones produced domestically. Second, the safeguard duty was levied only on products from China, so that imports were diverted to other foreign suppliers not subject to the duties, particularly Thailand and Indonesia. This episode illustrated once again the porous nature of administered protection, as discussed in chapters 11 and 12.

When Republicans gained control of the House in the 2010 midterm election, effectively blocking any further domestic initiatives by the president, the Obama administration began to turn to trade as one issue on which they could work together. The Republicans pushed the president to resurrect the trade agreements with Colombia, Korea, and Panama that had languished since 2008. The administration reluctantly supported the Colombia agreement (owing to controversy over human rights violations and questions about the suppression of labor unions) and asked Korea for more concessions (particularly on auto parts and beef), but eventually went forward in seeking the congressional approval. With mainly Republican support, the House and Senate passed the agreements with Panama, Colombia, and Korea in October 2011. Democratic support was marginally higher than it had been for CAFTA only because funding for trade adjustment assistance was part of the package.

In its second term, the Obama administration began to overcome its reluctance to champion new trade agreements. While small bilateral agreements like those undertaken by the Bush administration were out, and the Doha Round of multilateral negotiations had stalled (and was declared dead in 2015), larger regional agreements were back in play. Ever since 1989, under the aegis of the Asia-Pacific Economic Cooperation (APEC) forum, the United States and countries in the Asia-Pacific region had been discussing ways of further integrating the region's economies. Previous discussions to bring freer trade to the region had made little progress. In 1994, for example, leaders attending an APEC summit in Bogor, Indonesia, declared that they would achieve free trade and investment in the region by 2020. The Asian financial crisis in 1997–98 set back those efforts for a decade. When some countries later began to move forward with the discussions, the Bush administration announced in late 2008 that the United States would participate, a commitment reaffirmed by the Obama administration in late 2009.

In November 2011, the United States helped launch the Trans-Pacific Partnership (TPP) negotiations. (What used to be called "trade agreements" in the 1930s became "free-trade agreements" in the 1980s and then were labeled "partnerships" in the 2010s due to the negative connotation that "free trade" now had in many quarters.) Although it continued to view trade agreements as a political liability, the Obama administration could not avoid participating in a major initiative to open trade in the Asia-Pacific region. The administration's foreign policy "pivot" to Asia was another reason to promote trade cooperation in the region. The TPP would ultimately bring together twelve countries as disparate as Chile, New Zealand, Malaysia, Peru, Vietnam, and Japan in a single trade agreement, with the notable absence of China. The TPP negotiations demonstrated just how far trade discussions had moved away from tariff rates to non-tariff barriers and regulatory issues. The negotiating agenda included competition policy, capacity-building, cross-border services, e-commerce, environment, financial services, government procurement, intellectual property, investment, labor, legal issues, market access for goods, rules of origin, sanitary and phytosanitary standards, technical barriers to trade, telecommunications, temporary entry, textiles and apparel, and trade remedies. The goal of the agreement was to improve regulatory coherence and trade facilitation as a way of increasing market access and competition.

In his 2014 State of the Union address, Obama asked Congress to give his administration trade-promotion authority to conclude such an agreement. When Democratic leaders in Congress demurred, Obama repeated his request in 2015. "Look, I'm the first one to admit that past trade deals haven't always lived up to the hype," he said, "but 95 percent of the world's customers live outside our borders, and we can't close ourselves off from those opportunities."[138] Once again, Democrats balked, but the Republican majorities managed, with some difficulty, to secure trade-promotion authority for the administration in June 2015. Later that year, the TPP negotiations were concluded.

In 2013, the Obama administration also agreed to start trade negotiations with the European Union on the Transatlantic Trade and Investment Partnership (TTIP). Like the TPP, the idea of a US-EU trade agreement had been floating around for decades, but TTIP emerged out of the failed Doha Round and the fears of protectionism during the 2008 financial crisis. However, the negotiations proceeded much more slowly than those for the

TPP did, owing in part to European opposition to changing agricultural policy and fears about regulatory sovereignty.

Thus, although the Obama administration was initially reluctant to get involved in matters of trade policy, it played a major role in moving forward with two substantive trade negotiations with countries across the Pacific and the Atlantic. Much as NAFTA had done two decades earlier, however, the conclusion of the TPP near a presidential election made it an issue in the 2016 campaign. Republican Donald Trump and Democrat Bernie Sanders called past and prospective trade agreements "disastrous" for destroying jobs and hurting the middle class. The Democratic nominee, Hillary Clinton, who as Obama's secretary of state had endorsed the TPP, was forced to oppose it during the campaign.

The unexpected election of Donald Trump marked a sharp change in presidential tone on trade policy, and potentially a significant change in the substance of policy as well. Ever since World War II, American presidents had spoken favorably about international trade and supported multilateral and bilateral agreements to reduce trade barriers, often pulling a reluctant Congress along. Now a president was elected who had been openly and harshly critical of such agreements. During the campaign, Trump had slammed NAFTA and PNTR with China as bad deals that hurt American workers, even threatening to impose a 45 percent tariff on goods from China and a 35 percent tariff on goods from Mexico.

In his inaugural address, Trump did not soften these criticisms. "For many decades, we've enriched foreign industry at the expense of American industry," he stated. "One by one, the factories shuttered and left our shores, with not even a thought about the millions upon millions of American workers left behind." Trump promised an "America First" trade policy that would bring back jobs that had been lost to other countries. "We must protect our borders from the ravages of other countries making our products, stealing our companies, and destroying our jobs. Protection will lead to great prosperity and strength."[139] No president since Herbert Hoover had spoken so forcefully about the need for protection against foreign competition.

Upon taking office, one of Trump's first acts was to withdraw the United States from the TPP, meaning that it would not be submitted to Congress for approval. This was followed by steps to begin the renegotiation of NAFTA, along with threats aimed at companies moving jobs overseas. Although China was not immediately named as a currency manipulator, his administration was also expected to take tough actions against imports from China, a country that he had railed against on the campaign trail. Trump and his administration also viewed trade deficits as very bad for the country, taking them as an indication that the United States was "losing" from trade. Yet such deficits were not the result of previous trade deals, but foreign capital inflows, and it was not clear what the administration would do about it.

Because of his strong nationalist rhetoric, Trump was often branded a "protectionist" who could start a trade war, yet he sometimes maintained that he just wanted "fair trade" and a "better deal" from trading partners. For example, while he shelved the TPP, he also pledged to pursue bilateral trade agreements with the countries involved, although it was unclear how separate bilateral agreements would be an improvement over a single regional agreement. In fact, at least initially, the administration did not specify what provisions in existing trade agreements were so objectionable and should be changed, or how the agreements that it promised to reach would be different. After meeting with administration officials in February 2017, Senator Ron Wyden (D-OR) stated that officials offered "few details about the administration's objectives on trade and no strategy for how it plans to achieve them,"[140]

Whether the Trump administration marks a turning point in US trade policy, or just one with strong posturing on trade issues, remains to be seen. This book has emphasized the deep structural factors that have in the past prevented any big changes in the direction of trade policy from occurring. In chapter 7, we saw that Woodrow Wilson succeeded for a short time in reducing tariffs significantly, but this proved to be a brief interlude during the restriction period in which tariff levels generally remained high. In an unusual break from previous patterns, the American president was now more critical of the country's existing trade arrangements than many members of Congress. Some members began to speak up in defense of NAFTA, the WTO, and other agreements, particularly members from states with agricultural exports whose constituents would be at risk if other countries retaliated against new US import restrictions. Even if no major protectionist measures were introduced, the Trump administration portended a loss of US international economic leadership.

To some extent, Trump's election reflected deep frustration with government and the performance of the economy. The stagnation in real wages since the late 1990s and the steady rise in income inequality since 1979 led to a renewed debate over whether the average American was helped or hurt by increased globalization and technological change. While educated white-collar workers seemed to have done well, blue-collar and less-well-educated workers felt left behind. The slow economic recovery from the 2008 financial crisis and the increase in economic insecurity allowed the antitrade message to resonate with many voters. At the same time, a Gallup poll in early 2017 indicated that a record 72 percent viewed trade as an opportunity and only 23 percent viewed it as a threat.[141] This positive view of trade, however, did not necessarily translate into support for trade agreements themselves. As they were on so many other issues, Americans remained divided over trade policy.

Conclusion

As this book has shown, US trade policy has always been the subject of intense political controversy. Different economic interests, located in different regions of the country and working through political parties and elected representatives, have fought either to expand exports or restrict imports. The tension between those groups that benefit from or are harmed by international trade has been constant throughout American history.

And yet, on top of this conflict has been stability. The United States has passed through three different periods in which a different objective of trade policy—revenue, restriction, or reciprocity—has taken priority. Within each of these periods, trade policy has been relatively stable and resistant to change, despite the ever-present conflict over its direction. This stability has come about in part because the American political system makes it difficult to change the status quo. As a result, one way to characterize US trade policy is "stability despite conflict."

For example, from 1860 to 1934, when imports were restricted by high tariffs, trade policy was bitterly contested, but the same policy remained basically intact throughout this seventy-five year period. Opponents of existing policy had only two opportunities to reduce tariffs, one of which was squandered, and the other quickly reversed. Similarly, in the reciprocity period since 1934, which has now lasted for more than eighty years, the debate has been whether to approve trade agreements that reduce tariff and non-tariff barriers further or to maintain the status quo—not whether to return to the era of high tariffs. When put in historical perspective, the range of policies being considered at any given point in time is usually quite narrow.

If one focuses only on the immediate conflict, one might miss the longer-term stability. In the early 1960s, Jacob Viner warned that "in Congress . . . the tide is running in a protectionist direction." In the early 1970s, C. Fred Bergsten warned that "US trade policy has been moving steadily away from the liberal trade approach which has characterized it since 1934." And there were many more such warnings about the return of protectionism in the 1970s and 1980s, followed by claims about the impending reversal of globalization, and the end of free-trade policies in the 2010s. However justified at the time, these warnings seem, with the benefit of hindsight, to have been overstated.[1] Instead, despite some pauses and reverses, the period since 1934 appears to have been a fairly steady movement in the direction of reducing trade barriers. Only time will tell if the anti-trade rhetoric of Donald Trump in the 2016 election campaign will translate into policy action and alter this conclusion. While there may be an increase in trade friction with China, much like that with Japan in the 1980s, that does not necessarily mean a broad US retreat from open trade policies or the end of the "reciprocity" phase of trade policy.

In some sense, the emphasis on reciprocity since World War II represents US trade policy coming full circle. Reciprocity has been a long-standing policy objective and tradition in American trade politics. The Founding Fathers always wanted foreign trade to be conducted in an open and non-discriminatory way. After winning its independence, the United States was surprised to find itself facing many discriminatory policies against its trade and shipping once it left the British Empire. The difficult experience of the 1780s—the failed commercial-policy negotiations and the economic losses the country suffered from having been excluded from the markets of the colonial powers—left an indelible mark on American thinking about trade. Thomas Jefferson's *Report on Commercial Restrictions* in 1793 firmly argued that foreign "unfair" trade barriers should not be tolerated and should be either negotiated away or addressed with countervailing measures. This was a precursor to the "National Trade Estimate Report on Foreign Trade Barriers" issued annually by the US Trade Representative today.

The United States did not worry about reciprocity for much of the nineteenth century, because Britain, its leading trade partner, pursued a policy of unilateral free trade. During that period, trade policy was largely a matter of domestic politics. But the return of colonial trade preferences toward the end of the nineteenth century led to renewed interest in trying to establish world trade on an open and non-discriminatory basis. The "Open Door" notes of Secretary of State John Hay in 1899 reflect this thinking, as did President Woodrow Wilson's insistence after World War I that the

United States had a national interest in equal and non-discriminatory access to world markets. In both cases, no serious policy initiatives were
undertaken, but that changed with the dramatic deterioration in the world
trade environment during the Great Depression of the 1930s. The imposition of extreme trade restrictions and the reintroduction of tariff preferences by Britain and its dominions in the 1932 Ottawa Agreements helped
swing US trade policy toward the objective of eliminating preferential and
discriminatory policies against US exports.

That goal—seeking to conclude trade agreements to reduce trade barriers—has been the essence of US trade policy since the end of World War II.
"The overriding commitment of this administration in trade policy has
been to open markets and expand trade—multilaterally where possible,
and bilaterally where necessary—and to enforce trade laws against unfair
trade practices by other trading nations."[2] This declaration came from the
Clinton administration in 1993, but it could have described the trade policy of almost any presidential administration over the past eighty years.
The statement reflects the basic continuity of purpose in US trade policy.

By helping to create the GATT and WTO, the United States has gone
a great distance toward achieving the original goal of the 1780s, namely
open and non-discriminatory trade around the world. Trade negotiations
have brought down the import tariffs imposed by developed countries to
low levels. US import tariffs, which have been the primary focus of this
book, are also at historic low levels. In 2016, the average tariff on total imports stood at 1.5 percent, and the average tariff on dutiable imports stood
at 5.0 percent. While there is a zero lower bound in terms of tariffs, these
figures have not fallen much in recent years, and there is little chance that
they will be eliminated anytime soon. Of course, the United States, along
with other countries, continues to have many non-tariff barriers to trade.
Still, when put in historical perspective, the United States is currently
very open to trade; about 70 percent of imports currently enter duty free.

To continue this process of reducing trade barriers, the era of reciprocity has depended on presidential leadership. The natural inclination
of Congress is to do nothing about an issue unless it perceives there is
an important political problem to be solved. Because changes in trade
policy always generate domestic controversy, Congress needs to be given
a compelling reason to take action to reduce trade barriers. It has to be
convinced that a trade agreement can solve a significant economic problem. Every major trade initiative in the reciprocity era—the first GATT
negotiation in 1947, the Kennedy Round in the 1960s, and the Uruguay
Round in the 1980s—arose as a way of dealing with significant obstacles

facing US exporters: imperial preferences in the 1930s and the creation of the European Economic Community in the 1950s, and then European agricultural subsidies and the lack of intellectual property protection in the 1980s. In each case, a broad political consensus emerged that solving the problems facing exporters through negotiations with trade partners was in the national economic interest.[3] The lack of a compelling case that foreign trade policies are significantly impeding exports, or that foreign-policy considerations are enough to warrant action, has meant that gaining Congressional support for new trade agreements has been more difficult in recent years.

Perhaps a greater challenge facing US trade policy in this reciprocity phase is that new forms of protectionism are constantly arising. In the aftermath of the Great Recession of 2009, many countries around the world have used subtle forms of regulatory discrimination to protect and support domestic firms. These "grey area" measures are much less transparent than tariffs and other border measures, and hence much more difficult to negotiate away. Furthermore, the trade agreements of today are now as much about the harmonization of regulations, the establishment of product standards, and the protection of intellectual property as they are about traditional trade barriers, such as tariffs, quotas, and subsidies. As such, they become more intrusive in the domestic economy and are likely to be met with political resistance. The growing use of regulatory protectionism and the growing disenchantment with complex trade agreements makes the outlook for trade policy more uncertain today than in the past.

Still, there is a temptation to end a long book on history by projecting forward and making a prediction about future policy. If "stability despite conflict" is a lesson from past experience, one can easily be led to conclude that the future will look much like the past and that the reciprocity period will continue for some time to come. If it took the Civil War and the Great Depression to bring about a major shift in US trade policy in the past, it is hard to anticipate the next political or economic jolt that might put it onto a different track, the election of President Trump notwithstanding.

Yet a cautionary tale against such complacency comes from E. E. Schattschneider and his classic book on the Hawley-Smoot tariff, *Politics, Pressures, and the Tariff*. Schattschneider (1935, 283) concluded by saying that "a survey of the pressure politics of the revision of 1929–1930 shows no significant concentration of forces able to reverse the policy and bring about a return to a system of low tariffs or free trade." Unfortunately, this book was published the year after the passage of the Reciprocal Trade

Agreements Act, which marked the transition from restriction to reciprocity as the main objective of trade policy. That act eventually led to the lowest tariffs in US history. In light of that example, perhaps the only thing that can be said with confidence is that, as James Madison predicted long ago, many new clashes are sure to arise over the future of US trade policy.

ACKNOWLEDGMENTS

This book has been a long time in coming, and I have racked up large debts in the process of bringing this project to completion. Michael Bordo gets my first thanks for having, unwittingly, in a phone call in 1994, put me onto the subject of the history of US trade policy. Barry Eichengreen has been a role model for anyone working at the intersection of international economics and economic history, and I am grateful for his support and the example of his scholarship. I also give thanks to Jagdish Bhagwati and Ronald Findlay for indelibly influencing the way I think about international trade and commercial policy.

The National Bureau of Economic Research, under the leadership of Martin Feldstein and James Poterba, has provided an important venue in which I have presented many of the research papers that have been integrated into this volume. My thinking has been shaped and sharpened by participating in the research meetings of the NBER's Development of the American Economy Program, headed by Claudia Goldin, and the International Trade and Investment Program, headed by Robert Feenstra. Many participants at the NBER conferences and program meetings have given valuable feedback over the years. I particularly appreciate Price Fishback's enthusiastic encouragement and Claudia Goldin's long-standing support for this project.

A few heroic individuals took the time to read the entire manuscript—sometimes twice!—and provide detailed comments: Anne Krueger, Steve Meardon, Chad Bown, Mac Destler, and Doug Nelson. I cannot thank them enough for their time and effort in helping improve the manuscript, although I am sure the book would have been better if I had taken all of their advice. J. Michael Finger provided helpful comments on several chapters, and Susan Aaronson gave valuable early feedback. Long ago, I benefited from two manuscript review sessions, one at Dartmouth (including Robert Baldwin, Doug Nelson, Steve Meardon, and Nina Pacvnik) and the other at the University of California at Berkeley (organized by Barry Eichengreen and including Barry Weingast, Christina Romer, Brad DeLong, Judith Goldstein, Gavin Wright, Andrew Guzman, Alan Taylor, John Wallis, and Robert Feenstra).

A fellowship from the John Simon Guggenheim Memorial Foundation gave me extra time that allowed me to make great progress on this book, as did a sabbatical leave at the Hoover Institution at Stanford University.

At Dartmouth, I am deeply grateful to Michael Mastanduno and Nancy Marion for providing support that was absolutely essential to the completion of this book. Meir Kohn has long provided wise and needed advice as I struggled with this project. This book could not have been written without the superb collection of government documents and other materials in the Dartmouth College library. I thank John Cocklin for his many years of expert assistance with government documents. Dartmouth has a large collection of first-rate international economists, and my colleagues, especially Nina Pavcnik, have offered valuable comments, as have colleagues in the history department. For his superb assistance with the maps, I thank Jonathan Chipman, Director of the Citrin Family GIS/Applied Spatial Analysis Laboratory at Dartmouth College. Kory Hirak and Kristine Timlake saved me huge amounts of time in dealing with various aspects of the manuscript drafts. Finally, I am delighted to thank several generations of Dartmouth students for their invaluable research assistance: William Congdon, Amie Sugarman, Elise Waxenberg, Kristin Ricci, Maha Malik, Konrad von Moltke, Andres Isaza, Robert Klingenberger, Taylor Ng, Emma Ratcliffe, and April Liu.

My interest in trade policy was cultivated long ago by Bernard Gordon and fostered by Jagdish Bhagwati and Ronald Findlay. It was further stimulated by my spending an exciting year at the Council of Economic Advisers in 1986–87, where I worked on many of the issues discussed in chapter 12. This year gave me an amazing opportunity to see how the trade-policy process works in the federal government, and I learned an enormous amount from those at the CEA, the Office of the US Trade Representative, and the Office of Management and Budget, especially Thomas Dorsey. I am particularly grateful to Steven Husted and Gordon Rausser for their guidance and for letting me attend policy meetings above my level on trade and agriculture during that year. I also learned a tremendous amount from Michael Mussa then and thereafter.

I am saddened that Robert Baldwin, Michael Mussa, and Colin Campbell passed away before I could complete this book. Their encouragement help me stick with it.

This book is dedicated to my wife, Marjorie Rose. We met at the very moment that we both first reported for work at the Council of Economic Advisers. We have been together ever since, and she has patiently tolerated my obsession with trade policy and arcane history. Without her mantra "structure and purpose," you would not be reading these words or holding this book. I am forever grateful to her.

INTRODUCTION

1. *PJM* 10:265–66.

2. Martis (1988) points out that sectionalism has been a feature of congressional voting from the very beginning of the country.

3. For surveys of work by economists on the political economy of trade policy, see Rodrik 1995; Gwande and Krishna 2003; and McClaren 2016. The widely cited Grossman and Helpman (1994) model of "protection for sale" focuses on the determinants of tariff rates across industries, whereas this book focuses more on the average tariff rate, something captured by an exogenous parameter in their model: the weight that politicians put on social welfare.

4. Works on trade policy by political scientists include O'Halloran 1994; Hiscox 2002; Destler 2005; and others. For works by historians on trade policy, see Stanwood 1903; Ratner 1972; Dobson 1976; and Eckes 1995.

5. The Export-Import Bank was created in the 1930s to provide credit guarantees for exporters, but overall its financial support for exports has been small. For a history of the Export-Import Bank, see Becker and McClenahan 2003. Export subsidies were also used in the 1980s to deal with surplus agricultural production.

6. There are many other aspects of trade policy that we will not be able to consider, such as trade sanctions against particular countries and embargos on the export of particular products for national security purposes.

7. Import quotas can also be used to limit the quantity of particular foreign goods allowed to enter the market, but the United States did not start using them until the 1930s, and then mainly for agricultural goods.

8. Irwin 1998a.

9. These measures, calculated by dividing customs revenue by the value of total and dutiable imports, have several shortcomings, as discussed in Anderson and Neary 2005. They construct a trade-restrictiveness index that addresses many of the usual problems. Despite these shortcomings, the average tariff is still a useful measure. Irwin (2010) calculates a trade-restrictiveness index for US tariffs from 1867 to 1961 and shows

that it is highly correlated with the standard average tariff measures. Furthermore, the United States has not used many non-tariff barriers, such as import licenses, foreign exchange restrictions, and discriminatory regulations, to restrict imports that would make the average tariff measure misleading.

10. The distinction between revenue and protective duties is not always sharp. Revenue duties do not discriminate in favor of domestic producers; they tend to be levied on products that are not produced at home or that are subject to domestic taxes equal to the import tariff. Protective duties discriminate in favor of domestic producers; Johnson (1960) defines protection as "any policy that raises the price received by domestic producers of an importable commodity above the world market price."

11. See Corden 1974 for an introduction to the theory of commercial policy.

12. The Foraker quote is from Morgan 1965, 227, and the Reed quote is from Morgan 1969, 167.

13. By increasing the domestic price of imported goods, a tariff reduces the demand for imports and shifts demand toward domestically produced substitutes, leading domestic producers to increase their output. This is a description of the partial equilibrium "imperfect substitutes" trade framework developed by Baldwin (1976). See also Rousslang and Suomela 1988.

14. See Kim 1995 and Holmes and Stevens 2004. As Holmes and Stevens (2004, p. 2008) note, "For industries producing nontradable goods or services like retail, there is little [geographic] specialization, while for tradable goods like manufactures, mining output, and agricultural products, there is a substantial amount of specialization across regions."

15. After the 1950s, Holmes and Stevens (2004, p. 2000) report that "US manufacturing moved out of this northern region and into other parts of the country" and that "certain areas of the South have become quite specialized in manufacturing, in effect fashioning a new manufacturing belt."

16. See Lerner 1936. However, an across-the-board tariff on imports does not reduce all exported goods to the same degree.

17. See Bensel 1984 on sectionalism and American political development.

18. See Baldwin 1984a for this industry-based approach, as well as Grossman and Helpman 1994, both of which are implicitly based on the specific-factors model of Jones (1971) and Samuelson (1971).

19. The famous Stolper-Samuelson theorem focuses on the economic interests of the underlying factors of production that produce output rather than industries themselves. See Rogowski 1989 and Hiscox 2002 on this theme. See Deardorff and Stern 1994 for an overview of the Stolper-Samuelson theorem.

20. If trade-policy decisions were made via public referendum, Mayer (1984) shows how the preferences of the median voter would influence the outcome.

21. "The members of the Senate and House are the advocates and representatives of different local interests all of which naturally seek to influence the transactions of the government on their own behalf," noted Senator Thomas Bayard (D-DE) (quoted in Rothman 1966, 81).

22. This point relates to Mancur Olson's (1965) theory of collective action.

23. For example, if representatives from Pennsylvania want to impose higher

tariffs on steel, and representatives from South Carolina want to enact higher tariffs on apparel, the legislators from each state could agree to support each other's proposal. The benefits to Pennsylvania of higher steel tariffs would far exceed any loss it would incur from higher apparel tariffs, and a similar calculation holds for South Carolina. See Grossman and Helpman 2005 for a theoretical analysis of the protectionist bias in majoritarian politics.

24. See Fernandez and Rodrik 1991 on the certain losers and the uncertain winners, and Tullock 1975 on the transitional gains trap. The imposition of a tariff may generate short-run or transitional gains for the protected industry, but not permanent gains, because the initial benefits eventually get capitalized into asset values or eroded due to expanded production and the entry of new producers. At this point there is no apparent benefit of the tariff for incumbent firms, but its removal would force them to incur large capital losses—hence their strong opposition to any change.

25. Destler 1986, 3.

26. *CQA* 1988, 223.

27. Quoted in Binkley 1962, 222. There were some exceptions: President Woodrow Wilson was a strong party leader who actively helped shape the 1913 tariff.

28. On this switch, see Keech and Pak 1995.

29. McGillivray (1997), Brady, Goldstein, and Kessler (2002), and Weller (2009) show that political parties have an impact on trade-policy outcomes beyond constituent economic interests.

30. Of the 77 Congresses from 1867 to 2019, there have been 21 unified Democratic governments, 22 unified Republican governments, and 34 divided governments. Since the enactment of the Reciprocal Trade Agreements Act of 1934, divided government has been less of a problem for trade policy, since Congress no longer considered tariff legislation; see Karol 2000 and Sherman 2002.

31. Goldstein (1993) makes the case for the role of ideas in shaping US trade policy.

32. Remini 1997, 223.

CHAPTER 1

1. Pereira and Flores de Frutos 1998.

2. See Lindert and Williamson 2016, as well as Gallman 2000 and McCusker 2000.

3. As Shammas (1982, 268) points out, "How can communities that spent a quarter of per capita income on goods imported from outside the colony be described as practicing local self-sufficiency?"

4. Shepherd and Walton 1972.

5. Ibid.

6. Shammas 1982.

7. The nominal GDP of colonial America in 1774 is estimated to have been between $142 million (McCusker 2000, table 2) and $164 million (Lindert and Williamson 2013, table 4). The nominal value of exports from England and Scotland to the thirteen colonies was £2.953 million in 1774, or $13.1 million after translating into dollars at the par exchange rate of $4.44 per pound (McCusker 1971).

8. Harper 1939, 35.

9. The estimates by Thomas (1965) spawned a large literature that probed the methods and figures used. See Walton 1971 and Sawers 1992 for references.

10. Ransom 1968.

11. *PTJ* 1:123.

12. Egnal and Ernst 1972, 30.

13. As Baack (2004) points out, land was another source of contention: the Proclamation of 1763 prevented the colonists from settling in or trading west of the Allegheny Mountains.

14. Mitchell 1988, 579.

15. See Thomas 1987 and Calloway 2006.

16. Breen 2004.

17. Thomas 1975, 151.

18. US Bureau of the Census 1975, Z-227–28.

19. Olson 1992.

20. Witkowski 1989.

21. Thomas 1987, 169–70.

22. Mitchell 1988, 494.

23. See Ragsdale 1996 and Holton 1999. Southern colonies accounted for 84 percent of the nearly £3 million in debt owed to British merchants in 1776 (Sheridan 1960, 167).

24. Thomas 1987, 246–54.

25. Labaree 1964.

26. From the Journal of the Continental Congress, available online at http://www.loc.gov/teachers/classroommaterials/presentationsandactivities/presentations/timeline/amrev/rebelln/rights.html (accessed July 11, 2016).

27. *PJA* 3:190.

28. Ibid., 4:57.

29. See Lint 1978 and Clarfield 1979.

30. Cheney 2006.

31. Article 2 of the treaty stated that the two countries "engage mutually not to grant any particular favour to other nations, in respect of commerce and navigation, which shall not immediately become common to the other Party, who shall enjoy the same favour, freely, if the concession was freely made, or on allowing the same compensation, if the concession was conditional." See Malloy 1910, 1:468. Setser (1933) finds that the conditional MFN clause was due to the French negotiators.

32. Buel 1998, 178.

33. See Ritcheson 1969; Olson 1992; Crowley 1993.

34. Bjork 1964; see also Shepherd and Walton 1976.

35. Nettles 1962, 49.

36. McCusker 2001.

37. Massachusetts produced about 125 ships a year before the revolution, but just 4 ships in 1784. Nettles 1962, 52; Marks 1973, 64.

38. Nettles 1962, 49, 51.

39. *PJM* 8:314–16.

40. *WJA* 8:383.

41. Ibid., 313.

42. Ibid., 101

43. Ibid., 299.

44. *PJA* 17:390.

45. *PAH* 3:75–76.

46. Baack 2001; see also Ferguson 1961.

47. *PJM* 6:144–45.

48. Ibid., 9:294–95.

49. In a series of articles, Zornow (1954–56) investigated the tariff laws of seven states during the 1780s. For Rhode Island, Connecticut, Pennsylvania, and Maryland, see Shepherd (1993).

50. See McGillivray 2001 and Giesecke 1910.

51. Marks 1973, 82.

52. Ibid., 83, 68.

53. *PTJ* 9:399–400.

54. *PJM* 8:333.

55. Davis 1977, 91–92.

56. *PTJ* 8:215, 296.

57. Davis 1977, 92–93.

58. *PJM* 8: 407.

59. Davis 1977, 85.

60. *PJM* 8:344.

61. Ibid., 334–35.

62. Marks 1973, 68.

63. *PJM* 8:502.

64. Ibid., 9:96.

65. *LJM* 4:251.

66. *PJM* 10:29.

67. On voting patterns at the convention, see McGuire 2003, Heckelman and Dougherty 2007, and Pope and Treier 2015.

68. Farrand 1911, 3:126, 327.

69. Ibid., 2:441.

70. See Finkelman 1987; Goldstone 2005; and Baack, McGuire, and Van Cott 2009.

71. Farrand 1911, 2:374.

72. *PJM* 8:340.

73. Farrand 1911, 2:360, 306.

74. Ibid.

75. Ibid., 371.

76. Ibid., 374–75.

77. Ibid., 450, 453.

78. Ibid., 449–450.

79. Ibid., 449. Maryland's Luther Martin, who opposed the constitution, also confirmed this vote trade, stating that "the *eastern* States, notwithstanding their *aversion to slavery*, were very willing to indulge the southern States, at least with a temporary liberty to prosecute the *slave trade*, provided the southern States would in their turn gratify them, by laying no *restriction* on *navigation* acts; and after a very little time the

committee, by a very great majority, agreed on a report by which the general government was to be prohibited from preventing the importation of slaves for a limited time, and the restrictive clause relative to navigation acts was to be omitted." Ibid., 3:210.

80. McClendon 1931.

81. *PAH* 4:340.

CHAPTER 2

1. As McCoy (1980, 86–87) explains, "Many republicans eagerly embraced an eighteenth century ideology of free trade, whose leading spokesmen included Montesquieu, Hume, Adam Smith, and the French physiocrats. According to these writers, foreign as well as domestic commerce should be freed from all restraints so that it might flourish and, in the process, humanize men by refining their manners and morals. . . . Given their hostility to Britain and the mercantilist model, it is not surprising that many Americans in the early years of independence embraced this outlook and tied it directly to the spirit of their revolution."

2. *PBF* 35:83.

3. *PTJ* 8:332; Jefferson 1955 [1785], 176.

4. *PBF* 39:344.

5. As Thomas Jefferson advised a correspondent in 1790, "In political economy, I think Smith's *Wealth of Nations* is the best book extant" (*PTJ* 16:449). Cowin (1999) and Fleischhacker (2002) examine the influence of Adam Smith on the founding fathers.

6. *PJM* 12:71. Fisher Ames (1854, 1:49), one of the leading Federalists of the period, noted, "One of his [Madison's] first speeches in regard to protecting commerce, was taken out of Smith's 'Wealth of Nations.' The principles of the book are excellent, but the application of them to America requires caution. I am satisfied, and could state some reasons to evince, that commerce and manufactures merit legislative interference in this country much more than would be proper in England."

7. *PAH* 3:76.

8. For more on Smith and trade policy, see Irwin 1996b.

9. *PTJ* 27:527.

10. Ibid., 8:633.

11. *PJM* 8:333–334.

12. *WTJ* 3:269.

13. "Were I to indulge my own theory, I should wish them [Americans] to practice neither commerce nor navigation, but to stand with respect to Europe precisely on the footing of China. We should thus avoid wars, and all our citizens would be husbandmen." Jefferson recognized that "this is theory only, and a theory which the servants of America are not at liberty to follow" (*PTJ* 8:633).

14. *PGW-CS* 3:299–300.

15. *PTJ* 8:633.

16. Bordewich 2016.

17. *PJM* 12:64–65.

18. AC, 4/9/1798, 114.

19. *PJM* 12:69–70.

20. *PJM* 20:70–71.

21. Ibid., 71–72.

22. Ibid., 72–73.

23. See Edling and Kaplanoff 2004. Peskin (2003, 91) notes that the federal tariff rates were roughly double those of New York, but were generally lower than those imposed by Pennsylvania and Massachusetts.

24. Balinky 1958, 57.

25. Brown 1993, 238–39.

26. Edling and Kaplanoff 2004.

27. Riley 1978.

28. *PAH* 7:232.

29. Irwin 2003.

30. Richardson 1903, 1:65.

31. On the *Report*, see Cooke 1975; Nelson 1979; and Irwin 2004.

32. *PAH* 10:262–63.

33. Ibid., 266.

34. Ibid., 3:75.

35. Ibid., 10:266.

36. Ibid., 10:68.

37. Ibid., 299.

38. Ibid., 301.

39. *PJM* 14:195.

40. *PAH* 10:302–04.

41. *PTJ* 23:172–73.

42. Ibid., 24:187.

43. Ibid., 214, 353.

44. See Elkins and McKitrick 1993, 277.

45. See Clarfield (1975).

46. *PAH* 11:139.

47. AC, 1/27/1792, 349–51. This portion of the debate is clearly misplaced as it refers to events that occurred after January; it almost surely took place in late April.

48. Stanwood 1903, 1:102; Irwin 2004.

49. Elkins and McKitrick (1993, 261) argue that it would be "misleading to connect Hamilton too closely with the protective-tariff theorists of the early nineteenth century, much as they may have looked to him for inspiration. His ends were more complex than theirs, and went well beyond simple protection. (Indeed, a nineteenth-century Hamilton would in all likelihood have been a free trader: he did not think it well that any interest should become too settled and comfortable.)"

50. *PAH* 3:78–79.

51. Ibid., 4:477.

52. Ibid., 10:301.

53. See also Shankman (2003). This is not to say that protectionist pressures were strong, because the number of manufacturers was very small, and many of them had

divided interests. For example, Peskin (2003, 109) points out that iron producers and iron users (nail and horseshoe producers) were deeply divided: the former wanted high duties, and the latter wanted low duties on imported iron.

54. *PAH* 11, 141.

55. *AC*, 5/4/1789, 238.

56. *WTJ* 8:405. See Peterson (1965) on Jefferson's trade-policy views and McCoy (1974) and McCoy (1980) for an overview of the economic views of the Republicans.

57. *AC*, 5/4/1789, 256.

58. *PGW PS* 3:323–24.

59. *PAH* 5:488–89.

60. Ibid., 7:426.

61. Ibid., 424.

62. *PTJ* 20:236, 353–54.

63. Goldin and Lewis (1980) conclude that the favorable improvement in terms of trade translated into an increase in the growth rate of per capita income of about a quarter of a percentage point, from about 1.07 percent to 1.32 percent a year. By their calculations, American national income would have been about 3 percent lower had there been no American trade boom as a result of the European conflict.

64. Even though some ships and cargoes were confiscated, there were relatively few direct losses from the European war. As Nettles (1962, 324) points out, "The political and diplomatic quarrels of the time may give the impression that losses to American shippers all but ruined their business and drove their vessels from the sea. Actually, they prospered as never before. Ships that completed voyages greatly outnumbered those that fell prey to belligerents."

65. *AC*, 5/6/1806, 557.

66. Adams 1980.

67. See *PTJ* 27:567–78.

68. Ibid., 574.

69. Ibid., 560.

70. Ibid., 561–63

71. Ibid., 562.

72. In 1792, Hamilton drafted a reply to Jefferson's impending report, which began by noting, "The commercial system of Great Britain makes no discriminations to the *prejudice* of the UStates as *compared* with other foreign powers" and "There is therefore no ground for a complaint on the part of the UStates that the system of G Britain is particularly *injurious* or *unfriendly* to them" (*PAH* 13:412).

73. Ibid., 16:271–72.

74. *AC*, 1/13/1794, 196, 203, 202. According to Jefferson, "I am at no loss to ascribe Smith's speech to its true father. Every tittle of it is Hamilton's except the introduction. There is scarcely anything there which I have not heard from him in our various private tho' official discussions. The very turn of arguments is the same . . . the style is Hamilton's. The sophistry is too fine, too ingenious even to have been comprehended by Smith, much less devised by him" (*PTJ* 28:49).

75. *PAH* 16:275.

76. Mitchell 1988, 494.

77. *PAH* 16:274–76.

78. *PTJ* 27:560.

79. See Bemis 1923; Combs 1970; and Estes 2006.

80. *WGW* 35:233, 235.

81. Nettles 1962, 325.

82. Richardson 1903, 1:322.

83. Lambert 2005.

84. Davis and Engerman 2006.

85. Hickey 1987.

86. *WTJ* 5:64.

87. Latimer 2007, 20.

88. *PJM SSS* 16:322. On Jefferson's commercial policy, see Peterson 1965; Spivak 1979; and Ben-Atar 1993.

89. *WTJ* 5:265.

90. Richardson 1903, 1:433.

91. On the embargo, see Jennings 1921; Sears 1927; Spivak 1979; Frankel 1982; and Irwin 2005b.

92. British figures for the calendar year show the "official value" of British exports to the United States fell from £7.9 million in 1807 to £4.0 million in 1808, a decline of 49 percent, while the official value of British imports from the United States fell from £2.8 million in 1807 to £0.8 million in 1808, a decline of 71 percent (Mitchell 1988, 499).

93. Irwin 2005b.

94. Bailey 1980, 126.

95. Wolford 1942.

96. Fry 2002, 34.

97. Sears 1921.

98. Irwin 2011a.

99. *WTJ* 5:271.

100. Gallatin 1879, 1:389.

101. Mannix 1979.

102. *WTJ* 9:202.

103. Ibid., 237.

104. Ibid., 239, 245; *WTJ* 12:56.

105. Frankel 1982.

106. *ASP FR* 1:256.

107. *WTJ* 9:237.

108. See Mannix 1979 and Stuart 1982.

109. Stagg 1983, 24; Spivak 1979, 153.

110. *AC*, 11/28/1808, 538, 541.

111. *WTJ* 9:244.

112. *AC*, 1/31/1809, 1249.

113. Ketcham 1971, 465.

114. *PTJ RS* 2:537.

115. Ibid., 533–34.

116. In 1825, Jefferson recalled that John Quincy Adams had told him about talk

in New England about secession because of the embargo: "However reluctant I was
to abandon the measure (a measure which persevered in a little longer, we had subsequent and satisfactory assurance would have effected its object completely), from that
moment, and influenced by that information, I saw the necessity of abandoning it, and
instead of effecting our purpose by this peaceable weapon, we must fight it out, or break
the Union. I then recommended to yield to the necessity of a repeal of the Embargo,
and to endeavor to supply its place by the best substitute, in which they could procure a
general concurrence" (*WTJ* 7:424–26).

117. "In the course of those consultations, I learned the whole policy of Mr. Jefferson; and was surprised as well as grieved to find, that in the face of the clearest proofs of
the failure of his plan, he continued to hope against facts. . . . The very eagerness with
which the repeal was supported by a majority of the Republican party ought to have
taught Mr. Jefferson that it was already considered by them as a miserable and mischievous failure" (Story 1851, 1:185).

118. *PTJ RS* 2:506; *WTJ* 9:521; 10:354. "Despite overwhelming evidence to the
contrary," Ben-Atar (1993, 171) argues, Jefferson "continued until the end of his public
life, to hold on to an inflated assessment of the strength of the United States and its
commerce."

119. *PAH* 16:275.

120. *PJM PS* 2:322.

121. Latimer 2007.

122. Hickey 1981, 521.

123. Buel 2005.

124. Risjord 1961, 205.

125. Gilji 2013.

126. *AC*, 12/31/1811, 599–600.

127. *AC*, 12/9/1811, 424.

128. *AC*, 12/31/1811, 601.

129. *PHC* 1:842.

130. Latimer 2007, 31.

131. Perkins 1961, 326.

132. Ibid., 339.

133. As Perkins (1961, 339–40) writes, "The [British] depression of 1810, totally
unconnected with events in America, secured for the United States what Jefferson's
Embargo had been unable to obtain."

134. Hickey 1981, 523.

135. Dudley 2003.

136. Lebergott 1984, 124.

137. "From Thomas Jefferson to Marie-Joseph-Paul-Yves-Roch-Gilbert du Motier,
marquis de Lafayette, 24 February 1809," Founders Online, National Archives (http://
founders.archives.gov/documents/Jefferson/99-01-02-9871 [last update: 2015–12–30]).

138. Richardson 1903, 1:476.

139. *ASP-F* 2:430–31.

140. *PJM PS* 3:52.

141. Irwin and Davis 2003.

142. *PTJ* RS 5:563.

143. *WTJ* 4:521–23.

CHAPTER 3

1. North 1966, 242; Davis 2004.

2. Hansard's *Parliamentary Debates* 33, 1099.

3. Brougham viewed this trade as a mistake rather than a deliberate attempt to sabotage American producers, but it is easy to understand why Brougham's comments seemed to confirm a predatory intent on the part of British manufacturers. See Viner 1923, 42.

4. Richardson 1903, 1:553.

5. Ibid., 1:567.

6. *ASP-F*, 3:90.

7. Ibid.

8. *PHC* 2:179.

9. *AC*, 1/16/1816, 687.

10. *AC*, 4/4/1816, 1330.

11. On the South's support for the bill, see Preyer 1959.

12. In 1832, Madison wrote that he still believed in free trade "as a theoretic rule, and subject to exceptions only not inconsistent with the principle of it," but that "theories are the offspring of the closet; exceptions to them, the lessons of experience." *LJM* 4:259.

13. US Bureau of the Census 1975, series K-554.

14. *ASP-F*, 2:426, 430. See also Ware 1926.

15. Jeremy 1981, 101. According to Zevin (1971, 141), "The principal motive for introducing the power loom was a desire to regain competitive viability by cutting costs. The stimulus which brought this desire to the fore was the traumatic pressure which material and product price movements put on the manufacturers' gross margins. The result of adopting the power loom was to lower direct operating costs by a very substantial margin."

16. Jeremy 1981, 101.

17. Ware 1931, 75.

18. Rosenbloom (2004) argues that it is premature to dismiss an important role for the tariff if there were external economies of scale at work in the industry.

19. Taussig (1931, 68) notes that "no strong popular movement for protection can be traced before the crisis of 1818–19." On the panic, see Rothbard 1962 and Dupre 2006.

20. As Peart (2013, 97) notes, "Carey played a pivotal role in this expansion, offering advice and encouragement to allies all over the Union through an extraordinary volume of personal correspondence."

21. In 1820, a special committee of the Pennsylvania Senate concluded that the underlying economic problem was "to be found chiefly in the abuses of the banking system" and their "universally bad administration. . . . The want of protection to domestic manufacturers, although it may apply in a great degree to the operations of manufacturing towns, yet it is not valid as relates to the great mass of people of the

commonwealth, who can perceive in the banking institutions the immediate cause of their embarrassments" (see Eiselen 1932, 45).

22. As Rothbard (1962, 172) observed, "While the protectionists devoted a great deal of attention to the depression, the 'free traders' in opposition devoted little space to the depression, since they could not counter with a simple remedy of their own. Free traders generally concentrated on general political economic questions, such as the benefits of international trade and the division of labor, the danger of monopoly, the injustice of special privilege, and the morals of factory life."

23. Richardson 1903, 2:45.

24. Ibid., 61.

25. On tariff politics surrounding the Baldwin bill, see Peart 2013.

26. *AC*, 4/26/1820, 2116, 2131.

27. Kennon and Rogers 1989, 86.

28. *AC*, 4/26/1820, 2036.

29. Vipperman 1989, 204.

30. Setser 1937.

31. Richardson 1903, 2:192.

32. *PHC* 3:685, 687.

33. Ibid., 692.

34. Ibid., 688.

35. Ibid., 694.

36. Ibid., 726.

37. Ibid., 701.

38. Ibid., 704.

39. Ibid., 723–24.

40. *AC*, 4/2/1824, 2028.

41. *AC*, 4/6/1824, 2206.

42. *AC*, 4/1/1824, 2010.

43. *AC*, 4/30/1824, 649, 623.

44. *AC*, 4/15/1824, 3359.

45. *AC*, 4/30/1824, 649.

46. As Jefferson noted to a correspondent, "Congress has done nothing remarkable except the passing of a tariff bill by squeezing majorities, very revolting to a great portion of the people of the States, among whom it is believed it would not have received a vote but of the manufacturers themselves" (*WTJ* 10:304).

47. Paskoff 1983, 76. See also Pincus 1977, 58–61.

48. Another attendee was Friedrich List, a German newspaper editor from Reading, Pennsylvania, who later achieved fame for writing *The National System of Political Economy* in 1841, a book that defended protectionist policies and was widely seen as the best rebuttal to the free-trade doctrines found in Adam Smith's *Wealth of Nations*. See Henderson 1983.

49. The quotations are from Bartlett 1993, 145, and Dangerfield 1952, 409. See also Remini 1958 and Stanwood 1903, 1:243–90.

50. Remini 1981, 70.

51. "Whether the [Adams] Administration, which was already ruined, was worth such an elaborate stratagem was another question" that Dangerfield (1952, 406) asks.

52. Pincus 1977, 50.

53. Dangerfield 1952, 406.

54. *RD*, 3/4/1828, 1750.

55. Daniel Webster attributes this phrase to Smith in *RD*, 5/9/1828, 756.

56. *PHC* 7:95, 136.

57. *Weekly Register*, 9/20/1828, 52.

58. Remini 1958, 913.

59. "Adams's signature meant only that he believed the bill to be Constitutional: like his predecessors, he did not consider himself justified in vetoing a piece of legislation merely because it was inexpedient" (Dangerfield 1952, 409).

60. *RD*, 5/9/1828, 746.

61. *PJC* 13:459–60.

62. *CG*, 5/30/1844, appendix, 747.

63. *RD*, 4/21/1828, 2472.

64. *PJC* 12:61.

65. *PHC* 10:125.

66. Richardson 1903, 2:414.

67. *PJC* 10:402–03.

68. Of course, a revenue tariff would have some protective effects on certain industries, but such protection was an incidental by-product of the duties, and the promotion of certain industries was not intentional. As Rep. John Letcher of Virginia admitted in 1857, "It is utterly impossible to arrange it [a revenue tariff] as to avoid incidental protection" (*CG*, 2/5/1857, appendix, 190). Of course, others wanted just the opposite. Sen. Simon Cameron of Pennsylvania stated, "I am in favor of protection as the *object* and revenue as the *incidence*" (*CG*, 6/15/1860, 3019).

69. Peskin 2003, 208–9. See also Prince and Taylor 1982.

70. Meyer 2003. On Pennsylvania's role in trade politics during the nineteenth century, see Eiselen 1932.

71. See Tiegle 1942.

72. See Larson 2001 and Irwin 2008.

73. See Baxter 1995 and Ha 2015.

74. *CG* 5/27/1846, 936. As Sellers (1991, 290) put it, "The logrolling genius of Clay's American System linked protectionism with internal improvements. Northwestern entrepreneurs backed high tariffs to provide revenue for roads and canals, while northeastern manufacturers supported transportation appropriations to sop up surplus revenues that might force tariff reductions."

75. *PHC*, 6:654.

76. Larson 2001, 165–66.

77. Feller 1984, 136.

78. *RD*, 2/9/1832, 339–40.

79. *PJC* 10:456–57.

80. Ibid., 450.

81. Huston 1994, 532–33.

82. *PJC* 10:482.

83. *PHC* 10:328.

84. *AC*, 3/31/1824, 1994.

85. "That a Tariff for the encouragement of Manufactures may be abused by its excess, by its partiality, or by a noxious selection of its objects, is certain. But so may the exercise of every constitutional power," Madison noted. "If mere *inequality*, in imposing taxes, or in other Legislative Acts, be synonymous with *unconstitutionality*, is there a State in the Union whose constitution would be safe? Complaints of abuse are heard in every Legislature, at every session" (*PJM* 9:287).

86. Ibid., 431–32.

87. Forsyth 1977, 82.

88. Lindert and Williamson 2013. See also Russel 1924.

89. Ratcliffe 2000, 17.

90. Freehling 1965, 118.

91. *AC*, 1/30/1824, 1308.

92. *PJC* 11:299.

93. Huston 2003, 27; Gundersen 1974, 922.

94. *PJC* 10:398.

95. *RD*, 3/5/1832, 501–2.

96. *AC*, 3/31/1824, 1979.

97. *AC*, 2/2/1832, 278.

98. *LJM* 4:261–62.

99. *PJC* 11:227.

100. Ibid., 10:402–3.

101. Ibid., 444–46.

102. *PAJ* 9:78.

103. Parton 1861, 3:295.

104. Feller 1984, 141.

105. Ratcliffe 2000, 11.

106. Richardson 1903, 2:525.

107. The statement is reprinted in Taussig 1892, 127–28. See Belko 2012 for details on the Philadelphia Free Trade Convention.

108. Richardson 1903, 2:556.

109. The minority on the committee dissented, arguing that "the protecting system is interwoven with the best interests of the country" (Stanwood 1903, 1:374–75).

110. *MJQA* 8:443, 446.

111. *PHC* 8:125. In March 1832, James Madison pleaded with Clay to work out a compromise (*PHC* 8:479).

112. *MJQA* 8:445.

113. *RD*, 2/2/1832, 266.

114. *RD*, 2/13/1832, 367.

115. Freehling 1965, 248.

116. *PHC* 8:551.

117. *RD*, 2/13/1832, 367. See also Miller 1975.

118. *PJC* 12:62 and *PJC* 11:603.

119. See Pease and Pease 1981; Ochenkowski 1983; and Ford 1988.

120. Benton 1854, 1:297.

121. Freehling 1965, 262.

122. Richardson 1903, 2:643, 645.

123. Ibid., 652.

124. Bassett 1926, 4:498, 504, 502.

125. See Bergeron 1973; Latner 1977; and Ellis 1987.

CHAPTER 4

1. Richardson 1903, 2:598.

2. Ibid.

3. *PHC* 8:621–22.

4. Ibid., 617. Years later, when asked to explain why he endorsed the compromise, Clay said that he had two motives. First, he sought to "avert the calamity of civil war, the fire of which, having been lighted up in South Carolina, threatened to extend its flames over the whole Union." Second, he sought to "preserve from utter destruction the system of protection" because "if the compromise act had not been adopted, the whole system of protection would have been swept by the board by the preponderating influence of the illustrious man then at the head of Government [President Jackson]" (*PHC* 9:660).

5. On the compromise, see Peterson 1982.

6. *PHC* 12:41.

7. Benton 1854, 1:311.

8. Kennon and Rogers 1989, 113.

9. *RD*, 2/25/1833, 729–42.

10. *RD*, 1/14/1833, 1040.

11. *PHC* 8:630 and 628.

12. *RD*, 2/26/1833, 1792.

13. *RD*, 2/12/1833, 468.

14. *PHC* 8:626–27.

15. *CG*, 3/12/1838, 638.

16. Timberlake 1993. Also see Rousseau 2002 and Wallis 2001 on the origins of the panic.

17. See Egnal 2001.

18. Richardson 1903, 4:43. On Tyler and the tariff, see Monroe 2003, chap. 5.

19. Richardson 1903, 4:82.

20. *PJC* 16:171.

21. *CG*, 6/15/1842, 635.

22. Johnson and Porter 1973, 9, 3.

23. Polk 1969, 7:264.

24. Richardson 1903, 4:378–79.

25. Polk 1910, 2:28.

26. Ibid., 44. Sellers 1966, 462; Shenton 1961, 74.

27. Richardson 1903, 4:405–6.

28. S. Doc. No. 2-29, at 8 (1845).

29. *PHC* 10:286.

30. S. Doc. No. 20-29, at 11 (1845).

31. James and Lake 1989.

32. Richardson 1903, 5:18.

33. *CG*, 7/21/1846, 1124.

34. See Taylor 1951, 451.

35. Lebergott 1966, table 1.

36. See Irwin 2010 for the 1859 calculation. In 1830, the import share was about 7 percent of GDP, and the average import duty was about 60 percent, yielding a dead-weight loss of 1.3 percent of GDP. This calculation ignores the variance in tariff rates across goods, which usually increases the deadweight loss by a factor of two or more. Thus, a very crude guess at the deadweight loss would place it around 2.5 percent of GDP in 1830.

37. Irwin 2003c.

38. Gallman 1960, table A-1.

39. Meyer 2003.

40. As early as 1825, even Hezekiah Niles conceded that coarse American cotton fabrics did not need protection from imports. Taussig (1931, 136) and Ware (1931, 106) both conclude that domestic producers of coarse goods did not need protection by the early 1830s at the latest.

41. Irwin and Temin (2001) find only a weak relationship between domestic production and import prices even before 1830, consistent with domestic and foreign producers specializing in different products. Their empirical results suggest that the 1846 Walker tariff reduction would have reduced domestic production of cotton textiles by just 7 percent, and elimination of the tariff in 1820, when the tariff rate was much lower, would have reduced domestic production by about 9 percent.

42. Davis and Irwin 2008; Warren 1973, 11, 13.

43. Pincus 1977, 32.

44. See Engerman 1971 and Davis and Irwin 2008.

45. Richardson 1903, 4:285.

46. For example, the Senate rejected a reciprocity agreement with the German Zollverein in 1844. Similarly, Louisiana blocked a reciprocity agreement with Hawaii in 1855 out of fear of sugar imports. The Senate also stopped a trade agreement with Mexico in 1859. The one exception was the negotiation of a limited reciprocity agreement with Canada in 1855. Under this agreement, most bilateral trade in raw materials was given duty-free treatment in both countries. The United States and Canada also agreed to share the Atlantic fisheries off of Newfoundland, and the United States received permission to navigate the St. Lawrence River. The Senate approved this pact. Trade quickly tripled between the two countries, and Canada became the second-largest trading partner of the United States. The United States abrogated the treaty in 1866. See Officer and Smith 1968 and 1971.

47. Richardson 1903, 4:338.

48. Calomiris and Schweikert 1991.

49. Richardson 1903, 4:458.

50. Ibid., 521.

51. See Pitkin 1940 and Flaherty 2001, 108.

52. Luthin 1944, 626.

53. *CG*, 5/10/1860, 2053.

54. Magness 2009. See also Hofstadter 1938.

55. Flaherty 2001, 111.

56. Johnson and Porter 1973, 33.

57. *WAL* 3:487.

58. *WAL* 4:252. As James Blaine (1884, 198–99) explained, "The convention which nominated Mr. Lincoln met when the feeling against free-trade was growing, and in many States already deep-rooted. A majority of those who composed that convention had inherited their political creed from the Whig party, and were profound believers in the protective teachings of Mr. Clay. But a strong minority came from the radical school of Democrats, and, in joining the Republican party on the anti-slavery issue, had retained their ancient creed on financial and industrial questions. . . . The convention therefore avoided the use of the word 'protection,' and was contented with the moderate declaration" mentioned above.

59. Although the South had already decided to leave the Union, Morrill worried about the political ramifications of the tariff: "Our tariff bill is unfortunate in being launched at this time, as it will be made the scape-goat of all difficulties. In fact the southern Confederacy would have made a lower tariff had we left the old law in force and precisely the same troubles would have been presented" (Sherman 1895, 1:183).

60. Magness 2009, 325, 315.

61. Lee 1957, 299.

62. Luthin 1944, 625.

63. *WAL* 4:211.

64. See Huston 2003, 27; and Gunderson 1974.

65. This estimate is from Goldin and Lewis 1975. As Goldin (1973) points out, the cost of buying out slaves from their owners as an alternative to war would have been expensive as well. She estimates the cost of purchasing the freedom of slaves at about $2.7 billion, which would have required tripling federal expenditures, even if spread out over twenty-five years.

66. *CG*, 3/12/1862, 1196.

67. *CG*, 7/1/1862, 3053.

68. *CG*, 6/2/1864, 2672.

69. Lincoln is often thought to have made the statement that the United States gets a good but loses the money when it imports, but it gets the good and keeps the money with protection. Taussig (1920, 34–48) finds no evidence that Lincoln ever said that.

70. McGuire and Van Cott 2002, 429.

71. Bensel 1990, 175.

72. Carlander and Majewski 2003.

73. Burdekin and Langdana 1993, table 2.

74. Davis and Engerman 2006, 144. Although the price of cotton in Liverpool soared from 6 pence per pound in 1860 to 27 pence in 1864, the British government did not offer much support for the Confederate government.

75. Lebergott 1983, 69.

76. Lebergott 1983, 67; and Burdekin and Langdana (1993).

77. "Given Southern unwillingness to be taxed or pay taxes due, and given planter unwillingness to restrict their sale of cotton to support Confederate bond sales, the Confederacy was left with only one financial policy—confiscation" via inflation, Lebergott (1983, 70) notes.

78. Lebergott 1981, 883, and Hetherington and Kower 2009. In addition, by raising the cost of trade, the blockade affected the composition of Confederate imports in a way that was detrimental to the South's war effort. Merchants were given an incentive to import high-valued luxuries (such as coffee and tea) rather than bulky but essential war material. See Lebergott 1981, 873 and Ekelund and Thornton 1992. On the northern blockade in general, see Surdam 2001 and Davis and Engerman 2006.

79. Easterlin 1961, 86; see also Sellers 1927.

CHAPTER 5

1. US Bureau of the Census 1975, Y-493.

2. McGuire 1990.

3. *CG*, 6/29/1866, 3499.

4. *CG* 6/29/1866, 3499.

5. *CG*, 6/29/1866, 3500.

6. *CG*, 7/10/1866, 3719.

7. Joyner 1939, 44.

8. H.R. Exec. Doc. No. 12-39(December 1866).

9. Ferleger 1942, 178.

10. Wells's change in outlook was probably triggered by the intense lobbying surrounding the earlier Morrill bill. Meardon (2007) considers some of the reasons for Wells's intellectual conversion.

11. H. R. Rep. No. 72-41, at 33, 63, 65 (1869).

12. *CG*, 1/19/1869, 452.

13. Tarbell 1912, 67.

14. *CG*, 4/1/1870, 270–71.

15. Richardson 1903, 7:107.

16. *CG*, 3/28/1872, 2017–18.

17. Morgan 1969, 167.

18. Johnson and Porter 1973, 42.

19. Richardson 1903, 7:293.

20. Johnson and Porter 1973, 54, 50.

21. Morgan 1969, 167.

22. Ibid., 116.

23. *Harper's Weekly*, 11/13/1880, 731.

24. Richardson 1903, 8:49.

25. Tariff Commission 1882, 1.

26. Taussig 1931, 249.

27. Richardson 1903, 8:134–36.

28. This is described in Stanwood (1903, 2:207–218). See also Hendrickson and Roberts 2016.

29. *CR*, 5/9/1890, 4431.

30. See Bensel 2000, 495.

31. Quoted in Tedesco 1985, 127.

32. Kennon and Rogers 1989, 187.

33. Thompson 1985.

34. Hoogenboom 1995, 493–5.

35. Richardson 1997, 105.

36. *CR*, 5/3/1882, 3577.

37. Wright 1910.

38. Because of their willingness to do so during this period, Smith (1954, 165) notes that "outside of the cotton South and apart from the period 1830–1860, American farmers have contributed virtually nothing to the cause of a liberal trade policy."

39. Morgan 2003, 168. See also Calhoun 1996, 300–301, and Richardson 1997.

40. Leiter 1961.

41. Skocpol 1993; Holcombe 1999.

42. Bensel 1984, 70.

43. Thompson 1985, 187.

44. Morgan 1969, 170.

45. *CR*, 4/17/1888, 3058.

46. *CR* 5/9/1872, 3234.

47. *CR*, 5/17/1888, 4352. "The whole history of our national experience shows a constantly decreasing price as the effect of increased home competition," one Republican report explained. "A reduction of duties which destroys our production and competition as inevitably results in putting up the price demanded by our foreign rivals."

48. *CR*, 3/25/1870, Appendix, 209

49. Palen 2013, 217.

50. Oddly, Carey favored massive immigration into the United States, which he argued would raise wages by adding to the diversity of employment. See Morrison 1986 and Meardon 2011.

51. While applauding his policy conclusions, Justin Morrill gently conceded that Carey was unpopular because his argumentation was too "diffuse" (Huston 1983, 51).

52. Mill [1848] 1909, 922; *JSM* 17:1589.

53. Morrison 1986, 2.

54. On Wells, see Terrill 1969. Best known for his advocacy of a land tax, Henry George attacked trade restrictions in *Protection or Free Trade* (1886), while William Graham Sumner, a Yale professor and social Darwinist, wrote *Protectionism: The-ism Which Teaches that Waste Makes Wealth* (1885). Arthur L. Perry of Williams College was active with the American Free Trade League and even debated tariff policy with Horace Greeley.

55. *CG*, 4/1/1870, 268.

56. *CR*, 1/10/1877, 555.

57. *CR*, 2/1/1894, 1781.

58. See Corden 1971 and Anderson 1998. Hawke 1975 calculates effective rates of protection for various US industries in the nineteenth century.

59. Most studies of this period put the level of US prices higher than in Britain. In 1910, the nominal dollar-sterling exchange rate was £4.86, but Williamson (1995) calculates that the purchasing-power parity exchange rate was 30 percent higher, at £6.35, reflecting trade impediments and the higher prices of non-traded goods in the United States. Similarly, Ward and Devereux (2003, 832) report that the prices of services (housing, domestic service, and transportation) were roughly 25 percent higher in the United States than in Britain during the late nineteenth century, despite the similar income levels in the two countries.

60. See O'Rourke and Williamson 1999.

61. This "specific factors" model is due to Jones (1971) and Samuelson (1971), and the "neo-classical ambiguity" is analyzed in Ruffin and Jones 1977.

62. As Ward and Devereux (2003, 833) show, surveys of consumers in the 1870s and 1880s indicate expenditure shares of about 42 percent for food, 10 percent for tobacco and alcohol, 18 percent for housing, 20 percent for clothing, and 10 percent for other items.

63. Irwin 2010.

64. However, the collection costs in levying import duties were higher than the costs of internal taxes. The Treasury Department reported that the operating costs (as a percentage of revenue collected) were about 3 percent for both import tariffs and internal taxes in the 1880s, but the costs for internal taxes fell to about 1 percent by about 1900 (Lindert 2014, 487).

65. Irwin 2014.

66. With a perfectly elastic supply of imports, the domestic price of imports would be expected to fall 25 percent, calculated as $(1 + \tau_{1870})/(1 + \tau_{1869})-1$, or $(1.20/1.60)-1 = -0.25$, where τ is the tariff rate.

67. As Smith (1926, 119–120) puts it, "The consensus of opinion among economic historians is that the tariff was not the predominant influence in shaping the course of events in the wool growing industry during the years covered by this chapter."

68. McGuire 1990.

69. James 1984, 193.

70. H.R. Rep. No. 792-48 (1884).

71. Porter and Johnson 1956, 65.

72. Ibid., 72–3.

73. In relating this story, Allan Nevins (1932, 280) adds, "Cleveland might well have expressed his comparative ignorance, but it is unlikely that he did it with this sentimental gesture."

74. Cleveland vetoed hundreds of private pension bills that were pure patronage. Cleveland marveled at "the ingenuity developed in the constant and persistent attacks upon the public Treasury by those claiming pensions and the increase of those already granted is exhibited in bold relief by this attempt to include sore eyes among the results of diarrhea" (Bensel 1984, 65).

75. Richardson 1903, 8:341.

76. Ibid., 509–10.

77. Ibid., 581.

78. Ibid., 584.

79. Ibid., 588.

80. Ibid., 590.

81. Ibid., 590.

82. See H.R. Rep. 1496-50, at 15 (1888).

83. *CR*, 7/19/1888, 6519.

84. *CR*, 6/7/1888, 4401/4403, 4:3591, 5:4107.

85. Johnson and Porter 1973, 78.

86. Ibid., 80.

87. "There is no question that the tariff was the central issue of the election of 1888," Reitano (1994, 108) argues. See also Calhoun 2008.

88. Baumgardner 1984.

89. To date, there has been no systematic analysis of voting patterns in the 1888 election, but see Reitano 1994, 127–28 and Kleppner 1979, 361–62.

90. Richardson 1903, 8:774–76.

91. McCarty, Poole, and Rosenthal (2002) discuss how territorial expansion helped to boost Republican support in Congress for tariff protection.

92. Richardson 1903, 9:39.

93. Morgan 2003, 109. See also Morgan 1960.

94. Quoted in Frieden 1997, 387.

95. *CR*, 5/7/1890, 4253.

96. *CR* 5/8/1890, 4318.

97. H.R. Rep. No. 1466-51, at 1–2 (1890).

98. Stanwood 1903, 2:268.

99. H.R. Rep. No. 1040-52, at 2 (1890).

100. Conybeare (1991) examines the economic basis for the political support given to the McKinley tariff.

101. Morgan 2003, 113.

102. Josephson 1938, 454.

103. Morgan 2003, 113–14.

104. Rogers 2007; Palen 2010; Palen 2016.

105. The infant industry argument usually relies on learning by doing, in which initial production costs fall rapidly with production experience. If production experience is an important determinant of a firm's (or an industry's) costs, temporary protection can enable it to reduce its costs in order to compete successfully against established foreign incumbents. Sutthiphisal (2006) finds little evidence of learning-by-doing in three industries—shoes, textiles, and electrical equipment—in the late nineteenth century.

106. As Irwin (1996b) points out, the infant industry doctrine has a long intellectual history and was endorsed by no less an authority than John Stuart Mill. Baldwin (1969) points out that import tariffs do not provide the right incentives to help infant industries mature.

107. Even James Swank, the stalwart protectionist of the American Iron and Steel Association, did not claim the industry was a newcomer that needed protection on infant industry grounds; see Tedesco 1985, 191.

108. See Berglund and Wright 1929, 195 and Hogan 1971, 357. Taussig (1915, 151) argued that "the same sort of growth [in iron and steel] would doubtless have taken place eventually, tariff or no tariff; but not so soon or on so great a scale."

109. The assumption of no international technology transfer is hard to sustain in view of a 1901 report by a visiting party of British iron officials, which noted that "a considerable number of the heads of the American iron industry of today acquired their training, their knowledge, and their experience in British works" (Berthoff 1953, 67). See also Hyde 1991.

110. Irwin 2000b.

111. For example, using a basic formula for the effective rate of protection, if iron and steel account for two-thirds of the cost of producing tinplate, and the tariff on iron and steel was 40 percent, then a nominal tariff on tinplate of 25 percent implies an effective rate of protection of –56 percent!

112. See Berthhoff (1953, 69).

CHAPTER 6

1. *Statistical Abstract of the United States* 1903, 549; League of Nations 1945, 13.

2. The commonly used figures by Maddison (1995), which have the United States overtaking Britain in per capita income around the turn of the century, are increasingly questioned. Ward and Devereux (2003, 2005) suggest that the United States always had a higher per capita income than Britain, which is consistent with the work of Lindert and Williamson (2016) on the late eighteenth and early nineteenth centuries. On 1910, see Woltjer 2015.

3. *CR* 5/7/1890, 4255.

4. "The effect of alternative commercial policies on the rate of growth may well be the quantitatively significant issue in the free trade versus protection debate," Harry Johnson (1960, 339–40) once wrote. "If the cost of protection is a small proportion of the level of national income at any point of time, and if protectionists happen to be correct in their claim that protection increases an economy's rate of growth, the increase does not have to be very great for its effect in raising national income to counterbalance the reduction due to the cost of protection within relatively few years." See Bairoch 1993, 52–53, and O'Rourke 2000 for statements noting a positive relationship between tariffs and economic growth during this period. This section of the book draws on Irwin 2001.

5. Unfortunately, there is relatively little research that tries to explain the structure of late nineteenth-century tariffs across industries. Baack and Ray (1983) find that tariff rates by industry are not strongly related to skill intensity of labor in production or the capital-labor ratio.

6. Haines 2000, 153.

7. Hatton and Williamson (1998) find that immigration to the United States was highly cyclical and depended upon the wage gap between the two continents as well as business-cycle movements. These migration cycles are uncorrelated with movements

in the tariff; for example, the reduction in protective duties in the Walker Tariff of 1846 was followed by a huge wave of migration to the United States.

8. See Davis and Gallman 1978 and Davis and Gallman 1994. James (1984) found indirect evidence that the government's fiscal surpluses, devoted largely to reducing Civil War debt, promoted domestic investment by reducing interest rates (i.e., fiscal surpluses "crowded in" private investment).

9. Jaremski 2014.

10. De Long (1998, 369) notes that "the tariff made a wide range of investment goods—from British machine tools and steam engines to steel rails to precision instruments—more expensive." The higher prices of foreign and domestic capital goods depressed the rate of capital accumulation. "The damaging effects of the tariff on investment were extremely important for nineteenth century growth," De Long (1998, 370) concludes. "In the long run, a reduction in the real investment share of national product of 2 to 4 percent carries with it a reduction in the capital-output ratio of 10 to 20 percent—and a reduction in productivity and real wages of 5 percent or more."

11. Kravis 1972, 403. The late nineteenth century saw the rise of big business enterprises, but they were not yet large multinational corporations capable of sizeable foreign investments. Wilkins (1989) examines the role of foreign investment in the US economy prior to World War I. See also Lipsey 2000.

12. See Lewis 1979, as well as Dennis and Iscan 2009 and Alvarez-Cuadrado and Poschke 2011.

13. Weiss 1993.

14. Cochran (1961) and others have shown that the Civil War did not provide a boost to manufacturing.

15. Data from the US Bureau of the Census (1975), series P-5, P-10, U-223–224.

16. "The impact of the international economy upon American economic growth during this period was clearly less significant than in earlier periods," North (1960b, 199) notes. If the contribution of import-substitution to late nineteenth-century economic growth was negligible, that period was certainly not one of "export-led" growth either (Kravis 1972).

17. As Taussig (1915, 29) points out, "All the general indications from the economic history of the United States are that protective duties in the great majority of cases have not served to bolster up antiquated establishments or to retard improvements; though it may not be so clear that they have so often actually simulated improvement in the way and to the extent contemplated by the [infant] industries argument."

18. Chandler (1959, 31) argues that "*the* major innovation in the American economy between the 1880s and the turn of the century was the creation of the great corporations in American industry." This innovation "was a response to the growth of a national and increasingly urban market that was created by the building of a national railroad network—the dynamic force in the economy in the quarter century before 1880."

19. Hirschman and Mogford 2009.

20. "Within a decade of the initial transfer of Bessemer steel technology to the USA, American Bessemer plants were decidedly superior to British plants, in terms of output levels and productivity," Hyde (1991, 67) notes.

21. *LTR* 1:104. In Stanwood's (1903, 2:294) view, "The result seemed to be, and in a certain real sense it was, an emphatic rejection of the protection system by the voters of the country." The perception that high tariffs protected monopolistic big businesses and trusts also contributed to the unpopularity of the McKinley act. In Taussig's (1931, 317) view, "The outcry against trusts and monopolies, though in fact it describes an exception rather than the normal working of protective duties, was probably the most effective argument in bringing about the public verdict against the McKinley act."

22. In Cannon's view, any revision of the tariff (up or down) harmed the economy because it generated uncertainty for business. For an analysis, see Clarke, Jenkins, and Lowande 2016.

23. Johnson and Porter 1973, 93.

24. Ibid., 87.

25. Richardson 1903, 9:392.

26. Friedman and Schwartz (1963) attribute the loss of gold reserves to the fear that silver interests would force the United States to abandon the gold standard. It was not until the Republican election victory in 1896 that such fears were set aside, gold returned to the United States, and the economy began to recover. On the economic depression during this period, see Steeples and Whitten 1998.

27. See Miron and Romer 1990 and Romer 1986.

28. Richardson 1903, 9:458–60.

29. As Kennon and Rogers (1989, 237) note, "The public hearings were merely pro forma—the real work occurred behind closed doors. The Wilson bill was as much of a 'dark lantern' measure as the Mills bill of 1888. After the formal hearings, the committee moved to the virtually inaccessible Census Committee room in the labyrinthine Capitol basement. The subcommittee met with Treasury Department officials and businessmen, some of whom came only on the condition that they could remain anonymous. The committee continued to draft the bill in its subterranean chamber."

30. Cleveland had earlier resurrected the party's call for free raw materials for manufacturers: "The world should be open to our national ingenuity and enterprise. This cannot be while Federal legislation through the imposition of high tariffs forbids to American manufacturers as cheap materials as those used by their competitors. It is quite obvious that the enhancement of the price of our manufactured products resulting from this policy not only confines the market for these products within our own borders, to the direct disadvantage of our manufacturers, but also increases their cost to our citizens" (Richardson 1903, 9:459).

31. Joseph 2004. See also Mehrotra 2004.

32. *CR*, 2/1/1894, 1781.

33. Ibid., 1792.

34. Ibid., App., 205.

35. Summers 1953, 186.

36. Stanwood 1903, 2:341.

37. Morgan 1969, 474.

38. *CR* 7/23/1894, 7082.

39. *CR*, 8/28/1894, App., 1535.

40. Ratner 1942, 184–92; Joseph 2004.

41. Johnson and Porter 1973, 98.

42. Ibid., 107.

43. Rove 2015.

44. Richardson 1903, 10:13.

45. Morgan 1965, 227.

46. Morgan 2003, 212.

47. Kennon and Rogers 1989, 242.

48. Palen 2013.

49. *CR*, 6/14/1898, 5903.

50. La Croix and Grandy 1997.

51. See Pérez 2003, 74.

52. In his book *The Tragedy of American Diplomacy*, William Appleman Williams argued that the United States was trying to create an informal empire based on economic expansion, sometimes called the "Open Door" thesis. Yet, as Herring (2008, 334) notes, "The original Open Door Notes, while important, amounted to much less than has been attributed to them. . . . The notes had little immediate impact for China or the United States" and seemed merely to reiterate the US interest in non-discrimination. See also Palen 2016.

53. Lipsey 2000; Lipsey 1963, 144.

54. US Bureau of the Census 1975, U 213–18; Lipsey 1963, 144.

55. Lewis 1957, 579; League of Nations 1945, 13; Eysenbach 1976, 6.

56. Lipsey (1963, 59) observed that the composition of manufactured exports had been "changing ceaselessly since 1879 in a fairly consistent direction—away from products of animal or vegetable origin and toward those of mineral origin." Examining the factor content of US trade in manufactured goods from 1879–1940, Wright (1990) found that net exports were intensive in non-reproducible natural resources.

57. Warren 1973, 116.

58. On the international competitiveness of the steel industry, see Allen 1979; Allen 1981; and Irwin 2003a.

59. Wolman 1992, 82; *Statistical Abstract of the United States* 1904, 218, 522.

60. Findlay and Jones 2001.

61. Wolman 1992, xvii.

62. Kenkel 1983, 44.

63. Terrill 1973, 168.

64. Healey 2001, 165–66.

65. *CR*, 6/19/1890, 6256–59.

66. *CR*, 5/9/1890, 4397.

67. Johnson and Porter 1973, 87. In their election platform, Republicans defended the provision: "We point to the success of the Republican policy of reciprocity, under which our export trade has vastly increased and new and enlarged markets have been opened for the products of our farms and workshops. We remind the people of the bitter opposition of the Democratic party to this practical business measure, and claim that, executed by a Republican administration, our present laws will eventually give us control of the trade of the world" (ibid., 93).

68. *FRUS* 1899, 130.

69. Johnson and Porter 1973, 107.

70. Morgan 1965, 226.

71. On Kasson, see Younger 1955.

72. US Tariff Commission 1919.

73. Richardson 1903, 10:210.

74. Ibid., 240.

75. Younger 1955, 378–79.

76. Richardson 1903, 10:394–96.

77. For example, the domestic price of raw sugar dropped more than 20 percent on the day the duty was abolished by the McKinley tariff of 1890 and rose immediately when the sugar duty was increased in 1894 and 1897. See La Croix and Grandy 1997; Irwin 2015.

78. Tarbell 1912, 266, 261.

79. Stapleford 2009.

80. Wolman 1992, xvii; Lamoreaux 1985.

81. *CR*, 4/24/1888, 3305.

82. *CR* 12/2/1902, 8.

83. As Havemayer stated, "Economic advances incident to the consolidation of large interests in the same line of business are a great incentive to their formation [i.e., trusts], but these bear a very insignificant proportion to the advantages granted in a way of protection under the customs tariff" (*Literary Digest*, June 24, 1899, 720).

84. As Taussig (1931, 310) pointed out, one "needs no great acquaintance with economic history, and no great skill in general reasoning, to show that the tendency to combination has deeper causes than protective legislation, and presents problems more complicated, and in their social importance more weighty, than those involved in the tariff controversy."

85. Bittlingmayer (1985) argues that antitrust enforcement was responsible for the merger wave. "Without the Sherman Act and these judicial interpretations [of the 1890s], the cartels of small family firms owning and operating single-function enterprises might well have continued into the twentieth century in the United States as they did in Europe," Chandler (1977, 375) noted.

86. Chandler (1977) attributes the growth of firm size to changes in technology, as well as falling transportation and information costs due to the spread of the railroad and telegraph, which allowed firms to exploit economies of scale and transformed the United States into a national, integrated market served by large-scale businesses.

87. Gould 1978, 65.

88. Williamson 1995.

89. Irwin 2002.

90. For some evidence on this contention, see Liu and Meissner 2015.

91. Roosevelt apparently had been an enthusiastic advocate of free trade as a Harvard undergraduate, and he began his career sympathetic to the idea of free trade. In an address to the Free Trade Club of New York in 1883, Roosevelt stated that he favored "a gradual and progressive modification of the import duties in the direction of a tariff for revenue only." He added that "there is certainly reaction in public sentiments against our doctrines, but this should not encourage cowardice in the ranks. It should rather

make the advocates of free trade more persistent in their efforts to bring about the desired reform." He even predicted that the complete success of free-trade doctrines was merely a matter of time (*NYT*, 5/29/1883, 5). Yet he soon repudiated these beliefs in order to advance in the Republican party; see Baker 1941. At the same time, Roosevelt (1924 16:338) wrote that the problem with the tariff was "that it puts a premium upon the sacrifice of the general welfare to the selfish interests of particular individuals and particular business or localities, and the most forceful plea advanced for a policy of low tariff is that it does away with this scramble of greedy and conflicting interests."

92. *LTR* 1:408.

93. Ibid., 312–13. At another point, he wrote, "The question is simply whether the gain to be accomplished by a reduction of some of the duties is sufficient to offset the trouble that would be caused by a change in the tariff. Personally I do not believe that any important interest is being harmed in the least by the present tariff, nor, on the other hand, do I think that any special benefit or special harm will come so far as material things are concerned by a reduction" (ibid., 471–72).

94. *LTR* 4:1100.

95. Richardson 1903, 10:428.

96. Roosevelt timidly approached a reciprocity agreement with Cuba in which the State Department had offered concessions on its sugar and tobacco duties. After encountering opposition from Republicans backed by domestic sugar beet and cane producers and tobacco farmers, Roosevelt backed down: "I do not wish to split my own party wide open on the tariff question unless some good is to come" (Gould 1978, 35).

97. *LTR* 3:580.

98. *LTR* 4:1039–40.

99. Ibid., 1056.

100. Ibid., 1052–53.

101. Ibid., 1028.

102. Goodwin 2013, 309.

103. *LTR* 4:1062–63.

104. *LTR* 5:367. The brief financial panic of 1907 set back any prospects of reform. Roosevelt maintained that the "country is definitely committed to the protective system and any effort to uproot it could not but cause widespread industrial disaster. In other words, the principle of the present tariff law could not with wisdom be changed" (Richardson 1903, 14:7083).

105. Johnson and Porter 1973, 158.

106. Solvick 1963, 425–26.

107. Anderson 1981, 169–70.

108. Johnson and Porter 1973, 146.

109. *CR*, 3/4/1909, 3.

110. H.R. Rep. No. 1-61, at 2 (1909).

111. The bill also granted free trade to Philippines, although it limited the amount of sugar and tobacco it could export.

112. *CR*, 3/22/1909, 139.

113. H.R. Rep. No. 1-61, at 3 (1909).

114. Goodwin 2013, 592.

115. *CR*, 5/4/1909, 1716; *CR*, 5/5/1909, 1742.

116. Harrison 2004, 178.

117. Goodwin 2013, 593.

118. Sarasohn (1989, 64) notes, "However divided and uncertain the Democrats appeared in their attempts to lower the tariff, the insurgent Republicans seemed to be aiming at something else entirely. No insurgent would begin a tariff speech without first reaffirming his belief in the protective system."

119. Ibid.

120. *CR*, 5/5/1909, 1744.

121. Goodwin 2013, 593.

122. Chauncey Depew (R-NY) called the income tax movement "the most direct possible attack upon the protective system" and said that such a tax would be unjustifiable except in times of war. "Perhaps you would like to reduce revenues for the purpose of imposing an income tax and thus taking the first steps for the destruction of the protective system," Aldrich remarked to the proponents of tariff cuts (*CR*, 4/19/1909, 1379).

123. *CR*, 6/16/1909, 3344.

124. On Taft's role, see Solvick 1963 and Barfield 1970.

125. Goodwin 2013, 593.

126. Anderson 1981, 174.

127. The Tariff Board was to be an executive advisory group, not an arm of Congress, and could also provide advice on other tariff matters. The chairman of the Tariff Board was Henry C. Emery, a professor of political economy from Yale University.

128. *WHT* 3:177. See also Lake 1988, 144.

129. *CR*, 4/4/1911, 7.

130. Anderson 1981, 178.

131. Kenkel 1983, 81.

132. See Percy, Norrie, and Johnston 1982, and Beaulieu and Emery 2001.

CHAPTER 7

1. Johnson and Porter 1973, 184–85.

2. Ibid., 184–85, 168–69.

3. See Burdick 1968. Speaking before the commission, Wilson argued that high tariffs fostered monopolies, were detrimental to domestic welfare, and would harm relations with other countries. He was not impressed by the commission, calling it a "much ridiculed body of incompetencies" (*PWW* 2:140–43, 285–86).

4. Wilson 1909, 554.

5. "By 1909, that compelling sense of destiny which so infused the campaign days of 1896 had long since vanished, and the Democrats seemed dedicated to the lesser goals of scrambling for office, logrolling for favors, and searching for convenient issues with which to embarrass the Republicans," notes Barfield (1970, 308–9).

6. Johnson and Porter 1973, 168.

7. Ibid., 180–81.

8. *PWW* 27:150.

9. Underwood (1928, 217) was a strong Southern advocate for lower tariffs who

believed that "protective tariff bills are written to protect manufacturers' profits rather than to sustain wages or labor's standard of living."

10. Link 1956, 37–38.

11. Historically, high duties on raw wool meant that woolen manufacturers demanded higher compensatory duties to offset the higher costs of the raw material. Essentially, the tariff on raw wool established a high floor that prevented any reductions in the woolens tariffs. To end this practice of tariff escalation, Wilson insisted on putting wool on the free list. Under pressure, the Ways and Means Committee agreed. Woolen manufacturers also supported this move, and thus Wilson succeeded in splitting the wool producers from the woolens manufacturers. As Willis (1914, 15) notes, "The testimony showed that the manufacturers were very desirous in most instances of securing free raw materials, and that they had hesitated to urge removal of duties only because they feared that they might thereby break up the 'unholy alliance' which had long existed between themselves and the shepherds, thus losing the support of the latter and sacrificing the votes of the senators from the sheep-growing states. When, however, it became evident that no amount of manipulation would probably suffice to 'hold the party in line,' so that a genuine revision of the wool and woolen schedule was assured, manufacturers hastened to seek the remission of duties which they had long desired."

12. *PWW* 23:270–71.

13. H.R. Rep. No. 5-63, at ii–iii, xii (1913).

14. Ibid., at lv.

15. *CR*, 5/6/1913, 1247.

16. Link 1956, 187.

17. Burdick 1968. "The committee found little actual wrongdoing . . . and no evidence of lobbying by the great interests that had led the fight for high tariffs twenty years before," notes Link (1956, 190). See *Maintenance of a Lobby to Influence Legislation: Hearings Before the Senate Judiciary Committee*, 63rd Congress (1913) 4 vols.

18. See Holt 1967. Despite having criticized the excesses of the Payne-Aldrich tariff, the insurgents now attacked the Democratic tariff reduction. Progressive Republicans insisted that they were more interested in "tariff equity" than "tariff reduction." To them, tariff equity meant a rebalancing of duties so that those on industrial goods fell, while those on agricultural and raw materials rose. Progressive Republicans viewed the across-the-board Democratic approach to tariff cutting as reckless, and they particularly assailed the tariff reductions on farm goods, especially meat and grain.

19. Link 1956, 194.

20. Saunders 1999, 230.

21. Joseph 2004. On the political economy of the income tax, see Baack and Ray 1985, Anderson and Tollison 1993, Holcombe and Lacombe 1998, and Mehrotra 2004.

22. US Bureau of the Census 1975, Y-352–53.

23. Congress established the Federal Reserve System in December 1913 as the new central bank of the United States, but the country remained on the gold standard.

24. Miron and Romer 1990.

25. Brownlee 1982.

26. As McAdoo reported, "The Republican leaders are most anxious to make the tariff an issue in the coming campaign. In the Spring of 1915 they made consistent and

persistent attacks upon the Democratic tariff act, alleging that the business depression existing at that time was due wholly to its enactment and Democratic incompetency, when, as a matter of fact, the chief cause of the depression was the European war. When prosperity began to return [in the fall of 1915], they changed their line of attack and said [prosperity] would disappear as soon as the war ended; that American manufacturers would then begin to feel the deadly effects of the Underwood tariff law because it would permit European nations to 'dump' such extraordinary quantities of their manufactured products upon the American market, at any sort of prices, that the home manufacturer would be seriously hurt, if not destroyed by this competition" (PWW 35:475).

27. Schnietz 1998.

28. PWW 35:477.

29. During the Senate consideration of the 1913 tariff, an amendment to create a bipartisan Tariff Commission failed by a vote of 32–37, with Republicans in favor and Democrats opposed.

30. Link 1956, 342.

31. See Taussig 1916. The memo is reprinted in Taussig 1920, 180–93.

32. Houston pitched the idea of a Tariff Commission to Wilson three times before the president relented. As Houston (1926, 196–97) recalled, "I stated that I was not foolish enough to think that the tariff or any other form of taxation could be taken out of politics," but he thought it "could be of great service by gathering reliable data for the information of the President, of Congress, and, above all, of the public."

33. PWW 35:312–16.

34. PWW 36:12–13.

35. PWW 35:510–52, 526–27. Schnietz (1998, 25) notes that the draft legislation that Wilson sent to the Ways and Means Committee was similar to the draft prepared by Taussig for Houston and McAdoo, except that the Wilson draft explicitly gave the Tariff Commission the power to investigate dumping.

36. Johnson and Porter 1973, 205, 195.

37. Fordham (2007) contends that the German threat to the wartime export boom may have influenced the decision to enter World War I.

38. League of Nations 1945, 13.

39. PWW 45:537.

40. As Wilson explained, "I, of course, meant to suggest no restriction upon the free determination of any nation of its own economic policy, but only that whatever tariff any nation might deem necessary for its own economic service, be that tariff high or low, it should apply equally to all foreign nations; in other words, that there should be no discriminations against some nations that did not apply to others" (PWW 51:476).

41. Ibid.

42. Diamond 1943, 183. Indeed, the initial drafts of a League of Nations charter did not include any provision for equality of trade conditions, although the United States later began drafting proposals to limit new preferences and discriminations (including on colonial trade) in trade policy and to create an International Trade Commission under the auspices of the League. Despite these tentative steps, Temperley (1921, 5:68) finds that "there is no evidence that the suggestions of the American advisers were ever seriously urged or even seriously discussed" at the conference.

43. Temperley (1921, 5:69–71) explains the lack of action on trade policy as reflecting the greater focus on political issues after the war.

44. The Republican Congress cut funding for the Tariff Commission to prevent it from undertaking studies that might bring into question the principle of tariff protection. After Taussig resigned as chairman in 1919, the position remained vacant for two years until Republican president Warren Harding appointed a well-known protectionist, Thomas O. Marvin, the former president of the Home Market Club, to the post.

45. *PWW* 59:294.

46. *PWW* 64:108–9.

47. Another policy with trade implications was Prohibition, which went into effect in January 1920. The Eighteenth Amendment to the Constitution prohibited the manufacture, sale, and transport of alcohol, and gave rise to illicit trade. British distillers began shipping whiskey and other alcoholic beverages to the Bahamas, where it could be smuggled into the United States. Bahama's imports of liquor jumped from 27,000 gallons in 1918 to 567,940 gallons in 1921, allowing the island to eliminate its public debt in two years, dredge Nassau harbor, and pay for other public works (Spinelli 1989, 3). When a US-UK treaty limited this illicit trade, Canada became the major headquarters for smuggling operations until Prohibition was repealed in 1933.

48. Johnson and Porter 1973, 216, 235.

49. Meltzer 2003, 91.

50. The severity of the post–World War I recession is disputed. The official Commerce Department series for real GNP falls 14 percent between 1919 and 1921, whereas Romer's (1988) revised series declines just 3 percent between those two years. To judge by industrial production, the recession was intense but short, both on the downturn and the upswing. The business-cycle peak was January 1920, and the trough was in July 1921, according to the National Bureau of Economic Research.

51. H.R. Rep. No. 1139-66, (1920).

52. *CR*, 3/3/1921, 4498–99.

53. Kennon and Rogers 1989, 262.

54. *CR*, 3/4/1921, 7.

55. *CR*, 3/12/1921, 170.

56. "In practically no case did prices rise immediately after the passage of the act," the US Tariff Commission (1922, 1–2) concluded. "In some cases a decrease of imports, as well as a continued decline in agricultural prices in this country, preceded the enactment of the emergency tariff law."

57. Goldin 1994.

58. Kenkel 1983, 152.

59. H.R. Rep. No. 248-67 (1921).

60. Ibid., at 44, 49

61. *CR*, 9/21/1921, 13105; *CR* 9/13/1922, 12508.

62. *CR*, 7/14/1921, 3835, 3840.

63. Hoff 1971, 76.

64. *CR*, 12/6/1921, 37.

65. *CR*, 4/20/1922, 5673–74.

66. When Frank Kellogg (R-MN) complained that many rural Republicans might

lose their seats over the tariff, Fordney snapped, "Well I would rather see the Senate lose you than American industry suffer" (Murray 1969, 277).

67. Senator Reed Smoot (R-UT) noted in his diary for February 28, 1922, "We disposed of some of the most difficult paragraphs in the tariff bill today. Among them pocket knives, scissors and shears, buttons and clasps and razors. We provided rates so high the President need not act to increase duties" (Smoot 1997, 495–96).

68. Dollar 1973.

69. The memo is reproduced in Culbertson 1937, 209. See also Gersting 1932.

70. On Culbertson, see Snyder 1968 and Snyder 1980.

71. CR, 12/6/1921, 37.

72. Because Smoot was an Old Guard Republican, the two were odd bedfellows. As Culbertson noted, "If anyone had told me six months ago that I would now be sympathetically working with Senator Smoot, . . . I would have rolled over and croaked" (Leffler 1979, 46–47).

73. McClure 1924, 50–51.

74. In 1928, the Supreme Court upheld the constitutionality of the flexible tariff provision in the case of J. W. Hampton, Jr. & Co. v. the United States. In this case, an importer contested the imposition of a duty of six cents per pound on barium dioxide, two cents more than in the 1922 statute, after a 1924 proclamation by President Calvin Coolidge. The Supreme Court ruled that the delegation of authority was constitutional because the president was carrying out of the will of Congress in changing the duty.

75. Many members of Congress would support higher tariffs regardless of what a "cost of production" investigation would reveal. As Senator Aldrich stated, "If it was necessary, to equalize the conditions and to give the American producer a fair chance for competition, other things being equal of course, I would vote for three hundred per cent as cheerfully as I would for fifty" (CR, 5/17/1909, 2182).

76. CR, 8/10/1922, 1192–93.

77. Kelley 1963, 18–19.

78. US Tariff Commission 1930, 24–25.

79. Greenbaum 1971.

80. From Costigan's resignation letter, reprinted in the CR, 3/15/1928, 4735.

81. See Goodykoontz 1947 and Snyder 1968.

82. CR, 5/29/1928, 10546–52. The full report is S. Rep. No. 1325-70 (1926).

83. Kenkel 1983, 175. For Taussig's reaction, see Taussig 1926.

84. CR, 9/12/1929, 3549.

85. H.R. Rep. No. 79-67, at 1–2 (1921).

86. Baldwin 1998, 301.

87. Viner 1924.

88. Wilson argued that the United States should be capable of protecting its commerce against discrimination in foreign countries and should work toward establishing equal treatment in world trade. Currently, the United States had "no weapon of retaliation in case other governments should enact legislation unequal in its bearing on our products as compared with the products of other countries," Wilson noted. "Though we are as far as possible from desiring to enter upon any course of retaliation, we must frankly face the fact that hostile legislation by other nations is not beyond the range of

possibility, and it may have to be met by counter legislation." The Tariff Commission report "has shown very clearly that we lack and that we ought to have the instruments necessary for the assurance of equal and equitable treatment" (*PWW* 59:295–96).

89. *CR*, 4/24/1922, 5881.

90. Culbertson 1937, 245.

91. *FRUS* 1923, 1:122.

92. Ibid., 126–27.

93. Ibid., 128–29.

94. In August 1923, Hughes sent a confidential circular to American diplomatic officers notifying them that the president had "authorized the secretary of state to negotiate commercial treaties with other countries by which the contracting parties will accord to each other unconditional most-favored-nation treatment" (Ibid., 1:131).

95. "Because the United States conditional MFN policy resulted in relatively little discrimination," Kelley (1963, 35) notes, "the adoption of an unconditional MFN policy in 1923 would not be of such major significance had the United States tariff continued to be virtually non-negotiable."

96. *CR*, 12/6/1923, 97.

97. *CR*, 12/23/1924, 54.

98. *CR*, 12/7/1926, 29.

99. Johnson and Porter 1973, 245.

100. Benedict 1953, 168–72.

101. Alston 1983.

102. See Hansen 1991.

103. Tontz 1958.

104. "There was practically no direct attack upon the principle of a high tariff by the national farm organizations," such as the American Farm Bureau Federation and the National Grange, Conner (1958, 37–38) notes. "Instead, the basic approach of these groups was an attempt to secure parity in tariff rates with industry. . . . The thinking of organizational leaders was developed within the framework of a high tariff structure, the emphasis being upon raising agricultural rates to obtain parity with industry, rather than upon lowering any or all rates."

105. *CR* 7/14/1922, 3835, 3840.

106. See Kelley 1940 and Benedict 1953.

107. Benedict 1953, 216.

108. The Old Guard Republican establishment had always been rather dismissive of farmers. "Well, farmers never had made money," Coolidge reportedly remarked about their plight. "I don't believe we can do much about it" (Sundquist 1983, 187).

109. *CR*, 5/23/1928, 9524–27.

110. Malin 1930, 114–15.

111. *NYT*, 1/1/0/1928.

CHAPTER 8

1. Johnson and Porter 1973, 272, 285.

2. Ibid., 272.

3. "For the first time in at least three generations, the platform contained no explicit attack upon the GOP theory of a high protective tariff as the best guarantee of high wages and prosperity," notes Craig (1992, 158–59). "The Democratic party, which for over a century had upheld the principle of tariffs for revenue only as the chief distinguishing factor between it and the GOP, had now committed itself to the principle of a protective tariff."

4. *NYT*, 11/4/1928, 132.

5. Johnson and Porter 1973, 282.

6. *NYT*, 11/4/1928, 132.

7. *PPP* 1929, 75.

8. *CR*, 4/15/1929, 25.

9. *PPP* 1929, 79.

10. H.R. Rep. No. 7-71, at 11 (1929).

11. *CR*, 5/9/1929, 1073–74.

12. H.R. Rep. No. 7-71, at 11 (1929).

13. *CR*, 5/28/1929, 2127.

14. Under the plan, an exporter of farm goods would receive a debenture (certificate) equal to half of the value of the import tariff on the good. For example, if the tariff on wheat was 42 cents per bushel, a farmer would receive a certificate for 21 cents for every bushel of wheat exported. Even if the tariff did not really protect wheat farmers from imports, because the United States exported much of its crop, the debenture would be valuable to the farmer. The certificate was like cash and could be sold at something close to face value to importers, who could use it to pay import duties.

15. *CR*, 5/25/1929, 1951.

16. *CR*, 5/13/1929, 1201.

17. *CR*, 6/14/1929, 10762.

18. *NYT*, 5/29/1929, 1.

19. Empirical studies of the House vote on the Hawley bill have sought to determine some of the underlying political and economic factors behind the legislation. See Eichengreen 1989 and Callahan, McDonald, and O'Brien 1994.

20. Merrill (1990, 288) writes that "there is no evidence that any apparent fact, any argument, any introspection even faintly disturbed the certainty of his knowledge and belief in the benefits of protectionism, or weakened his unalterable opposition to any reduction." In Taussig's (1930, 184) view, Smoot "was not only an out-and-out protectionist of the most intolerant stamp, but was strongly interested in his own region and its own product, beet sugar; not regarded as an impartial or disinterested person, and not entitled to be so regarded."

21. *CR*, 9/19/1922, 12906.

22. *CR*, 9/26/1929, 3971.

23. *CR*, 9/12/1929, 3549.

24. Ibid., 3542.

25. *CR*, 11/6/1929, 5239.

26. *NYT*, 11/1/1929, 1. Historians have subsequently criticized Hoover for this indifference. "Had Hoover exercised his election mandate and exerted more legislative

leadership during these early months of his presidency," Ritchie (2007, 48) argues, the ensuing tariff mess could have been avoided. See also Koyama 2009.

27. A *New York Times* editorial explained why: "It is a mistake to suppose that the rebellious coalition wants to write a bill of its own. Its chief desire is to destroy the bill of the Senate Finance Committee. If the leaders of the coalition were locked up in a committee room and told not to come out until they had produced a measure satisfactory to all their supporters, they would never come out. If the door was burst open, they would doubtless be found lying about wounded after bloody rows with each other" (*NYT*, 11/11/1929, 20).

28. In a widely noted claim, Jude Wanniski (1978) argued that a small, critical Senate vote on a particular tariff produced the stock market crash of Black Thursday and Black Tuesday, October 24 and 29, 1929. On the other hand, Alfred Eckes (1998) suggests that it was the coalition's effort to reduce industrial tariffs that may have led to the stock market crash because business supported higher duties. Kindleberger (1986, 125) dismissed as "farfetched" the idea that "the stock market crash of October 24, 1929, was a response to the action of a Senate subcommittee, reported on an interior page of the *New York Times*, in rejecting an attempt of some members to hold down a proposed increase in a tariff on carbide." After careful study, White (1990, 173) found "no evidence to support the view that the Smoot-Hawley tariff significantly contributed to the crash."

29. *CR*, 3/24/1930, 5976–77.

30. *CR*, 3/20/1930, 5669.

31. *CR*, 3/24/1930, 5977.

32. They concluded that the tariff would be fully effective on flax, olive oil, soybean oil, sugar, and wool; partially effective on buckwheat, butter, casein, milk and cream, sheep, lamb, and mutton, Swiss cheese, and high-protein wheat; and ineffective on barley, molasses, cheddar cheese, coconut oil, corn, cotton, jute, cottonseed oil, eggs, oats, rye, and other wheat (*CR*, 11/11/1930, 1439–47).

33. *CR*, 1/10/1930, 1368.

34. See Hayford and Pasurka 1992; Cupitt and Elliott 1994; and Irwin and Kroszner 1996.

35. *NYT*, 3/30/1930, 22.

36. As Hoover (1951–52, 295–96) recalled, "I learned on May 24 that the conferees had overridden Senator Smoot and Congressman Hawley and had watered the flexible provision down to about nothing. I wrote out the provision I wanted. I sent word that unless my formula was adopted, the bill would be vetoed. The result was a complete victory for the flexible tariff in the conference report."

37. *CR*, 6/14/1930, 10760.

38. *CR*, 6/12/1930, 10546.

39. *CR*, 6/14/1930, 10762.

40. Ibid., 10764.

41. In 1929, the president of the American Federation of Labor reaffirmed that the organization had "never committed itself to the support of a protective tariff or free trade. We have avoided most scrupulously and carefully that controversial field" (Leiter 1961, 56).

42. Leuchtenburg 2009, 92.

43. Scroggs 1930.

44. Steel 1980, 288.

45. Burner 1979, 298.

46. Morison 1960, 312.

47. Snyder 1973.

48. *CR*, 5/5/1930, 8327–30. The statement was organized by Clair Wilcox of Swarthmore College and Paul H. Douglas of the University of Chicago (and later a senator from Illinois). For the origins of the statement, see Fetter (1942). Rep. David O'Connell (R-NY) said, "I have no patience with the economists that are consistently raising flimsy objections to this legislation" (*CR*, 5/5/1930, 8383). Senator Henry Hatfield (R-WV) stated, "Cloistered in colleges as they are, hidden behind a mass of statistics, these men have no opportunity to view the practical side of life in matters pertaining to our industrial welfare as a nation." He scorned these "intellectual free traders, who seem to be more concerned with the prosperity of foreigners than they are with the well-being of our own American people" (*CR*, 5/28/1930, 9704).

49. *PPP* 1930, 232–33.

50. Ibid.

51. The Tariff Act of 1930 is sometimes popularly known as the Smoot-Hawley tariff, both because it sounds better than Hawley-Smoot and because Smoot was more closely associated with the legislation than Hawley. However, we follow the standard convention that the first name of a tariff act is the chairman of the House Ways and Means Committee and the second name is the chairman of the Senate Finance Committee.

52. Tariff Act of 1930, H.R. Doc. No. 476-71, at 43, 2 (1930).

53. *NYT*, 11/10/1929, 11.

54. These examples and many more are in Bidwell 1930.

55. Irwin 2011b, 95.

56. The average tariff on dutiable imports reached its highest rate of 61.7 percent in 1830, shortly after the enactment of the Tariff of Abominations in 1828. Of course, the average tariff on total imports was much lower in 1932 (at 19.6 percent) than in 1830 (at 57.3 percent) because many imports were duty-free in 1932.

57. US Bureau of the Census 1975, U-237.

58. Irwin 1998a.

59. *NYT*, 11/10/1929, 21.

60. Archibald et al. (2000) calculate that the Hawley-Smoot tariff actually reduced the effective rate of protection received by agricultural producers.

61. *CR*, 6/14/1930, 10762.

62. Conner 1958, 40.

63. Schattschneider 1935, 136.

64. US Bureau of the Census 1975, series U 225, 237.

65. This finding is supported by Hall's (1933) contemporary estimates of the tariff's impact on trade.

66. Quarterly GDP is available in Gordon 1986, appendix B.

67. These data are from the US Bureau of the Census 1975 and *Statistical Ab-*

stract of the United States 1934, 283, 703. Quarterly real GDP is from Gordon 1986, appendix B.

68. See Fishback 2013 for a recent survey.

69. See Eichengreen 1992; Irwin 2012–13; and Sumner 2015.

70. Working with a Keynesian type model, Eichengreen (1989) suggests that the expenditure-switching effect from the Hawley-Smoot tariff could have increased domestic output by 5 percent in the absence of foreign retaliation. After incorporating limited foreign retaliation into his Keynesian model, Eichengreen (1989) finds a smaller but still positive net expansionary effect from Hawley-Smoot of about 2 percent of GDP.

71. If this decline in exports was due to foreign retaliation, then that could have more than offset any positive, expansionary influence coming from the tariffs themselves; see Dornbusch and Fischer 1986, 469.

72. See Irwin 2011b, 123.

73. Irwin (2010) estimates that the deadweight welfare losses associated with the tariff structure increased by 0.1 percent of GDP between 1929 and 1933.

74. Alston 1983.

75. Archibald and Feldman 1998.

76. Carey 1999.

77. *CR*, 6/9/1930, 10291–98.

78. *CR*, 9/12/1929, 3548.

79. McDonald, O'Brien, and Callahan 1997.

80. *NYT*, 9/17/1930, 26.

81. Irwin 2011b, 158.

82. League of Nations 1942.

83. Jones 1934, 53.

84. Gordon 1941, 54–55.

85. Eichengreen and Irwin 2010.

86. Jones 1934, 238.

87. MacDougall and Hutt 1954.

88. On the spread of protectionism across Europe, see Kindleberger (1989), Eichengreen and Irwin (2010), and Irwin (2012b).

89. "There is a widespread belief among the people of the United States that by reason of the high and exorbitant rates of the tariff act of 1930, we have incurred the hostility of many nations throughout the world. They believe that this hostility has resulted in the enactment of many retaliatory tariffs against us, the results of which are causing uneasiness and concern to all thoughtful minds" (H.R. Rep. No. 29-72, at 6 [1931]).

90. *PPP* 1932, 205–7.

CHAPTER 9

1. See Ritchie 2007.

2. Johnson and Porter 1973, 343.

3. When accused by a Democratic official of supporting high tariffs, Raskob denied it, responding that the Hawley-Smoot tariff was "the most atrocious law every put on our statute books. . . . The impression seems to have gone abroad that I am in favor of

high tariffs," he said; "such is not the case at all." Instead, he wanted to reassure the industrial East that the party would not "destroy industry" but rather be "in favor of the lowest tariffs that will adequately protect and restore prosperity to American industry." See Craig 1992, 196.

4. Ibid., 199.

5. Johnson and Porter 1973, 331.

6. Rosen 1977, 344.

7. Ibid., 345.

8. *PPP* 1928–32, 1:702.

9. Leuchtenburg 2009, 141.

10. Moley 1939, 51.

11. Neither Smoot nor Hawley returned to Congress. Smoot was defeated for reelection in the 1932 campaign, while Hawley was an unsuccessful candidate for his party's nomination that year.

12. *PPP* 1933, 2:14.

13. As Temin and Wigmore (1990, 485) put it, "The devaluation of the dollar was the single biggest signal that the deflationary policies implied by adherence to the gold standard had been abandoned; . . . the devaluation of April–July 1933 was the proximate cause of the [US economic] recovery." See Taylor and Neumann 2016. A large body of research has demonstrated that worldwide economic recovery from the Depression began once countries left the gold standard and began pursuing more expansionary monetary policies; see Eichengreen 1992 in the international context and Sumner 2015 for the United States. Romer (1992) argues that monetary expansion was the driving force behind the US economic recovery after 1933.

14. *Survey of Current Business*, July 1951, 27.

15. Steward 1975, 14.

16. Even John Maynard Keynes strongly objected to the attempt to raise prices by reducing output. These policies impeded the recovery because reducing output was not a way to increase employment.

17. Others products covered by quotas included coconut oil and cordage from the Philippines, red cedar shingles, Douglas fir and western hemlocks from Canada, cattle, cream, and white seed potatoes. Some of these quotas were nonbinding (Whittlesey 1937).

18. Kelley 1963.

19. On Hull's views on trade policy, see Butler 1998 and Allen 1953.

20. Butler 1998, 37.

21. *NYT*, 4/30/1933.

22. Assistant Secretary of State Francis Sayre (1957, 158), who worked closely with Hull in the 1930s, said, "He had a singular devotion to his ideals, and was firm as a rock in allegiance to his underlying principles. His long experience in Congress gave him strength on 'the Hill'; in case of Congressional tangles he could always pick up the telephone and talk to his former associates in the intimacy of comradeship. Everywhere he was respected. He had high qualities of leadership and was recognized throughout the country as the strongest member of the Roosevelt Cabinet."

23. Schatz 1972, 499.

24. Acheson (1969, 55) noted that Hull was so focused on trade to the exclusion of other issues that "whatever the occasion" and regardless of the issue of the day, any speech that Hull gave "was apt to turn into a dissertation on the benefits of unhampered international trade and the true road to it through agreements reducing tariffs."

25. As Francis Sayre (1939, 41–42) put it, "Unilateral tariff reduction on our part would have left untouched the mounting trade barriers which had been erected all over the world as a result of aggressive economic nationalism, and which were effectively barring American surpluses from world markets. If we were to regain our vanishing export markets for American surpluses, obviously the only sound and effective method lay in lowering trade barriers simultaneously at home and abroad."

26. *FRUS* 1933, 1:727–731.

27. Ibid., 924.

28. *CR*, 3/2/1934, 3580.

29. Hull (1948, 356) notes that the original State Department draft of the legislation was longer and more complicated. Ironically, his soon-to-be opponent within the administration, George Peek, suggested that the proposal would stand a better chance of passage if it were only two or three pages long, a suggestion with which Hull agreed. See Peek 1936, 197–99.

30. Schnietz 2000, 431 and *CR*, 6/14/1930, 10761.

31. *Reciprocal Trade Agreements: Hearings Before the Committee on Ways and Means*, 73rd Cong. 2, 5 (1934).

32. H.R. Rep. No. 1000-73 (1934).

33. See Berglund 1935 on the RTAA's passage through Congress.

34. In a press conference in June 1933, Roosevelt remarked that "Congress would never give me complete authority to write tariff schedules," to which a reporter replied, "Well, they have given you everything else" (Haggard 1988, 96). But Roosevelt was right about Congress's reluctance to grant too much power over trade policy to the executive branch.

35. *CR*, 3/24/1934, 5356.

36. Trubowitz 1998, 163.

37. *CR*, 5/29/1934, 9803, 9805.

38. *CR*, 6/4/1934, 10383.

39. Ibid., 10378–79.

40. Although cotton and wheat farmers supported the bill, textile firms, toy makers, and many other small and medium-sized producers opposed it (Schnietz 2000, 428). Despite this lack of participation, interest groups were affected by the legislation. Schnietz (2003) finds that export-dependent firms experienced a positive and significant stock return of nearly 4 percent when Roosevelt requested the RTAA, and that highly protected firms experienced a significant stock return decline of nearly 5 percent when the RTAA was reported out of the Senate Finance Committee.

41. The text of the RTAA is in Tasca (1938, 306–8). Other contemporary studies of the trade agreements program include Larkin (1940) and Beckett (1941).

42. Studies about the political economy of the RTAA include Haggard 1988; Nelson 1989; Lohmann and O'Halloran 1994; Bailey, Goldstein, and Weingast 1997; Gilligan 1997; Irwin and Kroszner 1999; Hiscox 1999; Schnietz 2000, and Schnietz 2003. For a

general study of Congress's relation to the executive in foreign economic policy, see Pastor 1980.

43. *NYT*, 2/13/1936.

44. For a history of the Export-Import Bank, see Becker and McClenahan 2003.

45. Annex A of Irwin, Mavroidis, and Sykes 2008 reproduces the 1941 trade agreement template.

46. See Miller 2003.

47. Butler 1998, 25.

48. Similarly, Francis Sayre (1957, 159), to whom Hawkins reported, wrote that he "was a rare and splendid man whose whole heart and soul, like Secretary Hull's, were in this work of reducing excessive trade barriers. I suspect that, apart from Secretary Hull, the success of the trade agreements program was due more to Harry Hawkins than to any other single man." Likewise, Henry Grady (2009, 56) wrote that Hawkins was "one of the ablest men, and his resourcefulness, particularly in the working out of the basic principles of our agreements, was essential. To him as much as to any one person is due the success of this great but difficult government enterprise. For years he gave under Secretary Hull the most excellent direction to the [trade agreements] program."

49. Varg 1976.

50. See O'Brien and McDonald 2009 for the change in Canada's policy during this period.

51. *Extension of the Reciprocal Trade Agreements Act*, 1:38, H.R., Committee on Ways and Means, 76th Cong., (1937).

52. Schatz 1970, 100.

53. Rooth 1993, 303. On the Anglo-American trade agreement, see Kottman 1968, Schatz 1970, and Drummond and Hillmer 1989. US documents relating to the negotiations appear in *FRUS* 1938, 2:1–71.

54. Cantril 1951, 842.

55. See Durand 1937 for an early quantitative assessment of the RTAA's impact on the pattern of US trade.

56. Hart 2002.

57. Tasca 1938, 188.

58. This calculation implies that the RTAA reduced the tariff by 12.8 percent, quite close to the Tariff Commission's estimate of 13 percent. Thus, two-thirds of the overall tariff reduction during 1934–39 can be attributed to negotiated tariff reductions, and one-third to higher import prices (Irwin 1998a).

59. *Survey of Current Business*, July 1951, 27.

60. *FRUS* 1937, 1:842.

61. See also Grady 2009, 49, 51–52. Hawkins (1944) describes the implementation of the trade agreements program.

62. *CR*, 2/5/1937, 925.

63. *Department of State Bulletin*, January 13, 1940, 34–35. Hull complained about the misrepresentation of the agreements by critics: "Frequently, allegations of injury are made with respect to commodities on which existing duties have not been reduced, or with respect to commodities which were left on the free list even by the authors of the Hawley-Smoot tariff. In my entire experience, I do not recall a more flagrant and

unscrupulous suppression and misuse of material facts on an issue which is of vital significance to every citizen, every home, every farm, and every factory."

64. *NYT*, 1/21/1938, 12.

65. In Francis Sayre's (1939, 95–96) view, "While we are in the very midst of these hair-trigger negotiations, seeking to win an agreement with real profit for both sides, high-powered lobbyists make their voices heard throughout the country, using every device to prevent the giving of concessions in the particular commodities in which they are interested or to defeat or upset the agreement. Pressure is brought against members of Congress; Washington is deluged with inspiring letters and telegrams. The country rings with the protests of special interests; unhappily few seem sufficiently concerned to speak for the interests of the consumer or of the Nation."

66. As Brenner (1977, 151) notes, "The change in institutions had sharply reduced the effectiveness of these interests' influence, . . . and they knew it."

67. *NYT*, 1/14/1939.

68. Johnson and Porter 1973, 363.

69. Ibid., 368. Hull (1948, 486) was "dumbfounded" by the last section of the platform.

70. *CR*, 2/5/1937, 925.

71. "In talking it over with the President, I found he favored making the bill permanent, instead of limiting it to three years," Hull (1948, 518) recalled. "I also preferred the permanent idea, but seriously doubted our ability to pass it. . . . The bill went up to the House as the president wanted it, but the House Ways and Means Committee inserted the three-year limitation."

72. *Extending Trade Agreements Act: Hearings Before the Senate Finance Committee*, 75th Cong. 1:14 (1937).

73. H.R. Rep. No. 166-75, at 19 (1937).

74. *CR*, 2/23/1937, 1502.

75. Schatz 1972.

76. Schatz 1970, 86–87. A memorandum he sent to diplomatic officers in July 1937 provides an excellent summary of his philosophy; see *FRUS* 1937, 1:841–45.

77. Blum 1959, 1:524.

78. Quoted in Patrick 2009, 124. Schatz (1970, 102–3) offers a useful assessment.

79. Gallup 1972, 206.

80. *Department of State Bulletin*, 3/2/1940, 231.

81. *NYT*, 2/4/1940.

82. "Hull had persuaded about one dozen wavering representatives to support reciprocal trade, while [Assistant Secretary of State Breckinridge] Long had consulted privately with administration leaders in the House and had made certain that practically all Democrats were in Washington on the roll call date" (Porter 1980, 51).

83. Ibid., 53. Vice President John N. Garner, who did not support deep tariff reductions, was secretly working against the administration by recruiting votes for an amendment that would limit the president's negotiating authority to just one year.

84. Ibid., 55. Of course, Republicans continued to attack the RTAA. Senator James Davis of Pennsylvania called it a "guerrilla attack on American trade protection," while Arthur Vandenberg criticized the "despotic secrecy" with which the agreements were

reached and called it "a grossly unconstitutional delegation of legislative power to the executive branch" (*CR*, 3/25/1940, 3341; *CR*, 3/26/1940, 3495).

85. Porter 1974.

86. The State Department lobbied hard to convince western Democrats to support the renewal, and apparently converted two of them just hours before the final roll call vote (Porter 1980, 57). "We were fighting a losing battle from the start," Pittman wrote. "We had three votes in the majority the night before the vote. The power exerted was too strong for us to hold these votes. You can understand the power when you realize that Schwartz of Wyoming and Schwellenbach of Washington voted against us. The fight is not ended" (Israel 1963, 130).

87. Porter 1980, 58.

88. Johnson and Porter 1973, 392.

89. For an overview of US international transactions during the war, see Bach 1946 and US Department of Commerce 1948.

90. *State Department Bulletin*, 1943, 329, 333.

91. See Long 1966, 305.

92. Zeiler 1999, 18.

93. However, it was not until 1945 that Vandenberg gave his famous speech renouncing isolationism; see *CR*, 1/10/1945, 166. See also Kaplan 2015.

94. *CR*, 5/24/1943, 4796, 4795.

95. *CR*, 5/11/1943, 4200.

96. As Breckinridge Long (1966, 311) wrote, "It is attributable in part to antagonism against the Administration and the rest is Republican desire to reassume authority—to terminate grants of power to the Executive—partly anti-Roosevelt and partly anti-Democrat. . . . The vote is *not* on the merits of the bill. It is just a manifestation of political strength and a warning to this and to all other Governments that America will probably slip back into its shell again after this war as it did in the last, return to an 'isolation' point of view and withhold cooperation in a wholehearted manner after this war. I see the signs I saw in 1918. I hope not to see the consequences."

97. *CR*, 5/12/1943, 4310.

98. H.R. Rep. No. 403-78, at 10 (1943).

99. *State Department Bulletin* 1943, 169.

CHAPTER 10

1. In December 1940, Roosevelt wrote to Treasury Secretary Henry Morgenthau, "I have been thinking very hard on this trip about what we should do for England, and it seems to me that the thing to do is to get away from the dollar sign" (Reynolds 1982, 157).

2. See Notter 1949.

3. In May 1941, President Roosevelt gave the State Department the principal responsibility for negotiating a Lend-Lease agreement with Britain (*FRUS* 1941, 2:5).

4. Notter 1949, 45–46.

5. *FRUS* 1945, 4:74–5.

6. As the State Department saw it, "Britain under the Ottawa Agreements granted

special low tariff duties and signed long-term bulk-purchasing agreements with empire trading partners in order to monopolize their raw materials and make sure that they took only British-manufactured products," writes Woods (1990, 18). "Imperial preferences could be used, then, not only to monopolize the trade of a particular nation or region; it also could be used to isolate and punish political and military rivals. In a political as well as an economic sense, the structure established by the Ottawa Agreements seemed the antithesis of multilateralism."

7. "The Foreign Office advised stalling on any suggestion for commitment on post-war policy," Pressnell (1986, 31) notes. "This firm stonewalling reflected British optimism that either there would be no Consideration at all or that it might be largely and acceptably non-economic."

8. *FRUS* 1941, 3:15.

9. Ibid., 11.

10. See Acheson's minutes of the meeting in *FRUS* 1941, 3:12.

11. Ibid., 11. However, Keynes came around: "At the end of our talk he seemed more reconciled to the Article, but by no means wholly so," Acheson reported. After he had calmed down, Keynes wrote to Acheson, "My so strong reaction against the word 'discrimination' is the result of my feeling so passionately that our hands must be free to make something new and better of the postwar world; not that I want to discriminate in the old bad sense of that word—on the contrary, quite the opposite. . . . But the word calls up, and must call up—for that is what it means, strictly interpreted—all the old lumber, most-favored-nation clause and the rest which was a notorious failure and made such a hash of the old world. We know also that won't work. It is the clutch of the dead, or at least the moribund, hand" (*FRUS* 1941, 3:16–17).

12. Harrod 1951, 512.

13. An economic official at the US Embassy in London, E. F. Penrose (1953, 18), later said, "At that time and later I did my best to impress on Mr. Keynes and other government economists that the desire for freer and for non-discriminatory trade in the State Department should not be written off as the product of a nineteenth century laissez-faire attitude toward economic affairs, untouched by recent economic thought and experience. . . . In conversations in Washington both Acheson and Hawkins showed themselves progressive in outlook and under no illusion that freer trade alone was panacea for all economic ills. However, it soon appeared that the contrary view had been expressed to British officials in Washington by some US officials outside the State Department."

14. Wilson 1991, 164.

15. Ibid., 163–72.

16. Woods 1990, 18.

17. *FRUS* 1942, 1:535–36.

18. On the misinterpretation, see Pressnell 1986.

19. Pressnell (1986) provides the background. Meade's memorandum is reproduced in Irwin, Mavroidis, and Sykes 2008. "If any one event can be designated as marking the origin of the International Trade Charter and the International Trade Organization proposed at Havana in 1947, it took place in Whitehall in the latter part of 1942," wrote Penrose (1953, 89–90). "If any one person can be described as the originator of the move-

ment for an International Trade Organization, it is James Meade." Meade was a remarkable economist whose views on postwar trade policy were similar to those held by the
State Department. He had enormous respect for Keynes but rejected his views on trade
policy. In 1940, Meade published a short book entitled *The Economic Basis of a Durable
Peace*, in which he examined the principles that might serve as the basis for a postwar
international economic order.

20. See Cairncross and Watts (1989), and Culbert (1987).

21. On Anglo-American cooperation on trade policy during the war, see Gardner
1956, Culbert 1987, Ikenberry 1992, Zeiler 1999, and Irwin, Mavroidis, and Sykes 2008.
The finance discussions led to the Bretton Woods conference in 1944 that established
the International Monetary Fund and the postwar system of fixed exchange rates.

22. Hawkins could not guarantee that the State Department would embrace it.
Indeed, Meade was warned by a member of Hawkins' staff that "Hawkins was a coura-
geous and disinterested man who was running a terrific risk with his personal career in
taking the grand line he was taking in favour of a multilateral approach to Commercial
Policy, because the Secretary of State is an ultra-cautious man" (Howson and Moggridge
1990, 139).

23. Notter 1949, 622.

24. *FRUS* 1944, 2:71–72, 87.

25. Johnson and Porter 1973, 403.

26. Ibid., 411.

27. Fossedal 1993, 136.

28. Gallup 1972, 505.

29. US Tariff Commission 1948, 2:14.

30. *FRUS* 1945, 6:27–28.

31. E. F. Penrose (1953, 106–07) later recalled, "The outcome of the discussion on
this question was determined, not by economic reasoning, nor on grounds of equity, but
by what the Assistant Secretaries in the State Department believed it possible to pass
through Congress."

32. "Recommendation for Renewal of the Trade Agreements Act," *State Department Bulletin*, April 1, 1945, 532–33.

33. Fossedal 1993, 152.

34. "1945 Extension of Reciprocal Trade Agreements Act," 79th Congress, 1st Session, 1:20.

35. The majority report stated, "If after this war, the nations are again persuaded
by the urgings of minority interest, or are deceived by the false doctrines of economic
nationalism, into following the short-sighted economic policies which divided them,
economically and politically, after the last war, the economics of all nations will suffer, and the political unity essential to world security will be endangered" (H.R. Rep.
No. 594-79, at 4 (1945).

36. *CR*, 5/22/1945, 4871–72.

37. Ibid., 4878, 4981, 4884–85.

38. *CR*, 5/26/1945, 5124.

39. Ibid., 5148. Acheson (1969, 107) had written the letter the night before, got the

president to sign it that morning, and quickly gave it to Speaker Rayburn "who used it with great dramatic effect. . . . This stopped the Old Guard just short of victory."

40. *CQA* 1945, 314.

41. *CR*, 6/19/1945, 6256.

42. Drury 1963, 444.

43. Irwin and Kroszner 1999.

44. Hawkins and Norwood 1963, 104–05.

45. *FRUS* 1945, 4:57.

46. Ibid., 6:63.

47. Ibid., 64, 72–73.

48. Ibid., 74–76.

49. US Department of State 1945, 12.

50. Ibid., 3.

51. *FRUS* 1946, 1:1307.

52. Ibid., 6:1311–12; Diebold 1993, 36.

53. The US delegation was headed by Clair Wilcox, the director of the State Department's Office of International Trade Policy, with Harry Hawkins, the minister-counselor for economic affairs at the US Embassy in London, as his principal deputy. Wilcox was a professor of economics on leave from Swarthmore College.

54. *Report of Committee II: General Commercial Policy, Preparatory Committee of the International Conference on Trade and Employment*, United Nations Economic and Social Council, E/PC/T/30, 24 November 1946, 5.

55. "I am not opposed to any and all tariff reductions," Butler explained to the Senate. "But I am opposed to wiping out, almost at one blow, the system that has made America great. I am opposed to one-sided disarmament on our economic protection" (*CR*, 2/7/1947, 892). On Truman's relationship with the Republican Congress, see Hartmann 1971.

56. The exchange of letters was published in the *Department of State Bulletin*, 1/26/1947, 161–163.

57. Kaplan 2015.

58. *CR*, 2/10/1947, 912.

59. *CR*, 2/26/1947, 1411.

60. Ibid., 1413.

61. In fact, the escape clause was first developed and inserted into the template reciprocal trade agreement in 1941 by the State Department. They did so in response to congressional concerns, expressed during the 1940 renewal of the RTAA, about the possible impact of trade disruptions on US producers after World War II.

62. "With this agreement in his pocket, Senator Vandenberg then persuaded a number of influential and uncommitted Republican leaders to come out publicly in support of the Trade Agreements program (not including Senator Taft, who broke with Vandenberg openly on the question)," Jones (1955, 99) notes. Indeed, Taft (2003, 242–43) wrote, "I do not agree with the proposal made by Senators Vandenberg and Millikin to accept the reciprocal trade program with certain amendments, but at least they have secured the agreement of the State Department to put a cancellation clause in every agreement made."

63. *Department of State Bulletin* 1947, 483.

64. *FRUS* 1947, 1:914.

65. For the early history of the GATT, see Brown 1950; Kock 1969; Zeiler 1999; and Irwin, Mavroidis, and Sykes 2008.

66. World Trade Organization 1999, 424.

67. Canada's lead negotiator, Dana Wilgress (1967, 153–54), later wrote, "Much frustration was experienced in getting the tariff negotiations started; each country had a good excuse for putting them off. . . . Some of the countries had come to the conference intending to obtain all they could in the way of concessions without giving too much in return. The United States . . . found it necessary to be very tough, and this toughness brought forth recriminations, particularly from the Cubans."

68. As a result of a commodity loan program designed to increase wool production during the war, the Commodity Credit Corporation had accumulated more than 460 million pounds of wool, but could not dispose of the surplus without incurring a large financial loss, because the government-established parity price was much higher than the market price. Because imports kept the domestic price of wool below the parity level, the House considered imposing a 50 percent tariff on wool so that the CCC could sell the surplus without incurring a loss.

69. Zeiler 1999, 102; see also Hussain 1993.

70. *PPP* 1947, 309. See Hussain (1993) for details. Wool growers did not go away empty-handed. In the end, the Congress passed legislation allowing the CCC to dispose of the surplus wool at world market prices. Thus, the government absorbed the financial loss, and there was no adverse impact on wool growers.

71. Toye 2003b.

72. In June, the US delegation in Geneva reported, "We are convinced [the British negotiator] desires face-saving charter draft and trade agreement but has no intention making serious modification in system of Empire preference. We believe he wishes to place responsibility on us for failure of conference to achieve purposes contemplated" (*FRUS* 1947, 1:953).

73. Ibid., 965, 975. As Toye (2003b, 923) concludes, "There was some truth in Clayton's allegation that the British were not playing ball. They were not making all possible efforts to secure waivers from Commonwealth countries; rather the reverse."

74. Ibid., 979. Some context is needed to appreciate the sources of the intransigence on both sides. From Clayton's perspective, his personal credibility was at stake. In many statements before Congress, from the 1945 RTAA renewal to the British loan, he assured lawmakers that the British Empire would be cracked, and the Geneva meeting would mark the end of Britain's discriminatory tariffs. Believing that Britain had agreed to eliminate imperial preferences as far back as the Atlantic Charter in 1941, he overestimated his ability to deliver on these promises. In fact, Britain had never committed itself to abandoning the preferences. The State Department staff had a more realistic view of what could be achieved and tried to soften Clayton's view. They even had to persuade Clayton not to abandon the Geneva conference simply because Britain refused anything more than token compromises on preferences.

75. Ibid., 978.

76. As Lovett cabled Clayton, "We are attempting to give UK every assistance in

getting over this difficult period and in avoiding irretrievable damage to their long-run position. Believe course of action leading to rupture trade negotiations inconsistent with policy we are following regarding financial agreement. (President referred to inconsistency our position if we should take alternative (3).) Important from point of view of successful relaxation convertibility and nondiscrimination provisions that some progress, even though slight, be made in commitment to reduce trade barriers. Believe alternative (3) likely to lead to strong resentment British public and considerable confusion and criticism in US. Would make more difficult consideration by Congress further assistance UK and Europe generally. As you know, UK Govt now under intense pressure from left wing members Labor party to curtail sharply UK foreign commitments, reduce arm forces and to withdraw British forces from Greece and Italy. We are concerned over likelihood that USSR will exploit fully any such differences between US and UK just as they are now trying to capitalize on British weakness by increasing pressure throughout Eastern Europe and Near East. Consequently best course seems to be to get best agreement possible in present highly unfavorable circumstances and reserve part of our negotiating position for use at more propitious time by trimming our offers correspondingly. From standpoint of public and congressional opinion here thin agreement of this kind we believe better than none, especially if made clear that present agreement only an initial stage in dealing with this problem" (Ibid., 981).

77. Gardner 1956, 360; see also Fossedal 1993, 253.

78. *PPP* 1947, 480.

79. *NYT,* 10/31/1947.

80. Canada, *House of Commons Debates,* 12/9/1947, 99.

81. *NYT* 10/31/1947, 99.

82. *NYT,* 11/20/1947.

83. Ibid.

84. US Bureau of the Census 1975, series U-226.

85. According to official calculations, had the duties negotiated at Geneva been in effect in 1947, the average tariff on dutiable imports would have been 15.3 percent instead of the actual 19.4 percent, a reduction of 4 percentage points, or 21 percent (US Tariff Commission 1948, 19). On the impact of import prices, see Irwin 1998a. Since import prices rose 60 percent between 1944 and 1950, 0.60 x –0.67 = –0.40.

86. For details on this calculation, see Irwin 1998a. The average tariff in 1948 turned out to be 13.9 percent, not the 15.3 percent predicted by the Tariff Commission, and higher import prices fully account for the difference. Import prices rose 10.5 percent in 1948, enough to reduce the tariff by about 6.7 percent. Applying both the 21.1 percent reduction due to the GATT negotiations and the 6.7 percent reduction due to higher import prices to the 19.4 percent average tariff in 1947 yields 14.0 percent, close to the actual figure of 13.9 percent. The Tariff Commission (1948, 18) recognized at the time that the erosion of specific duties by inflation during the 1940s had contributed significantly to tariff reduction, noting that "prices of import goods have risen greatly during the last two decades, and this fact alone would have cause a marked reduction in the average rate of duties actually collected in recent years compared with earlier years because of the effects of higher prices on the ad valorem equivalents of the specific and compound duties."

87. Irwin (1998a) calculates that the RTAA and GATT would have reduced the tariff by 32 percent between 1931 and 1948, while higher import prices would have reduced the tariff by 38 percent.

88. General Agreement on Tariffs and Trade 1949, 11.

89. Bown and Irwin 2015.

90. Subramanian and Wei 2007.

91. *CR*, 9/8/1949, 12655.

92. As Curzon (1965, 70) put it, "Countries believing that quantitative restrictions would be a permanent feature of the post-war world gave sham but very substantial reductions on their tariff rates in exchange for real reductions from the only country not applying quotas on manufactured goods, i.e., the United States."

93. MacDougall and Hutt 1954.

94. Johnson and Porter 1973, 454.

95. Sen. Paul Douglas (1972, 476) described the postwar political lineup this way: "The Eastern international finance section of the Republican party was finally compelled by the logic of the situation to change its position, although it did so in a somewhat shame-faced fashion. However, the dominant legislative wing of the party, based on textiles, steel, and chemicals, was still strongly protectionist and sought to reverse the Hull policy. In the main, the Democratic party continued to be loyal to its historic position, although as manufacturing moved southward there was some weakening. The export of raw cotton and tobacco still served as a low-tariff force in the South."

96. *CR*, 6/14/1948, 8049–50.

97. Lewis 1957, 579.

98. US Department of Commerce 1950, 28.

99. Taylor, Basu, and McLean 2011.

100. Mitchell 1970; Donohue 1993.

101. Foster 1983, 94. In May 1945, a survey by the American Institute of Public Opinion found that when informed voters were asked whether the trade agreements program should be continued, 75 percent answered yes, 7 percent answered no, and 18 percent were uncertain. When asked whether it was a good idea to reduce US tariffs under the trade agreements program, 57 percent said yes, 20 percent said no, and 23 percent were uncertain (Bauer, Pool, and Dexter 1963, 81).

102. According to Foster (1983, 94), "Less than 30 newspapers, out of 150 examined, registered out-right opposition to the legislation."

103. Watson 1956, 964.

104. Leddy and Norwood 1963, 128.

105. *Administration and Operation of Customs and Tariff Laws and the Trade Agreements Program: Hearings Before the House Committee on Ways and Means*, 84th Cong. pt. 2, 915 (1956).

106. *CQA* 1958, 173.

107. Leffler 1984, 364.

108. See Fordham 1998a; 1998b. Bailey (2003) shows how public concerns about national security affected congressional votes on trade policy.

109. "The delayed recovery of the German economy increased Europe's dependence

on the dollar area as a source of imports of foodstuffs and capital goods. This dependence was further accentuated by the disintegration of western Europe's trade with
Eastern Europe, prior to the war a major supplier of grain imports," Brusse (1997, 124)
notes.

110. *PPP* 1949, 366.

111. See Milward 1984; Killick 1997 and Eichengreen 2006.

112. *FRUS* 1947, 3:230.

113. While economists still debate how critical Marshall Plan aid was to Europe
at this time, DeLong and Eichengreen (1993) argue that it relieved resource constraints
that otherwise would have put European economic policy on a different, less market-
oriented track.

114. *FRUS* 1947, 1:955.

115. Zeiler 1999, 137.

116. *CQA* 1958, 169.

117. H.R. Rep. No. 594-79, at 38–39 (1945).

118. On the ITO charter, see Wilcox 1949 and Brown 1950; both were trade negotiators for the United States.

119. The US delegation noted the "irreconcilable opposition" of Argentina in particular, cabling back to Washington, "There has been disconcerting absence [of] interest
in supporting US positions or suggestions. Absence particularly noticeable in view [*sic*]
practice Latin American Dels rushing to support one another even where issue is of no
importance whatsoever country giving support. . . . Habana haunted by resurgence extravagant claims ITO 'violation national sovereignty' and insistence [on] maintenance
[of] complete freedom national economic determination . . . Generally accepted by most
Dels, Argentine goal is to prevent successful Conf and organization ITO" (*FRUS* 1948,
1:830–31).

120. Ibid., 824, 829 and Toye 2003a. In February 1948, Wilcox reported that representatives from the major developed countries were "buried in gloom. Wilgress [of
Canada] saw no hope at all. Coombs [of Australia] was saying that we should adjourn
the Conference and put the whole project on ice for a year or more" (Ibid., 872–73).

121. The Havana delegation included two Republican members of the Foreign Affairs Committee, but this did little to win their support.

122. *PPP* 1948, 168.

123. The State Department was also accused of being soft on Communism. As
Congressman Daniel Reed (R-NY) asked, "Can it be to the interest of our Republic to
entrust the future of hundreds of domestic industries, many of them founded on blood
and sweat, to a handful of Communist-minded self-admitted internationalists" at the
State Department? (*CR*, 5/26/1948, 6513).

124. H.R. Rep. No. 2009-80 (1948). Robert Doughton, the former Democratic chair
of the Ways and Means committee, decried the renewal: "The present law is such an
improvement over the old log-rolling, back-slapping, monopoly-breeding, enemy-mak-
ing method of dealing with the tariff" (*CR* 5/26/1948, 6505).

125. *PPP* 1948, 385.

126. Republicans strenuously objected to the removal of peril points, which they

believed were essential to prevent "possible but unnecessary disaster through any ill-advised tariff reduction, because the findings of the Commission are based on economic realities" (H.R. Rep. No. 19-81, at 5 (1949).

127. *PPP* 1949, 234.

128. *NYT*, 5/10/1948, 33.

129. Diebold 1952, 20–21.

130. Gardner 1956, 376.

131. See Aaronson 1996 for a discussion of the ITO debate in Congress.

132. Toye 2003, 294.

133. *FRUS* 1950, 1:780–81.

134. Ibid., 783–85.

135. Department of State Bulletin 1950, 977.

136. For an analyses of the failure of the ITO, see Diebold 1952; Aaronson 1996; Odell and Eichengreen 1998; and Zeiler 1999.

137. See Diebold 1952, 14.

CHAPTER 11

1. Wilkinson (1960) provides a thorough review of Congress and trade policy during the late 1940s through the 1950s. Watson (1956) analyzes Congressional voting on trade bills during this period and finds that regional patterns replaced partisan ones. Bauer, Pool, and Dexter (1963) also provide a comprehensive survey of political support and opposition to the trade agreements program during the 1950s.

2. See Stiles 1995. According to Koch (1969, 82, 84), the passivity reflected the "feeling that the United States had given away concessions without any real corresponding benefit, as the European countries were slow in eliminating their discrimination against dollar goods" and had failed to dismantle their colonial preferences as well.

3. *PPP* 1951, 340.

4. Schulman 1991, 153.

5. See Leddy 1963, 187.

6. Kane 1988.

7. See Fordham 1998a, 1998b, and Bailey 2003.

8. Johnson and Porter 1973, 499.

9. As Senator Paul Douglas (1972, 478) put it, the Republicans "could do what they wanted. But they did not know what that was. They were divided between their internationalists from the East and their economic and political nationalists of the Middle West and mountain states."

10. See Wilkinson 1960 and Kaufman 1982 for overviews of trade policy during the Eisenhower administration. Eisenhower (1963, 499) recalled that "the problem of trade was constantly on my mind."

11. *PPP* 1953, 164.

12. Wilkinson 1960, 84.

13. *PPP* 1954, 363.

14. *CR*, 2/17/1955, 1678.

15. The 1955 vote was the first in which members of Congress from textile-

producing regions in New England and the South joined forces to strengthen the peril points and escape-clause provisions for the express purpose of protecting the textile industry from Japanese imports. As Rep. Styles Bridges (R-NH) put it, "I cannot go along with a trade policy that can create boomtowns in Japan and ghost towns in New England" (*CQA* 1955, 296).

16. In the case of the United States, the tariff concessions applied to just 16 percent of dutiable imports and resulted in a weighted average tariff reduction of just over 2 percent. According to Kreinin (1961), the tariff reductions increased US imports by $200 million (at a time when total imports were about $12 billion) and may have displaced at most twenty thousand workers, or about 0.03 percent of the labor force. This figure was based on the calculation of Salant and Vaccara (1961) that the displacement of $1 million of domestic production by imports would be responsible for the loss of 115 domestic jobs at that time.

17. About half of the signatories to the GATT invoked Article 35 of the agreement and denied Japan the full benefits of non-discriminatory treatment. It was not until the mid-1960s that Japan normalized its trade relationship with other GATT participants; see Forsberg 1998. On the politics of GATT accession in the Cold War era, see McKenzie 2008.

18. Keesing and Wolf 1980.

19. See Leddy 1963.

20. Kelley 1963, 107.

21. *PPP* 1955, 397–98. Eisenhower reminded Congress of the importance of the OTC in his January 1956 State of the Union message, and the Ways and Means Committee agreed to hold hearings. Business groups and labor groups (such as the AFL-CIO) endorsed US participation, while opponents questioned how the Congress could authorize participation in the OTC when it had not even approved the GATT. Despite a favorable report from the Ways and Means Committee, the Democratic House majority leader declined to bring it to a vote on the grounds that it could never pass. Republicans were opposed to the measure by a two-to-one margin, and many Democrats remained uneasy about it as well. As a result, the matter was dropped.

22. Bohi and Russell 1978, 23.

23. See Bohi and Russell 1978 for an analysis of the oil-import quota scheme.

24. Kaufman (1982, 91) notes that "it might be conveniently argued that it contributed to the energy crisis of the 1970s and 80s by helping to deplete the nation's oil reserves at a time when foreign oil was both cheap and plentiful."

25. Mitchell 1970.

26. During the Annecy negotiations in 1951, the Tariff Commission found that the tariff was too low on imported petroleum from Venezuela, while in the 1955–56 Geneva negotiations the Tariff Commission recommended that duties be increased on certain tungsten alloys and on violins and violas. The president took no action in either case. However, the peril points did hamper trade negotiations with the European Economic Community in the 1960–62 Geneva negotiations, when the United States could not match the degree of tariff-cutting offered by the EEC (Leddy and Norwood 1963, 143–46).

27. Murray and Egmand 1970, 406.

28. In addition, the old flexible tariff authority (Section 315 of the Fordney-

McCumber tariff, or Section 336 of the Hawley-Smoot tariff) was also infrequently used. See Kelley 1963, 22–23.

29. Fordham 1998b.

30. In the president's view, "The enactment of this legislation—unencumbered by amendments of a kind that would impair its effectiveness—is essential to our national economic interest, to our security, and to our foreign relations" (PPP 1955, 10).

31. Asbeek Brusse 1997, 127.

32. World Trade Organization 1999, 458. On the compatibility of the EEC with the GATT, see McKenzie 2010.

33. The negotiating round was named for Douglas Dillon, an undersecretary of state in the Eisenhower administration and Treasury secretary in the Kennedy administration.

34. The 1960 Democratic platform stated that "world trade is more than ever essential to world peace. In the tradition of Cordell Hull, we shall expand world trade in every responsible way. Since all Americans share the benefits of this policy, its costs should not be the burden of a few. We shall support practical measures to make the necessary adjustments of industries and communities which may be unavoidably hurt by increases in imports" (Johnson and Porter 1973, 577).

35. PPP 1962, 74.

36. As Meany himself put it, "There is no question whatever that adjustment assistance is essential to the success of trade expansion. And as we have said many times, it is indispensable to our support of the trade program as a whole" (Charnovitz 1986, 158).

37. Diebold 1962, 361.

38. NYT, 1/18/1962, 12.

39. Zeiler 1987.

40. Bauer, Pool, and Dexter 1963, 363.

41. Talbot 1978.

42. Gallup 1972, 3:1761.

43. "There were many other acts of discrimination, about which the State Department blandly professed indifference," Douglas (1972, 481, 485) later recalled. "I could understand the anger of the protectionists and their later demand for retaliatory action. . . . I asked the State Department for instances of trade discrimination against us, but although I was fighting its battle in the Finance Committee, it never helped. When their guard was down, . . . I was shocked to hear them often refer to these other countries as their 'clients.' International alliances seemed more important than the mutual benefits of two-way economic cooperation. . . . With some pain I finally concluded that the State Department could not be trusted to represent the Congress in economic matters."

44. Douglas (1972, 482–83) proposed that the United States "should have greater power to retaliate if discriminated against, by going back to the old Smoot-Hawley rates or beyond. I hoped that we would never have to use this weapon, but in view of the European treatment of us, I felt that we needed a stick as well as the carrot."

45. PPP 1962, 759–60.

46. On the Kennedy Round endgame, see Lee 2001.

47. Dryden 1995, 94. The 1964 Republican platform pledged "a determined drive,

through tough, realistic negotiations, to remove the many discriminatory and restrictive trade practices of foreign nations" and attacked the Johnson administration for having "proved itself inept and weak in international trade negotiations, allowing the loss of opportunities historically open to American enterprise and bargaining away markets indispensable to prosperity of American farms" (Johnson and Porter 1973, 760).

48. See Zeiler 1992 on American trade politics in the 1960s.

49. Johnson and Porter 1973, 727.

50. Ibid., 760.

51. See Matusow 1998 for an overview of trade politics during the Nixon administration.

52. Ibid., 120.

53. Destler, Fukui, and Sato 1979.

54. The bill worried economists enough so that 4,390 of them signed a statement urging Nixon to veto the measure should it pass (*NYT*, 9/19/1970, 1). Paul Douglas, one of the original sponsors of the 1930 petition, also helped organize this effort. Douglas (1972, 607) called the House measure "far worse than Smoot-Hawley" because it would use quotas and not tariffs to limit trade. The petition was ultimately signed by 5,025 economists.

55. Maddison 2001, 261; Maddison 1989, 139.

56. Bernhofen, El-Sahli, and Kneller 2016.

57. See Levinson 2006a, b.

58. Van Cott and Wipf 1983.

59. *Statistical Abstract of the United States* 1978, 873.

60. Adams and Dirlam 1964. At various times, Presidents Truman and Kennedy clashed with the steel industry over its rigid pricing policies.

61. Crandall 1981, 35.

62. Commission on International Trade and Investment Policy 1971, 2.

63. *WP*, 4/26/1971, A4.

64. Magee 1972, 692.

65. *CR*, 9/17/1962, 19591.

66. *NYT*, 3/28/1972, 59.

67. Ruttenberg 1971, 62.

68. Saloom 1972, 121.

69. As George Meany, the president of the AFL-CIO, argued, "This displacement of industrial production means the loss of American jobs. It threatens the decline of America's economic strength. The narrowing of America's industrial base means that this country is now on the road to becoming a second or even third-rate industrial power, if these huge and rapid losses of American production and jobs are not halted" (Saloom 1972, 122–23).

70. Ruttenberg 1971, 123.

71. A former legislative assistant to Senator Hartke stated, "It is an open secret that much of the impetus for this legislation came from organized labor; . . . the bill was drafted under the auspices of the AFL-CIO" (Saloom 1972, 115).

72. Ibid., 99.

73. See Eichengreen 2000 and Bordo and Eichengreen 1993.

74. The exact wording of this statement has been reported in several different ways. See Reeves 2001, 341, Odell 1982, 263, and James 1996.

75. "The Japanese are still fighting the war, only now instead of a shooting war, it's an economic war," Connally told the president. "They have built up tariff arrangements, they have built up trade restrictions against US goods. . . . The people themselves, frankly, are more industrious than we are, as they work harder than we do. . . . The simple fact is that in many areas other nations are out-producing us, out-thinking us and out-trading us." Nixon replied, "We'll fix those bastards." But the president also believed that "the US cannot build a fence around itself and expect to survive as a great nation" (Reeves 2001, 341).

76. Gowa (1983) and Irwin (2012a) discuss the domestic politics behind the August 1971 action.

77. Odell 1982, 252 and *FRUS* 1969–76, 3:424–25.

78. Commission on International Trade and Investment Policy 1971, 37. The idea that a uniform import tariff and export subsidy was equivalent to a currency devaluation is often attributed to John Maynard Keynes.

79. James 1996, 217–18.

80. Ohlmacher 2009, 9.

81. Gowa (1983, 150n) writes, "Most, although not all, of the administration's economic officials believed that the surcharge coupled with the suspension constituted overkill, dangerous because it invited retaliation by other nations. Camp David participants generally adhere to the view that the surcharge would not have been imposed had Connally not been secretary." Connally was the key figure who wanted the import surcharge; see Volcker and Gyohten 1992, 76.

82. Volcker later recalled that "the only really active debate about the program was over the import surcharge. As I remember it, the discussion largely was a matter of the economists against the politicians, and the outcome wasn't really close. I think the president had been convinced that it was both an essential negotiating tactic and a way to attract public support" (Volcker and Gyohten 1992, 78).

83. Safire 1975, 513.

84. *PPP* 1971, 889.

85. Harris Survey 1975, 184.

86. Volcker assumed that countries would agree to US demands: "In my naïveté, I thought we could wrap up an exchange rate realignment and start talking about reform in a month or two. . . . Instead, I got a fast lesson in big-league negotiations. . . . What we found, even after we shut the gold window, was fierce resistance by key countries to their currencies floating upward against the dollar" (Volcker and Gyohten 1992, 80).

87. Angel 1991, 128.

88. Initially "agnostic" about the August 15 measures, Kissinger (1979, 955, 957) recognized that the administration "would have to tread a narrow path between maintaining enough pressure to provide an incentive for the adjustments we were seeking, and evoking a trade war as well as jeopardizing political relationships built up over decades." The National Security Council believed that the bargaining value of the surcharge deteriorated the longer it was in place (*FRUS* 1969–76, 512–515). On September 20, Kissinger pressed this foreign-policy argument with the president, suggesting that

the surcharge be dropped. Nixon shot down this appeal: "The difficulty is the surcharge, Henry, it's so popular domestically, we just can't end it until we get something for it. That's the, hell, the surcharge is supported by 85 percent of the people. Good God, you just can't give it away" (Ohlmacher 2009, 23).

89. Angel 1991, 257; Volcker and Gyohten 1992, 97.

90. *PPP* 1971, 1195–96.

91. Irwin 2012a.

92. White House international economic adviser Peter Peterson agreed that "had we not taken that very vigorous action on the dollar, it was the sure road to protectionism" (Stein 2010, 49).

93. See Destler, Fukui, and Sato 1979.

94. See Crandall (1981).

95. *CQA* 1974, 836.

96. Destler 1980, 169.

97. Laird and Yeates 1990, 316.

98. "Fast track enables us to be a trade negotiating partner with [Congress having] the ultimate power to say yes or no," House Minority Leader Robert H. Michel (R-Ill.) said. Senator John C. Danforth (R-Mo.) stated, "It is the overwhelming opinion of people who know anything about international trade that without fast track there is no possibility of a trade agreement. It is just not going to happen." On fast track, see Shapiro 2006.

99. Baldwin (1985a) examines some of the constituency factors that shaped Congress's vote.

100. In October 1972, as part of Nixon's policy of détente, the United States signed a trade agreement with the Soviet Union whose implementation hinged on the United States granting the country MFN status. This was not given automatically because the Soviets were not a party to the GATT.

101. In the 1962 legislation, the escape clause had a three-part test: imports had to be entering the United States in increased quantity, the increase in imports had to be attributable in "major part" to a concession made in a trade agreement, and the increased imports had to cause or threaten to cause serious injury. The escape clause proved to be a difficult vehicle for receiving temporary respite from import competition because the "major" attribution requirement was the legal obstacle in the Tariff Commission (Murray and Egmand 1970). For example, in 1971 three labor unions in the television industry had filed for escape-clause relief, but the petition was rejected because the increased imports had to be "a result in major part of concessions granted under trade agreements." While the tariff on imported televisions had fallen from 10 percent in 1962 to 6 percent in 1971, that modest reduction could not be held responsible for the enormous increase in imports of television sets from Japan.

102. A representative of the United Steel Workers concurred: "Trade adjustment assistance is an idea whose time has passed. . . . [It] cannot be an adequate substitute for an effective trade policy" (Charnovitz 1986).

103. Similar authority had been granted earlier, in Section 252 of the Trade Expansion Act of 1962, but only used twice, once to retaliate against the EEC's variable import levy on poultry in the "chicken war" of 1962 and then against Canada for its barriers against US beef exports.

104. As Winham (1980) noted, these provisions pushed constituent and interest group lobbying further away from Congress and toward the executive branch and administrative agencies. In Destler's (1980) words, this system of administered protection was a way of "providing protection for Congress" so that it would not have to deal with all the trade concerns of constituents.

105. Congress had long wanted the Tariff Commission to be more responsive to its concerns in making injury determinations in escape-clause and dumping cases. In late 1960s, Sen. Russell Long (D-LA) stated, "It is to the Congress, and not the Executive, that the Tariff Commission is expected to be responsive" (Baldwin 1984, 16).

106. Winham (1986) provides an overview of the Tokyo Round negotiations and agreements.

107. Quoted in Baldwin 1970, 2.

108. The United States also finally agreed to abolish the American Selling Price for chemicals, a holdover from the Kennedy Round. Specific agreements were also reached regarding trade in bovine meat, dairy products, and civil aircraft.

109. Hufbauer 1983, 332.

110. Minchin 2013, 80.

111. *PPP* 1978, 2:2008.

112. As Destler (1980, 202) notes, five of the eleven votes against the legislation came from Wisconsin, whose representatives opposed concessions to cheese imports that might harm the dairy industry.

113. The success of the bill in Congress was "an enormous tribute to the colossal skills of Bob Strauss," Rep. Bill Frenzel (R-MN) observed. "Without Bob we'd have had all kinds of difficulties putting this thing together." See Winham 1980.

114. Millstein 1983, 123.

115. From 1970 to 1976, Krueger (1980) found that, in ten of nineteen industries in which employment declined, import-related losses exceeded those attributable to changes in domestic demand or productivity in only one case, leather products. Over the period from 1967 to 1979, Grossman (1987) found that only one industry of the nine examined experienced a large reduction in employment as a result of imports (radio and television production).

116. US General Accounting Office 1987.

117. The industries that were denied relief included asparagus, ferrocyanide blue pigments, honey, mushrooms, cast-iron stoves, bolts, nuts and screws, high carbon ferrochromium, stainless steel flatware, copper, bicycle tires or tubes, fishing tackle, and leather apparel. When presidents declined to give escape-clause relief, Congress sometimes intervened on behalf of the domestic industry. For example, in 1976, in a Section 201 case involving non-rubber footwear, President Ford granted adjustment assistance, but not the import relief proposed by the ITC. Congress urged reconsideration of the case, so the footwear industry filed another petition. In 1977, the ITC again determined that the industry was seriously injured and recommended a stringent, five-year tariff-rate quota. This time, President Carter opted to negotiate orderly marketing arrangements (OMAs) with Taiwan and South Korea.

118. In 1977, the mix of South Korea's shoe exports to the United States was 70 per-

cent non-rubber and 30 percent rubber. In 1978 those proportions were exactly reversed (Mutti and Bale 1981).

119. Canto and Laffer 1983.

120. Aggarwal 1985.

121. Indeed, European countries fought over such subsidies themselves, because the state-owned industries in France, Belgium, the United Kingdom, and Italy received government assistance to cover their operating losses, to the detriment of private firms in Germany and the Netherlands.

122. The TPMs covered seventy different product categories and covered 85 percent of steel imports in 1979. See Eichengreen and van der Ven 1984.

CHAPTER 12

1. For overviews of trade-policy developments during the decade, see Destler 1991, Richardson 1994, Destler 1995, and Krueger 1996.

2. The US economy experienced two recessions during this period, one from January to July 1980 and another from July 1981 to November 1982, according to the National Bureau of Economic Research. The economy was generally weak throughout this period, although the second recession was much more severe than the first.

3. Eichengreen 1996.

4. Fukoa 1990.

5. *Statistical Abstract of the United States* 1988, 768.

6. Lawrence 1984, 44.

7. As Kletzer (2002, 129) puts it, "While we can be certain that exports are produced by US workers, we cannot be certain that an industry import directly substitutes for a domestic good."

8. *Handbook of US Labor Statistics* 2001, table 2.1.

9. See Addison, Fox, and Ruhm (1995). Kletzer (1998, 455) also concludes that "increasing foreign competition across industries accounts for a small share of job displacement" across industries because there are "high rates of job loss for industries with little trade." Davis, Haltiwanger, and Schuh (1995, 48–49) concluded that there is "no systematic relationship between the magnitude of gross job flows and exposure to international trade. . . . On balance, the evidence is highly unfavorable to the view that international trade exposure systematically reduces job security."

10. Revenga (1992) found that a 10 percent decline in industry import prices was associated with a 2.5–4.0 percent reduction in industry employment but only a 0.5–1.0 percent fall in industry wages. This implies that when import prices fell 19 percent between 1980 and 1985, wages fell by about 2 percent in import-sensitive industries, while employment fell 5–8 percent. Freeman and Katz (1991) similarly found that a 10 percent increase in imports reduced industry employment by 5–6 percent and industry wages by 0–0.6 percent.

11. Jacobson (1978) found that the earnings of workers displaced from their jobs in the automobile and steel industries in the early 1970s fell by more than 40 percent in the first two years after displacement, and in the subsequent four years were still about 10 to 15 percent below the earnings of those who remained employed in the industry.

12. See Jacobson (1978) and Bednarzik (1993). Workers displaced from non-unionized industries with relatively low wages (for example, women's clothing, television receivers, toys, cotton weaving) experienced less of an initial earnings loss (about 10 percent), and some actually earned more than they previously had; workers in cotton weaving earned nearly 12 percent more in the four years after displacement. In most of these cases, about half of these losses were due to the period of unemployment rather than subsequently earning lower wages.

13. "Policymakers often ascribe the declining share of industrial employment to a lack of manufacturing competitiveness brought on by inadequate productivity growth," noted Krugman and Lawrence (1994). "In fact, the shrinkage is largely the result of higher productivity growth, at least as compared with the service sector." Several industry studies reached similar conclusions. In the 1970s, Lawrence (1984, 54) found that in six of nine industries where overall employment fell more than 10 percent, employment due to trade actually increased; only in footwear and apparel was the loss due to trade greater than that due to changing domestic use. In the case of the steel industry, Grossman (1986) found that the secular decline in employment was responsible for five times more job losses than imports. Over the shorter period 1979–83, imports and secular factors were equally important, but he noted that "the injury due to import competition during this period is entirely the results of the more than 30 percent real appreciation of the US dollar."

14. See Revenga 1992. C. Fred Bergsten (1985, 138) was one of the leading contemporary voices arguing that Reagan economic policy "has also been plagued by a fundamental contradiction between its trade policy and its monetary policy."

15. Though President Jimmy Carter was from the South, he was not viewed as a friend to the textile and apparel industry after vetoing a bill that would have exempted it from tariff cuts in the Tokyo Round. In a September 1980 letter to Sen. Strom Thurmond (R-SC), Reagan noted that the textile and apparel industry provided 2.3 million jobs and pledged that "the Multifiber Arrangement "needs to be strengthened by relating import growth from all sources to domestic market growth. I shall work to achieve that goal" (Oversight of US Trade Policy: Joint Hearings, Before the Subcommittee on International Trade, Committee on Finance, and Subcommittee on International Finance and Monetary Policy, Committee on Banking, Housing and Urban Affairs, 97th Cong., pt. 1, 19 (1981).

16. As Reagan stated in the 1983 State of the Union message, "As the leader of the West and as a country that has become great and rich because of economic freedom, America must be an unrelenting advocate of free trade. As some nations are tempted to turn to protectionism, our strategy cannot be to follow them, but to lead the way toward freer trade" (PPP 1983, 1:108).

17. Oversight of US Trade Policy: Joint Hearings, 19.

18. For example, in the mid-1970s, Reagan gave a talk at the Hoover Institution at Stanford University in which he criticized foreign dumping of goods in the US market. When an economist who replied that consumers benefited from the low prices of dumped goods, Reagan countered that it also increased unemployment and led to plant closures. When another economist suggested that the economy would eventually adjust to this setback, Reagan got a puzzled look and said, "That may very well be. But in the

meantime what will happen to the American worker? How will he and his family get along?" See Hook 1987, 598–99.

19. For an inside account, see Niskanen 1988.

20. Hufbauer, Berliner, and Elliott 1986, 21.

21. This section draws on Krueger 1996, which provides industry case studies of trade policy.

22. Destler 1980, 196–97.

23. As Reagan (1990, 253–54) wrote in his memoirs, "As I listened to the debate, I wondered if there might be a way in which we could maintain the integrity of our position in favor of free trade while at the same time doing something to help Detroit and ease the plight of its thousands of laid-off assembly workers." According to Reagan, when he asked if anyone had suggestions about how to strike a balance between the two positions, Vice President George H. W. Bush chipped in, "We're *all* for free enterprise, but would any of us find fault if Japan announced without any request from us that they were going to *voluntarily* reduce their export of autos to America?" Stockman (1986, 157) blamed presidential adviser Edwin Meese for planting this idea, saying that Meese was "quietly pounding square pegs into round holes, convincing himself and the president that all we had to do to maintain our free trade position was to convince the Japanese 'voluntarily' to restrict their own exports. Under the Meese formulation, our hands would be clean; the Japanese would do the dirty work themselves." See also Dryden 1995, 267–75.

24. See McClenahan 1991. For a general analysis of VERs, see Jones 1994.

25. For differing assessments of the steel industry, see Crandall 1981 and Howell et al. 1988. See also Moore 1996.

26. As Destler (1991, 262) notes, "US steelmakers jointly delivered to the Commerce Department, on a single day, 494 boxes containing 3 million pages of documentation, for 132 countervailing duty and antidumping petitions."

27. *PPP* 1984, 2:1312.

28. Between 1966 and 2001, domestic shoe production fell from 639 million pairs to 129 million, and full-time employment fell from 233,400 to 28,900, almost entirely due to plant closures, even as consumption was rising. Import penetration rose from 13 percent of domestic consumption in 1966 to almost 97 percent in 2001 (Freeman and Kleiner 2005).

29. Minchin 2013, 99.

30. Before House vote, Jenkins implored the House that "we have to have some action to save basic industry in the United States." Opponents such as Sam Gibbons (D-FL) responded that "no nation has ever risen its standard of living by restricting its imports" (Minchin 2013, 116).

31. *PPP* 1988, 2:1486.

32. The MFA-IV was scheduled to be in effect for five years until 1991, although it was later extended to 1995. The MFA had grown from covering the exports of eighteen countries in 1977 to forty-one countries by 1991, mainly small, developing countries.

33. Gardner 1996.

34. *CQA* 1986, 187.

35. Organization for Economic Cooperation and Development 2014.

36. Graham 1983, 130.

37. See Krueger 1990b and Marks and Maskus 1993.

38. Maskus 1989, 96.

39. See Finger, Hall, and Nelson 1982. A former staff economist at the ITC, John Suomela (1993), provides an insider perspective on some cases.

40. US General Accounting Office 1987. Hollings is quoted in *CR*, 11/13/1985, S15315.

41. Irwin 2005a, Baldwin 1998, Congressional Budget Office 1994.

42. Congressional Budget Office 1994, 50.

43. Economists and lawyers frequently criticized the Commerce Department for using questionable methods that seemed designed to guarantee a finding of dumping and to inflate the calculated dumping margin. See, for example, Boltuck and Litan 1991 and Finger 1993.

44. Congressional Budget Office 1994, 58.

45. Ibid., 50.

46. The figures come from US International Trade Commission 1995, 3–1 and Congressional Budget Office 2001, 41.

47. Gallaway, Blonigen, and Flynn 1999.

48. These economists were employed by the Federal Trade Commission, the International Trade Commission, and the Congressional Budget Office. For example, see Morkre and Tarr 1980 and Tarr and Morkre 1984, as well as Rousslang and Suomela 1988.

49. The United States also could have captured the quota rent by auctioning off the quota rights to sell in the US market. For such a proposal, see Bergsten et al. 1987.

50. This estimate is similar to $12.3 billion in 1986 by Trela and Whalley (1990). Hufbauer and Elliott (1994, 15) found the welfare cost of the MFA was $3 billion in 1984 and $8.6 billion in 1990, using a partial equilibrium model. Another partial equilibrium estimate by Cline (1990, 191) came to $8.1 billion, due largely to differences in the estimated quota premium. De Melo and Tarr (1992, 105–106) explain the differences in these figures, which hinge on better estimates of the quota-induced premium.

51. In 1987, the restraints on foreign textile and apparel exports had the same effect on the volume of imports as an additional tariff of 22 percent on textiles and 28 percent on apparel, on top of the existing 10 percent tariff on textiles and 18 percent on apparel (US International Trade Commission 1989).

52. De Melo and Tarr (1992, 89–90) calculated that the MFA protection allowed 247,000 more workers to remain employed in the industry than otherwise, or 12 percent of industry employment. Cline (1990, 193–94) concluded that the MFA saved 234,000 textile and apparel jobs, almost all of them in apparel. The US International Trade Commission (1989) estimated that eliminating trade barriers would reduce employment in the textile and apparel industry by 233,000–291,000 jobs, or roughly 15 percent.

53. Cline (1990, 95) found that "even in their worst period (1982–86) [import's] negative contribution to textile employment change was only about one-sixth as large as the negative contribution from productivity growth." In the case of textiles, McKenzie and Smith (1987) found that technological change was the major source of job loss, not imports.

54. To keep 224,700 jobs in textiles and apparel, Cline (1990, 192) calculated that the annual consumer cost per job saved was $134,686 per textile worker and $81,973 per apparel worker. "Considering that average wages in textiles and apparel are in the range of $12,000 annually," he concluded, "consumers pay nearly seven times as much to sustain apparel jobs through protection as it would cost them to provide permanent vacations at full salary to the workers involved, and for textile jobs the multiple is even higher."

55. Feenstra (1988) estimates that the VER was only binding in 1983 and 1984, and increased the price of a Japanese automobile by 17 percent, putting the welfare cost of the VER as $2.3 billion in 1984–85. Dinopoulos and Kreinin (1988) added that the VER shifted US demand to European cars and resulted in an additional welfare loss of $3.4 billion, due to the increased price of cars imported from Europe.

56. Thus, Collard-Wexler and De Loecker (2015) conclude that the main reason for the rapid productivity growth and the associated decline in employment was not a decline in steel consumption or the growth of imports but the displacement of the older technology used by vertically integrated producers by the more efficient mini-mills.

57. As Baldwin (1985b, 109) wrote, "Import-restricting measures frequently turn out to be an ineffective form of government regulation that does not bring the employment and equity benefits which the protected industries and the general public expect." "They result in a much smaller reduction in imports and a much smaller increase in domestic output and employment than anticipated and, what is more, in equity terms they often do not help the most deserving groups in a society."

58. The company's management conceded that Harley's production process was far behind the cutting-edge Japanese manufacturing practices at the time the Section 201 petition was filed, as Reid (1990) notes. See Kitano and Ohashi 2009, and Irwin 2015.

59. See Kahn 1999.

60. Feyrer, Sacerdote, and Stern 2007. In particular, each steel or auto job lost in a county led to a net decrease in population of 1.8 persons. Although some Rust Belt counties recovered quickly in terms of unemployment and per capita income, other local attributes (crime rates, public libraries, and restaurants) did not improve over time and may have worsened. One silver lining of the decline of manufacturing in the Rust Belt was the improved environmental quality, especially the significant drop in airborne particulate matter (Kahn 1999).

61. As Trubowitz (1998, 219) notes, "In contrast to the 1930s, when much of the industrial Northeast had a stake in freer trade, by the 1980s the northern core was strongly protectionist, much as it had been in the late nineteenth and early twentieth centuries. By contrast, the West, the bedrock of trade protectionism of the 1930s, had become the most free-trade-oriented region, surpassing the South, which on balance stood somewhere between the protectionist Northeast and the free-trade West."

62. See Lande and VanGrasstek 1986.

63. President Reagan, who was from California, rejected out of hand a proposal pushed by his adviser Edwin Meese (also from California) to protect the wine industry from foreign competition (Stuart Auerbach, "Reagan Rejects Meese's Plea to Back Bill Aiding Wineries," *WP* 2/17/1984, A2).

64. Caroline Herron and Michael Wright, "A Race for Import Curbs," *NYT*, 9/22/1985, A4.

65. Destler and Henning 1989, 104–5.

66. Destler (1986, 84) reports that, of the 634 bills, "99 were directly and seriously protectionist, and 77 more were potentially so, in that they would make quasi-judicial trade relief easier to obtain."

67. Destler (1991, 279) notes that the resolution was clearly aimed at the Reagan administration, not Japan. As he reports, when asked why the Senate was so anti-Japan, a Senate aide replied, "You don't understand. The target isn't the Japanese; it's the White House!"

68. Destler 1995, 272.

69. *CR* 10/4/1988, H9497.

70. See Graham 1992. Most economists rejected the idea of having an industrial policy. Charles Schultze (1983, 4), former chairman of President Carter's Council of Economic Advisers, wrote that "reality does not square with any of the four premises on which the advocates of industrial policy rest their case. America is *not* de-industrializing. Japan does *not* owe its industrial success to its industrial policy. Government is *not* able to devise a 'winning' industrial structure. Finally, it is *not* possible in the American political system to pick and choose among individual firms and regions in the substantive, efficiency-driven way envisaged by advocates of industrial policy."

71. Shoch 2001, 97.

72. *CQA* 1985, 254.

73. Steven V. Roberts, "The President's Hard Sell on Free Trade," *NYT*, 9/29/1985, A1.

74. For assessments of US trade policy with Japan, see Porges 1991, Schoppa 1997, and Kunkel 2003.

75. Zinsmeister 1993.

76. Lincoln 1990, 16.

77. See Krugman 1991 for the debate among economists about the distinctiveness of Japan's trade pattern.

78. CQ 1984, 157.

79. The United States also objected to remaining import quotas on beef, citrus, tobacco, and leather, and these became the subjects of bilateral negotiations. In 1986 another round of MOSS talks was initiated for transportation machinery (auto parts): these talks broke new ground by focusing on *keiretsu* and other private business practices, and on US firms' sales to Japanese-owned firms, even in the United States.

80. Greaney 2001.

81. See Prestowitz 1988 for a discussion of these battles from the perspective of a Commerce Department trade negotiator.

82. "The disparity between the strong dollar and weak foreign currencies gave foreign competitors a big advantage over companies in the United States," Baker (2006, 427) wrote in his memoirs. "This contributed to our growing trade deficit and sparked demands for high tariffs, import quotas, and other protectionist measures."

83. Volcker later wrote that "the exchange rate of the dollar had plainly become so high as to be deeply troublesome, whether or not the administration wanted to recognize it. Surely, it did not look sustainable either on economic or political grounds."

Baker and his deputy Richard Darman "did not need to be Ph.D. economists to relate that [protectionist] pressure to the strength of the dollar" (Volcker and Gyohten 1992, 228–29, 241).

84. Destler and Henning 1989; Bergsten and Green 2016.

85. *PPP* 1985 2:1127–28.

86. The use of Section 301 was controversial; critics called it "aggressive unilateralism." See Bhagwati and Patrick 1990.

87. This section follows Irwin 1996a.

88. Prestowitz 1988 provides a vivid description of this episode and a fascinating discussion of the difficulties faced by US negotiators with Japan.

89. The text of the letter is published in Irwin 1996a.

90. Odell and Matzinger-Tchakerian 1993.

91. Bayard and Elliott 1994, 14.

92. Stuart Auerbach, "Baker Calls US Late in Attacking Trade Gap," *WP*, 9/15/1987.

93. *CQA* 1986, 344.

94. *PPP* 1986:1, 689.

95. *CQA* 1986, 343.

96. *CQA* 1987, 640.

97. On the 1988 legislation, see Schwab 1994 and Grinols 1989. See Nollen and Quinn 1994 on voting patterns in Congress over the various elements of the bill.

98. Laird and Yeates 1990, 312. See also Nogués, Olechowski, and Winters 1986.

99. Low 1993, 76.

100. Aho and Bayard 1982 is another pessimistic piece from the period.

101. The Dunkel quotes are from Wolff 1983, 363 and Croome 1995, 11.

102. The declaration also called for countries "to make determined efforts to ensure that trade policies and measures are consistent with GATT principles and rules and to resist protectionist pressures in the formation and implementation of national trade policy and in proposing legislation; and also to refrain from taking or maintaining any measures inconsistent with GATT and to make determined efforts to avoid measures which would limit or distort international trade" (*NYT* 11/30/1982, D25).

103. For example, the 1982 report on the trade agreements program stated that "the United States remains committed to the multilateral system of the GATT as the primary vehicle for the realization of its own interests and those of other trading nations." The 1986 report reiterated that "the United States remains committed to GATT and the multilateral negotiating process," but added that "multilateral negotiations are not an end in themselves" and that "America has decided to pursue trade liberalization opportunities wherever and whenever they exist, whether in a multilateral, plurilateral or bilateral context" (Richardson 1994, 641).

104. *PPP* 1985, 2:1129.

105. Israel's goal in concluding the agreement was to solidify its ties with the United States and secure its export access to the US market; even though 90 percent of Israeli goods exported to the United States entered duty-free, this access was contingent on Congress's approval of the GSP and other programs. With a free-trade agreement, Israel could extend and guarantee this access.

106. For this reason, all previous discussions of a bilateral trade agreement (in 1854,

1911, and 1947) had been initiated by Canada. The 1854 agreement was only in effect until 1866, when it was abrogated by the United States. In 1911, an agreement was reached and was approved by the Senate, only to be rejected by Canada's Parliament after the speaker of the House said that it would lead the way to the annexation of Canada.

107. As the chief of staff of the Canadian prime minister, and later Canadian ambassador to the United States, Derek Burney (2005, 109) put it, "We now realized fully the extent to which the priority for free trade was vastly different in the two capitals. Free trade had become an all-consuming issue in Canada, debated intensely, heatedly, and in highly partisan fashion nationally, provincially, and even municipally. In Washington it barely raised a ripple. The biggest problem we had was trying to get the US administration to recognize the political priority of the issue for the Canadian government and to treat it accordingly."

108. For a detailed discussion of the negotiation from the Canadian perspective, see Hart 1994, Ritchie 1997, and Burney 2005.

109. Murphy basically ran an interagency process in which the Commerce Department and others would nitpick about particular details of the agreement. As Prime Minister Mulroney (2007, 566) put it in his memoirs, "Peter Murphy was an able enough negotiator but, without a political champion above him in the administration, he concentrated on 'irritants' identified by officials from various US agencies or key congressmen, and gave the lowest common denominator replies to Canadian overtures."

110. Gotlieb 2006, 486.

111. Canadian officials were unimpressed by the haphazard US negotiating process, but praised Baker. In his diary, Ambassador Gotlieb (2006, 490–91) wrote, "The Yankees behaved abominably. Assholes on the Hill . . . pressured the administration, and the administration lost its way. It showed no sense of history. Baker is the only man of larger spirit." Gotlieb feared that his country had wasted two years planning for the negotiations. "The Americans showed themselves to be shallow-minded and leaderless, the Canadian ministers to be divided and erratic."

112. As Baker said, "I had to break a lot of china. I had to override [USTR] Clayton [Yeutter]. He was against it. I had to call a half-dozen senators and various congressmen. I know I'm in deep trouble proposing this. I've taken a big risk for Canada" (Gotlieb 2006, 491). As an example of his decisive leadership, when a Justice Department memo suddenly appeared and stated that the dispute-settlement mechanism would be unconstitutional, Baker replied "This is nonsense. Get me the attorney general" and worked it out. The memo turned out to have been hatched by Commerce Department officials who did not want their trade-remedy rulings reviewed by an independent panel (Gotlieb 2006, 492).

113. As Gibbon put it, "I can't say there's great enthusiasm" for the agreement. Rep. John LaFalce (D-NY) confessed that "members of Congress are rather indifferent to the US-Canada relationship" (CQA 1987, 662).

114. Singleton 1990.

115. CQA 1990, 144.

116. Congressional Budget Office 1991.

117. PPP 1990 2:1364–65.

118. Hufbauer and Elliott 1994, 15.

119. Noland (1997) concluded that that USTR was "chasing phantoms" because it used Section 301 to focus on countries with large trade surpluses rather than those with clearly identifiable unfair trade practices.

120. The SSI focused on deeply embedded policies and practices and sought changes to Japan's distribution system, public works spending, land reform, exclusionary *keiretsu* business practices, and anti-monopoly policy enforcement.

121. See Kunkel 2003 and Lincoln 1999.

122. Kunkel 2003, 167.

123. Kunkel (2003, 173) points out that "Japanese officials were wary of any terminology—indicators, benchmarks, standards, yardsticks, targets—which could be interpreted as a government commitment enforceable under US trade law." The policy instrument was even given a name, a "voluntary import expansion" (or VIE), the counterpart to the voluntary export restraint. See Bhagwati 1987 and Irwin 1994.

CHAPTER 13

1. *PPP* 1985, 2:1129.

2. *PPP* 1988 1:88. During the 1980 election campaign, Reagan floated the idea of a North American pact between the United States, Canada, and Mexico to promote trade and investment between them.

3. Mexico had slowly begun to open up its tightly controlled economy with unilateral trade reforms in the early 1980s and the decision to join the GATT in 1986. Jaime Serra Puche noted that Mexico had the advantage of exporting under the Generalized System of Preferences (GSP), but such exports were capped. For example, the country could export up to 100,000 microphones to the United States under GSP, but if it exported one more than that it would lose the preferences on all the microphones exported. See Boskin 2014, 20.

4. According to Jaime Serra Puche, the Mexican Secretary of Commerce: "At the end of one evening, very late at night, Salinas came to my room [in Davos] and said, 'We have to do something. We are not on the map for foreign direct investment. Why don't we start thinking about this idea of trade with the US?' See ibid., 19–20.

5. The fact that many high-level Bush administration officials came from Texas helped the Mexicans get attention from the administration (Mayer 1998, 41). For studies on the origins of NAFTA and its negotiation, see Mayer 1998 and Cameron and Tomlin 2000. For a Mexican perspective on the negotiations, see Van Bertrab 1997.

6. Having recently fought a difficult general election campaign over the issue of free trade with the United States, Prime Minister Brian Mulroney and his aides at first thought that Canada had free-trade fatigue and should not participate. While many Canadian officials were reluctant to join, they soon recognized that they had little choice but to participate to protect their interests in the US market.

7. They viewed NAFTA as a massive expansion of the *maquiladora* program, which allowed American manufacturers to locate assembly operations in Mexico, send components into Mexico for assembly duty-free, and then reexport the final goods to the

United States also without paying a tariff because of the offshore assembly provision in the US tariff code. Although the Mexican *maquiladora* program had been operational since 1965, Mexican exports under the program only began to grow rapidly in 1980s.

8. Preeg 1995, 129.

9. Ironically, the sponsors of the anti-fast-track resolutions were more interested in blocking the prospective GATT agreement than in blocking NAFTA; Rep. Byron Dorgan (D-ND), because of the reduction in agricultural subsidies; and Sen. Ernest Hollings (D-SC), because of the elimination of the Multifiber Arrangement.

10. As Mayer (1998, 69–70) points out, "In the case of NAFTA, however, free trade threatened few economic sectors. Farmers of certain agricultural products, most notably citrus fruit, sugar cane and sugar beets, and warm weather vegetables such as tomatoes, and manufacturers in currently protected labor-intensive sectors such as apparel, brooms, and glass were rightly concerned about increased competition. Compared to the collection of industries who stood to gain from free trade, however—banks and other financial institutions, the big three automakers, corporate agriculture, virtually the whole of American big business—these potential losers did not look like much of a political threat. Where necessary, too, the blow could be softened with promises to negotiate longer transition periods or other measures to deal with special circumstances. The significant opposition, therefore, came not from the traditional source—protectionist producers—but rather from a new coalition of labor unions, environmentalists, and grassroots groups." See also Aaronson 1996.

11. Shikher 2012.

12. As Mayer (1998, 142–43) reports, "When informed of the US concession, Ford CEO Harold 'Red' Poling was furious. He called [chief US negotiator] Jules Katz in a rage. Poling thought they had agreed on 65 percent. Trying to calm him down, Katz reminded him, 'We're talking about a 2.5 percent difference on a 2.5 percent tariff.'"

13. Cameron and Tomlin (2000, 40–41) note the irony that Mexico, which wanted NAFTA in order to encourage foreign investment, was reluctant to open its market to foreign investment, whereas the United States, which was worried about an outflow of investment to Mexico, was pressing for Mexico to open its market for such investment.

14. Mayer 1998, 229.

15. In 1991, when some Democratic supporters questioned the political wisdom of his support of freer trade and open markets, Clinton replied, "If you guys want me to run as an isolationist or a protectionist, you need another candidate. I'm not going to do it" (*WSJ*, 11/2/1993).

16. See Grayson 1995, 121–22. The endorsement did not come easily. As Harris (2005, 95) put it, "Intellectually, Clinton, an adherent of free trade, supported it enthusiastically. Politically, it was agony for him. . . . A year earlier, the problem of what candidate Clinton should say about NAFTA had briefly paralyzed the campaign. He had backed the agreement, but slathered his support with a thick mayonnaise of qualifications that rendered his commitment almost meaningless."

17. *PPP* 1993, 1:209ff.

18. Ibid., 210.

19. In negotiating the side agreements, however, the administration could not push too hard. Not only did Canada and Mexico resist making strong commitments on labor

and the environment, but effective side agreements might cost some Republican votes, even if it won some Democratic votes. Business groups and Republicans warned that their support for NAFTA might weaken if the side agreements were too stringent and created new regulatory burdens. With Democrats divided at best, Republican votes were essential to passing NAFTA. Thus, the Clinton administration had a difficult balancing act: If the side agreements were too weak, they might not mollify opponents or win the support of marginal Democrats; if they were too strong, some Republican support might be lost.

20. Mayer 1998, 179, 224.

21. Ibid., 144–45.

22. Grayson 1995, 180.

23. Mayer 1998, 253.

24. Grayson 1995, 177.

25. Minchin 2013, 195.

26. Orden 1996.

27. Mayer 1998, 220–21.

28. *NYT*, 9/17/1993.

29. See Mayer 1998, 341–42.

30. The Clinton administration tried to win Gephardt's support, but he never quite indicated what specific provisions the agreement would have to have to win his support (Mayer 1998, 201).

31. In private conversations at the time, Clinton described NAFTA as "good policy and bad politics." The president believed that the opposition to NAFTA was "beyond rational" since the agreement promised to open up Mexico's market for US goods more than the United States would open up its market for Mexican goods (Branch 2009, 49–50).

32. *PPP* 1993, 2:1489.

33. While the president was diplomatic in his remarks, former President Carter ripped into Ross Perot, saying, "Unfortunately, in our country now, we have a demagogue who has unlimited financial resources and who is extremely careless with the truth who is preying on the fears and the uncertainties of the American public" (*NYT*, 9/15/1993).

34. Michael Duffy and Laurence I. Barrett, "Secrets of Success," *Time*, 11/29/1993, 26.

35. Engel and Jackson 1998.

36. Grayson 1995, 211. A Gallup poll taken before the debate showed that 34 percent of respondents supported NAFTA and 38 percent opposed it. A poll of the same respondents taken after they had watched the debate showed that now 57 percent supported it, and 36 percent opposed it (Gallup 1994, 194–97).

37. Mayer 1998, 315.

38. See Box-Steffensmeier, Arnold, and Zorn 1997.

39. Clinton told Kantor to "open the candy store" to get the votes from Florida, which included relaxing some environment rules for agriculture. In conversations with Branch (2009, 83–84), "the president described how his negotiators averted disaster in Florida, where twenty-one of twenty-three Democrats were against NAFTA until changes placated citrus growers.

40. Mayer 1998, 317.

41. *CR* 11/17/1993, 29936.

42. Ibid., 29947.

43. Branch 2009, 83. In his memoirs, Clinton (2004, 557) recalled, "Our whole team had won a great economic and political victory for America, but . . . it came at a high price, dividing our party in Congress and infuriating many of our strongest supporters in the labor movement."

44. The president of International Union of Electronic Workers remarked that Clinton "screwed us, and we won't forget it" (Susan B. Garland and Richard S. Dunham, "Sweet Victory," *Business Week*, 11/24/1993, 34).

45. Branch 2009, 60. According to Al From, the chairman of the Democratic Leadership Council, "Three-quarters of the Democratic caucus believe Clinton is right, but they are afraid to vote yes" (*NYT*, 11/17/1993). Rep. Jim Kolbe (R-AZ) said that "if people were voting their conscience, this thing would pass handily. . . . Privately, most members recognized NAFTA's virtues." As Mickey Kantor recalled, the president asked the undecided representatives, "'If you could vote secretly, how would you vote?' Well, everyone said, 'Of course, we'd be for it.' He said, 'Doesn't that tell you something?'" (Boskin 2014, 26).

46. See, for example, Kahane 1996; Holian, Krebs, and Walsh 1997; Uslaner 1998; and Baldwin and Magee 2000.

47. See Burtless et al. 1998, 57.

48. See Romalis 2007. Caliendo and Parro (2015) found that NAFTA increased intra-bloc trade by 118 percent for Mexico, 41 percent for the United States, and 11 percent for Canada. They also found that the agreement increased real wages in the United States and Mexico with an overall welfare increase of 1.3 percent in Mexico and 0.08 percent in the United States. In general, Shikher (2012) reports that the economic models used to predict the impact of NAFTA significantly understated the impact on trade but were more accurate in suggesting modest impacts on income and employment.

49. *PPP* 1993, 2:2180.

50. For histories of the Uruguay Round, see Croome 1995, Preeg 1995, Paemen and Bensch 1995, and VanGrasstek 2013.

51. Organization for Economic Cooperation and Development 2014.

52. Croome 1995, 138.

53. Sell 2003.

54. The United States pushed particularly hard in the TRIPs negotiations. According to the top European negotiator, "If the Americans showed themselves to be insensitive to Europe's wishes [on intellectual property], when it came to the concerns of the Third World, they were downright dismissive. . . . Whether born of insensitivity or a simple lack of awareness, the Americans' highly uncooperative attitude did not prevent their delegation from moving heaven and earth" to establish a stronger system of intellectual property rights for pharmaceutical, entertainment, and software producers (Paemen and Bensch 1995, 167).

55. The GATT reported that 236 export-restraint agreements in effect in 1989 were operating outside GATT disciplines (Low 1993, 76). Of these, the United States was involved in sixty-seven and the EEC in one hundred twenty-seven.

56. See Destler 2005, 161, 217.

57. Croome 1995, 144.

58. See Bhagwati 1993, 25. For the debate over Section 301, see Bhagwati and Patrick 1990. As VanGrasstek (2013, 52) points out, "It would be difficult to exaggerate the priority that other participants in the Uruguay Round placed on ending the practice by which Washington defined and enforced it rights" through Section 301 and retaliation rather than through the GATT. "The [European] Community had from the first pushed strongly in the dispute settlement negotiations for a clear prohibition on unilateral action on matters covered by multilateral rules."

59. See Jackson 1990, 94. Jackson came to be called the "father of the WTO" (Van-Grasstek 2013, 57–68).

60. Croome 1995, 273.

61. Preeg 1995, 114.

62. Ibid., 118.

63. In particular, France was adamantly opposed to any subsidy reduction. For a vivid description of Europe's isolation on the issue, see Paemen and Bensch 1995, 182–189.

64. A year later, Arthur Dunkel, the director-general of the GATT, circulated what became known as the "Dunkel draft" of an agreement that clarified the state of the negotiations by taking stock of all the progress that had been made and splitting the difference on agricultural subsidies. This was a bold move for a director-general to take, since he had no authority to act as a mediator between the government negotiators themselves, but it was later viewed as an important step in moving the round forward.

65. *PPP* 1992–93, 1:77.

66. The chief European negotiator stated that "had it not been for the tenacity of the Americans, the negotiations never would have taken place" (Paemen and Bensch 1995, 91).

67. Senator Ernest "Fritz" Hollings (D-SC) opposed the Uruguay Round agreement because the abolition of the MFA threatened textile jobs in his state. Holding up the bill in committee, Hollings forced the scheduling of a rare lame-duck session of Congress to vote on the package before fast-track authority expired. Ironically, by forcing the vote to be held after the election, he may have enabled it to receive more congressional support than otherwise.

68. Democrats did not fear retribution by labor unions, as they did when considering NAFTA, if they voted for the Uruguay Round. Meanwhile, some Republicans objected to the creation of the WTO, fearing that it would compromise America's sovereignty and put WTO panels in the position of judging domestic laws and trade-policy decisions.

69. On the tariff concessions, see Finger, Ingco, and Reincke 1996. The OECD sponsored research in which the market-access provisions of the Uruguay Round agreement were projected to add $184 billion in static welfare gains, or about 0.5 percent to 1.0 percent of world GDP. (This came from a general equilibrium model that did not include dynamic gains or imperfect competition, both of which would increase the calculated benefits.)

70. MacDonald and Vollrath 2005. The United States was also obligated to reduce the average tariff on clothing from 17.2 percent in 1994 to 15.2 percent in 2004.

71. The sharp price decline was evidence of quality downgrading (Harrigan and Barrows 2009). As we saw in chapter 12, just as export quotas led to quality upgrading (exporters would sell the highest-priced, highest-quality goods if the quantity they could sell was limited), the newly unconstrained exporters were now selling cheaper, lower-quality goods.

72. Ingco 1996.

73. Organization for Economic Cooperation and Development 2014.

74. See US General Accounting Office 2001.

75. Labor unions were still smarting from their NAFTA defeat and followed through on their threat to punish pro-NAFTA Democrats by withholding campaign contributions (Engel and Jackson 1998).

76. *PPP* 1997, 1:115.

77. In 1974, 1979, 1984, and 1988, fast track had been embedded within a larger trade bill that had many provisions that Congress supported. In 1991, when fast track was voted on as a stand-alone measure, it encountered stiff resistance. This was the case in 1997 as well.

78. Quoted in Devereaux, Lawrence, Watkins 2006, 227. See also Schneitz and Nieman 1999, and Bardwell 2000.

79. *CQA* 1998, 23–9.

80. As Han and Brady (2007, 506) note, "The recent period of polarization mirrors patterns of polarization that have prevailed throughout most of Congressional history. In fact, the truly unusual historical period is the bipartisan era immediately following the Second World War." The rise in partisanship was not due to redistricting, according to DeVault (2013), because "changes in party affiliation have a much greater impact on voting behavior than changes in district characteristics."

81. Conley (1999) finds that constituency pressures (measures of labor strength) were driving opposition to Clinton's bid for fast track in 1997.

82. *CR* 9/25/1998, H22154; *CR* 9/25/1998, H8797.

83. Turnover among Democrats also contributed to the increased opposition to trade agreements. Older Democrats who came of age during the Cold War era were more sympathetic to a liberal trade policy, whereas younger Democrats hewed more closely to their constituents' views.

84. Bureau of Labor Statistics 2015. Online at http://www.bls.gov/news.release/union2.nr0.htm.

85. Rep. Dennis Kucinich (D-OH) complained that the executive branch cared more about the barriers faced by Chiquita Brands International (an US-headquartered company operating in Central America) in selling bananas in the European Union (EU) than American steel firms: "Bananas did not build America. Steel did. Such a trade policy [of neglecting steel] is, in a word, bananas." *CQA* 1999, 23–20.

86. Steel's failure did not mean that there was no room for creative congressional assistance. In 2000, Senator Robert Byrd (D-WV) inserted into a bill (that was completely unrelated to trade) a requirement that the revenues generated by antidumping

and countervailing duties be distributed to the petitioning firms rather than the US Treasury. Over the next few years, more than $1 billion of tariff revenue worth was paid to domestic steel producers and other recipients of antidumping and countervailing duties under the Byrd amendment. The European Union and other countries denounced the policy, which they argued constituted an unjustifiable subsidy in violation of WTO rules. In 2002, a WTO panel sided with the complainants, and soon other countries were permitted to retaliate against the United States unless the payments were terminated. The George W. Bush administration finally persuaded Congress to repeal the Byrd amendment in 2005.

87. *NYT* 12/3/1999, 1.

88. In December 1994, at the Summit of the Americas in Miami, the United States and thirty three other countries in the Western Hemisphere committed to complete negotiations on the Free Trade Areas of the Americas by 2005. However, several Latin American countries, notably Argentina and Brazil, were suspicious of the project. By 2003, the prospect of an FTAA had disappeared.

89. World Trade Organization, *International Trade Statistics*, various years.

90. Every year from 1990 to 2001, the House voted on legislation to revoke China's temporary MFN status, and these votes succeeded in 1990, 1991 and 1992. The Senate did not concur.

91. Hufbauer and Rosen 2000.

92. Jackson and Engel 2003.

93. Like NAFTA, many representatives wanted PNTR to pass but did not want to vote for it if they knew it would pass. USTR Barshefsky said that "the vast majority of members know this is absolutely the right thing for us to do," but added that "doesn't necessarily mean . . . they will vote affirmatively" (*CQA* 2000, 20–5).

94. The agriculture lobby was nearly as important in increasing votes for PNTR as labor contributions were in taking votes away (Gilbert and Oladi 2012).

95. The US General Accounting Office (1994, 3) found that US firms "cited uncertainty surrounding the annual renewal of China's most-favored-nation trade status as the single most important issue affecting US trade relations with China." Handley and Limão (2015) find that the elimination of this uncertainty explains nearly a quarter of the import growth during this period.

96. Over the three years 2001–3, manufacturing production fell but then recovered, whereas employment failed to rebound at all. Pierce and Schott (2016) found that imports from China grew more rapidly in goods where the threat of higher tariffs (if China had not been granted continued market access) was higher, and employment losses were also larger in those industries. See also Acemoglu et al. 2016.

97. Autor, Dorn, and Hanson (2016). Other studies blamed the trade deficit with China for even larger job losses, but they rely on suspect methodologies. According to the Economic Policy Institute, the trade deficit with China was responsible for the loss of 3.2 million US jobs from 2001 to 2014 (Scott and Kimball 2014). However, using the dollar value of imports from China to calculate the effect on employment overstates its impact on the US labor market. The Chinese content in the consumer electronics exports tends to be relatively small (it imports the components and exports the assembled

goods). The EPI study assumes that if the United States did not import these goods from China, they would be produced in the United States, thereby creating jobs, rather than imported from other developing countries.

98. Field and Graham 1997.

99. Charles, Hurst, and Notowidigdo 2016.

100. Lawrence 2014, 86.

101. Hicks and Devaraj 2015, table 4.

102. See Lawrence Katz's comments in Krugman 2008.

103. "After 2000, the share of imports from non-OPEC developing countries continued to grow rapidly, while the share of imports from developed countries actually declined. . . . Yet this was a period of slow wage growth for almost all workers, with very little additional inequality" (Lawrence 2008, 31, 34).

104. For an analysis of China's current account surplus during this period, see Yang (2012).

105. See Goldstein and Lardy 2008. As Michael Mussa (2008, 281), a former chief economist at the IMF, pointed out, "Beyond any reasonable doubt, the renminbi's exchange rate has become substantially undervalued and is being kept in this position by Chinese policies that powerfully resist, and are intended to resist, significant appreciation."

106. US Department of Treasury 2016. The IMF Articles of Agreement obligate members to "avoid manipulating exchange rates or the international monetary system in order to prevent effective balance of payments adjustment or to gain unfair advantage over other members." Although it was responsible for exchange-rate surveillance of its members, the IMF did not call attention to China's policy. In 2006, the IMF said the renminbi was "undervalued" but did not say it was manipulated. Mussa (2008, 281) called the IMF's inaction "gross misfeasance, malfeasance, and nonfeasance."

107. The import shock had no effect on the reelection rates of incumbents, who strategically adjusted their votes on trade bills but did not change their voting on other bills (Feigenbaum and Hall 2015).

108. When the MFA expired in 2005, the Bush administration agreed on a memorandum of understanding between the United States and China establishing twenty-one quotas covering thirty-four categories of US imports of textiles and apparel products. These temporary quotas failed to slow the rapid growth in apparel imports from China and expired in 2009.

109. Koopman, Wang, and Wei 2012.

110. Bown and McCulloch 2009.

111. The Congressional Budget Office (2008, 9) found that "roughly one-third of the increase in the share of imports from China in US markets from 1998 through 2005 was offset by reduced growth and, in some cases, declines in the shares of imports from other countries," an offset that was even higher prior to 1998.

112. In signing the Trade Act of 2002, for example, Bush argued that "Free trade is also a proven strategy for building global prosperity and adding to the momentum of political freedom. . . . And greater freedom for commerce across the borders eventually leads to greater freedom for citizens within the borders" (*PPP* 2002, 1356).

113. Eun-Kyung Kim, "Candidates Stump in Key Swing States," Associated Press,

10/28/2000. The origin of this promise is purported to be campaign adviser Karl Rove's calculation that a pledge to help the steel industry might tip West Virginia's electoral votes to the Republicans. In fact, Rove may have been right: Bush won West Virginia—the first time a Republican had done so since 1984 and only the fourth time in eighteen elections since 1932—and he would have lost the election without it.

114. Prior to a key meeting, Treasury Secretary Paul O'Neil and Federal Reserve Chairman Alan Greenspan urged Vice President Cheney to reject steel tariffs on the grounds "that the largely bipartisan consensus on free trade was one of the great victories of the last decade; that the President would confuse many constituencies by flouting that consensus"; and that the action might violate WTO rules. Drawing on his experience as the CEO of Alcoa, O'Neill proposed an international agreement to reduce excess capacity in the world steel market, to essentially form a global steel cartel to manage production (Suskind 2004, 216). Presidential adviser Karl Rove thought that steel protection might help swing Pennsylvania and Michigan to the Republican side in the 2002 midterm elections. In February 2002, at a meeting in the White House situation room, the economic and diplomatic policy principals of the Bush administration met to make a final decision about the ITC ruling. According to Suskind, Cheney and US Trade Representative Robert Zoellick favored imposing the safeguard action, while most other participants were skeptical but not strongly opposed. Zoellick believed that relief would help secure the passage of fast track in the Senate, which had yet to vote on the measure.

115. See Hufbauer and Goodrich 2003, Bown 2013, and Finger 2012.

116. Read 2005.

117. See Zoellick (2000). The term "competitive liberalization" was first used by Bergsten (1996) to describe the process of trade liberalization in Asia during the early 1990s. See Evenett and Meier 2008.

118. *Nomination of Robert Zoellick: Hearings Before the Committee on Finance, US Senate*, 107th Cong. 13 (2001).

119. Blustein 2009.

120. Zoellick portrayed trade liberalization as a patriotic imperative, suggesting that opposition to TPA was coming from "protectionists" or members of Congress who were "held back for other rather narrow interests, reasons, some of them related to the understandable politics of where they get their money." This remark rankled Charles B. Rangel (D-NY), the ranking Democrat on the Ways and Means Committee, who promptly delayed consideration of the fast-track bill and demanded a "public apology." "There's no question that Zoellick crossed the line," added Rep. Robert T. Matsui (D-CA), a supporter of open trade. "I was very disappointed" (CQA 2001).

121. Two key Republicans—Jim DeMint of South Carolina and Robin Hayes of North Carolina—were persuaded to vote in favor with promises to prevent the trade preferences given to African, Caribbean, and Andean countries from harming textile dyeing and finishing producers in their districts. Hayes came from a textile family and owned a hosiery mill in North Carolina, but was put under enormous pressure not to vote against TPA. He voted in favor and broke down in tears on the House floor after casting the vote (Foer 2002).

122. DeVault 2010b.

123. The Senate later approved TPA in the context of a vote on Andean trade preferences in May 2002, and negotiating authority finally cleared Congress in July 2002.

124. Shapiro 2006, 29.

125. On the travails of the Doha Round, see Blustein 2009. Many developing countries expected non-reciprocal market access to be granted to them, believing they were owed such treatment by developed countries as a result of the Uruguay Round and the promises made at Doha. Of course, developed countries continued to insist on reciprocity, in which both sides had to make concessions to each other.

126. See Minchin 2013, 305.

127. As the International Trade Commission (2004) pointed out, the CAFTA economies were just 2 percent of the size of the American economy, imports from CAFTA countries were $16.8 million—about 80 percent of which already entered duty-free under the GSP—at a time when total US imports were $1.263 billion. The ITC expected that the value of US imports would increase by 0.07 percent (mainly in textiles and apparel and sugar) after the full phase-in of the tariff elimination, but the additional imports would largely displace those coming from other suppliers, so net imports would be only slightly higher. Aside from sugar, there would be hardly any discernible impact on domestic producers. The ITC also estimated that the elimination of trade barriers in the CAFTA countries would increase US exports by 0.16 percent.

128. *CQA* 2005, 17–4.

129. For example, Robin Hayes (R-NC), whose district had lost thousands of jobs in textiles and apparel, had announced his opposition before the vote. "I am flat-out, completely, horizontally opposed to CAFTA," Hayes stated. "It's not in the best interests of the core constituency I represent," he said. "Every time I drive through Kannapolis and I see those empty plants, I know there is no way I could vote for CAFTA." But under pressure from House Speaker Dennis Hastert (R-IL), who promised measures to restrict imports of clothing from China, Hayes was persuaded to switch his vote just before midnight. "I was minding my own business" in the House cloakroom, Hayes recalled. "All of a sudden, the speaker came around and said, 'We have to have your vote. In return for your vote, we will do whatever is necessary to help the people in the 8th District.'" Hayes barely won reelection in 2006 (*NYT*, 7/29/2005).

130. DeVault (2010a) finds that campaign contributions did not play a big role in congressional voting patterns on CAFTA. Furthermore, Guisinger (2009) finds that there was little electoral punishment of incumbents because of the low salience of the issue among constituents.

131. Magee (2010) later calculated that neither TPA in 2001 nor CAFTA-DR in 2005 would have been approved by Congress under a Democratic president, because more Republican votes would have been lost than Democratic votes gained.

132. The House vote was 224–195, with Democrats voting 218–10 in favor, and Republicans voting 185–6 against.

133. *PPP* 2008, 497–98.

134. Peter Engardio, "Refighting NAFTA," *Business Week*, 3/31/2008, 58.

135. Just 2 percent (0.2 percentage points) of the decline was due to increased protectionism (Kee, Neagu, and Nicita 2013; Henn and McDonald 2014). Although temporary

trade barriers (antidumping and countervailing duties) did increase during the crisis, they were invoked far less than anyone expected (Bown and Crowley 2014).

136. Monitoring by the WTO and USTR showed no major increase in trade restrictions during the crisis, although some analysts pointed to the spread of murky protectionism, such as discriminatory government procurement rules and health and safety regulations that burdened foreign firms to the advantage of domestic firms.

137. See Hufbauer and Lowry 2012 for an analysis of the case.

138. Barack Obama, 2015 State of the Union address, online at the American Presidency Project, http://www.presidency.ucsb.edu/ws/index.php?pid=108031 (accessed September 14, 2016).

139. "Inaugural Address: Trump's Full Speech." Online at CNN Politics, http://www.cnn.com/2017/01/20/politics/trump-inaugural-address/

140. William Mauldin and Siobhan Hughes, "Congress Tests Trump Officials on Trade," *WSJ* 2/17/2017.

141. "In US, Record-High 72% See Foreign Trade as Opportunity." Online at the Gallup website, http://www.gallup.com/poll/204044/record-high-foreign-trade-opportunity.aspx?

CONCLUSION

1. These quotations and many others like them come from Pastor (1983), who refers to it as the "cry and sigh" syndrome.

2. *PPP* 1993, 2:2198.

3. See Dür 2010.

REFERENCES

ABBREVIATIONS

AC   *Annals of Congress*

ASP   *American State Papers* (F–Finance, FR–Foreign Relations)

CG   *Congressional Globe*

CQA   *Congressional Quarterly Almanac*. Washington, DC: CQ Press, 1945–.

CR   *Congressional Record*. To 1875, search the Library of Congress
        (https://memory.loc.gov/ammem/amlaw/lawhome.html); after 1875, search
        ProQuest Congressional at (http://congressional.proquest.com/
        profiles/gis/search/advanced/advanced?accountid=10422). Site usage requires
        membership.

FRUS   US Department of State, *Foreign Relations of the United States*. Washington,
        DC: Government Printing Office.

JSM   *Collected Works of John Stuart Mill*, edited by John M. Robson. 33 vols.
        Toronto: University of Toronto Press, 1963–1989.

LJM   *Letters and Other Writings of James Madison*. 4 vols. Philadelphia: Lippin-
        cott, 1865.

LTR   *Letters of Theodore Roosevelt*, edited by Elting E. Morison. 8 vols. Cam-
        bridge: Harvard University Press, 1951–54.

MJQA   *Memoirs of John Quincy Adams*, edited by Charles Francis Adams. 12 vols.
        Philadelphia: J. B. Lippincott, 1874–77.

NYT   *New York Times*

PAH   *Papers of Alexander Hamilton*, edited by Harold C. Syrett. 26 vols. New York:
        Columbia University Press, 1961–.

PAJ   *Papers of Andrew Jackson*, edited by Sam B. Smith and Harriet C. Owsley.
        10 vols. Knoxville: University of Tennessee Press, 1980–.

PBF   *Papers of Benjamin Franklin*, edited by Leonard W. Labaree. 41 vols. New
        Haven, CT: Yale University Press, 1959–.

PGW CS *Papers of George Washington, Colonial Series*, edited by W. W. Abbott.
        10 vols. Charlottesville: University of Virginia Press, 1985–.

PGW PS   *Papers of George Washington, Presidential Series*, edited by W. W. Abbott.
19 vols. Charlottesville: University of Virginia Press, 1987–.

PHC   *Papers of Henry Clay*, edited by James F. Hopkins. 10 vols. Lexington: University Press of Kentucky, 1959–91.

PJA   *Papers of John Adams*, edited by Robert J. Taylor. 18 vols. Cambridge, MA: Harvard University Press, 1977

PJC   *Papers of John Calhoun*, edited by Robert L. Meriwether. 28 vols. Columbia: University of South Carolina Press.

PJM   *Papers of James Madison*, edited by William T. Hutchinson and William M. E. Rachal. 17 vols. Chicago: University of Chicago Press, 1962–1991.

PJM PS   *Papers of James Madison, Presidential Series*, edited by Robert Rutland. 8 vols. Chicago: University of Chicago Press, 1984–.

PJM SSS   *Papers of James Madison, Secretary of State Series*, edited by Robert Brugger. 10 vols. Chicago: University of Chicago Press, 1986–2014.

PPP   *Public Papers of the President*, Washington, DC: Government Printing Office.

PRT   *Papers of Robert Taft*, edited by Clarence E. Wunderlin. 4 vols. Kent, OH: Kent State University Press, 1997–2006.

PTJ   *Papers of Thomas Jefferson*, edited by Julian P. Boyd. 42 vols. Princeton, NJ: Princeton University Press, 1950–.

PTJ RS   *Papers of Thomas Jefferson, Retirement Series*, edited by J. Jefferson Looney. 12 vols. Princeton, NJ: Princeton University Press, 1994– .

RD   *Register of Debates*. Search the Library of Congress online at https://memory.loc.gov/ammem/amlaw/lawhome.html.

WAL   *Collected Works of Abraham Lincoln*, edited by Roy T. Basler. 9 vols. New Brunswick, NJ: Rutgers University Press, 1953–55.

WHT   *Collected Works of William Howard Taft*, edited by David H. Burton. 8 vols. Athens, OH: Ohio University Press, 2001–4.

WJA   *Works of John Adams*, edited by Charles F. Adams. 10 vols. Boston: Little, Brown, 1850–1856.

WTJ   *Writings of Thomas Jefferson*, edited by Paul Leicester Ford. 10 vols. New York: G. P. Putnam's Sons, 1892–99.

WP   *Washington Post*

WSJ   *Wall Street Journal*

Aaronson, Susan Ariel. 1996. *Trade and the American Dream: A Social History of Postwar Trade Policy*. Lexington: University Press of Kentucky.

Acemoglu, Daron, David Autor, David Dorn, Gordon H. Hanson, and Brendan Price. 2016. "Import Competition and the Great U.S. Employment Sag of the 2000s." *Journal of Labor Economics* 34:S141–S198.

Acheson, Dean. 1944. "Post-War International Economic Problems." Department of State *Bulletin* 11:656–63.

———. 1969. *Present at the Creation: My Years in the State Department*. New York: W. W. Norton.

Adams, Donald R., Jr. 1980. "American Neutrality and Prosperity, 1793–1808." *Journal of Economic History* 40:713–37.

Adams, Walter, and Joel B. Dirlam. 1964. "Steel Imports and Vertical Oligopoly Power." *American Economic Review* 54:626–55.

Addison, John T., Douglas A. Fox, and Christopher J. Ruhm. 1995. "Trade and Displacement in Manufacturing." *Monthly Labor Review* (April):58–67.

Aggarwal, Vinod K. 1985. *Liberal Protectionism: The International Politics of Organized Textile Trade.* Berkeley: University of California Press.

Aho, C. Michael, and Thomas O. Bayard. 1982. "The 1980s: Twilight of the Open Trading System?" *World Economy* 5:379–406.

Allen, Robert C. 1979. "International Competition in Iron and Steel, 1850–1913."*Journal of Economic History* 39: 911–37.

———. 1981. "Accounting for Price Changes: American Steel Rails, 1879–1910." *Journal of Political Economy* 89:512–28.

Allen, William R. 1953. "The International Trade Philosophy of Cordell Hull, 1907–1933." *American Economic Review* 43:101–16.

Alston, Lee. 1983. "Farm Foreclosures in the United States during the Interwar Period." *Journal of Economic History* 43:445–57.

Alvarez-Cuadrado, Francisco, and Markus Poschke. 2011. "Structural Change Out of Agriculture: Labor Push versus Labor Pull." *American Economic Journal: Macroeconomics.* 3:127–58.

Ames, Fisher. 1854. *Works of Fisher Ames.* Edited by Seth Ames. Boston: Little, Brown.

Anderson, Gary M., and Robert D. Tollison. 1993. "Political Influence and the Ratification of the Income Tax Amendment." *International Review of Law and Economics* 13:259–70.

Anderson, James E., and J. Peter Neary. 2005. *Measuring the Restrictiveness of International Trade Policy.* Cambridge, MA: MIT Press.

———. 1998. "Effective Protection Redux." *Journal of International Economics* 44:21–44.

Anderson, Judith Icke. 1981. *William Howard Taft: An Intimate History.* New York: W. W. Norton.

Angel, Robert C. 1991. *Explaining Economic Policy Failure: Japan and the 1969–71 International Monetary Crisis.* New York: Columbia University Press.

Ankli, Robert E. 1971. "The Reciprocity Treaty of 1854." *Canadian Journal of Economics* 4:1–20.

Appleton, Nathan. 1858. *The Introduction of the Power Loom and the Origins of Lowell.* Lowell, MA: Penhallow.

Archibald, Robert B., and David H. Feldman. 1998. "Investment during the Great Depression: Uncertainty and the Role of Smoot-Hawley Tariff." *Southern Economic Journal* 64:857–79.

———, David H. Feldman, Marc D. Hayford, and Carl A. Pasurka. 2000. "Effective Rates of Protection and the Fordney-McCumber and Smoot-Hawley Tariff Acts: Comment and Revised Estimates." *Applied Economics* 32:1223–26.

Asbeek Brusse, Wendy. 1997. *Tariffs, Trade, and European Integration, 1947–1957: From Study Group to Common Market.* New York: St. Martin's Press.

Autor, David H., David Dorn, and Gordon H. Hanson. 2013. "The China Syndrome: Local Labor Market Effects of Import Competition in the United States." *American Economic Review* 103:2121–68.

———, David Dorn, and Gordon H. Hanson. 2016. "The China Shock: Learning from Labor Market Adjustment to Large Changes in Trade." *Annual Review of Economics* 8:205–40.

Baack, Ben. 2001. "Forging a Nation State: The Continental Congress and the Financing of the War of American Independence." *Economic History Review* 54:639–56.

———. 2004. "British versus American Interests in Land and the American Revolution." *Journal of European Economic History* 33:514–54.

———, Robert A. McGuire, and T. Norman Van Cott. 2009. "Constitutional Agreement during the Drafting of the Constitution: A New Interpretation." *Journal of Legal Studies* 38:533–67.

Baack, Bennett D., and Edward J. Ray. 1983. "The Political Economy of Tariff Policy: A Case Study of the United States." *Explorations in Economic History* 20:73–93.

———, and Edward John Ray. 1985. "Special Interests and the Adoption of the Income Tax in the United States." *Journal of Economic History* 45:607–25.

Bach, G. L. 1946. "War Period Transactions of the Federal Government." *Survey of Current Business* 26:7–15.

Bailey, Michael A. 2003. "The Politics of the Difficult: The Role of Public Opinion in Early Cold War Aid and Trade Policies." *Legislative Studies Quarterly* 28:147–78.

———, Judith Goldstein, and Barry R. Weingast. 1997. "The Institutional Roots of American Trade Policy: Rules, Coalitions and International Trade." *World Politics* 49:309–39.

Bailey, Thomas A. 1980. *A Diplomatic History of the American People.* 10th ed. Englewood Cliffs, NJ: Prentice-Hall.

Bairoch, Paul. 1993. *Economics and World History: Myths and Paradoxes.* Chicago: University of Chicago Press.

Baker, James A. 2006. *Work Hard, Study . . . and Keep Out of Politics!* New York: G. P. Putnam.

Baker, Richard C. 1941. *The Tariff under Roosevelt and Taft.* Hastings, NE: Democrat Print Co.

Baldwin, Robert E. 1969. "The Case against Infant-Industry Tariff Protection." *Journal of Political Economy* 77:295–305.

———. 1970. *Nontariff Distortions of International Trade.* Washington, DC: Brookings Institution.

———. 1976. "The Trade and Employment Effects in the United States of Multilateral Tariff Reductions." *American Economic Review* 66:142–48.

———. 1982. "The Inefficacy of Trade Policy." Princeton Essays in International Finance, No. 150, December. International Finance Section, Princeton University.

———. 1984. "The Changing Nature of U.S. Trade Policy since World War II." In *The Structure and Evolution of Recent U.S. Trade Policy,* edited by Robert E. Baldwin and Anne O. Krueger. Chicago: University of Chicago Press.

———. 1985a. *The Political Economy of U.S. Import Policy.* Cambridge, MA: MIT Press.

———. 1985b. "Ineffectiveness of Protection in Promoting Social Goals." *World Economy* 8:109–18.

———. 1998. "Imposing Multilateral Discipline on Administered Protection." In *The WTO as an International Organization*, edited by Anne O. Krueger. Chicago: University of Chicago Press.

———, and Christopher S. Magee. 2000. "Is Trade Policy for Sale? Congressional Voting on Recent Trade Bills." *Public Choice* 105:79–101.

Balinky, Alexander. 1958. *Albert Gallatin: Fiscal Theories and Policies*. New Brunswick, NJ: Rutgers University Press.

Ball, George W. 1982. *The Past Has Another Pattern: Memoirs*. New York: W. W. Norton.

Bardwell, Kedron. 2000. "The Puzzling Decline in House Support for Free Trade: Was Fast Track a Referendum on NAFTA?" *Legislative Studies Quarterly* 25:591–610.

Barfield. Claude, E. 1970. "'Our Share of the Booty': The Democratic Party, Cannonism, and the Payne-Aldrich Tariff." *Journal of American History* 57:308–23.

Bartlett, Irving H. 1993. *John C. Calhoun: A Biography*. New York: W. W. Norton.

Bassett, John Spencer, ed. 1926. *Correspondence of Andrew Jackson*. 7 vols. Washington, DC: Carnegie Institute.

Bauer, Raymond A., Ithiel de Sola Pool, and Lewis Anthony Dexter. 1963. *American Business and Public Policy: The Politics of Foreign Trade*. 2nd ed. Chicago: Aldine-Atherton.

Baumgardner, James L. 1984. "The 1888 Presidential Election: How Corrupt?" *Presidential Studies Quarterly* 14:416–27.

Baxter, Maurice G. 1995. *Henry Clay and the American System*. Lexington: University Press of Kentucky.

Bayard, Thomas O., and Kimberly Ann Elliott. 1994. *Reciprocity and Retaliation in U.S. Trade Policy*. Washington, DC: Institute for International Economics.

Beale, Howard K. 1930. "The Tariff and Reconstruction." *American Historical Review* 35:276–94.

Beaulieu, Eugene and J. C. Herbert Emery. 2001. "Pork Packers, Reciprocity and Laurier's Defeat in the 1911 General Election." *Journal of Economic History* 61:1082–1100.

Becker, William H. 1982. *The Dynamics of Business-Government Relations: Industry and Exports, 1893–1921*. Chicago: University of Chicago Press.

———, and William M. McClenahan. 2003. *The Market, the State, and the Export-Import Bank of the United States, 1934–2000*. New York: Cambridge University Press.

Beckett, Grace. 1941. *The Reciprocal Trade Agreements Program*. New York: Columbia University Press.

Bednarzik, Robert W. 1993. "An Analysis of U.S. Industries Sensitive to Foreign Trade, 1982–87." *Monthly Labor Review* 116 (February), 15–31.

Belko, William S. 2012. *The Triumph of the Antebellum Free Trade Movement*. Gainsville: University Press of Florida.

Belohlavek, John M. 1994. "Economic Interest Groups and the Formation of Foreign Policy in the Early Republic." *Journal of the Early Republic* 14:476–84.

Bemis, Samuel F. 1923. *Jay's Treaty: A Study in Commerce and Diplomacy.* New York: Macmillan.

Ben-Atar, Doron S. 1993. *The Origins of Jeffersonian Commercial Policy and Diplomacy.* New York: St. Martin's Press.

Benedict, Murray R. 1953. *Farm Policies of the United States, 1790–1950.* New York: Twentieth Century Fund.

Bensel, Richard F. 1984. *Sectionalism and American Political Development, 1880–1980.* Madison: University of Wisconsin Press.

———. 1990. *Yankee Leviathan: The Origins of Central State Authority in America, 1859–1877.* New York: Cambridge University Press.

———. 2000. *The Political Economy of American Industrialization, 1877–1900.* New York: Cambridge University Press.

Benton, Thomas H. 1854. *Thirty Years' View: A History of the Working of the American Government for Thirty Years, from 1820 to 1850.* 2 vols. New York: Appleton.

Bezanson, Anne, Robert D. Gray, and Miriam Hussey. 1936. *Wholesale Prices in Philadelphia, 1784–1861.* Philadelphia: University of Pennsylvania Press.

Bergeron, Paul H. 1973. "Tennessee's Response to the Nullification Crisis." *Journal of Southern History* 39:23–44.

Berglund, Abraham. 1923. "The Tariff Act of 1922." *American Economic Review* 13:14–33.

———. 1935. "The Reciprocal Trade Agreements Act of 1934." *American Economic Review* 25:411–25.

———, and Philip G. Wright. 1929. *The Tariff on Iron and Steel.* Washington, DC: Brookings Institution.

Bergsten, C. Fred. 1985. "The Problem?" *Foreign Policy* 59:132–44.

———. 1996. "Globalizing Free Trade." *Foreign Affairs* 75:105–20.

Bergsten, C. Fred, et al. 1987. *Auction Quotas and United States Import Policy.* Washington, DC: Institute for International Economics.

———, and Russell A. Green. 2016. *International Monetary Cooperation: Lessons from the Plaza Accord after Thirty Years.* Washington, DC: Peterson Institute for International Economics.

Bernhofen, Daniel M., Zouheir El-Sahli, and Richard Kneller. 2016. "Estimating the Effects of the Container Revolution on World Trade." *Journal of International Economics* 98:36–50.

Berthoff, Rowland T. 1953. *British Immigrants to Industrial America, 1750–1950.* Cambridge, MA: Harvard University Press.

Bhagwati, Jagdish. 1987. "VERs, Quid Pro Quo DFI, and VIEs: Political-Economy Theoretic Analyses." *International Economic Journal* 1:1–14.

———. 1993. "The Diminished Giant Syndrome: How Declinism Drives Trade Policy." *Foreign Affairs* 72:22–26.

———, and Hugh Patrick, eds. 1990. *Aggressive Unilateralism: America's 301 Policy and the World Trading System.* Ann Arbor: University of Michigan Press.

Bidwell, Percy W. 1930. "The New American Tariff: Europe's Answer." *Foreign Affairs* 9:13–26.

Bierce, Ambrose. 1911. *The Devil's Dictionary*. Cleveland, OH: World Publishing.

Bierman, Harold. 2004. "The 1929 Stock Market Crash." In EH.net Encyclopedia of Economic and Business History, edited by Robert Whaples. Online at http://eh.net/encyclopedia/article/Bierman.Crash.

Binkley, Wilfred E. 1962. *American Political Parties: Their Natural History*. 4th ed. New York: Alfred A. Knopf.

Bittlingmayer, George. 1985. "Did Antitrust Policy Cause the Great Merger Wave?" *Journal of Law and Economics* 28:77–118.

Bjork, Gordon C. 1964. "The Weaning of the American Economy: Independence, Market Changes, and Economic Development." *Journal of Economic History* 24:541–60.

Blaine, James G. 1884. *Twenty Years in Congress: From Lincoln to Garfield*. Norwich, CT: Henry Bill.

Blum, John. 1959. *From the Morgenthau Diaries*. Boston: Houghton Mifflin.

Blustein, Paul. 2009. *Misadventures of the Most Favored Nations*. New York: Public Affairs.

Board of Governors of the Federal Reserve System. 1941. *Banking and Monetary Statistics. 1914–1941*. Washington, DC: Government Printing Office.

———. 1943. *Banking and Monetary Statistics. 1914–1941*. Washington, DC: Government Printing Office.

Bohi, Douglas R., and Milton Russell. 1978. *Limiting Oil Imports: An Economic History and Analysis*. Baltimore: Johns Hopkins University Press.

Boltuck, Richard, and Robert E. Litan, eds. 1991. *Down in the Dumps: Administration of the Unfair Trade Laws*. Washington, DC: Brookings Institution.

Bordewich, Fergus M. 2016. *The First Congress: How James Madison, George Washington, and a Group of Extraordinary Men Invented Government*. New York: Simon & Schuster.

Bordo, Michael D., and Barry Eichengreen. 1993. *A Retrospective on the Bretton Woods System*. Chicago: University of Chicago Press.

Boskin, Michael J., ed. 2014. *NAFTA at 20: The North American Free Trade Agreement's Achievements and Challenges*. Stanford, CA: Hoover Institution Press.

Bown, Chad P. 2013. "How Different Are Safeguards from Antidumping? Evidence from U.S. Trade Policies Toward Steel." *Review of Industrial Organization* 42:449–81.

———, and Meredith Crowley. 2014. "Import Protection, Business Cycles, and Exchange Rates: Evidence from the Great Recession" *Journal of International Economics* 90:50–64.

———, and Douglas A. Irwin. 2015. "The GATT's Starting Point: Tariff Levels circa 1947." NBER Working Paper No. 21782.

———, and Rachel McCulloch. 2009. "U.S.–Japan and U.S.–China Trade Conflict: Export Growth, Reciprocity, and the International Trading System." *Journal of Asian Economics* 20:669–87.

Box-Steffensmeier, J., L. Arnold, and J. Zorn. 1997. "The Strategic Timing of Position Taking in Congress: A Study of the North American Free Trade Agreement." *American Political Science Review* 91:324–38.

Brady, David, Judith Goldstein, and Daniel Kessler. 2002. "Does Party Matter? An Historical Test Using Senate Tariff Votes in Three Institutional Settings." *Journal of Law, Economics, and Organization* 18:140–54.

Branch, Taylor. 2009. *The Clinton Tapes: Wrestling History with the President.* New York: Simon & Schuster.

Breen, T. H. 2004. *The Marketplace of Revolution: How Consumer Politics Shaped American Independence.* New York: Oxford University Press.

Brenner, Steven R. 1977. *Economic Interests and the Trade Agreements Program, 1937–1940: A Study of Institutions and Political Influence.* PhD diss., Stanford University.

Broadberry, Stephen N. 1998. "How Did the United States and Germany Overtake Britain? A Sectoral Analysis of Comparative Productivity Levels, 1870–1990." *Journal of Economic History* 58:375–407.

Brown, Roger H. 1993. *Redeeming the Republic: Federalists, Taxation, and the Origins of the Constitution.* Baltimore: Johns Hopkins University Press

Brown, William A., Jr. 1950. *The United States and the Restoration of World Trade.* Washington, DC: Brookings Institution.

Brownlee, W. Elliot. 1982. "Wilson and Financing the Modern State: The Revenue Act of 1916." *Proceedings of the American Philosophical Society* 129:173–210.

Brusse, Wendy A. 1997. "Liberalizing Intra-European Trade." In *Explorations in OEEC History*, edited by Richard T. Griffiths. Paris: OECD.

Buel, Richard. 1998. *In Irons: Britain's Naval Supremacy and the American Revolutionary Economy.* New Haven, CT: Yale University Press.

———. 2005. *America on the Brink: How the Political Struggle over the War of 1812 Almost Destroyed the Young Republic.* New York: Palgrave Macmillan.

Burdekin, Richard C. K., and Farrokh K. Langdana. 1993. "War Finance in the Southern Confederacy, 1861–1865." *Explorations in Economic History* 30:352–76.

Burdick, Frank. 1968. "Woodrow Wilson and the Underwood Tariff." *Mid-America* 50:272–90.

Burner, David. 1979. *Herbert Hoover: A Public Life.* New York: Alfred A. Knopf.

Burney, Derek H. 2005. *Getting It Done: A Memoir.* Montreal: McGill-Queen's University Press.

Burtless, Gary, Robert Z. Lawrence, Robert E. Litan, and Robert J. Shapiro. 1998. *Globaphobia: Confronting Fears about Open Trade.* Washington, DC: Brookings Institution, Progressive Policy Institute, and Twentieth Century Fund.

Butler, Michael A. 1998. *Cautious Visionary: Cordell Hull and Trade Reform, 1933–1937.* Kent, OH: Kent State University Press.

Cairncross, Alec, and Nita Watts. 1989. *The Economic Section 1939–1961: A Study in Economic Advising.* London: Routledge.

Calhoun, Charles W. 1996. "Political Economy in the Gilded Age: The Republican Party's Industrial Policy." *Journal of Policy History* 8:291–309.

———. 2007. "The Political Culture: Public Life and the Conduct of Politics." In *The Gilded Age: Perspectives on the Origins of Modern America*, edited by Charles W. Calhoun. 2nd ed. Lanham, MD: Rowman & Littlefield.

———. 2008. *Minority Victory: Gilded Age Politics and the Front Porch Campaign of 1888.* Lawrence: University Press of Kansas.

Caliendo, Lorenzo, and Fernando Parro. 2015. "Estimates of the Trade and Welfare Effects of NAFTA." *Review of Economic Studies* 82:1–44.

Callahan, Colleen, Judith McDonald, and Anthony O'Brien. 1994. "Who Voted for Smoot-Hawley?" *Journal of Economic History* 54:683–90.

Calloway, Colin G. 2006. *The Scratch of a Pen: 1763 and the Transformation of North America*. New York: Oxford University Press.

Calomiris, Charles W., and Larry Schweikart. 1991. "The Panic of 1857: Origins, Transmission, and Containment." *Journal of Economic History* 51:807–34.

Cameron, Maxwell A., and Brian W. Tomlin. 2000. *The Making of NAFTA: How the Deal Was Done*. Ithaca, NY: Cornell University Press.

Canto, Victor, and Arthur B. Laffer. 1983. "The Effectiveness of Orderly Marketing Agreements: The Color TV Case." *Business Economics* 18:38–45.

Cantril, Hadley. 1951. *Public Opinion, 1935–1946*. Princeton, NJ: Princeton University Press.

Carey, Kevin. 1999. "Investigating a Debt Channel for the Smoot-Hawley Tariffs: Evidence from the Sovereign Bond Market." *Journal of Economic History* 59:748–61.

Carlander, Jay, and John Majewski. 2003. "Imagining 'A Great Manufacturing Empire': Virginia and the Possibilities of a Confederate Tariff." *Civil War History* 49:334–52.

Carnegie, Andrew. 1890. "Summing up the Tariff Controversy." *North American Review* 151:47–74.

———. 1908. "My Experience with, and Views upon, the Tariff." *Century Illustrated Monthly*. Reprinted in *Miscellaneous Writings of Andrew Carnegie*, edited by Burton J. Hendrick. Vol. 2. Garden City, NY: Doubleday, Doran, 1933.

Chandler, Alfred D. 1959. "The Beginnings of 'Big Business' in American Industry." *Business History Review* 33:1–31.

Chandler, Alfred D., Jr. 1977. *The Visible Hand: The Managerial Revolution on American Business*. Cambridge: Harvard University Press.

Charles, Kerwin Kofi, Erik Hurst, and Matthew Notowidigdo. 2016. "The Masking of the Decline in Manufacturing Employment by the Housing Bubble." *Journal of Economic Perspectives* 30:179–200.

Charnovitz, Steve. 1986. "Worker Adjustment: The Missing Ingredient in Trade Policy." *California Management Review* 28:156–73.

Cheney, Paul. 2006. "A False Dawn for Enlightenment Cosmopolitanism? Franco-American Trade during the American War of Independence." *William and Mary Quarterly* 63:463–88.

Clarfield, Gerard. 1975. "Protecting the Frontiers: Defense Policy and the Tariff Question in the First Washington Administration." *William and Mary Quarterly* 32:443–64.

———. 1979. "John Adams: The Marketplace, and American Foreign Policy." *New England Quarterly* 52:345–57.

Clarke, Andrew J., Jeffrey A. Jenkins, and Kenneth S. Lowande. 2016. "Tariff Politics and Congressional Elections: Exploring the Cannon Thesis." *Journal of Theoretical Politics* 29:382–414.

Clayton, William L. 1947. "The European Crisis." *Foreign Relations of the United States* 3 (May 27): 230–32.

———. 1963. "GATT, The Marshall Plan, and OECD." *Political Science Quarterly* 78:493–503.

Clements, Kenneth W., and Larry A. Sjaastad. 1984. *How Protection Taxes Exporters.* Thames Essay No. 39. London: Trade Policy Research Centre.

Cleveland, Grover. 1933. *Letters of Grover Cleveland, 1850–1908.* Selected and edited by Allan Nevins. New York: Houghton Mifflin.

Cline, William R. 1990. *The Future of World Trade in Textiles and Apparel.* Rev. ed. Washington, DC: Institute for International Economics.

Clinton, Bill. 2004. *My Life.* New York: Alfred A. Knopf.

Cochran, Thomas C. 1961. "Did the Civil War Retard Industrialization?" *Mississippi Valley Historical Review* 48:197–210.

Cole, Arthur H. 1938. *Wholesale Commodity Prices in the United States, 1700–186: Statistical Supplement.* Cambridge, MA: Harvard University Press.

Collard-Wexler, Allan, and Jan De Loecker. 2015. "Reallocation and Technology: Evidence from the US Steel Industry." *American Economic Review* 105:131–71.

Combs, Jerald A. 1970. *The Jay Treaty: Political Battleground of the Founding Fathers.* Berkeley: University of California Press.

Congressional Budget Office. 1984. *The Effects of Import Quotas on the Steel Industry.* Washington, DC: CBO.

———.. 1986. *Has Trade Protection Revitalized Domestic Industries?* Washington, DC: CBO.

———. 1987. *The GATT Negotiations and U.S. Trade Policy.* Washington, DC: CBO.

———. 1991. *Trade Restraints and the Competitive Status of the Textile, Apparel, and Nonrubber Footwear Industries.* Washington, DC: CBO.

———. 1994. *How the GATT Affects U.S. Antidumping and Countervailing Duty Policy.* Washington, DC: CBO.

———. 2001. *Antidumping Actions in the United States and Around the World.* Washington, DC: CBO.

———. 2008. "How Changes in the Value of the Chinese Currency Affect U.S. Imports." Washington, DC: CBO.

Conley, Richard S. 1999. "Derailing Presidential Fast-Track Authority: The Impact of Constituency Pressures and Political Ideology on Trade Policy in Congress." *Political Research Quarterly* 52:785–99.

Conner, James R. 1958. "National Farm Organizations and United States Tariff Policy in the 1920s." *Agricultural History* 32:32–43.

Conybeare, John A. C. 1991. "Voting for Protection: An Electoral Model of Tariff Policy." *International Organization* 45:57–81.

Cooke, Jacob E. 1975. "Tench Coxe, Alexander Hamilton, and the Encouragement of American Manufactures." *William and Mary Quarterly* 32:369–92.

Cooper, Richard. 2000. "Foreign Economic Policy in the 1960s: An Enduring Legacy." In *Economic Events, Ideas, and Policies: The 1960s and After*, edited by George L. Perry and James Tobin. Washington, DC: Brookings Institution.

Corden, W. M. 1971. *The Theory of Protection.* Oxford: Clarendon Press.

——. 1974. *Trade Policy and Economic Welfare*. Oxford: Clarendon Press.

Cowin, William P. 1999. "The Invisible Smith: The Impact of Adam Smith on the Foundation of Early American Economic Policy during the First Federal Congress, 1789–1791." In *Inventing Congress: Origins and Establishment of the First Federal Congress*, edited by Kenneth R. Bowling and Donald R. Kennon. Athens: Ohio University Press.

Craig, Douglas B. 1992. *After Wilson: The Struggle for the Democratic Party, 1920–1934*. Chapel Hill: University of North Carolina Press.

Crandall, Robert. 1981. *The U.S. Steel Industry in Recurring Crisis*. Washington, DC: Brookings Institution.

Croome, John. 1995. *Reshaping the World Trading System: A History of the Uruguay Round*. Geneva: World Trade Organization.

Crowley, John E. 1993. *The Privileges of Independence: Neomercantilism and the American Revolution*. Baltimore: Johns Hopkins University Press.

Crucini, Mario J., and James Kahn. 1996. "Tariffs and Aggregate Economic Activity: Lessons from the Great Depression." *Journal of Monetary Economics* 38:427–67.

Crucini, Mario J., and James Kahn. 2007. "Tariffs and the Great Depression Revisited." In *Great Depressions of the Twentieth Century*, edited by Timothy Kehoe and Edward Prescott. Minneapolis: Federal Reserve Bank of Minneapolis.

Culbert, Jay. 1987. "War-time Anglo-American Talks and the Making of the GATT." *World Economy* 10:381–99.

Culbertson, William S. 1923. "The Making of Tariffs." *Yale Review* 12:255–74.

——. 1937. *Reciprocity*. New York: McGraw-Hill.

Cupitt, Richard, and Euel Elliott. 1994. "Schattschneider Revisited: Senate Voting on the Smoot-Hawley Tariff Act of 1930." *Economics and Politics* 6:187–99.

Curzon, Gerard. 1965. *Multilateral Commercial Diplomacy: The General Agreement on Tariffs and Trade, and Its Impact on National Commercial Policies and Techniques*. London: Michael Joseph.

Dangerfield, George. 1952. *The Era of Good Feelings*. New York: Harcourt, Brace.

Davis, Joseph H. 2004. "An Annual Index of U.S. Industrial Production, 1790–1915." *Quarterly Journal of Economics* 119:1177–1215.

——, and Douglas A. Irwin. 2008. "The Antebellum U.S. Iron Industry: Domestic Production and Foreign Competition." *Explorations in Economic History* 45:254–69.

Davis, Joseph L. 1977. *Sectionalism in American Politics, 1774–1787*. Madison: University of Wisconsin Press.

Davis, Lance E., and Stanley L. Engerman. 2006. *Naval Blockades in Peace and War: An Economic History since 1750*. New York: Cambridge University Press.

——. and Robert E. Gallman. 1978. "Capital Formation in the United States during the Nineteenth Century." In *Cambridge Economic History of Europe*. Vol. 7. *The Industrial Economies: Capital, Labour, and Enterprise*. New York: Cambridge University Press.

——. and Robert E. Gallman. 1994. "Savings, Investment, and Economic Growth: The United States in the Nineteenth Century." In *Capitalism in Context: Essays on Economic Development and Cultural Change in Honor of R. M. Hartwell*, edited by John James and Mark Thomas. Chicago: University of Chicago Press.

Davis, Steven J., John C. Haltiwanger, and Scott Schuh. 1995. *Job Creation and Destruction*. Cambridge, MA: MIT Press.

De Melo, Jaime, and David Tarr. 1992. *A General Equilibrium Analysis of U.S. Foreign Trade Policy*. Cambridge, MA: MIT Press.

Deardorff, Alan V., and Robert M. Stern, eds. 1994. *The Stolper-Samuelson Theorem: A Golden Jubilee*. Ann Arbor: University of Michigan Press.

DeLong, J. Bradford. 1998. "Trade Policy and America's Standard of Living: An Historical Perspective." In *Imports, Exports, and the American Worker*, edited by Susan Collins. Washington, DC: Brookings Institution.

———. and Barry Eichengreen. 1993. "The Marshall Plan: History's Most Successful Structural Adjustment Program." In *Postwar Economic Reconstruction and Lessons for the East Today*, edited by Rudiger Dornbusch, Wilhelm Nölling, and Richard Layard. Cambridge, MA: MIT Press.

Dennis, Benjamin N., and Talan B. Iscan. 2009. "Engel versus Baumol: Accounting for Structural Change Using Two Centuries of U.S. Data." *Explorations in Economic History* 46:186–202.

Destler, I. M. 1980. *Making Foreign Economic Policy*. Washington, DC: Brookings Institution.

———. 1986. *American Trade Politics*. Washington, DC: Institute for International Economics.

———. 1991. "U.S. Trade Policymaking in the Eighties." In *Politics and Economics in the Eighties*, edited by Alberto Alesina and Geoffrey Carliner. Chicago: University of Chicago Press.

———. 1995. *American Trade Politics*. 3rd ed. Washington, DC: Institute for International Economics.

———. 2005. *American Trade Politics*. 4th ed. Washington, DC: Institute for International Economics.

———, Haruhiro Fukui, and Hideo Sato. 1979. *The Textile Wrangle: Conflict in Japanese-American Relations, 1969–1971*. Ithaca, NY: Cornell University Press.

———, and C. Randall Henning. 1989. *Dollar Politics: Exchange Rate Policymaking in the United States*. Washington, DC: Institute for International Economics.

DeVault, James M. 2010a. "CAFTA, Campaign Contributions, and the Role of Special Interests." *Economics and Politics* 22:282–97.

DeVault, James M. 2010b. "Swing Voting and Fast-Track Authority." *Southern Economic Journal* 77:63–77.

———. 2013. "Political Polarization, Congressional Redistricting, and Trade Liberalization." *Public Choice* 157:207–21.

Devereaux, Charan, Robert Z. Lawrence, and Michael D. Watkins. 2006. *Case Studies in US Trade Negotiation*. Vol. 1. *Making the Rules*. Washington, DC: Institute for International Economics.

Diamond, William. 1943. *The Economic Thought of Woodrow Wilson*. Baltimore: Johns Hopkins University Press.

Dickerson, Oliver M. 1951. *The Navigation Acts and the American Revolution*. Philadelphia: University of Pennsylvania Press.

Diebold, William, Jr. 1952. *The End of the ITO*. Essays in International Finance, No. 16. Princeton, NJ: International Finance Section, Princeton University.

———. 1962. "Trade Policies since World War II." *Current History* 42:256–61.

———. 1993. "Reflections on the International Trade Organization." *Northern Illinois University Law Review* 14:335–46.

———. 1999. "A Watershed with Some Dry Sides: The Trade Expansion Act of 1962." In *John F. Kennedy and Europe*, edited by Douglas Brinkley and Richard T. Griffiths. Baton Rouge: Louisiana State University Press.

Dinopoulos, Elias, and Mordechai E. Kreinin. 1988. "Effects of the U.S.-Japan Auto VER on European Prices and on U.S. Welfare." *Review of Economics and Statistics* 70:484–91.

Dobson, John M. 1976. *Two Centuries of Tariffs: The Background and Emergence of the United States International Trade Commission*. Washington, DC: US International Trade Commission.

Dollar, Charles M. 1973. "The South and the Fordney-McCumber Tariff of 1922: A Study in Regional Politics." *Journal of Southern History* 39:45–66.

Donohue, Peter. 1993. "'Free Trade' Unions and the State: Trade Liberalization's Endorsement by the AFL-CIO, 1943–1962." *Research in Political Economy* 13:1–73.

Dornbusch, Rudiger, and Stanley Fischer. 1986. "The Open Economy: Implications for Monetary and Fiscal Policy." In *The American Business Cycle: Continuity and Change*, edited by Robert J. Gordon. Chicago: University of Chicago Press for the National Bureau of Economic Research.

Douglas, Paul H. 1972. *In the Fullness of Time*. New York: Harcourt Brace Jovanovich.

Drummond, Ian M., and Norman Hillmer. 1989. *Negotiating Freer Trade: The United Kingdom, the United States, Canada, and the Trade Agreements of 1938*. Waterloo, Canada: Wilfrid Laurier University Press.

Drury, Allen. 1963. *A Senate Journal, 1943–1945*. New York: McGraw-Hill.

Dryden, Steve. 1995. *Trade Warriors: USTR and the American Crusade for Free Trade*. New York: Oxford University Press.

Dudley, Wade G. 2003. *Splintering the Wooden Wall: The British Blockade of the United States, 1812–1815*. Annapolis, MD: Naval Institute Press.

Dupre, Daniel S. 2006. "The Panic of 1819 and the Political Economy of Sectionalism." In *The Economy of Early America: Historical Perspectives and New Directions*, edited by Cathy Matson. University Park, PA: Penn State University Press.

Dür, Andreas. 2010. *Protection for Exporters: Power and Discrimination in Trans-Atlantic Trade Relations, 1930–2010*. Ithaca, NY: Cornell University Press.

Durand, E. Dana. 1937. "Measurement of Effects of Reciprocal Trade Agreements." *Journal of the American Statistical Association* 32:50–61.

Dye, Alan, and Richard Sicotte. 2003. "The U.S. Sugar Tariff and the Cuban Revolution of 1933." Working Paper, Barnard College.

Easterlin, Richard. 1961. "Regional Income Trends, 1840–1950." In *American Economic History*, edited by Seymour E. Harris. New York: McGraw-Hill.

Eckes, Alfred E., Jr. 1995. *Opening America's Market: U.S. Foreign Trade Policy since 1776*. Chapel Hill: University of North Carolina Press.

———. 1998. "Smoot-Hawley and the Stock Market Crash, 1929–1930." *International Trade Journal* 12:65–82.

Edling, Max M. 2007. "'So Immense a Power in the Affairs of War': Alexander Hamilton and the Restoration of Public Credit." *William and Mary Quarterly* 54:287–326.

———, and Mark D. Kaplanoff. 2004. "Alexander Hamilton's Fiscal Reform: Transforming the Structure of Taxation in the Early Republic." *William and Mary Quarterly* 61:713–44.

Egnal, Marc. 2001. "The Beards Were Right: Parties in the North, 1840–1860." *Civil War History* 47:30–56.

———, and Joseph A. Ernst. 1972. "An Economic Interpretation of the American Revolution." *William and Mary Quarterly* 29:3–32.

Eichengreen, Barry. 1989. "The Political Economy of the Smoot-Hawley Tariff." In *Research in Economic History*, edited by Roger Ransom. Vol. 12. Greenwich, CT: JAI Press.

———. 1992. *Golden Fetters: The Gold Standard and the Great Depression, 1919–1939.* New York: Oxford University Press.

———. 1996. *Globalizing Capital: A History of the International Monetary System.* Princeton, NJ: Princeton University Press.

———. 2000. "From Benign Neglect to Malignant Preoccupation: U.S. Balance of Payments Policy in the 1960s." In *Economic Events, Ideas, and Policies: The 1960s and After*, edited by George L. Perry and James Tobin. Washington, DC: Brookings Institution.

———. 2006. *The European Economy since 1945: Coordinated Capitalism and Beyond.* Princeton, NJ: Princeton University Press.

———, and Douglas A. Irwin. 2010. "The Slide to Protectionism in the Great Depression: Who Succumbed and Why?" *Journal of Economic History* 70:872–98.

———, and Hans van der Ven. 1984. "U.S. Antidumping Policies: The Case of Steel." In *The Structure and Evolution of Recent U.S. Trade Policy*, edited by Robert E. Baldwin and Anne O. Krueger. Chicago: University of Chicago Press.

Eiselen, Malcolm R. 1932. *The Rise of Pennsylvania Protectionism.* Philadelphia: University of Pennsylvania Press.

Eisenhower, Dwight D. 1963. *Mandate for Change: The White House Years.* Garden City, NJ: Doubleday.

Ekelund, Robert B., and Mark Thornton. 1992. "The Union Blockade and Demoralization of the South: Relative Prices in the Confederacy." *Social Science Quarterly* 73:890–902.

Elkins, Stanley M., and Eric McKitrick. 1993. *The Age of Federalism.* New York: Oxford University Press.

Ellis, Richard E. 1987. *The Union at Risk: Jacksonian Democracy, States' Rights, and the Nullification Crisis.* New York: Oxford University Press.

Engel, Steven T., and David J. Jackson. 1998. "Wielding the Stick Instead of the Carrot: Labor PAC Punishment of Pro-NAFTA Democrats." *Political Research Quarterly* 51:813–28.

Engerman, Stanley. 1971. "The American Tariff, British Exports, and American Iron

Production. 1840–1860." In *Essays on a Mature Economy: Britain after 1840*, edited by Donald N. McCloskey. Princeton: Princeton University Press.

Estes, Todd. 2006. *The Jay Treaty Debate: Public Opinion and the Evolution of Early American Political Culture.* Amherst: University of Massachusetts Press.

Evans, John W. 1971. *The Kennedy Round in American Trade Policy.* Cambridge, MA: Harvard University Press.

Evenett, Simon J., and Michael Meier. 2008. "An Interim Assessment of the U.S. Trade Policy of 'Competitive Liberalization.'" *World Economy* 31:31–66.

Eysenbach, Mary Locke. 1976. *American Manufactured Exports, 1897–1914.* New York: Arno Press.

Farrand, Max, ed. 1911. *Record of the Federal Convention of 1787.* 3 vols. New Haven, CT: Yale University Press.

Feenstra, Robert C. 1988. "Quality Change under Trade Restraints in Japanese Autos." *Quarterly Journal of Economics* 103:131–46.

Feigenbaum, James J., and Andrew B. Hall. 2015. "How Legislators Respond to Localized Economic Shocks: Evidence from Chinese Import Competition." *Journal of Politics* 77:1012–30.

Feis, Herbert. 1966. *1933: Characters in Crisis.* Boston: Little, Brown.

Feller, Daniel. 1984. *The Public Lands in Jacksonian Politics.* Madison: University of Wisconsin Press.

Ferguson, E. James. 1961. *The Power of the Purse: A History of American Public Finance, 1776–1790.* Chapel Hill: University of North Carolina Press.

Ferleger, Ronald. 1942. *David A. Wells and the American Revenue System, 1865–1870.* New York: Roosevelt Memorial Association.

Fernandez, Racquel, and Dani Rodrik. 1991. "Resistance to Reform: Status Quo Bias in the Presence of Individual-Specific Uncertainty." *American Economic Review* 81:1146–55.

Fetter, Frank W. 1933. "Congressional Tariff Theory." *American Economic Review* 23:413–27.

———. 1942. "The Economists' Tariff Protest of 1930." *American Economic Review* 32:355–56.

Feyrer, James D., Bruce Sacerdote, and Ariel Stern. 2007. "Did the Rust Belt Become Shiny? A Study of Cities and Counties That Lost Steel and Auto Jobs in the 1980s." In *Brookings-Wharton Papers on Urban Affairs*, 41–89. Washington, DC: Brookings Institution.

Field, Alfred J., and Edward M. Graham. 1997. "Is There a Special Case for Import Protection for the Textile and Apparel Sectors Based on Labour Adjustment?" *World Economy* 20:137–57.

Findlay, Ronald, and Ronald Jones. 2001. "Input Trade and the Location of Production." *American Economic Review* 91:29–33.

Finger, J. Michael. 1993. "The Origins and Evolution of Antidumping Regulation." In *Antidumping: How It Works and Who Gets Hurt*, edited by J. Michael Finger. Ann Arbor: University of Michigan Press.

———. 2012. "Flexibilities, Rules, and Trade Remedies in the GATT/WTO System."

In *The Oxford Handbook of the World Trade Organization*, edited by Amrita Narlikar, Martin Daunton, and Robert M. Stern. New York: Oxford University Press.

———, H. Keith Hall, and Douglas R. Nelson. 1982. "The Political Economy of Administered Protection." *American Economic Review* 72:452–66.

———, and Anne Harrison. 1996. "The MFA Paradox: More Protection and More Trade?" In Krueger 1996.

———, Merlinda D. Ingco, and Ulrich Reincke, 1996. *The Uruguay Round: Statistics on Tariff Concessions Given and Received*. Washington, DC: World Bank.

Finkelman, Paul. 1987. "Slavery and the Constitutional Convention: Making a Covenant with Death." In *Beyond Confederation: Origins of the Constitution and American National Identity*, edited by Richard Beeman, Stephen Botein, and Edward C. Carter II. Chapel Hill: University of North Carolina Press.

Fishback, Price. 2013. "U.S. Monetary and Fiscal Policies." In *The Great Depression of the 1930s: Lessons for Today*, edited by Nicholas Crafts and Peter Fearon. New York: Oxford University Press.

Flaherty, Jane. 2001. "Incidental Protectionism: An Examination of the Morrill Tariff." *Essays in Economic and Business History* 19:103–17.

Fleischacker, Samuel. 2002. "Adam Smith's Reception Among the American Founders, 1776–1790." *William and Mary Quarterly* 59:897–924.

Foer, Franklin. 2002. "Fabric Softener." *New Republic*, March 4/11, 19–21.

Fossedal, Gregory A. 1993. *Our Finest Hour: Will Clayton, the Marshall Plan, and the Triumph of Democracy*. Stanford, CA: Hoover Institution Press.

Ford, Gerald R. 1979. *A Time to Heal*. New York: Harper & Row.

Ford, Lacy K. 1988. *Origins of Southern Radicalism: The South Carolina Upcountry, 1800–1860*. New York: Oxford University Press.

Fordham, Benjamin O. 1998a. "Economic Interests, Party, and Ideology in Early Cold War Era U.S. Foreign Policy." *International Organization* 52:359–95.

———. 1998b. *Building the Cold War Consensus: The Political Economy of U.S. National Security Policy, 1949–51*. Ann Arbor: University of Michigan Press.

———. 2007. "Revisionism Reconsidered: Exports and American Intervention in World War I." *International Organization* 61:277–310.

Forsberg, Aaron. 1998. "The Politics of GATT Expansion: Japanese Accession and the Domestic Political Context in Japan and the United States, 1948–1955." *Business and Economic History* 27:185–95.

Forsythe, Dall W. 1977. *Taxation and Political Change in the Young Nation, 1781–1833*. New York: Columbia University Press.

Foster, H. Schuyler. 1983. *Activism Replaces Isolationism: U.S. Public Attitudes, 1940–1975*. Washington, DC: Foxhall Press.

Frank, Charles R., Jr. 1977. *Foreign Trade and Domestic Aid*. Washington, DC: Brookings Institution.

Frankel, Jeffrey A. 1982. "The 1807–1809 Embargo against Great Britain." *Journal of Economic History* 42:291–308.

Freehling, William W. 1965. *Prelude to Civil War: The Nullification Controversy in South Carolina, 1816–1836*. New York: Harper & Row.

Freeman, Richard B., and Lawrence Katz. 1991. "Industrial Wage and Employment

Determination in an Open Economy." In *Immigration, Trade, and the Labor Market*, edited by John Abowd. Chicago: University of Chicago Press.

———, and Morris M. Kleiner. 2005. "The Last American Shoe Manufacturers: Decreasing Productivity and Increasing Profits in the Shift from Piece Rates to Continuous Flow Production." *Industrial Relations* 44:307–30.

Frieden, Jeffry A. 1997. "Monetary Populism in Nineteenth Century America: An Open Economy Interpretation." *Journal of Economic History* 57:367–95.

Friedman, Milton, and Anna J. Schwartz. 1963. *A Monetary History of the United States*. Princeton, NJ: Princeton University Press.

Fry, Joseph A. 2002. *Dixie Looks Abroad: The South and United States Foreign Relations, 1789–1973*. Baton Rouge: Louisiana State University Press.

Fukoa, Mitsuhiro. 1990. "Liberalization of Japan's Foreign Exchange Controls and Structural Changes in the Balance of Payments." *Bank of Japan Monetary and Economic Studies* 8:101–53.

Gallaway, Michael P., Bruce A. Blonigen, and Joseph E. Flynn. 1999. "Welfare Costs of US Antidumping and Countervailing Duty Laws," *Journal of International Economics* 49:211–44.

Gallatin, Albert. 1879. *The Writings of Albert Gallatin*. Edited by Henry Adams. Philadelphia: Lippincott.

Gallman, Robert E. 1960. "Commodity Output, 1839–1899." In *Trends in the American Economy in the Nineteenth Century*. Vol. 24. *Studies in Income and Wealth*. Princeton, NJ: Princeton University Press for the National Bureau of Economic Research.

———. 2000. "Economic Growth and Structural Change in the Long Nineteenth Century." In *The Cambridge Economic History of the United States*, edited by Stanley L. Engerman and Robert E. Gallman. Vol. 2. *The Long Nineteenth Century*. New York: Cambridge University Press.

Gallup, George. 1972. *The Gallup Poll: Public Opinion, 1935–1971*. 3 vols. New York: Random House.

———. 1994. *The Gallup Poll: Public Opinion in 1993*. Wilmington, DE: Scholarly Resources.

Gardner, Bruce L. 1996. "The Political Economy of U.S. Export Subsidies for Wheat." In Krueger 1996.

Gardner, Richard N. 1956. *Sterling-Dollar Diplomacy: Anglo-American Collaboration in the Reconstruction of Multilateral Trade*. Oxford: Clarendon Press.

General Agreement on Tariffs and Trade. 1949. *The Attack on Trade Barriers: A Progress Report on the Operation of the GATT, January 1948–August 1949*. Geneva: GATT.

Gersting, John Marshall. 1932. *The Flexible Provisions in the United States Tariff, 1922–1930*. Philadelphia: University of Pennsylvania Press.

Giesecke, Albert A. 1910. *American Commercial Legislation before 1789*. Philadelphia: University of Pennsylvania Press.

Gilbert, John, and Reza Oladi. 2012. "Net Campaign Contributions, Agricultural Interests, and Votes on Liberalizing Trade with China." *Public Choice* 150:745–69.

Gilji, Paul A. 2013. *Free Trade and Sailors' Rights in the War of 1812.* New York: Cambridge University Press.

Gilligan, Michael. 1997. *Empowering Exporters: Reciprocity, Delegation, and Collective Action in American Trade Policy.* Ann Arbor: University of Michigan Press.

Goldin, Claudia. 1973. "The Economics of Emancipation." *Journal of Economic History* 33:66–85.

———. 1994. The Political Economy of Immigration Restriction in the United States, 1890 to 1921." In *The Regulated Economy: A Historical Approach to Political Economy,* edited by Claudia Goldin and Gary D. Libecap. Chicago: University of Chicago Press.

———, and Frank D. Lewis. 1975. "The Economic Cost of the American Civil War: Estimates and Implications." *Journal of Economic History* 35:299–322.

———. 1980. "The Role of Exports in American Economic Growth during the Napoleonic Wars, 1793–1807." *Explorations in Economic History* 17:6–25.

Goldstein, Judith L., Douglas Rivers, and Michael Tomz. 2007. "Institutions in International Relations: Understanding the Effects of the GATT and WTO on World Trade." *International Organization* 61:37–67.

———. 1993. *Ideas, Interests, and American Trade Policy.* Ithaca: Cornell University Press.

Goldstein, Morris, and Nicholas R. Lardy. 2008. *Debating China's Exchange Rate Policy.* Washington, DC: Peterson Institute for International Economics.

Goldstone, Lawrence. 2005. *Dark Bargain: Slavery, Profits, and the Struggle for the Constitution.* New York: Walker.

Goodwin, Doris Kearns. 2013. *The Bully Pulpit: Theodore Roosevelt, William Howard Taft, and the Golden Age of Journalism.* New York: Simon and Schuster.

Goodykoontz, Colin B. 1947. "Edward P. Costigan and the Tariff Commission, 1917–1928." *Pacific Historical Review* 16:410–19.

Gordon, Margaret S. 1941. *Barriers to World Trade.* New York: Macmillan.

Gordon, Robert J., ed. 1986. *American Business Cycle: Continuity and Change.* Chicago: University of Chicago Press for the National Bureau of Economic Research.

Gotlieb, Allan. 2006. *The Washington Diaries, 1981–89.* Toronto: McClelland & Stewart.

Gould, Lewis L. 1978. *Reform and Regulation: American Politics, 1900–1916.* New York: John Wiley & Sons, 1978.

Gowa, Joanne S. 1983. *Closing the Gold Window: Domestic Politics and the End of Bretton Woods.* Ithaca, NY: Cornell University Press.

Grady, Henry F. 1936. "The New Trade Policy of the United States." *Foreign Affairs* 14:283–96.

———. 2009. *The Memoirs of Ambassador Henry F. Grady: From the Great War to the Cold War,* edited by John T. McNay. Columbia: University of Missouri Press.

Graham, Otis L. 1992. *Losing Time: The Industrial Policy Debate.* Cambridge, MA: Harvard University Press.

Graham, Thomas R. 1983. "Global Trade: War and Peace." *Foreign Policy,* 50:124–37.

Grayson, George W. 1995. *The North American Free Trade Agreement: Regional Community and the New World Order*. Lanham, MD: University Press of America.

Greaney, Theresa M. 2001. "Assessing the Impacts of U.S.-Japan Bilateral Trade Agreements, 1980–85." *World Economy* 127–57.

Greenbaum, Fred. 1971. *Fighting Progressive: A Biography of Edward P. Costigan*. Washington, DC: Public Affairs Press.

Grinols, Earl L. 1989. "Procedural Protectionism: The American Trade Bill and the New Interventionist Mode." *Weltwirtschaftliches Archiv* 125:501–21.

Grossman, Gene M. 1986. "Imports as a Cause of Injury: The Case of the U.S. Steel Industry." *Journal of International Economics* 21:201–23.

———. 1987. "The Employment and Wage Effects of Import Competition in the United States." *Journal of International Economic Integration* 2:1–23.

———, and Elhanan Helpman. 1994. "Protection for Sale." *American Economic Review* 84:833–50.

———, and Elhanan Helpman. 2005. "A Protectionist Bias in Majoritarian Politics." *Quarterly Journal of Economics* 120:1239–82.

Guisinger, Alexandra. 2009. "Determining Trade Policy: Do Voters Hold Politicians Accountable?" *International Organization* 63:533–57.

Gunderson, Gerald A. 1974. "The Origins of the American Civil War." *Journal of Economic History* 34:915–50.

Gwande, Kishore, and Pravin Krishna. 2003. "The Political Economy of Trade Policy: Empirical Approaches." In *Handbook of International Trade*, edited by E. Kwan Choi and James Harrigan. Oxford: Basil Blackwell.

Ha, Songho. 2015. *The Rise and Fall of the American System: Nationalism and the Development of the Economy, 1790–1837*. New York: Routledge.

Haggard, Stephan. 1988. "The Institutional Foundations of Hegemony: Explaining the Reciprocal Trade Agreements Act of 1934." *International Organization* 42:91–119.

Haines, Michael R. 2000. "The Population of the United States, 1790–1920." In *The Cambridge Economic History of the United States*, Vol. 2. *The Long Nineteenth Century*, edited by Stanley L. Engerman and Robert E. Gallman. New York: Cambridge University Press.

Hall, Ray Ovid. 1933. "Smoot-Hawley Tariff Caused Only About $165,000,000 of 1931 Import Shrinkage." *The Annalist* (September 29): 403–404.

Han, Hahrie, and David W. Brady. 2007. "A Delayed Return to Historical Norms: Congressional Party Polarization after the Second World War." *British Journal of Political Science* 37:505–31.

Handley, Kyle, and Nuno Limão. 2015. "Policy Uncertainty, Trade and Welfare: Theory and Evidence for China and the U.S." *American Economic Review*, forthcoming.

Hansen, John Mark. 1991. *Gaining Access: Congress and the Farm Lobby, 1919–1981*. Chicago: University of Chicago Press.

Harley, C. Knick. 1992. "The Antebellum American Tariff: Food Exports and Manufacturing." *Explorations in Economic History* 29:375–400.

Harper, Lawrence A. 1939. "The Effects of the Navigation Acts on the Thirteen Colonies." In *The Era of the American Revolution*, edited by Richard B. Morris. New York: Columbia University Press.

Harrigan, James, and Geoffrey Barrows. 2009. "Testing the Theory of Trade Policy: Evidence from the Abrupt End of the Multifiber Arrangement." *Review of Economics and Statistics* 91:282–94.

Harris Survey. 1975. *Yearbook of Public Opinion in 1971.* New York: Lewis Harris & Associates.

Harris, John F. 2005. *The Survivor: Bill Clinton in the White House.* New York: Random House.

Harrison, Robert. 2004. *Congress, Progressive Reform, and the New American State.* New York: Cambridge University Press.

Harrod, Roy. 1951. *The Life of John Maynard Keynes.* New York: Harcourt Brace.

Hart, Michael. 1989. "Almost but Not Quite: The 1947–48 Bilateral Canada-U.S. Negotiations." *American Review of Canadian Studies* 6:25–58.

———. 1994. *Decision at Midnight: Inside the CanadaUS Free-Trade Negotiations-.* Vancouver: University of British Columbia Press.

———. 2002. *A Trading Nation: Canadian Trade Policy from Colonialism to Globalization.* Vancouver: University of British Columbia Press.

Hartmann, Susan M. 1971. *Truman and the 80th Congress.* Columbia: University of Missouri Press.

Hatton, Timothy J., and Jeffrey G. Williamson. 1998. *The Age of Mass Migration: An Economic Analysis.* New York: Oxford University Press.

Hawke, G. R. 1975. "The United States Tariff and Industrial Production in the Late Nineteenth Century." *Economic History Review* 28:84–99.

Hawkins, Harry C. 1944. "Administration of the Trade Agreements Act." *Wisconsin Law Review* 1:3–14.

———, and Janet L. Norwood. 1963. "The Legislative Basis of United States Commercial Policy." In *Studies in United States Commercial Policy*, edited by William B. Kelley Jr. Chapel Hill: University of North Carolina Press.

Hayford, Marc, and Carl A. Pasurka. 1992. "The Political Economy of the Fordney-McCumber and Smoot-Hawley Tariff Acts." *Explorations in Economic History*, 29:30–50.

Head, Keith. 1994. "Infant Industry Protection in the Steel Rail Industry." *Journal of International Economics* 37:141–65.

Healy, David. 2001. *James G. Blaine and Latin America.* Columbia: University of Missouri Press.

Heaton, Herbert. 1941. "Non-Importation, 1806–1812." *Journal of Economic History* 1:178–98.

Heckelman, Jac C., and Keith L. Dougherty. 2007. "An Economic Interpretation of the Constitutional Convention of 1787 Revisited." *Journal of Economic History* 67:829–48.

Henderson, William O. 1983. *Friedrich List: Economist and Visionary, 1789–1846.* London: F. Cass.

Hendrickson, Scott A., and Jason M. Roberts. 2016. "Short-Term Goals and Long-Term Effects: The Mongrel Tariff and the Creation of the Special Rule in the U.S. House." *Journal of Policy History* 28:318–41.

Henn, Christian, and Brad MacDonald. 2014. "Crisis Protectionism: The Observed Impact." *IMF Economic Review* 64:77–118.

Herring, George C. 2008. *From Colony to Superpower: U.S. Foreign Relations since 1776*. New York: Oxford University Press.

Hetherington, Bruce W., and Peter J. Kower. 2009. "A Reexamination of Lebergott's Paradox about Blockade Running during the American Civil War." *Journal of Economic History* 69:528–32.

Hickey, Donald R. 1981. "American Trade Restrictions during the War of 1812." *Journal of American History* 68:517–38.

———. 1987. "The Monroe-Pinkney Treaty of 1806: A Reappraisal." *William and Mary Quarterly* 44:65–88.

———. 1989. *The War of 1812: A Forgotten Conflict*. Urbana: University of Illinois Press.

Hicks, Michael J., and Srikant Devaraj. 2015. "The Myths and Realities of Manufacturing in America." Muncie, IN: Center for Business and Economic Research, Ball State University.

Hirschman, Charles, and Elizabeth Mogford. 2009. "Immigration and the American Industrial Revolution from 1880 to 1920." *Social Science Research* 38:897–920.

Hiscox, Michael. 1999. "The Magic Bullet? The RTAA, Institutional Reform, and Trade Liberalization." *International Organization* 53:669–68.

———. 2002. *International Trade and Political Conflict: Commerce, Coalitions, and Mobility*. Princeton, NJ: Princeton University Press.

Hoff, Joan. 1971. *American Business and Foreign Policy, 1920–1933*. Lexington: University Press of Kentucky.

Hofstadter, Richard. 1938. "The Tariff Issue on the Eve of the Civil War." *American Historical Review* 44:50–55.

Hogan, William T. 1971. *Economic History of the Iron and Steel Industry in the United States*. Lexington, MA: D.C. Heath.

Holcombe, Randall. 1999. "Veterans Interests and the Transition to Government Growth: 1870–1915." *Public Choice* 99:311–26.

———, and Donald Lacombe. 1998. "Interests versus Ideology in the Ratification of the 16th and 17th Amendments." *Economics and Politics* 10:143–59.

Holian, D., T. Krebs, and M. Walsh. 1997. "Constituency Opinion, Ross Perot, and Roll-Call Behavior in the U.S. House: The Case of the NAFTA." *Legislative Studies Quarterly* 22:169–92.

Holmes, Thomas J., and John J. Stevens. 2004. "Spatial Distribution of Economic Activities in North America." In *Handbook on Urban and Regional Economics*, Vol. 4, edited by J. V. Henderson and J. F. Thisse. Amsterdam: North Holland.

Holt, Laurence James. 1967. *Congressional Insurgents and the Party System, 1909–1916*. Cambridge, MA: Harvard University Press.

Holton, Woody. 1999. *Forced Founders: Indians, Debtors, Slaves, and the Making of the American Revolution in Virginia*. Chapel Hill: University of North Carolina Press.

Hoogenboom, Ari Arthur. 1995. *Rutherford B. Hayes: Warrior and President*. Lawrence: University Press of Kansas.

Hook, Sidney. 1987. *Out of Step.* New York: Harper & Row.

Hoover, Herbert. 1951–52. *Memoirs.* 2 vols. New York: Macmillan.

Houston, David F. 1926. *Eight Years with Wilson's Cabinet, 1913 to 1920.* Garden City, NY: Doubleday, Page.

Howell, Thomas R., William A. Noellert, Jesse G. Kreier, and Alan W. Wolff. 1988. *Steel and the State: Government Intervention and Steel's Structural Crisis.* Boulder, CO: Westview Press.

Howson, Susan, and Donald Moggridge, eds. 1990. *The Wartime Diaries of Lionel Robbins and James Meade, 1943–45.* London: Macmillan.

Hufbauer, Gary C. 1983. "Subsidy Issues after the Tokyo Round." In *Trade Policy in the 1980s,* edited by William R. Cline. Washington, DC: Institute for International Economics.

———, Diane T. Berliner, and Kimberly Ann Elliott. 1986. *Trade Protection in the United States: Thirty-One Case Studies.* Washington, DC: Institute for International Economics.

———, and Kimberly Ann Elliott. 1994. *Measuring the Costs of Protection in the United States.* Washington, DC: Institute for International Economics.

———, and Ben Goodrich. 2003. "Steel Policy: The Good, the Bad, and the Ugly." International Economics Policy Briefs, 03–1. Washington, DC: Institute for International Economics.

———, and Sean Lowry. 2012. "U.S. Tire Tariffs: Saving Few Jobs at High Cost." Peterson Institute for International Economics Policy Brief, No. PB12–9, April.

———, and Daniel H. Rosen. 2000. "America's Access to China's Market: The Congressional Vote on PNTR." International Economics Policy Briefs, 00–3. Washington, DC: Institute for International Economics.

———, and Jeffrey J. Schott. 1993. *NAFTA: An Assessment.* Washington, DC: Institute for International Economics.

———. 2005. *NAFTA Revisited.* Washington, DC: Peterson Institute for International Economics.

Hull, Cordell. 1937. *Economic Barriers to Peace.* New York: Woodrow Wilson Foundation.

———. 1948. *Memoirs.* 2 vols. New York: Macmillan.

Hussain, A. Imtiaz. 1993. *Politics of Compensation: Truman, the Wool Bill of 1947, and the Shaping of Postwar U.S. Trade Policy.* New York: Garland.

Huston, James L. 1983. "A Political Response to Industrialism: The Republican Embrace of Protectionist Labor Doctrines." *Journal of American History* 70:35–57.

Huston, James L. 1987. *Panic of 1857 and Coming of the Civil War.* Baton Rouge: Louisiana State University Press.

———. 1994. "Virtue Besieged: Virtue, Equality, and the General Welfare in the Tariff Debates of the 1820s." *Journal of the Early Republic* 14:523–47.

———. 2003. *Calculating the Value of the Union: Slavery, Property Rights, and the Economic Origins of the Civil War.* Chapel Hill: University of North Carolina Press.

Hyde, Charles K. 1991. "Iron and Steel Technologies Moving Between Europe and the United States before 1914." In *International Technology Transfer: Europe, Japan, USA, 1700–1914,* edited by David J. Jeremy. Aldershot: Edward Elgar.

Ickes, Harold. 1953–54. *The Secret Diary of Harold L. Ickes.* 3 vols. New York: Simon & Schuster.

Ikenberry, G. John. 1992. "World Economy Restored: Expert Consensus and the Anglo-American Postwar Settlement." *International Organization* 46:289–321.

Ingco, Merlinda D. 1996. "Tariffication in the Uruguay Round: How Much Liberalization?" *World Economy* 19:425–46.

Irwin, Douglas A. 1994. *Managed Trade: The Case against Import Targets.* Washington, DC: AEI Press.

———. 1996a. "Trade Politics and the Semiconductor Industry." In Krueger 1996.

———. 1996b. *Against the Tide: An Intellectual History of Free Trade.* Princeton, NJ: Princeton University Press.

———. 1998a. "Changes in U.S. Tariffs: The Role of Import Prices and Commercial Policies." *American Economic Review* 88:1015–26.

———. 1998b. "Higher Tariffs, Lower Revenues? Analyzing the Fiscal Aspects of the 'Great Tariff Debate of 1888,'" *Journal of Economic History* 58:59–72.

———. 2000a. "Could the U.S. Iron Industry Have Survived Free Trade After the Civil War?" *Explorations in Economic History* 37:278–99.

———. 2000b. "Did Late Nineteenth Century U.S. Tariffs Promote Infant Industries? Evidence from the Tinplate Industry." *Journal of Economic History* 60:335–60.

———. 2001. "Tariffs and Growth in Late Nineteenth Century America." *World Economy* 24:15–30.

———. 2002. "Ohlin versus Stolper-Samuelson?" In *Bertil Ohlin: A Centennial Celebration, 1899–1999,* edited by Ronald Findlay, Lars Jonung, and Mats Lundahl. Cambridge, MA: MIT Press.

———. 2003a. "Explaining America's Surge in Manufactured Exports, 1880–1913." *Review of Economics and Statistics* 85:364–76.

———. 2003b. "New Estimates of the Average Tariff of the United States, 1790–1820." *Journal of Economic History* 63:506–13.

———. 2003c. "The Optimal Tax on Antebellum Cotton Exports." *Journal of International Economics* 60:275–91.

———. 2004. "The Aftermath of Hamilton's Report on Manufactures," *Journal of Economic History* 64:800–821.

———. 2005a. "The Rise of U.S. Antidumping Activity in Historical Perspective." *World Economy* 28:651–68.

———. 2005b. "The Welfare Costs of Autarky: Evidence from the Jeffersonian Embargo, 1807–1809." *Review of International Economics* 13:631–45.

———. 2007. "Tariff Incidence in America's Gilded Age." *Journal of Economic History* 67:582–607.

———. 2008. "Antebellum Tariff Politics: Regional Coalitions and Shifting Economic Interests." *Journal of Law and Economics* 51:715–42.

———. 2010. "Trade Restrictiveness and Deadweight Losses from U.S. Tariffs." *American Economic Journal: Economic Policy* 2:111–33.

———. 2011a. "Revenue or Reciprocity: Founding Feuds over Early U.S. Trade Policy." In *Founding Choices: American Economic Policy in the 1790s,* edited by Douglas A. Irwin and Richard Sylla. Chicago: University of Chicago Press.

———. 2011b. *Peddling Protectionism: Smoot-Hawley and the Great Depression.* Princeton, NJ: Princeton University Press.

———. 2012a. "The Nixon Shock after Forty Years: The Import Surcharge Revisited." *World Trade Review* 12:29–56.

———. 2012b. *Trade Policy Disaster: Lessons from the 1930s.* Cambridge, MA: MIT Press.

———. 2012–13. "The French Gold Sink and the Great Deflation of 1929-32." *Cato Papers on Public Policy* 2:141.

———. 2014. "Tariff Incidence: Evidence from U.S. Sugar Duties, 1890–1930." NBER Working Paper, No. 20635.

———. 2015. *Free Trade under Fire.* 4th ed. Princeton, NJ: Princeton University Press.

———, and Joseph H. Davis. 2003. "Trade Disruptions and America's Early Industrialization." NBER Working Paper, No. 9944.

———, and Randall S. Kroszner. 1996. "Log-Rolling and Economic Interests in the Passage of the Smoot-Hawley Tariff." *Carnegie-Rochester Conference Series on Public Policy* 45:173–200.

———, and Randall S. Kroszner. 1999. "Interests, Institutions, and Ideology in Securing Policy Change: The Republican Conversion to Trade Liberalization after Smoot-Hawley." *Journal of Law and Economics* 42:643–73.

———, Petros C. Mavroidis, and Alan O. Sykes. 2008. *The Genesis of the GATT.* New York: Cambridge University Press.

———, and Peter Temin. 2001. "The Antebellum Tariff on Cotton Textiles Revisited." *Journal of Economic History* 61:777–98.

Israel, Fred L. 1963. *Nevada's Key Pittman.* Lincoln: University of Nebraska Press.

Jackson, David J., and Steven T. Engel. 2003. "Friends Don't Let Friends Vote for Free Trade: The Dynamics of the Labor PAC Punishment Strategy over PNTR." *Political Research Quarterly* 56:441–48.

Jackson, John H. 1978. "The Crumbling Institutions of the Liberal Trade System." *Journal of World Trade Law* 12:93–106.

———. 1990. *Restructuring the GATT System.* New York: Council on Foreign Relations.

Jacobson, Louis S. 1978. "Earnings Losses of Workers Displaced from Manufacturing Industries." In *The Impact of International Trade and Investment on Employment.* Washington, DC: GPO.

James, Harold. 1996. *International Monetary Cooperation since Bretton Woods.* New York: Oxford University Press.

James, John A. 1984. "Public Debt Management Policy and Nineteenth Century American Economic Growth." *Explorations in Economic History* 21.192-217.

James, Scott C., and David A. Lake. 1989. "The Second Face of Hegemony: Britain's Repeal of the Corn Laws and the American Walker Tariff of 1846." *International Organization* 43:1–29.

Jaremski, Matthew. 2014. "National Banking's Role in U.S. Industrialization." *Journal of Economic History* 74:109–40.

Jefferson, Thomas. 1955 [1785]. *Notes on the State of Virginia.* Edited by William Peden. Chapel Hill: University of North Carolina Press.

Jennings, Brendan. 2010. "The Rust Belt of the United States of America." Map republished in "Where Is the Rust Belt?" *Belt Magazine*, 9 December 2013. Retrieved from http://beltmag.com/mapping-rust-belt/.

Jennings, Walter W. 1921. *The American Embargo, 1807–1809*. Iowa City: Iowa State University Press.

Jensen, Merrill. 1969. "The American Revolution and American Agriculture." *Agricultural History* 43:107–24.

Jeremy, David J. 1981. *Transatlantic Industrial Revolution: The Diffusion of Textile Technologies between Britain and America, 1790–1830s*. Cambridge, MA: MIT Press.

Johnson, Donald B., and Kirk H. Porter. 1973. *National Party Platforms, 1840–1972*. 5th ed. Urbana: University of Illinois Press.

Johnson, Harry G. 1960. "The Cost of Protection and the Scientific Tariff." *Journal of Political Economy* 68:327–45.

Johnson, Lyndon B. 1971. *The Vantage Point: Perspectives on the Presidency, 1963–69*. New York: Holt, Rinehart, and Winston.

Jones, Joseph M. 1955. *The Fifteen Weeks*. New York: Viking.

———. 1934. *Tariff Retaliation: Repercussions of the Hawley-Smoot Bill*. Philadelphia: University of Pennsylvania Press.

Jones, Kent A. 1994. *Export Restraint and the New Protectionism: the Political Economy of Discriminatory Trade Restrictions*. Ann Arbor: University of Michigan Press.

Jones, Ronald W. 1971. "A Three-Factor Model in Theory, Trade and History." In *Trade, Balance of Payments and Growth*, edited by Jagdish Bhagwati, Ronald Jones, Robert Mundell, and Jaroslav Vanek. Amsterdam: North-Holland.

Joseph, Richard J. 2004. *The Origins of the American Income Tax: The Revenue Act of 1894 and Its Aftermath*. Syracuse, NY: Syracuse University Press.

Josephson, Matthew. 1938. *The Politicos*. New York: Harcourt Brace.

Joyner, Fred B. 1939. *David Ames Wells: Champion of Free Trade*. Cedar Rapids, IA: Torch Press.

Kahane, Leo H. 1996. "Congressional Voting Patterns on NAFTA: An Empirical Analysis." *American Journal of Economics and Sociology* 55:395–409.

Kahn, Matthew. 1999. "The Silver Lining of Rust Belt Manufacturing Decline." *Journal of Urban Economics* 46:360–76.

Kane, Nancy F. 1988. *Textiles in Transition: Technology, Wages, and Industry Relocation in the U.S. Textile Industry, 1880–1930*. New York: Greenwood Press.

Kaplan, Lawrence S. 2015. *The Conversion of Senator Arthur H. Vandenberg*. Lexington: University Press of Kentucky.

Karol, David. 2000. "Divided Government and U.S. Trade Policy: Much Ado about Nothing?" *International Organization* 54:825–44.

Kaufman, Burton I. 1982. *Trade and Aid: Eisenhower's Foreign Economic Policy, 1953–1961*. Baltimore: Johns Hopkins University Press.

Kee, Hiau Looi, Cristina Neagu, and Alessandro Nicita. 2013. "Is Protectionism on the Rise? Assessing National Trade Policies during the Crisis of 2008." *Review of Economics and Statistics* 95:342–46.

Keech, William R., and Kyoungsan Pak. 1995. "Partisanship, Institutions, and Change in American Trade Politics." *Journal of Politics* 57:1130–42.

Keesing, Donald B., and Martin Wolf. 1980. *Textile Quotas against Developing Countries*. London: Trade Policy Research Centre.

Kelley, Darwin N. 1940. "The McNary-Haugen Bills, 1924–1928: An Attempt to Make the Tariff Effective for Farm Products." *Agricultural History* 14:170–80.

Kelley, William B., Jr. 1963. "Antecedents of Present Commercial Policy, 1922–1934." In *Studies in United States Commercial Policy*, edited by William B. Kelley Jr. Chapel Hill: University of North Carolina Press.

Kendrick, John W. 1961. *Productivity Trends in the United States*. Princeton, NJ: Princeton University Press.

Kenkel, Joseph F. 1983. *Progressives and Protection: The Search for a Tariff Policy, 1866–1936*. New York: University Press of America.

Kennon, Donald R., and Rebecca M. Rogers. 1989. *The Committee on Ways and Means: A Bicentennial History 1789–1989*. Washington, DC: Government Printing Office.

Ketcham, Ralph. 1971. *James Madison: A Biography*. New York: Macmillan.

Keynes, John Maynard. 1979. *The Collected Writings of John Maynard Keynes*, edited by Donald Moggridge. Vol. 24. *Activities 1944–1946, The Transition to Peace*. London: Macmillan; Cambridge University Press, for the Royal Economic Society.

———. 1980. *The Collected Writings of John Maynard Keynes*, edited by Donald Moggridge. Vol. 26, *Activities 1941–1946, Shaping the Post-War World: Bretton Woods and Reparations*. London: Macmillan; Cambridge University Press, for the Royal Economic Society.

Killick, John. 1997. *The United States and European Reconstruction, 1945–1960*. Edinburgh: Keele University Press.

Kim, Sukkoo. 1995. "Expansion of Markets and the Geographic Distribution of Economic Activities: The Trends in U.S. Regional Manufacturing Structure, 1860–1987." *Quarterly Journal of Economics* 110:881–908.

Kindleberger, Charles P. 1986. *The World in Depression, 1929–1939*. Revised edition. Berkeley: University of California Press.

———. 1989. "Commercial Policy between the Wars." In *Cambridge Economic History of Europe from the Decline of the Roman Empire*. Vol. 8. Edited by Peter Mathias and Sidney Pollard. Cambridge: Cambridge University Press.

Kissinger, Henry. 1979. *White House Years*. Boston: Little, Brown.

Kitano, Taiju, and Hiroshi Ohashi. 2009. "Did US Safeguards Resuscitate Harley-Davidson in the 1980s?" *Journal of International Economics* 79:186–97.

Kleppner, Paul. 1979. *The Third Electoral System, 1853–1892: Parties, Voters, and Political Cultures*. Chapel Hill: University of North Carolina Press.

Kletzer, Lori G. 1998. "Trade and Job Displacement in U.S. Manufacturing: 1979–1991." In *Imports, Exports, and the American Worker*, edited by Susan Collins. Washington, DC: Brookings Institution.

———. 2002. *Imports, Exports, and Jobs: What Does Trade Mean for Employment and Job Loss?* Kalamazoo: W. E. Upjohn Institute for Employment Research.

Kock, Karin. 1969. *International Trade Policy and the GATT, 1947–1967*. Stockholm: Almquist and Wiksell.

Koopman, Robert, Zhi Wang, and Shang-jin Wei. 2012. "Estimating Domestic Content in Exports when Processing Trade Is Pervasive." *Journal of Development Economics* 99:178–89.

Kottman, Richard N. 1968. *Reciprocity and the North American Triangle, 1932–1938*. Ithaca, NY: Cornell University Press.

———. 1975. "Herbert Hoover and the Smoot-Hawley Tariff: Canada, A Case Study." *Journal of American History* 62:609–35.

Koyama, Kumiko. 2009. "The Passage of the Smoot-Hawley Tariff Act: Why Did the President Sign the Bill?" *Journal of Policy History* 21:163–86.

Kravis, Irving. 1972. "The Role of Exports in Nineteenth Century United States Economic Growth." *Economic Development and Cultural Change* 20:387–405.

Kreinin, Mordechai E. 1961. "The Effects of Tariff Changes on the Prices and Volumes of Imports." *American Economic Review* 51:310–24.

Krueger, Anne O. 1980. "Protectionist Pressures, Imports and Employment in the United States." *Scandinavian Journal of Economics* 82:133–46.

———. 1990a. "Asymmetries in Policy between Exportables and Import-competing Goods." In *The Political Economy of Trade Policy*, edited by Ronald Jones and Anne Krueger. Cambridge: Basil Blackwell.

———. 1990b. "The Political Economy of Controls: American Sugar." In *Public Policy and Economic Development: Essays in Honour of Ian Little*, edited by Maurice Scott and Deepak Lal. New York: Oxford University Press.

———, ed. 1996. *The Political Economy of American Trade Policy*. Chicago: University of Chicago Press.

Krugman, Paul, ed. 1991. *Trade with Japan: Has the Door Opened Wider?* Chicago: University of Chicago Press.

———. 1993. "The Uncomfortable Truth about NAFTA." *Foreign Affairs* 74:13–19.

———. 2008. "Trade and Wages, Reconsidered." *Brookings Papers on Economic Activity* (Spring): 103–37.

———, and Robert Z. Lawrence. 1994. "Trade, Jobs and Wages." *Scientific America* 270 (4): 22–27.

Kunkel, John. 2003. *America's Trade Policy towards Japan: Demanding Results*. New York: Routledge.

La Croix, Sumner J., and Christopher Grandy. 1997. "The Political Instability of Reciprocal Trade and the Overthrow of the Hawaiian Kingdom." *Journal of Economic History* 57:161–89.

Labaree, Benjamin W. 1964. *The Boston Tea Party*. New York: Oxford University Press.

Laird, Sam, and Alexander Yeats. 1990. "Trends in Nontariff Barriers of Developed Countries." *Weltwirtschaftliches Archiv* 126:299–325.

Lake, David A. 1988. *Power, Protection, and Free Trade: International Sources of U.S. Commercial Strategy, 1887–1939*. Ithaca, NY: Cornell University Press.

Lambert, Frank. 2005. *The Barbary Wars: American Independence in the Atlantic World*. New York: Hill & Wang.

Lamoreaux, Naomi R. 1985. *The Great Merger Movement in American Business, 1895–1904*. New York: Cambridge University Press.

Lande, Stephen L., and Craig Van Grasstek. 1986. *The Trade and Tariff Act of 1984: Trade Policy in the Reagan Administration*. Lexington, MA: D. C. Heath.

Larkin, John D. 1940. *Trade Agreements: A Study in Democratic Methods*. New York: Columbia University Press.

Larson, John L. 2001. *Internal Improvement: National Public Works and the Promise of Popular Government in the Early United States*. Chapel Hill: University of North Carolina Press.

Latimer, Jon. 2007. *1812: War with America*. Cambridge, MA: Harvard University Press.

Latner, Richard B. 1977. "The Nullification Crisis and Republican Subversion." *Journal of Southern History* 43:19–38.

Lawrence, Robert Z. 1984. *Can America Compete?* Washington, DC: Brookings Institution.

———. 2002. "International Trade Policy in the 1990s." In *American Economic Policy in the 1990s*, edited by Jeffrey Frankel and Peter Orzag. Cambridge, MA: MIT Press.

———. 2008. *Blue Collar Blues: Is Trade to Blame for Rising U.S. Income Inequality?* Washington, DC: Peterson Institute for International Economics.

———. 2014. "Adjustment Challenges for U.S. Workers." In *Bridging the Pacific: Toward Free Trade and Investment between China and the United States*, edited by C. Fred Bergsten, Gary C. Hufbauer, and Sean Miner. Washington, DC: Peterson Institute for International Economics.

League of Nations. 1932. *World Economic Survey*. Geneva: League of Nations.

———. 1933. *World Economic Survey*. Geneva: League of Nations.

———. 1942. *Commercial Policy in the Interwar Period: International Proposals and National Policies*. Geneva: League of Nations.

———. 1945. *Industrialization and Foreign Trade*. Geneva: League of Nations.

Lebergott, Stanley. 1966. "Labor Force and Employment, 1800–1960." In *Output, Employment, and Productivity in the United States after 1800*, edited by Dorothy Brady. New York: National Bureau of Economic Research.

———. 1981. "Through the Blockade: The Profitability and Extent of Cotton Smuggling, 1861–1865." *Journal of Economic History* 41:867–88

———. 1983. "Why the South Lost: Commercial Purpose in the Confederacy, 1861–1865." *Journal of American History* 70:58–74.

———. 1984. *The Americans: An Economic Record*. New York: W. W. Norton.

Leddy, James M. 1963. "United States Commercial Policy and the Domestic Farm Program." In *Studies in United States Commercial Policy*, edited by William B. Kelley Jr. Chapel Hill: University of North Carolina Press.

———, and Janet L. Norwood. 1963. "The Escape Clause and Peril Points under the Trade Agreements Program." In *Studies in United States Commercial Policy*, edited by William B. Kelley Jr. Chapel Hill: University of North Carolina Press.

Lee, Arthur M. 1957. "Henry C. Carey and the Republican Tariff." *Pennsylvania Magazine of History and Biography* 81:280–302.

Lee, Donna. 2001. "Endgame at the Kennedy Round: A Case Study of Multilateral Economic Diplomacy." *Diplomacy and Statecraft* 12:115–38.

Leffler, Melvyn P. 1979. *The Elusive Quest: America's Pursuit of European Stability and French Security, 1919–1939.* Chapel Hill: University of North Carolina Press.

———. 1984. "The American Conception of National Security and the Beginnings of the Cold War, 1945–48." *American Historical Review* 89: 346–81.

Legro, Jeffrey W. 2000. "The Transformation of Policy Ideas." *American Journal of Political Science* 44:419–32.

Leiter, Robert D. 1961. "Organized Labor and the Tariff." *Southern Economic Journal* 28:55–65.

Lemert, Benjamin F. 1933. *The Cotton Textile Industry of the Southern Appalachian Piedmont.* Chapel Hill: University of North Carolina Press.

Lerner, Abba. 1936. "The Symmetry between Import and Export Taxes." *Economica* 3:306–13.

Leuchtenburg, William E. 2009. *Herbert Hoover.* New York: Times Books.

Levinson, Marc. 2006a. *The Box: How the Shipping Container made the World Small and the World Economy Bigger.* Princeton, NJ: Princeton University Press.

———. 2006b. "Container Shipping and the Decline of New York, 1955–1975." *Business History Review* 80:49–80.

Lewis, Frank D. 1979. "Explaining the Shift of Labor from Agriculture to Industry in the United States: 1869 to 1899." *Journal of Economic History* 39:681–98.

Lewis, W. Arthur. 1957. "International Competition in Manufacturers." *American Economic Review* 47:578–87.

Lincoln, Edward J. 1990. *Japan's Unequal Trade.* Washington, DC: Brookings Institution.

———. 1999. *Troubled Times: U.S.-Japan Trade Relations in the 1990s.* Washington, DC: Brookings Institution.

Lindert, Peter D. 2014. "Private Welfare and the Welfare State." In *The Cambridge History of Capitalism.* Vol. 2. Edited by Larry Neal and Jeffrey Williamson. New York: Cambridge University Press.

Lindert, Peter H., and Jeffrey G. Williamson. 2013. "American Incomes Before and After the Revolution." *Journal of Economic History* 73:725–65.

———. 2016. "American Colonial Incomes, 1650–1774." *Economic History Review* 69:54–77.

Link, Arthur S. 1956. *Wilson: The New Freedom.* Princeton, NJ: Princeton University Press.

Lint, Gregg. 1978. "John Adams on the Drafting of the Treaty Plan of 1776." *Diplomatic History* 2:313–20.

Lipsey, Robert E. 1963. *Price and Quantity Trends in the Foreign Trade of the United States.* Princeton, NJ: Princeton University Press.

———. 2000. "U.S. Foreign Trade and the Balance of Payments." In *The Cambridge Economic History of the United States.* Vol. 2. *The Long Nineteenth Century,* edited by Stanley L. Engerman and Robert E. Gallman. New York: Cambridge University Press.

Liu, Dan, and Christopher M. Meissner. 2015. "Market Potential and the Rise of US Productivity Leadership." *Journal of International Economics* 96:72–87.

Lohmann, Susanne, and Sharyn O'Halloran. 1994. "Divided Government and U.S. Trade Policy: Theory and Evidence." *International Organization* 48:595–632.

Long, Breckinridge. 1966. *The War Diary of Breckinridge Long.* Edited by Fred L. Israel. Lincoln: University of Nebraska Press.

Low, Patrick. 1993. *Trading Free: The GATT and U.S. Trade Policy.* New York: Twentieth Century Fund Press.

Lowi, Theodore J. 1964. "American Business, Public Policy, Case-Studies, and Political Theory." *World Politics* 16:677–715.

Luthin, Reinhard H. 1944. "Abraham Lincoln and the Tariff." *American Historical Review* 49:609–29.

Lynd, Staughton, and David Waldstreicher. 2011. "Free Trade, Sovereignty, and Slavery: Toward an Economic Interpretation of American Independence." *William and Mary Quarterly* 68:597–630.

MacDonald, Stephen, and Thomas Vollrath. 2005. "The Forces Shaping World Cotton Consumption after the Multifiber Arrangement." US Department of Agriculture, Economic Research Service, CWS-05c-01, April.

MacDougall, Donald, and Rosemary Hutt. 1954. "Imperial Preference: A Quantitative Analysis." *Economic Journal* 64: 233–57.

Maclay, William. 1988. *The Diary of William Maclay and Other Notes on Senate Debates, March 4, 1789–March 3, 1791,* edited by Kenneth R. Bowling and Helen E. Veit. Baltimore: Johns Hopkins University Press.

Maddison, Angus. 1989. *The World Economy in the 20th Century.* Paris: OECD.

———. 1995. *Monitoring the World Economy, 1820–1992.* Paris: OECD.

———. 2001. *The World Economy: A Millennial Perspective.* Paris: OECD.

Madsen, Jakob B. 2001. "Trade Barriers and the Collapse of World Trade during the Great Depression." *Southern Economic Journal* 67: 848–68.

Magee, Christopher P. 2010. "Would NAFTA Have Been Approved by the House of Representatives under President Bush? Presidents, Parties, and Trade Policy." *Review of International Economics* 18:382–95.

Magee, Stephen P. 1972. "The Welfare Effects of Restrictions on U.S. Trade." *Brookings Papers on Economic Activity,* no. 3:645–707.

Magness, Phillip W. 2009. "Morrill and the Missing Industries: Strategic Lobbying Behavior and the Tariff, 1858–1861." *Journal of the Early Republic* 29:287–329.

Malin, James C. 1930. *The United States after the World War.* Boston: Ginn.

Malloy, W. M. 1910. *Treaties, Conventions, International Acts, Protocols and Agreements between the United State of America and other Powers.* 3 vols. Washington, DC: Government Printing Office.

Mannix Richard. 1979. "Gallatin, Jefferson, and the Embargo of 1808." *Diplomatic History* 3:151–72.

Marks, Frederick W. 1973. *Independence on Trial: Foreign Affairs and the Making of the Constitution.* Baton Rouge: Louisiana State University Press.

Marks, Stephen V., and Keith E. Maskus. 1993. *The Economics and Politics of World Sugar Policies.* Ann Arbor: University of Michigan Press.

Martis, Kenneth C. 1988. "Sectionalism and the United States Congress." *Political Geography Quarterly* 7:99–109.

Maskus, Keith E. 1989. "Large Costs and Small Benefits of the American Sugar Programme." *World Economy* 12:85–104.

Matusow, Allen J. 1998. *Nixon's Economy: Booms, Busts, Dollars, and Votes*. Lawrence: University Press of Kansas.

Mayer, Frederick W. 1998. *Interpreting NAFTA: The Science and Art of Political Analysis*. New York: Columbia University Press.

Mayer, Wolfgang. 1984. "Endogenous Tariff Formation." *American Economic Review* 74:970–85.

McCarty, Nolan M., Keith T. Poole, and Howard Rosenthal. 2002. "Congress and the Territorial Expansion of the United States." In *Party, Process, and Political Change in Congress: New Perspectives on the History of Congress*, edited by David Brady and Matthew D. McCubbins. Stanford, CA: Stanford University Press.

McClaren, John. 2016. "The Political Economy of Commercial Policy." In *Handbook of Commercial Policy*, edited by Kyle Bagwell and Robert W. Staiger. Vol. 1A. Amsterdam: North Holland.

McClenahan, William. 1991. "The Growth of Voluntary Export Restraints and American Foreign Economic Policy, 1956–1969." *Business and Economic History* 20:180–90.

McClendon, R. Earl. 1931. "Origin of the Two-Thirds Rule in Senate Action upon Treaties." *American Historical Review* 36:768–72.

McClure, Wallace. 1924. *A New American Commercial Policy*. New York: Columbia University Press.

McCoy, Drew R. 1974. "Republicanism and American Foreign Policy: James Madison and the Political Economy of Commercial Discrimination, 1789 to 1794." *William and Mary Quarterly* 31:633–46.

———. 1980. *The Elusive Republic: Political Economy in Jeffersonian America*. Chapel Hill: University of North Carolina Press.

McCraw, Thomas K. 1986. "Mercantilism and the Market: Antecedents of American Industrial Policy." In *The Politics of Industrial Policy*, edited by Claude E. Barfield and William A. Schambra. Washington, DC: AEI Press.

McCusker, John J. 1971. "The Current Value of English Exports, 1697 to 1800." *William and Mary Quarterly* 28:607–28.

———. 2000. "Estimating Early American Gross Domestic Product." *Historical Methods* 33:155–62.

———. 2001. *How Much Is That in Real Money? A Historical Commodity Price Index for Use as a Deflator of Money Values in the Economy of the United States*. 2nd ed. Worcester, MA: American Antiquarian Society.

———, and Russell R. Menard. 1985. *The Economy of British America, 1607–1789*. Chapel Hill: University of North Carolina Press.

McDonald, Judith A., Anthony Patrick O'Brien, and Colleen M. Callahan. 1997. "Tariff Wars: Canada's Reaction to the Smoot-Hawley Tariff." *Journal of Economic History* 57:802–26.

McGillivray, Fiona. 1997. "Party Discipline as a Determinant of the Endogenous Formation of Tariffs." *American Journal of Political Science* 41:584–607.

———. 2001. "Trading Free and Opening Markets." In *International Trade and Political
Institutions*, edited by Fiona McGillivray, Iain McLean, Robert Pahre, and Cheryl
Schonhardt-Bailey. Cheltenham: Edward Elgar.

McGuire, Robert A. 1990. "Deflation-Induced Increases in Post-Civil War US Tariffs."
Economic History Review 43:633–45.

———. 2003. *To Form a More Perfect Union: A New Economic Interpretation of the
United States Constitution*. New York: Oxford University Press.

———, and T. Norman Van Cott. 2002. "The Confederate Constitution, Tariffs, and the
Laffer Relationship." *Economic Inquiry* 40:428–38.

McKenzie, Francine. 2008. "GATT and the Cold War: Accession Debates, Institutional
Development, and the Western Alliance, 1947-1959." *Journal of Cold War Studies*
10:78–109.

———. 2010. "The GATT-EEC Collision: The Challenge of Regional Trade Blocs to the
General Agreement on Tariffs and Trade, 1950–67." *International History Review*
32:229–52.

McKenzie, Richard B., and Stephen D. Smith. 1987. "Loss of Textile and Apparel Jobs: Is
Protectionism Warranted?" *Cato Journal* 6:731–46.

Meardon, Steven. 2007. "Postbellum Protection and Commissioner Wells's Conversion
to Free Trade." *History of Political Economy* 39:571–604.

———. 2011. "Reciprocity and Henry C. Carey's Traverses on the 'Road to Perfect Freedom of Trade.'" *Journal of the History of Economic Thought* 33:307–33.

Mehrotra, Ajay K. 2004. "'More Mightly than the Waves of the Sea': Toilers, Tariffs, and
the Income Tax Movement, 1880–1913." *Labor History* 45:165–98.

Meltzer, Allan H. 1976. "Monetary and Other Explanations of the Start of the Great
Depression." *Journal of Monetary Economics* 2:455–71.

———. 2003. *A History of the Federal Reserve*. Vol. 1. *1913–1951*. Chicago: University of
Chicago Press.

———. 2009. *A History of the Federal Reserve*. Vol. 2, bk. 2. *1970–1986*. Chicago: University of Chicago Press.

Merrill, Milton R. 1990. *Reed Smoot: An Apostle in Politics*. Salt Lake City: Utah State
University.

Meyer, David R. 2003. *The Roots of American Industrialization*. Baltimore: Johns Hopkins University Press.

Mill, John Stuart. [1848] 1909. *Principles of Political Economy*. London: Longmans
Green.

Miller, James N. 2003. *Wartime Origins of Multilateralism, 1939–1945: The Impact of
the Anglo-American Trade Policy Negotiations*. PhD thesis, Emmanuel College,
University of Cambridge.

Miller, Richard G. 1975. "The Tariff of 1832: The Issue that Failed." *Filson Club History
Quarterly* 49:221–30.

Millstein, James E. 1983. "Declining in an Expanding Industry: Japanese Competition
in Color Television." In *American Industry in International Competition: Govern-

ment Policies and Corporate Strategies, edited by John Zysman and Laura Tyson. Ithaca, NY: Cornell University Press.

Milward, Alan S. 1981. "Tariffs as Constitutions." In *The International Politics of Surplus Capacity: Competition for Market Shares in the World Recession*, edited by Susan Strange and Roger Tooze. Boston: Allen & Unwin.

———. 1984. *The Reconstruction of Western Europe, 1945–1951*. Berkeley: University of California Press.

Minchin, Timothy J. 2013. *Empty Mills: The Fight against Imports and the Decline of the U.S. Textile Industry*. Lanham, MD: Rowman & Littlefield.

Miron, Jeffrey A., and Christina D. Romer. 1990. "A New Monthly Index of Industrial Production, 1884–1940." *Journal of Economic History* 50:321–37.

Mitchell, B. R. 1988. *British Historical Statistics*. New York: Cambridge University Press.

Mitchell, Daniel J. B. 1970. "Labor and the Tariff Question." *Industrial Relations* 9:268–76.

Moley, Raymond. 1939. *After Seven Years*. New York: Harper & Bros.

Monroe, Dan. 2003. *The Republican Vision of John Tyler*. College Station: Texas A&M Press.

Moore, Michael O. 1996. "The Waning Influence of Big Steel?" In Krueger 1996.

Morgan, H. Wayne. 1960. "Western Silver and the Tariff of 1890." *New Mexico Historical Review* 35:118–28.

———. 1965. "William McKinley and the Tariff." *Ohio History Journal* 74:215–31.

———. 1969. *From Hayes to McKinley: National Party Politics, 1877–1896*. Syracuse, NY: Syracuse University Press.

———. 2003. *William McKinley and His America*. Rev. ed. Kent, OH: Kent State University Press.

Morison, Elting Elmore. 1960. *Turmoil and Tradition: A Study of the Life and Times of Henry L. Stimson*. Boston: Houghton Mifflin.

Morkre, Morris E., and David G. Tarr. 1980. *Effects of Restrictions on United States Imports: Five Case Studies and Theory*. Washington, DC: Bureau of Economics, Federal Trade Commission.

Morrison, Rodney J. 1986. "Henry C. Carey and American Economic Development." *Transactions of the American Philosophical Society* 76:1–91.

Mulroney, Brian. 2007. *Memoirs, 1939–93*. Toronto: McClelland & Stewart.

Mundell, Robert A. 1957. "International Trade and Factor Mobility." *American Economic Review* 47:321–35.

Murray, Robert K. 1969. *The Harding Era: Warren G. Harding and His Administration*. Minneapolis: University of Minnesota Press.

Murray, Tracy W., and Michael R. Egmand. 1970. "Full Employment, Trade Expansion, and Adjustment Assistance." *Southern Economic Journal* 36:404–24.

Mussa, Michael. 2008. "IMF Surveillance over China's Exchange Rate Policy." In Goldstein and Lardy 2008.

Mutti, John H., and Malcolm D. Bale. 1981. "Output and Employment Changes in a 'Trade Sensitive' Sector: Adjustment in the U.S. Footwear Industry." *Weltwirtschaftliches Archiv* 117:352–67.

Nasaw, David. 2006. *Andrew Carnegie*. New York: Penguin Press.

Nelson, Douglas. 1989. "Domestic Political Preconditions of U.S. Trade Policy: Liberal Structure and Protectionist Dynamics." *Journal of Public Policy* 9:83–108.

Nelson, John R., Jr. 1979. "Alexander Hamilton and American Manufacturing: A Reexamination." *Journal of American History* 65:971–95.

Nettles, Curtis P. 1962. *The Emergence of a National Economy, 1775–1815*. New York: Harper.

Nevins, Allan. 1932. *Grover Cleveland: A Study in Courage*. New York: Dodd, Mead.

Niskanen, William. 1988. *Reaganomics: An Insider's Account of the Policies and the People*. New York: Oxford University Press.

Nogués, Julio J., Andrzej Olechowski, and L. Alan Winters. 1986. "The Extent of Nontariff Barriers to Industrial Countries' Imports." *World Bank Economic Review* 1:181–99.

Noland, Marcus. 1997. "Chasing Phantoms: The Political Economy of USTR." *International Organization* 51:365–87.

Nollen, Stanley D., and Dennis P. Quinn. 1994. "Free Trade, Fair Trade, Strategic Trade, and Protectionism in the U.S. Congress, 1987–88." *International Organization* 48:491–525.

North, Douglass C. 1960a. "The Balance of Payments of the United States, 1790–1860." In *Trends in the American Economy in the Nineteenth Century*. Studies in Income and Wealth, Vol. 24. Princeton, NJ: Princeton University Press for the National Bureau of Economic Research.

———. 1960b. "The United States in the International Economy, 1790–1950." In *American Economic History*, edited by Seymour Harris. New York: McGraw-Hill.

———. 1966. *The Economic Growth of the United States, 1790–1860*. New York: W. W. Norton.

Notter, Harley A. 1949. *Postwar Foreign Policy Preparation, 1939–1945*. Washington, DC: Government Printing Office.

O'Brien, Anthony Patrick, and Judith A. McDonald. 2009. "Retreat from Protectionism: R. B. Bennett and the Movement to Freer Trade in Canada, 1930–1935." *Journal of Policy History* 21:331–65.

O'Halloran, Sharyn. 1994. *Politics, Process, and American Trade Policy*. Ann Arbor: University of Michigan Press.

O'Rourke, Kevin H. 2000. "Tariffs and Growth in the Late 19th Century." *Economic Journal* 110:456–83.

———, and Jeffrey G. Williamson. 1999. *Globalization and History: The Evolution of a Nineteenth-Century Atlantic Economy*. Cambridge, MA: MIT Press.

Obama, Barak. 2006. *The Audacity of Hope*. New York: Crown.

Ochenkowski, J. P. 1983. "The Origins of Nullification in South Carolina." *South Carolina Historical Magazine* 83:121–53.

Odell, John S. 1982. *U.S. International Monetary Policy: Markets, Power, and Ideas as a Source of Change*. Princeton, NJ: Princeton University Press.

———, and Barry Eichengreen. 1998. "The United States, the ITO, and the WTO: Exit Options, Agent Slack, and Presidential Leadership." In *The WTO as an International Organization*. Chicago: University of Chicago Press.

———, and Margit Matzinger-Tchakerian. 1993. "European Community Enlargement and the United States." In *Talking Trade: U.S. Policy in Perspective*, edited by Robert S. Walters. Boulder, CO: Westview Press.

Officer, Lawrence H., and Lawrence B. Smith. 1968. "The Canadian-American Reciprocity Treaty of 1855 to 1866." *Journal of Economic History* 28:598–623.

Ohlmacher, Scott W. 2009. *The Dissolution of the Bretton Woods System: Evidence from the Nixon Tapes, August–December 1971.* Honors Thesis, University of Delaware.

Olson, Alison G. 1992. *Making the Empire Work: London and American Interest Groups, 1690–1790.* Cambridge, MA: Harvard University Press.

Olson, Mancur. 1965. *The Logic of Collective Action.* Cambridge: Harvard University Press.

Orden, David. 1996. "Agriculture ." In Krueger 1996.

Organization for Economic Cooperation and Development. 2014. *Agricultural Policies.* Paris: OECD.

Paemen, Hugo, and Alexandra Bensch. 1995. *From the GATT to the WTO: The European Community in the Uruguay Round.* Leuven, Belgium: Leuven University Press.

Palen, Marc-William. 2010. "Protection, Federation and Union: The Global Impact of the McKinley Tariff upon the British Empire, 1890–94." *Journal of Imperial and Commonwealth History* 38:395–418.

———. 2013. "The Civil War's Forgotten Transatlantic Tariff Debate and the Confederacy's Free Trade Diplomacy." *Journal of the Civil War Era* 3:35–61.

———. 2015. "The Imperialism of Economic Nationalism, 1890–1913." *Diplomatic History* 39:157–85.

———. 2016. *The 'Conspiracy' of Free Trade: The Anglo-American Struggle over Empire and Economic Globalization, 1846–1896.* New York: Cambridge University Press.

Pareto, Vilfredo. 1971. *Manual of Political Economy.* Translated by Ann S. Schwier. New York: A. M. Kelley. Orig. pub. 1909.

Parton, James. 1861. *Life of Andrew Jackson.* 3 vols. New York: Mason Bros.

Paskoff, Paul F. 1983. *Industrial Evolution: Organization, Structure, and Growth of the Pennsylvania Iron Industry, 1750–1860.* Baltimore: Johns Hopkins University Press.

Pastor, Robert A. 1980. *Congress and the Politics of U.S. Foreign Economic Policy, 1929–1976.* Berkeley: University of California Press.

Pastor, Robert. A. 1983. "The Cry and Sigh Syndrome: Congress and U.S. Trade Policy." In *Making Economic Policy in Congress*, edited by Allen Schick. Washington, DC: American Enterprise Institute.

Patrick, Stewart. 2009. *Best Laid Plans: The Origins of American Multilateralism and the Dawn of the Cold War.* Lanham, MD: Rowman & Littlefield.

Peart, Daniel. 2013. "Looking Beyond Parties and Elections: The Making of United States Tariff Policy during the Early 1820s." *Journal of the Early Republic* 33:87–108.

Pease, Jane H., and William H. Pease. 1981. "The Economics and Politics of Charleston's Nullification Crisis." *Journal of Southern History* 47:335–62.

Peek, George N. 1936. *Why Quit Our Own?* New York: Van Nostrand.

Penrose, Ernest F. 1953. *Economic Planning for the Peace.* Princeton, NJ: Princeton University Press.

Percy, Michael, Ken Norrie, and Richard Johnston. 1982. "Reciprocity and the Canadian General Election of 1911." *Explorations in Economic History* 19:409–34.

Pereira, Alfredo M., and Rafael Flores de Frutos. 1998. "Export Growth and Economic Development in Colonial British America." *Review of International Economics* 6:638–48.

Pérez, Louis A. 2003. *Cuba and the United States: Ties of Singular Intimacy.* Athens: University of Georgia Press.

Perkins, Bradford. 1961. *Prologue to War: England and the United States, 1805–1812.* Berkeley: University of California Press.

Peskin, Lawrence A. 2002. "How the Republicans Learned to Love Manufacturing: The First Parties and the 'New Economy.'" *Journal of the Early Republic* 22:235–62.

———. 2003. *Manufacturing Revolution: The Intellectual Origins of Early American Industry.* Baltimore: Johns Hopkins University Press.

Peterson, Merrill D. 1965. "Thomas Jefferson and Commercial Policy." *William and Mary Quarterly* 22:584–610.

———. 1970. *Thomas Jefferson and the New Nation.* New York: Oxford University Press.

———. 1982. *The Olive Branch and the Sword: The Compromise of 1833.* Baton Rouge: Louisiana State University Press.

Pierce, Justin, and Peter K. Schott. 2016. "The Surprisingly Swift Decline of U.S. Manufacturing Employment." *American Economic Review* 106:1632–62.

Pincus, Jonathan J. 1977. *Pressure Groups and Politics in Antebellum Tariffs.* New York: Columbia University Press.

Pitkin, Thomas M. 1940. "Western Republicans and the Tariff of 1860." *Mississippi Valley Historical Review* 27:401–20.

Polk, James K. 1910. *The Diary of James K. Polk during His Presidency, 1845–1849,* edited by Milo Milton Quaife. Chicago: McClurg.

———. 1929. *Polk: The Diary of a President, 1845–1849.* Edited by Allan Nevins. New York: Longmans, Green and Co.

———. 1969. *Correspondence of James K. Polk,* edited by Herbert Weaver. 12 vols. Nashville: Vanderbilt University Press.

———. 1989. *Correspondence of James K. Polk.* Edited by Wayne Cutler. Vol. VII, Jan.–Aug. 1844. Nashville: Vanderbilt University Press.

Pope, Jeremy C., and Shawn Treier. 2015. "Voting for a Founding: Testing the Effect of Economic Interests at the Federal Convention of 1787." *Journal of Politics* 77:519–34.

Porges, Amelia. 1991. "U.S.-Japan Trade Negotiations: Paradigms Lost." In Krugman 1991.

Porter, David L. 1980. *Congress and the Waning of the New Deal.* Port Washington, NY: Kennikat Press.

———. 1974. "Sen. Pat Harrison and the Reciprocal Trade Act of 1940." *Journal of Mississippi History* 36:363–76.

Porter, Kirk H., and Donald B. Johnson, eds. 1956. *National Party Platforms, 1840–1956.* Urbana: University of Illinois Press.

Preeg, Ernest H. 1995. *Traders in a Brave New World: The Uruguay Round and the Future of the International Trading System.* Chicago: University of Chicago Press.

Pressnell, L. S. 1986. *External Economic Policy since the War.* London: Her Majesty's Stationery Office.

Preston, Julia, and Samuel Dillon. 2004. *Opening Mexico: The Making of a Democracy.* New York: Farrar, Straus, and Giroux.

Prestowitz, Clyde V. 1988. *Trading Places: How We are Giving our Future to Japan and How to Reclaim It.* New York: Basic Books.

Preyer, Norris W. 1959. "Southern Support for the Tariff of 1816—A Reappraisal." *Journal of Southern History* 25:306–22.

Prince, Carl E., and Seth Taylor. 1982. "Daniel Webster, the Boston Associates, and the U.S. Government's Role in the Industrializing Process, 1815–1830." *Journal of the Early Republic* 2:283–29.

Ragsdale, Bruce A. 1996. *A Planters' Republic: The Search for Economic Independence in Revolutionary Virginia.* Madison, WI: Madison House.

Ransom, Roger L. 1968. "British Policy and Colonial Growth: Some Implications of the Burden from the Navigation Acts." *Journal of Economic History* 28:427–35.

Ratcliffe, Donald J. 2000. "The Nullification Crisis, Southern Discontents, and the American Political Process." *American Nineteenth Century History* 1:1–30.

Ratner, Sidney. 1942. *American Taxation.* New York: W. W. Norton.

———. 1972. *The Tariff in American History.* New York: Van Nostrand.

Read, Robert. 2005. "The Political Economy of Trade Protection: The Determinants and Welfare Impact of the 2002 US Emergency Steel Safeguard Measures." *World Economy* 28:1119–37.

Reagan, Ronald. 1990. *An American Life.* New York: Simon & Schuster.

Reeves, Richard. 2001. *President Nixon: Alone in the White House.* New York: Simon & Schuster.

Reid, Peter C. 1990. *Made Well in America: Lessons From Harley-Davidson on Being the Best.* New York: McGraw-Hill.

Reitano, Joanne R. 1994. *The Tariff Question in the Gilded Age: The Great Debate of 1888.* University Park: Pennsylvania State University Press.

Remini, Robert V. 1958. "Martin Van Buren and the Tariff of Abominations." *American Historical Review* 63:903–17.

———. 1981. *Andrew Jackson and the Course of American Freedom, 1822–1832.* New York: Harper & Row.

———. 1997. *Daniel Webster: The Man and his Times.* New York: Norton.

Revenga, Ana. L. 1992. "Exporting Jobs? The Impact of Import Competition on Employment and Wages in U.S. Manufacturing." *Quarterly Journal of Economics* 107:255–84.

Reynolds, David. 1982. *The Creation of the Anglo-American Alliance 1937–1941: A Study in Competitive Cooperation.* Chapel Hill: University of North Carolina Press.

Richardson, Heather Cox. 1997. *The Greatest Nation of the Earth: Republican Economic Policies during the Civil War.* Cambridge, MA: Harvard University Press.

Richardson, J. David. 1994. "Trade Policy." In *American Economic Policy in the 1980s*, edited by Martin Feldstein. Chicago: University of Chicago Press.

Richardson, James D., ed. 1903. *A Compilation of Messages and Papers of the Presidents, 1798–1902*. 10 vols. New York: Bureau of National Literature and Art.

Riley, James C. 1978. "Foreign Credit and Fiscal Stability: Dutch Investment in the United States, 1781–1794." *Journal of American History* 65:654–78.

Risjord, Norman K. 1961. "1812: Conservatives, War Hawks and the Nation's Honor." *William and Mary Quarterly* 18:196–210.

Ritcheson, Charles R. 1969. *Aftermath of Revolution: British Policy toward the United States, 1783–1795*. Dallas: Southern Methodist University Press.

Ritchie, Donald A. 2007. *Electing FDR: The New Deal Campaign of 1932*. Lawrence: University Press of Kansas.

Ritchie, Gordon. 1997. *Wrestling with the Elephant: The Inside Story of the Canada-- U.S. Trade Wars*. Toronto: Macfarlane Walter & Ross.

Rodrik, Dani. 1995. "Political Economy of Trade Policy." In *Handbook of International Economics*. Vol. 3. Edited by Gene M. Grossman and Kenneth Rogoff. Amsterdam: North Holland.

Rogers, Edmund. 2007. "The United States and the Fiscal Debate in Britain, 1873–1913." *Historical Journal* 50:593–622.

Rogowski, Ronald. 1989. *Commerce and Coalitions: How Trade Affects Domestic Political Alignments*. Princeton, NJ: Princeton University Press.

Romalis, John. 2007. "NAFTA's and CUSFTA's Impact on International Trade." *Review of Economics and Statistics* 89:416–35.

Romer, Christina D. 1986. "Spurious Volatility in Historical Unemployment Data." *Journal of Political Economy* 94:1–37.

———. 1988. "World War I and the Postwar Depression: A Reinterpretation Based on Alternative Estimates of GNP." *Journal of Monetary Economics* 22:91–115.

———. 1992. "What Ended the Great Depression?" *Journal of Economic History* 52:757–84.

Roosevelt, Theodore. 1924. *Roosevelt's Writings: Selections from the Writings of Theodore Roosevelt*. Edited by Maurice G. Fulton. New York: Macmillan.

Rooth, Tim. 1993. *British Protectionism and the International Economy: Overseas Commercial Policy in the 1930s*. New York: Cambridge University Press.

Rosen, Elliot. 1977. *Hoover, Roosevelt, and the Brains Trust: From Depression to New Deal*. New York: Columbia University Press.

Rosenbloom, Joshua L. 2004. "Path Dependence and the Origins of the American Cotton Textile Industry." In *The Fiber That Changed the World: Cotton Industry in International Perspective*, edited by Douglas Farnie and David Jeremy. New York: Oxford University Press.

Rothbard, Murray. 1962. *The Panic of 1819*. New York: Columbia University Press.

Rothman, David J. 1966. *Politics and Power: The United States Senate, 1869–1901*. Cambridge, MA: Harvard University Press.

Rousseau, Peter L. 2002. "Jacksonian Monetary Policy, Specie Flows, and the Panic of 1837." *Journal of Economic History* 62:457–88.

Rousslang, Donald J., and John W. Suomela. 1988. "Calculating the Welfare Costs of

Import Restrictions in the Imperfect Substitutes Model." *Applied Economics* 20:691–700.

Rove, Karl. 2015. *The Triumph of William McKinley: Why the Election of 1896 Still Matters.* New York: Simon & Schuster.

Ruffin, Roy, and Ronald Jones. 1977. "Protection and Real Wages: The Neoclassical Ambiguity." *Journal of Economic Theory* 14:337–48.

Russel, Robert R. 1924. *Economic Aspects of Southern Sectionalism, 1840–1861.* Urbana: University of Illinois Press.

Ruttenberg, Stanley H., & Associates. 1971. *Needed: A Constructive Foreign Trade Policy.* Washington, DC: Industrial Union Department, AFL-CIO.

Safire, William. 1975. *Before the Fall: An Inside View of the Pre-Watergate White House.* Garden City, NY: Doubleday.

Salant, Walter S., and Beatrice N. Vaccara. 1961. *Import Liberalization and Employment: The Effects of Unilateral Reductions in United States Import Barriers.* Washington, DC: Brookings Institution.

Saloom, Joseph A. 1972. Organized Labor and Adjustment Assistance. MSc Thesis, Sloan School of Business, MIT.

Samuelson, Paul A. 1971. "Ohlin Was Right." *Swedish Journal of Economics* 73:365–84.

Sanders, Elizabeth. 1999. *Roots of Reform: Farmers, Workers, and the American State, 1877–1917.* Chicago: University of Chicago Press.

Sarasohn, David. 1989. *The Party of Reform: Democrats in the Progressive Era.* Jackson: University of Mississippi Press.

Sawers, Larry. 1992. "The Navigation Acts Revisited." *Economic History Review* 45:262–84.

Sayre, Francis B. 1939. "The Constitutionality of the Trade Agreements Act." *Columbia Law Review* 39:751–75

———. 1939. *The Way Forward: The American Trade Agreements Program.* New York: Macmillan.

———. 1957. *Glad Adventure.* New York: Macmillan.

Schattsneider, E. E. 1935. *Politics, Pressures, and the Tariff.* New York: Prentice Hall.

Schatz, Arthur W. 1970. The Anglo-American Trade Agreement and Cordell Hull's Search for Peace 1936–1938. *Journal of American History* 57:85–103.

———. 1972. "The Reciprocal Trade Agreements Program and the 'Farm Vote,' 1934–1940." *Agricultural History* 46:498–514.

Schneitz, Karen E.1998. "Democrats' 1916 Tariff Commission: Responding to Dumping Fears and Illustrating the Consumer Costs of Protectionism." *Business History Review* 72:1–45.

———. 2000. "The Institutional Foundations of U.S. Trade Policy: Revisiting Explanations for the 1934 Reciprocal Trade Agreements Act." *Journal of Policy History* 12:417–44.

———. 2003. "The Reaction of Private Interests to the 1934 Reciprocal Trade Agreements Act." *International Organization* 57:213–33.

———, and Timothy Nieman. 1999. "Politics Matter: The 1997 Derailment of Fast-Track Negotiating Authority." *Business and Politics* 1:233–51.

Schoppa, Leonard J. 1997. *Bargaining with Japan: What American Pressure Can and Cannot Do*. New York: Columbia University Press.

Schulman, Bruce J. 1991. *From Cotton Belt to Sunbelt: Federal Policy, Economic Development, and the Transformation of the South, 1938–1980*. New York: Oxford University Press.

Schultze, Charles L. 1983. "Industrial Policy: A Dissent." *Brookings Review* 2:4–12.

Schwab, Susan C. 1994. *Trade-Offs: Negotiating the Omnibus Trade and Competitiveness Act*. Boston: Harvard Business School Press.

Scott, Robert E., and Will Kimball. 2014. "China Trade, Outsourcing, and Jobs." EPI Briefing Paper No. 385. Washington, DC: Economic Policy Institute.

Scroggs, William O. 1930. "Revolt against the Tariff." *North American Review* 230:18–24.

Sears, Louis M. 1921. "Philadelphia and the Embargo of 1808." *Quarterly Journal of Economics* 35:354–59.

———. 1927. *Jefferson and the Embargo*. Durham, NC: Duke University Press.

Select Committee on Investigation of the United States Tariff Commission. 1928. *Report: Investigation of the Tariff Commission*. Washington: Government Printing Office.

Sell, Susan K. 2003. *Private Power, Public Law: The Globalization of Intellectual Property Rights*. New York: Cambridge University Press.

Sellers, Charles G. 1966. *James K. Polk: Continentalist, 1843–46*. Princeton, NJ: Princeton University Press.

———. 1991. *The Market Revolution: Jacksonian America, 1815–1846*. New York: Oxford University Press.

Sellers, James. 1927. "Economic Incidence of the Civil War on the South." *Mississippi Valley Historical Review* 14, 179–91.

Setser, Vernon G. 1933. "Did Americans Originate the Conditional Most-Favored-Nation Clause?" *Journal of Modern History* 5:319–23.

———. 1937. *The Commercial Reciprocity Policy of the United States, 1774–1829*. Philadelphia: University of Pennsylvania Press.

Shammas, Carole. 1982. "How Self-Sufficient Was Early America?" *Journal of Interdisciplinary History* 13:247–72.

Shankman, Andrew. 2003. "'A New Thing on Earth': Alexander Hamilton, Pro-Manufacturing Republicans, and the Democratization of American Political Economy." *Journal of the Early Republic* 23:323–52.

Shapiro, Hal S. 2006. *Fast Track: A Legal, Historical, and Political Analysis*. Ardsley, NY: Transnational Publishers.

Shelburne, Robert C., and Robert W. Bednarzik. 1993. "Geographic Concentration of Trade-Sensitive Employment." *Monthly Labor Review* 116 (June): 3–13.

Shenton, James P. 1961. *Robert James Walker: A Politician from Jackson to Lincoln*. New York: Columbia University Press.

Shepherd, James F. 1993. "State Tariff Policies in the Era of Confederation." Unpublished paper, presented at Western Economic Association, Lake Tahoe, Nevada.

———, and Gary M. Walton. 1972. *Shipping, Maritime Trade, and the Economic Development of Colonial North America*. New York: Cambridge University Press.

———, and Gary M. Walton. 1976. "Economic Change after the American Revolution:

Pre- and Post-War Comparisons of Maritime Shipping and Trade." *Explorations in Economic History* 12:397–422.

Sheridan, Richard B. 1960. "The British Credit Crisis of 1772 and the American Colonies." *Journal of Economic History* 20:161–86.

Sherman, John. 1895. *Recollections of Forty Years in the House, Senate, and Cabinet.* 2 vols. Chicago: Werner Company.

Sherman, Richard. 2002. "Delegation, Ratification, and US Trade Policy." *Comparative Political Studies* 35:1171–97.

Shikher, Sergei. 2012. "Predicting the Effects of NAFTA: Now We Can Do It Better!" *Journal of International and Global Economic Studies* 5:32–59

Shoch, James. 2001. *Trading Blows: Party Competition and U.S. Trade Policy in a Globalizing Era.* Chapel Hill: University of North Carolina Press.

Singleton, Christopher J. 1990. "The 1987–88 Surge in Exports and the Rise in Factory Jobs." *Monthly Labor Review* (May), 42–49.

Sjaastad, Larry. 1980. "Commercial Policy, 'True Tariffs' and Relative Prices." In *Current Issues in Commercial Policy and Diplomacy*, edited by John Black and Brian Hindley. New York: St Martin's Press.

Skocpol, Theda. 1993. "America's First Social Security System: The Expansion of Benefits for Civil War Veterans." *Political Science Quarterly* 108:85–116.

Smith, Adam. 1976 [1776]. *An Inquiry into the Nature and Causes of the Wealth of Nations.* Oxford: Clarendon Press.

Smith, Howard R. 1954. "The Farmer and the Tariff: A Reappraisal." *Southern Economic Journal* 21:152–65.

Smith, Mark. 1926. *Wool and the Tariff.* New York: Macmillan.

Smith, Walter B., and Arthur H. Cole. 1935. *Fluctuations in American Business, 1790–1860.* Cambridge, MA: Harvard University Press.

Smoot, Reed. 1931. "Our Tariff and the Depression." *Current History* 35:173–81.

———. 1997. *In the World: The Diaries of Reed Smoot.* Edited by Harvard S. Heath. Salt Lake City, UT: Signature Books.

Snyder, J. Richard. 1968. "Coolidge, Costigan, and the Tariff Commission." *Mid-America* 50:131–48.

———. 1973. "Hoover and the Hawley-Smoot Tariff: A View of Executive Leadership." *Annals of Iowa* 41:1173–1189.

———. 1980. *William S. Culbertson: In Search of a Rendezvous.* Washington, DC: University Press of America.

Solvick, Stanley D. 1963. "William Howard Taft and the Payne-Aldrich Tariff." *Mississippi Valley Historical Review* 50:424–42.

Spinelli, Lawrence. 1989. *Dry Diplomacy: the United States, Great Britain, and Prohibition.* Wilmington, DE: Scholarly Resources.

Spivak, Burton. 1979. *Jefferson's English Crisis: Commerce, Embargo, and the Republican Revolution.* Charlottesville: University Press of Virginia.

Stagg, J. C. A. 1983. *Mr. Madison's War: Politics, Diplomacy, and Warfare in the Early American Republic, 1783–1830.* Princeton, NJ: Princeton University Press.

Stanwood, Edward. 1903. *American Tariff Controversies in the Nineteenth Century.* 2 vols. Boston: Houghton, Mifflin.

Stapleford, Thomas A. 2009. *The Cost of Living in America: A Political History of Economic Statistics, 1880–2000*. New York: Cambridge University Press.

Statistical Abstract of the United States. Various years. Washington, DC: Government Printing Office.

Steel, Ronald. 1980. *Walter Lippmann and the American Century*. Boston: Little, Brown.

Steeples, Douglas W., and David O. Whitten. 1998. *Democracy in Desperation: The Depression of 1893*. Westport, CT: Greenwood Press.

Stein, Judith. 2010. *Pivotal Decade: How the United States Traded Factories for Finance in the Seventies*. New Haven, CT: Yale University Press.

Steward, Dick. 1975. *Trade and Hemisphere: The Good Neighbor Policy and Reciprocal Trade*. Columbia: University of Missouri Press.

Stiles, Kendall W. 1995. "The Ambivalent Hegemon: Explaining the 'Lost Decade' in Multilateral Trade Talks: 1948–58." *Review of International Political Economy* 2:1–26.

Stockman, David A. 1986. *The Triumph of Politics: How the Reagan Revolution Failed*. New York: Harper & Row.

Stolper, Wolfgang, and Paul A. Samuelson. 1941. "Protection and Real Wages." *Review of Economic Studies* 41:58–73.

Story, Joseph. 1852. *The Miscellaneous Writings of Joseph Story*, edited by William W. Story. Boston: Little, Brown.

Strauss, Robert. 1987. "Foreword.: In *The Tokyo Round of Multilateral Trade Negotiations: A Case Study in Building Domestic Support for Diplomacy*, by J. E. Twiggs, Lanham, MD: University Press of America.

Strum, Harvey. 1994. "Rhode Island and the Embargo of 1807." *Rhode Island History* 52:58–67.

Stuart, Reginald C. 1982. "James Madison and the Militants: Republican Disunity and Replacing the Embargo." *Diplomatic History* 6:145–68.

Subramanian, Arvind, and Shang-jin Wei. 2007. "The WTO Promotes Trade, Strongly but Unevenly." *Journal of International Economics* 72:151–75.

Summers, Festus P. 1953. *William L. Wilson and Tariff Reform*. New Brunswick, NJ: Rutgers University Press.

Sumner, Scott. 2015. *The Midas Paradox: Financial Markets, Government Policy Shocks, and the Great Depression*. Oakland, CA: The Independent Institute.

Sundquist, James L. 1983. *The Dynamics of the Party System: Alignment and Realignment of Political Parties in the United States*. Washington, DC: Brookings Institution.

Suomela, John W. 1993. *Free Trade versus Fair Trade: The Making of American Trade Policy in a Political Environment*. Turku: Institute for European Studies.

Surdam, David. 2001. *Northern Naval Superiority and the Economics of the American Civil War*. Columbia: University of South Carolina Press.

Suskind, Ron. 2004. *The Price of Loyalty*. New York: Simon & Schuster.

Sutthiphisal, Dhanoos. 2006. "Learning-by-Producing and the Geographic Links between Invention and Production: Experience from the Second Industrial Revolution." *Journal of Economic History* 66:992–1025.

Taft, Robert A. 2003. *The Papers of Robert A. Taft*. Edited by Clarence F. Wunderlin. Vol. 3. Kent, OH: Kent State University Press.

Talbot, Ross B. 1978. *The Chicken War: An International Trade Conflict between the United States and the European Economic Community, 1961–1964*. Ames: Iowa State University Press.

Tarbell, Ida M. 1912. *The Tariff in our Times*. New York: Macmillan.

Tariff Commission. 1882. *Report of the Tariff Commission*. 2 vols. Washington, DC: Government Printing Office.

Tarr, David G., and Morris E. Morkre. 1984. *Aggregate Costs to the United States of Tariff and Quotas on Imports: General Tariff Cuts and Removal of Quotas on Automobiles, Steel, Sugar, and Textiles*. Washington, DC: Bureau of Economics, Federal Trade Commission.

Tasca, Henry J. 1938. *The Reciprocal Trade Policy of the United States*. Philadelphia: University of Pennsylvania Press.

Taussig, Frank W. 1892. *State Papers and Speeches on the Tariff*. Cambridge, MA: Harvard University Press.

———. 1915. *Some Aspects of the Tariff Question*. Cambridge, MA: Harvard University Press.

———. 1916. "The Proposal for a Tariff Commission." *North American Review* 203:194–204.

———. 1920. *Free Trade, the Tariff, and Reciprocity*. New York: Macmillan.

———. 1926. "The United States Tariff Commission and the Tariff." *American Economic Review* 16:171–81.

———. 1931. *The Tariff History of the United States*. 8th ed. New York: G. P. Putnam's Sons.

Taylor, George Rogers. 1951. *The Transportation Revolution, 1815–1860*. New York: Rinehart.

Taylor, Jason E., Bharati Basu, and Steven McLean. 2011. "Net Exports and the Avoidance of High Unemployment During Reconversion, 1945–1947." *Journal of Economic History* 71:444—54.

Taylor, Jason E., and Todd C. Neumann. 2016. "Recovery Spring, Faltering Fall: March to November 1933." *Explorations in Economic History* 61:54–67.

Tedesco, Paul H. 1985. *Patriotism, Protection, and Prosperity: James Moore Swank, the American Iron and Steel Association, and the Tariff: 1873–1913*. New York: Garland.

Temin, Peter, and Barrie A. Wigmore. 1990. "The End of One Big Deflation." *Explorations in Economic History* 27:483-502.

Temperley, H. W. V.. ed. 1921. *A History of the Peace Conference of Paris*. London: Frowde, Hodder & Stoughton.

Terrill, Tom E. 1969. "David A. Wells, the Democracy, and Tariff Reduction, 1877–1894." *Journal of American History* 56:540–55.

———. 1973. *The Tariff, Politics, and American Foreign Policy, 1874–1901*. Westport, CT: Greenwood Press.

Thomas, P. D. G. 1975. *British Politics and the Stamp Act Crisis: The First Phase of the American Revolution 1763–1767*. New York: Clarendon Press.

———. 1987. *The Townshend Duties Crisis: The Second Phase of the American Revolution, 1767–1773*. New York: Oxford University Press.

Thomas, Robert P. 1965. "A Quantitative Approach to the Study of the Effects of British Imperial Policy upon Colonial Welfare: Some Preliminary Findings." *Journal of Economic History* 25:615–38.

Thompson, Margaret S. 1985. *The "Spider Web": Congress and Lobbying in the Age of Grant*. Ithaca, NY: Cornell University Press.

Thorp, Willard L. 1926. *Business Annals*. New York: National Bureau of Economic Research.

Tiegle, Joseph G., Jr. 1942. "Louisiana and the Tariff, 1816–1846." *Louisiana Historical Quarterly* 25:24–148.

Timberlake, Richard. 1993. *Monetary Policy in the United States: An Intellectual and Institutional History*. Chicago: University of Chicago Press.

Tocqueville, Alexis de. 2004 [1848]. *Democracy in America*. Translated by Arthur Goldhammer. New York: Library of America.

Tontz, Robert L. 1958. "Origin of the Base Period Concept of Parity: A Significant Value Judgment in Agricultural Policy." *Agricultural History* 32:3–13.

Toye, Richard J. 2003a. "Developing Multilateralism: The Havana Charter and the Fight for the International Trade Organization, 1947–1948." *International History Review* 25:282–305

———. 2003b. "The Attlee Government, the Imperial Preference System, and the Creation of the GATT." *English Historical Review* 98:912–39.

Trela, Irene, and John Whalley. 1990. "Global Effects of Developed Country Trade Restrictions on Textiles and Apparel." *Economic Journal* 100:1190–1205.

Trubowitz, Peter. 1998. *Defining the National Interest: Conflict and Change in American Foreign Policy*. Chicago: University of Chicago Press.

Tugwell, Rexford G. 1968. *The Brains Trust*. New York: Viking.

Tullock, Gordon. 1975. "The Transitional Gains Trap." *Bell Journal of Economics* 6:671–78.

Tully, John. 1996. "Coal Fields of the Conterminous United States." USGS Open-File Report OF 96–92. Reston, VA: US Geological Survey.

US Bureau of the Census. 1975. *Historical Statistics of the United States: Bicentennial Edition*. Washington, DC: Government Printing Office.

———. Various years. *Census of Manufactures*. Online at https://www.census.gov/programs-surveys/decennial-census/library/publications.html.

US Department of Commerce. 1948. *International Transactions of the United States during the War, 1940–45*. Washington, DC: Government Printing Office.

———. 1950. *The Balance of International Payments of the United States, 1946–1948*. Washington, DC: Government Printing Office.

US Department of State. 1945. *Proposals for Expansion of World Trade and Employment*. Washington, DC: Government Printing Office.

US Department of the Treasury 2016 (April 29). *Foreign Exchange Policies of Major Trading Partners of the United States*. Available online at https://www.treasury.gov/resource-center/international/exchange-rate-policies/Pages/index.aspx.

US General Accounting Office. 1987. "Activity under Section 201." GAO/ NSIAO-87–96FS.

———. 1994. *International Trade: U.S. Government Policy Issues Affecting U.S. Business Activities in China.* GGD-94–94. Washington, DC: GAO.

———. 2001. "World Trade Organization: U.S. Experience in Dispute Settlement System: The First Five Years." July. Washington, DC: GAO.

US International Trade Commission. 1982a. *Economic Effects of Export Restraints.* Publication No. 1256. Washington, DC: USITC.

———. 1982b. *The Effectiveness of Escape Clause Relief in Promoting Adjustment to Import Competition.* Publication No. 1229. Washington, DC: USITC.

———. 1989. *The Economic Effects of Significant U.S. Import Restraints, Phase I: Manufacturing.* Publication No. 2222. Washington, DC: USITC.

———. 1993. *Potential Impact on the U.S. Economy and Selected Industries of the North American Free Trade Agreement.* Publication No. 2596. Washington, DC: USITC.

———. 1995. *The Economic Effects of Antidumping and Countervailing Duty Orders and Suspension Agreements.* Publication No. 2900. Washington, DC: USITC.

———. 2004. *U.S.-Central America-Dominican Republic Free Trade Agreement: Potential Economy-wide and Selected Sectoral Effects.* Publication No. 3717. Washington, DC: USITC.

———. 2016. *Economic Impact of Trade Agreements Implemented under Trade Authorities Procedures, 2016 Report.* USITC Publication Number 4614.

US Tariff Commission. 1919. *Reciprocity and Commercial Treaties.* Washington, DC: Government Printing Office.

———. 1922. "Operations of Rates in the Emergency Tariff Act." Senate Document No. 224, 67th Congress, 2d Session.

US Tariff Commission. 1930. Annual Report. Washington, DC: Government Printing Office.

———. 1948. *Operation of the Trade Agreements Program, July 1934 to April 1948, Part 1. Summary.* Washington, DC: Government Printing Office.

Underwood, Oscar W. 1928. *Drifting Sands of Party Politics.* New York: The Century Co.

Uslaner, E. 1998. "Let the Chips Fall Where They May? Executive and Constituency Influences on Congressional Voting Behavior on NAFTA." *Legislative Studies Quarterly* 23:347–71.

Van Bertrab, Hermann. 1997. *Negotiating NAFTA: A Mexican Envoy's Account.* Westport, CT: Praeger.

Van Cott, T. Norman, and Larry J. Wipf. 1983. "Tariff Reduction via Inflation: U.S. Specific Tariffs, 1972–79." *Weltwirtschaftliches Archiv* 119:724–33.

Vandenberg, Arthur. 1952. *The Private Papers of Senator Vandenberg.* Boston: Houghton Mifflin.

VanGrasstek, Craig. 2013. *The History and Future of the World Trade Organization.* Geneva: World Trade Organization.

Varg, Paul A. 1976. "The Economic Side of the Good Neighbor Policy: The Reciprocal Trade Program and South America." *Pacific Historical Review* 45:47–71.

Viner, Jacob. 1923. *Dumping: A Problem in International Trade.* Chicago: University of Chicago Press.

———. "The Most Favored Nation Clause in American Commercial Treaties." *Journal of Political Economy* 32:101–129.

Vipperman, Carl J. 1989. *William Lowndes and the Transition of Southern Politics, 1782–1822.* Chapel Hill: University of North Carolina Press.

Volcker, Paul A. 1978–79. "The Political Economy of the Dollar." *Federal Reserve Bank of New York Quarterly Review* 3 (Winter): 1–12.

———, and Toyoo Gyohten. 1992. *Changing Fortunes: The World's Money and the Threat to American Leadership.* New York: Times Books.

Walker, Robert J. 1845. *Report of the Secretary of the Treasury.* Senate Doc. No. 21, 28th Congress, 2nd session.

Wallis, John J. 2001. "What Caused the Crisis of 1839?" NBER Historical Working Paper No. 133, April.

Walton, Gary M. 1971. "The New Economic History and the Burdens of the Navigation Acts." *Economic History Review* 24:533–42.

Wanniski, Jude. 1978. *The Way the World Works.* New York: Basic Books.

Ward, Marianne, and John Devereux. 2003. "Measuring British Decline: Direct versus Long-Span Income Measures." *Journal of Economic History* 63:826–51.

———. 2005. "Relative British and American Income Levels during the First Industrial Revolution." *Research in Economic History* 23:255–92.

Ware, Caroline F. 1926. "The Effect of the American Embargo, 1807–1809, on the New England Cotton Industry." *Quarterly Journal of Economics* 40:672–88.

———. 1931. *The Early New England Cotton Manufacture.* Boston: Houghton Mifflin.

Warren, Kenneth. 1973. *The American Steel Industry, 1850–1970: A Geographical Interpretation.* Oxford: Clarendon Press.

Watson, Richard A. 1956. "The Tariff Revolution: A Study of Shifting Party Attitudes." *Journal of Politics* 18:678–701.

Weiss, Thomas. 1993. "Long-Term Changes in U.S. Agricultural Output Per Worker, 1800–1900." *Economic History Review* 46:324–41.

Weller, Nicholas. 2009. "Trading Policy: Constituents and Party in U.S. Trade Policy." *Public Choice* 141:87–101.

Wells, David. 1867. "Report of the Special Commissioner of the Revenue." Senate Executive Documents, No. 2, 39th Congress, 2nd session. Washington, DC: Government Printing Office.

———. 1869a. "Report of the Special Commissioner of the Revenue [1868]." House Executive Documents, No. 16, 40th Congress, 3rd session. Washington, DC: Government Printing Office.

———. 1869b. "Report of the Special Commissioner of the Revenue [1869]." House Executive Documents, No. 27, 41st Congress, 2nd session. Washington, DC: Government Printing Office.

White, Eugene N. 1990. "When the Ticker Ran Late: The Stock Market Boom and Crash of 1929." In *Crises and Panics: The Lessons of History,* edited by Eugene N. White. Homewood: Dow Jones–Irwin.

Whittlesey, C. R. 1937. "Import Quotas in the United States." *Quarterly Journal of Economics* 52:37–65.

Wilcox, Clair. 1949. *A Charter for World Trade.* New York: Macmillan.

Wilgress, Leolyn Dana. 1967. *Memoirs*. Toronto: Ryerson Press.

Wilkins, Mira. 1989. *The History of Foreign Investment in the United States to 1914*. Cambridge, MA: Harvard University Press.

Wilkinson, Joe R. 1960. *Politics and Trade Policy*. Washington, DC: Public Affairs Press.

Williamson, Jeffrey G. 1995. "The Evolution of Global Labor Markets since 1830: Background Evidence and Hypotheses." *Explorations in Economic History* 32:141–96.

Willis, H. Parker. 1914. "The Tariff of 1913: I." *Journal of Political Economy* 22:1–42.

Wilson, Theodore A. 1991. *The First Summit: Roosevelt and Churchill at Placentia Bay, 1941*. Rev. ed. Lawrence: University Press of Kansas.

Wilson, Woodrow. 1909. "Tariff Make-Believe." *North American Review* 190:535–56.

Winham, Gilbert R. 1980. "Robert Strauss, the MTN, and the Control of Faction." *Journal of World Trade Law* 14:377–97.

———. 1986. *International Trade and the Tokyo Round Negotiation*. Princeton, NJ: Princeton University Press.

Witkowski, Terrence H. 1989. "Colonial Consumers in Revolt: Buyer Values and Behavior during the Nonimportation Movement, 1764–1776." *Journal of Consumer Research* 16:216–26.

Wolff, Alan W. 1983. "The Need for New GATT Rules to Govern Safeguard Actions." In *Trade Policy in the 1980s*, edited by William R. Cline. Washington, DC: Institute for International Economics.

Wolford, Thorp L. 1942. "Democratic-Republican Reaction in Massachusetts to the Embargo of 1807." *New England Quarterly* 15:35–61.

Wolman, Paul. 1992. *Most Favored Nation: The Republican Revisionists and U.S. Tariff Policy: 1897–1912*. Chapel Hill: University of North Carolina Press.

Woltjer, Pieter. 2015. "Taking Over: A New Appraisal of the Anglo-American Productivity Gap and the Nature of American Economic Leadership c. 1910." *Scandinavian Economic History Review* 63:280–301.

Woods, Randall B. 1990. *A Changing of the Guard: AngloAmerican Relations, 1941–1946*. Chapel Hill: University of North Carolina Press.

World Trade Organization. 1999. *The Legal Texts: The Results of the Uruguay Round of Multilateral Trade Negotiations*. New York: Cambridge University Press.

Wright, Chester W. 1910. *Wool-Growing and the Tariff*. Cambridge, MA: Harvard University Press.

Wright, Gavin. 1990. "The Origins of American Industrial Success, 1879–1940." *American Economic Review* 80:651–68.

Yang, Dennis Tao. 2012. "Aggregate Savings and External Imbalances in China." *Journal of Economic Perspectives* 26:125–46.

Younger, Edward. 1955. *John A. Kasson: Politics and Diplomacy from Lincoln to McKinley*. Iowa City: State Historical Society of Iowa.

Zeiler, Thomas W. 1987. "Free Trade Politics and Diplomacy: John F. Kennedy and Textiles." *Diplomatic History* 11:127–42.

———. 1992. *American Trade and Power in the 1960s*. New York: Columbia University Press.

———. 1999. *Free Trade, Free World: The Advent of GATT*. Chapel Hill: University of North Carolina Press.

Zevin, Robert B. 1971. "The Growth of Cotton Textile Production After 1815." In *The Reinterpretation of America's Past*, edited by Robert Fogel and Stanley Engerman. New York: Harper & Row.

Zinsmeister, Karl. 1993. "MITI Mouse." *Policy Review* 64:28–35.

Zoellick, Robert B. 2000. "A Republican Foreign Policy." *Foreign Affairs* 79:63–78.

Zornow, William F. 1954. "Georgia Tariff Policies, 1775–1789." *Georgia Historical Quarterly* 37:1–10.

———. 1954. "Massachusetts Tariff Policies, 1775–1789." *Essex Institute Historical Collections* 90:194–215.

———. 1954. "New Hampshire Tariff Policies, 1775–1789." *The Social Studies* 45:252–256.

———. 1954. "The Tariff Policies of Virginia, 1775–1789." *Virginia Magazine of History and Biography* 62:306–319.

———. 1955. "North Carolina State Tariff Policies, 1775–1789." *North Carolina Historical Review* 32:151–164.

———. 1955. "Tariff Policies of South Carolina, 1775–1789." *South Carolina Historical and Genealogical Magazine* 56:31–44.

———. 1956. "New York Tariff Policies, 1775–1789." *New York History* 37:40–63.

Additional series titles (continued)

Samuel H. Preston and Michael R. Haines
Fatal Years: Child Mortality in Late Nineteenth-Century America
(Princeton University Press, 1991)

Barry Eichengreen
Golden Fetters: The Gold Standard and the Great Depression, 1919–1939
(Oxford University Press, 1992)

Ronald N. Johnson and Gary D. Libecap
The Federal Civil Service System and the Problem of Bureaucracy: The Economics and Politics of Institutional Change (University of Chicago Press, 1994)

Naomi R. Lamoreaux
Insider Lending: Banks, Personal Connections, and Economic Development in Industrial New England (Cambridge University Press, 1994)

Lance E. Davis, Robert E. Gallman, and Karin Gleiter
In Pursuit of Leviathan: Technology, Institutions, Productivity, and Profits in American Whaling, 1816–1906 (University of Chicago Press, 1997)

Dora L. Costa
The Evolution of Retirement: An American Economic History, 1880–1990
(University of Chicago Press, 1998)

Joseph P. Ferrie
Yankeys Now: Immigrants in the Antebellum U.S., 1840–1860 (Oxford University Press, 1999)

Robert A. Margo
Wages and Labor Markets in the United States, 1820–1860 (University of Chicago Press, 2000)

Price V. Fishback and Shawn Everett Kantor
A Prelude to the Welfare State: The Origins of Workers' Compensation
(University of Chicago Press, 2000)

Gerardo della Paolera and Alan M. Taylor
Straining at the Anchor: The Argentine Currency Board and the Search for Macroeconomic Stability, 1880–1935 (University of Chicago Press, 2001)

Werner Troesken
Water, Race, and Disease (MIT Press, 2004)

B. Zorina Khan
The Democratization of Invention: Patents and Copyrights in American Economic Development, 1790–1920 (Cambridge University Press, 2005)

Dora L. Costa and Matthew E. Kahn
Heroes and Cowards: The Social Face of War (Princeton University Press, 2008)

Roderick Floud, Robert W. Fogel, Bernard Harris, and Sok Chul Hong
The Changing Body: Health, Nutrition, and Human Development in the Western World since 1700 (Cambridge University Press, 2011)

Stanley L. Engerman and Kenneth L. Sokoloff
Economic Development in the Americas since 1500: Endowments and Institutions (Cambridge University Press, 2012)

Robert William Fogel, Enid M. Fogel, Mark Guglielmo, and Nathaniel Grotte
Political Arithmetic: Simon Kuznets and the Empirical Tradition in Economics (University of Chicago Press, 2013)

Price Fishback, Jonathan Rose, and Kenneth Snowden
Well Worth Saving: How the New Deal Safeguarded Home Ownership (University of Chicago Press, 2013)

Howard Bodenhorn
The Color Factor: The Economics of African-American Well-Being in the Nineteenth-Century South (Oxford University Press, 2015)

Leah Platt Boustan
Competition in the Promised Land: Black Migrants in Northern Cities and Labor Markets (Princeton University Press, 2017)